DATABASE

Principles
Programming
Performance

The Morgan Kaufmann Series in Data Management Systems

Series Editor: Jim Gray, Microsoft Research

4/2007

Second Edition

DATABASE

Principles
Programming
Performance

PATRICK O'NEIL
University of Massachusetts at Boston

ELIZABETH O'NEIL
University of Massachusetts at Boston

MORGAN KAUFMANN PUBLISHERS
AN IMPRINT OF ACADEMIC PRESS
A Harcourt Science and Technology Company
SAN FRANCISCO   SAN DIEGO   NEW YORK   BOSTON
LONDON   SYDNEY   TOKYO

Senior Editor	Diane D. Cerra
Director of Production and Manufacturing	Yonie Overton
Senior Production Editor	Cheri Palmer
Editorial Coordinator	Belinda Breyer
Text and Cover Design	Ross Carron Design
Cover Photograph	© Will McIntyre; Deni McIntyre/AllStock/PictureQuest
Composition	Nancy Logan
Illustration	Lineworks, Inc.
Copyeditor	Carol Leyba
Proofreader	Jennifer McClain
Indexer	Ty Koontz
Printer	Courier Corporation

Designations used by companies to distinguish their products are often claimed as trademarks or registered trademarks. In all instances where Morgan Kaufmann Publishers is aware of a claim, the product names appear in initial capital or all capital letters. Readers, however, should contact the appropriate companies for more complete information regarding trademarks and registration.

ACADEMIC PRESS
A Harcourt Science and Technology Company
525 B Street, Suite 1900, San Diego, CA 92101-4495, USA
http://www.academicpress.com

Academic Press
Harcourt Place, 32 Jamestown Road, London, NW1 7BY United Kingdom
http://www.hbuk.co.uk/ap/

Morgan Kaufmann Publishers
340 Pine Street, Sixth Floor, San Francisco, CA 94104-3205, USA
http://www.mkp.com

Library of Congress Cataloging-in-Publication Data

O'Neil, Patrick.
   Database--principles, programming, and performance / Patrick O'Neil, Elizabeth O'Neil.--2nd ed.
      p. cm.
   Includes bibliographical references and index.
   ISBN 1-55860-438-3 -- ISBN 1-55860-580-0 (pbk.)
   1. Database management. I. O'Neil, Elizabeth. II. Title.
QA76.9.D3 O489 2001
005.74--dc 21   99-089041

This book is printed on acid-free paper.

Foreword

by Jim Gray, *Microsoft Research*
Series Editor, Morgan Kaufmann Series in Data Management Systems

Since its first appearance in 1994, the O'Neil database book has become a standard text and reference for anyone learning, designing, or managing relational database applications. The book carefully presents both the theory and practice of database design and implementation. It covers relational theory, database design, database implementation, and performance-tuning issues. In all cases it starts with the general concept and then translates the ideas into specific examples demonstrated by real systems.

This revised edition reflects the substantial progress and ferment in the database field in the six years since the first edition. It places major emphasis on the object-relational model; it presents many new concepts now common in systems like Oracle, DB2, and Informix; it updates the presentation of isolation techniques; and it modernizes the presentation of performance issues. The object-relational presentation is especially noteworthy: this is widely considered the most important change to the SQL database language since the original standard. The book presents the SQL-99 design and relates that design to the principle ideas and to the major commercial products.

Professors Pat and Elizabeth O'Neil have an unusually broad and deep view of the database design issues and have been active contributors to the database field for three decades. They have taught generations of students, they have written many of the seminal research papers in the field, they have worked on the development of several products, and they have consulted with most of the vendors. They continue to innovate to this day—this book is an attempt to provide a unified view of the many disparate ideas and trends in the database area. The revision gives a modern view of the scene.

Database: Principles, Programming, and Performance makes an excellent text for anyone just approaching database systems. It is an accessible refresher for those of us who have not been paying careful attention to developments in this area and is a useful reference for designers and implementors who need just-in-time education.

Contents

Contents

Contents

Contents

Contents

Preface

Of making many books, there is no end; and much study is a weariness of the flesh.
—Christian Bible, Ecclesiastes 12:12.

Before I came here I was confused about this subject. Having listened to your lecture, I am still confused, but on a higher level.
—Enrico Fermi

The goal of this text in its first edition was to introduce the reader to the fundamental principles of database theory, together with an understanding of the connections (and gaps) between theory and commercial practice. The authors believe that the high pace of change in the various commercial database system products over the last five years has made it all the more important to provide readers with an up-to-date understanding of current database practice. While a number of important changes in the database field have driven the development of this second edition, we have tried not to lose sight of the fundamental aims of this text.

As in the first edition, we provide an up-to-date introduction to SQL and to practical applications created in real commercial database systems. Whether you are an Interactive SQL user, an application programmer, a database administrator (DBA), or a student interested in learning about the field, this book was written with you in mind. The combination of practical information with underlying principles has been extended, providing what past readers have considered to be the fundamental strength of this book.

Practitioners need an introduction to database application programming that is more than the simple listing of Embedded SQL features so often seen in texts. Vendor manuals sometimes give an excellent introduction to SQL and database programming but lack the intellectual grounding in fundamental principles that students and professionals need to adapt to future changes in database systems and languages. Some principles that are not well covered in many introductory database texts or manuals are these: implication of deadlock aborts (the need to retry), entity-relationship modeling and normalization (as well as the translation of database design into actual tables), problems of user interaction during transactions that access popular data (interaction while a transaction is active is dangerous), and finally, considerations of indexing and query optimization in terms of how they affect query performance, an important consideration for database administrators.

This book can be thought of as a solid introduction to the skills needed by a database administrator, application programmer, or sophisticated SQL user. Although the needs of a database administrator may be broader than those of an application programmer, programmers are more effective when they have a grasp of the general concepts that a DBA finds essential. The same can be said for serious Interactive SQL users. In addition to a firm grounding in SQL, an understanding of logical database design, physical layout of data, indexing, security, and cost-performance will benefit anyone working with a database system.

The authors are professors of computer science, with extensive experience consulting with database companies and database-intensive applications. See our home pages, www.cs.umb.edu/~poneil and ~eoneil.

Use of This Book

This book was developed over a period of several years for an introductory database course and a subsequent, more advanced course offered at the University of Massachusetts at Boston. The first course is an introduction to database principles. Roughly the first six chapters of the text contain the material from that course. The second course deals with more advanced database concepts, with a focus on cost-performance concerns. This material is covered in Chapters 7 through 10.

It is not necessary to proceed through the book sequentially, and the chapters have been prepared to accommodate a variety of reader interests and course plans. Depending on your experience and objectives, chapters can be read briefly or in a sequence different from the order offered by the book. For example, readers who have a familiarity with basic concepts may want to begin with their specific interest in the later chapters, referring to Chapters 1 through 6 only when needed (see Figure 1 for chapter dependencies). The book has been written so that new concepts are only introduced when previous concepts have been mastered. For this reason, experienced readers can begin with the subject most appropriate to their needs.

We've intended this book either as a tutorial and reference for the professional, or as a one- or two-term introductory course in colleges and universities. The presentation moves from basic theory and concepts to the most recent developments in the field. The text introduces basic SQL simultaneously with the fundamentals of relational databases.

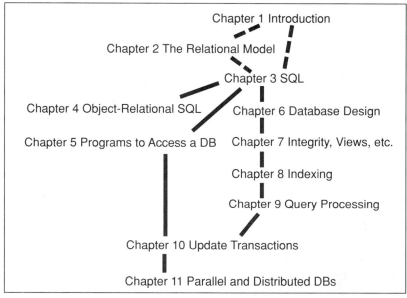

Figure 1   Chapter Dependencies for Planning Reading Order

Examples from **ORACLE, INFORMIX, DB2,** and others are used to illustrate the concepts and to clarify the cost-performance issues by comparing the differing approaches used in these successful systems. The key issues in each chapter are reinforced by programming examples and exercises. Three appendices provide additional background. As an aid to self-study, solutions to selected exercises are included in the back of the book.

Discussion of New Coverage: Object-Relational Model

Since the first edition was published, the SQL language has added a number of new features, and these are covered in new sections of Chapter 3. More fundamentally, the object-relational model has become the new database standard; and while all new ORDBMS products are backward compatible so that the relational model continues to be supported, it is our contention that this change is in the process of revolutionizing the industry. Table design and SQL access to the data can be expected to develop in new and relatively unexpected ways.

The history of how the object-relational model has entered the mainstream is instructive. In 1996, **INFORMIX** Corporation purchased the Illustra product and has been working since then to consolidate object-relational features into **INFORMIX**. (Illustra, then called Montage, was covered in Section 3.11 of our first edition, but we have modified and greatly extended this material to create a new Chapter 4 for the current edition.) In 1997, **ORACLE** Corporation shipped **ORACLE** release 8, which supported a set of new object-relational features that was considered revolutionary by many. With this event, the conversion from the relational to the object-relational model in the database industry was confirmed. Most recently, IBM's **DB2 UDB**, which has had an excellent programming interface for object-relational programming for some time, has begun to incorporate the object-relational data model at the design and interactive layers. (See [2] in the "Suggestions for Further Reading" at the end of this preface.) Unfortunately, all of these products are quite different in syntax, and a portable application is still impossible: no meaningful standardization of object-relational SQL has occurred as yet. Thankfully, the ANSI SQL-3 effort, after an extremely long process of development, released a final version of its object-relational standard in 1999. This new standard is known as SQL-99 (see [3]).

There is a tremendous pedagogical challenge to introducing new students to a field that is fragmented between two distinct models of data representation. At the present time (2000), most commercial database applications use the pure relational model. This means that object-relational concepts will be confusing to many users unless the introduction of these concepts is carefully segregated from relational concepts. We have decided in our second edition to keep our first edition introduction to the relational model in Chapter 2, and to merely bring up to date the relational SQL presentation in Chapter 3. We then expand the object-relational coverage of Section 3.11 of our first edition to a rather long Chapter 4, where we introduce **ORACLE** and **INFORMIX** object-relational conventions. Because the two products are so different, we break each section of Chapter 4 into two parts, to introduce **ORACLE** and **INFORMIX** concepts in parallel. We do not give **DB2 UDB** object-relational syntax equal weight in the current edition because the **DB2** object-relational model was still in development at the time we wrote Chapter 4.

After a thorough introduction to object-relational concepts and product usage in Chapter 4, the following chapters remain basically independent of these concerns. There are a number of reasons for this. Some of the topics covered in later chapters, such as logical database design in Chapter 6, are not well understood for the object-relational model at the present time, and for other coverage, such as update transactions in Chapter 10, object-relational concepts (aside from the introduction to PL/SQL and SPL in Chapter 4) seem largely irrelevant. A practitioner who reads through Chapter 4 carefully will be able to use object-relational SQL to augment most of the coverage of the following chapters, and for those readers who do not yet deal with object-relational products, we didn't want to confuse later issues with terminology they might wish to avoid for now. Thus we see in Figure 1 that there is no follow-on dependency on Chapter 4: the concepts of that chapter stand alone. (Chapter 7 does have coverage of catalog tables for object-relational schema objects, but this can be skipped if desired.) It is likely that the next edition will deal with object-relational concepts in all chapters of the text because it will likely be used nearly universally, but we feel that the time for that has not yet arrived.

To write the second edition, a number of difficult decisions had to be made, the most difficult being the selection of the database products and product categories to be covered in this text. We have avoided OODBMS coverage because we had to leave something out, and the potential commercial growth in the OODBMS field, which has been heralded for so many years, has never materialized; OODBMS products remain a niche category. We also decided reluctantly against providing an introduction to the Microsoft

SQL Server product, in spite of the great interest it has engendered. We made this decision because our major thrust in the second edition has been to introduce the new object-relational product features, and SQL Server doesn't yet support these features. We also decided to discontinue coverage of **INGRES**, which was central to our first edition because it was the most common database product in college use. Many other popular database products are now offering inexpensive versions for the college market, and we have therefore dropped **INGRES** in the second edition.

A Chapter-by-Chapter Outline of Changes

We outline some of the new material that has been included for the first time in the current edition in the following chapter descriptions.

Chapter 1   Introduction. New discussion of the object-relational model.

Chapter 2   The Relational Model. Aside from clarifying details from the first edition, this chapter is essentially unchanged, in keeping with our decision to cover the relational model in Chapters 2 and 3 and putting off object-relational features until Chapter 4.

Chapter 3   Basic Query Language SQL. There are a number of new features added to SQL that are covered for the first time in the second edition. Section 3.6 introduces some "Advanced SQL Syntax" not supported by all database products. This includes the INTERSECT [ALL] and EXCEPT [ALL] operations, and the new *tableref* definition of Figure 3.11, which provides for new Join Forms such as [INNER |{LEFT | RIGHT | FULL} [OUTER]] Joins, and joins ON search conditions. Since no SQL standard has been uniformly adopted by the vendors, the second edition provides a general form we call "Basic SQL," which provides the set of features we found commonly adopted by all database products under consideration.

Chapter 4   Object-Relational SQL. This is an entirely new chapter, and we provide here an extended table of contents of the sections and subsections of the chapter. Once features of **ORACLE** and **INFORMIX** are covered, a side-by-side comparison of features ends each section.

    4.1   Introduction: Definitions and Object-Relational History

    4.2   Object types in **ORACLE**; row types in **INFORMIX**; use of object (row) types for table definitions; object nesting; dot notation to access columns; lack of encapsulation of object data; coverage of REFs in **ORACLE** but not in **INFORMIX**; type inheritance in **INFORMIX** but not in **ORACLE**.

4.3 Collection Types. **ORACLE** has two collection types: nested tables (a column value can be a table) and VARRAYs (array type column value). **INFORMIX** has three collection types: sets, multisets (unordered, like sets, with duplicates allowed), and lists (ordered). Both allow ad hoc queries to retrieve data from collections, and to insert and update collections.

4.4 User-Defined Functions (UDFs) and Methods. **ORACLE** has a procedural SQL language PL/SQL and **INFORMIX** has one called SPL. In both products, UDFs can be written in this procedural language (or an Embedded SQL language such as Java), which can be called like built-in functions within SQL. Methods are UDFs supported in **ORACLE** that are defined as part of an object type.

4.5 External Functions and Packaged User Defined Types (UDTs). We survey the database systems' capabilities of "packaging" user-defined types with a set of external functions, which are UDFs written in a language like C and made available to the database server. Such a package is called a Cartridge in **ORACLE**, a DataBlade in **INFORMIX**, and an Extender in **DB2 UDB**.

The following chapter numbers increment by one the chapter numbers of the first edition because of the addition of the new Chapter 4.

Chapter 5 Programs to Access a Database. More programming examples have been provided, in particular, on transactions. We have also improved the coverage of error handling. **ORACLE** syntax has been brought up to date, in particular the **ORACLE** Dynamic SQL syntax, including SQLSTATE. **DB2 UDB** is also covered now (replacing **INGRES** in the first edition).

Chapter 6 Database Design. This is logical database design, including the E-R model and normalization. A number of definitions and proofs have been clarified and illustrations added.

Chapter 7 Integrity, Views, Security, and Catalogs. A number of standard clauses of the Create Table and Alter Table statements have been brought up to date. The section on triggers has been rewritten with real examples from **ORACLE** and **DB2 UDB**. The restrictions on updatable views have been updated significantly, and there are no longer any restrictions on querying views. The section on system catalogs has been slightly expanded and now includes a subsection on object-relational catalog coverage.

Chapter 8 Indexing. Figures for disk access speed, disk capacity, disk cost, and memory cost have been updated. The **ORACLE** Create Tablespace statement has been

updated. All specialized **INGRES** indexing capabilities (ISAM, hashing, etc.)
have been dropped, and **ORACLE** index-organized tables and table clusters,
in particular hash clusters, are now covered. The discussion of overflow
chaining has been modified to deal with the new **ORACLE** hash clusters
architecture. **DB2 UDB** index structures are now covered.

Chapter 9   Query Processing. While the earlier parts of this chapter have been brought
up to date to deal with newer product features, at the insistence of a number
of reviewers, the coverage of the IBM mainframe **DB2** query features leading
up to Set Query benchmark results from the first edition have been retained.
Because most of these **DB2** query capabilities are still state-of-the-art, and
performance is explained at a level of detail that would be hard to duplicate
today, this material can still be used to teach students important concepts
about how queries perform. In fact, the coverage of the query processor is
still relevant to the current mainframe **DB2** product, **DB2 for OS/390**.

Chapter 10   A number of improvements have been made in definitions and proofs of this
chapter. In Section 10.5, the Levels of Isolation definitions have been modified to take into account newly discovered facts in [1].

Chapter 11   Very minor changes have been made.

Support on the World Wide Web

The home page for this book is http://www.mkp.com/books_catalog/1-55860-438-3.asp.
This page will link to the authors' Web site and will provide database create and load
scripts for several products, current errata for the text, example programs, and slides to
use in lectures. Instructors will also be able to obtain solutions to non-dotted exercises.
Electronic mail on suggestions, contributions of teaching materials, or errata should be
addressed to poneil@cs.umb.edu or eoneil@cs.umb.edu.

Acknowledgments

It is our pleasure to acknowledge the help of many people who gave suggestions and help
in producing this book. A number of students helped by pointing out errors in the first
edition text and notes for the second edition. The most prominent among these are
Christian Junghanss, Dimitrios Liarokapis, and Usha Rao. Several colleagues also provided valuable help for the second edition, including Michael Carey, Don Chamberlin,
Andrew Eisenberg, Jim Gray, Berl Hartman, Rick Martin, Jim Melton, Betty Salzberg,
Mike Ubell, and Gerhard Weikum, as well as numerous reviewers that read over drafts of
the manuscripts for Morgan Kaufmann. We received help during our work from **IBM**,
INFORMIX, and **ORACLE**. We are also grateful for past help from Henry Etlinger, Goetz

Graefe, Fred Korz, Edward Omiecinski, Eugene O'Neil, Julie Pabst, Bryan Pendleton, Donald Slutz, Bruce Spatz, David Spooner, Toby Teorey, Gottfried Vossen, and Yun Wang. We would also like to acknowledge the excellent work of the editors at Morgan Kaufmann—Diane Cerra, Belinda Breyer, Cheri Palmer, and others.

Patrick O'Neil and Elizabeth O'Neil
University of Massachusetts at Boston
poneil@cs.umb.edu, eoneil@cs.umb.edu

Suggestions for Further Reading

[1] Hal Berenson, Phil Bernstein, Jim Gray, Jim Melton, Elizabeth O'Neil, and Patrick O'Neil. "A Critique of ANSI SQL Isolation Levels." *ACM SIGMOD Proceedings*, May 1995, pp. 1–10.

[2] Michael Carey, Don Chamberlin, et al. "O-O, What Have They Done to DB2?" *Proceedings of the 1999 VLDB Conference.*

[3] Andrew Eisenberg and Jim Melton. "SQL:1999, formerly known as SQL3." *SIGMOD Record*, vol. 28, no. 1, March 1999, pp. 131–138.

Introduction

In the beginning was information.
—Translation of the first sentence of the Christian Bible in the Book of John 1:1, by J. Peters, 1967

This chapter introduces the central ideas and definitions covered in the text. We describe basic database concepts and profile the typical database users. Then we give an overview of the concepts and features we cover about database management systems.

1.1 Fundamental Database Concepts

A *database management system*—or, simply, a *database system* or a *DBMS*—is a program product for keeping computerized records about an enterprise. For example, a wholesale business would normally use a DBMS to keep records about its sales (the *operational data* of the business), and a university would use a DBMS to keep student records (tuition payments, grade transcripts, and so on). Most large libraries use a database system to keep track of library inventory and loans, and to provide various types of indexing to material by subject, author, and title. All airlines use database systems to manage their flights and reservations, and state motor vehicle departments use them for drivers' licenses and car registrations. Tower Records has a database system to keep track of its stock, as well as all records and CDs in print, and to provide a query facility to customers searching for specific recordings. The collection of records kept for a common purpose such as these is known as a *database*. The records of the database normally reside on *disk* (a slow access medium where information will persist through power outages), and the records are normally retrieved from disk into computer memory only when they are accessed.

A DBMS may deal with more than one database at a time. For example, a university might maintain one database for enrolled students and a second database to keep track of the books in its library. The library database contains no records in common with the student records database (although there might be some duplication of information, since some library borrowers are also students), but both databases can be accessed, by different users, through the same DBMS.

History of Database Systems

A number of different approaches have been developed for structuring access to information in a database. Historically, two early products provided what were later recognized as distinct *data models* for structuring information: IBM's IMS (Information Management System), released in 1968, and Cullinet Software's IDMS, released in the early 1970s. IMS provided what came to be known as the *hierarchical data model*, where different kinds of records relate to one another in a hierarchical form. For example, a database for a bank might place a corporate entity record at the top, with information such as the corporate headquarters' address and telephone number; below that the bank might place records for the banking branches; and below that records for tellers and other employees at each branch. To process information about a particular teller, a program would normally navigate down through the appropriate hierarchical layers. The IDMS product, on the other hand, was conceived as a result of the 1971 CODASYL report of an industry database task group and provided what came to be known as the *network data model*, a generalization of the hierarchical model where a set of records in one layer might have two different containing hierarchies at the next layer up.

Naturally both the IMS and IDMS products had a variety of features that we are not mentioning. To oversimplify somewhat, the hierarchical model structured data as a directed tree, with a root at the top and leaves at the bottom, while the network model structured data as a directed graph without circuits, a slight generalization that allowed the network model to represent certain real-world data structures more easily. The main drawback with these products was that queries against the data were difficult to pose and execute, normally requiring a program written by an expert programmer who understood what could be a complex navigational structure of the data. Both products are still in use at a large number of companies, and IMS in particular is still an important source of revenue for IBM. However, the IMS and IDMS products that are running in most companies today are what are called *legacy systems*. It is very difficult to switch from a legacy system to a more modern data model, and the original system might be perfectly adequate to do its job. But any company planning to install a new system would choose a DBMS with a more modern kind of data model.

The Relational and Object-Relational Models

By far the most commonly used data model for database system products purchased over the last 18 years or so is the *relational model*, which provides a flexible capability to allow non-programmers to pose general queries quickly and easily. A DBMS that utilizes the relational model is known as a *relational DBMS*, or *RDBMS*. Over the last few years, an even newer data model, known as the *object-relational model*, has been replacing the relational model in many products. A DBMS that utilizes the object-relational model is referred to as an *ORDBMS* product. Since the object-relational model is actually an evolutionary extension of the relational model, a product that falls in the ORDBMS category will also support relational data from its earlier RDBMS incarnation. Some writers therefore refer to such a product as an *RDBMS/ORDBMS* type, and when we do not wish to distinguish we will simply continue to refer to it as a DBMS.

In this book we will study a body of concepts and techniques that has been developed to create, maintain, and use a database within a DBMS system. The techniques covered are surprisingly general in application, although there is a strong distinction drawn between RDBMS and ORDBMS features. Since the RDBMS data model is still the one that is most generally used, we segregate the object-relational concepts in a separate chapter (Chapter 4) and cover relational concepts almost exclusively in the rest of the text. Most new concepts of both models are illustrated with detailed commands from a number of different commercial DBMS products and standards. While the command syntax for the more complex ORDBMS features will change from one product to another, many of the basic RDBMS capabilities provided by any one DBMS are shared by the others.

The Database Systems Covered

The commercial database systems covered in this book, in order of extent of coverage, are

◆ ORACLE Server, denoted **ORACLE**. Runs on almost all UNIX systems, plus Windows NT and some older operating systems. See www.oracle.com.

◆ DB2 Universal Database, denoted **DB2 UDB**. Runs on most UNIX systems, plus Windows NT, OS/2, and OS/390. See www.ibm.com/db2.

◆ Informix Dynamic Server 2000, denoted **INFORMIX**. Runs on most UNIX systems, plus Windows NT. See www.informix.com.

◆ DB2 for OS/390, the original IBM mainframe DB2, denoted **DB2**. Runs on OS/390. See www.ibm.com/db2.

A Relational Database Example

To begin to illustrate some fundamental concepts, Figure 1.1a shows an example of a relational database representing student enrollment *records* in a university. The database is quite small for simplicity of illustration. A more realistic university enrollment database would contain tens of thousands of records, with many more *fields* in each record.

In a relational database, all information is represented in the form of named *tables* with labeled *columns*. For example, the students table of Figure 1.1a has the following column names: sid, which is a unique student ID number; lname and fname, which are the last name and first name of the student; class is the student year, 1 for freshman through 4 for senior; and telephone is the student's home telephone number. In a full-size database, there would be more columns for student address, tuition status, GPA, and

4

students

sid	lname	fname	class	telephone
1	Jones	Allan	2	555-1234
2	Smith	John	3	555-4321
3	Brown	Harry	2	555-1122
5	White	Edward	3	555-3344

enrollment

sid	cno	major
1	101	No
1	108	Yes
2	105	No
3	101	Yes
3	108	No
5	102	No
5	105	No

courses

cno	cname	croom	time
101	French I	2-104	MW2
102	French II	2-113	MW3
105	Algebra	3-105	MW2
108	Calculus	2-113	MW4

Figure 1.1a   Relational Student Enrollment Database

so on. The student records in this table are the individual rows of the students table—for example, the first row (just below the column names) represents a student named Allan Jones in the sophomore year, whose student ID is 1 and home telephone number is 555-1234. A table can be roughly pictured as a disk file of records (one record to a row), although many database theorists stress important differences between a table and a disk file. For intuitive presentation we use the following terms interchangeably: disk file and table, rows and records, columns and fields.

The courses table in Figure 1.1a lists the set of courses offered, with course number given by cno, course name by cname, the room where the course meets by croom, and the days and period it meets by time. The time column values are encoded: for example, MW2 means Monday and Wednesday during period 2. The enrollment table has only three columns: each row of the table pairs up a student with given student ID, sid, and a course that the student is taking, represented by cno, together with whether (Yes or No) the course is in the student major, major. For example, student 1 has a declared major in mathematics and student 3 has a major in modern languages. The three tables of Figure 1.1a together represent a relational database. Note that we use lowercase names (in monofont type) for tables and column names, but many other texts use uppercase names.

A number of other concepts governing the tabular representation of data in the relational model will be covered starting in Chapter 2, but we mention one concept now, known as the *first normal form rule*: in the relational model, a column of a table must contain a single, unstructured value. The unstructured value constraint implies, for example, that we cannot place both the last name and first name as separate values that can be separately set and retrieved in a single column: that is, we cannot create a column that looks like a C struct or Java class (e.g., a name column with parts name.lname and name.fname). Of course, we could create a name column that would contain a single character string value that concatenates two name parts with some kind of separator, such as "Allan.Jones", but that isn't the same thing. The part of the rule requiring a column to contain a *single* value constrains us in a different way: we can't, for example, create an enrollment column in the students table, so that each student row contains a *set* of (cno, major) pairs for courses taken by the student, obviating the need for the enrollment table. For an example of what such a column would look like, see Figure 1.1b, which depicts a student enrollment database as it could appear in an object-relational database system.

An Object-Relational Database Example

In an object-relational database, information is still represented as in the relational model in the form of named tables with labeled columns, but the column values are no longer restricted by the first normal form rule. We see an example of an object-relational database equivalent to the relational database of Figure 1.1a in Figure 1.1b. The relational model is sometimes described as being a "fill-in-the-form, one-fact-in-one place" model. In the object-relational model, we drop the "one-fact-in-one-place" limitation.

students

sid	name		class	telephone	enrollment	
	lname	fname			cno	major
1	Jones	Allan	2	555-1234	101	No
					108	Yes
2	Smith	John	3	555-4321	105	No
3	Brown	Harry	2	555-1122	101	Yes
					108	No
4	White	Edward	3	555-3344	102	No
					105	No

courses

cno	cname	croom	time
101	French I	2-104	MW2
102	French II	2-113	MW3
105	Algebra	3-105	MW2
108	Calculus	2-113	MW4

Figure 1.1b Object-Relational Student Enrollment Database

In Figure 1.1b, the column called name in the students table has a new kind of structured type to contain components that can be separately set and retrieved: name.lname and name.fname, both of them appearing as components under the upper-level name column. Object-relational database systems have not yet adopted a common standard, so the various products we study each support different features and nomenclature for their object-relational tables. In **ORACLE** a structured type for the name column is called an *object type,* in **INFORMIX** it is called a *row type,* and in **DB2 UDB** (and the new standard, ANSI SQL-99) it is called a *user-defined type,* or *UDT.*

The enrollment column of Figure 1.1b associates a *collection* of row type values with each row in the students table. Thus by looking at the row for student 1, Allan Jones, it is clear that Jones is taking two courses: course 101, which is not in Jones's major field, and course 108, which is. Once again, because of the lack of a standard, the enrollment column type that allows sets of structured values has different names in the different products we study. In the SQL-99 standard, such a column type is called a *collection type.* Because the enrollment column in the students table now contains all the information that was contained in the enrollment table in Figure 1.1a, there is no enrollment table needed in Figure 1.1b.

1.2 Database Users

One of the most important features of a DBMS is that relatively inexperienced users, called *end users,* are empowered to retrieve information from the database. The user poses a *query* at the keyboard, requesting the database system to display the answer on a monitor screen or on a printed sheet. At Tower Records, for example, the customers attempt to locate desired recordings through a sequence of menu interaction queries. As a result of these queries, lists of recordings appear on a monitor screen. A paper list can be printed to help the customers locate the items in the store.

This easy accessibility to data requires a good deal of work by specialists before end users can pose their queries. Unlike some other program products, a database system is not ready for use as soon as it is operational on the computer platform. The database of interest must still be designed and loaded (and later kept up-to-date), then application programs must be written to provide a simple menu interface to inexperienced end users. The specialists who perform these tasks can also be thought of as *users* of the database system. The idea of *user friendliness* in a relational database management system must be conditioned by the understanding that there are several types of users. The specialist users are responsible for providing an environment in which higher-level users can work, and each type of user has demands for ease of use. Here is a list of common terms describing the different types of users, followed by a description of each user type.

◆ End users—Interactive users
   Casual users—Users accessing the DBMS with SQL queries
   Naive users—Users accessing the DBMS through menus

◆ Application programmers—Programmers who write menu applications

◆ Database administrators—Specialists who supervise the DBMS

End users. A *casual user* is expected to have some facility with the *SQL* language, the standard query language for relational database systems. Facility with SQL is not a trivial skill, as we shall see in later sections. The term *casual* as used here implies that the user has changing requirements from one session to the next, so that it is not economical to try to write a menu-based program application for each such (casual) use. Queries that are formulated on the spot to answer some immediate need are known as *interactive queries* or *ad hoc queries*. (Ad hoc is a Latin term, meaning roughly "for this specific purpose.") A *naive user* is one who performs all database applications through menu applications and thus avoids having to construct queries in SQL syntax. Bank clerks and airline reservation specialists use such applications to perform their duties, but the term *naive* is perhaps misleading. Even database system implementors, perfectly capable of constructing SQL queries at need, would use menu applications to retrieve (say) bug report records fitting various criteria while performing program maintenance. The mental effort required to keep track of all the tables and column names and to write valid SQL query syntax introduces inappropriate complexity that detracts from a specialist's concentration on the real work to be performed.

Application programmers. An *application programmer,* in the sense used with database management systems, writes the menu applications used by naive users. The programs must foresee the needs of the users and be able to pose SQL queries during execution to retrieve desired information from the database. Note that programmers are experienced at dealing with complex concepts and difficult problems of syntax—it is appropriate for the application programmer to spend long periods deriving the correct query syntax to answer some question that might be posed by a naive user. In addition to saving the user effort, the programs provide more confidence that there is no subtle mistake in the query that might make it give the wrong answer. As we will see, the more complex SQL queries are difficult to construct in an ad hoc fashion without some risk of error.

Database administrators. The final type of DBMS user listed is known as a *database administrator,* or *DBA*. A DBA is a computer professional responsible for the design and maintenance of the database. Typically the DBA decides how the data will be broken down into tables, creates the database, loads the tables, and performs a large number of behind-the-scenes tasks to implement various policies about data access and update. These policies include areas such as security (e.g., which users are empowered to access what data) and integrity constraints (e.g., a savings account balance should not be allowed to fall below $0.00). In addition, the DBA is responsible for the physical layout of the database on secondary storage (disk) and the index structures to achieve best performance.

In this book, our goal is to give a basic grounding in the skills necessary to be a sophisticated casual user, a good application programmer, or a DBA. A sophisticated end user of SQL does not need to know how to write programs but can benefit from many of the other topics covered in this text. A lead application programmer should understand all the skills required by the DBA in order to plan efficient programs and to give the feedback that the DBA needs to provide appropriate tuning. The topics that make up the duties of a database administrator are the most all-embracing and form the subjects of most of the chapters that follow. The DBA deals with some of the most advanced features of a DBMS and must be fully conversant with the needs of other users on the scene, ideally having the ability to follow the technical details of application programs. The decisions made by the DBA will affect these programs in many ways, including the forms of SQL statements and program performance.

Note that another type of specialist is associated with databases, known as a *database system implementor*. This is a systems programmer who writes the programs that perform the internal work by which a DBMS provides its features. Some of the more advanced database textbooks concentrate on concepts of database internals. Because the database field is a large one, this text concentrates on understanding how a database system is used, a crucial goal before embarking on the task of implementing a system. In any event, a good database administrator understands the workings of the DBMS at quite a deep level of detail. As we shall see, such detail is sometimes necessary to properly tune system performance.

1.3 Overview of Relational and Object-Relational DBMS

Up until now, we have discussed only one major feature of an RDBMS—the ability to pose queries to retrieve information from a database. Many other features are commonly supplied, some of them sufficiently specialized that it is difficult to appreciate their value without first having had a certain amount of experience in use. Nevertheless we attempt to give some idea of these features and their significance. In this way, the details to come will be more easily placed in a global context.

In the sections that follow, we provide a short explanation of topics in the order that they are presented in the text. This is a good time to note that some of the smaller and less expensive database management systems provided for personal computers will not have all of the features outlined below. For example, the concerns that arise in multi-user systems are often of no interest on a PC database system that is meant to be accessed by only a single user.

Chapter 2: The Relational Model

Starting in Chapter 2, we cover several concepts and rules of the relational model that have governed the representation of data for a number of years. A rather careful definition is useful, to make it clear what features a user can expect and when a commercial product is offering a feature that is not a standard part of the model. As we have already mentioned, there is a rule that a value of a table cannot be multi-valued. Thus a hobby column in the students table cannot have several values (chess, hiking, skeet shooting) on the same row of the table. Such a multi-valued column was offered in some earlier data models, a feature known as *repeating fields*, but it is forbidden in relational tables. As we have already indicated, multi-valued columns are allowed again in the object-relational model, which seems to be the next evolutionary step. Relational rules served an important purpose of standardizing the various product offerings in the early days of the relational model, so that issues of database design were the same in all cases. Even so, as we will see, certain rules were frequently broken even in the relational model, without grave harm (although the first normal form rule was never broken prior to acceptance of the new object-relational model).

Following this, we characterize the relational model from a different aspect, the standard query power inherent in the *relational algebra*. This algebra consists of a set of operations performed on tables to produce other tables (much as multiplication or addition of real numbers produces other real numbers). The concepts of relational algebra are valuable in later chapters, since answers to many database queries can be represented as relational algebra expressions—query answers always have table form in the relational model. Relational algebra is not available to answer computerized queries on commercial DBMS products, which provide the SQL language for that purpose. However, the relational algebra has a virtue when compared with relational SQL. It has only a small number of operations, and they are extremely simple to describe and transparent in their effect. All operations of relational algebra must be possible in any acceptable query language such as SQL, and a study of the algebraic operations is thought to be valuable because it offers important insights in a much simpler form than SQL. Unfortunately, no analogous *object-relational algebra* is currently known.

Chapter 3: Basic SQL Query Language

In Chapter 3, the industry standard relational query language, SQL, is covered in a good deal of depth. Since the industry standard SQL, Core SQL-99, is not uniformly adopted by all database products, we provide something we call a Basic SQL syntax for features that have been adopted by all major relational products and an Advanced SQL syntax for features that are not yet generally adopted. We defer until Chapter 4 features that relate to the object-relational model. All syntax in Chapter 3 relates only to relational capabilities. An example of a relational SQL query posed on the student records database of Figure 1.1a, together with the tabular form of the answer retrieved, is given in Figure 1.2.

It is easy to validate the answer in Figure 1.2 by looking at the students table in Figure 1.1a and checking the names and student IDs of rows with class equal to 2. Figure 1.3 shows a somewhat more complex query.

Looking at Figure 1.1a, it should be clear that we need information from both the students and enrollment tables to answer the query of Figure 1.3. If we look at students alone, we don't know what courses students take, and if we look at enrollment alone, we don't know student names. We can look at the enrollment table and note the sid values matched with cno 101, then look up the names for these sid values in the students table. The SQL statement in Figure 1.3 reflects this approach.

Retrieve the sid and lname for all sophomores.

```
SQL: select sid, lname from students
     where class = 2;
```

answer

sid	lname
1	Jones
3	Brown

Figure 1.2   An SQL Query on the Student Records Database

Retrieve the sid and lname of students taking course number 101.

```
SQL: select students.sid, lname from students, enrollment
     where students.sid = enrollment.sid
     and enrollment.cno = 101;
```

answer

sid	lname
1	Jones
3	Brown

Figure 1.3   A Second SQL Query on the Student Records Database

The fact that the answers to the two queries of Figure 1.2 and 1.3 are identical does not, of course, imply that the two queries have the same meaning. There is no reason to believe that the set of students taking French 1 (course number 101) is always identical with the set of sophomores (class = 2) in the school. Rather we see it as an accident that these two queries happen to have the same answer for the current term—the answers would very likely be different for the two queries with a different enrollment table of a new term. This illustrates an important concept: the columns of a table are designed by the person creating the database and are expected to be stable over time, whereas the rows of the table, which correspond to the data records held in the table, are expected to change without warning. Two query forms represent the same concept only if they can be shown to have the same result for *all possible* row contents of the tables involved.

The SQL language also contains statements to insert new rows into a table, delete existing rows from a table, and update some column values of existing rows in a table (see Figure 1.4). It is perhaps inaccurate to refer to the SQL language as simply a *query language*, and to refer to SQL statements as *queries* when they are really Update, Insert, and Delete statements, but it is commonly accepted to use this broad meaning for the term "query." (Some authors try to be more accurate by referring to SQL as a *data manipulation language*, or simply as a *database language*.) Another common practice is

```
Insert the row (6, Green, John, 1, 555-1133) into the students table.

    SQL: insert into students values (6, Green, John, 1, 555-1133);

Delete all junior class members from students.

    SQL: delete from students where class = 3;

Change room number 2-113 to 2-121 where it appears in courses.

    SQL: update courses set croom = '2-121' where croom = '2-113';
```

Figure 1.4   SQL Statements to Delete, Insert, and Update

to group SQL Update, Insert, and Delete statements under the single term, *update statements*. We will follow these rather loose conventions, becoming more specific only when a distinction is important.

Chapter 4: The Object-Relational Model

In Chapter 4, we introduce the features of the object-relational model in detail, starting with the new user-defined types to allow us to create tables such as students in Figure 1.1b, with columns having structured values and collection values. The SQL language we covered in Chapter 3 requires a number of syntax extensions to retrieve data from such tables, and we refer to the object-relationally extended SQL as ORSQL. Unfortunately, the different products we study, **ORACLE**, **INFORMIX**, and **DB2 UDB**, each have different syntax for these extensions, so we need to cover the first two of the products in separate sections. Since the industry SQL standard, SQL-99, only fixed on syntax features when it was released in 1999 after several years of uncertainty, we can hope that the disparate ORSQL dialects of the different products will eventually converge on this standard. But clearly things are changing fast for a textbook such as ours, which tries to cover commercial syntax, and you are advised to connect to our text homepage for the latest developments, http://www.cs.umb.edu/~poneil/dbppp.html.

Not surprisingly, queries against object-relational tables such as Figure 1.1b that involve only columns as they would appear in a relational table, are unchanged from Chapter 3. For example, the relational query of Figure 1.2 will work in ORSQL as well, with only one change, namely, replacing lname with name.lname, since the last name is now part of the name column rather than being a column on its own. However, the query of Figure 1.3, which involves a join in relational SQL with the enrollment table of Figure 1.1a, which becomes a column in the object-relational students table, changes significantly, as we see in Figure 1.5.

In Figure 1.5, the Select clause in parentheses assembles all the cno's for one student into a set of rows, using the enrollment collection for that student. The where 101 in then checks if 101 is in the student's cno set, and if so, returns TRUE to the top Select, allowing this student's sid and name.lname to be printed out.

Retrieve the `sid` and `lname` of students taking course number 101.

```
SQL: select sid, name.lname from students
     where 101 in
       (select cno from table(students.enrollment));
```

answer

sid	name.lname
1	Jones
3	Brown

Figure 1.5   An ORSQL Query on the Student Records Database

Insert the row for John Green into the `students` table.

```
SQL: insert into students values
     (6, Green, John, 1, 555-1133, set(row(101,'No'),row(108,'Yes')));
```

Delete all students who are enrolled only in class 101, outside their major.

```
SQL: delete from students where students.enrollment = set(row(101,'No'));
```

Change the enrollment for student 1 to class 105, outside of major, and 107, in major.

```
SQL: update students set enrollment = set(row(105,'No'),row(107,'Yes'))
         where sid = 1;
```

Figure 1.6   ORSQL Statements to Delete, Insert, and Update

The ORSQL similarly generalizes Insert, Delete, and Update. See the examples in Figure 1.6. These simple examples treat the collection as a whole. It is also possible to scan through the collection and make changes to individual rows.

In the final few sections of Chapter 4, we learn how to increase the power of object-relational SQL by writing arbitrarily complex user-defined functions, UDFs, that can be used in non-procedural SQL statements to perform any programmatic action desired.

Chapter 5: Programs to Access a Database

In our examples of SQL queries outside of the last section of Chapter 4, we have concentrated on the situation where a user interactively types an SQL query into the database system (a query interface), and then the system prints the resulting answer table to the user's monitor screen. This is indeed one approach for queries to be answered, but it is not the only one. As we discuss in Chapter 5, most queries, in fact, are posed through an application program interface. Here an application programmer writes a program in some higher-level language such as C or Java or sometimes a special type of *procedural SQL language* provided with the DBMS. When the program is executed, it interacts with a monitor user (there may be many users executing the program simultaneously), usually

```
Library Database Selector Menu
   Author last name: Asimov
   Author first name: Isaac
   Title:
   Subject: robotics
```

Figure 1.7   An Example of a Menu Interaction for Database Lookup

by displaying a menu form. The user performs some menu selections, after which the program may respond by performing one or more SQL queries to execute tasks posed by the menu selection. All activity is controlled by the monitor user through selections from one displayed form or another—at no time does the monitor user actually construct an SQL query. We give an example of such a menu interaction in Figure 1.7.

In this figure, the user is trying to locate all books written by the author Isaac Asimov on the subject of robotics. For ease of use, various wildcard characters provided by the SQL language might also be used. For example "Asim%" might retrieve either "Asimov" or "Asimoff" if the user is unsure of the spelling. The keyword choice in the **Subject** category might be provided as a list in alphabetical order. This means extra work for the application, but how else would the user know whether to use "robotics" or "robot" or "robots"?

Note a crucial point here: an SQL query (or other type of SQL statement) can be written to execute inside a program. However, an SQL query is not a valid statement in most types of higher-level language such as C or Java, so a special form is used (in the C program of Figure 1.8 an initial code phrase exec sql) to designate such SQL statements. The program is then run through a preprocessor, where these special forms are turned into valid calls to C functions in the database function library, and after this the C compiler produces a working program.

The practice of placing SQL statements inside a higher-level language program is known as *Embedded SQL programming*. Anyone who has created programs to write C structs to a disk file and then retrieve them again must be extremely struck by how much simpler this becomes with SQL. In particular, Embedded SQL makes it relatively easy to perform one of the most difficult tasks programmers encounter: to look up information in a file following retrieval prescriptions that users find easy and flexible to pose. As we will see, the DBMS uses a number of disk-based data structures to make access to the data efficient, but the program logic can remain unaware of this, referencing only the structure of the tables and the column values they contain. It is also not necessary for the program logic to keep track of modes of access, positions in files, record structure, and so on. All of this detail is handled by the DBMS, a feature known as *program-data independence*. The value of program-data independence becomes particularly apparent as changes in table structure occur with the passage of time. Columns may be added to some tables, the number of rows in a table may grow to a point that it no longer fits on a single disk and must be split over several disks, and such growth can entail the need for new data structures to

```
exec sql begin declare sections;        /* C variables known to SQL      */
    char lname[18];                     /* author last name variable     */
    char fname[14];                     /* author first name variable    */
    char title[20];                     /* book title variable           */
    char subject[24];                   /* book subject variable         */
exec sql end declare section;

exec sql declare c1 cursor for          /* define cursor for query       */
    select alname, afname, title, subject from library
        where alname = :lnamev and afname = :fnamev
        and title = :title and subject = :subject;

menu(lname,fname,title, subject);       /* function to display menu      */
exec sql open c1;                       /* begin query, start cursor     */
exec sql whenever not found goto alldone; /* set up for loop termination  */
while (TRUE) {                          /* row by row printout           */
    exec sql fetch c1 into :lname,:fname,:title,:subject; /* get row values */
    displayrow(lname,fname,title,subject); /* print them out             */
}
alldone:                                /* reached when loop is done     */
```

Figure 1.8 A (Simplified) Program Fragment for Database Access

speed access to rows by some column values (comparable to looking up library books through a card catalog). None of this needs to affect application program logic on a properly designed database. In fact, the property of program-data independence is important enough that we offer the only formal definition of this overview.

DEFINITION 1.3.1 *Program-data independence* is a feature of a properly constructed database that makes application logic immune to changes in storage structure and access methods. ∎

Chapter 6: Database Design

A DBA deals with a database in every aspect of its creation and subsequent life. To begin with, it is the function of the DBA to make an in-depth study of the enterprise to be represented in a relational database. The DBA studies basic properties and inter-relationships among data objects in the real world that are part of the enterprise to be modeled. The aim is to provide a faithful representation of such objects as columns in relational tables. As part of this representation, the DBA creates rules, known as *integrity constraints*, that limit possible updates that can be performed on the data. This early phase of DBA responsibility is known as *logical database design,* or simply *database design.* Database design is an extremely complex field of study, in that it requires the DBA to recognize many different types of data relationships that reflect reality, an almost philosophical approach to taxonomy of data classes with an intensely practical aim. We

study two basic design approaches in this text. One is based on intuitive recognition of
certain real-world data classifications and is known as the *entity-relationship model,* or
the *E-R model.* The second approach, which complements the first, is known as *database
normalization.* These design approaches are covered in detail in Chapter 6.

Analyzing a large enterprise such as a university, we identify numerous pieces of data
that must be represented as column names in tables. We clearly need some guiding principle to decide how these column names might be related, when they should be placed
together in the same table, and when they should be placed in distinct tables. This is the
basic problem of logical design. To begin, we try to distinguish objects known as *entities.*
An *entity,* sometimes referred to as an *entity set* or an *entity type,* is a class of objects that
really exist and are distinguishable among themselves. As an example, we consider the set
of students at the university and name this entity Students. Associated with each entity
is a set of *attributes* that describe and distinguish the objects. In Figure 1.1a we materialized the Students entity as a relational table (which we named students), containing a
group of column names (attributes) that describe a student: sid, lname, fname, class,
and telephone. A second differentiable class of objects that clearly must be kept track of
in a university is the Courses entity, and Figure 1.1a contains a courses table, with
attributes describing individual courses: cno, cname, croom, and time.

The third table, enrollment, that appears in Figure 1.1a does not represent an
entity, but rather a *relationship* between entities, named as a verb form, enrolls_in, in
the entity-relationship diagram of Figure 1.9. Each student takes a number of courses,
and conversely each course contains some number of students. In the E-R diagram of Figure 1.9, an entity is represented as a rectangle, an attribute by an oval, and a relationship
between entity sets as a diamond. Lines connect entities with their associated attributes
and relationships with the entities to which they relate.

The entity-relationship viewpoint allows a designer to make sense of the collection
of data items encountered in designing a new database for a large enterprise. As each
entity is identified, it becomes clear that a number of data items are simply attributes
describing this entity. Thus a relational table and a number of columns are identified. As
the DBA studies this entity further, additional attributes to model the enterprise may be
identified that had not been obvious before. Designing tables associated with relationships is somewhat more complex, since relationships have a number of important properties that are outside the scope of this overview. It turns out that some relationships do

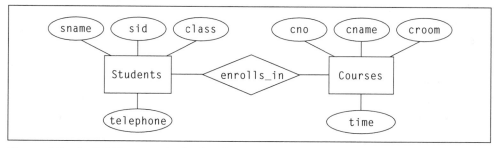

Figure 1.9 An E-R Diagram of a Student Records Database

not translate into tables of their own but are represented rather as columns known as "foreign keys" in entity tables. There are many details of logical design from an E-R viewpoint that we put off until Chapter 6.

Chapter 7: Integrity, Views, Security, and Catalogs

After the DBA has performed the logical design of a database, there are a number of physical actions required to translate the design into a computerized representation that users can access. Below we explain a number of SQL commands and other database utilities used by the DBA to create database tables, then to load the tables with data contained in operating system input files, and finally to maintain the database under changing conditions. Most aspects of these commands are quite straightforward. You are expected to master a simple version of the Create Table command at an early stage, preparatory to performing SQL queries. However, the tables created at this early stage are quite simple default forms, without any of the properties introduced in later chapters, such as integrity constraints, data views, security restrictions, and index structures to facilitate high performance access. In the following paragraphs we give a short description of the values of some of these properties. They are detailed further in Chapter 7.

Integrity Constraints

As part of the process of logical design, the DBA has identified a number of *integrity constraints* on the data. These are rules that are considered important for the database to obey at all times. For example, there might be a rule that every row of the courses table has a unique cno value (the same course number cannot be used by two different courses). Other examples are that the sid column in the enrollment table must reference a real sid on some row of the students table (what we call a referential integrity constraint), or that the balance column in a row of a savings_accounts table cannot fall below $25.00 (minimum account balance). It is clear that, if these integrity constraints originally hold for a table, then the only way they can later fail is as a result of some SQL Update statement—for example, an SQL statement that inserts a new row into the courses table with a duplicate cno value.

If we make an agreement that ad hoc SQL updates to the data are not permitted, then we could presumably guarantee all these integrity rules by careful enforcement of guidelines within our application program logic (". . . the programmer should always check that cno is not duplicated before inserting a new courses row . . ."). However, leaving the enforcement to the programmer is *not* the approach that is taken by relational database management systems. Instead, the constraints are created as distinct entities by the DBA, and they are thereafter enforced automatically by the DBMS, so that it is actually impossible for any constraint to be unwittingly broken. This has the advantage that even ad hoc updates or bad application logic created by an inexperienced programmer cannot harm the validity of the data. In Figure 1.10, an example is given of the syntax used to impose an integrity constraint in the SQL dialect of the **ORACLE** database product.

Add an integrity constraint to the `students` table to assure that the `class` column always has a value between 1 and 4, inclusive. Note that this is an SQL statement valid on the **ORACLE** database product.

```
SQL: alter table students modify
     (class smallint check(class >= 1 and class <= 4));
```

Figure 1.10 A Command to Create a New Integrity Constraint in **ORACLE**

Centralized Control of Data and Database Security

It is important to realize that the decision to place information in two different databases has a significant effect: a query cannot retrieve data from two databases at once. Consider, for example, the separate student records database and university library database mentioned earlier. If a student is holding an overdue book, the program that prints a reminder letter and mailing label for the library cannot make use of the student address kept in the student records database. This means that the university library database must keep *its own copy* of the student address. This is known as *data redundancy* (duplication of data—possibly unnecessarily). It is not a very good alternative, since it is easy for the library version of the student address to become out of date, even while the registrar's version in the student records database is methodically updated. To put it another way, there are ways of keeping addresses up-to-date by requesting change of address information from the post office with relatively frequent mailings and having a clerk maintain records based on these corrections. Given that this expense has been entailed by the registrar's office, it seems a shame that the library has to forgo this information or else duplicate the expense, simply because it has structured its tables in a separate database.

This discussion points out the advantages to be gained in asking a DBA to combine databases with related information, imposing *centralized control of data* to reduce data redundancy, a well-known database principle. But it would seem that there are some disadvantages to centralization as well. For example, we might not want our student librarians to be able to update (or even view) some of the student record fields involving grades, fee payments, and personal health history. The DBA can guarantee such constraints with a set of *security* commands, using security in conjunction with the ability to create views on the data. Security commands act in the same way as integrity constraints, in that they are enforced automatically by the DBMS at a low level. They make it impossible for certain tables or fields within tables to be accessed or updated by any SQL statement performed on behalf of a user, *unless that user is explicitly given permission by the DBA*. Security is standardized in SQL with the Grant statement, available on almost all relational database products. The Grant statement has well-developed and flexible features. For example, it is possible to deny update access to a table by a certain group of users while permitting read access. An example of the syntax used to impose an integrity constraint in standard SQL is provided in Figure 1.11.

Grant permission to select, update, or insert, but not to delete, rows on the
students table to user poneil.

    SQL: grant select, update, insert on students to poneil;

Figure 1.11   The Standard SQL Grant Statement

Database Views

A less obvious problem that arises from centralized control is the logical complexity associated with combining databases with related information. As a result of this, a simple application to validate insurance payments for university students may have to deal with dozens of tables to access needed column information; furthermore, many of these tables may have names and uses completely unrelated to health insurance. Thus it can become quite difficult to train new application programmers to navigate among the many tables of a combined database. It should also be clear that it is often impossible in a large organization to combine all related databases from the beginning—we must allow for phased implementation, where the benefits of centralization accrue in a number of steps as new databases are combined. This raises the specter of having to rewrite old applications as newer tables appear, with new columns that must be accessed in place of older columns, to eliminate data redundancy. Ideally we would like some way to assure that growing numbers of tables do not cause a training problem and also that old application code does not have to change as old tables are rearranged to eliminate redundant data.

Surprisingly, both of these problems are addressed by a single DBMS feature known as *database views*. A view command allows us to create an imaginary, or virtual, *view table*, which contains rows defined by an SQL Select statement in terms of other tables. Some of these other tables may also be views, but all rows in a view table are ultimately based on *base tables* that actually exist as files on disk. In Figure 1.12, we provide an example of the standard SQL syntax used to create a view table.

The tremendous power of views comes from the fact that (theoretically) all SQL Select statements can access a view table as if it were real. Thus the DBA can combine the fields from several (new) tables into a virtual copy of an (old) table that is frequently accessed by existing application code. The view approach also allows the DBA to simplify the database environment for training purposes, creating a view with only that aspect of the total database that is relevant to a particular application mission. Views can also be used to make security seamless, so that the user is actually unaware of fields and

Create a view table, called studentcourses, that lists student names and sid
values with course names and cno values for courses in which they are enrolled.

    SQL: create view studentcourses (lname, sid, cname, cno)
        as select s.lname, s.sid, c.cname, c.cno
        from students s, courses c, enrollment e
        where e.cno = c.cno and e.sid = s.sid;

Figure 1.12   The Standard SQL Command to Create a View Table

tables that he or she is not authorized to access. Clearly the concept of a view extends the
concept of program-data independence, in that not only is application logic immune to
changes in *physical* storage structure, but even to *logical* changes in the structure of base
tables.

Unfortunately, the view concept as currently implemented in the commercial SQL
standard falls short of the sort of theoretical power we have been discussing. While it is
possible to create a relatively general view table based on a number of base tables, there
are limitations on the SQL statements that can access this view table. In particular, certain Select statements and most updates to a view are not permitted in many useful cases.
It turns out there are theoretical limitations on certain Update statements on views (that
is, SQL Update statements, Insert statements, and Delete statements) where it is difficult
to translate the view update into updates of the base tables that the user intends. We
could do without statements of this theoretically intractable kind, but a number of other
useful updates have also been excluded by the commercial standard in order to make system implementation simpler. We can expect to see less restrictive views in the future, but
for now we must deal with numerous artificial limitations.

Chapter 8: Indexing

A major responsibility of a DBA is to decide how base tables are to be laid out on disk,
and what indexes should be created to optimize access to the data required by the applications and ad hoc uses at the installation. This is known as *physical database design*.
Chapter 8 explores design options, discussing data storage and indexing issues in relation
to actual database systems.

Indexes and Table Layout

We start with some of the capabilities for physical design offered by the three major
RDBMS products under study, **ORACLE**, **DB2 UDB**, and **INFORMIX**, and we focus on
indexing. When an index is placed on some column value of a table, for example, on the
column lname of the students table in Figure 1.1a, it is analogous to a card catalog
being created in a library to locate book volumes on the shelves. As a result, the query

```
select sid, class from students where lname = 'Smith';
```

can be performed by the system through the lname index. The lname value 'Smith' is
located quickly in the index, and the index entry then gives the location of the students
table row with lname = 'Smith' (or rows, as there may be many different ones). Of
course, with the extremely small number of students rows given in our example of Figure 1.1a, query performance would not improve as a result of such an index. But with a
more realistic table containing several thousand rows, the major alternative to looking
up rows in an index is to examine each row individually to see if it should be retrieved by
the query; thus an index offers important performance savings. It is also possible with
some products to place the rows themselves in position by the values of some index, a
practice known as *clustering*, comparable to ordering books on library shelves by author.

20

Clustering can only be done with a single index, however, so additional indexes will still be necessary for efficient access.

The text details a number of different types of disk-based structures for row access, such as hashed and B-tree structures, together with a number of properties of such structures with which a DBA needs to be conversant, such as disk space utilization. There are also trade-offs to consider in using a large number of indexes for large tables: as in a library catalog system, we get high performance for additional queries with more indexes, but there is also more effort involved in keeping the indexes up-to-date as new rows are inserted or old rows deleted.

Chapter 9: Query Processing

After the detailed introduction to indexing concepts provided in Chapter 8, we investigate in Chapter 9 the concept of *query optimization,* a process performed by the database system. For some of the more sophisticated SQL queries, it becomes a difficult problem to decide what step-by-step access strategy should be used to optimize performance, given that multiple indexes on different columns and different tables can be involved in the query, and that a range of different access techniques can be chosen at successive stages. SQL query syntax possesses an important property, known as *non-procedurality.* This means that the SQL query syntax allows the user to specify *what* is desired as an answer without specifying in any way *how* the answer is to be achieved, that is, without specifying the step-by-step access plan to be performed. Because of the non-procedural nature of SQL queries, it is possible to leave the determination of the access strategy to the query optimization module of the DBMS. This is yet another aspect of program-data independence mentioned earlier as a feature of modern relational database management systems. The programmer writing an SQL query can be totally unaware of the physical layout of the data and table indexes.

The text provides rather complete coverage of most aspects of query optimization in **DB2**, that is, IBM mainframe **DB2** for OS/390. We concentrate on a single database product to reduce confusion, since query optimization variations among products are quite difficult to present. In any event, **DB2** has excellent query optimization capabilities, subsuming most features of other products. After this, we provide an extended example of query performance by explaining the detailed results from the Set Query benchmark. A benchmark is an industry standard test to determine the relative cost-performance of different hardware-software (DBMS) product combinations for a particular type of use. The Set Query benchmark was created to measure cost-performance for common query applications arising in industry. The concept of *cost-performance* was developed to find some common measure of comparison across hardware-software platforms. It is often the case that the features of one kind of platform (**DB2** on an IBM mainframe) are difficult to compare with the features of a platform produced by different vendors (**ORACLE** on a Sun Solaris machine). Each set of vendors claims that their own features are superior, and thus we are left with a problem in trying to compare the two. The concept of cost-performance deals with this problem by trying to codify a certain type of work that has common use in industrial applications. Units are invented for this work, such as a *query* unit (actually an average of a large number of different query types), and we measure on different platforms the *dollar cost* ($COST) to achieve a standard rate of work in terms of *queries per minute* (QPM). The final rating in $COST/QPM is claimed to be a fair measure of value for the hardware-software platforms measured.

Chapter 10: Update Transactions

It turns out that the concepts and skills that go into understanding database query access are rather different from those that are needed to properly deal with database updates. When updates are performed on a database, we need some way to guarantee that a set of updates will succeed all at once or not at all—it is unacceptable, for example, that a transfer of money from one account to another should succeed in taking money out of the first account, but then, perhaps because of a system crash, fail in adding the transferred quantity into the second account. It is also important that a pure query retrieval application doesn't sum the balances in these two accounts while the transfer is "in flight," so that money has been taken out of one account but not yet added into a second. Such an event might lead to an invalid idea of the total assets of some individual, merely because he or she was in the act of transferring money. To guarantee that problems such as these don't arise, the concept of *database transaction* has been developed: a transaction draws a set of record reads and updates together into an indivisible package. We say that a transaction has the property of *atomicity,* meaning that other operations can only access any of the rows involved in transactional access either before the transaction occurs or after the transaction is complete, but never while the transaction is partially complete.

Understanding how a set of operations is packaged together in a transaction requires a number of other sophisticated concepts. Beginning with our discussion of Embedded SQL, we cover a preliminary set of SQL transactional commands available to application programmers on three different database products, including how to start and end (or *commit*) a transaction. While we put off the most detailed consideration of update transactions until Chapter 10, we need a certain amount of understanding of the transactional concept just to write query applications when updates might be taking place concurrently. Interactive update applications are an important area of concentration in database systems, often referred to as *transaction processing* or *OLTP* (for online transaction processing). A number of transactional concepts have important implications for an application writer—for example, the idea of *transactional abort*. It turns out that while trying to maintain atomicity of the transaction, the DBMS sometimes has no alternative but to give up trying to make forward progress, roll back all updates performed so far, and notify the application logic of this event. As a result, the application must be able to handle such an event by attempting to *retry* the transaction.

We explore the underlying theoretical concept of *concurrency* in transactional systems in Chapter 10. Concurrency deals with the need to make transactions atomic with respect to other, simultaneous user transactions that may attempt to access the same records—what is called *concurrent access*. The performance motivation for concurrent access is made clear. Then the problem arising from concurrency is expressed in the most general possible form, and a well-known theoretical approach to avoiding the problem is explained. This leads in practice to a scheme known as *two-phase locking*, whereby records accessed by a transaction are locked against access by concurrent users, generally speaking until the transaction is complete. This two-phase locking has a number of implications for later concepts of performance tuning.

After looking carefully into concurrency, the text considers the problem of what to do about a partial set of transactional record updates that have already been written to disk in the event that a system crash destroys the memory contents, so that the system loses the state of the transaction in the application logic. This is known as the problem of *database recovery*, and it is solved by a technique whereby the system writes notes to itself on disk so that it will remember after a crash how to reverse any record updates belonging to uncompleted transactions.

After these considerations have become clear, we deal with performance considerations in transactional processing. Some of the database administration commands for system tuning are explained, and we introduce the industry standard OLTP benchmark created by the Transaction Processing Performance Council, known as TPC-A. A number of cost-performance considerations of transaction processing are different from those we have already seen with query processing. These new concepts are explained in detail in Chapter 10.

Chapter 11: Parallel and Distributed Databases

Finally, in Chapter 11 we introduce the concepts of parallel and distributed database processing. The idea here is that a database can be partitioned so that one part of it sits on disks attached to one computer and another part sits on disks attached to a different computer. Any number of different computers can be involved. In spite of the partitioning, we wish to be able to perform queries and updates that require access to data on more than one computer at a time. Some of the concepts that motivate this approach to distributed databases are the following. First, we expect cost-performance to improve if we allow geographically distinct sites to store their data locally rather than having most sites access all information over long-distance communication lines. Centralized control of data, however, is still of crucial importance. For example, a large company depends on being able to place orders through company warehouses in a different city when it runs out of goods locally. *Reliability* is also an important consideration, especially since as the number of disks and computer processors involved in a database system increases, the expected *mean time to failure* (or *MTTF*) becomes worse—that is, smaller—with each new component added. The solution to the reliability problem is to replicate data on different disks and make it available through independent computers of the system. Many of these considerations are relatively new and only beginning to have their first expression in mission-critical applications.

1.4 Putting It All Together

We have now introduced the fundamental concepts and definitions discussed in this book. The coming chapters will provide a more in-depth understanding of how to create, maintain, and use a relational database. Our goal is an understanding of database theory along with a perception of practical details in existing database standards and products.

The Relational Model

The purpose of models is not to fit the data but to sharpen the questions.
—Samuel Karlin

A *database model,* or *data model,* is a set of definitions describing how real-world data is conceptually represented as computerized information. It also describes the types of operations available to access and update this information. As explained in Chapter 1, this book concentrates on the *relational model* and the *object-relational model.* The relational model is the classical one that has been in use since the late 1970s, but most database system vendors (such as **ORACLE, DB2 UDB,** and **INFORMIX,** which we cover in this text) have begun supporting the object-relational model in their recent releases; probably all serious vendors will be doing this before long. In both models, a collection of related information known as a *database* is represented as a set of *tables.* These "tables" are quite disciplined in their conceptual structure. There is much to learn about how various structures within the table are named (e.g., the *heading* of the table), the structural *rules* they follow (e.g., two rows cannot be identical in all columns), and a number of other concepts used in data access that are ramifications of these rules (e.g., the *primary key* for a table is a set of columns that identifies rows uniquely). The first four sections of this chapter will present some structural considerations of the relational model, with a few mentions of how the object-relational model differs. Details of the object-relational model will not be covered until Chapter 4.

Starting with Section 2.5, we introduce *relational algebra,* a collection of fundamental relational operations that can be used to create new tables from old ones, much as arithmetic calculation creates new numbers using operations such as addition and multiplication. Relational algebra is an abstract language, which means that it will not be possible to execute queries formulated in relational algebra on an actual computer. We introduce relational algebra in the current chapter in order to express, in the simplest form, the set of operations that any relational database query language must perform to answer English-language queries about the information in a database. All of these basic

26

concepts will prove very useful in later chapters, where we explain the meaning of various constructs in SQL, the standard computerized query language for relational database systems.

Chapter 2 has a rather abstract approach (with mathematical definitions and theorems), compared with some of the later chapters that deal with computerized query languages. There are a number of reasons for this. Certainly, it is appropriate to be as precise as possible when introducing the fundamental concepts of a field of study. But even more important, the serious database practitioner will find a need to be able to move back and forth from one style of presentation to another. Most commercial database products, such as **DB2 UDB**, **ORACLE**, and **INFORMIX**, provide extremely well-written manuals that explain practical database concepts in a most approachable way. However, there are invariably a number of deeper concepts that such manuals do not attempt to cover in depth. To master these, the practitioner will often find it necessary to read reference books or even original research papers that take a much more abstract viewpoint. (For example, see "Suggestions for Further Reading" at the end of this chapter.) Here we try to prepare you for encounters with these more abstract references, without losing the simple presentation of the manuals in situations where this approach is appropriate.

2.1   The CAP Database

As we explained in Section 1.1, a *database* is a collection of computerized records maintained for a common purpose. In the following chapters we refer frequently to a specific example, which we call the CAP database (for the table names CUSTOMERS, AGENTS, and PRODUCTS). This database, illustrated in Figure 2.2, is used by a wholesale business to keep track of its *customers,* the *products* it sells to these customers, and the *agents* who place *orders* for products on behalf of these customers.

The tables and columns in the CAP database of Figure 2.2 are described in Figure 2.1. The customers listed are themselves retail businesses that order large quantities of various products from the wholesale company for resale. Distinct customers in the CUS-TOMERS table are uniquely identified by values in the cid (customer identifier) column. Customers phone in orders to agents (uniquely identified by the aid value in the AGENTS table) based in cities nationwide to purchase products (identified by pid in the PRODUCTS table). Each time an order is placed, a new row is inserted in the ORDERS table, uniquely identified by an ordno value. For example, the order identified in the ORDERS table by ordno 1011 was taken in the month of January (jan) from customer c001 by agent a01 for 1000 units of product p01 at a dollar cost of $450. Figure 2.1 provides definitions of all the tables and columns of the CAP database, and the database content of a given moment is shown in Figure 2.2. (The content can change from one moment to the next.)

Note that the database administrator for the CAP database created the cid column to be a unique customer identifier (as described in Figure 2.1) because it was believed that no other single column properly filled this need. For example, the column cname can

CUSTOMERS	A table containing information about customers
cid	Unique identifier for a customer/row—note there is no customer corresponding to cid = 'c005'
cname	Name of a customer
city	City where the customer (headquarters) is located
discnt	Each customer has a negotiated discount on prices
AGENTS	A table containing information about agent employees
aid	Unique identifier for an agent/row
aname	Last name of agent
city	City where agent is based
percent	Percentage commission each agent receives on each sale
PRODUCTS	A table containing information about products for sale
pid	Unique identifier for a product/row
pname	Descriptive name of product
city	City where this product is warehoused
quantity	Quantity on hand for sale, in standard units
price	Wholesale price of each unit product

Note that the same column name, city, appears in all three tables defined so far. This is not a coincidence.

ORDERS	A table containing information about orders
ordno	Unique identifier for this order
month	Month the order was placed; assume that orders started in January of this year
cid	This customer . . .
aid	. . . purchased through this agent . . .
pid	. . . this specific product . . .
qty	. . . in this total quantity. . .
dollars	. . . at this dollar cost

Figure 2.1 Table and Column Definitions for the CAP Database

have duplicate values on different rows (and in fact the name "ACME" is duplicated). In a similar fashion, the aid, pid, and ordno columns have been created to act as unique identifiers of their respective tables. Note that the dollars value in any ORDERS row can be calculated separately by multiplying the qty value in that row by the corresponding price for that pid, and then taking a discount for the customer, as determined in the discnt column for the CUSTOMERS row with that cid. We do not also subtract the percent commission for the agent, since dollars is supposed to represent the total cost to the customer.

    This example CAP database is quite artificial. It fits snugly on a page and is used here to illustrate our ideas. To be closer to reality we would need to consider more tables, and larger ones. To begin with, we would need more columns. There should be a first name to

CUSTOMERS

cid	cname	city	discnt
c001	TipTop	Duluth	10.00
c002	Basics	Dallas	12.00
c003	Allied	Dallas	8.00
c004	ACME	Duluth	8.00
c006	ACME	Kyoto	0.00

PRODUCTS

pid	pname	city	quantity	price
p01	comb	Dallas	111400	0.50
p02	brush	Newark	203000	0.50
p03	razor	Duluth	150600	1.00
p04	pen	Duluth	125300	1.00
p05	pencil	Dallas	221400	1.00
p06	folder	Dallas	123100	2.00
p07	case	Newark	100500	1.00

AGENTS

aid	aname	city	percent
a01	Smith	New York	6
a02	Jones	Newark	6
a03	Brown	Tokyo	7
a04	Gray	New York	6
a05	Otasi	Duluth	5
a06	Smith	Dallas	5

ORDERS

ordno	month	cid	aid	pid	qty	dollars
1011	jan	c001	a01	p01	1000	450.00
1012	jan	c001	a01	p01	1000	450.00
1019	feb	c001	a02	p02	400	180.00
1017	feb	c001	a06	p03	600	540.00
1018	feb	c001	a03	p04	600	540.00
1023	mar	c001	a04	p05	500	450.00
1022	mar	c001	a05	p06	400	720.00
1025	apr	c001	a05	p07	800	720.00
1013	jan	c002	a03	p03	1000	880.00
1026	may	c002	a05	p03	800	704.00
1015	jan	c003	a03	p05	1200	1104.00
1014	jan	c003	a03	p05	1200	1104.00
1021	feb	c004	a06	p01	1000	460.00
1016	jan	c006	a01	p01	1000	500.00
1020	feb	c006	a03	p07	600	600.00
1024	mar	c006	a06	p01	800	400.00

Figure 2.2 The CAP Database (Content at a Given Moment)

go with aname in the AGENTS table; each city column needs to have added columns for street address, state, and zip code; we would want to keep track of agents' total commissions for the most recent month, just as we keep track of quantity on hand for products; we would need the name of a person to contact at each customer company, the name of a person in charge of each warehouse, and the person's address and telephone number, and so on. We need a more complete date and perhaps a timestamp for each order (month alone is insufficient) and some way of keeping track of payments (wholesale customers

have to be billed). There are probably additional employees not on agent commission   **29**
(warehouse managers are one type), and we have to keep track of their salaries, tax with-
holdings, and so on. We would also expect to see a lot more rows in each of the tables.

2.2 Naming the Parts of a Database

Two different standard terminologies are (unfortunately) used in databases. One terminology refers to tables, columns, and rows, and the other refers to *relations* (the counterpart of tables), *tuples* (corresponding to rows), and *attributes* (for columns). We'll use
both sets of terms so you can learn to recognize them easily. Thus we will frequently refer
to the column names of a table as the *attributes* of that table (for instance, the attributes
of the table CUSTOMERS are cid, cname, city, and discnt) or to rows as *tuples*.

A *database* is defined to be a set of named *tables*, or *relations*. For example, the CAP
database consists of the set of tables

        CAP = {CUSTOMERS, AGENTS, PRODUCTS, ORDERS}

We define the *heading* of a table to be the set of columns whose names appear at the top
of the table, above the first row. We denote the heading of a table T by Head(T). For
example, we have

        Head(CUSTOMERS) = {cid, cname, city, discnt}

In specifying the set of columns in a heading, there is a common convention to dispense
with the standard set notation ({x, y, . . .}) and simply list the attributes, separated by
spaces. Thus we will commonly write

        Head(CUSTOMERS) = cid cname city discnt

The heading of a table is also referred to as a *relational schema,* the set of attributes making up a relation; the set of all relational schemas for a database is known as a *database
schema.*

The set of rows, or tuples, in a table is referred to as the *content* of the table, and the
number of such rows is sometimes referred to as the *cardinality* of the table. For example, the PRODUCTS table in Figure 2.2 contains seven rows. It is important to understand
that the table name and heading are meant to be long-lived properties of a table, but the
precise set of rows in the table is expected to change from one moment to the next in
number and detailed values; this is why we refer to the content of a table "at a given
moment" in Figure 2.2. The reader familiar with programming in languages such as C or
Java should know that tables like the ones represented in Figure 2.2 can be thought of as
(and are usually stored as) files of records, or structures. Each row of a table normally
corresponds to a record in a file (or possibly several files), and the structure of fields
within the record is determined by the heading of the table. However, in a relational

database the application programmer is insulated from such details of storage by the principle of program-data independence, defined in Section 1.3, and the database can theoretically store the rows of a table in an entirely different type of disk structure.

Domains and Datatypes

A table must be *created* in a computerized database system (i.e., the structure of the empty table must be declared), just as a file and the records (structs) it contains need to be declared in C or Java. In current database system products such as **ORACLE, DB2 UDB**, and **INFORMIX**, each column in the table is declared to have a certain *type*. For example, we might define the CUSTOMERS table so that the column discnt has type *real* (a floating point number occupying 4 bytes), and the column city has type *char(13)* (a character string of length 13). In the more theoretical literature it has become common to say that an attribute A of a table T takes on values from a set D known as a *domain*. A domain is usually defined in such cases to contain the *exact* set of constants that can appear as values for the attribute, and thus a domain corresponds to the concept of enumerated type that is provided in some programming languages. For instance, the domain of the attribute city, designated by CITY, might be the set of all character strings corresponding to cities in the United States (assuming that our firm does business only with U.S. customers). On the other hand, the domain of the discnt column, DISCNT, might be defined as consisting of all real numbers between 0.00 and 20.00, with at most two non-zero digits after the decimal point (assuming that this is the range of possible discounts offered by our wholesale company to its customers).

Most commercial database systems support explicit accuracy after the decimal point (as with DISCNT) but do not support types consisting of enumerated sets (as with CITY). We usually have to be satisfied in such systems with saying that the values that may occur in the column named city belong to a generic type such as char(13). However, it is possible to restrict a domain such as char(13) to an enumerated set of values that appear in the column of another table; we can achieve this by using a type of *constraint*, known as *referential integrity*, which we will learn about in Chapter 7.

The significance of declaring a column of a table to have a particular type (or domain) is that the ability to compare the values of two different columns rests on this declaration. For example, if the city column of the CUSTOMERS table were declared to be char(13), and the city column of the AGENTS table were declared to be char(14), we could not be confident of being able to answer the request to print out all agent-customer pairs in the same city; it is theoretically justifiable for the system to refuse to compare columns of different types.

Tables and Relations

We start by reviewing a mathematical concept known as the *Cartesian product*.

DEFINITION 2.2.1 Cartesian Product. The Cartesian product of a sequence of k sets S_1, $S_2, \ldots, S_k$ is represented by $S_1 \times S_2 \times \ldots \times S_k$, and consists of all possible k-tuples (e_1, e_2,

..., e_k), where e_1 is any element in S_1, e_2 is any element in S_2, ..., and e_k is any element in S_k. ■

Consider the sets `CID`, `CNAME`, `CITY`, and `DISCNT`, which denote the domains of the attributes in the `CUSTOMERS` table, `cid`, `cname`, `city`, and `discnt`, respectively. The domain of an attribute A is denoted by Domain(A). Thus for example, Domain(`cid`) = `CID`, and if c is a value that occurs in the `cid` column, we must have c ∈ `CID`. Now consider the Cartesian product of the sets `CID`, `CNAME`, `CITY`, and `DISCNT` denoted by

```
CP = CID x CNAME x CITY x DISCNT
```

The Cartesian product, `CP`, consists of the set of all possible 4-tuples, t = (c, n, t, d), where c is a customer identification number from `CID`, n is a customer name from `CNAME` (not necessarily corresponding to the customer whose identification number is c), t is some U.S. city in the set `CITY`, and d is some discount value in `DISCNT`. As an example, the Cartesian product `CP` contains such tuples as

t = (c003, Allied, Dallas, 8.00)

and

t' = (c001, Basics, Oshkosh, 18.20).

Now a *relation* is a mathematical construct, defined as a subset of a Cartesian product. As an example, the table `CUSTOMERS` is a subset of `CP` = `CID` × `CNAME` × `CITY` × `DISCNT`. All rows (that is, all 4-tuples) of the table `CUSTOMERS` are contained in the set of tuples of the Cartesian product `CP`. On the other hand, not all tuples of the Cartesian product correspond to rows from the `CUSTOMERS` table. For instance, in the example above, t is contained in `CUSTOMERS`, while t' is not. The table `CUSTOMERS` is therefore a *proper subset*— that is, a subset that does not contain all elements—of the Cartesian product. Since not all component values sit with all other component values on a tuple of a relation, those that do are said to be *related*, and from this we get the term *relation*, which is used in mathematics. Note particularly that while each single row of a table relates the values of the different columns, it is the complete *set* of rows in a table that is called a relation.

As noted in Figure 2.1, each customer is supposed to have a distinct `cid` value, so it would not even make sense to have a `CUSTOMERS` table contain all the rows of the Cartesian product. At least two rows in the Cartesian product would have the same value from `CID` (as long as at least one of the domains `CNAME`, `CITY`, and `DISCNT` contained more than one value), but the `CID` value is supposed to be unique for each row.

EXAMPLE 2.2.1

Using the terminology just introduced, you should be able to see that if we define a table T that has a heading given by

Head(T) = $A_1 \ldots A_n$

then T is a subset of the Cartesian product of the sets: Domain(A_1), ..., Domain(A_n). ■

As mentioned earlier, the heading of the table is a relatively stable part, which prescribes the structure of the rows of the table. It is not common to add or delete columns, and we would not expect to do so in the normal course of everyday business. In creating the column layout, we must plan ahead with a thorough analysis of the needs we will have for our database; as explained earlier in Chapter 1, this process is known as logical database design.

On the other hand, the *content* of the table changes frequently over time. New rows can be added or deleted easily: we expect to add new rows as we acquire new customers and to delete rows as we lose them, for example. It would be impossible to keep track mentally of these changes in a large wholesale company: some tables might have millions of rows. But the number of columns is generally limited to the number of concepts a user can become familiar with. Query languages are created so that the user can retrieve information about the rows of one or more tables, with no advance knowledge except the names and characteristics of the columns. It would be a mistake, in most cases, to form a preconception of the precise answer to a query based on what you believe is the content of the tables involved in the query. Small examples such as the CAP database are an exception: you can often use knowledge of the content of the CAP tables to validate query results as a check on whether the queries have been properly posed. However, the ultimate test for query correctness must be whether the query would retrieve the correct result after any possible change to the content of the table.

2.3   Relational Rules

A few well-known defining characteristics, or *rules,* of the relational model tell us what variations in table structure are permitted and limit possible retrieval operations. These relational rules serve the important purpose of pointing out areas to standardize in the various commercial product offerings, so that issues of logical database design (which we will study in Chapter 6) are the same for all products. Many commercial database products have purposely broken a number of relational rules, and the new object-relational model specifically breaks many of them. Because of this it is important that you become sensitive to the issues addressed, while remaining flexible to the variations you can expect to encounter in commercial systems.

RULE 1: First Normal Form Rule. In defining tables, the relational model insists that columns that have multi-valued attributes (sometimes called repeating fields) or have any internal structure (like a record) are *not* permitted! A table that obeys this is said to be in *first normal form.* ∎

As an example, consider the table EMPLOYEES in Figure 2.3, which contains rows corresponding to the employees of a company. This table has a unique employee identification column eid, an ename column with the employee name, the position the employee holds in the company, and a multi-valued field (or attribute) listing the dependents for

EMPLOYEES

eid	ename	position	dependents
e001	Smith, John	Agent	Michael J.
			Susan R.
e002	Andrews, David	Superintendent	David M. Jr.
e003	Jones, Franklin	Agent	Andrew K.
			Mark W.
			Louisa M.

Figure 2.3 An EMPLOYEES Table with a Multi-Valued dependents Attribute

EMPLOYEES

eid	ename	position	dependent1	dependent2	. . .
e001	Smith, John	Agent	Michael J.	Susan R.	. . .
e002	Andrews, David	Superintendent	David M. Jr.	. . .	. . .
e003	Jones, Franklin	Agent	Andrew K.	Mark W.	. . .

Figure 2.4 An EMPLOYEES Table with Multiple Dependent Names on Each Employee Row

that employee. For example, John Smith, with employee ID e001, has two dependents, Michael J. and Susan R., listed on separate lines, while David Andrews has one dependent and Franklin Jones has three.

Relational RULE 1 states that repeating fields of dependents in Figure 2.3 are not permitted in relational tables. This is a real restriction in design, since if we now try to place the dependent names in a unique employee row of the EMPLOYEES table (as in Figure 2.4), we have to create separate column names for the maximum number of dependents that an employee might possibly have—for example, dependent1, dependent2, . . . , dependent20.

This is usually not feasible because it wastes space and makes queries difficult, so the approach taken instead is to *factor* the EMPLOYEES table into two parts, creating a separate table called DEPENDENTS that consists of two columns, eid and dependent (Figure 2.5).

We populate the table of Figure 2.5 with one row for each dependent, giving the eid of each employee-dependent name pair. As we will see, any relational query language will allow us to connect an employee row to each of the dependent rows with the same eid.

The first normal form rule also states that column values must be simple types, with no internal structure. For example, the column ename in the EMPLOYEES table of Figure 2.5 consists of a simple character string, and a certain amount of parsing is needed to construct the last name (all text before the comma). We could not construct a table with a column named ename that had three components: ename.fname, ename.lname, and ename.mi (first name, last name, and middle initial) because this assumes a structure in column values that is not permitted in first normal form.

EMPLOYEES

eid	ename	position
e001	Smith, John	Agent
e002	Andrews, David	Superintendent
e003	Jones, Franklin	Agent

DEPENDENTS

eid	dependent
e001	Michael J.
e001	Susan R.
e002	David M. Jr.
e003	Andrew K.
e003	Mark W.
e003	Louisa L.

Figure 2.5 EMPLOYEES and Associated DEPENDENTS Tables

We simply mention that the first normal form rule can be broken by tables defined in any object-relational database system product. Such tables are non-first normal form, or NFNF. We will defer discussion of the details of the object-relational model until Chapter 4, but the way in which the model breaks the first normal form rule is by permitting a new object column type that can contain a *set* of values of a *complex type*. For example, you could create a type for person_name containing component character strings: fname, lname, and mi. Then you could create a dependent_names type by declaring it: setof(person_name). Thus a column declared of type dependent_names could contain sets of complex names.

RULE 2: Access Rows by Content Only Rule. A second rule of the relational model states that we can only retrieve rows by their *content*, the attribute values that exist in each row.

∎

So far as user queries are concerned, RULE 2 implies that there is no order on the rows. Thus there is no way that a query in a (pure) relational language can ask, for example, to retrieve the third row of the ORDERS table. Instead the query would need to refer to the row with the value 1019 in the ordno column, a unique row, as implied by the definition of ordno in Figure 2.1. In this sense the picture that is presented in Figure 2.2, with its physical layout on paper of the ORDERS table, is misleading. According to this rule, the ORDERS table does not have a first row, or a second row, or a third. The set of rows making up the content of a table are unordered elements of a set. In the more abstract mathematical nomenclature, this simply says that a relation is a set of tuples. Another implication of RULE 2 is that you cannot create a "pointer" to a row to retrieve it at a later time. Such pointers are not permitted.

Many commercial database systems have always broken RULE 2, providing a method to retrieve a row of a table by its row identification number (RID, pronounced as in "get RID of"), sometimes called the ROWID (row-eye-dee), or tuple identification number (TID, tee-eye-dee). Usually the RID is easily calculable from the number of the row as it was loaded into the table. Commercial database systems seem to be saying that RULE 2 is sometimes an inappropriate rule, and that a new standard is called for. To justify access by RID value, it is important to realize that the rows of a database need to be stored on some nonvolatile medium, such as disk, in some real order. (*Nonvolatile* means that the medium retains the data when the power supply to the machine is interrupted.) The order of storage is predictable and, as we will see in Chapter 7, retrieval by RID is sometimes useful to a database administrator (DBA) in examining situations where it is suspected that the rows of the table are not stored in the proper way. Current technology of disk storage usually means that rows stored close to each other are more quickly retrieved in sequence than they would be if they were stored far apart. We will use this fact in considerations of performance later in the book. All in all, the RID values are sometimes useful because we do not consider the order of row storage to be totally immaterial. At the same time, there are reasons for most users not to perform normal queries in terms of saved RID values, since RIDs are subject to change when tables are updated in certain circumstances.

The object-relational model permits column values in one row to point at other rows. This is a very serious departure from the relational rules.

It is worth mentioning here that the relational model also states that there should be no order to the *columns* of a relation, so once again our mental model of a table is slightly misleading. This rule is broken, however, by the standard SQL language, as we will see in Chapter 3.

RULE 3: The Unique Row Rule. A third rule of the relational model is that two tuples in a relation (rows in a table) cannot be identical in all column values at once. A relation can be thought of as a *set of tuples* in the relational model, and of course a set never contains two identical elements; each tuple of the set must be unique. Furthermore, since a pure relational query language is able to distinguish rows only in terms of their column values (RULE 2), this is another way of saying that there must be a way of distinguishing any single row from all others in terms of these values, so that a query language statement can retrieve it uniquely.   ∎

In commercial database systems, a good deal of work is required to ensure that a newly inserted row in a table does not duplicate an existing row. While the unique row rule is a reasonable aim in most cases, the SQL Create Table statement formats don't make this guarantee except in tables with special constraints (which are more costly to maintain). The current chapter deals with the relational model in which the unique row rule has important implications, so in what follows, we assume that RULE 3 is obeyed by all tables unless we specify otherwise. This will cease to be the case once we begin talking about tables in commercial systems.

What is the motivation for the relational rules? These rules (and others) were laid down in a series of journal articles by E. F. Codd, the inventor of the relational model. The rules reflect certain mathematical assumptions that have important implications for the good behavior of relational structures; numerous examples will be covered in the following chapters. For example, RULE 3, which requires unique rows, simply reflects the mathematical idea that a relation is a set of tuples and a set never contains two identical elements. RULE 1, which requires first normal form, has certain important implications for the design of database tables, as seen in Figures 2.3 through 2.5. RULE 2, which requires that rows can be accessed by content only, simply guarantees that the methods provided a bit later in the chapter to retrieve rows will be the *only* methods permitted. Thus older pre–relational database products couldn't simply define tables to hold their data in, keep their original navigational access methods, and call the product relational. As mentioned earlier, relational rules serve the important purpose of standardizing the various product offerings so that issues of database design are the same in all cases. The reason for the new object-relational model is that many people believe that these mathematically motivated relational rules are too rigid to accommodate some valuable ideas, many of which first arose in object-oriented programming languages. By allowing new behavior, the object-relational model provides a number of natural extensions that are valuable in certain commercial situations. For the remainder of this chapter on the relational model, we shall assume all relational rules hold, unless otherwise specified.

2.4 Keys, Superkeys, and Null Values

Relational RULE 3 states that two rows in a table cannot be identical in all their column values. This is the same as saying that any two distinct rows of a table can be distinguished by differences in some column value; or, looking at it a different way, that the set of all columns distinguishes any two rows. Is it possible that some *subset* of the columns distinguishes any two rows? Yes. For example, in the CUSTOMERS table, the single cid column distinguishes between any two rows. (Recall that in Figure 2.1 we defined the cid identifier to be a customer identifier, unique for each row.) We say that cid is a *superkey* for the CUSTOMERS table, meaning that any two rows in the table will always have distinct values in this (singleton) set of columns. The cid column is in fact a *key* for the CUSTOMERS table, which is a somewhat more restrictive thing, meaning that no subset of the set of columns making up the key is itself a superkey.

Now a very important question: Is pname a superkey for the PRODUCTS table? *Even though every row has distinct pname values in the example table of Figure 2.2, the answer is no!* This is because when we say that a superkey is a subset of columns that distinguishes between any two rows of the table, we mean this to be the *intention* of the database designer, who is usually the DBA. But we never intended in our design that pname be a unique identifier for rows of the PRODUCTS table. We created the pid column as a unique row identifier (as explained in Figure 2.1) to allow duplicates in other columns when adding future rows. The fact that there are no duplicate values for pname in Figure 2.2 is simply an accident, based on *the content of the table at a given moment.* This might change in the next moment. For example, we might want to create a new row with pid value 'p08', and pname 'folder'; the two rows named folder, identified by their pid values p06 and p08, might have different sizes.

We could build size into the name (half-inch folder), but this might not be sufficient. The two folders might then have the same size and different colors, or have different types of closing clasps or be made of different materials. All of these distinctions could be clearly spelled out in other columns of a more realistic table (color, size, material, etc.), but it is easy to imagine that after the table is defined, a new product is offered that is identical to some other product in all existing column values. To distinguish the rows for these two products, the pid column is needed. It is also efficient to have a single column identifier to distinguish rows in PRODUCTS, and for this reason we decide to define a unique identifier pid and then depend on the pid value alone.

A key or superkey for a table is required to *remain* a key or superkey as new rows are added—that is, a key reflects the *intention* of the designer under all future conditions, rather than simply being something we notice about the accidental contents of the current table. In what follows, we give some definitions to make the ideas of key and superkey more precise.

Given a table T with attributes represented by subscripted letters, $\text{Head}(T) = A_1 \ldots A_n$, and a tuple t in T, we define the *restriction* of the tuple t to a subset $\{A_{i_1}, \ldots, A_{i_k}\}$ of $\{A_1, \ldots, A_n\}$, denoted $t[A_{i_1}, \ldots, A_{i_k}]$, as the k-tuple of values of t in the columns named. For instance, the restriction of the tuple

$$t = (c003, \text{Allied}, \text{Dallas}, 8.00)$$

from the table CUSTOMERS to the set that consists of the columns cid and cname is denoted by $t[\text{cid}, \text{cname}] = (c003, \text{Allied})$.

Using this notation, we can formalize the notion of key.

DEFINITION 2.4.1 Table Key. Given a table T, with $\text{Head}(T) = A_1 \ldots A_n$. A *key* for the table T, sometimes called a *candidate key*, is a set of attributes, $K = A_{i_1} \ldots A_{i_k}$, with two properties:

[1] If u, v are distinct tuples of T, then by designer intention $u[K] \neq v[K]$; that is, there will always exist at least one column, A_{i_m}, in the set of columns K such that $u[A_{i_m}] \neq v[A_{i_m}]$.

[2] No proper subset H of K has property 1. ∎

Property 1 is just a mathematical way of saying that the values any row u takes on for the set of attributes K are *unique*. We refer to a set of attributes that fulfills property 1 but not necessarily property 2 as a *superkey*. Property 2 ensures that a key is a *minimal* set of attributes with property 1. Thus a key is always a superkey, but a key has the additional property that no proper subset is a superkey. The fact that a singleton attribute with property 1 is always minimal follows from the fact that the empty set of attributes, φ, does not distinguish two rows: we say that $u[\varphi] = v[\varphi]$ for all rows u and v.

In a computerized database system, the person acting as database designer, who is usually a DBA, can define keys for a table using a syntax to be covered later in the text. Once such keys are defined, it becomes impossible for normal updates of the table (inserting new rows or updates of column values of existing rows) to cause the uniqueness condition for such keys to fail. Note too that when we speak of "designer intention," this might not be something that originates with the designer. For example, it is

38

standard for a DBA to stipulate that column socsecno is a key for an EMPLOYEES table, even though the designer has created a specific eid column for employee identification. However, the social security number is known to be unique, and duplicate values would mean an error in the table.

A table can have more than one key, as we see in the following example.

EXAMPLE 2.4.1

Consider the table T given by

T

A	B	C	D
a1	b1	c1	d1
a1	b2	c2	d1
a2	b2	c1	d1
a2	b1	c2	d1

As we have explained, the content of a table at a given instant does not tell us what keys the table has, since these depend on the intentions of the table designer. However, for purposes of illustration we want to calculate the keys of T from a given content, so we impose an unusual condition: that *the content of this table is intended by the designer to remain constant for the life of the database.* As a result of this database designer intention, an unusual one in real life, we can derive the keys of T by determining what combinations of columns make all rows unique.

To begin with, note that no single attribute in the table T can be a key, since in each column we have at least two equal entries. On the other hand, no set S of columns can be a key if it includes D, since D gives absolutely no help in distinguishing rows of T, and therefore S − D would also distinguish all rows of T. Therefore S would be a *superkey,* not a key. Next consider all pairs of attributes from T that do not contain D: AB, AC, and BC. All rows of T are distinguished by each of these pairs. Any other set of attributes either contains D or one of the sets AB, AC, or BC as a proper subset (just list all other sets to check this), and is therefore a superkey. Consequently, AB, AC, and BC are the complete set of keys for the table T. ∎

Since Relational RULE 3 assures us that the set of all columns distinguishes any two distinct rows, at least one key must exist for any relation. The proof of this gives a good illustration of how the definitions we have introduced are meant to be used.

THEOREM 2.4.2 Every table T has at least one key.

PROOF. Given a table T with Head(T) = $A_1 \ldots A_n$, we consider the attribute set S_1 with all these attributes. Now we know that the set S_1 is a "superkey," meaning that no two rows u and v of T have identical values in all the columns of S_1. For any u and v that are not the same row, there is an attribute (column) A_i in S_1 such that $u[A_i] \neq v[A_i]$. In what follows, we assume that we know the intentions of the table designer and can identify sets of attributes that will be superkeys. Now either the set S_1 is a key, or there is another set S_2, a proper subset of S_1, that is also a superkey. Given this, either S_2 is a key or there is another set S_3, a proper subset of S_2, that is also a superkey. Continuing in this fashion, we find a chain of sets: $S_1, S_2, \ldots, S_i, S_{i+1}, \ldots$, such that each set in the chain is a proper subset of the one preceding it, and all sets in the chain are superkeys. To show that a key exists, we merely keep going as long as possible, and claim that such a chain of sets comes to an end: there must be a final set S_k, which is contained in all the sets that have come before and has no smaller subset with the required property of being a superkey.

We can show that the chain comes to an end as follows. Represent by $\#S_i$ the number of attributes in the set S_i. Now S_1 has the n attributes in Head(T) = $A_1 \ldots A_n$, so $\#S_1 = n$. In addition, we see that $\#S_i > \#S_{i+1}$, since each successive set in the chain is a proper subset of the one preceding. Finally, each of the sets has a positive number of attributes, since a negative number is meaningless and the empty set is not a superkey. Therefore the chain given above is a descending sequence, given by: $n = \#S_1 > \#S_2 > \ldots > \#S_i > \#S_{i+1} > \ldots > 0$, and there must be a minimum number in this sequence corresponding to the final set in the chain, S_k. Then S_k has no proper subset that is a superkey and therefore must be a key for the table. Note that we have appealed to the fact that we can find a minimum element of a finite set of distinct integers. A pure mathematician might ask us to prove even this by mathematical induction. ∎

Rigorous proofs will not usually be required in this text. However, you should be sure that you understand why *some* demonstration was necessary for the existence of S_k. It is as if we were proposing a program loop to eventually determine a key set of columns and needed to be sure the loop would always terminate. This is a valid concern.

The various keys of a relation are often known as *candidate keys;* the name implies a selection process whereby one of the candidates will be designated as the *primary key.*

DEFINITION 2.4.3 Primary Key of a Table. A *primary key* of a table T is the candidate key chosen by the database designer to uniquely identify specific rows of T. ∎

Usually the primary key identifier is used in references from other tables, as in Figure 2.5, with the eid column in DEPENDENTS referencing the primary key column eid in EMPLOYEES. In the CAP database, the ORDERS table identifies each row by the ordno value. An extended PRODUCTS table might have another candidate key (in addition to pid) consisting of the set of columns specifying the name, size, color, and material of each part. It would be rather clumsy to use all these columns as an identifier in rows of ORDERS, however, so we would probably continue to choose pid as the primary key. The AGENTS table might have another candidate key, socsecno (i.e., Social Security number). While this would seem to be a good primary key to use, most companies still assign their own employee ID (like eid or aid) for all employees, possibly because some employees start work without a Social Security number but must be identified immediately.

Null Values

Suppose that a new stapler product is to be added to our PRODUCTS table, and we have not yet determined the quantity that has been stored at our warehouse, or even the warehouse city where it resides. We do know, however, that we have enough staplers on hand to start taking orders for the product, and we want to go ahead and start doing this. (We expect that the orders will be shipped at a later time, after we know the quantity on hand, so the inventory quantity can be kept up-to-date as we ship the product.) To record the information we have about staplers in the PRODUCTS table, we use a special value, known as a *null value*, in the city and quantity columns of the new PRODUCTS row:

pid	pname	city	quantity	price
p07	stapler	null	null	3.50

The null value used here should be interpreted as *unknown* or *not yet defined*, meaning that when we know more we intend to fill in the value. A slightly different meaning for null occurs when a field value is *inapplicable*, as when we fill in the manager name column in an employee table for the president of the company (who has no manager), or the percent commission for an employee who does not receive a commission. It is important to realize that the null value has different properties than those of the number 0 (for a numeric attribute) or a blank or null string (for a character attribute). As an example, if we were to query the average quantity on hand of all products in the PRODUCTS table, a zero value for the stapler product would bring down the average. However, the null value implies a more appropriate default behavior, in that the quantity for the stapler product is *left out* of the average.

Recall that a primary key for a table is used to identify individual rows of that table. We argue now for another relational rule requiring that a primary key cannot take on a null value. For example, we have placed a new product named 'stapler' in the PRODUCTS table before knowing the warehouse city and quantity stored, so that we could start accepting orders for the product. But we wouldn't have such motivation for storing this row if it hadn't yet been assigned a pid value, since we need to be able to list in the ORDERS table the pid of any product ordered. Basically, we are arguing that since the pid value is the *designated identifier* for the row, until we have the identifier *value* settled we will not allow the row to be stored in the table.

A primary key is just a specially designated candidate key, which may contain more than one column. We generalize the null restriction above to state the entity integrity rule.

RULE 4: Entity Integrity Rule. No column belonging to a primary key of a table T is allowed to take on null values for any row in T.   ■

We will discuss more properties of null values in later chapters.

2.5   Relational Algebra

Relational algebra was introduced by E. F. Codd in a series of journal articles that first appeared in 1970 and reached approximately the current form in 1972. The aim was to demonstrate the potential for a query language to retrieve information from a relational database system, although it was understood that several other languages were possible and perhaps even preferable for normal use. Information is stored in a relational system in the form of tables, so it seems natural to express the results of a query in table form. Relational algebra can be thought of as a collection of methods for building new tables that constitute answers to queries. The methods themselves are referred to as the *operations of relational algebra.*

Relational algebra is an abstract language, by which we mean that we will not execute queries formulated in relational algebra on an actual computer. We introduce relational algebra here to give a simple idea of the set of operations that any relational database query language must perform. These basic operations are very useful in understanding the considerations of the next chapter, where we explain how to perform queries in SQL, the standard computerized query language for relational database systems.

For the remainder of the text, we will use the CUSTOMERS-AGENTS-PRODUCTS (or CAP) database introduced in Section 2.1 to illustrate various operations. We supplement tables in CAP with a few others.

Fundamental Operations of Relational Algebra

We distinguish two types of operations in relational algebra: set-theoretic operations that make use of the fact that tables are essentially sets of rows, and native relational operations that focus on the structure of the rows. Given two tables R and S where Head(R) = $A_1 \ldots A_n$ and in many cases Head(S) is the same, we will define the following set of eight fundamental operations building on R and S to provide new tables. The keyboard form given below is for use on keyboards that do not contain the indicated special symbols. In addition to these operations, we will define a method of saving intermediate results, comparable to an assignment statement in a programming language such as C or Java.

SET-THEORETIC OPERATIONS			
NAME	SYMBOL	KEYBOARD FORM	EXAMPLE
UNION	$\cup$	UNION	R $\cup$ S, or R UNION S
INTERSECTION	$\cap$	INTERSECT	R $\cap$ S, or R INTERSECT S
DIFFERENCE	$-$	$-$ or MINUS	R $-$ S, or R MINUS S
PRODUCT	$\times$	TIMES	R $\times$ S, or R TIMES S

```
NATIVE RELATIONAL OPERATIONS

                                    KEYBOARD
     NAME          SYMBOL           FORM             EXAMPLE
     PROJECT       R [  ]           R [  ]           R [A_{i_1} . . . A_{i_k}]
     SELECT        R where C        R where C        R where A_1 = 5
     JOIN          ⋈                JOIN             R ⋈ S, or R JOIN S
     DIVISION      ÷                DIVIDEBY         R ÷ S, or R DIVIDEBY S
```

2.6   Set-Theoretic Operations

We assume in this section that tables are defined as sets of rows, so Relational RULES 1, 2, and 3 apply: tables have simple column values, they do not contain duplicate rows, and the order of the rows is immaterial.

You are expected to be familiar with such set operations as union, intersection, difference, and Cartesian product (Cartesian product was defined in Definition 2.2.1). These are the set-theoretic operations on which the first four relational algebra operations are based. For sets of rows to be involved in unions, intersections, or differences and to form new tables, the rows in different sets must have the same heading structure. A little reflection shows that we cannot, for example, create a new table consisting of the union of a table containing information about customers and a table containing information about products, since it would be impossible to accommodate in any meaningful way rows from CUSTOMERS and rows from PRODUCTS under the same table heading. Therefore we introduce the following definition.

DEFINITION 2.6.1 Compatible Tables. Tables R and S are *compatible* if they have the same headings; that is, if Head(R) = Head(S), with attributes chosen from the same domains and with the same meanings. ∎

The Union, Intersection, and Difference Operations

Only tables that are compatible can be involved in unions, intersections, and differences.

DEFINITION 2.6.2 Union, Intersection, Difference. Let R and S be two compatible tables, where Head(R) = Head(S) = $A_1 . . . A_n$. The *union* of R and S is the table $R \cup S$, with the same heading, consisting of all rows that are in R or in S or in both. Similarly, the *intersection* of R and S is the table $R \cap S$, consisting of those rows that are in both R and S. The *difference* of R and S is the table R – S, consisting of all rows that appear in R but do not appear in S. ∎

Note that $R \cup S = S \cup R$ and $R \cap S = S \cap R$, but $R - S$ is in general different from $S - R$. Note too that all relational operations can be applied recursively, so that the tables R and S in Definition 2.6.2 can themselves be the results of other relational algebra expressions. We can place parentheses around any such expressions without changing its meaning; for instance, we can write $(R - S)$ rather than $R - S$. This is useful to indicate order of evaluation. As in normal mathematical expressions, sub-expressions inside the deepest nesting of parentheses are meant to be evaluated first. Thus the expression $R - (S - R)$ means that we first evaluate $S - R$, and if we call the result T, we then evaluate $R - T$ to arrive at the final table indicated.

EXAMPLE 2.6.1

Consider the tables R and S:

R

A	B	C
a1	b1	c1
a1	b2	c3
a2	b1	c2

S

A	B	C
a1	b1	c1
a1	b1	c2
a1	b2	c3
a3	b2	c3

Then $R \cup S$ has five rows:

$R \cup S$

A	B	C
a1	b1	c1
a1	b1	c2
a1	b2	c3
a2	b1	c2
a3	b2	c3

Note that rows occurring in both R and S occur only once in the union, $R \cup S$. $R \cap S$ has two rows:

$R \cap S$

A	B	C
a1	b1	c1
a1	b2	c3

R – S has only one:

R – S

A	B	C
a2	b1	c2

while S – R has two:

S – R

A	B	C
a1	b1	c2
a3	b2	c3

∎

EXAMPLE 2.6.2

The operations of intersection, union, and difference are often pictured schematically using *Venn diagrams*, as illustrated below.

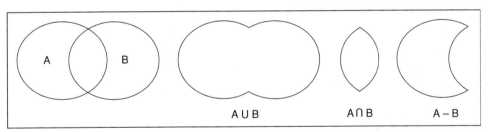

This form of illustration can sometimes serve as a demonstration of some principle of equivalence, as we will see a bit later.   ∎

Assignment and Alias

During evaluation of relational algebra expressions, it is sometimes useful to be able to save certain intermediate results. We next introduce a notation meant to add this capability to relational algebra.

DEFINITION 2.6.3 Assignment, Alias. Let R be a table and let Head(R) = $A_1 . . . A_n$. Assume that $B_1 , . . . , B_n$ are n attributes such that Domain(B_i) = Domain(A_i) for all i, $1 \leq i \leq n$. We define a *new table* S, whose heading is Head(S) = $B_1 . . . B_n$, by writing the assignment

$$S(B_1, . . . , B_n) := R(A_1, . . . , A_n).$$

The content of the new table S is exactly the same as the content of the old table R—that is, a row u is in S if and only if a row t exists in R such that $u[B_i] = t[A_i]$ for i, $1 \leq i \leq n$. The symbol := used in this assignment is called the *assignment operation*.

We've caused ourselves extra effort by requiring that the assignment operation allow a redefinition of all the attribute names in the heading of the original table. We will see the value of this shortly. For now, we note that a redefinition of attributes is not always necessary, and when all attributes are identical between the two tables, $B_i = A_i$ for all i, $1 \leq i \leq n$, we refer to S as an *alias* of the table R and simply write

S := R ∎

Note that the table R on the right can result from an evaluation of a relational algebra expression, and thus gives us an opportunity to "save" intermediate results of evaluation, much as we do with assignment statements used in programming languages. The table S on the left of the assignment operation must always be a named table, however; it cannot be an expression.

EXAMPLE 2.6.3

Consider the tables R and S given in Example 2.6.1. Using the assignment operation, we can define a new table:

T := (R ∪ S) – (R ∩ S)

This has the form

T

A	B	C
a1	b1	c2
a2	b1	c2
a3	b2	c3

We could also have defined the table T by first defining two intermediate tables:

T1 := (R ∪ S)
T2 := (R ∩ S)
T := T1 – T2 ∎

Note that in Example 2.6.3, the two intermediate tables T1 and T2 are not mandatory, because expressions in relational algebra allow arbitrary nesting. If we are given an expression expr1 involving T1, and T1 is represented through an assignment as an expression expr2 involving other tables, then we can substitute expr2 for every occurrence of T1 in expr1 to achieve the same result. The major motivation for the assignment operation in the following sections will be to display intermediate results of a complex expression to improve human understanding.

The Product Operation

The *product* operation of relational algebra is based on the set-theoretic operation of the Cartesian product. In what follows, we will generally assume that R and S are two tables with Head(R) = $A_1 \ldots A_n$ and Head(S) = $B_1 \ldots B_m$. Taking the product of R and S allows us to create a new table with rows containing all possible associations between the rows of the two tables. If r is a row in R consisting of the tuple of values $(r(A_1), \ldots, r(A_n))$, and s is a row in S with the tuple of values $(s(B_1), \ldots, s(B_m))$, then the usual definition of the Cartesian product would imply that the product of R and S contains all *pairs* of tuples from R and S, with the form $((r(A_1), \ldots, r(A_n)), (s(B_1), \ldots, s(B_m)))$. This distinction between columns of R and columns of S—that their values fall in separate component tuples of a set of Cartesian pairs—doesn't jibe with our definition of a relational table, which makes all columns indistinguishable. Thus we need a more relationally oriented definition.

DEFINITION 2.6.4 Product. The *product* of the tables R and S is a table T whose heading is Head(T) = $R.A_1 \ldots R.A_n\ S.B_1 \ldots S.B_m$. We say t is a row in T if and only if there are two rows u in R and v in S such that t is the concatenation of u with v, u ∥ v. To define this idea of concatenation in a more basic fashion, we say that t is a row in T if and only if there are two rows u in R and v in S such that $t(R.A_i) = u(A_i)$ for $1 \le i \le n$ and $t(S.B_j) = v(B_j)$ for $1 \le j \le m$. The product T of R and S is denoted by $R \times S$.   ■

We refer to attribute names of the form W.A (where W is a name of one of the tables involved in the product) as *qualified attribute names* or simply as *qualified attributes*. The heading of a product consists of qualified attributes, and we may use such attributes whenever we need to emphasize the table from which these attributes originated, usually because the same column name appears in both tables of the product, and confusion might otherwise result. If an attribute name appears in only one table, we can refer to it using its unqualified name.

EXAMPLE 2.6.4
Consider the tables R and S, and the product R × S given below:

R

A	B	C
a1	b1	c1
a1	b2	c3
a2	b1	c2

S

B	C	D
b1	c1	d1
b1	c1	d3
b2	c2	d2
b1	c2	d4

R × S

R.A	R.B	R.C	S.B	S.C	S.D
a1	b1	c1	b1	c1	d1
a1	b1	c1	b1	c1	d3
a1	b1	c1	b2	c2	d2
a1	b1	c1	b1	c2	d4
a1	b2	c3	b1	c1	d1
a1	b2	c3	b1	c1	d3
a1	b2	c3	b2	c2	d2
a1	b2	c3	b1	c2	d4
a2	b1	c2	b1	c1	d1
a2	b1	c2	b1	c1	d3
a2	b1	c2	b2	c2	d2
a2	b1	c2	b1	c2	d4

In the table R × S, the attributes A and D are unique and may be referred to without qualification, whereas the attributes R.B and S.B, for example, must be distinguished by their *qualifier names* (or simply *qualifiers*), R and S. In Table R × S, given above, all column names are qualified. ∎

This example shows that we can use the product operation to build large tables starting from tables that are relatively small. For instance, the product of two tables that have one thousand rows each is a table having one million rows!

A special situation arises if we intend to compute the product of a table with itself. Note that if we consider taking the product R × R, then Definition 2.6.4 implies we would have a problem with the qualifier names, since R × R would have the heading $R.A_1 \ldots R.A_n\ R.A_1 \ldots R.A_n$. With these names it would not be possible to tell apart similarly named attributes of the two factors, and so this product, R × R, is clearly unacceptable. Such a situation must be avoided by creating an *alias* of the table R, using the assignment S := R, and then performing the product between R and its alias: R × S.

2.7   Native Relational Operations

We define four native operations that deal specifically with the relational structure of tables. The native operations of relational algebra are projection, selection, join, and division.

As in the definition of the product operation, we deal with tables R and S having headings $Head(R) = A_1 \ldots A_n$ and $Head(S) = B_1 \ldots B_m$.

The Projection Operation

The operation of *projection* acts on a table by deleting some of its columns, both in the heading and in the corresponding column values of the table content. We say that we project the table *onto* the set of columns that remain undeleted. Note that different rows of a table R, when projected onto a subset of columns, may become identical, because distinguishing values between the rows existed in columns that were deleted. When this happens, the projection operator will also delete duplicate rows, until only one copy of each duplicate set of rows is present in the result. Here is a somewhat more rigorous definition.

DEFINITION 2.7.1 Projection. The projection of R on attributes $A_{i_1}, \ldots, A_{i_k}$, where $\{A_{i_1}, \ldots, A_{i_k}\} \subseteq \{A_1, \ldots, A_n\}$, is a table T whose heading is $\text{Head}(T) = A_{i_1} \ldots A_{i_k}$, with the following content. For every row r in the table R there will be a single row t in the table T such that $r[A_{ij}] = t[A_{ij}]$ for every A_{ij} contained in $\{A_{i_1}, \ldots, A_{i_k}\}$. The projection of R on $A_{i_1}, \ldots, A_{i_k}$ is denoted by $R[A_{i_1}, \ldots, A_{i_k}]$.   ■

The projection operation wipes out the columns of a table that are *not* named in the list of attributes enclosed in square brackets.

EXAMPLE 2.7.1
Suppose that we wish to post a list of customer names from the CUSTOMERS table of Figure 2.2 but not include their identification numbers, cities, and discounts. This can be accomplished in relational algebra by writing

```
CN := CUSTOMERS[cname]
```

The resulting table CN shown below is a "vertical" section of the table CUSTOMERS consisting of the column cname.

CN

cname
Tiptop
Basics
Allied
ACME

Note that two rows with duplicate ACME values in Figure 2.2 have become a single row in the projection.   ■

This is the first time we have created a relational algebra expression to answer an English-language request for data. We call such an expression a *relational algebra query*, or simply a *query*.

The Selection Operation

The next operation defined is *selection*, which creates a new table by selecting from a given table only those rows that satisfy a specified criterion. The general form of the condition that specifies this criterion is the subject of the following definition.

DEFINITION 2.7.2 Selection. Given a table S with Head(S) = $A_1 . . . A_n$, the selection operation creates a new table, denoted by

```
S where C
```

with the same set of attributes, and consisting of those tuples of S that obey the *selection condition*, or simply *condition*, denoted by C. A condition of selection determines, for each given tuple of the table, whether that tuple is *qualified* to remain in the set of selected rows making up the answer. The form a condition C can take is defined recursively as follows.

[1] C can be any comparison of the form $A_i \propto A_j$, or $A_i \propto a$, where A_i and A_j are attributes of S having the same domain, a is a constant from Domain(A_i), and $\propto$ is one of the comparison operators <, >, =, <=, >=, and <>. (Note that a comparison using the operator <> is true when the two values compared are unequal.) The table S where $A_i \propto A_j$ consists of all rows t of S with the property that $t[A_i] \propto t[A_j]$; the table S where $A_i \propto a$ contains all rows t of S with the property $t[A_i] \propto a$.

Examples in the case of the CUSTOMERS table of Figure 2.2 include city = 'Dallas', and discnt >= 8.00. Note that a character constant is placed between quotes when written in a condition. There are no pairs of attributes in CUSTOMERS that we would expect to have the same value, but an example of such a condition would be city > cname, where the operator > in the case of character constants means that the first operand comes later in alphabetical order than the second.

[2] If C and C' are conditions, then new conditions can be formed by writing C AND C', C OR C', and finally NOT C, possibly enclosing any such newly formed conditions in parentheses. If U := S where C_1, and V := S where C_2, then we have

- The AND connector: S where C_1 and C_2 means the same as U ∩ V.
- The OR connector: S where C_1 or C_2 means the same as U ∪ V.
- The NOT connector: S where not C_1 means the same as S − U.

Thus the table denoted by "S where C" contains all rows of S that obey condition C. A condition is evaluated for a row by testing sub-expression comparisons of the form given in part 1 of Definition 2.7.2, and then checking whether the combined logical statement is true. ∎

EXAMPLE 2.7.2

In order to find all customers based in Kyoto, we need to apply the following selection:

```
CUSTOMERS where city = 'Kyoto'
```

The result of this query, assuming the content seen in Figure 2.2, is the table

cid	cname	city	discnt
c006	ACME	Kyoto	0.00

As another example, suppose that we need to find the products stored in Dallas that cost more than $0.50. This can be accomplished by the selection

```
PRODUCTS where city = 'Dallas' and price > 0.50
```

And the query gives the following result:

pid	pname	city	quantity	price
p05	pencil	Dallas	221400	1.00
p06	folder	Dallas	123100	2.00

■

The operations introduced so far can be combined to solve more complicated queries.

EXAMPLE 2.7.3

It is simple to form a relational algebra expression to retrieve all agents who have a percentage commission of at least 6%. We use selection and define the table L:

```
L := AGENTS where percent >= 6
```

The table resulting from this query with the table content of Figure 2.2 is given in Figure 2.6. Now assume that we want to retrieve all pairs of agents, both with a percentage commission of at least 6%, and both stationed in the same city. We can accomplish this by using the product operator, but we need to be careful not to specify the product L × L, which, as we explained at the end of Section 2.6, is unacceptable. Therefore we start with another alias definition.

```
M := AGENTS where percent >= 6
```

aid	aname	city	percent
a01	Smith	New York	6
a02	Jones	Newark	6
a03	Brown	Tokyo	7
a04	Gray	New York	6

Figure 2.6 `L:= AGENTS where percent >= 6`

And now we can create a solution expression.

```
PAIRS := (L x M) where L.city = M.city
```

With the table M, identical to L except in having a different name, we are able to specify a condition on the product L × M to qualify rows only if the two agent cities are identical. The result of the PAIRS expression based on Figure 2.2 is the following:

PAIRS

L.aid	L.aname	L.city	L.percent	M.aid	M.aname	M.city	M.percent
a01	Smith	New York	6	a01	Smith	New York	6
a01	Smith	New York	6	a04	Gray	New York	6
a02	Jones	Newark	6	a02	Jones	Newark	6
a03	Brown	Tokyo	7	a03	Brown	Tokyo	7
a04	Gray	New York	6	a01	Smith	New York	6
a04	Gray	New York	6	a04	Gray	New York	6

This table contains a lot of redundant information. Actually only one distinct pair of aid values has the property we seek, (a01, a04), but the relational algebra expression for PAIRS also presents the pair in the opposite order, (a04, a01), and pairs of identical agents, such as (a01, a01). It is straightforward to create a more restrictive selection condition that will retrieve distinct pairs of agents only once.

```
PAIRS2 := (L X M) where L.city = M.city and L.aid < M.aid
```

The table resulting from this expression is given by

PAIRS2

L.aid	L.aname	L.city	L.percent	M.aid	M.aname	M.city	M.percent
a01	Smith	New York	6	a04	Gray	New York	6

■

EXAMPLE 2.7.4

We notice in the final answer, PAIRS2 of Example 2.7.3, that there is only a single row, and looking at Figure 2.2 we see why: only two agents are in the same city, and this city is New York. Now we ask the following question. Can we replace the query defined by PAIRS2 with a slightly different query, PAIRS3, where we specify the city of New York instead of specifying equal cities? That is, can we replace

```
PAIRS2 := (L X M) where L.city = M.city and L.aid < M.aid
```

with

```
PAIRS3 := (L X M) where L.city = 'New York' and M.city = 'New York' and L.aid < M.aid
```

If not, why not, since the two queries give the same answer?

This question illustrates a common error that was mentioned earlier, and it is important to become sensitive to this issue. In fact the two queries are quite different, even though they seem to give the same answer. The two queries are guaranteed to give the same answer *only for the content at the given moment* of Figure 2.2. Recall that we made a point in the example of Figure 2.2 that the content of these tables might change quickly, and that our queries should give the right answer without any user knowledge of their contents. If we were suddenly to add to the AGENTS table of Figure 2.2 a new agent tuple, (a07, Green, Newark, 7), then the result of PAIRS2 would change because there is now another pair of agents, (a02, a07), with a percent commission of at least 6%, both in the same city (Newark). This is what we asked to retrieve, and it is appropriate for the answer to change. However, the result of the PAIRS3 query would not change, because we misguidedly substituted for a desired condition (L.city = M.city) a condition that depended on the accidental contents of AGENTS in Figure 2.2 (L.city = 'New York' and M.city = 'New York'). Be careful to avoid this kind of error, known as a *content dependency,* when creating your own relational algebra query expressions to answer questions in the exercises. The fact that two query formulations have the same result for a table of a given content is not sufficient to guarantee that the two formulations are equivalent; they must give the same result for *all possible* contents of the tables involved.   ■

Precedence of Relational Operations

Note that in the expressions of Example 2.7.4 defining PAIRS2 and PAIRS3, the product of L and M is enclosed in parentheses before the where clause is applied. This is because the expression $(L \times M)$ where C has the effect of taking the Cartesian product first and then performing the selection implied by the where clause on this product, whereas $L \times M$ where C has the implied effect of first creating the selection M where C and then taking the Cartesian product with L. Thus the form $L \times M$ where C has the same meaning as if we had written $L \times (M$ where C). In fact the example PAIRS2 would be undefined if we took the second form, since $L \times (M$ where L.city = M.city and L.cid < M.cid) has a where clause that refers to columns not in the table (M) that is the object of selection.

$L \times M$ where C has the same effect as $L \times (M$ where C) because relational algebra operations have an implicit *precedence*, or *binding strength*, that determines which operations are performed first in an expression with no parentheses. Parentheses in an expression override the implicit precedence, so that sub-expressions contained in parentheses are always evaluated first. An example of this in normal (numerical) algebra is the expression $5 \star 3 + 4$. It is probably obvious to you that the value of this expression is 19, because you recognize intuitively that multiplication ($\star$) has a greater precedence than addition ($+$). Writing $5 \star 3 + 4$ is the same as writing $(5 \star 3) + 4$. However, we can override the precedence by placing the parentheses differently: $5 \star 3 + 4$ is 19, but $5 \star (3 + 4)$ is 35. In a similar manner, relational algebra operations have their own precedence, and now that we have seen most of the operations and are starting to combine them in more complex expressions, it's a good time to make this precedence clear.

DEFINITION 2.7.3 Precedence of Relational Operations. The order of precedence for the relational operators is given in Figure 2.7. The table includes the relational operators of join and divide, which will be covered shortly.   ■

Precedence	Operators	Symbols
Highest	PROJECT	R [ ]
	SELECT	R where C
	TIMES	×
	JOIN, DIVIDEBY	⋈, ÷
	INTERSECTION	∩
Lowest	UNION, DIFFERENCE	∪, −

Figure 2.7   Precedence Rules for the Relational Operations

EXAMPLE 2.7.5

Suppose that we wish to determine those cities where we have either customers who have a discount of less than 10% or agents who make a commission of less than 6%. This is accomplished by the following relational algebra expression:

```
(CUSTOMERS where discnt < 10) [city]
    ∪ (AGENTS where percent < 6) [city]
```

Note that the union operator is absolutely required here. We cannot replace it by using an OR connector of Definition 2.7.2 in a selection condition, because the cities in the result come from different tables entirely, with different criteria for inclusion in the final answer. ∎

The Join Operation

The purpose of the *join operation* is to create a table that relates the rows of two given tables that have equal values in identically named columns. For example, when we join the ORDERS table with the CUSTOMERS table, with common column name cid, the resulting table contains order information contained in ORDERS as well as additional information from CUSTOMERS about the customer placing each order. The join operation defined here is also known as *equijoin* or *natural join*.

DEFINITION 2.7.4 Join. Consider the tables R and S, with headings given by

$$\text{Head}(R) = A_1 \ldots A_n B_1 \ldots B_k \text{ and Head}(S) = B_1 \ldots B_k C_1 \ldots C_m$$

where n, k, m are the number of attributes of each category, A, B, and C. We define $B_1 \ldots B_k$ to the complete subset of attributes shared by these two tables, and this subset may possibly be empty if k = 0. Similarly $A_1 \ldots A_n$ are the attributes in R that are not in S, and $C_1 \ldots C_m$ are the attributes in S that are not in R, and either set can also be empty if n = 0 or m = 0. The *join* of the tables R and S is the table represented as R ⋈ S, with a heading $\text{Head}(R \bowtie S) = A_1 \ldots A_n B_1 \ldots B_k C_1 \ldots C_m$. A row t is in the table R ⋈ S if and only if there are two rows u in R and v in S, such that $u[B_i] = v[B_i]$ for all i, $1 \leq i \leq k$; then column values on the row t are defined as follows: $t[A_i] = u[A_i]$ for $1 \leq i \leq n$, $t[B_i] = u[B_i] = v[B_i]$ for $1 \leq i \leq k$, and $t[C_i] = v[C_i]$ for $1 \leq i \leq m$. When the rows u in R and v in S give rise to a row t in T, the two rows are said to be *joinable*.

We refer to $B_1 \ldots B_k$ as the attributes on which the tables R and S are joined. One of the rules of the relational model (which we merely mentioned in passing following RULE 2) states that the ordering of the columns of a table is not significant. In particular, it is not important that the attributes $B_1 \ldots B_k$ appear as a sequence at the end of table R and the beginning of table S, so long as they appear in some position in both tables. ■

EXAMPLE 2.7.6

Consider the following tables R and S:

R

A	B1	B2
a1	b1	b1
a1	b2	b1
a2	b1	b2

S

B1	B2	C
b1	b1	c1
b1	b1	c2
b1	b2	c3
b2	b2	c4

As we see, the second row of table R matches no row in S in the two columns B1 and B2 simultaneously; therefore, it gives rise to no row in R ⋈ S. On the other hand, the first row of the table R can be joined with two rows of S and, therefore, will generate two rows in R ⋈ S. The third row of the table R also matches a single row on the table S. We note that the fourth row in S matches no row in R in the two columns B1 and B2, therefore giving rise to no row in R ⋈ S. The new table R ⋈ S is the following:

R ⋈ S

A	B1	B2	C
a1	b1	b1	c1
a1	b1	b1	c2
a2	b1	b2	c3

■

If the two tables R and S being joined have no common attributes, then the content of the join coincides with the content of the (Cartesian) product of the two tables. That is, if $B_1 \ldots B_k$ is an empty set, k = 0, then R ⋈ S is the same as R × S. On the other hand, if R and S are compatible so that all attributes are in common, then the join of the two tables corresponds to the intersection of the two tables. Restated, if $A_1 \ldots A_n$ and $C_1 \ldots C_m$ are both empty sets, n = m = 0, then R ⋈ S is the same as R ∩ S. These equivalencies will be given as exercises at the end of the chapter, but you might give some thought to them now as an aid to understanding the definition.

Let us consider a few examples that involve the CAP database.

EXAMPLE 2.7.7

We wish to find the names of the customers who have ordered product p01. It should be clear that we need to use information from two tables to answer this question, since order information is in the ORDERS table, but the ORDERS table does not contain the customer name; for that value (cname) we need to go to the CUSTOMERS table. It turns out that the natural way to pose this query in relational algebra is to perform a join of the ORDERS and CUSTOMERS tables, so let us start by doing that and then look at the result. If we define CUSTORDS := CUSTOMERS ⋈ ORDERS, Figure 2.8 pictures the table result corresponding to the content of Figure 2.2.

CUSTORDS

cname	city	discnt	ordno	month	cid	aid	pid	qty	dollars
TipTop	Duluth	10.00	1011	jan	c001	a01	p01	1000	450.00
TipTop	Duluth	10.00	1012	jan	c001	a01	p01	1000	450.00
TipTop	Duluth	10.00	1019	feb	c001	a02	p02	400	180.00
TipTop	Duluth	10.00	1018	feb	c001	a03	p04	600	540.00
TipTop	Duluth	10.00	1023	mar	c001	a04	p05	500	450.00
TipTop	Duluth	10.00	1022	mar	c001	a05	p06	400	720.00
TipTop	Duluth	10.00	1025	apr	c001	a05	p07	800	720.00
TipTop	Duluth	10.00	1017	feb	c001	a06	p03	600	540.00
Basics	Dallas	12.00	1013	jan	c002	a03	p03	1000	880.00
Basics	Dallas	12.00	1026	may	c002	a05	p03	800	704.00
Allied	Dallas	8.00	1015	jan	c003	a03	p05	1200	1104.00
Allied	Dallas	8.00	1014	jan	c003	a03	p05	1200	1104.00
ACME	Duluth	8.00	1021	feb	c004	a06	p01	1000	460.00
ACME	Kyoto	0.00	1016	jan	c006	a01	p01	1000	500.00
ACME	Kyoto	0.00	1020	feb	c006	a03	p07	600	600.00
ACME	Kyoto	0.00	1024	mar	c006	a06	p01	800	400.00

Figure 2.8 CUSTORDS := CUSTOMERS ⋈ ORDERS

The only column with a common name between the CUSTOMERS and ORDERS tables is the cid column. Recall that the cid column is a key for the CUSTOMERS table, meaning that the cid value is unique on each row. At the same time, the ORDERS table has a specific cid value on each row listing the customer making the order (duplicate cid values from one row of ORDERS to another is of course possible). The effect of joining the two tables is to extend each row of the ORDERS table with information on a unique row of the CUSTOMERS table with the given cid value. This is clearly an important operation, since we need to be able to relate information about the cid value in ORDERS with information in the CUSTOMERS table for that given cid. We can do the same thing with pid and aid, extending the information on ORDERS rows by providing information about the products and agents, by joining ORDERS with the PRODUCTS or AGENTS tables.

The solution to the problem to find the names of the customers who have ordered product p01 is given by the relational algebra query

```
CNP01 := (CUSTOMERS ⋈ ORDERS where pid = 'p01') [cname]
```

Note that by the precedence rules of relational algebra, there is an implied parentheses around ORDERS where pid = 'p01'. This expression gives us the rows of ORDERS involving sales of product p01. Then the join with CUSTOMERS takes place, extending the information about ORDERS involving product p01 to include cname, and finally the projection on cname takes place so that only the cname column will appear in the answer, CNP01. The final answer is given by

CNP01

EXAMPLE 2.7.8

Now we wish to pose a query to get names of customers who order at least one product costing $0.50. This can be accomplished by first writing

```
CHEAPS := (PRODUCTS where price = 0.50) [pid]
```

to extract the product numbers of products that cost 50 cents. Then, by computing

```
((ORDERS ⋈ CHEAPS) ⋈ CUSTOMERS) [cname]
```

we retrieve those ORDERS involving 50-cent products in ORDERS ⋈ CHEAPS, and we find the names of the customers who placed these ORDERS by joining this intermediate result with the CUSTOMERS table. We can, of course, avoid an assignment statement by combining the two steps above:

```
((ORDERS ⋈ (PRODUCTS where price = 0.50) [pid]) ⋈ CUSTOMERS) [cname]
```

A very important point is that it is *necessary* to project products costing 50 cents onto pid in creating CHEAPS. The expression

```
((ORDERS ⋈ PRODUCTS where price = 0.50) ⋈ CUSTOMERS) [cname]
```

does *not* properly solve the problem, since an extra unforeseen column in the second join is common to the two tables: this expression forces the city of the product to coincide with the city of the customer placing the order for that product. One of the exercises asks you to display the result of this latter query, together with the results obtained by the original relational algebra expression. The moral here is that projection must sometimes be performed to avoid undesired side effects in the join. ∎

Both the product and join operations are *associative*. In other words, if R, S, T are any three tables, we have

$$(R \times S) \times T = R \times (S \times T)$$
$$(R \bowtie S) \bowtie T = R \bowtie (S \bowtie T).$$

Also, product and join are *commutative;* that is, $R \times S = S \times R$ and $R \bowtie S = S \bowtie R$ for all tables R and S. We discuss this and other properties of join in the exercises.

The Division Operation

To introduce division, the last of the native relational operations, consider two tables R and S, where the heading of S is a subset of the heading of R. Specifically, assume that

$$\text{Head}(R) = A_1 \ldots A_n B_1 \ldots B_m, \text{ and } \text{Head}(S) = B_1 \ldots B_m.$$

DEFINITION 2.7.5 Division. The table T is the result of the *division* $R \div S$ (which is read as "R DIVIDEBY S") if $\text{Head}(T) = A_1 \ldots A_n$ and T contains exactly those rows t such that for *every* row s in S, the row resulting from concatenating t and s can be found in table R. (See Definition 2.6.4 for what it means to concatenate t and s.) ■

There are no columns in common between S ($\text{Head}(S) = B_1 \ldots B_m$) and $T = R \div S$ ($\text{Head}(T) = A_1 \ldots A_n$), but since $\text{Head}(R) = A_1 \ldots A_n B_1 \ldots B_m$, we see that S and T have the proper headings, so that it is possible that $T \times S = R$ (or $T \bowtie S = R$, the same thing when there are no columns in common between T and S). This is exactly the sort of division operation we want to define, the *inverse* of the product operation.

THEOREM 2.7.6   We are given two tables T and S, where $\text{Head}(T) = A_1 \ldots A_n$ and $\text{Head}(S) = B_1 \ldots B_m$. If the table R is defined by $R = T \times S$, then it is true that $T = R \div S$.

PROOF. Since $R = T \times S$, we have $\text{Head}(R) = A_1 \ldots A_n B_1 \ldots B_m$. If we denote by W the table resulting from $R \div S$, then by Definition 2.7.5, $\text{Head}(W) = A_1 \ldots A_n$, and W has the same heading as T. Now by the definition of product, if the row t exists in table T we see that for every row s in S, t ‖ s (t concatenated with s) exists in $R = T \times S$. But that is exactly the condition specified in Definition 2.7.5 that will make the row t exist in $W = R \div S$. Thus $T \subseteq W$. By a similar argument we can demonstrate that $W \subseteq T$. ■

Unfortunately the possibility exists that we might start with contents for a table R and a table S so that it is not possible that $R = T \times S$, for any possible choice of T. However, the definition of T implies that when $T = R \div S$, the table T contains the *largest possible set of rows* such that $T \times S \subseteq R$. This is comparable to integer division in C or Java, writing $x = y/z$; we find x is the largest number such that $x * z = y$. We will see more about this in the exercises at the end of the chapter.

EXAMPLE 2.7.9

Suppose that we start with the table R given by

R

A	B	C
a1	b1	c1
a2	b1	c1
a1	b2	c1
a1	b2	c2
a2	b1	c2
a1	b2	c3
a1	b2	c4
a1	b1	c5

We list a number of possible tables S and the resulting table T := R ÷ S.

S

C
c1

T

A	B
a1	b1
a2	b1
a1	b2

In the case above, note that all of the rows in S × T are in R. There couldn't be any larger set of rows in T for which this is true, because only three rows in R have a c1 value in column C.

S

C
c1
c2

T

A	B
a1	b2
a2	b1

Note again that all of the rows in S × T are in R and that there couldn't be any larger set of rows in T for which this is true, as can be seen by looking at rows in R with C value c2.

S

C
c1
c2
c3
c4

T

A	B
a1	b2

Once again the rows in S × T are in R, and by looking at the rows in table R with C values c3 and c4, we see why T has the maximal content with this property.

S

B	C
b1	c1

T

A
a1
a2

Here we see an example of dividing R with three columns by a table S with two columns, resulting in a table T with a single column. Note that there are only two rows in R with B = b1 and C = c1, and these two rows have A = a1 and A = a2, respectively; thus T is maximal.

S

B	C
b1	c1
b2	c1

T

A
a1

You should be able to explain why T is maximal in this case.   ∎

Next we give an example to see why we use division—what kind of question it answers about the data.

EXAMPLE 2.7.10

Suppose that we extract the list of product numbers for products ordered by customer c006. This list is stored in the table PC6

PC6

pid
p01
p07

and can be obtained using the query

```
PC6 := (ORDERS where cid = 'c006')[pid]
```

We are interested in finding the customers who have placed orders for *all* these products. We can extract from ORDERS the customer numbers, together with the products they order, by writing CP := ORDERS[cid, pid]. The query we wish to pose, to retrieve the customers (cid value will identify them) who have placed orders for all parts in PC6, can be solved by applying division. The resulting table CP ÷ PC6 is

CP ÷ PC6

cid
c001
c006

You should draw the lesson from this example that whenever the word "all" is used in a retrieval request, the query expression to use may very well include the division operation. ∎

Note that it is absolutely necessary in Example 2.7.10 to project ORDERS onto the two columns cid, pid before dividing by PC6, rather than projecting on cid after division. Otherwise, we would be asking for additional column values in the ORDERS table to be constant in concatenation with the two pid values of PC6. To illustrate this point, consider the following tables R and S.

R

A	B	C
a1	b1	c1
a2	b1	c1
a3	b2	c1
a1	b1	c2
a2	b2	c2
a3	b3	c2

S

C
c1
c2

By the definition of division, R ÷ S has a heading with columns A B and a single row with values (a1, b1). Thus (R ÷ S)[A] has a single row with value a1. On the other hand, if we first project R on columns A C, R[A, C] has six distinct rows, and R[A, C] ÷ S is a table with the single column A and three rows with values a1, a2, and a3. You should always ask yourself what columns of the table being divided need to be held constant in concatenation with all rows of the divisor.

EXAMPLE 2.7.11

We answer the request to get names of customers who order all products by writing

    ((ORDERS[cid, pid] ÷ PRODUCTS[pid]) ⋈ CUSTOMERS)[cname].

Once again it is necessary to project ORDERS on the attributes [cid, pid] so that the resulting table has only the attribute cid. There is a single customer, c001, corresponding to cname Tip-Top, who orders all products, so that will be the content of the solution table. ∎

Several of the relational operators defined in Section 2.7 are provided simply for added convenience, in the sense that the full power of relational algebra could be achieved with a smaller subset of the operations. We claim that a minimal set of *basic operations* consists of union, difference, product, selection, and projection, together with the assignment operator, which allows us to redefine attribute names. To justify this claim we need to show how the remaining operations—intersection, join, and division—can be expressed using the operations mentioned above. The first two, intersection and join, are easy to demonstrate.

THEOREM 2.8.1 Let R and S be two compatible tables, where Head(R) = Head(S) = A_1 . . . A_n. The intersection operation can be defined in terms of subtraction alone:

$$A \cap B = A - (A - B)$$

PROOF. We demonstrate this by Venn diagrams.

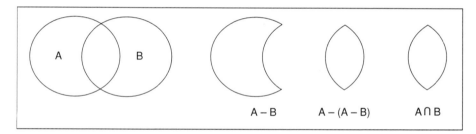

This demonstration can easily be translated into English, if desired. ■

THEOREM 2.8.2 The join of two tables R and S, where Head(R) = A_1 . . . A_n B_1 . . . B_k and Head(S) = B_1 . . . B_k C_1 . . . C_m and n, k, m ≥ 0, can be expressed using product, selection, and projection, together with the assignment operator.

PROOF. To show this, consider the table

T := (R × S) where R.B_1 = S.B_1 and . . . and R.B_k = S.B_k

constructed by using product and selection. This has the appropriate association of rows in R and S to make a join. Now we simply cross out the undesired duplicate columns using projection and redefine the column names using assignment.

T1 := T[R.A_1, . . . , R.A_n, R.B_1, . . . , R.B_k, S.C_1, . . . , S.C_m]
T2(A_1, . . . , A_n , B_1, . . . , B_k, C_1, . . . , C_m) := T1

The table T2 is identical to R⋈ S. ■

The demonstration that division can be expressed in terms of more basic operations is not as simple to grasp, and the proof is starred, meaning that you are not expected to follow it to have a good understanding of the course material. The proof is included for curious readers with a strong mathematics background.

THEOREM 2.8.3* [HARD] Division can be expressed using projection, product, and difference.

PROOF. Consider two tables R and S, where $\text{Head}(R) = A_1 \ldots A_n B_1 \ldots B_m$ and $\text{Head}(S) = B_1 \ldots B_m$. We can prove that

$$R \div S = R[A_1, \ldots, A_n] - ((R[A_1, \ldots, A_n] \times S) - R)\,[A_1, \ldots, A_n].$$

To demonstrate this, suppose that u is a tuple from $R[A_1, \ldots, A_n] - ((R[A_1, \ldots, A_n] \times S) - R)\,[A_1, \ldots, A_n]$. This means that u is in $R[A_1, \ldots, A_n]$ and that u is not a member of the table $((R[A_1, \ldots, A_n] \times S) - R)\,[A_1, \ldots, A_n]$. Suppose that there is a tuple s in S such that u concatenated with s is not in R. Since u is in $R[A_1, \ldots, A_n]$, this is another way of saying that u is a member of $((R[A_1, \ldots, A_n] \times S) - R)\,[A_1, \ldots, A_n]$, which is contradictory. Therefore, for every tuple s in S, u concatenated with s is in R and this means that u belongs to the table $R \div S$.

Conversely, if u is a tuple in the division $R \div S$, clearly u is in $R[A_1, \ldots, A_n]$. On the other hand, u is not in the table $((R[A_1, \ldots, A_n] \times S) - R)\,[A_1, \ldots, A_n]$, for this would mean that there exists a tuple s in S such that u concatenated with s would be in $R[A_1, \ldots, A_n] \times S$ but not in R. Therefore u belongs to the table $R[A_1, \ldots, A_n] - ((R[A_1, \ldots, A_n] \times S) - R)\,[A_1, \ldots, A_n]$, which concludes our argument. You may want to work this out for specific tables, using the division example just given. ∎

Naturally, this leads us to wonder whether the set of basic relational operations (union, difference, product, selection, and projection) is in fact a minimal set. In other words, can we find an even smaller set of operations (among those five) such that we would be able to express all remaining operations with operations from the smaller set? It turns out that these five operations do indeed form a minimal set, and the mathematically inclined reader may wish to consider how this can be proven.

The *power,* or *expressive power,* of a relational query language such as relational algebra or SQL is the ability of that language to create new tables to answer queries from an existing set of tables. In a paper written in 1972, E. F. Codd compared relational algebra with that of another language known as *tuple calculus,* which was based on symbolic logic, and showed that the two are equivalent in power. This became the test of a relational language, that it must have at least the expressive power of relational algebra. A language that passes this test is said to be *complete,* or *relationally complete,* and all modern query languages (such as SQL) have this power. A certain school of thought maintains that the expressive power of relational algebra is insufficient, and we will discuss this later in the chapter.

2.9 | Illustrative Examples

Consider for a moment the power relational algebra gives us to pose queries on the data. We can retrieve any set of column values (projection) from any number of tables, where the rows of the different tables are concatenated into single rows (product) and then restricted by conditions on the different columns (selection). Even ignoring the operations of union and difference, which add certain technical capabilities, this broad-brush outline seems to give us a good deal of power, when we consider how it matches with the English-language requests we might make. The current section explores some of this capability.

In this section we will always derive a final query expression that does not depend on intermediate result tables created by the use of an alias. In general, it is always preferable to give a final answer in the form of a single self-contained expression; we will require single expression solutions in the exercises, in cases where an alias is not absolutely needed. Note, however, that the following set of alias definitions can be used freely as shorthand for the CAP tables.

```
C := CUSTOMERS, A := AGENTS, P := PRODUCTS, O := ORDERS.
```

EXAMPLE 2.9.1

We want to get the names of customers who order at least one product priced at $0.50. The usual way to tackle a problem like this is to build the query inside out. First, start with products priced at $0.50.

```
P where price = 0.50
```

Now how do we find the customers who order the products? Join with ORDERS!

```
(P where price = 0.50) ⋈ O
```

The result gives us a subset of the ORDERS table for the appropriate products, with extended columns containing product information. Unfortunately we do not yet have names of customers, only cid values of customers who order these products. The natural idea is to join with the CUSTOMERS table, but first we have to get rid of the city column in the expression developed so far. The best way to do that is to go back to the first PRODUCTS selection and project out everything but pid. Then we join the result with CUSTOMERS and project the final expression on cname, for the final answer.

```
(((P where price = 0.50)[pid] ⋈ O) ⋈ C)[cname]
```

Note that (P where price = 0.50) is placed in parentheses before projecting on [pid] because otherwise, by the Precedence Table in Figure 2.7, projection would precede selection, so the selection condition on price would be meaningless. After being joined with O, the resulting expression, (P where price = 0.50)[pid] ⋈ O, is enclosed in parentheses again before joining with C. This is because we have only defined join as a binary operation; X ⋈ Y ⋈ Z is not defined yet, and we must write (X ⋈ Y) ⋈ Z. One of the exercises will ask you to show that join is associative: (X ⋈ Y) ⋈ Z = X ⋈ (Y ⋈ Z), so that we can define the expression X ⋈ Y ⋈ Z to stand for either one of these forms. Finally, the expression ((P where price = 0.50)[pid] ⋈ O)

⋈ C is placed in parentheses before projecting on cname; otherwise, the expression ((P where price = 0.50)[pid] ⋈ O) ⋈ C[cname] would project C onto cname before performing the join (precedence, Figure 2.7), and we would lose the join column cid.   ∎

EXAMPLE 2.9.2

We wish to find cids of all customers who do not place any order through agent a03. We can begin by determining those customers who do place some orders through agent a03 by

```
(ORDERS where aid = 'a03') [cid]
```

Now the request originally posed can be solved either by writing

```
ORDERS[cid] − (ORDERS where aid = 'a03') [cid]
```

or

```
CUSTOMERS[cid] − (ORDERS where aid = 'a03') [cid],
```

depending on the nature of the answer we expect. In the first query we retrieve only cid values of customers who place at least *one* order but none through agent a03; in the second query we also retrieve cid values of customers who do not place any orders at all. We should ask ourselves if we want to include such "inactive" customers in our solution. In the absence of any intuition about this (if we are posing an English query request that has been written down by somebody else, and we can't ask that person questions), the latter solution seems preferable, since it contains more information.   ∎

EXAMPLE 2.9.3

Let us now retrieve customers who place orders *only through* agent a03. The query request can be solved by determining initially the customers who place an order through an agent other than a03, and then eliminating these customers from the list of customers who place some orders through a03:

```
ORDERS[cid] − (ORDERS where aid <> 'a03')[cid].
```
  ∎

EXAMPLE 2.9.4

Suppose that we need to find products that have never been ordered by a customer based in New York through an agent based in Boston. It is obviously simpler to find initially those products that violate this condition—that is, products that *have* been ordered by a customer based in New York through an agent based in Boston:

```
(((C where city = 'New York')[cid] ⋈ ORDERS)
    ⋈ A where city = 'Boston') [pid]
```

As before, it is important that the C selection is projected on the cid column before the join with the A selection takes place, so that the join doesn't require matching city values between CUSTOMERS and AGENTS. All we need to do now is to remove this list of products from the list of all products:

```
PRODUCTS[pid] −
(((C where city = 'New York')[cid] ⋈ ORDERS)
    ⋈ A where city = 'Boston') [pid]
```

Once again, we have a choice of starting with PRODUCTS[pid], which might include inactive products that have never been ordered, or ORDERS[pid], which will list only products ordered at least once, and as in Example 2.9.2 we choose the alternative that gives more information. Note that the correct way to handle this in real life is to determine which alternative the user wants. ∎

EXAMPLE 2.9.5

Get names of customers who order all products priced at $0.50. To get the cid values of these customers, we take our hint from the phrase, "who order *all* parts," and think of division to arrive at cid values of such customers:

    O[cid, pid] ÷ (P where price = 0.50)[pid]

To get the names of these customers, we need to join with CUSTOMERS and project on cname.

    ((O[cid, pid] ÷ (P where price = 0.50)[pid]) ⋈ C)[cname] ∎

EXAMPLE 2.9.6

Get cids of customers who order all products that anybody orders. This is division again, and the divisor, the list of "all" products, must be projected from ORDERS rather than PRODUCTS.

    O[cid, pid] ÷ O[pid]

If the divisor were P[pid] instead, we might include a few newly listed products that no one orders yet, and therefore the resulting cid list of the answer would certainly be empty. ∎

EXAMPLE 2.9.7

Get aids of agents who take orders on at least that set of products ordered by c004 (and possibly more). Requests that seem difficult may only need to be rephrased. Try the request: get aids of agents who take orders on all products ordered by c004.

    O[aid, pid] ÷ (O where cid = 'c004')[pid] ∎

EXAMPLE 2.9.8

Get cids of customers who order *both* products p01 *and* p07. Note that the following relational algebra expression does *not* answer this request.

    O where pid = 'p01' and pid = 'p07'   **WRONG EFFECT **

The problem is that each row of ORDERS has only one value for pid, and that value may either be equal to 'p01' or to 'p07', but not to both at once. The proper query to pose is

    (O where pid = 'p01')[cid] ∩ (O where pid = 'p07')[cid]

using intersection to require that customers order both products in distinct ORDERS rows. ∎

EXAMPLE 2.9.9

Get cids of customers who place an order through at least one agent who places an order for product p03. In Figure 2.9, the customers to be retrieved are represented in the rightmost circle, with connections only to the agents in the center circle. Note in particular that the cids retrieved might not place orders for product p03 themselves. In the ORDERS table of Figure 2.2, we see on the fourth row that c001 places an order through a06 for p03; also, on the fourth row

66

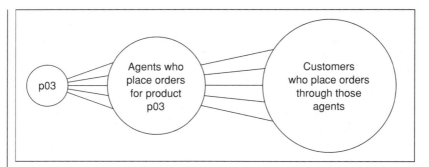

Figure 2.9   Sets of Objects and Their Connections to One Another in Example 2.9.9

from the bottom, c004 places an order through a06 for product p01; therefore, c004 should be included in our answer, since it places an order through at least one agent (a06) who places an order for p03. However, it is easy to check that c004 never places an order for p03.

The correct way to pose this query is by proceeding from the inside out; starting with the middle circle of Figure 2.9, we retrieve the agents who place an order for product p03.

```
(O where pid = 'p03')[aid]
```

The answer we want to achieve is represented in the rightmost circle of Figure 2.9, and we need to retrieve cids of customers who place an order through one of these agents. This implies another use of the ORDERS table, and to be on the safe side we will use a different alias, X := ORDERS, so that there is no confusion of column names in an expression where the same table is used twice:

```
(X ⋈ (O where pid = 'p03')[aid])[cid]
```

It is usually overkill to use different aliases of the same table in expressions where there is no product operation, but we take this approach to simplify the job of composing a query.   ■

EXAMPLE 2.9.10

Get cids of all customers who have the same discount as any customer in Dallas or Boston. This is a counterexample to the idea that the division operation must be used whenever the word *all* is mentioned. In fact the phrase *all customers* early in this request is misleading. The request can be rephrased as follows to be analogous with other requests we have seen: "Get cids of customers who have the same discount as any customer in Dallas or Boston." The point is that when we ask for the cids of customers who have some property, naturally we want to retrieve all such customers; but this doesn't imply that division should be used. To answer this query, we start by finding all the discounts of customers in Dallas or Boston.

```
(C where city = 'Dallas' or city = 'Boston')[discnt]
```

Next, to find all cids of customers with this set of discnt values, we use join. First we create a new alias, D := CUSTOMERS, and then write

```
((C where city = 'Dallas' or city = 'Boston')[discnt] ⋈ D)[cid]
```

These cid values from the rows of table D that join with this set of discnt values give us the desired answer.   ■

EXAMPLE 2.9.11

Suppose that we have a rather complex query to pose. We wish to list pids of products that are ordered through agents who place orders for (possibly different) customers who order at least one product from an agent who has placed an order for customer c001. The secret of creating such a query is to remain calm and work from the inside out.

Working backward, we can determine immediately the agents who have placed some order for customer c001:

```
(O where cid = 'c001')[aid]
```

In turn, the customers who order products through these agents can be determined by

```
(X ⋈ (O where cid = 'c001')[aid])[cid],
```

where X := ORDERS. Given that Y := ORDERS, agents who place ORDERS for these customers can be listed by

```
(Y ⋈ (X ⋈ (O where cid = 'c001')[aid])[cid])[aid]
```

Finally, with Z := ORDERS, the products ordered through these agents are

```
(Z ⋈ (Y ⋈ (X ⋈ (O where cid = 'c001')[aid])[cid])[aid])[pid]
```

This is the answer to our original request.   ∎

EXAMPLE 2.9.12

Get pids of products not ordered by any customer living in a city whose name begins with the letter D. How can we find customers in cities with names beginning with the letter D? Recall that inequalities for character strings reflect alphabetical order, and the following expression suggests itself.

```
C where city >= 'D' and city < 'E'
```

Now products that are not ordered by such customers can be discovered by starting with all products and subtracting the set of ORDERS that are ordered by them.

```
P[pid] - (O ⋈ (C where city >= 'D' and city < 'E'))[pid]
```
                                                                               ∎

2.10 Other Relational Operations

The fundamental set of operations discussed so far is basically an attempt to provide a small collection of useful operations in order to make it possible to pose most English-language queries in relational algebra. There is a theoretical basis for claiming that a useful level of computational power is available to pose queries with the basic operations named. Additional operations can make the job much simpler, however, as we saw when we tried to express the division operation in terms of basic operations.

Next we discuss two additional useful relational operations that are not in the standard set, outer join and theta join (or θ-join). The usage of these operations appears in the following table.

NAME	SYMBOL	KEYBOARD FORM	EXAMPLE
OUTER JOIN	$\bowtie_0$	OUTERJ	R $\bowtie_0$ S, or R OUTERJ S
LEFT OUTER JOIN	$\bowtie_{LO}$	LOUTERJ	R $\bowtie_{LO}$ S, or R LOUTERJ S
RIGHT OUTER JOIN	$\bowtie_{RO}$	ROUTERJ	R $\bowtie_{RO}$ S, or R ROUTERJ S
THETA JOIN	$\bowtie_{A_i \theta B_j}$	JN($A_i \theta B_j$)	R $\bowtie_{A_1 > B_2}$ S, or R JN($A_2 > B_2$) S

The outer join in particular has significant ability to simplify queries in commercial database applications. The capability to perform such a join easily was originally left out of many computer-based query languages, but is now being added. Both of these operations can be expressed in terms of the basic five operations, but the expression for outer join, for example, is not easy to use in practice.

Outer Join

To introduce the outer join we will use two tables, the AGENTS table we have dealt with up to now, and a new table known as SALES. SALES contains two columns, the agent aid that appears in the ORDERS table and a total column giving the dollar total of ORDERS taken by each such agent. If an agent has placed no ORDERS yet, we assume that the aid value for that agent *will not appear* in the SALES table. Now we wish to print a table (as a report to a sales manager) that provides all agent names, their aid, and their total sales (the sales manager is familiar with all agent names and prefers that form, using aid only to distinguish duplicate names). You would think that we need simply to write the relational algebra expression (AGENTS $\bowtie$ SALES)[aname, aid, total]. However, this falls short of the aim described in one important case: if the agent has placed no ORDERS, then we have assumed that the agent's aid will not show up in the SALES table, and therefore it will not show up in the resulting report (no aid value is in SALES to join with the aid value in AGENTS). The sales manager who poses this query will certainly not want an agent's name to disappear from the resulting report when no sales have been made; indeed, this might be a good reason for personnel action. We might also conceivably encounter a situation where a new agent named Beowulf, with aid value a07, has been hired and has taken an order that shows up in the SALES table before any information on the agent appears as a row in the AGENTS table. Then once again the expression (AGENTS $\bowtie$ SALES)[aname, aid, total] would fail to provide needed information to the sales manager, since the aid column in SALES finds no match in AGENTS. The outer join operation, denoted by $\bowtie_0$, is meant to solve problems of this kind. If we write instead

```
(AGENTS ⋈₀ SALES)[aname, aid, total]
```

we will get a table that has *all* values in both tables appearing. In the case of an agent who has made no sales, we would obviously not have a total value in SALES to correspond with this name; therefore, the corresponding total value would be filled in with a null value. The same holds for an agent who has made a sale but whose name is not known in AGENTS. For example, we might see this result:

OJRESULT

aname	aid	total
Smith, J	a01	850.00
Jones	a02	400.00
Brown	a03	3900.00
Gray	a04	null
Otasi	a05	2400.00
Smith, P.	a06	900.00
null	a07	650.00

Note that all unmatched column values show up in the outer join result. Agent Gray, a04, has no sales (no rows in SALES) so the total column is null. Agent Beowulf, a07, has taken an order and thus has a total value, but has no row in the AGENTS table yet, and thus has a null in the aname column.

To define outer join, consider the tables R and S, where $Head(R) = A_1 \ldots A_n B_1 \ldots B_k$ and $Head(S) = B_1 \ldots B_k C_1 \ldots C_m$, where n, k, m $\geq$ 0.

DEFINITION 2.10.1   Outer Join. The *outer join* of the tables R and S is the table $R \bowtie_0 S$, where $Head(R \bowtie_0 S) = A_1 \ldots A_n B_1 \ldots B_k C_1 \ldots C_m$. A row t is in the table $R \bowtie_0 S$ if one of the following situations occurs:

[1] Two rows u and v are joinable in R and S, respectively, so that $u[B_i] = v[B_i]$ for all i, $1 \leq i \leq k$; in this case we define t by setting $t[A_l] = u[A_l]$ for $1 \leq l \leq n$, $t[B_i] = u[B_i] = v[B_i]$ for $1 \leq i \leq k$, and $t[C_j] = v[C_j]$ for $1 \leq j \leq m$.

[2] A row u is in R such that no v in S is joinable with u. In this case, $t[D] = u[D]$ for every D in $Head(R)$ and $t[D]$ is null for every D in $\{C_1, \ldots, C_k\}$.

[3] A row v is in S such that no u in R is joinable with v. In this case $t[D] = v[D]$ for every D in $Head(S)$ and $t[D]$ = null for every D in $\{A_1, \ldots, A_n\}$.   ∎

We say that the outer join preserves unmatched rows, in the sense that a row from a table on one side of the outer join, with unmatched join column values in the table on the other side, will still show up in the outer join result. The idea of the *left outer join* and *right outer join* operators is that we might wish to preserve unmatched rows on one side only. The left outer join operator preserves unmatched rows in the table on the left of the operator, filling in nulls for missing row values from the table on the right, and the right outer join does the opposite, preserving unmatched rows from the table on the right. For example, assume we have a table named SPECIAL_AGENTS, compatible with the AGENTS table but containing only rows for agents on a special list (say, a01, a04, and a06). We want to see the same kind of report for these agents as was given in OJRESULT. Now if we use the expression

(SPECIAL_AGENTS $\bowtie$ SALES)[aname, aid, total],

we will not see the null sales total for agent a04, whereas if we use the expression

(SPECIAL_AGENTS $\bowtie_0$ SALES)[aname, aid, total],

we will see all agents, not just a01, a04, and a06, in the result, with nulls for the aname values not in SPECIAL_AGENTS, as follows:

OJRESULT2

aname	aid	total
Smith, J	a01	850.00
null	a02	400.00
null	a03	3900.00
Gray	a04	null
null	a05	2400.00
Smith, P.	a06	900.00
null	a07	650.00

This is the full outer join using SPECIAL_AGENTS instead of AGENTS. But all we really want is a report for the agents in SPECIAL_AGENTS. In a company with thousands of agents, receiving all this unwanted extra information would be quite a serious problem. In order to get what we really want, we would use the left outer join operator in the expression

(SPECIAL_AGENTS $\bowtie_{LO}$ SALES)[aname, aid, total],

with the resulting table:

LORESULT

aname	aid	total
Smith, J.	a01	850.00
Gray	a04	null
Smith, P.	a06	900.00

This is the result of a left outer join, displaying exactly the information we want. As an example of the use of a right outer join, we would get the same result as this from the expression

(SALES ⋈$_{RO}$ SPECIAL_AGENTS)[aname, aid, total]

We leave it as an exercise for you to determine how Definition 2.10.1 of an outer join must change in order to provide a valid definition of left outer join and right outer join.

Theta Join

The idea of a theta join, or θ-join, is that we might wish to join two tables where equality of attributes with the same name is not what is desired. The symbol θ stands for the comparison operator that will relate columns of different tables in the definition of the θ-join; it may be one of >, <, >=, <=, =, <>.

DEFINITION 2.10.2 Theta Join. Let R and S be two tables, with Head(R) = $A_1 \ldots A_n$ and Head(S) = $B_1 \ldots B_m$. We admit the possibility that any column A_i in Head(R) might have the same column name as a column B_j in Head(S), but we do not specify any columns in common. Suppose that the attributes A_i and B_j have the same domain and the relational operation θ is one of the set { >, <, >=, <=, <> }. If A_i and B_j are different names, the *θ-join* of the tables R and S is the table T := R ⋈ $_{A_i \theta B_j}$ S, where

$$\text{Head}(R \bowtie_{A_i \theta B_j} S) = A_1 \ldots A_n B_1 \ldots B_m.$$

Otherwise, if A_i and B_j are the same names, we must qualify the θ-join of the tables R and S, T := R ⋈ $_{R.A_i \theta S.B_j}$ S. We will assume unqualified names in what follows.

The rows of the new table have the form t = $(a_1, \ldots, a_n, b_1, \ldots, b_m)$, where

$a_i \theta b_j$, $(a_1, \ldots, a_n)$ is in R, and $(b_1, \ldots, b_m)$ is in S.

It is easy to see that θ-joins can be expressed using the basic operations of relational algebra.   ∎

EXAMPLE 2.10.1

Find all ordno values for orders whose order quantity exceeds the current quantity on hand for the product. This is solved by the theta join

(ORDERS ⋈ $_{ORDERS.qty \, > \, PRODUCTS.quantity}$ PRODUCTS)[ordno]

This is equivalent to the relational algebra expression

((ORDERS x PRODUCTS) where ORDERS.qty > PRODUCTS.quantity)[ordno]   ∎

The condition ORDERS.qty > PRODUCTS.quantity is referred to as the *θ-condition*. A common way of referring to the θ-join of this example is to say that it is a *greater-than join*. You will recall that the standard join operator is referred to as an *equijoin* or, sometimes, a *natural join*.

Suggestions for Further Reading

The relational model has many ramifications that we have not touched on in this short introduction. An excellent and quite advanced theoretical presentation is by David Maier [2]. The founding paper on the relational model, by E. F. Codd, is contained in Section 1.2 of *Readings in Database Systems* [1]. A number of other papers in these *Readings* may also be of interest.

[1] E. F. Codd. "A Relational Model of Data for Large Shared Data Banks." In *Readings in Database Systems*, 3rd ed. Michael Stonebraker and Joseph M. Hellerstein, editors. San Francisco: Morgan Kaufmann, 1998.

[2] David Maier. *The Theory of Relational Databases*. New York: Computer Science Press, 1983.

Exercises

One must learn by doing the thing; though you think you know it, you have no certainty until you try.
—Sophocles, 495–406 BC

Some of the following exercises have solutions at the end of the book in "Solutions to Selected Exercises." These exercises are marked with the symbol •.

[2.1] Assume that the tables of this exercise are like Example 2.4.1, in that they have *all the rows they are ever going to have,* so that we can figure out the intentions of the designer regarding keys for the table by merely looking at the contents of the rows.

T1

A	B	C	D
a1	b1	c1	d1
a2	b3	c1	d2
a3	b4	c2	d2
a4	b2	c2	d1

(a)• Consider the table T1, above. Find the three candidate keys for this table. One of the keys has two columns.

(b) Consider the table T2, following:

T2

A	B	C	D	E
a1	b1	c1	d1	e1
a2	b1	c1	d1	e2
a3	b1	c2	d1	e1
a4	b2	c1	d1	e1

Find the two candidate keys for this table.

(c)• Create an example of a table as in exercise (a) that has four columns and *only four rows,* but has only one candidate key, consisting of the first three columns. Be careful that *no pair* of the first three columns distinguishes all rows.

(d) Create an example of a table as in exercise (b) that has five columns, A B C D E, and only five rows, with only one candidate key consisting of the first four columns. Give an informal argument why no other set of columns in this table forms a key.

[2.2] Consider a database for the telephone company that contains a table SUBSCRIB-ERS, whose heading is

```
name ssn address city zip information-no
```

Assume that "information-no" is the unique 10-digit telephone number, including area code, provided for subscribers. Although one subscriber may have multiple phone numbers, such alternate numbers are carried in a separate table; the current table has a row for each distinct subscriber (but note that husband and wife, subscribing together, can occupy two rows and share an information number). The DBA has set up the following rules about the table, reflecting design intentions for the data:

◆ No two subscribers (on separate rows) have the same Social Security number.

◆ Two different subscribers can share the same information number (for example, husband and wife). They are listed separately in the SUBSCRIBERS table. However, two different subscribers with the *same name* cannot share the same address, city, and zip code *and* also the same information number. For example, if Diane and David Isaacs who live together and share the same information number wish to both be listed as D. Isaacs, they will be asked to differentiate their two names, say, by spelling out at least one of them.

(a)• Identify all candidate keys for the SUBSCRIBERS table, based on the assumptions given above. Note that there are three such keys; one of them contains the information-no attribute and a different one contains the zip attribute.

(b) Which of these candidate keys would you choose for a primary key? Explain why.

[2.3]   Recall that in Section 2.2, under the heading "Tables and Relations," we defined the Cartesian product: CP = CID X CNAME X CITY X DISCNT. In the paragraph just before Example 2.2.1, we pointed out that it would not make sense to have the CUSTOMERS table contain all the rows of this Cartesian product, because if any of the domains CNAME, CITY, and DISCNT contained more than one value, there would have to be at least two rows in the Cartesian product with the same CID value. Give an example to illustrate this, and explain why this implication is always true as long as any rows at all exist in CP.

[2.4]   Solve in relational algebra the following queries involving the CAP database. These problems are basic and meant as a warm-up for the following exercise.

(a)• Find all (ordno, pid) pairs for orders of quantity equal to 1000 or more.

(b) Find all product names of products priced between $0.50 and $1.00, inclusive.

(c)• Find all (ordno, cname) pairs for orders of dollar value less than $500. Use one join here.

(d) Find all (ordno, aname) pairs for orders in March. Use one join here.

(e)• Find all (ordno, cname, aname) triples for orders in March. Use two joins here.

(f) Find all the names of agents in New York who placed orders of individual dollar value less than $500.

(g)• Find all product names of products in Duluth ordered in March.

[2.5]   Solve in relational algebra the following queries involving the CAP database. (These requests will be used again in the next chapter to demonstrate capabilities of the computer-based query language SQL.) NOTE: In all requests that follow, you should pose the query as a single, self-contained relational algebra expression that does not depend on any intermediate results created by means of an alias, except where absolutely necessary.

(a)• Find all (cid, aid, pid) triples for customer, agent, product combinations that are all in the same city. Nothing about orders is involved in this selection.

(b) Find all (cid, aid, pid) triples for customer, agent, product combinations that are *not* all in the same city (any two may be).

(c)• Find all (cid, aid, pid) triples for customer, agent, product combinations, *no two of which* are in the same city.

(d) Get cities of agents booking an order from customer c002.

(e)• Get product names ordered by at least one customer based in Dallas through an agent based in Tokyo.

(f) Get pids of products ordered through any agent who makes at least one order for a customer in Kyoto. NOTE: The request posed here is not the same as asking for pids of products ordered by a customer in Kyoto.

(g)• Display all pairs of aids for agents who live in the same city.

(h) Find cids of customers who did not place an order through agent a03.

(i)• Find cids of customers who have the largest discount; separately, find those who have the smallest discount. NOTE: This is quite hard with the operations provided in relational algebra.

(j) Find cids of customers who order all products.

(k)• Find pids of products ordered through agent a03 but not through agent a06.

(l) Get pnames and pids of products that are stored in the same city as one of the agents who sold these products.

(m)•Get aids and anames of agents with aname beginning with the letter "N" who do not place orders for any product in Newark.

(n) Get cids of customers who order both product p01 and product p07.

(o)• Get names of agents who place orders for all products ordered by customer c002.

(p) Get names of agents who place orders for all products that are ordered by any customer at all. (Hint: The phrase "any customer at all" means the same as "some customer.")

(q)• Get (cid, aid, pid) triples for customer, agent, product combinations so that *at most two* of them are in the same city. (Is this equivalent to any of the first three queries of this exercise, (a), (b), or (c)?)

(r) Get pids of products ordered by all customers who place any order through agent a03.

(s)• Get aids of agents who place individual orders in dollar value greater than $500 for customers living in Kyoto.

(t) Give all (cname, aname) pairs where the customer places an order through the agent.

(u)• [HARD] Get cids of customers who order all their products through only one agent.

[2.6]   (a)   Given the tables R and S in Example 2.6.1, display the table for R JOIN S.

(b)• Demonstrate why it is true (prove) that if Head(R) ∩ Head(S) = Ø (there are no columns in common), then the tables R × S and R ⋈ S are equal. Here and elsewhere in this book, two tables are said to be equal if they have the same column headings and content: the order of the rows does not change the content. Even if you do not give a mathematically perfect proof, you should be able to explain why R × S and R ⋈ S are equal here.

[2.7]• Let R and S be two relations with no attributes in common, as in 2.6. Show that

R ⋈ S ÷ S is equal to R

[2.8]   Recall that Theorem 2.8.2 shows how the expression R ⋈ S can be expressed in terms of product, selection, and projection (using assignment as well).

(a)• Show how outer join can be expressed in terms of other operations. You are allowed to use normal join, union, product, selection, and projection.

(b)   Show how theta join can be expressed in terms of product, selection, and projection.

[2.9]   Explain why, for any tables R, S, and T, the following formulas always hold.

(a)• (R ⋈ S) ⋈ T = R ⋈ (S ⋈ T)

(b)   R ⋈ S = S ⋈ R

[2.10]   Show that R ⋈ S = R ∩ S if and only if R and S are compatible.

NOTE: The following exercises require some mathematical training.

[2.11]• Show that for any conditions C_1, C_2 on the table R, the following queries are equivalent in meaning:

(R where C_1) where C_2

(R where C_2) where C_1

R where (C_1 and C_2)

[2.12]   Prove that for any table R, attribute A of R, and value a in the domain of A, there always exists a table S_a such that the selection (R where A = a) can be expressed as R ⋈ S_a. Note that S_a is independent of R.

[2.13]• Let R, S be two compatible relations. If R and S are regarded as sets of tuples, then we can use the notation for set inclusion and write R ⊆ S if every tuple of the relation R is also a tuple of the relation S. Prove that, if R ⊆ S, then R ⋈ T ⊆ S ⋈

T; also, if U and V are tables with appropriate headings, then $U \div R \supseteq U \div S$ and $R \div V \subseteq S \div V$. If C is a condition, then (R where C) $\subseteq$ (S where C).

[2.14] Let R, S be two relations, where Head(R) = H and Head(S) = K. Prove that the following equalities hold:

$$(R \bowtie S) [H] = R [H] \bowtie S[H \cap K] = R \bowtie S[H \cap K].$$

The common value of these relations is called the *semijoin* of R and S; it is denoted by $R \ltimes S$.

Note that in general $R \ltimes S$ is distinct from $S \ltimes R$. The semijoin $\ltimes$ plays an important role in distributed databases.

[2.15] Let R, S be two compatible relations and let H be a set of attributes that is a subset of a common heading. Prove or disprove the following equalities:

(a) $(R \cap S)[H] = R[H] \cap S[H]$

(b)• $(R \cup S)[H] = R[H] \cup S[H]$

(c) $(R - S)[H] = R[H] - S[H]$

When you disprove one of these equalities, show that one side is included in the other.

Basic SQL Query Language   3

SQL really is great, compared with older-style database languages such as DL/I. . . .
The stories regarding ease of application development, ease of maintenance,
improved productivity, etc., really do have a significant basis in fact. Nevertheless,
the picture is not quite as rosy as some people have tried to paint it. . . .
—C. J. Date, What's Wrong with SQL?

This chapter introduces the *Basic form* of the database language known as SQL, a language that allows us to query and manipulate data on computerized *relational* database systems. SQL has been the lingua franca for RDBMS since the early 1980s, and it is of fundamental importance for many of the concepts presented in this text. The SQL language is currently in transition from the relational form (the ANSI SQL-92 standard) to a newer object-relational form (ANSI SQL-99, which was released in 1999). SQL-99 should be thought of as extending SQL-92, not changing any of the earlier valid language. The *Basic form* of SQL (or *Basic SQL*) introduced in the current chapter includes all the *relational* capabilities of the SQL-92 and SQL-99 standards that are available on most major database products. Usually, the Basic SQL we define matches most closely the ANSI SQL standards basic subsets, called *Entry SQL-92* and *Core SQL-99*, respectively. However, we also include a few features outside Entry SQL-92 and Core SQL-99 that are commonly implemented; our touchstone in defining Basic SQL is to provide a syntax that is fully available on most of the major RDBMS products. Chapter 4 will cover the newer *object-relational* syntax, which extends Basic SQL in a new direction. In both chapters, we will give frequent illustrative examples from commonly used database products.

3.1   Introduction

We begin with an overview of SQL capabilities, then we explain something about the multiple SQL standards and dialects and how we will deal with these in our presentation.

SQL Capabilities

In Chapter 2 we saw how relational algebra queries could be constructed to answer English-language requests for information from a database. In Chapter 3 we will learn how to pose comparable queries in SQL, using a form known as the *Select statement*. As we will see, the SQL Select statement offers more flexibility in a number of ways than relational algebra for posing queries. However, there is no fundamental improvement in power, nothing that couldn't be achieved in relational algebra, given a few well-considered extensions. For this reason, experience with relational algebra gives us a good idea of what can be accomplished in SQL. At the same time, SQL and relational algebra have quite different conceptual models in a number of respects, and the insight drawn from familiarity with the relational algebra approach may enhance your understanding of SQL capabilities.

The most important new feature you will encounter with SQL is the ability to pose queries interactively in a computerized environment. The SQL Select statement is more complicated and difficult to master than the relatively simple relational algebra, but you should never feel lost or uncertain as long as you have access to computer facilities where a few experiments can clear up uncertainties about SQL use. The interactive SQL environment discussed in the current chapter allows you to type a query on a monitor screen and get an immediate answer. Such *interactive queries* are sometimes called *ad hoc queries*. (*Ad hoc* is a Latin phrase meaning "for this specific purpose.") This term refers to the fact that an SQL Select statement is meant to be composed all at once in a few typewritten lines and not be dependent on any prior interaction in a user session. The feature of not being dependent on prior interaction is also known as *non-procedurality*. SQL differs in this way even from relational algebra, where a prior alias statement might be needed in order to represent a product of a table with itself. The difference between SQL and procedural languages such as Java or C is profound: you don't need to write a program to try out an SQL query, you just have to type the relatively short, self-contained text of the query and submit it.

Of course, an SQL query can be rather complex. In Figure 3.1 we illustrate the full form of the Basic SQL Select statement. A limited part of this full form, known as a *Subquery*, is defined recursively, and the full Select statement form has one added clause. You shouldn't feel intimidated by the complexity of the Select statement, however. The fact that a Select statement is non-procedural means that it has a lot in common with a menu-driven application, where a user is expected to fill in some set of choices from a menu and then press the Enter key to execute the menu choices all at once. The various clauses of the Select statement correspond to menu choices: you will occasionally need all these clauses, but don't expect to use all of them every time you pose a query.

In addition to the ability to pose queries with an SQL Select statement, a relational database system must provide the means to perform a variety of other operational and housekeeping tasks. At the beginning of this chapter, we learn how to perform certain simple *data definition statements*, such as a limited version of the SQL *Create Table statement* that we need to create the tables in the CAP database. Housekeeping tasks of this kind are usually performed by a database administrator (DBA). We put off until

```
subquery ::=
    SELECT [ALL | DISTINCT] { * | expr [[AS] c_alias] {, expr [[AS] c_alias]...}}
        FROM tableref {, tableref...}
        [WHERE search_condition]
        [GROUP BY colname {, colname...}]
        [HAVING search_condition];


    | subquery {UNION [ALL]| INTERSECT [ALL] | EXCEPT [ALL]} subquery

select statement ::=
    subquery [ORDER BY result_column [ASC|DESC] {, result_column [ASC|DESC]...}]
```

Figure 3.1 General Form of the Basic SQL Subquery and Select Statement

Chapter 7 most other SQL statements used by a DBA for data definition purposes, such as creating views of the data, as well as more complex features of the Create Table statement required to impose integrity constraints on data updates. Investigation of the complex Select statement takes up most of the current chapter, and only in Section 3.10 do we present the other *data manipulation statements* of SQL. With these new statements we will be able to perform all needed update operations on database tables: inserting new rows into a table, deleting existing rows from the table, and changing column values in existing rows. All of Chapter 3 deals with SQL statements that can be posed by the user in the interactive environment we have described. In Chapter 5 we will consider how to write programs to execute these SQL statements and numerous others. One form of SQL that is used in programs is known as *Embedded SQL,* which is somewhat different from the interactive form.

SQL History—Standards and Dialects

The first SQL prototype was developed by IBM researchers during the 1970s. The prototype was named SEQUEL, an acronym for Structured English QUEry Language. The SQL language that followed this prototype is still pronounced "sequel" by many, although the official pronunciation according to the ANSI SQL Committee is "ess cue ell." Several relational database system products using SQL dialects were released in the early 1980s, and since that time SQL has become the international standard database language (although the "standard" SQL is a moving target, as we will see). As SQL became the standard, a number of older languages fell into disuse when the commercial database system vendors that supported them rushed to introduce SQL dialects of their own. Notwithstanding the great similarity among most product dialects of SQL, the number of differences that do exist can be confusing to the beginner. For this reason, the current text concentrates on introducing our own "standard" SQL, which we have been calling Basic SQL (distilling a current target language out of a number of existing standards), and then tracks important differences from that standard in a few major database

82

system products: **ORACLE** release 8.1.5, **INFORMIX** release 9.2, and **DB2 Universal Database** version 6 (which we will refer to as **DB2 UDB** to differentiate it from other versions, for example, from the older DB2 system that runs only on OS/390. Occasional references are also made to other important products, such as **SYBASE** and **MICROSOFT SQL Server**. The reader who goes on to work with database systems will quite likely be using one of these.

Let us expand on the idea of an SQL standard. Several SQL "standards" are currently being referenced by database products and in course texts. The specification adopted by the American National Standards Institute (ANSI) in 1989 to replace the earlier 1986 standard, is known as SQL-89, and this was also adopted by the International Standards Organization (ISO). SQL-86 and SQL-89 were both missing a number of important DBA capabilities and formed a sort of minimal standard—a common denominator that most relational database products were already able to meet years ago. This amounted to a lack of guidance on newer product features, which were developed incompatibly and detracted from interoperability (that is, it became difficult to write a program using SQL that would operate on different database products). The X/Open standard was put forward by an open systems consortium, initially consisting of UNIX SQL vendors, to develop a common set of extensions to the ANSI/ISO standard and allow greater portability of SQL applications between products.

During the same period, the ANSI and ISO committees were taking a new direction. The approach adopted was to leapfrog existing versions and provide an SQL standard to anticipate future needs, so that vendors could develop new features without being plagued by the incompatibility problems that had arisen earlier. While this approach was under development, suggested future capabilities were assigned to two different revision lists, code-named SQL2 and SQL3. In 1992, the SQL2 version was released by ANSI/ISO, with the standard name SQL-92. There were a number of levels of compliance for SQL-92, from "Entry," which represents minimal extensions from SQL-89, to "Intermediate" and "Full." It has become obvious that major vendors will probably never comply with the higher levels of SQL-92, so that some of these features will never be adopted in practice. The SQL-99 revision, completed in 1999, had even more advanced features (including object-relational capabilities). Even before SQL-99 was finalized, some of the database products had already implemented features that anticipated this standard. SQL-99 moves away from the idea of "levels of compliance" and instead creates a "Core" level of features that everyone agrees are important, with additional feature sets that vendors can support for particular application uses.

As we can see, the SQL standard is a moving target, and the term "standard" comes near to losing its meaning (although the ANSI SQL Standards Committee intends that SQL-99 obsoletes SQL-92, and upward compatibility of features from SQL-92 to SQL-99 is impressively thought out). In the current chapter, we will concentrate on SQL-99, with reference to the X/Open standard when this seems relevant. As we have said, it is likely that some features in the broader SQL-99 (and the older Full SQL-92) standard will never be implemented by some vendors, while the X/Open standard makes a strong point of portability between systems and would not include features that member vendors have not agreed to adopt. In this chapter, we will introduce the relational SQL-99 features that have already been implemented in some products, but we put off a consideration of object-relational capabilities to Chapter 4. The current chapter introduces Basic SQL, which includes features from SQL-92 and SQL-99 that have been implemented by all the major vendors we study, and Chapter 4 will cover the object-relational features that are now supported by some database products.

Now for a short history of the commercial database products covered here. Note that it is the current vogue to refer to database products as *relational*, even when the most recent version of the product supports the *object-relational* model. This may change in the future.

The database product currently enjoying the largest sales is **ORACLE**, a product famous for its portability between different platforms, but probably most prominent on UNIX and Windows NT systems. In late 1997, **ORACLE** release 8 was the first release providing object-relational capabilities.

The **DB2** product was originally released by IBM for use on the MVS Operating System on IBM mainframe machines in 1983. IBM's commitment to the relational model was the driving force that made the relational model victorious over the older *prerelational* products, such as IMS and IDMS. (IMS is still in heavy use, however, because so many commercial companies had written their operational data processing systems assuming this architecture.) In 1997, IBM announced a new object-relational version known as **DB2 Universal Database**, version 5 **(DB2 UDB)**, which ran on PC and UNIX platforms. It now runs on OS/390 as well.

INFORMIX is the third database vendor with object-relational capabilities, having purchased the Illustra product in 1996. The Illustra product was developed specifically to encourage the object-relational standard, and it was extremely successful.

On a historical note, the **INGRES** product was developed at the University of California at Berkeley on DEC VAX and UNIX systems, and was adopted by many computer science departments throughout the world. **INGRES** was covered in some detail in our first edition, but most universities have moved on to other database systems, and the current edition no longer provides this coverage.

There are many versions of each of the products we've just mentioned, since a new version is put out every year or so, and at present the difference from one version to the next is quite significant. We will be dealing in this text with **ORACLE** release 8.1.5 (the object-relational version), **INFORMIX Dynamic Server (INFORMIX)**, version 9.2, and **DB2 Universal Database (DB2 UDB)**, version 6. In general, all database product releases have "upward compatibility," meaning that later releases may offer new features but should also support all features from earlier releases. Thus this text should be usable with later releases of all the products mentioned above.

From all this discussion of new database models with unreleased standards and significant changes from one release to another in major commercial products, you will receive the impression that database systems are in a state of flux. This is very true. Although the database field has made a great deal of progress in the 40 or so years since its beginning, we are currently in a development stage that hasn't been seen in more mature scientific disciplines since the 17th century, shortly after the scientific method was first proposed. A number of important principles of current database systems will

84

certainly remain valid far into the future, but we can also expect to see major changes in the coming years. In this text, we emphasize basic principles and point out limitations in current software practice where they exist.

3.2 | Setting Up the Database

At the end of this section, Exercise 3.2.1 provides a computer assignment based on the SQL data definition statements introduced here and in Appendix A. You will be asked to create database tables to duplicate the customers-agents-products database (the CAP database) of Figure 2.2. Later computer assignments will assume that this database exists and ask you to perform SQL data manipulation statements to retrieve and update data in these tables.

To begin, you will need to get an account on your computer system—a user ID and password to log in to the computer—and a separate account on the database system itself to enable you to enter the database system. Your instructor will tell you how to accomplish this. Once you have these accounts, the tutorials in Appendix A will instruct you in some of the fundamental product-specific skills you will need in the **ORACLE** and **INFOR-MIX** database systems. Skills covered in these tutorials include how to enter the database system from the operating system level, how to create tables or delete tables from the database, how to load data from an operating system file into an already defined table of the database, and how to perform SQL commands interactively. Typing sqlplus (all lowercase) to enter **ORACLE** or dbaccess to enter **INFORMIX** will result in an interactive environment with a number of commands that allow you to compose SQL statements, edit them, save them to operating system files and then read them back, submit them to the database system for execution, and so on.

To create the CUSTOMERS table of the CAP database in **ORACLE** (using the lowercase table name customers we adopt to differentiate SQL from relational algebra), you would enter the monitor and issue the SQL statement below:

```
[3.2.1]   SQL >    create table customers (cid char(4) not null,
          2        cname varchar(13), city varchar(20), discnt real,
          3        primary key(cid));
```

Notice that after performing a carriage return on the first line, the **ORACLE** SQL*Plus environment prints a prompt for the second line, 2. The prompt for the third line is 3, and so on. There is no limit to the number of lines you can type. The system doesn't attempt to interpret what you have written until you end a line with a semicolon (;). A semicolon is used to terminate all SQL statements.

The result of this Create Table statement is the creation of an empty customers table with column names cid, cname, city, and discnt, and a primary key consisting of the single column cid. The *type* or *datatype* of each attribute (discussed as the *domain* of the attribute in Chapter 2) follows each attribute name specified. Thus cname is of type var-

```
CREATE TABLE tablename (colname datatype [NOT NULL]
    {, colname datatype [NOT NULL] ...}
    [, PRIMARY KEY (colname {, colname ...})]);
```

Figure 3.2   Limited Form of Create Table Statement

char(13) (a variable-length character string with a maximum of 13 characters), and discnt is of type real (the ANSI datatype for a 4-byte real number, equivalent to the C language type float). Appendix A, Section 3 contains a number of other possible datatypes that can be used in defining table columns. The *not null* clause coming after the cid column name and type means that a null value cannot occur in this column: any SQL data manipulation statement that would result in a null value in this column will fail and give a warning to the user. Recall from Section 2.4 that a null value represents an undefined or inapplicable value. But since the DBA has decided that the cid column should be a unique identifier for each row (a *key* for the table), a null value is not permitted. A number of other features of the Create Table statement can be used to guarantee additional integrity properties of the data, comparable to the NOT NULL clause. However, we do not need all the power of the Create Table statement until a later chapter. For the present purposes of defining the tables of the CAP database, a limited form of the Create Table command is given in Figure 3.2.

Standard Typographical Conventions

Consider the SQL statement forms of Figures 3.1 and 3.2. Uppercase terms in statement forms are to be typed exactly as written (except that an uppercase term is normally brought to lowercase in specific examples; see, for example, statement [3.2.1] based on the form of Figure 3.2). Lowercase terms in these forms, such as tablename in Figure 3.2, describe terms that are named or chosen by the user. Thus every command of the form in Figure 3.2 begins with the words create table, while the word tablename is not literally entered and should be filled in with a desired table name, such as customers.

There are a number of special characters that are not used in SQL statements, including left and right braces, { }, left and right brackets, [ ], and vertical bar, |. Since these forms never appear in SQL statements, we can use them in SQL statement forms, together with the ellipsis, . . . , three periods in a row, to indicate syntactic features.

Recall that all special characters not in our list, and especially commas and parentheses, ( ), appearing in a statement form are to be typed *exactly as written* and have no typographical meaning. Thus in Figure 3.2, after tablename there is a left parenthesis followed by a sequence of comma-separated column definitions, and then a closing parenthesis. The actual number of columns that can be defined in a table has an upper limit on all systems, but we don't take account of such limits in these SQL statement forms.

When a phrase occurs in square brackets, [ ], it means that the phrase is optional. Thus we see that the phrase NOT NULL in Figure 3.2 may or may not occur following any column name and datatype description. Similarly it is optional to define a primary key,

86

and a primary key can have one or more columns. Look at statement [3.2.1] again as an example of the form specified in Figure 3.2.

Vertical bars, |, are used to indicate a choice between a number of possible phrases. The choice may be mandatory when exactly one of the phrases *must* occur, and in that case the form syntax would show (for three choices): choice1 | choice2 | choice3, or (using braces for "grouping" the choices) {choice1 | choice2 | choice3}. The enclosing braces in the second alternative are used to clarify where the choices begin and end. For example, the form

```
term1 term2 | term3
```

is ambiguous. Are we offering a choice between term1 term2 and term3? Where does the choice between alternatives begin? Note how this question disappears when we write instead

```
term1 {term2 | term3}
```

This form implies we can write term1 and then the braces in "grouping" form offer a choice between term2 and term3, so the phrase term1 term3 has become possible.

This "grouping" use of enclosing braces is *not* the form being used in Figure 3.2. Instead we use the convention that placing a phrase in braces, { }, ending with an ellipsis, . . . , such as { , colname . . . } in the last line of Figure 3.2, indicates that the phrase (initial comma and some chosen colname) may occur zero or more times in actual use. This implies that the syntax of Figure 3.2 requires a table to have one or more colname definitions, since we see the phrase colname datatype [NOT NULL] once, and then again in braces, with an initial separating comma, followed by an ellipsis.

Vertical bars can also be used inside square brackets, when only one of the phrases separated by vertical bars may be chosen, but the entire phrase is optional (i.e., maybe *none* of the phrases will appear). If this is the case and one of the phrases involved is underlined, this means that choosing no phrase is the equivalent of choosing the underlined phrase. As an example, look at Figure 3.1, which begins

```
SELECT [ALL | DISTINCT] select_list
```

Here ALL means that all rows resulting from the query will be placed in the result table (even if there are duplicate rows), whereas DISTINCT means that duplicate rows will not be placed in the result table. If no option in [ALL | DISTINCT] is chosen, the default will be ALL, to allow duplicates.

A Practical Exercise

If you are using the **ORACLE** or **INFORMIX** database products, you should at this point read Appendix A, which provides a tutorial on the skills you need to set up the CAP database. Even if you are using a different product, Appendix A will give you an idea of the skills required and the sequence of relatively standard Create Table commands you will need. (Note that the authors may in the future provide additional product tutorials on the homepage for this text, at the URL http://www.cs.umb.edu/~poneil/dbppp.html.)

EXERCISE

[3.2.1] After reading Appendix A for a description of **ORACLE** or **INFORMIX** use, create a database, if this has not already been done for you, with the name *dbname* consisting of (up to) the first six characters of your login ID, for example, poneil. Next, create and load into your database the tables pictured in Figure 2.2—customers, agents, products, and orders. You should create command procedure files with monitor commands to do as much of the work as possible: for example, see the form given for custs.ctl, in Appendix A.1 for **ORACLE**, and try to replicate this for additional CAP tables, with the file names agents.ctl, prods.ctl, and orders.ctl. You should then type in the data files to use in loading—custs.dat, agents.dat, prods.dat, and orders.dat—and then give the commands to create and load the tables. When the files have been created and loaded, use the appropriate database command to display the layout of the tables, as it is known to the database system, and then display the contents of each table with a Select statement.

3.3 Simple Select Statements

Queries are performed in SQL using the *Select* statement. The general form of the Select statement is quite complex, and we develop an explanation of the various features over the next several sections. In this section we introduce some of the most basic features of SQL queries, corresponding to the relational algebra operations of selection, projection, and product. As in the case of relational algebra, the result of a Select statement query is itself a table. We also give a brief idea of how a simple Select statement might be implemented by the database system as an *access plan,* a loop-oriented program hidden from the user to access the needed data of the query on a computerized database and to generate the desired solution.

EXAMPLE 3.3.1

Suppose that we wish to find the aid values and names of agents that are based in New York. In relational algebra this query can be expressed as

```
(AGENTS where city = 'New York')[aid, aname]
```

To solve the same problem in SQL, and to display the retrieved rows, we use the statement

```
select aid, aname from agents where city = 'New York';
```

The reserved words of this statement, appearing literally in all SQL Select statements, are SELECT, FROM, and WHERE. To execute this Select, the SQL interpreter starts with the table following the word FROM, performs the selection specified after the word WHERE, and then extracts the projection defined by the field name(s) that follow the word SELECT (we refer to this as the *select list*). Note that the table names are specified in lowercase (since they were defined that way in the Create Table command), and the constant 'New York' is enclosed in single quotes. (Double quotes can also be used in some database system products, but single quotes are always acceptable and are part of the recommended standard.) ∎

EXAMPLE 3.3.2

In Appendix A, an example of a Select statement is given that displays all the values in every row of the customers table in order to check that the table load has taken place properly:

```
select * from customers;
```

The symbol "*" in the select list is a shorthand symbol meaning *retrieve all fields*. That is to say, there is no projection onto a limited set of fields in this case. Furthermore, all rows are printed in this case, since there is no selection restriction (the WHERE clause is missing). ∎

The Select statement does not automatically cast out duplicate rows in the result; it is necessary to specifically request this service.

EXAMPLE 3.3.3

Retrieve all pid values of parts for which orders are placed. If we submit the query

```
select pid from orders;
```

the result will have a large number of duplicate pid values, one for each row where the corresponding pid appears in the orders table of Figure 2.2. For example, p01 will appear five times because of the appearances on rows of the orders table with ordno values 1011, 1012, 1021, 1016, 1024. In order to guarantee that each row in the result is unique, we need to give the query

```
select distinct pid from orders;
```

Note that the reserved word *distinct* actually guarantees that each *row* retrieved is unique (in comparison with other rows). Thus if we were to submit the query

```
select distinct aid, pid from orders;
```

we would only guarantee unique (pid, aid) pairs rather than unique pid values. Thus a01, p01 would appear only once in the result, although this pair appears on rows of the orders table with ordno values 1011, 1012, and 1016. ∎

The Select statement permits duplicate result rows when the DISTINCT keyword is not used; this implies that Relational RULE 3, the unique row rule, is not obeyed by default. To cast out duplicate rows is extra effort, after all, and results in an actual loss of information: the fact that the pid value p01 occurs five times in the initial Select statement of Example 3.3.3 could conceivably be of great interest to the user.

If we intend to emphasize that all rows of a result are printed, that duplicates are *not* to be dropped, we can use the reserved word ALL before the select list to convey the opposite meaning from DISTINCT:

```
select all pid from orders;
```

Since ALL is the default option, we don't need to type it except for better human under-standing. Notice how this standard SQL behavior provides an alternative to Relational RULE 3 of Section 2.3, since rows occurring in a result might not be unique.

Consider now a query that requires retrieval from several tables.

EXAMPLE 3.3.4

Let us specify a relational algebra expression to retrieve all customer-agent name pairs, (cname, aname), where the customer places an order through the agent. We need to involve tables CUSTOMERS, ORDERS, and AGENTS, since the cname column is in CUSTOMERS, the aname column is in AGENTS, and ORDERS keeps track of orders placed. In relational algebra we can solve this query by specifying the following expression:

```
((CUSTOMERS[cid, cname] ⋈ ORDERS) ⋈ AGENTS)[cname, aname]
```

Recall that it was important in relational algebra to project the CUSTOMERS table onto the col-umns [cid, cname] in order to get rid of the city column, since we didn't want to require joined rows between (CUSTOMERS ⋈ ORDERS) and AGENTS to have the same city value. Alter-natively, we could use a relational algebra query involving the product operation rather than the join:

```
(((CUSTOMERS x ORDERS) x AGENTS) where CUSTOMERS.cid = ORDERS.cid
    and ORDERS.aid = AGENTS.aid)[cname, aname]
```

In this product form, we restrict rows by specifically naming the columns that must have equal values, which happens automatically in the join. Now the normal way to perform this query in SQL is

```
select distinct customers.cname, agents.aname
    from customers, orders, agents
    where customers.cid = orders.cid and orders.aid = agents.aid;
```

The syntax of the SQL Select statement is equivalent to the product form of the two relational algebra solutions above. The Select statement results in the following (conceptual) steps.

[1] Compute the product of the tables mentioned in the list that appears after the word FROM (this is known as the *FROM clause* of the Select statement).

[2] Apply the selection specified by the condition that follows WHERE (the *WHERE clause*).

[3] Project the resulting table on the attributes that appear in the *select list*. We see here that SQL also has the capability of using qualified attribute names, such as customers.cid, when more than one table is involved. However, the SQL standard says that it is not neces-sary that a column name be qualified in a relational product retrieval such as this when the column name occurs in only one of the tables involved. Thus instead of writing

```
select distinct customers.cname, agents.aname . . .
```

in the first line above, we could have written instead

```
select distinct cname, aname . . .
```                                                                          ■

The SQL-99 and Full SQL-92 standards provide for join operations to be performed in the FROM clause of the SQL Select statement (see Section 3.6), but this capability is still not implemented in most commercial products. Without this feature, it is always necessary to emulate a join by taking the product (writing a comma-separated list of tables making up the product in the FROM clause) and including specific equate conditions to identify joinable column values in the WHERE clause.

It is possible to write a Select statement query that performs calculations, and to print the resulting values in the select list.

EXAMPLE 3.3.5

Retrieve a "table" based on the orders table, with columns ordno, cid, aid, pid, and profit, where profit is calculated from quantity and price of the product sold by subtracting 60% for wholesale cost, the discount for the customer, and the percent commission for the agent.

```
select ordno, x.cid, x.aid, x.pid,
    .40*(x.qty*p.price) - .01*(c.discnt + a.percent) * (x.qty*p.price)
    from orders as x, customers as c, agents as a, products as p
    where c.cid = x.cid and a.aid = x.aid and p.pid = x.pid;
```

Note that the letters x, c, a, and p are associated with the orders, customers, agents, and products tables because they appear in the FROM clause as table aliases, analogous to the relational algebra aliases that would be created by writing x := orders, c := customers, a := agents, p := products. A table alias is defined in a Select statement by following the table name with the optional keyword AS and then the desired table alias, without an intervening comma. A comma is used to indicate that a new table name follows. Note that if the word AS is left out, SQL will still be able to recognize a table alias by the fact that there are two identifiers in a row without an intervening comma. A table alias is associated with a table only within the context of the single Select statement where it is defined; therefore, the same table alias can be defined for different purposes in different Select statements. Table aliases are used in this query to create a short form of qualification for column names. We have used qualified names in this Select statement for x.qty, p.price, c.discnt, and a.percent for ease of understanding, although qualification of these unique column names is not strictly necessary.

The select list of this query illustrates an important feature: we can calculate the value of an expression with terms that are either constants (such as .01) or values from the various columns of the current joined row (such as p.price). The standard arithmetic operators (+, −, *, /) are supported, and scalar functions can also be used, such as mod(n, b) (remainder of n when divided by b), provided in **ORACLE**, **DB2 UDB**, and **INFORMIX**, but not part of the standard, except in Full SQL-99, which has abs( ) and mod( )), as well as string functions such as lower(c) (which returns a char variable with all characters in c brought to lowercase). Additional details of such expressions are covered in Section 3.9. For now, note that there is implicit type conversion taking place, so that c.discnt (float type) adds to a.percent (integer type) to give a float type result. The value of the calculated expression does not have a well-defined column name, and different products handle the naming of the calculated column in different ways. This query results in the following answer in **ORACLE**:

ordno	cid	aid	pid	.40*(x.qty*p.price) − .01*(c.discnt + a.percent) *(x.qty*p.price)
1011	c001	a01	p01	120.00
1012	c001	a01	p01	120.00
1013	c002	a03	p03	210.00
1014	c003	a03	p05	300.00
1015	c003	a03	p05	300.00
1016	c006	a01	p01	170.00
1017	c001	a06	p03	150.00
1018	c001	a03	p04	138.00
1019	c001	a02	p02	48.00
1020	c006	a03	p07	198.00
1021	c004	a06	p01	135.00
1022	c001	a05	p06	200.00
1023	c001	a04	p05	120.00
1024	c006	a06	p01	140.00
1025	c001	a05	p07	200.00
1026	c002	a05	p03	184.00

■

Note that the table aliases x, c, a, and p, used in Example 3.3.5, are referred to by a number of names in different commercial products. **ORACLE** and **INFORMIX** use the term *alias* or *table alias*, and it appears in all help text in these products. **DB2 UDB** and the ANSI SQL standards use the term *correlation name*. The term *range variable* or *tuple variable* is also used occasionally, for reasons explained below. Nomenclature of this kind is important if you want to be able to get around in the manuals provided by the various commercial database products. For example, in the *ORACLE Server SQL Language Reference Manual,* the term *alias, table* is listed in the index, whereas the term *correlation name* is not to be found. In the *INFORMIX Guide to SQL Syntax, alias* is the standard. And in the *DB2 Universal Database SQL Reference,* the term *correlation name* is used, and the term *alias,* when it appears, refers to yet another syntactic element!

A number of different approaches are taken by commercial database products regarding the column name displayed for the expression column of Example 3.3.5 representing profit, where there is no simple column name inheritance from a table. This variation among the commercial database system products results from the fact that earlier standards did not define a unique approach. In **ORACLE**, the full text of the symbolic expression would be copied and used as the column name, as we saw in the result table of Example 3.3.5. Starting with the SQL-92 standard, users are allowed to supply an ad hoc name for an expression column in the Select statement. In the ANSI SQL standards documents, this is called a *column-name* (meaning it becomes the column name of the result); in **ORACLE** it is called a *column alias*, as differentiated from the table alias that we have already seen; in **INFORMIX** it is called a *display label*; and in **DB2 UDB** it is called simply "a column name in the Select clause" (basically following the ANSI SQL standards). In **ORACLE**, we could write

```
select. . . , expr [[as] c_alias], . . .
```

to give a name, *c_alias*, to the column in a select list where an expression *expr* is displayed. Renaming such a calculated column is now possible in all major database products. Thus in **ORACLE**, for example, we could write the query of Example 3.3.5 as

```
select distinct x.ordno, x.cid, x.aid, x.pid, .40*(x.qty*p.price)
    −.01*(c.discnt + a.percent)*(x.qty*p.price) as profit          -- column alias
    from orders x, customers c, agents a, products p
    where c.cid = x.cid and a.aid = x.aid and p.pid = x.pid;
```

to create a table with the heading

x.ordno	x.cid	x.aid	x.pid	profit

Note that two consecutive hyphens (--) can be used on any SQL statement line to indicate that the text following the hyphens is a comment.

EXAMPLE 3.3.6
Suppose that we are asked to determine all pairs of customers based in the same city. To solve this query in relational algebra, we would start by computing the product of two copies of the CUSTOMERS table, then use an appropriate Select condition:

```
C1 := CUSTOMERS, C2 := CUSTOMERS
(C1 x C2) where C1.city = C2.city and C1.cid < C2.cid
```

We need two different names for CUSTOMERS, C1 and C2, so that columns in the product will be uniquely qualified. As we saw in Example 2.7.3, the restriction C1.cid < C2.cid allows us to drop redundant pairs of customers (two of the same, or the same unequal pair twice). In SQL this query can be performed with the following Select phrase:

```
select c1.cid, c2.cid
    from customers c1, customers c2
    where c1.city = c2.city and c1.cid < c2.cid;
```

This is an example of an SQL query where table aliases are necessary in order to consider pairs of rows in the same table. Without such names, we would not be able to qualify the identically named columns of the product. Note that uppercase table aliases C1 and C2 are also perfectly acceptable in SQL; however, we use lowercase names as a general rule. The name C1 is equivalent to c1 in the SQL standard (case is irrelevant). ∎

```
FOR c1 FROM ROW 1 TO LAST OF customers
    FOR c2 FROM ROW 1 TO LAST OF customers
        IF (c1.city = c2.city and c1.cid < c2.cid)
        THEN PRINT OUT SELECT_LIST VALUES: c1.cid, c2.cid
    END FOR c2
END FOR c1
```

Figure 3.3 Nested-Loop Access Plan Pseudo-Code for the Select Statement of Example 3.3.6

As mentioned in Example 3.3.4, the conceptual sequence of events to evaluate the Select statement in Example 3.3.6 is this: first the FROM clause equates tables c1 and c2 to the customers table and takes their product; then the WHERE clause limits the rows of the product; and finally the values from this set of rows are projected on the select list. This gives us a correct *conceptual* view of the order of evaluation, but it would be surprising if this were the procedure actually followed by a database system in answering our query. To foreshadow an area of study known as *query optimization,* we explain a different algorithmic method, known as an *access plan,* that a database system might use to physically retrieve the data of the query. This method also illustrates a different conceptual point of view that has some value in helping us picture what is happening. We start by thinking of the table aliases c1 and c2 as they appear in the FROM clause as *range variables*—that is, variables that take on row position values in the customers table. The range variables c1 and c2 range *independently* over the rows of the customers table, as in a nested loop, and we can think of the results of the above query as being generated by the pseudo-code of Figure 3.3.

The values retrieved in Figure 3.3 will be identical to the ones we expect from the SQL Select statement of Example 3.3.6. This *nested-loop* algorithm generates the same pairs of rows from c1 × c2 that would arise if we actually created the product of these two tables. Indeed a nested loop of this kind would be the only way we could go about generating the rows of a product table. But in the logic of Figure 3.3, instead of placing these rows in a temporary table, we short-circuit the process by performing the next conceptual phase of the Select statement and applying the selection condition of the WHERE clause. As a result, the nested-loop approach is much more economical in terms of space utilization than the approach that would physically create the table product as a first step.

The nested-loop algorithm is only one of a number of algorithms that might be chosen as an access plan for a Select statement where a product of tables is involved. Other approaches exist—for example, to make use of *indexed lookup* efficiencies that can improve performance immensely. However, the nested-loop algorithm represents another useful conceptual viewpoint to help us understand the Select statement. We see why *range variable* is a common term for variables such as c1 and c2, representing looping variables for row positions in the nested loop; each pair of row positions corresponds to one row of the table product. Clearly we can generalize this approach to any number of range variables defined on different or identical tables. Note that in cases where there is no alias for a named table, the table name itself may be thought of as a range variable that takes on specific row values. Consider again the query result of Example 3.3.4:

```
select distinct customers.cname, agents.aname
    from customers, orders, agents
    where customers.cid = orders.cid and orders.aid = agents.aid;
```

Here we can picture the Select statement as having three independent range variables, customers, agents, and orders. The values that arise as these three independent variables take up row positions in a triply nested loop in their respective tables are exactly the ones that would show up in a relational algebra product of the three tables. The restrictions in the WHERE clause basically select the rows that would come out of a join of the three tables, except that equality in the city column between customers and agents is not requested.

EXAMPLE 3.3.7

Suppose that we need to find pid values of products that have been ordered by at least two customers. We can solve this problem using table aliases:

```
select distinct x1.pid
    from orders x1, orders x2
    where x1.pid = x2.pid and x1.cid < x2.cid;
```

The best way to think about this query is that x1 and x2 each range over the rows in the orders table (sometimes they represent the same row). The condition x1.cid < x2.cid assures us that these two rows represent orders by distinct customers, each pair once, while the condition x1.pid = x2.pid assures us that both customers are ordering the same product. We print out all products having the property that two different customers order them. ∎

It is important in the above analysis that a product ordered by three customers, on different lines of the orders table, x, y, and z, not appear three times in the result: once for x and y, once for x and z, and once for y and z. To drop duplicate rows we need to use the reserved word DISTINCT introduced in Example 3.3.3. Often the keyword DISTINCT adds effort to the procedure that carries out the query. Usually the access plan requires the resulting rows to be placed in sorted order by the columns retrieved and successive rows to be tested for equivalence to avoid duplication. If the user knows that no duplication is possible, it may improve overall performance to avoid this extra effort. However, it is not always a simple matter to know when duplicates might exist in a join query and in some of the other forms that follow. We will return to this question in the exercises at the end of the chapter.

EXAMPLE 3.3.8

Get cid values of customers who order a product for which an order is also placed by agent a06. The important insight needed to frame this query is one we have encountered before in relational algebra (see Example 2.9.9). We must realize that this request is not asking for cid values of customers who place an order through a06—it is more indirect than that. See Figure 3.4, where the set of rows we wish to retrieve is contained in the circle on the far right.

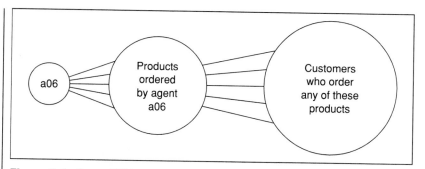

Figure 3.4 Sets of Objects and Their Connection to One Another in Example 3.3.8

First, consider the products for which an order is placed by agent a06, the set of rows contained in the middle circle of Figure 3.4.

```
select x.pid from orders x where x.aid = 'a06';
```

The set of product IDs retrieved by this query from the `orders` table of Figure 2.2 is {p03, p01}. Now we want to retrieve the customers who have placed an order for at least one of these products. We need to consider entirely different rows in the `orders` table to list such customers. For example, order number 1017 shows that p03 is ordered through agent a06, and at the same time this order row shows that customer c001 orders part p03. However, order number 1013 shows that c002 also orders p03, although the order does not occur through agent a06. We need to consider both order rows at once to show that c002 is in the select list for the request given above. We can put the whole thing together with the query

```
select distinct y.cid
    from orders x, orders y
    where y.pid = x.pid and x.aid = 'a06';
```

Here we see that the customer `cid` c002 is retrieved when the range variable x corresponds to the `orders` row with ordno = 1017 (since x.aid = a06 and x.pid = p03) and the range variable y corresponds to the `orders` row with ordno = 1013 (since y.pid = x.pid and y.cid = c002). This query returns the following table:

cid
c001
c002
c004
c006

To review, this query form represents an extremely important concept, where two differently named range variables on the `orders` table are needed simultaneously to connect the `cid` values retrieved to the agent with `aid` a06. ∎

```
SELECT [ALL | DISTINCT] { * | expr [[AS] c_alias] {, expr [[AS] c_alias]...}}
    FROM tablename [[AS] corr_name] {, tablename [[AS] corr_name]...}
    [WHERE search_condition];
```

Figure 3.5 Select Statement Syntax Introduced through Section 3.3

In this section we have introduced a limited form of the Select statement, illustrated in Figure 3.5. The vertical line in the form [ALL | DISTINCT] means that the user can choose one of the two literal terms ALL or DISTINCT; the fact that this choice is contained in square brackets ([ ]) means that the entire phrase is optional, whereas the fact that ALL is underlined means that this is the default term that takes effect if the phrase is omitted. The search_condition object of the WHERE clause turns out to be quite complex in itself, and will be the subject of discussion in a number of sections of this chapter.

3.4 Subqueries

Each Select statement query results in a table, but Select statements cannot be arbitrarily nested in the way we were able to nest relational algebra expressions in Chapter 2. The most telling limitation is the requirement that a table listed in the FROM clause of a Select statement cannot itself be the result of an arbitrary Select statement (the Full SQL-92 and SQL-99 standards have removed this limitation, but this capability is not fully available in current database products). This is an important point of divergence from relational algebra, because it means that the Select statement, having lost some of the nesting capability of relational algebra, must make up for it by adding power elsewhere. We find this added power in the search_condition of the WHERE clause. As we will see, we are allowed to nest certain forms of Select statement in a search_condition.

A Select statement form appearing within another Select statement is known as a *Subquery*. The general form of a Subquery is missing some syntax elements of a full Select statement, but it will be some time before we encounter these elements, and the form of Figure 3.5 is acceptable as a Subquery. For now we can think of the two forms, Select statements and Subqueries, as being identical. A Subquery can appear in the search_condition of a WHERE clause for another Select statement in numerous ways. In the current section we study a number of *predicates*, logical conditions with TRUE-FALSE values, that allow us to perform meaningful tests on Subqueries. To start with we consider the IN predicate, which tests membership in a set.

The IN Predicate

Suppose that we wish to determine the cid values of customers who place orders with agents in Duluth or Dallas. It is possible to do this in SQL using a relational product of tables, but we are concerned here with illustrating the use of the IN predicate and the new Subquery syntax.

3.4 Subqueries

EXAMPLE 3.4.1

Get `cid` values of customers who place orders with agents in Duluth or Dallas. We start by finding all agents based in Duluth or Dallas. We can do this with the query

```
select aid from agents
    where city = 'Duluth' or city = 'Dallas';
```

This Select statement can be used to represent a *set of values* (a Subquery) in a larger Select statement that solves the original problem:

```
select distinct cid from orders
    where aid in (select aid from agents
    where city = 'Duluth' or city = 'Dallas');
```

Conceptually, we regard the Subquery (the *inner* Select surrounded by parentheses) as returning a set of values to the *outer* Select WHERE clause: ". . . where aid in (set)". The outer Select WHERE clause is considered true if the aid value of the orders row under consideration in the outer Select is an element of the set returned by the inner Select (the aid value is *in* the set). Specifically, for the database content of Figure 2.2, the set of aid values returned by the Subquery is a05 and a06. Then, in the outer Select, rows of the orders table are restricted to those whose aid values are members in this set, and the cid values for the resulting rows are printed. The solution of this query is

cid
c001
c002
c004
c006

■

Membership can be tested not only against the set provided by a Subquery but also against sets that are explicitly defined, as we see in the following example.

EXAMPLE 3.4.2

We wish to retrieve all information concerning agents based in Duluth or Dallas (very close to the Subquery in the previous example). This can be done by the following:

```
select * from agents
    where city in ('Duluth', 'Dallas');
```

As we see, a set can be constructed from a comma-separated list of constant values enclosed in parentheses. This query returns the table

aid	aname	city	percent
a05	Otasi	Duluth	5
a06	Smith	Dallas	5

The query above has the same effect as one that uses logical OR:

```
select * from agents
    where city = 'Duluth' or city = 'Dallas';                         ■
```

As we see in the following example, multiple levels of Subquery nesting are allowed.

EXAMPLE 3.4.3
Suppose we now wish to determine the names and discounts of all customers who place orders through agents in Duluth or Dallas. We use the following form:

```
select cname, discnt from customers
    where cid in (select cid from orders where aid in
        (select aid from agents where city in ('Duluth', 'Dallas')));
```

Note that the `city` column named in the innermost Subquery is unambiguously associated with the `agents` table, the most local "scope" for this column name, rather than with the `customers` table of the outermost Select. This query returns the table

cname	discnt
TipTop	10.000
Basics	12.000
ACME	8.000
ACME	0.000

■

The Subqueries considered in the examples so far deliver a set of rows to the outer Select phrase without receiving any input data. These are known as *uncorrelated Subqueries*, because the inner Subquery is completely independent of the outer one. More generally, we can provide an inner Subquery with data that originates in the outer Select.

EXAMPLE 3.4.4
Suppose we need to find the names of customers who order product p05. Of course, we can solve this query using a straightforward Select statement:

```
select distinct cname from customers, orders
    where customers.cid = orders.cid and orders.pid = 'p05';
```

However, we are interested here in a solution where a Subquery receives data from the outer Select:

```
select distinct cname from customers where 'p05' in
    (select pid from orders where cid = customers.cid);
```

This query returns the table

cname
TipTop
Allied

If the DISTINCT keyword did not appear in these Select statements, it would retrieve the cname value 'Allied' on two different rows. In the exercises at the end of this chapter, you are asked to verify a number of rules that will help you to predict when a Select statement without the DISTINCT keyword will produce duplicate rows. *Note carefully* that the unqualified cid reference in the Subquery of the second Select statement above refers to the local orders table. When a Subquery involves a single table, it does not require a qualified reference to a *local* column name. But the Subquery reference to customers.cid is to a table in the *outer* Select, so a qualifier is needed in that case.   ∎

A Subquery using data from an outer Select is known as a *correlated Subquery*. Such a Subquery usually has the property that it cannot be evaluated once and for all before the outer Select is started, and as a result it is more difficult to optimize performance. For example, in the Subquery form of Example 3.4.4, we cannot determine the set of pid values retrieved in the inner Subquery without making a determination of the value of customers.cid, and this value changes for every row of the outer Select.

Although variables from *outer* Selects can be used in *inner* Subqueries, the reverse is not true. We can think of this as a kind of *scoping rule*, comparable to scope locality we see in a number of programming languages such as C. In SQL, a local variable of a Subquery is undefined until the Subquery has been entered.

EXAMPLE 3.4.5

If we wanted to get the names of customers who order product p07 from agent a03, the following query form would not be legal:

```
select cname from customers
    where orders.aid = 'a03' and 'p07' in -- ** ILLEGAL SQL SYNTAX
    (select pid from orders where cid = customers.cid);
```

The illegal syntax is due to the reference to orders.aid outside its proper scope.   ∎

The general form of an IN predicate expression so far has two alternate forms:

```
expr in (Subquery) | expr in (val {, val...})
```

The expr token stands for a character string expression or numeric expression of the kind we saw in the select list of Example 3.3.5, most often a simple column name or constant; however, an expr can also be an "expression list" as we see below in Example 3.4.6, a comma-separated list of expressions. The val token stands for a constant value, such as 17 or 'Duluth', or possibly a comma-separated list of such values.

EXAMPLE 3.4.6

Suppose we want to retrieve `ordno` values for all orders placed by customers in Duluth through agents in New York. The following Subquery form that tests a pair of values for inclusion in a Subquery is supported in Basic SQL.

```
select ordno from orders
    where (cid, aid) in
    (select cid, aid from customers c, agents a
        where c.city = 'Duluth' and a.city = 'New York');
```

Full SQL-92 and SQL-99 allow comma-separated expression lists, pairs, or longer tuples, enclosed in parentheses as shown, to be tested for inclusion. You may be using a product that does not yet support this extended capability. (At the time of writing, the capability is present in **ORACLE** and **DB2**, but not in **INFORMIX**.) An alternative standard SQL form that will work with such products is this:

```
select ordno from orders x where exists
    (select cid, aid from customers c, agents a
        where c.cid = x.cid and a.aid = x.aid and c.city = 'Duluth' and a.city = 'New York');
```

∎

The idea behind the expr IN (Subquery) format—a set of values is returned from the evaluation of the Subquery and then a test for membership is performed by the outer Select—is quite striking. It is important to realize that again this is only the *conceptual* course of events; it is frequently *not* the approach taken by the system in creating an access plan. As we will see later in this chapter, the SQL Select statement is *nonprocedural*, meaning that the user stating the query is not dictating the algorithm to be used by the system in answering it. As we have already hinted, a part of the system known as the *query optimizer* performs transformations on a posed query to a number of different forms, and then it chooses the form that gives the result most efficiently. One of the exercises at the end of this chapter asks you to show that all queries so far introduced involving the use of the IN predicate on Subqueries can be transformed into an alternate form where the Subqueries are replaced by a product of tables in the FROM clause. This is the sort of transformation form that may be executed.

In addition to an IN predicate, there is also a NOT IN predicate. For example, the clause

```
expr NOT IN (Subquery)
```

is true if and only if the evaluated value of the expr is not found in the set returned by the Subquery. The NOT IN predicate can also be used with the form that tests membership in a set of constant values, so the general form of this predicate now is seen in Figure 3.6, with an optional NOT preceding the IN keyword.

```
expr [NOT] IN (Subquery) | expr [NOT] IN (val {, val...})
```

Figure 3.6 The General Form of an IN Predicate Expression

```
expr θ{SOME|ANY|ALL} (Subquery)
    where θ is some operator in the set {<, <=, =, <>, >, >=}
```

Figure 3.7 The General Form of a Quantified Predicate

The Quantified Comparison Predicate

A *quantified predicate* compares the simple value of an expression with the result of a Subquery. The general form is shown in Figure 3.7.

Eighteen predicates fit this general form, with SOME and ANY synonymous; SOME is the new preferred form available in the recent versions of most database products.

Here is the definition of the quantified predicate. Given a comparison operator θ, representing some operator in the set {<, <=, =, <>, >, >=}, the equivalent predicates, expr θsome (Subquery), and expr θany (Subquery), are TRUE if and only if, for *at least one* element s returned by the Subquery, it is true that expr θ s; the predicate expr θall (Subquery) is TRUE if and only if expr θ s is true for *every one* of the elements s of the Subquery. Here are examples that illustrate two of these predicates.

EXAMPLE 3.4.7
We wish to find aid values of agents with a minimum percent commission. This can be accomplished with the query

```
select aid from agents where percent <=all (select percent from agents);
```

The Subquery returns the set of all percent values from the agents table and then the quantified comparison predicate <=ALL requires that the percent value of a row selected be less than or equal to ALL rows returned by the Subquery; therefore, the percent value for a row selected will be a minimum value of this kind. ∎

EXAMPLE 3.4.8
We wish to find all customers who have the same discount as that of any of the customers in Dallas or Boston. (Note that while there are no customers in Boston in the example of Figure 2.2, the correct form of a query to answer a user request is not dependent on the "accidental" table contents at a given moment.) We use the query

```
select cid, cname from customers
    where discnt =some (select discnt from customers
        where city = 'Dallas' or city = 'Boston');
```

The discnt value for a row selected must therefore be equal to at least one discnt retrieved by the Subquery, and therefore have the same discnt as that of some customer in Dallas or Boston. Note that the predicate =SOME . . . *has exactly the same effect* as the predicate IN. . . . This is a relatively startling fact, and we will discuss it later in this section. ∎

Note that, while the predicate expr =SOME (Subquery) means the same as expr IN (Subquery), the form expr NOT IN (Subquery) is not the same as expr <>SOME (Subquery). Instead, NOT IN (Subquery) is identical to expr <>ALL (Subquery), as you should verify.

The ANSI SQL standards define ANY and SOME identically, supporting a transition to replace use of the predicate θANY with the predicate θSOME. This is done because the word "any" can have an extremely misleading English use.

EXAMPLE 3.4.9

Get `cid` values of customers with `discnt` smaller than those of any customers who live in Duluth. If we were feeling a bit sleepy when we were given this request, we would be very likely to write the following Select statement, which does *not* have the desired effect:

```
select cid from customers
    where discnt <any  -- ** WRONG EFFECT
        (select discnt from customers where city = 'Duluth');
```

Applied to the `customers` table of Figure 2.2, the Subquery above returns the set of `discnt` values {10.00, 8.00} for the two `customers` with `cid` values c001 and c004. Now by definition, a `discnt` value of 8.00 results in a TRUE value for the predicate `discnt <any` {10.00, 8.00}. This is because 8.00 < 10.00 (i.e., expr < s is TRUE for at least one element s of the Subquery). Therefore the full Select statement will return the `cid` values {c003, c004, c006}. But this isn't what we really wanted. The request for `cid` values of customers with `discnt` less than those of *any* customers who live in Duluth could be rephrased to ask for the `cid` values of customers with `discnt` less than those of *all* customers who live in Duluth. The English meaning of the term *any* in the original phrasing was misleading. The proper Select statement to achieve our aim is

```
select cid from customers
    where discnt <all (select discnt from customers
        where city = 'Duluth');
```

If we didn't have a predicate involving the word *any*, but only one using the word *some*, we would be much less likely to fall into this trap.

All commercial products support this set of quantified predicates, except that some products might still fail to recognize the new form using SOME. We have taken our naming conventions from the SQL-92 and SQL-99 standards; see, among the list of references at the end of this chapter: *Understanding the New SQL*, by Jim Melton and Alan R. Simon, which indexes this topic under "quantified comparison predicate." The *ORACLE Server SQL Language Reference Manual* refers to them separately as "ALL comparison operator," "ANY comparison operator," and "SOME comparison operator." There is no entry in the *ORACLE SQL Manual* for "quantified predicate," or even "predicate"; the term "condition" is used instead. *The INFORMIX Dynamic Server Guide to SQL: Syntax* also refers to what we call "predicate" as a "condition." Most other references index this topic under the term "quantified comparison predicate," including the *DB2 Universal Database SQL Reference Manual*.

The EXISTS Predicate

The EXISTS predicate tests whether the set of rows retrieved in a Subquery is non-empty. The general form is shown in Figure 3.8.

```
[NOT] EXISTS (Subquery)
```

Figure 3.8 The General Form of the Exists Predicate

The predicate EXISTS (Subquery) is TRUE if and only if the Subquery returns a non-empty set (if there *exists* an element in the set). The predicate NOT EXISTS (Subquery) is TRUE if and only if the returned set is empty.

EXAMPLE 3.4.10

Retrieve all customer names where the customer places an order through agent a05. The idea is to see whether an orders row exists that connects the cname with the agent.

```
select distinct c.cname from customers c
    where exists (select * from orders x
        where c.cid = x.cid and x.aid = 'a05');
```

Note that the Subquery has * in its select list, rather than any single attribute; this is the simplest way of testing whether the result of the Subquery is empty. The customer names retrieved from the tables of Figure 2.2 are the ones associated with cid values c001 and c002, TipTop and Basics. Note that the correlation variable x in the query above is not needed, but it is included only for ease of comparison with the following alternate solution:

```
select distinct c.cname from customers c, orders x
    where c.cid = x.cid and x.aid = 'a05';
```

This query also solves the problem posed. Note that if the keyword DISTINCT is not included in the two queries, duplicate names will be displayed in the case of identically named customers who separately qualify. ∎

We see that the second query form is very close to the first one, which uses the EXISTS predicate. To compare the two, consider the following. The first query in the example explicitly requires the *existence* of a row x in orders that connects the row c in customers to the agent a05; the second query makes use of such a row, x, but doesn't say anything about it: it simply appears in the WHERE clause with a reference in the search_condition. Now a range variable that appears in the WHERE clause without being used in the select list is analogous to what is called an *unbound variable* in mathematical logic. It is reasonable to ask: What circumstances must occur in such a case that will make the WHERE clause TRUE? The answer, which we have been assuming intuitively all along, is that the WHERE clause will be TRUE if there *exists* a row for the unbound variable that makes the WHERE clause TRUE. In the case above, there must exist a row x such that c.cid = x.cid and x.aid = 'a05'. Thus the unbound variable x has the same meaning as if it were *bound* with the predicate exists(select * from orders x ...).

This whole discussion has shown that the EXISTS predicate, used in its positive sense, is not needed to pose queries; an unbound variable would do as well. In solutions to exercises you are urged to avoid complex forms in a Select statement; in particular, don't use EXISTS when it isn't needed.

EXAMPLE 3.4.11

Recall Example 2.9.8, a request that required the relational algebra intersection operation to get cid values of customers who order both products p01 and p07. The query used was

```
(O where pid = 'p01')[cid] ∩ (O where pid = 'p07')[cid]
```

It seems natural to use the EXISTS predicate in the positive sense to achieve this in SQL:

```
select distinct cid from orders x
    where pid = 'p01' and exists (select * from orders
        where cid = x.cid and pid = 'p07');
```

However, it is also possible to achieve this without a Subquery:

```
select distinct x.cid from orders x, orders y
    where x.pid = 'p01' and x.cid = y.cid and y.pid = 'p07'
```

∎

The NOT EXISTS predicate, on the other hand, *does* provide power that is new to us.

EXAMPLE 3.4.12

Retrieve all customer names where the customer does *not* place an order through agent a05. This query should retrieve exactly those customer names that were not retrieved by the query resulting from Example 3.4.10. Note that simple negation of the search_condition in the second Select statement of Example 3.4.10 (implicit EXISTS) will have the wrong effect.

```
select c.cname from customers c, orders x
    where not (c.cid = x.cid and x.aid = 'a05');   -- ** WRONG EFFECT
```

What rows c in customers make the condition not (c.cid = x.cid and x.aid = 'a05') TRUE? Consider customer c where c.cid = 'c001', and the first row x in orders where x.cid = 'c001' and x.aid = 'a01'. For these values of c and x, it is NOT TRUE that x.aid = 'a05', and therefore the condition not (c.cid = x.cid and x.aid = 'a05') is TRUE. As a result the cname value 'TipTop' will be returned, even though TipTop *does* place an order with agent a05. Because the implicit EXISTS on the unbound variable x above sits outside the clause beginning with not, the effect is to make the condition TRUE because there *exists* an x such that not (c.cid = x.cid and x.aid = 'a05'); that is, there *exists* an x such that c.cid <> x.cid OR x.aid <> 'a05'. Both of these conditions are easy to fulfill (we found one where c.cid = x.cid but x.aid = 'a05'). What we really wanted was to return a cname when there *did not exist* an x such that (c.cid = x.cid and x.aid = 'a05'). For this, we have to be explicit about the EXISTS predicate:

```
select distinct c.cname from customers c
    where not exists (select * from orders x
        where c.cid = x.cid and x.aid = 'a05');
```

This query solves the problem posed.   ∎

The NOT EXISTS predicate as used in Example 3.4.12 seems to offer a new kind of power in phrasing queries. It turns out that we already had this power for many requests using the NOT IN predicate and the equivalent <>ALL predicate.

EXAMPLE 3.4.13

We repeat the query of Example 3.4.12, retrieving all customer names where the customer does not place an order through agent a05, but using the two equivalent NOT IN and <>ALL predicates in place of NOT EXISTS. Here are the two queries:

```
select distinct c.cname from customers c
    where c.cid not in (select cid from orders where aid = 'a05');
```

and

```
select distinct c.cname from customers c
    where c.cid <>all (select cid from orders where aid = 'a05');
```

The question naturally arises whether the NOT EXISTS predicate has any power that the NOT IN and <>ALL predicates do not. This question is explored in the exercises at the end of this chapter.

■

NOT EXISTS can be used to implement the MINUS operator from relational algebra.

EXAMPLE 3.4.14

In Example 2.9.2 we formulated a relational algebra expression for the request to find cid values of customers who do not place any order through agent a03. Recall that there were two possible solutions. The first solution only retrieved customers who had placed *some* order:

```
ORDERS[cid] - (ORDERS where aid = 'a03')[cid]
```

Corresponding to this we have the following SQL statement:

```
select distinct cid from orders x
    where not exists (select * from orders
        where cid = x.cid and aid = 'a03');
```

The table printed as a result of this query is

cid
c004

The alternative solution in Example 2.9.2 that would include customers who place *no* orders is

```
CUSTOMERS[cid] - (ORDERS where aid = 'a03')[cid]
```

We can parallel this in SQL with

```
select cid from customers c
    where not exists (select * from orders
        where cid = c.cid and aid = 'a03');
```

There is no difference between the two solutions in retrieving from the content of the database in Figure 2.2, because there are no customers who fail to place an order.

■

Note that there is a new operator in Advanced SQL (to be covered in Section 3.6), something called the EXCEPT operator, which directly copies the effect of the MINUS operator. Many of the products we are studying don't have this operator yet, however. We will cover new SQL operators in Section 3.6 of this chapter.

In general, if R and S are two compatible tables (with Head(R) = Head(S) = $A_1 \ldots A_n$), then the difference R – S can be computed by the following SQL statement:

```
select A₁ . . . Aₙ from R
    where not exists (select * from S
        where S.A₁ = R.A₁ and . . . and S.Aₙ = R.Aₙ);
```

A Weakness of SQL: Too Many Equivalent Forms

We are beginning to see one of the reasons that the SQL language is controversial: there are often a large number of different ways to pose the same query.

EXAMPLE 3.4.15
Consider the request to retrieve the `city` names containing customers who order product p01. There are four different major Select statement formulations:

```
select distinct city from customers where cid in
    (select cid from orders where pid = 'p01');

select distinct city from customers where cid =any
    (select cid from orders where pid = 'p01');

select distinct city from customers c where exists
    (select * from orders where cid = c.cid and pid = 'p01');

select distinct city from customers c, orders x
    where x.cid = c.cid and x.pid = 'p01';
```

In addition, there are a number of less obvious alternatives, such as

```
select distinct city from customers c where 'p01' in
    (select pid from orders where cid = c.cid)
```

∎

Since the predicate IN is identical to =ANY, it seems reasonable to ask why we need both. It might be a good idea to dispense with the predicate IN, for example, since many people find a large number of alternate forms confusing. As a matter of fact, it is perfectly feasible to do without the IN predicate and all the quantified (any-or-all) predicates, as long as we are left with the predicate [NOT] EXISTS. In the early 1970s, an IBM group advocated the multiplicity of predicates as being more user-friendly than the EXISTS predicate alone. This is certainly debatable. An important disadvantage of all these different forms is that it seems difficult on first encounter to mentally make an exhaustive search of the alternatives available in posing a query. A common mental trick in searching for a way to pose a new query in relational algebra is to say something like, "Well, I *know* I will have to join these three tables to get this answer." But now that we have Subqueries, we have to worry what new power is available that we couldn't get out of a simple join. In fact some other part of the SQL language might be more powerful still: so many forms are available and a number of them are yet to be discussed. To help with these problems, a complete general form for the Select statement is presented in a later section to allow you to do an exhaustive search of all the forms allowed in SQL. Furthermore, we indicate in the text and also in the exercises when a new SQL form adds additional descriptive power to the language and when it does not. Luckily, the set of concepts we need to learn is not limitless, although it might seem at first to be confusingly large.

3.5 UNION Operators and FOR ALL Conditions

In Section 3.3 we saw how the SQL Select statement is capable of implementing the relational algebra operations of projection, selection, and product. In Section 3.4, we developed the power of the search_condition, providing a number of new predicate tests to create search_conditions involving Subqueries, and adding ways to emulate the relational operators of difference and intersection to our bag of tricks for the Select statement. In the current section, we will see how to perform union and division (which are new capabilities). This completes the set of relational operators, so it seems we can now express any relational algebra query in SQL form. However, in the next section we will introduce some new SQL operators for performing intersection, difference, and special join operations.

The UNION Operator

To provide the ∪ (UNION operator) of relational algebra, SQL requires a new type of Select syntax. Any number of Subqueries (syntax given in Figure 3.5) that produce compatible tables can be combined with repeated use of the UNION syntax of Figure 3.9.

We must be very careful about where we use the UNION operator. In many current products, you may use the UNION form in full Select statements, but *not* in the predicates having Subquery forms. That is, in Subqueries appearing in the IN, quantified comparison, and EXISTS predicates of Figures 3.6, 3.7, and 3.8, a UNION form of the Subquery cannot be used. Core SQL-99 allows UNION anywhere a Subquery is specified. **DB2 UDB** allows this now, and other products will probably follow.

```
Subquery UNION [ALL] Subquery
```

Figure 3.9 UNION Form of the Subquery

EXAMPLE 3.5.1

We wish to create a list of cities where *either* a customer *or* an agent, *or both*, is based. This can be accomplished by the following Select statement:

```
select city from customers
    union select city from agents;
```

It is conceivable that we would want to see the same city named twice if it fills both roles (more information is in such a result), and in that case we would use the statement

```
select city from customers
    union all select city from agents;
```

Note that there is no way that this query could be performed, retrieving a single city column, from a Product of the two tables, customers and agents.

As usual, we allow parentheses around any expressions, and parentheses might be needed to differentiate between UNION and UNION ALL where three Subqueries or more are involved. For example, consider the query

```
(select city from customers
    union select city from agents)
    union all select city from products;
```

In this case, if the city Chicago appears in customers and products but not in agents, it will appear twice in the result. But it would not appear twice in a Select statement, with the parentheses moved.

```
select city from customers
    union (select city from agents
    union all select city from products);
```
■

Division: SQL "FOR ALL . . ." Conditions

Suppose that we need to find the cid values of customers who place orders with all agents based in New York. In relational algebra this query is solved by the following expression involving division:

```
ORDERS[cid, aid] DIVIDEBY (AGENTS where city = 'New York')[aid]
```

Unfortunately, there is no equivalent DIVIDEBY operator in SQL, and we are not going to suddenly reveal a special new SQL syntax as we did for UNION. Note that this DIVIDEBY query cannot be posed using the quantified predicate forms <ALL, <=ALL, =ALL, and the like, because no comparison operation is being performed involving attributes of agents based in New York. We are going to be forced to use an entirely new approach in SQL to perform this query, one that merits a slow and painstaking introduction because of its innate difficulty.

The approach we use is based on mathematical logic and the concept of mathematical proof. We start by asking: How would we go about proving or disproving that a specific customer row, represented by c.cid for some range variable c, places orders with all agents based in New York? Clearly we could *disprove* this by finding a counterexample: an agent based in New York that does *not* take an order for c.cid. If we designate this agent by a.aid, we can represent this counterexample as an SQL search_condition (we label this cond1 for ease of reference, although this is not acceptable SQL syntax):

```
cond1:    a.city = 'New York' and
          not exists (select * from orders x
          where x.cid = c.cid and x.aid = a.aid)
```

This states that the agent represented by a.aid is in New York and that no row in orders connects c.cid to a.aid; that is, c.cid does not place an order through a.aid.

Now to prove that the specific customer represented by c.cid *does* place orders with all agents based in New York, we would have to come up with a condition guaranteeing that *no counterexample exists* of the kind we have just constructed. That is, we need to guarantee that there is no agent a.aid that makes cond1 TRUE. We can state this as a search_condition also, designated by cond2:

```
cond2:    not exists (select * from agents a where cond1)
```

Or writing it out in full:

```
cond2:    not exists (select * from agents a where a.city = 'New York'
          and not exists (select * from orders x
          where x.cid = c.cid and x.aid = a.aid))
```

This is a very difficult condition to grasp, so we need to think about cond2 for a moment. The logic says that there does *not* exist an agent a.aid in New York that fails to place an order for c.cid (the range variable in c.cid is still unspecified). Certainly this means that *all* agents in New York do place an order for c.cid. If you agree that cond2 has this meaning, then we are almost home, because all we need now is to retrieve all cid values that have the property of cond2. We bring this all together in the following example.

EXAMPLE 3.5.2

Get the cid values of customers who place orders with all agents based in New York. By the foregoing discussion, the answer to this request is given by

```
select cid from customers where cond2;
```

Or writing it out in full:

```
select c.cid from customers c where           -- select c.cid if...
    not exists (select * from agents a         -- ...there is no agent a.aid
    where a.city = 'New York' and              -- ...living in New York
    not exists (select * from orders x         -- ...where no order row
    where x.cid = c.cid
        and x.aid = a.aid));                   -- ...connects c.cid and a.aid
```

110 This query should return the following table:

cid
c001

We have nothing but sympathy for readers who are encountering this rather complex construct of symbolic logic for the first time. This is certainly the most difficult concept that exists in SQL queries. The proper way to approach it is to take an organized step-by-step approach, mastering the reason for each step until the concepts involved become second nature.

Whenever we are faced with an English-language query to retrieve some set of objects that obey a condition where the word "all" is fundamental, we proceed with the following steps.

[1] Give a name to the object considered for retrieval and consider how we would state a counterexample in English for a candidate considered for retrieval, where one of "all" the objects mentioned earlier fails to obey its required condition.

[2] Create a Select search_condition to select all counterexamples created in step 1. (Steps 1 and 2 will certainly refer to objects that are selected externally, so we need to be flexible in how we reference them, even to what tables they come from.)

[3] Create a containing search_condition, stating that no counterexample of the kind specified in step 2 exists. This will involve a NOT EXISTS predicate.

[4] Create the final Select condition, retrieving the objects desired, with a condition reflecting step 3.

EXAMPLE 3.5.3
Get the aid values of agents in New York or Duluth who place orders for all products costing more than a dollar. To proceed with step 1 above, we say that a.aid is an agent considered for retrieval (but we remain flexible about the range variable and say ?.aid to allow a containing table other than agents) and pose the counterexample:

"There is a product costing over a dollar that is not ordered by ?.aid."

Now (step 2) we state a Select search_condition that collects all counterexamples for ?.aid:

```
cond1:   select pid from products p where price > 1.00 and not exists
         (select * from orders x where x.pid = p.pid and x.aid = ?.aid)
```

Following step 3, we now create a condition stating that no such counterexample exists:

```
cond2:   not exists (select pid from products p where
         price > 1.00 and not exists (select * from orders x
         where x.pid = p.pid and x.aid = ?.aid))
```

Finally, following step 4, we create the final Select condition. Note that, unlike Example 3.5.2, the condition reflecting step 3 is only *one* of the conditions needed for agents retrieved:

```
select aid from agents a
    where (a.city = 'New York' or a.city = 'Duluth')
    and not exists (select p.pid from products p
        where p.price > 1.00 and not exists (select * from orders x
            where x.pid = p.pid and x.aid = a.aid));
```

This Select statement results in the following table:

aid
a05

The condition occurring first in the above (`a.city = 'New York' or a.city = 'Duluth'`) is placed in parentheses because the AND connector has a higher precedence than the OR connector, and natural precedence would lead to an unintended grouping: `... where a.city = 'New York' or (a.city = 'Duluth' and not exists . . .)`. The answer then would be

aid
a01
a04
a05

■

Note that this sequence of steps typically leads to a pair of nested Subqueries of the form

```
select ... where not exists (select ... where not exists (select ... ));
```

It would have been a lot easier if the designers of SQL had included a FOR ALL predicate, similar to the EXISTS predicate, but unfortunately they did not.[1] This means that we need to create the equivalent predicate using other conditional operators that do exist. For readers who are familiar with mathematical logic, the approach we are taking, wherein we use the NOT EXISTS predicate twice, is based on the following tautology:

[3.5.1] $\forall_z (\exists_y p(z, y)) \leftrightarrow \neg\exists_z (\neg\exists_y p(z, y))$

To restate [3.5.1] in words, the following two statements are equivalent: (1) for all z, there exists a y such that the statement p(z, y) depending on z and y is true, and (2) it is false there exists a z such that no y exists with p(z, y) true. In Example 3.5.2, z is a row in

---

[1] At one time, a FOR ALL quantifier was proposed for standard ANSI SQL, but the proposal failed. Note that in mathematical logic, the FOR ALL operator, $\forall$, and the EXISTS operator, $\exists$, are known as quantifiers rather than predicates. We use the term predicate to comply with current ANSI SQL standard conventions.

the agents table, with city New York; y is a row in the orders table; and p(z, y) says the agent in row z is connected by the order in row y to the customer c (existing outside this Subquery part). The best way to think of the statement in [3.5.1] is that the form on the left is the FOR ALL predicate we wish to create and the form on the right is the non-existence of a counterexample, as explained in Example 3.5.2. Note that there are two nested NOT EXISTS predicates in the expression on the right of tautology [3.5.1].

EXAMPLE 3.5.4

Find aid values of agents who place orders for product p01 as well as for all products costing more than a dollar. Note that the answer to this query is an empty table, given the CAP content of Figure 2.2, which was loaded into our Example database in Exercise 3.2.1. Of course we still have to create a Select statement that will act correctly if the content of the CAP database should change, so the answer becomes non-empty. The query statement given is a minor variant of Example 3.5.3, where we asked for agents in New York or Duluth who place orders for all products costing more than a dollar. We can use the FOR ALL condition of this prior solution without change, by finding a way to specify the new first condition:

```
select a.aid from agents a where a.aid in
    (select aid from orders where pid = 'p01')
    and not exists (select p.pid from products p
        where p.price > 1.00 and not exists (select * from orders x
            where x.pid = p.pid and x.aid = a.aid));
```

A somewhat more natural solution would arise from satisfying the first condition with the statement

```
select y.aid from orders y where y.pid = 'p01' and . . .
```

This means the reference to the range variable a inside the FOR ALL condition must be altered:

```
select y.aid from orders y where y.pid = 'p01' and
    not exists (select p.pid from products p
        where p.price > 1.00 and not exists (select * from orders x
            where x.pid = p.pid and x.aid = y.aid));
```

Recall that in step 2 of our four-step procedure to create a FOR ALL condition, we said that the condition we create "will certainly refer to objects that are selected externally, so we need to be flexible in how we reference them, even to what tables they come from." This is an example of a situation where a.aid must become y.aid.   ∎

EXAMPLE 3.5.5

Suppose we are asked to find cid values for customers with the following property: if customer c006 orders a particular product, so does the customer under consideration. It is not immediately obvious how to create a Select statement to fill this request, and it would be even more puzzling if we were not in the middle of a section on how to pose FOR ALL conditions. Here we see the need to think in terms of rephrasing English-language statements. We rephrase this request to the following: find cid values for customers who order *all* products ordered by customer c006. We proceed as before in steps. In step 1, above, we say that c.cid is a customer considered for retrieval and pose the English counterexample:

"There is a product ordered by customer c006 that is not ordered by `c.cid`."

Now we state this as a `search_condition`, step 2. We will give the name `p.pid` to the product ordered by c006, but remain flexible:

```
cond1:  p.pid in (select pid from orders x where x.cid = 'c006')
            and not exists (select * from orders y
                where y.pid = p.pid and y.cid = c.cid)
```

Following step 3, we now create a condition stating that no such counterexample exists:

```
cond2:  not exists (select p.pid from products p
            where p.pid in (select pid from orders x
                where x.cid = 'c006') and
                not exists (select * from orders y
                    where y.pid = p.pid and y.cid = c.cid))
```

Finally, following step 4, we create the final Select condition.

```
        select cid from customers c
            where not exists (select p.pid from products p
                where p.pid in (select pid from orders x
                where x.cid = 'c006') and
                not exists (select * from orders y
                where y.pid = p.pid and y.cid = c.cid));
```

An obvious variant of this is

```
        select cid from customers c
            where not exists (select z.pid from orders z
                where z.cid = 'c006' and
                not exists (select * from orders y
                where y.pid = z.pid and y.cid = c.cid));
```

As a result we obtain the table

cid
c001
c006

∎

After sufficient practice, it becomes possible in simple situations to write down the FOR ALL condition that no counterexample exists and from this immediately create the SQL statement required. It is generally possible to say that the innermost Subquery is to select an `orders` row that connects two rows listed in outer Select and Subqueries.

114

EXAMPLE 3.5.6

Find `pid` values of products supplied to all customers in Duluth. What we need to say is that there does *not* exist a customer in Duluth who fails to order the `pid` we want to retrieve.

```
select pid from products p              -- Retrieve product p.pid if
    where not exists
    (select c.cid from customers c      -- ... there is no customer
        where c.city = 'Duluth'         -- ... in Duluth
        and not exists
        (select * from orders x         -- ... where no row in orders
            where x.pid = p.pid         -- ... connects p.pid
            and x.cid = c.cid));        -- ... and c.cid              ■
```

We can conclude at this point that SQL is capable of computing everything that can be computed by relational algebra. The accepted term for this is that SQL is *relationally complete*. As we will see in the next few sections, SQL goes beyond what relational algebra can do. But this is a good point at which to pause and work through the initial set of exercises at the end of the chapter (3.1–3.7), which reflects the Select statement features we have covered so far.

3.6   Some Advanced SQL Syntax

In Sections 3.1 through 3.5, we introduced the necessary SQL power to perform all relational algebra queries. All of the Basic SQL syntax presented in these sections, with only a very few exceptions, is implemented by all the major database vendors. *In the current section we introduce some advanced SQL operators that are not uniformly available on all database systems, and are not part of Entry SQL-92.* On the other hand, almost all of them are in Core SQL-99, so they probably will be adopted in the future. None of the syntax introduced in this section qualifies as Basic SQL. You will need to read carefully to see what features from the current section are available in the database product you are using. Much of this advanced syntax simply provides alternate ways to perform relational query capabilities we have already seen. However, there are a few new added capabilities, such as the ability to perform a query in the FROM clause, that provide a good deal of added power.

We start by explaining SQL operators duplicating the relational operations of intersection and difference. Later, we'll introduce a new syntax for what can occur in the FROM clause of a Select statement, including a wide range of Join operators.

The INTERSECT and EXCEPT Operators in Advanced SQL

To emulate the ∩ (INTERSECT) and – (DIFFERENCE) operations of relational algebra, Full SQL-92 and SQL-99 provide two new operators, INTERSECT and EXCEPT. These operators are used in the same way as the UNION operator, diagrammed in Figure 3.9.

```
subquery {UNION [ALL]| INTERSECT [ALL] | EXCEPT [ALL] subquery}
```

Figure 3.10   Advanced SQL Subquery Form with UNION, INTERSECT, and EXCEPT

Indeed, Figure 3.9 presented the Entry SQL-92 syntax. Figure 3.10 has a larger subset of the Full SQL-92 syntax, covering the use of the set operations UNION, INTERSECT, and EXCEPT, which some products currently support. Of these, Core SQL-99 requires UNION [ALL] and EXCEPT.

Figure 3.10 indicates that two Subquery terms can be connected by a UNION, INTERSECT, or EXCEPT operator to produce a new Subquery (which can be used as a full Select statement or within certain predicates). Later, this resulting Subquery can recursively take the place of one of the Subqueries of the Figure 3.10 form, so that any number of Subqueries can be connected by these operators. As always, parentheses can be used to keep order of operations unambiguous. The INTERSECT operator is self-explanatory for tables considered as sets of rows, and the EXCEPT operator emulates the DIFFERENCE operator of relational algebra.

We have already seen from examples of UNION ALL on two Subquery terms with identical rows that the resulting UNION will contain two of these rows. This is another way of saying that the ALL keyword causes UNION to take counts of duplicate rows into account. The result of two UNION ALL operations could have three duplicate rows, and so on. Consider performing INTERSECT ALL on two Subquery terms, Q1 and Q2:

```
Q1 INTERSECT ALL Q2
```

Since the two Queries Q1 and Q2 could have resulted from any number of UNION ALL operations, there may be three identical rows in Q1 and two identical rows in Q2 that match the first three. Then the result of INTERSECT ALL will take account of the number of duplicates on both sides, and in this case will contain two duplicates of these rows (the minimum number in the two operands—this jibes with how we expect a count of zero in the result for rows that do not appear at all in one of the Subquery terms of the INTERSECT). On the other hand, if the ALL keyword is left out, we simply say that the row in question is in both Q1 and Q2 (we allow no counts except 0 and 1), and therefore the row is in the result.

Similarly, the EXCEPT ALL operator will take the count of duplicate rows into account:

```
Q1 EXCEPT ALL Q2
```

If Q1 contains three identical rows and Q2 contains two rows that are also identical to these, the result of the EXCEPT ALL Subquery will have one row of this form. That is, the count in the result of an EXCEPT ALL will be the number of occurrences of the row in Q1 minus the number in Q2 (but with a minimum of zero). If the ALL keyword is left out, the row will exist once in both Q1 and Q2, and thus not be present in the result. Note that EXCEPT ALL is not in Core SQL-99, only the simple EXCEPT is.

Two tables derived from Subqueries can be operands in UNION, INTERSECT, or EXCEPT operations if they have the same number of columns, and the datatypes of the columns passing from left to right in the Create Table statements of both tables are *compatible*. This allows, for example, comparison between a column declared of type char(5) with one of type char(10). The result of the operator will have the more general datatype, char(10).

The INTERSECT and EXCEPT operators don't add power to the Select statement (we already had the capability of performing such operations by using the NOT IN or NOT EXISTS predicates) but the ALL keyword does add power, which may or may not be useful.

EXAMPLE 3.6.1

Recall Example 3.4.11, requesting cid values of customers who order both products p01 and p07. There are a number of possible query forms that will solve this problem:

```
select distinct cid from orders x
    where pid = 'p01' and exists (select * from orders
        where cid = x.cid and pid = 'p07');
```

and

```
select distinct cid from orders x
    where pid = 'p01' and cid in (select cid from orders
        where pid = 'p07')
```

However, it is also possible to achieve this without a Subquery:

```
select distinct x.cid from orders x, orders y
    where x.pid = 'p01' and x.cid = y.cid and y.pid = 'p07';
```

The new INTERSECT operator gives us another solution:

```
select cid from orders where pid = 'p01'
    intersect select cid from orders where pid = 'p07';
```

■

Next, we give an example of how the EXCEPT predicate alone adds no new power.

EXAMPLE 3.6.2

Retrieve all customer names where the customer does *not* place an order through agent a05. This query can be performed using the new EXCEPT predicate:

```
select c.cname from customers c
    except
    select c.cname from customers c, orders x
        where c.cid = x.cid and x.aid = 'a05';
```

But we provided a different solution in Example 3.4.12. The NOT EXISTS predicate could be replaced with NOT IN or <>ALL in this solution:

```
select c.cname from customers c
    where not exists (select * from orders x
        where c.cid = x.cid and x.aid = 'a05');
```

Many database vendors have not yet implemented INTERSECT and EXCEPT. The X/Open standard supports UNION [ALL] but not INTERSECT [ALL} or EXCEPT [ALL]. (See "Suggestions for Further Reading" at the end of the current chapter for X/Open and other documentation.) **ORACLE** provides UNION, UNION ALL, INTERSECT, and MINUS (a variant name for EXCEPT), but not INTERSECT ALL or MINUS ALL. **DB2 UDB**, version 5, implements all of these forms: {UNION | INTERSECT | EXCEPT} [ALL]. **INFORMIX**, version 9.2, supports UNION [ALL].

Join Forms in Advanced SQL

In the ANSI SQL-89 standard, the FROM clause was extremely basic, as follows:

```
FROM tablename [corr_name] {, tablename [corr_name]...}
```

Entry SQL-92 duplicates the SQL-89 form. All major products except **ORACLE** have extended this form to allow the optional AS keyword before the correlation name, as was previously shown in Figure 3.5 and adopted as Basic SQL.

```
FROM tablename [[AS] corr_name] {, tablename [[AS] corr_name]...}
```

But Full SQL-92 and SQL-99 have extended this syntax considerably more, as we see in Figure 3.11. Note that Figure 3.11 starts by defining a general form called *tableref* and then defines the FROM clause in terms of this (simply the word FROM followed by a comma-separated list of tablerefs). *Once again, you are warned that the syntax presented in Figure 3.11 is not yet supported by most commercial DBMS products.* We believe Figure 3.11 gives insight into future syntax for most database products, but complete conformance to this syntax may never be implemented on all database systems. You need to read the text carefully to see which products support which features of Figure 3.11. You might also wish to refer to Appendix C, where SQL statement syntax for specific DBMS products is presented.

```
tableref::= tablename [[AS] corr_name [(colname {, colname ...})]] --simple form
    | (subquery) [AS] corr_name [(colname {, colname...})]          --subquery as table
    | tableref1 [INNER |{LEFT|RIGHT|FULL} [OUTER]] JOIN tableref2  --join forms
        {ON search_condition | USING (colname {, colname ...})}

FROM Clause ::= FROM tableref {, tableref...}
```

Figure 3.11 SQL-99 Recursive Definition of `tableref`, and FROM Clause Using `tableref` Form

Note that the definition of tableref in Figure 3.11 is recursive, and that `tableref` objects formed following this prescription can then be used recursively in any position that a `tableref` object occurs in the form. A Subquery (or Select statement) can use any form of the FROM clause of this figure. Parentheses are allowed around a JOIN form.

The first new SQL capability offered in Figure 3.11, on line 1 of the `tableref` definition, is to allow all columns retrieved FROM a table to be renamed in a parenthesized list: `[(colname {, colname...})]`. If this list is used, these column names must also be employed in the select list retrieving FROM this table. On line 2, we allow a `tableref` to be a Subquery, and this will give us the freedom in a Subquery or Select statement to retrieve data FROM a Subquery. Note that on line 2, unlike line 1, the correlation name is required, since we need a name to refer to the table retrieved in the Subquery. Once again, the named set of columns on line 2 is optional and gives us an alternative to providing column aliases for all elements of the Subquery select list.

While it has always been the case that the result of a Select statement was itself a table, it is only with Full SQL-92 and SQL-99 (in the extended features) that a Subquery could appear in the FROM clause of another Subquery. The fact that we can repeat any `tableref` after FROM in Figure 3.11 an arbitrary number of times means that we can list several `tableref`s of different kinds in sequence, taking a relational product of all `tableref`s listed, just as we have been doing up to now with named tables. Some database systems we deal with don't currently allow a Subquery in the FROM clause: **INFORMIX DS** version 9.2 does not, while **ORACLE** as of release 8 and **DB2 UDB** as of version 5 do allow it. However, **ORACLE** does not currently support the `[(colname {, colname...})]` syntax after, nor the AS keyword prior, to the `corr_name` in the `tableref` form. Subqueries after FROM are part of Full SQL-99 as a named extended feature; that is, this feature is not part of Core SQL-99.

EXAMPLE 3.6.3
Retrieve all customer names where the customer places at least two orders for the same product. This could be done in a number of ways, but here is one using a Subquery as a table to select from.

```
select cname from (select o.cid as spcid from orders o, orders x where o.cid = x.cid
    and o.pid = x.pid and o.ordno <> x.ordno) y, customers c
    where y.spcid = c.cid;
```

Note in this query that we provide an alias y (as we are required to do) for the Subquery result, and provide the colname selected in the Subquery an alias (spcid). We need these names to restrict the rows of the relational product of the table y with the customers table by setting y.spcid to c.cid. ∎

We will now talk about the various Join operators listed on lines 3 and 4 of Figure 3.11. Most database products have not yet implemented all of these Join operators.

The keyword INNER appears in line 3 of Figure 3.11, with INNER appearing as the default alternative to {LEFT | RIGHT | FULL} OUTER, prior to the required keyword JOIN. In fact an INNER JOIN is simply the type of join we originally learned about in relational algebra, the opposite of (FULL) OUTER JOIN. INNER JOIN is what is assumed if we use only the keyword JOIN. We will look at some INNER JOIN examples first, but we won't bother to use the INNER keyword, because we don't need it.

If JOIN (or, equivalently, INNER JOIN) is used from line 3 of Figure 3.11, then the two `tablerefs` on either side of the JOIN will need a specification of *how* they are to be joined, that is, a specification of what columns are the join columns. When the JOIN keyword is used, exactly one of the keywords ON or USING must appear to specify the join columns. The ON form is more general than the USING form, but the USING form is slightly more compact. The ON form can handle the case that a join column has a different name in the two joined tables.

We call it a *condition join* when two or more arbitrarily named columns are to be compared in an ON clause. For example, if we had a `cities` table with columns named `cityname`, `latitude`, and `longitude`, we could write:

```
select cname, city, latitude, longitude
    from customers c join cities x on c.city = x.cityname;
```

EXAMPLE 3.6.4

We wish to retrieve all customers who purchased at least one product costing less than $0.50. (Note that there are no rows in the CAP database of Figure 2.2 that will satisfy this query, but of course this is not relevant.) The following solution would not work:

```
((ORDERS ⋈ PRODUCTS where price < 0.50) ⋈ CUSTOMERS) [cname]
```

This is because this triple join requires product rows to match `customers` rows on `city`, a requirement we did not intend. Because of this, we restricted the first join in the expression, as follows:

```
((ORDERS ⋈ (PRODUCTS where price <0.50) [pid]) ⋈ CUSTOMERS) [cname]
```

But in SQL, we specify the join columns explicitly, and we have two methods to choose from. We can perform a *Condition Join* by naming all the columns to be joined with an ON `search_condition`:

```
select distinct cname from (orders o join products p on o.pid = p.pid)
    join customers c on o.cid = c.cid where p.price < 0.50;
```

Or we can restrict the columns used in the join by a *Column Name Join*, with a USING clause naming a subset of the commonly named columns of two tables to be used in the join:

```
select distinct cname from (orders join products using (pid))
    join customers using(cid) where price < 0.50;
```
∎

Obviously there is some redundancy among these capabilities. Given that we have the ON clause capability, for example, we certainly don't need the USING clause—this just handles a special case where we want to join on a subset of identically named columns. Indeed, you can ask whether any of the capabilities added in this section actually add new SQL power. Didn't we claim we had all needed relational power in the SQL features presented through Section 3.5? Clearly the ANSI SQL-92 committee was adding new syntax to make things "simpler" to do. Things are not simpler for a beginner, however, who has to learn to recognize all of these syntactic forms. The ANSI SQL Standards Committee continued this effort by making all the JOIN forms part of Core SQL-99 except for the FULL keyword.

OUTER JOIN

We are now going to discuss some syntax from Figure 3.11 that actually provides new power to SQL, because the operations provided by the syntax are not offered by classical relational algebra. These operations are the different forms of OUTER JOIN.

```
[{LEFT | RIGHT | FULL} [OUTER]] JOIN
```

We originally introduced OUTER JOIN (what we call here FULL OUTER JOIN) in Section 2.10, at the end of the relational algebra introduction. As with INNER JOIN, exactly one of the keywords, ON, or USING, must appear to determine what columns are involved with any type of OUTER JOIN.

As a first example, assume that we have two tables, S and T, with the following content:

S

C	A
c1	a1
c3	a3
c4	a4

T

A	B
a1	b1
a2	b2
a3	b3

Then the FULL OUTER JOIN of S and T will give the following result:

```
select * from
S full outer join t using (A);
```

C	A	B
c1	a1	b1
c3	a3	b3
c4	a4	null
null	a2	b2

The FULL OUTER JOIN has all the normal rows of a natural INNER JOIN plus rows derived from rows in S and T that do not match up, and these have nulls in the unmatched columns. If the FULL keyword is not supported (it is not required for Core

SQL-99), you can still compute the FULL OUTER JOIN by using something like the following Core SQL-99 Subquery:

```
select * from S left join T using (A) union select * from S right join T using (A);
```

Note that the JOIN operators work *inside* the tableref (see Figure 3.11) whereas the UNION works at the Subquery level (see Figure 3.10), so you need to select * from the joined table to create a Subquery before you can combine the sets of rows with UNION.

As another example, assume (as we did in Section 2.10) that we have a table named sales that contains two columns, the agent aid that appears in the orders table and a total column giving the dollar total of orders taken by each such agent in the orders table. Note that if an aid value doesn't appear in orders, we assume it will not appear in the sales table either. What we want to do now is to report agents and their corresponding sales, basically the aid values and totals from the sales table, but for ease of understanding we need to include the names of the agents along with aid. This seems to imply the need for a join, as follows:

```
select aname, aid, total from sales join agents using (aid);
```

The problem with the natural join used here arises in two cases: when we have an agent in the agents table who doesn't have any rows in the orders or sales table (because the agent hasn't placed any orders), and when we have an agent aid that has made sales, but there seems to be no aid to go with it in the agents table (this would probably be due to an error or delay in data entry). To deal with this problem, we use the FULL OUTER JOIN operator, which will preserve in the answer all rows from either table being joined, even if they have no matching row in the other table, and will display nulls for values that correspond to unmatched values in one of the two tables:

```
select aname, aid, total from sales full outer join agents using (aid);
```

Note that the three words FULL OUTER JOIN need not be used; the phrase FULL JOIN alone can be used according to the SQL-99 standard (Figure 3.11), but not OUTER JOIN alone. Similarly, LEFT OUTER JOIN can be written LEFT JOIN, and RIGHT OUTER JOIN can be written RIGHT JOIN. The result of this query might be the following table.

In this table, agent a04, Gray, has made no sales, and agent a07, who has made sales, doesn't have an aname value in the agents table (and might not have an aid value either—this must be checked).

A LEFT OUTER JOIN will only preserve rows in the left-hand table in the result, even if there is no join with a row of the right-hand table, but will not do this for unmatched rows in the right-hand table.

```
select aname, aid, total from sales left outer join agents using (aid);
```

122

aname	aid	total
Smith, J	a01	850.00
Jones	a02	400.00
Brown	a03	3900.00
Gray	a04	null
Otasi	a05	2400.00
Smith, P.	a06	900.00
null	a07	650.00

In this case, the row (null, a07, 650.00) will appear in the result, but not (Gray, a04, null).

A RIGHT OUTER JOIN will only preserve rows in the right-hand table in the result when there is no join with a row of the left-hand table.

```
select aname, aid, total from sales right outer join agents using (aid);
```

Here, the row (Gray, a04, null) will appear in the result, but not (null, a07, 650.00).

Join Forms Implemented in Database Systems

Most database vendors have not yet implemented all of these join operations. **DB2 UDB** implements everything we have covered except for the (redundant) USING clause. **ORACLE** provides only left and right outer join, using a different syntax than the ANSI SQL standards provide. In **ORACLE**, an outer join is indicated by special conditions in the WHERE clause, for example,

```
SELECT . . . FROM T1, T2 WHERE {T1.c1 [(+)] = T2.c2 | T1.c1 = T2.c2 [(+)]}
    AND search_cond;
```

Only one of the two tables T1 and T2 can have a plus in parentheses, (+), following it, and what this means is that the other table of the join will preserve all its rows, even rows that do not satisfy the Join condition. Note that if there are two or more Join conditions between the two tables, the (+) notation must be uniformly applied to the same table in both cases, for example, T1.c1 = T2.c2 (+) and T1.c3 = T2.c4 (+). Note too that in joining N tables, it is possible for N − 1 of those tables to have the (+) property. An interesting point is that we can compare a table column to a constant with (+) notation following the constant (select T1.c1 where T1.c2 = const1(+)) to allow **ORACLE** to return rows with the given constant value *or null values* in the column compared.

INFORMIX, version 9.2, also provides only left and right outer join, just as **ORACLE** does, but with slightly different notation. Instead of placing (+) after a table in the WHERE clause, it places the keyword OUTER before the second table named in the

FROM clause. In **INFORMIX** terminology, this makes the table a subservient table, and the rows of the other table, the dominant table, are preserved when the join is preserved. The equivalent of LEFT and RIGHT OUTER JOIN can be achieved by reversing the tables on the right and left, with an OUTER keyword on the right-hand one, in the FROM clause. As with **ORACLE**, only one of the two tables involved in a join condition can have this property.

3.7 Set Functions in SQL

We return now to features that have been implemented for some time by all serious database vendors. SQL provides five built-in functions that operate on sets of column values in tables: COUNT, MAX, MIN, SUM, and AVG. With the exception of COUNT, these *set functions* must operate on sets that consist of *simple values*—that is, sets of numbers or sets of character strings, rather than sets of rows with multiple column values.

> **EXAMPLE 3.7.1**
>
> Suppose that we wish to determine the total dollar amount of all orders. We can write
>
> ```
> select sum(dollars) as totaldollars from orders;
> ```
>
> The answer printed for our example database will be the one-entry table
>
> | totaldollars |
> | --- |
> | 9802.00 |
>
> ■

Like many other terms in use in the database field, there is some variation in terminology concerning set functions. The X/Open standard, and the ANSI SQL standards refer to the five *set functions*; C. J. Date, in his texts, and **INFORMIX** documents refer to *aggregate functions* (*to aggregate* means "to bring together a number of different elements into a single measure, or amount"); **ORACLE** speaks of *group functions*; and the IBM product, **DB2 Universal Database**, uses the term *column functions*. You should have no difficulty being understood if you use the term *set function* in talking with people familiar with other products. Figure 3.12 describes the set function syntax of Basic SQL and the Core SQL-99 standard.

Note in particular that MAX and MIN, when applied to a set of character type arguments, return the smallest and largest of the arguments in alphabetical order. Also, the AVG of some numeric quantity over a set of values is the same as the SUM divided by the COUNT (as long as the quantities in both cases are well defined, without floating point overflow).

Name	Argument type	Result type	Description
COUNT	any (can be *)	numeric	count of occurrences
SUM	numeric	numeric	sum of arguments
AVG	numeric	numeric	average of arguments
MAX	char or numeric	same as arg	maximum value
MIN	char or numeric	same as arg	minimum value

Figure 3.12   The Set Functions in SQL

EXAMPLE 3.7.2

To determine the total quantity of product p03 that has been ordered, we can use the function SUM and restrict its application to the set of rows satisfying the appropriate restriction:

```
select sum(qty) as TOTAL
    from orders where pid = 'p03';
```

The answer is the table consisting of a single row

. . . the sum of 600, 1000, and 800.   ■

The set functions should not be confused with the scalar functions, such as upper, and substr, which can occur in expressions in the select list of a Select statement. These built-in scalar functions take single row values as arguments and return a single value associated with *each row*. Set functions, on the other hand, combine values from a table expression to return a value. Thus the Select statement

```
select sum(dollars) as TOTAL
    from orders where pid = 'p03';
```

returns a single value, whereas the statement

```
select upper(cname) as UPCNAME from customers
    where discnt >= 10;
```

returns a column of values, *one value for each row* in the customers table, where discnt >= 10. We provide a list of built-in functions in Section 3.9.

EXAMPLE 3.7.3

The query to find the total number of customers uses the COUNT function and need not confine itself to a set of simple values. Either of the following forms is valid:

```
select count(cid)
    from customers;
```

or

```
select count(*)
    from customers;
```

The first Select statement counts the number of values that occur under the column cid. Note carefully that null values in a column are *not counted*. The two statements give the same answer in our case, because the Create Table statement did not allow null values in the cid column of the customers table. ∎

The set functions can be required to act on *distinct* values fitting some description.

EXAMPLE 3.7.4

Get the number of cities where customers are based. The Select statement

```
select count(distinct city)
    from customers;
```

produces the number of *distinct* cities where customers are based; once again, null values are not counted. Since two customers exist in Dallas as well as two in Duluth in the CAP database of Figure 2.2, the result of the query in this case will be three, quite different from the result of the same query without the DISTINCT keyword:

```
select count(city)
    from customers;
```

The result in this second case is five. Note that the English-language request to get the number of cities in which customers are based would normally be interpreted as meaning the number of distinct cities, so the second form is somewhat misleading. ∎

The Basic SQL general form for a set function reference in the select list of a query is

```
SET_FUNCTION_NAME([ALL | DISTINCT] colname) | COUNT(*)
```

Either ALL or DISTINCT can be placed before a colname, but ALL is the default.

Note that there is no value in using the DISTINCT keyword with a MAX or MIN function, since a single value from the set is chosen without taking duplication into account in any event. Additionally, a query of the form

```
select sum(distinct dollars) from orders where . . .
```

126

would be an *unusual* request, insisting as it does that the dollar amounts to be added should be distinct; this is not normally a meaningful consideration in taking a SUM or AVG.

An important restriction is that set functions are not allowed to appear in comparisons of a WHERE clause unless they are in the select list of a Subquery.

EXAMPLE 3.7.5

List the cid values of all customers who have a discount less than the maximum discount. The following approach is invalid:

```
select cid from customers
    where discnt < max(discnt);  -- ** INVALID SQL SYNTAX
```

A rationale for this rule is that the Select statement given contains only a single range variable (with the name "customers") that ranges once over the rows of the table; in order for max(discnt) to have a meaningful value, there must have been a prior loop in which all discnt values of the customers table were considered. Providing a second disconnected loop is just not part of the Select philosophy. The user can request this information in a different way:

```
select cid from customers
    where discnt < (select max(discnt) from customers);
```

Note that two distinct range variables have the name customers here, and the Subquery is evaluated first to provide the needed value for the outer Select. The Subquery returns only a one-element set, so we are able to use a comparison consisting of a single *less-than* (<). We could also have used the <ANY or <ALL comparison operators, since these mean the same thing for a Subquery that returns a set with one element.   ∎

EXAMPLE 3.7.6

Recall the query solved in Example 3.3.7 to find products ordered by at least two customers. We can now solve this problem in a way that generalizes easily to more than two customers.

```
select p.pid from products p
    where 2 <= (select count(distinct cid) from orders
        where pid = p.pid);
```

This query returns the table

pid
p01
p03
p05
p07

∎

Handling Null Values

The concept of null values was introduced in Section 2.4, but we have waited for the definition of set functions before giving details of the ideas involved. A null value is a special scalar constant (meaningful in either a numeric or character string type column) that stands for a value that is undefined (inapplicable) or else one that is meaningful but unknown at the present time. As an example, when we are inserting a new row in an employees table, we might prefer to have a null value in the salary column because the salary is not yet determined; alternatively, a percent (commission) column for an employee may be null because the job category is 'librarian', and no sales commission is provided for employees in this job category (thus the value is undefined, or inapplicable). The concept of null, as it is currently implemented on most commercial systems, does not differentiate between these two cases (although proposals have been made to do this).

NOTE: Some older database systems did not properly implement null values. Where a null occurs in what follows, we would expect to see in older systems a blank value for character types or a zero for numeric types; we will see that this has significant consequences.

Although we will not investigate the full syntax of SQL Insert statements for a while yet, it is appropriate to give a small foreshadowing here, to show how null values appear in a table.

EXAMPLE 3.7.7
Add a row with specified values for columns cid, cname, and city to the customers table. Recall from Figure 2.2 that a fourth column, discnt, is in the customers table, but we are assuming that this value is not known at the time that we wish to insert the new row—that is, it has not yet been negotiated.

```
insert into customers (cid, cname, city)
    values ('c007', 'WinDix', 'Dallas');
```

Since the discnt column is not mentioned in the column names or the values list of the Insert statement, it defaults to the null value for this row. Note that it is possible in most database products to specify a null value literally as NULL in an Insert Values clause; this became standard with SQL-92. ∎

A null value in a table has a number of important properties. First of all, the null value appearing in any normal comparison predicate of a search_condition makes that predicate evaluate to a special Boolean value, UNKNOWN, that is neither TRUE nor FALSE. For a row to be retrieved by a Select statement, the compound predicate in the WHERE clause must evaluate to TRUE, so this UNKNOWN value has essentially the same effect as FALSE in most cases.

EXAMPLE 3.7.8

After adding the row (c007, Windix, Dallas, null) to the customers table in Example 3.7.7, the row will *not* be retrieved by the following Select statement.

```
select * from customers where discnt <= 10 or discnt > 10;
```

This is surprising! Although this WHERE clause seems to cover all the bases, it has value UNKNOWN if the value null appears in a comparison to be less than 10, equal to 10, or greater than 10. The only way a row with null value in discnt can be retrieved by a predicate on dis-cnt is by using the special predicate IS NULL:

```
select * from customers where discnt is null;
```

It is also possible to use the specially provided predicate, discnt is not null, but variants, such as discnt = null, although acceptable Basic SQL syntax, have the **WRONG EFFECT**. It would be easier to avoid this pitfall if the statement were rejected as bad syntax, but as in any programming environment, the SQL system will sometimes give results you don't intend. ■

To reiterate this important point: if a null value appears in any normal comparison predicate, it will make that predicate evaluate to UNKNOWN. (We will discuss more details of this special Boolean value in Section 3.9.) This rule holds even in an equality predicate of the form col1 = col2, where both column values col1 and col2 in a row have null values; the predicate still evaluates to UNKNOWN. The only exception to this rule is the special predicate IS NULL.

Note that no normal values, such as 0, or the empty string, represented by two single quotes in succession (''), have the property demonstrated in Example 3.7.8. A column value of the empty string will be less than 'a' (in alphabetical order), the value zero will be less than 10, and rows that are assigned genuine values will always be retrieved by some range predicate. But this is sometimes inappropriate. A new employee with a null value for salary is not necessarily a candidate for the poverty program, as would certainly be the case if the salary were 0. Another problem arises as well. If we are trying to calculate the average salary in a department, it is inappropriate to average in the new employee's salary as zero. Better to leave the employee out of consideration entirely, and this is exactly what is done with null values.

EXAMPLE 3.7.9

After inserting the row (c007, Windix, Dallas, null) to the customers table in Example 3.7.7, assume that we wish to find the average discount of all customers.

```
select avg(discnt) from customers;
```

In this SQL statement, the null value is discarded before the average is calculated. ■

Similar considerations hold for the other set functions as well. As we mentioned in the discussion following Figure 3.12, avg( ) = sum( )/count( ), so it is clear that the sum( ) and count( ) functions must also ignore null values. Here is another interesting question: What value is returned by a set function acting on an empty set of values (no relevant rows exist)? The answer depends on the function: count( ) returns zero for an empty set, but sum( ), avg( ), max( ), and min( ) return the null value.

3.8	Groups of Rows in SQL

SQL allows Select statements to provide a kind of natural "report" function, grouping the rows of a table on the basis of commonality of values and performing set functions on the rows grouped. As an example, consider the query

[3.8.1]
```
select pid, sum(qty) as total from orders
    group by pid;
```

The GROUP BY clause of the Select statement will result in a set of rows being generated as if the following loop-controlled query were being performed:

```
FOR EACH DISTINCT VALUE v OF pid IN orders;
    select pid, sum(qty) as total from orders where pid = v;
END FOR;
```

The result of the GROUP BY clause in the Select statement of [3.8.1] is the table

pid	total
p01	4800
p02	400
p03	2400
p04	600
p05	2900
p06	400
p07	1400

A set function occurring in the select list aggregates for the set of rows in each group and thus creates a single value for each group. It is important that all of the attributes named in the select list have a single atomic value, for each group of common GROUP BY values. For example, the following Select phrase is invalid:

```
select pid, cid, sum(qty) from orders
    group by pid;  -- ** INVALID SQL SYNTAX
```

We cannot print multiple different cid values on a single line corresponding to a group of rows with the same pid value; for instance, the first group involving product p01 produces a set of cid values: {c001, c004, c006}. However, the GROUP BY clause of a Select statement *can* contain more than one column name. For example, we can GROUP BY two ID attributes from the orders table and thus retrieve both in the select list.

EXAMPLE 3.8.1

Let us create a query to calculate the total product quantity ordered of each individual product by each individual agent. We group the table orders on pid and aid in the following Select statement:

```
select pid, aid, sum(qty) as TOTAL from orders
     group by pid, aid;
```

As a result of this query we obtain the following table:

pid	aid	TOTAL
p01	a01	3000
p01	a06	1800
p02	a02	400
p03	a03	1000
p03	a05	800
p03	a06	600
p04	a03	600
p05	a03	2400
p05	a04	500
p06	a05	400
p07	a03	600
p07	a05	800

■

We can select from a product of tables using the WHERE clause together with the GROUP BY clause.

EXAMPLE 3.8.2

Print out the agent name and agent identification number, and the product name and product identification number, together with the total quantity each agent supplies of that product to customers c002 and c003.

```
select aname, a.aid, pname, p.pid, sum(qty)
     from orders x, products p, agents a
     where x.pid = p.pid and x.aid = a.aid and x.cid in ('c002', 'c003')
     group by a.aid, a.aname, p.pid, p.pname;
```

The default table returned by **ORACLE** for this query is

aname	aid	pname	pid	sum(qty)
Brown	a03	pencil	p05	2400
Brown	a03	razor	p03	1000
Otasi	a05	razor	p03	800

Note that since a.aname and p.pname are in the select list, it is necessary in the GROUP BY clause to include a.aname as well as a.aid, and p.pname as well as p.pid, in order to guarantee to the system that all columns in the select list will be single values for each group. In fact, a.aid is a unique identifier for rows of agents and p.pid for rows of products, so including a.aname and p.pname in the GROUP BY list will not cause any further subdivision of the groups considered. However, most database systems remain unaware of this fact, and they will complain if the a.aname and p.pname columns are left out of the GROUP BY clause. ∎

Note that the GROUP BY clause is written following the WHERE clause. You should conceive of the following *conceptual* order of events in evaluating a Subquery (with no UNION, INTERSECT, or EXCEPT operations).

◆ First the relational products of all tables in the FROM clause are formed.
◆ From this, rows not satisfying the WHERE clause are eliminated.
◆ The remaining rows are grouped in accordance with the GROUP BY clause.
◆ Finally, expressions in the select list are evaluated.

As explained in the discussions following Examples 3.3.6 and 3.4.6, you are cautioned that the *conceptual* order of evaluation may be quite different from the *actual* order that a database product uses to execute a Select statement. Recall that null values are ignored in a set function and considered to fail all tests of equality and inequality in a search_condition, even a test that one null value is equal to another null value. However, null values in a column that is an object of a GROUP BY clause *do* cause the corresponding rows to be grouped together. We will explore this further in the exercises at the end of the chapter.

If we wanted to eliminate rows from the result of a Select statement where a GROUP BY clause appears, for example, eliminating result rows when an aggregate such as sum(qty) in the select list was too small, we could *not* do this by using a restriction in the WHERE clause.

```
select pid, sum(qty) from orders    -- ** INVALID SQL SYNTAX
    where sum(qty) > 1000
    group by pid;
```

For one thing, recall that a set function cannot occur in the WHERE clause except in the select list of a Subquery (as illustrated in Example 3.7.5). Even more important, we have just finished saying that the WHERE clause conceptually eliminates rows *before* the GROUP BY clause performs the grouping of the rows remaining; this means that the condition in the WHERE clause cannot be aware of the aggregate quantities in the select list, since these quantities depend on the exact groups determined. To create a condition that depends on knowledge of this grouping, SQL Select statements are provided with a *new* restriction clause, known as the HAVING clause, which is evaluated after the GROUP BY.

EXAMPLE 3.8.3

Print out all product and agent IDs and the total quantity ordered of the product by the agent, when this quantity exceeds 1000.

```
select pid, aid, sum(qty) as TOTAL from orders
    group by pid, aid
    having sum(qty) > 1000;
```

Note that the action of the HAVING clause follows the action of the GROUP BY, but it precedes evaluation of expressions for the select list. This query prints out the rows in the table resulting from query (3.8.1) that exceed 1000 in the right-hand column:

pid	aid	TOTAL
p01	a01	3000
p01	a06	1800
p05	a03	2400

■

The HAVING clause can only apply tests to values that are single-valued for groups in the Select statement (that is, values that could legally appear in the select list). The general form of a Subquery as it now stands is given in Figure 3.13. This is the final form; no new clauses will be defined for a Subquery, although a new clause is still to be specified for the full Select statement.

```
subquery ::=
    SELECT [ALL | DISTINCT] { * | expr [[AS] c_alias] {, expr [[AS] c_alias]...}}
        FROM tableref {, tableref...}
        [WHERE search_condition]
        [GROUP BY colname {, colname...}]
        [HAVING search_condition];
    |   subquery UNION [ALL] subquery
```

Figure 3.13 General Form of Basic SQL Subquery (Usable as Select Statement)

For this Basic SQL Subquery form, the `tableref` in the FROM clause is the simple form from the first line of Figure 3.11 in Section 3.6:

```
tableref::= tablename [[AS] corr_name]
```

We are not using the more general tableref syntax of Figure 3.11 in our Basic SQL general form. Also note that the Basic SQL general form includes only the UNION [ALL] operator, not INTERSECT and EXCEPT. The HAVING clause here gives us yet another way of solving a problem already solved in two entirely different Select statements in Examples 3.3.7 and 3.7.6.

EXAMPLE 3.8.4

Provide pid values of all products purchased by at least two customers.

```
select pid from orders
    group by pid
    having count(distinct cid) >= 2;
```

It feels risky to even mention cid in the above Select statement since the cid column is not single-valued in grouping by pid value: the HAVING clause needs to apply to values that could appear in the select list, and these values must therefore be single-valued in the group. However, the set function value COUNT(cid) is single-valued by pid within the GROUP BY, and since it could appear in the select list, it can also appear in the HAVING clause. This results in the following table:

pid
p01
p03
p05
p07

■

Note that we would normally not use the HAVING clause unless a GROUP BY clause was present—if the GROUP BY clause is omitted, then the HAVING clause applies to the entire result as a single group. Thus in Example 3.8.4, if group by pid was missing but the HAVING clause was still there, nothing would be printed unless there were at least two values for cid in the orders table.

The Basic SQL Select statement general form we have been covering does not give us the ability to *nest* set functions, providing the AVG of a set of MAX elements, for example. However, the more general syntax provided in Section 3.6 does provide a means to accomplish such a nesting.

EXAMPLE 3.8.5

We would like to be able to pose a query to find the average, over all agents, of the maximum dollar sales made by each agent. In Basic SQL, there is no way to put one set function inside another, as shown below:

```
select avg(select max(dollars) from orders  -- ** INVALID SQL SYNTAX
    group by aid);
```

This SQL statement is invalid because a Subquery is not allowed inside a set function in Basic SQL, and in any event there is no natural table for the FROM clause of the outer Select statement. However, if we employ the extended syntax of Figure 3.11 (Section 3.6), we are able to place a Subquery in the FROM clause (which we are unable to do in Basic SQL). By renaming the table and naming the column to be aggregated, we are able to perform the desired query, as follows.

```
select avg(t.x) from (select aid, max(dollars) as x   -- ** ADVANCED SQL, Fig. 3.11
        from orders group by aid) t;
```

Here the FROM clause renames the Subquery result table as t (as required), and the aggregated column retrieved is given the column name x in the select list. The outer Select statement is then able to average t.x. This query will be accepted in **ORACLE** and **DB2 UDB**. The result of the *Subquery* above is the following table:

aid	max(dollars)
a01	500.00
a02	180.00
a03	1104.00
a04	450.00
a05	720.00
a06	540.00

The average of these values, returned by the outer Select statement, is 582.33.   ∎

3.9   A Complete Description of SQL Select

The general form of the Basic SQL Select statement that we provide is given in Figure 3.14, and we define new syntactic elements in the paragraphs that follow. At the end of this section, you should feel confident that no new SQL syntax remains to be introduced.

As we see in this general form, the ORDER BY clause is not allowed to appear in Subquery forms, but only in full Select statements. The ORDER BY clause is new, and it allows us to place rows of the final answer in order by one or more result_columns (column names or column aliases) appearing in the select list. When more than one result_column is specified, the rows are ordered first by the initial result_column, and only when the order of rows is identical in the first j result_columns specified does a later result_column appearing in position j + 1 need to be taken into account. For extra flexibility, the result_column can be specified in the ORDER BY clause by one of the column numbers 1 through n, where n columns occur in the select list. The column number option is for occasions when result_columns have no valid names, as when an expression is evaluated with no column alias created. Another occasion occurs when Select is a union of a number of different Subqueries, since we cannot assume that corre-

```
subquery ::=
    SELECT [ALL | DISTINCT] { * | expr [[AS] c_alias] {, expr [[AS] c_alias]...}}
        FROM tableref {, tableref...}
        [WHERE search_condition]
        [GROUP BY colname {, colname...}]
        [HAVING search_condition]
    |  subquery UNION [ALL] subquery

Select statement ::=
    Subquery [ORDER BY result_column [ASC | DESC] {, result_column [ASC | DESC]...}]
```

Figure 3.14 General Form of the Basic SQL Subquery and Select Statement

sponding columns have the same qualified names in all cases. In the [ASC | DESC] choice (ascending order or descending order), ASC is the default and means that smaller values come earlier as rows of the answer table.

Note that when null values appear in a column that is the object of an ORDER BY clause, the corresponding rows of output are placed in the same collating position, either larger ("high") or smaller ("low") than all non-null values in the column. The precise collating position for nulls is product dependent, since the various standards do not specify this: in **ORACLE** and **DB2 UDB**, null values sort "high," but in some other products, including **INFORMIX**, null values sort "low." Of course it is possible to avoid retrieving rows with nulls in some column by using an IS NOT NULL predicate for that column in the WHERE clause.

In the general form of Figure 3.14, the order of clauses in the Select statement is meant to carry over to the conceptual order of evaluation, as we see in Figure 3.15. The new steps in this conceptual order are perfectly reasonable, since evaluation of the ORDER BY clause to place resulting rows in sequence by column values is clearly a final step before display. The reader is once again reminded that the conceptual order of evaluation may be quite different from the actual order chosen by a query optimizer.

◆ First the relational product of all tables in the FROM clause is formed.
◆ From this, rows not satisfying the WHERE condition are eliminated.
◆ The remaining rows are grouped in accordance with the GROUP BY clause.
◆ Groups not satisfying the HAVING clause are then eliminated.
◆ The expressions of the SELECT clause select list are evaluated.
◆ If the keyword DISTINCT is present, duplicate rows are now eliminated.
◆ Evaluate UNION, INTERSECT, and EXCEPT for Subqueries up to this point.
◆ Finally, the set of all selected rows is sorted if an ORDER BY is present.

Figure 3.15 Conceptual Order of Evaluation of a Select Statement

EXAMPLE 3.9.1

List all customers, agents, and the dollar sales for pairs of customers and agents, and order the result from largest to smallest sales totals. Retain only those pairs for which the dollar amount is at least equal to 900.00.

```
select c.cname, c.cid, a.aname, a.aid, sum(o.dollars) as casales
    from customers c, orders o, agents a
    where c.cid = o.cid and o.aid = a.aid
    group by c.cname, c.cid, a.aname, a.aid
    having sum(o.dollars) >= 900.00
    order by casales desc;
```

In **ORACLE**, this query returns the following:

cname	cid	aname	aid	casales
Allied	c003	Brown	a03	2208.00
TipTop	c001	Otasi	a05	1440.00
TipTop	c001	Smith	a01	900.00

Note the syntax at the end: order by casales desc. The DESC keyword was used because we wanted to order the results with the largest sales totals first. Note that an ORDER BY form such as order by sum(o.dollars) would not work in all databases in the Select statement above. To work in all databases, the result_columns in the ORDER BY clause must be given in terms of column names or aliases in the select list or by position number.   ■

We have reached a good point to define more precisely the basic syntax objects that are combined to make up a search_condition. Much of what follows is a review of concepts we have already covered, but from a somewhat more rigorous standpoint.

Identifiers

Normal SQL identifiers (tablenames, columnnames, aliases, etc.) are caseless. In effect, SQL turns all identifiers into uppercase as it uses them. Thus you may type select PID from Customers; or even select PiD from CuStOmErS and get the same results. An identifier must start with a letter, and after that consists of letters, digits, and underscores. Entry SQL-92 and Core SQL-99 limit the number of characters in an identifier to 18. SQL keywords (select, from, etc.) are also turned into uppercase before being interpreted.

If you want to maintain a certain pattern of case or use special symbols, you can use the alternative format for identifiers called *delimited identifiers*, available in Entry SQL-92 and Core SQL-99. These are enclosed in double quotes, and the double quotes ensure that the name must be taken literally. Although normal SQL identifiers cannot have spaces or other special characters (except for underscores), delimited identifiers are allowed them. In this text we do not utilize this delimited method, but one place that is particularly handy to use it is for column aliases used in printing out results, as in:

```
select sum(qty) as "Total quantity of product p01" from orders where pid = 'p01';
```

Expressions, Predicates, and the search_condition

The search_condition is the condition used in the WHERE clause to eliminate rows and in the HAVING clause to eliminate groups: rows are retained in step 2 and groups in step 4 of Figure 3.15 exactly when the corresponding search_condition evaluates to TRUE.

We start by describing the syntax object known as an *expression (expr)*: that is, a numeric value expression (*numexpr*), a string value expression (*strvexpr*), and, if supported in a product, other types of expressions such as datetime value expression (*datexpr*), and so on. We say that expr ::= numexpr | strvexpr | datexpr | .... Numeric value expressions and string value expressions are the ones that occur most frequently and are part of Basic SQL. Expressions commonly appear in search_conditions. For example, in comparing an attribute value (of a row) to a constant, x.dollars > 100, both x.dollars and 100 are simple expressions. Expressions defined below can also appear in the *select list* of a Select statement. A numexpr is an arithmetic expression, made up of constants, table attributes, arithmetic operators, built-in arithmetic functions, and set functions. Constants are also called *literals*. A recursive definition is given in Figure 3.16a.

We see a few new syntax items in Figure 3.16a. The entries inside dotted boxes are unavailable as yet in some important products and are not part of what we have been calling Basic SQL (and thus are part of Advanced SQL). However, since they are part of Core SQL-99, they are likely to be available soon in the major database products. On line 1, :percent stands for a program variable that can be used when a program executes an SQL statement. The colon is placed before the variable name as a hint to the SQL precompiler that the name represents a program variable.

numexpr	Examples
1. val: constant or variable	`6, 7.00, :percent`
2. colname	`dollars, price, percent`
3. qualifier.colname	`orders.dollars, p.price`
4. numexpr arith_op numexpr	`7.00 + p.price`
5. (numexpr)	`(7.00 + p.price)`
6. numv_function(expr)	`sqrt(7 + a.percent), char_length(str)`
7. set_function(numexpr)	`sum(p.price)`
8. (Subquery with one value)	`(select max(percent) from agents)`
9. cast expression	`cast(substring(cid from 2 for 3) as integer)`
10. case expression	`case when price > 1.00 then price else 0 end`

Figure 3.16a Recursive Definition of a Numeric Value Expression (numexpr)

On line 6 of Figure 3.16a, we display two numeric value functions (the returned value is numeric), sqrt and char_length. We list various functions returning other types of values below. Functions that apply to numeric and character arguments, sometimes known as *scalar functions* to differentiate them from set functions, are not fully standardized in SQL-99. The string-related functions in Core SQL-99 are char_length, substring, and so on; none were required for Entry SQL-92. The products commonly call char_length just *length* and substring *substr*. Functions that accept and return numeric values, often called *mathematical functions*, remain largely product specific; only abs( ) and mod( ) are standardized in SQL-99, but as extended features. See Figure 3.17 for examples.

The subquery in parentheses on line 8 of Figure 3.16a must return a single value of numeric type to qualify as a numeric expression. Entry SQL-92 did not require this form for expression, and some products may not support it in all places that expressions can be used. Thus it is not in Basic SQL. We will discuss this further under the heading "Scalar Subqueries as Expressions" after Figure 3.19, which displays important details of WHERE clause forms.

The cast expression on line 9 of Figure 3.16a takes an argument of one type and converts it explicitly to another type. This is done in C and Java by writing (cast) value, where cast is a typename.

The case expression is reminiscent of the C or Java switch statement, except that it results in a single value. The general form is as follows:

```
CASE
    WHEN search_condition1 THEN result1
    WHEN search_condition2 THEN result2
    . . .
    WHEN search_conditionN THEN resultN
    ELSE result(N+1)
END
```

Neither CAST nor CASE is yet in Basic SQL, but they are becoming fairly commonly available and are part of Core SQL-99. Note that the explicit value NULL does not qualify as an expression. However, in some places where expressions are used, the value NULL may also be used. Figure 3.16b defines a string expression, *strvexpr*, just as Figure 3.16a did for *numexpr*.

The concatenate operator (| |) of line 4 in Figure 3.16b is not standard until Full SQL-92 and Core SQL-99, but it is commonly available. In Figure 3.17 we list a few mathematical functions that are provided by the products we cover in this text. See specific product documentation listed at the end of this chapter for more complete listings (usually indexed under "functions").

In addition to the examples in Figure 3.17, all three products have trigonometric, exponential, logarithmic, and power functions, and round(n). **ORACLE** and **DB2 UDB** also have ceil(n), floor(n), and sign(n), among others. A listing of standard and product-

strvexpr	Examples
1. val: constant or variable	`'Boston', 'TipTop', :cityname`
2. colname	`cid, aname`
3. qualifier.colname	`orders.cid, a.city`
4. strvexpr op strvexpr	`o.cid ||'Boston' (concatenate two strings with ||)`
5. (strvexpr)	`(o.cid ||'Boston')`
6. strv_function(expr)	`substring(o.cid ||'Boston' from 7 for 4) (= 'ston')`
7. set_function(strvexpr)	`max(o.cid)`
8. (Subquery with one value)	`(select max(city) from agents)`
9. cast expression	`cast(o.qty as char(10))`
10. case expression	`case when city > 'Atl' then city else 'Atlanta' end`

Figure 3.16b Recursive Definition of String Value Expression (strvexpr)

Name	Description	Result datatype
`abs(n)`	Absolute value of n, n a numeric datatype	All numeric types
`mod(n, b)`	Remainder of n after division by b, n and b integers	Integer
`sqrt(n)`	Square root of n, n integer or float	Float

Figure 3.17 Some Mathematical Functions in **ORACLE, INFORMIX**, and **DB2 UDB**

specific string-handling functions (functions acting on string arguments) is given in Figure 3.18.

String-handling functions in Figure 3.18 have different names in the different products to accomplish most of the same functions. Probably the Core SQL-99 forms will become available in most products before very long. Two of these functions return integers and thus are numeric-valued functions (numv_function in Figure 3.16a); the rest are string-valued functions (strv_function in Figure 3.16b). **INFORMIX** provides a substring *operation*, called *subscripting*, as well as a a substring *function*. For example, to obtain the substring consisting of the last three characters of c.cid, in positions 2 through 4, we would use c.cid[2,4]. In addition to the tabulated functions, **ORACLE, DB2 UDB**, and **INFORMIX** have functions to replace substrings in strings and pad strings with blanks or other characters.

Description and Form in Core SQL-99	ORACLE	DB2 UDB	INFORMIX
Returns length of string (integer number of characters), CHAR_LENGTH(str)	length(str)	length(str)	length(str), char_length(str)
Returns substring from string str, from char m to end [or for length n], SUBSTRING(str FROM m FOR n)	substr(str,m [,n])	substr(str,m [,n])	substr(str,m [,n]); substring(str from m for n)
Returns string with spaces (or any of a set of characters) trimmed off the left or right end of str, TRIM([[LEADING | TRAILING | BOTH] [set] FROM] str)	trim([[leading | trailing | both] [set] from] str), ltrim(str [,set]), rtrim(str [,set])	ltrim(str), rtrim(str)	trim([[leading | trailing | both] [set] from] str)
Returns position (integer) of occurrence of string str2 in str1; search starts at beginning of str1, or at position n, if specified, POSITION(str1 IN str2)	instr (str1,str2 [,n])	posstr(str1, str2 [,n])	
Returns string with alphabetic chars in lowercase, LOWER(str)	lower(str)	lcase(str)	lower(str)
Returns string with alphabetic chars in uppercase, UPPER(str)	upper(str)	ucase(str)	upper(str)

Figure 3.18   Some Standard and Product-Specific String-Handling Functions

Our Basic SQL standard (and that of Core SQL-99) has seven kinds of *predicates*, the simplest forms of logical clauses. These predicates are listed in Figure 3.19. They take on values TRUE (T), FALSE (F), or UNKNOWN (U) when evaluated in the GROUP BY or HAVING clause. We will explain the motivation for the UNKNOWN value shortly.

We have encountered most of these predicates before; the new ones are explained below. Wherever you see *expr* in Figure 3.19, NULL may also be used, in Basic SQL, but it almost certainly doesn't mean what you want it to, as we saw in Example 3.7.8. Recall that NULL does not qualify by itself as an expression. Refer again to Figures 3.16a and 3.16b to see what does qualify as an expression, for numeric and string datatypes. Line 1 of those figures defines what a *val* is in Figure 3.19, that is, a constant or a variable from an embedded program (covered in Chapter 5).

In some cases, what qualifies as an expression depends on whether the database system has implemented the newer features of lines 8, 9, and 10 in Figures 3.16a and 3.16b, that is, Subqueries returning one value and CAST and CASE. A single experiment or consultation of the SQL manual can determine for you whether your database system supports CAST or CASE. The tricky one is the Subquery.

Predicate	Form	Example
comparison predicate	expr1 θ {expr2 I (Subquery)}	p.price > (Subquery)
BETWEEN predicate	expr1 [NOT] BETWEEN expr2 and expr3	c.discnt between 10.0 and 12.0
quantified predicate	expr θ [ALL I ANY] (Subquery)	c.discnt >=all (Subquery)
IN predicate	expr [NOT] IN (Subquery) (see Example 3.4.6 for variant form)	pid in (select pid from orders) (cid, aid) in (select cid, aid...
	expr [NOT] IN (val {, val...})	city in ('New York', 'Duluth')
EXISTS predicate	[NOT] EXISTS (Subquery)	exists (select * ...)
IS NULL predicate	colname IS [NOT] NULL	c.discnt is null
LIKE predicate	colname [NOT] LIKE val [ESCAPE val]	cname like 'A%'

Figure 3.19 Standard Predicates Valid for All Products (i.e., for Basic SQL)

Scalar Subqueries as Expressions: Advanced SQL

A scalar subquery is a Subquery that returns a single value rather than a set of more than one row or more than one column. As indicated in Figures 3.16a and 3.16b, a scalar subquery is treated in Advanced SQL (and Core SQL-99, but not Basic SQL, yet) as a full-fledged expression building block, and we are looking forward to being able to use this new power in several ways.

◆ A scalar subquery as an *expression in a select list*, as is currently allowed in **DB2 UDB**, **INFORMIX**, and **ORACLE**, for example,

```
select cid, (select max(qty) from orders o where o.cid = c.cid)
    from customers c;
```

◆ A scalar subquery as an *expression in a WHERE clause* not allowed by Basic SQL (Figure 3.19), for example:

```
select cid from customers
    where (select max(qty) from orders o where o.cid = c.cid) > 100;
```

Note the six other places where *expr* shows up in Figure 3.19 that can be similarly treated. This second form is currently allowed in **DB2 UDB** and **ORACLE**. As a final note, compare this Advanced SQL *expression* syntax with the Advanced SQL *tableref* syntax of Figure 3.11, also involving (Subquery) but in that case the Subquery is allowed to return a whole set of rows, a "derived table."

search_condition	Example
predicate	o.pid = 'p01', exists (Subquery)
(search_condition)	(o.pid = 'p01')
NOT search_condition	not exists (Subquery)
search_condition AND search_condition	not (o.pid = 'p01') and o.cid = 'c001'
search_condition OR search_condition	not (o.pid = 'p01') or o.cid = 'c001'

Figure 3.20 Recursive Definition of search_condition

Given the predicates of Figure 3.19, we can define a search_condition recursively as shown in Figure 3.20.

We have now described all the predicates in SQL and the logical search_condition that uses predicates as building blocks. When we have completely explained the meaning of these predicates, you should be able to create any possible search_condition.

Basic SQL versus Advanced SQL: Summary

In this chapter, we have defined Basic SQL, a syntax for SQL that is available in most serious DBMS products, including **ORACLE**, **DB2 UDB**, and **INFORMIX**. Basic SQL corresponds quite closely to the Entry SQL-92 and X/Open version 2 standards (see "Suggestions for Further Reading" at the end of the chapter). The Core SQL-99 standard extends Entry SQL-92 slightly beyond our defined level of Basic SQL, giving database vendors some guidance for future features, but our guiding principle is current availability. Basic SQL includes all the SQL syntax presented in this chapter, *except* for the coverage of Advanced SQL features; these features are part of the SQL-99 standard, perhaps not in Core SQL-99, but are already adopted by some vendors. Advanced SQL syntax is covered in Section 3.6, "Some Advanced SQL Syntax," as well as in the forms of expressions in dotted boxes in Figures 3.16a and 3.16b, and the subsection just past, "Scalar Subqueries as Expressions: Advanced SQL." More information on syntax extensions is available in Appendix C. Basic SQL is quite portable between products: the only variations in syntax that we have had to document are differently named functions for string manipulations (Figure 3.18) and the fact that while most products sort nulls high, some sort them low. The terminology used to describe syntax elements, "condition" versus "predicate," and so on, varies more from one product to another than the actual syntax.

A Discussion of the Predicates

Comparison Predicate

A comparison predicate takes the form

```
expr1 θ {expr2 | (Subquery)}
```

where θ is one of set {=, <>, >, >=, <, <=}. Note that in most database system products the notation for *not equal to* (<>) may also be indicated by (!=) or (^=), but we believe (<>) is the most generally accepted form. The Subquery on the right is only permitted provided that the result retrieved is known to either contain a single value or be an empty set. Core SQL-99 generalizes this form to `expr1 θ expr2`, where either or both of these expressions may contain Subqueries in parentheses, possibly along with other expression elements. However, few database products implement this general form at the time of this writing. The other Subquery forms listed in Figure 3.19 are not generalized in SQL-99.

EXAMPLE 3.9.2

Recall Example 3.7.5, in which we listed the `cid` values of all customers with a discount less than the maximum discount. We were able to use the query

```
select cid from customers
    where discnt < (select max(discnt) from customers);
```

because we knew that the Subquery retrieved only a single value. We could just as easily have used the predicates <ANY or <ALL. ∎

If the result of the Subquery on the right of a comparison predicate is an empty set, the comparison predicate of the form `expr1 q (Subquery)` evaluates to UNKNOWN (U). An UNKNOWN result also occurs if a null value appears on either side (or both sides) of a comparison predicate, as we saw in the Select statement of Example 3.7.8:

```
select * from customers where discnt <= 10 or discnt > 10;
```

where a row in the `customers` table had a null value for `discnt`. The motivation for this UNKNOWN Boolean value is explained in the next section.

Truth Values: TRUE (T), FALSE (F), and UNKNOWN (U)

A predicate can evaluate to the truth value UNKNOWN for a specific row being qualified in a WHERE clause (or a group in a HAVING clause, but we will assume a WHERE clause in what follows). What this basically means is that a null value or an empty Subquery has occurred in evaluating some row, so that if this predicate were the entire `search_condition`, the person posing the query would probably *not* want this row retrieved. For example, if we had a Select statement with the `search_condition`

```
select * from customers where discnt < (Subquery);
```

and the Subquery retrieved an empty set, or only a single null value, we probably wouldn't want to retrieve any rows. Since a `search_condition` must evaluate to TRUE for a row to be retrieved, a new truth value called UNKNOWN is equivalent to FALSE for this purpose.

However, UNKNOWN may not be equivalent to FALSE in all situations. Consider a `search_condition` that contains a predicate with an UNKNOWN value in logical

AND	T	F	U
T	T	F	U
F	F	F	F
U	U	F	U

OR	T	F	U
T	T	T	T
F	T	F	U
U	T	U	U

NOT	
T	F
F	T
U	U

Figure 3.21   The Behavior of UNKNOWN Truth Values under Logical Operations

combination. For example, consider what we should do if we changed the Select just mentioned to

```
select * from customers where not (discnt < (Subquery));
```

and the predicate `discnt < (Subquery)` still had an UNKNOWN result. We think of `not (discnt < (Subquery))` as having equivalent meaning to `discnt >= (Subquery)`, which should certainly evaluate to UNKNOWN again if `discnt < (Subquery)` does. But this explains why we need the UNKNOWN truth value, because if we had said earlier that the predicate `discnt < (Subquery)` evaluated to FALSE when the Subquery returned an empty set, then by normal rules of logic, `not (discnt < (Subquery))` would evaluate to TRUE! This is not the sort of behavior we want, so a new truth value UNKNOWN has been invented with the property that not(UNKNOWN) = UNKNOWN. In Figure 3.21, we present the complete rules of operation for the three truth values, TRUE (T), FALSE (F), and UNKNOWN (U), under logical operations.

In the current section, we indicate the situations where UNKNOWN truth values arise during the evaluation of the various predicates. This has rather surprising effects in certain Select statements, and we explore these effects in the exercises at the end of the chapter.

The BETWEEN Predicate

A BETWEEN predicate tests whether a value is within a range specified by two other values. It has the form

```
expr1 [NOT] BETWEEN expr2 and expr3
```

The meaning (leaving out the NOT) is exactly as if we had written

```
expr2 <= expr1 and expr1 <= expr3
```

When the keyword NOT is included, the resulting predicate is TRUE when the initial value is not in the range specified. The initial reason for providing this form was that an expression using the BETWEEN predicate was more efficiently evaluated than the equivalent AND of two comparison predicates. This is no longer true with all products, but it should be assumed for performance reasons whenever a restrictive range with two endpoints must be asserted and the question of portability from one product to another arises.

The Quantified Comparison Predicate

The meaning of the quantified predicate, with form

```
expr θ [SOME | ANY | ALL] (Subquery)
```

was covered in Section 3.4, but we still have to define special UNKNOWN evaluations.

The result of `expr θALL (Subquery)` is FALSE if and only if the comparison is FALSE for at least one value returned by the Subquery. Taking this definition to a logical conclusion, this means that the predicate evaluates to TRUE if and only if the comparison θ is TRUE for all values retrieved *or the Subquery results in an empty set.* However, if the expr value on the left or if one of the values returned by the Subquery is null, the result is UNKNOWN.

The result of `expr θANY (Subquery)` is TRUE if the comparison θ is TRUE for at least one value retrieved; the result is FALSE if the Subquery results in an empty set or the comparison is FALSE for every value returned. However, if the expr value on the left is null, or if one of the values returned by the Subquery is null with comparisons for all other returned values being FALSE, the result is UNKNOWN.

Let us illustrate, for example, why `expr θall (Subquery)` should be TRUE if the Subquery results in an empty set.

EXAMPLE 3.9.3

Retrieve the maximum discount of all customers. Clearly we could answer this with the following query:

```
select max(discnt) from customers;
```

but we want to illustrate a point about the θALL predicate, and so use the query

```
select distinct discnt from customers c
    where discnt >=all (select discnt from customers d
        where d.cid <> c.cid);
```

In words, we are retrieving the `discnt` value for a row (on the left) that is greater than or equal to all `discnt` values for customer rows different from the original row (a correlated Subquery). If there is only a single customer row, the Subquery retrieves an empty set. Clearly we want to retrieve the single `discnt` value since it is maximum, but that means that the predicate of the `search_condition` should be TRUE for a Subquery retrieving an empty set. ∎

The IN Predicate

The IN predicate has the form

```
expr [NOT] IN {(Subquery)|(val {, val...})}
```

Its use was covered in Section 3.4. The IN predicate has identical behavior to that of the predicate =ANY. See Example 3.4.6 for a generalization of the expr here to a multi-column row value. The `val` form is defined in line 1 of Figures 3.16a and 3.16b.

The EXISTS Predicate

The EXISTS predicate has the form

```
[NOT] EXISTS (Subquery)
```

It evaluates to TRUE exactly when the Subquery does not result in an empty set. The use of this predicate was covered in Section 3.4, and there are no conditions under which this predicate evaluates to UNKNOWN.

The IS NULL Predicate

The IS NULL predicate, introduced in Example 3.7.8, has the form

```
colname IS [NOT] NULL
```

There are no conditions under which this predicate evaluates to UNKNOWN.

The LIKE Predicate

The LIKE predicate is new. The general form is given by

```
colname [NOT] LIKE val [ESCAPE val]
```

The element represented by the first val is the pattern string, usually a quoted string of normal and special characters. (By the definition of val in Figure 3.16, it could also be a program variable, but we have not yet seen programs.) The pattern string forms a template for character string values fitting a certain description. The special characters, including *wildcard* characters, that can be used in a pattern string are the following:

Character in pattern	Meaning
Underscore (_)	Wildcard for any single character
Percent (%)	Wildcard for any sequence of zero or more characters
Escape character	Precedes quoted literal character (explained below)
All other characters	Represent themselves

EXAMPLE 3.9.4

Retrieve all data about customers whose cname begins with the letter 'A'. We write

```
select * from customers where cname like 'A%';
```

This returns the table

cid	cname	city	discnt
c003	Allied	Dallas	8.00
c004	ACME	Duluth	8.00
c006	ACME	Kyoto	0.00

∎

The convention by which the special pattern characters % and _ are quoted literally in a pattern string involves an *Escape* character that can be defined differently in each Select statement, using an *Escape clause* given in the general form of the LIKE predicate, above. When an Escape character is used in a pattern, the character that follows it is to be taken literally.

EXAMPLE 3.9.5

Retrieve cid values of customers whose cname does *not* have a third letter equal to '%'.

```
select cid from customers where cname not like '_ _\%%' escape '\';
```

Note that the final percent sign allows a trailing sequence of zero or more arbitrary characters.

∎

EXAMPLE 3.9.6

Retrieve cid values of customers whose cname begins "Tip_" and has an arbitrary number of characters following.

```
select cid from customers where cname like 'TIP\_%' escape '\';
```

Note that the final percent sign allows a trailing sequence of zero or more arbitrary characters.

∎

In the form of the LIKE predicate, if the colname on the left takes on a null value, the result for the row in question is UNKNOWN.

Note that some database products might use an older convention whereby some Escape character, such as +, is chosen by the system. With all Escape characters, if we desire to see the Escape character appear literally in the pattern string, we should use the Escape character twice in a row. Thus, if + is the Escape character, then __++ represents a pattern string with any two characters followed by the character +.

EXAMPLE 3.9.7

Retrieve cid values of customers whose cname starts with the sequence "ab\". We could write

```
select cid from customers where cname like 'ab\\%' escape '\';
```

or, alternatively, we could choose a different Escape character, or none:

```
select cid from customers where cname like 'ab\%';
```

Note that the final percent sign allows a trailing sequence of zero or more arbitrary characters.

■

3.10   Insert, Update, and Delete Statements

The three SQL statements—Insert, Update, and Delete—are used to perform data modifi-cations to existing tables. The Insert statement acts to insert new rows, the Update state-ment acts to change information in existing rows, and the Delete statement acts to delete rows that exist in a table. These three statements are often referred to collectively as *update statements*, since they all serve to update tables. There is some risk of confusion here, because the Update statement is the specific name of one of these three statements, and we need to take care to differentiate the two whenever confusion may result. For example, it should be clear that the *Update statement* is only one of the set of *update statements*. To perform an Update statement on a given table, the current user must be the user who created the table or else have been granted *update privilege* on the table. We will cover the process of granting privileges in a later chapter.

The Insert Statement

The *Insert statement* in SQL acts to insert new rows into an existing table. It has the gen-eral form as shown in Figure 3.22.

The Insert statement inserts new rows into the specified table. One of two forms must be used (symbolized by the "or bar," |): either the VALUES form, where a single row is inserted with specified values, or the Subquery form, where all rows that result from evaluating the Subquery (possibly involving a number of different tables) are inserted.

EXAMPLE 3.10.1
Add a row with specified values to the orders table, setting the qty and dollars columns null. There are two ways to perform this insert.

```
insert into orders (ordno, month, cid, aid, pid)
    values (1107, 'aug', 'c006', 'a04', 'p01');
```

Here, the values for qty and dollars are not known at the time of insert, so they are not men-tioned in the column names nor in the values list and will default to null.

```
INSERT INTO tablename [(colname {, colname...})]
    {VALUES (expr | NULL {, expr | NULL...}) | Subquery}
```

Figure 3.22   The General Form of the Basic SQL Insert Statement

```
insert into orders (ordno, month, cid, aid, pid, qty, dollars)
    values (1107, 'aug', 'c006', 'a04', 'p01', null, null);
```

In this case, we give explicit null values to the qty and dollars columns.   ■

EXAMPLE 3.10.2
Create a new table called swcusts of Southwestern customers, and insert into it all customers from Dallas and Austin.

```
create table swcusts (cid char(4) not null, cname varchar(13),
    city varchar(20), discnt real); -- same as customers

insert into swcusts
    select * from customers
        where city in ('Dallas', 'Austin');
```
                                                                              ■

This example shows how the specific columns to receive values need not be named in the Insert statement. Omitting the column names is equivalent to specifying all the columns in the table in the same order as they were defined in the Create Table statement. When the columns are named specifically, as in Example 3.10.1, they need not appear in that order. Note that in the Insert statement of Example 3.10.2, it is a *mistake* (in Entry SQL-92 and in many products) to surround the Subquery following the tablename swcusts with parentheses.

The ability to use a Subquery to create input to an Insert statement adds a great deal of power. Only one table receives new rows in an Insert statement, but the Subquery can be on any number of tables, as long as it produces the right number of columns of the right type to serve as new rows to be inserted.

The Update Statement

The SQL Update statement acts to change information in existing rows of a table. It has the Basic SQL general form (which is an extension of the Entry SQL-92 form) shown in Figure 3.23.

The Update statement replaces the values of the specified columns with the values of the specified expressions for all rows of the table that satisfy the search_condition. The expressions used above can reference only column values on the specific row of the table currently being updated.

```
UPDATE tablename
    SET colname = {expr | NULL | (subquery)}
        {, colname = {expr | NULL | (subquery)...}}
    [WHERE search_condition];
```

Figure 3.23   General Form of the Basic SQL Update Statement

EXAMPLE 3.10.3
Give all agents in New York a 10% raise in the percent commission they earn on an order.

```
update agents set percent = 1.1 * percent where city = 'New York';
```
■

The way to take values from other tables into account in deciding what columns are to be updated is to use a Subquery in the search_condition.

EXAMPLE 3.10.4
Give all customers who have total orders of more than $1000 a 10% increase in the discnt they receive.

```
update customers set discnt = 1.1 * discnt where cid in
    (select cid from orders group by cid having sum(dollars) > 1000);
```
■

Note that only one table can be the object of the Update statement. Some database systems do not accept qualified attributes in the SET clause:

```
update agents set agents.percent = ... -- ** MAY BE INVALID
```

The Entry SQL-92 form of the Update statement does not provide a Subquery in the SET clause. Thus we could not derive the values to put in the updated table by reference to other tables, as we could in the Insert statement. However, the Full SQL-92 standard, the Core SQL-99 standard, and the **ORACLE, INFORMIX,** and **DB2 UDB** products permit the extended syntax for the Update statement that addresses this problem, so we include this capability in our Basic SQL general form. In fact, since Core SQL-99 classifies a scalar subquery as an expression form in general, the | (subquery) alternative can be dropped from Figure 3.23 to describe Core SQL-99 syntax. Here is an example of the use of such syntax.

EXAMPLE 3.10.5
Update the discnt values in rows of the swcusts table created in Example 3.10.2 with more up-to-date discnt values from the customers table.

```
update swcusts set discnt = (select discnt from customers where cid = swcusts.cid);
```
■

The Delete Statement

The SQL Delete statement removes existing rows from a table. It has the Basic SQL general form shown in Figure 3.24.

```
DELETE FROM tablename
    [WHERE search_condition];
```

Figure 3.24   General Form of the Basic SQL Delete Statement

EXAMPLE 3.10.6

Delete all agents in New York.

```
delete from agents where city = 'New York';
```
∎

Once again, the search_condition can contain Subqueries, allowing us to use data from other tables to decide what rows to delete.

EXAMPLE 3.10.7

Delete all agents who have total orders of less than $600.

```
delete from agents where aid in
    (select aid from orders group by aid having sum(dollars) < 600);
```
∎

3.11 The Power of the Select Statement

A *procedural language* is one in which a program is written as an ordered sequence of instructions to accomplish some task. The order of statements is important because we can think of an earlier statement of a program having a long-term effect that is a precondition to the correct execution of a later statement. For example, if we wish to create a loop to sum a sequence of input variable values V, we might start by setting SUM = 0, then incrementally increase the sum with the statement SUM = SUM + V as the loop progresses. It is clearly important, for example, that we start with the statement SUM = 0, rather than executing this statement somewhere in the middle of the loop. The necessity to use a number of statements in a particular order to achieve a correct result can be thought of as demonstrating the *procedurality* of the language.

A *non-procedural language,* by contrast, is one in which a desired end is described all at once! This means that we must specify *what* is desired rather than *how* it is to be achieved, with no implied ordering of effects for a programmer to keep track of. A perfect example of this kind of non-procedural language is an interface consisting of a screen menu, where a user chooses a number of options to accomplish some task (with no order to the selection) and then presses the Execute key. Some of the early writers advocating the relational model held up non-procedurality as an extremely valuable goal. Database languages before that time usually required a kind of navigation to go from one piece of data to another. As a simple example, consider the program we just mentioned to sum a sequence of input values V. If we think of these values as existing in a file, then as we perform a loop to take the sum, we are keeping a kind of cursor while we navigate through the data from beginning to end—we know which values have been summed so far and which have not—and so there is a preexisting context for each program statement. The advocates of the relational model pointed out that many potential database users (such as financial specialists, real estate agents, and lawyers) might find it beyond their abilities to write program loops to acquire information. If the information they required was not provided by some program that had been prewritten for their needs, then they would be out of luck, and it seemed likely that many queries that they might want to perform could not be foreseen in advance. These were ad hoc queries, meaning that they arose from spur-of-the-moment needs and could not be anticipated with a program written in advance.

The stated goal was to provide a query language to handle ad hoc needs, offering the user the capability of asking a single question about the data. This single question might be rather complex, but even so the language should avoid procedural complexities that would require a programmer. It was pointed out that the study of symbolic logic seemed relevant to this goal of designing a database language and, as we mentioned in Chapter 2, it was shown by E. F. Codd that the relational algebra had all the power of a language based on a type of symbolic logic known as the *first-order predicate calculus*. From this result, a number of issues were raised in fixing on a standard database language. One issue is the question of just how non-procedural the language is—no complex language can be perfect in this regard, but some are better than others. A second issue is how much *power* the language has. Based on Codd's result, a language with the power of relational algebra is defined to be *complete* or *relationally complete*, and the implication is that this is an important milestone. However, we will describe a number of capabilities that are missing from the relationally complete language SQL, and there is an indication that a non-procedural approach may actually detract from the available power.

The Non-Procedural Select Statement

Let us start by examining the relative non-procedurality of two languages.

EXAMPLE 3.11.1
Recall the relational algebra query derived in Example 2.7.8, to retrieve the names of custom-ers who order products costing $0.50:

```
((ORDER ⋈ (PRODUCTS where price = 0.50)[pid]) ⋈ CUSTOMERS)[cname]
```
■

This query is accomplished in one statement, and thus it seems to have an important non-procedural advantage over using the assignment statement (:=) to hold intermediate results. However, this advantage is somewhat of an illusion. There *is* an important aspect of procedurality in this expression, since sub-expressions in parentheses must be evalu-ated first, and even in sub-expressions with no parentheses the precedence rules of Figure 2.7 place an order on the evaluation. Furthermore, the user clearly *intends* this order of evaluation. For example, it is necessary that (PRODUCTS where price = 0.50) should be projected on [pid] before the later join with CUSTOMERS, because we do not wish to require equal city values.

Now there are a number of equivalence rules in relational algebra, such as commuta-tivity and associativity, that allow us to pass from one expression to another equivalent form. Thus the precise parenthetical form of a given relational algebra query will not necessarily keep a query optimizer from finding a more efficient variant form. However, there can be no question that the expression in Example 3.11.1 implies a precise order of evaluation, and the query optimizer will find it difficult to take a higher-level view of how to achieve its objective efficiently as long as the query is stated in parenthesized form.

There is little difference between an expression with nested parentheses and a sequence of statements, with intermediate results created using the assignment statement. In other words, relational algebra is quite procedural. Consider the difference between this and the SQL equivalent.

EXAMPLE 3.11.2

Here is the analogous SQL statement to retrieve the names of customers who order products costing $0.50:

```
select cname from customers c, orders x, products p
    where c.cid = x.cid and x.pid = p.pid and p.price = 0.50;
```
■

If you recall the conceptual order of evaluation given in Figure 3.15 (near the beginning of Section 3.9), the Select statement of this example can be thought of as acting in the following way: in step 1, the relational product of the customers, orders, and products tables named in the FROM clause is formed; then, in step 2, rows not satisfying the WHERE search_condition are eliminated, and finally expressions in the select list (simple cname values) are evaluated and output as the answer.

Of course, this conceptual order is just a way of thinking of what will happen, and not necessarily the way a database query optimizer will actually decide to go about performing it. In particular, the query optimizer has the freedom to combine two or more steps that succeed one another in the conceptual order. For example, as we mentioned earlier, the computerized access strategy would probably *not* start by creating a new table that is the product of the three tables listed in the FROM clause. Instead, the strategy might be to perform a triple loop through independent rows of the three tables, testing the WHERE predicate as each new triple of rows is considered. Thus we are combining steps 1 and 2, performing the loop to create the relational product and before storing such rows, testing the WHERE search_condition to eliminate certain rows. Or an entirely different type of strategy might be used to combine steps 1 and 2, where we access all orders rows, one after another, and the cid and pid values allow us to "look up" in some efficient index structure the unique row in customers and the unique row in products with matching cid and pid values, as required by the join condition.

The point of all this is that *we are not expressing any presumptions about the strict order of evaluation when we write an SQL Select statement!* A Select statement is simply a *prescription* for *what* data is to be retrieved, rather than a *procedure* describing *how* it is to be retrieved. The conceptual order of evaluation provided in Figure 3.15 is simply an order the user can imagine that will always work: a product of tables in the FROM clause comes before eliminating rows with the search_condition in the WHERE clause because the search_condition often has no meaning before a product is taken (consider the predicates in Example 3.11.2); inappropriate rows must also be eliminated by the search_condition before the select_list results are evaluated. But an important technique in the process of query optimization is to evaluate a Select statement in something other than the conceptual order, combining steps or even reversing them when this seems to offer added efficiency without changing the result. For example, in the triple-loop approach mentioned above, full materialization of the product is deferred while row elimination takes place with successive rows, so these two steps have been combined. It is an important consideration that the triple-loop procedure can pause once a sufficient number of rows have been generated for immediate needs—for example, when a screen full of rows has been displayed and further output awaits a user request to continue. This combines all three steps and can result in important savings if the user decides to abort the display without going further. In the index approach, where we look up a row in customers (for example) based on the cid value in an orders row, we can even say that the WHERE elimination precedes taking the product of the FROM clause and obviates the need to consider all rows in the customers table.

We have just seen an important advantage of the non-procedural Select statement. When we specify a prescription of *what* data is to be retrieved rather than a procedure describing *how* to do it, we leave the decision on the exact access strategy up to the database system. The database *query optimizer* theoretically has the resources to make a very sophisticated decision about exactly how to navigate through the data to retrieve the desired information. This decision can often be superior to one that a programmer could make, simply because a programmer writes a query at a particular time and usually doesn't revisit it later (a programmer's time is quite valuable), so an access strategy determined by a programmer cannot be up-to-date about later developments of size and indexed access for tables. On the other hand, an unmodified Select statement can be recompiled at a later time and can result in a different access strategy if the query optimizer becomes aware of significantly changed conditions. We will talk more about query optimization in later chapters on indexing and performance.

Turing Power

Readers who have studied *automata theory*, used in formal languages, may have encountered the concept known as *Turing's thesis*. The mathematician Turing investigated a type of conceptual machine, similar to a modern computer in capability except that it has an infinite tape (or memory) to store intermediate results. He demonstrated to almost everyone's satisfaction that such a machine, which could execute simple procedural programs of finite length, had all the power necessary to perform any computational procedure that it was possible to describe in specific (algorithmic) terms. Thus the Turing machine could compute how to play a perfect game of chess (it might take a long time) or create any kind of report on data to which it had access, just as long as the person requiring the report is able to describe exactly how to create it in a finite number of steps. The ability to perform such computations in a given language is called *computational completeness,* or sometimes *Turing power*. All modern programming languages, such as C, have Turing power if we just make the assumption that they have an arbitrarily large (infinite) addressing space to store intermediate results. This then is the benchmark against which the power of other languages is to be measured.

No non-procedural language can have Turing power. If we think of the model of choosing options from a menu, we see that we are limited to a relatively small number of possibilities: we can choose any subset of these options. Some of the options may have parameters we can use to enlarge this choice (such as naming columns in the ORDER BY clause), but unless we start encoding arbitrarily long sequential programs into the parameters (which would defeat our purpose) there is no possibility of Turing power coming out of this model.

This lack of Turing power is not necessarily a great disadvantage. The human mind, for example, doesn't really have Turing power, since it presumably has finite ability to store intermediate results. However, it is a starting point in thinking about what SQL is capable of in querying a database, and what we think we could do with a programming language such as C that had access to the same data. In the next chapter on Embedded SQL, when we learn how to perform SQL calls from within a program, we will find that we can write programs with this capability that cannot be performed using non-procedural SQL. It seems likely that few database practitioners today would disagree with this point. Although early advocates of the relational model justified it in terms of giving nonprogrammers the ability to do everything through an interactive interface, a number of difficulties arise in practice, and programmed database applications are used today for almost all access. The value of the SQL language is now thought to reside in the flexibility and generality it has to benefit the programmer, rather than the end user.

Limited Power of the Basic SQL Select Statement

For now, let us investigate the limits of power of the Basic SQL Select statement we have introduced in this chapter by listing some examples of queries that Basic SQL is *not* able to perform. These examples are particularly interesting because many of them have served as motivation for the new object-relational SQL that will be covered in the next chapter. (Also, some of the Advanced SQL syntax of Section 3.6 extends the capabilities of Basic SQL to perform some of these queries.)

SQL and Non-Procedural Set Functions

Recall that relational algebra was once shown to have all the power of first-order predicate logic. Perhaps this will seem less intimidating when we realize that none of the Set functions of SQL exist in relational algebra. (They could be included, but historically have not been.) Thus we cannot answer, in relational algebra, the question: How many orders have dollar values greater than $500? In SQL we have added the set functions: sum, avg, max, min, and count. Can we think of any others?

EXAMPLE 3.11.3

The *median* is a type of statistical average, generally considered to be a more stable measure for certain statistics, such as monthly housing prices, than the mean average provided by the SQL set function avg( ). Given a sequence of n numbers, $a_1, a_2, \ldots, a_n$, with $a_i \leq a_{i+1}$, for i = 1, $\ldots, n - 1$, the *median* is defined to be the value a_k in the sequence such that k = FLOOR((n+1)/ 2)). Because the median is not defined as an SQL set function, we are unable to write a Select statement of the following kind:

```
select median(dollars) from orders; -- ** INVALID SQL SYNTAX
```

To illustrate how such a median function would work, we place all `dollars` values of rows in the `orders` table of Figure 2.2 in nondecreasing sequence to get {180.00, 450.00, 450.00, 450.00, 460.00, 500.00, 540.00, 540.00, 600.00, 704.00, 720.00, 720.00, 800.00, 880.00, 1104.00, 1104.00}, with 16 entries. The median value is therefore entry number FLOOR((16 + 1)/2), entry 8, or 540.00.

In fact, the median can be calculated with clever use of the Advanced SQL extension that allows Subquery results to be used as a FROM table. See Exercise 3.18. ∎

Other set functions that might be valuable in various circumstances are *mode* and *variance*. The mode for a set of numbers is the most commonly occurring number in the set, while variance is an important statistical measure, the mean square of differences of individual observations from the mean average, the result of the avg( ) set function. As a matter of fact, the **ORACLE** product does have a variance( ) set function. Statisticians commonly think of the sum of squares of a set of observations as the *second moment*. We can express the variance in terms of the second moment and the mean average, known as the *first moment*. But there is no limit to the number of set functions that could be requested, since third moment (mean of third powers), fourth moment (mean of fourth powers), and higher moments are used for some purposes. Note that all of these set functions can easily be calculated by a program that has access to the data, simply by looping through the values and performing the appropriate aggregation, sum of squares, and so on. However, in the non-procedural SQL model, if a set function isn't provided by the system, then we won't be able to evaluate the functional result. The ability to create new set functions within the SQL language by the use of something called *user-defined functions* is one of the motives that has driven the development of object-relational SQL, which will be covered in the next chapter. This capability is not yet available in most products, however.

Another capability missing in the Basic SQL we have been covering is the ability to *nest* set functions. However, we explained in Example 3.8.5 that this capability is part of the extended syntax of Figure 3.11 in Section 3.6 and is already offered in **ORACLE** and **DB2 UDB**.

EXAMPLE 3.11.4

We would like to be able to pose a query to find the average, over all agents, of the total dollar sales by agent. The type of form that would seem a natural method of nesting set functions is something like the following:

```
select avg(select sum(dollars) from orders -- ** INVALID SQL SYNTAX
    group by aid);
```

However, this SQL statement is invalid because a Subquery is not allowed inside a set function in SQL. If we are using a database system with the Advanced SQL capability to select from query results, we can do the query as follows.

```
select avg(totdollars) from
    (select sum(dollars) as totdollars from orders -- ** ADVANCED SQL SYNTAX
        group by aid) sumtab;
```

The Subquery in the above statements, using the `orders` table of Figure 2.2, yields the following table:

sum(dollars)
1400.00
180.00
4228.00
450.00
2144.00
1400.00

The average of these values is 1633.67. ∎

It turns out that there does exist a way in Basic SQL to find the average, over all agents, of the total dollar sales by agent. Since this average is the sum of the dollar totals by agent, divided by the number of agents, and since the sum of the dollar totals by agent is the sum of all dollar values, the desired result can be achieved with the statement

```
select sum(dollars)/count(distinct aid) from orders;
```

However, the fact remains that it is not possible to nest set functions in Basic SQL, and because of this we can list numerous requests that cannot be implemented by any Select statement in Basic SQL. For example, there is no way to find the total of all average dollar sales by agent, or the maximum of all total dollar sales by agent. We will see in the next chapter how such queries can be answered, using programs that access SQL data in a procedural way.

Non-Procedural Reports

The GROUP BY clause, another concept missing from relational algebra, permits a kind of reporting function. But we don't have to look very far to find a report that Basic SQL can't create. As in the case of the median, the Advanced SQL extensions do provide the power needed for the following example.

EXAMPLE 3.11.5

We wish to create a report in which we break down total sales by category, according to the dollar size of the sale. Say the categories, which we will call *ranges*, are 0.0 to 499.99, 500.00 to 999.99, and so on. We would like to be able to write something like

```
select range-start, sum(dollars) from orders    -- ** INVALID SQL SYNTAX
    group by dollars in ranges from 0.00 in blocks of 500.00;
```

The idea here is to find the total contribution to sales by each category of dollar sales range. A sales manager might wish to do this to determine which sales amounts provide the bread-and-butter volume. The result for the orders table of Figure 2.2 would be as follows:

range-start	sum(dollars)
0.00	2390.00
500.00	5204.00
1000.00	2208.00

For example, dollars values in the range 0.00–499.99 are 450.00, 450.00, 180.00, 450.00, 460.00, and 400.00, which sum to 2390.00. A report such as this cannot be generated with a single legal Basic SQL statement. It can be done using two Advanced SQL features, the CAST expression and the ability to use a query result as a FROM table in an outer query. See Exercises 3.18 and 3.19. ∎

Clearly a report of this kind would be possible with a procedural programming language. Indeed, we can imagine an infinite number of report formats (literally) that SQL is incapable of creating non-procedurally, but that could be accomplished with a program. There doesn't seem to be any way to address this weakness short of writing procedural programs that can access the database. We will cover how to do this in Chapter 5.

Transitive Closure

A well-known weakness of first-order predicate calculus is its inability to perform something called *transitive closure*. Consider a directed graph G on a set of nodes {a, b, c, . . . }; we say that a → b when an edge is directed from a to b. Then the graph is *transitive* if and only if the following property holds: whenever a → b and b → c, the edge a → c also exists. If we start with a graph G that is not transitive, we can fill in edges to make transitivity hold for all triples of nodes (a, b, c): if a → b and b → c, fill in a → c if it does not already exist. As we do this, we are basically saying that whenever c can be reached by a path of edges from a, there should be an edge from a to c. The result of this process of filling in edges is known as the *transitive closure* of the graph G. This kind of consideration comes up occasionally in real queries.

EXAMPLE 3.11.6
Let us create a table called employees, with the following Create Table command:

```
create table employees (eid char(5) not null, ename varchar(16),
    mgrid char(5));
```

The eid attribute stands for employee ID, a unique identifier for the employee represented on a row, and the mgrid attribute contains the employee ID of the manager of the represented employee. Assume we have loaded the following employees table:

employees

eid	ename	mgrid
e001	Jacqueline	null
e002	Frances	e001
e003	Jose	e001
e004	Deborah	e001
e005	Craig	e002
e006	Mark	e002
e007	Suzanne	e003
e008	Frank	e003
e009	Victor	e004
e010	Chumley	e007

Note here that employee e010, Chumley, reports to (has the manager) e007, Suzanne, and Suzanne reports to e003, Jose, who reports to e001, Jacqueline. Jacqueline has a null in the mgrid column because she is president and has no manager. We can easily write a Select statement to list all employees who report to any given employee (presumably a manager, or the list will be empty). For example, to retrieve all employees who report to Jacqueline, with employee id e001, we write

```
select e.eid from employees e where e.mgrid = 'e001';
```

This would give us employees e002, e003, and e004. Now we can also retrieve all employees who report to employees who report to this manager:

```
select e.eid from employees e where e.mgrid in
    (select f.eid from employees f where f.mgrid = 'e001');
```

This would give us everyone who reports to one of the employees returned by the Subquery, the same as the Select we just did, and so we would get e005, e006, e007, e008, and e009. Employee e010 is not included, because e010 reports to e007, rather than to one of the managers returned by the Subquery. No single SQL expression is guaranteed to list all employees *at all different levels* who have e001 as a manager at some level above them (not even in the Advanced SQL we presented in Section 3.6). This would list all employee IDs other than e001.

∎

If we say that the employees table represents a graph, with employee rows representing nodes and edges directed from mgrid to eid, then what we are pointing out in the above example is that we can list all employees with a Select statement that can be reached by a single edge from any specific eid such as e001; similarly, we can retrieve all employees that can be reached by paths of exactly two edges from any specific eid, such as e001. The query we are trying to pose will return all employees that can be reached from a specific eid by a path with an *arbitrary number* of edges. If the graph had the transitive closure property, then all employees reached by a path could be reached also by

160

a single edge. The ability to pose such a query is commonly known as transitive closure in a query language.

The **ORACLE** product already has the ability to pose a transitive closure query, using nonstandard Select clauses, the CONNECT BY and START WITH clauses. The query to retrieve all employees who have e001 as a manager at some level above them would have the following form in **ORACLE** SQL:

```
select eid from employees
    connect by prior eid = mgrid
    start with eid = 'e001';
```

There is also a feature in SQL-99 to support transitive queries, but we will not cover this in the current text.

Limited Power of Boolean Conditions

There is a general consensus in certain areas of information retrieval that the SQL language is seriously flawed, because the user is limited to Boolean conditions in posing queries. Gerard Salton, a founding author in the field of text retrieval, pointed out a number of examples where Boolean conditions do not provide the power needed to answer important questions. (See, for example [6], "Extended Boolean Retrieval Model, Fuzzy Set Extensions," Section 10.4.)

EXAMPLE 3.11.7
Assume we are given a table named documents, with rows representing text documents (such as journal articles) with primary key docid, and where each document has up to a hundred keyword values that identify the subject matter (e.g., magnetic resonance, superconductor, gallium arsenide). As we saw in explaining first normal form in Section 2.3, we need to implement this kind of relationship with a second table, keywords, having the two attributes keyword and docid. A simple example of this kind is given in Figure 3.25.

As we see in Figure 3.25, the keywords 'integer' and 'integral' occur in the 'Intro Math' document, the keyword 'SQL' appears in the 'Intro DB' document, and the keyword 'relation' occurs in both. We would normally expect to have hundreds of thousands of documents and many thousands of keywords, with a great deal of duplicate keyword use among documents. To retrieve all the keywords for a document, d12293, for example, we would use the query

```
select k.keyword from keywords k where k.docid = 'd12293';
```

To retrieve all documents with the keyword 'Xyz1', we would use the query

```
select * from documents d where d.docid in
    (select k.docid from keywords k where k.keyword = 'Xyz1');
```

A common approach to retrieving documents is to come up with a list of keywords we would like to see present. A query to retrieve all documents with ALL of a given set of six keywords (Xyz1, Xyz2, . . . , Xyz6) can be expressed, using the FOR ALL type of query we covered in Section 3.5, as follows:

documents

docid	docname	docauthor
d12272	Intro Math	Thomas
d23753	Intro DB	Gray
. . .	. . .	. . .

keywords

keyword	docid
integer	d12272
integral	d12272
integrity	d23753
. . .	. . .
relation	d12272
relation	d23753
SQL	d23753
. . .	. . .

Figure 3.25 The Documents and Keywords Database

```
select * from documents d              -- retrieve documents d
    where not exists
    (select * from keywords k          -- ... where no keyword
        where k.keyword in            -- ... in our list
        ('Xyz1','Xyz2','Xyz3',
        'Xyz4','Xyz5','Xyz6')
        and not exists
        (select * from keywords m      -- ... fails to equal
            where m.keyword = k.keyword  -- ... a keyword
            and m.docid = d.docid));    -- ... in the document d
```

In words, we select any document d where there does not exist a keyword in our list that fails to be a keyword for our document. This is a relatively complex (and inefficient) query for such a simple idea, but this is not the worst of our problems. More important, what if there were no documents that had all six of these keywords? How could we pose a query to retrieve documents that had any five of the six keywords? Or any four? There is no such syntax in SQL. Indeed we would require six queries to retrieve documents with any five of the attributes, and (6 * 5)/2 = 15 queries to retrieve documents with any four of them. ∎

It should be noted that this *fuzzy set* concept of retrieving all rows with a large subset of the desired properties is only the beginning of what is expected in the field of document retrieval. The different keywords are often weighted as to importance, terms of the query might also be weighted, and different measures of k dimensional distance are used to retrieve the closest matching set of documents. The user is also empowered to ask for a specific number of documents in descending order of closeness of match. Interfaces have been proposed and prototyped that provide enormous ease of use, by posing the query for the user and using feedback to alter the weighting terms of the query, using statistical analysis of user-perceived closeness of fit to the desired retrieval for documents already returned. Most of these capabilities seem ruled out by the limitations of Boolean search_conditions. We just consider one more of these capabilities in the familiar CAP

162

database setting, the ability to ask for a specific number of documents in descending order of closeness of match.

EXAMPLE 3.11.8

In our standard CAP database, assume that we have an extremely large number of agents, and we want to print out a list of the 20 agents with the highest total sales so that we can reward them with a vacation in Hawaii. In SQL there is no way to ask for the 20 agents with the largest sales. Of course it is possible to list all agents in decreasing order by total sales:

```
select aid, sum(dollars) from orders x group by aid
    order by 2 desc;
```

From this output we can stop retrieving after the first 20 lines to limit to the agents we are concerned with. Of course this implies that a procedure is being performed. ∎

In Chapter 5 we will see how to create programs to answer any of the questions that have arisen in this section, indeed any questions for which we can imagine an algorithmic approach. The fuzzy set problem of Example 3.11.7 will still be extremely challenging, however, since the relational model is simply not well suited to retrieval by keywords.

Suggestions for Further Reading

An introduction to the SQL-92 standard is given in a text by Jim Melton (who edited the SQL-92 standard) and Alan R. Simon [4]. The X/Open standard is introduced in [8]. **DB2 UDB** SQL is covered in [1] and [2]. **INFORMIX** SQL is covered in [3]. **ORACLE 8** SQL is covered in [5]. An excellent reference work on text retrieval is by Gerald Salton [6]. Practitioners in the field of information retrieval, subsuming text retrieval, generally avoid use of the SQL language as being too limited and inefficient for their needs. A number of founding papers on data models and prototype database systems are given in the *Readings* collection, [7].

[1] Don Chamberlin. *A Complete Guide to DB2 Universal Database*. San Francisco: Morgan Kaufmann, 1998.

[2] *DB2 Universal Database SQL Reference Manual*. Version 6. IBM, 1999. Available at *http://www.ibm.com/db2*.

[3] *INFORMIX Guide to SQL Syntax*. Version 9.2. Menlo Park, CA: Informix Press, 1999. *http://www.informix.com*.

[4] Jim Melton and Alan R. Simon. *Understanding the New SQL: A Complete Guide*. San Francisco: Morgan Kaufmann, 1993.

[5] *ORACLE8 Server SQL Reference*. Volumes 1 and 2. Redwood Shores, CA: Oracle. *http://www.oracle.com*.

[6] Gerald Salton. *Automatic Text Processing.* Reading, MA: Addison-Wesley, 1988.

[7] Michael Stonebraker and Joseph M. Hellerstein, editors. *Readings in Database Systems,* 3rd ed. San Francisco: Morgan Kaufmann, 1998.

[8] *Data Management: Structured Query Language (SQL).* Version 2. Berkshire, UK: X/ Open Company, Ltd., March 1996. Email: xospecs@xopen.co.uk.

Exercises

I hear, and I forget
I see, and I remember
I do, and I understand.
—Anonymous

Exercises with solutions at the back of the book in "Solutions to Selected Exercises" are marked with the symbol •.

STUDENT HOMEWORK: We suggest the following method for student submission of the executable SQL statements. The student creates SQL command files with names Q1A through Q1U, and so on, in an appropriate directory. These command files contain the correct (tested) queries. Then the student displays and runs these queries in a (script) mode that captures the results of the executions in a file that can be turned in. Note that a few of the early queries return an extremely large number of rows; in that case, the student should edit out most of those rows from the result file before turning it in.

NOTE: Exercises 3.1 through 3.7 deal only with SQL features covered through Section 3.5, features that offer the power provided by the relational algebra of Chapter 2.

[3.1] Create queries in SQL to answer the requests in Exercise 2.5 (a) through (u), at the end of Chapter 2.

[3.2] Use one of the All-or-Any predicates in (a) and (b) below.

(a)• Retrieve aid values of agents who receive more than the minimum percent commission (column name: percent).

(b) Retrieve aid values of agents who receive the maximum percent commission.

(c)• Explain why the following query fails to answer request (a) above, although it retrieves the right rows from the agents table of Figure 2.1: select aid from agents where a.percent > 5;

164

[3.3]   Recall that the two predicates IN and =SOME have the same effect (as explained in Example 3.4.8).

(a)• Given this, explain why the predicates NOT IN and <>ANY (not equal any) do not have the same effect, but that <>ALL must be used to have the effect of NOT IN.

(b)   Execute the two queries of Example 3.4.13 with predicates NOT IN and <>ALL. Then execute the query with the predicate <>ALL replaced by <>ANY and state in words what will be retrieved as a result.

(c)• Execute the query of Example 3.4.7, which uses the predicate <=ALL. What quantified comparison predicate would you substitute in this query to retrieve exactly those rows that are *not* retrieved using <=ALL? Demonstrate by execution that this query returns the proper rows.

(d)   Refer to the definitions of predicates <ANY and <ALL and explain why these predicates have the same meaning as < in the condition expr < (Subquery), when the Subquery returns a single element.

[3.4]   (a)• Compose an SQL statement that solves the problem of Example 3.4.1 without using a Subquery. (The FROM clause should reference all tables involved.)

(b)   Is it always possible to avoid using a Subquery as we did in part (a)? Assume that we have a table S with attributes $A_1, \ldots, A_n$, a table T with attributes $B_1, \ldots, B_m$, and constants c and k, where A_i and B_i are from the same domain, for i = 1, 2, 3, and c and k are both from the same domain as A_2 and B_2. Consider the query

```
select A1,..., An from S where A2 = k and
    A1 in (select B1 from T where B2 = c);
```

Rewrite this Select statement to get the same result but without using a Subquery. Don't forget to qualify attributes when needed.

(c)• Repeat part (b), rewriting without a Subquery, the query

```
select A1,..., An from S where A2 = k and
    A1 in (select B1 from T where B2 = c and B3 = S.A3);
```

[3.5]   [HARD] Consider the problem to find all (cid, aid) pairs where the customer does not place an order through the agent. This can be accomplished with the Select statement

```
select cid, aid from customers c, agents a
    where not exists (select * from orders x
        where x.cid = c.cid and x.aid = a.aid);
```

Is it possible to achieve this result using the NOT IN predicate in place of the NOT EXISTS predicate with a single Subquery? With more than one Subquery? Explain your answer and demonstrate any equivalent form by execution.

[3.6]   Look again at the pseudo-code in Figure 3.3.

(a)• Write comparable pseudo-code to show how the query of Exercise 3.4(b) can be evaluated *without* the use of nested loops. You should have two loops performed at distinct times (not one within another)—the first loop, corresponding to the Subquery, placing results (A, values) into a list of values L, and the second loop using a predicate to test if a value of A_1 is in L. We do not have a rigorous definition of what pseudo-code should look like, but try to make it clear what is happening, by analogy with the pseudo-code of Figure 3.3.

(b) Explain why we cannot avoid nested loops in pseudo-code for the query of Exercise 3.4(c). The reason is based on the fact that this query has what is known as a *correlated Subquery*.

[3.7]   How would we show that SQL Select actually offers all the power of relational algebra? Recall from Section 2.8 that all eight operations of relational algebra (listed at the end of Section 2.5) can be expressed in terms of the five basic operations: UNION, DIFFERENCE, PRODUCT, PROJECT, and SELECT. Consider any two tables R and S existing in an SQL database that have been created using the Create Table statement, which we will call *base tables*.

Explain how you would use SQL Select to retrieve any of the answer tables:

(a)• R UNION S

(b) R MINUS S, R TIMES S, R[subset of columns], R WHERE <condition> as in relational algebra. Use only the NOT EXISTS predicate for Subqueries. Assume that R and S have compatible headings where necessary.

(c)• [HARD] But we are not finished demonstrating the power of the SQL Select, because recursive expressions are possible in relational algebra where recursion is not possible in SQL Select. For example, if R, S, and T are all compatible base tables with headings $A_1 \ldots A_n$, then explain how we can express, using the SQL Select, the relational algebra expression (R UNION S) MINUS T.

(d) [VERY HARD; REQUIRES MATH BACKGROUND] Prove that if U and V represent any arbitrarily recursive relational algebra expressions achieved by SQL Select statements in terms of base tables, we can also achieve by SQL Select statements the deeper recursions:

U UNION V, U MINUS V, U TIMES V, U[subset of columns], U WHERE <condition>

(e)• [VERY HARD] Recall from Theorem 2.8.3 that R DIVIDEBY S can be expressed in terms of projection, difference, and product. Let R stand for the SQL statement "`select cid, aid from orders;`" and let S stand for "`select aid from agents where city = 'New York';`". Then R DIVIDEBY S gives the same answer as Example 3.5.2. Use the formula of 2.8.3 and express this in terms of an SQL Select, then execute the resulting statement and verify that it gives the right answer.

NOTE: The following three exercises require SQL features introduced in Section 3.6, features that expand on the power provided by the relational algebra of Chapter 2 but are not offered by many database products as yet. In general, you will only be able to perform these exercises on line with **ORACLE** version 8 and later, or with **DB2 UDB**. Also see Exercises 3.18 and 3.19 for more applications of Advanced SQL.

[3.8]   (a)• Write a Select statement with no WHERE clause to retrieve all customer `cids` and the maximum money each spends on any product. Label the columns of the resulting table: `cid, MAXSPENT`.

(b)   Write a query to retrieve the AVERAGE value (over all customers) of the MAXSPENT of query (a).

(c)   Is it possible to solve (b) without the new capabilities presented in Section 3.6?

[3.9]   The proof of [3.7] (d) from the text is much easier when we include the capabilities of Section 3.6. Explain why. It has to do with recursiveness. (Extra Credit: Prove it if you can.)

[3.10]   (a)• Assume we have a small subset C of `customers` rows (10 rows out of 500,000 customers) determined with a `search_condition`, WHERE C, and separately we have an `sporders` table for orders by customers that are approximately (but maybe not exactly) the same subset C. We want to print out a report giving: cid, cname, TOTDOLL, where TOTDOLL is the SUM(dollars) ordered by each customer in `sporders`. We want to be able to tell when a customer shows up in `sporders` but not in C (by showing a null cname); but we do *not* want to see customers (whether in C or not) who have made no orders in `sporders` (i.e., we very much want to avoid displaying approximately 500,000 – 10 customers with nulls in TOTDOLL). What SQL would you write?

(b)   Now assume that we *do* want to see all customers in the subset C who have not made sales in `sporders`, with nulls in TOTDOLL. What SQL would you write?

NOTE: Many of the exercises that follow require SQL features introduced after Section 3.6, features that expand on the power provided by the relational algebra of Chapter 2 and are in general use in all major database products.

[3.11] Compose and execute SQL statements to perform the following set of tasks, using the Basic SQL standard we have provided (outside of Section 3.6), and optionally note ways to write them using the extended features of Section 3.6.

(a)• For each agent taking an order, list the product pid and the total quantity ordered by all customers from that agent.

(b) We say that a customer x orders a product y in an average quantity A if A is avg(qty) for all orders rows with cid = x and pid = y. Is it possible in a single SQL statement to retrieve cid values of customers who order all the products that they receive in average quantities (by product) of at least 300?

(c)• Get aid values of agents not taking orders from any customer in Duluth for any product in Dallas.

(d) Get aid values of agents who order at least one common product for each customer who is based in Duluth or Kyoto.

(e)• Get cid values of customers who make orders only through agent a03 or a05.

(f) Get pid values of products that are ordered by all customers in Dallas.

(g)• Find agents with the highest percent (percent commission), using the max set function.

(h) In the agents table, delete the row with the agent named Gray, print out the resulting table in full, then put Gray back, using the Insert statement.

(i)• Use the Update statement to change Gray's percent to 11. Then change it back.

(j) Use a single Update statement to raise the prices of all products warehoused in Duluth or Dallas by 10%. Then restore the original values by rerunning the procedure that you originally used to create and load the products table.

(k)• Write an SQL query to retrieve cid values for customers who place at least one order, but only through agent a04. On the same line with each cid, your query should list the total dollar amount of orders placed.

(l) Write an SQL query to get aid and percent values of agents who take orders from all customers who live in Duluth. The aid values should be reported in order by decreasing percent. (Note that if percent is not retrieved in the select list, we cannot order by these values.)

(m)•Write an SQL query to get `pid` values of products ordered by at least one customer who lives in the same city as the agent taking the order.

[3.12] In this problem, you are asked to write down the answers that you would expect SQL to give before checking your answer by executing the query. The point here is to understand how SQL arrives at the answer.

(a)• In the following query, show how the answer is built up; that is, show all Subquery sets of elements created, then write out the final answer you would expect.

```
select city from customers where discnt >=all
    (select discnt from customers where city = 'Duluth')
union select city from agents where percent >any
    (select percent from agents where city like'N%');
```

(b) In the following query, explain in words how SQL arrives at the answer, then write out the final answer you would expect.

```
select cid, pid, sum(qty) from orders
    where dollars >= 500.00
    group by cid, pid having count(qty) > 1;
```

[3.13] Here is an exercise to investigate the question: What SQL queries are guaranteed to return answer tables with no duplicate rows without use of the DISTINCT keyword? This can be important, because using the DISTINCT keyword when it isn't necessary can cause unwanted resource use. We present a series of rules for queries that will not return duplicate rows and ask you to (i) explain why each rule works, and (ii) give an example of a query that returns duplicate rows when the rule fails. In parts (a) and (b), we consider only queries with no Subqueries and no GROUP BY clauses.

(a)• In a query with only one table in the FROM clause, there will be no duplicate rows returned if the column names in the select list form a superkey for the table.

(b) In a query with multiple tables in the FROM clause, there will be no duplicate rows returned if the column names in the select list contain subsets that form superkeys for each of the tables involved.

(c)• Is it true that no query with a GROUP BY clause will have duplicate rows? Explain why or give a counterexample.

(d) In Select statements that contain Subqueries in their WHERE clause, queries should be guaranteed unique rows in at least the same situations as (a) and (b) above. The transformation of Exercise 3.4(b) from a Subquery form to a join form without a Subquery may result in duplicate rows, however, unless the DISTINCT keyword is used before the select list. Give an example where a Select statement without duplicates gains duplicates during such a transformation.

[3.14] **(a)**• Rewrite the query of Example 3.9.4, using only comparison predicates and without any use of the partial Match Pattern form.

(b) Can you find another pattern that *cannot* be replaced with other predicate forms?

[3.15] Recall the definition of outer join from Section 2.10. Consider the (ordinary) join query:

```
select a.aname, a.aid, sum(x.dollars)
    from agents a,orders x
    where a.aid = x.aid group by a.aid, a.aname;
```

(a)• Rewrite this query in Basic SQL to implement an outer join (this will require a union of three Subqueries). An agent aname and aid should appear even if the agent takes no orders, and orders should appear (grouped by aid) even if there is no corresponding aid in agents listed. Supply constant values, nulls for aname, and for sum(x.dollars) when no proper value exists in a column (or blanks and zeros, if you cannot use a null constant on your system).

(b) To test your answer to part (a), add a new row to orders, (1027, 'jun', 'c001', 'a07', 'p01', 1000, 450.00), and a new row to agents, ('a08', 'Beowulf', 'London', 8), and then execute the query. When you are satisfied, delete the two rows you just added.

[3.16] The following exercise illustrates some of the special properties of null values. To perform this exercise, we add a few new rows to the agents table with null values in the percent column (and delete them again at the end of the exercise). We execute two Insert statements:

```
insert into agents (aid, aname, city)
    values ('a07', 'Green', 'Geneva');
insert into agents (aid, aname, city)
    values ('a08', 'White', 'Newark');
```

(a)• Predict the result of the following statement, then execute it and check your answer. The question is, how do nulls act in a GROUP BY clause?

```
select percent from agents group by percent;
```

(b) Predict the result of the following statement, then execute it. The question is, how do nulls act when placed in order with other values?

```
select aid, percent from agents order by percent;
```

(c)• Consider the following query.

```
select distinct aname from agents where percent >=all
    (select percent from agents where city = 'Geneva');
```

(i)   Put into words the effect of this query: "get names of agents . . ."

(ii)   Note that the Subquery here returns a single null value. In this case the result of the >ALL predicate will be unknown for all percent values of any row in agents. What, therefore, do you expect will be the result of this query? Execute the query to test your understanding.

(d) Similarly consider the following query, and do parts (i) and (ii) as in (c).

```
select distinct aname from agents a where not exists
    (select * from agents b
        where b.city = 'Geneva'
        and a.percent <= b.percent);
```

Does it seem to you that the effect of this query is the same as the effect of the query of problem (c)? But there is a surprise here, because the only row for which b.city = 'Geneva' has b.percent = null, and all other percent values compare to null with an UNKNOWN result. Therefore the Subquery returns a null set of values and NOT EXISTS is TRUE for all agents a. This is *not* the result from part (c).

[3.17] More on "ALL means no counterexamples." Suppose we modify Example 3.5.2 by changing New York to Los Angeles.

(a)• What is the answer now?

(b) Explain why.

[3.18] In Example 3.11.5, we saw that the specified report could be not done in a single Basic SQL query.

(a)• Show how to produce the specified report using multiple Basic SQL statements (that create tables for later use). Create blocks of width 500.00 by rounding down dollars/500.00 to an integer "bucket number." For example, 750.00/500.00 = 1.5 rounds down to bucket number 1. Use a Create Table statement to make a table btab of bucket numbers, with one integer column named bucket. In **ORACLE**, for example, you can use the floor( ) function that rounds off any fractional part of a numeric value to an integer. In **DB2 UDB** and **INFORMIX** systems, you can use a CAST expression to compute the bucket number from dollars. Now that these bucket numbers are materialized in btab, you can perform the necessary GROUP BY for the report by performing a join of orders with btab. (Note that some systems may round off rather than round down in performing CAST; in this case you need to use the expression: `cast((dollars+250.005)/500.00)-1 as inte-ger).)` The extra .005 ensures that 0 dollars is CAST to bucket number 0, 500.00 to 1, etc.)

(b) Write a single query using the Advanced SQL features of Section 3.6 (and available in **ORACLE** and **DB2 UDB**) to produce the report. Here the rounding-down operation can be done either with the floor( ) or CAST expression. The special Advanced SQL feature you need is that of placing a Subquery in the FROM clause.

[3.19] In Example 3.11.3, we saw that Basic SQL cannot compute the median in a single statement. Show how to compute the median by using multiple Basic SQL statements and a single (very long) Advanced SQL statement, as follows.

(a) Use multiple Basic SQL statements. Create a table `relhist` (for relative frequency histogram) of `dollars` values and the counts of their occurrences in the table `orders`. For example, `dollars = 720.00` has a count of 2. Make another table `cumhist` (for cumulative frequency histogram) of counts of occurrences of `dollars` values at or below each individual `dollars` value. For example, `dollars = 400.00` has an accumulated count of 2, one for the single 400.00 value and one for the value 180.00. Query the second table to find the median.

(b)• Write a single query using the Advanced SQL features to produce this report.

[3.20] **ORACLE** has the ability to do transitive closure type queries as explained in the notes. Create the `employees` table shown in Example 3.11.6. Then execute the CONNECT BY query given in the text just after the example.

Object-Relational SQL | 4

Object-Relational is the answer! What was the question?
—Michael Carey, SIGMOD 97

This chapter introduces the *object-relational* model for database management systems, abbreviated *ORDBMS*, and contrasts it with the older relational DBMS (RDBMS) model we have been studying up to now. ANSI/ISO SQL-99 has introduced an SQL language standard that supports the ORDBMS model, and the three major database products that we have been studying, **DB2 UDB**, **ORACLE**, and **INFORMIX**, have all adopted ORDBMS SQL language dialects (which, unfortunately, disagree on some basic syntax elements). While database vendors such as **MICROSOFT** and **SYBASE** have not released products that support ORDBMS at the time of this writing, the thrust of the future seems to be in this direction, and we give a thorough introduction to ORDBMS in the current chapter. Because ORDBMS products will also run RDBMS SQL, a feature known as *upward compatibility*, we sometimes refer to these products as being in the RDBMS/ORDBMS category.

While IBM's **DB2 UDB** has had a very strong object-relational programming interface for some time, it began to support some of the interactive ORDBMS SQL features a bit later than the others—after we had already started writing this chapter. Because of this, we will only be covering **ORACLE** and **INFORMIX** ORDBMS features in the current chapter. Since the ORDBMS model is so new, there will probably be other changes in the field before a new version of our text is released, so we recommend that readers connect to our text homepage for late-breaking material on ORDBMS and other topics. The URL for the homepage is http://www.cs.umb.edu/~poneil/dbppp.html.

4.1 Introduction

There are several different dialects of ORDBMS SQL at the present time. Each product has its own idiosyncratic dialect, and even the SQL-99 model and syntax saw dramatic changes in the final few years before its adoption. To use a generic term in our discussion, we will refer to the SQL language that represents concepts common to most of the ORDBMS SQL dialects as *ORSQL*. The terminology we use in speaking of ORSQL will not be accurate for all ORDBMS products.

We begin this section with an overview of ORSQL capabilities, including the multiple ORSQL standards and dialects and how we will deal with covering them in our presentation.

ORSQL Capabilities

The object-relational model of ORSQL supports a composite structured type the user can declare to define what are sometimes referred to as *objects*—what we have been used to thinking of as *rows*—that is, a grouping of typed data values that can be stored in a table. We refer to an *object type* in **ORACLE**, a *row type* in **INFORMIX**, and a *user-defined type*, or *UDT*, in **DB2 UDB** to be a format for a row (or object) and all its typed *attributes*. Since the term *user-defined type* is also used in the SQL-99 standard, we will adopt that terminology generically for ORSQL. A table can then be declared to contain rows (or objects) of a user-defined type. In addition, *a column within a table* can be declared to contain values of a user-defined type (i.e., a column can have row-like values).

Collection Types

Additionally, the object-relational model allows a column value (on a single row) to contain a *set* (or some other type of *collection*, such as an *array*) of row-like values. In some systems a single column value can itself hold a *table*, a feature known as *table nesting*. In other cases, collections of such objects can be *cast* to a table, so that SQL retrieval concepts will work on the collection. What this all adds up to is the most extreme possible departure from the first normal form rule of the relational model, Relational RULE 1. Below we reiterate this rule as it was stated in Section 2.3.

RULE 1: First Normal Form Rule. In defining tables, the relational model insists that columns that look like multi-valued fields (sometimes called repeating fields) or have any internal structure (like a record) are *not* permitted! A table that obeys this is said to be in *first normal form.*   ∎

By comparison, the object-relational model breaks the first normal form rule by permitting column values that contain multi-valued, structured data values. Figure 4.1 has an example of an object-relational `employees` table, where a single column, `dependents`, contains structure (two attributes, `dep_name` and `dep_age`) and multiple values per row (for example, employee e001, John Smith, has two dependents, Michael J. and Susan R.).

Methods and UDFs

In object-oriented languages such as Java, any *private data* in an object can be accessed only via object *methods*; such methods are functions that can be called to operate on one

employees

eid	ename	position	dependents	
			dep_name	dep_age
e001	Smith, John	Agent	Michael J.	9
			Susan R.	7
e002	Andrews, David	Superintendent	David M. Jr.	10
e003	Jones, Franklin	Agent	Andrew K.	11
			Mark W.	9
			Louisa M.	4

Figure 4.1 An employees Table with a Multi-Valued dependents Attribute

particular object. Normally, the set of methods for an object will deal with all properties of the object that can be treated in isolation. For a simple bank account object, we might have methods get_balance( ), make_deposit( ), and make_withdrawal( ), as well as methods to create and destroy bank account objects. Some methods, like get_balance( ), only read the object data and return information about it to the caller; others, like make_deposit( ) and make_withdrawal( ), modify the data in the object. In a pure object-oriented environment (where all data is private), the set of methods for a class of objects characterizes the class, since there is no other way to operate on the objects.

The objects we will study in this chapter always allow ORSQL to perform direct access to their component parts, so in ORDBMS all data is considered to be *public* rather than *private*. In the early sections below, we use general ORSQL access to work with objects. Later we explain how to write *object methods*, which are functions "attached" to an object, and the more general *user-defined functions* (UDFs), which are not so attached but can deal with multiple different objects as parameters of equal importance.

Form of Presentation for This Chapter

In this chapter we will be presenting object-relational concepts for two commercial products, **ORACLE** and **INFORMIX**. The two products are quite different in design and nomenclature, sufficiently different that we feel the introductions to the two products must be addressed separately. As a result, we intend to perform these introductions in separate numbered subsections. For example, in Section 4.2, "Objects and Tables," we will cover a number of basic definitions and examples: Subsection 4.2.1 covers "Object Types in **ORACLE**," and Subsection 4.2.2 covers "**INFORMIX** Row Types for Objects." You will note that Chapter 4 is the only instance of these numbered subsections in the book. This is an intentional distinction to address two distinctly different products.

A VERY IMPORTANT POINT: It is recommended that you read through successive sections of the text, covering both products in your reading, whether you work with both products or not. The different product concepts introduced in the alternate sections are important for a proper understanding of the object-relational model. Since **ORACLE** coverage introduces each section, the **INFORMIX** subsections might conceivably be skipped without loss of continuity, but a certain breadth of understanding will be sacrificed by studying only one product.

Object-Relational History

The object-relational model had a number of factors motivating its development. To begin with, interest in object-oriented programming languages such as Smalltalk and C++ led to a desire to create database systems that would interact naturally with such languages. In the mid-eighties a number of *object-oriented database system* (OODBS) products began to appear. Among other things, the OODBS products extended object-oriented programming languages by providing *persistent variables*. (The word *persistent* here is used in the same sense as the term *persistent storage*, storage that survives reboot of the system, i.e., disk storage.) The idea was that a variable J could be declared "persistent" in a language such as C++ and then updated in a natural way within the language, for example, by writing J = J + 1 as a line of code. Then the underlying OODBS would see to it that when the program that updated J completed, the new value would be automatically saved to persistent storage, and when such a program was executed again it could access the saved value of J. No SQL statements were necessary in the OODBS model, and *complex objects* such as *arrays* and *classes* (or *encapsulated structs*) could be used to contain the data. Such complex objects are particularly useful in applications such as machine parts design, where some machine parts have extremely detailed subassemblies with thousands of subparts. To model such designs in relational products can require a very large number of joins of different types of tables, with accompanying difficulty in coding and inefficiency in execution, whereas the more complex structures allowed in C++ can model such subassemblies much more naturally.

While the OODBS model was the best choice for certain applications, the idea of a "table" was absent, and queries in early OODBS products were rather primitive. Although a good deal of effort was put into fixing such shortcomings in later releases, many business customers who had adapted the "fill-in-the-form, one-answer-to-a-space" relational model many years before found that it fit their business needs reasonably well and wanted to avoid having to reimplement their business applications. As a result, the OODBS products (from companies such as Object Design, Versant, Gemstone, and Objectivity) have made up a "niche" market, with total dollar sales only a few percent of the total sales of RDBMS/ORDBMS products. Because of this, we will concentrate on the ORDBMS model entirely in the current text.

The ORDBMS model evolved to fill a number of needs. To begin with, the first normal form rule was early seen to be unnecessarily restrictive. A number of papers were published about non-first normal form models that would support "nested relations." IBM supported commercial research on this model, and various researchers started moving toward prototyping. Commercial users were seen to be willing to accept an evolutionary change from relational tables, where the "one-answer-to-a-space" restriction was removed, as long as old applications could continue to work in the new model. The most

important early prototype product on the object-relational scheme was POSTGRES, the **177**
brainchild of Michael Stonebraker, who was then at the University of California at
Berkeley. (See "Suggestions for Further Reading" at the end of this chapter for more
about POSTGRES and Stonebraker's views of the object-relational model.) POSTGRES
was then developed into a commercial product (under a series of names because of copy-
right challenges, ending with Illustra). The Illustra product was ultimately purchased by
INFORMIX in 1996, to form the basis of their ORDBMS offering, which we treat in this
text. **ORACLE** came out with an object-relational release, version 8, in 1997.

The ANSI/ISO SQL-99 standards effort, ultimately producing SQL-99 (more officially SQL:1999), was directed toward an object-relational standard since about 1994
but went through so many time-consuming modifications that database products with
object-relational features were developed and released prior to the final release in 1999.

4.2 Objects and Tables

In the **ORACLE** object-relational model we have a new kind of user-defined type, known
as an *object type*. We cover use of the new **ORACLE** object type in Section 4.2.1. In
INFORMIX, **ORACLE**'s object type has an analog known as a *row type*, and we cover this
in Section 4.2.2.

4.2.1 Object Types in **ORACLE**

We start by showing how to create an object type. We say that an object type has
attributes of various types, analogous to columns of a table. An object type is defined in
ORACLE with the Create Object Type statement, as shown in Example 4.2.1.

EXAMPLE 4.2.1

Create an object type name_t to represent a person's name, with last name, first name, and
middle initial. The example below is written in the form we would use in **ORACLE**'s Interactive
SQL environment, SQL*Plus.[1]

```
create type name_t as object   -- We call this a "Create Object Type" statement
    (
        lname   varchar(30),    -- last name
        fname   varchar(30),    -- first name
        mi      char(1)         -- middle initial
    );
    /                           -- for Sql*Plus, not part of SQL syntax
```

---

[1]When the Create Object Type statement of Example 4.2.1 is executed in the SQL*Plus environment introduced in Appendix A.1, the terminating semicolon (;) must be followed with a new line containing the
forward slash (/) character. If a final / line were included following previous statements we've introduced,
it would have caused the statement to be executed twice.

After this SQL statement is executed (after the / character is entered), the system has recorded a new database type, an *object type*. The *attributes* of name_t are lname, fname, and mi. The double dash mark (--) indicates that what follows on the line is a comment.   ∎

Example 4.2.1 creates the **ORACLE** object type name_t to hold people's names, in the same sense that a C struct definition declares a "struct type," but no object of this type has yet been created. For that, we need to create a table whose rows or columns can hold objects. We show a table with a column declared to be of object type in Example 4.2.2.

EXAMPLE 4.2.2
Create a table called teachers, with three columns: tid (a teacher identifier, of type int), tname (teacher name, of type name_t), and room (teacher homeroom number, of type int).

```
create table teachers
    (
        tid        int,
        tname      name_t,
        room       int
    );
```

This is an empty table, so we have still not created any objects of type name_t. But if we now perform Insert statements to populate the teachers table with rows, the column values in tname will take on object values of type name_t. An example of such an Insert statement is this:

```
insert into teachers values (1234, name_t('Einstein', 'Albert','E'), 120);
```
   ∎

The VALUES keyword used in the Insert statement above was defined as syntax in the general form of the Insert statement in Section 3.10, Figure 3.22. The second column being inserted uses a name_t(. . .) form to put together values of the attributes of name_t, lname, fname, and mi, and generate a value of object type name_t for the tname column. This object_type_name( ) form, which builds an object from values of its attributes, is called an *object constructor*. (For details, see the discussion of Figure 4.5 below.) Clearly the definition of the column tname in the table teachers breaks Relational RULE 1, which forbids internal structures within column values.

We use a form of "dot" notation to access attributes within the tname object column of the teachers table defined in Example 4.2.2. First here is a regular SQL statement dealing only with columns of teachers:

```
select t.tid from teachers t where t.room = 123;
```

Now here is one that deals with attributes within the name_t type column:

```
select t.tid, t.tname.fname, t.tname.lname from teachers t where t.room = 123;
```

Note that there are two dots used in t.tname.lname, the first one to indicate that tname is a column of the table t (alias of teachers) and the second to indicate that lname is an attribute of the object value for tname. While we were always able to do without a table alias in Chapter 3 (and did not use a table qualifier for columns when there was only one table named in the FROM clause), this is *not* the case in Select statements that access attributes. We will explain the details later, but for now you should always include a table alias and use it to qualify all column names of a Select statement when in doubt. In particular, because the following variant of the Select statement just mentioned lacks a table qualifier on the tname accesses, the Select statement *won't work!*

```
select tid, tname.fname, tname.lname from teachers where room = 123; ** DOESN'T WORK
```

One object type can be used for an attribute definition within another object type. In Example 4.2.3 we define an object type person_t for describing a person with a name_t attribute called pname, short for person-name.

EXAMPLE 4.2.3

Create an object type person_t to hold a person's Social Security number, name, and age, respectively. Start by using the Drop Type statement for person_t, to clear out any preexisting types of that name.

```
drop type person_t;
create type person_t as object (
    ssno      int,
    pname     name_t,
    age       int
);
```

As in Example 4.2.1, to make a Create Type statement execute in SQL*Plus, we would need to follow it with / on its own line.   ■

Note that name_t is a type that must already be defined in order for the definition of person_t to execute properly, and this is what is called a *dependency*: person_t is *dependent* on name_t. An attempt to drop a type on which another type is dependent will result in an error; we first need to drop all the dependent types. If we attempted to drop the name_t type after defining the person_t type of Example 4.2.3, we would need first to drop the person_t type, and possibly others that are dependent on name_t. Information on interdependencies of types and tables can be displayed from the catalog tables maintained by the database system. See the last section of Chapter 7.

A table in **ORACLE** is called an *object table* if its rows are of object type, that is, each of its rows consists of an object of that type. Example 4.2.4 creates a table with rows of type person_t.

EXAMPLE 4.2.4

Create an object table called `people` to contain `person_t` objects (rows). Use the Social Security number for the primary key.[2]

```
create table people of person_t
(
        primary key(ssno)
);
```

We have written this out on four lines for ease of reading but, as usual, the whitespace does not affect its meaning, so we could equally well write:

```
create table people of person_t(primary key(ssno));
```

An example of the `people` table just created is given in Figure 4.2.

people

nameless top-level column holding the row object					
named columns (also known as top-level attributes)	ssno	pname			age
attributes within pname		pname.lname	pname.fname	pname.mi	
row 1	123550123	March	Jacqueline	E	23
row 2	245882134	Delaney	Patrick	X	59
row 3	023894455	Sanchez	Jose	F	30

Figure 4.2   ORACLE Object Table `people` of Example 4.2.4, with Contents at a Given Moment

∎

Recall that the relational Create Table statement form (Figure 3.2 in Chapter 3) specified all the column names and datatypes as part of its definition. But in an object table, the object attributes provide the columns of the table. Thus the **ORACLE** Create Object Table statement of Example 4.2.4 (with a CREATE TABLE table_name OF type_name ... form) only needs to specify the object type (person_t) and an optional primary key; the person_t attributes, ssno, pname, and age, become column names for people, where they are sometimes referred to as *columns* and sometimes as *top-level attributes*. Since ssno is treated as a column, it can be specified as the primary key in the Create Object Table statement.

---

[2] A column with the PRIMARY KEY column constraint is implicitly defined to be NOT NULL (and provide a key), although the PRIMARY KEY clause and NOT NULL clause can be used together. In fact a number of older products required that a column declared PRIMARY KEY also had to be NOT NULL. Since only newer products have object-relational extensions, we use PRIMARY KEY without NOT NULL on the same column in this chapter.

In what follows we will refer to the Create Table statement form used to create a **181** relational table as the *Create Relational Table* statement and the form used to create an object table as the *Create Object Table* statement. When we do not wish to differentiate, we will refer to the *Create Table* statement.

The `people` table of Example 4.2.4 involves two types of objects. The `person_t` objects are called *row objects* of the table because they sit in table rows. Since the column-like attribute `pname` is itself of object type, `pname` values are called *column objects*. The attributes of `pname` are accessible within the `people` table, as they were in the `teachers` table of Example 4.2.2, by using dot notation, e.g., `p.pname.lname`, where `p` is an alias for `people`, but they are never referred to as columns, always as attributes. The "nameless top-level column" included in Figure 4.2 is meant to indicate we can refer to the entire row object of `people` using a VALUE( ) form (explained below, not to be confused with the VALUES keyword of the Insert statement), something we can't do in a non-object table. In general, we won't mention the nameless top-level column in figures of object tables.

Since top-level attributes of object tables act as columns, we can write simple queries in the usual way:

```
select p.age from people p where p.ssno = 123550123;
```

We can display the column object `pname` in the same manner, for example,

```
select p.pname from people p where p.age > 25;
```

The `name_t` objects in the `pname` column will be printed out in a format such as `name_t('Sanchez','Jose', 'F')`, as we will soon cover in more detail. Just as with normal tables, the * form in the select list of a Select statement

```
select * from people p where p.age > 25;
```

displays all the columns of the selected rows; with an object table, it displays all the top-level attributes, as shown in Figure 4.3.

In Figure 4.3, the non-object columns are displayed as expected. The column `pname` has a heading showing its attribute names, and its values are contained in the object constructor `name_t( )`. (On some systems, **ORACLE** will display the multiple columns of Figure 4.3 with a new line for each column of each row, one value under another. This seems to occur whenever one or more of the columns represent objects, but the display form may change with new releases of **ORACLE**.)

ssno	pname(lname,fname,mi)	age
245882134	name_t('Delaney','Patrick','X')	59
023894455	name_t('Sanchez','Jose','F')	30

Figure 4.3 ORACLE Output from a Select * Query, Displaying All Columns

```
value(p)       (ssno,            pname(lname, fname, mi),            age)

--------       -----------       --------------------------------    ------

person_t       (245882134,       name_t('Delaney', 'Patrick', 'X'),  59)
person_t       (023894455,       name_t('Sanchez', 'Jose', 'F'),     30)
```

Figure 4.4   ORACLE Output from Select value(p), Displaying Full Row Object

There is another way to display the same data as *full row objects*. This is one impli-cation of the nameless top-level column of Figure 4.2, namely, that we can retrieve all columns of an object table such as people as a single column value.

```
select value(p) from people p where age > 25;
```

(Once again, be careful not to confuse this value(p) form with the VALUES keyword used in the Insert statement.) The result of this query is shown in Figure 4.4.

In the output of Figure 4.4, we see the object constructor person_t( ) in the selected rows, along with its component parts. This is quite different conceptually from the Select * query result of Figure 4.3, and we will see how this ability to retrieve single object values from an object table provides new functionality in subsequent examples.

Figure 4.4 demonstrates how **ORACLE** displays column objects and row objects:

```
name_t('Delaney','Patrick','X')
person_t(023894455,name_t('Sanchez','Jose','F'),30)
```

Note the similarity of this display format to the form used in Example 4.2.2 to create a name_t column object to insert into the table teachers. **ORACLE** provides this general form of *object constructor* used for creating objects from attribute values and also for displaying objects of a given type. See Figure 4.5.

Example 4.2.5 provides another example of how to use an object constructor.

EXAMPLE 4.2.5
Display the full person_t object, including Social Security number and age, for Jose F. Sanchez.

```
select value(p) from people p
    where p.pname = name_t('Sanchez', 'Jose', 'F');
```

Note that it is the name_t( ) that is the object constructor here, not the value( ) form, which can only be used to retrieve the current row of a table (possibly in a search_condition); the value( ) form cannot be used to construct a new object. ∎

```
typename(argument [{,argument...}])
```

Figure 4.5   General Form of the **ORACLE** Object Constructor

In Example 4.2.6, we illustrate a query that uses nested dot notation to access an attribute of a column object, something that doesn't by itself qualify as a column.

EXAMPLE 4.2.6

Find the names and ages of all people whose first names start with "Pat" and are over 50 years of age.

```
select p.pname, p.age from people p
    where p.pname.fname like 'Pat%' and p.age > 50;
```

As before, the table alias p is required in this query. We finally explain this below. ∎

Nested dot notation can be used in any **ORACLE** SQL statement to access an attribute of an object that is an attribute of an object that is an attribute . . . of an object column x, up to some limited but large level of nesting. Specifically, to access attribute attr1 of object column x we use x.attr1; if x.attr1 is an object with an attribute attr2, we can use x.attr1.attr2 to access that attribute, and so on.

While the SQL of Chapter 3 did not require a qualifier for certain column references, SQL statements that access attributes of objects have different rules. Officially, **ORACLE** requires all attribute-accessing expressions to be fully qualified *by an alias*; that is, such expressions must start with a table alias (rather than the table name itself), followed by a dotted sequence of nested attributes, as in Example 4.2.6. Unofficially, **ORACLE** seems to support an exception, allowing top-level attributes of an object table (which are meant to act like columns) to be used without qualification. For example, consider accessing the top-level attribute pname and fname, its attribute:

```
select p.pname from people p;    -- table alias used, officially correct, works
select pname from people;        -- no table alias, not officially correct, but works
```

The rule is strictly enforced for attributes below the top level that require nested dot notation.

```
select pname.fname from people;        -- not a top-level attribute: doesn't work
select people.pname.fname from people; -- also doesn't work, since must use alias
```

Insert and Update statements can also use object constructors to specify values for new rows but with rather strict rules, as we see in the next two examples.

EXAMPLE 4.2.7

Create a table named scientists of object type name_t, and insert a row object for Albert Einstein into it.

```
create table scientists of name_t;
insert into scientists values ('Einstein', 'Albert','E');
```

Since we can create a name_t object with an object constructor, name_t('Einstein', 'Albert','E'), it might seem that the following Insert statement should work:

```
insert into scientists name_t('Einstein', 'Albert','E'); ** DOESN'T WORK
```

But it doesn't, for the simple reason that it doesn't fit the Insert general form of Figure 3.22, which requires the tablename to be followed by either a VALUES keyword or a Subquery. However, it would work to update `scientists`, replacing an entire row object with an object constructed value, for example,

```
update scientists s set s = name_t('Eisenstein', 'Andrew','F')
    where value(s) = name_t('Einstein', 'Albert','E');
```

We can insert the Einstein name object into `people`, using the VALUES keyword and an object constructor.

```
insert into people values (123441998, name_t('Einstein', 'Albert','E'), 100);
```

We could also insert all the `name_t` objects found in `people` into the `scientists` table.

```
insert into scientists select p.pname from people p;
```

      ■

A null value can also be assigned to objects, as we see below.

EXAMPLE 4.2.8

Add a row to `people` with `ssno` 321341223, null `pname`, and null `age`. We can do this in two ways:

```
insert into people values (321341223, null, null);
(this is equivalent to the following)
insert into people (ssno) values (321341223);
```

Since the syntax of Insert does not support table aliases, top-level attributes, such as `ssno` in the second example, are referenced in the column list without a qualifier. On the other hand, Update does allow a table alias, so fully qualified attribute expressions should be used.

Replace the null name in the last inserted row with 'Ben Gould'. We don't know his middle initial.

```
update people p set p.pname = name_t('Gould', 'Ben', null) where ssno = 321341223;
```

Updates can be used to replace a part of a complex-object column, for example, a single second-level attribute value. Replace the null middle initial of the row we have just inserted with 'C'.

```
update people p set p.pname.mi = 'C' where ssno = 321341223;
```

Recall that we can replace an entire row with an Update statement using a row object constructor. We can even modify the primary key `ssno` as we perform the update.

```
update people p set p = person_t(332341223, name_t('Gould', 'Glen', 'A'), 55)
    where ssno = 321341223;
```

      ■

Figure 4.6 lists the general forms we have introduced so far for creating and destroying object types and object tables. The datatypes for all attributes are specified in the Create Object Type statement, and the only attributes named in the Create Object Table

```
CREATE TYPE typename AS OBJECT
    (attrname datatype {, attrname datatype ...});
CREATE TABLE tablename OF typename
    ( [attrname NOT NULL] {, attrname NOT NULL ...}
        [, PRIMARY KEY (attrname {,attrname ...})]);
DROP TYPE typename;
DROP TABLE tablename;
```

Figure 4.6 Creating and Destroying Object Types and Object Tables in **ORACLE** (Covered So Far)

statement are those that need to be specified NOT NULL or included in a PRIMARY KEY specification.

Definition of the REF Object Reference

Objects that appear in object tables are called *row objects*, whereas objects that appear as table columns (or attributes within other objects) are called *column objects*. **ORACLE** provides all row objects (but not column objects) with a unique means of identification, known as an *object identifier*, and a column (or attribute) of a table can be declared to have a built-in datatype called a *REF* to allow it to "point to" a row object of a (possibly different) object table. A REF to a specific row object and the object itself are considered to have different (though related) datatypes. Column objects, unlike row objects, can be thought of as just convenient groupings of related attributes that are not important on their own; they don't "deserve" their own REFs.

In the CAP database of Figure 2.2, there were four tables: customers, agents, products, and orders. In Example 4.2.9, we recast these tables as object tables and use REFs to point from the order row object to the customer, agent, and product row objects for the order. We will see that we can use REFs to avoid what may be inefficient joins between orders and the other tables. We could *replace* the cid, aid, and pid columns in the orders table with the three object REFs, but it is hard to set the REF values without such columns. It turns out that it is best to keep all the old cid, aid, and pid columns, and just add the three object REF columns. As before, the cid, aid, and pid columns are primary keys in their own tables, customers, agents, and products.

EXAMPLE 4.2.9

Create the CAP database using object tables for customers, agents, products, and orders, keeping all the old columns in each table, and adding REFs from each order in the orders table to the customer, agent, and product row objects involved in the order.

```
create type customer_t as object (...);  -- attributes same as columns for customers
create type agent_t as object (...);      -- attributes same as columns for agents
create type product_t as object (...);    -- attributes same as columns for products
```

```
create type order_t as object
(
     ordno        int,
     month        char(3),
     cid          char(4),
     aid          char(3),
     pid          char(3);
     qty          int,
     dollars      double precision,
     ordcust      ref customer_t,    -- added column points to customers row object
     ordagent     ref agent_t,       -- added column points to agents row object
     ordprod      ref product_t      -- added column points to products row object
);
create table customers of customer_t (primary key (cid));
create table products of product_t (primary key (pid));
create table agents of agent_t (primary key (aid));
create table orders of order_t
(
     primary key (ordno),
     scope for (ordcust) is customers,
     scope for (ordagent) is agents,
vscope for (ordprod) is products
);                                                                          ■
```

Each orders row object has a cid column (as well as all other customers columns), because of the order_t attribute cid; a column such as this is often referred to as a *foreign key*, since it is used in a join to determine the appropriate (foreign table) customers row object with the same cid *primary key* value. Each orders row object also has an ordcust column, a REF to the customers row object with the same cid. Similarly, each orders row object has aid and ordagent, pid and ordprod columns. (Of course we are assuming here that all the tables above have been loaded and the ordcust, ordagent, and ordprod REF values set appropriately; for how this is done, see the last subsection of the current section, "Loading Tables with REFs.") The SCOPE FOR clauses that appear in the Create Table statement for orders in Example 4.2.9 are meant to ensure that the newly defined REF column values will always refer to objects in the table specified by the scope; naturally the table specified in the scope must be an object table. This scope determines the internal format to be assigned to the REF values; a REF that is not scoped for (i.e., restricted to point to) a particular table would require a longer format (since it would need to allow space for a Table ID as well). A REF can become invalid if the object it references is deleted, but to start with, we will assume all REFs have been created to reference appropriate objects.

We can use dot notation to follow a REF, which we call *dereferencing* a REF. Here is a query to print out all order numbers for dollar amounts over $200.00, together with the ordering customers' names:

```
select o.ordno, o.ordcust.cname from orders o where o.dollars > 200.00;
```

We have replaced a join query with a much simpler REF syntax, and the result is not only simpler syntax but the cname value is also more efficient to access (in this particular case, though not necessarily in all cases). More examples of this simplification follow.

EXAMPLE 4.2.10

As in Example 3.3.4, retrieve all customer-agent name pairs, (cname, aname), where the customer places an order through the agent.

```
select distinct o.ordcust.cname, o.ordagent.aname from orders o;
```

The original Example 3.3.4 required a three-way join. ∎

It is not the case that all queries involving the orders table simplify as nicely as this. A query that requires a self-join of orders with itself is not shortened, as we see in the next example.

EXAMPLE 4.2.11

As in Example 3.3.7, find pid values of products that have been ordered by at least two customers.

```
select distinct x1.pid
    from orders x1, orders x2
        where x1.pid = x2.pid and x1.ordcust < x2.ordcust;
```

Note in this query that we test the order of REFs, the ordcust values, to avoid duplicates in the results. Recall that Example 3.7.6 shows another way to perform this query. ∎

The REFs of Example 4.2.9 allow us to simplify any join on cid between customers and orders, on aid between agents and orders, or on pid between products and orders. These are arguably the most common joins used in practice, so this is a valuable simplification. In some cases, access through a REF is more efficient than access through a join, but we need to understand query plans (covered in Chapter 9) before we will be able to recognize these cases. For now we can say that retrieving a *single* orders row together with related information from customers, agents, and products will be more efficiently handled through a REF form than through a join of foreign key to primary key.

ORACLE provides a function REF( ) that can be used to derive the REF value of an object appearing in an SQL statement in some other connection. Here is an example.

EXAMPLE 4.2.12

As in Example 3.4.12, retrieve all customer names where the customer does *not* place an order through agent a05.

```
select c.cname from customers c
    where not exists (select * from orders x
        where x.ordcust = ref(c) and x.aid = 'a05');
```

Here we have avoided using cid explicitly by identifying the customer by the REF value instead. We can hope this is faster than searching for a match on cid, but this is not absolutely clear without an understanding of what query plan would be used in this case. At least it should be clear how the Subquery is dependent on the outer Select statement: this is a correlated Subquery. ∎

In the FOR ALL queries we met with in Section 3.5, we see some improvement in complexity from using REFs. The clutter of identifiers can be reduced, leaving the essential issues of connections between objects showing more clearly.

EXAMPLE 4.2.13

As in Example 3.5.2 (compare that solution), get the cid values of customers who place orders with *all* agents based in New York. Rewording as before, we get: "Find customers c for which no counterexample exists, that is, customer c for which we cannot find an agent a living in New York *with no orders x connecting a to c*." Here we can characterize a connecting order as one with REFs to a and c:

```
select c.cid from customers c where        -- select c if
    not exists (select * from agents a      -- there is no agent
        where a.city = 'New York' and       -- living in N.Y.
        not exists (select * from orders x   -- with no order connecting a and c
            where x.ordcust = ref(c) and x.ordagent = ref(a)));
```
∎

In the queries using REFs we have met with up to now, we have been assuming that all the REF-valued columns are non-null and reference the correct row of the correct object table. The SCOPE clause ensures that all non-null references point to the correct table when created, and we assume the REF values are set appropriately after the load (see the subsection below, "Loading Tables with REFs"), but as rows are deleted in the table referenced, REFs connected to those rows become what we call *dangling REFs*. We can query for abnormalities such as this by using a new IS DANGLING predicate.

EXAMPLE 4.2.14

Get the cid values of customers whose REFs in orders are dangling.

```
select o.cid from orders o where o.ordcust is dangling;
```

Similarly we can find null REFS with a predicate IS NULL. This is not the same as IS DANGLING, since a dangling reference can have a value, just not the right one. Another way to find such abnormalities is to use the orders.cid column as we would to determine the appropriate ordcust value.

```
select o.cid from orders o where o.ordcust <>
    (select ref(c) from customers c where c.cid = o.cid);
```
∎

A dangling REF is non-null but useless. If o.ordcust is null or dangling, then o.ordcust.cname is null, as well as any other attribute of the nonexistent customers row referenced. Thus a bad reference is not as deadly as a bad pointer in C, for example, since we can dereference it without causing an addressing exception that aborts the containing program. However, it can be confusing to retrieve an unexpected null value.

An object type cannot recursively contain a component of the same type, but it can contain a REF to another object of the same type. Consider the following definition of a `police_officers` table, where every officer is assumed to have a partner.

EXAMPLE 4.2.15

Create a type for a police officer with a partner attribute represented by a REF to another police officer object. Create an object table for these police officers.

```
create type police_officer_t as object
(
    pol_person       person_t,
    badge_number     integer,
    partner          ref police_officer_t
);
create table police_officers of police_officer_t
(
    primary key (badge_number),
    scope for (partner) is police_officers
);
```

■

EXAMPLE 4.2.16

Retrieve the last names of all police officers who have partners over sixty years of age.

```
select p.pol_person.pname.lname from police_officers p
    where p.partner.pol_person.age > 60;
```

■

ORACLE provides a DEREF function to allow SQL syntax to retrieve the full object being referenced from a given REF. Here is a query to retrieve all the information on all police officers and their partners.

```
select value(p), deref(p.partner) from police_officers p;
```

The last attribute of `value(p)` in the query above is `partner`, a REF value, and it will print out as a hexadecimal number.

REF Dependencies

A set of tables can have a complicated set of relationships expressed in REFs. For example, employees have departments, and departments have managers who are employees. We can create a REF column in the `employees` table pointing to a `departments` row object, and a REF column in the `departments` table pointing to the `manager employee` in the `employees` table. Because there is a circular dependency involved (departments have REFs to employees and employees have REFs to departments), it sounds impossible to create the types, since each Create Type statement refers to the other type. However,

ORACLE supports a technique of incomplete type definitions. You can *partially create* the employee_t type with the following statement (written for input to SQL*Plus by adding / at the end instead of a semicolon):

```
create type employee_t
/                    -- note no semicolon used in partial create
```

Then you can fully create department_t with a REF to employee_t and finally create a complete type employee_t with a REF to department_t. When we try to drop a set of tables and types that reference one another like this, we need to drop the tables before we drop the types. But because the types have REFs to one another, we find if we try to drop either type, an error will be returned. To avoid this, instead of the simple

```
DROP TYPE typename;
```

we must use

```
DROP TYPE typename FORCE;
```

for all types involved in the REF cycle among multiple tables.

Loading Tables with REFs

Loading tables with REF columns needs special consideration. In the case of the orders table, the REF columns are determined completely by the foreign key cid, aid, or pid column values in orders, since these columns are primary keys in their own tables. We can start by using the same load procedure with the same data as in the relational case, covered in Appendix A. Since the REF columns in orders are the last ones defined, this will result in null values for the REFs. Then we can set all the references by one Update as follows.

EXAMPLE 4.2.17
Replace any current REF values in orders with the correct REFs to customers, agents, and products.

```
update orders o set
    ordcust = (select ref(c) from customers c where c.cid = o.cid),
    ordagent = (select ref(a) from agents a where a.aid = o.aid),
    ordprod = (select ref(p) from products p where p.pid = o.pid);
```

Here we are using a scalar Subquery to retrieve the REF values, a form allowed by **ORACLE** and our general form of the Update statement, shown in Figure 3.23. ∎

EXAMPLE 4.2.18
Insert a new police officer into the table of Example 4.2.15, chosen from the people table with ssno 033224445, providing a badge number 1000. The new officer's partner is another officer, already in police_officers, with badge number 990, so the partner of the new officer can be set immediately.

```
insert into police_officers
    select value(p), 1000, ref(p0) from people p, police_officers p0
        where p.ssno = 033224445 and p0.badge_number = 990;
update police_officers set p.partner = (select ref(p0) from police_officers p0
    where p0.badge_number = 1000) where badge_number = 990;
```

In the Insert statement above, we used a Subquery to pick up the right row object out of people and the right REF into police_officers. An Update statement is required to set the REF
value for the police officer with badge_number 990.   ∎

4.2.2   INFORMIX Row Types for Objects

INFORMIX *row types* correspond closely with the *object types* we have been dealing with
in **ORACLE**. **INFORMIX** row types are defined with the Create Row Type statement, as
shown in Example 4.2.19. Note that the component parts that are called *attributes* in
ORACLE are called *fields* in **INFORMIX**.

EXAMPLE 4.2.19

Create a row type name_t with two varchar(30) fields, lname and fname, and one char(1) field,
mi. This is analogous to Example 4.2.1 for **ORACLE**.

```
create row type name_t
    (
        lname       varchar(30),
        fname       varchar(30),
        mi          char(1)
    );
```
                                                                                          ∎

We will call row type instances *objects*, or *row objects*, because they so closely parallel **ORACLE** *row objects*, and also because they satisfy some of the commonly encountered characteristics of objects. For example, they provide a user-defined type that has an
internal component structure of values but works like a built-in type in many ways.
INFORMIX does not use the *objects* terminology, but instead refers to *rows* or *instances*
of row types.

As with **ORACLE**, the name_t row (object) type definition of Example 4.2.19 doesn't
create any *instances* of this type, with values for lname, fname, and mi filled in. For that
we need to define a table whose rows or columns can contain such instances, as in Example 4.2.21 below.

One row type can be used in the definition of a field in another row type. In Example
4.2.20 we define an **INFORMIX** row type person_t, describing a person with a name_t
field called pname, short for person-name, as well as other fields. Example 4.2.20 is an
analog of Example 4.2.3 for **ORACLE**.

EXAMPLE 4.2.20

Create a row type `person_t` to hold a person's Social Security number, name, and age, respectively. Drop the row type first to clear out any preexisting ones with this name.

```
drop row type person_t restrict;
create row type person_t
    (
        ssno      int,
        pname     name_t,
        age       int
    );
```

The keyword "option" RESTRICT is required in all **INFORMIX** Drop Row Type statements. While it seems strange to have only one option that is required in all Drop Row Type statements, this behavior is explained below.   ■

Since name_t is used in the definition of person_t, person_t is said to have a *dependency* on name_t. As with **ORACLE**, we cannot drop the name_t row type once person_t is in existence. To drop both, we need to drop them in the "referencer first" order: drop person_t and then name_t.[3] Information on interdependencies of types and tables can be displayed from the catalog tables maintained by the database system. See the last section of Chapter 7.

A table in **INFORMIX** is called a *typed table* if its rows are of a named row type. An **INFORMIX** typed table corresponds with an **ORACLE** object table. Example 4.2.21 creates a table with rows of type person_t, analogous to Example 4.2.4 for **ORACLE**.

EXAMPLE 4.2.21

Create a table called `people` of `person_t` objects, with the primary key being the Social Security number.

```
create table people of type person_t
(
        primary key (ssno)
);
```
                                                                               ■

In what follows we will refer to the CREATE TABLE table_name OF TYPE typename . . . statement form used in Example 4.2.21 as a *Create Typed Table* statement, and the older syntax to create a relational table with a list of column names (as in Figure 3.2) as the *Create Relational Table* statement. When we do not wish to differentiate, we will refer to the *Create Table* statement. See Figure 4.10 for the general forms to Create and Drop row

---

[3]In the SQL-99 standard, a second option in addition to RESTRICT, called CASCADE, is also specified, to delete a user-defined type and all types that have a dependency on it as well. One of the two options, RESTRICT or CASCADE, must be specified in all such Drop statements, but the RESTRICT option is part of the Core SQL-99 standard while CASCADE is not, so **INFORMIX** having only RESTRICT as an option is appropriate. **ORACLE** provides a nonstandard capability to not require RESTRICT and provides an option FORCE, which is not the same as CASCADE.

types and typed tables. In particular you should note that, unlike **ORACLE**, **INFORMIX** defines NOT NULL fields in the Create Type statement rather than in the Create Typed Table statements.

The top-level fields of a row type used to define a typed table will work like columns in the table, corresponding to the treatment of top-level attributes in **ORACLE** object tables. Thus in effect, the table people of Example 4.2.21 has columns for ssno, pname, and age, the same model as was depicted in Figure 4.2. The typed table can be viewed as a table with one column of row type objects, or as a table with a sequence of named columns, just as in **ORACLE**. Thus we can query the **INFORMIX** typed table using the top-level field names ssno, pname, and age. The following Select statements work in the expected way:

```
select age from people where ssno = 123550123;
select pname from people where age > 25;
```

or equivalently using qualified column references

```
select q.pname from people q where q.age > 25;
```

Note that it is not necessary to have a qualified alias in Select statements from **INFOR-MIX**, as it is in **ORACLE**. Here the name_t objects will be printed out in a format like row('Sanchez', 'Jose', 'F'), as we will soon cover in more detail. The special * form of the select list

```
select * from people where age > 25;
```

causes all the columns to be displayed. There is some difference in the display format of the pname column object in Figure 4.7 compared with **ORACLE** in Figure 4.3, specifically in the use of a row( ) constructor instead of a name_t( ) object constructor form.

To display "integral" row objects (rather than the set of columns in the row objects), we can use the table alias itself as the only element in the select list; see query below and display in Figure 4.8. (Recall that in **ORACLE** we needed to use VALUE(p) in the select list of Example 4.2.5.)

```
select p from people p where age > 25;
```

Objects of row type can be constructed by the *row constructor* ROW( ), and then must be *cast* to have the appropriate row type. See Figure 4.9 for syntax of the cast

ssno	pname	age
245882134	row('Delaney', 'Patrick','X')	59
023894455	row('Sanchez', 'Jose','F',)	30

Figure 4.7 Output from **INFORMIX** SELECT * Query, Displaying All the Columns

194

```
p

row(245882134,row('Delaney', 'Patrick','X'),59)
row(023894455,row('Sanchez', 'Jose','F'),30)
```

Figure 4.8   Output from **INFORMIX** SELECT table_alias Query, Displaying Full Row Objects

```
ROW(expression {, expression...}).
CAST(ROW(expression {, expression...}) AS rowtype)
```

Figure 4.9   General Forms for **INFORMIX** Constructors of Untyped and Typed Row Objects

expression CAST(. . .), with its special use in this case. (Recall that in **ORACLE** we used object constructors such as name_t(...) and person_t(...) for this purpose, in Examples 4.2.5 and 4.2.8.)

```
cast(row('Delaney', 'Patrick','X') as name_t)
cast(row(023894455,cast(row('Sanchez', 'Jose','F') as name_t),30) as person_t)
```

EXAMPLE 4.2.22
Display the full person_t object for Jose Sanchez, using a name_t object for his name.

```
select p from people p
    where p.pname = cast(row('Sanchez', 'Jose','F') as name_t);
```

There is also an **INFORMIX** shortcut form for casting, row_expression::typename, of a ROW() function expression to the proper named type. Thus we could write the prior Select statement as

```
select p from people p
    where p.pname = row('Sanchez', 'Jose','F')::name_t;
```
■

Dot notation can be used to access fields within fields, nearly as it is used in **ORACLE** to access attributes within attributes. The only difference is that we are not required to use a table qualifier in these expressions as we are in **ORACLE**; if there is only one table in a Select statement, we have the choice of column.field or alias.column.field or even table.column.field to access a field within a column.

EXAMPLE 4.2.23
Find the names and ages of all people whose first names start with "Pat" and are over 50 years of age.

```
select pname, age from people
    where pname.fname like 'Pat%' and age > 50;
```

Here pname is the top-level field of the row object, and pname.fname is the fname field of pname. Note that this form would not work in **ORACLE** because there is no table alias (see Example 4.2.6). ■

Inserts and Updates can use row constructors. As with **ORACLE**, null is allowed for objects, since nulls are full-fledged data item values.

EXAMPLE 4.2.24

Insert a row object for Albert Einstein into table `people`, with Social Security number 123441998 and age 100. Then insert a row with a meaningful `ssno` but null pname and null age.

```
insert into people values (123441998, cast(row('Einstein', 'Albert', 'E') as name_t), 100)
insert into people values (321341223, null, null);
(or equivalently)
insert into people (ssno) values (321341223);
```

Replace the null name in the last inserted row with 'Ben Gould'.

```
update people set pname = cast(row('Gould', 'Ben', cast(null as char(1))) as name_t) where
ssno = 321341224;
```

Replace the null middle initial with 'C', keeping the rest of the name as already specified.

```
update people set pname = cast(row(pname.lname, pname.fname, 'C') as name_t)
    where ssno = 321341224;
```

Here the row constructor ROW( ) is building a row from non-constant expressions, `pname.lname` and `pname.fname`. Now create a table `scientists` of row type `name_t` and insert the names from `people` into it.

```
create table scientists of type name_t;
insert into scientists
    select pname.fname, pname.mi, pname.lname from people;
```                                                                              ∎

In Figure 4.10, we provide the general forms to create and drop row types and typed tables.

Figure 4.10 provides the general form for the Create Typed Table statement. (The Create Relational Table statement form is given in Figure 3.2. Since row types are full-fledged types, we can also create relational tables with columns of row type.) In a typed table, all the columns are based on fields defined in the Create Type statement, along with NOT NULL specifications if appropriate, leaving only the optional PRIMARY KEY specification for inclusion inside the parentheses of the Create Typed Table statement. Recall that **ORACLE** put the NOT NULL specifications in the Create Object Table statement rather than in Create Type. The Drop Table specification is unexceptional, but the Drop Row Type requires a RESTRICT clause at the end.

```
CREATE ROW TYPE rowtype
    (fieldname datatype [NOT NULL]{, fieldname datatype [NOT NULL] ...});
DROP ROW TYPE rowtype RESTRICT;
CREATE TABLE tablename OF TYPE rowtype
    ( [ PRIMARY KEY (column {,column ...})]);
DROP TABLE tablename;
```

Figure 4.10 INFORMIX General Forms to Create and Drop Row Types and Typed Tables

Absence of REFs in INFORMIX

An important variation from **ORACLE** in the current release of **INFORMIX** is the lack of REFs. It is expected that REFs will be added to **INFORMIX** in a future release, possibly by the time you read this text.

Type Inheritance in INFORMIX

INFORMIX also has a capability that is missing in **ORACLE**, known as *type inheritance* in a *hierarchy* of types. We need to define the idea of a *hierarchy* in terms of creating a new employee row type as a subtype of the person type, where the subtype inherits the data items and methods of the supertype and adds some of its own. Recall the definition of the person_t type:

```
create row type person_t
    (
        ssno        int,
        pname       name_t,
        age         int
    );
```

We can define a subtype of person_t, named employee_t, as follows:

```
create type employee_t
    (
        eid         int,
        salary      double precision,
        mgrid       int
    )
    under person_t;        -- says employee_t is subtype of person_t
```

The top-level fields of the employee_t type will now consist of a *union* of fields named in the type and subtype definitions: eid, salary, mgrid, ssno, pname, and age. And now a new type called manager_t can be defined as a subtype of employee_t.

```
create type manager_t
    (
        budget      double precision,
        groupname   varchar(30)    -- name of group managed
    )
    under employee_t;
```

Objects of type manager_t inherit all fields defined for employee_t. Now we can create a typed table containing objects of a subtype such as manager_t directly.

```
create table managers of type manager_t;
```

But to achieve some of the behavior that accompanies inheritance, we need to start with a table of the highest-level type and define subtables:

```
create table people of type person_t;

create table employees of type employee_t
    under people;                       -- employees table is subtable of people

create table managers of type manager_t
    under employees;                    -- managers table is subtable of employees
```

Now an important aspect of SQL behavior that comes with table inheritance is this: when a row is inserted into the managers table, it automatically becomes a row in the employees table as well. Thus the query

```
select pname.fname, pname.lname, eid from employees
    where salary > 50000;
```

will retrieve not only information from qualified employees that have been inserted in the employees table, *but also qualified employees that have been inserted in the* managers *table*. At the same time, the managers table is still a distinct entity, so if we write

```
select pname.fname, pname.lname, eid from managers
    where salary > 50000;
```

we will retrieve only qualified rows that have been inserted in managers. Finally, if we wanted to retrieve only non-managerial employees in the query above, we would rewrite the select statement as

```
select pname.fname, pname.lname, eid from only (employees)
    where salary > 50000;
```

This behavior marks the difference between creating a stand-alone managers table of type manager_t, and creating it as a subtable of the employees table.

4.2.3   Objects and Tables: Summary

We have seen how to create object (row) types, and tables containing objects of those types, either as rows or column values, in two major products. Aside from some keyword and terminology differences, they are very much alike.

Similarities between ORACLE and INFORMIX Objects

Both products

◆ allow the programmer to build a *composite* object (row) type out of database types;

◆ allow the user to provide a new object datatype for general use, for example, datatypes used in columns for otherwise ordinary tables;

◆ allow objects to be nested within objects;

◆ access attributes (fields) using dot notation in queries, and allow multiple nesting;

◆ allow an object to fill a whole row of a table, and in this case allow the top-level attributes to work as columns for the table;

◆ do not support encapsulation of object data (i.e., data is not hidden from external view; see explanation in the subsection below, "Object Orientation").

Differences between ORACLE and INFORMIX Objects

◆ **ORACLE** provides the capability to use REFs, while **INFORMIX** does not yet do so.

◆ **INFORMIX** provides type hierarchies and inheritance, while **ORACLE** does not yet do so.

Object Orientation

One of the major motivations for bringing the object model into database type systems was a desire to support some of the concepts of object-oriented programming languages (such as Java and C++). In 1989, a paper entitled "The Object-Oriented Database System Manifesto," written by six highly respected practitioners in the field, attempted to prioritize features in the object-oriented database system (OODBS) model. (See "Suggestions for Further Reading" at the end of this chapter: [1], Chapter 1). The Manifesto listed 13 mandatory features, or "Golden Rules" for an OODBS, and the object-relational system has adopted some of these features and avoided others. Here we present a selection of features relevant to ORDBMS.

In object-oriented terminology, *objects* combine the concepts of data structures and functions (known as *user-defined functions* in ORSQL) that can act on that data. The user-defined functions involving an object are also called *methods* of the object if they are an implicit part of the object's definition. In object-oriented terminology, an object is said to *encapsulate* data and methods if the user (or programmer) normally cannot access data within the object *except through the methods provided*. However, ORSQL objects do not support true encapsulation, since methods are just one way to access the data: direct SQL query and update access to the data is also allowed. (It can be argued that encapsulation that does not support arbitrary SQL access defeats the purpose of a database query language.)

Objects with a specific structure and set of methods are said to belong to an object *class* in OODBS (objects belong to a class just as data variables in programming languages are declared to be of a given *type*). The ORDBMS community prefers to use the word *type* for its objects, rather than the OODBS term *class*.

Finally, the OODBS model allows new classes to be created that extend the description of a previous class, what we have referred to as *type hierarchy,* and any such new *subtype* is said to *inherit* the data items and methods of the type on which it is defined.

Object-Oriented Feature	**ORACLE** Object Types	**INFORMIX** Row Types	SQL-99 User-Defined Types (UDTs, not Core)
Encapsulation	No	No	No
User-defined functions	Yes, including methods	Yes	Yes, including methods
Object references	Yes	Planned	Yes
Inheritance	No	Yes	Yes

As we have seen, **INFORMIX** allows row types to be created within inheritance hierarchies. A manager is an employee with extra information attached, and the row type definition for a manager_t type needs only the explicit listing of the extra fields, plus the phrase under employee_t. Object references, or REFs, are not available in **INFORMIX** version 9.2, but are scheduled for version 9.3.

ORACLE allows method functions to be defined for object types, as we will explain in Section 4.4. **INFORMIX** has user-defined functions that are not bound to individual objects or object hierarchies, but can work like methods. **ORACLE** allows a row object to be pointed to by a REF (object reference, another datatype) from another object attribute or table column.

The new SQL-99 standard has *user-defined types* (or *UDTs*) that are similar to **ORACLE** object types and **INFORMIX** row types. However, they are not part of the basic Core of the standard. The UDTs have methods and references like **ORACLE** and inheritance like **INFORMIX**, and like both products, no encapsulation. The lack of encapsulation probably kept the standards body from calling them *objects,* and they ended up with the neutral and colorless name *user-defined types*.

While **ORACLE** doesn't support inheritance of objects and **INFORMIX** version 9.2 doesn't support object methods, neither of these is a huge handicap for normal use.

4.3 Collection Types

Collection types allow us to put multiple values (*collections* of values) in a column of an individual row, thus circumventing Relational RULE 1, which disallows multi-valued attributes. For example, collection types allow us to represent the set of dependents for an employee in one column of an EMPLOYEES table, as illustrated in Figure 4.11 (duplicating Figure 2.3 of Chapter 2).

EMPLOYEES

eid	ename	position	dependents
e001	Smith, John	Agent	Michael J. Susan R.
e002	Andrews, David	Superintendent	David M. Jr.
e003	Jones, Franklin	Agent	Andrew K. Mark W. Louisa M.

Figure 4.11   An EMPLOYEES Table with a Multi-Valued dependents Attribute

It turns out that the treatment of collection types in the different database products we deal with is not yet fully standardized. We will cover **ORACLE**'s nested tables and arrays in Section 4.3.1 and **INFORMIX**'s sets, lists, and multisets in Section 4.3.2, then conclude with a general discussion in Section 4.3.3.

4.3.1   Collection Types in **ORACLE**

There are two collection types in **ORACLE**: *table types* and *array types*. Each collection type describes collections containing items all of the same type, the *element type*. An element type can be any built-in or object type, but an element type in **ORACLE** cannot be a collection type. The collection types are full-fledged datatypes in the system and, with appropriate conversions, can be interpreted as tables in queries. We will cover table types first, then array types. This coverage assumes **ORACLE** 8.1.5 or later. **ORACLE** 8.0 has collection type support, but large syntax changes occurred from 8.0 to 8.1.5, so some queries shown here will not work in 8.0.

Table Types and Nested Tables

We define a *table type* that can be used to implement a multi-valued attribute.

EXAMPLE 4.3.1
Create a table type called dependents_t to hold tables of person_t objects.

```
create type dependents_t as table of person_t;
```

Now we can create a relational table employees with columns for eid, eperson, and dependents, the last of which can take on multiple values. We make eid the primary key.

```
create table employees
(
    eid             int,
    eperson         person_t,
    dependents      dependents_t,
    primary key     (eid)
)   nested table  dependents store as dependents_tab;
```

Note that by first creating a type employee_t with the appropriate columns, we could create an object version of the employees table.

■

The Create Table statement of Example 4.3.1 creates a standard relational table, except that it has a table type column dependents, and a NESTED TABLE clause, with the form

```
NESTED TABLE colname STORE AS tablename
```

The capitalized words, as usual, are required keywords. In Example 4.3.1, this clause specifies a tablename, dependents_tab, to contain multiple person_t objects that can occur in the dependents column of employees. Thus two database tables will be created by this one Create Table statement, table employees as the top-level table and table dependents_tab for the dependents table data, containing all the dependent person_t objects for all the employees. Figure 4.12 illustrates an employees table of Example 4.3.1 with two employees rows, one employee with two dependents and the other with just one.

We see that the two dependents of employee 101 can be said to conceptually constitute a small object table, as does the single dependent of employee 102, although in fact all dependents objects lie in the single dependents_tab table. Nevertheless, the conceptual tables occurring as column values in each individual row of employees are called *nested tables*.

Figure 4.13 displays the syntax for the Create Relational Table statement with a NESTED TABLE clause in Example 4.3.1. We have only seen an example of a relational table with one nested table column so far, but it is easy to construct tables with several nested table columns, and in that case, we need one NESTED TABLE clause for each such column.

We note that the Create Object Table forms of Figure 4.6 can be extended in the same way as in Figure 4.13, adding NESTED TABLE clauses, one for each table type attribute (the attribute having a TABLE OF clause) at some level of nesting within the table's object type. For example, in Example 4.3.1 we could define an employees_t type with an attribute dependents of type dependents_t, then define an object table employees of type employees_t. While a table type cannot contain a table type attribute in

employees

eid	eperson	dependents
101	person_t(123897766,name_t('Smith', 'John', 'P'),45)	person_t(322456776,name_t('Smith', 'Michael',' 'J'),8)
		person_t(123822332,name_t('Smith', 'Susan','R'),12)
102	person_t(432112233,name_t('Andrews', 'David', 'S'),32)	person_t(565534555,name_t('Shaw', 'David','M'),3)

Figure 4.12 ORACLE employees Table with Column dependents of Nested Table Type

```
CREATE TABLE tablename (columnname datatype [NOT NULL]
        {, columnname datatype [NOT NULL]...}
        [, PRIMARY KEY (columnname {, columnname...})])]
    [NESTED TABLE columnname STORE AS tablename
        {, NESTED TABLE columnname STORE AS tablename...}];
```

Figure 4.13   Create Relational Table Syntax with Nested Table Storage Specification(s) in **ORACLE**

ORACLE, it is perfectly all right for multiple levels of normal object type nesting to ultimately contain a table type attribute. Thus, for example, we could create an object type workhistory_t that contained attributes for a person's current company name and employee information (in an attribute of type employees_t); then we could create an object table named workhists of type workhistory_t, using a NESTED TABLE clause for the dependents_t attribute that appears at a second level of nesting.

ORACLE nested tables can be queried interactively, but there are limitations. We have already seen that nested tables are held in their own database tables (what we will refer to as *child* tables), existing separately from the table in which they are nested (their *parent* table). But the data of a child table can only be accessed via the parent table. After the Create Table of Example 4.3.1, a Select statement with dependents_tab in the FROM clause will fail, with an error message indicating that the user must access the parent table.

We provide some examples of accessing nested tables.

EXAMPLE 4.3.2
Retrieve the nested table of all dependents of employee 101.

```
select dependents from employees where eid = 101;
```

This displays one line for the employee, with dependents listed as one *scalar* nested table value, as shown in Figure 4.14. We did not use a qualifier in this query, providing an alias e for employees and then writing e.dependents, although we could have. Qualifiers are only required for object attribute references, and dependents is (surprisingly) a non-object column of a relational (non-object) table. Note too that the scalar nested table value retrieved *represents* a table containing two different rows—but is *not itself* a table containing two rows. As we will see, this limitation has important implications.

```
dependents(ssno,pname(fname,minitial,lname),age)
----------------------------------------------------------------------------------
dependents_t(person_t(322456776,name_t('Smith','Michael','J'), 8), person_t(123822332,
name_t('Smith', 'Susan', 'R'), 12))
```

Figure 4.14   ORACLE Output of Two Dependents, from Example 4.3.2

■

In Figure 4.14, note the similarity of the nested table output format to the object-type display format of Figure 4.3, that is, type name, followed by a parenthesized list of the component parts.

EXAMPLE 4.3.3

Retrieve the nested tables of all `dependents` of all `employees`.

```
select dependents from employees;
```

This displays one line for each employee, with the `dependents` listed as one scalar nested table value in the format shown in Figure 4.14. ∎

EXAMPLE 4.3.4

Retrieve the `eids` of `employees` with more than six dependents.

```
select eid from employees e
    where 6 < (select count(*) from table(e.dependents));
```

This is the first time we have seen a nested table column in a FROM clause, and we note that we must cast the scalar nested table column value `e.dependents` as a table, using the new `TABLE( )` form, in order to perform a Select statement on it. Without such conversion, the `e.dependents` scalar value retrieved will not give a table of `person_t` objects that can be queried. We are not required to put the Subquery on the right-hand side of the comparison predicate here: **ORACLE** supports the Advanced SQL comparison predicate that allows a Subquery on either side. ∎

To find an `employees` row with a certain set of dependents, we might try a query of the form

```
select eid from employees e where e.dependents = . . .
```

using some form of set constructor on the right to specify the set desired. But it turns out that **ORACLE** *does not support equal match predicates between nested tables*, as it does between built-in types or simple objects of the same object type. In what follows, we define a *simple object* as one that does not have a collection type object at any level of nesting within its attributes.

To find an employee with one specific dependent, the IN predicate can be used.

EXAMPLE 4.3.5

List `eids` of `employees` (there should be only one) with a dependent having Social Security number 3451112222.

```
select eid from employees e
    where 3451112222 in
        (select d.ssno from table(e.dependents) d);
```

Since **ORACLE** supports equality match on simple objects, we can also retrieve `eids` with dependents that have name given by `name_t('Lukas', 'David', 'E')`.

```
FROM TABLE(collection_expr)
```

Figure 4.15   ORACLE TABLE( ) Form

```
select eid from employees e
        where name_t('Lukas', 'David', 'E') in
            (select d.pname from table(e.dependents) d);                    ■
```

Again we have used the TABLE( ) form in the FROM clauses of Subqueries of Example 4.3.5. The syntax of the TABLE( ) form is given in Figure 4.15.

Note that the syntax of Figure 4.15 requires a specific row on which a column collection value can be specified. Therefore the TABLE( ) form cannot be used to provide the only table in the FROM clause of the *outermost Select statement*, since we cannot determine a specific row for TABLE( ) to act on in that situation:

```
select ssno from table(employees.dependents); -- Invalid: employees row undetermined
```

Another way we might want to bring a nested table into a query is given in Example 4.3.6.

EXAMPLE 4.3.6
Retrieve the number of dependents of employee 101. The following might seem like a reasonable approach:

```
select count(*) from
    (select e.dependents from employees e where e.eid = 101); -- ** UNEXPECTED RESULT
```

Unfortunately, the Subquery here retrieves a scalar nested table value, e.dependents, rather than a table with person_t objects for each dependent, so the result of the count will be one (or zero if there is a null e.dependents value for the desired employee). To fix this, we need to convert the e.dependents value into a table, but we cannot do this with the TABLE( ) form in the select list, changing the Subquery to

```
    (select table(e.dependents) from employees e where e.eid = 101); -- ** BAD SYNTAX
```

since the Subquery's job is to deliver scalar values for individual rows, not whole tables. To fix this, we need to convert the e.dependents value into a table *after* it has been delivered by the Subquery, and this can be done with TABLE( ) form as follows:

```
select count(*) from
    table (select e.dependents from employees e where e.eid = 101);
```

With this syntax, we obtain the actual number of dependents for this single employee. First, the Subquery selects the employee with eid equal to 101 and retrieves the e.dependents as a scalar nested table value; then TABLE( ) turns that value into a set of rows of person_t objects, and COUNT(*) in the outer Select counts these rows.   ■

In general, the TABLE keyword can be thought of as removing the "collection container" from a nested table value resulting from a Subquery or collection expression value, revealing all the table rows within it. The action of dissolving the collection value of the Subquery into its contents is called *unnesting* the collection.

In Example 4.3.6, we might have been tempted to try a different approach:

```
select count(e.dependents) from employees e where e.eid = 101;
```

Here we would hope to get COUNT( ) to count the dependents for this row. But once again the e.dependents expression in the Select statement represents a single nested table value for the row, so we would just be counting zero or one, the null or non-null scalar value e.dependents selected from the appropriate row of the employees table. But in fact for this query **ORACLE** will return an error, "inconsistent datatypes," since there is a rule that COUNT( ) cannot take a collection-valued argument. This is a good rule, as it avoids confusion. But as we shall see in the next subsection, **INFORMIX** gives us a new form to take the place of COUNT( ) in this case, known as CARDINALITY( ), and this form can be quite useful.

EXAMPLE 4.3.7

Instead of counting the dependents of the employee with eid 101 as we did in Example 4.3.6, we could display all their Social Security numbers, from that same nested table of dependents, as follows:

```
select d.ssno from
    table(select e.dependents from employees e where e.eid = 101) d;
```

Here, as in Example 4.3.6, the Subquery selects the dependents nested table for employee 101, and then the TABLE( ) operator unnests it into a table of person_t objects. In this case, the table is given the alias d, for dependents, and d.ssno in the select list selects the table's ssno column for display. ∎

Two Techniques for Retrieving from a Table of Tables

It turns out that trying to retrieve ssno column values from *all* the dependents of *all* employees is not a simple problem. We need to select from multiple nested tables, one for each employee, and report on all their rows at once, rather than retrieving just the rows of one nested table as we have been doing. We end up needing to retrieve ssno column values from a *table of tables*, because each nested table is no longer one collection value but has been turned into a table of person_t row objects. In Example 4.3.3, we managed to retrieve *all* the data in the dependents columns, as *scalar values*, but it is more difficult to treat the dependents values as tables in their own right.

To address this problem of handling tables within tables, **ORACLE** designers have come up with two different mechanisms: the *table product* of the two levels of tables and the *nested cursors* facility.

Unnesting via Table Products

The table product of employees and their dependents can be used as follows to unnest the dependents and produce a display of all employee identifiers and their dependents' ssno values:

```
select e.eid, d.ssno from employees e, table(e.dependents) d;
```

This would display a table with two columns, eid and ssno, and one row for each (eid, ssno) combination. The employees with no dependents would not show up in this result. To see a row for an employee with no dependents, with a null ssno, add a (+) to the dependents side, as follows.

```
select e.eid, d.ssno from employees e, table(e.dependents) (+) d;
```

This (+) notation derives from similar notation for **ORACLE**'s outer join, presented at the end of Section 3.6. In both cases, the (+) marks the side where nulls will be filled in to preserve rows of the *other* table.

Recall the general model of query execution from the beginning of Section 3.9 and summarized in Figure 3.15. First the relational product of the FROM tables is formed. For the table product above involving table(e.dependents), we have a modified relational product operation. The normal relational product matches each row in the first table with each row in the second table. In the table product involving unnesting, each row in the first table is matched with each row of *its own* collection column value (converted to a table.)

Specifically, here we have a table employees with a typical row x (say) and table alias e. Row x has a collection column named dependents with a typical row y and table alias d. This relational product step produces a table of rows of the form x||y for all x and y, that is, a typical result row is an employee row filled out by one of its dependents rows. Each such composite row retains knowledge of its particular employee (x row, symbolized by the current value of e) and particular dependent of that employee (y row, symbolized by the current value of d.) Thus we may use e.colname for any column of employees and d.colname for any column of the dependents table without ambiguity in the query. The following execution steps (WHERE clause processing, etc.) proceed based on these unambiguous values. In particular, e.dependents, the collection column value itself, has a clear meaning and can be the subject of TABLE( ) wherever we need to further query the set of dependents for a particular employee, as we will see in Example 4.3.9.

Nested Cursors

The other way of displaying the tables of tables is by use of *nested cursors*. A *cursor* is like a loop control variable that moves through a set of rows as the query executes. The top-level Select standardly provides a cursor-like loop over its FROM tables to generate the rows to retrieve. The nested cursor syntax, CURSOR( ), then allows us to add a second loop (or more loops if there is multiple nesting) to scan the nested tables within each row as they are encountered in the outer Select loop. Here is an example.

EXAMPLE 4.3.8

Display all eid values of rows in the employees table, and for each eid the Social Security numbers of any dependents of that employee under 16 years of age.

Since we need to display multiple rows from multiple nested tables, we need to use unnesting by table products or the CURSOR form. We first show the query that uses table products to do the unnesting of the dependents:

```
select e.eid, d.ssno as dep_sso from employees e, table(e.dependents) d
    where d.age < 16;
```

The output for this query is shown in Figure 4.16.

Secondly, we retrieve the same information using a nested cursor:

```
select e.eid, cursor(select d.ssno as dep_ssno
        from table(e.dependents) d where d.age < 16) dep_tab
    from employees e;
```

Here the SELECT sets up a loop over the employees table, and the CURSOR sets up a secondary loop over the nested table of dependents of each employees row retrieved. Figure 4.17 shows the display for the employees table pictured in Figure 4.12: the outer loop finds eid 101, and then the inner loop finds two ssnos for that employee row, and then the outer loop finds eid 102, and its inner loop finds one ssno.

```
       EID        DEP_SSNO
-------------- ----------------
       101       322456776
       101       123822332
       102       565534555
```

Figure 4.16   ORACLE SQL*Plus Output for a Table Product Query, for Example 4.3.8

```
         EID DEP_TAB
-------------- --------------------
        101 CURSOR STATEMENT : 2
CURSOR STATEMENT : 2
    DEP_SSNO
--------------
  322456776
  123822332
        102 CURSOR STATEMENT : 2
CURSOR STATEMENT : 2
    DEP_SSNO
--------------
  565534555
```

Figure 4.17   ORACLE SQL*Plus Output for a Nested Cursor Query, for Example 4.3.8

```
cursor_expression ::= cursor(Subquery)
```

Figure 4.18   ORACLE General Form for the CURSOR( ) Expression

Note that the display of Figure 4.17 is not in relational form, because it contains lines of two different formats, with accompanying headings. The nested cursor causes a scan through the nested table while the outer Select scans the parent table. First the outer scan displays EID and under it 101, then DEP_TAB is an alias for the cursor expression (CURSOR STATEMENT : 2) under which the elements of the inner CURSOR( ) scan outputs a table labeled dep_ssno (the column alias created in the query) and the two ssno values for dependents of eid 101. Column aliases such as dep_ssno are important for readability in nested cursor retrievals. Once this has been done, the outer scan displays another eid, 102, and another dep_ssno table, this time with only one dependent ssno.

The general form of the CURSOR( ) expression is given in Figure 4.18. The Subquery may return either a single nested table column value as in Example 4.3.8, or a normal relational set of rows. Both of these types of Subqueries can be used with CURSOR( ), and in the case of the relational set of rows, CURSOR( ) will move through all the rows of the Subquery.

In Figure 4.18, the CURSOR( ) is classified as an expression, but it is usable only in a top-level select list, that is, as one of the expressions in the following form:

```
select expression, expression, .... from ... ;
```

Additionally, a second CURSOR( ) can be used *inside another one* if there is a nested table or rowset encountered within the scan of the outer CURSOR( ). We see that CURSOR is a novel facility, one that produces table-of-table data that can be very useful for display in queries acting on nested tables.

Note that until now all Select statements retrieved data in relational form, that is, each displayed row has had the same pattern of datatypes (e.g., two strings and then a number). Even the results of collection queries in this section, prior to the introduction of CURSOR( ), were pure tables once we allowed collection-object values as acceptable values for table cells. But the CURSOR( ) results are not in relational form because some displayed rows describe the progress of the outer loop and others the progress of the inner loop, with different numbers and types of data values in each case.

On the other hand, the table product query retrieves data in relational table form, as shown in Figure 4.16. If you don't mind having multiple rows for a single employee, the report is simpler and certainly better looking.

EXAMPLE 4.3.9

List names and eids of employees along with the first name of the oldest dependent (if one exists).

```
select eid, cursor(select d1.pname.fname from table(employees.dependents) d1
    where d1.age = (select max(d2.age) from table(employees.dependents) d2))
    from employees;
```

Note that the syntax of TABLE( ) given in Figure 4.15 and the discussion following it implies that a clause such as

```
select fname from table(employees.dependents) d1
```

can be problematical, because TABLE( ) must take as an argument a single nested table column value, and `employees.dependents` in an outer Select clause has no restriction to a single row. However, in the current case, `employees.dependents` falls inside a Subquery in a CURSOR( ) expression, and refers back to the `employees` qualifier of the outer Select loop, which is always stabilized on a single row of `employees` before the CURSOR( ) begins looking at a nested table of the row.

To do this without a nested cursor, we use the TABLE( ) form twice, once to form a table product and another time to form a table over which we can compute the maximum dependent age for a certain employee.

```
select eid, d.pname.fname from employees e, table(e.dependents) d1
    where d1.age = (select max(d2.age) from table(e.dependents) d2);
```
∎

EXAMPLE 4.3.10

In Example 4.3.6, we counted the dependents for a certain employee. We can also retrieve a multi-row answer where we count the number of dependents individually belonging to each employee:

```
select eid, cursor(select count(*) from table(e.dependents))
    from employees e;
```

The nested cursor runs through the nested table for each `employee` row of the outer Select, and it counts the number of rows in the `dependents` table. The inner tables (like the ones for `dep_ssno` in Figure 4.17) are absent in the output, since there is no data to display for *each* dependent.

Alternatively, we can drop the CURSOR( ) here and use the resulting scalar Subquery in the select list, an Advanced SQL feature:

```
select eid, (select count(*) from table(e.dependents))
    from employees e;
```

Finally, we can unnest with a table product:

```
select eid, count(*) from employees e, table(e.dependents)
    group by eid;
```
∎

Example 4.3.10 shows various ways to query for the number of dependents for each employee. To count all the dependents regardless of employee, we must use the table product to do the unnesting because it is the only form that gives us a seamless set of rows across employees. We write

```
select count(*) from employees e, table(e.dependents);
```

Array Types for VARRAYs

The second collection type for **ORACLE** is the array type, declared as *VARRAY*, standing for "varying-length array." Each array type declaration has a name, an element type, and a maximum number of elements the VARRAY object can contain. (The size of a VARRAY object will not be proportional to the maximum but to the *actual* number of elements contained, just as with a varchar string type.) Unlike the nested table type, elements of VARRAY type are held in a specific order.

> **EXAMPLE 4.3.11**
> Set up a simple phone book in a table: each person has a VARRAY of up to four integer phone extensions. The first number is the extension callers should try first, followed by the second extension, and so on. Since phone extensions after the first might belong to co-workers, order is important so that co-workers will not be bothered unnecessarily.
>
> ```
> create type extensions_t as varray(4) of int;
> create table phonebook
> (
>     phperson    person_t,
>     extensions  extensions_t
> );
> ```
> ∎

Unlike nested tables, VARRAY data is normally held directly in the containing row of the table. Because of this, no special storage clause is needed in this Create Table statement, as was required with nested tables in Example 4.3.1. For special purposes, VARRAY data can be held externally, but we will not cover this case. Also note we don't have a primary key clause here, so it could be possible to have two rows for the same person in this table. Or we could create a primary key based on the ssno attribute of the phperson column, by adding the following line to the Create Table statement:

```
primary key (phperson.ssno)
```

Figure 4.19 depicts a small phonebook table with two extensions for John Smith and one for David Andrews.

phonebook

phperson	extensions
person_t(123897766, name_t('Smith', 'John', 'P'), 45)	extensions_t(345, 989)
person_t(432112233, name_t('Andrews', 'David', 'S'), 32)	extensions_t(123)

Figure 4.19 The phonebook Table with **ORACLE** VARRAY Column extensions of Integers

EXAMPLE 4.3.12

Retrieve the first name and VARRAY of extensions for the person with Social Security number 123897766.

```
select pb.phperson.pname.fname, pb.extensions from phonebook pb
    where pb.phperson.ssno = 123897766;
```

This displays one line for each person, with the extensions listed as below as a scalar VARRAY value. The result is shown in Figure 4.20.

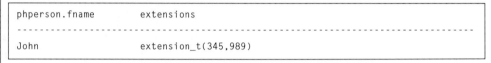

phperson.fname	extensions
John	extension_t(345,989)

Figure 4.20 **ORACLE** Output of VARRAY Column Value for Query of Example 4.3.12

■

Note that there is actually no way in SQL to access a subscripted element of a VARRAY declared object, such as by writing pb.extensions[1] in the select list of Example 4.3.12. (You can CAST a VARRAY as a nested table and access individual rows, but the relative order of rows isn't guaranteed.) We can't access the *first* extension, or any other numbered subscript extension, except by displaying the entire collection value and asking the reader to count from left to right. When we consider programming language interfaces to SQL in Chapter 5, a VARRAY that is retrieved from a row will be mapped into a programming language array, and only then will it be possible to access elements of a VARRAY by subscript.

In a query, the TABLE( ) form may be applied to a VARRAY value just as it was to a nested table.

EXAMPLE 4.3.13

Find the number of extensions the person with Social Security number 123440011 has in the phonebook table

```
select (select count(*) from table(pb.extensions)) from phonebook pb
    where pb.phperson.ssno = 123440011;
```

or, using a table product

```
select count(*) from phonebook pb, table(pb.extensions)
    where pb.phperson.ssno = 123440011;
```

■

EXAMPLE 4.3.14

List the people in the phonebook table who have extension 104.

```
select phperson from phonebook pb
    where 104 in (select * from table(pb.extensions));
```

■

```
collection_cast_expression :: =
    CAST(collection_valued_expr AS collection_type)
    |CAST((collection_valued_subquery) AS collection_type)
    |CAST(MULTISET(rowset_valued_subquery) AS collection_type)
```

Figure 4.21   ORACLE General Form of CAST Expression Collection Types

Sometimes we need to CAST from one collection type to another or from a set of rows to a collection value. For example, we could have a nested table of person_t as a column value and use it to update a column of type VARRAY of person_t. Or we could use relational data from a Subquery to fill in for a collection value. Figure 4.21 gives the general form of the CAST expression for collection types. The collection_type form below must always be replaced by either a nested table type (such as dependents_t) or a VARRAY type (such as extensions_t). The CAST expression allows expressions or Subqueries with values that are nested tables or VARRAYs to be cast to other nested table or VARRAY type values. This is particularly useful in performing a CAST from a VARRAY type to a nested table type, or vice versa.

Note that the MULTISET( ) form in the last line of Figure 4.21 is used to contain a Subquery returning a set of rows that we wish to CAST as a VARRAY or nested table. A set of rows returned by a traditional relational query will be called a *rowset* in what follows, since *multiset* has a different meaning in **INFORMIX**.

As an example of MULTISET, we can redo Example 4.3.8 by collecting together all the dependent ssnos into a collection type:

```
create type ssno_set as table of int;
select e.eid, cast(multiset(select d.ssno from table(e.dependents) d
        where d.age < 16) as ssno_set) as dep_ssno
            from employees e;
```

This query will output one row per employee with eid and an ssno_set( ) nested table value. We see that MULTISET( ) is the opposite of TABLE( ). TABLE unnests collection values into rowsets. MULTISET nests rowsets into collection values. The above query unnests the dependents, picks out the ssno values, and nests them back into a collection value.

SQL Syntax for Collections in ORACLE

The problem facing RDBMS vendors and SQL standards bodies who wish to include collection types into ORDBMS SQL syntax is trickier than it might seem at first. The goal is to be able to query the contents of nested tables with a natural extension of relational query syntax. Clearly the tableref syntax, the clause that follows the FROM in the FROM clause, as shown with SQL-99 extensions in Figure 3.11, is one place to generalize syntax to include nested tables, which is exactly what **ORACLE** did.

```
tableref::=    {tablename | (rowset_valued_subquery)
               | TABLE (collection_expr)}       -- collection-valued subquery, etc.
               [corr_name]                      -- "AS" keyword not allowed in ORACLE
```

Figure 4.22 ORACLE Syntax for `tableref` Subquery Forms (Compare with Figure 3.11)

The new `tableref` syntax of Figure 4.22 has two relational forms (the basic form `tablename` and `rowset_valued_subquery`, the first two forms in Figure 3.11) and one new collection form. Note that the `tableref` is always immediately preceded by FROM, so the new form for queries are FROM TABLE( ).

Recall the display format from Example 4.3.2, shown in Figure 4.14:

```
dependents_t(person_t(322456776,name_t('Smith','Michael','J'), 8),
             person_t(123822332, name_t('Smith', 'Susan', 'R'), 12))
```

Syntax such as this can also be used as a *nested table constructor* to build a specific nested table from expressions of appropriate types. Similarly,

```
extensions_t(395,667)
```

is a VARRAY constructor by which we can build a VARRAY of type `extensions_t`. In fact, both the nested table constructor and the VARRAY constructor mirror the **ORACLE** object constructor syntax already displayed in Figure 4.5. These collection constructors can be used in Inserts and Updates in the same way that object constructors are used.

Note that according to Figure 4.22, FROM TABLE(. . .) can convert a *collection expression* to a rowset. A collection expression can be any of the following ways to specify a single nested table or VARRAY value:

◆ Collection-valued Subquery: a Subquery returning a single scalar collection value
  Example: `(select e.dependents from employees e where eid = 101)`
◆ Column or attribute expression. Example: `e.dependents`
◆ CAST expression resulting in a collection value
◆ Function returning a collection value

Inserts and Updates in ORACLE

Simple Inserts and Updates use collection constructors to compose new rows or new column values for rows.

EXAMPLE 4.3.15
Insert a row in `employees` for John Smith, as in Figure 4.12.

```
insert into employees values (101, person_t(123897766, name_t('Smith', 'John', 'P'), 45),
    dependents_t(person_t(322456776,name_t('Smith', 'Michael', 'J'), 8),
        person_t(123822332, name_t('Smith', 'Susan','R'),12)));
```

Insert a row in phonebook for John Smith as in Figure 4.19.

```
insert into phonebook values (person_t(123897766, name_t('Smith', 'John', 'P'), 45),
        extensions_t(345,989));
```

Update the list of extensions in phonebook for John Smith to be 345 and 999.

```
update phonebook pb set extensions = extensions_t(345,999) where pb.phperson.ssno
= 123897766;                                                                      ■
```

In **ORACLE**, we may insert or update the elements of a nested table that already exists in a row, with the help of the syntax form TABLE(nested_table_subquery) to turn a scalar nested table value into an ordinary table.

EXAMPLE 4.3.16
Insert a new dependent for employee John Smith to commemorate a blessed event.

```
insert into table(select e.dependents from employees e
    where e.eperson.ssno = 123897766)
    values (344559112, name_t('Smith', 'Diane', null), 0);
```

Note that this ability to insert new dependents in a nested table is a relatively surprising capability. The Insert statement here will *add* to the rows of the nested table dependents that are specified by the Subquery for the specified employee John Smith, then wrap the set of rows up in a nested table collection container again to complete the Insert. This capability of manipulating rows of a nested table is quite useful.

Next we show how to update all the dependents of a certain employee, in this case by changing the last names of all dependents to uppercase.

```
update table(select e.dependents from employees e where e.eid = 101) d
    set d.pname.lname = upper(d.pname.lname); -- convert last name to uppercase
```

Note that we can't update the dependents of all employees with a single Update statement. CURSORs work only for Select statements, so we can't CURSOR through the set of all dependents of all people in a single Update statement.   ■

Although we can use TABLE(subquery) to specify a nested table for insert or update, we cannot do the same for VARRAYs. Thus we cannot insert or update individual elements of VARRAYs as we did with nested tables in Example 4.3.16 above. In Example 4.3.15, we saw how to replace the whole VARRAY of extensions of an individual phonebook row with an Update statement.

In the following example we see how we can use Subquery to focus on a dependents collection for a particular employee while selecting a set of dependents from a collection of another table.

EXAMPLE 4.3.17
Insert all the rows from the table people into John Smith's dependents table. (This sounds like a very bad thing to have happen to John Smith.)

```
   insert into table(select e.dependents from employees e
      where e.eperson.ssno = 123897766)
         select * from people;
```

■

4.3.2   Collection Types in INFORMIX

In **INFORMIX**, there are three collection types: *set*, *multiset*, and *list*. Given any type x_t, we can make it an element type in a collection type: SET(x_t), MULTISET(x_t), and LIST(x_t). Sets of sets are allowed, and sets of lists, and so on. We will investigate sets and lists in this section. Multisets are like sets in that they are unordered collections of elements, but a multiset will allow duplicate elements, which a set will not. Be careful not to confuse the collection type of multiset in **INFORMIX** with the **ORACLE** MULTISET( ) form we introduced in Figure 4.21.

As in mathematics, a set is an unordered collection of elements; they must all have the same type with no duplicates among the elements. The SET type can appear anywhere a built-in type could appear, in a type or table definition. For example, a single column of a table may be of SET type. Sets correspond roughly to **ORACLE** nested tables, as we shall illustrate below.

A list is an *ordered* collection (sequence) of elements with duplicates allowed. For example, addresses take different numbers of lines in different circumstances, so a list of strings is a convenient way to hold them. Lists correspond to **ORACLE** VARRAYs, except that there is no maximum to the number of elements in a list as there is in each VARRAY.

Sets in INFORMIX

Following our examples for **ORACLE**, we will use examples providing a SET(person_t) type for dependents as a column in an employees table, and a LIST(int) type for telephone extensions in a phonebook table. As in the corresponding **ORACLE** examples, we will use traditional relational tables (not typed tables) for employees and phonebook, but typed tables could be used instead.

EXAMPLE 4.3.18
Create a relational table for employees, with an eid column of type int, an eperson column of row type person_t, and a dependents column to contain a SET of person_t elements.

```
create table employees
(
      eid          int,
      eperson      person_t,
      dependents   set(person_t not null)
);
```

employees

eid	eperson	dependents
101	row(123897766, row('Smith', 'John', 'P'),45))	set{row(322456776, row('Smith', 'Michael',' 'J'),8), row(123822332, row(' Smith', 'Susan',' R'),12)}
102	row(432112233,row('Andrews', 'David', 'S'),32)	set{row(565534555,row(' Shaw','David','M'),3)}

Figure 4.23 INFORMIX employees Table with Set Column dependents of Row Type person_t

Recall that in **ORACLE**, we first defined a type dependents_t for the nested table of dependents, and then used it in a Create Table statement. In **INFORMIX**, we don't need to name the collection type; we simply use SET to define a set collection type in the Create Table statement. Note that in the SET type specification SET(person_t NOT NULL), the keyword phrase NOT NULL is (rather surprisingly) required.   ∎

Figure 4.23 shows the employees table of Example 4.3.18 with a content of two employees rows, one with two dependents and the other with just one.

EXAMPLE 4.3.19
Retrieve the set of all dependents of employee with eid 101.

```
select dependents from employees where eid = 101;
```

This displays one line for the employee, with the dependents listed as one collection value as shown in Figure 4.24. Similarly, the query

```
select * from employees;
```

displays one such dependents set per employee, along with the other columns.

```
    dependents
  set{row(322456776, row('Smith','Michael','J'), 8), row(123822332, row('Smith',
  'Susan', 'R'), 12)}
```

Figure 4.24 INFORMIX Output for Query of Example 4.3.19 with Set-Valued Column

∎

INFORMIX also allows us to count the elements in a set using a CARDINALITY( ) form.

EXAMPLE 4.3.20
Count the dependents of employee 101.

```
select cardinality(dependents) from employees where eid = 101;
```

Retrieve the `eids` of employees with more than six dependents.

```
select eid from employees
    where cardinality(employees.dependents) > 6;
```
■

INFORMIX supports set equality testing, unlike **ORACLE**. Here is an example.

EXAMPLE 4.3.21

Find all the different employees with the same `dependents` sets. List each pair only once.

```
select el.eid, e2.eid from employees el, employees e2
    where el.eid < e2.eid and el.dependents = e2.dependents;
```
■

The IN predicate is extended in **INFORMIX** to test for a specific element in a collection. A particular element of the `dependents` set is a `person_t` row type object. We can construct such an object using the row constructor expression ROW(. . .) with the result CAST to the appropriate type, as covered in Section 4.2.2.

EXAMPLE 4.3.22

List `eids` of employees with David Shaw as a dependent, using a match on a `person_t` object.

```
select eid from employees
where cast(row(565534555,cast(row('Shaw', 'David','M') as name_t),3) as person_t)
    in employees.dependents;
```
■

Starting with version 9.2, **INFORMIX** has the collection-derived table form TABLE( ), which works like the **ORACLE** TABLE( ), as shown in Figure 4.22. The **INFORMIX** TABLE( ) form acts on an argument collection value specified by an expression (most commonly a simple column name), or a Subquery that returns a single collection value, and turns it into a table of rows consisting of the collection's elements. Here are some examples.

EXAMPLE 4.3.23

List `eids` of employees (there should be only one) with a dependent having Social Security number 322456776.

```
select eid from employees e
    where 322456776 in
        (select d.ssno from table(e.dependents) d);
```
■

EXAMPLE 4.3.24

Display all Social Security numbers of the dependents of employees with `eid` 101 (compare Example 4.3.7, in **ORACLE**).

```
select d.ssno from
    table (select e.dependents from employees e where e.eid = 101) d;
```

Here the Subquery selects the dependents nested table for employee 101, and then the TABLE( ) form flattens it into a table of person_t objects. In this case, the table is given the alias d, for dependents, and d.ssno in the select list selects the table's ssno column for display.

∎

EXAMPLE 4.3.25

Display all eid values of rows in the employees table, and for each eid, the count of dependents of that employee under 16 years of age (compare Example 4.3.8, in **ORACLE**).

```
select e.eid, (select count(*) from table(e.dependents) d
       where d.age < 16)
    from employees e;
```

Here the SELECT sets up one loop over the employees table, and the Subquery sets up a secondary loop over the nested table of dependents of a certain employee.   ∎

Note that **INFORMIX**, like **ORACLE**, allows a Subquery that returns a single value in the select list. This capability was exploited in Example 4.3.25 for **INFORMIX** and in Example 4.3.10 for **ORACLE**. However, by using **ORACLE**'s CURSOR( ) syntax or specialized table product in Example 4.3.8, we were able to list the specific Social Security numbers of the dependents under 16 years of age for all employees. This type of tables-of-tables scan cannot be executed in a single **INFORMIX** SQL statement that puts different Social Security numbers on different lines of output. It can be done by collecting all the Social Security numbers for each employee's dependents into a collection object and then displaying those collection objects, like the **ORACLE** query following Figure 4.21.

```
select e.eid, multiset(select item ssno from table(e.dependents)
       where age < 16)
    from employees e;
```

It can also be done using **INFORMIX** user-defined functions and other forms of procedural programming. We will cover **INFORMIX** user-defined functions in Section 4.4.2.

Lists in INFORMIX

In **INFORMIX** collection types, lists and multisets are like sets in that they have IN and CARDINALITY to work with elements, and the TABLE( ) form to convert collections to tables that can be queried. Thus all collection types are very similar in terms of use within queries. Lists are different from sets in that they keep an order to the elements, and allow duplicates, like VARRAYS in **ORACLE**. However, the order in a list is lost when it is converted by TABLE( ).

EXAMPLE 4.3.26

As in **ORACLE** Example 4.3.11, set up a simple phonebook table. Each person in the phonebook table has a LIST of integer phone extensions, and order is important: the first number is the primary extension, followed by the secondary, and so on.

phonebook

phperson	extensions
row(123897766, row('Smith','John', 'P'),45)	list{345,989}
row(432112233,row('Andrews','David', 'S'),32)	list{123}

Figure 4.25 The **INFORMIX** phonebook Table with List-Valued Column extensions of Integers

```
create table phonebook
(
    phperson    person_t,
    extensions  list(int not null)
);
```

Note we don't have a primary key clause here, so it could be possible to have two rows for the same person in this table. In the **ORACLE** case, we were able to use phperson.ssno for the primary key, but this is not supported in **INFORMIX**. Of course, if we wished, we could add a top-level ssno column and declare that as the primary key. ∎

Figure 4.25, like Figure 4.19 using **ORACLE** VARRAYs, depicts a small phonebook table with two extensions for John Smith and one for David Andrews. Extension 345 is the primary extension for Smith, and 989 is his secondary extension.

EXAMPLE 4.3.27
Retrieve the first name and list of extensions for all persons over 30 years of age.

```
select phperson.pname.fname, extensions from phonebook
    where phperson.age > 30;
```

This displays one line for each person, with extensions listed as a single collection value. See Figure 4.26, where the *list constructor* format uses curly braces ({ }) rather than the parentheses **ORACLE** uses in VARRAY constructor forms.

```
fname           extensions

John            list{345,989}
David           list{123}
```

Figure 4.26 **INFORMIX** Output of Query from Example 4.3.27, with List-Valued Column

∎

We can generally use the capabilities for lists that we did for sets, including equality testing, though we note that order matters for the list elements as it did not for the set elements.

220

EXAMPLE 4.3.28

Find the number of extensions person 123897766 has in the phonebook.

```
select cardinality(extensions) from phonebook
    where phperson.ssno = 123897766;
```

List the people who have extension 123.

```
select phperson from phonebook
    where 123 in extensions;
```

List the pairs of people who have the same extension lists.

```
select pb1.phperson, pb2.phperson from phonebook pb1, phonebook pb2
    where pb1.extensions = pb2.extensions and pb1.phperson <> pb2.phperson;
```

The output here would list each pair twice, since we only require a row type inequality between the phperson values. If we knew the Social Security numbers were all non-null, we could eliminate the duplicates with pb1.phperson.ssno < pb2.phperson.ssno instead of the inequality predicate on the phperson objects.   ∎

EXAMPLE 4.3.29

Retrieve the person who has extension 123, and no others.

```
select phperson from phonebook
    where phperson.extensions = list{123};
```

Here we are using a list constructor to define a list containing a single integer constant. Starting with **INFORMIX** 9.2, double quotes around "list{123}" are no longer required.   ∎

SQL Syntax for Collections in INFORMIX

Collection-valued expressions in **INFORMIX** have various forms listed in Figure 4.27. There are no operators to combine collections in an expression in the sense that multiplication combines integers, for example. Compare Figure 4.27 to the numexpr definition of Figure 3.16.

collvexpr	Examples
1. val: constant or variable	"set{'a', 'b'}", "list{1,2}", :citylist
2. collection constructor expr	set{'a', 'b'||'c'}, list{1+5,2*age}
3. colname	dependents
4. dotted expression	ph.extensions, a.b.mycollection
5. (Subquery) returning one collection	(select dependents from employees where eid = 101)
6. case expr	case when cardinality(extensions) > 0 extensions else list {1000}

Figure 4.27 INFORMIX Definition of Collection-Valued Expression (collvexpr), Following Figure 3.16

```
CARDINALITY(colname)              -- an extension to numvexpr
IN collvexpr                      -- an extension to the IN predicate
TABLE(collvexpr)                  -- in place of a tablename in FROM ...
```

Figure 4.28   General Forms for **INFORMIX** SQL for Collections

In **INFORMIX** queries, any collection-valued expressions can be used in a select list, an equality comparison predicate, or an IN predicate. See Figure 4.28 for related syntax extensions to SQL. Note that CARDINALITY( ) cannot take a general collvexpr as an argument; it requires a colname of collection type.

EXAMPLE 4.3.30
We noted at table-create time that the lack of a primary key clause would mean possible duplicate rows for the same person. Retrieve the duplicated people.

```
select pb.phperson from phonebook pb
    group by pb.phperson
    having count(*) > 1; -- remove unduplicated people
```

This query using full person objects works fine but the corresponding query on pb.phperson. ssno does not; **INFORMIX** does not fully support fields in GROUP BYs in version 9.2.   ■

Inserts and Updates in INFORMIX

Inserts and Updates use collection constructors to place collection values into tables. In the case of the dependents, we have a set of person_t row types.

EXAMPLE 4.3.31
Insert a row in phonebook for John Smith of Figure 4.25.

```
insert into phonebook values
    (cast(row(123897766,cast(row('Smith','John','P') as name_t),45) as person_t),
    list{345,989});
```

Insert a row in employees for John Smith of Figure 4.23.

```
insert into employees values (1,
    cast(row(123897766, cast(row('Smith','John','P') as name_t),45) as person_t),
    set{row(322456776,row('Smith','Michael', 'J'),8), --NOTE NO CASTS HERE
        row(123822332,row('Smith','Susan','R'),12)});
```

The row constructors ROW(. . .) *within* the set constructor SET( ) may not be cast to their appropriate row types, name_t and person_t, in version 9.2.
    Update the list of extensions in phonebook for John Smith to be 345 and 999.

```
    update phonebook set extensions = list{345,999} where eid = 101;
```
■

In Example 4.3.16, dealing with **ORACLE** syntax, we went on to insert a new dependent for employee John Smith, and made all the last names of dependents uppercase. We cannot perform such manipulations of collection elements in interactive **INFORMIX**; we would need to write procedural code to do this, as we will explore in Section 4.4.2.

4.3.3   Collection Types: Summary

Collection types and database products. We see much more variation between **ORACLE** and **INFORMIX** in collection types than we did with user-defined types covered in Section 4.2. Both products support true collection types that allow us to break Relational RULE 1 and put multiple data objects of almost any datatype in a column of a single row. Both allow interactive queries that run through scalar collection values converted to table form. Beyond that, however, everything is different. **ORACLE** has a first-class collection type in nested tables and requires a second-class VARRAY collection type to be cast as a nested table before it can be queried. **INFORMIX** treats sets, lists, and multisets more uniformly, and they can all be queried in the same way through the TABLE( ) form. **ORACLE** does not allow nested tables within nested tables, but **INFORMIX** allows sets within sets and other forms of collection type nesting. **ORACLE** expects the user to name all collection types, while **INFORMIX** does not use names for the collection types, instead using generic forms such as SET(elementtype) as the set type specifier. By use of the special CURSOR( ) syntax, **ORACLE** allows displays of all the elements of a collection for every row in a table, whereas **INFORMIX** cannot do this at the current time.

Collections and database design. The lack of uniformity between products means that if you use collections in a database design, you will have a hard time porting your application from one product to another. Furthermore, the decision to use collections for a certain kind of data must be made carefully. For example, in the employees table we studied, each row has scalar collection values of dependents, which can be queried for any individual row. However, the set of *all* dependents is broken up into many separate tables and is not easy to deal with. In **ORACLE** we can use a table product to expand a table to include a row for each collection element, but in **INFORMIX** there is no corresponding facility. In both cases, we must access the collection elements via the parent table rows. Thus for good database design, it is important not to relegate any important object to be stored in collections. Only attributes of the parent row with no independent interest should live in collections. Collections containing REFs are available in **ORACLE** and planned for **INFORMIX**. Thus in the future the actual objects will be able to live in an independent object table and be referred to in collection values by other objects via REFs.

Collections and SQL-99. The SQL-99 working group clearly wrestled with the collections syntax. Each version of the evolving standard has had significant changes in this area, and in the final version the only collection type supported was the array, with provisions for extensions to other collection types. In the final version of SQL-99 the tableref has a new form, UNNEST( ), that works like the TABLE( ) form in **ORACLE** and **INFOR-MIX**. Note, however, that arrays are not part of Core SQL-99.

4.4 Procedural SQL, User-Defined Functions (UDFs), and Methods

Recall from Section 3.11 that a *procedural language* is one in which a program is written as an ordered sequence of instructions to accomplish some task, whereas a *non-procedural language,* such as the interactive SQL language, requires that the desired task be described all at once. Non-procedurality was touted as an important feature of SQL at the time of its introduction, not least because it made the language easier for non-programmers to use. But in Section 3.11, the point was made that any non-procedural language lacked *Turing power* (also known as *computational completeness*), which means there are perfectly simple tasks (such as printing out a customized report in any of a very large number of possible formats) that will always be outside the reach of non-procedural SQL.

This problem was addressed in 1987, when the Sybase SQL Server product introduced a Procedural SQL language called T-SQL (Transactional SQL). Since that time, most other vendors have introduced their own proprietary Procedural SQL languages, such as **INFORMIX**'s SPL and **ORACLE**'s PL/SQL. Procedural SQL supports memory-resident variables, conditional and loop constructs (IF . . . THEN . . . ELSE, WHILE, and FOR), procedures and functions, and the ability to execute SQL statements in a program. Functions written in Procedural SQL can be used in non-procedural SQL statements (select list expressions, for example) in the same way as built-in functions.

Procedural SQL also has the potential to improve performance in client-server applications. Such applications are usually written in a language such as C or Java to execute on the client personal computer and a server, which usually runs on a different processor. The SQL statements execute on the server, and improved performance comes from the fact that a Procedural SQL function can execute like a custom SQL statement on the server, performing a good deal of application logic without constant interaction with the client, thus reducing the number of time-consuming data interchanges between the client and server. When a function is written in a Procedural SQL language to execute on the server, it can be called a *stored procedure*. It is registered in the database catalog tables of the server with the Create Function statement of SQL. Even the code of the (PL/SQL or SPL) function is in the catalog tables. Thus it is fair to say that the function is *stored* in the server. The Procedural SQL language has been standardized in SQL-99 as SQL-99/PSM, the "Persistent Stored Module" feature.

In Chapter 7, we will also consider a feature known as *triggers*, which are Procedural SQL blocks that can be performed whenever some event occurs, such as an insert of a new row to a table, and can be used to implement customized constraints or customized default behavior.

User-defined functions (UDFs) are functions written in Procedural SQL (or a language such as C or Java) that can be called like built-in functions from Interactive SQL or from the database system's Procedural SQL language. Some UDFs are as simple as computing a numeric formula and are not object-relational. But others take objects or collections as arguments, or return them from the function to the caller. In this section, we will show how UDFs can be implemented in PL/SQL (for **ORACLE**) and in SPL (for **INFORMIX**).

Methods are user-defined functions that are defined along with a user-defined type. With the ability to define methods, **ORACLE** objects come closer to the sorts of objects supplied in object-oriented programming languages. However, we will see that objects without methods are still useful. **INFORMIX** row types do not have methods, but user-defined functions with row type parameters have the same general power (in fact they are a bit more flexible). We will show how to use UDFs in **INFORMIX** to provide a row type with the same object operations as we provide in the corresponding **ORACLE** case.

4.4.1   ORACLE PL/SQL Procedures, UDFs, and Methods

We provide a simple introduction to **ORACLE** PL/SQL in the next subsection, and then demonstrate how to use it to implement the program logic needed for UDFs and methods. Readers who want a more complete understanding of the language syntax are referred to **ORACLE**'s *PL/SQL User's Guide and Reference* and the *ORACLE Server Application Developer's Guide* (see "Suggestions for Further Reading" at the end of the chapter). We assume in what follows that you are already familiar with some of the concepts of the C language.

PL/SQL: ORACLE's Procedural SQL Language

PL/SQL is an extension of Interactive SQL in a procedural sense. It provides a way to perform procedural logic, declaring memory variables and performing loops and conditional execution, while at any point SQL statements can be used to access the database. However, these SQL statements, especially the Select statements, are complicated by the fact that results must be stored in memory variables: a Select statement retrieving multiple rows cannot simply display results to the user. PL/SQL memory variables can also be used in place of constants in the SQL statement search_conditions.

A PL/SQL program *block* has three parts: a DECLARE part where memory variables are declared, followed by a BEGIN-END part where executable statements appear. After all the executable statements and before the END statement, a third EXCEPTION part can occur, but we will not explain the EXCEPTION part here. We will begin by giving an example of a program that performs a simple calculation and stores the answer in a table named result.

EXAMPLE 4.4.1

Write a program block in PL/SQL to add up the integers from 1 to 100.

```
declare
    i       integer;              -- local variable without an initial value
    total   integer:= 0;          -- local variable with an initial value
```

```
begin
    for i in 1..100 loop
        total := total + i;
    end loop;
    insert into result(rvalue) values (total); -- insert answer into database table
end;
```

This code may be entered and run in SQL*Plus. As with a Create Type statement, you must follow it with a final line containing / alone. Note that this program block does not output anything to the user, but successful execution will print out the message: "PL/SQL procedure
successfully completed." We assume the `result` table has been created with a single column
`rvalue` of type integer.   ∎

Example 4.4.1 shows several important features. We see the DECLARE keyword
and the BEGIN and END keywords defining those parts of the program block. Comments have the SQL form, beginning with a double dash (--). The assignment operator is
:=, to leave = for comparison, as is standard in SQL. A simple loop can be set up with the
following structure:

```
FOR counter IN [REVERSE] lower_bound..higher_bound LOOP
    -- sequence of statements
END LOOP
```

Between the FOR LOOP and END LOOP are one or more statements to form the loop
body; every statement ends in a semicolon, as in C or Java. In Example 4.4.1 we just
have one assignment statement. Iteration proceeds from the lower_bound to the
higher_bound unless the optional keyword REVERSE reverses the order of iteration.
    A different form of loop that ends with some arbitrary chosen condition rather than
because of a count limit being reached has the following form:

```
LOOP
    -- sequence of statements
    -- exit loop at any point with: EXIT WHEN condition;
END LOOP
-- flow of control resumes here after EXIT WHEN occurs within loop
```

For example, we could rewrite the program of Example 4.4.1 as follows:

```
declare
    i        integer:= 0; -- local variable, with an initial value
    total  integer:= 0; -- local variable, with an initial value
begin
    loop
        i := i + 1;
        total := total + i;
        exit when i >= 100;
    end loop;
    insert into result(rvalue) values (total); -- insert answer into database table
end;
```

After executing either of these programs, the user can select from the table result to display the answer. These programs will only calculate the sum of integers from 1 to 100. A more flexible approach is to place the logic in a PL/SQL *function*; this is a function that can be used in an SQL statement in the same way as built-in functions like sqrt( ) and substr( ).

EXAMPLE 4.4.2

Write a function in PL/SQL to add up the integers from 1 to n, for any integer n. Call it from SQL.

```
create function sum_n(n integer) return integer is
    i              integer;
    total          integer:= 0;
begin
    for i in 1..n loop
        total := total + i;
    end loop;
    return total;                  -- return result to SQL or PL/SQL caller
end;
```

Note that the DECLARE part of the function program block simply follows the Create Function line, without the keyword DECLARE. To make this work in SQL*Plus you must follow it with / alone on a new line. You should see the acknowledgement "Function created." If not, use the SQL*Plus command

```
show errors
```

This will display errors noted in compilation, with line numbers where the errors occurred. ∎

After a Create Function statement has been executed as in Example 4.4.2, the function will be a long-lived schema object, like a table or view. The function can be called from SQL with an argument that is any integer expression, for example,

```
select sum_n(10) from orders;
```

This Select statement is rather strange. It never actually uses the orders table—the table is there simply to satisfy the syntax requirement that a Select statement have a table in the FROM clause. *However, this select statement will return multiple values in columnar form!* There will be one value for each row in orders, clearly an undesirable result! To address this problem, **ORACLE** provides a special table called dual, with one row and one column, for use when any single-row table will do. Thus we can write:

```
select sum_n(10) from dual; -- use Oracle's provided table (not actually accessed)
```

We can, of course, use actual column values in the expression we place in the function sum_n:

```
select qty, sum_n(qty), 2*sum_n(qty*qty) from orders where aid = 'a04';
```

Note that sum_n( ) is a scalar function and is *not* comparable to SQL set functions such as sum( ) and count( ) (called *group functions* in **ORACLE**). The function sum_n( ) we have defined takes one value from each row and returns one value, whereas the set function sum( ) scans groups of values (the entire table if there is no GROUP BY) and returns one value. The most recent Select statement above will return one line for each order placed by agent a04.

Example 4.4.2 introduces the Create Function statement and the RETURN statement. PL/SQL uses the same datatype syntax for its memory variables as SQL does for its named columns (see the discussion in Section 3.9, the subsection "Expressions, Predicates, and the `search_condition`") and has access to the same built-in functions, such as sqrt( ) and substr( ). All the column datatypes for **ORACLE** given in Appendix A.3 can be used as memory variable types in the DECLARE part of any program block.

A function call from SQL is not supposed to change the database; it can only compute a value. In Example 4.4.1, we performed an Insert into a table. If we had such an Insert in the function of Example 4.4.2, when we attempted to call that function from SQL we would see the runtime error "Function sum_n does not guarantee not to update database." Of course, we could execute the function from a PL/SQL program block (like that of Example 4.4.1), with a line of code such as

```
x := sum_n(100);
```

The Select statement does not change any database data, so it can be used in a function called from SQL, as in the following example.

EXAMPLE 4.4.3

Write a function that finds the `cname` and `city` in table `customers` for a given `cid` and returns the information in a formatted string such as 'Tiptop (Duluth)'.

```
create function namecity(custid char) return char is
    custname char(20); -- maximum size, gets trimmed back below
    custcity char(20);
begin
    select cname, city into custname, custcity from customers where cid = custid;
    return rtrim(custname)||" ("||rtrim(custcity)||')'; -- trim extra space at right
end;
```

Note that it is a mistake to put a length for char (or varchar) types on the first line (`custid char` and `return char`), since the system will adapt to arguments and return values of any length. The `namecity` function can be called from SQL. ∎

Example 4.4.3 uses a Select Into that returns a single row, a very simple case. PL/SQL can also handle multiple-row Selects with the help of a CURSOR construct, not covered in our text.

In many languages such as C, you can safely modify any parameter variable within the code of a function because of *call-by-value* behavior, meaning that parameters in the called function are just *copies* of the actual arguments used in the call statement: the original value of any argument variable will not change. In PL/SQL, however, parameters are not copies but the actual argument variables used in the function call, and the compiler rejects code that tries to modify them. If you try to change a variable that stands for a parameter within the logic of the function, the Create Function will fail. Thus, you must learn not to use a parameter variable as a place to perform intermediate calculations within the function logic. For example, consider this small function that increments its formal parameter x:

```
create function increment(x int) return int is
begin
    x := x + 1;        -- change x, a parameter variable **ERROR - WON'T COMPILE**
    return x;          -- (we should have written "return x+1")
end;
```

This function gives the summary **ORACLE** error message "Function created with compilation errors." If you try to use it, you will see "Package or function INCREMENT is in an invalid state."

There is a way to make a parameter variable updatable, and we could do that in the Create Function statement above by writing increment(x in out int) instead of increment(x int). But then it would not be possible to use this function in an arbitrary SQL statement, since SQL expressions (and function calls are parts of expressions) are not supposed to change data. Thus if such a function were used in an **ORACLE** SQL statement, the system would interpret our updatable parameter as possibly changing its arguments and would return a different error message. This argument against updatable parameters applies to expressions for values to be used in Insert and Update statements as well as expressions in queries. We need to live with read-only parameters for our user-defined functions to keep them usable from both Interactive SQL and PL/SQL.

Since parameter variables must be read-only, we often need to declare local variables to hold intermediate and final results. We can create a local object by using an object constructor, as we see for the local variable nper in Example 4.4.4.

EXAMPLE 4.4.4
Write a function that adds one to a person_t object's age. Set up the return value in a local person_t object type variable with age increased by one from the parameter x.

```
create function inc_age(x person_t) return person_t is
    nper person_t:= person_t(x.ssno, x.pname, x.age); --clone x to local object nper
begin
    nper.age := x.age + 1; --change age in LOCAL VARIABLE, not PARAMETER
    return nper;
end;
```

Here we need to use the object constructor person_t( ) to create a local object to modify. We specify all the arguments to person_t( ) by using the attributes of the x object (its ssno, pname, and age), so the new object is a clone of x. We can't just use x in the object constructor on the right: person_t(x); we need to specify the attributes separately. The assignment nper := x would work, but a prior call to the constructor person_t( ) to create the variable nper would still be needed.

To use this function, we display all the `person_t` objects in `people` with their updated ages.

```
select inc_age(value(p)) from people p;
```

Here no table data is updated; the increment affects the displayed value only. To get incremented ages into the table, we need to use an Update statement.

```
update people p set p = inc_age(value(p)) where p.age < 40;
```

Note that when we evaluate a row object in any *expression* (as in the clause after SET p = of this Update statement), we need to use the VALUE( ) form: `value(p)`. But in the Update statement *before* the equals sign, we use the table alias itself to represent the row object to be replaced.

■

The syntax for the two types of FOR loop we have already introduced is shown in Figure 4.29. In the counted loop, the loop variable is a local integer variable (declared at the beginning of the code) that takes on values starting from lower_bound (an integer expression) and increasing by one for each pass of the loop in turn, until the loop terminates after the pass with value higher_bound (another integer expression). If higher_bound is less than lower_bound in value, no passes are made. We also introduce a new form in Figure 4.29, the IF-THEN-ELSE form, which can be used in PL/SQL.

Using PL/SQL to Implement Methods in ORACLE

Methods are just functions that belong to a certain object type. Every call to a method is a call that can reference a particular object of that type, and when execution reaches the code for the method, the referenced object is called simply `self`, and it is a variable of the object type.

```
FOR counter IN [REVERSE] lower_bound..higher_bound LOOP
    -- sequence of statements
END LOOP


LOOP
    -- sequence of statements
    -- exit loop at any point with: EXIT WHEN condition;
END LOOP
-- flow of control resumes here after EXIT WHEN occurs within loop


IF condition THEN
    statements
[ELSE
    statements...]
END IF
```

Figure 4.29 Forms for Loops and IF Statement, in **ORACLE** PL/SQL

EXAMPLE 4.4.5

Define object types `point_t` for points and `rectangle_t` for rectangles. Declare methods `area( )` and `inside(point_t)` for `rectangle_t`. The `area( )` method returns the area of the underlying rectangle object (no argument is needed), and the `inside(point_t)` method returns 1 if the point argument is inside or on the boundary of the underlying rectangle object, and 0 otherwise.

```
create type point_t as object
(
    x int,                           -- horizontal coordinate of the point
    y int                            -- vertical coordinate of the point
)    ;


create type rectangle_t as object
(
    pt1 point_t,                     -- lower left-hand corner of rectangle
    pt2 point_t,                     -- upper right-hand corner of rectangle
    member function inside(p point_t) -- method to test if point is inside rectangle
        return int,                  -- return 1 if point inside, else 0
    member function area             -- method for area of rectangle
        return int                   -- area value will always be an integer
);
```
∎

In Example 4.4.5, the `rectangle_t` object type includes two methods, `area` and `inside`, which are parts of this object type in the same sense as the two attributes `pt1` and `pt2`. These methods, also known as *member functions* because of the syntax of their definition, have not yet been provided any code to perform the necessary logic, for example, to multiply the length and width of the rectangle to calculate the area. The Create Type statement itself contains only enough information to be able to *call* the code for the method, like a C prototype or Java interface definition. The code will be provided in a separate statement, the *Create Type Body* statement, which we won't see until Example 4.4.8 after we have looked at some queries. Until then, we will assume that code has been supplied and works as desired in the examples that follow. For now, simply note that the Create Type for `rectangle_t` has, for each of its methods, the following declarative elements:

◆ the method name: `area` and `inside`
◆ the method return type: integer in both cases
◆ the method parameter(s): none for `area`, a `point_t` object named p for `inside`

If you are new to programming with objects, you may wonder how an `area` function can exist without parameters. The answer is that all methods belong to a specific object type and can be called only for an object of that type. Here, the `area` method belongs to `rectangle_t` and can only be called for an actual `rectangle_t` object. We can picture each `rectangle_t` object having an area value *attached*, a value like a data attribute that happens to be calculated by a method. Locating the method `area` is like finding the object's `pt1` attribute. Thus if `rect1` is an object of type `rectangle_t`, the value of `rect1.pt1` will represent the `pt1` attribute of `rect1`, and the value of `rect1.area( )` will represent the area of `rect1`. Of course, `rect1.area( )` is calculated by a method that computes the value from other attributes, but this calculation is invisible to the caller: `area( )` just acts like an attribute of the object. The `inside` method, on the other hand, is designed to handle the case where there is a `rectangle_t` object and a `point_t` object (for example, `pt1`) and we want to determine if the point is inside the rectangle. The rectangle's `inside` method then must pass the point as the argument, and it will do it with the format `rect.inside(pt1)`.

EXAMPLE 4.4.6

Create object tables of type `point_t` and `rectangle_t` and insert some values into them.

```
create table points of point_t (primary key (x, y));
create table rects of rectangle_t (primary key (pt1.x, pt1.y, pt2.x, pt2.y));
insert into rects values (point_t(1,2),point_t(3,4));
insert into rects values (point_t(1,1),point_t(6,6));
insert into points values (2,3);
insert into points values (1,4);
insert into points values (4,4);
```
■

We see from Example 4.4.6 that the addition of methods to the object types does not change any of the capabilities introduced in Section 4.2.1. As before, we can construct object tables out of types `point_t` and `rectangle_t` and use object constructors such as `point_t( )` in a VALUES form of Insert statement to insert rectangles (or points) built up out of constants. Similarly we can reference the various attributes in Select statements. But we now have additional capabilities through the use of the `area` and `inside` methods, as seen in the next example.

EXAMPLE 4.4.7

We start by providing a Select statement query to retrieve the area of all rectangles in the table `rects` and one to determine if the point (4,2) is in each rectangle.

```
select value(x), x.area() from rects x;
select value(x), x.inside(point_t(4,2)) from rects x;
```

Recall from Figure 4.4 that `value(x)` in the select list retrieves the entire object (row) of the alias x ranging over `rects`, in object constructor format. In the first query, `x.area( )` calls the area method and returns the value for each row in `rects`, exactly as `x.pt1` would be returned if it took the place of `x.area( )` in the select list. In the second query, `x.inside(point_t (4,2))` will call the `inside` method with a `point_t` argument constructed from the coordinates 4 and 2, to determine if the point lies in each row encountered by the alias X in `rects`.

Next we write a query to list all the points in the table `points` that are inside *some* rectangle in table `rects`.

```
select distinct p.x, p.y from points p, rects r
    where r.inside(value(p)) > 0;
```

It would be neater to write `select distinct value(p)...` here, but **ORACLE** does not support DISTINCT processing, GROUP BY, or ORDER BY on full objects unless we supply a special ordering method.[4] We will avoid this problem by referencing the attributes when we need to compare whole objects.

Having point p in all rectangles means there is no rectangle r for which `r.inside(p)` = 0, as expressed in the query

```
select value(p) from points p where not exists
    (select * from rects r where r.inside(value(p)) = 0);
```

Finally, to illustrate an Update, for all rectangles currently having area below 24, change pt2 by adding 1 to both its x and y values.

```
update rects r set pt2 = point_t(r.pt2.x+1, r.pt2.y+1)
    where r.area() < 24
```

We need to use a table alias here because of a rule that attributes (and methods!) must be referenced through dotted notation that starts with a table alias. ∎

See Figure 4.30 for syntax details of the Create Type statement, as covered so far. We have already seen the Create Type statement in Section 4.2.1 and its Figure 4.6; to this we have now added the MEMBER FUNCTION clause.

EXAMPLE 4.4.8
Implement the methods `area( )` and `inside(point_t)` for the `rectangle_t` object type, declared in Example 4.4.5. We use a new type of statement, a Create Type Body statement.

```
create type body rectangle_t as
    member function area return int is      -- all logic is in PL/SQL
    begin
        return (self.pt2.x-self.pt1.x)*(self.pt2.y-self.pt1.y); -- The calculated area
    end;
    member function inside(p in point_t) return int is
    begin
        if (p.x >= self.pt1.x) and (p.x <= self.pt2.x) and  -- inside on x coordinate
           (p.y >= self.pt1.y) and (p.y <= self.pt2.y) then -- inside on y coordinate
            return 1;     -- p is inside rectangle (including the boundary)
        else
            return 0;     -- p is outside rectangle
        end if;
    end;
end;
```
∎

---

[4]That is, we would need to define an "order" method to tell the system how to compare two objects. See the *ORACLE8 Server Application Developer's Guide*.

```
CREATE TYPE typename AS OBJECT
    (attrname datatype {, attrname datatype ...}
    MEMBER FUNCTION methodname [(param type {, param type ...})]
        RETURN datatype,
    {, MEMBER FUNCTION methodname [(param type {, param type ...})]
        RETURN datatype ...});
```

Figure 4.30 General Form for **ORACLE** Create Object Types with Methods, Covered So Far

This Create Type Body statement is related to the earlier Create Type statement for the same type, rectangle_t (see Example 4.4.5) and provides the implementation code for the methods declared there. Note how the special built-in variable self is used to stand for the object of type rectangle_t on which these methods operate, whereas inside(p in point_t) declares a typed argument for the method inside referenced by the name p.

The self object works as an *invisible parameter for a member function*. As discussed above, parameters (by default, and to provide SQL-callable functions) are read-only, and this applies to self as well. We should create a local object whenever we need a place to store results in an object. Don't forget to call the object constructor for a new local object. See Example 4.4.4 for use of an object constructor.

See Figure 4.31 for syntax details of the Create Type Body statement. Note the use of the optional OR REPLACE syntax. With this option, we don't need to use Drop Type Body before re-creating a type.

Suppose the rectangles we have been studying represent regions on the earth's surface. We have a large number of these rectangles, and the task is to find the smallest-area rectangle that covers (encloses) each of a given set (i.e., table) of points. See Figure 4.32.

```
CREATE [OR REPLACE] TYPE BODY type {AS|IS}
    MEMBER FUNCTION methodname [(param type [{, param type, ...}])]
        RETURN type IS
        BEGIN                       -- BEGIN PL/SQL statements
            implementation statements
        END;                        -- END PL/SQL statements
    {MEMBER FUNCTION methodname [(param type [{, param type, ...}])]
        RETURN type IS
        BEGIN                       -- BEGIN PL/SQL statements
            statements
        END;                        -- END PL/SQL statements
    ...}
END;
```

Figure 4.31 Syntax for **ORACLE** Create Type Body Statement, as Covered So Far

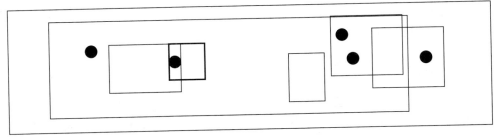

Figure 4.32 Example 4.4.9: Points and Rectangles

EXAMPLE 4.4.9

If all we wanted were the minimum areas of the covering rectangles for each point (but not to display which rectangles have those areas), the following would suffice:

```
select p.x, p.y, min(r.area()) from rects r, points p
    where r.inside(value(p)) > 0
    group by p.x, p.y;
```

Notice that there is exactly one row in each group of the GROUP BY clause, since the (x, y) coordinates form a primary key. However, we still need the GROUP BY clause to guarantee that the min( ) set function runs over one point at a time and not the entire set of points.

We can identify the minimal rectangles as well by using a correlated Subquery to calculate the minimal area rectangle for a point and use that in the outer Select.

```
select value(p), value(r), r.area() from rects r, points p
    where r.area() =
        (select min(r1.area()) from rects r1-- minimal area rectangle...
            where r1.inside(value(p)) > 0)   -- ...containing the point p
        and r.inside(value(p)) > 0
    order by p.x, p.y;
```

The outer Select may find more than one rectangle of the same minimal size, for some points. The ORDER BY clause collects such cases together and also puts all the results in a useful order.

∎

An object purist would say that a Select statement is "properly object-oriented" if it has no direct references to object attributes, but instead uses only methods for all accesses to objects. See Section 4.2.3 for a discussion of object orientation. We note that the final query of Example 4.4.9 is almost properly object-oriented in this sense, since the only direct references to the attributes are in the final ORDER BY clause, and we could do without this clause and still get all the data.[5] In the object-oriented methodology, the attributes are said to provide the *internal representation* of the object and would never be directly accessed from outside the object.

However, we do not usually attempt in ORSQL to limit ourselves to accessing tables through methods, because the natural model of querying we've been using is to be aware

---

[5]As explained in an earlier footnote, we could also arrange to use value(p) in the ORDER BY clause by defining an "order" method for rectangle_t.

of the column names of a table and use those columns to search for the data desired. Since there is no equivalent model for creating and making a user aware of all necessary methods to access a table in a generic way, we continue to access internal columns whenever necessary. Of course we could create methods that access these columns and thus provide properly object-oriented queries, but this type of direct mapping of column values to methods gains us nothing.

One of the exercises at the end of the current chapter shows that the final query of Example 4.4.9 can be performed in Interactive SQL, without use of methods, but the query is extremely long and complicated. The reason that the methods we have introduced for `rectangle_t` objects didn't actually extend the power of the queries is that the logic of the methods is so simple that it can be expressed directly in non-procedural SQL. This would not be true if we performed loops in a method that Interactive SQL couldn't duplicate.

EXAMPLE 4.4.10

We demonstrate how to create an object type, `wordset_t`, that will represent a nested table of words (for example, a set of keywords). An attribute of this type in the `documents` table of Example 4.4.11 will allow us to look up documents by any subset of keywords in the set.

```
create type wordtbl_t as table of varchar(30); -- nested table type of [key]words
create type wordset_t as object (          -- [key]word set object type with methods
    words     wordtbl_t,                    -- attribute is nested table of [key]words
    member function wordcount return int, -- return count of words in self object
    member function subset(x in wordset_t) return int,  -- is self a subset of x?
    member function superset(x in wordset_t) return int -- is self a superset of x?
);
create or replace type body wordset_t as
    member function wordcount return int is
    begin
        return self.words.count;       -- built-in collection method counts words in
        wordset_t
    end;
    member function subset(x in wordset_t) return int is
        matches int; i int; j int;
    begin
        for i in 1..self.words.count loop    -- loop through all words in self.words
            matches := 0;
            for j in 1..x.words.count loop  -- loop through x.words; nested table..
                if self.words(i) = x.words(j) then -- rows found by index no.
                                                   -- in PL/SQL
                    matches := matches + 1; -- found match, count it
                end if;
            end loop;                        -- end for loop on x.words
            if matches = 0 then
                return 0;                    -- self.words not subset of x.words
            end if;
        end loop;
        return 1;                            -- we found all self.words in x.words
    end;
    member function superset.           -- similar to subset (reverse x and self)
end;
```

Note we have left out the superset( ) method definition for reasons of space. The code is very much like what we see in subset( ).   ∎

In Example 4.4.10, the member function (method) definition of wordcount determines the number of elements of the nested table object self.words by using a built-in **ORACLE** method count in the expression self.words.count. Note that the right-hand ( ) is not required for a built-in method. Unfortunately, this built-in method is not available in Interactive SQL.

In the subset method definition, we need to work with the elements of the nested table in the wordset_t object. The entire set of elements in the nested table is brought into memory and made available to the PL/SQL code in an *array-like* structure. The elements are addressable as self.words(1), self.words(2), and so on. We use an outer loop over our words and an inner for loop to count matches of our word against the words of the other wordset_t object x. Note that the code would be more efficient if it were optimized to exit from the inner loop on the first match.

In Example 3.11.7 of Chapter 3, we considered the problem of how to perform a query to retrieve all documents having a number of specified keywords. We can revisit this now as a nice illustration of object-relational capabilities. To begin with, instead of factoring documents into two tables. as we must with the relational model, we will define a single table named documents containing nested tables for the sets of keywords of each document.

EXAMPLE 4.4.11
Create an object type document_t with an identifier attribute docid, name docname, author person_t, and keyword set object attribute keywords of type wordset_t. Create an object table to documents with primary key docid to contain objects of type document_t.

```
drop table documents;                          -- drop old table (depends on type below)
create or replace type document_t as object-- and old type, before re-creation
(
      docidint,                                -- unique id of document
      docname varchar(40),                     -- document title
      docauthor person_t,                      -- document author
      keywords wordset_t                       -- keyword set for document
);
create table documents of document_t           -- this is the object table of documents
(
      primary key(docid)
) nested table keywords.words store as keywords_tab;  -- nested table of keywords
                                                      -- for documents          ∎
```

Next we provide examples of how to retrieve rows from the documents table with appropriate keywords.

EXAMPLE 4.4.12

After loading rows in `documents`, find the documents with the keyword 'boat'.

```
select docid from documents d
    where 'boat' in (select * from table(d.keywords.words));
```

This first query doesn't require the methods we created in Example 4.4.10. But if we ask for the total number of keywords for all the documents, this task is impossible in **ORACLE**'s Interactive SQL without using the `wordcount( )` method.

```
select sum(d.keywords.wordcount()) from documents d;
```
■

EXAMPLE 4.4.13

Retrieve documents that have all three keywords: 'boat', 'Atlantic', and 'trip'. This requires us to use another method from Example 4.4.10.

```
select docid, docname from documents d
    where d.keywords.superset(wordset_t(wordtbl_t('boat', 'Atlantic', 'trip')))>0;
```

Compare the above with the relational query of Example 3.11.7. The expression above

```
wordtbl_t('boat', 'Atlantic', 'trip')
```

is a nested table constructor, introduced in the discussion following Figure 4.22. This table is passed into the object constructor `wordset_t( )`. Finally the constructed object is compared by the `superset` method to see if the keywords in the `document` object are its superset.

   Next we show how to retrieve documents with exactly the three keywords 'boat', 'Atlantic', and 'trip'. We would be tempted to try to use `where d.keywords = wordset_t(wordtbl_t ('boat', 'Atlantic', 'trip'))`, but although `d.keywords` is an object, and simple-enough objects can be compared, ones with collections cannot.

```
select docid, docname from documents d
    where d.keywords.superset(wordset_t(wordtbl_t('boat', 'Atlantic', 'trip')))>0
    and d.keywords.subset(wordset_t(wordtbl_t('boat', 'Atlantic', 'trip')))>0;
```
■

Update Methods

So far our discussion of methods has focused on read-only tasks. But while read-only methods are important, it can be even more important to create methods that perform updates to objects. The programmer writing such update methods has the time and experience to guard against unpleasant side effects of an update, whereas unplanned modifications of an ad hoc nature have a potential to leave data in an inconsistent state because of some unexpected oversight. The current subsection will explain how to create methods to update data objects.

   Let us return to our example of points and rectangles to illustrate update methods. Suppose we want to allow a rectangle to be expanded or contracted by changing its `pt2` value via a method. Consider adding a method to the `rectangle_t` object type of Example 4.4.5:

```
member function resize(npt2 point_t) return...
```

Here, npt2 is the new pt2 value we want to set for the rectangle. Note that this kind of modification could result in an invalid rectangle, one with its upper right-hand corner below or to the left of its lower left-hand corner, so it is important to guard against that possibility in the code we write for the method.

In the discussion following Example 4.4.3 we point out that a function cannot modify any of its parameters if it is to be usable in SQL statements. For the same reason, methods should not modify their self object. The resize( ) method is attached to the rectangle_t object, and the fact that we cannot modify self means that in communicating the result back to the caller, we will need to *return* an object of type rectangle_t. We see this worked out in Example 4.4.14.

EXAMPLE 4.4.14

Implement resize as discussed above. What follows is part of the Create Or Replace Type Body statement for rectangle_t.

```
member function resize(p point_t) return rectangle_t is
    newrect rectangle_t := self;                -- clone self to local object
begin
    if p.x > self.pt1.x and p.y > self.pt1.y then -- check new rectangle is valid
        newrect.pt2 := p;                       -- OK, update pt2 for return rectangle
    end if;
    return newrect;                             -- no change if pt2 was illegal
end;
```

Note in Example 4.4.14 how we clone the self rectangle to a local variable newrect. This local variable can then be modified and returned to the caller who wants to see the new rectangle. If the new rectangle with pt2 set equal to p is not a valid one, the old rectangle value is returned.

EXAMPLE 4.4.15

Display all rectangles in rects as they would look after being resized to have a new pt2 corner at (10,10), assuming this is a valid rectangle form; otherwise, retain the current form of the rectangle.

```
select r.resize(point_t(10,10)) from rects r;   -- display resized rectangles
```

No rectangles in rects are actually modified in Example 4.4.15, since we are merely displaying the returned values from resize. But of course we *do* want to use resize( ) to change database values. The SET clause of the Update statement is just what we need to put a resized rectangle in place, as follows.

EXAMPLE 4.4.16

Apply the resizing operation to all rectangles in rects with pt1 at (2,1) to increment pt2.x and pt2.y by 1.

```
update rects r
    set r = r.resize(point_t(r.pt2.x + 1,r.pt2.y + 1))
        where r.pt1 = point_t(2,1);
```

4.4.2   INFORMIX User-Defined Functions

INFORMIX does not have object *methods*, in the sense that functions belonging to the object type are automatically defined to act on objects of that type, but its user-defined functions have the same general power and even a bit of added flexibility. We will look at user-defined functions in **INFORMIX**'s procedural language SPL, which is quite similar to **ORACLE**'s PL/SQL. We provide a short introduction to SPL syntax elements in what follows. Figure 4.35 at the end of this section summarizes the basic language element syntax in PL/SQL and SPL. More information on the language can be found in *INFORMIX Guide to SQL: Tutorial* (see "Suggestions for Further Reading" at the end of the chapter).

SPL: INFORMIX's Procedural SQL Language

SPL is an extension of Interactive SQL in a procedural sense. It provides a way to perform procedural logic in a function or procedure. Like **ORACLE**'s PL/SQL, SPL programming involves declaring memory variables and performing loops and conditional execution; at any point, SQL statements can be used to access the database.

In SPL, all code is contained within a function (or procedure, not covered here.) A stand-alone block of code of the kind we saw in **ORACLE** Example 4.4.1 is not supported. Each function starts with CREATE FUNCTION and ends with END FUNCTION and is made up of *blocks* of code. An SPL program block starts with a sequence of DEFINE statements, where memory variables are declared, followed by a sequence of executable statements; DEFINE statements cannot appear after any executable statement. The whole block is surrounded with either a CREATE FUNCTION/END FUNCTION pair (when the block is the entire function) or a BEGIN/END pair (we can have multiple blocks within a function). Variables defined within a block are not accessible outside their block. In other words, the whole function definition works as an implicit code block, but we are allowed to create blocks within it to define local variables. We will begin by giving an example of a function that performs a simple calculation.

EXAMPLE 4.4.17

Write a function in SPL to add up the integers from 1 to n, for any integer n.

```
create function sum_n(n int) returning int;
    define i int;
    define total int;
    let total = 0;
    for i = 1 to n
        let total := total + i;
    end for;
    return total;   -- return result to SQL or SPL caller
end function;
```

Compilation errors will be displayed automatically along with line numbers. To execute the function, we can use the following special **INFORMIX** SQL statement:

```
execute function sum_n(10);
```

We could also use the function in any SQL statement:

```
select sum_n(10) from orders;
```

However, this Select statement will return multiple values in columnar form! There will be one value for each row in orders, clearly an undesirable result! In **INFORMIX**, we simply use the Execute statement above, when we don't want to return multiple values. We can, of course, use actual column values in the function sum_n:

```
select qty, sum_n(qty), 2*sum_n(qty*qty) from orders where aid = 'a04';
```

Note that sum_n( ) is a scalar function and is *not* comparable to SQL set functions such as sum( ) and count( ).   ∎

Example 4.4.17 shows several important features. We see the CREATE FUNCTION and END FUNCTION keywords delimiting the program block. Comments have the SQL form, beginning with a double dash (--). The assignment statement is let target = expression, unlike the target := expression form in PL/SQL. SPL uses the same datatype syntax for its memory variables as SQL does for its named columns (see the discussion in Section 3.9, the subsection entitled "Expressions, Predicates, and the search_condition") and has access to the same built-in functions, such as sqrt( ) and substring( ).

After a Create Function statement has been executed as in Example 4.4.17, the function will be a long-lived schema object, like a table or view. The general form for the Create Function statement is given in Figure 4.33.

A simple loop can be set up with the following syntax:

```
FOR counter = lower_bound TO higher_bound [STEP increment]
    -- sequence of statements
    -- exit loop at any point with EXIT FOR condition
END FOR;
-- flow of control resumes here after EXIT FOR occurs within loop
```

```
CREATE FUNCTION funtionname ([param [{, param ...}]]) RETURNING datatype;
    statements
end function;
param :: = paramname datatype
```

Figure 4.33   INFORMIX Syntax for User-Defined Functions in SPL (Covered So Far)

Between the FOR and END FOR are one or more statements to form the loop body; every statement ends in a semicolon, as in C or Java. In Example 4.4.17 we have just one assignment statement in the loop body. Iteration proceeds from the first-specified bound to the later bound, even if the STEP increment value is negative, for example, for 10 to 1 step -1.

A different form of loop that ends with some arbitrary chosen condition rather than because of a count limit being reached has the following form:

```
WHILE condition
    -- sequence of statements
    -- exit loop at any point with: EXIT WHILE condition;
END WHILE;
-- flow of control resumes here after EXIT WHILE occurs within loop
```

For example, we could rewrite the program of Example 4.4.1 as follows:

```
create function sum_n2(n int) returning int;
    define i integer;
    define total integer;
    let i = 0;
    let total = 0;
    while TRUE                          -- could instead write while i <= n
        let total := total + i;
        let i := i + 1;
        exit while i > n;               -- exit while clause
    end while;
    delete from result;                 -- delete all old rows from database table
    insert into result (rvalue) values (total); -- insert answer into a database
                                        -- table
end function;
```

After executing this function, the user can select from the table result to determine the answer or see the answer displayed by using the Execute statement. See Figure 4.35 at the end of this section for the various programming constructs, including loop syntax, in both **INFORMIX** and **ORACLE**.

Surprisingly enough, the second function defined above, sum_n2( ), cannot be called successfully from SQL, although it works fine with Execute Function. Instead, when used from SQL, it generates the error "Illegal SQL statement in stored procedure." The illegal statement is the Insert statement. As in **ORACLE**, functions called from SQL may not change database data because a function call from SQL counts as an expression (which just calculates a value from other values).

Since Select does not change the database data, it can be used in a function callable from SQL, as in the following example.

EXAMPLE 4.4.18

Write a function that finds the cname and city in table customers for a given cid and returns the information in a formatted string such as 'Tiptop (Duluth)'.

```
create function namecity(custid char(10)) returning char(20)
    define custname char(20);    -- make local string big enough (it gets trimmed below)
    define custcity char(20);
    select cname, city into custname, custcity from customers where cid = custid;
    return trim(custname) || '(' || trim(custcity) || ')';  -- trim extra spaces off
end;
```

This function can be called from SQL the same way the function sum_n( ) was. ∎

Example 4.4.18 uses a Select that returns a single row, a very simple case. SPL can also handle multiple-row Selects with the help of a CURSOR construct, not covered in our text.

As mentioned earlier, in many languages such as C, you can safely modify any parameter variable in the code of a function because of *call-by-value* behavior, as parameters in the called function (numbers, characters, etc.) are just *copies* of the actual arguments used in the call statement: the original value of any argument variable will not change. Although SPL uses call-by-value, there are obscure coding rules regarding when parameter variables can be used in a RETURN statement. The safest approach is to treat SPL like PL/SQL, as call-by-reference. That means we should avoid changing the parameter variables and create new local variables for calculating the return value; this will keep us from breaking the special coding rules about return values in SPL. Here is an example that breaks our rule against changing the parameter variables (although the real crime in SPL is to return the updated parameter value).

EXAMPLE 4.4.19

Write a function that updates one of its (string) parameters.

```
create function x_out(s varchar(80)) returning varchar(80);
    let s[1,3] = 'XXX'; -- change the parameter **DON'T DO THIS!!**
    return s;            -- return updated parameter variable
end;
```

Note the use of the special **INFORMIX** substring syntax mentioned just after Figure 3.18 in Section 3.9. Here s[1,3] stands for the substring from position 1 to position 3. This function compiles and (often, but not always) works fine for both the Execute Function and more complex calls from SQL:

```
select x_out(cname) from customers;
```

However, the x_out( ) function updates a parameter variable, in violation of our coding rule, so we should rewrite it to do the update to a string in a local variable, as follows:

```
create function x_out(s varchar(80)) returning varchar(80);
    define newstr varchar(80);
    let newstr = s;          -- clone parameter string to local variable newstr
    let newstr[1,3] = 'XXX'; -- change newstr's first three chars to 'XXX'
    return newstr;           -- return updated LOCAL string
end;
```
■

Note that the SPL compiler does not report violations of its return-parameter coding rule, but the resulting function can execute incorrectly in an intermittent fashion—sometimes correctly and sometimes not. Thus to be safe, we will *make changes to local variables only*, as we did in PL/SQL.

We often need to declare local variables to hold intermediate and final results. We can create a local row type by using a row constructor, as we see for the local variable nper in Example 4.4.20, an analog of the PL/SQL Example 4.4.4.

EXAMPLE 4.4.20

Write a function that adds 1 to a person_t object's age. Set up the return value in a local person_t row type variable with age increased by one from the parameter value x.

```
create function inc_age(x person_t) returning person_t;
    define nper person_t;                                 -- local variable nper
    let nper = cast(row(x.ssno, x.pname, x.age) as person_t);-- clone x to nper
    let nper.age = nper.age + 1;                          -- change age
    return nper;                                          -- return local nper
end;
```

Here we have created a local row type variable nper to modify in the logic. We specify all the arguments to the row constructor on the second line by using the fields of the x object (its ssno, pname, and age fields), so the new local variable is a clone of x. Unfortunately, row(x) does not work; we need to specify the fields separately. The assignment nper := x would work, but a prior call to the constructor row( ) to create the variable nper would still be needed. This whole function body is so simple it could be reduced to one line as

```
return cast(row(x.ssno, x.pname, x.age+1) as person_t);    -- construct and return
```

To use this function, we can display all the person_t objects in people with their updated ages with

```
select inc_age(p) from people p;
```

Here no table data is updated; the increment affects the displayed value only. To update table data, we need to use an Update statement. Unfortunately, in **INFORMIX** we cannot Update a whole row object at once, so we cannot show a simple example updating the table people with inc_age( ); instead we would need to update each of its fields (ssno, pname, age) as columns.
■

244

Using SPL to Implement UDFs in INFORMIX

As in the **ORACLE** Example 4.4.5, we implement user-defined functions area( ) and inside( ) for points and rectangles. Since these are not methods, we need to call them using an explicit rectangle argument. The function calls, for a rectangle r and point p, are area(r) and inside(r,p).

EXAMPLE 4.4.21

We create **INFORMIX** row types point_t and rectangle_t for rectangles, then implement user-defined functions area(r) and inside(r,p).

```
drop function area;
drop function inside;
drop row type rectangle_t restrict; -- Note we must drop objects depending...
drop row type point_t restrict;     -- ...on these types before dropping the types
create row type point_t
(
    x int,                          -- horizontal coordinate of point
    y int                           -- vertical coordinate
);
create row type rectangle_t
(
    pt1 point_t,                    -- point at lower left-hand corner of rectangle
    pt2 point_t                     -- point at upper right-hand corner of rectangle
);

create function area (r rectangle_t) returning int;
    return (r.pt2.x-r.pt1.x)*(r.pt2.y-r.pt1.y);  -- area of rectangle r
end function;

create function inside (r rectangle_t, p point_t) returning boolean;
    if (p.x >= r.pt1.x) and (p.x <= r.pt2.x) and (p.y >= r.pt1.y) and (p.y <= r.pt2.y)
        then return 't';             -- return True if p inside r
    else
        return 'f';                  -- return False if p not inside r
    end if;
end function;
```

We see that the SPL syntax to create a UDF is very close to that of **ORACLE** PL/SQL syntax for Create Type Body, where code for a method is defined. **INFORMIX** supports the Boolean type for the return value of inside; this will make the queries a little prettier. ∎

EXAMPLE 4.4.22

Create typed tables for the rectangles and points and insert some values into them.

```
insert into rects values (cast(row(1,2) as point_t),cast(row(3,4) as point_t));
insert into rects values (cast(row(1,1) as point_t),cast(row(6,6) as point_t));
insert into points values (2,3);
insert into points values (1,4);
insert into points values (4,4);
```

To check your work, write simple queries to compute the area of each rectangle and see if the point (4,2) is in each rectangle.

```
select area(x) from rects x;
select inside(x,cast(row(4,2) as point_t)) from rects x;
```

The results will be as expected.

■

See Figure 4.33 for the **INFORMIX** Create Function syntax and Figure 4.35 at the end of this section for the various programming constructs we are using in both **INFORMIX** and **ORACLE**.

We now consider keywords and documents covered in Example 4.4.10 for **ORACLE**. This example is particularly important, because **INFORMIX** lacks the Interactive SQL Cursor capability of **ORACLE** to access multiple collections across rows of a table, or to insert or update individual elements in collections. But with the help of SPL functions, we can search through multiple collections, element by element, and modify the elements if desired.

We start to prepare for this in Example 4.4.23 by creating a user-defined function to implement the subset operation, like the method of Example 4.4.10. Note that we don't need the wordcount function of that example, since **INFORMIX** provides CARDINAL-ITY( ) as a built-in function for collections, and we also don't need the superset operation because our UDF has no implied order determined by one of the two arguments being referred to as self.

EXAMPLE 4.4.23

For SETs of varchar(30) elements, write a user-defined function subset(wdset1, wdset2) to return TRUE if wdset1 is a subset of wdset2.

```
create function subset(wdset1 set(varchar(30) not null),
      wdset2 set(varchar(30) not null)) returning boolean;
   define matchcnt int;          -- local variable for count of word matchcnt
   define wd1 varchar(30);       -- local variable for word from wdset1
   define wd2 varchar(30);       -- local variable for word from wdset2
   foreach cursor1 for           -- loop through elements of wdset1; see Fig. 4.34
      select * into wd1 from table(wdset1) -- select 1 element at a time from cursor1
      let matchcnt = 0;          -- initialize count of matchcnt for wd1 in wdset2
      foreach cursor2 for        -- loop through elements of wdset2
         select * into wd2 from table(wdset2)
         if (wd2 == wd1) then
            let matchcnt = matchcnt + 1;  -- count match of wd1 in wdset2
         end if;
      end foreach;
      if (matchcnt==0) then
         return 'f';             -- this wd1 not in wdset2, fail
      end if;
   end foreach;
   return 't';                   -- all wdset1 words were found in wdset2
end function;
```

■

```
FOREACH cursorname FOR
    SELECT * INTO element_var FROM TABLE(collection_var)
    statements
END FOREACH;
```

Figure 4.34 INFORMIX SPL Syntax for Cursor Loop over Collection Variable

Figure 4.34 shows the collection-looping syntax used in Example 4.4.23. To use it, it is necessary to DEFINE a local variable of the type of the collection element argument (the local variable is called element_var in Figure 4.34) and use it with a Select Into statement, selecting from the collection_var argument cast as a TABLE. On each pass of the loop over the collection, the Select Into fills in the element variable from the next element of the collection.

In Example 4.4.11, we defined the documents table needed for queries in **ORACLE** to retrieve all documents having a number of specified keywords. In Example 4.4.24, we similarly define a single table named documents in **INFORMIX** containing SETs of keywords for each document.

EXAMPLE 4.4.24
Create a row type document_t with identifier docid, document name docname, author person_t, and keywords set of varchar(30). Create a typed table documents of type document_t.

```
drop table documents;
drop row type document_t restrict; -- all objects dependent on type must be dropped
create row type document_t
(
    docid       int,                        -- unique id of document
    docname     varchar(40),                -- document title
    docauthor   person_t,                   -- document author
    keywords    set (varchar(30) not null)  -- keyword set for document
);
create table documents of type document_t
(
    primary key(docid)
);
```
■

EXAMPLE 4.4.25
After loading a few rows, find the documents with the keyword 'boat'.

```
select docid from documents
    where 'boat' in keywords; -- note IN doesn't require a Subquery in INFORMIX
```

As with Example 4.4.12, this query doesn't need any functions at all. As a second task, we retrieve the total number of keywords for all the documents.

```
select sum(cardinality(keywords)) from documents;
```
■

EXAMPLE 4.4.26

Retrieve documents with all the keywords: 'boat', 'Atlantic', and 'trip'.

```
select docid, docname from documents
    where subset(set{'boat','Atlantic','trip'},keywords);
```

Next, we retrieve documents with *exactly* the three keywords 'boat', 'Atlantic', and 'trip'. We would have needed to test for both subset and superset in **ORACLE**, because PL/SQL did not support equality testing on nested tables, but **INFORMIX** supports equality testing on sets, so we have the following simple query:

```
select docid, docname from documents d
    where d.keywords = set{'boat','Atlantic','trip'};
```
■

Suppose we create a requests table, each row of which has a column named wds of type SET of varchar(30) holding a set of keywords to find in some document, as well as an integer ID reqid. The following Select matches documents to requests:

```
select d.docid, r.reqid from documents d, requests r
    where subset(r.wds, d.keywords);
```

A document with a lot of keywords would be found by most requests. To be more selective, we could report, for each request, the document that has all the keywords and has a minimal total number of keywords.

```
select d.docid, r.reqid, cardinality(d.keywords) from documents d, requests r
    where cardinality(d.keywords) =
        (select min(cardinality(d1.keywords)) from documents d1
            where subset(r.wds, d1.keywords)) and subset(r.wds, d.keywords);
```

Update Functions

User-defined functions provide the only means to change individual elements of a collection in **INFORMIX**. As in **ORACLE**, we create functions that return modified collections, and we can use them to modify any column of that datatype.

EXAMPLE 4.4.27

Write a function addword that adds a word to a SET of words of type varchar(30), by returning a newly constructed set with the one additional word.

```
create function addword(wdset set(varchar(30) not null), wd varchar(30))
        returning set(varchar(30) not null);
    define newset set(varchar(30) not null);
    let newset = wdset;                      -- clone parameter set for return value
    insert into table(newset) values (wd);   -- add new element
    return newset;
end function;
```
■

EXAMPLE 4.4.28

Use `addword` to add 'bird' to the keyword list of the document with `docid` 200 in the documents table.

```
update documents set keywords = addword(keywords,'bird')
    where docid = 200;
```
∎

Similarly we could write a function to add a whole set of words to the keyword set of some document. Then we would need a cursor scanning the Insert set, and for each element we would perform an Insert into the expanding set.

EXAMPLE 4.4.29

Write a function `delword` that deletes a specified word from a SET of words of type varchar(30), by returning a newly constructed set with the one fewer words.

```
create function delword(wdset set(varchar(30) not null),wd varchar(30))
        returning set(varchar(30) not null);
    define wd1 varchar(30);                    -- for Select into use in cursor
    define newset set(varchar(30) not null);
    let newset = wdset;                        -- clone set for return value
    foreach cursor1 for                        -- scan set, looking for wd to delete
        select * into wd1 from table(newset)
        if wd1 = wd then                       -- found wd, delete it
            delete from table(newset) where current of cursor1;
            exit foreach;                      -- only one to delete, so leave loop now
        end if;
    end foreach;
    return newset;                             -- return set, possibly one element smaller
end function;
```
∎

Note the special SPL statement form:

```
delete from table(wdset) where current of cursor1;
```

The function `delword( )` is used in the same way `addword( )` was.

4.4.3   User-Defined Functions: Summary

We have studied **ORACLE** methods and **INFORMIX** user-defined functions, or UDFs. In fact **ORACLE** methods are a type of UDF and **ORACLE** supports non-method UDFs as well, written in PL/SQL or else externally in C. Thus we could implement the subset( ) function as a separate UDF in **ORACLE** and call it with subset(s1,s2) as we did in the **INFORMIX** case.

Language Element	**ORACLE** PL/SQL	**INFORMIX** SPL
local variable declaration	varname datatype [:= initval];	DEFINE varname datatype;
Assignment	varname := expr;	LET varname = expr;
Boolean equals	=	=

IF	IF boolean_expr THEN
	statements
	[ELSE
	statements]
	END IF;
		IF boolean_expr THEN
		statements
		[ELSE
		statements]
		END IF;

FOR LOOP	FOR var IN first..last LOOP statements END LOOP;	FOR var IN (first TO last) statements END FOR;
RETURN	RETURN expr;	RETURN expr;
LOOP over COLLECTION x	i int; --local variable: ... FOR i in 1..x.count LOOP statements using element x(i) END LOOP;	DEFINE e elementtype;--local var ... FOREACH cursorname FOR SELECT * INTO e FROM TABLE(x) statements using element e END FOREACH;
object/row type constructor	objecttype(expr,...)	row(expr,...)
SELECT INTO	SELECT expr INTO varname FROM ...	SELECT expr INTO varname FROM ...

Figure 4.35 Elements of Procedural SQL Languages: **ORACLE** PL/SQL and **INFORMIX** SPL

We note the following similarities between PL/SQL and SPL. (See Figure 4.35 for a comparison of elements in the two languages.)

◆ Datatypes are specified as in Create Type or Create Row Type.
◆ Arithmetic operations are the same as in Interactive SQL.
◆ Dot notation is used to access attributes/fields.
◆ Local variables of object/row type need initialization by an object/row constructor (or a Select Into statement) before use.
◆ RETURN expr; is allowed anywhere in the function body.

4.5 External Functions and Packaged User-Defined Types (UDTs)

So far in this chapter we have studied object-relational techniques that allow us to directly and relatively easily implement our own objects and collection types. In this section we will survey object-relational extensions, namely, UDTs and their functions, that

250

are more challenging to implement, usually with code in C or Java that can perform heavy computations more efficiently than Procedural SQL languages. But once implemented, the new UDTs are just as easy to use as the ones we have studied. Clearly this situation provides opportunity for tool builders to write general-purpose UDTs and sell them to the database community. The database vendors have recognized this activity and have provided mechanisms to "package up" UDTs for easy installation. These UDT packages are called *DataBlades* in **INFORMIX**, *Cartridges* in **ORACLE**, and *Extenders* in **DB2 UDB**.

For example, a text retrieval package makes it much easier to write applications that involve finding patterns of words in documents. When such a package is installed, new UDTs appear, ready for use. Note that we still call them UDTs, since to the database server they are add-ons, even if they are sold by the vendor of the database itself. If the functions are implemented in a language not supplied as part of the database, such as C or Java, they are called *external functions*.

Packaged UDTs typically support "multimedia" data, that is, mixes of non-traditional datatypes, often involving large amounts of data: images, text documents, sound tracks, video clips, and the like. To be capable of handling these large objects, a database needs to support BLOBs, Binary Large OBjects, to hold the raw data. BLOBs are further discussed below. A common implementation technique is to take a BLOB and possibly a few built-in datatypes and compose from them a UDT. For example, an image could have a BLOB with data holding the pixels, and integer height and width. The height and width could be part of the BLOB, or (depending on the database) could be held in separate table values.

To understand this topic, we need to introduce several concepts used in packages of this kind: binary data and BLOBs, external functions, encapsulation, and distinct types.

Binary Data and BLOBs

The ability to store "raw data," long strings of bits to the database, is essential for providing storage for images, sound tracks, and other large data objects. **ORACLE, INFORMIX,** and **DB2 UDB** all support BLOBs. For a 2-MB BLOB, you would use datatype BLOB in **INFORMIX** and **ORACLE** and BLOB(2M) in **DB2 UDB**. In all three products, the BLOBs grow as needed until the needed resources run out. In **ORACLE**, the maximum BLOB length in bytes is 4 GB – 1, in **INFORMIX**, 4 TB (terabytes), and in **DB2 UDB**, 2 GB – 1.

SQL-99 with the named extended feature "Basic LOB data types" specifies the *binary string* type BINARY LARGE OBJECT, or BLOB. For example, BLOB(100) provides 100 bytes of storage, and BLOB(10G) provides 10 GB of storage (assuming this size is supported by the database). Similarly K and M can be used to represent kilobytes and megabytes. These BLOBs can be assigned literal values with a string of hexadecimal digits, such as X'104ABF'. With another named SQL-99 feature, "Extended LOB support," parts of a BLOB can be accessed in SQL using the binary string function SUBSTRING, and queries can perform pattern matching using POSITION and LIKE. The full power of BLOBs, however, is realized in their use with external functions. External functions can load them from files, perform specialized computations on their data, and deliver back important results to the SQL caller.

External Functions

An external function is a function implemented in a language not stored in the database but callable from SQL. After the function is implemented, the compiled code must be placed in a file accessible to the database server. Then the external function is registered with the server using a Create Function statement. This statement specifies the function name, parameters, return value type, and location of the compiled code. External functions and stored procedures (with code stored in the database) are both registered with Create Function, but with different arguments.

ORACLE, **INFORMIX**, and **DB2 UDB** all support external functions allowing parameters that can be BLOBs and the standard numeric and string types, among others. In all three products, parts (substrings) of a BLOB can be accessed from the code of the external functions. They all use a Create Function statement to register an external function in the database, although the syntax details vary somewhat among the products.

Core SQL-99 specifies external functions (SQL-92 does not), called *SQL-invoked functions,* and Full SQL-99 also specifies external methods, an external function attached to a user-defined type. These are all registered by using the Create Function statement.

Encapsulation

Strong encapsulation exists when a programmer cannot access data in an object except through methods or user-defined functions associated with that object. An example of this is **INFORMIX** opaque types. See Section 4.2.3 for more discussion of encapsulation as an object-oriented concept.

Distinct Types

A new type that duplicates an existing type can be made from any other type, built-in or not, by the *distinct type* capability. Once defined, it is treated as a separate type, so that, for example, if type U is a distinct type based on type T, you cannot compare objects of these two types without a cast (a way to explicitly change the type). The idea of distinct types is to provide the advantages of type checking, to catch errors such as comparing prices to percent commissions, or a price in U.S. dollars with one in Japanese yen.

BLOB Objects

In general, if a database has BLOB support, and external functions that can pass BLOBs and most other useful types, the database can support a function-accessed UDT, that is, an encapsulated object, at least for read accesses to the objects. Providing BLOB object *Update* functions for use in Insert and Update turns out to be difficult in many cases. Consider how we had to clone a local object to pass back to the caller in our inc_age( ) function, in Examples 4.4.4 and 4.4.20. In general we cannot *ever* clone a local BLOB, because it might be larger than memory. Thus unless the database vendor has made sure there is a way to reference the return BLOB directly (as **DB2 UDB** has), returning a BLOB value may be impossible. Without this capability, you may need to write special-purpose

BLOB object loaders or updaters in C (or another procedural language) that know which columns of which tables to load or update. In most cases this should not be a serious problem.

For a small example of a BLOB object application, think of our rectangles from Section 4.4. We can store the four integers for the two points defining a rectangle in a 16-byte-long BLOB. We can write an external function area( ) that accepts a BLOB, gets the four numbers out of it, and computes the area, implemented in C or Java. Similarly we can implement the inside( ) function. Then in SQL, we can set up a table with a BLOB column and use these functions very much the same way we did the user-defined functions in Section 4.4.2. We may need to load the rectangles into the BLOB column using a special-purpose program.

Although we would want to name this type rectangle_t, in some products we may be stuck with BLOB as the official type name. If the database supports distinct types, this capability allows us to rename the BLOB type to rectangle_t. But even without a distinctive type name, the BLOB with its functions has the important characteristics of an object type. Let us call an object implemented this way a *BLOB object*.

Of course to be realistic, we should consider much more complicated shapes than rectangles to hold in a BLOB. In fact, it would be doing it the hard way to work with rectangles this way. We should only use BLOBs when they are needed for their huge capacity. Also, note that although the BLOB setup in SQL is very similar across products, the BLOB programming interface used from the C implementation code varies quite a bit.

Although it is useful to discuss BLOB objects in general, there are a lot of product-specific details to cope with, and some competitors to BLOB objects demand our attention. Let us now look at three specific products.

Packaged UDTs and Other Encapsulated UDTs

INFORMIX has the deepest historical roots in this field and the most UDTs available as packages. These UDT packages are called DataBlades and can be installed by a DBA to support a specialized type of data access, such as to geographic data or images. Database programmers can write their own DataBlades, with *database module datatypes*. These types are often based on the built-in BLOB type. Function and type registration for Data-Blades are handled by a special DataBlade Manager.

Individual UDTs known as *opaque types* are somewhat simpler to implement and are fully documented for the database programmer. The opaque types are based on the lvarchar proprietary type. They must be small enough to be brought into program memory, so they are normally limited to under 1 GB. They are defined by the Create Opaque Type statement and are fully encapsulated. They can contain embedded BLOB references (called *locators*), managed by the functions of the opaque type. Input functions for opaque types can be written to be used in SQL Insert, and functions can be written for comparison, bulk load, and many other database operations as well.

The functions for an opaque type must be in C, and thus they are external functions. Each function is registered with the database using the Create Function statement, with syntax given in Figure 4.33. In the case of an external function, the SPL function body of the Create Function statement (the statements line in Figure 4.33) is replaced by an EXTERNAL NAME clause specifying the compiled code file, and a LANGUAGE C clause for the C language.

ORACLE has "Cartridges" for packaged UDTs, corresponding to **INFORMIX**'s Data-Blades. For example, Virage, Inc. offers its image retrieval software as both an **INFORMIX** DataBlade and as an **ORACLE** Cartridge. Database programmers can write PL/SQL or external functions in C accessing BLOBs to set up a BLOB object. In the PL/SQL or C code, the BLOB may be accessed via a substring function and other read-only functions (read-only to maintain our ability to call it from SQL). Either type of function is registered with the database with a Create Function statement, like the member function declarations covered in Section 4.4.2. In the case of an external function, the PL/SQL function body (the part after AS or IS) is replaced by an EXTERNAL LIBRARY clause to specify where the compiled code is held, and various optional clauses. Although BLOBs can be passed to external functions, objects and collections cannot. This is not usually a serious problem because usually we would have an object with a BLOB attribute. You can pass the BLOB, plus any other attributes needed, as various parameters to an external function. You will need to write special-purpose BLOB loading programs.

DB2 UDB has had structured user-defined types, like **ORACLE** objects or **INFORMIX** row types, since version 5.2 (1998). Like **INFORMIX**, these types may be arranged in an inheritance hierarchy, and like **ORACLE**, they may be pointed to by REFs. However, the UDTs are not fully integrated into the database type system. For example, you cannot have a column of type UDT, although a column can hold a REF to a UDT. For a much longer time, **DB2 UDB** has had external functions and BLOB capabilities to implement BLOB objects, each with a user-specified name, using **DB2 UDB**'s distinct type capability. Packages of these UDTs are called Extenders. The external functions implementing the operations on the UDT can be implemented in C or Java (or C++ or other languages capable of using C function calling conventions).

In **DB2 UDB**, user-defined table functions are supported, that is, a programming interface that allows rows to be returned one by one from a user function to the system, in a form that appears as a table. Thus any sort of tabular data can be made to look like a table using user-defined table functions, a very convenient way to extend the database. **DB2 UDB** does not have collection types at the time of this writing.

Summary

Clearly we can support multimedia data with any of these databases. They are compared feature-by-feature in Figure 4.36. Each database system has basic ways to write external functions that access (read-only) the data and are callable from SQL. We can buy a product, an **INFORMIX** DataBlade, an **ORACLE** Cartridge, or a **DB2 UDB** Extender, and use the provided UDTs and functions to access the data. The number of such packages is growing; consult the database vendor web sites for current status. See the URLs for the three products: www.oracle.com, www.informix.com, and www.ibm.com/db2.

	ORACLE	INFORMIX	DB2 UDB
User-defined types (UDTs) in SQL	Yes, structured "object types"	Yes, structured "row types," distinct types	Yes, structured UDTs and distinct types
Inheritance	No	Yes	Yes
UDT REFs	Yes	Not yet, planned	Yes
Collection types in SQL	Yes, nested tables, VARRAYs	Yes, Sets, Multisets, Lists	No
User-defined functions (UDFs)	Yes, including methods for object types, in PL/SQL, C, Java	Yes, in SPL (Procedural SQL), C, Java	Yes, in C, Java
Encapsulated UDTs (unpackaged)	BLOB objects	BLOB objects, opaque types	BLOB objects
Packaged UDTs	Cartridges	DataBlades	Extenders
BLOB maxsize	4G-1	4T	2G-1
BLOB sub-strings	Access from UDFs	Access as part of opaque type, from UDFs	Access using SQL or from UDFs

Figure 4.36 Summary of Object-Relational and Related Features of Three Products

Suggestions for Further Reading

A number of founding papers on data models and prototype systems to replace relational systems is given in Stonebraker and Hellerstein's *Readings* [9]. A more complete set of papers on object-oriented and object-relational data models is to be found in the *Readings* collection of Zdonik and Maier [10]. Reference [1] concentrates on the various aspects of a specific OODBMS, known as O$_2$, and contains the "Object-Oriented Database System Manifesto" in its first chapter. All the rest of the references here are for specific products with object-relational capabilities: **DB2 UDB** ([2] and [3]), **INFORMIX** ([4] and [5]), and **ORACLE** ([6], [7], and [8]).

[1] François Bancilhon, Claude Delobel, and Paris Kanellakis, editors. *Building an Object-Oriented Database System, The Story of O$_2$.* San Mateo, CA: Morgan Kaufmann, 1992.

[2] Don Chamberlin. *A Complete Guide to DB2 Universal Database.* San Francisco: Morgan Kaufmann, 1998.

[3] *DB2 Universal Database SQL Reference Manual.* Version 6. IBM, 1999. Available at http://www.ibm.com/db2.

[4] *INFORMIX Guide to SQL Syntax*. Version 9.2. Menlo Park, CA: Informix Press, 1999. (Includes SPL syntax.)

[5] *INFORMIX Guide to SQL: Tutorial*. Version 9.2. Menlo Park, CA: Informix Press, 1999.

[6] *ORACLE8 PL/SQL User's Guide and Reference*. Redwood City, CA: Oracle. http://www.oracle.com.

[7] *ORACLE8 Server Application Developer's Guide*. Redwood City, CA: Oracle. http://www.oracle.com.

[8] *ORACLE8 Server SQL Language Reference Manual*. Volumes 1 and 2. http://www.oracle.com.

[9] Michael Stonebraker and Joseph M. Hellerstein, editors. *Readings in Database Systems,* 3rd ed. San Francisco: Morgan Kaufmann, 1998.

[10] Stanley B. Zdonik and David Maier, editors. *Readings in Object-Oriented Database Systems*. San Mateo, CA: Morgan Kaufmann, 1990.

Exercises

Some of the following exercises have solutions at the end of the book in "Solutions to Selected Exercises." These exercises are marked with the symbol •. Exercises can be performed in **ORACLE** or **INFORMIX** except as noted.

[4.1]   Here are some simple queries on the table people.

   (a)• Find the ssnos of people with null middle initials.

   (b)   Find the ssnos of people with null names.

   (c)• Find all the pairs of ssnos of people with the same names, using object equality testing on the names.

   (d)   Find everything about the oldest person, displayed as a person object.

[4.2]   Suppose a student_t type should have a person_t type within it, as well as an integer student ID, an email name, and an expected year of graduation, an integer. The person_t object should be non-null.

   (a)• Define the student_t type, and a table students (object table in **ORACLE** or typed table in **INFORMIX**) using the student ID as the primary key.

   (b)   Show an Insert of a student with name Susan A. Morris, age 25, Social Security number and student ID both 231458888, email "samorris," expected to graduate 2001.

[4.3] (**ORACLE** only) Consider the queries of Exercise 2.5. Determine which ones can be done with REFs and write them out. You may use the extensions of Entry SQL-92 described in Section 3.6 that are available in **ORACLE**. Note that the dotted parts of the problem are answered for this chapter as well as for Chapter 2.

[4.4] Queries on collections:

(a)• Find the dependents that are only dependents of employees.

(b) Check if any employee is listed in employees as his/her own dependent, and if so, print out the eid. Use object compare.

(c)• Count the people in phonebook with phone extension 100.

[4.5] Advanced queries on collections:

(a)• Find eids of employees with the same first name as one or more of their dependents.

(b) Find employees with dependents older than themselves.

(c)• Find and display the oldest dependent of employee 100.

(d) Display ssnos of people in phonebook with extensions over 1000.

(e)• Display ssnos of people with any extensions between 800 and 900.

[4.6] User-defined functions and methods:

(a)• Find the points that are inside more than three rectangles, and display them and their count of enclosing rectangle, ordered by highest count first.

(b) Find the rectangles containing the most points.

(c)• Find the points contained in the largest-area rectangle.

(d) List the rectangles by area, largest first.

[4.7]• (**ORACLE** only) Although we hope you feel that the query of Example 4.4.9 shows some of the power and ideas of object methods, it has to be admitted that the methods are not necessary to do the query. Write the same query with all the logic in Interactive SQL.

[4.8] (**ORACLE** only) Consider an "above" operation between points and rectangles: a point is above a rectangle if its y value is greater (>=) than the y values of either rectangle points and is between (inclusively) the x values of the rectangle. Turn this operation into a method.

[4.9] Set up a table requests. Each row of the requests table has a column named wds of type SET of varchar(30) holding the match set of words as well as an integer request ID reqid.

(a) Compose and try out the Select that matches documents to requests, that is, finds documents that have all the keywords in the request.

(b) Implement the intersectcount function or member and compose a query that finds partial keyword matches, in particular, ones that match up at least half of the requested keywords.

Programs to Access a Database

5

Tim Collins's Laws of Software Maintenance:
First Law: Other people's code tends to look like undecipherable junk.
Second Law: Your own code will look like someone else's code after six months.

One of the motivations for developing the SQL language was that end users would be able to use it to pose ad hoc database queries. Previous query capabilities had depended on application programs, and there was a backlog in most data processing centers, so that new programs took months of waiting. Recall that, in the terminology of Chapter 1, an end user who accesses a database through Interactive SQL is known as a *casual user.* For a number of reasons, it turns out that the number of end users who now access data directly through SQL is not as great as originally conceived; instead, most users still work with data through an application program interface. The term *naive user* is commonly taken to refer to an end user who performs all database access through a menu application, offering fill-in-the-form choices on a monitor screen, and so avoids having to deal with the syntax of the SQL Select statement. A *menu application* or *form application* is a program written by an *application programmer* for this purpose. From the standpoint of the programmer, the application program logic interacts with the end user through a *form* interface to determine the user's desires and then executes SQL statements programmatically to carry out these desires. Most workers who deal with data, such as bank clerks and airline reservation agents, use form applications to perform their duties.

The dialect of SQL that can be executed from within a program is known as *Embedded SQL,* a name that signifies the SQL statements are "embedded" among the regular statements of a programming language, or *host language,* such as C, Java, COBOL, or Fortran. Much of the early promise of the SQL language is achieved in this form, because application programmers find Embedded SQL a much easier platform from which to access data than those that existed before the relational model. Standard Embedded SQL in Java is called *SQLJ* and is available in **ORACLE**, **INFORMIX**, and **DB2 UDB**. SQL can also be accessed from Java using JDBC, a part of standard Java designed to connect it to any database or databases. In this chapter we will concentrate on Embedded SQL programs written in the C language. If you are not completely familiar with the C language, this should not present an insurmountable obstacle, as long as you have good programming experience in some other language, since the programs we'll consider are rather simple. Copying program formats from the text (or from examples given on line), with only occasional original contributions in the form of different logical decisions, input names, or output formats, should suffice to get you through most assignments. At the same time, you may notice an acceleration in the pace of new concepts being introduced in the current chapter, especially if you lack a background in C, and you will probably need to make a special effort to grasp the details. A number of excellent C books are available for reference. Particularly recommended as an introductory text is *The C Programming Language*, by Kernighan and Ritchie [4].

Let us consider some of the reasons that customized form applications are preferred to Interactive SQL for most common database tasks. To begin with, the mental effort required to keep track of all the tables and column names and to write appropriate SQL syntax detracts from a specialist's concentration on the real work to be performed. Imagine an airline reservation clerk trying to compose ad hoc SQL statements to make connecting reservations, book flights, make seat assignments, place customers on a waiting list, handle various modes of payment, and so on. Even the most knowledgeable database system programmers commonly use form applications to perform support work such as tracking bug reports; it is simply a less demanding interface to deal with than ad hoc SQL.

A second point in favor of application programs over ad hoc SQL is that many tasks we think of as single units of work cannot be performed non-procedurally with single SQL statements. Instead, some sort of programmatic looping is frequently required. For example, suppose you need to find the median of a set of column values. The median m of a set S of values is that value such that at least half of the values in the set are less than or equal to it and at least half are greater than or equal to it. Since there is no built-in aggregate function named MEDIAN, this value cannot be returned by any single Select statement. In the current chapter we will see how such a task can be implemented by a simple program using Embedded SQL. In the same vein, certain tasks require sets of statements to read a number of different rows and then possibly update some of them on the basis of what has been read; a guarantee is needed that interfering updates from other users will not spoil the results. We need to tie together sets of statements in special indivisible packages called *transactions,* and the procedural capabilities of Embedded SQL turn out to be crucial in this area as well.

A third point in favor of programmatic usage is this: it should be clear from some of the complex syntax we have encountered in SQL (such as the forms used to implement FOR ALL conditions) that the process of phrasing queries can be quite prone to error. In many business situations, an incorrect query (or worse, an incorrect Update statement) can have horrendous results. It is clearly preferable to leave such syntax to professional programmers, who have both the time and the skill to create statements that accomplish exactly what is intended. Since these statements are used over and over in the same situations, we also gain a consistency that is extremely important in most business situations.

On the other hand, there are occasionally situations where Interactive SQL is preferred. Certain types of users need to perform unusual and complex queries, which no general-purpose programming interface can foresee and provide for. An example is a research librarian at the Library of Congress making custom searches for desired books, where mechanical search methods have already proved ineffective. A somewhat less rarefied use for Interactive SQL is to provide tools for users in special situations where form applications have not yet been written, because of the application backlog mentioned earlier. However, the risk of erroneous results is always a major concern in such situations, and application programs to handle such special cases should always be a goal.

Before plunging into the detailed features of Embedded SQL, let us pause for a moment to consider what we wish to achieve. The aim of this chapter is to provide you with the skills you need to implement any conceivable algorithm in an Embedded SQL program. As we make progress toward this goal, a number of considerations arise that require increasingly sophisticated techniques. To avoid getting lost in a welter of detail, you should keep in mind that these techniques are not ends in themselves: it is important to identify the value of each new feature of Embedded SQL syntax in the context of what capability it offers to implement programs that access a database. In Section 5.1 we introduce some of the basic syntax needed to access data within a program using the Select statement; a slight variation of the Select (retrieving rows through a declared *cursor*) is required to allow a program to access multiple rows in a loop. In Section 5.2 we learn how to handle various error returns and also to recognize other types of conditions, such as an end-of-loop condition, when retrieved rows from a cursor run out, or conditions that say when null values appear in columns of a row retrieved. In Section 5.3 we specify the general form of a number of Embedded SQL statements, including new Update statement forms that can be used within a program.

In Section 5.4 we consider a number of details of the transaction concept mentioned earlier, where a set of executed statements are tied together in a special indivisible package. Several examples of tasks that cannot be accomplished with non-procedural SQL are implemented as programs in Section 5.5.

In Section 5.6 we present *Dynamic SQL*. In earlier sections on *Static SQL*, all Embedded SQL statements need to exist as literal statements in the program source file before compilation. Dynamic SQL offers greater flexibility, permitting Embedded SQL statements to be built up in character string variables, so that statements that were not foreseen in detail at the time of program compilation can be created and executed dynamically in response to changing user needs. Dynamic SQL is rather complicated to learn, however, which is why we defer it until later.

In this chapter you will also encounter some differences among two of the database systems under study, **ORACLE** and **DB2 UDB**. All other major DBMS products also support Embedded SQL. We will try to make it clear when our descriptions apply to a specific system. If a description of an Embedded SQL capability contains no such warning, it is meant to be part of Basic SQL. (See the first paragraph of Chapter 3 for a discussion.) The Basic Embedded SQL covered in this chapter is close to that of X/Open, SQL-92, and SQL-99, and the only difference (as we cover it) is the appearance of the WITH

HOLD clause for cursors, discussed at the end of Section 5.4. The different SQL statement forms are also gathered together in alphabetical order in Appendix C, to serve as a reference that is not dependent on the narrative order of the next few chapters. You should take an occasional glance at Appendix C as you progress through the following introduction to Embedded SQL. Appendix B covers product-specific issues related to building embedded programs, for **ORACLE** and **DB2 UDB**.

5.1   Introduction to Embedded SQL in C

When a programmer writes an Embedded SQL statement in a host language source file, the SQL statement is preceded by the phrase exec sql; the resulting EXEC SQL statement may extend over several lines of the file. For example, here is an Embedded SQL statement in C:

[5.1.1]
```
exec sql select count(*) into :host_var
        from customers;
```

Note that C language source files are normally written in lowercase, and we will follow this convention, although uppercase SQL statements are used in many texts. Free-form statements on multiple lines, ending with a semicolon, are the norm in the C language. In COBOL, where statements are not normally multiline free-form as in C, the Embedded SQL statement would end with the phrase end-exec.

In what follows, we describe the features needed to implement a very simple Embedded SQL program, execute a single Select statement, and print the result.

A Simple Program Using Embedded SQL

We start with descriptions of a number of general language features and lead up to the program illustrated in Example 5.1.1. Note that C language compilers are not generally constructed to recognize EXEC SQL statements of Embedded SQL, so the source file is typically run first through a *precompiler* that converts such embedded statements into C function calls into the database engine.

The Declare Section

In an Embedded SQL program, the program logic is able to use normal program variables, referred to as *host variables*, to represent some syntax elements in SQL statements. For example, we might want to declare program variables to contain retrieved values for customer name, cname (using a variable cust_name, the structure of which is explained below), and discnt (using a variable cust_discnt), as well as one for a value normally provided by the user in the WHERE clause for customer cid (using the variable cust_id). We can then perform a retrieval with the Embedded SQL statement

[5.1.2]
```
exec sql select cname, discnt into :cust_name, :cust_discnt
      from customers where cid = :cust_id;
```

Note the new INTO clause of this Select statement and also the colon (:) that always precedes host variables when they are used in Embedded SQL statements. When this Select statement is executed, if the character string in cust_id has been set to the string c001 earlier in the C program, the variables cust_name and cust_discnt will now be filled in with values 'TipTop' and 10.000 from the customers table of Figure 2.2.

In order to use these host variables in an Embedded SQL statement, they must first be declared, including a declaration to the precompiler (which needs special treatment). This is accomplished with a special Embedded SQL Declare section of the C program where all such declarations are performed. Here is an example that declares the variables needed in the Select statement of [5.1.2].

[5.1.3]
```
exec sql begin declare section;
      char cust_id[5] = "c001";  /* declare and initialize cust_id          */
      char cust_name[14];
      float cust_discnt;
exec sql end declare section;
```

The declarations of these three variables are normal C declarations, occurring between the Begin Declare statement and the End Declare statement, and end up being understood in the same form by both the precompiler and the C compiler. It is important that host variables used in Embedded SQL statements have datatypes that are known to the database system. A certain amount of type conversion is possible for database values retrieved into host variables. For example, if we changed the declaration of cust_discnt in [5.1.3] so that it could only accept integer values

```
int cust_discnt;
```

and then executed the Select statement of [5.1.2], the value retrieved into cust_discnt would be 10 instead of 10.00. However, any fractional accuracy would be lost, so that if customer c009 had discnt 11.3, and this discnt value was retrieved by the Select statement of [5.1.2], the resulting cust_discnt value would be 11. All of this is reasonably familiar, but the forms of C variables that accept character strings used in Embedded SQL statements require a good deal more explanation. We defer this explanation until we have had a chance to look at the first program example.

SQL Connect and Disconnect

At the beginning of an Embedded SQL program, the program logic is faced with the same problem as any interactive user: how to connect with the SQL database management system and the right database. In what follows, we will provide examples in SQL-99 and in **ORACLE** and **DB2 UDB**. Connecting to the SQL database is accomplished in Full SQL-99 as follows:

```
EXEC SQL CONNECT TO target-server [AS connect-name] [USER username];
```

or

```
EXEC SQL CONNECT TO DEFAULT;
```

The "target-server" is a literal character string name that would be supplied by your DBA or instructor; the "connect-name" is a name you yourself give to the connection for later reference (it is possible to have more than one connection open at once), and "user-name" is a literal character string identifying you as user. The CONNECT TO DEFAULT form can be used when you don't need to reference the connect-name later in the program, that is, when you will only have one connection open. The Connect statement is not part of Entry SQL-92 or Core SQL-99, because of the variability in user identification and authorization needs of different platforms. However, the SQL-99 Connection Management feature provides a standard usage for the Connect statement, as we show below.

In **ORACLE** and **DB2 UDB**, a constant character string is not normally used as an argument for the Connect statement. We require the following declarations:

```
exec sql begin declare section;
    . . .                       /* unallied declarations            */
    char user_name[10], user_pwd[10];
exec sql end declare section;
```

Assuming a password "XXXX", we would initialize the variables above with the statements

```
strcpy(user_name, "poneilsql");   /* set user_name string          */
strcpy(user_pwd, "XXXX");         /* set user password string      */
```

Then the Embedded SQL Connect statement in **ORACLE** is

```
exec sql connect :user_name identified by :user_pwd;    -- ORACLE form of Connect
```

and in a database system such as **DB2 UDB** compliant with the SQL-99 Connection Management feature, with the same declarations, we would write

```
exec sql connect to mydb user :user_name  using :user_pwd;
```

to connect to database mydb. The database name may be supplied via a declared string variable as well. **DB2 UDB** also allows a shorter form without user or password where these are not needed. Note the colons used to identify the host variables as arguments for this SQL syntax. To disconnect from the database, the SQL Disconnect statement from Basic SQL is

```
exec sql disconnect connect-name;
```

\

or

```
exec sql disconnect current;
```

However, before the Disconnect statement can be used, it is necessary to use the Commit statement, for successful completion, or the Rollback statement, to undo any partial work in an unsuccessful task. Otherwise the Disconnect will fail. We will cover the Commit and Rollback statements in more detail in Section 5.4. At this point, we simply note that the important combinations are (using the simpler form of Disconnect), for successful task termination,

```
exec sql commit work;
exec sql disconnect current;
```

and for unsuccessful task termination,

```
exec sql rollback work;
exec sql disconnect current;
```

ORACLE has one statement to perform both a Commit and a Disconnect:

```
exec sql commit release;        -- ORACLE form of success Disconnect
```

This form of Disconnect is required beginning with **ORACLE** release 7. If the Disconnect follows a serious error, we use the following form (Rollback and Disconnect) instead:

```
exec sql rollback release;      -- ORACLE form of failure Disconnect
```

DB2 UDB has the SQL-99 forms, and its own combination form, as follows:

```
exec sql connect reset;         -- DB2 UDB form of success Disconnect
```

Example 5.1.1 illustrates the Embedded SQL features introduced up to now, together with a number of new concepts. For simplicity, here and in most examples of the text, we will ignore possible errors in program execution resulting from program bugs, invalid database information, or inappropriate user entry. In the program of Example 5.1.1, we deal with potential errors in executing Embedded SQL statements with two statements: exec sql include sqlca and exec sql whenever sqlerror goto report_error. At the beginning of a program, exec sql include sqlca allocates space for certain errors and statistics to be communicated by the database system monitor, a *communication area*. It should not be required for true SQL-99–compliant systems but is commonly needed in current systems. The statement exec sql whenever sqlerror goto report_error sets up an error trap condition to cause a jump to code that prints out the database's error message for the error condition. Section 5.2 covers treatment of SQL error handling.

EXAMPLE 5.1.1

Consider the Embedded SQL program illustrated in Figure 5.1. The program prompts a user repeatedly for a customer cid and replies by printing the customer name and discount, halting when the user inputs an empty string.

Most of the syntax of this figure has already been covered. The character string variable formats used are explained in the next subsection; the prompt( ) function that interacts with the user is explained in the second subsection following. Note that the statement at the end of the main loop of main( ), exec sql commit work, is used after a sequence of reads from a table, before any user interaction such as printing results. As explained later in this chapter, a lock is taken on any row when it is read, to keep other users from performing updates and perhaps giving the reader an inconsistent view of the data. We need to find some point in the main loop to release read locks, so they don't accumulate indefinitely and make it impossible for other users to update rows that have been read in the distant past. One good time for this is just before user interaction.

The function print_dberror( ) prints out the database system's error message, for example, "ORA-00942: table or view does not exist" for **ORACLE**. The code for the print_dberror( ) function is given in Appendix B.2, for **ORACLE** and **DB2 UDB**.

Note that only the lines with comments starting with ORACLE... are using **ORACLE**-specific syntax, that is, the Connect and Disconnect statements. All the other exec sql ... lines are extremely portable across database systems. For **DB2 UDB**, and database abc, replace the Connect statement with

```
exec sql connect to abc user :user_name  using :user_pwd;      -- DB2 UDB Connect
```

or if your database uses user authorization provided by the operating system, use the simpler form:

```
exec sql connect to abc;      -- DB2 UDB Connect, simple form
```

Replace the **ORACLE** successful Disconnect with

```
exec sql connect reset;      -- DB2 UDB success Disconnect
```

or the SQL-99

```
exec sql commit work;
exec sql disconnect current;
```

Finally, replace the failure Disconnect with the same two lines with rollback replacing commit.
∎

Character Strings in Database Systems and in C

Here we provide an explanation of character string handling that we see in the program of Figure 5.1. This handling is complicated because character strings are treated differently in C than they are in character database types.

A character string in C is represented as a sequence of char type values, 8-bit integers—bytes—that represent individual character codes, terminated with a null character (all 8 bits 0). For this reason, C character strings are sometimes referred to as *null-terminated strings*. Most character code values in C can be represented by characters enclosed in single quotes ('). The character code 'c', for example, represents the integer

```
#include <stdio.h>
/* header for prompted-input function                                        */
#include "prompt.h"
/* header for database system's SQLCA structure                              */
exec sql include sqlca;
char cid_prompt[] = "Please enter customer id: ";   /* declaration unknown to SQL   */

int main( )
{
    exec sql begin declare section;             /* declare SQL host variables   */
        char cust_id[5], cust_name[14];         /* character strings            */
        float cust_discnt;                      /* host var for discnt value    */
        char user_name[20], user_pwd[20];       /* for Connect                  */
    exec sql end declare section;

    exec sql whenever sqlerror goto report_error;   /* error trap condition     */
    exec sql whenever not found goto notfound;      /* not found condition      */
    strcpy(user_name, "poneilsql");
    strcpy(user_pwd, "XXXX");
    exec sql connect :user_name
        identified by :user_pwd;                /* ORACLE Connect               */
    while((prompt(cid_prompt, 1, cust_id, 4)) >= 0){ /* main loop: input cid    */
        exec sql select cname, discnt
            into :cust_name, :cust_discnt       /* retrieve cname, discnt       */
                from customers where cid = :cust_id;
        exec sql commit work;                   /* release read lock on row     */
        printf("Customer's name is %s and discount is %5.1f\n", /* print values */
            cust_name, cust_discnt);            /* NOTE: no initial colons      */
        continue;                               /* back to top of loop          */
    notfound: printf("Can't find customer %s, continuing\n",cust_id); /* loop again */
    }                                           /* end of main loop             */
    exec sql commit release;                    /* ORACLE Disconnect from database */
    return 0;                                   /* indicate success of program  */
report_error:
    print_dberror( );                           /* print out error message      */
    exec sql rollback release;                  /* ORACLE Disconnect in error   */
    return 1;                                   /* indicate failure of program  */
}
```

Figure 5.1   ORACLE Embedded SQL Program (Illustrates Example 5.1.1)

value 99 in the ASCII character encoding, while the character code '0' represents the integer value 48. The null character is represented by '\0' and has integer value 0. (You should not confuse the null character, '\0', with the SQL null value.) By convention, all C library string functions expect null-terminated strings. The initialization statement in [5.1.3], which declares and initializes the array of 5 chars cust_id[5] with the C string "c001", creates the following array of char values:

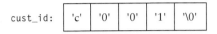

A constant string such as "c001", enclosed in double quotes, represents a *pointer* to a null-terminated string built by the C compiler, and similarly an array name such as user_name is a pointer to its contents. In general, strings in C are handled via their string pointers. The strcpy( ) function used in the program of Figure 5.1,

```
strcpy(user_name, "poneilsql");
```

copies all characters in sequence from the right-hand string argument to the left-hand string argument (which is simply an uninitialized array of chars), up to and including the terminal '\0'. A function call to copy or print out a character string that does not have a terminal null character will attempt to interpret all memory bytes starting at the string position pointed to, until it encounters some byte with 8 zero bits (a null, or '\0', character).

Database systems normally use an entirely different format to represent character strings in columns declared in Create Table statements with type char(n) or varchar(n). The cid column in the customers table, with type char(4), takes up exactly four characters with no null terminator. If we were to place the C string value "c9" into the char(4) type column cid for a new row of customers (we will see how to do this a bit later in this chapter), then the actual characters stored in cid would be 'c', '9', ' ', ' ', where the last two characters are filled in with blanks, and no terminal null character is needed to mark the end of the string because the string length is known by the database in advance. A varchar column type in a database column, such as cname in customers, does not have a constant string length; instead the varchar format begins with a 2-byte integer count of characters to follow. Since this count is provided, no terminal null character is needed to mark the end of the string.

Now when an Embedded SQL statement retrieves a character column value into a C variable array, most database systems will convert the column value into a null-terminated string, so that the C language will be able to deal with the string normally. This implies that the C variable arrays intended to hold character column values from SQL must always contain enough array entries to hold every character of the corresponding table column, together with a terminal '\0' character. Thus where the Create Table statement [3.2.1] of Chapter 3 defines the table customers so that the column cid has type char(4), the declaration for cust_id in the Begin Declare Section statement [5.1.3] above allows an extra character and is declared as follows:

```
char cust_id[5]
```

It is possible that some database systems may not perform this conversion. If you have trouble with "garbage" being printed out after strings fetched from your database, look into proper conversion rules for your system.

Prompted User Interaction

We explain the prompt( ) function used in Example 5.1.1 to perform prompted interaction with the user. (The C code for this function is given in Appendix B.1.) The beginning of the main loop of Example 5.1.1 is this:

```
while((prompt(cid_prompt, 1, cust_id, 4)) >= 0)
```

The prompt( ) function here will print out to the user the message contained in the cid_prompt array initialized earlier in the example:

```
Please enter customer id:
```

Any line typed in by the user in response to a prompt can be interpreted (parsed) as a succession of *tokens* separated by *whitespace*. Whitespace consists of one or more blanks (spaces), tabs, or newlines, denoted by ' ', '\t', and '\n', respectively, in C. Tokens are character strings with no embedded whitespace. Multiple tokens in an input string are separated by whitespace, normally blanks. In Example 5.1.1, the prompt ( ) function is expecting a single token (since the second argument is 1) and will read it into the array cust_id (the third argument), which has room for 4 chars (the fourth argument) plus 1 for the null terminator. Thus if the user types

```
c003
```

after seeing the prompt, cust_id will be filled with a C string "c003". But if the user types

```
c003 wxyzabcdef
```

cust_id will have the same value. The prompt( ) function is only looking for one token here and will only see the first one returned. Now if the user types a simple carriage return on the prompted line, or else a character string that is too long to fit in the array (more than four characters), the result will be less than 0 and the condition of the While statement that runs the main loop will be FALSE, so the loop will terminate. *Typing a carriage return on the prompted line is a recommended way of ending a prompt loop of this kind.*

The prompt( ) function can also be used to accept multiple tokens from the user. For example, the program in Figure 5.13 prompts for two account number strings and a dollar amount. See Appendix B.1 for information on the more complicated uses of the prompt( ) function and its source code.

Precompilation and Compilation Procedures

As we mentioned earlier, a C language compiler won't recognize the syntax of an embedded exec sql statement, so the source file is typically run first through a *precompiler*, which converts such embedded statements into appropriate statements in C. For more information, see Appendix B.3.

Selecting Multiple Rows with a Cursor

The form of Embedded SQL Select statement dealt with in Example 5.1.1 can be used only when the Select is guaranteed to retrieve *at most one row* into a single set of column variables. How do we handle multiple row retrieval in a program? It is all very well with interactive queries to retrieve multiple rows in table form to a screen, but in a program we must specify exactly where each column of every row is to be placed, so we can refer to it by name. Conceivably we could declare arrays and then retrieve all rows of data "into" those arrays, but this is *not* a good idea—we can't generally know in advance how big the arrays should be, nor even that the data to be retrieved will all fit at once in a memory-based array. In fact, you should take this as a principle of Embedded SQL programming.

One-Row-at-a-Time Principle. Whenever an unknown number of rows is to be retrieved in an Embedded SQL program, the programmer should assume that these rows cannot all fit at one time in any conceivable array that can be declared, and the design of the program should reflect this assumption.

The problem of how to deal with an unknown number of rows reminds us of processing an unknown number of input values from a file, which we usually do one value at a time in a loop. It's clear that we're going to have to look at the rows from a Select statement one at a time anyway, since programs work in a sequential, one-step-at-a-time fashion. As we perform a Select on an unknown number of rows, retrieving the rows one at a time, we need a *cursor* to keep track of where we are.

Given a specific customer, identified by the cid and provided interactively by the user, we want to retrieve rows listing aids of agents who placed orders for that customer, together with the dollar sum of orders placed for cids by each agent. We declare a cursor with the name agent_dollars to take the place of a simple Select statement as follows:

```
exec sql declare agent_dollars cursor for
    select aid, sum(dollars) from orders
    where cid = :cust_id group by aid;
```

A Declare Cursor statement is a declaration in the usual sense, and it is usually placed early in a program. After the cursor has been declared, it is still not in active use. Before the program can begin to retrieve information, an Embedded SQL statement must be executed to *open* the cursor. After the cursor is open, the program can then retrieve one row at a time from the cursor using a *fetch* operation; when the program is finished fetching, it should *close* the cursor once again. First, the statement to open the cursor:

```
exec sql open agent_dollars;
```

When the Open Cursor statement is encountered during program execution, a call is made to the database system monitor, which prepares to execute the Select statement of the agent_dollars cursor. If the evaluation of the query is dependent on any host variables (cust_id in our case), *the values of these variables will be evaluated at this time.* It is important to realize that changing the value of cust_id at a later time will have no effect on successive rows retrieved. Once the cursor has been opened, we can begin to retrieve successive rows in the query, using the following Fetch statement:

```
exec sql fetch agent_dollars into :agent_id, :dollar_sum;
```

The INTO clause appeared earlier in the Select statement, which retrieved a single row. In the case of multiple row retrieval, the INTO clause is attached to the Fetch statement, rather than being declared as part of the cursor. This is to give us as much flexibility as possible, since it is conceivable that we might want to fetch row values from a single cursor into more than one set of variables in different circumstances. Clearly the INTO clause belongs with the Fetch statement, which actually retrieves values from the row. After all Fetch statements on a cursor have been executed, a Close Cursor statement should be executed, since there is a limit on the number of cursors that can be open at once. When the program terminates, all open cursors will be closed.

A cursor can usually be thought of as pointing to *the row that has most recently been retrieved*, or in the case when the cursor is first opened, to a position *just before* the first row. In successive calls to fetch, the cursor position is first incremented, then values in that row are retrieved into the host variables specified. It is possible that a new fetch will increment the cursor to find that there are no rows left to retrieve; a condition indicating this event is returned to the program. This behavior is entirely analogous to many program situations where an arbitrary number of values are to be retrieved from a file. For example, in C the function getchar( ) retrieves characters from the standard input file, which acts like a disk file but reads input from the keyboard by default. If the standard input file has been redirected to input from a normal disk file, the getchar( ) function returns a special EOF value when it runs out of characters in the file it is reading. It is the responsibility of the programmer to test each value returned and proceed to new logic when EOF is encountered. In the case of the SQL Fetch statement, the condition to indicate that an end of cursor has been reached is returned, not in functional return values, but through special condition-handling methods covered in the next subsection.

The SQL Communication Area: SQLCA

The *SQL Communication Area*, or SQLCA, is a declared memory structure (a struct in C) containing member variables used to communicate information between the database system monitor and the program. The SQLCA structure has been deprecated by the SQL standards since the early 1990s (i.e., phased out), but the SQLCA structure is still widely used in commercial database products (in particular, **ORACLE** and **DB2 UDB** support the use of the SQLCA), so we will include the following statement at the top of our programs. The SQLCA is declared in embedded C programs, usually before any other external declaration statements, by writing the Include statement

```
exec sql include sqlca;
```

The following example and accompanying program illustrate some of these concepts.

EXAMPLE 5.1.2
Figure 5.2 shows a program to retrieve multiple rows, a GROUP BY Select statement listing agent ID values and sum of dollar orders by these agents for any customer ID provided by the user. Unlike in Example 5.1.1, this program is written in **DB2 UDB** form. It is easy to convert to **ORACLE** form by changing just the Connect and Disconnect statements. ■

5.2 Condition Handling

The Whenever statement allows us to control execution in the face of errors and other conditions such as out-of-data. It has the general form

```
EXEC SQL WHENEVER condition action;
```

An example of such a statement, which we used in Examples 5.1.1 and 5.1.2, is as follows:

[5.2.1] `exec sql whenever sqlerror goto report_error;`

The effect of the Whenever statement is to set up a "condition trap" so that all subsequent runtime calls to the database system resulting from EXEC SQL statements will be automatically tested for an error condition on return. If an error condition exists, the action is taken; in the case of [5.2.1], this is the GOTO action (see below).

Here is an explanation of conditions and actions that can occur in a Whenever statement.

CONDITIONS
◆ SQLERROR. Tests for errors following each EXEC SQL . . . call that is covered by the Whenever statement. Such errors often arise from a programming error. Error code significance is dependent on the specific DBMS. **ORACLE** error codes are found in the *ORACLE Error Messages* [6]; for example, a possible error return from exec sql connect is this: "–02019: database (link) does not exist."[1]

---

[1] This condition was in Entry SQL-92, but is not in SQL-99, which has SQLEXCEPTION instead (although this is not part of Core SQL-99). This represents one of the very few cases where upward compatibility fails in these standards.

```
#define TRUE 1
#include <stdio.h>
#include "prompt.h"
exec sql include sqlca;
exec sql begin declare section;
    char cust_id[5], agent_id[4];
    double dollar_sum;                          /* double float variable        */
exec sql end declare section;

int main( )
{
    char cid_prompt[] = "Please enter customer ID: ";
    exec sql declare agent_dollars cursor for
        select aid, sum(dollars) from orders    /* cursor for select            */
        where cid = :cust_id group by aid;      /* note: depends on cust_id     */

    exec sql whenever sqlerror goto report_error; /* error trap condition       */
    exec sql connect to testdb;                 /* DB2 UDB Connect, simple form  */
    exec sql whenever not found goto finish;    /* end of cursor trap condition  */
    while (prompt(cid_prompt, 1, cust_id, 4) >= 0) { /* main loop, get cid from user */
        exec sql open agent_dollars;            /* cust_id value used in open cursor */
        while (TRUE)   {                        /* loop to fetch rows            */
            exec sql fetch agent_dollars        /* fetch next row and ...        */
                into :agent_id, :dollar_sum;    /* ... set these variables       */
            printf("%s %11.2f\n",               /* print out latest values       */
                agent_id, dollar_sum);
        }                                       /* end fetch loop                */
finish:  exec sql close agent_dollars;          /* close cursor when done        */
        exec sql commit work;                   /* end locks on fetched rows     */
    }                                           /* end of main loop              */
    exec sql disconnect current;                /* Disconnect from database      */
    return 0;
report_error:
    print_dberror( );                           /* print out error message       */
    exec sql rollback work;                     /* failing, undo work, end locks */
    exec sql disconnect current;                /* Disconnect from database      */
    return 1;
}
```

Figure 5.2 DB2 UDB Program to Retrieve Multiple Rows (Illustrates Example 5.1.2)

◆ NOT FOUND. Tests when no rows are affected following some SQL statement such as Fetch, Insert, Update, or Delete. This condition is in Entry SQL-92 and Core SQL-99.

◆ SQLWARNING. Tests for a non-error but notable condition, other than the NOT FOUND condition. Note that the SQLWARNING condition is not part of Full SQL-92 and it is not required by the X/Open SQL standard, but it is defined as an extended feature of SQL-99; however, it is widely implemented in various database products, including **ORACLE**, **DB2 UDB**, and **INFORMIX**. You may need exec sql include sqlca in your program to use SQLWARNING (this is not normally needed for SQLERROR). Examples of warning conditions are "at least one null value was eliminated in evaluating a set function" and "a truncated column value was assigned to a host variable in a Select Statement."

ACTIONS

◆ CONTINUE. This means that no action should be taken on the basis of the associated condition—normal flow of control continues.

◆ GOTO label. This has the same effect as a "goto label" statement in C. Note that the label named must be within the scope of all subsequent EXEC SQL statements up to the point where another Whenever statement is encountered for the same condition.

◆ STOP. This action terminates execution of the program, rolls back the current transaction, and disconnects from databases it is connected to. It does not print out an error message, so the exit from the program can seem mysterious. This action is defined in **ORACLE** and **INFORMIX** but not in **DB2 UDB** or Basic SQL.

◆ DO function (**ORACLE**), CALL function (**INFORMIX**). The condition causes a named C function to be called. On return from this function, flow of control continues from the statement after the EXEC SQL statement that raised the condition. This action is not defined in **DB2 UDB** or Basic SQL.

Whenever Statement: Scope and Flow of Control

We can picture that the precompiler implements the condition trap of a Whenever statement with any action other than Continue by inserting tests after every *subsequent* runtime database system call. These tests compare either the SQLCODE (product-specific) or the SQLSTATE (portable, standardized) to various values. After a Whenever statement is encountered, the precompiler performs a simple statement-by-statement search and insertion as it passes through successive lines of code in the *source file,* changing its action only when a subsequent overriding Whenever statement is encountered. In particular, note that the action *does not follow the flow of control* if an intervening Whenever statement overrides the original prescription.

EXAMPLE 5.2.1
Consider the following sequence of statements in a program file.

```
main( )
{
exec sql whenever sqlerror stop;          /* first whenever statement          */
. . .
```

```
    goto s1
    . . .
    exec sql whenever sqlerror continue;        /* overrides first whenever        */
    s1: exec sql update agents set percent = percent + 1;
        . . .

    }
```

The action for an sqlerror condition in force at label S1 is continue (the effect of the second Whenever statement), even though this Update statement has been reached by a Goto statement in the scope of the first Whenever statement. This is because the precompiler placed a test at label S1 under the influence of the second Whenever; the controlling factor is statement position in the file, not flow of control, of which the precompiler is unaware.   ∎

Note that the default action when no Whenever statements have occurred is Continue, meaning that no special action is taken and the normal flow of control continues. No test after a runtime call to the database is necessary to achieve this action. The default action can be specifically reestablished to override a Whenever statement with a different action, as in Example 5.2.1:

```
    exec sql whenever sqlerror continue.
```

We must be careful when using the Whenever statement to avoid infinite loops.

EXAMPLE 5.2.2 Avoiding Infinite Loops.
The following code fragment sits inside a function that is called to create a table in Embedded SQL:

```
    exec sql whenever sqlerror goto handle_error;
    exec sql create table customers
        (cid char(4) not null, cname varchar(13), . . .);
```

If the Create Table command fails because of some error (for example, an error return indicating insufficient disk space), the flow of control passes to the following labeled fragment:

```
    handle_error:
        exec sql whenever sqlerror continue;
        exec sql drop customers;
        exec sql disconnect;
        fprintf(stderr, "Could not create customers table\n");
        return -1;                          /* return error condition        */
```

The exec sql whenever sqlerror continue statement is important here, because an error might result from the call to drop the customers table—in fact, this is quite likely if we didn't succeed in creating the table. If the original Whenever statement were still in effect, the result would be to goto the handle_error label again, repeating the Drop statement attempt and looping indefinitely. The new Whenever statement overrides the Goto action, so a loop does not occur.

Note that when an error occurs within a C program function, proper exit handling is important. After the Disconnect statement above, the `return -1` statement returns an error from this level, as compared to returning 0 (success) to indicate the function had completed successfully. Appropriate behavior on receiving a return of –1 is up to the programmer. It is barely possible that there is some alternative action to take in the event that a Create Table statement is unsuccessful, so in that case a normal return with a warning value will indicate the need for that action. ∎

Explicit Error Checking

Underlying the Whenever mechanism is a system of error codes that provides much more information about the conditions. Unfortunately, there is no fully portable way to use these codes. Products that support the SQLCA fill in `sqlca.sqlcode` (a member of the SQLCA struct) or a variable called SQLCODE with product-specific error codes. As mentioned earlier, the SQL-92, SQL-99, and X/Open SQL standards have been attempting to deprecate the SQLCA approach, to move the standard to a new method of error reporting known as SQLSTATE, but some products do not yet use it or require non-default settings to support it. In particular, **ORACLE** requires its preprocessor to be run with the option MODE=ANSI to enable SQLSTATE support. As we saw in Example 5.2.3, **DB2 UDB** provides the SQLSTATE as a member of the SQLCA. In the standard and in all products that support it, the SQLSTATE is encoded in a 5-char string, with a 2-char "class code" and a 3-char "subclass code." For example, "00000" is no-error, and "82100" is "out-of-memory," and is the same for all products. You will want to look up SQLSTATE, SQLCA, and SQLCODE in the index of the Embedded SQL reference guide for the database system product you are using to determine all major error conditions and how they are reported.

If there is a need to recognize explicit error conditions at a particular point in execution, this will normally not be possible if a Whenever statement is in force with any action other than CONTINUE. We see why this is so in Example 5.2.3.

EXAMPLE 5.2.3 Explicit Error Checking.
Consider the following **ORACLE** code fragment:

```
exec sql begin declare section;
    char SQLSTATE[6];                       /* 5-char SQLSTATE needs 6-char C array */
exec sql end declare section;
exec sql whenever sqlerror goto handle_error;   /* this is in force below        */
. . .
exec sql create table custs
    (cid char(4) not null, cname varchar(13), . . .);
if (strcmp(SQLSTATE,"82100")==0)                /* ORACLE, out of disk space?    */
    <call procedure to handle this condition>   /** NEVER REACH THIS           **/
```

Note that the preprocessor implements the Whenever statement by placing a test for sqlerror (`if (errcode < 0) goto handle_error`, for example) immediately after the Create Table statement. Therefore it should be obvious that the strcmp test will never see the condition on the line following. The Whenever condition has gotten in first and short-circuited our intended test. It turns out that if we want to recognize an explicit error condition, we need to drop our GOTO action for SQLERROR beforehand, modifying the logic above as indicated below in italics.

```
exec sql whenever sqlerror goto handle_error;    /* this is in force below    */
. . .
exec sql whenever sqlerror continue;             /* but this overrides it     */
exec sql create table custs
    (cid char(4) not null, cname varchar(13),....); /* as above               */
if (strcmp(SQLSTATE,"82100")==0)/                /* ORACLE, out of disk space? */
    <call procedure to handle this condition>    /* now this works            */
else if (strcmp(SQLSTATE,"00000")!=0) {          /* another error?            */
    goto handle_error;                           /* yes, handle it            */
exec sql whenever sqlerror goto handle_error;    /* again in force below      */
```

In **DB2 UDB**, SQLSTATE value is available in the SQLCA, in `sqlca.sqlstate`, assuming the program has exec sql include sqlca in effect. We do not need a Declare section for it, but need to be careful with comparisons because char array in the SQLCA has only five character positions in it. We need to use strncmp rather than strcmp to make the comparison stop after five characters:

```
if (strncmp(sqlca.sqlstate,"82100",5)==0)        /* DB2 UDB, out of disk space? */
    <call procedure to handle this condition>     /* now this works             */
else if (strcmp(sqlca.sqlstate,"00000")!=0) {     /* another error?             */
    goto handle_error;                            /* yes, handle it             */
```

■

Advantages of the Whenever Statement

One major value of the Whenever statement lies in the fact that a condition trap can greatly reduce the number of lines of code written to handle error returns. Another advantage is that the Whenever syntax is extremely portable across different database systems. For example, the condition NOT FOUND is commonly needed in Fetch loops and Update statements whose effects are uncertain, but the condition has different `sqlca.sqlcode` values in different products. (The value is often 100 for historical reasons.) The Whenever statement will always be triggered in the appropriate situation.

On the other hand, for specific database products it is possible to detect any of the standard Whenever conditions by carefully inserting tests on the SQLSTATE, SQL-CODE, or `sqlca.sqlcode` value after all database runtime calls. Indeed, such tests allow a greater flexibility in recognizing special conditions and often in specifying an action to take.

Handling Errors: Getting Error Messages from the Database

It is often valuable for debugging purposes for programs to access the system-generated error message associated with an error return. To exemplify this, we expand the handle_error code fragment of Example 5.2.2. The exact code sequence required to extract an error message is dependent on the database system in use. An attempt to standardize these methods was made in SQL-92 (duplicated in SQL-99), but the complicated method specified was never adopted by major database vendors. Each product should have some method comparable to the following **ORACLE** code sequence, used in the print_dberror( ) function we have been using in examples. See Appendix B.2 for the code for print_dberror( ) for **ORACLE** and **DB2 UDB**.

EXAMPLE 5.2.4 Printing Error Messages in ORACLE.
To start with, we need a few declarations:

```
#define ERRLEN 512        /* maximum length of an ORACLE error message    */
int errlength = ERRLEN;   /* size of buffer                               */
int errsize;              /* to contain actual message length             */
char errbuf[ERRLEN];      /* buffer to receive message                    */
```

ORACLE extracts the error message with a call to sqlglm and returns the actual message length in errlength. Note that the error message is not null-terminated. We can use this in a printf by using the * feature to fill in the format width at runtime with the value of the second argument:

```
char errbuf[ERRLEN];                   /* buffer to receive message        */
sqlglm(errbuf, &errlength, &errsize);
printf("%.*s\n",errsize,errbuff);      /* print just errlength chars from string */
```

■

Indicator Variables

Recall from Chapter 3 that column values in a table can take on null values (unless they have been declared with the *not null* clause in the Create Table statement), and these null values are outside the range of normal values for the type declared. In Example 3.7.8 we pointed out that the statement

```
select * from customers where discnt <= 10 or discnt > 10;
```

would not retrieve a row from the customers table that has a null value in the discnt column. This is relatively surprising, since it would seem that all possible values are either less than, equal to, or greater than 10, but it is exactly the kind of behavior that null values are supposed to supply. Recall that the null value represents an unknown or undefined quantity. If a customer doesn't yet have a discnt value assigned, we don't want to count that customer as one who has discnt value <= 10, nor as a customer who has discnt value > 10. Now assume that we retrieved the discnt value of a row from customers into a host variable declared as int cust_discnt (and perhaps other column values into other variables), with the following Embedded SQL Select statement:

```
exec sql select discnt, . . . into :cust_discnt, . . .
    from customers where cid = :cust_id;
```

Consider what would happen if the discnt value is null in the row selected. Most modern database products will not perform a retrieval of a null value into a variable cust_discnt, but if it were permitted, then certainly the C variable cust_discnt would retrieve some pattern of bits. Now consider the following test:

```
if (cust_discnt <= 10 || cust_discnt > 10) . . .
```

(The || operator is the logical OR in C.) The If statement in this test would evaluate to TRUE, since any pattern of bits in cust_discnt obeys one of these two conditions. But this is the wrong behavior if the value is null, since the value is uncertain and neither less than, equal to, nor greater than 10. In recognition of this problem, most current database systems (e.g., **ORACLE** and **DB2 UDB**, as well as **INFORMIX** with an -icheck option for the compilation command) follow the SQL-99 standard and give an error when a null value is read into an ordinary host variable (one like :cust_discnt that has no indicator variable, as explained below).

We would like to mimic the logic of SQL as closely as possible in our C decisions, and this conceptual example shows a problem. To handle possibly null column values better, what we need is some way to distinguish when a returned variable value is null, so we can write

```
if (not-null(cust_discnt) && (cust_discnt <= 10)  ...     /** INVALID **/
```

(The && operator is the logical AND in C.) However, there is no actual function named "not-null( )". Our intent is clear, though: we want a test that will *not* evaluate to TRUE when a null value is retrieved in cust_discnt. Unfortunately, there is not enough significance in the cust_discnt variable to tell us whether the retrieved value is null—all useful significance would be taken up with the integer values retrieved from a non-null discnt attribute. Thus we need some other way to remember that cust_discnt has retrieved a null value, and the standard approach used in SQL is to declare an *indicator variable* to go with cust_discnt. We will name this indicator variable cd_ind. Here is the declaration we use:

```
exec sql begin declare section;
    float cust_discnt;
    short int cd_ind;
    . . .
exec sql end declare section;
```

Now in the Select statement, we would replace the :cust_discnt reference by the pair :cust_discnt :cd_ind, as follows:

```
exec sql select discnt into :cust_discnt :cd_ind
    from customers where cid = :cust_id;
```

Basic SQL allows an optional keyword indicator between the colon-prefixed names to emphasize what is happening, so an alternative form is

```
exec sql select discnt into :cust_discnt indicator :cd_ind
    from customers where cid = :cust_id;
```

In the case that the keyword indicator is not used, **ORACLE** (but not **DB2 UDB**) requires the two host variables to be written with no spaces between them, as follows:

```
exec sql select discnt into :cust_discnt:cd_ind        /* ORACLE form            */
    from customers where cid = :cust_id;
```

Clearly the most portable syntax is to use the indicator keyword, and we will do that in what follows. Following this retrieval, a value of −1 (minus one) in the cd_ind variable means that the variable cust_discnt has a null value, whereas a value of 0 (zero) means that cust_discnt has a normal integer value. Now the logical test we suggested earlier, not-null(cust_discnt), can be implemented with a test of this indicator variable. We write

```
if ((cd_ind >= 0) && cust_discnt <= 10). . .
```

The test of c_ind will evaluate to TRUE only for non-null values retrieved from the attribute discnt into the pair :cust_discnt indicator :cd_ind.

We can always represent a null value with an indicator variable of −1, even when updating the database rather than retrieving from it. For example, to set the discnt value to null in a specific row of customers, we can write

```
cd_ind = -1;
exec sql update customers
    set discnt = :cust_discnt indicator :cd_ind where cid = :cust_id;
```

There is one other standard use for the indicator variable. The database system will set the indicator variable to a positive value (ind > 0) if the associated host variable holds a character string (in one of the two formats explained earlier) and the SQL statement truncates the length of the string value it retrieves from the database to make it fit in the host variable. Typically, the value of the positive indicator variable after truncation is the length of the database string value that had to be truncated. Thus the possible values for indicator variables in standard use are

= 0   A database value, not null, was assigned to the host variable.

> 0   A truncated database character string was assigned to the host variable.

= −1   The database value is null, and the host variable value is not a meaningful value.

Clearly it is possible to expand on values retrieved in the indicator variable. The **DB2 UDB** product, for example, assigns a value of –2 if a null value is retrieved because of an error rather than as a stored value of the database (special steps have to be taken to guarantee this, however).

5.3 Some Common Embedded SQL Statements

In this section we provide general forms of various Embedded SQL data manipulation statements, starting with a complete description of the Embedded SQL Select statement.

The Select Statement

Recall that a Select statement can be executed in a program without use of a cursor, *but only when no more than one row is to be retrieved* (zero or one row is permitted). If more than one row is found by a Select, a runtime error will be returned. The syntax of the Select statement in Embedded SQL is given in Figure 5.3. See Chapter 3 for explanations of most of the syntax elements, including the definition of a valid search_condition. Note that the host-variable referred to in Figure 5.3 can contain an indicator variable as a part of it.

Since only a single row can be retrieved by an Embedded Select statement, the Interactive SQL GROUP BY, HAVING, UNION, and ORDER BY clauses are not included in this general form. The variables named in the INTO clause must be in one-to-one correspondence with the expressions retrieved; they need to have appropriate types, since automatic conversion cannot always do everything you might think reasonable. In **ORACLE** a varchar string with the SQL value '1234' will be converted into numeric form by the database system when it is retrieved into a C variable of type int or short int. Also, the predicate qty = '1000' (where qty is an integer column and '1000' is a string constant) is accepted in Interactive or Embedded SQL by **ORACLE** because it is willing to convert the string into an integer. Such conversions between strings and numeric types is not standardized for all database products, however. If you intend to depend on such conversions, you should become familiar with what is supported by the database system you are using. When the Select statement of Figure 5.3 results in no row being retrieved, the values of SQLSTATE and SQLCODE will be set to an appropriate warning value, and a Whenever Not Found action will be triggered.

```
EXEC SQL SELECT [ALL|DISTINCT] expression {, expression...}
    INTO host-variable {, host-variable...}
    FROM tableref [corr_name] {, tableref [corr_name]...}
    [WHERE search_condition]
```

Figure 5.3   Basic Embedded SQL Select Form (Single-Row Select)

Basic SQL type	ORACLE type	DB2 UDB type	C datatype
char(n)	char(n)	char(n)	char arr[n+1]
varchar(n)	varchar(n)	varchar(n)	char array[n+1]
smallint	smallint	smallint	short int
integer, int	integer, int, number(10)	integer, int	int (**DB2 UDB** requires long int)
real	real	real	float
double precision, float	double precision, number, float	double precision, double, float	double

Figure 5.4   Type Correspondences: Basic SQL, **ORACLE**, **DB2 UDB**, and C

In the Select statement and other statements covered below, host variables that have been declared in an EXEC SQL DECLARE . . . section can be used in the INTO clause to receive target list variables retrieved. Figure 5.4 gives a partial list of normal type correspondences between column datatypes specified in the Create Table command and C variable datatypes. A larger table of SQL datatypes is in Appendix A.3. Note that *float* means different things in C and SQL; that is, *float* in SQL corresponds to *double* in C. Also, although an SQL int is compatible with a C int for **ORACLE**, **DB2 UDB** requires us to use a *long int* in C to match with an SQL int, to make sure it is large enough.

Host variables that have been declared in an EXEC SQL DECLARE section can also be used in any `search_condition` syntax of an Embedded SQL statement. However, host variables in the `search_condition` can only be used to represent numerical or character string constants in an expression. In particular, host variables cannot hold character strings meant to represent more complex syntax elements, such as names of columns or tables or logical conditions in expressions, which would require compiler attention at runtime after the host variable value is set. The ability to use host variable character strings to represent such elements and even entire statements will be covered in a later chapter as "Dynamic SQL."

The Declare Cursor Statement

The core syntax of the Basic SQL Declare Cursor statement is given in Figure 5.5. Most of this syntax is basically the same as the interactive Select syntax of Figure 3.13. The Subquery form permits GROUP BY and HAVING clauses, for example, and can also contain host variable expressions. However, most database system products do not provide a column alias for an expression retrieved in the target list: such a feature is less valuable because there is no default table display in the embedded case, although it is sometimes used to provide a named column for use in the ORDER BY clause. However, an integer is commonly allowed in the result_column, to specify a column by its position in the result table.

The optional forms in the final line of Figure 5.5 specify the cursor to be READ ONLY or FOR UPDATE. If neither is specified, the cursor defaults to READ ONLY if

```
EXEC SQL DECLARE cursor_name CURSOR FOR
    Subquery
    [ORDER BY result_column [ASC | DESC] {, result_column [ASC | DESC]...}]
    [FOR {READ ONLY | UPDATE [OF columnname {, columnname...}]}];
```

Figure 5.5 Embedded SQL Declare Cursor Syntax

ORDER BY is used and FOR UPDATE otherwise. In **DB2 UDB** (and in Core SQL-99), it is necessary to choose at most one of the two final clauses in this syntax, ORDER BY or FOR UPDATE. **ORACLE** allows both forms to be used simultaneously. (However, **ORACLE** uses the keyword clause WITH READONLY *prior to* the ORDER BY clause, instead of FOR READ ONLY after it.) The FOR UPDATE clause should be included with the cursor declaration if the program logic intends to update or delete a row through the cursor (as explained in the next two subsections). If FOR UPDATE is used without a column list, all selected columns are assumed updatable. A READ ONLY clause should be used where possible to allow the database to optimize queries. When you use READ ONLY, the logic is promising *not to* Update or Delete rows through the cursor. **ORACLE** and **DB2 UDB** allow an expression in the ORDER BY clause, not just a column name.

Note that a cursor as defined above can only move forward through a set of rows. This limitation disappears with the SQL-99 *scrollable cursor* feature covered in Section 5.7. However, this feature is not yet supported by **ORACLE** or **DB2 UDB**, and this means you will need to close and reopen a cursor in order to fetch a row a second time. The same cursor may be opened and closed successive times in a single program. It generally must be closed, however, before it can be reopened (**ORACLE** permits an exception to this rule, as explained below).

The Delete Statement

There are two forms of the Delete statement, the *Positioned Delete,* which deletes the current row (most recently fetched row) of a cursor, and the *Searched Delete,* which has the same sort of form we have already seen in Interactive SQL in Section 3.9. Figure 5.6 gives the syntax that describes the two forms of Delete.

The Positioned Delete uses a special CURRENT OF cursor_name syntax. Only one of the two WHERE forms can be used; if neither is used, all rows of the table will be deleted. The corr_name is for use in the search_condition and may cause a runtime error condition in some products if used with a Positioned Delete. Following a Searched Delete, the long int variable sqlca.sqlerrd[2] contains the number of rows affected in

```
EXEC SQL DELETE FROM tablename [corr_name]
    [WHERE search_condition | WHERE CURRENT OF cursor_name];
```

Figure 5.6 Embedded Basic SQL Delete Syntax

systems using the deprecated SQLCA. If no rows are affected, the NOT FOUND condition of the Whenever statement arises.

In the Positioned Delete, after the delete is executed the cursor points to a new position, following the row deleted but just preceding the next row, if any. This is in the same sense that after an OPEN of a cursor, the cursor points to a position just before the first row in the Select; this behavior is carefully chosen to work well with loops (as we see in Example 5.3.1). If the cursor is not pointing to a row when a delete is executed (that is, if it is pointing just before some row, or else Fetch has already returned a NOT FOUND condition and is pointing to a position after all the rows), a runtime error will be returned. For the Positioned Delete to work at all, the cursor stipulated in the delete must be already open and pointing to a real row, and the FROM clause of the delete must refer to the same table as the FROM clause of the cursor select. In addition, the cursor in use must be an updatable cursor, that is, it must not have been declared as a READ ONLY cursor.

EXAMPLE 5.3.1

Delete all customers from the customers table who live in Duluth and have made no orders (do not appear in the orders table). We can do this simply, with a Searched Delete, using the following statement:

```
exec sql delete from customers c where c.city = 'Duluth' and
    not exists (select * from orders o where o.cid = c.cid);
```

We could also use a cursor to perform this delete:

```
exec sql declare delcust cursor for
select cid from customers c where c.city = 'Duluth'
    and not exists (select * from orders o where o.cid = c.cid)
    for update of cid;            /* must declare cursor for update      */
whenever not found goto skip;     /* label "skip" lies later in code     */
exec sql open delcust;
while (TRUE) {                    /* TRUE has value 1: loop forever      */
    exec sql fetch delcust into :cust_id;  /* if not found, goto skip: out of loop */
    exec sql delete from customers
        where current of delcust;  /* delete row under cursor            */
}
. . .
```

Note that after the Delete statement in the while(TRUE) loop, the cursor points to a position just before the following row. The Fetch statement at the beginning of the loop is needed to advance the cursor through each of the rows selected, whether or not a delete is performed. In cases where the delete may or may not be performed, depending on some complex logical condition, this is valuable default behavior because we can always depend on requiring a fetch at the top of the loop. ∎

It is possible to modify the program of Example 5.3.1, creating a cursor that retrieves `city` and `cid` for all `customers` who have made orders and then performing the test `if(strcmp(city,"Duluth")==0)` in the program logic to decide whether the row should be deleted. However, this approach would be a mistake, for performance reasons. It is always best to provide as much of a selection criterion as possible to SQL, because that way SQL can perform a test without the extra overhead of having to extract the values from the table and send them back to the program, often a very time-consuming action. Indeed it is usually preferable to leave as much of the intended action as possible to SQL. The Searched Delete appearing at the top of Example 5.3.1 is more efficient than the loop below to perform equivalent Positioned Deletes through the cursor.

The Update Statement

As with Delete, there are two versions of the Update statement, a *Searched Update* analogous to the multi-row Interactive Update statement, and a *Positioned Update,* which acts through a cursor. The Searched Update (Figure 5.7) is virtually identical to the interactive version presented in Section 3.9, and it contains no elements we haven't explained earlier:

Following a Searched Update, the long int variable `sqlca.sqlerrd[2]` contains the number of rows affected (i.e., deleted). If no rows are affected, the NOT FOUND condition of the Whenever statement arises.

As with Delete, for the Positioned Update statement (Figure 5.8) to work properly the cursor must be open, the table named in the Update and in the Declare Cursor statement must be identical, and the cursor must be pointing to a valid row, rather than to a position just before or after some row. In addition, the cursor must be an updatable cursor and declared FOR UPDATE on all the columns changed by the Update statement. If any of these conditions are not valid, a runtime error will be returned from the Positioned Update statement execution.

```
[EXEC SQL] UPDATE tablename
    SET columnname = expr | NULL| (subquery)
        {, columnname = expr | NULL | (subquery)...}
    [WHERE search_condition];
```

Figure 5.7   Embedded Basic SQL Searched Update Syntax

```
EXEC SQL UPDATE tablename
    SET columnname = expr | NULL| (subquery)
        {, columnname = expr | NULL | (subquery)...}
    WHERE CURRENT OF cursor_name;
```

Figure 5.8   Embedded Basic SQL Positioned Update Syntax

```
EXEC SQL INSERT INTO tablename [(columnname {, columnname...})]
        {VALUES (expr {, expr}) | Subquery};
```

Figure 5.9   Embedded Basic SQL Insert Syntax

The Insert Statement

The Insert statement has only a single form, identical to the interactive version of the Insert statement presented in Section 3.9. The Insert statement syntax is given in Figure 5.9. Nevertheless, there are two Insert forms, one that inserts a single row with specified values and one that may possibly insert multiple rows, derived from a general Subquery statement as specified earlier in this section. Following an insert derived from a Subquery, the long int variable sqlca.sqlerrd[2] will contain the number of rows affected. If no rows are affected (e.g., the Subquery returns no rows), the NOT FOUND condition of the Whenever statement will arise.

Let us consider for a moment why there is no positioned insert INSERT ... WHERE CURRENT OF cursor_name;. As we will learn in later chapters, a newly inserted row usually cannot be placed into a table at a designated position, but only at a position determined by the disk structure of the table. The phrase WHERE CURRENT OF cursor_name would thus overdetermine the problem to be solved by the database system in deciding where to place a newly inserted row.

Cursor Open, Fetch, and Close

The statement to open a previously defined cursor has the form shown in Figure 5.10. When the Open statement is executed, the database system evaluates expressions in the WHERE clause of the cursor specification for cursor_name and identifies a set of rows that becomes the active set for subsequent Fetch operations. Any host variables used in the cursor definition are evaluated *at the time the Open statement is executed*. If these values later change, this does not affect the active set of rows. For many database products, the cursor cannot be opened again if it is already open. **ORACLE** allows an exception to this rule, since an already open cursor can be reopened, redefining the active set of rows.

The statement to fetch a row from an active set of rows from an opened cursor has the form illustrated in Figure 5.11. Executing the Open Cursor statement positions the cursor, cursor_name, to a position just before the first row of an active set of rows. Each successive Fetch statement repositions cursor_name to the next row of its active set and assigns column values from that row (named in the Declare Cursor statement) to the host variables named in the Fetch statement. In order for a Fetch statement to work,

```
EXEC SQL OPEN cursor_name;
```

Figure 5.10   Embedded Basic SQL Open Cursor Syntax

```
EXEC SQL FETCH cursor_name
         INTO host-variable {, host-variable};
```

Figure 5.11 Embedded Basic SQL Fetch Syntax

```
EXEC SQL CLOSE cursor-name;
```

Figure 5.12 Embedded Basic SQL Close Cursor Syntax

cursor_name must already be open and the number of host variables must match the number of columns in the target list of the Define Cursor. The NOT FOUND condition of the Whenever statement arises when a Fetch statement is executed on an active set of rows that is empty, or when the cursor is positioned after the last active row.

The statement to close a cursor has the form shown in Figure 5.12. This statement closes the cursor so that the active set of rows is no longer accessible. It is an error to close a cursor that is not open.

Other Embedded SQL Operations

A number of other Embedded SQL statements will be explained in the following sections. Here is a list of ones we have already seen:

```
exec sql create table
exec sql drop table
exec sql connect
exec sql disconnect
```

The syntax for these and other statements can be found in Appendix C. While most of them have quite simple syntax, the Create Table statement has many syntax elements that have not yet been introduced and that require careful explanation. This will be covered in Chapter 6.

5.4 Programming for Transactions

In Chapter 3, we dealt only with ad hoc Interactive SQL statements. It is not surprising that a number of new considerations arise with the ability to create procedures that use several SQL statements in sequence to accomplish a single task. In this section we introduce the concept of *database transactions*. We show that there is sometimes a need to group several SQL statements together into a single indivisible, all-or-nothing transactional package, and that this concept has important ramifications for the way we write our programs.

The Concept of a Transaction

Most database systems allow multiple users to execute simultaneously and to access tables in a common database. You have probably seen situations where a large number of users on different monitors interacted with a single computer (students in a terminal room connected to a time-shared computer, bank clerks at their monitors, airline reservation agents, etc.). A major task of a computer operating system is to keep track of these users, all running different work streams known as *user processes*. The database system cooperates with this user process concept by permitting multiple processes to access data at the same time. This is known as *concurrent access*, or *concurrency*.

It turns out that without adequate controls on concurrent access, it is possible for a user process to view a collection of data elements that should never exist simultaneously.

EXAMPLE 5.4.1 Inconsistent View of Data.

Assume that a depositor has two bank accounts in a table A, represented as distinct rows with unique account ID values, aid, equal to A1 and A2. We represent A.balance where A.aid = An by An.balance, for short (note that this is not Basic SQL notation), and assume that we start with A1.balance containing $900.00 and A2.balance containing $100.00. Now assume that process P1 attempts to move $400.00 from account A1 to A2, to even out the balances. In order to do this, it must perform two row updates, first subtracting $400.00 from A1.balance, then adding $400.00 to A2.balance. Thus we have three "states" in which we can find the two row balances.

S1   A1.balance == $900.00, A2.balance == $100.00
      Values before any change has taken place.

S2   A1.balance == $500.00, A2.balance == $100.00
      Values after subtracting $400.00 from the balance of account A1.

S3   A1.balance == $500.00, A2.balance == $500.00
      Values after adding $400.00 to the balance of account A2.

Now let's say another process, P2, is running simultaneously to perform a credit check on this depositor, requiring a total of at least $900.00 before the depositor will be allowed to take out a credit card. To do this, process P2 must read the two rows with aid values A1 and A2 and add the account balances. If it does this while the two balances are in state S2, then the sum will be $600.00, and the depositor will fail the credit check; it would have passed the credit check if there had been $1000.00 in the two accounts. Here is a schedule of operations that could lead to this view of the balance total by P2:

Process P1	Process P2
	`int bal, sum = 0.00;`

`Update A set balance = balance - $400.00`
`    where A.aid = 'A1';`
(Now balance = $500.00.)	

	`select A.balance into :bal from A`
	`    where A.aid = 'A1';`
	`sum = sum + bal;` (Now sum = $500.00.)

	`select A.balance into :bal from A`
	`    where A.aid = 'A2';`
	`sum = sum + bal;` (Now sum = $600.00.)

	(Credit card issuance refused.)

`Update A set balance = balance + $400.00`
`    where A.aid = 'A2';`
(Now balance = $500.00. Transfer complete.)	

But the $600.00 total balance in state S2 seen by process P2 is actually an illusion. The depositor started with $1000.00 and process P1 was not trying to withdraw money, only to transfer it. The fact that state S2 exposes a balance of $600.00 is known as an "inconsistent view." We say there are certain consistency rules that are being observed (money is neither created nor destroyed by process P1, so the total of account values should not change), but in order to achieve the correct final state, the logic of process P1 must go through possibly inconsistent states along the way (e.g., state S2). We would like to keep other processes (such as P2) from viewing these temporary inconsistent states. ∎

To avoid inconsistent views and a number of other difficulties that can arise with concurrent access, database systems provide a feature called *transactions*. Each process is able to package together a series of database operations that make up a consistent change in state (such as the two updates of process P1) or an attempt at a consistent view (such as the two reads of process P2); such a package of database operations is called a *transaction*. Note that many transactions require a consistent view of the data as a basis for updates; for example, each of the two updates of process P1 can be thought of as a read followed by a write, and the two reads must be consistent or we may make an error in the final amounts stored in these balances. We will have more to say about this later. (However, it should be noted that while each of these updates can be thought of as a read followed by a write, an Update statement applied to a single row in a DBMS is itself indivisible: it is impossible for any other operation to interfere with the row between the read and the write of such an update. In this sense, an Update statement for a single row is already transactionally indivisible.)

A database system that supports transactions provides guarantees to programmers of a number of transactional properties that make the programming job easier. The most important guarantee for the current discussion is known as *isolation*. Isolation guarantees that even though transaction T1 (which might be the one that packages the two updates of process P1) and T2 (which might package the two reads of process P2) execute concurrently, it appears to each that it has operated on the database in isolation from the effects of the other. When we say *in isolation*, we mean that it appears that either T2 executes *before* T1 has begun making any changes, or T2 executes *after* T1 has completed; T2 sees state S1 or state S3 of Example 5.4.1, but never state S2, and thus cannot take an inconsistent view.

How Transactions Are Specified in Programs

Immediately after connecting to a database, a program has no active transaction in progress. A program that has no active transaction can begin one by executing any SQL statement that operates on rows of the database (such as Select, Open Cursor, Update, Insert, or Delete). The transaction remains active during a number of such executed statements, and the program ends the transaction by executing one of the following two Embedded SQL statements:

◆ EXEC SQL COMMIT [WORK]; This statement causes the transaction to end successfully; all row updates made during the transaction become permanent in the database and visible to concurrent users. All rows read during the transaction once again become available to concurrent users for update.

◆ EXEC SQL ROLLBACK [WORK]; This statement causes the transaction to end unsuccessfully (to *abort*); all row updates made during the transaction are reversed and the prior versions of these rows are put in place and become visible again to concurrent users. All rows read during the transaction become once again available to concurrent users for update.

Although the WORK keyword is optional starting with SQL-92, it was required in SQL-89 and thus it might be best to use it for transportability to older database systems. After a transaction ends as a result of a Commit or Rollback, the next SQL statement that operates on rows of the database will begin a new transaction, which once again will remain active until the next Commit or Rollback statement.

If neither a Commit nor a Rollback statement is executed for a transaction in progress before a program terminates, a product-dependent default action (Commit or Rollback) is performed. We saw the Commit statement used in the two examples at the beginning of this chapter, Examples 5.1.1 and 5.1.2, to release locks taken on the rows that had been read during the transaction. These locks are used to implement the transaction isolation guarantee, as we will see shortly. A transaction usually consists of the set of database operations (Select statements or Update statements or both) that takes place between one Commit statement and the next—a Rollback is less common. A typical way for an application program to behave is for each concurrent user process to loop around through a large number of statements, alternately requesting input from the user and then performing a set of database operations on the user's behalf. As we will see, it is a bad idea to keep a transaction active across user interactions, so a Commit statement is usually performed before requesting input. However, there might be more than one transaction for each user interaction, so it isn't safe to assume that transactions extend from one user input to the next, although that is the most typical case.

It should be clear in the situation just outlined that it is up to the programmer to specify to the system when a transaction ends—the system cannot guess. A transaction involving database updates (including Inserts and Deletes) is a set of updates that should either all succeed or all fail as a unit. The situation of Example 5.4.1 can be extended to a transfer of money between a large number of account balances, coming out even at the end, so that money is neither created nor destroyed. But the system is unable to tell when such a balance has been achieved (it doesn't follow the math performed) unless the programmer says so with a Commit statement. After the Commit, all row updates performed during the transaction become permanent and visible to concurrent users. After Rollback, all updates are reversed, and the (old) values likewise become visible. A transaction T2 involving only database reads (a read-only transaction) must never see a temporary inconsistent state in a sequence of updates performed by transaction T1—the kind of problem that might arise in Example 5.4.1, where transaction T2 (representing process P2) reads some account values *before* they have been updated by T1 (representing process P1) and other account values *after* they have been updated by T1. It turns out that a read-only transaction T2 must freeze all the data it touches as of a given instant, and this sets up a tension with update transactions that want to perform updates. Therefore we need to end a read-only transaction when we have completed our task, and once again the system is unable to guess when this should happen. The programmer needs to indicate the transaction end with a Rollback or Commit statement. In the case of read-only transactions, there is no difference in effect between Rollback and Commit, since no updates were attempted.

The Rollback statement is extremely convenient for an application programmer writing an *update transaction*. Consider the example of the last paragraph, where money is transferred between a large number of account balances. Assume that withdrawals will be made from the first N − 1 account balances, and the sum of these withdrawals will be added to the final account balance. The simplest method of programming this is to read each new account row, check that the balance is sufficient to cover whatever withdrawal is needed and, assuming that the answer is yes, make the withdrawal from this row balance, then pass on to the next account row, finally committing after updating the last row to receive the sum of the prior withdrawals. No other transaction is able to view these intermediate updates until the transaction commits, so there is no danger that other users will see updates while we are still uncertain of success. But assume now that some account balance in the series has insufficient funds, so that we cannot complete the transaction. Rather than read backward through the series of rows already updated and reverse the withdrawals (an error-prone programming task), the program can simply execute the Rollback statement. A common synonym for rolling back is that the transaction *aborts*. All updates made so far are reversed automatically by the system, and it is as if the updates we were trying to form into a transaction had never occurred.

This ability of the database system to roll back (abort, reverse, undo) all updates performed by a partial transaction illustrates another guarantee (like isolation) that is made by the system, a guarantee called *atomicity*. Atomicity guarantees the programmer that the set of row updates performed in a transaction is "atomic," that is, indivisible: either all updates occur or none of them occur. In order to support atomicity, to know what row updates in the database must be reversed when a transaction aborts, the database system must have some way of noting row updates and storing these notes for later access. This all-or-nothing update guarantee holds even in the presence of a system crash, where memory is lost and it becomes impossible to remember what the program was doing, what updates it had made, or why it had made them.

The fact that a transaction that has successfully committed is resilient to system crash is called *durability*, a third guarantee of the database system to the programmer, along with isolation and atomicity. To support durability, the database system must make additional notes to remind itself of its intentions and see that they are placed on disk, so it can recover from memory loss. We see that the transactional guarantees have a number of implications, but we won't discuss many of the complexities until we deal with update transactions in a later chapter. In the current section we discuss updates only in the depth necessary to shed light on consistent views in a sequence of reads; we concentrate in the remainder of this section on read-only transactions and the isolation guarantee.

A Transaction Example

Figure 5.13 illustrates an example of a banking transaction program to transfer money between accounts as requested by a bank teller. Recall that a transaction begins with the first SQL statement that operates on rows of the database, so the early Declare section, the Connect statement, and the loop containing the prompt in the program of Figure 5.13 are not part of any transaction. The prompt to the user requests account identifiers for accounts named *from* and *to*, which specify the two accounts between which the transfer is to be made and the dollar amount of the transfer. The sscanf( ) function is used to convert the text form of the dollar amount (contained in the dollarstr[ ] array) to the double (float) form of the dollar amount (placed in the dollars variable). To understand this section of the code, you should read Appendix B.1. Following this, the *Set Transaction statement*, SET TRANSACTION ISOLATION LEVEL SERIALIZABLE, is a boilerplate statement you don't need to understand for now; it will be explained when we return to transactions in depth in Section 10.5.

The statements of the transaction that operate on rows of the database are the two Update statements. If no errors are returned by these statements, the transaction is committed and the program terminates. If an error occurs, control jumps to do_rollback, and the transaction is rolled back. In this case, if the first Update had already occurred, all modifications would be reversed by the database system to restore the state of the database to be as if this transaction had never run.

Normally a program such as this would be performed inside a function call, with a loop at a higher level to give the teller a choice between transferring money from one account to another, withdrawing money from an account, depositing money to an account, checking account balances, and so on. In Figure 5.13, the part of the program performing the transaction has been placed in a loop to make this repetitive property

```c
#include <stdio.h>
#include "prompt.h"
int main( )        /* note no #include SQLCA, since SQL-99 deprecates this      */
{
    exec sql begin declare section;
        char acctfrom[11], acctto[11];
        double dollars;
    exec sql end declare section;
    char dollarstr[20];

    exec sql connect to default;              /* (not part of transaction)      */
    exec sql set transaction isolation level serializable;
    while (1) {        /* loop forever: simplified teller-program loop           */
        while ((prompt("Enter from, to accounts and dollars for transfer:\n",
               3, acctfrom, 10, acctto, 10, dollarstr, 10)) < 0) ||
               (sscanf(dollarstr,"%lf",&dollars) != 1)) {     /* convert to double   */
            printf("Invalid input. Input example: 345633 445623 100.45\n");
        } /* Above, print out error msg until input is acceptable               */
        exec sql whenever sqlerror goto do_rollback;

        /* transaction starts here--                                            */
        exec sql update accounts set balance = balance - :dollars
            where acct = :acctfrom;
        exec sql update accounts set balance = balance + :dollars
            where acct = :acctto;
        exec sql commit work;                  /* transaction ends here...       */
        printf("Transfer complete\n");
        continue;
do_rollback:
        exec sql rollback work;                /* ... or here                    */
        printf("Transfer failed\n");
    }
    exec sql disconnect current;
    return 0;
}
```

Figure 5.13 Simple Program to Transfer Money between Accounts (SQL-99)

clear and emphasize the importance of using a Commit or Rollback statement at the end of each transfer pass; otherwise old transactions would remain in force when the next transaction was initiated on behalf of an entirely different customer, and eventually all the account rows would be locked against use by other tellers.

Note that several different processes (acting for different tellers) can be executing this same program concurrently, and a transaction acting under one process might be transferring money from account A1 to account A2 while a second transaction is transferring money from account A2 to account A1. The surprising thing here is that even if there were no transactions containing each pair of Update statements in this program, the transactions would not interfere with each other: the same transfers would be accomplished even if the Update statements were interleaved in surprising ways. This is because each of the single-row Update statements acting alone is indivisible and accomplishes the required task to subtract or add a dollar amount to whatever the account balance is at the moment. But while a transaction enclosing the two Updates is not required for the transfers of Figure 5.13 to succeed, a transaction is required to ensure that a concurrent transaction returns the sum of balances from two accounts in a valid way. (See Example 5.4.1; the exercises have more detail on this.)

Note in the program of Figure 5.13 that user interaction (the prompt( ) loop) is performed completely outside the scope of any transaction. There is a good reason for this since in this way the transactional task can be performed quickly, so that locks or other resources held by this transaction to ensure isolation will not have a long-term negative effect on other transactions. This will be discussed further below.

The Transaction Isolation Guarantee and Locking

The isolation property guarantees that when transactions T1 and T2 execute concurrently, it appears to each that it has operated on the database in isolation from the effects of the other. More precisely, it seems that all database operations belonging to T2 occur before T1 starts or else after T1 has completed. A different way of saying this is that any set of concurrently executing transactions acts as if they are executing in some *serial* order; that is, for any two transactions in the set, one of them must complete all its operations before the other begins. This property of transactions, that they act as if they were occurring in serial order, is also called *serializability*, a property we will study in depth in a later chapter. Serializability is equivalent to isolation for our purposes.

If we think of T1 as a read-only transaction executing concurrently with a *set* of Update transactions, the definition of the last paragraph means that T1 sees only consistent states of a database, after some number (possibly zero) of these concurrently executing Update transactions have completed. The most common approach taken by database systems to implement the isolation guarantee is known as *database row locking*. The somewhat simplified set of locking rules shown in Figure 5.14 helps to support transaction isolation.

The more general locking approach, which will be covered in Chapter 10, differentiates between read access locks (R locks) and update, or write access, locks (W locks); but for now the simplified approach of exclusive locks in all cases gives a reasonable picture.

---

[1] When a transaction accesses a row R, it must begin by locking that row in an exclusive mode.

[2] All locks taken by a transaction are held until that transaction ends (commits or aborts).

[3] If T1 has locked a row R and a different transaction, T2, attempts to access the row, then T2 also attempts to lock R exclusively before accessing it and is refused, because a lock by T2 of R conflicts with the lock already held by T1.

[4] The usual approach with such a conflict is for the system to make T2 WAIT until T1 commits or aborts and releases its lock on R, after which T2 can be granted its lock request and proceed with further execution.

Figure 5.14 Simplified Rules of Database Row Locking to Guarantee Isolation

The somewhat simplified set of locking rules shown in Figure 5.14 helps to support transaction isolation.

EXAMPLE 5.4.2 Locking and Inconsistent Views.
Consider the sequence of events in Figure 5.15, a restatement of Example 5.4.1, where the balance for account A1 starts at $900.00 and for A2 at $100.00:

Transaction T1 (update transaction)	Transaction T2 (read-only transaction)
	`int bal, sum = 0.00;`

`Update A set balance = balance - $400.00`
    `where A.aid = 'A1';`
(Now balance = $500.00.)	

	`select A.balance into :bal from A`
	    `where A.aid = 'A1';`
	`sum = sum + bal;` (Now sum = $500.00.)

	`select A.balance into :bal from A`
	    `where A = 'A2';`
	`sum = sum + bal;` (Now sum = $600.00.)

`Update A set balance = balance + $400.00`
    `where A.aid = 'A2';`
(Now balance = $500.00.)	

	`commit work;`
`commit work;`	

Figure 5.15 No Locks Held for the Transaction: View of Inconsistent Data

This sequence of events corresponds to Example 5.4.1, which allowed process P2 to get an inconsistent view of the two balances of accounts A1 and A2. In this schedule, transaction T1

Transaction T1 (update transaction)	Transaction T2 (read-only transaction)
	`int bal, sum = 0.00;`

`Update A set balance = balance - $400.00`
`    where A.aid = 'A1';`
(This row is now locked, balance = $500.00.)	

	`select A.balance into :bal from A`
	`    where A.aid = 'A1';`
	(Same row as T1 just locked; must WAIT.)

`Update A set balance = balance + $400.00` `    where A.aid = 'A2';` (This row now locked) (Now balance = $500.00; transfer complete.)	
`commit work;` (Releases locks)	

	(Prior select can now achieve needed lock.)
	`select A.balance into :bal from A`
	`    where A = 'A1';`
	`sum = sum + bal;` (Now sum = $500.00.)

	`select A.balance into :bal from A`
	`    where A = 'A2';`
	`sum = sum + bal;` (Now sum = $1000.00.)

	`commit work;`

Figure 5.16   Transaction Locks Fix Inconsistent View of Data of Figure 5.15

represents process P1 and transaction T2 represents process P2; row accesses on later lines come later in time, so the accesses of the two transactions are interleaved. To start, there is a `balance` of $900.00 in account A1 (`A.aid = 'A1'`) and a `balance` of $100.00 in A2.

In Figure 5.15, transaction T2 has seen an inconsistent view of the two rows A1 and A2, the view associated with state S2 in Example 5.4.1. But now consider how these rows would be locked in the approach outlined above. In Figure 5.16, we see that T1 would start by locking row A1 before updating it. Thereafter, when transaction T2 attempts to lock row A1 before reading it through a Select statement, it would not be granted the lock and would have to wait until transaction T1 completed its work and committed. This would have the effect that all operations of transaction T2 would be delayed until both updates of T1 are complete, and T2 would proceed with its reads and see the consistent state S3. This sequence of events is pictured in Figure 5.16.

This is only an example, naturally, and does not constitute a proof that the isolation property is guaranteed in all situations by row locking. There are in fact a few other details that must be addressed to achieve such a guarantee (in particular, there is a problem associated with a set of rows activated by an Open Cursor statement), but row locking is the basic approach used by most database systems to guarantee isolation, and we assume in what follows that such locking takes place in all data accesses. ∎

Special Considerations in Transactions

With the guarantee of isolation there is a potential problem: what to do when the accesses of two transactions deadlock against each other. We also explain in what follows why it is usually necessary to avoid user interaction during a transaction.

Deadlock

A somewhat surprising concomitant of database row locking to guarantee isolation is the potential that arises for deadlock. A deadlock occurs when two (or more) transactions are waiting for resources of others and none of the transactions can proceed unless one of the transactions gives up (rolls back or aborts).

EXAMPLE 5.4.3 Transaction Deadlock.

Let us recapitulate Example 5.4.2 but reverse the order of data access attempted by transaction T2. See the schedule of Figure 5.17.

In this example, T1 starts by locking row A1 before updating it. Then transaction T2 successfully locks row A2 before reading it through a Select statement. But now transaction T2 tries to lock row A1, which is already locked by T1, and it fails. As a result the system causes transaction T2 to WAIT until T1 commits and releases its locks. Following this, transaction T1 tries to lock A2, which is already locked by T2, and fails. Now the system would normally cause T1 to WAIT until T2 commits and releases its locks, but in this case the system needs to recognize a deadlock situation. T1 cannot proceed until T2 commits and releases its locks, but that's never going to happen because T2 is waiting for T1 to complete and release its own locks. Neither can proceed until the other releases its locks. In this situation, the system has only one course available if it doesn't want to leave these transactions hanging forever. It chooses one of the two transactions to *abort* (roll back). This is called a *deadlock abort*. All updates that have been made by the aborted transaction are undone, the process running the transaction receives an error message return from the latest data access statement, and the process logic continues from that point. One avenue open to the process with the aborted

Transaction T1	Transaction T2
	`int bal, sum = 0.00;`

`Update A set balance = balance - $400.00`
    `where A = 'A1';`
(Lock achieved.)	

	`select A.balance into :bal from A`
	    `where A = 'A2';`
	`sum = sum + bal;` (Lock achieved.)

	`select A.balance into :bal from A`
	    `where A = 'A1';`
	(Conflict with T1: WAIT.)

	. . .

`Update A set balance = balance + $400.00`
    `where A = 'A2';`
(Conflict with T2: WAIT).
	. . .

. . .	. . .
. . .	. . .

Figure 5.17   Transaction Deadlock

transaction is to *retry* the transaction (that is, to attempt to run it again). Note that not only are all row updates by the aborted transaction undone, but also any row values that were read are untrustworthy (some of them might have been changed by a different update transaction after the locks were released), so the only safe approach is to run the transaction over again from scratch.   ∎

The deadlock abort condition has important implications for application programming in Embedded SQL. If the system aborts a partially completed chain of logic in a transaction to resolve a deadlock situation, the program needs to detect this situation and attempt to execute the transaction again, to *retry*. The retry approach was mentioned in Example 5.4.3, but it is often up to the program logic to actually implement it, and this may entail a good deal of complexity. Attempting a retry is appropriate because the earlier failure to complete was not a logical problem—rather it was merely a matter of bad timing—so we have a good hope that the transaction will complete if it is run again.

After beginning a transaction, the program must be on the lookout for the "deadlock abort" error return in sqlca.sqlcode from certain SQL statements entailing data access. The sqlca.sqlcode error numbers corresponding to this condition in **ORACLE** and **DB2 UDB** products are shown in Figure 5.18. We also provide SQLSTATE error returns, which are supported (for example) by **ORACLE** acting in ANSI mode.

The deadlock abort error return can occur nearly any time an EXEC SQL statement attempts to read or update data in the database. A program should react to a deadlock abort return by repeating the transactional attempt a certain number of times. (We say that we *retry* the transaction.) If a deadlock continues to occur, some serious problem might be implied, and the program should advise the user to speak with the system manager (the end user generally lacks understanding of any details of transactions). Note that if you were to set up a condition handler such as whenever sqlerror stop in advance of the statement where you detect the deadlock abort error, the error would never be detected. As we saw in Section 4.2, the Whenever statement reacts to the error before explicit tests for an error (unfortunately, there is no Whenever condition associated with deadlock abort). Therefore it is important to have the default CONTINUE action in place for error returns before attempting to trap deadlock abort errors.

EXAMPLE 5.4.4   Deadlock Abort Detection.
In the following program fragment, we write a transaction to contain the multiple row changes of a Searched Update statement and *retry* the transaction when a deadlock occurs. The symbolic constant for a deadlock abort error return is the one used by **ORACLE**. An alternative and potentially more portable version of this code would use the SQLSTATE value.

```
 . . .
#define DEADABORT -60
#define TRUE 1
exec sql whenever sqlerror continue;
int count = 0;
```

```
while (TRUE) {                          /* loop over deadlock-abort retries      */
    exec sql update customers
        set discnt = 1.1*discnt where city = 'New York';
    if (sqlca.sqlcode == DEADABORT) {
        count++;                        /* count up deadlock aborts              */
        if (count < 4) {                /* retry up to four times                */
            exec sql rollback work;
            /* here, call operating system to wait for a second                  */
        } else break;                   /* too many retries                      */
    else if (sqlca.sqlcode < 0)
        break;                          /* non-deadlock error                    */
}
if (sqlca.sqlcode < 0)  {               /* over-retried deadlock or other error  */
    print_dberror( );                   /* print error message                   */
    exec sql rollback work;
    return -1;                          /* return error                          */
} else return 0;                        /* return success                        */
```

Note that other transactional errors—such as time-out on a lock request—can occur, but dead-lock abort is the one where it seems most reasonable to retry the transaction. ∎

One other important consideration is associated with performing transaction retry. It is possible that the program has reset local program variables in memory during the course of the transaction, before the deadlock abort. These local variables might represent flags for products to be ordered, for example, which are turned off as the appropriate products are taken from the database; another possibility is that a local variable represents the dollar total ordered by the user. After the deadlock abort occurs, all *database* information is rolled back to the point that the program logic first found it. However, local program variables in memory are not under the control of the database, so the programmer should take care that these variables return to their original values as well. If the original state is difficult to reestablish, the programmer should go as far as copying, before starting the transaction logic, all status variables that might change in the course of the transaction, and then copy the original values back again if a deadlock abort occurs.

No User Interaction during Transactions

One of the more important points of database row locking is that any lock that has been taken by a transaction continues to be held while the transaction remains active—that is, until a Commit or Rollback statement has been executed in the program. This places a

	Variable	Value	Description
Basic SQL	SQLSTATE	'40001'	Serialization Failure
ORACLE	sqlca.sqlcode	-60	
DB2 UDB	sqlca.sqlcode	-911	

Figure 5.18 Deadlock Abort Errors. **ORACLE** (in ANSI mode) and **DB2 UDB** also support SQLSTATE.

limit on the appropriate duration of a transaction. Every second that goes by could be holding up other users who wish to access the same row. One cardinal rule is that a user interaction should never be initiated while a transaction is in progress (the user might get involved in a conversation or wander off to get a cup of coffee while crucial data remains inaccessible). However, there seem to be numerous situations in which a program would like to confer with the user in the midst of a transaction.

EXAMPLE 5.4.5 User Interaction during a Transaction.
Consider the program fragment of Figure 5.19, where we are taking orders from an agent and updating the quantity column in the products table, which represents the number of product units still available at the warehouse. The fragment interacts with an agent to test that an order can be filled, and it is not bulletproofed against all possible errors.

Note that when the user interaction in the While loop is occurring, a read of the products row has already been performed by the Select statement: a transaction has begun and a row in products is locked. No other agent can order this product while the agent confers with the customer about the size of the order desired. Performing user interaction while rows are locked is not a database system runtime error—the database system has no knowledge of user interaction in the example above—but it is a practice that should be avoided in any program where the row locked is likely to be accessed by another user.

```
/*  Interaction with agent taking product order for pid given by req_pid    */
exec sql select price, quantity into :price, :qoh
    from products where pid = :req_pid;       /* get info for later use       */
while (TRUE) {                /* loop until we get a quantord that fits in qoh */
    printf("We have %d units on hand at a price of %d each\n", qoh, price);
    if (prompt("How many units?\n", 1, quantordstr, QUANTORDLEN) < 0 ||
            (sscanf(quantordstr,"%d",&quantord) != 1)) {/* get int from string */
        printf("Please enter a decimal number.\n");
        continue;                            /* start over pass in loop        */
    }
    if (quantord <= qoh)
        break;                    /* break out of loop if quantord fits in qoh */
    else printf("There are not enough units to fill your order.\n");
}  /* end get-quantord loop                                                    */
exec sql update products                     /* reflect new order             */
    set quantity = quantity - :quantord      /* now know this fits            */
    where pid = :req_pid;
/* now insert new order in orders table                                       */
. . .
exec sql commit work;                        /* transaction complete          */
. . .
```

Figure 5.19   Program Fragment with Poorly Placed User Input (Illustrates Example 5.4.5)

A surprising problem can arise when transactions don't span user interactions.

EXAMPLE 5.4.6 User Interactions without Enclosing Transaction.   301

Consider the program fragment of Figure 5.20, a rewrite of the fragment in Figure 5.19, to avoid user interaction during a transaction.

This seems a straightforward modification of the logic in Example 5.4.5 to avoid having a lock held across a user request. However, if we look carefully, we note that something strange can happen. After retrieving the price and quantity of the product selected, we now commit the transaction before asking the agent what quantity is desired. We no longer hold a lock on the row while the agent responds (this was our aim), but this means that the quantity value for the row with this given pid value might be changed by some other transaction between the time we first read it and the time we try to update the row with the agent response. Therefore we cannot trust the qoh value we print out to the agent to remain valid. We must test the quantity ordered (quantord) *in the Update statement itself,* to be certain that the update of products.quantity will take place only if subtracting quantord does not bring quantity below zero. If no rows are affected by the update (NOT FOUND condition), the order is rejected because the quantity ordered is excessive. The surprising thing is that we might reject the order *even though the quantity ordered is less than the quantity we printed out as being on hand just a moment before.* For example, we might have printed out that there were 500 on hand, asked for an order, then rejected an order for 400, saying, "Sorry, there are not enough units on hand to fill your order." What is worse, if we execute a second pass of the While loop, select the new quantity value into qoh, print this, saying that (for example) 300 product units are on hand, and the customer now tries to order 300, we may reject the order again!

```
/* Interaction with agent for product req_pid-Version 2              */
while (TRUE) {                              /* loop until update succeeds   */
    exec sql select price, quantity into :price, :qoh
        from products where pid = :req_pid;     /* get info for later use   */
    /* shouldn't hold lock during user interaction, so need to Commit       */
    exec sql commit work;
    printf("We have %d units on hand at a price of %d each\n", qoh, price);
    if (prompt("How many units?\n", 1, quantordstr, QUANTORDLEN) < 0) ||
        (sscanf(quantordstr,"%d",&quantord) != 1)) {  /* get int from string */
        printf("Please enter a decimal number\n");
        continue;                               /* start over pass in loop   */
    }
    exec sql whenever not found goto unitsgone;
    exec sql update products                    /* new type of update with... */
        set quantity = quantity - :quantord
        where pid = :req_pid
        and quantity - :quantord >= 0;          /* ...new test that quantord fits*/
            /* insert new order in orders table                             */
    exec sql commit work;                       /* transaction complete      */
    break;                                      /* break out of loop         */
unitsgone:                        /* if no row selected, quantord didn't fit */
    printf("There are not enough units to fill your order.\n");
    exec sql rollback work;                     /* unneeded: no lock held    */
}   /* try-update loop                                                       */
. . .
```

Figure 5.20 Program Fragment (Illustrates Example 5.4.6)

■

This type of inconsistency is rare, and it is one we usually need to accept in writing transactional systems. You may even have encountered events like this in booking seats on an airplane flight: the agent starts by saying, "There's a window seat; I'll try to get it for you," and then a little later, "Oh, I'm sorry, someone else got it!"

Cursors and Transactions

Normally when a transaction is completed by a Commit or Rollback statement, all the open cursors are closed. This default reflects the usual mode of programming where a cursor is doing detailed work in a loop that should be performed as an atomic transactional unit. However, sometimes the program needs to commit many times in a loop. For example, suppose a program loops through all the employees to give them a 4% raise. If we perform the entire loop prior to committing, we will eventually lock all the rows of the table so they cannot even be read. To keep the number of row locks down, we would normally commit after counting some number of employees, say, 100. This would allow us to perform enough processing in the loop so the commit overhead doesn't take ten times as long as the logic processing, but if we lost the position of our cursor every time we committed, we would need a good deal of overhead to find the position again. For such cases, Core SQL-99 has specified the optional WITH HOLD clause for the Declare Cursor statement:

```
EXEC SQL DECLARE cursor_name [WITH HOLD] CURSOR FOR
    Subquery
[ORDER BY result_column [ASC | DESC] {, result_column [ASC | DESC]...}]
[FOR {READ ONLY | UPDATE [OF columnname {, columnname ...}]}];
```

When this option is in force, the cursor is kept open across commits, and thus remembers where it is in the employees table. Of course records not in the current locked range can change while this scan is in progress, and this is a good thing! If we make a rule that the salary column is only updated by one application at a time, and no new employees who don't deserve a raise are inserted while this process is in progress, the updates will be valid. We can enforce such a rule by having a special table with a row that all such updates and inserts must lock for update before they perform their other work.

This WITH HOLD feature is new to the SQL standards, but its presence in Core SQL-99 should mean that it will become generally available in serious database products soon. **DB2 UDB** has provided this feature starting from release 5 (1997). **ORACLE** doesn't have this clause and closes all cursors mentioned in CURRENT OF clauses at Commit or Rollback time under MODE=ORACLE, the default; it also closes all cursors belonging to the connection under MODE=ANSI, following the SQL standards when there is no WITH HOLD clause in effect.

From this description of **ORACLE**'s behavior, we see a way to avoid losing the cursor position at Commit time by avoiding the use of CURRENT OF actions. We can hold the position of a row by retrieving the pseudo-column ROWID in our Fetch loop through the cursor, then use it for any needed update by performing a Searched Update: where rowid = :row_id instead of one that is where current of cursor. Access through ROW-

IDs provides fast access. See Chapter 8, Section 8.2, for more information on ROWIDs, and the *ORACLE8 Programmer's Guide to the Pro*C/C++ Precompiler* [7] for more information on accessing RIDs.

5.5 | The Power of Procedural SQL Programs

In this section we show how tasks that could not be performed with non-procedural Basic SQL statements, as shown in Section 3.11, can now be achieved with a procedural approach. (Note that some of the Advanced SQL syntax of Section 3.6 can also extend the capabilities of Basic SQL to perform tasks of this kind.)

Customized Set Functions

In Example 3.10.3, it was pointed out that SQL lacks the median set function. We can now overcome this limitation programmatically.

EXAMPLE 5.5.1 Simulating a Median Set Function.

The program in Figure 5.21 repeatedly requests the user to input a `cid` value, then prints out the value that would be retrieved if we could write the SQL statement:

```
select median(dollars) from orders where cid = :cid;
```

The approach used in Figure 5.21 to find the median value is to count the number of `dollars` values in `orders` rows selected, then to fetch halfway through this count of orders rows, `ocount`. The final row retrieved above will be row number `(ocount+1)/2`—for example, row number 1 for 1 or 2 rows, row number 2 for 3 or 4 rows, and so on. If `ocount` is odd, this yields the perfect median position. If `ocount` is even, the row retrieved will be one of two equally valid median positions, row 2 for 4 rows, for example. Note that it is important that the count( ) function is performed in the same transaction as the Open Cursor and Fetch loop, to guarantee that no changes by concurrent transaction inserts will invalidate the median calculation. The treatment of null values of `dollars` needs to be thought out carefully, because we don't want to count null values in making our median determination. Note that the set function `count(dollars)` does not count null values, and the `where ... dollars is not null` clause used in defining `dollars_cursor` also ignores null values.

Also note that the variable name to hold the interactively returned `cid` value is itself `cid`, so we see a search condition: ... `where cid = :cid`. There is nothing wrong with this, since the colon (:) clearly differentiates the host variable from the column name. ∎

EXAMPLE 5.5.2 Transitive Closure.

Given the `employees` table of Example 3.10.6, we wish to prompt the user for an `eid` and then retrieve all employees who eventually report to an employee with the `eid` specified (through any number of intermediate managers). The hard part about doing this in Embedded SQL is rather surprising. We can create a cursor listing all the employees who report directly to the given `eid`, then for any direct report create a cursor for all second-level reports, and so on. But we don't know the total number of reporting levels, and since we need to declare all simultaneously used cursors in the beginning, this is a serious problem if we need one cursor for each

```
#include <stdio.h>
#include "prompt.h"
exec sql include sqlca;
char custprompt[] = "Please enter a customer ID: ";

int main( )
{
    exec sql begin declare section;
        char cid[5],user_name[20], user_pwd[10];
        double dollars; int ocount;
    exec sql end declare section;
    exec sql declare dollars_cursor cursor for        /* to calculate median      */
        select dollars from orders where cid = :cid and dollars is not null
        order by dollars;
    int i;
    exec sql whenever sqlerror goto report_error;
    strcpy(user_name, "poneilsql");
    strcpy(user_pwd, "XXXX");
    exec sql connect :user_name identified by :user_pwd; /* ORACLE Connect        */

    while (prompt(custprompt, 1, cid, 4) >= 0) {       /* main loop: get cid       */
        exec sql select count(dollars) into :ocount  /* count orders by cid       */
            from orders where cid = :cid;
        if (ocount == 0) {
            printf("No orders retrieved for cid value %s\n", cid);
            continue;                                  /* do outer loop again      */
        }
        /* open cursor and loop until midpoint of ordered sequence                 */
        exec sql open dollars_cursor;
        for (i = 0; i < (ocount+1)/2; i++)             /* fetch at least once      */
            exec sql fetch dollars_cursor into :dollars;
        exec sql close dollars_cursor;
        exec sql commit work;                          /* release locks            */
        printf ("Median dollar amount = %f\n", dollars);
    }                                                  /* end main loop            */
    exec sql commit release;                           /* ORACLE Disconnect        */
    return 0;
report_error:
    print_dberror( );
    exec sql rollback release;                         /* ORACLE Disconnect in error*/
    return 1;
}
```

Figure 5.21   ORACLE Program to Retrieve Median (Illustrates Example 5.5.1)

level. We get around this limitation by performing a rather tricky doubly recursive breadth-first search of the employee tree.

Note that all the accesses to database data are done in the breadth_srch function, so that is where the Whenever SQLERROR statement is placed. If we had accesses in both functions, we would need to have a separate label like "report_error" to GOTO in *each* function, or the program would not compile, since the GOTO target must be in the same function as each SQL data-access statement.

In the program of Figure 5.22, each time the function breadth_srch is entered with argument cursor_open == 1, it means we are moving from left to right on an already existing cursor level of employee reports. Thus breadth_srch fetches the next employee on this level, prints out the eid and ename, then saves the eid value in a local value and nests to a deeper level by calling itself for the next employee (to the right) on the same cursor. On return from the nested call, the implication is that all subtrees of eids to the right have been explored; now breadth_srch reestablishes the local eid value and opens a cursor once more to look at the *next level down*, and recursively explore subtrees of those eids. When all lower-level employees of the current subtree have been visited, the nested breadth_srch returns, either to explore subtrees of remaining eids on this level or, if eids on this level are exhausted, to the function that initiated the breadth_srch on this level. Eventually we return to main, which commits all work and disconnects from the database. ∎

5.6 Dynamic SQL

Recall that in the discussion in Section 5.3.1 of the syntax for the embedded Select statement, we said that the host variables named in a Declare section could be used only as *constant* values in a search condition; the variables could not contain character strings meant to represent more complex expression, that is, parts of statements requiring compiler parsing. In the current section, we learn a new approach, known as *Dynamic SQL*, which allows us to construct a character string in a host variable to be used as an SQL statement. All the Embedded SQL statements we have seen up to now are known as *Static SQL*. Dynamic SQL allows us to create new SQL statements that were not foreseen in detail at the time of program compilation and to execute them dynamically in response to changing user needs.

Execute Immediate

There are a number of advantages to being able to parse new statements dynamically in a program; but before going into the advantages, we need an example.

EXAMPLE 5.6.1 Execute Immediate.

The program of Figure 5.23 illustrates a program where a character array, sqltext[ ], is filled in with a character string representing an SQL statement and then is parsed and executed using a new Embedded SQL statement, Execute Immediate. The current example sets the contents of sqltext[ ] from a constant string, but it is more normal to build up such a string in response to expressed user wishes in a menu interaction. The example given here illustrates an immediate execution of a Delete statement, but other statements, such as Update and

```
#include <stdio.h>
#include "prompt.h"
exec sql include sqlca;
int breadth_srch(char *start_eid, int cursor_open);
int main( )
{
    char eid_prompt[] = "Enter Employee ID to see all lower level reports: ";
    char start_eid[6];
    exec sql connect to testdb;                    /* DB2 UDB Connect, simple form   */
    while(prompt(eid_prompt, 1, start_eid, 5) >= 0) { /* loop for eids              */
        breadth_srch(start_eid, 0);                /* recurse: retrieve subtree      */
        exec sql commit work;
    }
    exec sql disconnect current;
    return 0;
}   /* end main                                                                      */

exec sql begin declare section;
    static char eid[6], ename[17];
exec sql end declare section;
exec sql declare dirrept cursor for select eid,   /* cursor over direct reports     */
    ename from employees where mgrid = :eid;       /* ... of given employee eid      */

int breadth_srch(char *start_eid, int cursor_open)
{
    char save_eid[6];                              /* saved eid for recursion        */
    exec sql whenever sqlerror goto report_error;
    if (!cursor_open) {                            /* reached new report subtree     */
        strcpy(eid, start_eid);                    /* eid is at head of subtree      */
        exec sql open dirrept;                     /* get direct reports of eid      */
    }
    exec sql whenever not found goto srch_done;    /* return from here when done     */
    exec sql fetch dirrept into :eid, :ename;      /* next direct report             */
    printf ("%s %s\n", eid, ename);                /* print current ename, eid       */
    strcpy(save_eid, eid);                         /* save this eid                  */
    if (breadth_srch(eid, 1)<0) return -1;         /* get other emps, this level     */
    exec sql close dirrept;                        /* this level is exhausted        */
    return breadth_srch(save_eid, 0);              /* recurse: retrieve subtree      */
srch_done: return 0;
report_error: print_dberror( );
    exec sql rollback work;
    return -1;
}
```

Figure 5.22   DB2 UDB Program to Perform Transitive Closure

Insert, are also possible. However, a Select statement cannot be executed using this syntax; Select statements require another approach, to be explained shortly.

```
#include <stdio.h>
exec sql include sqlca;

exec sql begin declare section;
    char user_name[] = "scott"; char user_pwd[] = "tiger";
    char sqltext[] = "delete from customers where cid = \'c006\'";
exec sql end declare section;
int main( )
{
    exec sql whenever sqlerror goto report_error;
    exec sql connect :user_name identified by :user_pwd; /* ORACLE Connect        */
    exec sql execute immediate :sqltext;            /* execute immediate     */
    exec sql commit release;                        /* ORACLE Disconnect     */
    return 0;
report_error:
    print_dberror( );
    exec sql rollback release;                      /* ORACLE Disconnect in error  */
    return 1;
}
```

Figure 5.23 ORACLE Program with Execute Immediate SQL Statement (Illustrates Example 5.6.1)

The general form of the Basic SQL Execute Immediate statement is very simple:

```
EXEC SQL EXECUTE IMMEDIATE :host_variable;
```

The character string contents of the host_variable array must represent a valid SQL statement of the following types that we have so far encountered: Create Table, Delete (either Searched or Positioned), Drop Table, Insert, and Update (either Searched or Positioned).

Consider a menu interaction that allows a user to delete rows from the customers table of the CAP database, when the rows obey some set of user-specified conditions. The conditions can be identified in plain English through the menu interface, as shown in Figure 5.24.

```
Delete customer rows with ALL of the following properties:
Y _N X  Customer orders all products stored in city _____
Y _N X  Customer headquarters is in city _____
Y _N X  Customer discount is in range from _____ to _____
   . . . (and so on)
```

Figure 5.24 Example Menu to Delete Rows from the customers Table

The menu user can fill in an X following the Y choice (meaning "yes," overriding the default "no" choice), and then provide related parameters on the right. The program should accept these choices, create the appropriate sqltext[ ] to perform the desired Delete statement, and then immediately execute that statement. For example, consider the case where only a single line in the menu of Figure 5.24 was designated Y, as follows:

> Y X N _   Customer headquarters is in city _Duluth_____

The Y alternative has been chosen and the city name filled in with the name "Duluth." Assume the program has read this city name into an array cname2[ ]. The program must also initialize the sqltext[ ] array to contain the beginning of the Delete statement, with plenty of space left over:

```
char sqltext[256] = "delete from customers where ";
```

The program now fills in the rest of the sqltext[ ] Select statement, using the strcat( ) C library function to concatenate new strings onto sqltext[ ]:

```
strcat(sqltext, "city = \'");    /* concatenate string: city = '   */
strcat(sqltext, cname2)          /* concatenate cityname: (Duluth)  */
strcat(sqltext, "\'");           /* concatenate quote character: '  */
```

Note that the single quote character (') must be preceded by an escape character (\) within a C character string. The result of all this is as if we had written

```
char sqltext[256] = "delete from customers where city = \'Duluth\'";
```

To make sure the sqltext[ ] array is not overfilled, use strncat( ) instead of strcat( ).

Clearly an Execute Immediate with this string will now accomplish what the user requested. Of course we might want to perform some preliminary processing and user interaction to confirm that we are doing the desired thing, especially where updates are concerned. For example, we could start by counting the number of rows to be deleted and ask the user if it seems appropriate to delete this number of rows. For simplicity we ignore such confirmations in what follows.

But why do we need an Execute Immediate statement at all? We already have the ability to perform a Delete with the Searched Delete statement, which we could embed in the program as

```
exec sql delete from customers where city = :cname2;
```

How does the Execute Immediate statement add to our flexibility? To see the answer, look again at Figure 5.24, where three different options are listed for the user and more are suggested by the last line, ". . . (and so on)". Clearly we would need an entirely different Delete form if the user were to fill in line 3; for example,

```
exec sql delete from customers
    where discnt between :lowval3 and :hival3;
```

where the values for `lowval3` and `hival3` have been input from the two fill-ins of line 3. This seems OK: we could declare a different Delete statement for each line of the menu in our Embedded SQL program. But that is not enough! What if both line 2 and line 3 were selected? It would be necessary to create still another Embedded Delete statement in our Embedded program. Since there might be (say) 15 options in such a menu, and we have to allow for any possible subset of options being selected (2^{15} options), clearly it is impossible to foresee all conceivable user desires by providing statements in static SQL. We simply refuse to place 2^{15} different Select statements in a source program. Instead we need to be able to build statements "on the fly" with Dynamic SQL, to react flexibly to user requests.

Prepare, Execute, and Using

Instead of using the Execute Immediate statement, it is possible to use two distinct Dynamic SQL statements, Prepare and Execute, to accomplish the same task. This method allows host variables to be used as parameters in the SQL statement (accomplished with the USING clause of the Execute statement) and also improves performance of statements that will be executed repeatedly in a particular form by performing the compilation in advance of execution.

> **EXAMPLE 5.6.2 Prepare, Execute, and Using.**
> Figure 5.25 illustrates a program where the Prepare statement on the fifth line of the main program has the effect of parsing the character string in `sqltext[ ]` into a compiled form with the name `delcust`. Following this the Execute statement causes `delcust` to execute. Note that the `sqltext` variable has been initialized with a text SQL statement containing a *dynamic parameter* (represented by `:dcid`). Successive dynamic parameters in the Prepare statement can be filled in by host variable values specified in the USING clause of the Execute statement.
>   This program uses **DB2 UDB**/SQL-99 syntax in the Connect and Disconnect statements, and also for the form of the dynamic parameter "?". In **ORACLE**, in addition to the usual changes needed for the Connect and Disconnect statements, you need to change the "?" marking the dynamic parameter to an identifier prefixed with a colon, for example, `:dcid`, as follows:
>
> ```
> strcpy(sqltext, "delete from customers where cid = :dcid");    /* ORACLE form    */
> ```
>
> Since these parameters are replaced in positional order by the USING clause in the Execute statement, there is no real need for a specific name like `:dcid`, and the standard "?" seems preferable. ∎

The Execute Immediate approach provides much of the same functionality as the approach where we Prepare-Execute. The SQL statements that are accepted by Prepare are the same as those that can be used by Execute Immediate, so we gain no flexibility there. The USING clause is not available with Execute Immediate, but this is not a serious defect since the variable values can usually be converted to text and concatenated

310

```
#include <stdio.h>
exec sql include sqlca;

exec sql begin declare section;
    char cust_id[5], sqltext[256];
exec sql end declare section;
char cidprompt[] = "Name customer cid to be deleted: ";

int main( )
{
    /* The ? in the following line marks the dynamic parameter         */
    strcpy(sqltext, "delete from customers where cid = ?");
    exec sql whenever sqlerror goto report_error;
    exec sql connect to testdb;

    exec sql prepare delcust from :sqltext;              /* prepare for loop      */
    while((prompt(cidprompt, 1, cust_id.arr, 4)) >= 0) { /* loop for cid          */
        exec sql execute delcust using :cust_id;         /* using clause ...      */
                                                         /* ...replaces "?" above */
        exec sql commit work;                            /* commit the delete     */

    }
    exec sql disconnect current;
    return 0;
report_error:
    print_dberror( );
    exec sql rollback work; exec sql disconnect current;
    return 1;
}
```

Figure 5.25   DB2 UDB Program Using Prepare and Execute Statements (Illustrates Example 5.6.2)

into the text statement for immediate execution. The Prepare-Execute approach is probably simpler if several nontext variable values exist; it is easier to place these variables in a USING clause than to convert and concatenate them into the text. A more common reason for preferring the Prepare-Execute approach is performance, in the case that a statement must be created dynamically but will be executed repeatedly. The Prepare phase of compilation can consume significant resources, and it is good to get it out of the way before repeated execution of the compiled form. The Execute Immediate form must recompile a new statement each time.

Dynamic Select: The Describe Statement and the SQLDA

We have still not introduced a way to dynamically create and execute a Select statement. The problem with a dynamically created Select statement is that the number of *column* values to be retrieved may be unknown in advance of compilation. Therefore the rather simple-minded INTO clause syntax used in static SQL won't work in general. Consider the statement

```
exec sql select cname, discnt into :cust_name, :cust_discnt
    from customers where cid = :cust_id;
```

It works perfectly well in this case to declare two host variables cust_name and cust_discnt of known type to receive the values from the two columns retrieved. But to provide dynamic flexibility, we have to allow for *any* set of columns being retrieved, four columns, or perhaps twelve, and of arbitrary type. In order to handle such arbitrary retrieval sets, we need to consider a new type of structure, known as the *SQL Descriptor Area*, or *SQLDA*. To begin with, we illustrate a Dynamic Select in the **ORACLE** database product and later consider the SQLDA details. Then we will cover the corresponding material for **DB2 UDB**. Since the **ORACLE** and **DB2 UDB** SQLDA areas have significantly different data structures, we cannot consider any use of the SQLDA as part of Basic SQL.

EXAMPLE 5.6.3

Consider the **ORACLE** program of Figure 5.26. The exec sql include sqlda statement near the top of Figure 5.26 includes a header file that defines the SQLDA struct. (The header file itself is presented in Figure 5.28.) The first statement after the Connect statement initializes the program's SQLDA pointer to point to an initialized SQLDA struct by calling an **ORACLE** library function, sqlald( ). (This program is so full of **ORACLE**-specific constructs that we have abandoned our convention of marking each such line with a comment starting with **ORACLE** and have simply called it an **ORACLE** program.)

A constant text string sqltext[ ] with an SQL Select statement is constructed. A constant string such as this would not normally be dynamically executed: we know the full syntax in advance, and it would be much easier to use an Embedded Select statement. However, we deal with this simple case in order to provide an easily understood concrete example.

When the Prepare statement is executed to prepare the sqltext[ ] Select statement, the compilation process calculates the number and types of the column values to be retrieved (the Select statement lists two, cname and city, which are defined in the Create Table statement (3.2.1) as varchar(13) and varchar(20), respectively). For the program to learn this information, it executes the Describe statement, which places information for all columns retrieved into the SQLDA variable struct. Note that before executing Describe, the program sets sqlda->N to MAX_COLS, allowing for the maximum number of columns possible; this is actually unnecessary here, since sqlda->N was properly initialized by the sqlald( ) function, but in a loop that reused the SQLDA struct, this step would be crucial. After the Describe statement has been executed, the program should set sqlda->N to the actual number of dynamic columns returned by the Describe, sqlda->F.

The sqlda->T[ ] array has been filled in with type specifications for each column by the Describe statement. However, these type specifications each have a null flag (whether null values are allowed in the column) that needs to be cleared by calling **ORACLE**'s sqlnul( ) function on each element of T[ ], leaving a pure type value. This function also returns the null flag to the caller; it is TRUE if the column can have null values.

Each dynamic column needs memory areas for its column value and indicator value. These memory areas are specified by setting pointers to them in the provided V[ ] and I[ ] arrays in the SQLDA. Here we are providing that memory with the C library function malloc( ). Note that malloc( ) is relatively costly in terms of CPU, and when this is a consideration, the programmer should malloc space for an array of column values at once, when possible.

Finally, a cursor named crs is declared. Although in this case we know that only one row will be retrieved, a cursor must *always* be used for a Dynamic Select.

```
#define MAX_COLS 100
#define MAX_NAME 20
#include <stdio.h>
#include <malloc.h>
exec sql include sqlca;
exec sql include sqlda;
SQLDA *sqlald(int, int, int);
exec sql begin declare section;
    char sqltext[256];
    char user_name[20], user_pwd[10];
exec sql end declare section;
int main( )
{
    int i, null_ok; SQLDA *sqlda;
    exec sql whenever sqlerror goto report_error;
    strcpy(user_name, "poneilsql"); strcpy(user_pwd, "XXXX");
    exec sql connect :user_name identified by :user_pwd;

    sqlda = sqlald(MAX_COLS, MAX_NAME, 0);      /* allocate sqlda var        */
    strcpy(sqltext,
        "select cname, city from customers where cid = \'c003\'");
    exec sql prepare stmt from :sqltext;
    sqlda->N = MAX_COLS;                        /* before describe, set to max   */
    exec sql describe stmt into sqlda;
    sqlda->N = sqlda->F;                        /* reset N to described #cols    */

    for (i = 0; i < sqlda->N; i++) {            /* loop through 2 cols       */
        /* clear out null flag from T[i], return it in null_ok variable    */
        sqlnul(&(sqlda->T[i]),&(sqlda->T[i], &null_ok);
        /* allocate space for the column value plus a null terminator      */
        sqlda->V[i] = malloc((int)sqlda->L[i]+1);
        sqlda->I[i] = malloc(sizeof(short));    /* alloc space for indicator     */
    }
    exec sql declare crs cursor for stmt;
    exec sql open crs;
    exec sql fetch crs using descriptor sqlda; /* only 1 row: no loop       */
    printrow(sqlda);                            /* print out row (Fig 5.27)      */
    exec sql close crs;
    for (i = 0; i < sqlda->N; i++) {
        free(sqlda->V[i]);                      /* free col data space       */
        free(sqlda->I[i]);                      /* free indicator space      */
    }
    exec sql commit release;
    return 0;
report_error:
    print_dberror( );                           /* See Appendix B for code       */
    exec sql rollback release;
    return 1;
}
```

Figure 5.26   ORACLE Program to Perform Dynamic Select   ∎

```
/* printrow( ): print two varchar cols in sqlda, for ORACLE                    */
#include <stdio.h>
exec sql include sqlda;
void printrow(SQLDA *sqlda)
{
    char *s;
    int i, length;

    for (i = 0; i < sqlda->N; i++) {          /* loop through columns            */
        if (*(sqlda->I[i])) {                 /* if actually null ...            */
            printf("null\n");                 /* ... display null                */
        } else {
            s = (char *)sqlda->V[i];          /* point to column string value    */
            length = sqlda->L[i];
            printf("%*s\n", length, s);       /* print non-null string in column */
        }
    }
}
```

Figure 5.27   An **ORACLE** Printrow Function to Handle Multiple Varchar Columns

The printrow( ) function in Figure 5.27 provides a general-purpose function to print any number of column variables of character string type. It is simple enough to extend the printrow( ) function to print out multiple different column types. To do this we would need to read the datatype of each column, from sqlda->T[i], and perform a C switch statement to handle each of the types. If desired, types may be coerced (i.e., converted) to a different type by replacing the database type T[i] with 1 for character representation, 3 for int, and so on. Almost all types can be coerced to character data. Naturally, in this case V[i] must point to sufficient memory to hold the converted representation. In addition, L[i] needs to be updated to reflect the size of the memory area.

Example 5.6.3 uses Dynamic SQL to retrieve data from the database into program variables. Your program might also need a dynamic method for describing an arbitrary number of host variables to be used in a search condition where the number of clauses with constant values to be filled in is not known in advance. In this case you would need to "bind" these host variables to the search_condition, using a *Describe Bind Variables* statement. See the **ORACLE** *Programmer's Guide to the Pro*C/C++ Precompiler,* reference [7] at the end of this chapter, for more details.

Figure 5.28 provides the contents of the SQLDA header file read in by the **ORACLE** statement

```
exec sql include sqlda;
```

The **ORACLE** SQLDA keeps information on columns in array entries of multiple arrays, including the arrays V[ ], L[ ], T[ ], I[ ] that were used in Example 5.6.3. Note

```
struct sqlda
{
    long        N;          /* maximum # of columns handled by this SQLDA      */
    char        **V;        /* pointer to array of pointers to col values      */
    long        *L;         /* pointer to array of lengths of column values    */
    short       *T;         /* pointer to array of types of columns            */
    short       **I;        /* pointer to array of ptrs to ind variables       */
    long        F;          /* actual number of columns in this SQLDA          */
    char        **S;        /* pointer to array of pointers to column names    */
    short       *M;         /* pointer to array of max lengths of col names    */
    short       *C;         /* pointer to array of actual lengths of col names */
    char        **X;        /* pointer to array of addresses of ind var names  */
    short       *Y;         /* pointer to array of max lengths of ind var names */
    short       *Z;         /* pointer to array of actual lengths of ind var names */
};
```

Figure 5.28   ORACLE Definition Read in by exec sql include sqlda

that the codes for the various datatypes pointed to by the T[ ] array (in space allocated by **ORACLE**) are not defined in this header file; they must be defined instead in the source file using them.

DB2 UDB has very similar capabilities in Dynamic SQL. The names of the parts of the SQLDA structure are different, the Include files need to be changed, and a few other minor changes need to be made, along with the usual standardization of Connect and Disconnect statements. The same sequence of Prepare, Describe, Declare Cursor, Open, Fetch, and Close statements are used, as specified in the SQL standards (Full SQL-92 and SQL-99, but not in Core SQL-99).

What the SQL standards do not specify is the SQLDA data structure, and so this part tends to vary between database products. Where **ORACLE**'s SQLDA has parallel arrays of numbers and pointers to describe the columns and values, **DB2 UDB**'s SQLDA has an array of structs holding the same information, one sqlvar struct for each value that is being transferred from the database to the program (or vice versa.) Thus, for example, the pointer to the ith data value is referenced as sqlda->V[i] in **ORACLE**, the ith array element of the V pointer array within the SQLDA, whereas in **DB2 UDB**, it is referenced as sqlda->sqlvar[i].sqldata, the sqldata member of the ith sqlvar struct in its array in the SQLDA. See Figure 5.29 for the most important parts of the declaration header, sqlda.h, for **DB2 UDB**. The SQL-92 and SQL-99 standards replace the SQLDA used by the products with more SQL keywords and syntax, in an attempt to make them independent of the embedding language. However, this approach does not seem to have influenced database product development as yet.

Example 5.6.4 presents the code and a detailed explanation of it, for the same Dynamic SQL program we showed for **ORACLE** in Example 5.6.3.

```
struct  sqlvar                           /* Variable Description            */
{
    short        sqltype;                /* Variable data type             */
    short        sqllen;                 /* Variable data length           */
    char         *sqldata;               /* Pointer to variable data value */
    short        *sqlind;                /* Pointer to Null indicator      */
    struct       sqlname;                /* Variable name                  */
};
struct  sqlda
{
    char         sqldaid[8];             /* Eye catcher = 'SQLDA '          */
    long         sqldabc;                /* SQLDA size in bytes=16+44*SQLN  */
    short        sqln;                   /* Number of SQLVAR elements       */
    short        sqld;                   /* # of columns or host vars.      */
    struct sqlvar sqlvar[1];             /* first SQLVAR element            */
};
/* macro for allocating SQLDA                                              */
#define   SQLDASIZE(n) (sizeof(struct sqlda) + \
                       ((long) n-1) * sizeof(struct sqlvar))
```

Figure 5.29 Part of sqlda.h for **DB2 UDB**

EXAMPLE 5.6.4
Consider the **DB2 UDB** program of Figure 5.30, corresponding to the **ORACLE** program of Figure 5.26. The inclusion of sqlenv.h near the top of Figure 5.30 defines the SQLDA struct by its own inclusion of sqlda.h (part of the sqlda.h file is presented in Figure 5.29). The first statement after the Connect statement initializes the program's SQLDA pointer to point to an uninitialized SQLDA struct by calling the C library function malloc( ).

When the Prepare statement is executed to prepare the sqltext[ ] Select statement, the compilation process calculates the number and types of the column values to be retrieved (the Select statement lists two, cname and city, which are defined in the Create Table statement (3.2.1) as varchar(13) and varchar(20), respectively). For the program to learn this information, it executes the Describe statement, which places information for all columns retrieved into the SQLDA variable struct. Note that before executing Describe, the program sets sqlda->sqln to MAX_COLS, allowing for the maximum number of columns possible. After the Describe statement has been executed, the actual number of dynamic columns returned by the Describe is available as sqlda->sqld.

The sqlda->sqlvar array has been filled in with sqlvar structs for each column by the Describe statement. In particular, after Describe, sqlda->sqlvar[0].sqllen gives the length of the 0th column value, and sqlda->sqlvar[1].sqlname is a structure describing the column name for the first column value.

Each dynamic column needs memory areas for its column value and indicator value. These memory areas are specified by setting pointers to them in the provided sqlvar structs in the SQLDA. Here we are again providing that memory with malloc( ). Note that malloc( ) is relatively costly in terms of CPU, and when this is a consideration, the programmer should malloc space for an array of column values at once, when possible.

```
#define MAX_COLS 100
#include <sqlenv.h>
#include <stdio.h>
exec sql include sqlca;                             /* communication area          */
void printrow(struct sqlda *);
exec sql begin declare section;
   char sqltext[256];
exec sql end declare section;
int main( )
{
   int i; struct sqlda *sqlda;
   exec sql whenever sqlerror goto report_error;
   exec sql connect to testdb;                      /* DB2 UDB Connect, simple form */

   sqlda = (struct sqlda *)malloc(SQLDASIZE(MAX_COLS));/* allocate sqlda area       */
   strcpy(sqltext, "select cname, city from customers where cid = \'c003\'");
   exec sql prepare stmt from :sqltext;             /* compile select statement    */
   sqlda->sqln = MAX_COLS;                           /* set max # dynamic columns   */
   exec sql describe stmt into :*sqlda;              /* describe this statement     */

   for (i = 0; i < sqlda->sqld; i++) {               /* loop through 2 described cols */
     /* allocate space for the column value plus a null terminator              */
     sqlda->sqlvar[i].sqldata = malloc(sqlda->sqlvar[i].sqllen + 1);
     sqlda->sqlvar[i].sqlind = malloc(sizeof(short));   /* and for indicator      */
   }
   exec sql declare crs cursor for stmt;
   exec sql open crs;                                /* open cursor                 */
   exec sql fetch crs using descriptor :*sqlda;      /* only 1 row: no loop         */
   printrow(sqlda);                                  /* print out row (Fig 5.30)    */
   exec sql close crs;
   for (i = 0; i < sqlda->sqld; i++) {
     free(sqlda->sqlvar[i].sqldata);                 /* free col data space         */
     free(sqlda->sqlvar[i].sqlind);                  /* free indicator space        */
   }
   exec sql commit work; exec sql disconnect current;  /* or connect reset here     */
   return 0;
report_error:
   print_dberror( );                                 /* See Appendix B for code     */
   exec sql rollback work; exec sql disconnect current;
   return 1;
}
```

Figure 5.30   DB2 UDB Program to Perform Dynamic Select

Finally, a cursor named crs is declared. Although in this case we know that only one row will be retrieved, a cursor must *always* be used for a Dynamic Select.

Figure 5.31 shows the printrow function for this program, as it could be written in a separate file. It differs from its **ORACLE** counterpart only in the names of data structure parts. It also is easily extended to handle various datatypes by switching on the type information returned by Describe.

```
/* print two varchar cols currently in sqlda, for DB2 UDB                    */
#include <stdio.h>
#include <sqlenv.h>
void printrow(struct sqlda *sqlda)
{
    char *s; int i, length;

    for (i = 0; i < s->sqld; i++) {          /* loop through columns     */
        if (*(sqlda->sqlvar[i].sqlind)) {    /* if actually null . . .   */
            printf("null\n");                /* . . . display null       */
        } else {
            s = (char *)sqlda->sqlvar[i].sqldata + 2; /* point to string val   */
            length = sqlda->sqlvar[i].sqllen;    /* and find its length   */
            printf(%*s\n", length, s);           /* display non-null value */
        }
    }
}
```

Figure 5.31   DB2 UDB Printrow Function to Handle Multiple Varchar Columns

5.7 Some Advanced Programming Concepts

This section contains a short introduction to the concepts of scrollable cursors, cursor sensitivity, and other programming environments for databases.

Scrollable Cursors

A limitation of the Fetch statement under a standard cursor, mentioned in the discussion following Figure 5.5, is that a cursor can only move forward through a set of rows. This means that it is necessary to close and reopen a cursor in order to fetch a row for a second time. In Full SQL-92 and Full SQL-99, important generalizations of the Declare Cursor and Fetch statements are provided. The new Declare Cursor statement is given in Figure 5.32.

Basically the two Advanced SQL syntax elements are the keywords INSENSITIVE and SCROLL. These are not in Core SQL-99, but the rest of the syntax of Figure 5.32 is. We will talk about cursor sensitivity in a moment. When the SCROLL keyword is used in

```
EXEC SQL DECLARE cursor_name [INSENSITIVE] [SCROLL] CURSOR [WITH HOLD] FOR
    Subquery
    {UNION Subquery}
    [ORDER BY result_column [ASC | DESC]
        {, result_column [ASC |DESC]...}
    [FOR READ ONLY | FOR UPDATE OF columnname {, columnname}...];
```

Figure 5.32   The Advanced SQL Declare Cursor Statement

```
EXEC SQL FETCH
    [{NEXT | PRIOR | FIRST | LAST            -- advanced
    |{ABSOLUTE | RELATIVE} value_spec} FROM ] -- advanced
    cursor_name INTO host-variable {, host-variable...};
```

Figure 5.33   The Advanced SQL Fetch Statement

a cursor definition, the cursor is said to be *scrollable*, and the advanced capabilities of the SQL-99 Fetch statement can be exercised. This Advanced SQL Fetch statement is given in Figure 5.33

The specification of position movement (NEXT, PRIOR, . . .) is known as *orientation*. The current standard behavior is the default, NEXT, meaning "Retrieve the next row in sequence following the current position in the cursor." The PRIOR orientation means "Retrieve the row in sequence prior to the current position." The orientations FIRST and LAST retrieve the first or last row within the cursor sequence. The ABSOLUTE orientation, with value_spec given by an integer from 1 to the number n of rows in the cursor, retrieves that numbered row in the cursor sequence; ABSOLUTE 1 is equivalent to first. Negative numbers can also be used, from –1 down to –n; ABSOLUTE –1 is equivalent to last. The RELATIVE orientation means to retrieve the row, an integer number of rows away from the current position. Thus RELATIVE –1 is the same as PRIOR, RELATIVE 1 is the same as NEXT, and RELATIVE 0 retrieves the row just retrieved a second time.

Since neither **ORACLE** nor **DB2 UDB** supports this advanced syntax directly in its server SQL, we cannot consider it Basic SQL, and you might conclude it is not worth bothering with. However, it is supported under ODBC, the Open Database Connectivity API, an important C programming interface meant to provide interoperability between products. For more information on ODBC, see *The ODBC Solution*, by Robert Signore et al., [11] in "Suggestions for Further Reading" at the end of this chapter.

ODBC led directly to Java's database connectivity package JDBC (Java Database Connectivity API). JDBC version 2.0, included in Java version 1.2, has scrollable result sets, the equivalent of scrollable cursors. This JDBC distribution also supports the notion of sensitivity, covered next. For more information on JDBC, see www.sun.java.com. Some database products including **ORACLE** and **DB2 UDB** also provide SQLJ, Embedded

SQL in Java, which is considered easier to work with for simple applications on a single database.

Cursor Sensitivity

Recall that the concept of transaction was invented to isolate a stream of logic being performed by one user from the effects of concurrent updates by others on the data being accessed. We will learn more about transactions in Chapter 10, but certainly one implication of such isolation is that once a cursor is opened in a transaction, no rows in that cursor can be updated by any other concurrent user. Fine, but what can we say about updates to rows of the cursor that are side effects of updates made in the same transaction?

EXAMPLE 5.7.1

Assume that we are writing an application known as *ord_ship*, to actually ship products that were ordered earlier. Orders in the `orders` table have not yet been shipped, and `ord_ship` logic finds all orders in the `orders` table placed in the month of this_mo, calls the routine that ships this product to this customer, then deletes the current row from the `orders` table and places it in a table with identical columns known as `shipped_ords`. The cursor to access all the relevant rows in `orders` is the following:

```
declare cursor ship_em cursor for
    select * from orders for update of ordno
    where month = :this_mo;
```

Occasionally the routine to ship an order gives a return value that indicates the order can't be shipped because the product is out of stock. The normal thing to do under these circumstances is to create a back order, meaning that the order will be shipped when it comes back into stock. Let us say that the simple-minded way we have to do this is to simply backdate the order, calculating next_mo as the next month after this_mo, and replacing the `month` column value for relevant orders. Assume that we do this with the following statement:

```
update orders set month = :next_mo
    where pid = :ord_rec.pid;
```

where `ord_rec.pid` is the `pid` value of the product we have just found to be out of stock. Now assume that numerous other rows in the `ship_em` cursor are orders for the same `pid` value that we have just encountered. Are these rows still in existence in the cursor? The defining property for the `orders` rows of the `ship_em` cursor was that the `month` column had the value `:this_mo`, and now this is no longer true. Will they be encountered in the Fetch loop or not? Perhaps the user remembers that if we changed the value of this_mo after opening the cursor, that would not affect the rows selected; but this is a different thing, since we are actually varying the data that qualifies the rows for occupancy. If this answer seems straightforward, consider the following. What if instead of just updating the `month` of `orders` rows for the out-of-stock product, the proper approach was to put these `orders` rows in a different table and delete rows ordering that product from `orders`?

```
delete orders where pid = :ord_rec.pid;
```

Now what happens when we fetch one of these rows in the ship_em cursor? The row doesn't even exist anymore, so it doesn't seem that we can retrieve it. And there is no way for a Fetch statement to retrieve a nonexistent row, so we can't just point to where it used to be; presumably we will have to jump over the hole left by the former row. Of course it is possible that the system took a "snapshot" of the data when the cursor was originally opened, so that we have copies of the rows that have been deleted and can provide them for Fetch requests.   ■

The answer to the question of Example 5.7.1 is that there was no standard prior to SQL-92, and different products do different things. The answer might depend on whether the cursor in question was read-only, or on something else entirely. With Full SQL-92, however, this option becomes determined by the Declare Cursor syntax. Look again at the general form of Figure 5.32 and note the INSENSITIVE keyword. When that keyword is present, the cursor is said to be *insensitive*, and this means that the rows contained in the cursor will *not* change as a result of a Searched Update or Searched Delete outside the cursor itself. The effect is as if the system took a snapshot of rows under the cursor when the cursor was opened. (This would be an inefficient way to implement it, however.) Now the program logic can look at rows that are no longer there; but if an attempt is made to perform a Positioned Update or a Positioned Delete (using WHERE CURRENT OF CURSOR syntax), an error to show that the row no longer exists is returned. If the INSENSITIVE keyword is left out of a Select statement that complies with this Basic SQL feature, then Updates and Deletes outside the cursor are immediately reflected in the rows retrieved in the cursor. In the case of scrollable cursors, this means that a fetch with ABSOLUTE 23 might refer to different rows when called twice in a row.

Other Development Environments for Database Programming

A number of products, such as **ORACLE**, **INFORMIX**, and **SYBASE**, have procedural languages to extend SQL capabilities. See Section 4.4 for some coverage of the procedural languages of **ORACLE** (PL/SQL) and **INFORMIX** (SPL). These product-specific languages generally have local memory variables, if-then-else type statements, and the ability to create and call functions. In most cases there is also a method for constructing a friendly visual user interface, with quickly constructed forms, menus, the ability to scroll on retrieved cursors with point-and-click controls, and a myriad of other features that make developing simple applications easier. **DB2 UDB** is now providing Java as its new safer procedural language (safer than C/C++ and similar languages supported now) using SQLJ (Embedded SQL in Java) or Java's JDBC connectivity package.

The only difficulty with the procedural language interfaces, PL/SQL and SPL, is that they vary so much in detail: each product has its own dialect, and only recently with SQL-99/PSM (persistent stored modules, part of SQL-99) has there been any standard to adhere to.

Suggestions for Further Reading

A good guide to the C language is Kernighan and Ritchie's *The C Programming Language* [4]. The various SQL standards and individual product SQL reference manuals referenced in Chapters 3 and 4 continue to be useful. New reference manuals of use for Embedded SQL include manuals on general Embedded SQL constructs as well as special companion guides for SQL in the C language. The practitioner will also want to have access to the error code reference manuals for individual products.

[1] Don Chamberlin. *A Complete Guide to DB2 Universal Database*. San Francisco: Morgan Kaufmann, 1998. (Contains details of Embedded SQL, with C and Java language specifics.)

[2] *DB2 Universal Database Application Development Guide*. Version 6. IBM, 1999. Available at http://www.ibm.com/db2.

[3] *DB2 Universal Database SQL Reference Manual*. Version 6. IBM, 1999. Available at http://www.ibm.com/db2.

[4] Brian W. Kernighan and Dennis M. Ritchie. *The C Programming Language*. 2nd ed. Englewood Cliffs, NJ: Prentice Hall, 1988.

[5] Jim Melton and Alan R. Simon. *Understanding the New SQL: A Complete Guide*. San Francisco: Morgan Kaufmann, 1993. (This is a reference for SQL-92.)

[6] *ORACLE8 Error Messages*. Release 8.1.5. Redwood Shores, CA: Oracle. http://www.oracle.com.

[7] *ORACLE8 Programmer's Guide to the Pro*C/C++ Precompiler*. Redwood Shores, CA: Oracle. http://www.oracle.com.

[8] *ORACLE8 Server Concepts*. Volumes 1 and 2. Redwood Shores, CA: Oracle. http://www.oracle.com.

[9] *ORACLE8 Server SQL Reference*. Volumes 1 and 2. Redwood Shores, CA: Oracle. http://www.oracle.com.

[10] *Data Management: Structured Query Language (SQL) Version 2*. Berkshire, UK: X/Open Company, Ltd., 1996. Email: xospecs@xopen.co.uk.

[11] Robert Signore, John Creamer, and Michael Stegman. *The ODBC Solution*. New York: McGraw Hill, 1995.

Exercises

Exercises with solutions at the back of the book in "Solutions to Selected Exercises" are marked with the symbol •.

In writing the programs of these exercises, you should be aware that the executable files may be quite large because database code libraries are large and in some cases are bound into the individual application programs. Be careful to limit the number of executable files in your directories to save disk space.

NOTE: Exercises [5.1] and [5.2] deal only with Embedded SQL features covered through Section 5.1; they do not require bulletproofing except as specified.

[5.1]   Type the program of Example 5.1.2, making necessary modifications for the database product at your site, and run it.

[5.2]• Write a program to prompt a user in a loop to input a customer ID (cid) and product ID (pid), both on a single line. (Use the function prompt( ) explained after Example 5.1.1.) The program should then print out lines listing aids of agents who provide pid to cid, and the total of qty supplied by each agent. If a cid or pid value provided does not exist in the customers or products table, the program should simply return no lines. The program should terminate when the user types a blank line.

[5.3]   Write a program to prompt a user in a loop to input an agent ID (aid) and product ID (pid), both on a single line. (Use the function prompt( ) explained after Example 5.1.1.) The program should then print out lines listing cids of customers who order pid through aid, and the total of dollars ordered by the customer for each product through the agent. If the aid or pid value provided does not exist in the agents or products table, the program should simply return no lines. The program should terminate when the user types a blank line.

[5.4]   Modify the program assigned in Exercise 5.2 to notify the user and ask for a new input if a cid or pid input does not exist in the customers or products tables, respectively. Specifically request reentry of a bad cid, keeping a validly input pid, or reentry of a bad pid keeping a valid cid—that is, save user keystrokes as much as possible. NOTE: Don't go to the extreme of modifying prompt( ). If prompt( ) returns a negative value for the cid and pid user input, assume a blank line was input.

[5.5]   Here is a good-sized application program to write.

(a)   Write a main program that calls a menu( ) function, presenting three options to the user: (1) City Agent and Customers List, (2) Agent Performance, and (3) Exit This Program. The menu( ) function should return a value to the main program, which then calls a function city( ), or perform( ), or exit, according to user option. After option (1) or (2), the main program should loop for more menu( ) input. At all times in these programs you should create decently formatted I/O statements, so the user knows what is happening.

The function city( ) should request for input the name of some city (such as "Duluth"), and then return a list of customer cids and a list of agent aids who live in that city, and obey the following properties. (1) We want both lists clearly labeled and differentiated. (2) We do *not* want to return a cid from the given city unless the cid places at least one order through some aid in the same city. Similarly, we do not want to return an aid unless the aid places an order for some cid in the same city. (3) We do *not* want any aid to appear twice in its list or any cid to appear twice in its list. Test this by inserting a few rows into the orders table that might cause duplicates if we're not careful. In a large orders table, a huge number of duplicates might appear if this guarantee does not hold. Note that you will have to create *two* cursors in your program to guarantee this property—a single SQL statement probably cannot do it. Think of the city( ) function as being used by traveling executives of our wholesale company to invite customers and their agent contacts to dinner to meet each other when the executive is in town.

The function perform( ) should ask the user to input an agent aname and ensure uniqueness, *only* in case a duplicate aname exists in the agents table, by listing the city and aid values for two or more agents rows with that aname, asking the user to choose one by input of the aid. The function perform( ) should then calculate the total sales by that agent, the maximum of total sales for all agents, and finally the ratio of this agent's sales to that maximum.

(b) Here is another way of handling the task of discriminating which agent of the same name is wanted. Fetch rows and output a list of agents and their cities numbered 1, 2, 3, and so on, and ask the user to choose a number, performing a Commit before asking for user input. Then refetch the rows using the same cursor declaration (but a new Open of that cursor), count through the number of rows specified, and bingo—there's the desired agent. Explain why this is not guaranteed to work in a database where other users are performing concurrent updates. Is the method of part (a) safe in this sense? Explain.

NOTE: Many of the following program assignments deal explicitly or implicitly with transactions. In what follows, you should assume that there is no need to write error-handling routines to deal with transactional deadlock, unless the potential for deadlock is explicitly mentioned.

[5.6] (a) Write a program to input an order from an agent and enter it into the database. The main program should (repeatedly, in a loop) prompt for cid, the customer making the order; aid, the agent taking the order; pid, the product ordered; quantord, the quantity of the product being ordered; and the month of the order. Then it calls the function do_transaction to perform a transaction to place the order, with the user input values passed as arguments of do_transaction. Note that the user input values (cid, pid, etc.) are just ordinary program variables in main( ), so they will need to be copied into an SQL-declared area in do_transaction. To begin with, the transaction checks that pid exists in products, aid in agents, and cid in customers, and that subtracting quantord from products.quantity will not reduce products.quantity below zero. Given this, the transaction subtracts quantord units of this product and calculates the cost for these quantord units using products.price. Next the transaction adjusts cost by subtracting the customer discount. If any of the pid, cid, or aid do not exist (are null), or any other condition fails, the program should abort the transaction, then output an appropriate message and return from do_transaction. If all conditions are successful, the transaction inserts a new row into the orders table, placing the calculated cost value in the dollars column. The ordno value should be supplied by a special call that guarantees a new value to all executions of this program. For this exercise, write a function int fake_get_ordno( ) that uses a static var with initial value 1027 and increments and returns it on each call. Finally, the transaction should Commit. The program *should* be on guard against transactional deadlock abort and retry the transaction up to four times if such an abort occurs.

(b) Consider how to implement get_ordno( ), a function that returns a new ordno to each caller even if several programs are using it at the same time. Clearly we need to use the database itself to ensure consistent behavior. Set up a table ordno with just one row and column curordno containing the current ordno, and write short int get_ordno(char *errmsg) to access and update this table. It returns a new ordno or −1 on failure, in which case errmsg has an appropriate error string. Test this function with a simple driver. Assume that get_ordno will be called from within the order-entry transaction; because of this, it must not have its own commits or rollbacks. Explain why.

(c) Note that the ordno table of (b) will become a "hot spot" of a multi-user database, because every order-entry transaction accesses its one row. Explain why all concurrent transactions must wait for the Commit or Rollback of the one transaction that has the current ordno before they can get ordnos for their own work. One way to improve performance is to break out the ordno acquisition into a separate transaction before the order-entry transaction. In this case, get_ordno can and should have commits, rollbacks, and deadlock-retry logic. Explain why the resulting ordnos in the orders table will have skipped numbers—ordnos 1100, 1101, 1102, 1104, . . . , for example. Will this happen with the solution in (b)?

(d)• Explain why you should not have a Commit statement after the cid, aid, pid entry tests, and the test that there is enough quantity on hand to satisfy the request (the reading part of the transaction), and before the Update and

Insert statements (the writing part). Are there any places before the last read-write action (the insert) where a Commit would be a good idea?

[5.7] Consider the transfer program of Figure 5.13 with a transaction involving two Update statements.

(a) Imagine that there were no transactions containing the two single-row Update statements in this program. Then consider several processes running this modified program concurrently, with no other programs accessing the accounts table. Explain why the transactions still do exactly what they are supposed to, given that each individual Update on a single row is indivisible.

(b) Now suppose another process is running a program that adds the balances of two accounts to make a decision. Explain why you now need the serializability specification in the transfer program to obtain the desired results. Answer as in Example 5.4.1.

(c) A revised version of the transfer program is required to check that no account balance becomes negative as a result of the transfer. (Note that we assume the transfer amount in the dollars variable *can* be negative.) Explain how to make these changes to the program. Note the similar code in Figure 5.20.

(d) Is the argument of part (a) still valid for part (c)? That is, will processes running the program of part (c) without a transaction containing the test and Update statements still execute correctly? The revised single-row update is still indivisible if the update occurs, but the update may not occur at all. (Hint: It is important that the transfer amount can be negative in considering this question.)

[5.8] Write a program to repeatedly prompt the user for a customer ID and then print out the agent name, agent ID, and dollar orders placed by the different agents for that customer in their *median* dollar amount, as if we were performing the statement

```
select aname, aid, median(dollars)    /* INVALID SYNTAX */
    from orders
    where cid = :cid group by aname, aid;
```

[5.9] Write a program to print out the total of average dollar sales for all agents. Give a simple example to show that this is not the same as the average of total dollar sales for all agents.

[5.10]• Write a program to print out the report explained in Example 3.11.5.

[5.11] Create an employees table as given in Example 3.11.6 and write a program to repeatedly prompt for eid. Write out the sequence of managers to which eid ultimately reports, in ascending hierarchy position. Be careful to terminate properly.

NOTE: Treat the following problems as short-answer questions of the kind that might appear on an exam.

[5.12]   (a)• Write a code fragment in C beginning with exec sql begin declare section, to declare an array called city that will hold a city name from the agents table declared varchar(20).

(b)• Now declare cc as a cursor for an SQL query that retrieves exactly once all city names that contain agents who place orders for some part costing less than a dollar.

(c)• Now write a loop to retrieve successive cities into the array city, and print out each one. The loop should fall through as soon as there are no more cities to retrieve.

[5.13] Write the equivalent test (of an sqlcode) that you would place after executable SQL statements to take the place of the Whenever statement listed.

(a)•   exec sql whenever not found go to handle_error;

(b)•   exec sql whenever sqlerror go to handle_error;

[5.14] Consider the following SQL statement:

```
select c.city, cid, aid, pid
    from customers c, agents a, products p
    where c.city = a.city and a.city = p.city;
```

To begin with, we would like to make sure that all (cid, aid, pid) triples are grouped together (rows occur one after another) when they are from the same city (i.e., c.city).

(a)• How would you change the SQL statement above to guarantee that all triples with the same c.city occur one after another? (Hint: Use a non-procedural Select statement.)

(b)• If there are 30 rows in customers with c.cid = 'New York', 10 rows in agents with a.city = 'New York', and 20 rows in products with p.city = 'New York', how many rows in the SQL statement above will have c.city = 'New York'?

(c)• To restrict the amount of information to look at in situations such as part (b), we would like to write a report where *each* relevant city occurs once (in a header), followed by three labeled lists of cid, aid, and pid values that have that `city` value. Give pseudo-code to show how you would do this in Embedded SQL (declare the cursors carefully).

[5.15] Assume that we have 500 distinct `pid` values in the `products` table and that all these rows show up in the `orders` table. We want to list the *ten best sellers*—that is, the `pid` values of `products` with the biggest total dollar sales from the `orders` table, together with the `pname` values and the total dollar sales.

(a)• It is not possible to do what we want in non-procedural SQL, because there is no way of stopping at the ten biggest. We need to write an Embedded SQL program where we pick off the ten highest dollar sales from a cursor. Show how the cursor would be declared with a non-procedural SQL statement, so that all desired information appears as early as possible in the rows fetched.

(b)• In performing the loop to fetch rows from the cursor in (a), note that a problem might arise if we begin to fetch rows with a total of null `dollars` (nulls occur larger than non-null numbers when listed in order in some database products but occur smaller than non-nulls in others). Show how you would write a Fetch loop from the cursor of part (a) to skip over the early null values for totals in rows fetched.

[5.16]• Consider the following code fragment, where the two statements are meant to represent a single transaction:

```
      exec sql whenever sqlerror stop;
  begintx:
      exec sql update orders
          set dollars = dollars - :delta
          where aid = :agent1 and pid = :prod1 and cid = cust1;
      exec sql update orders
          set dollars = dollars + :delta
          where aid = :agent2 and pid = :prod1 and cid = cust1;
```

Rewrite this fragment, *modifying and adding statements,* to test for a deadlock abort error (see Figure 5.18) that might occur during the transaction, and then *have the program retry these two statements if a deadlock occurs.* Be careful that your tests actually work! Your rewrite should also commit the transaction after both statements above are complete; if a different error occurs instead, your logic should goto handle_err.

[5.17] In Dynamic SQL, assume a declaration of an **ORACLE** SQLDA of the kind given at the top of the program in Example 4.6.3. The variable sqlda is a pointer to a struct of type SQLDA.

(a)• After the Prepare statement, show how you could add code to provide column headings for the output data using, for **ORACLE**, the array of column name strings, and `sqlda->M[ ]`, the array of maximum column name string lengths. Similarly, for **DB2 UDB**, use `sqlda->sqlvar[i].sqlname.data` for the column name string and `sqlda->sqlvar[i].sqlname->length` for its short int length.

(b)• After a fetch from the dynamic cursor (in main), show what C test you would use to see if the second column retrieved has a null value, and call the function "handle_null( )" if this is the case.

[5.18] Write a program to loop as follows. Output a prompt SQL> and then accept a line of input from the user and execute it as a dynamic SQL statement, unless the line is empty, in which case you should exit the program. This is somewhat like the core loop of SQL monitors such as **ORACLE**'s SQL*Plus. However, this simple monitor cannot do Select statements. (Think about how you would extend the program to perform Select statements.)

[5.19] Suppose you need to change some product names in the `products` table, and you are given a file with lines containing a `pid` and new `pname` string, separated by whitespace, for each of the products to be renamed.

(a) Write a program that reads the file from standard input (stdin), line by line, and does the needed Updates; then execute the program with input redirection from a text file. You may use prompt( ) with a null-string prompt string to read each line of the file from standard input. Use Prepare and Execute for the Update statement needed here.

(b) Alternatively, use the load utility to load the lines of the file into rows of a table `pchanges` with `pid` and `pname` columns. Now perform the appropriate updates to the `products` table using the table `pchanges` and a single SQL statement.

[5.20] We wish to retrieve a set of columns from the `orders` table, where the columns to be retrieved are to be specified by a user. Write a program that prompts the user for which columns (by name) of the `orders` table to retrieve, one by one until a blank line is input. Then output data from these columns for all rows of the `orders` table, placing the columns from left to right in order of the user's input. You need to use fully Dynamic SQL as in Example 5.6.3 for **ORACLE**, or Example 5.6.4 for **DB2 UDB**. In **ORACLE**, for the `qty` and `dollars` columns, you can coerce the values to character by setting `T[i]` to 1 and `L[i]` (and the memory areas) to values large enough to hold the textual representation of the values. In **DB2 UDB**, you can use CAST in the SQL if you wish.

Database Design   6

No *human investigation can be called real science if it cannot be demonstrated mathematically.*
—Leonardo da Vinci

Until now we have dealt with databases made up of a number of distinct tables, without concerning ourselves very much with how the tables and their constituent columns were originally generated. *Logical database design,* also known simply as *database design* or *database modeling,* studies basic properties and interrelationships among data items, with the aim of providing faithful representations of such items in the basic data structures of a database. Databases with different data models have different structures for representing data; in relational databases the fundamental structures for representing data are what we have been calling *relational tables.* We concentrate on relational databases in the current chapter because design for the object-relational model is still in its infancy. Hopefully, we will have more to say about object-relational design in a later edition of this text.

It is the responsibility of the database administrator (DBA) to perform this logical database design, assigning the related data items of the database to columns of tables in a manner that preserves desirable properties. The most important test of logical design is that the tables and attributes faithfully reflect interrelationships among objects in the real world and that this remains true after all likely database updates in the future.

The DBA starts by studying some real-world enterprise, such as a wholesale order business, a company personnel office, or a college registration department, whose operation needs to be supported on a computerized database system. Often working with someone who has great expertise about the details of the enterprise, the DBA comes up with a list of data items and underlying data objects that must be kept track of (in college student registration, this list might include `student_names`, `courses`, `course_sections`, `class_rooms`, `class_periods`, etc.), together with a number of rules, or *constraints,* concerning the interrelatedness of these data items. Typical rules for student registration are the following:

◆ Every registered student has a *unique* student ID number (which we name sid).

◆ A student can be registered for *at most one* course section for a given class period.

◆ A classroom can house *at most one* course section for a given class period.

And so on. From these data items and constraints, the DBA is expected to perform the logical design of the database. Two common techniques covered in this chapter are used to perform the task of database design. The first is known as the *entity-relationship* approach (or *E-R* approach), and the second is the *normalization* approach. The E-R approach attempts to provide a taxonomy of data items to allow a DBA to intuitively recognize different types of data classification objects (entities, weak entities, attributes, relationships, etc.) to classify the listed data items and their relationships. After creating an E-R diagram that illustrates these objects, a relatively straightforward procedure allows the DBA to translate the design into relational tables and integrity constraints in the database system. The normalization approach seems entirely different, and perhaps less dependent on intuition: all the data items are listed, and then all interrelatedness rules (of a recognized kind, known as *dependencies)* are identified. Design starts with the assumption that all data items are placed in a single huge table and then proceeds to break down the table into smaller tables. In the resulting set of tables, joins are needed to retrieve the original relationships. Both the E-R modeling approach and the normalization approach are best applied by a DBA with a developed intuition about data relationships in the real world and about the way those relationships are ultimately modeled as relational tables. The two approaches tend to lead to identical relational table designs and in fact reinforce one another in providing the needed intuition. We will not attempt to discriminate between the two in terms of which is more applicable.

One of the major features of logical database design is the emphasis it places on rules of interrelationships between data items. The naive user often sees a relational table as made up of a set of descriptive columns, one column much like another. But this is far from accurate, because there are rules that limit possible relationships between values in the columns. Recall that in Section 2.2 we pointed out that the customers table, conceived as a relation, was a subset of the Cartesian product of four domains, CP = CID × CNAME × CITY × DISCNT. However, we also pointed out that in any legal customers table, two rows with the same cid value could not exist; this was because of the definitions in Figure 2.1 that described cid as a unique identifier for a customers row. Here is a perfect example of the kind of rule we wish to take into account in our logical database design. A faithful table representation enforces such a requirement by specifying that the cid column is a *candidate key* or the *primary key* for the customers table. Recall that a candidate key is a designated set of columns in a table such that two table rows can never be alike in all these column values, and where no smaller subset of the key columns has this property. A primary key is a candidate key that has been chosen by the DBA for external reference from other tables to unique rows in the table.

A faithful representation in a computerized database table of a candidate key or a primary key is provided when the table is created with the SQL Create Table statement. We will present a more complete syntax for this statement in Chapter 6, but a foreshadowing of the syntax is given in the declaration of Figure 6.1.

```
create table customers (cid char(4) not null, ssn integer not null unique,
      cname varchar(13), city varchar(20), discnt real, primary key (cid));
```

Figure 6.1 SQL Declaration of customers Table with Primary Key cid and candidate key ssn

The fact that the ssn column is declared as *not null unique* in a Create Table statement simply means that in any permitted customers content, two rows cannot have the same ssn value, and thus it is a candidate key. When cid is declared as a primary key in the Create Table statement, this is a more far-reaching statement, making cid the identifier of customers rows that might be used by other tables. Following either of the table definitions of 6.1, a later SQL Insert or Update statement that would duplicate a cid value or ssn value on two rows of the customers table is *illegal* and *has no effect*. Thus a faithful representation of the table key is maintained by the database system. Also a number of other clauses of the Create Table statement serve a comparable purpose of limiting possible table content, and we refer to these as *integrity constraints* for a table. The interrelationships between columns in relational tables must be understood at a reasonably deep level in order to properly appreciate some constraints. Although not all concepts of logical design can be faithfully represented in the SQL of today, SQL is moving in the direction of modeling more and more such concepts. In any event, many of the ideas of logical design can be useful as an aid to systematic database definition even in the absence of direct system support.

In the following sections, we first introduce a number of definitions of the E-R model. The process of normalization is introduced after some E-R intuition has been developed.

6.1 Introduction to E-R Concepts

The entity-relationship approach attempts to define a number of data classification objects; the database designer is then expected to classify data items by intuitive recognition as belonging in some known classification. Three fundamental data classification objects introduced in this section are *entities*, *attributes*, and *relationships*.

Entities, Attributes, and Simple E-R Diagrams

We begin with a definition of the concept of entity.

DEFINITION 6.1.1 Entity. An *entity* is a collection of distinguishable real-world objects with common properties.
∎

For example, in a college registration database we might have the following entities: Students, Instructors, Class_rooms, Courses, Course_sections, Class_periods, and so on. (Note that entity names are capitalized.) Clearly the set of classrooms in a college fits our definition of an entity: individual classrooms in the entity Class_rooms are distinguishable (by location—i.e., room number) and have other common properties such as seating capacity (not common values, but a common property). Class_periods is a somewhat surprising entity—is *MWF from 2:00 to 3:00* PM a real-world object?—but the test here is that the registration process deals with these class periods as if they were objects, assigning class periods in student schedules in the same sense that rooms are assigned. To give examples of entities that we have worked with a good deal in the CAP database, we have Customers, Agents, and Products. (Orders is also an entity, but there is some possibility for confusion in this, and we discuss it a bit later.) There is a foreshadowing here of entities being mapped to relational tables. An entity such as Customers is usually mapped to an actual table, and each row of the table corresponds to one of the distinguishable real-world objects that make up the entity, called an *entity instance,* or sometimes an *entity occurrence.*

Note that we do not yet have a name for the properties by which we tell one entity occurrence from another, the analog to column values to distinguish rows in a relational table. For now we simply refer to entity instances as being distinguishable, in the same sense that we would think of the classrooms in a college as being distinguishable, without needing to understand the room-labeling scheme used. In what follows we always write an entity name with an initial capital letter, but the name becomes all lowercase when the entity is mapped to a relational table in SQL.

We have chosen an unusual notation by assigning plural entity names: Students, Instructors, Class_rooms, and so forth. More standard would be entities named Student, Instructor, and Class_room. Our plural usage is chosen to emphasize the fact that each represents a *set* of real-world objects, usually containing multiple elements, and carries over to our plural table names, also somewhat unusual, which normally contain multiple rows. Entities are represented by rectangles in E-R diagrams, as you can see by looking at Figure 6.2.

Note that some other authors use the terminology *entity set* or *entity type* in referring to what we call an *entity.* Then to these authors, an *entity* is what we would refer to as an *entity instance.* We have also noticed occasional ambiguity within a specific author's writing, sometimes referring to an entity set and sometimes to an entity; we assume that the object that is represented by a rectangle in an E-R diagram is an entity, a collection of real-world objects, and authors who identify such rectangles in the same way agree with our definition. It is unfortunate that such ambiguity exists, but our notation will be consistent in what follows.

In mathematical discussion, for purposes of definition, we usually represent an entity by a single capital letter, possibly subscripted where several exist: E, or E_1, E_2, ... An entity E is made up of a set of real-world objects, which we represent by subscripted lowercase letters: E = {e_1, e_2, . . . , e_n}. As mentioned above, each distinct representative e_i of an entity E is called an entity *instance* or an entity *occurrence.*

DEFINITION 6.1.2 Attribute. An *attribute* is a data item that describes a property of an entity or a relationship (defined below). ∎

Recall from the definition of *entity* that all entity occurrences belonging to a given entity have common properties. In the E-R model, these properties are known as *attributes.* As we will see, there is no confusion in terminology between an attribute in the E-R model and an attribute or column name in the relational model, because when the E-R design is translated into relational terms the two correspond. A particular instance of an entity is said to have attribute values for all attributes describing the entity (a null value is possible). The reader should keep in mind that while we list distinct entity occurrences $\{e_1, e_2, \ldots, e_n\}$ of the entity E, we can't actually tell the occurrences apart without reference to attribute values.

Each entity has an *identifier,* an attribute, or set of attributes that takes on unique values for each entity instance; this is the analog of the relational concept of *candidate key.* For example, we define an identifier for the Customers entity to be the customer identifier, cid. There might be more than one identifier for a given entity, and when the DBA identifies a single key attribute to be the universal method of identification for entity occurrences throughout the database, this is called a *primary identifier* for the entity. Other attributes, such as city for Customers, are not identifiers but *descriptive attributes,* known as *descriptors.* Most attributes take on simple values from a domain, as we have seen in the relational model, but a *composite attribute* is a group of simple attributes that together describe a property. For example, the attribute student_names for the Students entity might be composed of the simple attributes lname, fname, and midinitial. Note that an identifier for an entity is allowed to contain an attribute of composite type. Finally, we define a *multi-valued attribute* to be one that can take on multiple values for a single entity instance. For example, the Employees entity might have an attached multi-valued attribute named hobbies, which takes on multiple values provided by the employee asked to list any hobbies or interests. One employee might have several hobbies, so this is a multi-valued attribute.

As mentioned earlier, E-R diagrams represent entities as rectangles. Figure 6.2 shows two simple E-R diagrams. Simple, single-valued attributes are represented by ovals, attached by a straight line to the entity. A composite attribute is also in an oval attached directly to the entity, while the simple attributes that make up the composite are attached to the composite oval. A multi-valued attribute is attached by a double line, rather than a single line, to the entity it describes. The primary identifier attribute is underlined.

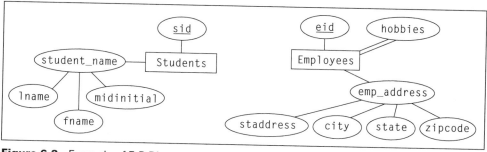

Figure 6.2 Example of E-R Diagrams with Entities and Attributes

Transforming Entities and Attributes to Relations

Our ultimate aim is to transform the E-R design into a set of definitions for relational tables in a computerized database, which we do through a set of transformation rules.

Transformation RULE 1. Each entity in an E-R diagram is mapped to a single table in a relational database; the table is named after the entity. The columns of the table represent all the single-valued simple attributes that are attached to the entity (possibly through a composite attribute, although a composite attribute itself does not become a column of the table). An identifier for an entity is mapped to a candidate key for the table, as illustrated in Example 6.1.1, and a primary identifier is mapped to a primary key. Note that the primary identifier of an entity might be a composite attribute, which therefore translates to a set of attributes in the relational table mapping. Entity occurrences are mapped to rows of the table. ∎

EXAMPLE 6.1.1

Here are the two tables, with one example row filled in, mapped from the Students and Employees entities in the E-R diagrams of Figure 6.2. The primary key is underlined.

students

<u>sid</u>	lname	fname	midinitial
1134	Smith	John	L.
...	...	...	...

employees

<u>eid</u>	staddress	city	state	zipcode
197	7 Beacon St	Boston	MA	02122
...	...	...	...	...

∎

Transformation RULE 2. Given an entity E with primary identifier p, a multi-valued attribute a attached to E in an E-R diagram is mapped to a table of its own; the table is named after the plural multi-valued attribute. The columns of this new table are named after p and a (either p or a might consist of several attributes), and rows of the table correspond to (p, a) value pairs, representing all pairings of attribute values of a associated with entity occurrences in E. The primary key attribute for this table is the set of columns in p and a. ∎

EXAMPLE 6.1.2

Here is an example database of two tables reflecting the E-R diagram for the Employees entity and the attached multi-valued attribute, hobbies, of Figure 6.2.

employees

eid	staddress	city	state	zipcode
197	7 Beacon St	Boston	MA	02102
221	19 Brighton St	Boston	MA	02103
303	153 Mass Ave	Cambridge	MA	02123
. . .	. . .	. . .	. . .	. . .

hobbies

eid	hobby
197	chess
197	painting
197	science fiction
221	reading
303	bicycling
303	mysteries
. . .	. . .

Relationships among Entities

DEFINITION 6.1.3 Relationship. Given an ordered list of m entities, E_1, E_2, . . . , E_m (where the same entity may occur more than once in the list), a *relationship* R defines a rule of correspondence between the instances of these entities. Specifically, R represents a set of m-tuples, a subset of the Cartesian product of entity instances $E_1 \times E_2 \times . . . \times E_m$. ■

A particular occurrence of a relationship, corresponding to a tuple of entity occurrences $(e_1, e_2, . . . , e_n)$, where e_i is an instance of E_i in the ordered list of the definition, is called a *relationship occurrence* or *relationship instance*. The number of entities m in the defining list is called the *degree* of the relationship. A relationship between two entities is known as a *binary relationship*. For example, we define teaches to be a binary relationship between Instructors and Course_sections. We indicate that a relationship instance exists by saying that a particular instructor teaches a specific course section. Another example of a relationship is works_on, defined to relate the two entities Employees and Projects in a large company: Employees works_on Projects.

A relationship can also have attached attributes. The relationship works_on might have the attribute percent, indicating the percent of work time during each week that the employee is assigned to work on each specific project (see Figure 6.3). Note that this percent attribute attached to the works_on relationship would be multi-valued if attached to either entity Employees or Projects; the percent attribute is only meaningful in describing a specific employee-project pair, and it is therefore a natural attribute of the binary relationship works_on.

A binary relationship that relates an entity to itself (a subset of $E_1 \times E_1$) is called a *ring*, or sometimes a *recursive relationship*. For example, the Employees entity is related to itself through the relationship manages, where we say that one employee manages another. Relationships are represented by diamonds in an E-R diagram, with connecting lines to the entities they relate. In the case of a ring, the connecting lines are often labeled with the names of the roles played by the entity instances involved. In Figure 6.3 the two named roles are manager_of and reports_to.

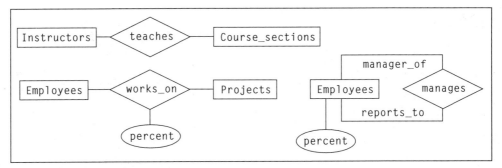

Figure 6.3   Examples of E-R Diagrams with Relationships

Note that we often leave out attributes in an E-R diagram to concentrate on relationships between entities without losing our concentration in excessive detail.

EXAMPLE 6.1.3   The orders **table in CAP does not represent a relationship.**
By Definition 6.1.3, the orders table in the CAP database is not a relationship between Customers, Agents, and Products. This is because (cid, aid, pid) triples in the rows of the orders table do not identify a subset of the Cartesian product, Customers × Agents × Products, as required. Instead, some triples of (cid, aid, pid) values occur more than once in the example of Figure 2.2, and this is clearly the designer's intention, since the same customer can order the same product from the same agent on two different occasions. Instead of a relationship, the orders table represents an entity in its own right, with identifier attribute ordno. This makes a good deal of sense, since we might commonly have reason to look up a row in the orders table for reasons unconnected to relating entity occurrences in Customers, Agents, and Products. For example, on request we might need to check that a past order has been properly billed and shipped (we are assuming attributes that are not present in the simple orders table of Figure 2.2). Thus the Orders occurrences are dealt with individually as objects in their own right. Of course the entity Orders is related to each of the entities Customers, Agents, and Products, as we will explore in the exercises at the end of the chapter.   ∎

Although the orders table doesn't correspond directly to a relationship, it is clear that there are any number of possible relationships we could define in terms of the orders table between the Customers, Agents, and Products entities.

EXAMPLE 6.1.4
Assume that we are performing a study in which we commonly need to know total sales aggregated (summed) from the orders table by customers, agents, and products for the current year. We might do this, for example, to study sales volume relationships between agents and customers as well as between customers and products, and how those relationships are affected by geographic factors (city values). However, as we begin to plan this application, we decide that it is too inefficient to always perform sums on the orders table to access the basic measures of our study, so we decide to create a new table called yearlies. We define this new table with the SQL commands

```
create table yearlies (cid char(4), aid char(3), pid char(3),
    totqty integer, totdoll float);
insert into yearlies
    select cid, aid, pid, sum(qty), sum(dollars) from orders
    group by cid, aid, pid;
```

Once we have the new `yearlies` table, the totals can be kept up-to-date by application logic: as each new order is entered, the relevant `yearlies` row should be updated as well. Now the `yearlies` table is a relationship, since the (`cid`, `aid`, `pid`) triples in the rows of the table iden-tify a *subset* of the Cartesian product, `Customers × Agents × Products`; that is to say, there are now no repeated triples in the `yearlies` table. Since these triples are unique, (`cid`, `aid`, `pid`) forms the primary key for the `yearlies` table.

∎

A relationship on more than two entities is called an *N-ary relationship*. The year-lies relationship on three distinct entities is also known as a *ternary relationship*. An N-ary relationship with N > 2 can often be replaced by a number of distinct binary relation-ships in an E-R diagram, and this is a good idea if the replacement expresses true binary relationships for the system. Binary relationships are the ones that are familiar to most practitioners and are sufficient for almost all applications. However, in some cases, a ter-nary relationship cannot be decomposed into expressive binary relationships. The year-lies relationship of Example 6.1.4 expresses customer-agent-product ordering patterns over a year, a ternary relationship that cannot be decomposed (exactly) into binary rela-tionships. We further explore ternary relationships in Exercises 6.4 and 6.21 at the end of this chapter.

In converting an E-R design to a relational one, a relationship is sometimes trans-lated into a relational table, and sometimes not. (We will have more to say about this in the next section.) For example, the `yearlies` relationship (a ternary relationship) is translated into a relational table named `yearlies`. However, the `manages` relationship between `Employees` and `Employees`, shown in Figure 6.3, does not translate into a table of its own. Instead this relationship is usually translated into a column in `employees` identifying the `mgrid` to whom the employee reports, as we saw in Example 3.11.6. This table is shown again in Figure 6.4.

Note the surprising fact that `mgrid` is *not* considered an attribute of the `Employees` entity, although it exists as a column in the `employees` table. The `mgrid` column is what is known as a *foreign key* in the relational model, and it corresponds to the actual man-ages relationship in the E-R diagram of Figure 6.3. We deal more with this in the next section, after we have had an opportunity to consider some of the properties of relation-ships. To summarize this section, Figure 6.5(a) and (b) lists the concepts introduced up to now.

employees

eid	ename	mgrid
e001	Jacqueline	null
e002	Frances	e001
e003	Jose	e001
e004	Deborah	e001
e005	Craig	e002
e006	Mark	e002
e007	Suzanne	e003
e008	Frank	e003
e009	Victor	e004
e010	Chumley	e007

Figure 6.4 A Table Representing an Entity, Employees, and a Ring (Recursive Relationship) manages

Classification	Description	Example
Entity	A collection of distinguishable real-world objects with common properties	Customers, Agents, Products, Employees
Attribute	A data item that describes a property of an entity or relationship	See below
Identifier (set of attributes)	Uniquely identifies an entity or relationship occurrence	customer identifier: cid, employee identifier: eid
Descriptor	Non-key attribute, describing an entity or relationship	city (for Customers), capacity (for Class_rooms)
Composite attribute	A group of simple attributes that together describe a property of an object	emp_address (see Figure 6.2)
Multi-valued attribute	An entity attribute that takes on multiple values for a single entity instance	hobbies (see Figure 6.2)

Figure 6.5(a) Basic E-R Concepts: Entities and Attributes

Classification	Description	Example
Relationship	Named set of m-tuples, identifies subset of the Cartesian product $E_1 \times E_2 \times \ldots \times E_m$	
Binary relationship	A relationship on two distinct entities	teaches, works_on (see Figure 6.3)
Ring, recursive relationship	A relationship relating an entity to itself	manages (see Figure 6.4)
Ternary relationship	A relationship on three distinct entities	yearlies (see Example 6.1.4)

Figure 6.5(b) Basic E-R Concepts: Relationships

6.2 Further Details of E-R Modeling

Now that we've defined some fundamental means of classification, let's discuss properties of relationships in the E-R method of database design.

Cardinality of Entity Participation in a Relationship

Figure 6.6 illustrates the concepts of *minimum* and *maximum cardinality* with which an entity participates in a relationship. Diagrams (a), (b), and (c) of that figure represent entities E and F on the left and right, respectively, by two sets; elements of the two sets are connected by a line exactly when a relationship R relates the two entity occurrences represented. Thus the connecting lines themselves represent instances of the relation R. Note that the diagrams of Figure 6.6 are *not* what we refer to as E-R diagrams.

The minimum cardinality with which an entity takes part in a relationship is the minimum number of lines that the DBA allows to be connected to each entity instance. Note that the diagrams of Figure 6.6 would normally only give examples of relationships at a given moment, and the line connections might change, just as the row content of a table can change, until some entity instances have different numbers of lines connected. On the other hand, the minimum and maximum cardinality properties of an entity are meant to represent rules laid down by the DBA for all time, rules that cannot be broken by normal database changes affecting the relationship. In diagram (a), the DBA clearly permits both entity sets E and F to take part in relationship R with minimum cardinality zero; that is to say, the DBA does not *require* a connecting line for each entity instance, since some elements of both sets have no lines connected to them. We symbolize this by writing min-card(E, R) = 0 and min-card(F, R) = 0. The maximum cardinality with which E and F take part in R is not obvious from diagram (a), however. No entity instance has more than one line connected to it, but from an example as of a given moment we have no guarantee that the line connections won't change in the future so that some entity

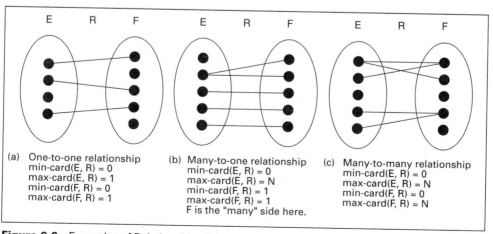

(a) One-to-one relationship
min-card(E, R) = 0
max-card(E, R) = 1
min-card(F, R) = 0
max-card(F, R) = 1

(b) Many-to-one relationship
min-card(E, R) = 0
max-card(E, R) = N
min-card(F, R) = 1
max-card(F, R) = 1
F is the "many" side here.

(c) Many-to-many relationship
min-card(E, R) = 0
max-card(E, R) = N
min-card(F, R) = 0
max-card(F, R) = N

Figure 6.6 Examples of Relationships R between Two Entities E and F

instances will have more than one line connected. However, we will assume for purposes of simple explanation that the diagrams of this figure are meant to represent exactly the cardinalities intended by the DBA. Thus since no entity instance of E and F in diagram (a) has more than one incident connecting line, we record this fact using the notation max-card(E, R) = 1 and max-card(F, R) = 1.

In diagram (b), assuming once again that this set of lines is representative of the designer's intention, we can write min-card(E, R) = 0, since not every element of E is connected to a line, but min-card(F, R) = 1, since at least one line is connected to every element of F, and our assumption implies that this won't change. We also write max-card(E, R) = N, where N means "more than one"; this means that the designer does not intend to limit to one the number of lines connected to each entity instance of E. However, we write max-card(F, R) = 1, since every element of F has exactly one line leaving it. Note that the two meaningful values for min-card are zero and one (where zero is not really a limitation at all, but one stands for the constraint "at least one"), and the two meaningful values for max-card are one and N (N is not really a limitation, but one represents the constraint "no more than one"). We don't try to differentiate numbers other than zero, one, and many. Since max-card(E, R) = N, there are multiple entity instances of F connected to one of E by the relationship. For this reason, F is called the "many" side and E is called the "one" side in this many-to-one relationship. (We will give a rigorous definition of a many-to-one relationship below, in Definition 6.2.2.)

Note particularly that the "many" side in a many-to-one relationship is the side that has *max-card value one!* In Figure 6.6(b), the entity F corresponds to the "many" side of the many-to-one relationship, even though it has min-card(F, R) = max-card(F, R) = 1. As just explained, the "one" side of a many-to-one relationship is the side where some entity instances can participate in multiple relationship instances, "shooting out multiple lines" to connect to *many* entity instances on the "many" side! Phrased this way the terminology makes sense, but this seems to be an easy idea to forget, and forgetting it can lead to serious confusion.

In diagram (c) we have min-card(E, R) = 0, min-card(F, R) = 0, max-card(E, R) = N, and max-card(F, R) = N. Starting with Definition 6.2.2, we explain the meaning of the terms used for the three diagrams: one-to-one relationship, many-to-one relationship, and many-to-many relationship.

EXAMPLE 6.2.1

In the relationship teaches of Figure 6.3, Instructors teaches Course_sections, the DBA would probably want to make a rule that each course section needs to have at least one instructor assigned to teach it by writing: min-card(Course_sections, teaches) = 1. However, we need to be careful in making such a rule, since it means that we will not be able to create a new course section, enter it in the database, assign it a room and a class period, and allow students to register for it, while putting off the decision of who is going to teach it. The DBA might also make the rule that at most one instructor can be assigned to teach a course section by writing max-card(Course_sections, teaches) = 1. On the other hand, if more than one instructor were allowed to share the teaching of a course section, the DBA would write max-card(Course_sections, teaches) = N. This is clearly a significant difference. We probably don't want to make the rule that every instructor teaches some course section (written as min-card(Instructors, teaches) = 1), because an instructor might be on leave, so we settle on min-card(Instructors, teaches) = 0. And in most universities the course load per instructor is greater than one in any given term, so we would set max-card(Instructors, teaches) = N.

∎

DEFINITION 6.2.1 When an entity E takes part in a relationship R with min-card(E, R) = x (x is either 0 or 1) and max-card(E, R) = y (y is either 1 or N), then in the E-R diagram the connecting line between E and R can be labeled with the ordered cardinality pair (x, y). We use a new notation to represent this minimum-maximum pair (x, y): card(E, R) = (x, y).

∎

According to Definition 6.2.1 and the assignments of Example 6.2.1, the edge connecting the entity Course_sections to the relationship teaches should be labeled with the pair (1, 1). In Figure 6.7 we repeat the E-R diagrams of Figure 6.3, with the addition of ordered pairs (x, y) labeling line connections, to show the minimum and maximum cardinalities for all entity-relationship pairs. The cardinality pair for the Instructors teaches Course_sections diagram follows the discussion of Example 6.2.1, and other diagrams are filled in with reasonable pair values. We make a number of decisions to arrive at the following rules: every employee must work on at least one project (but may work on many); a project might have no employees assigned during some periods (waiting for staffing), and of course some projects will have a large number of employees working on them; an employee who acts in the manager_of role (see discussion below) may be managing no other employees at a given time and still be called a manager; and an employee reports to at most one manager, but may report to none (this possibility exists because there must always be a highest-level employee in a hierarchy who has no manager).

In the Employees-manages diagram of Figure 6.7, the normal notation, card(Employees, manages) would be ambiguous. We say that there are two different *roles* played by the Employees entity in the relationship: the manager_of role and the

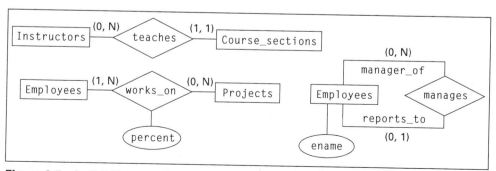

Figure 6.7 An E-R Diagram with Labels (x, y) on Entity-Relationship Connections

reports_to role. Each relationship instance in manages connects a *managed employee* (Employees instance in the reports_to role) to a *manager employee* (Employees instance in the manager_of role). We use the cardinality notation with entities having parenthesized roles to remove ambiguity.

```
card(Employees(reports_to), manages)= (0, 1)
```

and

```
card(Employees(manager_of), manages) = (0, N)
```

And from these cardinalities we see that an employee who acts in the manager_of role may be managing no other employees at a given time and still be called a manager; and an employee reports to at most one manager, but may report to none (because of the highest-level employee in a hierarchy who has no manager—if it weren't for that single person, we could give the label (1, 1) to the reports_to branch of the Employees-manages edge).

One-to-One, Many-to-Many, and Many-to-One Relationships

DEFINITION 6.2.2 When an entity E takes part in a relationship R with max-card(E, R) = 1, then E is said to have *single-valued* participation in the relationship R. If max-card(E, R) = N, then E is said to be *multi-valued* in this relationship. A binary relationship R between entities E and F is said to be *many-to-many*, or N-N, if both entities E and F are multi-valued in the relationship. If both E and F are single-valued, the relationship is said to be *one-to-one*, or 1-1. If E is single-valued and F is multi-valued, or the reverse, the relationship is said to be many-to-one, N-1. (See the note following: we do not normally speak of a 1-N relationship as distinct from an N-1 relationship.)   ∎

Recall that the "many" side in a many-to-one relationship is the side that has single-valued participation. This might be better understood by considering the relationship in Figure 6.7, Instructors teaches Course_sections, where card(Course_sections, teaches) = (1, 1), and the Course_sections entity represents the "many" side of the relationship. This is because one instructor teaches "many" course sections, while the reverse is not true.

In Definition 6.2.2, we see that the values max-card(E, R) and max-card(F, R) determine whether a binary relationship is many-to-many, many-to-one, or one-to-one. On the other hand, the values min-card(E, R) and min-card(F, R) are not mentioned, and they are said to be independent of these characterizations. In particular, the fact that min-card(F, R) = 1 in Figure 6.6(b) is independent of the fact that diagram (b) represents a many-to-one relationship. If there were additional elements in entity F that were not connected by any lines to elements in E (but all current connections remained the same), this would mean that min-card(F, R) = 0, but the change would not affect the fact that R is a many-to-one relationship. We would still see one element of E (the second from the top) related to two elements of F; in this case, the entity F is the "many" side of the relationship.

Although min-card(E, R) and min-card(F, R) have no bearing on whether a binary relationship R is many-to-many, many-to-one, or one-to-one, a different characterization of entity participation in a relationship is determined by these quantities.

DEFINITION 6.2.3 When an entity E that participates in a relationship R has min-card(E, R) = 1, E is said to have *mandatory participation* in R, or is simply called *mandatory* in R. An entity E that is not mandatory in R is said to be *optional,* or to have *optional participation.*

∎

Transforming Binary Relationships to Relations

We are now prepared to give the transformation rule for a binary many-to-many relationship.

Transformation RULE 3. N-N Relationships. When two entities E and F take part in a many-to-many binary relationship R, the relationship is mapped to a representative table T in the related relational database design. The table contains columns for all attributes in the primary keys of both tables transformed from entities E and F, and this set of columns forms the primary key for the table T. T also contains columns for all attributes attached to the relationship. Relationship occurrences are represented by rows of the table, with the related entity instances uniquely identified by their primary key values as rows.

∎

EXAMPLE 6.2.2

In Figure 6.7, the relationship works_on is many-to-many between the entities Employees and Projects. The relational design in Figure 6.8 follows Transformation RULE 1 to provide a table for the entity Employees (as specified in Example 6.1.2) and a table for the entity Projects; it also follows Transformation RULE 3, to provide a table for the relationship works_on.

We generally assume that the eid column in the employees table and prid column for the projects table cannot take on null values, since they are the primary keys for their tables and must differentiate all rows by unique values. Similarly, the (eid, prid) pair of columns in the works_on table cannot take on null values in either component, since each row must uniquely designate the employee-project pair related. This general observation was summed up in Relational RULE 4, (the entity integrity rule) at the end of Section 2.4, which says that no primary key column of a relational table can take on null values. Note that although we refer to this as the *entity integrity rule,* it applies as well to tables arising out of the relationships in the E-R model. Recall that the SQL Create Table command, introduced in Section 3.2, provides syntax to impose an integrity constraint on a table that guarantees this rule will not be broken, that no nulls will be assigned. For example, the SQL statement

```
create table projects (prid char(3) not null . . .);
```

guarantees that the prid column of the projects table cannot take on null values as a result of later Insert, Delete, or Update statements. There are other constraints as well that have this effect.

employees

eid	straddr	city	state	zipcode
197	7 Beacon St	Boston	MA	02102
221	19 Brighton St	Boston	MA	02103
303	153 Mass Ave	Cambridge	MA	02123
...	...	...	...	...

works_on

eid	prid	percent
197	p11	50
197	p13	25
197	p21	25
221	p21	100
303	p13	40
303	p21	60
...	...	...

projects

prid	proj_name	due_date
p11	Phoenix	3/31/99
p13	Excelsior	9/31/99
p21	White Mouse	6/30/00
...	...	...

Figure 6.8 Relational Design for Employees works_on Projects of Figure 6.7

Transformation RULE 4. N-1 Relationships. When two entities E and F take part in a many-to-one binary relationship R, the relationship will not be mapped to a table of its own in a relational database design. Instead, if we assume that the entity F has max-card(F, R) = 1 and thus represents the "many" side of the relationship, the relational table T transformed from the entity F should include columns constituting the primary key for the table transformed from the entity E; this is known as a *foreign key* in T. Since max-card(F, R) = 1, each row of T is related by a foreign key value to at most one instance of the entity E. If F has mandatory participation in R, then it must be related to exactly one instance of E, and this means that the foreign key in T cannot take on null values. If F has optional participation in R, then each row of T that is not related can have null values in all columns of the foreign key.

EXAMPLE 6.2.3

Figure 6.9 shows a relational transformation of the Instructors teaches Course_sections E-R diagram of Figure 6.7. Recall that we made the rule that one instructor can teach multiple course sections, but each course section can have only one instructor. The insid column in the course_sections table is a foreign key, relating a course_sections instance (row) to a unique instructors instance (row).

instructors

insid	lname	office_no	ext
309	O'Neil	S-3-223	78543
123	Bergen	S-3-547	78413
113	Smith	S-3-115	78455
...	...	...	...

course_sections

secid	insid	course	room	period
120	309	CS240	M-1-213	MW6
940	309	CS630	M-1-214	MW7:30
453	123	CS632	M-2-614	TTH6
...	...	...	...	...

Figure 6.9 Relational Design for Instructors teaches Course_Sections of Figure 6.7

The Create Table command in SQL can require a column not to take on null values; therefore it is possible to guarantee a faithful representation for mandatory participation by the "many" side entity in a many-to-one relationship. Here we can create the course_sections table so no nulls are allowed in the insid column. What we mean by "faithful" is that it becomes impossible for a user to corrupt the data by a thoughtless update, because SQL does not allow a course_sections row with a null value for insid. As we will see in the next chapter, SQL can also impose a constraint that the foreign key insid value in a row of the course_sections table actually exists as a value in the insid primary key column in the instructors table. This constraint is known as *referential integrity*. ∎

Unfortunately, it is not possible in standard SQL to guarantee a mandatory participation by the "one" side of a many-to-one relationship, or by either side of a many-to-many relationship. Thus in Example 6.2.3 there would be no way to provide a faithful representation in an SQL table definition that would guarantee that every instructor teaches at least one course.

Note that there are differences of opinion among texts on some of these E-R transformation rules for relationships. Reference [4] gives the equivalent to Transformation RULE 4 for N-1 relationships, but reference [1] provides an alternate transformation where the relationship is mapped onto a table of its own if the entity at the "many" side of the relationship has an optional participation. The reason for this is to avoid possibly heavy use of null values in the foreign key (insid in course_sections in Example 6.2.3); but since there seems to be nothing wrong with using null values, we follow the transformation of reference [4].

Transformation RULE 5. 1-1 Relationships, Optional Participation. Given two entities E and F that take part in a one-to-one binary relationship R, where participation is optional on either side, we wish to translate this situation into a relational design. To do this, we create a table S to represent the entity E, following the prescription of Transformation RULE 1, and similarly a table T to represent the entity F. Then we adjoin to the table T a set of columns (as a foreign key) constituting the primary key for table S. If we wish, we may also adjoin to table S a foreign key set of columns referring to the primary key of table T. For any relationship instance in R, a unique entity instance in E is related to a unique instance in F—in the corresponding rows of S and T, the foreign key column values filled in to reference the row in the other table arising from the instances related by R. ∎

Transformation RULE 6. 1-1 Relationships, Mandatory Participation on Both Sides. In the case of a one-to-one relationship with mandatory participation on both sides, it is most appropriate to combine the tables for the two entities into one, and in this way avoid any foreign keys. ∎

We do not present transformation rules for all possible N-ary relationships with N > 2. Usually such an N-ary relationship is transformed into a table of its own, but if all but one of the entities of the relationship participate with max-card = 1, then it is possible to represent the relationship with N – 1 foreign keys in the one table that participates with greater cardinality.

6.3 Additional E-R Concepts

In this section we introduce a number of additional concepts useful for E-R modeling.

Cardinality of Attributes

To begin with, we note that the min-card/max-card notation can be used to describe the cardinality of attributes attached to entities.

DEFINITION 6.3.1 Given an entity E and an attached attribute A, we write min-card(A, E) = 0 to indicate that the attribute A is optional, and min-card(A, E) = 1 to indicate that the attribute A is mandatory. An attribute that is mandatory should correspond to a column declared in the table representing the entity E with no nulls allowed. We write max-card(A, E) = 1 to indicate that the attribute is single-valued, and max-card(A, E) = N to indicate that the attribute is multi-valued. An attribute A is said to have card(A, E) = (x, y) when min-card(A, E) = x and max-card(A, E) = y. The (x, y) pair can be used to label an attribute-entity connection in an E-R diagram to indicate the cardinality of the attribute. ∎

Attributes that have unlabeled connectors in an E-R diagram can be assumed to have cardinality (0, 1) if they are descriptor attributes, and cardinality (1, 1) if they are identifier attributes. Figure 6.10 recapitulates Figure 6.2 with labeled attribute-entity connectors. (Note that these are not the default cardinalities we would have expected from Figure 6.2, which was left with unlabeled cardinalities only because of lack of notation.)

In Figure 6.10 we note that the attribute midinitial is optional (some people don't have middle names). The composite attribute student_names is mandatory for Students, but emp_address is optional for Employees. However, given that emp_address exists, all four simple attributes making up the address are mandatory. Both sid and eid have cardinality (1, 1); this is always the case for entity identifiers. The multi-valued hobbies attribute has max-card N, as we can also tell from the fact that it is connected to its

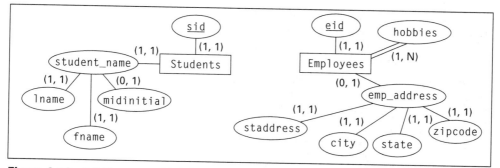

Figure 6.10 E-R Diagrams with Labeled Attribute-Entity Connectors

entity by a double line. The fact that min-card(hobbies, Employees) = 1 is somewhat surprising and indicates that the employee *must* name at least one hobby for inclusion in the database.

Weak Entities

DEFINITION 6.3.2 A weak entity is an entity whose occurrences are dependent for their existence, through a relationship R, on the occurrence of another (strong) entity. ∎

As an example, we have been assuming in our CAP design that an order specifies a customer, agent, product, quantity, and dollar cost. A common design variant that allows multiple products to be ordered at once will create an orders table that relates to customers and agents rows, as well as a line_items table containing individual product purchases; a number of rows in the line_items table relate to one master orders occurrence. The design of this in the E-R model is given in Figure 6.11.

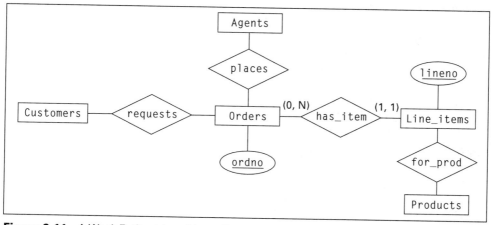

Figure 6.11 A Weak Entity, Line_items, Dependent on the Entity Orders

As we see, the entity Orders is optional in its relationship to Line_items, since each order must start without any line items. Line_items is mandatory in the relationship, because a line-item order for a product cannot exist without a master order containing it to specify the customer and agent for the order. If the Orders occurrence goes away (the customer cancels it), all occurrences of the weak entity Line_items will likewise disappear. A dead giveaway for a weak entity is the fact that the primary identifier for Line_items (lineno) is only meaningful within some order. In fact, what this implies is that the primary identifier for the weak entity Line_items must include the attributes in the primary identifier for the Orders entity. Attributes such as Line_items are known as *external identifier* attributes.

When the Line_items weak entity is mapped to a relational table line_items, an ordno column is included by Transformation RULE 4 to represent the N-1 has_item relationship; thus the primary key for the line_items table is constructed from the external attribute ordno and the weak entity identifier lineno. Note that it is also sometimes difficult to distinguish between a weak entity and a multi-valued attribute. For example, hobbies in Example 6.1.2 could be identified as a weak entity Hobbies, with an identifier hobby_name. However, Figure 6.11 obviously implies Line_items is a weak entity rather than a multi-valued attribute, since Line_items is separately related to another entity, Products.

Generalization Hierarchies

Finally, we introduce the concept of a *generalization hierarchy* or *generalization relationship*, the E-R concept that corresponds to the object-relational *inheritance* feature presented just prior to Section 4.2.3. The idea is that several entities with common attributes can be generalized into a higher-level *supertype entity* or, alternatively, a general entity can be decomposed into lower-level *subtype entities*. The purpose is to attach attributes at the proper level and thus avoid having attributes of a common entity that require a large number of null values in each entity instance. For example, assume that we distinguish between Managers and Non_managers as *subtype* entities of the *supertype* Employees (see Figure 6.12). Then attributes such as expenseno (for expense reports) can be attached only to the Managers entity, while non-manager attributes such as union status can be attached to Non_managers. Consultants might form another entity type sharing many properties with Employees, and we could create a new supertype entity named Persons to contain them both. An E-R diagram showing a generalization hierarchy normally has arrows (unnamed) directed from the subtype to the supertype entities.

The arrow relationship between the subtype entity and the supertype entity is often referred to as an *ISA relationship*, since a consultant *is a* person, a manager *is an* employee, and so forth. As we saw in Chapter 4, object-relational database systems express these concepts using *type inheritance*, where objects (rows) of a given subtype contain specific attributes but *inherit* all attributes of their *supertype*. In particular, **INFORMIX** and SQL-99 support inheritance of object types. See Section 4.2.3 for more information.

The relational model provides no support for the concept of generalization hierarchy, so it is necessary to reconfigure such a design element into simpler concepts. This

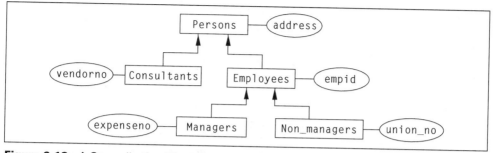

Figure 6.12 A Generalization Hierarchy with Examples of Attributes Attached

can happen either prior to transformation into relational tables or as part of the transformation. Here we give an idea of how to perform such a reconfiguration while remaining in the E-R model, before transformation into a relational representation. We consider one level of generalization hierarchy at a time and give two alternatives.

[1] We can collapse a one-level generalization hierarchy of subtype and supertype entities into a single entity by adding all attributes of the subtype entities to the supertype entity. An additional attribute must be added to this single entity, which will discriminate among the various types. As an example, the Employees entity of Figure 6.12 could be augmented to represent managers and non-managers as well, by affixing the attributes union_no, expenseno, and emptype to the Employee entity. Now the union_no attribute will be null when emptype has value 'Manager', and similarly expenseno will be null when emptype is 'Non-Manager'. The emptype attribute might also designate the supertype case, an important alternative when some entity instances in the supertype fall in none of the named subtypes.

[2] We can retain the supertype entity and all subtype entities as full entities and create explicit named relationships to represent the ISA relationships.

Alternative 2 is particularly useful when the various subtypes and supertype are quite different in attributes and are handled differently by application logic.

We do not investigate all concepts of the entity-relationship model in full depth here. See the references at the end of this chapter for a list of texts devoted to complete coverage of the E-R model and logical database design.

6.4 Case Study

Let us try to perform an E-R design from the beginning, ending up with a set of relational tables. Consider a simple airline reservation database handling (only) outgoing flights from one airline terminal. We need to keep track of passengers, flights, departure gates, and seat assignments. We could get almost arbitrarily complex in a real design, since a "flight" actually brings together a flight crew and an airplane, serviced by a ground crew, slotted into a regularly scheduled departure time with an assigned flight number on a specific date. But for simplicity, we will assume that we can represent flights with an entity Flights, having primary identifier flightno (unique identifier values, not repeated on successive days) and descriptive attribute depart_time (actually made up of date and time); other details will be hidden from us. Passengers are represented by another entity, Passengers, with primary identifier attribute ticketno; a passenger has no other attribute that we care about. We also need to keep track of seats for each flight. We assume that each seat is an entity instance in its own right, an entity Seats, identified by a seat number, seatno, valid only for a specific flight (different flights might have different airplane seat layouts, and therefore different sets of seat numbers). We see therefore that seat assignment is a relationship between Passengers and Seats, which we name seat_assign.

Now think about this specification for a moment. The Passengers entity is easy to picture, and so is the Flights entity. The depart_time attribute for Flights is composite, consisting of simple attributes dtime and ddate. We can add another entity Gates, with primary identifier gateno. We have already defined a Seats entity, but the entity seems to be a little strange: the seatno primary identifier for Seats is only meaningful when related to a Flights instance. This is what is referred to in the previous section as a weak entity, and thus there must be a relationship between Flights and Seats, which we name has_seat. The identifier for Seats is partially external, encompassing the identifier of the containing flight.

What other relationships do we have? If we draw the E-R diagram for what we have named up to now, we notice that the Gates entity is off by itself. But clearly passengers go to a gate to meet a flight. We model this as two binary relationships rather than as a ternary relationship: each passenger is related to a specific flight through the relationship Passengers travels_on Flights, and gates normally act as marshaling points for multiple flights (at different times) through the relationship Gates marshals Flights. Figure 6.13 shows the E-R diagram so far. The arrow from seatno to flightno symbolizes the fact that the primary identifier for Seats includes the identifier for the master entity Flights.

Now we need to work out the cardinalities with which the various entities participate in their relationships. Considering the marshals relationship first, clearly there is exactly one gate for each flight, so card(Flights, marshals) = (1, 1). A single gate might be used for multiple flights at different times, but there is no rule that a gate must be used at all, so card(Gates, marshals) = (0, N). Now each passenger must travel on exactly one flight, so card(Passengers, travels_on) = (1, 1). A flight must have multiple passengers to fly (the flight will be canceled and the gate reassigned if there are too few), but the database needs to hold information starting from no passengers, so we set a minimum of 0, and card(Flights, travels_on) = (0, N). A flight must have numerous seats for passengers, so card(Flights, has_seat) = (1, N), and each seat is on a unique flight, so card(Seats, has_seat) = (1, 1). Each passenger must have a seat, and only one, so card(Passengers, seat_assign) = (1, 1), and seats can be used by at most one passenger

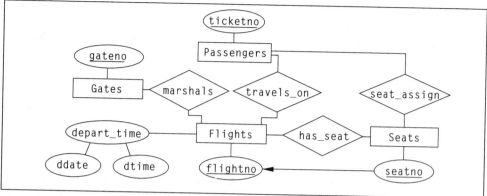

Figure 6.13 Early E-R Design for a Simple Airline Reservation Database

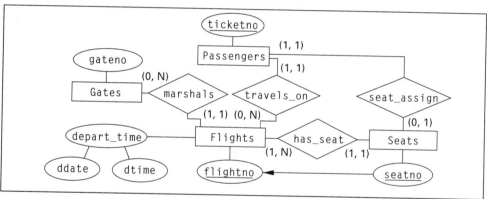

Figure 6.14 E-R Design with Cardinalities for a Simple Airline Reservation Database

and may go empty, so card(Seats, seat_assign) = (0, 1). The E-R diagram with these cardinality pairs added is pictured in Figure 6.14.

Now the E-R design is complete, and we need to transform the design into relational tables. We can begin by creating tables to map entities, even though this means that we might overlook some attributes that will be needed to represent foreign keys for relationships. We will simply have to return later when we consider the relationships and add attributes to these tables. To begin with, we notice with the Flights entity that we don't have multi-valued attributes in relational tables, so following the hint of Transformation RULE 1, we create columns for ddate and dtime in the flights table. All other tables are easily mapped, except for the seats table, where we take the easy way out and use the single column seatno, even though this is not a complete key for the table. Here are the tables so far:

passengers
<u>ticketno</u>
. . .

gates
<u>gateno</u>

flights		
<u>flightno</u>	ddate	dtime

seats
<u>seatno</u>

Now consider the relationship has_seat, which is N-1 in Figure 6.14, with Seats on the "many" side. By Transformation RULE 4, a foreign key in the seats table will connect each seats row to the appropriate flights row. This completes the primary key for the seats table, which represents a weak entity and therefore needs a foreign key to identify each row.

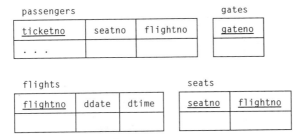

The seat_assign relationship is 1-1, with optional participation by Seats, so by Transformation RULE 5 we can represent this by adjoining to the passengers table a foreign key for seats (this requires two additional columns). We don't expect that we will ever need to look up the passenger for a given seat, so we place no additional foreign key on the seats table. The resulting table definitions are as follows:

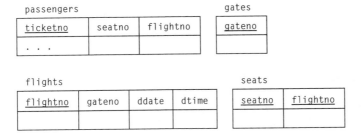

Now consider the marshals relationship. This is N-1, with Flights on the "many" side, so by Transformation RULE 4 a foreign key in the flights table, gateno, will connect each flights row to the appropriate gates row:

passengers

ticketno	seatno	flightno
. . .		

gates

gateno

flights

flightno	gateno	ddate	dtime

seats

seatno	flightno

Similarly the travels_on relationship is N-1, with Passengers on the "many" side, so by Transformation RULE 4 a foreign key, flightno, in the passengers table will connect each passengers row to the appropriate flights row. This column already exists in the passengers table, however, so the relational table design is complete.

6.5 Normalization: Preliminaries

Normalization is another approach to logical design of a relational database, which seems to share little with the E-R model. However, it will turn out that a relational design based on normalization and a careful E-R design transformed into relational form have nearly identical results, and in fact the two approaches reinforce each other. In the normalization approach, the designer starts with a real-world situation to be modeled and lists the data items that are candidates to become column names in relational tables, together with a list of rules about the relatedness of these data items. The aim is to represent all these data items as attributes of tables that obey restrictive conditions associated with what we call *normal forms*. These normal form definitions limit the acceptable form of a table so that it has certain desirable properties, thus avoiding various kinds of anomalous behavior. There is a series of normal form definitions, each more restrictive than the one before; the forms covered in the current chapter are first normal form (1NF), second normal form (2NF), third normal form (3NF), and Boyce-Codd normal form (BCNF). Other types of normalization, 4NF and 5NF, are less commonly considered and are not covered in detail in this text.

To begin with, a table in first normal form (1NF) is simply one that has no multi-valued (repeating) fields; that is, a table that obeys Relational RULE 1 from Section 2.3, the first normal form rule. The relational model and SQL language we studied in Chapters 2 and 3 accept this rule as basic, whereas the object-relational systems of Chapter 4 deviated in two ways, allowing composite types and collection types to sit in column values. *In what follows we assume that tables are in 1NF unless otherwise specified.* Second normal form (2NF) turns out to be of mainly historical interest, since no sensible designer would leave a database in 2NF but would always continue normalization until the more restrictive 3NF was reached. From an initial database containing data items that are all in the same table (sometimes referred to as a *universal table*) and relatedness rules on these data items, there is a procedure to create an equivalent database with multiple tables, all of which are in third normal form. (This is what we mean by having a database in 3NF—that all of its tables have 3NF form.) As we proceed through this chapter we will find that any table that does not obey third normal form can be factored into distinct tables in such a way that (1) each of the factored tables is in a valid third normal form, and (2) the join of all these factored tables contains exactly the information in the table from which they were factored. The set of 3NF tables resulting from the initial universal table is known as a 3NF *lossless decomposition* of the database.

There is a third desirable property that we can always provide with a 3NF decomposition. Note that when a new row is added to one of the tables in the 3NF decomposition (or an old row is updated), it is possible that an erroneous change might break one of the rules of data item relatedness, mentioned earlier as part of the design input. We wish to impose a constraint on Insert and Update operations so that such errors will not corrupt the data. The third property that we consider important in a decomposition, then, is (3) when a table Insert or Update occurs, the possible relatedness rules that might be broken can be tested by validating data items in the single table affected; there is no need to perform table joins in order to validate these rules. A 3NF decomposition constructed to have the three desirable properties just mentioned is generally considered an acceptable database design. It turns out that a further decomposition of tables in 3NF to the more restrictive BCNF is often unnecessary (many real-world databases in 3NF are also in BCNF), but in cases where further decomposition results, property (3) no longer holds in the result. Many database designers therefore settle on 3NF design.

We will need a good deal of insight into the details of the normalization approach before we are able to properly deal with some of these ideas. Let us begin to illustrate them with an example.

A Running Example: Employee Information

We need an example to clarify some of the definitions of database design that follow. Consider the data items listed in Figure 6.15, representing the employee information that must be modeled by the personnel department of a very large company.

The data items beginning with emp_ all represent attributes of what we would refer to in the E-R approach as the entity Employees. Other entities underlying the data items of Figure 6.15 include Departments where employees in the company work and Skills that the various employees need to perform their jobs. In the normalization approach, we leave the entity concept unnamed but reflect it in the data item interrelatedness rules that will be explained shortly, rules known as *functional dependencies*. The data item emp_id has been created to uniquely identify employees. Each employee works for some single department in the company, and the data items beginning with dept_ describe the different departments; the data item dept_name uniquely identifies departments, and each department normally has a unique manager (also an employee) with a name given in dept_mgrname. Finally, we assume that the various employees each possess some number of skills, such as typing or filing, and that data items beginning with skill_ describe the skills that are tested and used for job assignment and salary determination by the company. The data item skill_id uniquely identifies the skill, which also has a name,

```
emp_id
emp_name
emp_phone
dept_name
dept_phone
dept_mgrname
skill_id     ⎫
skill_name   ⎬  From one up to a large number
skill_date   ⎭  of skills useful to the company
skill_lvl
```

Figure 6.15 Unnormalized Data Items for Employee Information

skill_name. For each employee who possesses a particular skill, the skill_date describes the date when the skill was last tested, and skill_lvl describes the level of skill the employee displayed at that test.

Figure 6.16 provides a universal table, emp_info, containing all the data items of employee information from Figure 6.15. Because of first normal form, there can only be atomic values in each row and column position of a table. This poses a difficulty, because each individual employee might have any number of skills. As we argued in Section 2.3, it is inappropriate to design a table with unique rows for each emp_id and a distinct column for each piece of skill information—we don't even know the maximum number of skills for an employee, so we don't know how many columns we should use for skill_id-1,..., skill_id-n. The only solution that will work in a single (universal) table is to give up on having a unique row for each employee and replicate information about the employee, pairing the employee with different skills on different rows.

The intention of the database designer in the emp_info table of Figure 6.16 is that there is a row for every employee-skill pair existing in the company. From this, it should be clear that there cannot be two rows with the same values for the pair of attributes emp_id and skill_id. We have already introduced terminology to describe this state of affairs when we defined a table key in Definition 2.4.1. We claim that the table emp_info has a (candidate) key consisting of the set (pair) of attributes emp_id skill_id. Recall the shorthand notation of presenting a set of attributes by writing a list of attributes separated by spaces. We confirm that these attributes form a key by noting that the values they take on distinguish any pair of rows in any permissible content of the table (i.e., for any rows u and v, either $u(\text{emp\_id}) \neq v(\text{emp\_id})$ or $u(\text{skill\_id}) \neq v(\text{skill\_id})$), and that no subset of this set of attributes does the same (there can be two rows u and v such that $u(\text{emp\_id}) = v(\text{emp\_id})$, and there can be two rows r and s such that $r(\text{skill\_id}) = s(\text{skill\_id})$). We assume in what follows that emp_id skill_id is the primary key for the emp_info table.

emp_info

emp_id	emp_name	. . .	skill_id	skill_name	skill_date	skill_lvl
09112	Jones	. . .	44	librarian	03-15-99	12
09112	Jones	. . .	26	PC-admin	06-30-98	10
09112	Jones	. . .	89	word-proc	01-15-00	12
12231	Smith	. . .	26	PC-admin	04-15-99	5
12231	Smith	. . .	39	bookkeeping	07-30-97	7
13597	Brown	. . .	27	statistics	09-15-99	6
14131	Blake	. . .	26	PC-admin	05-30-98	9
14131	Blake	. . .	89	word-proc	09-30-99	10
. . .	. . .	. . .	. . .	. . .	. . .	. . .

Figure 6.16 Single Employee Information Table, emp_info, in First Normal Form

356   It turns out that the database design of Figure 6.16 is a bad one, because it is subject to certain anomalies that can corrupt the data when data manipulation statements are used to update the table.

Anomalies of a Bad Database Design

It appears that there might be a problem with the emp_info table of Figure 6.16 because there is replication of employee data on different rows. It seems more natural, with the experience we have had up to now, to have a unique row for each distinct employee. Do we have a good reason for our feeling? Let us look at the behavior of this table as SQL updates are applied.

If some employee were to get a new phone number, we would have to update multiple rows (all rows with different skills for that employee) in order to change the emp_phone value in a uniform way. If we were to update the phone number of only one row, we might *corrupt* the data, leaving some rows for that employee with different phone numbers than others. This is commonly known as an *update anomaly,* and it arises because of *data redundancy,* duplication of employee phone numbers and other employee attributes on multiple rows of emp_info. Calling this an "anomaly," with the implication of irregular behavior under update, may seem a bit extreme, since the SQL language is perfectly capable of updating several rows at once with a Searched Update statement such as

```
update emp_info set emp_phone = :newphone where emp_id = :eidval;
```

In fact, the consideration that several rows will be updated is not even apparent from this syntax—the same Searched Update statement would be used if the table had a unique row for each emp_id value. However, with this replication of phone numbers on different rows, a problem can still arise in performing an update with a Positioned Update statement. If we encountered a row of the emp_info table in fetching rows from a cursor created for an entirely different purpose, the program might execute the following statement to allow the user to correct an invalid phone number:

```
update emp_info set emp_phone = :newphone
    where current of cursor_name;
```

This would be a *programming error,* since an experienced programmer would realize that multiple rows need to be updated in order to change an employee phone number. Still, it is the kind of error that could easily occur in practice, and we would like to be able to create a *constraint* on the table that makes such an erroneous update impossible. It turns out that the best way to provide such a constraint is to reconfigure the data items into different tables so as to eliminate the redundant copies of information. This is exactly what is achieved during the process of normalization. We sum up the idea of an update anomaly in a definition that makes reference to our intuitive understanding of the E-R model.

DEFINITION 6.5.1 Update Anomaly. A table T is subject to an *update anomaly* when changing a single attribute value for an entity instance or relationship instance represented in the table may require that several rows of T be updated. ∎

A different sort of problem, known as the *delete anomaly,* is reflected by the following definition.

DEFINITION 6.5.2 Delete Anomaly, Insert Anomaly. A table T is subject to a *delete anomaly* when deleting some row of the table to reflect the disappearance of some instance of an entity or relationship can cause us to lose information about some instance of a different entity or relationship that we do not wish to forget. The *insert anomaly* is the other face of this problem for inserts, where we cannot represent information about some entity or instance without including information about some other instance of an entity or relationship that does not exist. ∎

For example, assume that a skill possessed by an employee must be retested after five years to remain current for that employee. If the employee fails to have the skill retested (and the skill_date column updated), the skill will drop off the emp_info list (an automatic process deletes the row with this emp_id and skill_id). Now consider what happens if the number of skills for some employee goes to zero in the emp_info table with columns of Figure 6.16: *no row of any kind will remain for the employee!* We have lost the phone number and the department the employee works in because of this delete! This is clearly inappropriate design. The other anomaly of Definition 6.5.2, known as the *insert anomaly,* exists in the emp_info table because we cannot enter a new employee into the table until the employee has acquired some skill; thus it becomes impossible to hire an employee trainee. Clearly this is just the other face of the delete anomaly, where information about an employee is lost when the employee loses his or her last skill.

Let us jump ahead to a solution for some of the problems mentioned so far. We simply factor the emp_info table and form two tables, the emps table and the skills table, whose column names are listed in Figure 6.17. Notice that the emps table has a unique row for each emp_id (and emp_id is the key for this table), while the skills table has a unique row for each emp_id skill_id pair, and this pair forms a key for the table. Since there are multiple skills associated with each employee, the emp_id column that we have included in the skills table acts as a foreign key, relating skills back to employees. When we form the natural join of these two tables, the result is exactly the emp_info table we started with. (We will need to demonstrate this fact in what follows, but for now you should take it on faith.) However, the delete anomaly is no longer a problem, since if we delete all rows corresponding to skills for any individual employee, this merely deletes rows in the skills table; the emps table still contains the information we want to retain about the employee, such as emp_phone, dept_name, and the like.

In the sections that follow we will learn how to perform normalization, to factor tables so that all anomalies are removed from our representation. Note that we haven't yet achieved this with the tables of Figure 6.17; as we will see shortly, a number of anomalies still exist. We will need a good deal of insight into the details of the normalization

```
┌─────────────────┐       ┌─────────────────┐
│ emps            │       │ skills          │
├─────────────────┤       ├─────────────────┤
│ emp_id          │       │ emp_id          │
│                 │       │                 │
│ emp_name        │       │ skill_id        │
│                 │       │                 │
│ emp_phone       │       │ skill_name      │
│                 │       │                 │
│ dept_name       │       │ skill_date      │
│                 │       │                 │
│ dept_phone      │       │ skill_lvl       │
│                 │       └─────────────────┘
│ dept_mgrname    │
└─────────────────┘
```

Figure 6.17   The `emp_info` Database with Two Tables

approach before we are able to properly deal with fundamental normalization concepts. In the following sections we present some needed mathematical preliminaries to database normalization. Because it is not always possible to show a real-life application for all these concepts as they are introduced, we ask the reader to be patient. The value of the concepts will become clear in the end.

6.6   Functional Dependencies

A *functional dependency* (FD) defines the most commonly encountered type of related-ness property between data items of a database. We usually only need to consider relat-edness between column attributes of a single relational table, and our definition reflects this. We represent rows of a table T by the notation $r_1, r_2, \ldots$, and follow standard convention by referring to attributes, rather than columns, of the table T. Individual attributes of a table will be represented by letters such as A, B, $\ldots$, and the letters X, Y, $\ldots$ will refer to subsets of attributes. We follow the notation of Chapter 2, that $r_i(A)$ represents the value of row r_i at attribute A.

DEFINITION 6.6.1 Given a table T containing at least two attributes designated by A and B, we say that A → B (read "A functionally determines B" or "B is functionally dependent on A"), if and only if it is the intent of the designer, for any set of rows that might exist in the table, that two rows in T cannot agree in value for A and disagree in value for B. A more formal way of saying this is: given two rows r_1 and r_2 in T, if $r_1(A) = r_2(A)$ then $r_1(B) = r_2(B)$. We will usually try to use the less formal statement in what follows. ∎

Definition 6.6.1 is comparable to the definition of a *function* in mathematics: for every element in the attribute A (which appears on some row), there is a unique corresponding element (on the same row) in the attribute B. See Figure 6.18 for a graphical representation of the functional dependency concept.

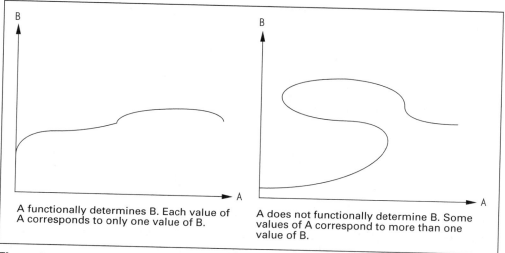

B

A

A functionally determines B. Each value of A corresponds to only one value of B.

B

A

A does not functionally determine B. Some values of A correspond to more than one value of B.

Figure 6.18   Graphical Depiction of Functional Dependency

EXAMPLE 6.6.1

In the emp_info table of Figure 6.16, the following functional dependencies hold:

    emp_id → emp_name
    emp_id → emp_phone
    emp_id → dept_name

In E-R terms, we know this is true because emp_id is an identifier for the Employee entity, and the other data items simply represent other attributes of the entity; once the entity is identified, all the other attributes follow. But we also recognize these facts intuitively. If we saw two rows in the single table emp_info design of Figure 6.16 with the same emp_id value and different emp_phone values, we would believe that the data is corrupted (assuming that every employee has a unique phone), but if we saw two rows with the same emp_phone value and different emp_id values, our first thought would be that they represented different employees who shared a phone. But the two situations are symmetric; it is simply our understanding of the data that makes the first one seem to imply corrupted data. We look to emp_id to break ties and uniquely identify employees. Note that what we are saying implies that, while emp_id functionally determines emp_phone, emp_phone does *not* functionally determine emp_id. We sometimes express this second fact with this notation:

    emp_phone ↛ emp_id

■

EXAMPLE 6.6.2

Here are three tables to investigate for functional dependencies between attributes (note that some of the tables break Relational RULE 3, the unique row rule, but we accept them as valid tables for purposes of illustration). In these tables we assume that it is the intent of the designer that *exactly* this set of rows should lie in each table—no changes will ever occur in the tables. Thus we can determine what functional dependencies exist by examining the data. This is *a very unusual situation*. Normally we determine functional dependencies from understanding the data items and rules of the enterprise (for example, each employee has a single phone number, employees can share a phone, etc.), as in Example 6.6.1. These rules exist before any data has been placed in the table.

T1 row #	A	B
1	x1	y1
2	x2	y2
3	x3	y1
4	x4	y1
5	x5	y2
6	x6	y2

T2 A	B
x1	y1
x2	y4
x1	y1
x3	y2
x2	y4
x4	y3

T3 A	B
x1	y1
x2	y4
x1	y1
x3	y2
x2	y4
x4	y4

In table T1 we can easily see that $A \rightarrow B$; we merely need to check that for every pair of rows r_1 and r_2, if $r_1(A) = r_2(A)$ then $r_1(B) = r_2(B)$. However, there is no pair of rows in T1 with equal values for column A, so the condition is trivially satisfied. At the same time, in T1, $B \nrightarrow A$ (read: "column B does *not* functionally determine column A"), since, for example, if r_1 is row 1 and r_2 is row 3, then $r_1(B) = r_2(B) = y1$, but $r_1(A) = x1 \neq r_2(A) = x3$. In table T2, we have $A \rightarrow B$ (we just need to check that rows 1 and 3, which have matching pairs of A values, also have matching B values, and similarly check rows 2 and 5), and $B \rightarrow A$. Finally, in table T3, $A \rightarrow B$ but $B \nrightarrow A$ (note that if r_1 is row 2 and r_2 is row 6, then $r_1(B) = r_2(B) = y4$, but $r_1(A) = x2 \neq r_2(A) = x4$). ∎

It is obvious how to extend the definition for functional dependency to its full generality, dealing with *sets* of attributes.

DEFINITION 6.6.2 We are given a table T with two sets of attributes, designated by X = $A_1 A_2 \ldots A_k$ and Y = $B_1 B_2 \ldots B_m$, where some of the attributes from X may overlap with some of the attributes from Y. We say that $X \rightarrow Y$ (read "X functionally determines Y" or "Y is functionally dependent on X"), if and only if it is the intent of the designer, for any set of rows that might exist in the table, that two rows in T cannot agree in value on the attributes of X and simultaneously disagree in value on the attributes of Y. Note that two rows agree in value on the attributes of X if they agree on *all of* the attributes of X, and they disagree in value on the attributes of Y if they disagree on *any of* the attributes of Y. More formally, given any two rows r_1 and r_2 in T, if $r_1(A_i) = r_2(A_i)$ for every A_i in X, then $r_1(B_j) = r_2(B_j)$ for every B_j in Y. ∎

EXAMPLE 6.6.3
We list here what we claim are all the functional dependencies (FDs) for the emp_info table of Figure 6.16 (with missing attributes in Figure 6.15). With this FD list, all the information needed for the normalization procedure has been provided.

(1) emp_id $\rightarrow$ emp_name emp_phone dept_name
(2) dept_name $\rightarrow$ dept_phone dept_mgrname
(3) skill_id $\rightarrow$ skill_name
(4) emp_id skill_id $\rightarrow$ skill_date skill_lvl

You should be able to interpret each of these functional dependencies and see if you agree with them. For example, FD (1) states that if we know the emp_id, then the emp_name, emp_phone, and dept_name are determined. Note that FD (1) is just another way of stating the FDs of Example 6.6.1. That is, if we know the FDs given there,

emp_id → emp_name, emp_id → emp_phone, and emp_id → dept_name,

we can conclude that FD (1) holds.

To say this in yet another way, the three FDs of Example 6.6.1 together imply FD (1). Similarly, from FD (1) we can conclude that the three FDs of Example 6.6.1 hold. A simple rule of FD implication is used to arrive at these conclusions, based on the FD definition. We will learn more about such rules shortly.

Because the FDs given in (1) through (4) are *all* the FDs for the emp_info table, we can conclude, for example, that the designer does *not* intend that skill_name be unique for a specific skill. Since skill_id is a unique identifier for the skill, to have a unique skill_name would presumably mean that skill_name → skill_id, the reverse of FD (3). However, this FD does not exist in the set, nor is it implied. (A quick test to see that it isn't implied is to note that skill_name does not occur on the left side of any FD in the set.) We also note that we do not have the FD dept_mgrname → dept_name, which presumably means that although each department has a unique manager, one manager might simultaneously manage more than one department. Finally, note that skill_lvl and skill_date are only meaningful as attributes of the *relationship* between an Employee entity and a Skill entity. If we said that a given employee had a skill level of 9, it would be necessary to ask, "For what skill?"; and if we said that we know there is a skill level of 9 for 'typing', we would wonder, "What employee?" Thus we need to name both the emp_id and the skill_id to determine these attributes. ∎

Logical Implications among Functional Dependencies

In Example 6.6.3 a number of conclusions were drawn that depended on understanding implications among functional dependencies. In what follows, we will derive certain rules of implication among FDs that follow directly from Definition 6.6.2. The reader needs to understand many such rules at both a rigorous and an intuitive level to properly appreciate some of the techniques of normalization that are presented in later sections. We begin with a very basic rule.

THEOREM 6.6.3 Inclusion Rule. We are given a table T with a specified heading (set of attributes, as defined in Section 2.2), Head(T). If X and Y are sets of attributes contained in Head(T), and $Y \subseteq X$, then $X \to Y$.

PROOF. We appeal to Definition 6.6.2. In order to show that $X \to Y$, we need only demonstrate that there is no pair of rows u and v that agree in value on the attributes of X and simultaneously disagree in value on the attributes of Y. But this is obvious, since two rows can never agree in value on the attributes of X and simultaneously disagree on a subset of those attributes. ∎

The inclusion rule provides us with a large number of FDs that are true for any table of attributes, irrespective of the intended content.

DEFINITION 6.6.4 Trivial Dependency. A *trivial dependency* is an FD of the form $X \rightarrow Y$, in a table T where $X \cup Y \subseteq \text{Head}(T)$, that will hold for any possible content of the table T. ∎

We can prove that trivial dependencies always arise as a result of the inclusion rule.

THEOREM 6.6.5 Given a trivial dependency $X \rightarrow Y$ in T, it must be the case that $Y \subseteq X$.

PROOF. Given the table T with a heading containing the attributes in $X \cup Y$, consider the set of attributes $Y - X$ (attributes in Y that are not in X). Since $X \rightarrow Y$ is a trivial dependency, it must hold for any possible content of the table T. We will assume $Y - X$ is non-empty and reach a contradiction. If the set $Y - X$ is non-empty, let A be an attribute contained in $Y - X$. Since $A \notin X$, it is possible to construct two rows, u and v in the table T, alike in values for all attributes in X, but having different values for the attribute A. But with these two rows in T, the dependency $X \rightarrow Y$ does not hold, since rows u and v agree in value on attributes of X and disagree on attributes of Y (because $A \in Y$). Since a trivial dependency is supposed to hold for any possible content of the table T, we have created a contradiction, and from this we conclude that the set $Y - X$ cannot contain an attribute A, and therefore $Y \subseteq X$. ∎

Armstrong's Axioms

The inclusion rule is one rule of implication by which FDs can be generated that are guaranteed to hold for all possible tables. It turns out that from a small set of basic rules of implication, we can derive all others. We list here three basic rules that we call Armstrong's Axioms (Figure 6.19). (Other sets of rules could be given just as easily—see the exercises at the end of the chapter.)

DEFINITION 6.6.6 Armstrong's Axioms. Assume in what follows that we are given a table T, and that all sets of attributes X, Y, Z are contained in Head(T). Then we have the following rules of implication.

[1] **Inclusion rule:**   If $Y \subseteq X$, then $X \rightarrow Y$.

[2] **Transitivity rule:**   If $X \rightarrow Y$ and $Y \rightarrow Z$, then $X \rightarrow Z$.

[3] **Augmentation rule:**   If $X \rightarrow Y$, then $X Z \rightarrow Y Z$.

Just as we list attributes with spaces between them in a functional dependency to represent a set containing those attributes, two sets of attributes in sequence imply a union operation. Thus the augmentation rule could be rewritten: if $X \rightarrow Y$, then $X \cup Z \rightarrow Y \cup Z$. ∎

We have already proved the inclusion rule in Theorem 6.6.3. Let us prove the augmentation rule and leave transitivity for the exercises at the end of the chapter.

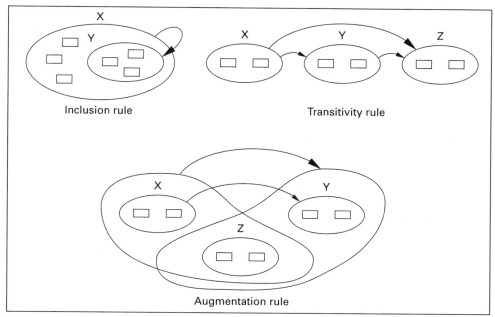

Figure 6.19 Armstrong's Axioms

THEOREM 6.6.7 Augmentation. We wish to show that if X → Y, then X Z → Y Z. Assume that X → Y, and consider any two rows u and v in T that agree on the attributes of X Z (i.e., X ∪ Z). We need merely show that u and v cannot disagree on the attributes of Y Z. But since u and v agree on all attributes of X Z, they certainly agree on all attributes of X; and since we are assuming that X → Y, then u and v must agree on all attributes of Y. Similarly, since u and v agree on all attributes of X Z, they certainly agree on all attributes of Z. Therefore u and v agree on all attributes of Y and all attributes of Z, and the proof is complete. ∎

From Armstrong's Axioms we can prove a number of other rules of implication among FDs. Furthermore, we can do this without any further recourse to the FD definition, using only the axioms themselves.

THEOREM 6.6.8 Some Implications of Armstrong's Axioms. Again we assume that all sets of attributes below, W, X, Y, and Z, are contained in the heading of a table T.

[1]	Union rule:	If X → Y and X → Z, then X → Y Z.
[2]	Decomposition rule:	If X → Y Z, then X → Y and X → Z.
[3]	Pseudotransitivity rule:	If X → Y and W Y → Z, then X W → Z.
[4]	Set accumulation rule:	If X → Y Z and Z → W, then X → Y Z W.

PROOF. We prove only [2] and [4], leaving the rest for the exercises. For [2], note that Y Z = Y ∪ Z. Thus Y Z → Y by the inclusion rule (axiom 1). By transitivity (axiom 2), X → Y Z and Y Z → Y implies X → Y. Similarly we can show X → Z, and the decomposition rule [2] has been demonstrated. For [4], we are given that (a) X → Y Z and (b) Z → W. Using axiom 3, we augment (b) with Y Z to obtain Y Z Z → Y Z W. Since Z Z = Z, we have (c) Y Z → Y Z W. Finally, by transitivity, using (a) and (c), we have X → Y Z W, and the set accumulation rule [4] has been demonstrated.   ∎

We state without proof the rather startling result that *all* valid rules of implication among FDs can be derived from Armstrong's Axioms. In fact, if F is any set of FDs, and X → Y is an FD that cannot be shown by Armstrong's Axioms to be implied by F, then there must be a table T in which all of the FDs in F hold but X → Y is false. Because of this result, Armstrong's Axioms are often referred to as being *complete*, meaning that no other rule of implication can be added to increase their effectiveness.

Recall that in Example 6.6.3 we pointed out that the three FDs from Example 6.6.1,

```
emp_id → emp_name, emp_id → emp_phone, and emp_id → dept_name
```

allowed us to conclude that FD (1) holds:

```
(1) emp_id → emp_name emp_phone dept_name
```

This fact follows from two applications of the union rule of Theorem 6.6.8. The inverse implication, that FD (1) implies the first three, follows from two applications of the decomposition rule in the same theorem. Whenever we have some set of attributes X on the left of a set of FDs, we can take a union of all sets of attributes on the right of these FDs and combine the FDs into one. For example, assume we have the attributes A B C D E F G in the heading of a table T, and we know that the following FDs hold:

B D → A, B D → C, B D → E, B D → F, and B D → G

Then we can combine these FDs into one by successive applications of the union rule:

[6.6.1]   B D → A C E F G

As a matter of fact, we can add the trivial dependency B D → B D and conclude

B D → A B C D E F G

However, we normally try to avoid including information in a set of dependencies that can be derived using Armstrong's Axioms from a more fundamental set. Thus we might want to return to the FD form of [6.6.1]. Note that if we had another attribute H in the heading of the table T not mentioned in any FD, we could conclude that in addition to the FD given in [6.6.1], the following FD holds:

$$B D H \rightarrow A C E F G H$$

But since this FD can be derived from FD [6.6.1] by using the augmentation rule, we would once again prefer the shorter FD [6.6.1].

EXAMPLE 6.6.4

List a minimal set of functional dependencies satisfied by the table T, below, where we assume that it is the intent of the designer that *exactly* this set of rows lies in the table. Once again, we point out that it is unusual to derive FDs from the content of a table. Normally we determine functional dependencies from understanding the data items and rules of the enterprise. Note that we do not yet have a rigorous definition of a minimal set of FDs, so we simply try to arrive at a minimal set in an intuitive way.

T

row #	A	B	C	D
1	a1	b1	c1	d1
2	a1	b1	c2	d2
3	a2	b1	c1	d3
4	a2	b1	c3	d4

Analysis. Let us start by considering FDs with a single attribute on the left. Clearly we always have the trivial FDs, $A \rightarrow A$, $B \rightarrow B$, $C \rightarrow C$, and $D \rightarrow D$, but we are asking for a minimal set of dependencies, so we won't list them. From the specific content of the table we are able to derive the following. (a) All values of the B attribute are the same, so it can never happen for any other attribute P (i.e., where P represents A, C, or D) that $r_1(P) = r_2(P)$ while $r_1(B) \neq r_2(B)$; thus we see that $A \rightarrow B$, $C \rightarrow B$, and $D \rightarrow B$. At the same time no other attributes P are functionally dependent on B since they all have at least two distinct values, and so there are always two rows r_1 and r_2 such that $r_1(P) \neq r_2(P)$ while $r_1(B) = r_2(B)$; thus $B \nrightarrow A$, $B \nrightarrow C$, and $B \nrightarrow D$. (b) Because the D values are all different, in addition to $D \rightarrow B$ of part (a), we also have $D \rightarrow A$ and $D \rightarrow C$; at the same time D is not functionally dependent on anything else since all other attributes have at least two duplicate values. So in addition to $B \nrightarrow D$ of part (a), we have $A \nrightarrow D$ and $C \nrightarrow D$. (c) We have $A \nrightarrow C$ (because of rows 1 and 2) and $C \nrightarrow A$ (because of rows 1 and 3). Therefore we can list all FDs (and failed FDs) with a single attribute on the left. (Letters in parentheses are keyed to the parts above that give us each fact.)

(a) $A \rightarrow B$	(a) $B \nrightarrow A$	(c) $C \nrightarrow A$	(b) $D \rightarrow A$
(c) $A \nrightarrow C$	(a) $B \nrightarrow C$	(a) $C \rightarrow B$	(a) $D \rightarrow B$
(b) $A \nrightarrow D$	(a) $B \nrightarrow D$	(b) $C \nrightarrow D$	(b) $D \rightarrow C$

By the union rule, whenever a single attribute on the left functionally determines several other attributes, as with D above, we can combine the attributes on the right: $D \rightarrow A B C$. From the analysis so far, we have the following set of FDs (which we believe to be minimal):

(1) $A \rightarrow B$, (2) $C \rightarrow B$, (3) $D \rightarrow A B C$

Now consider FDs with *pairs* of attributes on the left. (d) Any pair containing D determines all other attributes, by FD (3) above and the augmentation rule, so there is no new FD with D on the left that is not already implied. (e) The attribute B, combined with any other attribute P on the left, still functionally determines only those attributes already determined by P, as we see by the following argument. If $P \nrightarrow Q$, this means there are rows r_1 and r_2 such that $r_1(Q) \neq r_2(Q)$ while $r_1(P) = r_2(P)$. But because B has equal values on all rows, we know that $r_1(B\ P) = r_2(B\ P)$ as well, so $B\ P \nrightarrow Q$. Thus we get no new FDs with B on the left.

(f) Now the only pair of attributes that does not contain B or D is A C, and since A C has distinct values on each row (examine table T again!), we know that A C → A B C D. This is new. We can show most of this by inference rules: it is trivial that A C → A and AC → C, by inclusion, and we already knew that A → B, so it is easy to show that A C → B. Thus the only new fact we get from A C → A B C D is that A C → D, and we are searching for a minimal set of FDs, so that is all we include as FD (4) in the list below. If we now consider looking for FDs with triples of attributes on the left, we see that we can derive from the FDs we already have that any triple functionally determines all other attributes. Any triple that contains D clearly does, and the only triple not containing D is A B C, where A C alone functionally determines all other attributes. Clearly the same holds for any set of four attributes on the left.

The complete set of FDs implicit in the table T is therefore the following:

(1) A → B, (2) C → B, (3) D → A B C, (4) A C → D

The first three FDs come from the earlier list of FDs with single attributes on the left, while the last FD, A C → D, is the new one generated with two attributes listed on the left. It will turn out that this set of FDs is not quite minimal, despite all our efforts to derive a minimal set. We will see this after we have had a chance to define what we mean by a minimal set of FDs. ∎

Closure, Cover, and Minimal Cover

The implication rules for FDs derived from Armstrong's Axioms mean that whenever a set F of functional dependencies is given, a much larger set may be implied.

DEFINITION 6.6.9 Closure of a Set of FDs. Given a set F of FDs on attributes of a table T, we define the *closure* of F, symbolized by F^+, to be the set of all FDs implied by F. ∎

EXAMPLE 6.6.5
Consider the set F of FDs given by

F = {A → B, B → C, C → D, D → E, E → F, F → G, G → H}

By the transitivity rule, A → B and B → C together imply A → C, which must be included in F^+. Also, B → C and C → D imply B → D. Indeed, every single attribute appearing prior to the terminal one in the sequence A B C D E F G H can be shown by transitivity to functionally determine every single attribute on its right in the sequence. We also have trivial FDs such as A → A. Next, using the union rule, we can generate other FDs, such as A → A B C D E F G H. In fact, by using the union rule in different combinations, we can show A → (any non-empty subset of A B C D E F G H). There are $2^8 - 1 = 255$ such non-empty subsets. All FDs we have just derived are contained in F^+. ∎

Functional dependencies usually arise in creating a database out of commonsense rules. In terms of E-R concepts, it is clear that data items corresponding to identifiers of entities functionally determine all other attributes of that entity. Similarly, attributes of relationships are uniquely determined by the identifiers of entities that take part in the relationship. We would normally expect to start with a manageable set F of FDs in our design, but as Example 6.6.5 shows, the set of FDs that is implied by F could conceivably grow exponentially. In what follows, we try to find a way to speak of what is implied by a set F of FDs without this kind of exponential explosion. What we are leading up to is a way to determine a *minimal set* of FDs that is equivalent to a given set F. We will also provide an algorithm to derive such a minimal set in a reasonable length of time.

DEFINITION 6.6.10 FD Set Cover. A set F of FDs on a table T is said to *cover* another set G of FDs on T, if the set G of FDs can be derived by implication rules from the set F, or in other words, if $G \subseteq F^+$. If F covers G and G covers F, then the two sets of FDs are said to be equivalent, and we write $F \equiv G$. ∎

EXAMPLE 6.6.6

Consider the two sets of FDs on the set of attributes A B C D E:

$$F = \{B \rightarrow C\,D, A\,D \rightarrow E, B \rightarrow A\}$$

and

$$G = \{B \rightarrow C\,D\,E, B \rightarrow A\,B\,C, A\,D \rightarrow E\}$$

We will demonstrate that F covers G, by showing how all FDs in G are implied by FDs in F. In what follows we derive implications of FDs in F using the various inference rules from Definition 6.6.6 and Theorem 6.6.8. Since in F we have (a) $B \rightarrow C\,D$ and (b) $B \rightarrow A$, by the union rule we see that (c) $B \rightarrow A\,C\,D$. The trivial FD $B \rightarrow B$ clearly holds, and in union with (c), we get (d) $B \rightarrow A\,B\,C\,D$. By the decomposition rule, $B \rightarrow A\,B\,C\,D$ implies (e) $B \rightarrow A\,D$, and since (f) $A\,D \rightarrow E$ is in F, by transitivity we conclude (g) $B \rightarrow E$. This, in union with (d), gives us $B \rightarrow A\,B\,C\,D\,E$. From this, by decomposition we can derive the initial two FDs of the set G, and the third one also exists in F. This demonstrates that F covers G. ∎

In Example 6.6.1 a technique was used to find *all* the attributes functionally determined by the attribute B under the set F of FDs. (This turned out to be all the attributes there were.) In general we can do this for any set X of attributes on the left, finding all attributes functionally determined by the set X.

DEFINITION 6.6.11 Closure of a Set of Attributes. Given a set F of FDs on a table T and a set X of attributes contained in T, we define the *closure* of the set X, denoted by X^+, as the largest set Y of attributes functionally determined by X, the largest set Y such that $X \rightarrow Y$ is in F^+. Note that the set Y contains all the attributes of X, by the inclusion rule, and might not contain any other attributes. ∎

Here is an algorithm for determining the closure of any set of attributes X.

ALGORITHM 6.6.12 Set Closure. This algorithm determines X^+, the closure of a given set of attributes X, under a given set F of FDs.

```
I = 0; X[0] = X;                        /* integer I, attribute set X[0]    */
REPEAT                                  /* loop to find larger X[I]         */
    I = I + 1;                          /* new I                            */
    X[I] = X[I-1];                      /* initialize new X[I]              */
    FOR ALL Z → W in F                  /* loop on all FDs Z → W in F       */
        IF Z ⊆ X[I]                     /* if Z contained in X[I]           */
            THEN X[I] = X[I] ∪ W;       /* add attributes in W to X[I]      */
    END FOR                             /* end loop on FDs                  */
UNTIL X[I] = X[I-1];                    /* loop until no new attributes     */
RETURN X⁺ = X[I];                       /* return closure of X              */
```
■

Note that the step in Algorithm 6.6.12 that adds attributes to X[I] is based on the set accumulation rule, proved in Theorem 6.6.8: if $X \rightarrow Y Z$ and $Z \rightarrow W$, then $X \rightarrow Y Z W$.

In our algorithm we are saying that since $X \rightarrow X[I]$ (our induction hypothesis) and after finding $Z \rightarrow W$ in F with $Z \subseteq X[I]$, X[I] can be represented as Y Z (Y = X[I] − Z), so we can write $X \rightarrow X[I]$ as $X \rightarrow Y Z$. Now since F contains $Z \rightarrow W$, we conclude by the set accumulation rule that $X \rightarrow Y Z W$, or in other words, $X \rightarrow X[I] \cup W$, and our induction hypothesis is maintained.

Set closure is an important milestone in our development. It gives us a general way of deciding whether a given FD is implied by a set F of FDs, without worrying about the exponential explosion that Example 6.6.5 showed could occur in calculating F^+. For example, suppose we need to know if the FD $X \rightarrow A$ is implied by set F of FDs. We simply calculate X^+ under F by the set closure Algorithm 6.6.12, and determine if it contains A: if so, $X \rightarrow A$ is in F^+, that is, it is implied by F.

We will see that a key for a table is just a minimal set of attributes that functionally determine all the attributes of the table. To determine if X is a key, we just compute X^+ under F, the set of FDs for the table's attributes, and see if it includes all of them, then check that no subset of X does the same.

EXAMPLE 6.6.7 Set Closure and a Compact Derivational Notation for It.
In Example 6.6.6 we were given a set F of FDs, which we number below:

F: (1) B → C D, (2) A D → E, (3) B → A

Given X = B, we determined that X^+ = A B C D E. Using Algorithm 6.6.12, we start with X[0] = B. Then X[1] = B, and we begin to loop through the FDs. Because of (1) B → CD, we get X[1] = B C D. As a notational device to show that C and D were added after B because of FD (1), we write this as B C D (1). The next FD, (2) A D → E, does not apply at this time, since A D is not a subset of X[1]. Next, from (3) B → A, we get X[1] = A B C D (or, in our notation to reflect derivation order, B C D (1) A (3)). Now X[0] is strictly contained in X[1] (i.e., X[I − 1] ⊂ X[I]) so X[I − 1] ≠ X[I].

Thus we've made progress in the prior pass of the loop and go on to a new pass, setting X[2] = X[1] = A B C D (i.e., B C D (1) A (3)). Looping through the FDs again, we see all of them can be applied (but we skip the ones that have been applied before since they will have no new effect), with the only new FD, (2) A D → E, giving us X[2] = A B C D E, or in the derivational notation, B C D (2) A (3) E (2). At the end of this loop, the algorithm notes that X[1] ⊂ X[2]. Progress has been made, so we go on to create X[3] and loop through the FDs again, ending up this pass with X[3] = X[2]. Since all of the FDs had been applied already, we could omit this pass by noting that fact. Note that a different *ordering* of the FDs in F can change the details of execution for this algorithm. In exercises where the derivational notation is requested to demonstrate that the proper derivation was determined, the order is crucial: for example, the derivation above yields the compact notation

   B C D (1) A (3) E (2)

and *not*

   B C D (1) E (2) A (3).

■

Given a set F of functional dependencies on a table T, we use the following algorithm to determine a minimal set of dependencies M that covers F. The set M will be minimal in the sense that none of its FDs can be dropped in their entirety or changed by dropping any attributes on the left-hand side, without losing the property that it covers F.

ALGORITHM 6.6.13 Minimal Cover. This algorithm constructs a minimal set M of FDs that covers a given set F of FDs. M is known as the *minimal cover* of F—or, in some texts, as the *canonical cover* of F.

Step 1. From the set F of FDs, we create an equivalent set H of FDs, with only single attributes on the right side.

```
H = ∅;                          /* initialize H to null set      */
FOR ALL X → Y in F              /* loop on FDs in F              */
    FOR ALL A IN Y              /* loop on attributes in Y       */
        H = H ∪ {X → A};        /* add FD to H                   */
    END FOR                     /* end loop on attributes in Y   */
END FOR                         /* end loop on FDs in F          */
```

Since step 1 derives H by successive applications of the decomposition rule, and F can be reconstructed from H by successive applications of the union rule, it is obvious that F ≡ H.

Step 2. From the set H of FDs, successively remove individual FDs that are *inessential* in H. An FD X → Y is inessential in a set H of FDs, if X → Y can be removed from H, with result J, so that $H^+ = J^+$, or H ≡ J. That is, removal of the FD from H has no effect on H^+. See Figure 6.20 for an example of an inessential FD.

370

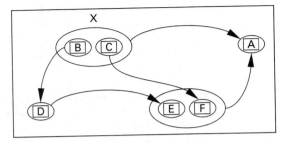

Figure 6.20   Example of an Inessential FD: $X \rightarrow A$

```
FOR ALL X → A in H              /* loop on FDs in H                        */
    J = H - {X → A};            /* try removing this FD                    */
    DETERMINE X⁺ UNDER J;       /* set closure algorithm 6.6.12           */
    IF A ∈ X⁺                   /* X → A is still implied by J             */
        H = H - {X → A};        /* ...so it is inessential in H            */
END FOR                         /* end loop on FDs in H                    */
```

Each time an FD is removed from H in step 2, the resulting set is equivalent to the previous, larger H. It is clear from this that the final resulting H is equivalent to the original. However, a number of FDs might have been removed.

Step 3. From the set H of FDs, successively replace individual FDs with FDs that have a smaller number of attributes on the left-hand side, as long as the result does not change H^+. See Figure 6.21 for an example of an FD that can be simplified in this manner.

```
HO = H                                      /* save original H                         */
FOR ALL X → A in H with #X > 1              /* loop on FDs with multiple attribute lhs*/
    FOR ALL B ∈ X                           /* loop on attributes in X                 */
        Y = X - {B}                         /* try removing one attribute              */
        J = (H - {X → A}) ∪ {Y → A};        /* left-reduced FD                         */
        GENERATE Y⁺ UNDER J, Y⁺ UNDER H;    /* set closure algorithm 6.6.12           */
        IF Y⁺ UNDER H = Y⁺ UNDER J          /* if Y⁺ is unchanged                      */
            UPDATE CURRENT X → A in H        /* this is X → A in outer loop            */
                SET X = Y;                   /* change X, continue outer loop          */
    END FOR                                 /* end loop of attributes in X             */
END FOR                                     /* end loop on FDs in H                    */
IF H <> HO                                  /* if FD set changed in Step 3            */
    REPEAT STEP 2 AND THEN GOTO STEP 4      /* retest: some FDs may be inessential now*/
```

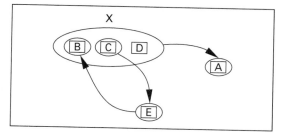

Figure 6.21 Example of an FD X → A Where B Can Be Dropped from the Left-Hand Side

Step 4. From the remaining set of FDs, gather all FDs with equal left-hand sides and use the union rule to create an equivalent set of FDs M where all left-hand sides are unique.

```
M = ∅;                              /* initialize M to null set        */
FOR ALL X → A in H                  /* loop on FDs in H                */
    IF THIS FD IS FLAGGED, CONTINUE;  /* if already dealt with, loop    */
    FLAG CURRENT FD;                /* deal with FDs with X on left    */
    Y = {A};                        /* start with right-hand side A    */
    FOR ALL SUCCESSIVE X → B in H   /* nested loop                     */
        FLAG CURRENT FD;            /* deal with all FDs, X on left    */
        Y = Y ∪ {B};                /* gather attributes on right      */
    END FOR                         /* gathering complete              */
    M = M ∪ {X → Y};                /* combine right sides of X → ?    */
END FOR                             /* end outer loop on FDs in H      */
```

We state without proof that this algorithm grows in execution time only as a polynomial in n, the number of attributes in the listed FDs of F (counting repetitions). Step 3 is the most costly, since we need to perform the set closure algorithm once for each attribute on the left-hand side of some FD in H. Note that if we performed step 3 before step 2, we would not have to go back and repeat step 2, as prescribed at the end of step 3 above; however, in general it would take more work for the costly step 3 without the cleanup action of step 2 occurring first. ∎

EXAMPLE 6.6.8
Construct the minimal cover M for the set F of FDs, which we number and list below.

   F: (1) A B D → A C, (2) C → B E, (3) A D → B F, (4) B → E

Note that it is important to *rewrite* the set of FDs as you begin each new step where the FDs have changed, so you can refer to individual ones easily in the next step.

Step 1. We apply the decomposition rule to FDs in F, to create an equivalent set with singleton attributes on the right-hand sides (rhs) of all FDs:

   H = (1) A B D → A, (2) A B D → C, (3) C → B, (4) C → E, (5) A D → B, (6) A D → F, (7) B → E.

Step 2. We consider cases corresponding to the seven numbered FDs in H.

(1) A B D → A is trivial and thus clearly inessential (since A B D$^+$ contains A), so it can be removed. The FDs remaining in H are (2) A B D → C, (3) C → B, (4) C→ E, (5) A D → B, (6) A D → F, and (7) B → E.

(2) A B D → C cannot be derived from the other FDs in H by the set closure algorithm, Algorithm 6.6.12, because there is no other FD with C on the right-hand side. (A B D$^+$, with FD (2) missing, will not contain C. We could also go through the steps of Algorithm 6.6.12 to demonstrate this fact. See also substep (6), below.)

(3) Is C → B inessential? Is it implied under the set of other FDs that would remain if this were taken out: {(2) A B D → C, (4) C → E, (5) A D→ B, (6) A D → F, (7) B → E}? To see if C → B is inessential, we generate C$^+$ under this smaller set of FDs. (We use the set closure Algorithm, 6.6.12, to generate X$^+$ in what follows, and use the derivational notation introduced in Example 6.6.7.) Starting with C$^+$ = C, FD (4) gives us C$^+$ = C E. To indicate the use of FD (4) notationally, we write C$^+$ = C E(4). Now with FD (3) removed, no other lhs of an FD is contained in the set C E, so we have reached the full closure of the attribute C. Since C$^+$ doesn't contain B, (3) C → B is essential and remains in H.

(4) C → E is inessential as shown by the working out of set closure on C with FD (4) missing: we get C$^+$ = C B (3) E (7). Thus since E is in C$^+$ after FD (4) is removed, we can drop FD (4). The FDs remaining in H are (2) A B D → C, (3) C → B, (5) A D → B, (6) A D → F, and (7) B → E.

(5) Is A D → B inessential under the set of FDs that remain with (5) missing: {(2) A B D → C, (3) C → B, (6) A D → F, and (7) B → E}? In the set closure algorithm, A D$^+$ = A D F(6) and nothing more. So FD (5) is essential and cannot be removed.

(6) Is A D → F inessential given the set of other FDs that would remain: {(2) A B D → C, (3) C → B, (5) A D→ B, (7) B→ E}? Clearly with this set of FDs we can derive A D$^+$ to contain A D B (3) C (2) E (7), all the attributes there are on the right except F, so we cannot derive A D → F without FD (6). Another way to say this is that with FD (6) removed, no FD has F on its rhs, so A D → F cannot be implied.

(7) Is B → E inessential under the set of other FDs that remains: {(2) A B D → C, (3) C → B, (5) A D→ B, (6) A D → F}? The answer is no, since deriving B$^+$ with this set of FDs gives only B.

We end step 2 with the set H = {(2) A B D → C, (3) C → B, (5) A D → B, (6) A D → F, (7) B → E}, which should be renumbered for ease of reference in step 3:

H = (1) A B D → C, (2) C → B, (3) A D → B, (4) A D → F, (5) B → E

Step 3. We start with FD (1) and note that there are multiple attributes on the left-hand side (lhs); we call this set on the lhs of FD (1), X = A B D. Therefore we need to try to reduce this set X by removing any single attributes and creating a new set J of FDs each time.

Drop A? We try to do away with the attribute A in FD (1), so the new set J is given by: (1) B D → C, (2) C → B, (3) A D → B, (4) A D → F, (5) B → E. To show that this reduction gives an equivalent set of FDs, we need to show that B D$^+$ (under H) is the same as B D$^+$ (under J). The risk here is that B D$^+$ under J will functionally determine *more than* B D$^+$ under H, since J has an FD with only B D on the left that H does not. We claim that the two sets H and J are equivalent FD sets if and only if B D$^+$ (under H) is the same as B D$^+$ (under J). So we calculate B D$^+$ under H to be B D E (5), and that's all. Under J, B D$^+$ is B D C (1) E (5). Since these are different, we can't replace (1) A B D → C with (1) B D → C.

Drop B? We repeat the method. Now J contains (1) A D → C, (2) C → B, (3) A D→ B, (4) A D → F, (5) B → E, and A D$^+$ under J is A D C (1) B (2) F (4) E (5). But under H, A D$^+$ = A D B (3) F (4) E (5) C (1). These are the same sets, but note the different order of generation. You need to use derivational notation with the proper order to show that the set closure algorithm is being applied on the proper FD set. Under H, FD (3) is the first one that expands the A D$^+$ closure, and FD (1) comes in the second pass. Under J, we can use each FD as we come to it in order on the first pass. In any event, since A D$^+$ under H is the same as A D$^+$ under J, we can reduce FD (1) to A D on the left-hand side, and the FD set H is now

    H = (1) A D → C, (2) C → B, (3) A D → B, (4) A D → F, (5) B → E

Drop D? We have already considered dropping A from the lhs of FD (1), A B D → C, and we don't need to repeat this now that B is dropped. But we must consider dropping D. Now J will contain: (1) A → C, (2) C → B, (3) A D → B, (4) A D → F, and (5) B → E, and we need to consider taking A$^+$ under H (A$^+$ = A) and under J (A$^+$ = A C (1) B (2) E (5)). Since they are different, we cannot remove D from FD (1).

We note FD (2) C → B cannot be reduced on the lhs, and (3) A D → B also cannot be reduced on the lhs, since A$^+$ and D$^+$ under H will contain only these attributes, whereas under the relevant J the closures will contain B. The argument that (4) A D → F cannot be reduced is similar.

Now since the set of FDs in H has changed in this pass through step 3, we need to return to step 2. When we reach FD (3) and consider dropping it, (3) A D → B, we find now that A D$^+$ under {(1) A D → C, (2) C → B, (4) A D → F, (5) B → E} gives A D C (1) B (2), so since A D$^+$ contains B with FD (3) missing, this FD is inessential and may be dropped. (Surprised? Repeating step 2 is a crucial step!) The final answer out of step 3 is

    H = (1) A D → C, (2) C → B, (3) A D → F, (4) B → E

This set is minimal. If you wish, you can perform step 2 and step 3 a final time to assure yourself there are no other changes.

Finally, step 4 leads to the final set of FDs:

    H = (1) A D → C F, (2) C → B, (3) B → E

      ■

To understand what we have accomplished, you might go through Example 6.6.8 and think about each change that was made in the set of FDs, then try to use Armstrong's Axioms to demonstrate that each change that was actually performed will result in the same FD closure. (Don't duplicate the set closure argument, but instead find a direct proof that the change is legal.)

EXAMPLE 6.6.9

The functional dependencies we derived in Example 6.6.4 turn out *not* to be minimal, despite our attempt to create a minimal set in the example. The demonstration of this is left as an exercise.

      ■

EXAMPLE 6.6.10

The set of functional dependencies stated in Example 6.6.3 for the emp_info database,

   (1) emp_id → emp_name emp_phone dept_name
   (2) dept_name → dept_phone dept_mgrname
   (3) skill_id → skill_name
   (4) emp_id skill_id → skill_date skill_lvl

already forms a minimal set; that is, the minimal cover Algorithm 6.6.13 will not reduce it further. We leave this derivation as an exercise.

      ■

The algorithm for finding a minimal cover of a set F of FDs will be crucial in later sections for algorithms to perform appropriate design by the method of normalization.

6.7   Lossless Decompositions

The process of normalization depends on being able to *factor* or *decompose* a table into two or more smaller tables, in such a way that we can recapture the precise content of the original table by joining the decomposed parts.

DEFINITION 6.7.1 Lossless Decomposition. For any table T with an associated set of functional dependencies F, a *decomposition* of T into k tables is a set of tables $\{T_1, T_2, \ldots, T_k\}$ with two properties: (1) for every table T_i in the set, Head(T_i) is a proper subset of Head(T); (2) Head(T) = Head(T_1) $\cup$ Head(T_2) $\cup \ldots \cup$ Head(T_k). Given any specific content of T, the rows of T are projected onto the columns of each T_i as a result of the decomposition. A decomposition of a table T with an associated set F of FDs is said to be a *lossless decomposition*, or sometimes a *lossless-join decomposition* if, for any possible future content of T, the FDs in F guarantee that the following relationship will hold:

$$T = T_1 \bowtie T_2 \bowtie \ldots \bowtie T_k$$ ∎

When a table T is decomposed, it is sometimes not possible to recover all the information that was originally present in some specific content of table T by joining the tables of the decomposition, not because we don't get back all the rows we had before, but because we get back other rows that were not originally present.

EXAMPLE 6.7.1 A Lossy Decomposition.
Consider the following table ABC:

ABC

A	B	C
a1	100	c1
a2	200	c2
a3	300	c3
a4	200	c4

If we factor this table into two parts, AB and BC, we get the following table contents:

AB

A	B
a1	100
a2	200
a3	300
a4	200

BC

B	C
100	c1
200	c2
300	c3
200	c4

However, the result of joining these two tables is

AB JOIN BC

A	B	C
a1	100	c1
a2	200	c2
a2	200	c4
a3	300	c3
a4	200	c2
a4	200	c4

This is *not* the original table content for ABC! Note that the same decomposed tables AB and BC would have resulted if the table we had started with was ABCX, with content equal to AB JOIN BC above, or either of two other tables, ABCY or ABCZ:

ABCY

A	B	C
a1	100	c1
a2	200	c2
a2	200	c4
a3	300	c3
a4	200	c4

ABCZ

A	B	C
a1	100	c1
a2	200	c2
a3	300	c3
a4	200	c2
a4	200	c4

Since we can't tell what table content we started from, information has been lost by this decomposition and the subsequent join. This is known as a *lossy decomposition,* or sometimes a *lossy-join decomposition.* ∎

The reason we lost information in the decomposition of Example 6.7.1 is that the attribute B has duplicate values (200) on distinct rows of the factored tables (with a2 and a4 in table AB and with c2 and c4 in table BC). When these factored tables are joined again, we get cross product rows that did not (or might not) exist in the original:

a2	200	c4

and

a4	200	c2

EXAMPLE 6.7.2 A Different Content for Table ABC.
Now let's say that table ABC started with a different content, one that had no duplicate values in column B:

ABC

A	B	C
a1	100	c1
a2	200	c2
a3	300	c3

The question is this: If we decompose this table ABC into the two tables AB and BC as we did in Example 6.7.1, is the resulting decomposition lossless? And the answer is no, because the definition of a lossless decomposition requires that the join of the factored tables recapture the original information for *any possible future content* of the original table. But the table ABC content we have just shown could change with the insert of a single row to give the content of Example 6.7.1. There doesn't seem to be any rule that would keep this from happening. ∎

What sort of rule would we need to limit all possible future content for table ABC so that the decomposition into tables AB and BC would be lossless? Of course functional dependencies spring to mind, because they represent rules that govern future content of a table. Notice that in Definition 6.7.1 of a lossless decomposition, a set F of FDs is considered to be part of the table T definition. We extend the database schema definition of Chapter 2.

DEFINITION 6.7.2 A database schema is the set of headings of all tables in a database, together with the set of all FDs that the designer wishes to hold on the join of those tables.

∎

EXAMPLE 6.7.3 Table ABC with a Functional Dependency.
Assume that table ABC is defined, which obeys the following functional dependency: $B \rightarrow C$. Now the table content of Example 6.7.2 is perfectly legal:

ABC

A	B	C
a1	100	c1
a2	200	c2
a3	300	c3

But if we tried to insert a fourth row to achieve the content of Example 6.7.1,

a4	200	c4

this insert would fail because it would break the FD B → C. A new row with a duplicate value for B must also have a duplicate value for C in order for B → C to remain true:

a4	200	c2

Is it true, then, that this new content for ABC can be decomposed and then rejoined losslessly? The answer is yes. Starting with

ABC

A	B	C
a1	100	c1
a2	200	c2
a3	300	c3
a4	200	c2

if we factor this table into two parts, AB and BC, we get the following table contents:

AB

A	B
a1	100
a2	200
a3	300
a4	200

BC

B	C
100	c1
200	c2
300	c3

Note that four rows are projected onto three in table BC because of duplicate values. Now when these two tables are joined again, the original table ABC with the FD B → C results. ∎

Because of the functional dependency B → C in table ABC of Example 6.7.3, the projection of ABC on BC will always have *unique values* for attribute B. Recall from

Definition 2.4.1 that this means attribute B is a *key* for table BC. The reason that the decomposition of ABC into AB and BC is lossless is that no cross terms can ever arise in joining them: although duplicate values for column B can occur in table AB, every row in table AB joins with a *unique* row in table BC (assuming that this B value exists in table BC, as it always would in an initial decomposition that projects rows from ABC). This is reminiscent of what happened with our CAP database when we joined ORDERS with CUS-TOMERS. We simply extended rows of ORDERS with more information about individual customers. While duplicate values can exist in the cid column of the ORDERS table, the cid values are unique in the CUSTOMERS table, so every row in ORDERS joins to exactly one row in CUSTOMERS.

We generalize the above discussion somewhat to deal with sets of attributes.

THEOREM 6.7.3 Given a table T and a set of attributes $X \subseteq$ Head(T), the following two statements are equivalent: (1) X is a superkey of T; (2) X $\rightarrow$ Head(T), that is, the set of attributes X functionally determines *all* attributes in T. Equivalently: X^+ = Head(T).

PROOF. (1) **Implies** (2). If X is a superkey of the table T, then by Definition 2.4.1, for any content of the table T, two distinct rows of T must always disagree on X; that is, distinct rows cannot agree in value on all attributes of X. But from this it is clear that two rows u and v cannot agree on X and disagree on some other column in Head(T) (since if two rows agree in X, then they both represent the same row), and this means that X $\rightarrow$ Head(T). (2) **Implies** (1). Similarly if X $\rightarrow$ Head(T), then for any possible content of T, two rows in T cannot agree in value on X and simultaneously disagree on Head(T). But if the two rows u and v don't disagree on any attributes of Head(T), then by Relational RULE 3, they must be the same row. Therefore this argument has shown that two distinct rows cannot agree in value on X, and therefore X is a superkey for T. ∎

We have reached a point where we can give a general rule for the kind of lossless decomposition we will need in performing normalization.

THEOREM 6.7.4 Given a table T with an associated set F of functional dependencies valid on T, a decomposition of T into two tables $\{T_1, T_2\}$ is a lossless decomposition of T if and only if Head(T_1) and Head(T_2) are both proper subsets of Head(T), Head(T) = Head(T_1) $\cup$ Head(T_2) (i.e., all attributes of T are duplicated either in T_1 or T_2), and one of the following functional dependencies is implied by F:

(1) Head(T_1) $\cap$ Head(T_2) $\rightarrow$ Head(T_1)

or

(2) Head(T_1) $\cap$ Head(T_2) $\rightarrow$ Head(T_2).

PROOF. We take as given the table T, its decomposition into T_1 and T_2, and FD (1), Head(T_1) $\cap$ Head(T_2) $\rightarrow$ Head(T_2). (The case with FD (2) is proven similarly.) In what follows, we denote by X the set of attributes Head(T$_1$) ∩ Head(T$_2$); Y is the set of attributes in Head(T$_1$) – Head(T$_2$), and Z is the set of attributes in Head(T$_2$) – Head(T$_1$). To begin, we note by the definition of decomposition (Definition 6.7.1) that T$_1$ and T$_2$ are projections of T, and Head(T$_1$) ∪ Head(T$_2$) = Head(T). From this we can demonstrate that T ⊆ T$_1$ ⋈ T$_2$. Every column of T appears in T$_1$ ⋈ T$_2$, and if u is a row in T, we say that the projection of u on Head(T$_1$) is given by y$_1$x$_1$, a concatenation of attribute values, where y$_1$ represents values for attributes in Y and x$_1$ represents values for attributes in X; similarly x$_1$z$_1$ is the projection of u on Head(T$_2$). Clearly the projection of u on Head(T$_1$) has the same values as the projection of u on Head(T$_2$) on all attributes in X = Head(T$_1$) ∩ Head(T$_2$), and by the definition of join (Definition 2.7.4), the row u, a concatenation y$_1$x$_1$z$_1$, will appear in T$_1$ ⋈ T$_2$.

Now we show under the given assumptions that T$_1$ ⋈ T$_2$ ⊆ T. Assume that from the row u in T, we get by projection a row y$_1$x$_1$ in T$_1$, as above. Similarly assume that from the row v in T, we get the row x$_2$z$_2$ in T$_2$, with x$_2$ representing values for attributes in X. Now assume that the two rows y$_1$x$_1$ and x$_2$z$_2$ in T$_1$ and T$_2$ are joinable, so that x$_1$ is identical in all attribute values to x$_2$, and y$_1$x$_1$z$_2$ is in T$_1$ ⋈ T$_2$. This is the most general possible form for a row in T$_1$ ⋈ T$_2$, and we have only to show that the row is also in T. We denote the additional attribute values of u that project on y$_1$x$_1$ in T by z$_1$, so that u = y$_1$x$_1$z$_1$, and claim that z$_1$ = z$_2$. This is because the row u is identical to v in the attributes of X, and X → Head(T$_2$), so in particular X → Head(T$_2$) – Head(T$_1$) = Z, and since u and v are alike on X, they must be alike on attributes of Z. Thus z$_1$ = z$_2$ and the row y$_1$x$_1$z$_2$ that is in T$_1$ ⋈ T$_2$ is identical to the row y$_1$x$_1$z$_v$ in T.

We defer to the exercises a proof that if Head(T$_1$) and Head(T$_2$) are both proper subsets of Head(T), Head(T) = Head(T$_1$) ∪ Head(T$_2$), and Head(T$_1$) ∩ Head(T$_2$) does *not* functionally determine either Head(T$_1$) or Head(T$_2$), then the decomposition T into T$_1$ and T$_2$ is not lossless. ∎

EXAMPLE 6.7.4

In Example 6.7.3, we demonstrated a decomposition of the table T with heading A B C and FD B → C, into two tables T$_1$ and T$_2$ with Head(T$_1$) = A B and Head(T$_2$) = B C. If we apply Theorem 6.7.4, we have Head(T$_1$) ∩ Head(T$_2$) → Head(T$_2$), that is, A B ∩ B C → B C, or B → B C, which is clear from B → C. ∎

EXAMPLE 6.7.5

Consider the table CUSTORDS from Example 2.7.7, created by joining CUSTOMERS with ORDERS. Clearly ordno is a key for CUSTORDS, since it has unique values, and the reader can also verify that we have the FD cid → Head(CUSTOMERS). Now we note that Head(CUSTOMERS) ∩ Head(ORDERS) = cid, the key for CUSTOMERS, so Head(CUSTOMERS) ∩ Head(ORDERS) → Head(CUSTOMERS). Thus by Theorem 6.7.4, CUSTORDS has a lossless join decomposition into CUSTS and ORDS, with the same headings as CUSTOMERS and ORDERS, respectively (we would need to verify that the rows projected from CUSTORDS onto CUSTS and ORDS give the same rows that we're used to in CUSTOMERS and ORDERS). The reason that this decomposition seems intuitive is that by joining CUSTOMERS and ORDERS, we extend each of the rows in the ORDERS table with columns from customers associated with the unique cid value in that row. It seems clear, therefore, that we don't lose any information by decomposing the join back onto the headings of CUSTOMERS and ORDERS. Of course we might have lost some information originally in creating CUSTORDS, if there were some customers who didn't place any orders, for example. But our lossless decomposition starts with the table CUSTORDS and guarantees that no information is lost in the decomposition.   ■

Theorem 6.7.4 shows how to demonstrate that a decomposition of a table T into two tables $\{T_1, T_2\}$ is a lossless decomposition. In cases where three or more tables exist in the decomposition, $\{T_1, T_2, \ldots, T_k\}$, with $k \geq 3$, we can demonstrate losslessness by using the two-table result in a recursive manner.

EXAMPLE 6.7.6 Lossless Join Decomposition with Multiple Tables.
Assume that we are given the table T with Head(T) = A B C D E F and the FD set given by (1) A B → C, (2) A → D, (3) B → E. Notice there is no FD for the attribute F, but A B forms a key for A B C D E, since its closure includes all these attributes. Therefore the key for the table T must be A B F, since the key must functionally determine everything in Head(T). A perfectly acceptable lossless decomposition of T is $\{T_1, T_2, T_3, T_4\}$ where Head(T_1) = <u>A B</u> C (the keys for these tables are underlined), Head(T_2) = <u>A</u> D, Head(T_3) = <u>B</u> E, and Head(T_4) = <u>A B</u> F. The union of these tables contains all the attributes in T, so we merely need to demonstrate losslessness. Note that if we join tables in the following order by pairs, each parenthesized table join so far will ensure a lossless decomposition with the table that is joined next by Theorem 6.7.4.

$$((T_1 \bowtie T_2) \bowtie T_3) \bowtie T_4$$

We note that Head(T_1) = A B C, Head(T_2) = A D, Head($T_1 \bowtie T_2$) = A B C D, Head(T_3) = B E, and Head(($T_1 \bowtie T_2$) $\bowtie T_3$) = A B C D E. Thus the following FDs yield losslessness for the multi-table join desired.

Head(T_1) ∩ Head(T_2) = A → Head(T_2) = A D, because of (2) A → D
Head($T_1 \bowtie T_2$) ∩ Head(T_3) = B → Head(T_3) = B E, because of (3) B → E
Head($T_1 \bowtie T_2$) $\bowtie T_3$) ∩ Head(T_4) = A B → Head(T_1) = A B C, because of (1) A B → C

Since the JOIN operator is associative, losslessness does not require a specific order of JOIN and we can remove the parentheses in the expression (($T_1 \bowtie T_2$) $\bowtie T_3$) $\bowtie T_4$.   ■

In the last few sections we have developed algorithms to determine a minimal set of FDs for a given set F and defined what is meant by a lossless decomposition. In the coming section, we learn how a minimal set of FDs helps us create an appropriate normal form decomposition for a database.

6.8 Normal Forms

Let us return now to the example of bad database design from Section 6.5 that motivated the long mathematical digression of the last two sections. Recall that we wish to create a database on a set of data items given in Figure 6.15, with rules of interrelatedness stated in the set of functional dependencies in Example 6.6.3. We repeat these here as Figure 6.22.

```
emp_id          dept_name        skill_id
emp_name        dept_phone       skill_name
emp_phone       dept_mgrname     skill_date
                                 skill_lvl


(1) emp_id → emp_name emp_phone dept_name
(2) dept_name → dept_phone dept_mgrname
(3) skill_id → skill_name
(4) emp_id skill_id → skill_date skill_lvl
```

Figure 6.22   Data Items and FDs for the Employee Information Database

```
emp_info
```

emp_id	emp_name	...	skill_id	skill_name	skill_date	skill_lvl
09112	Jones	...	44	librarian	03-15-99	12
09112	Jones	...	26	PC-admin	06-30-98	10
09112	Jones	...	89	word-proc	01-15-97	12
14131	Blake	...	26	PC-admin	05-30-98	9
14131	Blake	...	89	word-proc	09-30-99	10
...	...	...	...	...	...	...

```
(1) emp_id → emp_name emp_phone dept_name
(2) dept_name → dept_phone dept_mgrname
(3) skill_id → skill_name
(4) emp_id skill_id → skill_date skill_lvl
```

Figure 6.23   Employee Information Schema with a Single Table, emp_info

We started with a first normal form table, emp_info, that combined all these data items (see Figure 6.16) and noted a number of design problems, referred to as *anomalies*. In the following section, we perform a sequence of table factorizations, which are in fact lossless decompositions, to eliminate redundancies from the employee information database.

As explained in Definition 6.7.2, a database schema is the set of headings of all tables in a database together with a set of all FDs intended by the designer. The emp_info table in Figure 6.23, together with the FDs given, make up such a database schema.

A Succession of Decompositions to Eliminate Anomalies

One anomaly of the database represented in Figure 6.23 is that if the number of skills for some employee goes to zero in the emp_info table, no row of any kind will remain for

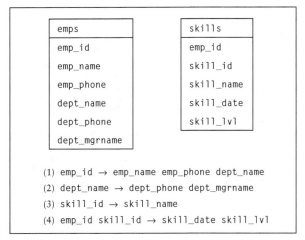

Figure 6.24 Employee Information Schema with Two Tables, emps and skills

the employee. We have lost the phone number and the department the employee works in because of deleting this skill. At the end of Section 6.5, we proposed a solution for this anomaly by factoring the emp_info table into two tables, the emps table and the skills table, whose column names were given in Figure 6.17 and are repeated in Figure 6.24.

When the emps table and the skills table were originally proposed, a number of features of this factorization were mentioned without justification. We are now in a position to demonstrate these points.

PROPOSITION 6.8.1 The key for the emp_info table is the attribute set emp_id skill_id. This is also the key for the skills table, but the emps table has a key consisting of the single attribute emp_id.

PROOF. By Theorem 6.7.3 we can determine a superkey for a table T by finding a set of attributes $X \subseteq \text{Head}(T)$ such that $X \rightarrow \text{Head}(T)$. Then, to show the set X is a key, we need merely show that no properly contained subset Y of X has this property. We start our search by finding the set closure of X for all attribute sets X found on the left-hand side of any of the FDs in Figure 6.23, repeated here.

    (1) emp_id → emp_name emp_phone dept_name
    (2) dept_name → dept_phone dept_mgrname
    (3) skill_id → skill_name
    (4) emp_id skill_id → skill_date skill_lvl

Starting with X = emp_id skill_id (the left side of FD (4) above), we use Algorithm 6.6.12 and the FD set F given to determine X^+. Starting from X^+ = emp_id skill_id and applying FD (4), we get X^+ = emp_id skill_id skill_date skill_lvl. Next, applying FD (3), since skill_id is in X^+, we add skill_name to X^+. Applying FD (1), since emp_id is in X⁺, we add the right-hand side of FD (1) to get X⁺ = emp_id skill_id skill_date skill_lvl skill_name emp_name emp_phone dept_name. Finally we apply FD (2), and since dept_name is now in X⁺, we add the right-hand side of FD (2) to get X⁺ = emp_id skill_id skill_date skill_lvl skill_name emp_name emp_phone dept_name dept_phone dept_mgrname. This final list contains all the attributes in emp_info, that is, Head(emp_info). By the definition of X⁺, this means that

[6.8.1] emp_id skill_id → Head(emp_info)

By Theorem 6.7.3 then, emp_id skill_id is a superkey for emp_info.

To show that emp_id skill_id is in fact a key for emp_info, we need only show that no subset (either emp_id or skill_id alone) functionally determines all these attributes. Let us take the closure of the set emp_id to find what attributes are functionally determined. We can immediately apply FD (1) to get emp_id → emp_id emp_name emp_phone dept_name. Next we can apply FD (2), and derive

[6.8.2] emp_id → emp_id emp_name emp_phone dept_name dept_phone dept_mgrname

Since skill_id is not in the right-hand set of [6.8.2], no other FDs can be applied, so this is the maximum right-hand set that is functionally determined by emp_id.

Finally starting with skill_id alone in the set X to be closed, FD (3) is the only one that can be applied, and we see that the maximum right-hand set functionally determined by skill_id is given as

[6.8.3] skill_id → skill_id skill_name

Neither [6.8.2] nor [6.8.3] contains all attributes of emp_info, and thus we can conclude from [6.8.1] that

[6.8.4] emp_id skill_id is a key for the emp_info table

In addition, we note from [6.8.2] that emp_id functionally determines all attributes in the emps table of Figure 6.24, and since no subset of a singleton set can be on the left side of an FD,

[6.8.5] emp_id is a key for the emps table

Finally we note that the skills table has attributes that are not functionally determined by either emp_id or skill_id individually, skill_lvl is not on the right-hand side in either [6.8.2] or [6.8.3], and therefore the only possible key for the skills table is emp_id skill_id:

[6.8.6] emp_id skill_id is a key for the skills table ∎

384

PROPOSITION 6.8.2 The factorization of the emp_info table into the emps table and skills table is a true lossless decomposition.

PROOF. To see that this is a valid decomposition, we note that Head(emps) ∪ Head(skills) = Head(emp_info). Furthermore Head(emps) ∩ Head(skills) = emp_id, and since functional dependency [6.8.2] shows that emp_id → Head(emps), by Theorem 6.7.4 the decomposition is lossless.   ■

From Proposition 6.8.2, we see that the decomposition that brings us from the emp_info table of Figure 6.23 to the emps table and skills tables of Figure 6.24 will always allow us to recapture any content of emp_info by a join of the two factored tables. But the real motivation for this decomposition was to deal with the various anomalies mentioned earlier.

How did the delete anomaly mentioned in Section 6.5 arise in the emp_info table of Figure 6.23? The basic reason is that the pair of attributes emp_id skill_id form the key for that table, but there are attributes that we wish to keep track of that are functionally determined by a single one of those two attributes, emp_id. If we delete the last skill_id value for some specific emp_id, we no longer have any (emp_id skill_id) pairs with that specific emp_id, *but we still have information that is dependent only on* emp_id, *which we don't want to lose!* Putting this in terms of the E-R model, employees are real entities whose attributes we want to keep track of (and so the employee identifier, emp_id, shows up on the left of a functional dependency). In the decomposition of Figure 6.24, we factored the emps table out of the emp_info table so that we wouldn't lose information in this way. With this new schema, we can keep a row for a given employee in the emps table even if the employee has no skills. Recall that the insert anomaly is the inverse face of the delete anomaly, making it impossible to insert a new employee without skills—a trainee—into the emp_info table. As before, this problem is solved by factoring out the emps table, since a new row can be inserted into emps that doesn't have any join to a row of the skills table. As far as the update anomaly is concerned, this problem arises in the emp_info table once again because attributes dependent only on emp_id are in a table with key emp_id skill_id; we can therefore have multiple rows with the same employee phone number in this table that must all be updated at once. Once again, factoring out the emps table solves this problem, because each employee is now represented by a single row.

The question now is this: Are there any more anomalies remaining in the database schema of Figure 6.24? The answer, perhaps unsurprisingly, is yes. There is another anomaly of the kind we have just analyzed in the skills table. This table has the primary key (skill_id emp_id), and we recall FD (3) of Figure 6.22:

[6.8.7] skill_id → skill_name

What this FD seems to be saying is that skills is an entity in its own right, that skill_id is an identifier for the entity, and that skill_name is a descriptor. (There might be two distinct skills with different skill_id values but the same skill_name, since skill_name → skill_id is not an FD that is implied by the list we presented.) But recall that the key we have discovered for the skills table is emp_id skill_id. This situation seems to be symmetric with the one that caused us to factor out the table emps from emp_info. Can we construct (for example) a delete anomaly of the kind that led to this step? The answer is yes, for if we assume that some skill is rare and difficult to master, and we suddenly lose the last employee who had it, we would no longer have any information about the skill at all, neither the skill_id nor the skill_name. We therefore need to factor out another table to solve this anomaly, and we see the result in Figure 6.25.

From examination of the new emp_skills table and skills table of Figure 6.25, it should be clear that these two tables form a lossless decomposition of the skills table of Figure 6.24. Indeed, the three tables of Figure 6.25 form a lossless decomposition of the single emp_info table we started with in Figure 6.23. Most importantly, we have dealt with the anomalies that arise from keeping attributes of skills entities in a table with a key of two attributes. In terms of the E-R model, what we have just done is to factor out the relationship emp_skills from the two entities Emps and Skills.

Consider now the three tables of Figure 6.25. Everything in the emps table, as we showed earlier in Proposition 6.8.1, is functionally determined by the singleton attribute emp_id; a similar situation holds with the skills table, as we see from the FD in [6.8.7]; in the emp_skills table, a glance at [6.8.2] and [6.8.3] makes it clear that no remaining attributes in this table are dependent on a subset of the (emp_id skill_id) key. We ask then if any further anomalies can remain in these tables. Once more, the answer is yes! To see how this is possible, consider what would happen if we had a large reorganization in the company, so that every employee in one department is to be transferred to other departments (even the manager will be transferred—presumably, at some later time, different employees will take their place in the department that has just been emptied). Now notice that when the last employee is removed, there remains no row in the emps table

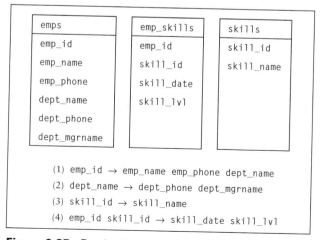

```
emps              emp_skills         skills

emp_id            emp_id             skill_id

emp_name          skill_id           skill_name

emp_phone         skill_date

dept_name         skill_lvl

dept_phone

dept_mgrname
```

    (1) emp_id → emp_name emp_phone dept_name
    (2) dept_name → dept_phone dept_mgrname
    (3) skill_id → skill_name
    (4) emp_id skill_id → skill_date skill_lvl

Figure 6.25   Employee Information Schema with Three Tables

386

containing information about the department: we have lost even the phone number of the department and the name it goes under! The solution to this problem is obvious: we must factor out a separate table for departments. This will result in the emp_info database of Figure 6.26; this database is in third normal form (3NF), or equivalently in this case, in Boyce-Codd normal form (BCNF). We will give definitions for these normal forms shortly.

With the factorization of the depts table of Figure 6.26, the update anomaly relating to department information will no longer trouble us. In terms of the E-R model, what we have done is to differentiate between the two entities Emps and Depts, between which there is a many-to-one relationship (represented by the foreign key dept_name in the emps table).

At this point, we claim that the database schema of Figure 6.26 is in some sense a final result—no anomalies remain in the representation to trouble us. For the rationale to justify this statement, we look to the four FDs listed that must be maintained in the database, which we refer to in what follows as the set F of FDs. In every case where we have noted an anomaly in earlier schemas, the underlying reason for the anomaly has turned out to hinge on the fact that some attribute (it could have been a set of attributes in a different schema) on the left-hand side of an FD in F might have multiple duplicate occurrences (or possibly zero occurrences) in the table where it appeared. The solution was to create a separate table, placing the attributes on the left-hand side of this FD, together with all attributes on the right-hand side in that table, while the attributes on the right-hand side were removed from the table where they previously appeared. Look carefully at the successive decompositions presented in Figures 6.23 through 6.26 to see that this is an accurate description of what was done. Since the attributes on the left-hand side of the FD are in both the old and the new tables and determine all other attributes in the new table, the decomposition is lossless. Thus FD (1) generates the emps table, FD (2) the depts table, FD (3) the skills table, and FD (4) the emp_skills table. Since no more FDs exist in F, we maintain that no more anomalies will arise, and therefore no further decomposition is necessary. Thus we have reached a final form.

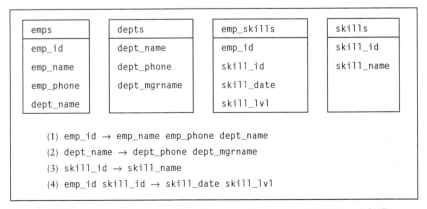

Figure 6.26 Employee Information Database Schema in 3NF (Also BCNF)

Normal Forms: BCNF, 3NF, and 2NF

The tables in the final schema of Figure 6.26 each have unique candidate keys, which we may think of as primary keys for the tables. One way to characterize why no further decomposition is needed to address anomalies in these tables is to say that all functional dependencies involving attributes of any single table in this schema arise from the table keys alone. We provide definitions to make this idea precise.

DEFINITION 6.8.3 Given a database schema with a universal table T and a set of functional dependencies F, let $\{T_1, T_2, \ldots, T_k\}$ be a lossless decomposition of T. Then an FD $X \to Y$ of F is said to be *preserved in* the decomposition of T, or alternatively the decomposition of T *preserves* the FD $X \to Y$, if for some table T_i of the decomposition, $X \cup Y \subseteq$ Head(T_i). When this is the case, we also say that the FD $X \to Y$ is *preserved in* T_i or that it *lies in* T_i or *is in* T_i. ∎

EXAMPLE 6.8.1

We have derived a number of successive decompositions of the Employee Information schema of Figure 6.23 with a universal table and a set F of FDs: a decomposition with two tables (Figure 6.24), three tables (Figure 6.25), and four tables (Figure 6.26). Each of these decompositions preserves all dependencies in F. For example, in the four-table decomposition of Figure 6.26, FD (1) lies in the emps table, FD (2) lies in the depts table, FD (3) lies in the skills table, and FD (4) lies in the emp_skills table. ∎

Because every FD in F is preserved in one of the four tables of Figure 6.26, whenever any single table in the schema is updated, it is possible to verify that any FD affected by the update is still valid by testing its validity in that single table, without any need for a join. This is the motivation for seeking to preserve functional dependencies in a decomposition.

DEFINITION 6.8.4 Boyce-Codd Normal Form. A table T in a database schema with FD set F is said to be in *Boyce-Codd normal form* (BCNF) when the following property holds. For any functional dependency $X \to A$ implied by F that lies in T, where A is a single attribute that is not in X, X must be a superkey for T. A database schema is in BCNF when all the tables it contains are in BCNF. ∎

Consider a table T, and let $X \to A$ be a functional dependency in T. If the BCNF property holds for this case, then X is a superkey, so for some set K of attributes representing a key for T, $K \subseteq X$. (Note that there might be a number of different sets K_1, K_2, . . . that are candidate keys for T, as we consider in Example 6.8.4 below.) If the BCNF property fails, then X does not contain a key set K, and K – X is non-empty for all K. Then two cases are possible: either (1) X – K is empty for some K, that is, $X \subset K$, and we say that some attributes of T are functionally determined by a *proper subset* X of a key K; or else (2) X – K is non-empty for all K, so some attributes are determined by a set X at least partially outside each K. In the second case, we say that some attributes of T are functionally determined by a *different* set of attributes that does not contain and is not contained in any key set.

EXAMPLE 6.8.2

In the emp_skills table of Figure 6.26, the only key consists of the set emp_id skill_id, as we can easily demonstrate by set closure arguments: any set of attributes that functionally determine all attributes in the emp_skills table must contain both of these attributes. We claim that the table is in BCNF and will demonstrate this in the next example. As we just pointed out, the BCNF property of Definition 6.8.4 implies that no attributes of this table are functionally determined by any *subset* of this key set, or any *different* set of attributes that does not contain this key set.

In the skills table of Figure 6.24, the unique key for this table consists of the two attributes emp_id skill_id, while the FD skill_id → skill_name also lies in the table. Clearly the left-hand side of this FD is a *subset* of the key emp_id skill_id. Because of this the BCNF property fails for this table (and we pointed out that an anomaly arose requiring us to perform further decomposition).

In the emps table of Figure 6.24 (identical to the emps table in Figure 6.25), the unique key for the table consists of the attribute emp_id, while the FD dept_name → dept_phone is implied by FD (2) of F and lies in the table. Since the left side of this FD is *different* from the key set (neither a subset nor a superset), the BCNF property fails, and further decomposition is necessary. Note, by the way, that a table emps2 containing all the attributes of emps except the attribute dept_phone would still not obey the BCNF property. Although the FD dept_name → dept_phone does not lie in the table emps2, the FD dept_name → dept_mgrname, which is also implied by FD (2), does lie in emps2. ∎

EXAMPLE 6.8.3

We claim that the database schema of Figure 6.26 is in BCNF. We need to show that for any FD X → A implied by F that lies in one of the tables of Figure 6.26, where A is an attribute not in X, then X contains a key for that table. We have shown in Example 6.8.1 that for the set of tables in Figure 6.26, one FD of F lies in each table, and this FD has as its left side the key for the table. This does not quite conclude the issue, however, because we also need to consider all FDs that are implied by F, that is, all FDs that are true in the schema. In Proposition 6.8.1, FDs [6.8.1], [6.8.2], and [6.8.3], we determined the closure of all sets X of attributes that fall on the left side of three FDs of F, and showed that these three sets form keys for three of the tables. For the fourth FD, we need merely take the closure of dept_name, which is easily seen to consist of the set dept_name, dept_phone, dept_mgrname, or Head(depts):

[6.8.8]   dept_name → Head(depts)

Now we claim that all attribute sets Z that do not contain one of these sets X, the left side of an FD in F and therefore a key for one of the tables of Figure 6.26, must have trivial closure $Z^+ = Z$. This follows from the fact that no FDs of the form X → Y exist with X ⊆ Z, and by Algorithm 6.6.12, no attributes will ever be added to the set closure of Z.

From this we can easily see that all of the tables in Figure 6.26 are BCNF, because if X → A holds and A is an attribute not contained in the attribute set X, then X → A X, and therefore X^+ is not identical to X. But we have just shown that any attribute set that does not contain a table key has a trivial closure, and this must mean that X contains some table key K. In that table, we have also included all attributes functionally determined by K, and therefore A is in that table as well. ∎

EXAMPLE 6.8.4

Suppose we changed the rules in the employee information database so that `dept_mgrname` was a second identifier of the `Departments` entity, duplicating the effect of `dept_name`. This would add a new FD to the set F: `dept_mgrname` → `dept_name`; by transitivity, since `dept_name` is a key for the `depts` table in Figure 6.26, `dept_mgrname` would also be a key. The question now is whether the `depts` table is still in BCNF. And the answer is yes, because the BCNF property was specially constructed not to require a unique key for the table. The only thing that has changed in the `depts` table is that there are now two keys, but any FD of the form X → Y in this table has the necessary property that X contains `dept_mgrname` or X contains `dept_name`.   ∎

Recall that every FD in F is *preserved* in one of the four tables of Figure 6.26, so that whenever any table in the schema is updated, it is possible to verify that an affected FD still holds by testing data items in that table alone. We would like to be able to guarantee that this property, preservation of FDs, can always be achieved starting from a universal table and proceeding to a lossless decomposition into BCNF. Unfortunately this is not true, because the BCNF criterion for a table is too strict.

EXAMPLE 6.8.5

We wish to add a number of attributes to the employee information database of Figure 6.22 to keep track of the full addresses of all employees (assumed to be living in the United States):

    emp_cityst, emp_straddr, emp_zip

Here `emp_cityst` reflects the city and state, `emp_zip` the zip code, and `emp_straddr` the street name, number, and apartment, if any. We find that when we reach the decomposition of Figure 6.26, the `emps` table contains all of these attributes in addition to the ones that are already there, as we see in Figure 6.27.

We assume that each employee is required to provide a single address, so it is clear that the `emp_id` value functionally determines all these new attributes, and FD (1) is modified accordingly:

    (1) emp_id → emp_name emp_phone dept_name emp_straddr emp_cityst emp_zip

No keys for any other tables of Figure 6.26 are affected, and the key for the `emps` table is still `emp_id`.

Figure 6.27   The `emps` Table Extended to Contain Employee Addresses

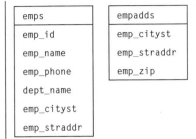

Figure 6.28   A 3NF Decomposition of Figure 6.27

But the post office has assigned zip codes to cover regions of a city (determined by street address) and never to cross city boundaries, so we also have the following new FDs to add to the set F:

(5)   emp_cityst emp_straddr → emp_zip   regions of city determine the zip code
(6)   emp_zip → emp_cityst   zip codes never cross city boundaries

Since the lhs of FD (5), emp_cityst emp_straddr, is not a superkey of the emps table, we need to perform a further decomposition to achieve the BCNF property. If we did not do this and deleted the last employee in some zip code, we would lose what information we have about that zip code, namely, what city and state it is associated with. Following the prescription explained in the discussion following Figure 6.26, we place the attributes on the left-hand side of FD (5), together with all attributes on the right-hand side of this FD in a separate table (empadds), while the attributes on the right-hand side are removed from the table where they previously appeared (emps). The result is given in Figure 6.28. This is a perfectly reasonable lossless decomposition of the previous table (lossless because of Theorem 6.7.4, since emp_cityst emp_straddr is a key for empadds, and this is also the intersection of the headings of the two tables). We note too that emp_zip emp_straddr is an alternate candidate key for empadds, since taking the closure of this set, we get emp_cityst by FD (6). Thus we have the new derived FD (7). It is easy to see by closure that no other candidate keys exist for empadds.

(7)   emp_zip emp_straddr → emp_cityst (FD derived from (5) and (6))

The emps table of Figure 6.28 is now in BCNF, since neither FD (5) nor (6) lies in emps, and the only remaining, FD (1), requires that any superkey for the table will contain emp_id. This decomposition also preserves FDs (5) and (6), which both lie entirely in the empadds table. However, at this point FD (6) forces us to perform further decomposition of empadds to achieve BCNF, since emp_zip → emp_cityst, and emp_zip does not contain either candidate key of empadds. Clearly this new decomposition must contain at most two attributes in each table, and we require one table (zipcit in Figure 6.29 below) to have heading emp_zip emp_cityst to contain FD (6). The other table only has two possible pairs of attributes for a heading, the lhs of FD (5) or the lhs of FD (7), both keys for the empadds table. Choosing the lhs of FD (5), emp_cityst emp_straddr, would not result in a lossless decomposition, since the only attribute it would have in common with zipcit is emp_cityst, and this wouldn't contain a key for either table. We therefore choose BCNF decomposition in Figure 6.29.

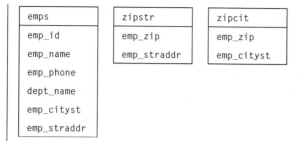

Figure 6.29 A BCNF Decomposition of Figure 6.28

The decomposition of Figure 6.29 is lossless for the following reasons: emp_zip is the key for the zipcit table, the intersection of Head(zipstr) and Head(zipcit), so that join is lossless; the union of the zipstr and zipcit table headings contains all the attributes of the previous empadds table, so zipstr and zipcit join to form the empadds table of Figure 6.28; the empadds table formed a lossless join with the emps table, so the three tables join losslessly. Furthermore, both new tables in Figure 6.29 are in BCNF form. The only FD in the zipcit table is FD (6), and emp_zip is the key. The zipstr table has no FD in it, so the unique key includes both attributes, emp_zip emp_straddr, which was also an alternate candidate key for the empadds table of Figure 6.28.

But the decomposition in Figure 6.29 does *not* preserve dependencies of the extended set F, since FD (5) does not lie in either table. This can have an unfortunate effect, in that we must perform programmatic checking to ensure that a given street address, city, state, and zip code being entered conforms with the post office assignment. ∎

It seems that we have gone too far in decomposition if we really want to preserve functional dependencies. What we'd like is a definition for normal form that allows us to stop at Figure 6.28 and not press on to Figure 6.29. In order to do this, we have to come up with a new definition for normal form (3NF, as it turns out). We achieve this with the following definitions.

DEFINITION 6.8.5 Prime Attribute. In a table T, an attribute A is said to be *prime* if and only if the attribute A exists in some key K for the table. ∎

DEFINITION 6.8.6 Third Normal Form. A table T in a database schema with FD set F is said to be in *third normal form* (3NF) under the following condition. For any functional dependency X → A implied by F that lies in T, where A is a single attribute that is not in X, one of the two following properties must hold: either (1) X is a superkey for T; or (2) A is a prime attribute in T. A database schema is in 3NF when all the tables it contains are in 3NF. ∎

EXAMPLE 6.8.6
Consider the database schema of Figure 6.29. Each of the tables in this schema is in BCNF, and therefore in 3NF. The BCNF prescription for a table requires that the table has property (1) of the 3NF definition, and it doesn't permit the "escape clause" of property (2). Therefore any table in BCNF is also in 3NF, but the reverse doesn't hold. ∎

EXAMPLE 6.8.7

Consider the empadds table of Figure 6.28. This table is in 3NF but not in BCNF. The reason we required a further decomposition of this table was that the empadds table of Figure 6.28 had as a key the attributes emp_cityst emp_straddr, and at the same time FD (6), emp_zip → emp_cityst lies in the table. This is an FD whose left-hand side does not contain a key of empadds, so the FD does not fulfill the BCNF property. However, we note that the attribute on the right of this FD does lie in some key and is therefore prime. Thus the FD does fulfill property (2) of the 3NF definition. ■

EXAMPLE 6.8.8

We are given a table T with Head(T) = A B C D, and FD set F as follows.

F: (1) A B → C D, (2) D → B

Clearly A B is a candidate key for T, and we see by closure that A D is another one: A D⁺ = A D B (2) C (1). It is easy to confirm that there are no others. Now we maintain that the table T is already in 3NF, because the only FD implied by F that does not contain A B on the lhs (and is not trivial) depends on FD (2) D → B, and since B is a prime attribute, the table T is 3NF by the "escape clause" of property (2).

   If we did wish to decompose T losslessly to a BCNF form, we would want to start by projecting on a table that contains FD (2), that is, the table T_2 with Head(T_2) = B D. Then we will want the table T_1 to contain a candidate key for T as well as the attribute C, but if we create T_1 with Head(T_1) = A B C, then the headings of T_1 and T_2 won't intersect in D and therefore won't join losslessly. Thus we must create the table T_1 with Head(T_1) = A D C. And so we have the BCNF decomposition {A D C, B D}. ■

In decomposing a database with a given set of functional dependencies F to achieve a normal form, the BCNF and 3NF forms are often identical, as we saw in Example 6.8.6. They differ exactly when there exist two nontrivial FDs implied by F, X → Y and Z → B, where Z ⊂ X ∪ Y and B ∈ X. In Example 6.8.8, FD (1) gave us A B → C D and FD (2) D → B, with D ⊂ C D and B ∈ A B. Further decomposition to achieve BCNF will cause dependencies not to be preserved. Many database designers aim for a 3NF design that preserves dependencies.

Another definition for a table property, known as *second normal form*, or *2NF*, is weaker than 3NF and of mainly historical interest since no advantage arises from stopping short of 3NF. From Definition 6.8.6 we see that when a table fails to be 3NF, it must contain a valid nontrivial functional dependency X → A, where A is non-prime and X is not a superkey for T. Recall from the discussion of BCNF following Definition 6.8.4 that if X is not a superkey for T, then two cases are possible: either X ⊂ K for some K and we say that some attributes of T are functionally determined by a proper subset X of a key K, or else X – K is non-empty for all keys K in T, and we say that some attributes of T are functionally determined by a different set of attributes that does not contain and is not contained in any key set. This latter case is also known as a *transitive dependency*, since we have K → X for any key K, and given X → A, the functional dependency K → A is implied by transitivity. A table in 2NF is not allowed to have attributes that are functionally determined by a proper subset of a key K, but it may still have transitive dependencies.

DEFINITION 6.8.7 Second Normal Form. A table T in a database schema with FD set F is said to be in *second normal form* (2NF) under the following condition. For any functional dependency $X \rightarrow A$ implied by F that lies in T, where A is a single attribute that is not in X and is non-prime, X is not a *proper subset* of any key K of T. A database schema is in 2NF when all the tables it contains are in 2NF. ∎

EXAMPLE 6.8.9

The database schema of Figure 6.25 is in 2NF. A demonstration of this is left for the exercises at the end of the chapter. ∎

An Algorithm to Achieve Well-Behaved 3NF Decomposition

For a number of technical reasons it turns out that the approach of successive decompositions to achieve a 3NF lossless join decomposition preserving functional dependencies is distrusted by many practitioners. This is the only approach we have seen, used in Figures 6.23 through 6.26. Problems can arise because the set F of functional dependencies used in the successive decompositions has not been carefully defined, and as we saw in Section 6.6 numerous equivalent sets F are possible. Algorithm 6.8.8 provides a straightforward method to create the desired decomposition.

ALGORITHM 6.8.8 This algorithm, given a universal table T and set F of FDs, generates a lossless join decomposition of T that is in third normal form and preserves all FDs of F. The output is a set S of headings (sets of attributes) for tables in the final database schema.

```
REPLACE F WITH MINIMAL COVER OF F;        /* use algorithm 6.6.13           */
S = ∅;                                     /* initialize S to null set       */
FOR ALL X → Y in F                         /* loop on FDs found in F         */
    IF, FOR ALL Z ∈ S, X ∪ Y ⊄ Z          /* no table contains X → Y        */
        THEN S = S ∪ Heading(X ∪ Y);      /* add new table Heading to S     */
END FOR                                    /* end loop on FDs                */
IF, FOR ALL CANDIDATE KEYS K FOR T         /* if no candidate Keys of T      */
        FOR ALL Z ∈ S, K ⊄ Z               /* are contained in any table     */
    THEN CHOOSE A CANDIDATE KEY K AND      /* choose a candidate key         */
        SET S = S ∪ Heading(K);           /* and add new table to S         */
```

Note that the function Heading(K) generates a singleton set containing the set K of attributes, which can then be added to the set S, which is a set of sets of attributes. ∎

EXAMPLE 6.8.10

To see why the choice of a candidate key might sometimes be necessary in Algorithm 6.8.8, consider the following small school database. We are given a universal table T with heading

```
Head(T) = instructor class_no class_room text
```

and FD set F given by

```
F = {class_no → class_room text}
```

In E-R terms, there is an entity Classes, identified by class_no, and the actual class holds all its meetings in the same classroom with a unique text. Whether or not there is an entity Class_rooms with identifier class_room is a matter of opinion. Since there is no FD with class_room on the left, such an entity would have no descriptor attributes and so no table exists for it in the relational model; thus we can think of class_room as a descriptor attribute for Classes if we like. The same argument can be applied to the text attribute in Head(T). But the instructor attribute in Head(T) is a different situation. Since the instructor attribute is not functionally determined by class_no, there can be several instructors for the same class, and since instructor does not determine class_no, this means that one instructor might teach several classes. From this it is clear that instructors have independent existence from classes, and in fact represent an entity, Instructors. Indeed, the table T contains a relationship between Instructors and Classes.

By standard BCNF/3NF normalization, since the attributes class_room and text are dependent on class_no alone in the table T, we need to factor T into two tables, T_1 and T_2, with

```
Head(T₁) = class_no class_room text

Head(T₂) = instructor class_no
```

But in Algorithm 6.8.8, only table T_1 will be created in the initial loop on FDs, since the instructor attribute does not figure in any FDs of F. However, it is clear from the standard set closure approach that the unique candidate key for T is class_no instructor. Therefore the loop on candidate keys in Algorithm 6.8.8 is necessary to create the table T_2 for the set S.   ∎

It is commonly said that the normalization approach and the E-R approach reinforce one another. Example 6.8.10 gives an example of this. Without considering functional dependencies, it is not clear why the instructor data item must represent an entity but the class_room data item might not. On the other hand, the E-R approach gives the motivation for why the loop on candidate keys in Algorithm 6.8.8 is appropriate to create table T_2. We need table T_2 to represent the relationship between the Instructors and Classes entities.

A Review of Normalization

In the normalization approach to database design, we start out with a set of data items and a set F of functional dependencies that the designer wishes to see maintained by the database system for any future content of the database. The data items are all placed in a single universal table T, and the set F is replaced by an equivalent minimal cover; then the designer determines a decomposition of this table into a set of smaller tables $\{T_1, T_2, \ldots, T_k\}$, with a number of good properties, as follows.

[1]   The decomposition is lossless, so that $T = T_1 \bowtie T_2 \bowtie \ldots \bowtie T_n$.

[2] To the greatest extent possible, the only FDs $X \rightarrow Y$ in tables T_i arise because X contains some key K in T_i; this is the thrust of the BCNF/3NF definitions.

[3] All FDs in F of the form $X \rightarrow Y$ are preserved in tables of the decomposition.

The value of property (2) is that we can avoid the various anomalies defined in Section 6.5. It is also important that with these normal forms we can guarantee that functional dependency will not be broken, so long as we guarantee the uniqueness of all keys for a table. In the beginning of the next chapter we will see that the Create Table statement of SQL gives us a way to define such keys K for a table, and the uniqueness of these keys will then be guaranteed by the system for all SQL table Update statements that follow (an update that breaks such a uniqueness constraint will result in an error). As we will see a bit later, such a uniqueness condition is a particularly easy condition to check with an index on the key columns involved, whereas a general functional dependency $X \rightarrow Y$ in a table T_i, where multiple rows with the same value for X can exist, is more difficult. Standard SQL does not provide a constraint to guarantee such general dependencies against update errors.

The value of property (3) should also be clear, since we want to guarantee that all functional dependencies provided by the designer hold for any possible content of the database. Property (3) means that FDs won't cross tables in the final database schema, so that if an update of one table occurs, only FDs in that table need to be tested by the system. On the other hand, the very decomposition we are providing does result in a certain amount of join testing, since the standard lossless join decomposition into tables T_1 and T_2 leads to a key for one table with attributes in both—that is, a key consisting of (Head(T_1) $\cap$ Head(T_2)). Standard SQL provides a constraint, known as *referential integrity*, that can be imposed with the Create Table statement to guarantee that these attribute values continue to make sense between the two tables they join, a constraint also known as a *foreign key condition*.

To sum up, the standard 3NF decomposition eliminates most anomalies and makes it possible to verify efficiently that desired functional dependencies remain valid when the database is updated.

Additional normal forms exist that are not covered here, 4NF and 5NF. In particular, fourth normal form, or 4NF, is based on an entirely new type of dependency, known as a *multi-valued dependency*. You are referred to references [4] or [5] for good descriptions of these.

We should mention at this point that *overnormalization*, factoring a database into more tables than are required in order to reach 3NF when this is the goal, is considered a bad practice. For example, if we factored the depts table into two tables, one with dept_name and dept_phone and a second with dept_name and dept_mgrname, we would certainly still have a 3NF database, but we would have gone further than necessary in decomposition. Unnecessary inefficiencies would arise in retrieving all department information together, because of the join that would now be required.

6.9 Additional Design Considerations

The E-R and normalization approaches both have weaknesses. The E-R approach, as it is usually presented, is extremely dependent on intuition, but if intuition fails there is little fallback. As we saw in Example 6.8.10, it can be difficult on the basis of intuition alone to determine whether a data item represents an entity or not. It helps to have the concept of functional dependency from normalization. Normalization is more mathematically based and mechanical in its application, but the idea that you can write down a complete set of FDs as a first step of logical database design is often a delusion; it may be found later that some have been missed. The intuitive exercise of trying to discover entities and relationships and weak entities and so on aids the designer in discovering FDs that might otherwise be overlooked.

Another factor affecting the normalization approach is that a certain amount of judgment might be needed to decide whether a particular functional dependency should be reflected in a final design. Consider the CAP database schema with tables listed in Figure 2.2. It might seem that all functional dependencies that hold for the database are reflections of the table key dependencies, so that all the tables are in BCNF. However, there is a rather unexpected FD of the following form:

[6.9.1]   qty price discnt → dollars

That is, for each order, from the order quantity, product price, and customer discount we can calculate the dollars charge for the order—this relationship is mentioned in the second-to-last paragraph of Section 2.1 and is expressed in the following SQL Insert statement [6.9.2]. Now the question is, does this FD make the set of tables in Figure 2.2 a bad design? Clearly the FD as it stands crosses tables, and therefore the decomposition does not preserve dependencies. Note that we can create another table, ddollars, that contains all the attributes on both sides of FD [6.9.1], qty price discnt dollars, and simultaneously remove the dollars attribute from orders. The result, a five-table schema for CAP including the ddollars table, is a 3NF design that would be arrived at by Algorithm 6.8.8. The unique key for the ddollars table is qty price discnt, and the only FD is given in [6.9.1]. There is a problem with this design, however. Whenever we want to retrieve the dollar cost for an order, we have to perform a join with products to get price, customers to get discnt, and ddollars to read off the dollars value for the given qty, price, and discnt. Is all this really necessary? The original design of Figure 2.2 seems preferable from this standpoint.

If we consider the original motivations for a decomposition such as this, we have two: to remove anomalies and to validate all FDs whenever changes are made in the data. But do we really want to validate this FD by a unique key constraint in normal form? Presumably when a new order is inserted, the program logic does a calculation of the dollars amount to store, something like this:

[6.9.2]
```
exec sql insert into orders
      values (:ordno, :month, :cid, :aid, :pid, :qty,
      qty*:price - .01*:discnt*:qty*:price;
```

With this Insert statement we guarantee the FD [6.9.1]; and more than that, we guarantee an exact numerical relationship that an FD is incapable of representing. The only validation that the ddollars table is capable of providing is this: if a previous row exists with a given qty, price, and discnt, then the calculated dollars value will be identical. This seems like a rather strange validation, since if there are a lot of products and customers, with real variation in order sizes and some limit on the number of orders tracked, we can expect to be adding many (qty, price, discnt) triples for the first time. Thus the unique key constraint offers no real value in verification: there is no old row with the same key to compare with it. You would much rather depend on the Insert statement [6.9.2] to perform the correct calculation. In this regard, it certainly makes sense to provide this insert in a tested function that must be used by all logic-performing inserts of new orders.

Now the delete and insert anomalies amount to saying that we don't want to lose track of any (qty, price, discnt) triples, but this is a questionable proposition given that we don't really value this method of validation. As for the update anomaly, we consider the case of needing to update all dollars values at once for a given (qty, price, discnt). Presumably this might happen if the price or discnt value needed to be changed for orders that were previously entered, perhaps because that value was originally entered erroneously and now has to be corrected. But this change would be so unusual and have such major ramifications for a wholesale business that it is unreasonable to assume that an inexperienced programmer might write code to correct a single row in orders by mistake. Indeed many designers would model the dollars column as an insert-only quantity that should not be updated at all (except to correct input errors). We are therefore willing to forgo the protection from the update anomaly.

We have gone into detail here to exemplify a type of situation that arises with some frequency in commercial applications, a need for *denormalization* to improve performance. Most design practitioners will agree that there is frequently a need for this.

Database Design Tools

A number of commercial products are aimed at providing environments to support the DBA in performing database design. These environments are provided by *database design tools*, or sometimes as part of a more general class of products known as *computer-aided software engineering* (CASE) tools. Such tools usually have a number of components, chosen from the following kinds. It would be rare for a single product to offer all these capabilities.

E-R Design Editor. A common component is an interface in which a designer can construct E-R diagrams, editing and making changes to the diagrams using the graphical drag-and-drop methods common to products such as the Apple Macintosh and Microsoft Windows.

E-R to Relational Design Transformer. Another common component of such tools is a transformer that automatically performs a transformation of an E-R design to a set of relational table definitions, following the steps outlined in Section 6.3 and exemplified in the case study of Section 6.4.

With database design tools, the flow of development usually starts with E-R design and proceeds to a relational table definition. However, a number of products deal with functional dependencies. One tool advises loading a small universal table and abstracts from this data the possible functional dependencies that might hold for the data. A transformation to BCNF/3NF for this set of FDs can then be automatically generated.

FD to E-R Design Transformer. Another type of component that is sometimes offered takes a set of FDs for the database and generates a valid E-R diagram to reflect the rules of the data.

As indicated in the previous section, a design that is theoretically perfect may also be inefficient in terms of performance. Thus a good design tool tries to analyze the performance implications of a design and accepts designer decisions to perform certain kinds of denormalization to improve performance. In addition, a tool must be forgiving of errors and omissions in FDs and entity classifications, in order to produce some kind of best guess at a design that the designer can picture while making corrections. This brings up another kind of standard tool component.

Design Analyzers. These components analyze design in the current stage and produce reports that might help the DBA to correct errors of various kinds.

For an excellent overview of database design tools, you are referred to the last chapter in reference [1] in "Suggestions for Further Reading."

Suggestions for Further Reading

Many variations in terminology are prevalent in the field of logical database design. The E-R approach is sometimes referred to as *semantic modeling*. The real-world objects known as *entity occurrences* in our notation are often referred to in the literature as *entities*, and the *entity* in our notation that makes up a category of entity occurrences then becomes an *entity type*, just like our *objects* and *object types* in Chapter 4. Attributes are also sometimes called *properties*.

Let us try to give an idea of what is meant by semantic modeling. In a programming language, the *syntax* of the language specifies how the statements are formed out of basic textual elements. The syntax does not associate any meaning with the statements, however. A specification of how programming language statements act under all possible conditions, what the statements mean in terms of their effect, is known as the *semantics* of the language. The term *semantic modeling* implies that in the E-R approach, we are getting into the topic of what data items *really mean* in order to model their behavior in terms of database structures such as relational tables.

References [1], [2], and [4] cover the topic of logical database design. Reference [1] also contains as its final section an article by David Reiner on commercial products used for database design, known as database design tools. References [3] and [5] also contain excellent coverage of many normalization concepts that are not covered in the current chapter. Reference [3], in particular, is extremely advanced and represents the state of the art in this field. Reference [6] is at the same level as this text and covers both entity-relationship and normalization.

[1] C. Batini, S. Ceri, and S. B. Navathe. *Conceptual Database Design*. Redwood City, CA: Benjamin-Cummings, 1992.

[2] C. J. Date. *An Introduction to Database Systems*. 6th ed. Reading, MA: Addison-Wesley, 1995.

[3] David Maier. *The Theory of Relational Databases*. New York: Computer Science Press, 1983.

[4] Toby J. Teorey. *Database Modeling and Design: The Fundamental Principles*. 2nd ed. San Francisco: Morgan Kaufmann, 1994.

[5] Jeffrey D. Ullman. *Database and Knowledge-Base Systems*. Volume 1. Rockville, MD: Computer Science Press, 1988.

[6] Jeffrey D. Ullman and Jennifer Widom. *A First Course in Database Systems*. Englewood Cliffs, NJ: Prentice Hall, 1997.

Exercises

For the things we have to learn before we can do them, we learn by doing them.
—Aristotle

Exercises with solutions at the back of the book in "Solutions to Selected Exercises" are marked with the symbol •.

[6.1]• In Figure 6.6, if we do not assume that the number of connectors of R in the three diagrams *precisely* represents the designer's intention, but instead that the number is accidental but falls within the limits of the designer's intention, we can still conclude in some cases the min-card and max-card values for E and F relative to R. List all such values for the three diagrams of Figure 6.6.

[6.2]• As pointed out in Example 6.1.3, the orders table does not represent a relationship, but rather an entity, Orders. The Orders entity is itself related by a binary relationship to each of the three entities Customers, Agents, and Products. The relationships are the following: Customers *requests* Orders, Agents *places* Orders, and Orders *ships* Products. Draw the E-R diagram for all these entities

400

and relationships and attach all relevant attributes, designating primary keys and labeling cardinalities. Note that the diagram of Figure 6.11 is quite different, with an Orders entity made up of multiple Line_items.

[6.3]   As in the case study of Section 6.4, create an E-R design and from this generate a relational table design for a database to represent a banking business. In the database, we need to keep track of customers who have accounts at branches (of the bank). Each account is held at a specific branch, but a customer may have more than one account and an account may have more than one associated customer. We identify account by acctid, with additional attributes acct_type (savings, checking, etc.) and acct_bal (the dollar balance of the account). Each branch has an identifier bno and attribute bcity. Customers are identified by ssn (Social Security number) and have attribute cname, made up of clname, cfname, and cmidinit.

In this E-R design, you should think about how to represent the customers-accounts-branches combination. Perhaps all three of these are entities and there is a ternary relationship between them. Or perhaps there are two binary relationships, for example, one between Customers and Accounts and one between Accounts and Branches. Or perhaps there are only two entities, Customers and Branches, and has_account is a relationship between them with its own attributes, where the relationship instance represents an account. More than one solution might be correct, but you should be able to rule out at least one of these alternatives. You should explore these three designs, decide which one you prefer, and *justify ruling out at least one of them.* Think about the following question in justifying your decision: Do all of these designs allow several customers to hold the same account jointly?

[6.4]   In Example 6.6.4, assume that the functional dependencies (FDs) derived from the content are true, but now new rows can be added (that must still obey these FDs). Which of the following rows can be legally added to the rows that already exist? If it cannot be added, specify the FD number in the example that makes it illegal to add it.

(a)• a5	b6	c7	d8

(b) a2	b2	c1	d8

(c)• a3	b1	c4	d3

(d) a1	b1	c2	d5

[6.5]• As in Example 6.6.4, list all functional dependencies satisfied by the following table T, where we assume that it is the intent of the designer that exactly this set of rows should lie in the table.

T

row #	A	B	C	D
1	a1	b1	c1	d1
2	a1	b1	c2	d2
3	a1	b2	c3	d1
4	a1	b2	c4	d4

[6.6] Repeat the previous exercise with the following table T:

T

row #	A	B	C	D
1	a1	b2	c1	d1
2	a1	b1	c2	d2
3	a2	b2	c1	d3
4	a2	b1	c2	d4
5	a2	b3	c4	d5

[6.7] [HARD] We expand on the idea of Example 6.6.4, of tables with fixed content where it is the intent of the designer that *exactly* that set of rows should lie in each table, so that the functional dependencies can be determined by examination. Notice that if we are presented with a table T having a given heading (set of attributes), but containing either zero rows or one row, examination seems to allow all possible FDs to hold. In order for Definition 6.6.2 of an FD to fail, there must be at least two rows in the table that match in some column values but not in others. An *Armstrong table* T is one that contains a minimum number of rows so that from its content a specific set of FDs F will be true (and of course all FDs in F^+ as well), but all FDs not in F^+ will be false. Thus if $X \to A$ is an FD that is not in F^+, it must be true that there are two rows in T such that $u[X] = v[X]$ and $u[A] <> v[A]$.

(a)• Is the table in Example 6.6.4 an Armstrong table? Explain. Can you give a table with fewer rows that determines the same set of FDs? (Maybe not.)

(b) Is the table given in Exercise 6.6 an Armstrong table? Support your answer as in part (a).

(c) Create an Armstrong table to represent the following set of FDs on the attributes A, B, C, D, and *no others*. If other FDs exist as well, the answer fails. Try to create a table with the smallest set of rows you can find that has this property.

(1) A B $\rightarrow$ D, (2) B C $\rightarrow$ A

(d) [VERY HARD] Specify an algorithm to generate an Armstrong table from a given set of FDs on a list of attributes. This algorithm shows that such an Armstrong table will always exist.

[6.8] Give a proof of the transitivity rule of Armstrong's Axioms in Definition 6.6.6, following the form of proof used for the inclusion rule in Theorem 6.6.3 and the augmentation rule in Theorem 6.6.7.

[6.9]• Use Armstrong's Axioms from Definition 6.6.6 to derive the rules listed in Theorem 6.6.8 for which no proof was given.

[6.10] Consider the following set of rules of inference for FDs, where X, Y, Z, and W are sets of attributes and B is an individual attribute.

[1] Reflexivity rule: It is always true that $X \rightarrow X$.

[2] Projectivity rule: If $X \rightarrow Y\,Z$, then $X \rightarrow Y$.

[3] Accumulation rule: If $X \rightarrow Y\,Z$ and $Z \rightarrow B\,W$, then $X \rightarrow Y\,Z\,B$.

Show how to derive the three rules of inference in Definition 6.6.6, Armstrong's Axioms, from these rules, and how these rules can be derived from Armstrong's Axioms. Since all rules can be derived using Armstrong's Axioms (because of completeness), these three rules form an alternate complete set of rules.

[6.11] [HARD] Given a set of attributes S and a set F of FDs, we say that a set X of attributes contained in S has a nontrivial set closure under F whenever $X^+ - X$ is non-null. Let F be a minimal set of dependencies, that is, where the minimal cover for F is F. We create a *nontrivial FD basis* B by forming set closures of all sets X_i on the left side of some FD in F, then creating the FD_i in B: $X_i \rightarrow (X_i^+ - X_i)$.

(a)• Show that if X is a set of attributes that does not contain the left-hand side X_i of some FD in F, then $X^+ = X$ under closure by FDs in F.

(b) It seems like a reasonable hypothesis that all FDs $W \rightarrow Z$ in F^+, where W and Z have no attributes in common, arise directly from the nontrivial FD basis B, so that if the attribute $A \in Z$, then $A \in (X_i^+ - X_i)$ for some FD_i in B of the form $X_i \rightarrow (X_i^+ - X_i)$, with $X_i \subseteq W$. However, this simplistic hypothesis is invalid. Construct a set S of attributes and a set F of FDs that constitute a counterexample. Only two FDs are needed in F.

[6.12] Use Armstrong's Axioms and the results of Theorem 6.6.8, together with the following set of FDs from Example 6.6.4:

(1) A → B, (2) C → B, (3) D → A B C, (4) A C → D

to derive the FDs labeled (a) through (c) below. Perform your derivation in a step-by-step manner, labeling each step with the rule from the above axioms.

(a)• D → A B C D

(b) A C → B D

(c) A C → A B C D

[6.13] As in Example 6.6.6 in the text, where it is shown that the set F of FDs covers the set G, show the reverse, that the set G covers the set F.

[6.14] (a)• Demonstrate the statement of Example 6.6.9, that the functional dependencies derived in Example 6.6.4 are *not* minimal, by going through the steps of finding a minimal cover.

(b) In part (a), only one FD derived in Example 6.6.4 needed to change to make a minimal cover. Explain the need for this change with a simple application of reasoning about FD implications.

[6.15]• In Algorithm 6.6.13, step 2, show that the test performed to determine that Y^+ is unchanged passing from the set of FDs H to the set J, as defined in the algorithm, also implies that H^+ is the same as J^+.

[6.16] (a) Go through Example 6.6.8 and think about each change that was made in the set of FDs. Then try to use Armstrong's Axioms to show that each change will result in the same FD closure.

(b) In Example 6.6.8, in step 3 after we have dropped B, demonstrate that if we consider dropping A again it will still be inappropriate.

(c) Can you find an argument to show why it is unnecessary to ever consider dropping a left-hand-side attribute a second time in step 3 after considering it once and then dropping a different attribute?

[6.17] Demonstrate the statement of Example 6.6.10, that the FDs given in Example 6.6.3 for the emp_info database (the set F) form a minimal set. Demonstrate this by going through the steps of finding a minimal cover. (Use the derivational notation introduced in Example 6.6.7.)

[6.18] (a) Assume we are given three tables T, T1, and T2, with T = T1 ⋈ T2, and Head(T1) ∩ Head(T2) → Head(T2). Then if T is decomposed (projected) onto S1 and S2, where Head(S1) = Head(T1) and Head(S2) = Head(T2), this guarantees that the set of rows in S1 is a subset of rows in T1, and similarly the set of rows in S2 is a subset of rows in T2. Give an example to show why we cannot conclude that S1 = T1 and S2 = T2.

(b) Replace Join by Outer Join in part (a), find a way to extend Definition 6.7.1 to handle Lossless Outer-Join Decomposition, and show that in the end of part (a), S1 = T1 and S2 = T2.

[6.19] (a) Consider the table T given below. First show that a decomposition of this content into two tables with Head(T1) = A B and Head(T1) = B C, when rejoined, gives back the original table. However, show that this decomposition is lossy by considering removing any single row from T and looking at the resulting decomposition.

A	B	C
a1	b1	c1
a1	b1	c2
a2	b1	c1
a2	b1	c2

(b)• Explain how the table contents of T above show the "only if" part of Theorem 6.7.4, for the case of no FDs for T and this proposed decomposition.

(c) Prove the unproven "only if" part of Theorem 6.7.4, that if Head(T1) and Head(T2) are both proper subsets of Head(T), Head(T) = Head(T1) ∪ Head(T2), and Head(T1) ∩ Head(T2) does not functionally determine either Head(T1) or Head(T2), then the decomposition T into T1 or T2 will not be lossless.

[6.20] Assume that we wish to construct a database from a set of data items {A, B, C, D, E, F, G} (which will become attributes in tables) and a set F of FDs given by

$$F = (1)\ B\ C\ D \rightarrow A,\ (2)\ B\ C \rightarrow E,\ (3)\ A \rightarrow F,\ (4)\ F \rightarrow G,\ (5)\ C \rightarrow D,\ (6)\ A \rightarrow G.$$

(a) Find the minimal cover for this set of FDs and name this set G. (Use the derivational notation introduced in Example 6.6.7.)

(b)• Start with the table T containing all these attributes, and perform a lossless decomposition into two tables, T_1 and T_2, that make up a 2NF decomposition. List carefully the keys for each table (T, T_1, and T_2) and the FDs that lie in each table.

(c) Continue decomposition to bring this database to 3NF. Is this decomposition also BCNF?

(d)• Use Algorithm 6.8.8 and the set G of FDs to achieve a lossless 3NF decomposition that preserves FDs of G. Is this the same as the decomposition in part (c)?

[6.21] Assume that we wish to construct a database from a set of data items {A, B, C, D, E, F, G, H} (which will become attributes in tables) and a set F of FDs given by

(1) A → B C , (2) A B E → C D G H, (3) C → G D, (4) D → G, (5) E → F.

(a) Find the minimal cover for this set of FDs and name this set G. (Use the derivational notation introduced in Example 6.6.7.)

(b) Start with the table T containing all these attributes and perform a lossless decomposition into a 2NF but not a 3NF schema. List carefully the keys for each table (T, T_1, and T_2) and the FDs that lie in each table. Justify the fact that the decomposition is lossless. Explain why it is 2NF but not 3NF.

(c) Continue decomposition to bring this database to 3NF. Is this decomposition also BCNF?

(d) Use Algorithm 6.8.8 and the set G of FDs from part (a) to achieve a lossless 3NF decomposition that preserves FDs of G. Is this the same as the decomposition in part (c)?

[6.22]• Repeat the relational design of the banking database of Exercise 6.3, but this time use a normalization approach. This will require you to come up with the proper set of FDs, and you should make sure that your answer makes sense. Compare your output to the E-R solution.

[6.23] Assume that we wish to construct a database from a set of data items {A, B, C, D, E, F, G, H, J}, which will become attributes in tables, and a set F of FDs forming a minimal cover given by

(1) A B → C D, (2) A → E, (3) B → F H, (4) C → G, (5) D → B, (6) G → C, (7) H → I.

(a) Create a lossless join decomposition of the table T that is 3NF and preserves all the FDs. Use the algorithm provided in the text to determine the headings for the tables of the decomposition and underline a key for each table.

(b) One or more of the tables from part (a) have two candidate keys. Find them and demonstrate that they are keys.

(c) Prove that the decomposition is lossless.

(d) Is the decomposition you have created a BCNF decomposition? Explain why or why not.

[6.24] Consider again the airline reservation database from the case study of Section 6.4. Note that passengers come together at gates to depart on flights; it might seem that we could replace the two binary relationships marshals and travels_on of Figure 6.14 with a ternary relationship, departs, that relates Passengers, Gates, and Flights. See below.

We note that the relationship is 1-N-N since one gate has many flights and many passengers, whose entity has max-card = 1 in the relationship. As mentioned at the end of Section 6.2, this means that we can represent the relationship by foreign keys in one of the entity tables. Specifically, since the Passengers entity participates with max-card = 1, we adjoin foreign keys for gates and flights to identify the unique gate and flight for a passenger.

(a) Translate the E-R design with the ternary relationship departs into relational tables.

(b) How does this relational table design differ from the design at the end of Section 6.4? Say which is preferable and justify your answer. (You might try to come up with a question like the one at the end of Exercise 6.3.)

(c) Create the proper set of FDs for the airline reservation database and then perform normalization, following Algorithm 6.8.8, to arrive at a relational table design. Does this shed any light on the question of part (b)?

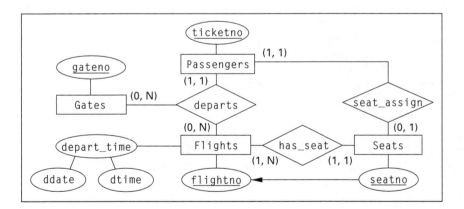

(d) If you created the right FDs, you should find that there is no distinct table for gates. One problem with having gateno as the attribute of another table is the delete anomaly: if the last flight leaves from some gate, we no longer have any record that the gate exists. But what the normalization process is saying is that there doesn't seem to be any *reason* to remember that the gate exists. We can imagine adding a new attribute to the design, gatecap, which represents the seat capacity for passengers waiting at a gate. Now a new attempt at normalization will come up with a separate table for gates. Explain why.

(e) Note that with the design of part (d) for gates and capacity, we can easily imagine program logic that assigns a gate for a flight that is not already assigned to a flight during the hour before departure, and that has seating capacity to hold passengers for the seats of the flight. But suppose that all gates have the same seating capacity. We might still want to assign gates to flights, and now the delete anomaly mentioned in part (d) is a real problem. What does this imply about the normalization approach?

Integrity, Views, Security, and Catalogs   7

Exact and careful model building should embody constraints that the final answer had in any case to satisfy.
—Francis Harry Compton Crick, 1988

In Chapter 6 we learned how to model an enterprise by designing a set of relational tables and the functional dependencies that represent it. The current chapter begins by detailing the steps the database administrator (DBA) must take to convert such a design into physical form, using new clauses of the Create Table statement to create relational tables. We concentrate on relational tables in the current chapter because the details of object-relational tables in Chapter 4 were presented as optional coverage. For some idea of how to extend the capabilities of the current chapter to the object-relational model, especially extension of Create Table to Create Object Table, you should refer to Appendix C, which provides a general reference to SQL statement syntax.

The first section of the current chapter concentrates on how to create physical (relational) tables and how to impose *integrity constraints* on the columns that will guarantee a *faithful representation*. Integrity constraints are meant to ensure that the data interdependencies identified during the logical design phase of Chapter 6 are not unwittingly broken by poorly posed SQL Update statements; that is, we wish to guarantee that the integrity of the data is preserved in the presence of update errors. In later sections of the current chapter, we also detail numerous other tasks the DBA must carry out for large, heavily accessed databases, before desired information can be easily and efficiently accessed by end users. The DBA must begin by creating the tables and constraints and loading the data. Then there is a facility, explained for the first time in this chapter, to provide *views* of the data, virtually restructuring the physical tables into variant table forms (which have no physical existence), to simplify access to data. The DBA must also provide for *security*, so that only authorized users are able to read or update certain confidential data. The structure of the various tables, views, and other objects of a database are made available to the DBA through a set of system-defined tables, called *system catalogs*, which are described at the end of this chapter. The DBA is also responsible for performance issues, providing indexes to speed up access to tables, and various other types of tuning; the details of such tuning are covered in the next chapter.

The DBA who deals with an enterprise-critical database has an extremely responsible position and must be aware of the needs of all database users supported by the system—end users as well as application programmers. One aim of this text is to provide a basic grounding in the concepts needed by a DBA. The current chapter introduces many of the commands and features a DBA needs to do his or her work. Throughout the text we concentrate on database concepts from an "operational" standpoint. This means that the emphasis is on material required to make intelligent trade-off decisions as a DBA, rather than on the details needed by a systems programmer to design and implement the internals of a database system software product. An operational approach does not imply a less rigorous coverage of concepts, but it does mean that we will concentrate on effects, say, of a B-tree data indexing structure, rather than on the details of programming a B-tree. It is probably fair to say that an operational understanding must precede most system programming considerations: a programmer writing database system code who doesn't have a clear understanding of the considerations important to a DBA is operating under a serious handicap.

We have already seen some of the commands that a database administrator uses to create and load a table. In Chapter 3 we introduced the SQL statement

```
create table customers (cid char(4) not null, cname varchar(13),
    city varchar(20), discnt real, primary key(cid));
```

As we will see, this example illustrates only a small part of the full syntax.

7.1   Integrity Constraints

An *integrity constraint* is a *rule,* usually formulated by the creator of a database table (the database administrator for important tables) from design considerations of the kind we saw in Chapter 6, that must be obeyed by all SQL Update statements. As an example, if we make the rule that the cid column in the customers table of our CAP database must be unique (making it a *candidate* or *primary key*), then it should be impossible for a future insert to the customers table to create a row that duplicates an existing value in its cid column. This is what is known as a *faithful representation*. Indeed, for the integrity constraints we will be introducing, any update action—Insert, Update, or Delete—that breaks the integrity constraint will fail to execute. As we saw in Chapter 6, a number of integrity constraints come out of the design process—for example, columns that are part of a key in a table cannot be null and the key must have unique values. Before discussing some of the virtues and limitations of integrity constraints, we need to explain how they are implemented on commercial database systems. We will begin by explaining something about SQL standards, which dictate that integrity constraints are specified in the Create Table command.

Integrity Constraints in the Create Table Statement

The Basic SQL Create Table statement is shown in Figure 7.1. Recall from Chapter 3 that we provide *Basic SQL* as a common standard, combining public standards such as X/Open and SQL-99. We limit Basic SQL syntax to capabilities that are available on most major database products. In particular, we provide a set of features common to the three products **ORACLE**, **DB2 UDB**, and **INFORMIX**. Note that a user who creates a table (often the DBA) becomes the *owner* of that table, and we will see that this has special implications when we discuss database security.

Referring to Figure 7.1, we see that an optional syntax element, [schema.], can appear before a tablename. See Section 7.4 for a description of *schemas*, which are used to differentiate identical object names in a database. Users are typically given schema names (the same as their user name) to qualify the names of tables and other objects they create within a database. For example, user eoneil might have a customers table, with full *schema-qualified name* eoneil.customers, in the same database as the table poneil.customers. When user eoneil uses the name customers, it refers to eoneil.customers, and likewise for user poneil, and in this way there is no ambiguity. If user

```
CREATE TABLE [schema.]tablename
    ({columnname datatype [DEFAULT {default_constant|NULL}] [col_constr {col_constr...}]
        | table_constr}-- choice of either columnname-definition or table_constr
    {,{columnname datatype [DEFAULT {default_constant|NULL}] [col_constr {col_constr...}]
        | table_constr}
    ...});                       -- zero or more additional columnname-def or table_constr
```

The col_constr form that constrains a single column value follows:

```
    {NOT NULL |                    -- this is the first of a set of choices
    [CONSTRAINT constraintname]    -- if later choices used, optionally name constraint
        UNIQUE                     -- the rest of the choices start here
        | PRIMARY KEY
        | CHECK (search_cond)
        | REFERENCES tablename [(columnname)]
            [ON DELETE CASCADE]}
```

The table_constr form that constrains multiple columns at once follows:

```
    [CONSTRAINT constraintname]
        {UNIQUE (columnname {, columnname...})         -- choose one of these clauses
        | PRIMARY KEY (columnname {, columnname...})
        | CHECK (search_condition)
        | FOREIGN KEY (columnname {, columnname...})   -- following is all one clause
            REFERENCES tablename [(columnname {, columnname...})]
                [ON DELETE CASCADE]}
```

Figure 7.1 Basic SQL Syntax for Create Table

`eoneil` has appropriate authorization, she can access a table that is not in her schema by using the schema-qualified name: `poneil.customers`.

We start below by defining some of the clauses of the Create Table statement in Figure 7.1, and then give an example for our CAP database. Following that, we explain special syntax extensions in **ORACLE** and **DB2 UDB**.

DEFINITION 7.1.1 Clauses of the Create Table Command. The Create Table command of Figure 7.1 begins by naming the table being created, by specifying a tablename with an optional schema name qualifier. If a schema name is not given in the Create Table statement, it will default to the name of the user executing the Create Table statement. After the tablename specification, the Create Table statement lists in parentheses a comma-separated sequence of column definitions or table constraints. Column definitions and table constraints can be freely mixed in any order. Each column definition contains columnname and datatype and an optional DEFAULT clause. This clause specifies the default value that the database system will supply for the column if the SQL Insert statement does not furnish a value. (Note that bulk-load commands such as Load are not covered by the SQL standards and are therefore not constrained to provide this value, although some do.) The default value supplied can be a constant of appropriate datatype supplied as `defaultvalue`, or NULL.

Each column definition is also allowed to have a list of *column constraints,* symbolized in Figure 7.1 by col_constr, which consists of a sequence of optional clauses explained below. ∎

DEFINITION 7.1.2 Column Constraints. The col_constr clauses appearing in the Create Table statement of Figure 7.1 are optional clauses associated with single columns.

The NOT NULL condition has already been explained; it means that null values cannot occur in this column. If NOT NULL appears in a col_constr, then the DEFAULT clause cannot specify NULL; if neither the DEFAULT clause nor the NOT NULL clause appears in a column definition, then DEFAULT NULL is assumed.

The CONSTRAINT constraintname clause allows us to specify a name for each constraint other than NOT NULL, so that we can later drop the constraint with an Alter Table statement we will introduce a bit later in this chapter, without re-creating the whole table.

The UNIQUE clause can be specified even if NOT NULL is not, and the column is then constrained so that all non-null column values in the table are unique, but multiple nulls can exist for this column. We say that a column on a table is a *candidate key* if it is declared both NOT NULL and UNIQUE.

The PRIMARY KEY clause specifies a column to be a primary key—that is, a candidate key referred to by default in another table in a REFERENCES clause (see below). A column with the PRIMARY KEY column constraint is implicitly defined to be NOT NULL and UNIQUE. There can be at most one PRIMARY KEY clause in any Create Table statement. The UNIQUE clause and PRIMARY KEY clause cannot both be used for a column, although the PRIMARY KEY clause and the NOT NULL clause can be used together. In fact, a number of older products required that a column declared PRIMARY KEY also had to be NOT NULL. This is no longer standard, but for robustness with older products we often follow this convention.

If the CHECK clause appears, then each row is constrained to contain a value in this column that satisfies the specified search_condition. (In the X/Open standard and **DB2 UDB**, this search_condition is only permitted to contain constant values and references to the specific column name value being constrained in the current row; no other column references or set functions are permitted. **ORACLE** allows references to other column names of the same row.)

For a column defined with a REFERENCES tablename [(columnname] clause, each value in the column must be either null or a value that appears in a column of the table referenced; the column of the table referenced is either the single-column primary key of that table or else the column specified in the optional column name included in the REFERENCES clause. Any specified column name of the table referenced must be unique, or else the Create Table statement containing this REFERENCES clause will fail. (Nulls in the column name referenced are permitted, however.) The optional ON DELETE CASCADE clause that follows the REFERENCES clause requires that when a row in the referenced table is deleted that is referenced by rows in the referencing table (the table with the REFERENCES clause), then those rows in the referencing table are deleted. If no ON DELETE clause appears, then such a delete of a referenced row will simply fail to execute because of this constraint.

■

EXAMPLE 7.1.1

Here is a possible Create Table statement for the customers table.

```
create table customers (cid char(4) not null unique, cname
    varchar(13), city varchar(20),
    discnt real constraint discnt_max check (discnt <= 15.0));
```

Note that the cid column is defined here to be a *candidate key* for the customers table because of the NOT NULL and UNIQUE clauses; while cid must have unique values on each row, it is not understood as a result of this statement to be a *primary key;* we will see what this means shortly. This Create Table statement also constrains any row of the customers table to have a discnt value that does not exceed 15.0. This constraint is named discnt_max so that later we can drop it by using the Alter Table statement. However, we will not be able to add it back, as we could with a named table constraint. As we will see, we can rewrite this constraint as a more general table constraint.

■

DEFINITION 7.1.3 Table Constraints. The table_constr clauses appearing in the Create Table statement of Figure 7.1 are listed below. The col_constr form is merely a special case of the table_constr form, except for the column-specific NOT NULL form.

The UNIQUE clause has the same meaning as UNIQUE in the case of a col_constr, except that it is possible to specify a set of columns that must be unique in combination. Therefore this is a way to specify a multi-column candidate key for a table (although we could specify only a single column and replace a column constraint with a table constraint in this way).

The PRIMARY KEY clause specifies a non-empty set of columns to be a primary key—that is, a candidate key referred to by default in another table in a REFERENCES clause (see below). Every column that participates in a PRIMARY KEY clause is implicitly defined to be NOT NULL. There can be at most one PRIMARY KEY clause in any Create Table statement, whether the clause is a column constraint or table constraint.

We say that a set of columns in a table is a *candidate key* if the set of columns is declared UNIQUE and every individual column in the set is declared NOT NULL.

The CHECK clause as a table constraint is similar to the column CHECK clause and limits acceptable values for a set of columns; the search_condition can refer to any column values in the same table, on the same row for which an Update or Insert statement is in process. As in the column analog, no Subqueries or set functions are allowed in the X/Open standard. A named feature extending SQL-99 beyond Core allows a Subquery in the CHECK clause and the expanded power is extremely significant, but most database products, including **ORACLE** and **DB2 UDB**, do not support this extension.

The FOREIGN KEY . . . REFERENCES . . . [ON DELETE . . .] clause is a single clause with keywords in this order. The FOREIGN KEY columnname list specifies a set of columns in the table being created whose values on each row, if none of them are null, are constrained to be equal to the values of a set of columns on some row of another table specified by the associated REFERENCES clause. When the columns in the other table being referenced form the primary key, the REFERENCES clause does not need to specify a list of columns. When one of the column values in the FOREIGN KEY column-name list is null on some row, no restriction whatsoever holds on the column values of that row.

The optional ON DELETE CASCADE clause specifies that deletion of a row in the *referenced* table that is actively being referenced by rows in the *referencing* table (with the ON DELETE CASCADE clause) causes deletion of all referencing rows in the referencing table. This action, although seemingly drastic, maintains the constraint. *Without this optional clause, attempted deletions of a referenced row will fail.*

A detailed discussion of the concepts of primary key, foreign key, and referential integrity is deferred until a later part of this section.   ∎

Here is an example to illustrate some of these concepts.

EXAMPLE 7.1.2
We provide appropriate Create Table statements for the customers and orders tables in the CAP database. See Figure 7.2 for the E-R diagram on which these Create Table definitions are based, a solution to Exercise 6.2 at the end of Chapter 6. Recall that the (x, y) pair labeling a connection between an attribute A and an entity E means that x = min-card(A, E) and y = max-card(A, E). In particular, a value x = 0 means that nulls are allowed in this column, and a value x = 1 implies *mandatory participation* and means that the column should be defined with a NOT NULL clause in the Create Table statement. The identifier attribute for each entity in the E-R diagram is underlined, and this generally translates to a PRIMARY KEY clause in the Create Table statement. We add a few CHECK clauses in the Create Table statement that have no counterpart in the E-R diagram. Discussion of the FOREIGN KEY . . . REFERENCES clause in the orders table is deferred until we explain referential integrity, a bit later in this section.

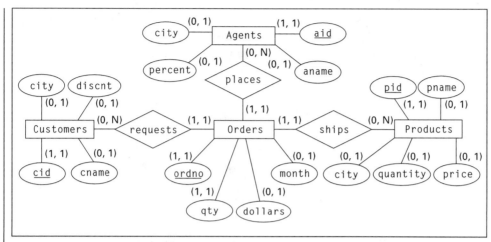

Figure 7.2 E-R Diagram for CAP Database

```
create table customers (cid char(4) not null, cname varchar(13),
    city varchar(20),
    discnt real constraint discnt_max check(discnt <= 15.0),
    primary key (cid));

create table orders (ordno integer not null, month char(3),
    cid char(4) not null, aid char(3) not null, pid char(3) not null,
    qty integer not null constraint qtyck check(qty >= 0),
    dollars float default 0.0 constraint dollarsck check(dollars >= 0.0),
    primary key (ordno),
    constraint cidref foreign key (cid) references customers,
    constraint aidref foreign key (aid) references agents,
    constraint pidref foreign key (pid) references products);
```

Constraints for the orders table are examined further in Example 7.1.3, when we discuss how the motivation for referential integrity arises from E-R transformations. ■

In the following subsections, we discuss variations from the Basic SQL standard of how constraints are imposed in the database products **ORACLE** and **DB2 UDB**.

Create Table Statement in ORACLE

The **ORACLE** Create Table statement supports all the integrity constraint clauses (col_constr and table_constr clauses) of the Basic SQL syntax in Figure 7.1, with additional ENABLE and DISABLE clauses as shown in Figure 7.3. **ORACLE** syntax also supports one minor variation from the Basic SQL syntax, in that it allows an optional constraint name to appear before NOT NULL, so that NOT NULL can be dropped as a column constraint by using the Alter Table statement. Further, NULL is allowed in **ORACLE** as well as NOT NULL.

```
CREATE TABLE [schema.]tablename
    (... as in Basic SQL, except with [NOT] NULL)
    [disk storage and other clauses (not covered, or deferred)]
| CREATE TABLE tablename
    (... as in Basic SQL, columnnames and datatypes can be left out if no
        constraints are specified)
    [disk storage and other clauses (not covered, or deferred)]
        AS subquery;
```

The col_constr form that constrains a single column value follows:

```
    ... as in Basic SQL
    [ENABLE and DISABLE clauses for constraints];
    [storage and transaction specifications];
```

The table_constr form that constrains multiple columns at once follows:

```
    ... as in Basic SQL
    [ENABLE and DISABLE clauses for constraints];
    [storage and transaction specifications];
```

Figure 7.3 ORACLE Relational Create Table Syntax (without Object-Relational Extensions)

Note in Figure 7.3 that there are two forms of the Create Table statement. Both forms refer to "disk storage and other clauses" that define, among other things, how rows of the table will be stored on disk. We defer consideration of these clauses until Chapter 8.

The second Create Table form of Figure 7.3, with the AS Subquery clause, lets the user create a table containing the result of a Subquery from other tables. The column names and datatypes of the new table can be inherited from the target list of the Subquery (assuming column aliases are used to give names to expressions), and thus the names and datatypes of the columns in the table created can be left out of this Create Table syntax. Note that column and table constraints are *not* inherited, not even from a Subquery from a single table, and column names must be specified if the user wishes to create such constraints as part of the Create Table specification (datatypes can still be left out, however).

Note the ENABLE and DISABLE clauses allow the user to define a constraint but then disable it before creating the table; ENABLE is the default if no clause appears to DISABLE the constraint. The constraint can be reenabled later by the Alter Table statement. The only problem with this ENABLE/DISABLE capability is that it is not portable to other products, so we will be using other capabilities in the Alter Table statement to achieve approximately the same functionality. For more details of the **ORACLE** Create Table statement, refer to Appendix C, or to the *ORACLE8 Server SQL Reference Manual* (see reference [13] in "Suggestions for Further Reading" at the end of this chapter).

Create Table Statement in INFORMIX

The **INFORMIX** Create Table statement supports all the Basic SQL clauses of Figure 7.1, with one minor variation: **INFORMIX** requires all of the column definitions to precede the table constraint definitions, whereas Figure 7.1 allows the two types of definitions to be mixed together in any order. As in Figure 7.3, the **INFORMIX** Create Table statement also has product-specific "disk storage and other clauses." There is also a form of ENABLE/ DISABLE for constraints as in **ORACLE**, but we do not document it here. For more details of the **INFORMIX** Create Table statement, refer to Appendix C, or to the *INFOR-MIX Guide to SQL: Reference* (see reference [8] in "Suggestions for Further Reading" at the end of this chapter).

Create Table Statement in DB2 UDB

The **DB2 UDB** Create Table statement supports all the Basic SQL clauses. It also has product-specific "disk storage and other clauses," which we will cover in Chapter 8. Finally the FOREIGN KEY REFERENCES clause of the table constraint has more options for actions (shown later in Figure 7.6). For more details of the **DB2 UDB** Create Table statement, refer to Appendix C, or to the *DB2 Universal Database SQL Reference Manual* (see reference [4] in "Suggestions for Further Reading" at the end of this chapter).

Primary Keys, Foreign Keys, and Referential Integrity

In this subsection we explain the FOREIGN KEY . . . REFERENCES clause in the Create Table statement of Figure 7.1, and how the implied integrity constraints (called referential integrity constraints) are enforced for ensuing update statements. We begin with an example from our CAP database to motivate the definition of referential integrity in Definition 7.1.4.

EXAMPLE 7.1.3 Referential Integrity.

In the E-R diagram of the CAP database pictured in Figure 7.2, we note that all relationships, requests, places, and ships, are many-to-one, with the Orders entity representing the "many" side of the relationship (see Definition 6.2.2). Each single customer requests many orders, each agent places many orders, each product is shipped in many orders, but each order has only one defining customer, agent, and product. Thus by Transformation RULE 4 in Section 6.2, the orders table needs to contain a foreign key column to represent each of the entity instances for Customers, Agents, and Products to which the Orders instance is related. For example, the orders table in the Create Table statement of Example 7.1.2 contains a foreign key cid to represent the Customers instance that requests the particular order represented by this row. Note in particular that the cid column in the orders table does not represent an *attribute* of the Orders entity, but actually represents an instance of the requests relationship.

This is such an important concept that we repeat it again in a slightly different way: each specific cid value in a row of orders actually corresponds to a relationship instance connecting an Orders entity and a Customers entity. The *referential integrity* constraint simply insists that we avoid "dangling" references in foreign keys to nonexistent primary keys in another table, so the relationship instance specified will always make sense for each row in the orders table. Thus a cid value in orders must also exist in customers. This constraint is guaranteed in Example 7.1.2 by the foreign key (cid) references customers clause in the Create Table statements for orders.

There is also a different constraint on cid, arising in Figure 7.2 from the fact that the Orders entity has mandatory participation in the requests relationship (because the label on the connecting link between Orders and requests has a min-card of 1). Given this, it is necessary that there is a non-null cid value in each row in orders (clearly different from referential integrity, which states that every non-null cid value in orders must reference a real cid value in customers). This mandatory participation constraint is imposed in Example 7.1.2 by the NOT NULL clause following the cid definition in the Create Table statement for orders. ■

To repeat: referential integrity implies a rule for the CAP database that no row in the orders table can contain a cid, aid, or pid value unless it refers to an existing value in the corresponding customers, agents, or products tables. This rule basically says that as we place rows in orders, we want to avoid an implicit statement of the form: "Trust me. Although I'm referring to a nonexistent agent (or product or customer) in this order, it will all make sense eventually when I have a chance to define a new row in the agents table." We are insisting that the agents row be inserted *first*, before the orders row that refers to it. The reason we are imposing the referential integrity rule comes from fundamental considerations of logical design, but it also works well in practice. We can now say that if an attempt is made to insert such a "nonreferential" value in orders, it probably means that an error has been made by someone typing data for the orders table. For example, consider a row such as the following to be added to the orders table with the content of Figure 2.2.

ordno	month	cid	aid	pid	qty	dollars
1011	jan	c001	a0@	p01	1000	450.00

There is no aid value "a0@" in the primary key for agents; this attempted row insert probably means that there was a slip in typing the digit 2 after the letters a0 in the orders column aid ("@" is the shift value of 2). It seems there is no good argument that a new cid, aid, or pid value should validly appear in orders for the first time; we are making a reasonable rule that a new customer, agent, or product must appear in the appropriate "home" table first, to give us a chance to catch important errors. Of course a referential integrity constraint comes at a certain cost in performance: the resources used to perform an insert to the orders table may be quite badly affected when three referential integrity rules such as this are imposed, since each insert of an order will require a lookup of a primary key value in three separate tables.

Now let us clarify our thinking to create a definition: a *referential integrity* constraint insists that values appearing in the foreign key of some table in a database must be matched by values in a primary key of another table (possibly the same one, as when rows in an employees table, with primary key eid, reference through the mgrid column the eid of some other employee). But what are we to do about null values? We know that a null value cannot exist in a primary key (see RULE 4, the entity integrity rule, at the end of Section 2.4, and the explanation of the PRIMARY KEY clause near the end of Definition 7.1.2). But what rule do we wish to adopt about nulls existing in a foreign key? We will see that one of the actions of the ON DELETE table constraint clause in **DB2 UDB** (Figure 7.6) is to set nulls in the foreign key when a row with that primary key value is deleted. So database products allow nulls to exist in a foreign key, and we need to give a careful definition.

DEFINITION 7.1.4 Foreign Key, Referential Integrity. A set of columns F in table T1 is defined as a *foreign key* of T1 if the combination of values of F in any row is required to either contain at least one null value, or else to match the value combination of a set of columns P representing a candidate or primary key of a referenced table T2. Saying this in a different way, a referential integrity constraint is in force if the columns of F in any row of T1 must either (1) have null values in at least one column that allows null values, or (2) have no null values and be equal to the value combination of P on some row of T2. ∎

Note that some of the columns of a foreign key for a table might figure in a candidate key or even a primary key for that same table and therefore not be *nullable*; that is, they appear in a NOT NULL or PRIMARY KEY clause of the Create Table statement. However, Definition 7.1.4 implies that if *optional participation* in a relationship is to be supported by the foreign key, then at least one column of a foreign key must be nullable and thus able to represent the *existence* of a relationship instance; if the relationship instance is no longer valid, possibly because of a delete of a primary key row with a SET NULL action on the candidate key, then a null value in such a nullable column means that the entire foreign key is invalid, that is, null.

EXAMPLE 7.1.4

Recall that in Section 2.2 we said that the *domain of an attribute* is usually considered to be an *enumerated* set of possible values from which column values can be drawn. However, no major database supports such enumerated datatypes. Thus for example, the city columns of customers, agents, and products are simply constrained to be character strings, and it is not possible to provide a datatype that enumerates valid city names. However, it is possible to provide the functionality of an enumerated type if we are willing to create a new table known as cities, containing all acceptable city names. (The same city name might appear numerous times in distinct states, and even in distinct countries, but assume that we don't care about that; we ignored states and countries for simplicity in our original example tables, and it is clear how to generalize, for example, to unique city-state pairs.)

```
create table cities (city varchar(20) not null,
    primary key (city) );
create table customers (cid char(4) not null, cname varchar(13),
    city varchar(20), discnt real check(discnt <= 15.0),
    primary key (cid),
    foreign key (city) references cities);
```

The city values in the cities table are unique and make an appropriate primary key, whereas the city value in customers is a secondary key that must match some (primary key) value in the cities table. This constraint ensures that no city value will occur in customers if it is not listed in the cities table, and therefore has the effect of an enumerated domain. ■

Recall that integrity constraints ensure that the integrity of the data is preserved in the presence of poorly posed Update statements. What restrictions on row updates are actually implied by foreign key constraints? What tests must be performed to guarantee conformance? Recall that in the ON DELETE clause of Figure 7.1, the CASCADE action specified that if a row of the referenced primary key table was deleted, rows would also be deleted in the table being created that had foreign key values that referenced that row. However, this is not the only situation that can arise. Consider the three SQL statements, Insert, Delete, and Update, that might be used to perform row updates, and the two columns that might be affected, the primary key of one table and the referencing foreign key of another table. A matrix of necessary tests to detect broken integrity constraints is shown in Figure 7.4.

It should be clear that the two cells in the matrix that specify "no test" represent cases that cannot conceivably cause the referential integrity constraint to fail. For example, given that all value combinations in a foreign key correspond to value combinations in the primary key, it is impossible that inserting a new row with new primary key values will invalidate this property. The cells in the matrix labeled test-1 through test-4, on the other hand, correspond to situations where the system needs to perform a test to ensure that an update of this kind does not invalidate referential integrity. For example, in deleting a row from a primary key (test-1), we might remove a primary key value that is referenced by some set of rows in the foreign key column (this is handled by the ON DELETE clause we have been discussing). An update of a primary key column (test-2) could also have the effect of removing a referenced primary key, and the ON DELETE actions of **DB2 UDB** (discussed below, see Figure 7.6) are extended to include this case. An ON UPDATE clause to control the response in this event is part of the Full SQL-99 standard, and **DB2 UDB** also offers such an ON UPDATE clause.

Clearly we must also test any new insert of a row in the foreign key table (test-3) to assure ourselves that it references a valid primary key, and an update of a foreign key column (test-4) to a new value also requires such a test. Both of these cases are understood to be performed when such an insert occurs, and the default action if this test fails is NO ACTION, that is, to disallow the insert or update that would create an invalid foreign key. From the types of tests being performed, efficiency must clearly be a primary consideration when determining to use referential integrity in a marginal case. For exam-

	Insert	Delete	Update
Primary key (referenced by a foreign key)	no test	test-1	test-2
Foreign key (referencing primary key)	test-3	no test	test-4

Figure 7.4 Matrix of Tests for Referential Integrity

	Insert	Delete	Update
Primary key (referenced by a foreign key)	No test needed	ON DELETE... or default of NO ACTION	ON DELETE... or ON UPDATE... or default of NO ACTION
Foreign key	Statement fails if necessary	No test needed	Statement fails if necessary

Figure 7.5 Referential Integrity Tests and SQL Clauses That Specify Resulting Actions

ple, when a new row is inserted in the `customers` table of Example 7.1.4, the system will need to look up the `city` value in a `cities` table that may contain many thousands of rows, a nontrivial additional responsibility. The functionality provided might be exactly what the DBA desires, but it is important to be aware of the cost in terms of diminished capacity of updates on any given hardware configuration. Figure 7.5 summarizes the SQL clauses and their relationship to the tests and actions we have been discussing.

Foreign Key Constraints: Product Variations

The major database products all support the Basic SQL FOREIGN KEY clause in Figure 7.1:

```
| FOREIGN KEY (columnname {, columnname...})
      REFERENCES tablename [(columnname {, columnname...})]
         [ON DELETE CASCADE]
```

The corresponding FOREIGN KEY clause for columns specifies only one column in the referenced table. In the discussion above, we noted that the default action when there is no ON DELETE clause can be called the NO ACTION option, meaning that attempted deletes that break the constraint will fail, resulting in no action at all. Figure 7.6 shows that X/Open, Full SQL-99, and **DB2 UDB** allow an explicit NO ACTION specification in the constraint, while **ORACLE** and **INFORMIX** offer it only through absence of the ON DELETE clause.

	ORACLE, INFORMIX	DB2 UDB	X/Open, Full SQL-99
ON DELETE...	CASCADE |SET NULL	NO ACTION |CASCADE |SET NULL |RESTRICT	NO ACTION |CASCADE |SET NULL |SET DEFAULT |RESTRICT (SQL-99 only)
Without ON DELETE	NO ACTION effect	NO ACTION effect	NO ACTION effect

Figure 7.6 ON DELETE Actions Available for Foreign Key Constraints, by Product and Standards

DB2 UDB supports all the ON DELETE syntax defined in Full SQL-99 except for SET DEFAULT. For example, consider the foreign key, cid, in the orders table that references the primary key of the customers table. What action should be taken in response to a Delete statement that removes a row from the customers table whose cid value is referenced as a foreign key from rows of the orders table? The four actions permitted in **DB2 UDB** are NO ACTION, CASCADE, SET NULL, and RESTRICT. With the CASCADE effect, when the customers row with a given cid value was deleted, all orders rows referring to that customer cid would also be deleted, and deletes would continue recursively for other rows with a cascaded foreign key dependency on other rows deleted. With the NO ACTION or RESTRICT effect, the delete of the customers row would be rejected (there is a very subtle distinction between the two); the NO ACTION effect is the default if none is specified. With the SET NULL effect, the customers row would be deleted and cid values in the orders table that refer to that row would be set to null. (The column cid in orders must therefore not be created with the NOT NULL or PRIMARY KEY specification.) If the ON DELETE clause is missing from this FOREIGN KEY specification, then the ON DELETE NO ACTION option is assumed. The ON DELETE NO ACTION specification is also the default action assumed by the SQL standards (and **DB2 UDB**), when no ON DELETE clause is provided.

The Alter Table Statement

The Alter Table statement allows the DBA to alter the structure of a table originally specified in a Create Table statement, adding or modifying columns, and adding or deleting various constraints as well. Anyone using an Alter Table statement must be the owner of the table in question (or have Alter privilege on it in some products), and may be required to have other privileges as well. We will cover privileges of this kind in a later section of this chapter.

The Alter Table statement was not defined in older standards. For this reason, the **ORACLE**, **DB2 UDB**, and **INFORMIX** products provide a number of features with slightly different syntax. Since no standard seems to provide a good picture of the Alter Table statement as it is implemented in practice, we will refrain from providing a Basic SQL standard form and simply display the vendor forms.

Note the usefulness of constraint names in the Alter Table forms of Figures 7.7, 7.8, and 7.9. If a table constraint is named, the table owner can DROP it by specifying the name. A new named table constraint can be added by using the ADD clause. A column constraint cannot be the subject of an ADD clause, but recall that column constraints are just short versions of table constraints, so most such constraints (other than NOT NULL) can be added that way. In **ORACLE**, you can enable and disable individual constraints, that is, turn them on and off, via the ENABLE and DISABLE clauses, while they remain defined in the database. We do not go into this feature here, however, because it isn't portable between products. A portable method would be to DROP a named constraint and later ADD the same constraint back.

ORACLE, **DB2 UDB**, and **INFORMIX** have nearly the same capabilities, but a number of differences in syntax. For example, the **ORACLE** form for Alter Table in Figure 7.7

```
ALTER TABLE tablename
    [ADD ({columnname datatype
            [DEFAULT {default_constant|NULL}] [col_constr {col_constr...}] | table_constr}
        {, {columnname datatype
            [DEFAULT {default_constant|NULL}] [col_constr {col_constr...}] | table_constr}
        ...})]                       -- zero or more added columnname-def or table_constr
    [DROP {COLUMN columnname | (columnname {, columnname...})}]
    [MODIFY (columnname data-type
            [DEFAULT {default_constant|NULL}] [[NOT] NULL]
        {, columnname data-type
            [DEFAULT {default_constant|NULL}] [[NOT] NULL]
        ...})]
    [DROP CONSTRAINT constr_name]
    [DROP PRIMARY KEY]
    [disk storage and other clauses (not covered, or deferred)]
    [any clause above can be repeated, in any order]
    [ENABLE and DISABLE clauses for constraints];
```

Figure 7.7   ORACLE Form for Alter Table Statement

```
ALTER TABLE tablename
    [ADD [COLUMN] columnname datatype
        [DEFAULT {default_constant|NULL}] [col_constr {col_constr...}]
    [ADD table_constr]
    [DROP CONSTRAINT constr_name]
    [DROP PRIMARY KEY]
    [repeated ADD or DROP clauses, in any order]
    [disk storage and other clauses (not covered, or deferred)];
```

Figure 7.8   DB2 UDB Form for Alter Table Syntax

```
ALTER TABLE tablename
    [ADD new_col | (new_col {, new_col...})]
    [DROP columnname | (columnname {, columnname...})]
    [ADD CONSTRAINT table_constr | (table_constr {, table_constr...})]
    [DROP CONSTRAINT constraintname | (constraintname {, constraintname...})]
    [repeated ADD or DROP clauses, in any order]
    [disk storage and other clauses (not covered, or deferred)];
```

The new_col form that constrains a single column value follows::
```
    columnname datatype
        [DEFAULT {default_constant|NULL}] [col_constr {col_constr...}]
```

Figure 7.9   INFORMIX Form for Alter Table Syntax

requires parentheses around one or more "columnname datatype" elements in the ADD and MODIFY clauses; the **INFORMIX** form of Figure 7.9 permits parentheses around a multi-element comma-separated list of this type, but also permits a single-element form without parentheses; but the **DB2 UDB** form in Figure 7.8 requires that parentheses *not* be used. The Drop column capability (a capability supported in all the modern standards) is provided in **ORACLE** (starting with release 8.1.5) and **INFORMIX** but not **DB2 UDB**. **ORACLE** has the capability to MODIFY a column. (**DB2 UDB** also has a means to modify a varchar column by changing its maximum length, but we do not include this syntax in Figure 7.8.)

An added constraint that does not originally hold, such as a PRIMARY KEY for a table or NOT NULL for a column containing nulls (this can only occur in a MODIFY clause for a column in **ORACLE**), normally results in a NO ACTION response—that is, the statement will not succeed. DROP PRIMARY KEY is available in **ORACLE** and **DB2 UDB** but not **INFORMIX**. However, if you name this constraint, you can drop it in any of these products.

Refer to the SQL reference manual for the specific product you are working with to determine the exact form of Alter Table statement options available.

Note that if a new column is added by an Alter Table statement, it must start by being assigned all null values or all default values, and therefore cannot be specified as NOT NULL unless it is provided with a default value. Adding new columns to a table has important implications for the physical storage of the rows, which must be expanded in size to a point where they might not fit in their current disk positions. Most products allow the DBA to alter the table and to assume null values in new columns without moving all rows of the table to new disk positions at that time, a task that can require tremendous computer resources for very large tables. There is a good deal of variation among the different database products in treating physical storage considerations.

Non-Procedural and Procedural Integrity Constraints: Triggers

The designers of SQL integrity clauses apparently tried to foresee all important rules that could arise from logical database design so they could be implemented as non-procedural constraints. The constraints would then be impossible to break, since they would be validated during any SQL Update statement execution, and this would guard against loss of data integrity resulting from erroneous updates. In the remainder of this section, we examine various aspects of these integrity constraints and contrast a procedural method of imposing active rules, known as *triggers*. As with the discussion of non-procedural SQL Select statements in Section 3.11, we claim that non-procedural constraints miss a good deal of power that is available if constraints can be procedurally specified. However, there is a trade-off in complexity of representation that we need to pay for this added power. We start with a short discussion of how triggers are implemented, so we have an idea of alternatives before considering pros and cons.

```
CREATE TRIGGER trigger_name {BEFORE | AFTER}
    {INSERT | DELETE | UPDATE [OF columnname {, columnname...}]}
    ON tablename [REFERENCING corr_name_def {, corr_name_def...}]
    [FOR EACH ROW | FOR EACH STATEMENT]
        [WHEN (search_condition)]
        {statement                                    -- action (single statement)
        | BEGIN ATOMIC statement; { statement;...} END  -- action (multiple statements)
```
The corr_name_def that defines a correlation name follows:
```
    {OLD [ROW] [AS] old_row_corr_name
    |  NEW [ROW] [AS] new_row_corr_name
    |  OLD TABLE [AS] old_table_corr_name
    |  NEW TABLE [AS] new_table_corr_name}
```

Figure 7.10 Advanced SQL Create Trigger Syntax

Procedural Constraints and Triggers

Relatively powerful triggered procedures have long been available in the **SYBASE** commercial database product and now exist in many other products, such as **ORACLE, DB2 UDB, INFORMIX**, and **MICROSOFT SQL SERVER**. SQL-92 offered no standard for triggers, and Melton and Simon [9] state that "the standards committees simply guessed wrong: they didn't realize how rapidly the demand for triggers and the implementations of triggers would come along. . . . However, most vendors have simply gone beyond SQL-92 and used the SQL-99 trigger specification as the basis for their implementation." We will study the Full SQL-99 Create Trigger syntax, shown in Figure 7.10.

The Create Trigger syntax creates a trigger database object named trigger_name. This name is used in error messages and in any later request to drop this trigger from the database:

```
    DROP TRIGGER trigger_name;
```

The trigger is *fired* (executed) either BEFORE or AFTER one of the events listed (INSERT, DELETE, or UPDATE, optionally limited to a set of named columns) takes place in the table specified by tablename. If the trigger is fired, the optional search_condition, if present, is executed to determine if the current row or set of rows affected should cause further execution. If so, the triggered *action,* given by a single statement or a sequence of statements in a statement block between BEGIN ATOMIC and END, is executed. The statements are generally executable SQL statements ending with semicolons (statements to open a connection or begin a session or transaction are not permitted), including the SQL-99 CALL statement to call a function *from SQL,* such as a stored procedure (in the SQL-99 Procedural SQL language SQL/PSM, or a product-specific procedural language) or a function in a language such as C or Java. The *granularity* of the action is either FOR EACH ROW or FOR EACH STATEMENT (the default), and this determines how frequently the action is executed—once for each row affected or else at the end of the statement. (Clearly we might execute a multi-row Update, Delete, or Insert statement, so there can be an important distinction here.)

In the case of a triggered UPDATE event, the sequence of statements in the action program may wish to access values in each row affected either *before* the update or *after* the update occurs. To achieve this we have an optional REFERENCING clause defining one or more "correlation names" for the affected row or for the whole table. Table correlation names (old_table_corr_name or new_table_corr_name) can be used with either granularity, but row correlation names (old_row_corr_name or new_row_corr_name) can be used only for the granularity FOR EACH ROW. A row correlation name can be used to qualify a column name in expressions in the WHEN clause or in the statements of the trigger *action*, and identifies whether the column value comes from the old row (before update) or the new row (after update). Correlation names for the whole table are used like tablenames and similarly identify which version is intended.

Because a trigger causes an action to be executed, a trigger is able to implement a *procedural constraint*. The DBA can specify a sequence of statements to perform a constraint-implementing procedural action (a relatively simple procedure is most common). Most major database products such as **SYBASE**, **ORACLE**, and **INFORMIX** provide Procedural SQL language extensions with memory-resident variables, looping control, and if-then-else logic. We gave a short introduction to the procedural languages for **ORACLE** (PL/SQL) and **INFORMIX** (SPL) in Chapter 4. **DB2 UDB** has a smaller set of such procedural extensions that it provides just for triggers. More complex procedural actions are implemented in C (for example) and called from the trigger action.

Because of this use of product-specific procedural language in specifying the trigger action, it is impossible to show a "Basic SQL" version of Create Trigger. However, there is enough similarity among the different products in the non-action part of the Create Trigger general forms that it should be straightforward to port *simple application* triggers from one product to another. (Application programs that depend on complex product-specific sequencing rules for multiple triggers firing on the same update event are harder to port.)

See Figure 7.11 for the Create Trigger syntax in **DB2 UDB**. It differs from the SQL-99 syntax in several minor ways. First, in a trigger that fires BEFORE some update event, **DB2 UDB** requires the keywords NO CASCADE, which guarantees that the triggered actions will never cause other triggers to fire. Second, the additional keywords MODE DB2SQL must appear, so that in the future **DB2 UDB** will be able to provide a new MODE keyword to provide new functionality without breaking the code written now. Finally, the keywords in the optional REFERENCES clause are slightly different from SQL-99, and one of the FOR EACH clauses *must* be specified (there is no default assumed). **DB2 UDB** supports FOR EACH STATEMENT only for AFTER triggers. In general, FOR EACH ROW triggers are more commonly implemented than FOR EACH STATEMENT triggers.

The **ORACLE** Create Trigger syntax is shown in Figure 7.12. One important difference from SQL-99 is that the trigger statement is specified completely in PL/SQL (including possible CALL statements to stored procedures and functions in languages such as C).

```
CREATE TRIGGER trigger_name {NO CASCADE BEFORE | AFTER}
    {INSERT | DELETE | UPDATE [OF columnname {, columnname...}]}
    ON tablename [REFERENCING corr_name_def {, corr_name_def...}]
    {FOR EACH ROW | FOR EACH STATEMENT} MODE DB2SQL
        [WHEN (search_condition)]
        { statement
        | BEGIN ATOMIC statement; {statement;...} END};
```

The corr_name_def that provides table or row correlation names follows:

```
    {OLD [AS] old_row_corr_name
    |NEW [AS] new_row_corr_name
    | OLD_TABLE [AS] old_table_corr_name
    | NEW_TABLE [AS] new_table_corr_name}
```

Figure 7.11 DB2 UDB Create Trigger Syntax

```
CREATE [OR REPLACE] TRIGGER trigger_name {BEFORE | AFTER | INSTEAD OF}
    {INSERT | DELETE | UPDATE [OF columnname {, columnname...}]}
    ON tablename [REFERENCING corr_name_def {, corr_name_def...}]
    {FOR EACH ROW | FOR EACH STATEMENT}
        [WHEN (search_condition)]
        BEGIN statement {statement;...} END;
```

The corr_name_def that provides row correlation names follows:

```
    {OLD old_row_corr_name
    |NEW new_row_corr_name}
```

Figure 7.12 ORACLE Create Trigger Syntax

IMPORTANT NOTE: In **ORACLE**, the optional WHEN search_condition cannot contain any Subqueries or calls to user-defined functions; however, such conditional coding can be performed in the trigger body.

The INSTEAD OF clause causes the trigger to fire and the INSERT, UPDATE, or DELETE triggering action not to execute. In addition, because there is no old_table_corr_name, we don't have access to the whole old table in an AFTER trigger, just the new version available under its regular name (and not always that: see the *ORACLE8 Server Application Developer's Guide,* reference [14] in the "Suggestions for Further Reading" at the end of the chapter).

In what follows we will use **ORACLE** syntax for the trigger statements and indicate the equivalent **DB2 UDB** form. We begin investigating triggers by duplicating a few integrity constraints we have seen provided by the Create Table statement.

EXAMPLE 7.1.5
Use a trigger to CHECK that the `discnt` value of a new `customers` row does not exceed 15.0.

```
create trigger discnt_max after insert on customers
    referencing new as x
    for each row when (x.discnt > 15.0)
        begin
            raise_application_error(-20003, 'invalid discount attempted on insert');
        end;
```

After each insert to the `customers` table, this trigger tests the search_condition of the WHEN clause, `discnt > 15.0`, to see if it is satisfied for any rows. If any are found, the trigger performs the RAISE_APPLICATION_ERROR statement, which rolls back any effects of the trigger and then causes an SQLERROR condition in the application that was doing the insert. The error condition rolls back any partially completed part of the statement being performed, backing out all newly inserted rows, and then returns the code –20003 in SQLCODE, while the SQL-STATE is set to '72000' for an SQL execution error. If the application is written in PL/SQL, the specific application error (here –20003) can be given a name and handled as a normal named exception.

A minor variant of this trigger can be used to restrict `discnt` values greater than 15.0 from arising in the `customers` table as a result of an *Update* statement; in fact, we can handle both events in one Create Trigger statement in **ORACLE**, by replacing the AFTER clause of the first line with

```
...after insert or update...
```
■

In Example 7.1.5, there is only one statement in the trigger action, the **ORACLE** statement form

```
RAISE_APPLICATION_ERROR(error_number, error_message_string);
```

Here the error_number must be between –20000 and –20999, where –20000 is meant to be used for non-specific application errors, and –20001 through –20999 are to be used for specific application errors the programmers define. The execution of this statement causes an SQLERROR condition in the application that caused the trigger to fire. The user-defined error number is available in the SQLCODE variable, whereas the SQL-STATE value has only the more generic value '72000' for SQL execution error. Note that SQL-99 does not provide an exception-raising statement like RAISE_APPLICATION_ERROR( ), so it is appropriate that this special user exception number be provided via the vendor-specific SQLCODE variable. On the other hand, there are portions of the SQLSTATE space reserved for implementation-defined codes, so it is also appropriate for a vendor to use this mechanism, as we will see in **DB2 UDB**. The error string obtainable by the **ORACLE** library function sqlglm( ) (and printed out by print_dberror( ) of Appendix B) contains the user-defined error_message_string specified as the second argument of RAISE_APPLICATION_ERROR( ), along with other information such as the name of the trigger that fired. (If the application is written in PL/SQL, the specific application error condition can be given a name and handled as a normal named exception.)

For **DB2 UDB** triggers, the corresponding trigger statement is

```
SIGNAL SQLSTATE_string (SQLCA_error_message_string);
```

Example 7.1.5 would be coded in **DB2 UDB** as follows:

```
create trigger discnt_max after insert on customers
   referencing new as x
   for each row when (x.discnt > 15.0)
      SIGNAL '70003' ('invalid discount attempted on insert'); -- DB2 UDB STATEMENT
```

This statement causes the statement to abort in error, with an error code specified by the 5-character SQLSTATE_string, '70003' in Example 7.1.5. The SQLCA_error_message_ string within the parentheses, 'invalid discount attempted on insert', is put in the SQLERRMC field of the SQLCA and can be printed out (from embedded C programs) by the print_dberror( ) function of Appendix B. For more information on SQLSTATE codes, see the subsection "Explicit Error Checking" in Section 5.2. All SQLSTATE codes starting with '7' are site-specific, by vendor convention (this is consistent with the SQL-99 standard, which specifies that all codes starting with digits between 5 and 9 or letters between I and Z are implementation-defined).

To implement a trigger implementing a simple FOREIGN KEY and a REFERENCES clause, we need to reference a second table in our trigger.

EXAMPLE 7.1.6

Here is how we would implement the policy known as ON DELETE SET NULL in the X/Open and Full SQL-99 standards, but not available yet as an ON DELETE option in the **ORACLE** product. In this strategy, applied to customers and orders, we handle a delete of a customers row by setting to null the cid references in the orders table that otherwise would be non-null and invalid.

```
create trigger foreigncid after delete on customers
   referencing old as ocust
      for each row
      begin
         update orders set cid = null where cid = :ocust.cid;
      end;
```

Note that we do not need this trigger in **DB2 UDB** since it has the ON DELETE SET NULL option. The above trigger works just as well as a BEFORE trigger, but according to **ORACLE** documentation, AFTER triggers run faster in general. ∎

The CASCADE policy turns out to be exceptionally difficult to implement procedurally (but is available as an ON DELETE option in **ORACLE** and **DB2 UDB**). For this and other reasons we will discuss shortly, the decision of the SQL-99 committee is that non-procedural actions (constraints) will be retained as preferred behavior even after a procedural capability is added.

Pros and Cons of Procedural and Non-Procedural Constraints

All the constraints we have been considering are intended to guard against accidental loss of data integrity due to erroneous SQL Update statements. This suggests a preoccupation with errors that might arise from ad hoc SQL updates by casual users, and historically the concept of integrity constraints did arise during a time when casual users were seen to be an important group. Today most practitioners agree that casual users should not be permitted to perform interactive updates on important tables. It is too easy for a casual user to erroneously change column values in some set of rows to reasonable-seeming values (thus obeying any conceivable constraints) that are, however, *totally wrong!* It is much more appropriate to only permit users updates of tables through a program interface, using programs that have been carefully designed so that erroneous changes in the data are unlikely to occur. This being the case, why don't we just rule out ad hoc SQL updates and leave constraints up to the program logic? Such logic is totally flexible and would seem to be ideally suited to guaranteeing whatever integrity rules the DBA wants.

The danger of course lies in *too much* flexibility. A new programmer who is not aware of all the rules, or even an experienced programmer who allows a subtle bug to slip through, is perfectly capable of subverting the very rules the programs are supposed to maintain. To avoid this, it is possible to develop a programmatic layer through which all database updates must be performed, which will reduce or even eliminate the possibility of such errors; that is, to update a table the application programmer cannot perform an Embedded SQL statement directly, but must call a function layer call, update_tblname( ). But providing a strong guarantee of integrity with a flexible and efficient programmatic layer is not a simple design task. The triggers feature was originally meant to provide this same capability in a procedural form that was totally transparent to the programmer.

Clearly non-procedural constraints that we see in the Create Table statements are of a limited number of types (CHECK constraint, UNIQUE value constraint, FOREIGN KEY–REFERENCES constraint, etc.). This limits their power, but also guarantees that they are more easily understood than an infinitely variable and complex set of procedural constraints. As we will see, the limited set of non-procedural constraints we use can be listed in the same way as data values in system catalog tables, a set of system-maintained tables listing defined database objects (explained later in this chapter), and such constraints can be extracted and even updated by a program in response to the needs expressed by someone with DBA privileges. This is an important consideration. All the rules for the system are automatically gathered in a single place and can be examined by the DBA as a whole in an easily understood data-like form.

Another common argument in favor of non-procedural integrity constraints over procedural triggers is that the non-procedural constraints, since they are known directly by the system, can be checked much more efficiently than is possible with procedural logic. This is probably true in many cases but may be overblown. Often the system needs to do approximately the same work as the procedural logic to implement a comparable constraint, and having the system in charge does not necessarily mean a great deal of performance savings.

Arguing against non-procedural system constraints are examples of the greater power available with procedural constraints. Here are two major areas where non-procedural constraints currently appear deficient.

Specifying Constraint Failure Alternatives. A major weakness of non-procedural constraints as they are currently implemented is that they do not aid in specifying what course the program is to take if the constraint fails. In a database that keeps track of employees, we might wish to create an integrity constraint to ensure that all employee ages are between 18 and 70. But if an automatic routine updates an employee's age to 71 on his or her birthday, we would certainly want to take some action other than simply making sure the update fails—we don't want the employee to continue working at the company, simply keeping the recorded age at 70 when the true age has increased. While the constraint makes the update refusal automatic, the alternative action to be performed must be supplied by the application programmer. The refusal shows up as an SQL exception with a certain error code, and the application code is required to test for such errors on each call rather than handling the problems once and for all in a trigger.

As another example, we might have a rule to accept only valid name and address data from order entry clerks—for example, to guarantee that the zip code is correct for the state named. (Zip codes do not cross state borders—this constraint could be implemented using referential integrity.) If such a check fails, however, we wouldn't want to simply refuse to accept the data. We would presumably want to call a routine that asked the clerk to re-enter the information, and if the error is repeated, accept it provisionally, possibly in a separate table. After all, data that is not totally accurate may still be of some value to an enterprise, and later analysis might correct the entry. In both of these examples, specifying the test for the non-procedural constraint is the simplest part of the job. The hard part is specifying the course to take if the test fails, and clearly a procedural approach is needed for this.

Guaranteeing Transactional Consistency. Another common example of an important constraint is that of *transactional consistency,* one of the guarantees made to the programmer in update transactions. For example, in moving money between different account records in a commercial transaction, a consistency rule might be that money should be neither created nor destroyed, and this will be maintained by concurrent transactions *as long as the program logic itself maintains the rule properly.* But of course errors can arise in program logic, and application programming managers who are responsible for such update transactions would be extremely happy at the prospect of a constraint capability to catch subtle consistency-breaking program bugs at runtime. However, no major commercial product provides constraints that apply to interactive effects between two or more updates at the end of a transaction.

With triggers, we can check the effects of multiple updates, or make one update happen automatically upon the execution of another. For example, suppose we want to maintain a count in each row of the orders table of the number of rows in the

432

line_items table associated with that order. We can provide a trigger that fires on the insert of a line_item and increments the count in the orders row. Then this count is maintained by triggers and does not need its own update in application program logic.

EXAMPLE 7.1.7
Here is how we would implement a line_item count for each order by using triggers. We assume the order is originally inserted with n_items set to zero.

```
create trigger incordernitems after insert on lineitems
    referencing old row as oldli
        for each row
        begin              -- for ORACLE, leave out for DB2 UDB
            update orders set n_items = n_items + 1 where ordno = :oldli.ordno;
        end;               -- for ORACLE
create trigger decordernitems after delete on lineitems
    referencing old row as oldli
        for each row
        begin
            update orders set n_items = n_items - 1 where ordno = :oldli.ordno;
        end;                                                                    ∎
```

As another example, suppose two accounts are tied together so that one can borrow from the other whenever needed to maintain a positive balance. We can write a trigger that does the borrow action when needed over a wide range of programmed actions. It can also raise an exception if the secondary account has insufficient resources.

Without a constraint capability to specify alternative actions and test consistency rules in transactional logic, it is natural to ask the following question: if we leave it up to the programmers to guarantee the complex rules and handle the difficult alternatives in program logic, why are we creating a separate mechanism for the simple cases? Presumably the answer is that we constrain against errors we understand well and hope that such constraints improve the dependability of our database applications.

A major value of procedurality has to do with convenience in implementing new ideas. While new constraints with a given functionality can be provided eventually at the system level in any commercial product, the delay in waiting for a system implementation in a future release is very disheartening. Referential integrity was not provided by many database vendors for several years after it was raised as an important benefit. This area of constraint specification is still in a state of development, and a complete answer to the questions raised in this section will probably not be possible until a more unified system is developed. Probably some of the constraints offered to the DBA in the database system of the future will be extremely common non-procedural ones, and some constraints to handle more complex situations will be procedural.

Listing Defined Triggers

The standard method of listing all accessible views in a database is to use a Select statement to retrieve trigger names from the system catalog tables, a set of system-maintained tables listing defined objects (explained later in this chapter). The different database products have different names and structures for their system catalog tables. In **ORACLE**, to find the triggers and the tables they apply to, we would write

```
select trigger_name, table_name from user_triggers;
```

For information on a particular trigger, we need to refer to it by an uppercase name:

```
select when_clause, trigger_body from user_triggers
    where trigger_name = 'DISCNT_MAX';
```

If the text of the trigger body is chopped short in answer to this query, the user should use the SQL*Plus command to reset the display length of these types of fields from the rather short default of 80, for example:

```
set long 1000
```

In **DB2 UDB**, to list triggers for user eoneil, we would write

```
select trigname, tabname, text from syscat.triggers where definer = 'EONEIL';
```

7.2 Creating Views

A table defined by the Create Table statement is often referred to as a *base table* in what follows. A base table contains rows that are actually stored on disk, normally in the form of physical records with contiguous fields of different types, as specified in the Create Table statement. Now an important property of the relational model is that data retrieved by any SQL Select statement is also in the form of a table, and from here it is a short step to defining the concept of a view table. A *view table* (sometimes referred to simply as a *view*) is a table that results from a Subquery, but which has its own name and can be treated in most ways as if it were a base table. Thus a view table is a logical window on selected data from the base tables of a database that can be named in the FROM clause of other Select statements and even updated in certain carefully limited cases.

EXAMPLE 7.2.1

Create a view table, called `agentorders`, that extends the rows of the `orders` table to include all information about the agent taking the order. This is done with the SQL Create View statement:

434

```
create view agentorders (ordno, month, cid, aid, pid, qty, charge, aname, acity, percent)
    as select o.ordno, o.month, o.cid, o.aid, o.pid, o.qty, o.dollars,
        a.aname, a.city, a.percent
        from orders o, agents a where o.aid = a.aid;
```

Note that we have given a new name, charge, to the retrieved o.dollars column. All column names in the Select target list except o.aid are unique to their containing table and therefore do not actually require the qualification used in the target list: o.ordno, a.city, etc.   ∎

When the Create View statement is executed, no data is retrieved or stored. Instead, the definition of the view is placed in the system catalogs as a distinct object of the database, to be retrieved later whenever a query or Update statement is issued with this view name used in the FROM clause. Recall that the Advanced SQL syntax of Figure 3.11 permits a Subquery to occur in the FROM clause of a Select statement; viewed in this context, a view simply gives a name to such a Subquery. The concept of a view table has been standardized for some time, however, unlike the Advanced SQL syntax of Figure 3.11, so all major database products support view capabilities. The database system can simply modify a query or Update statement that accesses a view—the definition of the view table is taken into account along with the intent of the statement—so that the modified query or update actually performs accesses on base tables. This approach is known as *query modification*.

EXAMPLE 7.2.2

Find the dollar sum of all orders taken by agents in Toledo, using the agentorders view table of Example 7.2.1. Here is the query the user would pose:

```
select sum(charge) from agentorders where acity = 'Toledo';
```

The database (at least conceptually) modifies this query to take account of the definition of the agentorders view table in Example 7.2.1, and the resulting modified query is the following (view definition elements substituted are underlined):

```
select sum(o.dollars) from orders o, agents a
    where o.aid = a.aid and a.city = 'Toledo';∎
```

It is extremely important to realize that a view is a *window* on the data of the base tables. We are not taking a snapshot of the data at the time a view is created, but only storing definitions that must be interpreted with each new query; thus queries on views are immediately responsive to changes in the underlying base table data.

The complete description of the Basic SQL standard Create View statement used in this text is shown in Figure 7.13. (It is identical to the X/Open and Core SQL-99 standards.)

```
CREATE VIEW viewname [(columnname {, columnname...})]
    AS subquery [WITH CHECK OPTION];
```

Figure 7.13   Basic SQL Create View Syntax

Recall that a Subquery, defined in Figure 3.13, is missing only the ORDER BY clause of the full Select statement, which basically imposes no restriction on the view tables we can define. The Create View command can be used as an Embedded SQL statement, but the Subquery statement of the view must not contain any host variables or dynamic parameters. The user creating the view becomes the *owner* of the view and is given update privileges on the view, assuming that the view is updatable (explained below) and that the user has the needed update privileges on the base table on which the view is defined (there will be only one such table).

The optional WITH CHECK OPTION clause specifies that Inserts and Updates performed through the view to result in base table changes should not be permitted if they result in rows that would be invisible to the view Subquery; see Example 7.2.4 for an explanation. If the optional column name list in Figure 7.13 is not specified, then the columns of the new view table will inherit names of single columns in the target list of the Subquery statement. However, names must be provided when any view columns represent expressions in the target list. (**ORACLE** and **DB2 UDB** will permit names for expressions created with column aliases in the Subquery, but this is not a portable solution since it is not currently supported in **INFORMIX**.) Note too that qualifiers to make column names unique in the target list are absent in the inherited view, so we need to create specific column names for a view if the original column names of a target list would become identical without qualifiers. This point is illustrated in Example 7.2.3.

EXAMPLE 7.2.3

Create a view table, called `cacities`, that lists all pairs of cities from the `customers` and `agents` tables, where the agent places an order for the customer. The following does not work, because it allows the two `city` columns in the resulting view to take on identical names.

```
create view cacities as
    select c.city, a.city              ** ILLEGAL VIEW DEFINITION
    from customers c, orders o, agents a
    where c.cid = o.cid and o.aid = a.aid;
```

The statement just given results in a runtime error. We need to specify distinct view `city` names:

```
create view cacities (ccity, acity) as
    select c.city, a.city
    from customers c, orders o, agents a
    where c.cid = o.cid and o.aid = a.aid;
```
■

Suppose a database system did not support the CHECK option in its Create Table statement. We can overcome this limitation using views.

EXAMPLE 7.2.4

We show how the functionality of the CHECK clause of the Create Table statement can be supplied by a WITH CHECK OPTION clause in a view, as long as all updates are then made through the view. We assume that the table `customers` has been created as in Example 7.1.2, but with no CHECK clause to ensure that `discnt <= 15.0`. We create the following view:

```
create view custs as select * from customers
    where discnt <= 15.0 with check option;
```

Now any update of `custs` that would result in a row in `customers` with `discnt > 15.0` fails, because the resulting row would be invisible to the view. Consider the update

```
update custs set discnt = discnt + 4.0;
```

This update fails for customer c002 on the basis of the values of Figure 2.2, because the resulting `discnt` value would be 16.0 and therefore invisible to the view. If the CHECK option fails for any row of an Update statement, an error occurs and no changes are made to the table. ∎

As we will explain shortly, not all views can accept updates and translate them into updates on the base tables. Views that permit this are called *updatable views*. Note that it is entirely possible to create a view based on other views—that is, to create nested view definitions.

EXAMPLE 7.2.5

Create a view table, called `acorders`, that gives all order information and the names of the agent and customer involved in the order:

```
create view acorders (ordno, month, cid, aid, pid, qty,
        dollars, aname, cname)
    as select ao.ordno, ao.month, ao.cid, ao.aid, ao.pid, ao.qty,
        ao.charge, ao.aname, c.cname
from agentorders ao, customers c where ao.cid = c.cid;
```

As we see, the view `agentorders` of Example 7.2.1 is used in the FROM list of the `acorders` view definition. ∎

Listing Defined Views

The standard method of listing all accessible views in a database is to use a Select statement to retrieve view names from the system catalog tables (see Section 7.4 for more details). For example, the X/Open standard would have us use the following statement to list views:

```
select tablename from info_schem.tables where table_type = 'VIEW';
```

The different database products have different names and structures for their system catalog tables. In **ORACLE**, we would write

```
select view_name from user_views;
```

For each such view, we can use the Describe statement to obtain further information on any table or view (and some other database objects as well), for example,

```
describe agentorders;
```

In **DB2 UDB**, to list views for user eoneil, we would write

```
select viewname from syscat.views where definer = 'EONEIL';
```

The **DB2 UDB** Describe command works for tables but not for views. However, information on the columns are available in syscat.columns. See Section 7.4 on system catalogs later in this chapter.

Dropping Tables and Views

The standard SQL statement used to delete a view definition from the system catalog tables is basically the same Drop statement form that is used to delete a table, and there are some aspects of the Drop Table statement that we haven't yet covered. We start with the complete description of the Drop Table and Drop View statements in X/Open and Full SQL-99 (Core SQL-99 has no CASCADE option).

```
DROP {TABLE tablename | VIEW viewname} {CASCADE|RESTRICT};
```

This form *requires* CASCADE or RESTRICT to be specified, whereas most products assume a default. In the case of the Drop Table statement, {CASCADE | RESTRICT} specifies the effect if a FOREIGN KEY constraint or a view table definition references the table being dropped: CASCADE implies that all such constraints and view tables are dropped, and RESTRICT implies that the Drop Table statement will fail in these cases. Similarly, in the case of a Drop View statement, CASCADE and RESTRICT define the effect if another viewed table is based on the viewed table being dropped. When a base table is dropped, all its rows are deleted automatically, but of course a view table owns no rows and so none are dropped.

Only the owner of a table or view (usually the original creator) is authorized to drop it. Most products use the Drop statement to delete other types of database objects from the system catalogs as well: tablespaces, indexes, and the like. We will deal with some of these other database objects in Chapter 8.

Interpreting Figure 7.14 in the case of **ORACLE**, we have

```
DROP TABLE tablename [CASCADE CONSTRAINTS];
DROP VIEW viewname;
```

	ORACLE	DB2 UDB	INFORMIX	X/Open, SQL-99
DROP TABLE tablename...	[CASCADE CONSTRAINTS]		[CASCADE |RESTRICT]	{CASCADE |RESTRICT}
DROP VIEW viewname...			[CASCADE |RESTRICT]	{CASCADE |RESTRICT}

Figure 7.14 Drop Table and Drop View Statement Options in Products and Standards

When **ORACLE** drops a table or view, it invalidates any views and triggers that depend on it. Later, if the table is re-created with the same relevant column names, the views and triggers can become usable again. In the Drop Table statement, the CASCADE CON-STRAINTS clause implies that any constraints referring to this table are dropped. Without it, the statement fails if any constraints refer to this table.

In **DB2 UDB** we have the following simple form implied by Figure 7.14:

```
DROP {TABLE tablename | VIEW viewname};
```

When **DB2 UDB** drops a table or view, it invalidates any views and triggers that depend on it. This retains their definitions in the system catalog, but such views and triggers are unusable until re-created. Constraints referring to this table are dropped.

When **INFORMIX** drops a table or view, it drops all the triggers that depend on it. If you specify CASCADE, it drops the views and referential constraints referencing the table, whereas if you specify RESTRICT, it fails if views or referential constraints depend on it.

Updatable and Read-Only Views

Views are not as flexible as base tables in every respect, since some views cannot be updated. The best reason for not accepting Update statements is that sometimes it is not clear how to translate an Update statement on a view into unique updates of the underlying base tables to reflect the intention of the view creator and the user posing the Update statement. However, some of the rules we will see that restrict updates on views go beyond this situation, to cases where a way to translate an update on the view could be translated to updates on the base tables. In particular, no view based on a join can ever be updated in most database products, although equivalent translation of updates to base tables through such views is often quite obvious for most columns involved. See the exercises at the end of the chapter for coverage of this.

In Basic SQL, we say that a view table is either *updatable* or *read-only*. Insert, Update, and Delete operations are permitted for updatable views and not permitted for read-only views (note that all base tables are considered updatable). Figure 7.15 gives the X/Open standard rules that must be followed for a view table to be updatable.

We illustrate the reason for some of these restrictions with examples.

EXAMPLE 7.2.6
Consider the following view definition, called colocated:

```
create view colocated as select cid, cname, aid, aname, a.city as acity
    from customers c, agents a where c.city = a.city;
```

This view lists customers and agents who are located in the same city, so they can be invited out and introduced by visiting executives. Assuming the CAP database content of Figure 2.2, two rows that exist in this view are

A view table is said to be *updatable* when the following conditions hold for its Subquery clause.

[1] The FROM clause of the Subquery must contain only a single table, and if that table is a view table it must also be an updatable view table.

[2] Neither the GROUP BY nor the HAVING clause is present.

[3] The DISTINCT keyword is not specified.

[4] The WHERE clause does not contain a Subquery that references any table in the FROM clause, directly or indirectly via views.

[5] All result columns of the Subquery are simple column names (that is, there are no arithmetic expressions such as avg(qty) or qty+100), and no column name appears more than once in distinct result columns.

Figure 7.15 X/Open Restrictions on the Subquery Clause for an Updatable View

```
    c002    Basics    a06      Smith    Dallas
```

and

```
    c003    Allied    a06      Smith    Dallas
```

However, the view definition breaks rule 1 above, in that there is more than one table in the FROM clause, and therefore the view table is restricted to being read-only, not updatable. Let us try to understand this restriction by investigating some Update statements as they would apply to the view. We start by asking this question: What update should occur on the base tables if we give the command to update the aname in the second row listed above (specified as the row with cid = 'c003' and aid = 'a06'), changing it from Smith to Franklin? Clearly if agent a06 changes his or her name to Franklin, the first row above will also change, so a row update on such a view can have unexpected side effects on other rows. This is not the sort of behavior we expect from a base table.

A slightly different consideration applies to performing a delete of the second row. Exactly what update needs to be applied to the base tables to achieve this? Do we need to delete the whole customers row for c003, or the whole agents row for a06, or change the city value of one of them (to what?), or something else entirely? Similarly if we try to insert a new row,

```
    c003    Allied    a12      Watanabe    Dallas
```

this insert seems to create a new row in the agents table, a12 Watanabe Dallas, with the percent field left null. Fine, but doesn't this have unexpected side effects in that we now also have to insert a row to pair customer c002 with agent a12 in our view?

To avoid complications of this kind, the standards restrict the FROM clauses to a single table. More sophisticated approaches are taken in a few database systems that allow limited updates on certain join views, and we deal with such considerations in the exercises. ∎

Here is another example to illustrate the reason for rule 2 in Figure 7.15.

EXAMPLE 7.2.7

Let us define a view table, called agentsales, whose rows contain aid values of agents who have taken orders, together with their total dollar sales:

```
create view agentsales (aid, totsales) as select aid, sum(dollars)
    from orders group by aid;
```

Rule 2 above implies that this view is not updatable since the GROUP BY clause is present. The reason for this restriction is that once again it is impossible to perform an update on this view that would be straightforwardly translated to a base table. For example, assume that we want to increment the total sales of agent a01 by $1000.00 through the agentsales table.

```
update agentsales
    set totsales = totsales + 1000.00;        /* ILLEGAL SYNTAX        */
```

The problem with this update is that we can't figure out how to add needed information to make the change "take" on the base table, orders. What are the cid and pid values for the order that was added to the orders table for agent a01? Is there indeed only a single order, or are there several? Or perhaps one or more of the dollars rows in orders was updated to larger values. We don't know. ∎

To reiterate, we cannot make updates "take" on a view if we can't figure out exactly what changes the update should create for some underlying base table. Thus rule 3, which restricts updatable tables to have no distinct keyword, is easily understood. If the resulting table view contains a single row where two or more existed in the base table, how are we to decide what to do with a request that updates one of the attributes of that specific row? Should we update one of the rows of the underlying base table, or all such rows?

There are some join views that are so well behaved that they can be safely updated. **ORACLE** allows updates to join views if the join is N-1 (many-to-one) and the table on the N side has a primary key (thus we have a lossless join). For example, the agent-orders view of Example 7.2.1 has these properties, so in **ORACLE** the agentorders view is updatable. But we can only update the columns that map one-to-one with the orders table, not the aname, acity, or percent columns, and also not the aid column by which the rows that join are determined. To display the rows that are updatable in this view, we can execute the following Select statement on the **ORACLE** data dictionary view user_updatable_columns:

```
select column_name, updatable from user_updatable_columns
    where table_name = 'AGENTORDERS';
```

The Value of Views

Chapter 1 mentioned some problems that arise out of centralized control of data. The first was logical complexity. For example, an application to validate insurance payments for university students may have to deal with dozens of tables to access needed column information, and many of these tables may have names and uses completely unrelated to health insurance. As a result, it can be quite difficult to train new application programmers to navigate among the many tables involved. A second aim of centralized control is a desire for phased implementation, where the benefits of centralization accrue in a number of steps as new databases are combined. We don't want to have to rewrite old applications to eliminate data redundancy as newer tables appear, with new column names that must be accessed in place of older columns. Ideally we would like some way to ensure that growing numbers of tables do not cause a training problem, and also that old application code does not have to change as old tables are rearranged to eliminate redundant data and new table columns appear to take their places. Views are generally used to handle both of these problems, and others as well.

[1] Views provide a way to make complex, commonly issued queries easier to compose. We saw this in Example 7.2.2, where we were able to pose the query

```
select sum(charge) from agentorders where city = 'Toledo';
```

instead of

```
select sum(o.dollars) from orders o, agents a
    where o.aid = a.aid and a.city = 'Toledo';
```

Rather than specify a join of tables and a complex search_condition in nearly every query, it is possible to hide this complexity in a view and depend on subsequent query modifications performed invisibly by the system. (In real applications, much greater complexity is frequently hidden in views.)

[2] Views allow obsolete tables, and programs that reference them, to survive reorganization. Imagine reorganizing the orders table as a new table, ords:

```
create table ords (ordno integer not null, month char(3),
    custid char(4) not null, agentid char(3) not null,
    prodid char(3) not null,
    quantity integer default null check(quantity >= 0),
    primary key (ordno),
    foreign key (custid) references customers,
    foreign key (agentid) references agents,
    foreign key (prodid) references products);
```

We have performed a few minor renamings of the cid, aid, and pid columns and done away with the dollars column from orders; we now intend to derive the dollars total for each orders row by multiplying the quantity value by the cost of the product ordered. If a large number of programs are accessing the old-style orders table, we can create a view for use by these programs defined in terms of the newly reorganized ords table and the products table.

```
create view orders (ordno, month, cid, aid, pid, qty, dollars) as
    select ordno, month, custid, agentid, prodid,
    m.quantity, m.quantity*price
    from products p, ords m where m.prodid = p.pid;
```

442

In this way we make the program's view of the data independent of changes in the physical structure, a feature known as *program-data independence,* which we mentioned in Chapter 1 (Definition 1.3.1). Note that the independence is not complete since the Subquery of the orders view contains two tables, and thus updates through the orders view are not possible; this means that program logic to enter new orders must be rewritten.

[3] Views add a security aspect to allow different users to see the same data in different ways. Centralized control of data provides support for an important principle of data management: there should be only one copy of any piece of information crucial to the enterprise. The risk is that with more than one copy, versions might get out of synchronization (the same stock might be listed with two different prices by a brokerage), and bad decisions might result. However, it is also the case that not everyone should have access to every piece of information. An employee row might have an office number and location, facts that should be available to fellow employees; salary data, which should be available only to managers, the human resources department, and accounting; and performance review ratings, which should be available only to managers and human resources.

We can create different views of the same employees table and associate security for different user classes to access these views: see the Grant statement for granting security authorization, discussed in the next section. In granting access to a view for a user class and restricting access to the underlying base tables, we automatically provide security for fields not named in the view.

7.3   Security: The Grant Statement in SQL

The Grant statement is an SQL command issued by the owner of a table (base table or view table) to authorize various kinds of access (select, update, delete, or insert) to the table by another user or class of users. It is a form of table access security, but column access can also be implemented through views. The other user must already be able to connect to the database containing the table, an authorization provided by the database administrator.

EXAMPLE 7.3.1
The owner of the customers table wishes to give select-only access to the user with login ID "eoneil".

```
grant select on customers to eoneil;
```
∎

The Basic SQL form of the Grant statement (equivalent to X/Open) is given in Figure 7.16.

```
GRANT {ALL PRIVILEGES | privilege {, privilege...}}
    ON [TABLE] tablename | viewname
    TO {PUBLIC | user-name {, user-name...} } [WITH GRANT OPTION]
```

Figure 7.16 The Basic SQL Form of the Grant Statement

The Grant command either grants all types of access privileges or else a comma-separated list of privileges from the following set:

```
SELECT
DELETE
INSERT
UPDATE [columnname {, columnname...}]
REFERENCES [columnname {, columnname...}]
```

The privileges named (SELECT, DELETE, . . .) give authorization to all present and future users (in the case of PUBLIC) or else to the list of user names specified, to use the corresponding SQL statement with this tablename/viewname as an object; the REFER-ENCES privilege gives a user authorization to create a foreign key constraint in another table that refers to this table. If a column name list is not specified with the UPDATE privilege, then authorization is given to update *all* present or future columns in the table. The optional WITH GRANT OPTION clause provides the user(s) receiving these privileges the additional authority to grant other users these same privileges. All the Basic SQL syntax for the Grant statement is supported in **ORACLE, DB2 UDB**, and **INFORMIX**. The Grant statement can be issued in Embedded SQL programs.

The owner of a table automatically has all privileges, and they cannot be revoked. To grant privileges on a viewed table to other users, the grantor must own the viewed table (and have necessary privileges on all tables from which the view is derived), or else must have been granted these privileges with a WITH GRANT OPTION clause. To grant the insert, delete, or update privilege on a viewed table, the table must be updatable.

EXAMPLE 7.3.2

Grant permission to select, update, or insert, but not to delete, to eoneil on the table orders. Then give eoneil authorization for all operations on the products table.

```
grant select, update, insert on orders to eoneil;
grant all privileges on products to eoneil;
```

■

We can combine the idea of creating views with use of the Grant statement to provide field security. A Grant statement to provide privileges on a view will have the desired effect without granting privileges on the underlying view or base table.

EXAMPLE 7.3.3

Grant permission to user eoneil on the `customers` table to insert or delete any row, update only the `cname` and `city` columns, and select all columns other than the `discnt` column. Since there is no field specification associated with the select privilege, the owner first creates a view, named `custview`:

```
create view custview as select cid, cname, city from customers;
```

Now the owner provides the necessary authorization on `custview`:

```
grant select, delete, insert, update (cname, city) on custview
    to eoneil;
```

Since eoneil has not been granted any privileges on the base table `customers`, the `discnt` column values cannot be selected by eoneil. ∎

It is also possible, using a view, to grant authorization on a selected subset of rows from a table.

EXAMPLE 7.3.4

Grant permission to user eoneil to perform all accesses on `agents` with `percent` greater than 5.

```
create view agentview as select * from agents where percent > 5;
grant all privileges on agentview to eoneil;                          ∎
```

The SQL statement to revoke privileges on a table has the following general form in X/Open SQL (the Basic SQL form would not currently support the {CASCADE | RESTRICT} clause).

```
REVOKE {ALL PRIVILEGES | privilege {, privilege...} }
    ON tablename | viewname
    FROM {PUBLIC | user-name {, user-name...} }
    {CASCADE | RESTRICT};        -- one of these is required in X/Open
```

The Revoke statement can revoke a subset of privileges earlier granted to a user. Unlike the Grant statement, the Revoke statement cannot specify specific column names in revoking update privileges. Recall that the owner of a table automatically has all privileges; they cannot be revoked. The Revoke statement can be issued in Embedded SQL, and an attempt to revoke privileges that were not previously granted results in an SQL-WARNING condition, not an SQLERROR, which is deprecated by the standards.

In X/Open, the effect of the CASCADE option is to drop views that depended on the privilege currently being dropped (to create a view, you must have a SELECT privilege on an underlying table), or to drop FOREIGN KEY constraints dependent on a REFER-ENCES privilege. The RESTRICT option varies from CASCADE by causing the Revoke statement to fail if there are such dependencies.

Note that neither **ORACLE** nor **DB2 UDB** implements the required CASCADE | RESTRICT clause as such, and **INFORMIX** has it as an optional clause with CASCADE as the default. **ORACLE** has instead an optional CASCADE CONSTRAINTS clause at the same spot in the syntax. This causes the system to drop only referential integrity constraints dependent on a REFERENCES privilege being revoked. **DB2 UDB** has no syntax to control the action, and views that depend on a revoked privilege in all three products default to become inoperative if the privilege is revoked.

Variations in Database Products

The **ORACLE, DB2 UDB,** and **INFORMIX** products support the X/Open SQL standard syntax for the Grant and Revoke statements except for the details of the CASCADE | RESTRICT clause just mentioned. However, all three products have a large number of additional privileges. For example, **ORACLE** has something called a *DBA* privilege that a user would need to execute most of the SQL commands in this chapter. In addition, a *connect* privilege in a database in **ORACLE** allows a user to enter a database, and the *resource* privilege permits the user to create database objects such as tables and indexes that take up disk resources. For details of such **ORACLE** capabilities, the user is referred to the *ORACLE8 Server SQL Reference Manual* [13] and *ORACLE8 Server Concepts* [12] listed in "Suggestions for Further Reading."

   DB2 UDB has an equally wide selection of additional privileges. It has DBADM authority for a database that provides the right to access and modify all the database tables, views, and so forth, CONNECT authority as in **ORACLE**, CREATETAB to create tables, and additional table-level privileges as well. See *A Complete Guide to DB2 Universal Database* [1].

7.4 System Catalogs and Schemas

All relational database systems maintain system catalogs, tables (or views) maintained by the system that contain information about objects defined in the database. Such objects include tables defined with the Create Table statement, columns, indexes, views, privileges, constraints, and so on. For example, in the X/Open standard, the INFO_SCHEM.TABLES catalog table contains one row with information about each table defined. Here are a few of the columns of the INFO_SCHEM.TABLES system view in X/Open:

INFO_SCHEM.TABLES

Column name	Description
TABLE_SCHEM	Schema name of the table (usually the owner's user name)
TABLE_NAME	Name of the table
TABLE_TYPE	'BASE_TABLE' or 'VIEW'

A DBA visiting from another site would reference catalog tables such as this to learn about the local database layout. The DBA would use normal SQL Select statements to retrieve this information—for example, select TABLE_NAME from TABLES. An application program executing Dynamic SQL might need to access catalog tables to make certain decisions—for example, to learn the number and names of columns defined in a specific table. The database system itself uses these catalog tables as a basis for translating queries on views and imposing constraints on runtime update statements. (We need to be careful in saying this, however, since the system may use a more efficient method for such purposes than access through a Select statement to character columns of the catalog tables. A catalog table can be thought of as an analog to program source code, where some type of compilation can be required for efficient execution—for example, to allow the system to respond to submitted dynamic Update statements by retrieving all constraints that can apply.)

Every commercial database system has a different set of catalog tablenames with different structures and refers to them with different terminology. **DB2 UDB** refers to *catalog tables;* **INFORMIX** to the *system catalog* (also containing tables); **ORACLE** to the *data dictionary* (which is a set of system-maintained views); and the X/Open standard to *system views*. The catalog tables are created at the time that a database is created, and the underlying base tables of the catalog are meant to be updated only by the system in response to data definition statements and a few other statement types. In general, the user is not supposed to update catalog tables directly, as this may compromise data integrity (for example, if a user were to delete a row in TABLES with a table object that has not been dropped). Many products give the user access to the catalogs only through read-only views (granted with only the SELECT privilege for PUBLIC) in order to guarantee that no updates can occur. However, some products (notably, **DB2 UDB**) permit DBA updates to modify statistics in catalog tables that will influence the query optimizer to choose desired query plans.

The information contained in catalog tables is sometimes called *metadata,* meaning that it is "data about data." The metadata is even self-descriptive, in that the TABLES catalog table contains a row for the table TABLES (possibly a view type of table if that is how TABLES is defined). In what follows, we give catalog tablenames in uppercase.

Note that all object identifiers are carried in the catalogs in uppercase in **ORACLE** and **DB2 UDB** and lowercase in **INFORMIX**.[1]

Thus if a user were to define the orders table with Create Table, the name would be entered into TABLES as ORDERS. The same rule holds if the user were to define the tablename in mixed case—Orders or OrdErs; the object cataloged would be ORDERS. This is important for users writing Select statements with object names in the WHERE clause.

---

[1]In fact, all SQL identifiers are caseless, as explained in the subsection "Identifiers," following Example 3.9.1. But when a *catalog query* specifies a tablename in lowercase, it is handled as *string data* by the query processor, which interprets strings literally and fails to match the uppercase version stored in the catalog table. **INFORMIX** doesn't hold tablenames in uppercase in its catalogs, but in lowercase.

Schemas

A *schema* in Core SQL-99 is a collection of tables, indexes, and other related database objects, typically intended for a single user. The full name of a table within a database catalog is schemaname.tablename (where the schemaname is usually a user name), and similarly for other named database objects. This naming system allows different users (such as students in a class) to employ the same tablename without ambiguity in the full database. In some database systems, besides a schema for each user, there are additional schemas used to hold related sets of tables and other objects for systemwide use, such as schema SYSCAT in **DB2 UDB** and schema PUBLIC in **ORACLE**.

In Core SQL-99 and in most current products, users are provided with a schema named after their user name when their database account is created, and they cannot then create other schemas. An extended feature of SQL-99 allows additional user schemas with user-assigned schema names and object ownership by the user. The following syntax shows the Create Schema statement for use in that case.

```
[EXEC SQL] CREATE SCHEMA
    {schemaname | AUTHORIZATION authorization_id}
        [{schema_element schema_element ...}];
```

X/Open has the same syntax, with an additional optional clause specifying the character set. The optional schema_elements are SQL statements in the following set for Core SQL-99 and X/Open: Create Table, Create View, Create Index, and Grant. They are used to provide initial contents to the new schema with appropriate ownership. A user would only need to specify the schema name, skipping the AUTHORIZATION and schema_element options, and subsequently create tables and other objects in the new schema. Of the three products we are covering, currently only **DB2 UDB** allows users to create additional schemas. For other products, you may see "schemaname" replaced by "ownername" or "username" in product documentation.

Catalog Variations in Database Products

Since each database product has different conventions for its catalog tables, the standards can only give an idea of what tables and columns *must* exist. This subsection contains short descriptions of the catalog tables in **ORACLE**, **DB2 UDB**, and **INFORMIX**. These descriptions are not by any means complete, and you are referred to the appropriate product manuals for details.

The ORACLE Data Dictionary

The **ORACLE** data dictionary consists of views, many of which have three different forms distinguished by their prefixes:

Prefix	Purpose
USER_	User's view (objects owned by the user, in the user's schema)
ALL_	Expanded user's view (objects that the user can access)
DBA_	DBA's view (subset of DBA objects that all users can access)

For example, the dictionary has the views USER_TABLES, ALL_TABLES, and DBA_TABLES. The ALL_TABLES and DBA_TABLES views contain over a dozen columns, many of which have to do with disk storage and update transaction clauses of the Create Table statement that we have deferred. Here are some of the columns of interest.

ALL_TABLES (or DBA_TABLES)

Column name	Description
OWNER	Owner of the table
TABLE_NAME	Name of the table
(Other columns)	Disk storage and update transaction information

The USER_TABLES view would differ from the ALL_TABLES view by not having the OWNER column, since the owner is the current user by definition. (In fact, the USER_TABLES view could be defined in terms of the ALL_TABLES view, with OWNER = current_user selected and the OWNER column left out of the result.)

Information about columns of all tables and views (and clusters, **ORACLE**-specific structures that are like tables) that is accessible to the user is kept in the ACCESSIBLE_COLUMNS view and in the identical synonym view ALL_TAB_ COLUMNS. The DBA_TAB_COLUMNS has the same structure, and USER_TAB_ COLUMNS is the same except for a missing OWNER column.

ALL_TAB_COLUMNS (or ACCESSIBLE_COLUMNS)

Column name	Description
OWNER	Owner of the table, view, or cluster
TABLE_NAME	Name of the table, view, or cluster containing the column
COLUMN_NAME	Column name
DATA_TYPE	Datatype of the column
DATA_LENGTH	Length of the column in bytes
(Other columns)	Other properties: nullable? default value? etc.

The primary key for ALL_TAB_COLUMNS clearly includes TABLE_NAME and COLUMN_NAME, since it is possible to have identical column names for different tables. It is also possible to duplicate tablenames for different users. To distinguish such names in SQL, the tables may be qualified by user names (also called schema names): username.tablename. Thus to access all column names in the orders table created by poneil (where you are not the user poneil, but have access to that orders table), we could use the Select statement

```
select column_name from all_tab_columns
    where owner = 'PONEIL' and table_name = 'ORDERS';
```

There is also a somewhat simpler way of describing the columns in a table the user has created, by giving the SQL*Plus command

```
describe orders;
```

The Describe command also works for user-defined views and system-defined tables and views, but **ORACLE** users of releases, prior to 8i (release 8.1.5 or earlier) must include a special prefix to decorate system-defined object names, such as

```
describe "PUBLIC".USER_TABLES;
```

Note that the prefix ("PUBLIC".) must be double-quoted and in capital letters (see the explanation of double-quoted strings in the "Identifiers" subsection following Example 3.9.1). **ORACLE** also has catalog views called ALL_TAB_COMMENTS and ALL_COL_COMMENTS (and associated USER_ and DBA_ variants) to contain *descriptions* of the tables and columns that explain their purpose and would be used by the hypothetical visiting DBA. The **ORACLE** language has a nonstandard SQL statement: COMMENT ON tablename | tablename.columnname IS 'text'. Using this, a text comment can be associated with any owned tables or columns.

In addition, **ORACLE** has the relatively standard catalog views: TABLE_PRIVILEGES (or ALL_TAB_GRANTS) and COLUMN_PRIVILEGES (or ALL_COL_GRANTS), listing privileges granted on accessible tables, as well as CONSTRAINT_ DEFS (or ALL_CONSTRAINTS), listing constraints on accessible tables. The DICTIONARY view lists all data dictionary table and view names (TABLE_NAMES) and descriptive comments (COMMENTS), and DICT_COLUMNS view lists all columns in such dictionary columns and views (TABLE_NAME, COLUMN_NAME as primary key), along with descriptive comments (COMMENTS column). A number of other objects that we have not yet covered, such as indexes, are also listed in the catalog. They will be explained as needed. Information about users and performance statistics are also contained in the data dictionary; we will cover performance statistics in Chapter 9.

To create a list of all system-defined views, the user can write the following SQL*Plus sequence:

```
spool view.names            -- or whatever file name you want to use
select view_name from all_views where owner = 'SYS'
    and view_name like 'ALL_%' or view_name like 'USER_%';
```

450

To find how a view such as `agentorders` was originally defined in **ORACLE**, you can write

```
select text from user_views where view_name = 'AGENTORDERS';
```

Recall that the need to set the display length for text of this sort was covered when we were discussing display of trigger definitions just prior to Section 7.2. You can increase the default length of 80 characters for text display by using the SQL*Plus `set long` command:

```
set long 1000
```

If the text for a column is too long, on the other hand, you can trim it down by using the SQL*Plus *Column command*; to make the view_name display fit in 20 columns, for the rest of your session, type

```
column view_name format a20;
```

For detailed information about the **ORACLE** data dictionary, see the *ORACLE8 Server Administrator's Guide* [10].

The DB2 UDB System Catalog Tables

The **DB2 UDB** product contains an almost overwhelming set of catalog tables and defined columns within those tables. The user can access these tables with a SYSCAT qualifier (this is a schema name) or by prefixing the table name by SYS and using the SYSIBM qualifier. Here are a few of the columns of SYSCAT.TABLES, or equivalently, SYSIBM.SYSTABLES:

SYSCAT.TABLES (or SYSIBM.SYSTABLES)

Column name	Description
DEFINER	Creator of the table or view
TABNAME	Name of the table or view
TYPE	'T'=TABLE, 'V'=VIEW
(Other columns)	Disk storage and update transaction information

DB2 UDB has catalog tables for tables (TABLES), columns within tables (COLUMNS), views (VIEWS), and privileges held on tables and views (TABAUTH). Various types of constraints are held in distinct tables—for example, table KEYCOLUSE contains one row for each column of every foreign key, primary key, or unique column. The table SYSCAT.COLUMNS has columns as follows:

SYSCAT.COLUMNS (or SYSIBM.SYSCOLUMNS)

Column name	Description
TABNAME	Name of the table or view containing the column
COLNAME	Column name
TYPENAME	Datatype of the column
LENGTH	Maximum length of the column in bytes
(Other columns)	Other properties: nullable? default value? etc.

For example, to list all columns in the orders table created by poneil, we would write

```
select colname from syscat.columns
    where definer = 'PONEIL' and tabname = 'ORDERS';
```

For more information on **DB2 UDB** system catalogs, see *A Complete Guide to DB2 Universal Database* [1] listed in "Suggestions for Further Reading" at the end of this chapter.

The INFORMIX System Catalog

INFORMIX has catalog tables for table objects (SYSTABLES), columns within tables (SYSCOLUMNS), views (SYSVIEWS), and privileges held on tables and views (SYSTAB-AUTH). SYSREFERENCES lists referential constraints, while SYSCONSTRAINTS lists column constraints. SYSDEPEND lists dependencies between tables and views. No qualifier is needed when performing Selects on these tables. Here are a few of the columns of SYSTABLES:

SYSCAT.TABLES (or SYSIBM.SYSTABLES)

Column name	Description
owner	Creator of the table or view
tabname	Name of the table or view
tabid	Unique identifier of the table
tabtype	'T'=TABLE, 'V'=VIEW
type_xid	If a typed table, the extended ID of table type, or 0

The table SYSCOLUMNS has the following important columns:

INFORMIX SYSCOLUMNS

Column name	Description
colname	Name of the column
tabid	Table identifier, as in SYSTABLES
coltype	0 = char, 1 = smallint, . . . ,19 = set, . . . , 4118 = named row type
extended_id	Unique identifier for the column type

The extended_id differentiates the different "named row types" (which are user-defined types in object-relational **INFORMIX**); the coltype value of 4118 (see SYSCOL-UMNS above) is only a generic type for all named row types, and each named row type is different. Note that SYSCOLUMNS and SYSTABLES both have column tabid. To find all the column names in the orders table, we could perform the following join using tabid:

```
select colname from syscolumns c, systables t
    where c.tabid = t.tabid and t.tabname = 'orders';
```

Note that unlike in **ORACLE** and **DB2 UDB**, we use lowercase representation of orders, because **INFORMIX** changes all names to lowercase instead of to uppercase. See the INFORMIX Guide to SQL: Reference [8] listed in "Suggestions for Further Reading" for more information on catalog tables.

Catalog Tables for Object-Relational Constructs: ORACLE and INFORMIX

When users create user-defined types and user-defined functions in a database, various catalog tables are updated to record not only the individual existence of these types and functions, but also their interdependencies. As you immediately learn when working with UDTs and UDFs, dealing with these dependencies can be a real nuisance in development. If your user-defined type A uses user-defined type B in its definition, and you want to change a detail of B's definition, you have to drop A's definition and start over. In fact, you not only need to drop type A, but all tables using A and B types, and so on.

One way to simplify your work is to create and maintain an SQL program to drop everything and rebuild it all from scratch. In database systems where a user has the needed privileges to drop and create databases, it is possible to skip the tedious task of dropping everything piece-by-piece by just dropping and re-creating the whole development database.

Even with the most careful implementation of a program of this kind, you are likely to find that one of your types will fail to drop at some point, because of some unreported dependency. This means you need to consult the catalog tables that track these interdependencies.

In **ORACLE**, the USER_TYPES catalog table provides a top-level view of each object type. Object tables are described in USER_OBJECT_TABLES (or ALL_ or DBA_), rather than in USER_TABLES. The dependencies we need to study are (thankfully) all brought together in one table, USER_DEPENDENCIES. The most important columns of these tables are shown here:

ORACLE USER_TYPES

Column name	Description
TYPE_NAME	Name of type
ATTRIBUTES	Number of attributes in the type
METHODS	Number of methods for the type
INCOMPLETE	'YES' or 'NO': whether type is incomplete

ORACLE USER_DEPENDENCIES

Column name	Description
NAME	Name of dependent schema object
TYPE	Classification: 'TABLE', 'TYPE', etc. of this object
REFERENCED_NAME	Name of parent object (object this one depends on)
REFERENCED_TYPE	Classification: 'TABLE', 'TYPE', etc. of parent object
DEPENDENCY_TYPE	'HARD' (normal) or 'REF' (via REF)

For example, recall Examples 4.2.3 and 4.2.4, where we set up the person_t object type to be dependent on its attribute type of object type name_t. Then we created the table people, an object table of type person_t, so that it was dependent on person_t and through person_t, on name_t as well. To investigate dependencies of the people table, we write

```
select referenced_name, referenced_type from user_dependencies
    where name = 'PEOPLE';
```

The output would be as follows:

referenced_name	referenced_type
STANDARD	PACKAGE
NAME_T	TYPE
PERSON_T	TYPE

From this output, we see that the USER_DEPENDENCIES table captures even the indirect dependency of table people on type name_t via type person_t. It has also recorded the fact that the table people has been assigned to the "standard" package, since the user has not set up a special user-named **ORACLE** package for it.

The same kind of query can find all the dependencies for a type just as easily as a table. Since collection types are also named types, they also fit into this dependency-tracking system. REFs that exist from orders to customers in Example 4.2.9 would show up in such a query on ORDERS; to distinguish REF dependencies from HARD dependencies (table or type dependencies), you should include the dependency_type column in the query. (See the **ORACLE** USER_DEPENDENCIES column descriptions, above.)

Additional tables are needed in **INFORMIX** to track type and table interdependencies, since the dependencies have not been brought together in one table. Further, numeric identifiers are used as join columns between the tables, rather than simply using the string names. The top-level table for user-defined types is SYSXTDTYPES. We need tables SYSCOLUMNS and SYSTABLES (described earlier in this section) to match up the numeric identifiers with tablenames and column names and their types. Finally we need table SYSATTRTYPES to connect field types to their enclosing row types. Here are the important columns of the catalog tables for types (row types and collection types), attributes of row types, and element types for collection types:

INFORMIX SYSXTDTYPES

Column name	Description
name	Name of the type, if a named row type
extended_id	Unique identifier for type
type	like coltype: 0 = char, . . . , 19 = set, 20 = multiset, 21 = list, 22 = unnamed row type, 4118 = named row type

INFORMIX SYSATTRTYPES

Column name	Description
extended_id	Unique identifier for the type containing the field
fieldname	Name of the field
xtd_type_id	Unique identifier for field's type

To list all the typed tables and their table types, we need to join SYSTABLES and SYSXTDTYPES, matching the unique identifier of the table types, called type_xid in SYSTABLES and extended_id in SYSXTDTYPES. Here we will list the table type of the people table:

```
select t.tabname, typ.name from systables t, sysxtdtypes typ
    where t.type_xid = typ.extended_id and tabname = 'people';
```

We now turn to the same example we gave in **ORACLE**, to find the types for which the table people of Example 4.2.4 has dependencies. The query just given will output the person_t type name for table people. To find the row types in use by table people (as column types), we need to join further with SYSCOLUMNS, as explored in Exercise 7.20. However, we still would miss attributes of attributes within a column type. Unfortunately, the full search for dependencies involves following chains of dependencies, a transitive closure computation. Transitive closures are discussed in Section 3.11 in Chapter 3. **ORACLE** has solved this problem for the user by providing the transitive closure result in the catalog table USER_DEPENDENCIES.

Collection types do not have specific type names in **INFORMIX**, and thus blank type names are output by the above queries. They do have specific extended identifiers, however, numbers that can be printed out and used to track the types.

Suggestions for Further Reading

The various SQL standards and individual product SQL manuals referenced in Chapters 3 and 5 continue to be useful.

[1] Don Chamberlin. *A Complete Guide to DB2 Universal Database.* San Francisco: Morgan Kaufmann, 1998.

[2] *DB2 Universal Database Message Reference.* IBM. Available at http://www.ibm.com/db2.

[3] *DB2 Universal Database Administration Guide.* IBM. Available at http://www.ibm.com/db2.

[4] *DB2 Universal Database SQL Reference Manual.* IBM. Available at http://www.ibm.com/db2.

[5] *Data Management Structured Query Language (SQL).* Version 2. Berkshire, UK: X/Open Company, Ltd. Email: xospecs@xopen.co.uk.

[6] Jim Melton and Alan R. Simon. *Understanding the New SQL: A Complete Guide.* San Francisco: Morgan Kaufmann, 1993.

[7] *INFORMIX Error Messages.* Version 9.2. Menlo Park, CA: Informix Press, 1999. http://www.informix.com.

[8] *INFORMIX Guide to SQL: Reference.* Version 9.2. Menlo Park, CA: Informix Press, 1999. http://www.informix.com.

[9] *INFORMIX Guide to SQL Syntax.* Version 9.2. Menlo Park, CA: Informix Press, 1999. http://www.informix.com.

[10] *ORACLE8 Server Administrator's Guide.* Redwood Shores, CA: Oracle. http://www.oracle.com.

[11] *ORACLE8 Server Error Messages.* Redwood Shores, CA: Oracle. http://www.oracle.com.

456

[12] *ORACLE8 Server Concepts.* Volumes 1 and 2. Redwood Shores, CA: Oracle. http://www.oracle.com.

[13] *ORACLE8 Server SQL Reference Manual.* Volumes 1 and 2. Redwood Shores, CA: Oracle. http://www.oracle.com.

[14] *ORACLE8 Server Application Developer's Guide.* Redwood Shores, CA: Oracle. http://www.oracle.com.

Exercises

Exercises with solutions at the back of the book in "Solutions to Selected Exercises" are marked with the symbol •.

In the following exercises, unless otherwise specified, you should always assume that Basic SQL form, or if there is none, the appropriate product syntax, is to be used for all SQL statements.

[7.1]   (a)• Provide a reasonable Create Table statement with integrity constraints for the agents table and products table to go with the customers and orders definitions of Example 7.1.2. You should make sure that percent remains between 0 and 10, and that quantity and price are always greater than zero (give zero values of the proper datatype form).

(b) Assume that the DBA wants the possible discnt values for customers to be between 0.00 and 10.00, with values that differ only by 0.02, so that acceptable values are 0.00, 0.02, 0.04, . . . , 9.96, 9.98, 10.00. Show how you would be able to achieve a constraint of this kind using appropriate Create Table statements. Note that it is *not* appropriate to try to use a CHECK clause for such a large number of possible values; you need to define and load another table to impose this constraint.

[7.2]   Provide Create Table statements to define the tables passengers, gates, flights, and seats at the end of Section 6.4. Try to create tables that faithfully represent the cardinalities of entity-relationship participation in Figure 6.14.

[7.3]• Fill in missing cardinalities of entity-relationship participation in Figure 6.11, then perform a relational table design, and finally give the Create Table statements you would use to faithfully represent this design.

[7.4]   In which of the following cases (a), (b), and (c) is it possible to faithfully represent mandatory participation of an entity in a relationship, using constraints provided in the Create Table statement?

(a)• When the entity is on the "one" side of an N-1 relationship.

(b) When the entity is on the "many" side of an N-1 relationship.

(c)• When the entity is on either side of an N-N relationship.

(d) With referential integrity, we can guarantee that a foreign key of a table (which might represent a relationship instance) refers to a real primary key in another table (which might represent an entity participating in that relationship). Unfortunately, referential integrity cannot be used to guarantee mandatory participation of the entity in the relationship. Can you describe a new (imaginary) type of integrity that you would invent to achieve this type of constraint?

[7.5] (a) Which of the following SQL statements are legal, given the X/Open restrictions for updating a view? (The example where the view is created is specified in parentheses.)

(i) `update agentorders set month = 'jun';` (Example 7.2.1)

(ii) `update acorders set month = 'jun' where pid = 'c001';` (Example 7.2.5)

(iii) `update agentsales set aid = 'axx' where aid = 'a03';` (Example 7.2.7)

(b)• Assume that we have failed to include an integrity constraint in the Create Table statement of Exercise 7.1(a), to limit the value of the `percent` column. Create a view, `agentview` on the table `agents`, that is updatable and will keep any user who updates `agentview` from changing the `percent` column to a value less than zero or greater than ten.

(c) Under the same assumption that we have a missing integrity constraint on the `percent` column for `agents`, there is a way in **ORACLE**, **DB2 UDB**, and **INFORMIX** to *add* this integrity constraint to the table without re-creating the table. Give the necessary command in some specific product.

(d)• We would like to issue a sequence of two statements to grant privileges to a user named Beowulf to be able to look at the `products` table columns `pid`, `pname`, `city`, and `quantity` (but not `price`), and update either of the columns `city` and `quantity` (but no others). Give the statements you would use to accomplish this.

[7.6] Answer the following true/false questions, and explain your answers. Try to cite a section of the text (definition, example, figure, or any discussion on a specified page) that supports your answer.

(a)• A row of a table is allowed to have a null value in one of the columns making up the primary key for the table. True or false?

(b) A row of a table is allowed to have a null value in one of the columns making up a foreign key defined for the table. True or false?

(c)• In the Basic SQL Create Table syntax, it is possible to impose the effect of a FOREIGN KEY . . . REFERENCES constraint by using a CHECK clause containing a particular Subquery. True or false?

(d) Although there is a way in Basic SQL to impose a constraint that defines a primary key, there is no way to define other candidate keys in a table. True or false?

[7.7] All of the database products allow the DBA to specify in their integrity constraints some alternative actions to take when a row is deleted from one table whose primary key value might be referenced by foreign key values of rows in another table. One of the products has more possible actions.

(a)• Name the actions that are possible by all products and by the one product.

(b) Name the action that is performed by default in SQL products.

(c) Referring to the CAP database content in Figure 2.2, state in words what would happen if there were an attempt to delete customer c001 and the action named in (b) were in effect.

[7.8] Suppose table customers was created as in Example 7.1.2. We wish to create customers1, an exact copy of customers, complete with its constraints and rows.

(a)• Give the **ORACLE** statement you would use to create the table customers1, complete with rows, all in one statement.

(b) Do the same thing using two statements in Basic SQL (with no AS Subquery clause).

(c)• Explain why the following Create Table statement will give an error when executed in **ORACLE**, and explain how to fix the error.

```
create table customers1(cid primary key, cname, city,
discnt check (discnt <= 15.0)
    as select c.* from customers c, orders o where c.cid = o.cid
    and o.qty > 1000;
```

[7.9] Assume that we have a table employees, with columns eid, ename, and mgrid, and the float columns salary1 and salary2, where there are two different kinds of salary (perhaps for different work projects). Note that in SQL, FLOAT is another name for DOUBLE PRECISION. Now assume a Create View' statement that creates a view emps:

```
create view emps (eid, ename, mgrid, totsal) as
    select eid, ename, mgrid, salary1 + salary2 from employees;
```

This is not an updatable view. What is the rule that is broken? Explain why this rule is a good idea by giving an example of an update on the emps view that is difficult to translate into changes on the base table employees (that is, the changes that should be made to the underlying employees table are not clear).

[7.10] [HARD] Example 7.2.6 shows us a view, colocated, where a join of two tables customers and agents by the city columns leads to unexpected results when we try to delete a row or update a column. But what if we defined a view, agentords, based on a join on the column aid between agents and orders (the natural foreign key to primary key join). We want to justify permitting updates on a natural view of this kind, by considering updates, deletes, and inserts on the resulting View table. Come up with a reasonable interpretation of what *should* happen to the base tables as a result of each operation on the view. Note that some difference of opinion is possible.

(a)• In the case of inserts, consider what happens if a new aid value is inserted or an old aid value is inserted, possibly with a different aname. (What do you think should happen, based on functional dependencies?)

(b) What should you do about deletes?

(c) In the case of updates, consider separately non-key columns that are part of agents and non-key columns that are part of orders, and key columns ordno, aid, cid, and pid.

Machine Assignments. Create procedures or programs for the following exercises.

[7.11] Here are some exercises on triggers.

(a) Create a trigger, named agent_city, to ensure that any new row added to the agents table must have a city that is one of the cities in the customers table. Note that this trigger must be defined AFTER INSERT in order to refer to the newly inserted agent_city. Even though the table is checked AFTER the insert, if the fired trigger calls an **ORACLE** raise_application_error, or a **DB2 UDB** signal function, the insert will fail. Demonstrate a test for your trigger—that it causes an insert to fail when it is appropriate and doesn't do so when it is inappropriate—using two different attempted Insert statements for this purpose.

(b) Create a trigger that will fire whenever a new order is added to the orders table, to automatically update the quantity column of the products table. The trigger should subtract the qty specified in orders from quantity of the appropriate row in products.

(c) Assume that a row insert will fail because of a non-procedural constraint. Will a BEFORE INSERT trigger ever be fired in such a situation? Display a simple experiment to justify your answer.

[7.12] In the interactive monitor for your class database system connected to the CAP database, give a command to list all views. You may need to query the system catalog. Now create a view, `custview`, based on the `customers` table, that selects rows with `discnt < 12.0`, and add the `with check option` clause to the view definition. List views again to see that `custview` has been added. Perform the Select statement `select * from custview`. Next try to update `custview` so that the customers row with `cid` equal to c001 gets a `discnt` equal to 13.0. Does the update "take"? Show that it doesn't by typing `select * from customers`. Now re-create the `custview` without the check option (you'll have to drop the old one first) and try the update again. Show that it works this time. Leave the `customers` table in this modified state for the time being.

[7.13] If you have an **ORACLE** database system to work with, perform the following exercise on joined views.

(a) Make sure that you have primary keys defined for all your CAP tables. Then create a view `prodords` that selects all columns from the joined tables products and orders, keeping only one `pid` column renamed `ppid` by an alias in the Subquery. Then execute the statement

```
select column_name, updatable from user_updatable_columns
    where table_name = 'PRODORDS';
```

Validate that you can update the view columns listed with YES in the UPD column of the answer, by updating one of them and then checking that the update was effective on the base table. Also validate that one of the columns in the view with NO for UPD cannot be updated.

(b) Repeat the relevant steps of part (a) for the view `colocated` from Example 7.2.6.

(c) Repeat the relevant steps of part (a) for the view `apords`, which selects all columns for the joined tables agents, products, and orders, keeping only one `aid` and one `pid` column and renaming them `aaid` and `ppid`, respectively, and renaming `a.city` and `p.city` as `acity` and `pcity`, respectively. Then repeat the relevant steps of part (a).

(d) Drop and create again the table products without a primary key (just use `not null unique` for the column `pid`); then reload the table. Now repeat the steps of part (a) for prodords.

(e) State a rule that fits the facts for when a column in a join view will be updatable.

When you have finished this exercise, reload all modified CAP tables.

[7.14]• In your SQL monitor, issue a command to list all integrity constraints. You may need to query the system catalog. We are assuming the row with `cid` equal to c001 has a `discnt` equal to 13.0, continuing from the previous problem. Now create an integrity constraint (a named constraint if your system supports named constraints) on the `customers` table to require that `discnt <= 12.0`. Does this work? What happens? Now update `customers` so that the `customers` row with `cid` equal to c001 has value 10.0, and try again to create the integrity constraint. Next try to update `customers` so that the `customers` row with `cid` equal to c001 has `discnt` equal to 16.0. Does the update "take"? Show that it doesn't by typing `select * from customers`. Now remove the constraint and try the update again, showing that it is successful this time. Finally perform the `customers` table load to bring all `customers` table values back to their original value.

[7.15] **(a)•** Insert a new row in the `orders` table: 1031, jul, c001, a01, p01, 1000, 450.00. Now create a view called `returns` based on `orders` that shows columns `ordno`, `month`, `cid`, `aid`, `pid`, `qty`, `dollars` and, in addition, `discnt` (from the `customers` table), `percent` (from `agents`), and `price` (from `products`). Show that `returns` exists as a view, using an SQL statement to consult the appropriate catalog table. Also determine what the column names are.

(b) Execute the statement `select ordno, qty, dollars, discnt, percent, price from returns where cid = 'c001'`. Then update the underlying base table `customers` by changing the `discnt` for c001 to 13.0. Now repeat the previous Select statement from `returns` again. Notice that updates in the base tables are reflected in the view. Change the `discnt` for c001 back to 10.0 at the end (or just reload `customers`).

(c)• Note that the `dollars` column in `returns` should be equal to `qty` times `price` minus the `discnt` percentage for this amount. Test your ability to write expressions in terms of the `returns` view by selecting columns `ordno`, `qty`, `dollars`, `discnt`, `percent`, and `price` of all rows, with an extra column in the Select statement calculating this expression. The extra expression column should give the same value as `dollars`.

(d) Now create a new view, `profits`, based on the `returns` view, with columns `ordno`, `cid`, `aid`, `pid`, and `profit`, where the `profit` column has been calculated in the Create View statement to equal `qty` times the `price` for that `pid`, minus 60% of this for wholesale cost, minus the `percent` royalty for the particular agent and the `discnt` for the customer in question. Be sure that the expression makes sense. Demonstrate the effectiveness of this by typing `select * from profits`.

[7.16] Given an assigned partner in the class, trade "privileges" with your partner. Grant privilege to your partner's database account to perform selects (only) on `customers` where `discnt < 10`. You will need a view, call it `custview`, to do this. Show that the view and privilege exist, using appropriate commands. Leave this permit in force and demonstrate your access to your partner's database. (You need to access that database account and type the statement: `select * from custview`.)

[7.17] Show how to retrieve all view names, then all base table names in your database from the system catalog tables. Then retrieve all column names from the returns view. Can you also use the catalog to retrieve the *definition* of the returns view?

[7.18] Write an Embedded SQL program to update customers, setting discnt in the row with cid c001 to the old value plus 1. Include a test to check if no rows are updated, and print out a user warning. Then place a constraint on customers that keeps discnt <= 15.0, and execute your program until the warning is printed.

[7.19] In the last subsection of Section 7.1, the text suggests developing a programmatic function layer to perform all database updates. The layer itself would guarantee any necessary constraints and would possibly do other things such as implementing alternative actions when constraints are broken. For this problem you should create a new table, ords, with all the columns of the orders table with the same datatypes, *but no constraints*, not even NOT NULL for ordno. The ords table should have one other column, named constrok, of type integer. Then you are to write a C function called insertords( ), declared

```
int insertords(int *ordnop, char *monthp, char *cidp,
    char *aidp, char *pidp, int *qtyp, double * dollarsp);
```

A program that wishes to insert a row in the ords table must call insertords, with pointers to each of the values to be inserted in the relevant columns. A null pointer indicates that no value is specified and that a null should therefore be placed. The insertords function should *test all eleven constraints* of the orders table given in Example 7.1.2. If the row to be inserted passes the test, the function should insert the row in ords, with a constrok column value of 1, and return the value 0. If the row fails any of the constraints, the function should print an indicative message to the user (for example, "Error: null ordno, continue? Enter Y or N"). If the row user answers anything but Y or N, a "Y or N, Please" message is printed and we take another input. If an N is input, then insertords returns without inserting a row, with value –1. If a Y is input, then insertords inserts the row as it stands (broken constraints and all) and sets the constrok flag to 0. It then returns the value 1. Your instructor will provide you with a driver, driveord.c, to test this function, and sample input for the driver program. Note that this method is not proposed to replace constraints, but rather to show their convenience compared with programming, and to show how to proceed if the database product does not support all the constraints you need.

[7.20]• (Object-Relational **INFORMIX**) Write a query on catalog tables SYSTABLES, SYSCOLUMNS, and SYSXTDTYPES to find the row types in use as column types by table people of Example 4.2.4. This query will find name_t, because it is considered to be a column type, but not `person_t`, the type of the entire row (and already found by a query in the text). We could UNION these two queries together, of course. Also it cannot find types of *attributes* of a row type column. To dig those out, write a query using the SYSATTRTYPES table as well (four tables in all).

Indexing   **8**

How Index-learning turns no student pale,
yet holds the eel of science by the tail.
—*The Dunciad*, Book 1, line 279

Somehow the verb "to hash" magically became standard terminology for key
transformation during the mid-1960s, yet nobody was rash enough to use such an
undignified word publicly until 1967.
—D. E. Knuth, *The Art of Computer Programming*, 1975

When an SQL query is submitted to a database system, a software module of the system known as the *query optimizer* analyzes the non-procedural prescription of the query to determine an efficient step-by-step method to retrieve the desired data. The resulting procedural sequence of steps to carry out the query is known as the *access plan* or *query plan*. We will go into detail in Chapter 9 about why a query optimizer arrives at an access plan; in the current chapter we lay a foundation by learning how query efficiency depends on the existence of *database indexes* that channel accesses to data in a table.

8.1   The Concept of Indexing

A *database index*, or simply *index*, is somewhat similar to the memory-resident data structures you have probably encountered in earlier studies. It is meant to improve the efficiency of data lookup to rows of a table by a *keyed access* retrieval method. This chapter assumes that you have some familiarity with memory-resident structures that support lookup of this type: *binary trees*, *2-3 trees*, and *hash tables*. (There are numerous texts covering these concepts: see "Suggestions for Further Reading" at the end of this chapter.) Database indexes differ from memory-resident structures in that they often contain more data than can be held in memory at one time. Thus, database index data is meant to reside on disk, being made partially memory resident only when it is accessed. There is another design advantage: when the computer is turned off, memory-resident data would be lost, but the data of a database index will *persist* like the rows in a table.

A database index consists of a sequence of *index entries* that are stored on disk. One index entry for each row exists in the index, and the index is responsive to future row updates. This means that if a row is to be accessed by the value in a column, and the index provides this access, then if the row is updated in this column value, the index will change to reflect it. Index entries look a little like rows of a table with two columns: the *index key*, consisting of the concatenation of values from certain column values in the row (often just one column), and a "row pointer" to the disk position of the row from which this specific entry was constructed. The index entries are placed on disk, usually in sorted order by index key (although hashed access is also possible), and are then used by the system to speed up certain Select statements. Standard lookup through an index locates one or more index entries with a given key value or range of key values, and follows the entry pointers to the associated rows. The fact that a database index normally resides on disk has far-reaching ramifications, because access to disk is extremely slow compared with memory access speeds. This fact has an important effect on the database index structures we will study, such as the B-tree. The most important aim in the design of a database index is to minimize the number of disk accesses needed to read desired data.

You can best picture an index to a database table by analogy to the old-style card catalogs in a library, which indexed the books on the shelves in various categories. One set of cards in the catalog might be placed in alphabetical order by book author, another in order by title, and a third in order by subject name (several subjects are possible). Each card in the catalog contains a call number to locate the book indexed, so that once we find a catalog entry for a book with the title *The Three Laws of Robotics*, we can immediately locate the book on the shelves. Now returning to the discussion of indexes on a table, consider what should happen when a database system receives the following SQL query:

[8.1.1]   `select * from customers where city = 'Boston'`
          `and discnt between 12 and 14;`

The query optimizer would now have to decide how to access the rows requested by this query from the `customers` table. One alternative that always exists is to perform a *table scan,* in which the system successively accesses all rows of the table and discards rows that don't satisfy the two ANDed predicates in the WHERE clause of query [8.1.1]. (In doing this, we say that we *qualify* the rows by direct inspection of the row data.) In the case where there are fewer than ten rows in the `customers` table, as in Figure 2.2, a table scan is probably the best strategy; direct examination of all the rows is quick when the table isn't extensive. In an analogous sense, looking up a book through a card catalog isn't as efficient as a direct scan when there are fewer than ten books on the shelves. In a table with 1 million rows, however, access by lookup through index directory structures can represent a very substantial performance advantage.

What is the proper course to take with such a large customers table, in performing query [8.1.1], assuming that there is no index associated with the column discnt but there is one on the column city? In this case, the system would probably decide to "look up" customers in Boston and then access all the customers rows in Boston through the index-supplied *row pointers* mentioned above, analogous to the call number of a library book. The total number of rows accessed would presumably be greatly reduced by limiting the query to customers in Boston, and we would only have to qualify the single remaining predicate, discnt between 12 and 14, by looking at the rows retrieved.

An end user or application programmer posing a query need not be aware of the underlying indexes that speed up access. When an application program executes an SQL request like the query in [8.1.1], the query optimizer determines how to fill the request, basing its judgment on factors (such as existing indexes) that may have been significantly different at the time the program was originally written. As a matter of fact, it is considered an important feature of the relational model that a programmer is insulated from this issue and can therefore write programs that don't depend on the existence of particular indexes (because the table scan method is always available). This is another aspect of *program-data independence,* which we have seen before (see Definition 1.3.1 in Chapter 1). In this way, the database administrator gains flexibility in being able to create and destroy indexes in response to changing disk availability. This, at any rate, is the theory. In practice, we can expect users to notice a difference between a query performed in 2 seconds that uses appropriate indexes and the same query taking 2 minutes without them. Removing existing indexes ceases to be an option when increased resource use significantly degrades the total performance of the system.

In considering the various aspects of indexing, we enter an area where the SQL standards have very little to say. To give an idea of what is to come, Figure 8.1 presents the X/Open standard specification of the Create Index statement.

The table specified by tablename in the Create Index syntax must be a base table that already exists at the time that the statement is issued and the column names specified must be unqualified. The statement of Figure 8.1 creates a sequence of index entries that are then stored on disk, one index entry for each row existing in the table specified by tablename. As mentioned earlier, index entries look like rows of a table with two columns: the index key, consisting of the concatenation of values from the columns named in the Create Index statement, and a row pointer to the disk position of the row from which this specific entry was constructed. When the UNIQUE clause is present, the index key values placed in the index will be unique, unless one of the column values concatenated into the key value is null: duplicate index key values are permitted in this case. The

```
CREATE [UNIQUE] INDEX indexname
      ON tablename (columnname [ASC | DESC] {, columnname [ASC |DESC]});
```

Figure 8.1 X/Open Syntax for the SQL Create Index Statement

index entries are placed on disk in sorted order by index key (hashed access is not supported in the standard), with ASC or DESC order for each component column, as in the ORDER BY clause of the Select statement. Lookup through an index locates a sequence of index entries with a given key value or range of key values and follows the entry pointers to the associated rows. Note that index entries automatically respond to changes in the table after the Create Index statement has been performed. When a row is inserted in the table, a new index entry is created in the index and placed in the appropriate index structure position for efficient lookup. Similarly row updates that change the index key value are reflected by a change in index entries: a delete of the entry with the old index key value and an insert of the entry with the new index key value in the appropriate position in the index.

EXAMPLE 8.1.1

Create an index on the `city` column of the `customers` table.

```
create index citiesx on customers (city);
```

Note that each index key value (i.e., `city` name) in the `citiesx` index can correspond to a large number of different `customers` rows. To delete the index `citiesx` after it has been created, we use the standard form:

```
drop index citiesx;
```
∎

Note carefully that the term *index key* has a significantly different meaning from the relational concept of a *table key*, that is, a *primary key* or *candidate key* for a table. An index key is created by concatenating a sequence of columns in a specific order, whereas a relational key has unordered columns. More basically, an index key is constructed with the aim of supporting efficient lookup, and it is perfectly possible to have multiple identical index key values for different rows of a table when the UNIQUE keyword of the Create Index statement is missing. We saw such duplicate index key values for `citiesx` in Example 8.1.1. On the other hand, the definition of a relational key says nothing about efficiency of lookup, and keys (candidate or primary) are created in the Create Table statement, with the NOT NULL and UNIQUE or PRIMARY KEY clauses, only to reflect the designer's intention that unique key values should exist on each row. We will carefully differentiate between these two concepts in what follows by always referring to an *index key* in distinction to a *table key* (or other specific terms for table key such as *primary key* or *candidate key)* when there can be any chance of confusion.

Of course it is perfectly possible to impose a uniqueness constraint on a set of columns of a table by specifying a unique index for them. Back before the UNIQUE and PRIMARY KEY constraints were part of the standard for the Create Table statement, a unique index was the accepted way in some database systems to guarantee a uniqueness constraint for a candidate key (there was no explicit primary key). Nulls could still occur in columns of a unique index, however, so it was necessary to include NOT NULL for all columns that were to be included in a candidate key, just as it is now that we have the UNIQUE constraint as part of the Create Table statement.

EXAMPLE 8.1.2

Assume we did not declare the `cid` column of the `customers` table to be UNIQUE or PRIMARY KEY. Create an index that guarantees each `customers` row has a unique `cid` value.

```
create unique index cidx on customers (cid);
```

When the `cidx` index is first created, the system tests whether duplicate `cid` values already exist in the `customers` table; if duplicates are found (aside from multiple null values), the index will not be created. After the index is created, any update to the table is immediately reflected in the index, and Insert or Update statements that would duplicate the unique index key will fail to execute.

∎

Now that Create Table UNIQUE and PRIMARY KEY constraints exist, it is preferable to use them rather than imposing a uniqueness constraint through an index: the query optimizer is able to take advantage of this, especially of knowing the primary key of a table. However, these Create Table uniqueness constraints are commonly supported by a system-created unique index in any event, since quick lookup is extremely valuable in guaranteeing a unique value for new row inserts or updates affecting the index key value.

The X/Open standard Create Index statement of Figure 8.1 is relatively simple compared to some of the statements supported by major database system products, but even this limited form was absent from the SQL-99 standard. The reason no standard has been attempted is that an indexing strategy deals with considerations of the internal architecture of the database system, including the explicit design for row access on disk, and there is no agreed-upon optimal approach to this design. There are actually a number of different types of indexes, and it is impossible to understand the advantages of some of these types without understanding some detailed properties of disk access, covered in the next section. For example, we will learn that a binary search algorithm, which we can show provides nearly optimal efficiency to find a key value in a sorted list of memory-resident key values, is *not* optimal for a disk-based structure. All of the commercial database system products have taken somewhat different—you might say almost idiosyncratically different—approaches to the exact structures used to place rows on disk, assign pointers of custom type to the rows for outside reference by indexes, and accomplish myriad other details covered in the following sections. At the same time, although there are many differences between the products, the product architectures have a lot in common, and we will present indexing details of two of our standard three commercial database products, **ORACLE** and **DB2 UDB**, with an emphasis on these common aspects. We do not present indexing details for **INFORMIX** because there is a different version of **INFORMIX**, known as **INFORMIX XPS** (for eXtended Parallel Server), with more sophisticated indexing capabilities. There are plans to integrate the two **INFORMIX** codelines, and we will try to provide details on **INFORMIX** indexing on our homepage, www://www.cs.umb.edu/~poneil/dbppp.html, when this happens.

470

8.2 | Disk Storage

Until now we have been content to say that the rows of base tables (as well as any indexes that are created) are stored on disk and read into memory when they are accessed. As mentioned in Chapter 1, the fact that the database must be persistent over time means that disk storage is the most practical storage medium available. We say that computer memory is *volatile storage,* meaning that although it can be accessed very efficiently, the data contents of memory do not persist when electrical power is turned off, or when certain kinds of system failures occur to cause a computer failure. Disk storage is referred to as *nonvolatile storage,* or sometimes *persistent storage,* meaning that it retains data through loss of electrical power—as everyone knows who has moved data on a diskette from one personal computer to another. Various software methods covered later in the text can also make disk storage resistant to other types of errors that arise from system failures and even disk failures, creating what we will refer to as *stable storage.* Disk storage is extremely cheap and therefore plentiful in most systems, but it is also very slow to access. As we will see, the extremely slow speed of access to disk storage dictates many details of database index structures.

Disk Access Is Excruciatingly Slow

As nearly everyone knows, computers have been getting faster and cheaper for decades. It has been said that if the auto industry had kept up with the computer industry since 1950, you would now be able to buy a car for $9 that would take you to the moon in an hour on a gallon of gas. Furthermore, this rate of progress seems to be continuing. A relatively inexpensive computer today can execute program logic with its central processing unit (CPU) at a rate of (say) 100 million instructions per second (100 MIPS). Of course different instructions take different lengths of time, but this rate is a rough measure of the average speed for a "standard" instruction mix on a relatively fast computer.

Disk access speed, an extremely important aspect of database system performance, has not kept pace with the enormous improvements in CPU execution speed. A *disk* is a rotating magnetic recording medium, typically several platters stacked one above another, with a current industry-standard rotation speed for a medium performance disk drive of about 120 *rps,* or *rotations per second,* and a disk arm that moves in and out like an old-style record player arm. (The rotational speed and disk arm movement speed have doubled in the last five years, and they are improving constantly as new commercial releases occur.) The disk arm terminates in a set of *read-write heads* that sit on the surfaces of the various platters. As the arm moves through its range of positions, the heads all move together to address successive concentric *cylinders* of data, made up of circles or *tracks* on the stacked set of surfaces. A track is broken up into a sequence of angular pieces, called *sectors,* typically containing 512 bytes. A typical disk unit today contains 10 GB of data (or 10 *gigabytes,* a gigabyte being a billion bytes). Each track might contain 200 sectors (the number actually varies, with more sectors on tracks of larger circumference), 512 bytes in each sector, with 10 surfaces (thus about 1 million bytes per cylinder), and about 10,000 cylinders on the disk unit. In order to read or write data on a disk, the disk arm must first move in or out to the appropriate cylinder position, then wait for the disk to rotate until the appropriate sector on one of the disk surfaces is just about to pass under the disk arm head. At this point the disk head reads the data from a sequence of sectors on one surface of the rotating medium, known as a *disk page*, or simply *page*. A disk page access is usually modeled as having three phases, based on this physical analysis:

Seek time	The disk arm moves in or out to the proper cylinder position.
Rotational latency	The disk platter rotates to the proper angular position.
Transfer time	The disk arm reads/writes the disk page on the appropriate surface.

Because a disk access requires physical action, the time needed to read in a random page of data from disk is enormous compared with a computer instruction execution; a disk access requires about .0125 seconds, or 1/80 of a second. This can be thought of as being amortized over the three phases as follows:

Seek time	.008 seconds
Rotational latency	.004 seconds
Transfer time	.0005 seconds (for a few thousand bytes of transfer)

The seek time is actually highly variable, depending on the starting position of the disk arm and how far the arm has to move before it arrives at the proper cylinder. If two successive reads from disk are close to one another on the disk medium, the seek time can be very small, zero for two reads from the same cylinder. The average seek time of .008 seconds is based on a model where successively accessed pieces of data occur with equal likelihood at any cylinder position between the two extreme disk arm extents. The rotational latency is equal to half a disk rotation at 120 rps, an average value assuming that the start sector can be anywhere on the track after the disk arm seek is completed.

Once the data has been brought into memory, it can be accessed by an instruction in .00000001 seconds (one 100-millionth of a second), or .01 μs (μs is the notation for a microsecond, or millionths of a second) by a machine with a speed of 100 MIPS. The disparity between time for memory access and disk access is enormous: we can perform 1,250,000 instructions in the time it takes to read or write a disk page. For an analogy, imagine yourself as Voltaire's secretary around the time of the American Revolution, with the duty of making copies of Voltaire's many letters to correspondents. If we assume that it takes you about a second to copy each word, you can picture writing a letter as analogous to executing a computer program of several hundred instructions, each taking .01 μs. Now say that you come to a word that you are unable to read in Voltaire's handwriting. Unfortunately, Voltaire is in St. Petersburg, so you need to take time out to write a letter to him, asking for the exact spelling of the word. (In the analogy, there is information on disk needed by the database system, and it executes a series of instructions to start a disk read.) You post the letter to him, go back to your office, and wait six weeks doing nothing until the letter reaches him in St. Petersburg and you receive his reply. This is analogous to the system waiting .0125 seconds for the disk read to bring the needed data into memory where it can be accessed directly by the system. Clearly we want to avoid performing more disk reads than are absolutely necessary.

It's important to realize that once the disk arm reaches the appropriate spot on disk, you don't want to ask for just a byte or so. It takes very little time for each additional byte returned. Most of the disk access time was to get the disk arm into position on the rotating disk medium, but after this is accomplished the transfer rate is millions of bytes per second. For this reason we find that all disk access is "page-oriented," a page being a long contiguous sequence of bytes: 2048 bytes, or 2 KB, is the standard page size for many products, such as **ORACLE**, while 4096 bytes, or 4 KB, is standard for others, such as **DB2 UDB**. (**DB2 UDB** and a few other products also support larger pages—8 KB, 16 KB, and 32 KB—but 4 KB is still the standard at most user sites.) Retrieving a 2- or 4-KB page from disk into memory, in the analogy we have been using, is like getting back a long letter from Voltaire that answers your question as well as several others you might have later: the cost for such an extensive letter is only a few additional hours of waiting. Similarly it's clearly worthwhile, after bringing back a page from disk and placing it in memory, to keep the page around (rather than throwing it away) in case we need to reference it again, so we won't have to access it from disk later. Figure 8.2 illustrates database system page buffering to keep such pages in memory.

In Figure 8.2, we see that the database system reads disk pages through an interface where it provides a *disk page address,* symbolized by *dp,* bringing the pages into memory *buffers* contained in memory space that was set aside when the database system was

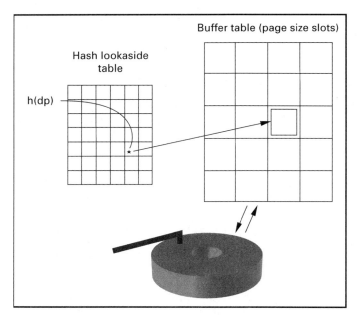

Figure 8.2   Disk Page Buffering and Lookaside

initiated. The dp values might be a logical succession of integers (1, 2, 3, . . .), or they might be constructed from the device number, cylinder number, surface number, and starting sector position of the page on disk. Each page that is read in has its disk page address hashed (h(dp)) into a small entry of a *hash lookaside table,* which points to the buffer slot where the page will reside. From that point on, every time a new page is to be read from disk we start by hashing the disk page address and looking in the hash lookaside table to see if the desired page is already in a memory buffer. If it is, we can skip the disk access step. Otherwise we will have to find a disk page to drop from memory buffers so that we can read in this new page. We try to drop a page that hasn't been referenced for a long time, so that we keep popular pages buffer resident.

Since we know we're going to be reading entire pages from disk, we try to structure all our access so that all useful information for any particular task tends to occur on the same page. As we will see, this has an important effect on index structures. The most important feature of an index is to minimize the total number of disk accesses to read desired data.

Since disk is so much slower than memory, it is natural to ask why we bother with disk at all: Why don't we just use memory for our accesses? Historically, of course, memory was volatile, so that updated data held in memory would be lost if the computer crashed for some reason. But one of the major aims of the transactional database field has been to ensure that data that gets updated in memory buffers will not be lost if the computer crashes. This feature is known as *transactional recovery,* and we will cover it in Chapter 10. Even so, two basic assumptions of transactional recovery are that the data itself is backed up on some nonvolatile medium, and special reminders called *recovery logs* can be written to a stable medium. At present, all major database systems use disks as the nonvolatile medium and parallel writes to two separate disks to simulate a stable medium. (This guards against loss of log information through any single disk failure.)

So we can't do without disk entirely in a database system, but that begs the question of why we use slow disk when CPU access to memory is so much faster. Why can't we bring all the data we need to access into an extremely large memory buffer of the kind we see in Figure 8.2 and then keep all data in memory while it is accessed? Indeed a good deal of database thought has gone into just that. The algorithms involved in doing buffer lookaside are extremely efficient, so required CPU time doesn't grow at all as the number of buffered pages increases, and a lot of large database users have been buying more and more memory to speed up access. But we have still not realized the potential of this approach. It wasn't so long ago that memory was simply too expensive for most enterprises to purchase several gigabytes to hold all their data, so that disk storage was the only alternative. There is still a surprising variation in the cost of memory for mainframe servers compared with personal computers, but simple cost is no longer a very large factor in choosing disk over memory. A rough idea of the difference in memory and disk costs can be gleaned from these very approximate rules of thumb from the PC industry:

Memory storage cost	About $4000 per gigabyte
Disk storage (disk arms attached) cost	About $100 per gigabyte

Thus we can still purchase 40 times as much disk storage for the same cost. Considering that a small company would be unlikely to use a database of much over a gigabyte (there might be a good deal more storage needed for backups and other data, but disk can be used for that), it seems unlikely that a $4000 charge will dissuade most users from buying the necessary memory if performance is important. On the other hand, the $4000 cost is a bit of a waste if performance is not important, and a small company with a small database will probably also have a relatively small number of transactions to perform each day, making performance a secondary consideration. Larger companies with more significant performance requirements will probably also have much larger databases, 10 GB or more, that they would need to buffer in memory. But before that can happen, computer designers will have to extend the memory address size, which is currently limited to 32 bits, or about 4 billion bytes of addressing on most processors. Some of the new massively parallel machine architectures have already started using 64-bit architecture, and IBM mainframes have been providing a means of switching between different 32-bit addressing spaces for several years. All of this seems to indicate that reasonably soon we will be driving to Mars in a few minutes in a car that costs 15 cents.

The DBA and Disk Resource Allocation in ORACLE

In Chapter 7, we were not yet ready to consider disk space allocation for tables, although this is in fact one of the most important tasks of the DBA. Unfortunately, this topic is extremely dependent on the specific database product being used, since the variety of different data architectures of commercial systems has so far defeated any standard SQL approach. However, most commercial systems deal with data allocation in the same *general* way, even though the details can be quite different. To give an idea of the considerations that arise, we provide in what follows a short description of the commands used in the **ORACLE** product to allocate disk storage resources. We will not try to be complete in describing equivalent capabilities for the other products. For additional details on the various products we have been covering, see "Suggestions for Further Reading" at the end of this chapter.

Before creating a database, the DBA might start by allocating a number of operating system files on disk, with names such as fname1, fname2, . . . , and so on. These are the same kind of files that a user would encounter when editing text or compiling C source files into executable program files. Various operating systems give the DBA the ability to specify the size of the file in bytes and the disk device on which the file is to be allocated. We say that disk storage is *contiguous* if it consists of sectors on disk as close together as possible—successive sectors on successive surfaces of a cylinder within a succession of adjoining cylinders. Keeping disk space contiguous minimizes seek time, as we have explained, and most systems try to allocate space to a file in long contiguous chunks. At the same time, most operating system files do not have the flexibility to span disk devices. Given these operating system files, the DBA might issue an **ORACLE** command of the following kind:

```
create tablespace tspace1 datafile 'fname1', 'fname2';
```

A *tablespace* is the basic allocation medium of an **ORACLE** database, out of which tables and indexes as well as other objects requiring disk space receive their allocations. A tablespace corresponds to one or more operating system files and can span disks. On most operating systems, **ORACLE** is perfectly capable of creating or extending operating system files on its own, although the administrator does lose some precision. Alternatively, a tablespace may be built from "raw disk partitions," that is, disk devices not part of the OS file system that **ORACLE** can use without going through the file system services. (While we avoid complexity in our text by not going into the syntax of using raw disk partitions, you should be aware that such partitions are extremely important at sites where high performance is a major consideration.) All database products have a disk resource construct like a tablespace to insulate users from specific operating system considerations: **DB2 UDB** also calls it a *tablespace*, while **INFORMIX** calls it a *dbspace*. In all cases it represents a usable chunk of disk, possibly spanning several disk devices.

Here is an example of a Create Tablespace statement in which it is left to **ORACLE** to create the files fname3 and fname4:

```
create tablespace tspace2 datafile 'fname3' size 200M,
    datafile 'fname4' size 300M;
```

The integer following the SIZE keyword can be given in bytes, in kilobytes (an integer followed by the letter K), or in megabytes (when followed with the letter M). Note that a kilobyte is actually 2^{10} = 1024 bytes, and a megabyte is 2^{20} = 1,048,576 bytes. Many **ORACLE** databases contain several tablespaces, including a special tablespace named SYSTEM, which is automatically brought into being when the Create Database command is issued (not covered here). The SYSTEM tablespace contains the *data dictionary* for the database (what we have been calling the system catalog tables) and may also be used to provide disk space for user-defined tables and indexes, as well as other objects. It is up to the DBA to decide whether to create multiple named tablespaces. Two advantages of having multiple tablespaces on large systems are: (1) better control over which disk devices are used for what purposes (load balancing), and (2) the ability to take some disk space off line without bringing down the whole database.

When a table or index is created by a DBA (or any user with the CREATE TABLE privilege), an optional clause of the Create Table or Create Index statement, known as the TABLESPACE clause, allows the creator to name the tablespace from which disk space will be allocated (see Figure 8.5 for an example in the Create Table syntax). If no tablespace is named, then the table is created in the user's default tablespace, which was set when the user was first granted a tablespace resource. When a table is created, its tablespace allocation is identified with an allocation object known as a *data segment*; when an index is created, it is identified with an *index segment*. There are other types of segments as well, each with common properties of allocation to subdivide a tablespace. See Figure 8.3.

When a data or index segment is first created, it is given an initial allocation of disk space from the tablespace, known as an *initial extent*. By default, an initial extent contains 10 KB (10,240 bytes) of disk storage. Each time a data segment comes close to

Database	CAP database							
Tablespaces (made up of OS files)	tspace1					SYSTEM		
	fname1		fname2			fname3		
Tables, indexes, etc.	customers	agents	products	orders	ordindx	. . .		
Segments	DATA	DATA	DATA	DATA	INDEX	. . .		
Extents								

Figure 8.3 Database Storage Structures

running out of space, it is given an additional allocation of space, known as a *next extent,* and numbered by an integer starting with 1. Figure 8.3 is a schematic diagram of the logical structures just named. Note that each extent lies totally in one data file, a fact that is difficult to represent in this diagram.

An extent must consist of contiguous disk space within a single file making up a tablespace, but a segment can have extents from multiple files. It is possible to specify a number of parameters in a tablespace definition to define how new extent allocation is to be handled. All segments that are defined within a tablespace inherit these parameters, but definitions of objects such as tables and indexes can also override these default values with their own parameters. Figure 8.4 contains the partial syntax form for the Create Tablespace statement.

As already explained, the tablespace is constructed from a set of operating system files named in the DATAFILE clause. If the SIZE keyword is omitted, the data file must already exist, and **ORACLE** will use the file with that name. If SIZE is defined, **ORACLE** will normally create a new file of that name, deleting any previous one. The REUSE keyword is only meaningful when the SIZE keyword also appears, and it allows **ORACLE**

```
CREATE TABLESPACE tblspacename
     DATAFILE 'filename' [SIZE n [K|M]] [REUSE] [AUTOEXTEND OFF
     | AUTOEXTEND ON [NEXT n [K|M] [MAXSIZE {UNLIMITED |n [K|M]}]
     {, 'filename' (repeat SIZE, REUSE, and AUTOEXTEND options) . . .}
  -- the following optional clauses can come in any order
  [ONLINE | OFFLINE]
     [DEFAULT STORAGE ([INITIAL n [K|M]] [NEXT n [K|M]] [MINEXTENTS n] [MAXEXTENTS {n|UNLIMITED}]
              [PCTINCREASE n]) (additional DEFAULT STORAGE options not covered)]
  [MINIMUM EXTENT n [K|M]]
  [other optional clauses not covered];
```

Figure 8.4 **ORACLE** Create Tablespace Statement Syntax

to reuse an existing file, first verifying that the file is of the appropriate size. Any old contents of the file are destroyed.

The AUTOEXTEND clause controls whether **ORACLE** can extend the size of a data file. In the case of AUTOEXTEND ON, the NEXT n [K|M] specification determines how large a size expansion will be each time a new extent is required. (Note that the expansion of the file might be a good deal larger than the extent required.) The MAXSIZE clause determines how large the file can grow during AUTOEXTEND, either to a limited number of bytes or UNLIMITED. Note that if UNLIMITED is chosen, there will still be some limit set by the file system itself.

A tablespace is created ONLINE by default, meaning that it is immediately available for use by the database system. If a tablespace is created OFFLINE, it cannot immediately be used for table creation. The tablespace can be brought ONLINE by the DBA for later use with the Alter Tablespace statement (not covered in this text). The SYSTEM tablespace, which is created by the Create Database statement, is never off line.

The DEFAULT STORAGE clause of Create Tablespace allows the tablespace creator to specify default parameters governing how allocation of disk extents should be handled in segments defined on this tablespace. Here are explanations of these parameters (note that they can actually come in any order):

INITIAL n [K|M]   The integer n specifies the size in bytes of the initial extent assigned. The default is the number of bytes in five data blocks, normally 10,240 = 10 K.

NEXT n [K|M]   The integer n specifies the size in bytes of the next extent to be allocated, numbered 1, with a default size of 5 data blocks and a minimum of 1 data block (2 K); the size of subsequent next extents may increase (but not decrease) if a positive PCTINCREASE value is specified.

MAXEXTENTS n   The integer n specifies the maximum number of extents, including the initial extent, that can ever be allocated. UNLIMITED is an alternate choice.

MINEXTENTS n   The number of extents to be allocated initially when the segment is created. Since extents must be contiguous, this allows for a large initial space allocation, even when the space available is not contiguous. The default is 1.

PCTINCREASE n   The percentage by which each successive next extent grows over the previous one. If the integer is zero, there is no increase. The default of 50 causes successive next extents to grow by a factor of one and a half times over the prior next extent.

All extent sizes are rounded up to an integral multiple of the number of bytes in a *data block* (which is **ORACLE**'s name for a disk page). The minimum size for an extent is 2048 bytes, and the maximum is 4095 MB. The MINIMUM EXTENT clause is a way to

```
CREATE TABLE [schema.]tablename
  ({columnname datatype [DEFAULT {default_constant|NULL}] [col_constr {col_constr. . .}]
     | table_constr}   -- choice of either columnname-definition or table_constr
  {, {columnname (repeat DEFAULT clause and col_constr list) | table_constr} . . .})
  [ORGANIZATION HEAP | ORGANIZATION INDEX (this has clauses not covered)]
  [TABLESPACE tblspacename]
  [STORAGE ([INITIAL n [K|M]] [NEXT n [K|M]] [MINEXTENTS n] [MAXEXTENTS {n|UNLIMITED}]
          [PCTINCREASE n]) (additional STORAGE options not covered)]
  [PCTFREE n] [PCTUSED n]
  [disk storage and other clauses (not covered, or deferred)]
  [AS subquery]
```

Figure 8.5   ORACLE Relational Create Table Statement Syntax with Partial Indexing Syntax

guarantee that a Create Table statement, in overriding the Create Tablespace default extent size, will not choose such a small size that excessive fragmentation results. The MINIMUM EXTENT n [K|M] specification guarantees that an extent of at least n bytes will be the smallest that will ever be allocated.

We have seen an earlier form of the **ORACLE** Create Table statement in Figure 7.3. A more complete syntax that takes storage allocation options into account is provided in Figure 8.5.

The new clauses of the Create Table statement begin with the optional choice between ORGANIZATION HEAP (the default) and ORGANIZATION INDEX. A HEAP-organized file is one where new rows are stored at any convenient location (typically in successive locations of successive data pages of successive extents). An INDEX organized file means that new rows are stored *within* an index, in order by the primary key value. We will discuss this further in Section 8.4, when we discuss the topic of *primary index*; note, however, that the current implementation of **ORACLE** INDEX organized files has a number of limitations that make it less useful than we might wish.

Note that the optional STORAGE clauses of this Create Table syntax allow the creator of a table to override the parameters for extent allocation associated with the tablespace in which the table is defined. The PCTFREE n clause determines how much space on each disk page can be used for inserts of new rows (see Figure 8.6 for a schematic of row layout on a disk page). The integer n varies from 0 to 99, with a default of 10; an n value of 10 means that new inserts to the page will stop when the page is 90% full, and a value 0 means that new inserts will continue until there is no room at all left on the page. Larger values of n leave more space on a page for possible increase in size of some of the rows, arising from longer varchar columns or possibly Alter Table statements that add new columns. The PCTUSED n clause specifies a condition for a data page where new inserts to the page will start again if the amount of space used by stored rows falls below a certain percentage of the total. The value must be an integer n from 1 to 99. The default value is 40. The sum of the PCTFREE and PCTUSED values must be less than 100, and together determine a range in which the behavior with respect to inserts on the disk page remains stable, depending on the last percentage value encountered.

For example, the default settings mean that pages fill to 90% full and are then marked "full" so they will not receive further inserts. Only when they fall to 40% full can they accept more inserts and start filling again. Thus pages are occasionally refilled during their lifetimes by a sequence of successive inserts. If inserts are frequent, these successive inserts to a single page can avoid individual page reads and writes, since the appropriate page will always be found in buffer for the next insert. If we consider the case PCTFREE 30, PCTUSED 60, a succession of inserts will only take the page from 60% full to 70% full. If we set PCTFREE = 20, PCTUSED = 90 (with a sum of 110, which should not occur), it would mean that once a page is marked full (at 80% full), it will immediately be considered fillable again because it is below the PCTUSED level. This would be an anomalous situation.

Data Storage Pages and Row Pointers: ORACLE and DB2 UDB

Once a table has been created and the initial extents of disk storage allocated, we are ready to load or insert rows into the table. In a HEAP organized table, the most common architecture, rows are simply inserted one after another on the first page of the first extent until the space on the first page is exhausted, after which the next page is used. When the initial extent allocation of pages runs out with repeated row inserts, the database allocates a new extent for the table and continues this process with additional extensions up to the maximum number of extents or pages that can be allocated. Each row placed on a disk page consists of a contiguous sequence of bytes containing column values of various types, and each row begins at a known offset in bytes from the beginning of a page. It is possible in some architectures for long rows to exceed the size that can be accommodated on a single disk page, but we defer consideration of this issue until later.

A typical data storage page layout is given in Figure 8.6, where we show N rows on a disk page. The header info section (which we usually refer to as a *page header*) might contain fields to show the page address (disk access identifier for the page), the type of segment (index, table), and so on. Each row is a contiguous sequence of bytes, starting at a specific byte offset within the page. (Recall that because of varchar(n) datatypes, the rows might have different lengths.) Entries in the row directory number the rows within a page and give the *byte offset* within the page to where each row begins. In the following sections, we usually refer to a row directory number within a page as a *slot* number. In the architecture shown in Figure 8.6, it is assumed that newly inserted rows are placed right to left in the disk page, and directory entries from left to right, leaving free space for future inserts in the space between. This implies that if a row is deleted from a disk page and its space reclaimed, then the remaining rows are shifted flush right in the page, and the row directory entries (which usually are not deleted) remain flush left, so that all free space remains in the middle. **ORACLE** and **DB2 UDB** can defer shifts of this sort, however, and this is only a simplified schematic structure for most products. Other types of information can also occur in the row directory area. For example, **ORACLE** allows rows from multiple tables to appear on the same disk page (recall that a disk page is called a *data block* in **ORACLE**, or sometimes simply a *page*), and in that case, a table directory is needed in the header info section to distinguish rows from the different tables.

Figure 8.6 Row Layout on a Disk Page

A row in a database table can be uniquely identified for access on disk by specifying the disk page address on which the row appears and the slot number of the row within the page. This is the form of row pointer we referred to earlier, which is used in indexes to point to rows that correspond to a given index key value. It turns out that we gain flexibility by pointing to a row using a logical slot number within a disk page, because of the *information hiding* that takes place. If instead we used the byte offset of the row within the page, then external row pointers used in indexes would need to change when rows had to be moved within a page reorganization, for example, to allow for a larger value in some varchar column, or to recover fragmented free space by shifting rows flush right. By using logical slot numbers in row pointers instead of byte offsets, external index references to the rows remain stable when the disk page row layout is reorganized, as long as the row directory entries themselves remain in place.

A row pointer has somewhat different names in different systems. In **ORACLE** it is called a *ROWID* and in **DB2 UDB** *RID*. When speaking generically, we will refer to such a row pointer as a ROWID. Remember that the concept of row pointer is not part of any standard, but the concept explained here is very common. To give a simple idea of a RID, we refer to an old definition, in the first edition of this text, for the TID (Tuple ID) row pointer in the **INGRES** product. **INGRES** was one of the earliest relational database system products marketed, and it is still available from Computer Associates. We make no claim that our definition of the TID is up-to-date, however. In **INGRES**, successive disk pages were allocated to a database table assigned an integer disk page number P, ranging from 0 to $2^{23} - 1$, requiring 23 bit positions, and a maximum of 8,388,608 pages. The architecture allowed at most 512 rows on a 2-KB page, so that a slot number S ranged from 0 to 511, and this can be expressed in 9 bits. A row pointer, or TID, in **INGRES** is calculated from the disk page number P and the slot number S for the particular row using the following formula:

$$TID = 512 * P + S$$

For example, the TID value for a row with slot number S = 4 on page P = 2 is calculated as 2 * 512 + 4 = 1028. The slot number within a page is not permitted to exceed the value 511, so the formula for a TID is always unique for rows on different pages. The slot number fits in 9 bits and the page number in 23, so the TID value is guaranteed to fit in 32 bits, a 4-byte unsigned integer. In addition to serving as a pointer to a row associated with a given index key value, it was also possible to retrieve an **INGRES** TID with a normal SQL Select statement as a "virtual" column value, as seen in the following example.

EXAMPLE 8.2.1

Assume that an **INGRES** DBA has just loaded a table named employees with 10,000 rows and believes each row of the employees table to be 200 bytes long, with little variation in size. This means that a disk page of 2048 bytes should contain about ten such rows. (The header info section and row directory represent overhead space common to most systems, and there is also a certain amount of overhead for various columns, which we assume has already been included in the 200-byte row length. Without descending into detailed calculations of overhead usage, ten rows of length 200 on a 2048-byte page should be about right, assuming that 2000 out of 2048 bytes on a page can be used for row data.) To test that the rows have been loaded ten to a page, the DBA can pose the following SQL query to retrieve the TID values for an initial sequence of rows:

```
select tid from employees where tid <= 1024;
```

The DBA expects to see a sequence of TIDs with values 0, 1, 2, 3, 4, 5, 6, 7, 8, 9, 512, 513, 514, 515, 516, 517, 518, 519, 520, 521, and 1024. Any other displayed sequence means that there are not ten rows on each page. ∎

A **DB2 UDB** record pointer RID also encodes the table page number and slot number into a 4-byte integer. However, a **DB2 UDB** RID is *not* available through a Select statement as a virtual column value in an arbitrary table. In addition, the internal structure of a **DB2 UDB** RID is not public knowledge, and IBM warns that this structure might be changed without warning at any time in the future.

In **ORACLE**, a ROWID is 6 bytes long and has two possible printed forms: a "restricted ROWID" form and an "extended ROWID" form. A restricted ROWID identifies a row within a given segment (i.e., table) and specifies the block (disk page) number on which the row falls, the row number (what we have been calling the slot number) within the block, and the number of the operating system file within which the block exists. The ROWID is displayed as a string of three components having the following layout, with letters in each component representing hexadecimal digits:

BBBBBBBB.RRRR.FFFF

Here BBBBBBBB represents the block number within the file, RRRR the row number, and FFFF the file number. For example, 0000000F.0003.0002 represents the row in slot 3 of block 15 within file number 2. A restricted ROWID takes up 6 bytes of storage, and it appears in index entries. The ROWID value for each row can be retrieved as a virtual column by an SQL Select statement on any table, as with the following query:

```
select cname, rowid from customers where city = 'Dallas';
```

which might return the following row information (if ROWID is in restricted form):

```
CNAME           CROWID
------------    --------------------
Basics          00000EF3.0000.0001
Allied          00000EF3.0001.0001
```

The alternative "extended ROWID" form is displayed as a string of four components having the following layout, with letters in each component representing a base-64 encoding:

OOOOOOFFFBBBBBRRR

Here OOOOOO is the data object number, and represents the database segment (e.g., a table). The components FFF, BBBBB, and RRR represent the file number, block number, and row number (slot number), as with the restricted ROWID. The encoding used for this representation is a base-64 representation, comparable to hexadecimal representation except that we have 64 digits. The digits are mapped to printable characters as follows:

```
DIGITS              CHARACTERS
-----------------   ------------------------
0 to 25             A to Z (capital letters)
26 to 51            a to z (lowercase letters)
52 to 61            0 to 9 (decimal digits)
62 and 63           + and / respectively
```

For example, AAAAm5AABAAAEtMAAB represents object AAAAm5 = 38 * 64 + 57, file AAB = 1, block AAEtM = 4 * 64^2 + 45 * 64 + 13, and slot 1. The query

```
select cname, rowid from customers where city = 'Dallas';
```

might return the following row information (different values than given for restricted ROWID):

```
CNAME           ROWID
------------    -------------------
Basics          AAAAm5AABAAAEtMAAB
Allied          AAAAm5AABAAAEtMAAC
```

Since an index is associated with a table, there is no need for the ROWID values in entries of the index to carry the object number of the unique table segment. However, the Select statement commonly displays the extended form. We use the **ORACLE** ROWID nomenclature generically in what follows to refer to record pointers in arbitrary database systems.

EXAMPLE 8.2.2

Consider the following Embedded SQL code to retrieve a row from a relation and, depending on a complex decision procedure, perform an update on the row to set a taxcode flag column to 1.

```
exec sql select * into :emprec
    from employee where eid = :empidval;      /* unique row                       */
decisionproc(&emprec, &yesno);                /* call decision procedure function */
if (yesno)                                    /* if flag was set to yes           */
    exec sql update employee set taxcode = 1  /* perform update                   */
        where eid = :empidval;
exec sql commit;
```

Note that the Update statement setting taxcode to 1 will need to perform a second lookup of the row, probably through a unique empid index, in order to update the desired employee column. This lookup could be avoided and performance improved by remembering the ROWID of the row from the initial Select statement. The original Select would have to be modified to read as follows (e.ROWID names the virtual column in **ORACLE**):

```
exec sql select e.*, e.ROWID into :emprec, :emprid
    from employee e where eid = :empidval;
```

The emprid variable would be declared to contain an 18-character string for **ORACLE** (a 19-character array, to include the null terminator). Now the final Update statement can be rewritten:

```
exec sql update employee set taxcode = 1
    where ROWID = :emprid;                    /* perform update    */      ∎
```

Recall that RULE 2 of the relational model in Section 2.3 states that rows can only be retrieved by their content. The existence of a ROWID value in SQL to retrieve a row by pointer value is a definite contravention of this rule, which was supported by many database products even before the REF capability was added in object-relational syntax. Retrieving a ROWID value from a table is considered useful, for at least two reasons:

◆ ROWIDs can be used to see how the rows of a table are stored on disk.
◆ A ROWID can be used as the fastest way to access a particular row.

Nevertheless, a ROWID cannot take the place of a primary key for a table, since a ROWID stored over an extended period for use in retrieval might become invalid. For example, various types of database reorganization can occur where rows are moved to new disk pages, thus invalidating their former ROWID values. When this happens, an outmoded ROWID value points to a nonexistent row, or worse, a new row that has taken the old one's place on that page and slot. An error in retrieving the wrong row associated with an outmoded ROWID value can be fatal. To be safe you should only hold a ROWID value within a single transaction; a ROWID held for the space of a single transaction will not be invalidated, because a lock is kept on the row accessed to keep it from being deleted or reorganized. Note that these considerations of invalidated ROW-IDs can affect object-relational REFs in the same way: REFs can be invalidated after reorganization of a table.

Another point that might make us wish to avoid heavy ROWID use is that the ROWID format is not portable from one system to another, nor is it necessarily supported by the database system in the same way as some other aspects of SQL.

Can Rows Extend over Several Pages? Product Variations

Different products have different rules about whether rows can extend over several pages. The maximum row size in **DB2 UDB** is limited basically to the size of a disk page. (The maximum row size is 4005 bytes for a 4-KB disk page; 4005 is what is left of a 4096-byte disk page after required space overhead.) When an existing row grows too large to fit on a page, **DB2 UDB** moves the row to another page and puts an overflow record (RID forwarding pointer) on the old page to point to the new location. **ORACLE**, however, allows rows to split between pages. If a row on some page grows to a point where no free space remains, then the row splits. Its ROWID remains the same and it leaves a row fragment in the original slot position on its original page, but a pointer at the end of that row fragment points to the ROWID of a continuation fragment. The continuation fragment is placed, just as a row is placed, on a new disk page with a slot position and a ROWID. However, the ROWID of the continuation fragment is not made available to any external access method; it is an internal property of row access to a row splitting between disk pages. If multiple splits occur, the original slot position is edited to point to the new location; no chain of forwarding pointers occurs.

Clearly we would like to avoid fragmented rows whenever possible. A fragmented row is analogous to sending a letter off to Voltaire without listing all your questions, saying that you will send another letter with more of the questions you have in mind after you receive a response. We try to minimize fragmentation in **ORACLE** by leaving extra free space on each page with the PCTFREE clause of the Create Table statement to handle most row enlargements. However, since **ORACLE** permits rows that cannot fit on a single page, extra free space on a page is not a general solution. While a row in **DB2 UDB** will move entirely to a new page when it grows too large for its prior slot, a certain kind of fragmentation exists even so, since a RID forwarding pointer must be left on the original page. (**DB2 UDB** does this to avoid changing all index entry pointers to the original row position.) Reducing fragmentation arising from forwarding pointers of this kind is one of the reasons that the database reorganization utilities mentioned earlier are valuable.

8.3 The B-Tree Index

A *B-tree* is a keyed index structure, comparable with a number of memory-resident, keyed lookup structures you have probably encountered in earlier reading, such as the

```
CREATE [UNIQUE | BITMAP] INDEX [schema.]indexname ON [schema.]tablename
    (columnname [ASC | DESC] {, columnname [ASC | DESC]. . .})
    [TABLESPACE tblspacename]
    [STORAGE ([INITIAL n [K|M]] [NEXT n [K|M]] [MINEXTENTS n] [MAXEXTENTS n]
        [PCTINCREASE n] ) ]
    [PCTFREE n]
    [other disk storage and transactional clauses not covered or deferred]
    [NOSORT]
```

Figure 8.7 ORACLE Create Index Statement Syntax

balanced binary tree, the *AVL-tree,* and the *(2-3)-tree.* The difference is that a B-tree is meant to reside on disk, being made partially memory resident only when entries in the structure are accessed. A number of other disk-based index structures, based on alternate access methods such as hashing, also offer performance advantages in certain applications; we cover some of these later in the chapter. However, the B-tree structure is the most commonly used index type in databases today.[1] It is the only index structure available on **DB2 UDB**, and it was the only one provided by **ORACLE** until release 7, when a facility known as *hash cluster* was added. In defense of **DB2 UDB**, which offers only the B-tree index, it should be said that the B-tree provides a good deal of flexibility for different types of indexed access, and the **DB2 UDB** implementation has a number of special features (such as sequential prefetch I/O, covered in the next chapter) that make it extremely competitive in performance for many applications.

The following subsections provide an extended introduction to the structure of a B-tree. The discussion is summarized in Definition 8.3.1, where the important properties of the B-tree are listed. To begin, Figure 8.7 provides the **ORACLE** syntax for a Create Index statement, which assumes a B-tree index. Hashed access is provided by **ORACLE** with the Create Cluster statement, covered later.

We will discuss the BITMAP keyword at a later point; in the following discussion, we assume that the BITMAP keyword is not present. Recall from the X/Open syntax of Figure 8.1 that the list of column names in parentheses on the second line specifies a concatenation of column values that make up an index key on the specified table. The ASC | DESC keywords actually have no effect, since it is easy to range through the index in either direction. When the **ORACLE** Create Index statement is issued, an initial set of extents is created in the named tablespace. Then an index entry of the form (keyval, ROWID) is extracted for each of the N rows of the table. This sequence of index entries is then placed on disk and sorted in order by key value:

(keyval1, ROWID1), (keyval2, ROWID2), ... , (keyvalN, ROWIDN),

---

[1] What we call a *B-tree* in this text is more precisely known as a B^+-*tree* in many references and represents a variation on the original published B-tree structure. All commercial products have adopted the B^+-tree variation, however, and the resulting structure is often referred to by the simpler name *B-tree.*

so that after the sort, keyval1 ≤ keyval2 ≤ . . . ≤ keyvalN. We will consider algorithms for sorting sequences of index entries (or rows) on disk in Chapter 9; a good deal of disk space and memory space as well as CPU and disk arm use can be required for this sort step. The TABLESPACE and STORAGE clauses determine disk allocation for the index in the same way they do with tables. We defer consideration of the PCTFREE option until we have had a chance to investigate the B-tree index node layout. The NOSORT option of Figure 8.7 indicates that the rows of the table have already been sorted by the key values of the index and lie on disk in that order. Thus index entries in increasing order can be extracted from successive rows of the table, and the effort of the sort step can be saved. **ORACLE** checks that the key values extracted are actually in increasing order and returns an error if the order is not as promised.

EXAMPLE 8.3.1 Special Binary Search in a Memory Array.
You are expected to have encountered a binary search in an earlier text on data structures, but the special algorithm given here is constructed to handle the case where multiple duplicate values exist in the sorted list. This is an important consideration for searches in non-unique indexes.

In the program of Figure 8.8, assume we have been given a table with seven rows (generalizable to N) and have brought a special index-like sorted list into a memory-resident array of structs, arr[7], so that the (keyvalK, ROWIDK) pair of values in the Kth entry is given by arr[K-1].keyval and arr[K-1].ROWID. (Recall that subscripts range from 0 to N − 1 with N

```
int binsearch(int x)              /* return K so that arr[K].keyval == x, or else -1 */
    /* if no match; arr assumed to be external, dimension 7 is wired in        */
{
    int probe = 3,                      /* start subscript K = 3              */
        diff = 2;                       /* difference to 2nd probe            */

    while (diff > 0) {                  /* loop until K to return             */
        if (probe <= 6 && x > arr[probe].keyval) /* if probe too low          */
            probe = probe + diff;       /* raise the probe position           */
        else                            /* otherwise                          */
            probe = probe - diff;       /* lower the probe position           */
        diff = diff/2;                  /* home in on answer, K               */
    }                                   /* we have reached final probe = K    */
    if (probe <= 6 && x == arr[probe].keyval)  /* have we found x?            */
        return probe;                   /* if so, return K                    */
    else if (probe + 1 <= 6
        && x == arr[probe+1].keyval)    /* might have undershot               */
            return probe + 1;           /* then return this K                 */
    else return -1;                     /* else, return failure               */
}
```

Figure 8.8   Function binsearch, with Seven Entries Wired In

entries.) If the structs in arr[ ] are ordered by the keyval component, so that arr[0].keyval ≤ arr[1].keyval ≤ . . . ≤ arr[6].keyval, the C function binsearch of Figure 8.8 implements a binary search to locate the subscript of the *leftmost* keyval equal to x, among the duplicate keyvals with this value.

Assume we were given the sequence of keyval values {1, 7, 7, 8, 9, 9, 10} at subscript positions 0–6. Then if x = 1, binsearch probes successive subscripts 3, 1, and 0 and returns 0. If x = 7, the successive subscript probes are 3, 1, 0, and then since 7 is not equal to arr[0].keyval, we test arr[1].keyval that has the value 7, and return 1. If x = 8, the successive probes are to 3, 1, 2, and then 3 is returned. With x = 9, we probe 3, 5, 4, and return 4. With x = 10, we probe 3, 5, 6, and return 6. Given duplicate values in the array, the binsearch logic of Figure 8.8 always returns the smallest subscript K such that x == arr[K].keyval. (One of the exercises at the end of the chapter asks you to demonstrate this fact.) The binsearch function generalizes easily: given N entries instead of 7, choose m so that $2^{m-1} \leq N < 2^m$; then initialize probe to $2^{m-1} - 1$ and diff to 2^{m-2}. Tests that probe <= 6 or probe + 1 <= 6 become probe <= N – 1 or probe + 1 <= N – 1.

∎

The number of passes through the binsearch loop to locate x in a sequence of N entries is m – 1, where 2^m is the smallest power of 2 that exceeds N (one for each value of diff, counting down in powers of 2 from 2^{m-2} to 2^0). Then there is a test with the final probe value and possibly with probe + 1. Another way to put this is that the number of probe tests is either m or m + 1, where we can calculate m as CEIL($\log_2$(N)). (Recall that the CEIL function rounds up to the next larger integer.) Although we can show that this is nearly the most efficient possible search in terms of the total number of comparisons performed, it is not optimal for disk-based lookup. It turns out that if we performed a binary search on a large sorted list placed in disk storage, we would probably perform more I/Os than necessary.

EXAMPLE 8.3.2 Binary Search of a Million Index Entries.
Assume that we have a million rows in our table, and therefore a million entries in our sorted list arr[ ]. A rather minimal assumption for entry size is 4 bytes for the ROWID and 4 bytes for the key value (appropriate for an integer key value; it could be much more for a character string index key). With 8 bytes for each entry, the number of entries we can fit on a 2-KB disk page is at most 2048/8 = 256, ignoring overhead. The pattern of binary search is to make a first probe to compare the value x sought to the keyval at entry number $2^{19} - 1 = 524,287$ of the sorted list. After this, the next pass moves left or right in the list by $2^{18} = 262,144$ entries, depending on how the comparison comes out. Each successive probe is a "distance" half as far from the previous one. Figure 8.9 shows the pattern of successive probes, that is, the distance moved in each case from the previous probe.

The point of all this is that on probe 13, for the first time there is a *chance* that the previously probed entry and the current entry lie on the same page! Recall that there are only 256 entries on a page, and for the first 12 probes binary search is jumping over numerous pages of entries between successive probes. If we assume that the pages accessed are not already resident in memory buffers from some prior reference, this means we need at least 12 I/Os to locate the desired entry.

Probe number	Distance from prior probe	Probe number	Distance from prior probe
1	(No previous probe)	8	4096 entries away
2	262,144 entries away	9	2048 entries away
3	131,072 entries away	10	1024 entries away
4	65,536 entries away	11	512 entries away
5	32,768 entries away	12	256 entries away
6	16,384 entries away	13	128 entries away
7	8192 entries away	. . .	. . .

Figure 8.9 Converging Distances between Probes in a Million-Entry Binary Search

We can improve on binary search from the standpoint of disk I/O with a B-tree structure.

EXAMPLE 8.3.3 B-Tree Structure for a Million Index Entries.
If we assume that 256 index entries will fit on a page, then the number of pages containing entries is CEIL(1,000,000/256) = 3907. These pages, containing index entries of the form (key-val, ROWID), are known as *leaf nodes* in a B-tree structure. Now let us create the most efficient possible *directory* entries to direct us to the right leaf node, given that we wish to locate an entry with arbitrary key value x. All we need is a pointer to each leaf node (a page number, which we refer to as a node pointer, np) and what we call a *separator* key value between pairs of such pointers. Figure 8.10 gives an example of such a structure with specific key values. Note that ROWID values of leaf-level entries are not shown.

In searching at the directory level for a node pointer to a leaf containing key value x, say, 305, we need merely find the leftmost (smallest) directory separator value S_1 such that $x \leq S_1$. The separator value 377 has this property in the example given, and we can then follow the node pointer on the left of that separator down to the leaf level. At the leaf level, we perform a separate search for the precise key value we are seeking. Since there are 3907 pages at the leaf level, the directory level above this requires only 3907 node pointers, with 3906 separator values to distinguish between the key value ranges contained on all the leaf nodes. We assume that each directory entry, analogous to a leaf-level index entry, contains a node pointer and a separator key value, (np, sepkeyval). Because the space needed for directory entries is about the same as that for the leaf entries, we see that these 3907 entries will fit on CEIL(3907/256) = 16 pages, which we call *index nodes* or *directory nodes* of the B-tree. The next step is to create an even *higher* directory level to guide us to the proper index node of the directory we have created above the leaf level! We can use the same approach in this higher-level directory, with

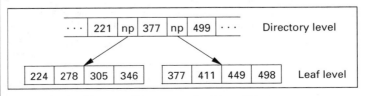

Figure 8.10 Directory Structure to Leaf-Level Nodes

key value separators and pointers down to nodes of the subsidiary directory level, and the number of entries we need at this new level is only 16! Certainly this small number of entries will fit on a single page, and this is called the *root* of the B-tree. Figure 8.11 shows a schematic picture of a three-level B-tree, such as we have just created.

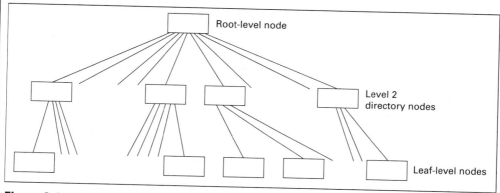

Figure 8.11 A Three-Level B-Tree

■

Note that a B-tree is built upside down, with the root at the top and the leaves at the bottom. We refer to all nodes above the leaf level, including the root, as *directory nodes*, or sometimes *index nodes*. Directory nodes below the root are sometimes called *internal* nodes of the tree. The root node is also known as level 1 of the B-tree, and successively lower levels are given successively larger level numbers, with the leaf nodes at the lowest level, level 3 in Figure 8.11. The total number of levels is called the *depth* of the B-tree. Now we can find our way down to any leaf-level entry by first reading in the root page, then finding our way to successive level directory pages, which ultimately direct us to the appropriate leaf page. We then examine the leaf page to find the leaf-level entry we want, assuming that it exists. In Figure 8.11, this means that we require a maximum of three I/Os to access the desired index entry, much fewer than the binary search for 1 million entries, which required 13 I/Os.

The relative I/O efficiency of a B-tree over binary search results from the fact that the B-tree is structured to get the most out of every disk page (B-tree node) read. All entries on a directory node page have real value in determining which lower-level node to access, and something like 256 lower-level nodes can be pointed to. In the binary search, only a binary decision is made, and only two nodes are accessed as a result. If we look at the tree of page accesses resulting from a binary search, we notice that the B-tree is *bushy*, whereas the binary search tree is *sparse*. The B-tree is flatter as a result, because we can reach as many as 256^3 leaf-level entries in a three-level tree. The B-tree is said to have a *fanout* of 256, compared to the fanout of two for the binary search. The leaf-level nodes of the tree also have their own large fanout, with 256 entry ROWID values pointing down to rows indexed. The rows of the table can be pictured as another level lying below the leaf level of a B-tree.

If we assume a B-tree with a fanout of f, we can access N entries at the leaf level in CEIL($\log_f(N)$) probes. Thus with the fanout of 256 we have been assuming, we can access 1 million leaf-level entries in CEIL($\log_{256}(1,000,000)$) = 3 probes. This compares to CEIL($\log_2(1,000,000)$) = 20 probes in the case of the binary search of Figure 8.8. Of course probes past a certain point in the binary search don't cause page I/Os. Furthermore in the case of a B-tree, multiple probes are made on each index node to locate the appropriate separator value to channel access down to the subordinate level. But the I/Os are what we are trying to minimize, so the multiple probes within a node page don't count. In fact, because of the relatively frequent access to the upper-level index nodes of an actively used B-tree and the fact that all database products buffer disk pages in memory as shown in Figure 8.2, it is likely that *upper-level pages will remain in memory buffers!* There are only 17 pages in the top two levels of Example 8.3.3, after all, not a lot of space when compared with the 3907 nodes at the leaf level. Buffering all the index node pages in this way would reduce the number of I/Os for an index entry lookup to only *one!* In the case of the binary search, we could cut out only the first 5 out of 12 probes by keeping a comparable number of (say) 31 memory-resident pages (31 = 1 + 2 + 4 + 8 + 16 counts the number of pages commonly branched to on the first five probe levels).

Dynamic Changes in the B-Tree

What we have been talking about so far is how to access entries at the leaf level through a multi-level B-tree directory. We also need to consider how inserts to the tree are handled, since we want to claim that a B-tree is an efficient self-modifying structure when new entries are inserted, pointing to new rows inserted in the indexed table. Note that a normal sorted list of entries on disk can always be reconstructed when a new entry is added, but only by moving all successive entries one position to the right to create the hole for the insert, implying an I/O for about half the pages holding entries in the list. But in any application with frequent inserts, such an approach is much too inefficient for a large index. With the 3907 leaf pages of Example 8.3.3, we would need to move about half of these pages—nearly 1953 disk page reads and 1953 disk page writes—which must occur separately if we are not to overwrite needed data. At 80 I/Os per second (assuming most of these pages are not resident in memory buffers), this will require about 4000/80 = 50 seconds. (Note that there are 4000 I/Os that must be performed, and the rate is 80 I/Os/second, so 4000/80 has units I/Os divided by I/Os/second, with the resultant units being seconds. Unit calculations such as this will be very useful in the next few chapters, where calculations are frequently called for.)

The means by which a B-tree is kept ordered (and balanced) as new entries are inserted at the leaf level, without too many pages being updated, is explained based on the example in Figure 8.12. The nodes of the B-tree at every level are generally assumed not to be "full" (we assumed full nodes earlier when calculating 256 entries per page). Instead, space is left so that inserts are often possible to a node at any level without new disk space being required. When a new entry is to be inserted, we follow the directory structure down to the leaf page where it would exist if we were simply looking it up. After the insert has been made, the directory structure will channel our lookup access to

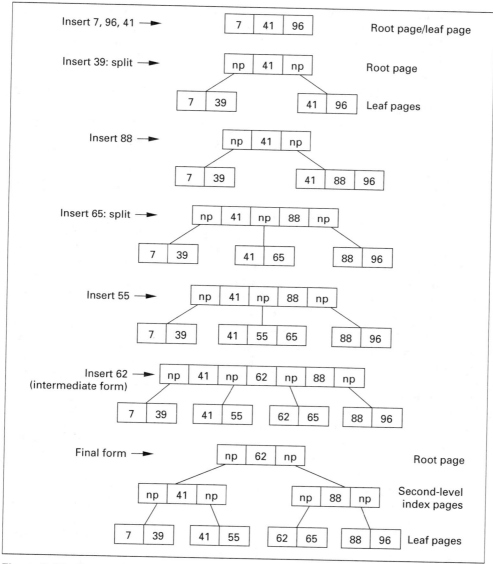

Figure 8.12   Growth of a B-Tree (ROWIDs in Leaf Entries Not Shown)

the same leaf node of the new entry key value. An insert of a new entry always occurs at the leaf level, but occasionally the leaf node is too full to simply accept the new entry. In this case, for additional space the leaf-level node is *split* into two leaf pages (the entries are kept in order, lower key values to the left split page, higher ones to the right). This means that the higher-level index node must be modified so that a new separator exists, along with a new pointer to the new page resulting from the split (the other page has simply been reused). Occasionally the modification of adding a new separator and pointer to the next higher level of index will exceed the space available on that index node. In that case the index node is split, just as the node at the leaf level was, with resulting changes at the next higher-level node of the index. Eventually an additional entry may be placed at the root level, and if the root splits, then a new root node is created at a higher level, having as its children the two split nodes resulting from the former root.

Now consider Figure 8.12. We are assuming that a B-tree leaf page will accept up to three entries, but not four. (This is much smaller than is realistic for disk pages, but keeping it small simplifies our explanation.) We also assume that higher-level index nodes have room for as many as three subordinate node pointers, designated by "np," but not four. (There are only two separator values associated with three pointers, but we equate index entries with the number of node pointers.) Such a structure is basically the same as a (2-3)-tree, a balanced memory-resident tree that is introduced in many data structure courses.

The B-tree starts out empty. As the first three entries are inserted into the B-tree, we have a simple structure, a leaf page that is also a root—that is, no higher-level directory entries are needed, since all entries fit on a single page, the initial page brought in from disk. Note that we dispense with showing ROWID values in leaf entries—it is assumed that each of the key values being inserted at the leaf level has a corresponding ROWID value. Higher-level node entries have visible pointers np to lower-level nodes. Now when the value 39 is added to the one-level B-tree in Figure 8.12, the root splits and a new root is created, with pointers to the two lower leaf-level pages. After this, the values 88 and then 65 are added, a new split occurs, and the new upper-level entry is accepted in the root node. Finally the insert of 62 causes a double split. First the leaf node splits, sending a new separator entry to the higher-level root node. This causes the root node to split and create a new root.

Note in particular that the only way in which the depth of a B-tree can increase is when the root node splits. Immediately after a root-node split, all leaf nodes increase their depth by one from the root node, and it is clear that there is no way in which two leaf nodes can ever come to be at different depths down from the root in a growing B-tree—the B-tree remains totally balanced.

Now what happens when entries are deleted from a B-tree in response to rows being deleted or column values updated in the indexed table? If we consider the final form of the B-tree of Figure 8.12, and imagine deleting the entry with key value 62 at the leaf level, it is clear that this would result in a leaf node with only a single entry, having key value 65. Looking to the right at the leaf level, we see that two leaf nodes now contain only three entries, and they could therefore be *merged* (the opposite of splitting) into a single node with three entries, 65, 88, and 96. At the directory-level node above, we no longer need two node pointers after these leaf nodes are merged, but only one. We also no longer need the separator 88; the separator 62 at the root serves perfectly well. Now with a little bit of thought, we can see how to merge this directory-level node (which has only one node pointer and no separators) with the directory node to its left; the separator from the root must move down to that merged node to distinguish the two node pointers in the standard way. This does away with the need for the root node, and the tree collapses one level to be comparable in structure (although not quite identical) to the B-tree of Figure 8.12 just prior to the insertion of the entry with key value 62.

An algorithm that performs the actions just outlined when entries are deleted from a B-tree could be used to keep a shrinking B-tree balanced and all nodes below the root at least half full. However, very few commercial database systems implement this algorithm for deleted entries. The logic to merge nodes is somewhat complicated, and it requires extra disk I/O during deletion rebalancing to keep nodes well populated. Most database systems architects have decided to allow nodes to become depopulated without automatic rebalancing. Nodes of the tree are released if they become completely empty, so that an index that grows on the right and gets deleted on the left (such as an index by calendar date/time for a scheduled meeting table for a group of employees) releases old nodes as it uses new ones. (However, starting with version 5, **DB2 UDB** supports merging of B-tree nodes whenever the percentage of free space in the nodes merits it. We will have more to say on this when we discuss the **DB2 UDB** Create Index statement of Figure 8.15.)

The major reason for concern over a sparsely populated index is not the disk space (which is cheap, as we have said), but the extra disk I/Os entailed in a range search for a number of entries spread on an unusually large number of leaf nodes (as might happen if we kept one row in 200 in the scheduled meeting table after the time for the meeting had passed). To deal with such inefficiencies, the various database systems provide utilities to *reorganize* the B-tree. Such utilities duplicate the work of the original index creation (though more efficiently) and result in a clean new copy with good disk utilization. We introduce a number of other disk storage considerations, such as free space and compression, in the following sections.

Properties of the B-Tree

Definition 8.3.1 describes the B-tree structure that we have discussed. The definition assumes that entry key values can have variable length, since variable-length column values can appear in the index key. Many definitions in the literature assume fixed-size entries, but this is unrealistic in practice. The definition also assumes that when a node split occurs, equal lengths of entry information are placed in the left and right split nodes. However, some products allow the nodes to split in an uneven fashion, for example, to optimize for a situation where rows are normally being inserted in increasing order by key value. Finally the definition assumes that rebalancing actions in the B-tree occur when entries are deleted (an uncommon situation, as explained in the previous subsection), or that delete operations are overwhelmed by insert operations, so that all the B-tree nodes grow in the number of entries they contain.

DEFINITION 8.3.1 Properties of the B-Tree (B^{+}-Tree) Structure. A B-tree has a tree-like structure with multi-way fanout from the root down to the leaves, so that the following properties hold:

[1] Every node is disk-page sized and resides in a well-defined location on the disk.

[2] Nodes above the leaf level contain directory entries, with $n - 1$ separator keys and n disk pointers to lower-level B-tree nodes.

[3] Nodes at the leaf level contain entries with (keyval, ROWID) pairs pointing to individual rows indexed.

[4] All nodes below the root are at least half full with entry information. (Recall that this is not often enforced after multiple deletes, except with **DB2 UDB**.)

[5] The root node contains at least two entries (except in the case where only one row is indexed and the root is a leaf node containing a single (keyval, ROWID) pair).

■

Index Node Layout and Free Space

A normal B-tree node page has a relatively simple structure. Figure 8.13 shows a possible schematic layout of a leaf-level node with unique key values. An index with multiple duplicate key values will usually have some way of compressing out the duplicate key values so as to list all the RIDs that will fit on a leaf page with the same key value in a row (as in Figure 8.17, below). Note that because an index with variable-length key values will have variable-length entries as well, some form of "entry directory" will exist in the nodes of Figure 8.13, comparable with the row directory slots in Figure 8.6. An entry directory also provides the capability to perform a binary search within the node, even though the keyval values are variable length.

Because of the splits that occur in a growing B-tree, the nodes of a tree that result from random insert activity will vary randomly from half full to full (except for the root, which may have as few as two subsidiary node pointer entries). The average node below the root level in an actively growing B-tree will be about 70.7% full, *not* three-quarters full, as might seem more intuitive. This fullness percentage can be derived by mathematical analysis, and matches well with empirical observations. The percentage holds for all nodes except the root, and it means that the earlier analysis of the number of leaf pages required for a million-row table is an underestimate if the B-tree results from a large number of randomly inserted rows.

EXAMPLE 8.3.4 Corrected B-Tree Structure for a Million Index Entries.

As in Example 8.3.3, we assume once again an index entry size of 8 bytes and a node page size of 2048 bytes. But now we allow 48 bytes for the header and assume that the average node below the root level is only 70% full (an approximation to 71% that we use for simplicity). This implies 1400 bytes of entries per node, and 1400/8 = 175 entries per node. With 1,000,000 entries at the leaf level, this means we will require CEIL(1,000,000/175) = 5715 leaf-node pages. With 5715 entries at the next higher index (directory) level, we will have CEIL(5715/175) = 33

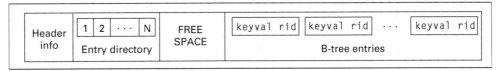

Figure 8.13   Layout of a B-tree Leaf-Level Node with Unique Key Values

page nodes there. Thus we have 33 directory entries at the root level, and we still have a B-tree of depth three. In general, we encourage rather rough calculations in sizings of this kind, for example, in the exercises for this chapter and the next. A header size of 48 bytes is probably incorrect for any particular product, but (with a fullness of 70%) this gives us a round number for our calculations. ∎

Recall that the purpose of a B-tree index is to minimize the number of disk I/Os needed to locate a row with a given index key value. The depth of a B-tree bears a close relationship to the number of disk I/Os used to reach the leaf-level entry where the ROWID is kept. As we mentioned earlier, it is common to estimate the fanout at each level to have the value n (rather than f, used earlier), where n is the expected number of entries that appear in each node. Assuming that there are n directory entries at the root node and every node below that, the number of entries at the second level is n^2, the number at the third level n^3, and so on. For a tree of depth K, the number of leaf-level entries is n^K just before a root split occurs in the tree to make it a tree of depth K+1. Putting this a different way, if we want to build a B-tree with entries for M rows, then we need to have K levels, where

$$K = CEIL(\log_n(M))$$

Thus the depth of the tree bears a logarithmic relationship to the number of rows to be indexed. The depth K is then taken to be the number of I/Os that must be performed to look up a key value entry at the leaf level. However, it turns out that both of these statements are misleading. Because of buffering, the upper levels of the B-tree are almost certain to be buffer resident for any B-tree that is commonly used (and we don't really care very much about performance of B-trees that are infrequently used). Generally an active B-tree of depth three has all nodes buffer resident above the leaf level, but very few leaf-level nodes resident, so the effective number of real I/Os that must be performed to look up a leaf entry is one, rather than three. At the same time, the logarithmic relationship of tree depth to number of entries indexed is misleading because the fanout n is so large as to be unintuitive. With the assumptions of Example 8.3.4, the average number of entries in each node is 175, and this is also the fanout n. Ignoring the fact that the number of entries in the root will be somewhat greater, this means that when a B-tree of depth two is about to have a root split, it contains 175^2 = 30,625 entries at the leaf level. We then have a B-tree of depth three, and there will not be another root split until we have 175^3 = 5,359,375 entries! This provides enough entries to index a 5-million-row table, and it is fairly unusual to have B-trees with more than three levels. The value of 175^4 is 937,890,625, so we would need nearly 1 billion rows in a table to require a five-level B-tree. (Of course, if the key values are extremely long, then there would be fewer entries to a page, and a five-level tree would occur with fewer rows.)

When creating indexes on a table with most database products, it is usually most efficient to first load the table with the initial set of rows and then to create the indexes. This is advantageous because the process used by Create Index to first extract the index entries, then sort the entries by key value, and finally load the sorted entries into the leaf level of the B-tree is extremely efficient. The nodes of the B-tree are all loaded in a left-to-right fashion, so that successive inserts normally occur to the same leaf node, which will be held consistently in memory buffer. When the leaf node splits, the successive leaf node is allocated from the next disk page of the allocated extent. Node splits at every level occur in a controlled way and allow us to leave just the right amount of free space on each page. On the other hand, as rows are inserted after the initial Create Index statement, this normally results in B-tree entries that are inserted to random leaf-level nodes, requiring much more I/O (because the B-tree leaf page affected is often not in buffer) and random node splits. Thus it is much more efficient to load the table and then create the index than to create the index and then load the table.

The Create Index Statement in ORACLE and DB2 UDB

It is of course possible that a B-tree index will remain unchanged after being created. This would occur if the table indexed is guaranteed to have no new row inserts or updates that affect the columns indexed. If no changes are envisioned, we should start with all B-tree nodes packed full. However, if new entry inserts are likely, it is a bad idea to have fully packed nodes in a newly created index. A small number of new inserts will cause a very large number of initial node splits (costly in I/O and CPU), with the result that the number of nodes quickly doubles and ends up only half full, an unfortunate waste of resources. In most database systems, we can control how full the index B-tree gets packed during its initial creation. In Figure 8.14, which repeats the syntax presented in Figure 8.7, we illustrate this with a clause provided with the **ORACLE** Create Index statement, known as the PCTFREE clause.

The value of n in the PCTFREE clause can range from 0 to 99, and this number determines the percentage of each B-tree node page (recall that a page is known as a *block* in **ORACLE**) that will be left unfilled when the index is first created. This space is then available for new index entry inserts when rows are inserted to the underlying table. The default value for PCTFREE is 10, and larger values permit more row insertions before node splits occur. A comparable parameter for leaving free space in index nodes is provided by **DB2 UDB**, as we see in Figure 8.15. Indeed **ORACLE** has historically made an effort to keep its syntax compatible with that of **DB2 UDB**, so we can expect identical naming conventions when differences in disk storage architecture don't require variations.

```
CREATE [UNIQUE | BITMAP] INDEX [schema.]indexname ON [schema.]tablename
    (columnname [ASC | DESC] {, columnname [ASC | DESC]})
    [TABLESPACE tblspacename]
    [STORAGE ([INITIAL n [K|M]] [NEXT n [K|M]] [MINEXTENTS n] [MAXEXTENTS n]
        [PCTINCREASE n] ) ]
    [PCTFREE n]
    [other disk storage and transactional clauses not covered or deferred]
    [NOSORT]
```

Figure 8.14 ORACLE Create Index Statement Syntax, with PCTFREE Clause

```
CREATE [UNIQUE] INDEX indexname ON tablename
    (columnname [ASC | DESC] {, columnname [ASC | DESC]})
    [INCLUDE (columnname [ASC | DESC] {, columnname [ASC | DESC]})]
    [CLUSTER]
    [PCTFREE n]
    [MINPCTUSED n]
    [ALLOW REVERSE SCANS];
```

Figure 8.15   The **DB2 UDB** Create Index Statement Syntax

The **DB2 UDB** Create Index statement of Figure 8.15 is missing the TABLESPACE clause of **ORACLE**, because the tablespace used for indexes is the same as that for the table in **DB2 UDB**. (The **DB2 UDB** Create Table statement is otherwise comparable with our Basic SQL form in terms of the syntax we have discussed up to now.) The INCLUDE clause can be used with a UNIQUE index to specify columns that can be stored in the index beyond those in the index key. These columns can later be accessed very quickly in what are known as INDEXONLY queries, where no table rows need to be accessed. The CLUSTER keyword will be explained later along with clustering indexes in general. The PCTFREE clause in **DB2 UDB** is identical in meaning to the **ORACLE** form. The MINPCTUSED clause sets a threshold level at which pages are merged together after record deletes have occurred. The ALLOW REVERSE SCANS clause (a new feature in **DB2 UDB** version 6) creates bidirectional leaf pointers, so that the query optimizer can plan scans in either direction through the index. **DB2 UDB** makes extremely efficient use of contiguous disk storage when doing index range retrievals, so it is especially important to keep leaf nodes as contiguous as possible on disk. We will explore this further in Section 8.4 and in Chapter 9.

Duplicate Key Values in an Index

In our discussion of B-tree structure so far, we have not assumed a unique restriction on the entry key values. Recall that in Example 8.3.1, when discussing binary search, we considered the possibility of duplicate key values and provided an algorithm to find the leftmost key value in a set of duplicates. The succession of key values inserted into the B-tree index of Figure 8.12 is 7, 96, 41, 39, 88, 65, 55, 62. These values have no duplicates, but looking at the final B-tree form at the bottom of this figure, we can easily imagine how we would handle a new row insert with a duplicate key value of 88. A new index entry with key value 88 would search for the first sepkey S_1 such that $88 \leq S_1$, and follow the np on its left down to the leaf with entries with key values 62 and 65, being placed as the third entry of that leaf. Now the ROWIDs (not pictured in Figure 8.12) of the two entries with key value 88 would have different ROWID pointers. Both the key value and the ROWID pointer are used to distinguish one entry from another.

What would happen now if we inserted another row with key value 88? The new entry for this row would be inserted in the same leaf page as the previous one, making

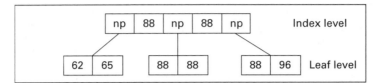

Figure 8.16 B-Tree Structure with Multiple Duplicate Key Values

four entries in all, 62, 65, and two entries for 88. In the example pictured, where no leaf-level node can contain more than three entries, this would require a leaf-node split, with the node containing key values 62 and 65 going to the left and a node with two key values 88 going to the right. This in turn means that the separator entry in the directory above the leaf needs to distinguish these two leaf-level nodes by using the separator value 88. See Figure 8.16.

Using two separator values of 88 seems a bit strange, and this value does not really distinguish key values in the two rightmost leaf nodes below. (There are key values of 88 in both nodes.) Therefore the system has to take this fact into account in answering queries, and this has already been done. Specifically, when the system processes a query to retrieve all rows with this key value equal to 88, it searches the index level to find the leftmost entry with value ≥ 88. Of course, we find an index entry sepkey value 88, and because we allow duplicates, we are aware there might be values 88 on the leaf node following the np to the left of this sepkey value in Figure 8.16. In this case there are none. (Note that if we had a unique index, we could look for the leftmost entry at each index entry with value > 88, and always be certain of going to the proper node below if the key value we are seeking exists.) After reaching the leaf level, we read through all leaf-level entries that have key value 88, jumping from one leaf node to the next if the possibility of another match exists on the successive leaf node. Note that this approach—retrieving successive duplicate entries on successive leaf pages—generalizes naturally to range retrieval (for example, finding all rows with key value between 88 and 120). To make this kind of successive retrieval easy, leaf nodes usually have *sibling pointers* in their header info segment that point to successive leaf nodes. (There should also be sibling pointers to the *prior* leaf node in the sequence, in case a Select request in descending order requires retrieval in that direction.)

Now consider the case where the number of key value entries of 88 increases to a point that we must have two duplicate separator values in the directory level above. Nothing is wrong with this as long as our directory search algorithm is intelligent about always finding the way to the leftmost entries at the leaf level, thus always following the leftmost directory pointer to a desired value. We will still be able to retrieve all entries with key value = 88 by starting at the left and proceeding through all successive entries with the same key value. An interesting situation arises, however, when we wish to delete a row that has key value 88. To properly complete the row delete, the associated entry from the B-tree leaf level must be removed as well; otherwise we are left with an index entry pointing to a nonexistent row. Since the entry is not uniquely identified by its key value, the system may have to read through a succession of entries, possibly on multiple leaf-node pages, to retrieve the entry with key value equal to 88 *that has the ROWID value of the row being deleted.* It is possible to keep the leaf-level lookup entries in order by ROWID within the key value and to allow directory separator values to carry this ROWID information as well. Then successive separators are unique, since they contain a unique ROWID suffix value, and a fast lookup of any particular ROWID with key value 88 can be performed through the B-tree directory. However, this approach is not implemented on some commercial database systems. A delete of a row that corresponds to a heavily duplicated key value can thus entail a long search through the leaf level of the B-tree.

Index RID lists

There is an opportunity when multiple duplicate key values are present to save a good deal of space in the leaf nodes. Because the same key value is repeated for a large number of rows, it is possible to list the key value only once for a long list of ROWID values. Because the key value is sometimes a relatively lengthy character string and the ROWID value is usually quite short, this can represent a large savings in I/O at retrieval time. In **DB2 UDB**, where the ROWID is referred to as a RID (pronounced like the word "rid" in "get rid of"), the leaf nodes of a B-tree index have somewhat different forms, depending on whether the key value is unique or has a number of duplicates. We have already seen in Figure 8.13 what the **DB2 UDB** leaf-node layout with unique key values looks like. Figure 8.17 shows the layout where multiple duplicate key values are present.

We see that where duplicate key values are the rule, **DB2 UDB** is able to represent the key value once, followed by a list of RID values. (We will call this a *RID list* or *ROWID list* in what follows.) In the **DB2 UDB** representation, there is a prefix of 2 bytes for each distinct RID-list logical block, represented by Prx in Figure 8.17. This block prefix contains the length of the logical block, including the prefix, from which the number of duplicates is easily determined. The number of RID values in a block has an upper limit of 255, but clearly it is possible to create a successive block with the same key value. If we assume a character string key value of length 10 bytes, then each unique key takes up 14 bytes (length of keyval + RID), and 100 unique key value entries take up 1400 bytes. On the other hand, 100 duplicate entries take up 2 + 10 + 100 * 4 = 412 bytes (length of Prx + keyval + 100 RID values), a significant savings. Clearly as the number of duplicates grows, the space needed for leaf-level indexes converges to the space needed for RID values alone.

Figure 8.17 Layout of a **DB2 UDB** Leaf Node with Duplicate Key Values on Different Rows

The ORACLE Bitmap Index

Recall the BITMAP keyword from the **ORACLE** Create Index statement syntax of Figure 8.7. A bitmap index is appropriate in situations where multiple rows have duplicate key values. For example, assume we are defining a table for the 100,000 employees of a large company:

```
create table emps (eid char(5) not null primary key, ename varchar(16),
    mgrid char(5) references emps, gender char(1), salarycat smallint,
    dept char(5));
```

Recall that the primary key column eid for this table automatically has a unique index defined for it. Since each row has a single eid key value, a bitmap index for this column is inappropriate. Indeed, the syntax of Figure 8.7 allows either an optional keyword UNIQUE or BITMAP, but not both. On the other hand, the columns named gender (values 'M' or 'F'), salarycat (values 1 through 10), and dept (12 values, 'ACCNT' through 'SWDEV') all have relatively few values (a different way of saying this is that the columns have small *cardinality*). Thus we expect that any particular value for any of these columns would have a lot of different ROWIDs following it in an index, and these columns are therefore appropriate keys for bitmap indexes.

```
create bitmap index genderx on emps(gender);
create bitmap index salx on emps(salrycat);
create bitmap index deptx on emps(dept);
```

We are now ready to introduce the idea of a bitmap. To begin with, a table with N rows on which bitmaps are to be created must have each row provided with an *ordinal number*: $0, 1, 2, \ldots, N - 1$. Successively numbered rows are, wherever possible, physically contiguous on disk, and there must be functions to convert from ordinal number to ROWID and back. Now a *bitmap* is a sequence of N bits (with values 0 or 1, eight bits to a byte), and can represent any list L of ROWIDs as follows: if the ROWID with ordinal number k is in the list L, set bit k of the bitmap of N bits to 1; otherwise set bit k to 0. For example, the bitmap

```
1001010001101101...
```

represents the list L of ROWIDs with ordinal numbers 0, 3, 5, 9, 10, 12, 13, 15, . . . , and so on. (Examine the bitmap yourself to determine that the left-to-right order of 1-bits matches the ordinal numbers in the list.) Each individual bitmap represents a ROWID list of the sort you would expect to find in a B-tree index associated with a single value; thus a *bitmap index* on a column will have one bitmap for each value in the column. For example, the bitmap index on the dept column of emps is a regular B-tree, with each key value having an associated list of ROWIDs, except that instead of having a ROWID list of the kind we see in Figure 8.17, we would use bitmaps, as in Figure 8.18. Note that just as **DB2 UDB** partitions the RID list in Figure 8.17 into logical blocks that fit on a disk

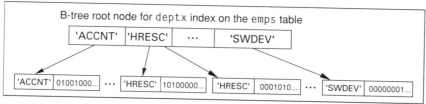

Figure 8.18 Bitmap Index on the dept Column of the emps Table

page, **ORACLE** partitions bitmaps into *segments* to fit on disk pages. Obviously a bitmap for a table with 100,000 rows will have 100,000 bits, or 100,000/8 = 12,500 bytes, and such a bitmap would need to be partitioned across at least seven 2-KB pages.

Density of Bitmaps

We say that a bitmap is *dense* if the proportion of 1-bits in the bitmap is large. The *bitmap density* is defined as the number of 1-bits divided by the number N of all bits in the bitmap. A bitmap index for a column with 32 values will have bitmaps with average density of 1/32 for each of its values. (This is because the column for the row with ordinal number k has exactly one value, so a 1-bit will appear in position k in exactly one of the index value bitmaps.) When there are 32 key values, the disk space to hold a bitmap index will be comparable to the disk space needed for a **DB2 UDB** RID-list index, which requires about 4 bytes, or 32 bits, for each RID present (and a small additional space for the key values, which is also required in the bitmap index). However, in a bitmap index with 320 values, there would be ten times as many bitmaps as there are in the 32-value case, and each (uncompressed) bitmap will take the same space as it did when there were 32 values. The density of each bitmap has dropped to 1/320 on the average, and so the size of a bitmap index (using uncompressed bitmaps) is proportional to the number of column values. But a RID-list index with any number of key values always has the same total number of RIDs, and remains about the same size as long as we continue to have many more RIDs than key values, so the key value lengths are a small fraction of the RID lengths.

When a bitmap has a relatively small density, we say that the bitmap is *sparse*, and it seems that when there are many key values, bitmap indexes must take a lot more disk space than RID-list indexes because of such sparse bitmaps. But **ORACLE** uses a special algorithm to *compress* a sparse bitmap in a bitmap index, and thus reduces its size. A sparse bitmap can be compressed, for example, by returning to the ROWID-list-like approach of providing a list of ordinal numbers where 1-bits occur. Clearly this would be an important savings in space in a bitmap with density 1/320. But **ORACLE** has a much more effective compression algorithm than this. To give an idea of its effectiveness, a compressed bitmap index on a large table will remain smaller than a RID-list index up to the point where there are only two rows for each key value (an extremely sparse bitmap indeed!). The advantage of the compressed bitmap index grows quickly as the number of key values goes down, until at some point the bitmaps become so dense that compression is no longer needed. In what follows, we will refer to an uncompressed bitmap as a *verbatim* bitmap, to differentiate it from a compressed bitmap.

Advantages and Disadvantages of Bitmap Indexes

There are at least two performance advantages that a bitmap index can have over a traditional RID-list index. First, a bitmap index is normally quite efficient in terms of I/O performance, since compression causes it to take up less space on disk than a ROWID-list index. Second, a bitmap index is quite efficient in performing Boolean operations (such as AND and OR) between two predicates that are represented on bitmap indexes. For example, assume we wished to answer the query

```
select eid from emps where salarycat = '10' and dept = 'ADMIN';
```

If both columns mentioned in the WHERE clause have a bitmap index, then the two equal match predicates will each correspond to a bitmap in that index. We claim we can perform the AND Boolean operation between two SQL predicates that are indexed in this way in a more efficient manner than can be done with traditional ROWID-list indexes. Furthermore, the advantage extends to compressed bitmap indexes as well as verbatim bitmap indexes, and becomes more and more effective as more predicates appear in a WHERE clause. In addition, special types of predefined bitmap indexes are valuable in performing join queries of the most common type, foreign-key-to-primary-key joins. For these reasons, bitmap indexes are commonly used in tables that experience a large number of complex queries.

On the other hand, bitmap indexes can be somewhat disadvantageous when many updates must be performed on a table that will affect the bitmap indexes. While bitmap indexes can accommodate updates, deletes, and inserts to a table, the modifications required are not necessarily easily done. This is especially true when the bitmap indexes that must be modified are in compressed form, since the bitmap affected must be uncompressed prior to the modification, which typically turns a bit on or off, and then compressed again in what might be a different way. Because of this disadvantage, bitmap indexes are normally not used for tables that have a large volume of updates performed that could affect the index representation.

8.4   Clustered and Non-Clustered Indexes

We saw in the discussion following Figure 8.5 how rows of a table are typically inserted on successive data storage pages on disk, one after another, in a heap structure (this is true for almost all database products: **ORACLE**'s default HEAP organization is typical). In a library, this would correspond to placing volumes on shelves in order by acquisition—an unusual procedure, admittedly, but one that would be feasible as long as various card catalog indexes allowed us to locate all books by any useful category. It is more common to place books on the shelves in order by Dewey decimal number for non-fiction and author's name for fiction. (Actually, the order for fiction books is usually determined by the concatenated index key: authlname || authfname || authmi || title.) The

advantage of such ordering on the shelves is convenience. If we want to locate all the   **503**
novels by Charles Dickens, we can look up any Dickens novel in the card catalog and
proceed to the shelves where all novels by Dickens are grouped together. This saves us
quite a few steps. Similarly, if we want to find books on building bridges, we will probably find them all clustered together under the appropriate Dewey classification (the classification is by the major topic of a nonfiction work).

Placing books on shelves—or rows on disk—in order by some common index key
value is called *clustering*. An index with referenced rows in the same order as its key values is known as a *clustered index*, or sometimes a *clustering index* in **DB2 UDB**. (The
cluster term also has another, slightly different meaning in **ORACLE** when we speak of
INDEX CLUSTER and HASH CLUSTER. We will treat these concepts a bit later in this
section.)

A slightly more general concept than a clustered index is a *primary index* for a table,
where the index specifically determines the placement of the rows on disk. In a primary
B-tree index—one example of a primary index—the rows actually sit in the leaf level of
the B-tree, taking the place of index entries with ROWIDs that merely point at the rows
in the indexes we have been discussing up to now. An index that contains ROWID pointers to the rows is now referred to as a *secondary index*, to distinguish it from a primary
index. There can be only one primary index for a table, and many database products,
such as **DB2 UDB**, do not support a primary index at all, while others, such as **ORACLE**,
provide a primary index with very limited capability. Note that a primary B-tree index
must be a clustered index, since the rows must be in order by the key values of the index.
However, another type of primary index exists that uses hashing, and in a hash primary
index the rows are placed on disk in order by hash value on the index key. Since the hash
values seem almost random, and there is no correlation between successive key values, it
is clear that there is no clustering taking place: rows with successive key values will tend
to appear far apart on disk.

The advantage of a clustered index in a database is that certain queries are more efficiently answered when the desired rows are close to one another. The average row takes
up only a small fraction of a page, so that when rows with common index key values are
clustered together and we read in the data page from disk containing one of the rows
with a given key value, other rows with the same key value are likely to lie on the same
page. Thus in accessing those other rows, we don't have to repeat the disk I/O required to
access the first row. Even if our database access method is relatively naive and accesses
the rows only one at a time on the basis of their ROWID values, we find that second and
successive rows in a clustered index lie on a page that is already in memory buffers (Figure 8.2), which were constructed to save I/O for accesses to popular pages. On the other
hand, a non-clustered index does not have this advantage. Successive index entries of a
non-clustered index reference rows on disk pages that are likely to be far apart, so there
is no savings from one row to another. It is as if we placed books on library shelves in
order by acquisition and then had to walk all over the library to retrieve all the novels by
Dickens. See Figure 8.19 for a schematic idea of a clustered versus a non-clustered index.

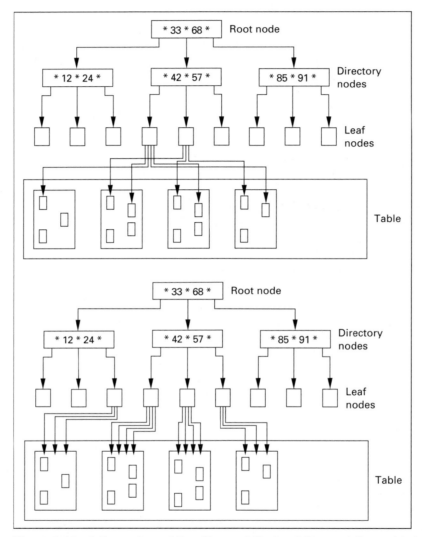

Figure 8.19   A Comparison of Non-Clustered (Top) and Clustered (Bottom) Indexes

EXAMPLE 8.4.1

A large department store with hundreds of branch stores has records of 10 million customers in the United States. The store has created the table customers, with columns named as follows: straddr, cityst, zipcode, age, incomeclass (values 1 to 10, from lowest to highest family income), hobby (50 different values, from acrobatics to zoology), major1dept, major2dept (the departments in the store where the customer has spent the most and second-most money), and numerous others as well. The main use for the customers table is to select prospective customers to whom mailings should be sent announcing sales by the store. Normally these sales take place in a specific region of the country or even a specific store (a very common need in merchandising, since different regions have different characteristics in terms of what sells well, and we don't always have enough of some item to support a sale in all stores in a region). Thus the store might need to generate mailing labels for a sale on sports equipment in the Boston area with the following Select statement:

```
select name, address, city, state, zip from customers
    where city = 'Boston' and age between 18 and 50 and hobby in ('racket sports',
    'jogging', 'hiking', 'bodybuilding', 'outdoor sports');
```

Of course, the fields would be formatted for mailing labels through an application program and the query would be performed in Embedded SQL through a cursor, but the I/O performance considerations are the same as in this ad hoc Select statement.

Now consider the best indexing to support queries of this form. First we would like to create a *clustered index* on the column zipcode, so that all rows in the Boston area, or indeed any geographic region, would fall in a contiguous segment of disk. We might find from statistics kept on the indexes that the Boston region has about 1/50 of our 10 million U.S. customers, or about 200,000 rows. If we are using a database system with 2-KB pages, and each customer row requires 100 bytes, we can conclude that each page contains 20 rows, so 200,000 rows will sit on 10,000 disk pages. If the predicates in the WHERE clause of the query above that do not involve the city column further restrict the number of rows retrieved to 1/5 of the customers in Boston, we will find that the 40,000 rows that are left still occupy most of the 10,000 disk pages used for Boston customers. But note that if we had *not* kept rows in clustered order, the Boston customer rows would have been spread across 500,000 disk pages (10 million rows divided by 20 rows per page), and nearly every one of the 40,000 rows in Boston would have then required a separate disk I/O. Thus clustering has reduced the number of I/Os we have to perform from 40,000 disk pages to 10,000 disk pages, and at 80 I/Os per second (recall this disk access statistic from Section 8.2), this is a difference between 500 seconds of disk arm use and 125 seconds of disk arm use, a significant variation in resource cost, and most likely in elapsed time as well. (Different disk arms can perform accesses simultaneously for a query, but if this is only one of multiple queries competing for resources, the elapsed time for the query can easily approach the number of seconds of disk arm use.)

If we added additional restrictions in the WHERE clause, such as mailing only to customers who have made large purchases in the sports department before (major1dept = 'sports' or major2dept = 'sports'), and to customers with a large family income (incomeclass in (9, 10)), we might limit the number of customers in the mailing to only 2000 (and thus save on mailing cost to target a more select group). Then at most 2000 disk pages would need to be accessed, *assuming we can evaluate all these predicates simultaneously in the WHERE clause to restrict the rows retrieved!* This can be done for all the major database systems we have been considering, assuming that we provide *secondary indexes* on all the attributes named above. If we do not have such secondary indexes, we will need to access all Boston area customers on 10,000 pages of disk, in order to determine which rows fit the other predicate restrictions. ∎

We made a large number of assumptions in arriving at the estimates of Example 8.4.1, but we will defer detailed considerations of such performance assumptions until the next chapter. For now, we simply say that the estimates we have just made are probably in the ballpark for most commercial applications, and the enormous variation in performance between clustered and non-clustered conditions makes the value of clustering obvious. We should add that we do not require a large number of duplicate key values in a table to see large differences between clustered and non-clustered performance. A query that uses a BETWEEN predicate, between keyval1 and keyval2 (one of the predicate forms referred to as a *range predicate*), can also benefit enormously from clustered indexes, even when key values are unique. Unfortunately, we can only cluster a table by one index at a time. Clearly we can't place nonfiction books on library shelves in order by Dewey decimal classification *and* by author name simultaneously—we must choose one or the other. The index we use to cluster the underlying data rows depends a great deal on the most common query types in use at a database site. The DBA usually makes this clustering decision in consultation with application managers and programmers who are aware of the most common query needs.

Clustering Indexes in DB2 UDB

The next question, of course, is: How do we create a clustered index? The approach to creating a clustered index differs from one product to another. As we saw in Figure 8.15, the **DB2 UDB** Create Index statement, which we repeat in Figure 8.20, has a special CLUSTER clause.

The **DB2 UDB** CLUSTER clause has no arguments, and only one index for a table can be identified as a CLUSTER index (referred to in what follows as a *clustering index*). When an index is identified as a clustering index for an empty table that is about to be loaded with new rows, you should sort the rows in the OS file in order by the CLUSTER key value before performing the **DB2 UDB** LOAD utility. If sorting the rows in advance is not convenient, you can load the rows in any order and then invoke the REORGANIZE action (utility). The result in **DB2 UDB** will look like the tree structure at the bottom of Figure 8.19, a B-tree index conceptually lying above a sequence of table rows placed in data pages in the same order. Indeed the entire structure looks a bit like a B-tree with an extra level, where the data rows, in order by key value, lie at the new leaf level, and the former leaf level of the index acts as a higher-level directory to the rows (not just the data pages, as would be the case for a true directory to the leaf level of a B-tree). This is the type of structure we might expect with a primary B-tree index.

```
CREATE [UNIQUE] INDEX indexname ON tablename
    (columnname [ASC | DESC] {, columnname [ASC | DESC]})
    [INCLUDE (columnname [ASC | DESC] {, columnname [ASC | DESC]})]
    [CLUSTER]
    [PCTFREE n]
    [MINPCTUSED n]
    [ALLOW REVERSE SCANS];
```

Figure 8.20   The **DB2 UDB** Create Index Statement Syntax with CLUSTER Clause

Unfortunately the analogy is somewhat inaccurate because the behavior of the structure as new rows are inserted does not conform to what we would expect with a primary index. **DB2 UDB** advises the table creator to leave free space on the data pages for the table (with a PCTFREE clause in the Create Table statement), so that successive row inserts can be directed by **DB2 UDB** to the free slots on the appropriate data page to maintain the clustering order for as long as this is feasible. However, when a data page runs out of slots and new rows are inserted that would normally be placed on such a page, the B-tree approach of *splitting* the leaf node does not take place on the data pages. Instead a new data page is allocated in the current extent if possible, or more likely when the current extent is full, in another extent at the end of the table. The longer we proceed with new inserts, the less clustered the index becomes because of latecomer rows that are entirely out of clustered sequence. Eventually the index can lose much of its clustering property, and the user is advised to invoke the REORGANIZE action again, so that the rows will be re-sorted in appropriate order and left with PCTFREE space on each data page again.

As we will see, **DB2 UDB** retrieves data through clustering indexes with extreme I/O efficiency. In the situation of Example 8.4.1, where a large fraction of the rows in Boston need to be retrieved from 10,000 consecutive pages, **DB2 UDB** will actually perform multi-page reads (known as *prefetch I/O*) to increase the number of disk pages that can be accessed each second. Recall from Section 8.2 that most of the time needed for an I/O is spent waiting for the disk arm to get to the right place, and only a very small fraction of the time is spent actually transferring the data once the head begins reading. If we perform a longer disk read after the disk arm is in position, to read in multiple relevant pages at full transfer rate, we will improve our I/O rate. The improvement can be as much as a factor of 10 in some cases, and such high performance for multi-page reads and writes is so far unmatched by any other DBMS products. We will cover this topic in greater detail in Chapter 9.

ORACLE Special Indexing Features

ORACLE has a number of special access structures by which tables can be indexed, including index-organized tables and indexed and hashed clusters, which we explain below.

ORACLE Index-Organized Tables

Recall that the **ORACLE** Create Table command of Figure 8.5 provides an optional ORGANIZATION INDEX clause.

```
CREATE TABLE [schema.]tablename
    ({columnname datatype . . .
    [ORGANIZATION HEAP | ORGANIZATION INDEX (this has clauses not covered)]
```

When this clause appears, the rows of the table created are placed in a *true primary key B-tree index*, in order by key value at the leaf level of the tree. As new rows are inserted, they are guided by the B-tree to proper order at the leaf level, and when no space remains at the leaf node, the leaf will split, with rows appearing in both split nodes in appropriate order. Thus all rows in an **ORACLE** index-organized table are clustered by key value and remain clustered in this way as new rows are inserted. While this might seem like an ideal situation, there is a limitation on an index-organized table that makes it somewhat less useful than it might be. The limitation is that the B-tree key value in an ORGANIZA-TION INDEX structure must be the primary key for the table.

Let us recall Example 8.4.1, where we explored appropriate indexing to support retrievals of customers by criteria such as hobbies and incomeclass, from geographically limited regions. A clustered index on the column zipcode was proposed, so that all rows in any geographic region would fall in a contiguous segment of disk. At the same time, various other secondary indexes on columns, such as hobby and incomeclass, were provided to restrict the rows prior to retrieval from disk.

In **ORACLE**, we would not be able to define an index-organized table on the zipcode column, because it is not a primary key for the table (it is not even a candidate key, since multiple rows will have the same zip code). We could instead use a primary key such as custid for the table custs, but it is unclear how to assign such numbers so as to maintain geographic locality. To provide a unique primary key ordered by geographic information, we need to use at least two columns such as: zipcode, custid. Then we would be able to define secondary indexes on hobby and incomeclass. (Index-organized tables became available with the release of **ORACLE** 8, but until the **ORACLE** 8i release, no ROWIDs were provided for rows in such a structure, and thus no secondary indexes could be defined. However, with **ORACLE** 8i, a new feature known as logical ROWIDs provided support for secondary indexes.)

ORACLE Table Clusters

An **ORACLE** *cluster* is a structure that normally contains rows from two or more tables joined on certain columns, usually in a foreign-key to primary-key manner. These join columns are used to define a *cluster key*, so that rows from both tables with the same values for this cluster key will be stored together on disk within the cluster. For example, an employees table and a departments table might both have a deptno column that is commonly used in joins between the two. This deptno column for the two tables would be used as the cluster key in the cluster that holds these two tables. All rows from the two tables for one key value of the cluster key would then be stored together on disk. For example, all the employees rows for deptno = 10 and the departments row for deptno = 10 would be stored together, on as few disk blocks as possible. The Create Cluster syntax is shown in Figure 8.21.

The Create Cluster statement of Figure 8.21 has many of the clauses that appear in a Create Table statement, but there are a number of differences. First, the columnname datatype sequence coming after the clustername definition does not define all columns of the tables contained in the cluster, but only lists the small number of columns in the cluster key. The table definitions will define all their own columns (and constraints), and

```
CREATE CLUSTER [schema.]clustername
    (columnname datatype {, columnname datatype ... }  -- this is the cluster key
        [cluster_clause { cluster_clause ...}];
```
The cluster_clauses that specify cluster characteristics are chosen from the following:
```
    [PCTFREE n] [PCTUSED n]
    [STORAGE ([INITIAL n [K|M]] [NEXT n [K|M]] [MINEXTENTS n] [MAXEXTENTS n]
        [PCTINCREASE n])]
    [SIZE n [K|M]]                                 -- defaults to one disk block
    [TABLESPACE tblspacename]
    [INDEX | [SINGLE TABLE] HASHKEYS n [HASH is expr]]
    [other clauses not covered];
```
To delete an existing cluster, the DROP CLUSTER statement is used:
```
DROP CLUSTER [schema.]clustername [INCLUDING TABLES [CASCADE CONSTRAINTS]];
```

Figure 8.21 ORACLE Create Cluster Statement Syntax

```
CREATE TABLE [schema.]tablename
    (column definitions as Basic SQL, see Figure 7.1 or Figure 8.5)
    CLUSTER clustername (columnname {, columnname...}) -- table columns map to cluster key
    [AS subquery];
```

Figure 8.22 Create Table Statement for Table to Be Contained in a Cluster

specify which of their columns match with the cluster key column names given in Figure 8.21. See Figure 8.22 for how this matching is specified. As before, if the AS subquery clause is used, the column definitions of the Create Table statement do not need to specify datatypes.

The PCTFREE and PCTUSED keywords of the Create Cluster statement of Figure 8.21 are used to specify the circumstances of how full a disk block can be when additional rows can be added to a cluster's disk block. This was explained in the discussion following the Create Table statement syntax of Figure 8.5, and the STORAGE clause was explained there as well. The SIZE parameter of Figure 8.21 is an estimate of the number of bytes that should be reserved for the rows with a single cluster key value that will be stored together in the cluster. We will call the disk space filled by the rows with a single cluster key value a *cluster slot*, or simply a *slot*. (This term is used only for convenience here and is not standard in **ORACLE**.) Thus the SIZE parameter is an estimate of how large a slot will be, and is used by **ORACLE** to determine the maximum number of slots that can be placed on a single disk block:

```
Number of slots in a disk block = CEIL(Number of usable bytes in a disk block/SIZE)
```

When the SIZE parameter exceeds the number of usable bytes in a disk block (i.e., the bytes not used for overhead), then the number of slots assigned to each disk block will be

1. If rows with a single cluster key value are added until the total bytes in the slot exceed the SIZE estimate, other bytes on the disk block may be used, borrowing from other slot space allocations, until the disk block is full. After this, new disk blocks will be allocated (in a heap fashion, within the containing tablespace) to handle the overflow, and the rows assigned to a specific slot will *chain* from one page to another. Overflow of this kind leads to inefficient disk access, however, so it is important to make SIZE estimates large enough that unforeseen overflow is rare. On the other hand, if the average number of bytes for rows in a slot falls well below the SIZE estimate, space will be wasted on all the disk blocks of the cluster. **ORACLE** will not add additional cluster key values to a disk block that already has the maximum number for a single disk block.

The [INDEX | HASHKEYS n [HASH is expr]] clause in Figure 8.21 indicates that there are two kinds of clusters, index clusters and hash clusters, with index clusters being the default. In both cases, all rows for one cluster key value are stored together in a single slot on disk. In index clusters, an additional index must be created *on the cluster* to provide indexed access to the rows with individual cluster key values. (Hash clusters do not need such an index.) The syntax for creating an index on an index cluster is identical to the Create Index syntax of Figure 8.14, except that the ON clause of the first line uses a clustername rather than a tablename, as follows:

```
CREATE [UNIQUE] INDEX [schema.]indexname ON CLUSTER [schema.]clustername
```

Unlike what we have encountered so far with tables, an index for an index cluster is essential for accessing the data in the clustered tables. Although the index can be dropped and re-created at any time, the data in the indexed cluster will be inaccessible in the meantime.

After the cluster index has been created for an index cluster, rows in the tables of the cluster can be inserted. Note that an index defined on a cluster is *not* a primary index. When each row of a table defined in a cluster is first stored on the block with a new cluster key value, a new slot for rows with that cluster key value will be allocated on a disk block of the cluster. The slots are assigned in a heap-organized fashion, first come first served, up to the maximum number of slots permitted on each page. Thus if the rows of the first table to be inserted in a clustered table are sorted in order by the clustered key value, the slots and all contained rows will be placed on the disk block in clustered order. However, if later rows are inserted with new cluster key values, the new slots created will fall on the rightmost disk block of the table in a typical heap-organized allocation.

We will deal with hash clusters in the next section. In a hash cluster, a hash function is used to calculate the disk page location of the cluster slot from the cluster key when the first row with that cluster key is inserted. Queries to retrieve a row with a given cluster key value use the same hash function to locate the disk page, potentially saving the I/Os of the B-tree lookup. We conclude this section with some examples of index clusters.

EXAMPLE 8.4.2

A typical example of an index cluster is one that clusters departments and employees within departments in a company. We assume that a common lookup task when accessing any employee is to access all employees in a given department. We start by creating the cluster, deptemp:

```
create cluster deptemp
    (deptno int)
    size 2000;
```

We note that this is an index cluster, since index is the default and we haven't used the HASH-KEYS keyword. Next we create the tables that lie inside the cluster:

```
create table emps
(   empno      int            primary key,
    ename      varchar(10)    not null,
    mgr        int            references emps,
    deptno     int            not null)
    cluster deptemp (deptno);

create table depts
(   deptno     int            primary key,
    dname      varchar(9),
    address    varchar(20))
    cluster deptemp (deptno);
```

And now we need to create the index for the cluster key on the cluster:

```
create index deptempx on cluster deptemp;
```

We note that we have set SIZE to 2000 bytes, which means that **ORACLE** will assign only one cluster slot per page. If we assume that a disk block has 2000 useful bytes, a row from depts takes up 40 bytes, and a row from emps takes up 28 bytes, then we can fit one depts row and $(2000 - 40)/28 = 70$ emps rows with a common deptno value on a single disk block. If we assume that the largest department has 1000 employees, then there will be a large number of continuation disk blocks for this slot. We note that $2000/28 = 71$ (rounded down) rows from emps will fit on each continuation page. Thus we will require $(1000 - 70)/71 = 14$ (rounded up) additional disk blocks to contain all these rows. While this might seem like a very large number of disk pages to access, it is acceptable if emps rows are normally accessed all at once in a join with the depts row of the same deptno. In fact, in that case we are placing the rows on the minimum possible number of pages. Furthermore, if we want to access emps rows directly by other attributes, such as empno or ename, it is possible to do this efficiently by creating secondary indexes on the emps tables for these attributes. (Note that in this case, since empno is a primary key, there is already an index created, so we need merely create an index for ename.)

```
create index enamex on emps (ename);
```

∎

8.5　A Hash Primary Index

Recall from the Create Cluster statement of Figure 8.21, the cluster_clauses that specify cluster characteristics:

```
[PCTFREE n] [PCTUSED n]
[STORAGE ([INITIAL n [K|M]] [NEXT n [K|M]] [MINEXTENTS n] [MAXEXTENTS n]
    [PCTINCREASE n])]
[SIZE n [K|M] ] -- defaults to one disk block
[TABLESPACE tblspacename]
[INDEX | [SINGLE TABLE] HASHKEYS n [HASH is expr]]
```

If the HASHKEYS keyword is present in the Create Cluster statement, the cluster created will be a hashed cluster large enough to contain at least HASHKEYS distinct slots for hashkey values (equating the keyword HASHKEYS with the quantity n that follows it). Then **ORACLE** should create a single initial extent large enough to contain a hash cluster with SIZE * HASHKEYS bytes. (Note, however, that if the STORAGE clause is present and has an INITIAL value that is larger than SIZE * HASHKEYS, then the larger initial extent will be used. It is a good idea to use an INITIAL extent allocation to guarantee that the initial disk allocation is as contiguous as possible.) Multiple tables can be included in a hash cluster, but starting with **ORACLE** 8i, the optional SINGLE TABLE keyword clause allows **ORACLE** to optimize for a single table. Any row of a table in a hash cluster will be placed in the cluster in a slot on a disk block, which is calculated by a hash function based on the row's key value columns. **ORACLE** provides a standard built-in hash function, but the DBA may provide a custom function by using the optional HASH is expr clause, where expr is an expression that calculates a numeric value, based on all the column values in the key value. Normally you shouldn't consider overriding the built-in hash function with a custom one of your own unless you have performed a great deal of prior analysis. However, for the sake of completeness, we now provide an example where a hash cluster is provided with a custom hash function.

EXAMPLE 8.5.1

We create a hash cluster named acctclust to contain a single table, accounts, where the 50,000 rows in accounts are checking-account master records for bank customers. (Note that a hash cluster, like an index cluster, can contain multiple tables clustered for efficient join operations on key value, but here we provide a single table with a unique key value.)

```
create cluster acctclust (acctid int)
    size 80
    single table
    hashkeys 100000 hash is mod(acctid, 100003);
```

Note that when HASHKEYS is specified to be n, **ORACLE** will create a hash cluster with the actual number of slots S equal to the next prime number larger than n. (**ORACLE** continues to refer to the actual number of slots S allocated as HASHKEYS.) In this case, where HASHKEYS is originally specified as 100,000, the actual number of slots S created will be 100,003; thus we create a hash function mod(acctid, 100003) that will calculate appropriate slot values based on acctid. Note that the actual number of slots S created (100,003 in this case) can be determined by creating a trial hash cluster with HASHKEYS 100000, and then performing the query

```
select hashkeys from user_clusters
    where cluster_name = 'ACCTCLUST';
```

Now we create the accounts table, rows of which are assumed to take up a maximum of 80 bytes:

```
create table accounts
(   acctid      integer     primary key,
    balance     integer     not null
    alname      varchar(12) not null,
    afname      varchar(12) not null,
    ami         char(1)     not null,
    apasswd     varchar(12) not null,
    straddr     varchar(12),
    city        varchar(10),
    state       char(2),
    zipcode     int)
    cluster acctclust(acctid);
```

You are not expected to create an index on a hash cluster key value.   ∎

Note that the accounts table in Example 8.5.1 has a primary key, acctid. This means that a B-tree index has been created to avoid duplicates of this key value, which is also the acctclust key value. However, the point of creating a hash cluster is to be able to access accounts rows without needing to pass through a B-tree directory. By including this table in a hash cluster, we have created a *hash primary index* for this table. A row is inserted in the accounts table by applying the hash function to the acctid key value, thus generating a *pseudo-random number* to determine the slot number. From the slot number, the system can calculate the disk block number and then access that disk block with a single I/O and place the row in that slot. (Note that there can be multiple rows in a single slot in a hash cluster.) There is no key value *directory* lying above the disk blocks in this access method as there is with a secondary B-tree index. The savings of not having to perform one or more I/Os in a large B-tree to look up the ROWID for an account row with a given acctid, and then a final I/O to access the disk block containing that row, is what hashing is all about. The I/O savings in going directly to the proper page and slot without a directory lookup can be quite valuable in a large application, for example, a teller application in a large bank with hundreds of account accesses per second.

While hashing can be very efficient for accessing rows with individual key values (a bank teller accessing a customer's account by acctid), there is no way to *order rows by key value* in such a structure to provide efficient retrieval within a range. We would expect two rows with successive key values to be located on entirely uncorrelated data pages, depending on the caprice of the pseudo-random hash function. Thus we say that the hash access structure here forms a *primary index* (the disk positions for rows on disk are determined by the key value and provide efficient retrieval by specific key value), but not a clustered index (in which rows lie on disk in the same order as their key values). As a result, SQL range retrievals such as

```
select acctid, afname, ami, alname from accounts
    where acctid between :low and :high;
or:
select acctid, afname, ami, alname from accounts
    where acctid >= :low and acctid <= :high;
```

might require a query plan that scans through all rows in the table. (In the particular case of Example 8.5.1, the unique index on acctid can be used to determine rows in the range.)

Tuning HASHKEYS and SIZE in a Hash Cluster

Let us review how **ORACLE** determines the number of slots and data pages for a hash cluster. When a Create Cluster statement of the kind given in Example 8.5.1 is issued, a certain number, S, of data page slots on a known sequence of pages is set aside for occupancy by rows of the table. **ORACLE** will set S to be the first prime number greater than or equal to the HASHKEYS parameter in the Create Cluster statement, a number we denote as PRIMECEIL(HASHKEYS) (note that there is no actual PRIMECEIL( ) function in **ORACLE** or any other database product):

```
S = Total number of slots = PRIMECEIL(HASHKEYS)
```

Next from the discussion following Figure 8.22, we can calculate B, the number of slots per disk block, as

```
B = Number of slots/disk block =
    MAX(FLOOR(Number of usable bytes per disk block/SIZE), 1)
```

The number of usable bytes in a disk block can differ among installations, but an example value on Sun Solaris 2.6 is 1962 bytes. We will use 2000 bytes in what follows as a basis for calculation in examples and exercises. Given S and B, we can calculate the total number of disk blocks D initially allocated to the hash cluster as

```
D = CEIL(S/B)
```

Thus the total number of disk blocks D initially allocated is equal to the total number of slots S divided by the number of slots per disk block B, rounded up. The number of slots S assigned to a hash cluster will never change, but the same is not true for the total number of disk blocks. While D is the initial allocation of disk blocks, the number can grow to exceed D if enough rows are added to cause significant overflow. To avoid fragmentation on disk, it is recommended that the DBA calculate D in advance and use the STORAGE clause of the Create Cluster statement to create an INITIAL extent to contain at least D pages (and perhaps an additional fraction, 1.1 * D or more, if overflow seems at all likely). We now need to discuss how hash overflow occurs.

Recall that each row is placed in a hash cluster on a slot determined by the hash function h applied to the cluster key value of the row. The slot a key value is hashed to has a slot number sn, $0 \leq sn \leq S - 1$. In particular, the system determines a specific slot number sn1 for a given keyval1 by

```
sn1 = h(keyval1)
```

The initially allocated disk blocks will each contain a constant number B of slots per disk block, so **ORACLE** can calculate disk block number b, and slot s within the page, that the slot sn1 corresponds to by the formula

```
b = sn1/B
s = MOD(sn1, B)
```

This is the way we calculate the block number b of the disk block containing the row or rows with a given keyval1. Given b, access to a row in a hash cluster can normally occur with a single I/O. The only exception to this is when rows overflow from the initial disk block.

EXAMPLE 8.5.2

Continuing Example 8.5.1, assuming 2000 usable bytes per page, we see that B = FLOOR(2000/80) = 25 slots/block and D = CEIL(100003/25) = 4001 blocks. We can use a STORAGE INITIAL specification of 8002 K or more to make sure the initial hash cluster will be contiguous on disk. The hash cluster might start at block 31244, and use blocks 31245, 31246, and so on as (relative) block numbers b = 0, 1, 2, . . . in the hash cluster. Then for an `acctid`, say, acctid = 2345678, we will have h(2345678) = MOD(2345678, 100003) = 45609. Thus account 2345678 will hash to slot 45609. This slot will lie in relative block b = 45609/25 = 1824 among the 4001 blocks of the initial hash cluster, or actual block number 31244 + 1824 = 33068. The row will be placed in slot s = MOD(45609, 25) = 9 among the 25 slots of this block. ∎

The idea of a hash function is to make each different key value hash to a different slot, but since there are only S different slot numbers sn, this will clearly be impossible if the actual number of distinct key values grows to exceed S. Indeed, even before this point is reached, there are likely to be two different key values that hash to the same slot. The hash function merely provides a pseudo-random slot number for each key value. Consider an analogous situation where we perform the experiment of asking students in a class their birthday (a pseudo-random number between 1 and 365). We can pretend we are *hashing* students into 365 slots. Then when the class size reaches a certain point (well under 365, or even 365/2) it becomes likely that two students in a class will have the same birthday. This phenomenon is known as the "birthday surprise problem" and we will see more of it in the exercises. When two different key values hash to the same slot, we say that there is a *hash collision*.

In Figure 8.23 we see a hash-clustered table with 7 stored rows sparsely filling 48 slots on 8 data pages. Six slots fit on each page, and a page is pictured as a sequence of 6 slots on each level of the figure. (In actuality, the number of slots would have to be a prime number in the current **ORACLE**, but we ignore that here.) A hash function h is being applied to the same key values that were inserted into the B-tree of Figure 8.12, and we show only the key values of the rows stored in the slots. In Figure 8.23, we are illustrating the situation when the seventh inserted key value, 55, hashes to the same slot as the prior key value 39, a hash collision. In this case, both key values end up in the same slot.

When a row with a new key value hashes to a slot that is already in use for a different key value, **ORACLE** will attempt to expand the space for the slot on the page to make room for the new row. Note that a hash cluster, like an index cluster, might have more than one table assigned to it, with a non-unique cluster key value for one of the tables. Consequently multiple rows might need to be stored in the same slot even when there is no hash collision. The rows hashed to a slot are not expected to be contiguous on the disk block page; they are simply chain-linked together. **ORACLE** tries to expand the slot for a newly inserted row to keep all rows on the same page, thus minimizing the number of I/Os needed to search through the chain for a single hashkey value. Only if we run out of space on the first disk block page is a slot continued (overflowed) to a succeeding page. (New pages will be allocated in the normal manner for a HEAP-organized table.) As the number of overflow pages increases, it takes longer and longer to insert new rows, since the entire chain must be searched in order, looking through multiple disk blocks.

To obtain good performance in a hash cluster, it is important to provide large enough HASHKEYS and SIZE parameters so that overflows between pages will be as rare as possible. Of course, if we are clustering depts and emps tables together as in Example 8.4.2, with a cluster key of deptno and hundreds of emps rows for each deptno value, there is no way to avoid a long overflow chain to multiple disk block pages for each occupied slot. But this is not the sort of situation that hash clusters were created for. In hash clusters where there is very little overflow, query plans will use hashing to access specific rows in the cluster, but the query optimizer will give up on hashed access and use secondary B-tree access when overflow is sufficiently common.

Consider the case of Example 8.5.1, where 50,000 accounts rows are placed in the 100,003 slots of acctclust. The average disk block will only be half full in this situation, and overflows between pages will be quite rare. (We will learn how to quantify the number of overflows as we study the mathematical foundations in the next section.)

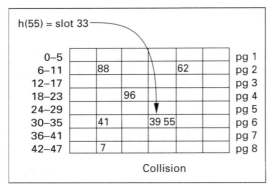

Figure 8.23   Hash-Structured Cluster Collision, Inserting a New Row with Key Value 55

However, if we place 500,000 `accounts` rows in the 100,003 slots, there will be tremendous overflow. An average of five rows will be hashed to each slot, the disk blocks will fill up with the first 100,000 rows (assuming that the SIZE parameter is just large enough for a single `accounts` row), and there will be overflow to new pages thereafter. With the large number of overflow pages, hashing will no longer be an efficient way to access the `accounts` rows. Instead, the query optimizer will choose to access rows through their secondary (unique) index on `acctid`, which exists because `acctid` was designated as a primary key for the table.

The usual rule of thumb in tuning hash clusters is to start with a Create Cluster statement with a HASHKEYS parameter that is at least twice the maximum possible number of cluster keys you ever expect to use. The SIZE parameter should be smaller than the disk block size for the most efficient access (although hash clusters do support larger SIZE values at lower performance), but large enough to hold all the maximum-length rows that will ever appear with an individual cluster key. Thus, the `emps-depts` cluster of Example 8.4.2 is essentially ruled out for hash clusters, unless we know an upper limit on the number of employees per department to guarantee that they will all fit on a disk block. It is quite common to use a single table in a hash cluster, with a unique cluster key value.

No Incremental Changes in the Number of Slots Used

We mentioned earlier that once the number of slots S in the hash data table has been specified, the number cannot be incrementally enlarged. The reason for this limitation is as follows. The hash function can be thought of as having two phases in its calculation. In the first phase, it generates a pseudo-random number x, based on the key value x = r(keyvalue), where x is a floating point number uniformly distributed in the range $0 < x < 1$. Next, the slot number h(keyvalue) resulting from the hash function is generated with the following formula:

$$h(keyvalue) = INTEGER\_PART\_OF(S * r(keyvalue))$$

The formula results in a random slot number from the sequence $0, 1, \ldots, S - 1$. Most hashing functions take this two-phase approach because in this way the generic function r can easily lead to a uniform distribution of integers from 0 to $S - 1$, for any given value of S. But note that if the total number of slots were to change, say, to S', we would now find that the hash function

$$h'(keyvalue) = INTEGER\_PART\_OF(S' * r(keyvalue))$$

would not give the same slot number for all slot placements previously calculated. For example, if r(keyvalue) is 0.33334, and S is 2, then

$$h(keyvalue) = INTEGER\_PART\_OF(2 * 0.33334) = 0$$

518

since 2 * 0.33334 is 0.66668, which is between 0 and 1. However, if S is 3, we would have

h'(keyvalue) = INTEGER_PART_OF(3 * 0.33334) = 1

since 3 * 0.33334 is 1.00002. This is the reason that we cannot incrementally enlarge the number of pages used for data in a hash-organized table.

Because of these considerations, if the number of hashed key values begins to surpass the HASHKEYS value you initially used in creating the hash cluster so that page overflows become common, you should plan to create a new hash cluster with a larger HASHKEYS value and move the rows from the old cluster to the new one to address this problem. One simple way to do this is to create a new hash cluster with the new desired number of HASHKEYS and then use the CREATE TABLE . . . AS form to bring all the rows from the old hash clustered table to a new one on the new hash cluster.

Advantages and Disadvantages of a Hash Primary Index

In order for a table (or set of tables) to be a good candidate for placement in a hash cluster, you need to identify a number of features.

◆ There is a lookup key that is used in a large proportion of queries to the table or tables, to retrieve a unique row or small set of rows for a constant value of that key. (In particular, this means that range queries don't figure as a big user of resources.)
◆ The small set of rows retrieved for a unique key value will fit easily on a single disk page.
◆ The total number of HASHKEYS needed for the cluster is easily predicted in advance, and doesn't change wildly over short periods once the table is loaded.

A large number of database texts analyze the advantage of a hash primary index over a B-tree index, in the case of an exact-match predicate, as being one of reduced I/O. This is the point we made earlier, since access through a B-tree structure requires passing through a number of higher-level directory nodes before the desired row is retrieved. For large tables where efficient keyed access becomes most important, there are usually three, sometimes four, levels of B-tree directory nodes. We should note, however, that many of these levels of access will not be relevant to I/O—the existence of memory buffers usually guarantees that some fraction of the levels is resident in memory, and often only one real directory page I/O is required for each random row access. Still the advantage of one I/O directly to data rows in the hash case over two I/Os in the B-tree case can be very important. However, another factor sometimes enters that makes B-tree indexes more efficient than you might think in advance. Consider the following two tables:

autodeposit   employees

eid
...

eid	bank	acctid	weeksal	...
...	...	...	...	...

The first table, called autodeposit, is a single-column list of employee IDs (eid) for individuals who have asked that their weekly checks be automatically deposited. The second table, employees, has the column eid, the bank and account numbers, and the weekly salary for each employee.

We now demonstrate an application where a B-tree index can perform better than a hash cluster when accessing rows in these two tables. A common type of application program, performed once a week, would read the eid values from the autodeposit table one after another and then use these eid values to access the rows of the employees table and make the desired automatic deposit in the appropriate account. In the B-tree index case, this appears to be a long sequence of indexed accesses to the employees table by an eid index, and we might decide to use a primary hash index on eid for the employees table instead, since this will give us the most efficient I/O access to these rows. However, this approach would be a mistake.

An alternate approach is to first load the employees table in an INDEX OR-GANIZED table in order by eid to provide a *clustered* organization. (An alternative is to sort the rows in advance in order by eid before loading them in a normal HASH ORGA-NIZED table, and place an index on eid. This has the advantage of permitting us to create secondary indexes for other columns in employees. However, new rows added to the table will not remain in eid order, so reorganization will be needed to retain the efficiency of clustering.) Now during our weekly deposit run, we are careful that the rows of the autodeposit table lie in the same increasing eid order we find in the employees table. We would then find that when looping through the autodeposit rows, the application makes all accesses to the employees table in order by the clustered eid key. In general, successive accesses to the employees table pass down through a directory through nodes that almost always remain in memory buffers from the prior access, and then to a row on a page that is also already in buffer.

The total number of employees pages involved in I/O for the whole application run is equal to the total number in the table. (We are assuming that a large proportion of employees receive autodeposit, so most employees table data pages will be involved.) On the other hand, in the hash cluster case, as each new row is accessed it can be expected to lie on a random page unrelated to the previous one, even though it is being accessed by a successive key. If there are, for example, an average of 10 rows on each hash data page for employees who desire direct deposit, there will be 20 times as many I/Os in the hash primary index case as in the B-tree clustered index case. We are assuming that there are too many hash disk blocks to remain in memory buffers between accesses, and that the B-tree pages are few in number compared with the data pages, both common assumptions.

Thus we see an example where the hash structure is not as I/O efficient for row access as other ordered structures. Of course we stacked the deck, since the eid references are not actually random. On the other hand, this is a common situation, and you should be aware how the order of the rows in a table can imply a big resource savings in access to the table.

8.6   Throwing Darts at Random Slots

In the current section, we will solve a probabilistic problem of a kind commonly encountered in performing database estimates. We refer to the general problem as *throwing N darts at M random slots*. We picture ourselves with some number N of darts and imagine that we are throwing them at a dartboard from a great distance, so that, although we always manage to hit the board, each cross-hatched slot on the dartboard is equally likely to be hit by any dart we throw. We might vary the problem a bit with further restrictions, and then ask some question about the eventual likely configuration of darts on the board. For example, we might ask:

> How many slots on the board have a dart in them?

Since some of these slots might contain multiple darts, this question probably doesn't have the simple answer N. It all depends on the restrictions on slot occupancy.

Unlimited Slot Occupancy: How Many Slots Are Occupied?

Let us solve the most standard problem for N darts in M slots, when there is no limit to the number of darts that will fit in each slot. After throwing the N darts, what is the expected number of slots that contain darts? We denote by S the number of slots containing one or more darts in any configuration resulting from this experiment, and by E(S) the expected number of such slots for a given N and M.

Probably the best way to picture this problem is to break it down into three cases:

◆ Case 1: There are only a few darts in comparison to the number of slots, signified by N << M.

◆ Case 2: The number of darts is comparable to the number of slots, written N ≈ M.

◆ Case 3: The number of darts is greater than the number of slots, or N > M.

We expect in Case 1, where the number of darts is quite small compared to the number of slots, that it is rare for many slots to be occupied by two or more darts. Therefore the number of occupied slots will be close to the number of darts, S ≈ N. (S will be just slightly less than N in most cases, allowing for slots with higher occupancy.)

We expect in Case 3, where the number of darts is somewhat greater than the number of slots, say, three times as great, that most slots will contain several darts (three on average). However, if there are a lot of slots, we expect some slots to still be empty. Therefore in this case we assume M − S << M, but probably M − S ≠ 0.

Finally in Case 2, the number of darts is about the same as the number of slots (to be precise, let us say N = M), and we certainly expect a reasonable number of slots with two darts and some with three or more. This means that a decent fraction of the slots will have no darts (M − S is some reasonable fraction of M, since there are just enough darts to go around once), but intuition fails us in trying to estimate the number of empty slots.

As we will see in a moment, with N = M we can estimate that $E(S) = M(1 - e^{-1})$, where e is the base of the natural logarithms, 2.71828. . . .

To begin our derivation of E(S) given N and M, consider the probability P that a particular slot s does *not* get hit by a specific thrown dart d. Since there are M slots and the dart will hit any particular slot with equal likelihood, the probability that a particular dart d hits slot s is 1/M and the probability that the slot s does *not* get hit is given by

Pr(slot s does not get hit by dart d) = $(1 - 1/M)$

This is a fairly large probability if we have a large number M of slots. But now let's say that we throw some number N of darts in succession, and ask the probability that the slot s does not get hit by any of these darts. Each dart throw is an independent event, and the probability that the slot never gets hit is given by the following conjunction of events: slot s does not get hit by dart 1 *and* slot s does not get hit by dart 2 *and* . . . *and* slot s does not get hit by dart N. The probability for this conjunction of events is the product of the probabilities for each of the individual events, so

Pr(slot s does not get hit by N darts thrown in succession) = $(1 - 1/M)^N$

Since there are M slots, each with the same probability, the expected number of slots that do not get hit is the number of slots times the probability that a specific slot will not be hit:

[8.6.1]   E(number of slots that do not get hit) = $M(1 - 1/M)^N$

Thus the number of slots that *do* get hit, E(S), is M minus the quantity just calculated:

[8.6.2] $E(S) = M(1 - (1 - 1/M)^N)$

From calculus, we know that the number represented by e is defined in a limit form as

$$e = \lim_{x \to 0} (1 + x)^{1/x}$$

If we assume that M is quite large, we can substitute x for $-1/M$ and derive the approximation for e:

$$e \approx (1 - 1/M)^{-M}$$

or

[8.6.3] $e^{-1} \approx (1 - 1/M)^M$

From [8.6.2], we see that

$$E(S) = M\ (1 - ((1 - 1/M)^N)) = M\ (1 - ((1 - 1/M)^M)^{N/M}\ )$$

and substituting (8.6.3), we get

[8.6.4] $E(S) \approx M\ (1 - e^{-N/M})$

Thus the expected number of slots hit by darts is approximated by $M\ (1 - e^{-N/M})$, and the expected number of slots not hit is

[8.6.5] $E(\text{slots not hit}) \approx M\ e^{-N/M}$

In the exercises we provide some examples using these formulas.

Slot Occupancy of One: Number of Retries (Rehash Chain)

Another approach used in some database systems for hashing rows to slots does not allow more than one row to be placed in any single slot. Successive rows that hash into a particular slot must find another slot to go to, and this is accomplished by *rehashing* the key value to a sequence of slots until an empty one is located. The succession of slots hashed to will always be the same for any particular key value, although collisions on any slot can occur between different key values as well. Naturally, every attempt is made to rehash collisions to different slots on the same page, but if none is found on the original page then slots on successive pages are tried in the rehash chain. You should note that this algorithm creates an absolute limit on the number of rows that can be successfully placed, no more than the total number of slots S that are initially created. The question we wish to ask is how many times rehashing must occur before an empty slot is located. In terms of the darts in slots approach, we can describe this problem with the following shorthand:

N darts in M slots. Slot occupancy 1. Retries until all darts in board.

What we mean by "Slot occupancy 1" is that each slot in the board is assumed to have room for only a single dart. If a second thrown dart tries to enter that slot, it bounces off. The phrase "Retries until all darts in board" means that each time a dart bounces off, we retrieve it and try again until it sticks in the target. Eventually all darts are in slots, so we must have $N \leq M$, since each dart lies in only one slot. In this case, the question of how many slots have a dart in them does have the simple answer N. But we are asking a different question:

In throwing dart N, what is the expected number of retries to get it in some slot?

The answer depends on the number $N - 1$ of darts already placed in M slots, and the following analysis provides a good approximation to the answer. We assume that M is large, and when we try to throw dart N to place it in a slot, the probability that any slot it hits is already occupied is $P = (N - 1)/M$. This means that the probability that the slot is empty is $(1 - P) = (1 - (N - 1)/M)$, and this is also the probability that we will be able to place the final record in the first position we come to. We call this a collision chain of length 1 (only one probe is necessary), and it is written as

$$\text{Pr(collision chain of length 1)} = (1 - P)$$

On the other hand, in order to have a collision chain of length 2, the first position hashed to must be full (with probability P) and the second position that we reach in the rehash sequence must be empty (with probability $(1 - P)$). Using the principle of multiplication by which we calculate the probability of two or more independent events happening together, we get

$$\text{Pr(collision chain of length 2)} = (1 - P)P$$

Now for a collision chain of length 3, we must start with full slots in the first two positions we reach (with probability $PP = P^2$) and then an empty slot in the third with probability $1 - P$. Simple extension of this argument gives

$$\text{Pr(collision chain of length 3)} = (1 - P)P^2$$
$$\text{Pr(collision chain of length 4)} = (1 - P)P^3$$
$$\cdots$$
$$\text{Pr(collision chain of length K)} = (1 - P)P^{K-1}$$

Now the *expected* length of the collision chain, $E(L)$, is given by the sum of all these probabilities times the associated lengths:

$$E(L) = (1 - P) + 2(1 - P)P + 3(1 - P)P^2 + 4(1 - P)P^3 + \ldots$$

or, factoring:

[8.6.6] $E(L) = (1 - P)(1 + 2P + 3P^2 + 4P^3 + \ldots)$

where the sum extends to some large number of terms, proportional to the maximum number of possible collisions in the table. Now we would like to provide a simple formula for this sum. To see how to do this, start by considering the function $f(x)$ given by the infinite series

$$f(x) = x + x^2 + x^3 + x^4 + \ldots$$

This is the well-known infinite geometric progression, $a + ar + ar^2 + ar^3 + \ldots$, where a and r are both x. The formula for the sum is known from algebra as $a/(1 - r)$, so we can give a closed-form solution for the infinite series $f(x)$:

[8.6.7] $f(x) = x + x^2 + x^3 + x^4 + \ldots = x/(1 - x)$

Now taking the derivative of all terms in the equations of [8.6.7], we get

[8.6.8] $f'(x) = 1 + 2x + 3x^2 + 4x^3 + \ldots = 1/(1 - x)^2$

Rewriting the formula of [8.6.6] for the expected length E(L) of a collision chain, we see that we can represent the infinite sum on the right with f'(P), replacing x with P in the left-hand equality of equation [8.6.8]:

[8.6.9] $E(L) = (1 - P)(1 + 2P + 3P^2 + 4P^3 + \ldots) = (1 - P)(f'(P))$

Now using the right-hand side of equation [8.6.8], we can replace f'(P) with $1/(1 - P)^2$, to get

[8.6.10] $E(L) = (1 - P)(f'(P)) = (1 - P)(1/(1 - P))^2 = 1/(1 - P)$

Thus we see that the expected length of the collision chain is the reciprocal of $(1 - P)$. Regarding the approximation we began with in terms of N and M, $(1 - P) = (1 - (N - 1)/M)$, we have

[8.6.11] $E(L) = 1/(1 - (N - 1)/M) = M/(M - N + 1)$

Let's consider a few examples. If the hash structure is 50% full $((N - 1)/M = 0.5)$, then $P = 0.5$ and $E(L) = 1/0.5 = 2$. If the table is 90% full, $((N - 1)/M = 0.9)$, then $P = 0.9$ and $E(L) = 1/0.1 = 10$. The graph of this relationship is given in Figure 8.24. The average collision chain length asymptotes to infinity as $(N - 1)/M$ approaches 1.

As we would expect, the more full we set the table, the longer the average collision chain. What might be surprising, however, is how quickly the average chain increases in length once the fillfactor comes close to 100. If we can fit 20 rows on a page and load a

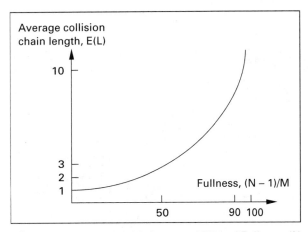

Figure 8.24 Relationship between E(L) and Fullness, (N − 1)/M

table half full, it seems unlikely that a collision chain of average length 2 will grow long enough (L = 21) to continue to a successive page. However, if the fillfactor is 95, the average length of a chain is 20, so about half the collision chains will continue to a new page. This shows how important it is to avoid having a very full table under these conditions. On the average, we would be able to find a row associated with a unique key value halfway through a collision chain, so significant overhead starts to occur when a significant number of entries begin to hash to position 21 or later in the chain. A hashed table containing duplicate key values tends to have longer collision chains, since equal-value rows are certain to collide. In our derivation, we assumed independent random positions for separate hash entries, which is obviously not the case when duplicate entries exist.

When Do Hash Pages Fill Up?

In calculating the possibility of chaining to a new page, the question of whether multiple rows can fit in the same page or in only one is immaterial. Both hashing algorithms of the last two subsections will use all the space on a page before chaining to a new page. The question is this: If we attempt to load a table only partially full, when will a hash chain continue to a new page anyway? Readers who have studied statistics can follow the rough argument that follows.

Assume a million-row table, where 20 rows fit on each page. If we try to load each page half full with 10 rows per page, we will require 2 million hash slots large enough to hold a row (in **ORACLE** this means HASHKEYS 2,000,000 and SIZE is the size of a row, which we assume doesn't vary much). Thus we will use 100,000 data pages. However, the occupancy is random, and we need to use the normal distribution function to estimate the probable number of rows that occupy an arbitrary page. For any page of the table, we calculate the probability that a particular row in the table hashes to this page as $1/100,000$, p = 0.00001. We denote by q = $(1 - p)$ = 0.99999 the probability that the slot is empty (a number so close to 1 that the difference in the calculations that follow is not significant). Then the expected number of rows hashed to the current page, E(r), is N $*$ p, where N is the total number of rows hashed:

$$E(r) = 0.00001 * 1,000,000 = 10$$

This is what we would expect, that the average page contains rows in 10 out of its 20 slots. Now the standard deviation for this probability distribution, σ, is given by the formula

$$\sigma = \sqrt{Npq} = \sqrt{1000000 * 0.00001 * 0.99999} \approx \sqrt{10} = 3.162$$

Then the likelihood that there are more than E(r) + σ = 13.162 rows on a page is a 1-sigma event, with a probability of $\Phi(1.0)$ = 0.158, as determined by the normal Φ function. To get 10 + 2 $*$ 3.162 = 16.324 rows is a 2-sigma event, with a probability of $\Phi(2.0)$ = .0228. In particular, the probability that more than 20 rows hash to this page is

526 $\Phi(10/3.162) = .000831$. Since there are 100,000 pages in the table, we can expect overflows for about 83 of them.

Readers with a bit of statistics experience and access to a normal distribution table will be able to apply these estimates to the table of their choice.

Suggestions for Further Reading

For an introduction to memory-resident data structures, such as hashing and 2-3 trees, the reader is referred to the text by Aho, Hopcroft, and Ullman [1]. The text by Knuth [5] that deals with this area is a classic reference work in *The Art of Computer Programming* series that helped to found rigorous computer science. The various product SQL reference manuals referred to in earlier chapters continue to be useful in understanding how to index tables. Reference manuals likely to be useful in understanding indexing capabilities in the various products are listed in bold type below.

[1] Alfred V. Aho, John E. Hopcroft, and Jeffrey D. Ullman. *Data Structures and Algorithms.* Reading, MA: Addison-Wesley, 1987.

[2] Don Chamberlin. *A Complete Guide to DB2 Universal Database.* San Francisco: Morgan Kaufmann, 1998.

[3] *DB2 Universal Database Administration Guide.* IBM. Available at http://www .ibm.com/db2.

[4] *DB2 Universal Database SQL Reference Manual.* Version 6. IBM. Available at http: //www.ibm.com/db2.

[5] Donald E. Knuth. *The Art of Computer Programming: Sorting and Searching.* Volume 3. Reading, MA: Addison-Wesley, 1997.

[6] *INFORMIX Guide to SQL: Reference.* Version 9.2. Menlo Park, CA: Informix Press, 1999. http://www.informix.com.

[7] *INFORMIX Guide to SQL Syntax.* Version 9.2. Menlo Park, CA: Informix Press, 1999. http://www.informix.com.

[8] *INFORMIX Performance Guide.* Version 9.2. Menlo Park, CA: Informix Press, 1999. http://www.informix.com.

[9] *ORACLE8 Server Administrator's Guide.* Redwood Shores, CA: Oracle. http:// www.oracle.com.

[10] *ORACLE8 Server Concepts.* Volumes 1 and 2. Redwood Shores, CA: Oracle. http:// www.oracle.com.

[11] *ORACLE8 Server SQL Reference Manual.* Volumes 1 and 2. Redwood Shores, CA: Oracle. http://www.oracle.com.

[12] ORACLE8 *Server Application Developer's Guide.* Redwood Shores, CA: Oracle. http://www.oracle.com.

Exercises

Exercises with solutions at the back of the book in "Solutions to Selected Exercises" are marked with the symbol •.

Assume disk pages of 2048 bytes in all questions that follow unless otherwise stated.

[8.1]   Assume that a DBA issued the following Create Table statement in **ORACLE**:

```
create table customers (cid . . .)
    storage (initial 20480, next 20480,
    maxextents 8, minextents 3, pctincrease 0);
```

(a)• How many bytes of disk space will be allocated to this file when it is first created?

(b)• What is the maximum space capacity (in bytes) of this table?

(c) How would the answer to (b) change if we changed from pctincrease 0 to pctincrease 100? Show calculations.

[8.2]   Consider the definition of the **INGRES** TID given just before Example 8.2.1. A TID must fit in an unsigned 4-byte integer, with values from 0 to $2^{32} - 1$. The TID allows for 512 slots on each 2048-byte disk page, although there will usually be fewer rows than this actually placed. For each row on a page, a 2-byte offset to the row is held in the row directory.

(a)• If we actually had 512 fixed-length rows on a 2048-byte page, what would be the maximum length of the row? (Don't forget about the row directory offsets.)

(b) How many rows of length 50 can be stored on a 2048-byte page?

(c)• What is the precise maximum number of disk pages that can be represented in a TID?

(d) What is the maximum number of rows of length 50 that can be stored in an **INGRES** table?

(e) Provide a different definition for a TID that would increase the maximum number of rows (of most sizes) that could be stored in an **INGRES** table. The TID definition for each table would depend on the minimum length m in bytes of a row in the table (calculated from the Create Table statement) and would use a more realistic estimate of the maximum number of rows that can be placed on a page.

[8.3]   Consider the function binsearch of Example 8.3.1. Generalize it to handle any size N sorted array and allow it to find nearest matches above x, if any, as follows:

```
int binsearch(int x, int N)
```

so that for a given x and N the K that is returned is the smallest K such that arr[K].keyval >= x, or −1 if x is larger than any keyval value.

[8.4]   Consider a table emp (for employees) with 200,000 rows of 100 bytes each, created with the statement

```
create table emp (eid integer not null, . . . ) pctfree 25;
```

where the PCTFREE n clause refers to the amount of free space that must be left on each data page in placing the rows on the page.

(a)• Assuming a small header so that 2000 bytes out of 2048 are usable, and only 2-byte offsets in the row directory, already counted in the 100 bytes for the row, make a *rough* calculation of the number of data pages needed to hold the rows of the table emp.

Now assume that the following command has been issued in **ORACLE** to create a unique index on emp (eid is the primary key for emp, but we forgot to mention this in the Create Table statement).

```
create unique index eidx on emp (eid) pctfree 20;
```

(b)   The **ORACLE** ROWID takes up 6 bytes (it would be 7 bytes for a non-unique key), and there is a 1-byte overhead per column of the key. Assume the int eid column value takes 4 bytes. Make a rough calculation of the number of index entries per leaf page and the total number of leaf-level pages there will be in the eidx B-tree. Notice the PCTFREE clause of Create Index.

(c)   Make a rough calculation of the number of node pages this B-tree will have at *each* higher directory level. Show all work. Assume that the byte length of an entry in the B-tree, (sepkeyval, np), is the same as an entry at the leaf level. The PCTFREE clause above still affects calculations in the directory.

(d)• How many I/Os are needed to perform the query select * from emp where eid between 10,000 and 20,000? Assume that the eid values have no gaps and range from 1 to 200,000. Do *not* assume that the rows of emp are clustered by eid. Assume that data pages are not buffered, so that each data page reference requires a disk read. Assuming 80 I/Os per second (ignore CPU time), how long will this query take to execute?

(e)   Repeat the calculation of (d) where you do assume that the rows of emp are clustered by eid. How long will this query take to execute in terms of I/O?

(f)• How many I/Os are needed to perform the query select count(*) from emp where eid is between 10,000 and 20,000? (Hint: The query optimizer doesn't pick up rows from the table unless it needs to.) How long will this query take to execute?

[8.5] Rework Example 8.3.4, assuming nodes 70% full, but with 4096-byte pages for an IBM machine and assuming the **DB2 UDB** index compression of Figure 8.17, with the usual RID length of 4 bytes. There are 1 million entries in the index, the index key is city declared char(16), and there are 200 different cities evenly distributed among the rows of the table. As always, *rough calculations* are acceptable. Assume that **DB2 UDB** does not use compression in the directory-level B-tree nodes.

[8.6] (a) Are the following statements true or false? Please justify your answer.

   (i)• **DB2 UDB** allows rows to split over several data pages.

   (ii) **ORACLE** ROWIDs are longer than **DB2 UDB** RIDs.

   (iii)• The binary search algorithm on a sorted list is inefficient in terms of disk I/O compared with that of a B-tree algorithm.

   (iv) A binary search will take ten probes to find one key value among a list of 1 million distinct key values.

   (v)• If we have a disk page memory buffer with 1000 pages and we are retrieving rows at random from 1 million pages, after sufficient time we will have one chance in a thousand with each retrieval that we do *not* have to perform a disk I/O.

   (b) Write an **ORACLE** storage clause (just the clause) for a Create Table statement to start the table with 10 KB of disk storage, and let the size increase in incremental jumps that double after the first two and stop with at least 5120 KB total (10 + 10 + 20 + 40 + . . . + 2560). Show calculations.

[8.7] In **ORACLE**, consider a table named students of 400,000 rows with 200 bytes each, and assume that the following command has been issued to load the students table.

```
create table students (stid char(7) not null primary
    key, . . . <other columns>)
    pctfree 20;
```

(a) How many pages will the rows of students sit on? Assume 2000 bytes per page, and ignore row directory offsets and page header. Show calculations in all parts that follow.

(b)• Assume an index on `stid` with PCTFREE = 25. Calculate the entry size assuming ROWID of 6 bytes, and 1 byte overhead for the single column key. Then calculate how many leaf-level pages there will be in the B-tree.

(c) Calculate how many pages exist on various upper levels of the B-tree.

(d) How many I/Os are needed to perform this query?

```
select * from students
    where stid between 'e000001' and 'e020000';
```

Assume that 1/20th of all students have `eid` values in this range, that the `stid` index is *not* a clustering index for students, and that we do not save any I/Os because of buffering.

(e)• Recalculate part (d) with the assumption that the `stid` index *is* a clustering index for the `students` table.

(f) Under the assumptions of part (e), calculate how many I/Os are required for the following query:

```
select count(*) from students
    where stid between 'e000001' and 'e020000';
```

[8.8] Assume that we are given a hash-organized table with slots for 20 rows on a page.

(a) Given 100,000 pages in the hash table, how many slots exist? Show calculations.

(b) Given 100,000 pages, assuming that 1 million rows are hashed into this table, calculate the probability on a single page that a hash chain of length 21 exists. Show calculations.

(c) We say that a page "overflows" when a row is hashed to the page, but there is no room for it on that page and it must be placed on a different page.

(i) Does the fact that a hash chain of length 21 exists on a page imply that the page overflows?

(ii) Does a page overflow imply that a hash chain of length 21 or more exists on the page?

[8.9] Assume as in Section 8.6 that we are throwing N darts at M slots with unlimited occupancy of darts in slots. We want to examine some of the formulas derived.

(a)• Use your calculator to determine the number of slots that get hit throwing 128 darts at 10,000 slots. Use both formulas [8.6.2] and [8.6.4]. Note that 128 is a power of 2, so formula [8.6.2] can be evaluated by successive squaring of $(1 - 1/M)$, and you should do it this way. Is the number of slots that do get hit close to 128 in both cases?

(b) Repeat problem (a), throwing 16,384 darts at 16,384 slots. Note that the number is a power of 2, so you can calculate by successive squaring again. Are the two numbers close? Is the fraction of slots that get hit close to $(1 - e^{-1})$?

(c) Use formula [8.6.5] to calculate the number of slots that do *not* get hit when there are 10,000 slots and 30,000 darts.

[8.10] (a)• When we throw one dart at a board, there is no chance that two darts will go in the same slot, and the probability remains low as the number of darts remains very small relative to the number of slots. However, for a given number of slots M, there is a first point in throwing darts (a number N) where the probability is greater than .50 that two darts will fall in the same slot. Calculate this point for 365 slots. (This is called the "birthday surprise point" because the number of people you need in a room for it to become likely that two people have the same birthday is surprisingly small.)

(b) [HARD] Calculate the "birthday surprise point" as a formula in terms of M.

[8.11] (a) Create a bitmap index on the month column of CAP's orders table. Make a script of this and include it in your answer file.

(b) What is the expected density of this index?

(c) How many bytes are needed to hold each bitmap?

(d) Write out the bitmap for 'feb' assuming the rows are given indexes in order of the rows in Figure 2.2.

[8.12] (a) See Figure 6.11 for an example of a database design where orders are for multiple items (unlike our CAP orders table, which have only single-item orders), and there is a Line_items weak entity connected to Orders by a has_item relationship. Also see Exercise 7.3 and its in-book solution. The CAP database has no line_items table, as it stands. You are asked to drop the tables of the CAP database and write a new script to create a table orders2, without the pid, qty, and dollars columns, but with all other normal orders columns. Your script should also create the regular CAP customers, agents, and products tables, *and* a table line_items with columns lineno, ordno, pid, qty, and dollars, with (ordno, lineno) as the primary key. Next make a copy of your loadcap files (as loadcap2; you want to be able to return to the regular CAP database later). Edit the loadcap files to provide rows for these tables, with most orders having only one line_item with value 1, but add a new line_item 2 for order 1011, for 1000 units of p04 (calculate the dollars amount properly). Create a script to show how this all works out.

(b) Once part (a) is working, drop the tables you have just created and loaded, and re-create the orders and line_item tables in an index table cluster called orderdata (leave customers and agents in the form they are already). Show a script of everything you have to do to end up with the tables loaded in this cluster. Explain how you figured out the SIZE to specify.

(c) Add a (secondary) bitmap index on month to the orders2 table.

[8.13] Continuing with the tables of Exercise 8.12, set up the tables as a hash cluster of 1000 hashkeys and perform the load. Give the size of the hash table **ORACLE** creates. Add a bitmap index on month.

Query Processing   9

Where is the wisdom we have lost in knowledge?
Where is the knowledge we have lost in information?
—T.S. Eliot, *The Rock*

Where is the information we have lost in data?
—A natural follow-on question

Recall query [8.1.1] from the beginning of Chapter 8:

```
select * from customers
    where city = 'Boston' and discnt between 12 and 14;
```

When a database system receives a query such as this, it goes through a series of *query compilation steps* before it begins execution. In the first phase, the *syntax-checking phase,* the system parses the query and checks that it obeys the syntax rules, then matches objects in the query syntax with views, tables, and columns listed in system tables, and performs appropriate query modification. During this phase the system validates that the user has appropriate privileges and that the query does not disobey any relevant integrity constraints. At this point the *query optimization phase* begins. Existing *statistics* for the tables and columns are located, such as how many rows exist in the tables, and relevant indexes are found with their own applicable statistics. A complex procedure now takes place, which we can think of as "figuring out what to do," and the result is a procedural *access plan* to perform the query. The access plan is then put into effect with the *execution phase,* wherein the indexes and tables are accessed and the answer to the query is derived from the data.

    The goal of this chapter is to explain some of the basic principles of query processing, with particular emphasis on the ideas underlying query optimization. There are normally a large number of competing access plans that will work to perform a given query, just as there are a large number of ways to play a chess game with the object of winning (or at least not losing). The system query optimizer tries to choose an access plan that will minimize runtime as well as various other types of resource use, such as the number of disk I/Os, CPU time, and so on. The query optimizer will probably not choose the best possible plan for a complex query, any more than a chess player plays the perfect game, but the objective is to spend enough effort in the optimization process to ensure a reasonably good choice. Basic issues in query optimization include how to use available indexes, how to use memory to accumulate information and perform intermediate steps such as sorting, how to determine the order in which joins should be performed, and so on. At the end of this chapter you should be able to display and analyze an access plan chosen by the database system for a specific query. You should also understand what constitutes a "good" or "bad" access plan. As a result, you will have a much better grasp of what "tuning" steps a DBA can take to improve query performance, such as indexes to be added, different clustering of rows by index, denormalization of tables, and so on.

The current chapter also explains many of the considerations that go into choosing an access plan for a given SQL query, but it is limited to explaining *why* a specific access plan should be chosen, based on the details of the possible alternatives, rather than *how* it is chosen by the query optimizer. In general, a query optimizer generates a number of alternative strategies from which it must select a plan, and choosing among these alternatives can become quite a complex problem. Because a computer program has no "intuition," the programmers responsible for writing the query optimizer have the difficult job of creating an efficient algorithmic decision procedure that will choose between competing access plans. Algorithmic procedures of this kind (such as *dynamic programming* techniques) are outside the scope of the current text. We will depend a great deal on your intuition to follow arguments as to why one access plan is better than another, and simply assume that the query optimizer comes to the same conclusion by using an algorithmic search. Such an approach is commonly used in texts that explain the effect of programming language statements, without detailing how the compiler achieves the effects.

DB2 for OS/390 and DB2 UDB. Up until now we have presented features from a number of different database products in parallel, but in the remainder of this chapter we concentrate on IBM's **DB2** products. In previous discussions, we have been covering **DB2 UDB**, the newer "Universal Database" system that runs on UNIX, Windows NT, and most recently, on IBM mainframes under OS/390. In discussing query optimization, we turn attention to the older "big brother" product, **DB2 for OS/390**, referred to simply as **DB2** in this chapter, that runs only on the IBM OS/390 operating system for IBM mainframe computers. We believe that architectural differences between unallied products are too all-encompassing for a successful presentation of query optimization details. Thus we will concentrate on **DB2** in this chapter and occasionally refer to **DB2 UDB** and **ORACLE**.

DB2 has an extremely sophisticated approach to query optimization and provides numerous advanced execution features that support high performance for queries. This is not to say that other products don't have important performance features of their own. Query optimization is a young field, dating from about the mid-1970s, and no single product has a monopoly on good ideas. Indeed a number of recent research results suggest new performance capabilities that have not yet been fully consolidated in any commercial products. The current chapter concentrates only on features that are already in commercial use. The final three sections of the chapter present a query *benchmark*, an industry-standard test of query performance that was reported in the first edition of this text for the **MVS DB2** product, the direct predecessor of **DB2 for OS/390**. The benchmark measurements and accompanying discussions of concrete query access plans have been an enormous aid in cementing readers' understanding of the query performance principles presented in earlier sections.

9.1 Introductory Concepts

We start by introducing some fundamental concepts as a preliminary to our discussion of query optimization. To begin with, we consider exactly what resource use the system is trying to minimize in optimizing a query. Ultimately this reduces to the question of saving money on computer equipment and the users' time (which can certainly be thought of as a money issue for the employer). We also consider special commands the DBA needs to tune the database system and to understand the plans output by the query optimizer.

Query Resource Utilization

The query optimizer attempts to minimize the use of certain resources by choosing the best of a set of alternative query access plans. The major resources considered are CPU time and the number of I/Os required. Computer memory is also an important resource, but memory capacity for various purposes is normally determined at system initialization time. For example, the number of buffers used to keep popular disk pages in memory is set in advance by the DBA. Since the query optimizer can have no effect on this, it usually reacts in a relatively simple way by choosing different types of behavior in query plans at various thresholds of memory availability. We will see examples later in the chapter.

By contrast, the CPU and I/O resources that can be used in a query can be whatever is necessary to perform the query under different alternatives. For each alternative access PLAN there is an associated *CPU cost*, with notation $COST_{CPU}(PLAN)$, and *I/O cost*, or $COST_{I/O}(PLAN)$. Whenever there are two incomparable costs it is possible that two query plans, $PLAN_1$ and $PLAN_2$, will be incomparable in resource use. See Figure 9.1.

	$COST_{CPU}(PLAN)$	$COST_{I/O}(PLAN)$
$PLAN_1$	9.2 CPU seconds	103 reads
$PLAN_2$	1.7 CPU seconds	890 reads

Figure 9.1 Two Query Plans with Incomparable I/O and CPU Cost Pairs

Clearly PLAN$_2$ is superior to PLAN$_1$ in terms of having smaller CPU cost, but PLAN$_1$ is superior in terms of smaller I/O cost. To provide a single measure that can be minimized unambiguously, the **DB2** query optimizer defines the *total cost* of an access PLAN, COST(PLAN), as the weighted sum of the I/O cost and the CPU cost.

[9.1.1] $COST(PLAN) = W_1 * COST_{I/O}(PLAN) + W_2 * COST_{CPU}(PLAN)$

Here W_1 and W_2 are both positive numbers, weighting the relative importance of the two measures in the total cost. The job of the optimizer is to choose the lowest value COST(PLAN) ranging over all alternative plans that answer a given query. In the following sections we discuss how to analyze alternative access plans to derive, relatively accurately, the associated I/O cost. It is not so easy from theoretical considerations alone to derive the associated CPU usage, since this depends on the details of the CPU instruction set and the efficiency of the database system implementation. (Of course, the query optimizer for a specific database system release is able to estimate CPU cost for a plan, using a tabulation of measured CPU times for internal functions required, but there is a great deal of uninteresting detail here that we don't want to have to address in the current chapter.) As a general rule, the CPU cost to perform a query does not vary as much from one access plan to another as does the I/O cost, except that often the CPU cost overhead associated with each I/O is an important contribution, so that minimizing the I/O will tend to minimize the CPU as well. This implies that the incomparable CPU and I/O cost pairs of Figure 9.1 are somewhat unusual. The following sections concentrate on quantitative estimates of the I/O cost and discuss CPU differences in a qualitative way only in circumstances where major variations are likely to arise.

The Workload of a System

We define the *workload* of a system as a mix of queries and the frequencies with which these queries are posed by the system users. For example, we might have a query system built to help a group of 5000 insurance adjusters perform their everyday work. It may be that the adjusters pose two types of queries, Q1 and Q2, in their work.

Q1 retrieves information from an accident claim form using the claim number.
Q2 retrieves all claim numbers, indexed by (lastname, firstname) of the insured.

When they are submitted, queries of these types have different specific values for claim numbers and insured names, but the CPU and I/O resources needed to answer such queries are approximately the same for any specific values of these parameters. From observing the adjusters during their peak work period we note that, on the average, a member of the group poses a query of type Q1 40 times each second and a query of type Q2 20 times each second. These frequencies are reflected in Figure 9.2. Of course this is a simplified example of a workload; in real life there would be more types of queries and fewer round numbers for submission rates.

Query type	RATE(query) in submissions/second
Q1	40.0
Q2	20.0

Figure 9.2 Simple Workload with Two Queries

For a given workload on a system, and the query execution plans generated by the query optimizer for the queries that make up the workload, the required CPU and I/O resource needs per second can be calculated. From this and a list of equipment costs we can translate the requirements into a measure that may seem more immediate: the dollar cost of the system to support the workload. For example, consider a workload with a large frequency of queries that performs about 1000 I/Os but uses very little CPU. To begin with, we note that we would expect relatively long response times (only about 80 random I/Os can be performed each second when successive I/O requests in a query plan must wait for the previous I/O to complete). We would probably need to purchase a large number of disks to provide the needed I/O access rate under this workload, although we could get along with a relatively inexpensive CPU. We normally have a good deal of freedom in choosing larger or smaller CPU systems; IBM mainframe computers, for example, tried for years to maintain (somewhat artificially) a linear price scale-up with increasing CPU power.

All of these purchases need to be worked out in advance, of course, which is why the DBA attempts to get some estimate of workload even before an application is implemented. Each query in the workload, depending on its peak frequency and resource utilization, translates to a specific dollar cost in computer hardware, using the "fair rent" on the equipment utilized. A high response time has a cost as well, in that the company needs to hire more employees to get the work done (employee time waiting for a response is usually wasted), and with long delays we might expect to see a high turnover rate as employees quit in frustration. Looking at it this way, it is clear that if we can improve the set of alternatives available to the query optimizer to make a better choice among alternative access plans, an immediate cost savings will result. This is an extremely important area of study for the DBA.

Gathering Statistics

A query optimizer of any sophistication needs to have knowledge about the statistics of the various tables, columns, and indexes it deals with. For example, recall the query

```
select * from customers
    where city = 'Boston' and discnt between 12 and 14;
```

If the customers table contains only three rows on a single data page, the query optimizer should certainly ignore any indexes that might exist and perform a table scan—a direct search of the rows—to qualify the two predicates. On the other hand, if there are

538

```
RUNSTATS ON TABLE username.tablename
    [WITH DISTRIBUTION [AND DETAILED] {INDEXES ALL | INDEX indexname}]
    [other clauses not covered or deferred]
```

Figure 9.3 DB2 RUNSTATS Command Syntax

```
ANALYZE {INDEX | TABLE | CLUSTER} [schema.] {indexname | tablename | clustername}
    {COMPUTE STATISTICS | other alternatives not covered}
        {FOR TABLE | FOR ALL [INDEXED] COLUMNS [SIZE n] | other alternatives not covered}
```

Figure 9.4 ORACLE Analyze Statement Syntax

100,000 rows on 10,000 data pages, the query optimizer would probably save resources by using an index on city or one on discnt, if such indexes exist. In order to evaluate resource costs at this point, the query optimizer would want to be able to estimate, for example, how many customers rows exist with city = 'Boston'. If it turns out there is only one value for the city column (with the value 'Boston'), then all rows have this city value and the query optimizer learns that this index is not of any use after all. We will consider specific statistics and their uses in the sections that follow.

Statistics are not automatically gathered when a table is loaded or an index is created. A special command must be given by the DBA, a utility command that gathers the needed statistics and puts the results in system tables. Later updates on the table can cause changes that are not reflected in the statistics, which then become obsolete, and inappropriate decisions by the query optimizer may result without sufficiently frequent reissuance of the statistics-gathering command.

DB2 uses the RUNSTATS command with the syntax given in Figure 9.3 to gather statistics into catalog tables. The simplest form of the RUNSTATS command (exemplified here for a CAP database table)

```
runstats on table poneil.customers;
```

will actually retrieve most of the statistics we need. Details will be covered in later sections.

ORACLE uses the Analyze statement to collect statistics into the data dictionary. The syntax for the Analyze statement is given in Figure 9.4.

Retrieving the Query Plan

A query optimizer builds an access plan, consisting of a sequence of *procedural access steps*, or simply *procedural steps* or *access steps*. These procedural steps are peculiar to the specific database system and are put together like a series of instructions in an object program created by a compiler to carry out the logic of a higher-level program (the nonprocedural SQL query, in our case). In the following sections we will discuss the access steps available in **DB2**, including

Tablespace scan (in **DB2**, or Table scan in **DB2 UDB**)
Index scan
Equal unique index lookup
Unclustered matching index scan
Clustered matching index scan
Index-only scan

Most database systems have analogous procedural steps. However, even steps with comparable names may have different effects in the different database systems, and thus require different procedural flow, quite analogous to machine instruction sets for different processors. While bitmap indexing and hashed access are not offered by **DB2**, the product has a sophisticated set of procedural steps and supports most access concepts available in other systems, with a number of valuable high-performance capabilities that are especially valuable in range retrievals.

A DBA is able to generate the query plan for a given query by using a command provided by the database system. In **DB2 UDB**, the DBA uses a special SQL statement of the form

```
EXPLAIN PLAN [SET QUERYNO = n] [SET QUERYTAG = 'string']
   FOR explainable-sql-statement;
```

This statement executes correctly on both (mainframe) **DB2** and on **DB2 UDB**. In the **DB2** case, it inserts rows into a user-created **DB2** table known as the plan_table, one row for each individual access step in the plan created for the explainable-sql-statement. In the **DB2 UDB** case, it inserts into a set of user-created tables known collectively as the explain tables. We will avoid discussion of the rather complex **DB2 UDB** explain tables in what follows, except to say that all the simple capabilities we will be covering for **DB2** have **DB2 UDB** (and **ORACLE**) counterparts. The queryno specified in an Explain Plan statement is a column of plan_table in **DB2**, so it can be used for later retrieval from the plan_table with the value n specified. Thus the DBA could execute the following statement to generate the query plan for the query we have been using as an example:

```
explain plan set queryno = 1000 for
   select * from customers
      where city = 'Boston' and discnt between 12 and 14;
```

Then to retrieve all rows associated with this query (only one in this case) from the **DB2** plan_table, the DBA (or interested user who owns the plan created) could then execute the statement

```
select * from plan_table where queryno = 1000;
```

The plan_table (which we sometimes refer to simply as the *plan table*) contains a large number of columns, indeed an almost overwhelming number on first encounter. We will explain the significance of many of these columns as they become relevant, but as an introduction we mention one important column named ACCESSTYPE. A *tablespace scan* step in a **DB2** plan will pass through a tablespace where rows of a single table of the query are stored (possibly with rows from other tables present on the same pages, as in an **ORACLE** cluster), and will validate the search condition of the WHERE clause relevant to that table. When this occurs, we will see an 'R' in the ACCESSTYPE column of plan_table, which we will symbolize in the following sections by writing ACCESSTYPE = R. Another column of plan_table will give the name of the table on which the scan is being performed.

Note that while the original Select statement might refer to view tablenames in the FROM clause, the access plan refers only to physical base tables. Most of the early plans we introduce consist of only a single step, and thus a single row appears in the plan table. (Each single-access plan step refers to only a single table, so a multi-step plan is required when more than one table is mentioned in the FROM clause, either because of a join or a sequence of subqueries.) Another ACCESSTYPE corresponds to a plan step where a single index is used to qualify rows of the table for retrieval—for example, a cityx index used to retrieve all rows satisfying the predicate city = 'Boston', while any predicates in the WHERE clause not restricted by that index (such as discnt between 10 and 12) are validated after qualified rows are accessed. For this type of plan we see ACCESSTYPE = I in the plan table.

In **ORACLE**, the plan for a specific query can likewise be placed in a default plan_table, or any other named table with identical columns, using a statement with the following syntax:

```
EXPLAIN PLAN [SET STATEMENT_ID = 'text-identifier'] [INTO [schema.]tablename]
    FOR explainable-sql-statement;
```

The Explain Plan statement is presented in the *ORACLE8 Server SQL Reference* [9]. For information on how to interpret the execution plan, refer to the *ORACLE8 Server Tuning Guide* [8], Chapter 21.

9.2 Tablespace Scans and I/O

To begin our study of procedural access steps, we consider the tablespace scan step in **DB2**. Recall that the row in the plan table representing a tablespace scan has the letter R in the ACCESSTYPE column, which we write as ACCESSTYPE = R.

EXAMPLE 9.2.1 Tablespace Scan Step.
A *tablespace scan* step in **DB2** is an algorithmic step wherein all the data in a table (the relevant data pages of a tablespace) is scanned and the rows are restricted by the relevant predicates in a search_condition of a WHERE clause. In the **DB2** architecture there are situations in which rows from different tables can be mixed on common extents of a tablespace, which is

why this is called a tablespace scan rather than a table scan. However, in what follows we assume that all pages referenced in a tablespace scan contain only rows from a single table.

Assume that we are given an employees table with 200,000 rows, each row 200 bytes in length, and that data pages have been loaded just 70% full. (In **DB2**, the PCTFREE specification that determines how full data pages are loaded by default is given in the Create Tablespace statement, and can be overridden in the Create Table statement.) We assume that each 4-KB page uses roughly 96 bytes for overhead, leaving 4000 bytes, and with data pages loaded 70% full we have 2800 available bytes, so 14 rows will fit on each page. Thus the total number of data pages needed for 200,000 rows is CEIL(200,000/14) = 14,286 pages. Now consider the following query:

```
select eid, ename from employees where socsecno = 113353179;
```

where an employee with a given Social Security number is to be retrieved. If we don't have an index on socsecno, then our only alternative is to scan the whole table with a tablespace scan, looking for all rows that fit the WHERE clause description. (We assume there is only one such row, but the query optimizer might not know this, depending on what statistics have been gathered.) Note that the data scan step is in fact the whole of the access plan, since the result of this step completely answers the query. There are 14,286 data pages in this table, so the I/O cost of this plan, COST$_{I/O}$(PLAN), is 14,286 R—that is, 14,286 random I/Os. Recall that we do not try to estimate COST$_{CPU}$(PLAN), but assume that the total cost is normally proportional to the I/O cost. ∎

The tablespace scan is also known under other names with other products, such as a *direct search, data scan,* or *table scan.* (In fact, it is known as a *table scan* in **DB2 UDB**, since each page contains rows from only one table.) We have mentioned before, for instance, in Example 8.4.1, about the elapsed time required to perform a large number of random I/Os. But now it is time to examine some of the assumptions we use in estimating elapsed time, and to introduce some new types of I/Os, known as *sequential prefetch I/O* and *list prefetch I/O.*

Assumptions about I/O

What implications can be drawn from an I/O cost of 14,286 R for the query plan of Example 9.2.1? To begin with, recall that a random I/O on a normal disk takes an expected elapsed time of approximately 0.0125 seconds (1/80 of a second), as we saw in Section 8.2. But of course that doesn't necessarily mean that 14,286 random I/Os in succession will require a total elapsed time of 14,286/80 = 178.6 seconds. Quite possibly these 14,286 data pages could be spread out over (say) ten different disks, and the system could then enlist the service of all ten disk arms moving simultaneously, so that each disk reads only one-tenth as many pages into memory (1429 pages per disk), in one-tenth the elapsed time (17.9 seconds). This approach to having multiple disk arms acting simultaneously in a query plan is known as *I/O parallelism.* Since the CPU time in a query plan is often much smaller than the elapsed time required for disk I/O, we expect the CPU to be able to keep up with retrieving appropriate rows from the data pages as quickly as the pages can be read from disk into memory buffers, overlapping CPU efforts with a large number of simultaneously moving disk arms. Certainly such read parallelism requires no additional CPU, and it significantly lowers the elapsed time for the query.

I/O Parallelism and Disk Striping

I/O parallelism is a feature offered by several database systems. For example, some systems offer the ability to *stripe* the data pages across (say) ten different disks, page 1 on disk 1, page 2 on disk 2, . . . , page 10 on disk 10, then page 11 on disk 1, page 12 on disk 2, and so on, with page N lying on the disk number $((N - 1)\%10) + 1$. ("X%Y" is the C language expression for "X MOD Y." See Figure 9.5.) When we stripe the pages in this way, the system reading successive pages from a table can make multiple I/O read requests into the future and thus keep all involved disk arms busy most of the time. Since we can easily predict future tablespace page requests when performing a tablespace scan, we merely need an architecture that supports striping, translating logical page addresses into physical device addresses on multiple disks and passing along future I/O requests to the appropriate devices. This is not at all difficult, since allocated extents in such a striping architecture must span multiple disks in a well-defined way.

There are a number of reasons why striping for parallel I/O is not more commonly used. Certainly it requires extra effort on the part of the DBA, who must allocate equivalent amounts of space on multiple disks. Balancing the disk arm load to gain maximum parallelism is also a complex problem: if one of the ten striped disks is extremely busy doing other I/O in a workload, that disk will become a bottleneck for a parallel access and possibly cause other disks in the striped tablespace to be underutilized. Also, many systems do not have enough disk devices or a large enough application, requiring parallel scans to make tuning of this kind possible.

Another point is that disk striping doesn't actually save any computer resource cost. We require the same total *number* of random I/Os, even though the workload is split up among several different disk devices. If we estimate the I/O cost of the 14,286 random I/Os of Example 9.2.1 by charging a fair rent on the disk devices during the time they are dedicated, then parallelism has no effect whatsoever on this cost; we are simply using more devices for a shorter time, paying the same ultimate rent. The savings we achieve with a reduced elapsed time for the query has to do with the employee costs mentioned earlier, reducing wasted time and turnover caused by the frustration of waiting for query responses. Because I/O parallelism is still relatively rare, we assume in the following discussion that we are always dealing with the alternative, sequential I/O, where one I/O

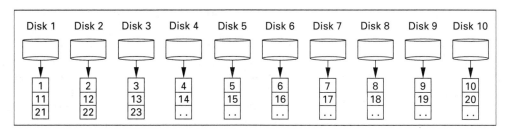

Figure 9.5   Successive Disk Pages on Striped Disks

request must be complete before a second request is made in a plan, unless we specify
otherwise. Sequential I/O still has an unrevealed trick to offer, however, that will actually
save a large amount of resource cost in performing a tablespace scan.

Sequential Prefetch I/O in DB2

We have been assuming implicitly that 14,286 R (random I/Os) when performed one
after another will require 14,286 times as long as a single random I/O. In Section 8.2, we
derived the fact that a single random I/O took an expected average time of about 0.0125
seconds, broken down as in Figure 9.6. (We make no modification for the 4-KB pages of
DB2 from the analysis of Section 8.2.)

Now let us return to the consideration of performing 14,286 random I/Os in a
tablespace scan. Because of the way extents are allocated on disk media, we will generally find that successive data pages in a table are contiguous on disk, with successive
pages on the same track. This seems to imply that successive data page I/Os from a table
usually have no seek time component during which a disk arm must move from one
cylinder to another. Recall from the discussion at the beginning of Section 8.2 that the
seek time of about .016 seconds is an average time for disk arm seek, where it is assumed
that successive accessed pages are scattered at random between the two extreme cylinder
positions. In our case there is usually no distance to move at all, and we should expect
the seek time to completely disappear. In fact, at first glance it would seem that the rotational latency should disappear as well, since we normally retrieve one disk page after
another in sequence. Thus there seems no reason why the normal time for bringing successive data pages into memory buffers can't proceed at the speed of full transfer rate,
about 0.00125 seconds per 4-KB page. There were a number of arguments against this
analysis in our first edition, since a request made for the next page on disk after the previous one has been returned will be too late to retrieve the next page without a complete
rotation of the disk, adding back a full rotational latency of about 8 ms. But recent
advances in database system parallelism by which successive requests can be made to the
controller without waiting for earlier requests to be filled has made it possible to achieve
this sort of high sequential I/O rate in most cases.

In fact, the analysis is reinforced by a common sort of buffering that disk controllers
now typically support. Whenever a disk page I/O is requested through such a controller,
an I/O is performed on the *entire track* containing the disk page requested. The data from
the track is buffered in memory owned by the disk controller, and the single page
requested is returned to the database server. However, if later requests for pages on the

Seek time	.0080 seconds
Rotational latency	.0040 seconds
Transfer time	.0005 seconds (for 4 KB of transfer)
TOTAL	.0125 seconds

Figure 9.6 Breakdown of Random I/O Elapsed Time for **DB2**

544

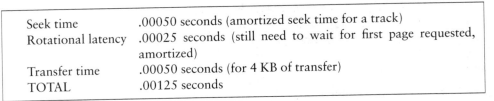

	Seek time	.00050 seconds (amortized seek time for a track)
	Rotational latency	.00025 seconds (still need to wait for first page requested, amortized)
	Transfer time	.00050 seconds (for 4 KB of transfer)
	TOTAL	.00125 seconds

Figure 9.7 Breakdown of Average Sequential I/O Elapsed Time

	Random I/O (in seconds)	Sequential prefetch I/O (in seconds)
Elapsed time per page	0.0125	0.00125

Figure 9.8 Comparison of Sequential Prefetch and Random I/O Elapsed Time

same track occur (as they would in the case of a tablespace scan), the data is read out of the disk controller buffer and returned to the database server immediately, without any need for access to the disk. Therefore the I/O speed after the first seek would be almost instantaneous. The disk controller is retrieving a track at a time, and this translates to an I/O rate for sequential I/O that is almost 10 times faster than random I/O! We show this speed-up of sequential I/O in Figure 9.7.

One problem with the disk controller habit of reading an entire track and buffering it all when a single disk page is requested is that this will *always* happen, even when it is counterproductive. Thus an elapsed time of 0.008 ms to read an entire track will also be added to every I/O performed by the database, even random I/Os to pick up rows where there is no intention of accessing the next page on the track.

The **DB2** system offers a more responsive type of I/O request, known as *sequential prefetch* I/O. The idea of sequential prefetch I/O is that the system specifies a large number of data pages in sequence to be read in from disk, most commonly 32 pages, but *only when it is needed*. As we will see a bit later, **DB2** also expends a good deal of effort to determine how to place I/O requests in order when this is possible. As a result, **DB2** is able to perform 32 page reads in sequence at the full rotational transfer rate of the disk, even if the disk controller track buffering capability is turned off. What this all boils down to is that retrieval of a large number of slots in sequence is a lot faster than random I/O, as we dramatize in Figure 9.8.

In what follows, we use the rough rule of thumb that sequential prefetch, in situations where it can be applied, proceeds ten times as fast as random I/O, at a rate of 800 I/Os per second, that is, 0.00125 seconds (or 1.25 ms) per I/O.

EXAMPLE 9.2.2 Tablespace Scan with Sequential Prefetch.

Recall the *tablespace scan* of Example 9.2.1, where the given Select statement has an I/O cost of 14,286 R (where R stands for random I/O). Under standard assumptions of random I/O (no parallelism), we calculated that the elapsed time for this query, during which one disk arm is completely utilized, is 14,286/80 = 178.6 seconds. But since in fact the disk page requests in a tablespace scan can be made in contiguous order, the I/O will take place a good deal more quickly. We write $COST_{I/O}(PLAN) = 14{,}286$ S. The letter S at the end of the number of pages to be read indicates that the pages are in sequence and in **DB2** sequential prefetch is to be employed. The resulting elapsed time for this query is 14,286/800 = 17.86 seconds. This is an important I/O cost savings, since the time spent by the disk arm has actually been reduced by a factor of ten, and the rent on the device is therefore reduced by a similar factor. Putting this a different way, we can perform ten times as many queries of this kind with sequential prefetch on the same disk equipment as we could with random I/Os.

  A query plan might make use of both sequential prefetch and random I/O. We use the elapsed time for total I/O as the best common measure, since the rental cost on a disk arm is directly proportional to the elapsed time the arm is in use, and in this important sense sequential prefetch I/Os are about ten times more effective than random I/Os.

  This is a good time to introduce another column of the **DB2** plan table, the PREFETCH column. When sequential prefetch is selected for a given access step, we see the letter S in the PREFETCH column for that row of the plan table, and we designate this by writing PREFETCH = S. Thus the tablespace scan step of Example 9.2.2 would be designated in the **DB2** plan table by ACCESSTYPE = R, PREFETCH = S. The plan table listing only these two columns is given in Figure 9.9.

List Prefetch

There is also another kind of prefetch available in **DB2**, known as *list prefetch,* in which the disk controller is provided in advance with a list of pages (usually 32) that need to be read in to memory buffers, but the pages are not necessarily in contiguous sequential order as with sequential prefetch. With list prefetch, the disk controller typically attempts to perform the most efficient possible sequence of movements it can determine to perform the successive reads (using something called the *elevator algorithm*). Thus the I/Os occur much more efficiently than they would with random I/O requests. The elapsed time for such a list prefetch does not follow a simple general rule, however, and the 0.00125 seconds elapsed time given in Figure 9.8 for a sequential prefetch is generally an unattainable optimum for a list prefetch. List prefetch is more efficient than random I/O (which we are assuming performs 80 I/Os per second) and less efficient than sequential prefetch I/O (which we are assuming performs 800 I/Os per second). The actual speed is determined by how far apart the pages are on disk, but as a rule of thumb in the problems that follow we will assume that list prefetch proceeds at 200 I/Os per second. We will use these approximate rates for random, sequential prefetch, and list prefetch I/Os a good deal in what follows, so Figure 9.10 tabulates the rules of thumb just mentioned.

ACCESSTYPE	PREFETCH
R	S

Figure 9.9 Plan Table for Example 9.2.2

Random I/O	Sequential prefetch I/O	List prefetch I/O
80 pages/second	800 pages/second	200 pages/second

Figure 9.10   Rules of Thumb for I/O Rates

Although these are rather rough figures, they usually give a reasonably good estimate for queries that occur in practice.

An access step in the plan table using list prefetch would be designated by PREFETCH = L—that is, a letter L in the PREFETCH column, analogous to the letter S when sequential prefetch is to be used. An access step that uses neither sequential prefetch nor list prefetch would have a blank value in the PREFETCH column.

More about Prefetch

We present a number of examples in the following sections to solidify these concepts. However, we do not consider list prefetch until we have had a chance to explain the **DB2** preconditions for list prefetch in Section 9.6. Until then, we act as if table rows are always read in from disk using random or sequential prefetch I/Os.

There are also a number of special cases involving prefetch I/O. When the number of pages that needs to be read from disk is less than 32, a prefetch I/O is still possible; indeed, a prefetch can be performed to read in as few as 4 pages. Naturally such small transfers will adversely affect the I/O rate given in Figure 9.10 since we have reduced the number of pages to amortize the seek time and rotational latency, but in the calculations that follow we generally ignore such effects. However, any time that 3 or fewer pages must be read in from disk, you should assume that random I/O is used, even if the preconditions for sequential or list prefetch are met.

It is clear that sequential and list prefetch are important capabilities. One of the important things about sequential prefetch in **DB2** is that the system has the freedom to choose whether to read in a single page with a normal random I/O or 32 such pages with a prefetch I/O. Any attempt to compromise, say, on an 8-page read for all purposes, will penalize some applications while it helps others. There is no value, for example, in reading in 8 pages around a B-tree node when all the desired information has been carefully placed on a single page node. Indeed such behavior penalizes everyone by wasting memory buffer space that should be applied to keeping other popular information in buffer.

9.3   Simple Indexed Access in DB2

As we noted in Chapter 8, columns of tables referenced in a Select statement can take part in indexes, and a query plan for the Select statement can sometimes make use of those indexes to limit rows selected and make the query execution more efficient. In the next several sections we consider basic indexed access step capabilities. To begin with we will consider only Select statements having a single table named in the FROM clause and no new tables named in Subqueries in the search_condition of the WHERE clause, thus avoiding considerations of join processing. We also confine our attention to the **DB2** query optimizer unless otherwise stated, and we refer to variations in the **ORACLE** product only parenthetically. In the following examples, tables are designated by the generic names T1, T2, . . . , and columns within these tables designated by C1, C2, C3, C4, ...

EXAMPLE 9.3.1 Matching Index Scan, Single-Column Index.
Assume that an index C1X exists on the column C1 of table T1 (this is always a B-tree index in **DB2**), and that the following query has been posed:

```
select * from T1 where C1 = 10;
```

This query is implemented in **DB2** by an access step known as a *matching index scan*. In execution, the B-tree index on column C1 is traversed down to the leaf level for the leftmost index entry that has the value 10 (recall the exercise to find the leftmost entry as a variation of the binsearch algorithm of Example 8.3.1). Then the row from table T1 pointed to by that entry is retrieved into the answer set. Following this, successive entries are retrieved from the leaf level of the index while the index value remains 10, passing from left to right in the entries and from one leaf node to the next, following leaf sibling pointers when necessary. For each entry, the corresponding row pointed to in T1 is retrieved into the answer set. When the index value first exceeds 10, the matching index scan is complete. Note in particular that only one traversal of the B-tree down to the leaf level was required. The rows retrieved during this scan may or may not have been found in clustered order by C1; we have made no assumption as to whether C1 is a clustered index. ∎

A matching index scan is a single-step query plan, sharing this property with the tablespace scan: when the step is complete the query has been answered. In the plan table, three columns of which are shown in Figure 9.11, a matching index scan such as that seen in Example 9.3.1 has ACCESSTYPE = I (this represents an index scan), ACCESSNAME = C1X (the name of the index being scanned), and MATCHCOLS = 1. MATCHCOLS gives the number of matching columns in the index; this value can be at most 1 for an index scan on an index with a single column.

Now consider the following query:

[9.3.1]
```
select * from T1
    where C1 = 10 and C2 between 100 and 200 and C3 like 'A%';
```

Recall that the search_condition of a WHERE clause is made up of a number of logical predicates, listed in Figure 3.19 of Section 3.9, connected by logical operators such as AND, OR, and NOT, as defined in Figure 3.20. The Select statement of [9.3.1] above

ACCESS TYPE	ACCESS NAME	MATCH COLS
I	C1X	1

Figure 9.11 Plan Table for Example 9.3.1

contains three predicates connected by logical operators AND: (1) a comparison predicate involving the column C1 (this is a special type of comparison predicate known as an
equal match predicate), (2) a BETWEEN predicate involving the column C2, and (3) a
LIKE predicate involving the column C3. In each of these cases an index on the associated column can be used efficiently in a **DB2** query plan to limit the rows considered for
retrieval. These predicates are said to be *indexable* in **DB2**. Not all predicates are indexable, however, which means that although it might still be possible to use an index to
limit the rows retrieved, the index will not be used efficiently. For example, the predicate
C1 <> 10 is not indexable, and the query

```
select * from T1 where C1 <> 10;
```

while it *can* use index scan on a C1X index, is more likely to use a tablespace scan, which
is always available as a fallback. We give a detailed list of indexable and non-indexable
predicates later in this chapter, in Figure 9.15. For now, we want to study how multiple
predicates in a WHERE clause such as we see in the Select statement of [9.3.1] might all
be used simultaneously to restrict the rows retrieved.

EXAMPLE 9.3.2 Matching Index Scan, Single-Column Index, Additional Predicates to Be Verified.

As before, assume that an index C1X exists on the column C1 of table T1, but this time the
query of [9.3.1] has been posed:

```
select * from T1
    where C1 = 10 and C2 between 100 and 200 and C3 like 'A%';
```

We assume that there are no indexes involving the columns C2 and C3. As before, this query is
implemented in **DB2** by a single *matching index scan* access step. The B-tree index on column
C1 is traversed down to the leaf level for the leftmost index entry that has the value 10; the
entries at the leaf level with index value 10 are traversed left to right. Successive rows from
table T1 pointed to by these entries are then accessed, and tests are performed on the rows to
validate the other two predicates: C2 between 100 and 200 and C3 like 'A%'. Rows that pass
these tests are retrieved into the answer set.   ■

The matching index scan step introduced in Examples 9.3.1 and 9.3.2 is defined as a
step where a *single index* is used to retrieve all the rows from a table that satisfy some
(set of) predicates in a WHERE clause. In the case of an index on a single column, a
matching index scan usually represents a single contiguous range of column values, corresponding to exactly one predicate such as C1 = 10 (with an index C1X on C1), C2
between 100 and 200 (with an index C2X on C2), or C3 like 'A%' (with an index C3X
on C3). A noncontiguous set of column values can also be retrieved with a special case of
the matching index scan, known as an *IN-LIST index scan,* on a predicate such as C4 in
(1, 2, 3) (with an index C4X on C4). It is also possible to satisfy several predicates at
once through a single index in a matching index scan. Consider the index C123X, created with the following Create Index statement:

```
create index C123X on T1 (C1, C2, C3) . . . ;
```

In the Select statement of Example 9.3.2, with only the index C1X available, we notice that the two later predicates do not reduce the number of rows accessed from T1. We can only use the first predicate to limit to rows with C1 = 10, and then access each of these rows from the table to validate the other predicates. But with the index C123X available, we can restrict all three predicates at once (C1 = 10 and C2 between 100 and 200 and C3 like 'A%') by recourse to this single index. To give an analogy, it is as if we were looking in a library catalog for all books with the last name James (C1 = 10), first name beginning with the letters H through K (C2 between 100 and 200), and title beginning with the letter A (C3 like 'A%'). It should be obvious that we will be able to restrict the number of books to be retrieved quite effectively by examining the cards alone.

In a second type of situation, separate indexes exist on each of the columns under discussion. Thus we might have an index C1X on C1, an index C2X on C2, and an index C3X on C3. The method by which three different indexes of this sort can be employed to answer the query of Example 9.3.2 may not be immediately obvious. By analogy, it involves extracting a list of catalog cards from *each* associated catalog that satisfies *one* of the given predicates, sorting each list of cards in order by call number (RID), and then performing a merge-intersect of the three lists of cards so that we end up only with books that obey all three predicates. This multiple-step approach is known as *multiple index access*; we cover it in detail after we have had a chance to look at some of the more basic concepts of indexed access.

Equal Unique Match Index Access

Experience shows that many readers tend to picture columns that have unique values when first introduced to indexed retrieval. This is actually a relatively uninteresting case, but we give an example to place the situation in context.

EXAMPLE 9.3.3 Index Scan Step, Unique Match.
Consider the employees table introduced in Example 9.2.1, with a unique index, eidx, on the column eid. We are given the following SQL query:

```
select ename from employees where eid = '12901A';
```

If we assume a **DB2** index (see Figure 8.15 for **DB2 UDB**'s Create Index, the same as **DB2**'s for our purposes) with PCTFREE = 30, we have about 2800 bytes on each page of the index available for index entries. Assume the eid column requires 6 bytes. Since we know the RID requires 4 bytes, we can assume 10 bytes per entry. Thus there are 2800/10 = 280 entries on each index page, and with 200,000 rows, we require CEIL(200,000/280) = 715 pages at the leaf level, CEIL(715/280) = 3 pages at the next directory level up, and a single root page above this. Accessing the unique row with a given eid value requires an access through three levels of B-tree nodes and then an access to one of the 14,286 data pages to retrieve the ename value from the designated row. Therefore it seems that the I/O cost of this Select statement is 4 R. But recall that we keep popular disk pages in memory buffers to reduce the number of real disk I/Os. The $COST_{I/O}(PLAN)$ figure calculated by the query optimizer is meant to be in terms of real I/Os; a page that is already resident in memory buffer entails only a minor CPU cost for lookaside. As we will explain in detail in Chapter 10 (see Example 10.10.2), it is the economically correct decision to purchase enough memory to keep in memory all disk pages that are accessed again within a few minutes (we assume 120 seconds, to be specific on the IBM **DB2** platforms). That's what we mean when we say we are keeping popular pages buffer resident.

Now we need to ask how often the eidx B-tree index is accessed. If the answer is once each second with a random eid value, then we should expect to find the root node of the tree and all three nodes at the next directory level already buffered in memory. On the other hand, the expected time between accesses to leaf-level nodes is 715 seconds, more than the 120-second threshold, so we would *not* expect to find the leaf nodes of the B-tree in buffers. Clearly we would also not expect to find the 14,286 data pages buffer resident. Thus the proper I/O cost for this query plan, under reasonable buffering assumptions, should be 2 R, representing the I/Os to read from disk the leaf node of the B-tree and the data page. Note that all the foregoing analysis has assumed a perfect world—that the proper amount of memory has been purchased and that the buffering scheme will keep all the B-tree directory nodes in memory buffers.

The row of the plan table corresponding to this unique match index scan has ACCESSTYPE = I (implies an index scan), ACCESSNAME = eidx (the name of the index being scanned), and MATCHCOLS = 1. The plan does not mention that a unique match is expected; this is a property that we can predict by noting that the eid column was defined to be unique. ∎

Clustered versus Non-Clustered Indexing

Recall from Section 8.4 that a clustered index has an ordinary B-tree index directory structure, in one area of disk, referencing *rows stored in key order* on contiguous or nearly contiguous disk pages, possibly in a quite different area of disk.

We introduce a table named prospects for use in examples that follow. The prospects table is modeled on tables used by organizations that perform direct-mail applications (mail advertising). The prospects table has 50 million rows corresponding to people in the United States who are potential customers for new products. Information on prospects is often gathered from warranty questionnaires. (It is assumed that people who fill out such warranties expect to have their demographic data kept on record for possible future mailings.) The rows of the prospects table are clustered in **DB2** by an index, addrx, representing the address of the prospect:

```
create index addrx on prospects (zipcode, city, straddr) . . .
    cluster . . . ;
```

Recall that a zip code determines the state (zip codes do not cross state boundaries), and usually corresponds to a district of a large city. Many direct mailings, such as sales announcements at area stores, are to small geographical districts consisting of a few zip code regions, and we will see that clustering by addrx permits extremely efficient queries.

We assume that PCTFREE = 0 for the prospects table and all indexes, because we don't expect any inserts, or even updates, to the prospects table during its lifetime. New households are added to the prospects table infrequently. Typically new prospects would be added only once every week or so by doing a complete reload of the table to ensure optimal retrieval efficiency. Given that rows of the prospects table contain 400 bytes, we can fit 10 rows on each 4-KB page, and a 50-million-row table requires 5 million pages.

At the leaf level of the addrx index B-tree, we assume that the zipcode column can be represented as an integer in 4 bytes, city requires 12 bytes, straddr 20 bytes, and of course the RID for each entry requires 4 bytes. Thus an entry in the addrx index requires 40 bytes. (We assume for simplicity that there are no duplicate index values—that is, two or more prospects with the same address. We thus avoid needing to take into account the type of **DB2/DB2 UDB** index compression covered in Figure 8.17.) We can fit 100 40-byte entries in a 4-KB page that is 100% full. With 50 million total entries, this means 500,000 node pages at the leaf level of the tree. The next directory level up contains 5000 nodes, the one above that contains 50 nodes, and the root page lies above that. This is a four-level B-tree.

The prospects table also has a large number of non-clustering indexes. Consider one possible index, on the attribute hobby, provided by the prospect on the questionnaire as a hobby of major interest.

```
create index hobbyx on prospects (hobby);
```

Assume that 100 distinct hobbies are listed in the form the prospect filled out (. . . card games, chess, coin collecting, . . .). We say that the *cardinality* of the hobby column, the number of different attribute values, is 100:

CARD(hobby) = 100

This is a type of statistic used by **DB2** in calculating the I/O cost of a query plan, and it also gives us an idea of the amount of index compression present in the hobbyx index. In the same way, we can assume that there are 100,000 distinct zipcode values in the addrx index, from 00000 to 99999. (This is actually an overestimate, used for simplicity.) Basically, the small number of hobbies means that we can assume that the length of the hobby column is irrelevant for leaf-level index entries, because from the **DB2** index compression of Figure 8.17 we see that the index key appears only once for every few hundred RID values. Thus the leaf-level entries can be taken as being 4 bytes in length, 1000 entries per page. This is because we have about 500,000 prospects rows for every one of the 100 hobbyx values, and **DB2** index compression can be applied in its most effective form, with 255 RIDs amortizing each key value. With 50 million entries at the leaf level and 1000 entries fitting on a page, we have 50,000 leaf pages. At the next level up, the index key separators appear with each entry (there is no compression). If we assume entries of 12 bytes, we fit 333 entries to a page and thus have 50,000/333 = 151 nodes. The next level up is the root. These calculations are summarized in Figure 9.12. We are now ready for a few more illustrative examples.

EXAMPLE 9.3.4 Matching Index Scan Step, Unclustered Match.
Consider the following SQL query:

```
select name, straddr from prospects where hobby = 'chess';
```

To answer this query, the query optimizer considers an index scan step on the index hobbyx. This is comparable to the matching index scan step of Example 9.3.1, except that this time we will be making I/O estimates. The root node of the hobbyx B-tree is read first, followed by the next node down along the proper path until the leaf node is read corresponding to the leftmost of the hobbyx entries with value = 'chess'. The next step is to retrieve successive entries from the leaf level until the hobbyx value that follows 'chess' is encountered. As noted earlier, there are only 100 different values for hobbyx. If we assume that each of the values is equally likely, this means that there are 500,000 entries corresponding to the value 'chess'. To traverse across 500,000 entries with 1000 entries per leaf node requires 500 leaf page I/Os, and these I/Os can be performed using sequential prefetch I/O. Now for each of these 500,000 'chess' index entries, we must perform a random page I/O to access the appropriate row of the prospects table and return the name and straddr values. With 5,000,000 data pages and 500,000 rows, we expect each row to be on a separate page (this is actually one of the cases of the "N darts in M slots" problem, discussed earlier in Section 8.6, which will be the subject of exercises at the end of the chapter). In any event, we have no reason to think that rows retrieved are close together on data pages, since hobbyx is an unclustered index. Thus each row retrieval requires its own random I/O, and the total number of I/Os needed to resolve this query is 2 R for index directory nodes, 500 S for index leaf nodes, and 500,000 R for data pages.

The elapsed time to read 500 pages with sequential prefetch at 800 pages a second is 500/800 = 0.625 seconds; the elapsed time to read 500,000 pages using random I/O, at 80 I/Os per second, is 500,000/80 = 6250 seconds, or somewhat less than 2 hours. Clearly the I/Os to descend the hobbyx B-tree and even to traverse the entries at the leaf level are insignificant by comparison with the data page I/Os. ■

In exercises involving elapsed time for I/O, you should generally assume that index directory pages are buffer resident and that index leaf pages are not, unless instructed otherwise. You may ignore index I/O in your answers when these sum to less than 5% of the total. However, you should be careful to include index I/O calculations, to demonstrate why you consider them insignificant.

If instead the query of Example 9.3.4 is performed with a tablespace scan, we see that to retrieve 5,000,000 pages using sequential prefetch I/O, this will require 5,000,000/800 = 6250 seconds elapsed time—*nearly the same elapsed time as required by the index scan*. This is a fairly surprising result, and demonstrates the value of a query optimizer to compare costs of competing plans. Basically what is happening is that with

prospects table	addrx index	hobbyx index
50,000,000 rows	500,000 leaf pages	50,000 leaf pages
5,000,000 data pages	5,000 level 3 nodes	151 level 2 nodes
	50 level 2 nodes	1 root node
	1 root node	
	CARD(zipcode) = 100,000	CARD(hobby)=100

Figure 9.12 Some Statistics for the prospects Table

sequential prefetch I/O, approximately ten times as many pages can be read in the same amount of time as is the case with random I/O. Since the unclustered index scan of this example reads 500,000 pages to retrieve the same number of prospects with a single hobby, and the data scan reads 5,000,000 pages with prefetch I/O, the two methods are actually quite close in elapsed time and indeed in I/O disk arm rent. If we had more hobbies for our prospects table, and thus a smaller number of rows per index value, the unclustered index scan would certainly be used, and with fewer hobbies a data scan would probably be more appropriate.

In Example 9.3.4 we used the fact that CARD(hobby) = 100 to conclude that the predicate hobby = 'chess' retrieves about 1/100 of the rows of the prospects table. This fraction is known as the *filter factor* of the predicate; we will frequently meet such filter factors in what follows.

EXAMPLE 9.3.5 Matching Index Scan Step, Clustered Match.
Consider the following SQL query:

```
select name, straddr from prospects
    where zipcode between 02159 and 03158;
```

Recall our assumption that there are 100,000 distinct zipcode column values making up the first component of the addrx index on which the data rows are clustered. The index scan step here performs its search by reading down to the leftmost entry of the addrx B-tree having zipcode 02159 (other values in the concatenated key value are immaterial), then examining entries from left to right until the first zipcode value outside the range is encountered. We see that approximately the same number of leaf-level index entries are processed here as were processed from the hobbyx index of the last example. The filter factor of hobby = 'chess' was 1/100, but here we are retrieving a range of 1000 values from the zipcode index with 100,000 distinct values. While the filter factor of zipcode = 02159 would be 1/100,000, the factor for the range predicate with 1000 values is 1000/100,000 = 1/100. The number of leaf-level pages of addrx that is read in with 500,000 entries, at 40 bytes per entry, 100 entries per page, is 5000; and since sequential prefetch can be used, this means an I/O cost of 5000 S. (A simple check on this is that the number of pages at the leaf level of addrx, as shown in Figure 9.12, is 500,000, and we will be processing 1/100 of these pages.)

Now we will retrieve the same number of rows from the prospects table, or 500,000 rows, as we did in Example 9.3.4. However, since the rows in prospects are *clustered* by zipcode, where they were not by hobbyx, the 500,000 rows in the contiguous retrieved range of zipcodes are *packed together* in the table data pages, 10 to a page. We can therefore assume that we need to retrieve only 50,000 table pages, and that we can accomplish this using sequential prefetch I/O, so the I/O cost is 50,000 S. (Note that we required 5000 S to retrieve an equivalent number of addrx entries, 40 bytes in length, and these rows are 400 bytes in length, so this is a check on our work.) The total elapsed time for 5000 S + 50,000 S is 55,000/800 = 66.8 seconds, a little over 1 minute, compared to nearly 2 hours of the previous example. This is a dramatic example of the advantage of clustering! ∎

Looking at Example 9.3.5, we note that the query optimizer chooses to examine each index entry in the range before retrieving the row indexed, even though the rows themselves are clustered by the index values. It might seem to be an I/O savings to ignore the index entries once the left end of the range of rows has been located, and thereafter to look only at the rows within the sequence of data pages for the range selected. However, this is not done in **DB2**. One important reason index entries are always examined is that the clustering property breaks down after a number of new row inserts have filled up data pages. When this occurs, future rows inserted in a range of values are placed on data pages that lie entirely out of the local data page sequence, and the only way to retrieve such rows in a range is to examine the index entries. Although we do not intend to insert new rows into the prospects table until the table is reorganized, **DB2** is unaware of this and therefore always examines index entries before retrieving the rows.

Index-Only Retrieval

Another interesting observation from Example 9.3.5 is that the index entries retrieved in the desired range entail an I/O cost of 5000 S and the data rows retrieved entail an I/O cost of 50,000 S. Since the index entries involved are 40 bytes in length and the data rows are 400 bytes in length, the multiple of ten in I/O cost seems natural. This observation, together with some of the other examples we have seen, allows us to categorize the retrieval advantages of index entries over data rows in terms of the following properties:

[1] The index has a directory structure that allows us to retrieve a range of values efficiently.

[2] Index entries are always placed in sequence by value on contiguous disk pages, and therefore the system can use sequential prefetch I/O to achieve low retrieval cost.

[3] Index entries are shorter than data rows and require proportionately less I/O.

We could conceivably place a directory structure on clustered rows, where the rows take the place of entries at the leaf level of a B-tree, and thus achieve properties 1 and 2 on the clustered row structure. Of course we can only cluster the rows by one set of values, while we can create numerous indexes for different indexing values. We see a special advantage from property 3 in the following example.

EXAMPLE 9.3.6 Concatenated Index, Index-Only Scan.
Consider again the SQL Select statement of Example 9.3.5:

```
select name, straddr from prospects
    where zipcode between 02159 and 03158;
```

Recall that the addrx index was used in Example 9.3.5 to access rows of the prospects table in the desired range of zipcodes, where addrx was created with the statement

```
create index addrx on prospects (zipcode, city, straddr) . . .
    cluster . . . ;
```

But now let us assume—for the current example only—that an alternative index, naddrx, has been created with the statement

555

```
create index naddrx on prospects (zipcode, city, straddr, name)
     . . . cluster . . . ;
```

As we will see, the fact that the index naddrx is a *clustered* index for the prospects table is not crucial to this example, since the Select statement at the beginning of this example can be answered by reference to components of the values in naddrx *without any reference to the* prospects *table.* The concatenated key value of the naddrx index has the conceptual form

```
naddrx key value: zipcodeval.cityval.straddrval.nameval
```

so that each of the individual component values can be read out of an index entry retrieved in the desired range, and retrieved into the select list of the Select statement. To answer the Select statement we started with, the index entries of naddrx in the range of zipcode are accessed as they were in Example 9.3.5; but then instead of referencing the associated row pointed to by the entry RID, the name and straddr values in the select list of the Select statement are retrieved from the fourth and third components, respectively, of the naddrx key value. This type of index scan is known as an *index-only scan.*

What is the I/O cost of this retrieval? Assume that the index entries in naddrx are 60 bytes in length, 50% longer than the 40-byte addrx entries, because of the addition of the name column. In Example 9.3.5, the addrx index entry retrieval had an I/O cost of 5000 S, so we would expect the naddrx cost to be 7500 S with these larger entries. Since there is no other I/O cost in this index-only retrieval, we would expect an elapsed time for this query of 7500/800 = 9.4 seconds. This compares with the elapsed time of 66.8 seconds for the same query in Example 9.3.5.

∎

Index-only retrieval occurs for a Select statement when the elements retrieved in the select list can be generated from the entries of the index used, without recourse to data rows. Note in particular that any Select statement from a single table where count(*) is the only element of the select list can be performed with index-only retrieval whenever an index scan can totally resolve the WHERE clause search_condition; the entries retrieved only need to be counted to supply the answer. When EXPLAIN is used to generate query plan steps in the plan table, an index-only scan step is characterized by the plan column ACCESSTYPE = I, and by a new column we mention for the first time, INDEXONLY = Y. In previous examples we have had INDEXONLY = N.

Example 9.3.6 demonstrates a valuable advantage in using concatenated indexes to permit index-only retrieval (and an even greater advantage compared with non-clustered index retrieval). However, it is often difficult to create a set of concatenated indexes to foresee all query needs. For example, consider what would happen in the query of Example 9.3.6 if we wished to retrieve some other prospects attribute into the select list as well:

```
select name, straddr, age from prospects
    where zipcode between 02159 and 03159;
```

Then the concatenated index naddrx would be insufficient to answer the query with an index-only scan, and it would be necessary to read in the table rows after all, except that now the naddrx index to be used requires more I/O than the simpler addrx index we started with. If we try to foresee all needs in a single concatenated index, the index entries become longer and longer, until we are receiving less advantage over reading in the rows (at least in the clustered case). Furthermore it costs something to create multiple indexes. For one thing, there is increased disk media cost, although this is usually an unimportant cost. Another overhead cost occurs in situations where new rows are commonly inserted to the table, because the inserts take more resources to update additional indexes. Even in the read-only database case, there is additional cost in the initial load time, a nontrivial consideration for large tables such as prospects. Still you should be aware that there are numerous examples of read-only tables—such as the prospects table—where nearly all single columns of the table have a corresponding index.

9.4 | Filter Factors and Statistics

As we pointed out in the introduction to Example 9.3.3, indexed retrieval on a column with unique values is actually a relatively uninteresting case. Indeed, an extremely important feature introduced in relational query languages such as SQL that was missing from earlier database models is the capability to retrieve information based on compound (usually ANDed) predicate conditions. Clearly if a predicate such as C1 = 10 were to identify a unique row of the containing table, there would be no point in considering compound predicates such as C1 = 10 and C2 between 100 and 200. If the first predicate identifies a unique row, the second predicate can only rule out that row and return an empty answer set. In what follows, we usually assume instead that a single predicate restriction, such as C1 = 10, results in a large subset of rows from the table, and the second predicate, C2 between 100 and 200, filters that set, bringing the number down to a smaller quantity for row retrieval. We speak of the *filter factor* of a predicate P, *FF(P)*, as the fraction of rows from a table resulting from the predicate restriction P. We normally estimate the filter factor of a predicate by making a number of statistical assumptions, including uniform distribution of individual column values and independent joint distributions of values from any two unallied columns. We will discuss variations from these assumptions a bit later.

For example, we said that the number of distinct zipcode values was assumed to be 100,000, symbolized by CARD(zipcode) = 100,000. Assuming that all zipcode values are equally represented in the prospects table (the uniform distribution assumption), we can estimate the filter factor of an equal match predicate, zipcode = const, as follows:

```
FF(zipcode = const) = 1/100,000 = .00001
```

The same assumption allows us to estimate the filter factor of the BETWEEN predicate of Example 9.3.5:

```
FF(zipcode between 02159 and 03158) = 1000(1/100,000) = 1/100 = .01
```

Similarly the cardinality of the hobby column was given as CARD(hobby) = 100, which together with the uniform distribution assumption gives us

```
FF(hobby = 'chess') = 1/100 = .01
```

The joint distribution of values from two unallied columns is taken to be independent, meaning that the filter factors for compound ANDed predicates multiply, so that

```
FF(hobby = 'chess' and zipcode between 02159 and 02658) =
    (1/100)(500/100,000) = .00005
```

A set of predicates, each with a relatively nonrestrictive (large) filter factor, can have a significant effect in ANDed combinations.

> **EXAMPLE 9.4.1 Filter Factor Calculation.**
> Consider a query that might be used by a police department in tracing a car involved in a serious hit-and-run accident: find all drivers who own a red 1997 Oldsmobile 88 registered in Ohio:
>
> ```
> select * from autos where license = 'Ohio' and color = 'red'
>     and year = 1997 and make = 'Olds' and model = '88';
> ```
>
> Under quite reasonable assumptions, we can expect that the predicates of this clause will filter the number of rows retrieved from an autos table of 40 million rows down to a much more manageable set of a few hundred rows. This would occur if 1/50 of all autos are registered in Ohio, 1/10 of all cars are red, 1/8 have year 1997, 1/6 have make Olds, and of these 1/8 have model 88. Except for the dependent pair Olds-88, we assume that these properties are independent—for example, that driving an Olds 88 does not predispose the owner toward buying a red car—and we multiply the filter factors for each of the predicates to arrive at the filter factor for the entire WHERE clause search condition:
>
> ```
> FF(search_cond) = (1/50)(1/10)(1/8)(1/6)(1/8) = 1/192,000
> ```
>
> The number of rows retrieved by the Select statement is therefore approximated statistically by (1/192,000)(40,000,000) = 208.33, or roughly 208 rows. Given a solution set of this size, it is reasonable to take the investigation further by speaking with the car owners and inspecting the cars for physical signs of damage. ∎

The filter factor terminology is from **DB2**, which bases its query optimizer estimates on statistics gathered by the RUNSTATS utility.

DB2 Statistics

Figure 9.13 lists some of the statistics gathered by the RUNSTATS utility that are used by the **DB2** query optimizer for access plan determination. For each statistic we list (1) the name of the **DB2** catalog table in which it appears, and (2) the statistic name, which is the

Catalog name	Statistic name	Default value	Description
SYSTABLES	CARD NPAGES	10,000 CEIL(1+CARD/20)	Number of rows in the table Number of data pages containing rows
SYSCOLUMNS	COLCARD HIGH2KEY LOW2KEY	25 N.A. N.A.	Number of distinct values in this column Second highest value in this column Second lowest value in this column
SYSINDEXES	NLEVELS NLEAF FIRSTKEY-CARD FULLKEY-CARD CLUSTER-RATIO	0 CARD/300 25 25 0% if CLUSTERED = 'N' 95% if CLUSTERED = 'Y'	Number of levels of the index B-tree Number of leaf pages in the index B-tree Number of distinct values in the first column, C1, of this key Number of distinct values in the full key, all components—for example, C1,C2,C3 Percentage of rows of the table that are clustered by these index values

Figure 9.13 Some Statistics Gathered by RUNSTATS Used for Access Plan Determination

column name under which the statistic appears in the specified catalog table. Each of these statistics also has a default value for cases when RUNSTATS has not yet been run. Note that a number of the index statistics assume a concatenated index of several components, which we assume to be the columns (C1, C2, C3).

Refer back to Figure 9.12 for statistics of the prospects table. Within SYSTABLES, we see a row for the prospects table, as follows, after RUNSTATS has been executed.

SYSTABLES

NAME	CARD	NPAGES
. . .	. . .	. . .
prospects	50,000,000	5,000,000
. . .	. . .	. . .

Within SYSCOLUMNS, rows for the hobby and zipcode columns described before Figure 9.12 would have NAME column values 'hobby' and 'zipcode'. Since column names are not unique across tables, the containing tablename for these columns is given in the TBNAME column.

SYSCOLUMNS

NAME	TBNAME	COLCARD	HIGH2KEY	LOW2KEY
. . .	. . .	. . .	. . .	. . .
hobby	prospects	100	Wines	Bicycling
zipcode	prospects	100,000	99,998	00001
. . .	. . .	. . .	. . .	. . .

Finally in SYSINDEXES (below), we see rows for the two indexes listed in Figure 9.12.

SYSINDEXES

NAME	TBNAME	NLEVELS	NLEAF	FIRSTKEY CARD	FULLKEY CARD	CLUSTER RATIO
. . .	. . .	. . .	. . .	. . .	. . .	. . .
addrx	prospects	4	500,000	100,000	50,000,000	100
hobbyx	prospects	3	50,000	100	100	0
. . .	. . .	. . .	. . .	. . .	. . .	. . .

For the `zipcode` column, which makes up the first column in the `addrx` index, we assume values from 00000 to 99999, so COLCARD = 100,000, LOW2KEY (the second-lowest value) is 00001, and HIGH2KEY = 99998. (Recall that this is inaccurate, but assumed for simplicity.) For the `addrx` index, FIRSTKEYCARD = 100,000 and FULLKEYCARD = 50,000,000, since we assumed in the paragraph preceding Figure 9.12 that `addrx` key values have unique RIDs.

The CLUSTERRATIO in the rightmost column of SYSINDEXES above is a measure of how well the clustering property holds for the rows of a table with respect to a given index: the closer this value is to 100%, the more row retrieval through the index will occur as in the bottom diagram of Figure 8.19. Recall that an index created with a CLUSTER clause may cease to have a high CLUSTERRATIO value after updates have caused a significant number of rows to be moved or inserted out of cluster order on the data pages. The significance of this statistic for the query optimizer is that an index scan will use sequential prefetch to retrieve data pages through an index exactly when the CLUSTERRATIO value is 80% or higher for that index.

Figure 9.14 contains a list of predicate types and the corresponding formulas for filter factor calculations performed by the query optimizer. Note that no filter factor calculations are given in Figure 9.14 for predicates involving Subqueries. In fact, predicates involving noncorrelated Subqueries can be used for indexed retrieval, but their filter factors are not predictable by a simple formula. We will deal with Subqueries later in the chapter, at the same time that we cover joins.

Filter Factors in DB2

It is commonly pointed out that the uniform distribution assumption explained earlier is not always valid. For example, consider a `gender` column on a table containing residents at a boys' school. Although there are occasional residents with gender = 'F', staff and faculty members, for example, it is clear that a filter factor calculated in terms of 1/(CARD(gender)) = 1/2 is misleading, and a query optimizer that uses this assumption may very well make incorrect decisions. For this reason, **DB2** and a number of other database systems, such as **ORACLE**, provide statistics on individual column values that deviate strongly from the uniform assumption. In the interest of brevity, however, we will

Predicate type	Filter factor	Notes
Col = const	1/COLCARD	"Col <> const" same as "not (Col = const)"
Col ∝ const	Interpolation formula	"∝" is any comparison predicate other than equality; an example follows
Col < const or Col <= const	$\dfrac{(\text{const} - \text{LOW2KEY})}{(\text{HIGH2KEY} - \text{LOW2KEY})}$	LOW2KEY and HIGH2KEY are estimates for extreme points of the range of Col values
Col between const1 and const2	$\dfrac{(\text{const2} - \text{const1})}{(\text{HIGH2KEY} - \text{LOW2KEY})}$	"Col not between const1 and const2" same as "not (Col between const1 and const2)"
Col in list	(List size)/COLCARD	"Col not in list" same as "not (Col in list)"
Col is null	1/COLCARD	"Col is not null" same as "not (Col is null)"
Col like 'pattern'	Interpolation formula	Based on the alphabet
Pred1 and Pred2	FF(Pred1) * FF(Pred2)	As in probability
Pred1 or Pred2	FF(Pred1) + FF(Pred2) − FF(Pred1) * FF(Pred2)	As in probability
Not Pred1	1 − FF(Pred1)	As in probability

Figure 9.14   Filter Factor Formulas for Various Predicate Types

not discuss these statistics further, and assume in what follows that the uniform distribution assumption is generally applicable.

9.5   Matching Index Scans, Composite Indexes

Assume that a **DB2** index named mailx has been created for the prospects table, using the statement

```
create index mailx on prospects (zipcode, hobby, incomeclass, age);
```

This is an index that we might construct to handle common types of mailing requests efficiently (we will see what this means shortly), and we assume that it is not a clustered index. Here incomeclass is a smallint variable defining a range of income, with 10 values from 1 to 10, distributed approximately equally on the prospects rows (thus equal match predicates have a filter factor of 1/10), and age is a smallint variable with (say) 50 values from 16 to 65. Given the CARD of each column, we can therefore calculate the potential number of distinct key values for this index as

```
CARD(zipcode) * CARD(hobby) * CARD(incomeclass) * CARD(age) =
    100,000 * 100 * 10 * 50 = 5,000,000,000
```

Since we have only 50,000,000 rows, we can picture the assignment of rows to mailx values as placing 50,000,000 darts in 5,000,000,000 slots. Very few slots will have two darts, and so we will assume essentially unique key values (FULLKEYCARD = 50,000,000), with no duplicate key value handling at the leaf level of the kind illustrated in Figure 8.17. Now the entries in the mailx index have length given by 4 (integer zipcode) + 8 (hobby attribute) + 2 (incomeclass) + 2 (age) + 4 (RID) = 20 bytes. We can therefore fit FLOOR(4000/20) = 200 entries per page. The leaf level of the index then has 50,000,000/200 = 250,000 leaf pages (NLEAF = 250,000). The next level up has 1250 nodes, the next level up has 7, and above this is the root (NLEVELS = 4). The relevant column values in the SYSINDEXES row for the mailx index are shown in the following table.

SYSINDEXES

NAME	TBNAME	NLEVELS	NLEAF	FIRSTKEY CARD	FULLKEY CARD	CLUSTER RATIO
. . .	. . .	. . .	. . .	. . .	. . .	. . .
mailx	prospects	4	250,000	100,000	50,000,000	0
. . .	. . .	. . .	. . .	. . .	. . .	. . .

EXAMPLE 9.5.1 Concatenated Index, Matching Index Scan.
Consider the SQL query

```
select name, straddr from prospects
    where zipcode = 02159 and hobby = 'chess' and incomeclass = 10;
```

Although the concatenated index mailx doesn't enable us to resolve the query in index only, as in Example 9.3.6, it still offers an important advantage in that all three predicates in the WHERE clause, zipcode = 02159, hobby = 'chess', and incomeclass = 10, can be *resolved* in this single index (that is, the needed columns can all be retrieved from the index). Filter factors of the three equal match predicates are each calculated as 1/COLCARD and give 1/100,000 = .00001 (for zipcode = 02159), 1/100 = .01 (for hobby = 'chess'), and 1/10 = 0.1 (for incomeclass = 10). The three ANDed attributes together give a filter factor (1/100,000)(1/100)(1/10) = (1/100,000,000), so we expect there will be (1/100,000,000)50,000,000 = 0.5 rows selected. (For example, one row might be returned half the time and no rows the other half.) We estimate that the I/O cost for data access is 0.5 R, requiring an elapsed time of 0.5/80 = .006 seconds.

The index scan step performs its search by reading down to the leftmost entry of the B-tree with zipcode = 02159 and hobby = 'chess' and incomeclass = 10. Then it reads entries from left to right, following leaf sibling pointers if necessary, until the last entry with these values has been processed. You need to convince yourself that all desired entries (even if there are more than one) are in one contiguous scan of the leaf level of the mailx index. We only expect 0.5 entries of this kind, so we expect all entries to lie on a single index leaf page. Assuming that the top two levels of the index are kept in buffer, we estimate the I/O cost of the index scan to be 2 R for the third-level index page and the leaf page. ∎

The query of Example 9.5.1 is being performed with a matching index scan on a composite index. What *matching* means is that the predicates in the WHERE clause match the *initial* attributes in the index. Whenever we are dealing with equal match predicates on initial attributes, the portion of the index in which selected RID values are found is a contiguous subrange of the entire index leaf level. By analogy, assume that in the metropolitan New York telephone directory, subscribers are alphabetized by lastname, firstname, borough or town, and finally street. Then the query of Example 9.5.1 is like looking up a telephone number by lastname and firstname, without knowing the street, borough, or town.

EXAMPLE 9.5.2 Concatenated Index, Matching Index Scan.

Consider the SQL query

```
select name, straddr from prospects
    where zipcode between 02159 and 04158
    and hobby = 'chess' and incomeclass = 10;
```

Again, all three predicates in the WHERE clause, zipcode between 02159 and 04158, hobby = 'chess', and incomeclass = 10, can be resolved in the mailx index. We calculate the filter factor for the predicate zipcode between 02159 and 04158 by using an interpolation formula (see filter factor for the BETWEEN predicate in Figure 9.14):

$$(04158 - 02159)/(\text{HIGH2KEY} - \text{LOW2KEY}) = 1999/99,998$$

which we approximate as 2/100 = .02. The other two predicates are approximated by 1/COLCARD as before, and give 1/100 = .01 (for hobby = 'chess') and 1/10 = 0.1 (for incomeclass = 10). The three ANDed attributes together give the filter factor (2/100)(1/100)(1/10) = (1/50,000) = .00002. Thus there will be (2/100,000)50,000,000 = 1000 rows selected on the average. Because the index is not clustered, and successive rows are far apart on disk, the I/O cost for data access is 1000 R, requiring an elapsed time of 1000/80 = 12.5 seconds. (The reason that list prefetch cannot be used here will be explained in Example 9.6.5, based on material not yet presented.)

The index scan step performs its search by reading down to the leftmost entry of the B-tree with zipcode = 02159 and hobby = 'chess' and incomeclass = 10, then reading in leaf pages from left to right following the sibling pointers until the last entry with values satisfying this WHERE clause has been processed. However, in this case it is *not* true that all desired entries are in one contiguous scan of the leaf level of the mailx index. There will be entries with other hobby values, for example, intervening between index entries with zipcode = 02159 and hobby = chess and entries with zipcode = 02160 and hobby = chess. This is still a matching index scan, but the only index component matched from the concatenated index is the zipcode range, zipcode between 02159 and 04158. This means that we need to read 2000/100,000 = 1/50 of the leaf level from the mailx index, or (1/50)(250,000) = 5000 pages. We can do this with sequential prefetch at a cost of 5000 S in elapsed time of 5000/800 = 6.25 seconds. The total elapsed time for the query is therefore 6.25 seconds for index scan + 12.5 seconds for data page retrieval = 18.75 seconds. ∎

Example 9.5.2, in terms of the analogy we used earlier, looks up everyone in the New York metropolitan telephone directory with last name starting with "Sm" and first name "John." There are a lot of entries to scan to retrieve this set of subscribers. But things can get even worse. If the attributes in the WHERE clause don't include the initial attribute of the index, we need to consider a *non-matching* index scan. This is comparable to finding everyone with the first name "John" in the borough of the Bronx from the New York metropolitan telephone directory, with no idea of the last name, a difficult task. We can't use the alphabetical order of the directory to any effect, since we never know under what last name the first name "John" might show up, and thus we have to look through the whole directory. Still, it is preferable to use the telephone directory for such a search (a non-matching index scan) than to go out and canvas the entire town from door to door looking for everyone named John who owns a phone (a table scan, to stretch the analogy somewhat).

> **EXAMPLE 9.5.3 Concatenated Index, Non-Matching Index Scan.**
> Again we assume that the `mailx` index exists. Consider the SQL query
>
> ```
>     select name, straddr from prospects
>         where hobby = 'chess' and incomeclass = 10 and age = 40;
> ```
>
> We recall that the cardinality of the `hobby` column is 100, the `incomeclass` column is 10, and the `age` column is 50, so we calculate the filter factor of the compound selection predicate as $(1/100)(1/10)(1/50) = (1/50,000) = .00002$. This is the same filter factor we calculated in Example 9.5.2, so we still retrieve 1000 rows from `prospects` at an I/O cost of 1000 R, in 12.5 seconds of elapsed time. But the index scan situation is totally different. Because this is a non-matching index scan, we need to read in every one of the 250,000 `mailx` leaf pages. The I/O cost is 250,000 S, and the elapsed time is $250,000/800 = 312.5$ seconds, more than 5 minutes.
>
> ∎

Definition of a Matching Index Scan

We have mentioned the idea of an indexable predicate before, when we studied single-column indexes. It is time to give a careful description of what it means to perform a matching index scan. This requires a series of definitions.

DEFINITION 9.5.1 A *matching index scan* retrieves rows from a table after matching a number of predicates to column components of a single index. At least one indexable predicate must refer to the initial column of the index; this is known as a *matching predicate*. A set of indexable predicates can match a *sequence* of initial columns of a composite index, and they are all then known as matching predicates. ∎

For example, consider index C1234X on table T, a composite index on columns (C1, C2, C3, C4). The following compound predicate matches all columns of the C1234X index:

```
C1 = 10 and C2 = 5 and C3 = 20 and C4 = 25
```

The compound predicate

```
C2 = 5 and C3 = 20 and C1 = 10
```

matches the first three columns of C1234X (note that the predicates don't need to be in the same order as the columns). This is analogous to the matching index scan we saw in Example 9.5.1, three ANDed equal match predicates on the first three columns of a four-column composite index, mailx. The compound predicate

```
C2 = 5 and C5 = 22 and C1 = 10 and C6 = 35
```

has two matching predicates on the first two columns of C1234X. The columns C5 and C6 are not part of the index and therefore cannot be matching. The compound predicate

```
C2 = 5 and C3 = 20 and C4 = 25
```

is not a matching index scan, since it has no matching predicates. This is analogous to the situation we saw in Example 9.5.3, three ANDed equal match predicates on the second, third, and fourth columns of a four-column composite index.

Note that in Example 9.5.3, where there were no matching predicates, this doesn't mean that the filter factors of the non-matching predicates have no effect. As we saw in that example, the predicates still have the role of filtering 50,000,000 rows down to a 1000-row answer set. Because this was a non-matching scan, however, the entire index needed to be examined to perform this filtering. In a matching index scan, by comparison, we usually end up with only a small contiguous range of leaf-level entries in the index that need to be considered. (As we will see, there is an exception when the IN-LIST predicate is involved, but this is rather special.)

Predicate Screening and Screening Predicates

When **DB2** makes use of the filter factors of *non-matching predicates*, as in Example 9.5.3, it ranges through a large number of leaf-level entries of the index before it accesses any data rows, and it discards entries that do not obey the predicates. This practice is known as *predicate screening*, and the non-matching predicates involved are known as *screening predicates*. In predicate screening, column values available in a concatenated index that are *not* involved in matching predicates, but that still correspond to predicates to be evaluated, are used to decide on keeping or dropping entries. All rows corresponding to the entries remaining after this screening are candidates to be retrieved, but the number of such rows is often much smaller after this type of screening takes place.

As we saw in Example 9.5.3, the use of predicate screening can lead to a situation where the elapsed time to perform disk I/O reading index entries is much larger than the elapsed time to read in rows in the answer set. The difference between screening predicates and matching predicates is an important one; as we will see, there are situations in index access where predicate screening is not performed by **DB2**. However, matching predicates are always used.

This whole concept of matching index scans is rather complex, so let's review what we have covered up to now. Assume that we are given a composite index C1234X on columns (C1, C2, C3, C4) and a compound predicate involving predicates P1, P2, . . . , Pk.

DEFINITION 9.5.2 Basic Rules of Matching Predicates.   **565**

[1]   A *matching* predicate must be an *indexable* predicate.

Figure 9.15 provides a list of indexable predicates: equal match and comparison predicates, BETWEEN predicates, LIKE predicates, IN-LIST predicates, and IS NULL predicates are indexable. In general, attaching the NOT logical operator to an indexable predicate gives a non-indexable result.

[2]   Matching predicates must match successive columns C1, C2, . . . of an index.

Here is a procedure to determine them. Look at the index columns from left to right. For each column, if there is at least one indexable predicate on that column, we have found a matching column and a matching predicate. If no matching predicate is found for a column, this terminates the procedure. (There are other rules as well, which will be covered in Definition 9.5.4.)

[3]   A non-matching predicate on a column in an index can still be a screening predicate.

There might be a matching index scan on one index to answer a query and a non-matching index scan on a different index with a much better filter factor that is more efficient. The query optimizer must consider all index possibilities in arriving at the access plan.   ∎

In the case of a matching index scan on the leading K columns of an index such as C1234X, the EXPLAIN command creates a plan table row with ACCESSTYPE = I, ACCESSNAME = C1234X, and MATCHCOLS = K. In particular, for a non-matching index scan, we see MATCHCOLS = 0.

From point 1 of Definition 9.5.2, we see that a matching predicate must be an indexable predicate. In fact, the term "indexable predicate" means exactly this and no more.

DEFINITION 9.5.3 An *indexable predicate* is defined as a predicate that can be used to match a column in a matching index scan, currently the set of predicates in Figure 9.15. ∎

The term "indexable predicate" is rather confusing, since it seems to imply that predicates that are not indexable cannot be used in an index to filter the rows to be retrieved. But this is not true: non-indexable predicates can still be used as screening predicates in an index scan—they simply cannot be used for matching, as we describe in more detail after formally defining matching predicates in Definition 9.5.1. A better term to replace "indexable predicate" would be "matchable predicate," but unfortunately, the earlier term is firmly embedded in the database vocabulary at this point.

In the case of a single-column index, a non-indexable predicate that functions as a screening predicate is unusual, but not impossible. The possibility depends on whether the filter factor makes the query optimizer think it is worthwhile. Since a common non-indexable predicate is Col <> const, with a filter factor $(1 - 1/\text{COLCARD})$, the filter

Predicate type	Indexable	Notes
Col ∝ const	Y	∝ stands for >, >=, =, <=, <, but <> is *not* indexable
Col between const1 and const2	Y	Must be last in matching series (see rules of matching)
Col in list	Y	But only for one matching column (see rules of matching)
Col is null	Y	
Col like 'pattern'	Y	No leading % in pattern
Col like '%xyz'	N	With leading %
Col1 ∝ Col2	N	Col1 and Col2 from same table
Col ∝ *Expression*	N	For example, C1 = (C1 + 2)/2
Pred1 and Pred2	Y	Pred1 and Pred2 both indexable, refer to columns of the same index
Pred1 or Pred2	N	Except (C1 = 3 or C1 = 5), which can be thought of as C1 in (3, 5)
Not Pred1	N	Or any equivalent: not between, not in list, <>, not like pattern

Figure 9.15   Indexable Predicates on a Single Table

factor is likely to be close to 1 and to seem to offer very little cost savings in reducing the number of rows retrieved to make up for the cost of reading through a large fraction of the index.

Things get a bit more complex in matching columns when we deal with indexable predicates that are not equal match predicates. We repeat the prescription of the second point of Definition 9.5.2 and add a number of other rules.

DEFINITION 9.5.4 Advanced Rules of Matching Predicates.

[1] Look at the index columns of the concatenated index from left to right. For each column, if at least one indexable predicate is found for that column, it is a *matching column* with a *matching predicate*.

[2] If no matching predicate is found for a column, this terminates the search. However, the search may terminate earlier for a number of reasons.

[3] When a matching *range predicate* (comparison of the form <, <=, >, >=, LIKE predicate, or BETWEEN predicate) is used for a column, the search terminates at that point.

[4] At most one IN-LIST predicate can be used in a set of matching predicates. A second column matching of an IN-LIST will cause the search to terminate before the column involved is made part of the matching list. ∎

If we assume that the idea of a matching index scan is to end up with a contiguous range of leaf-level index entries, it is easy to see why a range predicate terminates the search for matching predicates. Recall that in Example 9.5.2, the three ANDed predicates of the query refer to the first three columns from the `mailx` index. However, the predicate on the first column, `zipcode between 02159 and 04158`, is a range predicate and thus the remaining predicates are not part of the matching index scan. The reason is that once we limit to the index entries for the range predicate, the entries that satisfy the remaining two predicates appear in 2000 separated intervals, satisfying `hobby = 'chess'` and `incomeclass = 10` for each of the 2000 `zipcode` values 02159, 02160, 02161, . . . , 04158. The index scan simply finds it easiest to scan through all entries that obey the range predicate and treat the remaining two predicates as screening predicates. Thus we have a relatively large index scan to perform, requiring an elapsed time of 12.5 seconds even with sequential prefetch, compared to a relatively small row I/O cost of 25 seconds with random I/O.

The IN-LIST predicate is the only one that breaks the rule of requiring the final range of leaf-level index entries to be contiguous. Given the C1234X index and the compound predicate

[9.5.1]   `C1 in (6, 8, 10) and C2 = 5 and C3 = 20`

we have a matching predicate on all three columns, even though we do not end up with a single contiguous range of leaf-level entries. Instead there are three contiguous ranges, one for the leading column selection C1 = 6, one for C1 = 8, and one for C1 = 10. You can picture a matching index scan with an IN-LIST predicate in just this way, as a series of scans with equal match predicates substituted for the IN-LIST. But **DB2** stops short of allowing a second IN-LIST predicate into the matching scan. Thus the compound predicate

[9.5.2]   `C1 in (6, 8, 10) and C2 = 5 and C3 in (20, 30, 40) and C4 = 25`

would have only two matching predicates. Matching stops before the second IN-LIST predicate on C3. When an IN-LIST predicate is used in a matching index scan, the plan table row contains a special value, ACCESSTYPE = N. We would have MATCHCOLS = 3 for the first such compound predicate above, and MATCHCOLS = 2 for the second.

EXAMPLE 9.5.4 Query Optimization and Composite Index Scans.

Assume that we are given a table T with columns C1, C2, . . . and the indexes C1234X on (C1, C2, C3, C4); C56X on (C5, C6); and C7X, a unique index on the key column C7. Consider the following queries:

 (1) `select C1, C5, C8 from T where C1 = 5 and C2 = 7 and C3 <> 9;`

This results in a matching index scan on the two columns C1 and C2. The predicate C3 is not indexable (but it would be used as a screening predicate). In the plan table we see ACCESSTYPE = I, ACCESSNAME = C1234X, MATCHCOLS = 2.

(2) `select C1, C5, C8 from T where C1 = 5 and C2 >= 7 and C3 = 9;`

We see a matching index scan on the two columns C1 and C2. Although the third predicate is indexable, we stop short because the predicate on C2 is a range predicate. The plan table is the same as (1).

(3) `select C1, C5, C8 from T`
    `    where C1 = 5 and C2 = 7 and C5 = 8 and C6 = 13;`

There is a type of multiple index use we haven't seen yet in which we can combine filter factors of predicates from more than one index; this approach would be used here. If that alternative were not present, the query optimizer would consider a choice between using a matching index scan of two columns on C1234X and a matching index scan of two columns on C56X. We would learn what happens from the plan table, ACCESSTYPE = I, ACCESSNAME = C56X, MATCHCOLS = 2.

(4) `select C1, C4 from T`
    `    where C1 = 10 and C2 in (5, 6) and (C3 = 10 or C4 = 11);`

This is a matching index scan on the first two columns. ACCESSTYPE = N (because of the IN-LIST predicate), ACCESSNAME = C1234X, and MATCHCOLS = 2. The third predicate, (C3 = 10 or C4 = 11), is not indexable, but it would be used as a screening predicate in the scan. (We do not see screening predicates mentioned in the plan table, but all predicates of the query must be used to filter, and predicates that involve columns of the index chosen are certainly used for screening.) The scan would also have INDEXONLY = Y, a very important factor in determining the cost.

(5) `select C1, C5, C8 from T`
    `    where C1 = 5 and C2 = 7 and C7 = 101;`

Because the C7X index is unique, the query optimizer would certainly choose ACCESSTYPE = I, ACCESSNAME = C7X. The plan table does not reveal that this retrieval is unique (returns zero or one rows).

(6) `select C1, C5, C8 from T`
    `    where C2 = 7 and C3 = 10 and C4 = 12 and C5 = 15;`

This query can be handled either by a non-matching index scan on C1234X, columns C2, C3, C4, or by a matching index scan on C56X, column C5. (For reasons to be covered shortly, multiple index use mentioned in (3) above is not an alternative.) We might see the following result in the plan table: ACCESSTYPE = I, ACCESSNAME = C1234X, MATCHCOLS = 0. ∎

Indexable Predicates and Performance

Pattern-match search. A *pattern-match search*, `C1 like 'pattern'`, with a leading % wildcard in the pattern, is comparable to a non-matching scan of a concatenated index. The predicate may have a small filter factor, but the search is analogous to using a normal dictionary to look up all words that end in "action." An index on the column C1 must be totally scanned to retrieve the set of RIDs pointing to the appropriate rows. Special dictionaries exist that alphabetize words in reverse, and a DBA having a workload with a large number of pattern-match searches with leading % wildcards should consider creating indexed columns with reverse spellings. Thus if column C2 is created to contain the text of C1 spelled backward, the specification `%action` on C1 becomes `noitca%` on C2, a much easier search.

Expressions. The non-indexable predicate, Col $\propto$ *Expression* given in Figure 9.15, is only one example of a class of non-indexable predicates. Basically, any comparison involving an expression is non-indexable. For example, consider the query

```
select * from T where 2 * C1 <= 56;
```

The query optimizer is unable to use an index to resolve this predicate. However, you can rephrase the predicate

```
select * from T where C1 <= 28;
```

(dividing both sides by 2), and now the index can be used.

One-fetch access. A certain class of queries is particularly efficient in **DB2**, providing what is called *one-fetch (index) access*, with ACCESSTYPE = I1 in the plan table. An example of such a query is

```
select min(C1) from T;
```

where an index exists with leading column C1. Clearly the query optimizer in this case can simply search down to the leftmost entry at the leaf level of the index and retrieve the C1 value, which is why this is termed "one-fetch access." It is possible to apply this principle in a more general situation. Assume that we have an index C12D3X on T, with columns (C1, C2 DESC, C3). Then, for example, the following queries can be answered by a one-fetch access step:

```
select min(C1) from T where C1 > 5;
```

(Note that C1 > 5 doesn't necessarily mean that the min value for C1 is 6. Index use is important here.) Other examples with one-fetch access are

```
select min(C1) from T where C1 between 6 and 10;
select max(C2) from T where C1 = 5;
select max(C2) from T where C1 = 5 and C2 < 30;
select min(C3) from T where C1 = 6 and C2 = 20 and C3 between 9 and 14;
```

Each successive matching equal match predicate reduces the range of values for the index key. In the final example above, **DB2** walks down the C12D3X index to find the first entry key value >= 6.20.9.

9.6   Multiple Index Access

Assume that the following indexes are the only ones defined on the table T: C1X on (C1), C2X on (C2), and C345X on (C3, C4, C5). Now consider the following query:

[9.6.1]   `select * from T where C1 = 20 and C2 = 5 and C3 = 11;`

With the matching index scans we have studied up to now, the query optimizer would need to choose a single one of the three indexes, each of which matches only one of the three predicates in query [9.6.1]. Thus we would have the benefit of only one of the three predicate filter factors to extract RID values from an index before retrieving rows from the data, and the query plan would need to test the truth of the remaining two predicates to restrict the rows retrieved.

But this could be a tremendously inefficient course of action. If we assume that each of the predicates has a filter factor of 1/100 and the table T contains 100 million rows, then a single predicate only reduces the number of rows retrieved to 1 million. All three predicates together would have a combined filter factor of 1/1,000,000 and reduce the number of rows retrieved to 100. We ask, therefore, if there is a way to combine the filter factors of predicates matching different indexes before retrieving the rows selected.

There is in fact a way to do this, and it provides our first example of a multiple-step plan. Basically this approach extracts from each index the list of RIDs that satisfies the matching predicate. Then the lists of RIDs for the distinct indexes are intersected (ANDed), so that the final RID list corresponds to rows that satisfy all predicates indexed. The sequence of steps from the **DB2** plan table resulting from an EXPLAIN of query [9.6.1] might be the plan displayed in Figure 9.16. (Only selected columns of the plan table are shown. The following paragraphs provide descriptions for the steps of Figure 9.16.)

- ◆ **MIXOPSEQ = 0.** This plan row with ACCESSTYPE = M indicates that multiple index access processing is about to begin on table TNAME = T. The PREFETCH = L

TNAME	ACCESSTYPE	MATCHCOLS	ACCESSNAME	PREFETCH	MIXOPSEQ
T	M	0		L	0
T	MX	1	C1X	S	1
T	MX	1	C2X	S	2
T	MX	1	C345X	S	3
T	MI	0			4
T	MI	0			5

Figure 9.16   Plan Table Rows of a Multiple Index Access Plan for Query [9.6.1]

value means that list prefetch I/O (which we covered near the end of Section 9.2) is used to retrieve rows from that table T, after the final calculated RID list has been generated.

♦ **MIXOPSEQ = 1.** This plan row with ACCESSTYPE = MX indicates that the entries of the index with ACCESSNAME = C1X that satisfy the matching predicates of the query are to be scanned, using sequential prefetch I/O. In this case MATCHCOLS = 1, and the matching predicate in query [9.6.1] is C1 = 20. As the entries from C1X are encountered, the RIDs are extracted and placed into what we call a RID *candidate list* (or simply a RID *list)*, in a memory area known as the RID *pool*. At some point after all RIDs have been extracted from this C1X access step, the RID candidate list is placed in sorted order to make the later intersection step easier to perform.

♦ **MIXOPSEQ = 2 and MIXOPSEQ = 3.** These steps perform the same MX function on the indexes C2X and C345X as in MIXOPSEQ = 1, generating their own RID candidate lists for the matching predicates of these indexes. We can think of successive generated RID candidate lists as being pushed on a stack as in a reverse Polish calculator: lists generated more recently are closer to the top of stack and are acted on first by later calculator operations.

♦ **MIXOPSEQ = 4.** The ACCESSTYPE = MI indicates that a RID *candidate list intersection* (AND) will take place. The two most recently generated RID lists are popped from the top of stack (first the list generated from C345X, then the list generated from C2X); they are intersected to provide a new RID list (an intermediate result that **DB2** names IR1) and this list is pushed back on the stack. Since the RIDs of both lists are in sorted order, the intersection is easily performed by creating two cursors pointing to the initial RID in each list, then repeatedly advancing the list cursor pointing to the lower-valued RID. Whenever a tie occurs we have found an intersection element. We place this RID value into the IR1 list, then advance one of the two cursors to look for the next intersection element. The process is complete when one of the cursors being advanced goes off the end of the list.

♦ **MIXOPSEQ = 5.** This final step also has ACCESSTYPE = MI, and this pops the top two RID lists from the stack, IR1 and the list generated from C1X. The lists are intersected to form a new RID list named IR2 that is pushed back on the stack, and this is the *final RID list* generated. This final RID list is then used to retrieve rows from the table T, using list prefetch I/O, as mentioned in the initial M step of the plan.

There is one other type of access step used in multiple index access. A row with ACCESSTYPE = MU indicates a step that will pop the two RID lists on the stack, perform a *RID candidate list union* (OR) of the two lists, and push the new intermediate result back on the stack. For example, with the same table and index assumptions seen above, EXPLAIN applied to the query given in [9.6.2] might result in rows of the plan table of Figure 9.17.

[9.6.2]   select * from T where C1 = 20 and (C2 = 5 or C3 = 11);

TNAME	ACCESSTYPE	MATCHCOLS	ACCESSNAME	PREFETCH	MIXOPSEQ
T	M	0		L	0
T	MX	1	C1X	S	1
T	MX	1	C2X	S	2
T	MX	1	C345X	S	3
T	MU	0			4
T	MI	0			5

Figure 9.17   Plan Table Rows of a Multiple Index Access Plan for Query [9.6.2]

Figure 9.17 differs from Figure 9.16 only in the row with MIXOPSEQ = 4, where an MU step is performed to take the union (OR) of the RID lists for predicates C2 = 5 and C3 = 11 instead of intersecting (ANDing) them. This union is then ANDed with C1 = 20 in the final step with MIXOPSEQ = 5.

Note that in both Figures 9.16 and 9.17, successive steps of multiple index extraction into RID lists have been generated to follow the physical order of predicates in the query. Naturally the order of evaluation is independent of the query syntax. The multiple index access steps are actually generated by the query optimizer in an order that uses the RID pool most efficiently, and this *usually* means that there are a minimum number of RID lists in existence at any one time; that is, operations to combine RID lists are executed as early as possible to minimize memory use. What this implies for the query of [9.6.2] is a rearrangement of the rows in Figure 9.17 to the following plan.

TNAME	ACCESSTYPE	MATCHCOLS	ACCESSNAME	PREFETCH	MIXOPSEQ
T	M	0		L	0
T	MX	1	C2X	S	1
T	MX	1	C345X	S	2
T	MU	0			3
T	MX	1	C1X	S	4
T	MI	0			5

This new plan has the same effect as the one in Figure 9.17, but it has the property that there are never more than two RID lists in existence at once.

EXAMPLE 9.6.1 Multiple Index Access.

Consider the `prospects` table and the `hobbyx` and `addrx` indexes with the statistics outlined in Figure 9.12, and assume that the only other indexes available on `prospects` are the `agex` index on the `age` column and the `incomex` index on the `incomeclass` column. A little thought will convince you that these indexes have nearly the same statistics as the `hobbyx` index, since there is so much index compression at the leaf level that the length of the index key is superflu-ous in the entry length dominated by multiple RID entries of 4 bytes (thus NLEAF is the same); and at higher levels where the key length is more relevant there will not be enough variation to change the NLEVELS statistic in SYSINDEXES (see Figure 9.13). Now consider the query that we dealt with in Example 9.5.1:

```
select name, straddr from prospects
    where zipcode = 02159 and hobby = 'chess' and incomeclass = 10;
```

In that example, we had a concatenated index mailx on which an index scan was performed. With the single indexes assumed above, this query can be performed with the multiple index access plan outlined in Figure 9.18.

Let us calculate the I/O cost of the step with MIXOPSEQ = 1. This step scans the hobbyx index for the predicate hobby = 'chess'. Since FF(hobby = 'chess') = 1/100, and NLEAF for hobbyx = 50,000, this entails a scan across 1/100 of the 50,000 leaf-level pages (ignoring I/Os to walk the directory), at an I/O cost of 500 S. The list of RIDs from these leaf-level entries is extracted and pushed on the stack.

For MIXOPSEQ = 2 we scan the addrx index to resolve the predicate zipcode = 02159 and extract the RID values into a list. Since FF(zipcode = 02159) = 1/100,000 and NLEAF = 500,000 for addrx, the number of leaf pages scanned from left to right to resolve this predi-cate is (1/100,000)(500,000) = 5 S. With MIXOPSEQ = 4 the predicate incomeclass = 10 has a filter factor of 1/10, and with 50,000 leaf-level pages the I/O cost to extract the RIDs is 5000 S.

Now the ACCESSTYPE = MI list intersection steps with MIXOPSEQ = 3 and 5 require no I/O, since all RIDs are already memory resident. Multiplying the filter factors of the three predicates as we did in Example 9.5.1, we see again that we expect only 0.5 rows to be retrieved from the table. This is a probabilistic estimate, of course.

However many rows are retrieved, they most likely all lie on separate disk pages, and the system retrieves them with a list prefetch (as we saw in MIXOPSEQ = 0, where PREFETCH = L). The I/O cost for retrieving 0.5 pages by list prefetch is designated by 0.5 L. As we mentioned in the rule of thumb for I/O rate in Figure 9.10, list prefetch proceeds at 200 I/Os per second. A list prefetch of 0.5 pages is below the lower limit of this rule of thumb approximation (4 pages), but in any event the time involved to pick up an expected half row is insignificant.

The total elapsed time for the query, based on I/O cost, is therefore calculated from 500 S + 5 S + 5000 S + 0.5 R as (5505)/800 + 0.5/80, or about 6.9 seconds.

TNAME	ACCESSTYPE	MATCHCOLS	ACCESSNAME	PREFETCH	MIXOPSEQ
prospects	M	0		L	0
prospects	MX	1	hobbyx	S	1
prospects	MX	1	addrx	S	2
prospects	MI	0			3
prospects	MX	1	incomex	S	4
prospects	MI	0			5

Figure 9.18 Plan Table Rows of Multiple Index Access Plan (Illustrates Example 9.6.1)

■

EXAMPLE 9.6.2 Multiple Index Access.

Under the index assumptions of Example 9.6.1, we examine the query considered earlier in Example 9.5.2:

```
select name, straddr from prospects
     where zipcode between 02159 and 04158
     and hobby = 'chess' and incomeclass = 10;
```

For this query, the BETWEEN predicate on zipcode causes a matching index scan on addrx with a filter factor of (2000/100,000) = 1/50. Since NLEAF = 500,000 for addrx, the scan to extract RID values for this predicate entails a cost of 10,000 S. The costs of resolving the predicates on hobby and incomeclass are unchanged from Example 9.6.1, 500 S and 5000 S.

   The total number of rows retrieved by this query is calculated in the same way it was done in Example 9.5.2: (1/50)(1/100)(1/10)(50,000,000) = 1000 rows, likely to all be on separate pages. However, because ordered RID lists were intersected to arrive at this sequence of rows, the RIDs are in order and List Prefetch will save us time in the I/O of these 1000 disk pages. The total I/O cost for this query is therefore given by 10,000 S + 500 S + 5000 S + 1000 L, and the elapsed I/O time is 15,500/800 + 1000/200 = 19.4 + 5 = 24.5 seconds. This compares to the 18.75 seconds we derived in Example 9.5.2, where we assumed that the 1000 data page I/Os were retrieved using random I/O (1000 R), and therefore took 12.5 seconds, rather than list prefetch I/O (1000 L), which takes 5 seconds.   ■

List Prefetch and the RID Pool

If list prefetch is more efficient than random I/O, why would we ever perform random I/O? The answer, as we suggested at the end of Section 9.2, is that certain rather special preconditions need to be met before list prefetch can occur in **DB2**, conditions that are presented in this subsection as "Rules for RID-List Use." However, before proceeding it seems appropriate to make a disclaimer to prevent possible misunderstanding.

   Up until now, most of the query access principles we have introduced have been quite general purpose, and although our examples have referred to **DB2** features, we expect to see equivalent features now or in the near future in most relational database products. For example, all relational products you are likely to encounter in education or industry have query optimizers that make use of data statistics, calculate and compare filter factors, and generate query access plans that contain steps such as table scans and various types of index-aided scans. The idea of matching scans on composite indexes and the specific types of predicates that can be matched or used for screening are usually implemented in a less sophisticated form on most non-**DB2** products. (*Matching scan* is actually **DB2**-specific nomenclature.) The same goes for the multiple index access feature (sometimes made more efficient by bitmap indexing) and for the concept of a memory-resident RID list (or final foundset bitmap). The *ideas* are implemented on many (not yet all) relational products, but generally with less flexibility. The topic of the current subsection, list prefetch and its dependency on RID-list rules, crosses the border from general principle to product-specific design. These concepts are important for a good understanding of **DB2** query optimization, but you should be warned that there is nothing fundamental about them; indeed a number of the rules are somewhat arbitrary, and it is quite likely that other database products might choose a different (and perhaps superior!) approach in determining what RID lists (or bitmaps) to materialize in memory.

To return to the topic at hand, what limits the use of list prefetch in **DB2**? The rule is that list prefetch is only performed when retrieving rows from data pages, when indexing allows the query evaluator to predict rows that will need to be accessed well into the future. For a list prefetch to be possible, the RIDs for the rows to be retrieved must already have been extracted from an index scan into a memory storage area known as the RID pool, then sorted into ascending page number order (implied by ascending RID order). The list prefetch mechanism needs such a RID list so it can ask the disk controller to retrieve blocks, up to 32 pages at a time, by the most efficient predetermined movements in a small region of the disk. As we mentioned in Example 9.6.1, we assume a rate of 200 I/Os per second as a rule of thumb for list prefetch, although the rate actually varies depending on the proximity of the pages fetched.

List prefetch is always used to access data pages in multiple index access (which we sometimes refer to as *MX access* for short), since the sorted RID list must exist during the plan. In composite index scans, such as the scan of Example 9.5.2 where 1000 rows are retrieved, it would seem that we are also likely to use list prefetch so as to speed up the data page retrieval. The limiting factor in choosing list prefetch is usually a matter of space in the RID pool, and since each RID is 4 bytes in length, a list of 1000 RIDs will take up only 4000 bytes, about the size of one disk page in memory buffer. But there are other limitations on the use of RID lists, which are discussed in Definition 9.6.1.

The size of the RID pool memory area is based on the size of the buffer pools chosen by the DBA (there are actually multiple buffer pools in **DB2**, but for simplicity we usually refer to a single pool and assume that other pools are not used). The size of the RID pool defaults to half of the combined sizes of the buffer pools, except that it cannot exceed 200 MB in version 2. This limit has been increased to 1000 MB in version 5, the current version, but we will use the older value to correspond to the benchmark data presented later in the chapter. (Note that this discussion of sizes does *not* mean that the RID pool is part of the buffer pool; the two pools are distinct memory areas.) The memory for the RID pool is not actually allocated until it is needed, and grows as needed in 16-MB increments up to the system's configured limit. The RID pool is used concurrently by a number of different processes performing queries, and it is doled out rather parsimoniously. Every effort is made to minimize the use of the pool space by the following restrictive rules.

DEFINITION 9.6.1 Rules for RID-List Use. The following rules govern the use of RID lists by the query optimizer.

[1] When the query optimizer constructs a plan for a query (known as *bind time*) involving RID-list generation, the predicted number of RIDs active at any time in the plan cannot require more than 50% of the RID pool. If it does, then an alternate plan is created that does not call for the creation of RID lists. If predictions of RID use turn out to be wrong at runtime after RID-list extraction has

already begun, so that RID list generation is actually inappropriate, the plan is aborted and another access method used to answer the query.

[2] No screening predicates can be used in an index scan that extracts a RID list.

[3] An IN-LIST predicate cannot be used in an index scan that extracts a RID list.

The above rules are true for **DB2** version 2.3, corresponding to performance data quoted later in this chapter. In **DB2** version 5, rules [2] and [3] are documented, but [1] is not, possibly simply because it is now considered as an internal concern. ∎

EXAMPLE 9.6.3 RID-List Size Limit.

Consider again the prospects table with the indexes of Example 9.6.1, addrx, hobbyx, and incomex. We add a new index, called genderx, on a column of prospects named gender, with two values, 'M' and 'F', where we assume that the two column values appear with equal frequency. Consider the query

```
select name, straddr from prospects
    where zipcode between 02159 and 04158
    and incomeclass = 10 and gender = 'F';
```

Because of index compression, we see that the leaf level of the genderx index must contain approximately 50,000 pages, the same as the hobbyx index. To review this reasoning, there are 50,000,000 rows in prospects, and the average leaf-level entry (because of compression of duplicate key values) takes up approximately 4 bytes for the RID. Therefore 1000 entries fit on a leaf page, and 50 million entries require 50,000 leaf pages. Now consider the size of the RID list we would extract from the index genderx to satisfy the matching predicate, with FF(gender = 'F') = 1/2. This scan would traverse half of the 50,000-page leaf level and extract all the RIDs, a 25,000-page RID list, since nearly all of the space on the leaf level is made up of RIDs. But by rule 1 of Definition 9.6.1, we would not be able to construct a 25,000-page RID list unless we had a 50,000-page RID pool—that is, 200 MB, the absolute limit (in **DB2** version 2.3, our reference release). Given that there must be another RID list from the plan in existence at the same time to intersect with, we see that the predicate gender = 'F' probably cannot have its RID list extracted. Since we suppose that gender = 'F' extracts RIDs for half of the 50 million rows of the prospects table, it is clear that we cannot have an MX step for this predicate. The multiple index plan must make do with the other two predicates and their filter factors, and proceed from there to retrieving the data rows. ∎

Even in simple matching index scans, list prefetch access is not always a foregone conclusion.

EXAMPLE 9.6.4 RID-List Size Limit, Again.

Consider again the prospects table with the hobbyx index and the query evaluated in Example 9.3.4:

```
select name, straddr from prospects where hobby = 'chess';
```

Since FF(hobby = 'chess') = 1/100, the dominating I/O cost of Example 9.3.4 was to retrieve (1/100)(50,000,000) = 500,000 rows in unclustered order from the prospects table. The cost of

500,000 R in elapsed time is 500,000/80 = 6250 seconds, or about 2 hours. Clearly list prefetch would be enormously preferable, since 500,000 L would be performed in 500,000/200 = 2500 seconds, about 42 minutes. But in order for list prefetch to take place, the RID list for this predicate must be extracted into the RID pool. There are 500,000 entries scanned, resulting in 500,000 RIDs, which take up 2 MB in the RID pool. This means there must be a 4-MB RID pool by rule 1 of Definition 9.6.1, since any plan can use only half of the RID pool. Because the RID pool is half the size of the buffer pool, a disk buffer size of 8 MB (containing 2000 4-KB disk pages) must be present. If the buffer pool is smaller than that, list prefetch cannot be used for this query. But such a small buffer pool is very unlikely with systems in use today. ∎

The RID pool rules use rather coarse heuristics to set resource bounds. The number of users active in the system is not taken into account, and if we had a single user performing this query of Example 9.6.4 with a buffer pool size of 100 MB, it seems inappropriate to limit ourselves to using only half of the 50-MB RID pool and fail to perform list prefetch when there is no other user competing for the RID space. On the other hand, if there were several users active at once performing queries of this kind, we note that the queries do not result in large sets of popular pages requiring buffering, and thus we would like to be able to "convert" some of the buffer space into RID space to support more list prefetch.

A very important limitation on RID lists is rule 3, which states that index screening cannot be performed to generate a RID list. In particular, a non-matching index scan cannot result in list prefetch in the data row retrieval phase. Further, since MX processing requires RID lists, MX processing cannot utilize non-matching predicates. We will discuss this further after an example.

EXAMPLE 9.6.5 List Prefetch and Index Screening.
Recall the query of Example 9.5.2, where only the mailx index (zipcode, hobby, incomeclass, age) was present on prospects, and how this query was repeated in Example 9.6.2 with different indexes:

```
select name, straddr from prospects
    where zipcode between 02159 and 04158
    and hobby = 'chess' and incomeclass = 10;
```

With the mailx index, the index scan was matching on the zipcode column but not on the later columns hobby and incomeclass, so that hobby = 'chess' and incomeclass = 10 were used as screening predicates. It was calculated that the index scan of mailx would traverse (1/50)(250,000) = 5000 leaf pages of the index, at a cost of 5000 S and an elapsed time of 5000/800 = 6.25 seconds, and that 1000 data pages would be retrieved at a cost of 1000 R and an elapsed time of 1000/80 = 12.5 seconds. Since screening predicates were used to achieve this small composite filter factor, we cannot extract a RID list for these 1000 pages (because of rule 3). It is impossible to perform these 1000 data page reads using list prefetch. Therefore a data page I/O of 1000 L in 5 seconds elapsed, as we saw in Example 9.6.2, is not possible using this concatenated index. ∎

There doesn't seem to be any theoretically important reason why filter predicates and IN-LIST predicates cannot be used for RID-list extraction, as stated in rules 3 and 4, except that the RID list would be in use for a somewhat extended period while the filtering was carried out on a large set of index pages. Presumably the designers were looking for limitations on RID-list extraction to preserve the valuable RID pool space for more deserving applications and hit on these rules. Various details of query optimization can change from one release to another, however.

Point of Diminishing Returns in Multiple Index Access

Another rule about RID-list extraction in multiple index access is not so much a limitation as a rule of optimization. A scan on an index, with an I/O cost for leaf page traversal, will only be performed if it will pay for itself by reducing the I/O cost of data page retrieval by a larger amount. To determine the indexes that will be scanned with an MX step in a multiple index access plan, the query optimizer follows steps something like the ones that follow.

DEFINITION 9.6.2 Steps to Determine the Point of Diminishing Returns in MX Access.

[1] List indexes with matching predicates in the WHERE clause of the query. For simplicity, we assume in what follows that each index has a disjoint set of matching predicates.

[2] Place the indexes in order by increasing filter factor value for matching scans. We will choose an initial sequence of indexes on which MX steps will be performed, with smallest filter factors first. This means we start by considering predicates with smaller index I/O costs and larger effects on saving data page I/O, and the approach can be proved to have optimal results.

[3] For successive indexes listed, perform MX steps only if the I/O cost for the index scan to extract the RID list will pay for itself with a reduced cost of data page scan for final row retrieval. The simplest formulation example of this rule is that once we are down to a few rows, we don't read several hundred pages of a new index to get the number of rows down to one!   ∎

Actually things are somewhat more complex than this. For example, in step 3 the first index considered may not pay for itself in I/O savings compared to a tablespace scan, so the procedure might have to consider using two indexes before a savings is evident. As an example, a filter factor of 1/20 for the first index doesn't save much I/O if there are 20 rows on a page. However, a second index with filter factor 1/15 results in a large I/O savings.

EXAMPLE 9.6.6
We refer again to the prospects table with the indexes addrx, hobbyx, agex, and incomex. Consider the query

```
select name, straddr from prospects
    where zipcode between 02159 and 02658
    and age = 40 and hobby = 'chess' and incomeclass = 10;
```

We assume that multiple index access is used, and try to figure out which predicates will pay for themselves. The filter factors of these clauses are as follows (in ascending order):

(1) FF(zipcode between 02159 and 02658) = 500/100,000 = 1/200
(2) FF(hobby = 'chess') = 1/100
(3) FF(age = 40) = 1/50
(4) FF(incomeclass = 10) = 1/10

Applying the filter factor for predicate (1) to 50 million rows, we get (1/200)(50 M) = 250,000 rows retrieved, unclustered of course, and thus likely all to be on distinct pages of the 5 million data pages and retrieved with list prefetch. The elapsed time for 250,000 L is 1250 seconds. We ignore the index cost.

Applying predicate (2) after predicate (1), the scan of the index hobbyx for the predicate hobby = 'chess' entails a number of leaf page I/Os, calculated by (1/100)(50,000) = 500, so the cost is 500 S, taking elapsed time 500/800 = 0.625 seconds. As a result, we reduce the number of data pages scanned from 250,000 (resulting from the previous step) to (1/100)(250,000) = 2500, and 2500 L takes elapsed time 2500/200 = 12.5 seconds. With an investment of 0.625 seconds for the hobbyx index scan we have gone from a data scan of 2500 seconds to one of 12.5 seconds, obviously worthwhile.

Applying predicate (3) after predicates (1) and (2), the scan of the agex index (discussed in Example 9.6.1) for age = 40 entails a number of leaf page I/Os, calculated by (1/50)(50,000) = 1000, at cost 1000 S, taking elapsed time 1000/800 = 1.25 seconds. As a result, we reduce the number of data pages scanned to (1/50)(2500) = 50, and 50 L takes elapsed time of 0.25 seconds. With an investment of 1.25 seconds for the agex index scan we have gone from a data scan of 12.5 seconds to one of 0.25 seconds, obviously worthwhile.

Applying predicate (4) after predicates (1), (2), and (3), the scan of the incomex index for incomeclass = 10 entails a number of leaf page I/Os, calculated by (1/10)(50,000) = 5000, so the cost is 5000 S, taking elapsed time 5000/800 = 6.25 seconds. As a result, we reduce the number of data pages scanned to (1/10)(50) = 5, and 5 L takes elapsed time of 0.025 seconds (approximately). With an investment of 6.25 seconds for the agex index scan, we have gone from a data scan of 0.25 seconds to one of 0.025 seconds. This is *not* worthwhile, and the incomex index will not be scanned with an MX step in the multiple index access plan. ■

9.7 Methods for Joining Tables

In this section we study three algorithms currently used by **DB2** for joining two tables. The algorithms are known as *nested-loop join, merge scan join,* and *hybrid join.* (**DB2 UDB** currently implements the nested-loop join and merge scan join, while only **DB2 for OS/390** has the hybrid join.) Each of these methods has performance advantages in a certain class of situations that can arise in performing a join. Other methods have been developed for performing joins that are not used by **DB2** but nevertheless provide performance advantages in special circumstances—for example, the method known as *hash* *join*—but we will restrict our attention to the join methods provided by **DB2**. The terminology used to describe **DB2** join methods is fairly universal, and some of these concepts are implemented in most database products.

We define a *join* of two tables to be a process in which we combine rows of one table with rows of another to answer a query. By this definition, a join occurs whenever two or more tables appear in the FROM clause of a Select statement. Even if we are taking a simple Cartesian product of rows from the two tables (a table *product*), we refer to it as a join. As we will see, a Select statement with a single table in the FROM clause, and a WHERE clause that contains a Subquery from a different table, is often converted by the query optimizer to an equivalent query statement that joins tables. To begin with, we consider only the situation where exactly two tables appear in the FROM clause.

A join of two tables in **DB2** usually occurs in two steps. During the first step, only one table is accessed; this is referred to as the *outer table*. In the second step, rows of the second, *inner table* are combined with rows of the first, outer table. Other predicates, involving columns of the two tables that have not been retrieved through an index, are used to qualify rows as they are retrieved. As a result of all this, a *composite table* is generated that contains all the qualified rows of the join. If a join with a third table is now necessary, the composite table becomes the outer table for the succeeding join step. Otherwise specified columns of the composite table provide the answer to the query. Although it is simplest to think of the composite table result of a join being fully materialized in a disk workfile, it is important to realize that we may be able to avoid such wasteful materialization. For example, if a user is only likely to look at the first 20 or 30 rows of the resulting output, it would be terribly inefficient to materialize a million-row composite table. Thus in Embedded SQL, when a cursor on a join query is first opened and the first row is retrieved, we avoid materializing tables where possible.

Nested-Loop Join

Consider the following query:

[9.7.1]   select T1.C1, T1.C2, T2.C3, T2.C4 from T1, T2
           where T1.C1 = 5 and T1.C2 = T2.C3;

In a nested-loop join, the table referred to as the *outer table* corresponds to the "outer loop" in a nested pair of loops, as we see in the pseudo-code of Figure 9.19. Assuming that the table T1 in the Select statement of [9.7.1] is the outer table, the first step of the nested join determines rows in T1 that satisfy the relevant predicate(s) on T1—in this case, T1.C1 = 5. If we assume that an index C1X exists on column C1 of table T1, then the first step of the join would give rise to a row in the plan table with the following relevant column values:

PLAN NO	METHOD	TAB NO	ACCESS TYPE	MATCH COLS	ACCESS NAME	PREFETCH	SORTN_ JOIN
1	0	1	I	1	C1X	L	N

```
R1: FIND ALL ROWS T1.* IN THE OUTER TABLE T1 WHERE C1 = 5;
    FOR EACH ROW T1.* FOUND IN THE OUTER TABLE;
R2:     FIND ALL ROWS T2.* IN THE INNER TABLE WHERE T1.C2 = T2.C3;
        FOR EACH ROW T2.* FOUND IN THE INNER TABLE
            RETURN ANSWER: T1.C1, T1.C2, T2.C3, T2.C4;
        END FOR;
    END FOR;
```

Figure 9.19 Pseudo-Code for Nested-Loop Join (Illustrates Query [9.7.1])

This row of the plan table indicates the following. We are employing the first step of a multi-step plan (PLANNO = 1). No join method has yet been employed (METHOD = 0), and we are extracting rows from the first table of the join (TABNO = 1), using an index scan step with one matching column on index C1X. We are able to retrieve rows from the table T1 using list prefetch.

Now that the rows of the outer table have been determined (they have not actually been extracted yet), a loop is performed to retrieve each of these rows. For each qualified row of the outer table, a retrieval is performed on the second, *inner* table, T2, and all rows of T2 are retrieved that satisfy the join predicate that connects the two tables, T1.C2 = T2.C3. Note that because the row of T1 is fixed for this retrieval, we can treat the value T1.C2 as if it were a constant, K. Then the rows retrieved from T2 are exactly those that satisfy a predicate of the form T2.C3 = K, and an index C3X on column C3 of table T2 will make this retrieval efficient. This second step of the nested-loop join, using the C3X index, has the following row in the plan table:

PLAN NO	METHOD	TAB NO	ACCESS TYPE	MATCH COLS	ACCESS NAME	PREFETCH	SORTN_ JOIN
2	1	2	I	1	C3X	L	N

This row of the plan table indicates the second step of a multi-step plan (PLANNO = 2). The join method being employed is nested-loop join (METHOD = 1); we are extracting rows from the second table of the join (TABNO = 2), using an index scan step with one matching column on index C3X. The second table is in fact T2, and we are retrieving rows from this table using list prefetch. Figure 9.19 contains procedural pseudo-code for the two-step method just explained. Figure 9.20 illustrates the method of nested-loop join for query [9.7.1], using specific tables T1 and T2.

Note that the R1 and R2 labels of Figure 9.19 designate retrievals in the join processing. Additional predicates limiting the rows of either table can be added to the relevant retrievals. Either retrieval can be performed using an index scan (which we have assumed above) or a table scan. The outer table has only one retrieval, while the inner table has a number of retrievals equal to the number of qualifying rows in the outer table. The I/O cost of the join is therefore given by the following formula:

582

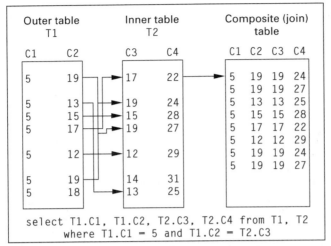

```
select T1.C1, T1.C2, T2.C3, T2.C4 from T1, T2
        where T1.C1 = 5 and T1.C2 = T2.C3
```

Figure 9.20   Nested-Loop Join (Illustrates Query [9.7.1])

$$\text{COST}_{I/O}(\text{NESTED-LOOP JOIN}) = \text{COST}_{I/O}(\text{OUTER TABLE RETRIEVAL}) +$$
$$\text{NUMBER OF QUALIFYING ROWS IN OUTER TABLE} * \text{COST}_{I/O}(\text{INNER TABLE RETRIEVAL})$$

For the nested-loop join to be an appropriate algorithm to join large tables, we would normally expect to see an index on the matching columns of the inner table to guarantee efficient retrieval. Nested-loop join is particularly efficient when only a small number of rows qualify from the outer table after limiting predicates are applied, or when the inner table is small enough that all index and data disk pages become resident in memory buffers after being accessed once during the join.

EXAMPLE 9.7.1
Assume that we are given two tables, TABL1 with columns C1 and C2, and TABL2 with columns C3 and C4, each with 1 million rows of 200 bytes each. We wish to estimate the I/O cost of the following query performed using a nested-loop join:

```
select T1.C1, T1.C2, T2.C3, T2.C4 from TABL1 T1, TABL2 T2
        where T1.C1 = 5 and T2.C4 = 6 and T1.C2 = T2.C3;
```

We assume that a non-clustering index C1X exists on column C1 of TABL1, and on TABL2 we have the index C3X on C3 and C4X on C4. Assume also that the filter factors for these predicates are given as follows: FF(C1 = const) = FF(C4 = const) = 1/100; FF(C2 = const) = 1/250,000; and FF(C3 = const) = 1/500,000. We start with the question: How many rows are retrieved by this query? It turns out that it is best to have a specific join method in mind before we try to answer this question, as we see in the following analysis of I/O cost.

We will evaluate the I/O cost in terms of elapsed time for a possible nested join plan to answer this query, where the outer table is T1 (referring to the shorter alias for TABL1) and the inner table is T2 (the alias for TABL2). The plan we consider consists of the following steps. (1) Using the C1X index, retrieve all rows from T1 where T1.C1 = 5. (2) For each row retrieved from the outer table T1, think of T1.C2 as a constant, renamed K. Using the C3X index, retrieve all rows in the inner table T2 such that T2.C3 = K. As the rows from this index scan are retrieved, further restrict the rows by verifying the predicate T2.C4 = 6. (Note that there is no way to use the index C4X here since, as we explain below, we are only retrieving two rows with the T2.C3 = K clause, and a further use of the C4X index would hit the point of diminishing returns.) (3) Print out T1.C1 and T1.C2 from the outer table row and T2.C3 and T2.C4 for the qualified inner table row.

The following table shows the rows in the plan table for this strategy.

PLAN NO	METHOD	TAB NO	ACCESS TYPE	MATCH COLS	ACCESS NAME	PREFETCH	SORTN_ JOIN
1	0	1	I	1	C1X	L	N
2	1	2	I	1	C3X	L	N

Using the filter factor and the number of rows in T1, the number of rows retrieved from T1 in step (1) is about (1/100)(1,000,000) = 10,000 rows, likely to be all on different pages. The row for PLANNO = 1 tells us that list prefetch is being used. The index I/O cost for this retrieval is assumed to be insignificant next to the data page I/O cost. We therefore assume that $COST_{I/O}$ (OUTER TABLE RETRIEVAL) = 10,000 L, with elapsed time of 10,000/200 = 50 seconds.

For each outer table row qualified, we assume that the value T1.C2, renamed K, is in the range of values for the column T2.C3. Since FF(C3 = const) = 1/500,000, we expect to retrieve two rows out of a table of 1 million rows. This requires for each new value of T2.C3 one random I/O to the leaf level of the C3X index (assuming that upper-level directory nodes are in memory buffers) and then two I/Os (average) to retrieve the two pages containing the two rows. Thus the I/O cost for the 10,000 different inner loop steps is 10,000 * (1 R + 2 R). We would normally perform a list I/O to retrieve the data pages in this situation, but recall that it is quite misleading to think of a list prefetch of two pages as taking place in 2/100 seconds, since there are too few pages retrieved to amortize the arm seek time and rotational latency. It is much more reasonable to think of this retrieval as equivalent to 2 R, and therefore the elapsed time for the inner loop is calculated from 10,000 * (3 R), or 30,000/80 = 375 seconds. The elapsed time, then, is 50 seconds + 375 seconds = 425 seconds.

Now to determine how many rows are retrieved in the query, we see that there are 10,000 rows retrieved from T1 and for each row in T1 there are two rows joined to it (on the average) from table T2. Therefore there are about 20,000 rows retrieved at this point, after which a qualification test takes place to see if T2.C4 = 6 for the rows retrieved. With a filter factor of 1/100, the final number of rows retrieved is (1/100) 20,000 = 200.   ∎

Merge Join

Merge join is also known in other texts as *merge scan join* or *sort merge join*. Consider again the query of Example 9.7.1, with the same index assumptions.

[9.7.2]   select T1.C1, T2.C2, T1.C3, T2.C4 from TABL1 T1, TABL2 T2
                where T1.C1 = 5 and T2.C4 = 6 and T1.C2 = T2.C3;

The merge join method scans two tables only once, in the order of their join columns. In the Select statement of [9.7.2], **DB2** would start by applying the non-join predicates and creating intermediate tables. We first evaluate select C1, C2 from T1 where T1.C1 = 5 order by C2, placing the output rows in an intermediate table IT1 with columns C1 and C2, and rows sorted in order by C2. Then we evaluate select C3, C4 from T2 where C4 = 6 order by C3, to get an intermediate table IT2 with columns C3 and C4 and rows sorted in order by C3. Note that these intermediate tables, IT1 and IT2, are usually too large to hold in memory. They are written to disk workfiles as temporary tables, and the sort of the rows is a disk base sort, explained later.

We are now prepared to perform the merge process from which the merge join algorithm takes its name. To perform a merge join on IT1 and IT2, we associate a pointer with each intermediate table, pointing initially to the first row of each. As the algorithm proceeds, the two pointers move forward in such a way that any matching C2/C3 values for rows in the two tables are detected. Except for cases where multiple identical C2 values in IT1 match multiple identical C3 values in IT2, both pointers move steadily forward through the rows of both tables, and detect all matching values IT1.C2 = IT2.C3 that exist. In the pseudo-code of Figure 9.21 the C2 value of the row in table IT1 pointed to by pointer P1 is represented by P1 → C2, and similarly for P2 → C3 in table IT2.

```
      CREATE TABLE IT1 AS: SELECT C1, C2 FROM T1 WHERE C1 = 5 ORDER BY C2;
      CREATE TABLE IT2 AS: SELECT C3, C4 FROM T1 WHERE C4 = 6 ORDER BY C3;
      SET P1 POINTER TO FIRST ROW OF IT1;              /* OUTER TABLE              */
      SET P2 POINTER TO FIRST ROW OF IT2;              /* INNER TABLE              */
MJ:   WHILE (TRUE) {                                   /* LOOP UNTIL EXIT MJ LOOP  */
          WHILE (P1 -> C2 > P2 -> C3) {                /* IF P2 NEEDS TO ADVANCE   */
              ADVANCE P2 TO NEXT ROW IN IT2;           /* ADVANCE IT               */
              IF (P2 PAST LAST ROW) EXIT MJ LOOP;      /* OUT OF ROWS, EXIT        */
          }
          WHILE (P1 -> C2 < P2 -> C3) {                /* IF P1 NEEDS TO ADVANCE   */
              ADVANCE P1 TO NEXT ROW IN IT1;           /* ADVANCE IT               */
              IF (P1 PAST LAST ROW) EXIT MJ LOOP;      /* OUT OF ROWS, EXIT        */
          }
          IF (P1 -> C2 == P2-> C3) {                   /* FOUND MATCH ON JOIN      */
              MEMP = P2;                               /* REMEMBER P2 START POINT  */
              WHILE (P1 -> C2 == P2 -> C3) {           /* LOOP                     */
                  RETURN ANSWER: IT1.C1, IT1.C2, IT2.C3, IT2.C4;
                  ADVANCE P2 TO NEXT ROW IN IT2;       /* ADVANCE P2               */
              }    /* LOOP CONTINUES IF P2 -> C3 IS UNCHANGED                      */
          }                                            /* DONE WITH JOIN MATCH     */
          /* SINCE FELL THROUGH, P2 -> C3 IS NEW OR BEYOND END OF TABLE           */
          ADVANCE P1 TO NEXT ROW IN IT1;               /* ADVANCE P1               */
          IF (PAST LAST ROW) EXIT MJ LOOP;             /* OUT OF ROWS, EXIT        */
              IF (P1 -> C2 == MEMP -> C3)              /* IF NEXT P1-> C2 IS SAME  */
                  P2 = MEMP;                           /* START OVER WITH P2       */
      }                                                /* END OF MJ LOOP           */
```

Figure 9.21 Pseudo-Code for Merge Join (Illustrates Query [9.7.2])

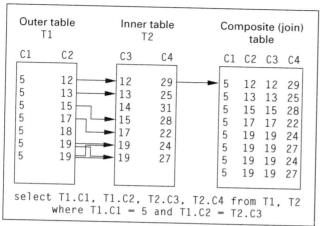

$$\text{select T1.C1, T1.C2, T2.C3, T2.C4 from T1, T2}$$
$$\text{where T1.C1} = 5 \text{ and T1.C2} = \text{T2.C3}$$

Figure 9.22 Merge Join (Illustrates Query [9.7.1])

Figure 9.22 illustrates the method of merge join for query [9.7.1], using specific tables T1 and T2. Once a match is found in the pseudo-code of Figure 9.21, we keep P1 fixed and advance P2 through all duplicate values. Then we advance P1; if we find a duplicate, this is the only situation in which a pointer moves backward, where we set P2 = MEMP to run through all duplicates of P2 again. Clearly if there are a lot of occurrences where C2 and C3 have the same value, a large number of rows will be joined, and this innermost loop will have an enormous effect. However, it is more common that there will be only a small number of rows in one table matching more than one row with another, since we don't normally perform joins on columns with a large number of duplicate values (see Section 6.7 on lossy and lossless decompositions). In any event, the query optimizer can determine the likely number of duplicates facing each other using existing statistics, and it is likely that most computer resources will be used in finding any match at all.

EXAMPLE 9.7.2

We repeat the join query of Example 9.7.1 using a merge join:

```
select T1.C1, T1.C2, T2.C3, T2.C4 from TABL1 T1, TABL2 T2
    where T1.C1 = 5 and T2.C4 = 6 and T1.C2 = T2.C3;
```

We have all the same assumptions: non-clustering indexes C1X still exists on column C1 of TABL1, with C3X and C4X on C3 and C4 of TABL2. The tables both contain 1 million rows of 200 bytes each, and we still have filter factors FF(C1 = const) = FF(C4 = const) = 1/100, FF(C2 = const) = 1/250,000, and FF(C3 = const) = 1/500,000. In the nested join of Example 9.7.1, we used the indexes C1X and C3X.

The strategy for answering query [9.7.2] with a merge join consists of the following steps: (1) Using the index C1X, retrieve all rows from T1 where T1.C1 = 5 (again there will be 10,000 rows), output the C1 and C2 values to IT1, and sort the result by C2 value. (2) Using the index C4X, retrieve all rows from T2 where T2.C4 = 6 (10,000 rows also), output the resulting C3 and C4 values to IT2, and sort them.

Then perform the merge join step, following the pseudo-code above. The merge join plan is shown in the following table. Note the SORTN_JOIN column, which shows that a sort is required to achieve IT1 and IT2.

PLAN NO	METHOD	TAB NO	ACCESS TYPE	MATCH COLS	ACCESS NAME	PREFETCH	SORTN_ JOIN
1	0	1	I	1	C1X	L	Y
2	2	2	I	1	C4X	L	Y

As before, step (1) requires a read of 10,000 entries from the T1.C1 leaf-level index, which we treat as insignificant, followed by an I/O cost of 10,000 L to retrieve the indexed rows from the data pages. If we assume that each of the C1 and C2 values extracted requires 10 bytes, the materialized table IT1 requires 200,000 bytes, or about 50 pages. It is appropriate to think of this sort taking place completely in memory, so the total I/O cost of step (1) is 10,000 L. The same considerations apply to step (2). The total cost for the plan is therefore 20,000 L, with an elapsed time of 100 seconds, an improvement over the nested-loop join of Example 9.7.1, which required 425 seconds. The advantage comes from using index C4X in merge join for more efficient batch retrieval from TABL2. ∎

Note that it is not always necessary to extract the rows from a table such as T1 into an intermediate table IT1. If there were an index on T1 that allowed us to qualify the rows of T1 with the predicate T1.C1 = 5 and still access the qualified rows in order by T1.C2, **DB2** would certainly take that option. This would be possible, for example, if T1 had an index C12X on (C1, C2): the matching scan through the index with the given predicate would provide rows of T1 in order by C2. The same considerations hold for T2.

The merge join is not always a superior strategy.

EXAMPLE 9.7.3
Consider the following join query:

```
select T1.C5, T1.C2, T2.* from TABL1 T1, TABL2 T2
    where T1.C5 = 5 and T1.C2 = T2.C3;
```

We assume that indexes C2X, C3X, and C5X exist on the corresponding columns of tables T1 and T2, with filter factors as in Examples 9.7.1 and 9.7.2, FF(C2 = const) = 1/250,000 and FF(C3 = const) = 1/500,000, and a new filter factor FF(T1.C5 = const) = 1/1000. Thus the I/O cost for a nested-loop join with T1 as the outer table can be calculated as follows. With 1000 rows to look up in T1 having T1.C5 = 5, we have an index lookup cost of 1 R (for index) + 1000 L (for data pages). For each row in the outer table T1, we set T1.C2 = K, then look up rows in the inner table having T2.C3 = K, about two rows, requiring 1 R for the index leaf entry lookup and 2 R for the row retrievals. The I/O cost for the inner loop is calculated as 1000 * (3 R) = 3000 R. Thus the total nested loop join cost is 3001 R + 1000 L, with elapsed time of 3001/80 + 1000/200, or approximately 42.5 seconds.

For merge join, we calculate costs as follows. We can easily calculate that the extraction of IT1 requires 10 seconds for I/O, but as we will see, this is insignificant in comparison to elapsed time for the loop join. Since there were no independent limiting predicates on T2 such as we had in Example 9.7.2 (T2.C4 = 6), we have a choice between accessing the rows from T2 in order by the index C3X to perform the merge, or materializing and sorting the entire table T2 as intermediate table IT2. In the first case, we would access all rows of T2 through an unclustered index, at a cost for data page access alone of 1,000,000 R, clearly not a good strategy. (We can't use prefetch I/O here, because we don't want to retrieve the rows in RID order.) In the second case, we need to materialize a table IT2 with 1 million rows of 200 bytes each (note that all columns of T2 are in the select list) and sort the resulting rows by C3. We defer consideration of disk sort, but it is reasonable to point out that a disk sort of these rows would probably require two passes through the disk pages, writing out the results of the first pass and then reading in these results for the second pass, an I/O cost of over 100,000 S, with an elapsed time of 100,000/800 = 125 seconds. Clearly the nested-loop strategy is superior. ∎

Hybrid Join

The hybrid join method, METHOD = 4 in the IBM taxonomy, is used less frequently than nested-loop join and merge join, and for brevity we merely give a verbal description of the algorithm used.

Description of the Hybrid Join Algorithm. A hybrid join of two tables has an outer and an inner table, just as the nested-loop and merge join algorithms do. The first step is the same as that of merge join for the outer table. The table is scanned once in join column order, either through an index or after extracting a set of rows restricted by some predicates into an intermediate table IT1. As rows of the outer table are being scanned in join column order, matching join column values of the inner table are looked up through an index on the join column. The rows of the inner table are not accessed yet, however; instead the rows from the outer table, with an additional column giving the RID value of each matching join row in the inner table, are written to an intermediate table IT2. Rows of IT2 are then sorted in RID order, and list prefetch is used to pick up rows from the inner table to join with outer table rows.

EXAMPLE 9.7.4
Consider again the join query of Example 9.7.3:

```
select T1.C5, T1.C2, T2.* from TABL1 T1, TABL2 T2
    where T1.C5 = 5 and T1.C2 = T2.C3;
```

As in Example 9.7.3, we assume that indexes C2X, C3X, and C5X exist on the corresponding columns of tables T1 and T2, with filter factors as in Examples 9.7.1 and 9.7.2, FF(C2 = const) = 1/250,000, FF(C3 = const) = 1/500,000, and FF(T1.C5 = const) = 1/1000. The I/O cost for a hybrid join with T1 as the outer table can be calculated as follows. With 1000 rows to look up in T1 having T1.C5 = 5, we see an index lookup cost of 1 R (for index) + 1000 L (for data pages). We only need to extract C2 and C5 from T1 for each of these 1000 rows to write into IT1, about 8000 bytes, so creating IT1 and the following sort by C2 should cost no I/O. For each row in the outer table IT1, we set T1.C2 = K, then look up index entries in the C3X index for T2.C3 = K, requiring 1 R of index leaf I/O for each entry, at a cost of 1000 R.

As we perform this lookup, we create rows of the form (T1.C2, T1.C5, RID) in intermediate table IT2. This table will contain about 2000 rows of 12 bytes each, about 24,000 bytes or buffer space for six disk pages, so once again we assume that no I/O is needed for creating IT2 and the following sort by RID values. Finally, we pass through the rows of IT2, using the sorted RID values in IT2 as a kind of RID list to retrieve the rows from the inner table T2, and matching the C5 and C2 values of T1 with all columns of T2 to generate the target-list rows. We are retrieving 2000 rows from T2, likely all to be on separate pages, at an I/O cost of 2000 L. Therefore the total I/O cost for this method is 1000 L (extracting rows from T1) + 1000 R (index entries from C3X) + 2000 L (extracting rows from T2). The elapsed time is (1000 + 2000)/200 + 1000/80 = 5 + 10 + 12.5 = 27.5 seconds, an improvement on the nested-loop join calculated in Example 9.7.3, which was superior to merge join. ∎

The advantage gained over nested-loop join arises from the fact that all row retrievals from the inner table can be performed using list prefetch I/O with large blocks.

Multiple Table Joins

In **DB2** and most database systems, joins of three or more tables are performed by joining two tables at a time; the composite result of the first two joins is written to an intermediate table and then joined with the third table. The resulting composite may be joined with a fourth table, and so on. The order of joins is not determined by the non-procedural SQL Select, but is left up to the query optimizer. The proper choice is very important.

Consider a three-table join of the form:

[9.7.3]   select T1.C1, T1.C2, T2.C3, T2.C4, T2.C5, T3.C6, T3.C7
          from T1, T2, T3
          where T1.C1 = 20 and T1.C2 = T2.C3 and T2.C4 = 40
          and T2.C5 = T3.C6 and T3.C7 = 60;

The query plans available for such a join have a number of different degrees of freedom. We can start by performing either of the joins $T1 \bowtie T2$ or $T2 \bowtie T3$. Assuming that we start with $T1 \bowtie T2$, we can use a nested-loop join or a hybrid join with either T1 or T2 in the outer loop, or a merge join (the decision on inner and outer tables in the merge join is immaterial). Once the table $T4 := T1 \bowtie T2$ has been (at least conceptually) materialized, we need to perform the join $T4 \bowtie T3$, once again using either a nested-loop join, a hybrid join, or a merge join. The query optimizer needs to consider all such plans to discover the most efficient one, and it is here that efficient algorithms for query optimization begin to become important. For joins involving multiple tables, query optimization can require a great deal of computational effort.

Note that in the plan just mentioned, joining T1 and T2 to create T4, then joining T4 to T3, if the query optimizer decides to perform the join $T4 \bowtie T3$ by a nested-loop algorithm, the intermediate table $T4 := T1 \bowtie T2$ does not need to be physically materialized before starting the final join step. As each row of T4 is generated from $T1 \bowtie T2$, the next iteration of the nested-loop join of $T4 \bowtie T3$ can be immediately performed. The technique whereby successive rows output from one step of an access plan can be fed as input into the next step of the plan is known as *pipelining*. Pipelining minimizes the physical disk space needed for materialization. Even more important, in cases where only a small fraction of initial rows from the query are ever required (perhaps because the user ceases scrolling through the cursor after getting a look at a few screens of information), minimal materialization by pipelining often saves a great deal of effort. However, pipelining is not always possible: if the query optimizer chooses a merge join to evaluate T4 = T1 ⋈ T2, and then another merge join to evaluate T4 ⋈ T3, where the T4 ⋈ T3 join columns dictate a different sort order than the join columns output from T1 ⋈ T2, then the intermediate table T4 must be fully materialized before the initial sort of the next join step can be performed.

Transforming Nested Queries to Joins

It is possible to transform most nested queries into equivalent queries involving only table joins. This is an important technique for the query optimizer.

EXAMPLE 9.7.5
Consider the query

```
select * from T1 where C1 = 5
    and C2 in (select C3 from T2 where C4 = 6);
```

Conceptually we think of this query as being performed in two steps. First the subquery is evaluated, extracting a set of values for the C3 select list into an intermediate table IT1, then the outer query, select * from T1 where C1 = 5 and C2 in IT1, is evaluated, with a condition on the C2 column that it have a value in the IT1 list just created. The most efficient way to do this, given that there is no index created on IT1, is probably as a merge join: select * from T1 where C1 = 5 is extracted into an intermediate table IT2, the rows are ordered by the T1.C2 value, and then the merge join process of Figure 9.21 is performed between IT2 and IT1. Possible duplicate rows must now be removed, as explained below. This procedure puts us in mind of the following *join form:*

```
select distinct T1.* from T1, T2
    where T1.C1 = 5 and T2.C4 = 6 and T1.C2 = T2.C3;
```

The Subquery at the beginning and this join query give identical results, and the equivalent join form allows the query optimizer to use other algorithms that are not obvious in the nested form. For example, it is now possible to perform a nested-loop join with T2 as the outer table.

The need for the DISTINCT keyword in transforming the nested query to the join form arises from the following observation: if a row r1 of T1 obeys the condition of the join query, then r1.C1 = 5 and there must exist a row r2 in T2 so that r2.C4 = 6 and r1.C2 = r2.C3. But nothing is said about the columns C3 and C4 forming a relational key of T2, so it is perfectly possible that there is a second row r3 in T2 that has the same values for C3 and C4 as r2. Then in the select list of the join query without a DISTINCT keyword, the row r1 would appear twice. This would clearly not happen in the original nested form of the query, since each single row of T1 is conceptually considered only once and qualified or not by the predicates C1 = 5 and C2 in IT1. Thus the DISTINCT keyword in the join form merely casts out duplicates that would not appear in the nested form. ∎

The value of a transformation such as this is that it reduces the number of different types of predicates the query optimizer needs to consider to achieve optimal efficiency. Once the nested query of Example 9.7.5 has been rewritten as an equivalent join query, it is reduced to a problem previously solved, and the query optimizer can use any of the join methods we have already introduced. The next example considers the case of a correlated Subquery.

EXAMPLE 9.7.6

Consider the query

```
select * from T1
    where C1 = 5
    and C2 in (select C4 from T2 where C5 = 6 and C6 > T1.C3);
```

Because this nested form contains a correlated Subquery, it is not possible to evaluate the Subquery until the outer product row is fixed so that T1.C3 can be evaluated. From this consideration, it seems that the only valid approach is to start by looping on rows of T1 and then for each row in T1 find all rows in T2 through an index on C4, where T2.C4 is equal to the outer T1.C2, and then resolve the clause T2.C6 > T1.C3. Now notice that the nested query above gives the same result as the join query:

```
select distinct T1.* from T1, T2
    where T1.C1 = 5 and T1.C2 = T2.C4 and T2.C5 = 6 and T2.C6 > T1.C3;
```

It is much easier to picture the strategy of performing a merge join with the query in this form. Extract rows from T1 where T1.C1 = 5 into intermediate table IT1, and sort by T1.C2. Then sort T2 in order by column C4 into table IT2. Now merge join IT1 and IT2 on matching values for T1.C2 and T2.C4 (casting out duplicates), and qualify rows matched by making them obey the predicate T2.C6 > T1.C3. This strategy might be superior to the nested-loop join that seemed most natural for the query in nested form.   ∎

Theorem 9.7.1 gives a general form covering the cases described above.

THEOREM 9.7.1   The following two query forms give equivalent results:

```
select T1.C1 from T1 where [Set A of predicates on T1 and] T1.C2
    is in (select T2.C3 from T2 [where Set B of predicates on T2, T1]);
```

and

```
select distinct T1.C1 from T1, T2
    where T1.C2 = T2.C3 [and Set A of predicates on T1]
    [and Set B of conditions on T2, T1];
```

Note that Set A of conditions can be empty, as can Set B. Note too that if no conditions in Set B from the nested query refer to table T1 in the outer query, the entire nested query is noncorrelated. The forms given above can be generalized to multiple tables in the outer and inner queries.   ∎

DB2 performs this transformation only under certain conditions, including the following:

[1]   The Subquery select list is a single column, guaranteed by a unique index to have unique values.

[2]   The comparison operator connecting the outer query to the Subquery is either IN or =ANY (with the same meaning).

Thus for example, all nested queries involving the NOT EXISTS predicate are not transformed into join predicates. But most nested queries have equivalent join forms, and it turns out that the **DB2** query optimizer usually finds a more efficient execution plan if the query is posed in the join form. This is true even if the transformation into a join plan doesn't take place under **DB2** rules of transformation and implies that the person writing queries should make some effort to create a join form rather than the equivalent nested form query if possible. Given that a nested form query is used, it is possible to tell from the output of the EXPLAIN command if a transformation into join form has been performed. A join is indicated by a METHOD column value of 1, 2, or 4.

9.8   Disk Sorts

There are a number of situations in query processing in which a sort of a set of objects too large to fit in memory must be performed. Recall that RID lists are assumed to lie completely in memory in the RID pool. As a result, the method used to sort the RIDs can be any one of the efficient memory sorts you have probably already encountered in a data structure programming course, such as merge sort. However, when the set of objects being sorted does not fit entirely in memory, the problem becomes a good deal more difficult. The database system needs to use methods that minimize disk I/O, a problem that probably never arose in earlier programming courses. We refer to a sort of data, some of which must be disk resident, as a *disk sort*. In the analogy of keyed lookup, the most efficient lookup structure for memory-resident data (allowing arbitrary inserts and range finds) is a balanced binary tree or 2-3 tree, whereas for data that is disk resident the most efficient structure is the B-tree.

DB2 must be ready to employ an efficient disk sort during merge join and hybrid join processing, where the intermediate tables IT1 and IT2 are sorted by join column or by RID. (Sorts must be performed unless an index is used for accessing the original tables that already has the right order.) These tables are often small enough to retain in memory, but **DB2** cannot depend on that, and so a disk sort is used. The disk sorts used in merge join and hybrid join processing are assumed to take place during the second step of these two-step join plans (PLANNO = 2, METHOD = 2 or 4), and the sort is reflected in the plan row by two new column values, SORTN_JOIN = Y and SORTC_JOIN = Y. There are a number of other plan table columns that are used to indicate when disk sort steps are being performed, and for what purpose. These plan columns include SORTC_ ORDERBY (generally triggered when an ORDER BY clause is used in the Select statement); SORTC_GROUPBY (to gather terms together in response to a GROUP BY clause); and SORTC_UNIQ (generally used when a DISTINCT keyword is used in the select list). The columns contain value 'Y' when the sort is being performed and otherwise contain value 'N'. Note that there are three columns in the plan table that are never used in the current release of **DB2**, and therefore always contain the value 'N'; these columns are SORTN_GROUPBY, SORTN_UNIQ, and SORTN_ORDERBY.

The N-Way Merge Disk Sort Algorithm

In what follows we refer to a *table* of *rows* to be sorted by some *sortkey* column. Note that we are not necessarily referring to a relational table, but to any list of record-structured objects that the database system cannot hold entirely in memory. A disk sort takes place in a series of *passes*. In each pass the algorithm makes progress toward producing a sorted result on disk, which is as much progress as possible given the limitations of memory space in comparison to the total size of the table to be sorted. If by chance the table to be sorted and all temporary sort information can be held totally in memory during the sort, then a single pass will produce a completely sorted list. Otherwise the first pass sorts the largest possible fraction of the table into ascending order and writes this out to disk as a sorted block, then repeats this process until all rows in the table have been written out in a sequence of sorted blocks. Each successive pass performs successive *merges* of N blocks into new, longer blocks containing sequences of ordered rows, until all rows are sorted. The N-way merge sort is a generalization of the memory-resident two-way merge sort often taught in data structure classes, in the same way that a B-tree is a generalization of a binary tree, and for the same reason. By increasing N we can greatly reduce the number of passes, where each pass must read all information in the table from disk and write it back again. Thus the I/O is minimized.

To be more specific, assume that we are given a table of short rows of data to be sorted that takes up a number D of disk pages (we assume that the disk pages are contiguous on disk, so that sequential prefetch I/O can be used), and that we have $M + 1$ disk buffer pages of memory, $M \leq D$, that we are allowed to use during our sort. We wish to illustrate the procedure of an N-way merge sort. As we will see, if $M \geq D$, then we can perform the sort entirely in memory. It turns out that the exact length of the rows isn't important, as long as all rows always lie entirely within a disk page (rows cannot cross pages). To have some numbers to work with for purposes of illustration, let us assume that $D = 10,000$ pages and $M = 2$ pages. In what follows we will perform an M-way merge sort—that is, since $M = 2$, it is a two-way merge sort. All calculations that follow can be generalized back to arbitrary values for D and M.

To begin with, we say that the rows to be sorted are originally stored on 10,000 contiguous disk pages known as area A1, and for simplicity we assume that we have a second disk area of 10,000 contiguous pages known as area A2. Successive passes in the merge sort move pages from A1 to A2 and back again. In reality we don't need so much extra space, but the algorithm is easier to explain with these two distinct areas. We start by assuming that there is no order whatsoever to the rows and proceed to describe pass 1 of the M-way merge sort. Note that in describing passes of the M-way merge sort, we won't consider any sequential prefetch I/O optimizations. Later, when sequential prefetch I/O is considered, we will describe a slightly more general N-way merge sort, with N < M.

Pass 1. The sort module reads the first block of M pages of the table to be sorted, represented as pages 1, 2, . . . , M, from disk area A1 into memory; sorts the rows within the buffered area by a method to be described later (we assume that the sorted rows can be placed on M pages again after sorting so that no row laps across a page boundary—this is simple if all rows have the same length); and writes out these M pages as a *sorted block* to the corresponding positions on area A2, pages 1, 2, . . . , M. This process is repeated with successive blocks of M pages (possibly less for the final block, if M does not divide D). The module reads from area A1 the pages numbered $M * i + 1, M * i + 2, . . . , M * i + M$, sorts the rows in this block, and writes the resulting pages out to area A2, block B_{i-1}. Since we have fixed on the value M = 2 (an unrealistically small number, used for purposes of illustration), we can schematically picture the result of the first pass written to area A2 as follows:

Page	1 2	3 4	5 6	7 8	9 10	11 12	13 14	15 . . .	. . .	D – 1 D
Block	B_0	B_1	B_2	B_3	B_4	B_5	B_6	B_7		$B_{(D-1)/2}$

The pages are numbered 1, 2, 3, 4, . . . , D – 1, D, and they are blocked into pairs by blocks B_0, B_1, . . . , meaning that within each block (consisting of a pair of pages) all rows are in sorted order. We assume here that D is even, and the last two pages in area A2, D – 1 and D, are odd and even, respectively. If instead the last disk page D were an odd number, then the final block $B_{(D-1)/2}$ would be only a single disk page in length. In pass 1 we have initialized the disk sort process, but successive passes are where actual merges take place.

Later passes. Each merge pass reads in initial pages from groups of (up to) M blocks from the most recent pass completed and merges these blocks into a larger block, writing out one page at a time to the new block on the alternate area not containing input. As an example, pass 2 for the M = 2 example above takes the output from pass 1 on area A2, merges pairs of blocks containing two pages each, and writes the resulting ordered sequence of rows to blocks four pages in length on area A1.

Page	1 2 3 4	5 6 7 8	9 10 11 12	13 14 15 . . .	. . .	. . . D – 1 D
Block	B_1	B_2	B_3	B_4		$B_{(D-1)/4}$

Consider carefully how the I/O for this merge takes place. The merge pass begins by reading in the first page of block B_1 and the first page of block B_2. Both B_1 and B_2 are in sorted order, so it is clear that we only need to look at the first page of each block to find the smallest row contained in the two blocks. In fact, once these initial block pages have been read into memory, we only have to look at the initial row on each of these pages, comparing the two sortkey values to find the smallest row in sort order. Now we merge the two blocks to a larger output block, moving merged rows to a sort output page in buffer and performing disk reads and writes as necessary.

In the general case, we read in the first page from each of M blocks from the previous pass and place cursors pointing to the initial row in each page. We then determine the smallest row under any cursor and place it at the beginning of a buffer page set aside for sort output. (Recall that there are M + 1 pages of buffer available, one for a page in each block being merged and one for output.) At this point it is necessary to advance the cursor pointing to the row just merged to the next row in that block. If there are no more rows in the current page, we read in the next page from the containing block. If there are no more pages in the block, we drop this cursor and continue merging rows from the remaining cursors until all rows have been merged. Whenever the sort output page fills up, we write it out to the next page of the output block. At the end of this process, all rows in the M input blocks, b pages in length, have been merged into sort sequence on a new output block containing M * b pages. We continue merging M blocks at a time from the prior pass, until all rows have been merged into new longer blocks and the pass is complete. We perform successive passes until the size of the block output by a pass would exceed D; at this point the sort is complete.

EXAMPLE 9.8.1 Example of a Two-Way Merge Sort.

Assume a sequence of 2000-byte rows, two on each disk page, to be sorted in order by the key values of the following sequence, which represents the initial order of the rows.

57 22 99 64 12 29 46 7 91 58 69 17 65 36 33 28 77 6 54 63 88 95 38 44

After pass 1 of a two-way merge sort, we have (four rows to each two-page block):

22 57 64 99	7 12 29 46	17 58 69 91	28 33 36 65	6 54 63 77	38 44 88 95

After pass 2, we have (four-page blocks):

7 12 22 29 46 57 64 99	17 28 33 36 58 65 69 91	6 38 44 54 63 77 88 95

After pass 3, we have (eight-page blocks; the final block has no pair to merge with):

7 12 17 22 28 29 33 36 46 57 58 64 65 69 91 99	6 38 44 54 63 77 88 95

And finally, after pass 4, we have the sorted sequence:

6 7 12 17 22 28 29 33 36 38 44 46 54 57 58 63 64 65 69 77 88 91 95 99

∎

Pass number	Block size	I/Os in pass
1	2	20,000
2	4	20,000
3	8	20,000
4	16	20,000
5	32	20,000
6	64	20,000
7	128	20,000
8	256	20,000
9	512	20,000
10	1024	20,000
11	2048	20,000
12	4096	20,000
13	8192	20,000
14	16,384	20,000

Figure 9.23 Sequence of Passes for Disk Sort of 10,000 Pages Using Two-Way Merge Sort

It is clear that all nonterminal blocks increase by a factor of M in size during each pass of an M-way merge sort. Each page from blocks of the prior pass needs to be read in only once, and an equivalent number of pages written out during the pass to create these longer blocks. Thus pass 1 requires 2D page I/Os, and each successive merge pass requires 2D pages also. Figure 9.23 gives output block sizes and I/Os required for successive passes of the two-way merge algorithm, assuming 10,000 pages of data.

Recall that when the block size exceeds the number of pages in the table, the table has been successfully sorted. This means that the table has been successfully sorted with pass 14, using 14 * 20,000 = 280,000 I/Os. More generally, after K passes, we have achieved a block size of 2^K, and we complete our sort when $2^K \geq D$, or in other words when $K = \text{CEIL}(\log_2(D))$. Thus the total number of I/Os required to perform a two-way merge sort of D pages is $2\text{CEIL}(\log_2(D)) * D$.

The two-way merge sort is not an optimal disk sort, of course, given that a reasonably large amount of buffer space exists. An M-way merge sort increases block length by a factor of M with each pass. Thus we will complete our sort after K passes, where $M^K \geq D$, or in other words where $K = \text{CEIL}(\log_M(D))$. Each pass still requires only 2D page I/Os, so the total number of I/Os required for an M-way merge sort of D pages is $2\text{CEIL}(\log_M(D)) * D$.

This change, from $\log_2(D)$ to $\log_M(D)$ as a factor of the needed I/Os, is quite important. Figure 9.24 gives output block sizes and I/Os required for successive passes of the 4-way merge algorithm, assuming 10,000 pages of data. Figure 9.25 gives these figures for a 100-way merge sort.

EXAMPLE 9.8.2 Example of a Three-Way Merge Sort.
Given the same sequence as that of the previous example, demonstrate a three-way merge sort. We start with the initial order:

Pass number	Block size	I/Os in pass
1	4	20,000
2	16	20,000
3	64	20,000
4	256	20,000
5	1024	20,000
6	4096	20,000
7	16,384	20,000

Figure 9.24   Sequence of Passes for Disk Sort of 10,000 Pages Using Four-Way Merge Sort

Pass number	Block size	I/Os in pass
1	100	20,000
2	10,000	20,000

Figure 9.25   Passes for Disk Sort of 10,000 Pages with 100-Way Merge Sort

57 22 99 64 12 29 46 7 91 58 69 17 65 36 33 28 77 6 54 63 88 95 38 44

After pass 1, we have three-page blocks:

12 22 29 57 64 99	7 17 46 58 69 91	6 28 33 36 65 77	38 44 54 63 88 95

After pass 2, we have

6 7 12 17 22 28 29 33 36 46 57 58 64 65 69 77 91 99	38 44 54 63 88 95

And with pass 3, we have the same sorted order that we got with a two-way merge sort:

6 7 12 17 22 28 29 33 36 38 44 46 54 57 58 63 64 65 69 77 88 91 95 99

■

EXAMPLE 9.8.3 Two-Step Plan Requiring Sort.
Recall Example 9.3.6, in which we used the naddrx index for the prospects table, created by the command

```
create index naddrx on prospects (zipcode, city, straddr, name) . . . ;
```

and needed to find a plan for the query (modified slightly here to require a sort):

```
select name, straddr from prospects
    where zipcode between 02159 and 04158
    order by name, straddr;
```

The query plan performs an INDEXONLY step, where the range of leaf-level entries with zip-code values from 02159 to 04158 is accessed using sequential prefetch, and the name and straddr values are extracted. Given that FF(zipcode between 02159 and 04158) is approximately 2/100, the index scan step to extract these values needs to access 1 million entries of 60 bytes each, 15,000 disk pages, so the I/O cost is about 15,000 S, requiring 15,000/800 = 18.75 seconds.

A sort must be performed to place the output (name, straddr) rows into the proper order for output, so we begin by finding the length of the temporary table IT1 created to hold these rows. We have assumed that both the name and straddr columns are 20 bytes in length, so the rows are 40 bytes long and can fit 100 on a page. We need to materialize a table of 1,000,000 rows, requiring 10,000 disk pages.

Assume that we can only spare 11 memory buffer pages to perform the sort (an unrealistically small number, used for purposes of illustration). We can therefore perform a ten-way merge sort. After pass 1 we have blocks of size 10; after pass 2, size 100; after pass 3, size 1000; after pass 4, size 10,000, and we are done. Now it is important to realize that there is no opportunity to perform sequential prefetch I/O in the I/Os we are performing during block merge I/O. Therefore passes 1 through 4 each require 5000 page reads and 5000 writes, a total of $4 * 2 * 5000 = 40,000$ R. The final pass does not need to perform disk writes, since the rows are now in the right order to be returned to the user. We will materialize the rows in the final pass on buffered pages and output them as quickly as possible to the user and then deallocate the pages so the final writes are not needed. Therefore the I/O cost of the final pass is 5000 R, and the total I/O cost for the sort is 45,000 R, requiring 45,000/80 = 562.5 seconds.

Note that the final pass of the sort step never has a cost for page writes unless a subsequent step requires a materialized table for input. It is much more common to pass off the output from one step to the input of the next step without materializing the rows passed. You should be sensitive to this "end-game" efficiency in the last pass of a sort.   ∎

In modern database systems the number of buffer pages available for a sort is large enough so that a two-pass sort is probably the longest anyone will see. We make a rough assumption that 100-page sorts occur entirely in memory and all other sorts occur in two passes.

9.9   Query Performance Benchmarks: A Case Study

A *software benchmark* is a prescription for a set of measurements to evaluate some category of software capability, usually performance. A good benchmark allows an administrator to make a purchase decision for a hardware/software platform based purely on cost-performance considerations. Alternatively if the purchase is to be made based on other considerations, such as compatibility with existing systems, the administrator may wish to ensure that there are no cost-performance problems serious enough to alter this decision. Benchmarks also offer a good quality assurance test for software developers, allowing them to plan and implement their new product releases to improve performance in critical areas.

598

The *Set Query benchmark* presented in the next few sections measures database system performance for a wide range of queries. The queries are defined in terms of SQL, but can be implemented in other query languages as well and are meant to be portable to as many platforms as possible—for example, **DB2** on an IBM OS/390 mainframe, **ORACLE** on a Sun Solaris UNIX system, or FoxPro on a Windows PC. The measurements reported here resulted from a benchmark in which **DB2** version 2.3 was run on a small IBM system/390.

It is hoped that these concrete results, and the accompanying discussion of the query plans from which they arose, will solidify in your mind an appreciation for the way **DB2** performs queries that could not be achieved by discussion of theory alone. However, a great deal of detail is reported in the following sections, and mastery of these details may not come easily. You are encouraged to proceed with care to avoid confusion, to take the details that follow one at a time, and to refer to the exercises at the end of the chapter for a test of understanding. All of the basic principles needed to follow the discussion have already been presented, but frequent references to earlier sections for supporting details may be necessary.

IMPORTANT NOTE: OLD DISK I/O RATES ARE IN USE IN THIS SECTION. In this section, we will use disk I/O rates typical of the early 1990s when this data was collected. These rates are just half the rates quoted in Figure 9.10, that is, 40 pages/second for random I/O, 100 pages/second for list prefetch, and 400 pages/second for sequential I/O. Considering the length of time elapsed, disks have not progressed much in access speed to pages. In the same period, their typical disk storage capacity has risen from 500 MB to 10 GB, a factor of 20.

Note that the Set Query benchmark has a difficult task comparing database performance of the many different architectures with which it must deal, and it achieves this comparison by imposing a simple unifying criterion by rating each platform with a single figure: dollar cost per query per minute ($/QPM). The dollar cost of the system represents the cost for hardware, software, and maintenance over a five-year period. (Software and maintenance are often licensed on a monthly or yearly basis, even when the hardware is purchased all at once. At the end of five years, it is common to assume that the system is totally depreciated and to replace it with a newer, faster, and cheaper one.) The "query per minute" (QPM) rating for the system is a measurement of throughput for a specific query *workload* (see Section 9.1), all queries of the benchmark receiving equal weight. Although this may seem rather limiting, a more sophisticated approach is possible where the QPM rating for an arbitrary workload can be derived from published detailed timings, required by the benchmark, for each of the individual queries measured. This is an extremely flexible capability, and theoretically it allows the DBA to compare performance on different platforms for the specific workload for which the DBA is responsible.

In Chapter 10 we will cover a different benchmark, known as the TPC-A benchmark, which measures database performance for update transactions; but for now we concentrate on **DB2** query performance to round out our coverage of query optimization.

The BENCH Table

The Set Query benchmark performs all its queries on a single table, known as the BENCH table, which is specified in great detail so that everyone performing the benchmark will get the same results. The default BENCH table contains 1,000,000 rows of 200 bytes each, and the disk pages containing the rows should be loaded 95% full. (A BENCH table with more than 1,000,000 rows is possible within the framework of the specification, but we do not consider this variation in what follows.) To offer indexed predicates with a range of filter factors, the BENCH table has 13 indexed columns with integer values, assumed to be 4 bytes in length. To start with, we have the KSEQ column, a key column with values 1, 2, . . . , 1,000,000, in the same order as the loaded rows. We see best performance if KSEQ is a column with perfect clustering, meaning that the rows in sequence by KSEQ, and the pages on which the rows lie, are all blocked together in successive order on disk. This can usually be achieved, even with database products that do not support clustering indexes, by using a freshly initialized disk to hold the data and sorting the rows in KSEQ order before loading them. All the other columns contain natural integer values with cardinality suggested by their name; for example, column K2 has only values 1 and 2, and K4 has values 1, 2, 3, and 4. Figure 9.26 gives a list of all indexed columns in the BENCH table.

Note that the letter K appearing at the end of a column name, as in K40K, represents a factor of 1000. Thus K40K has values from 1 to 40,000. All indexed columns of the BENCH table other than the KSEQ column have randomly generated integer values in the appropriate range specified in Figure 9.26. The random number generation function assigning values to the columns is provided in the benchmark specification to ensure identical results for different sites performing the benchmark. Of course the numbers are

Column name	Range of values contained in the column
KSEQ	1, 2, . . . , 1,000,000 in sequential order
K2	1, 2 at random
K4	1, 2, 3, 4 at random
K5	1, 2, 3, 4, 5 at random
K10	1, 2, . . . , 10 at random
K25	1, 2, . . . , 25 at random
K100	1, 2, . . . , 100 at random
K1K	1, 2, . . . , 1000 at random
K10K	1, 2, . . . , 10,000 at random
K40K	1, 2, . . . , 40,000 at random
K100K	1, 2, . . . , 100,000 at random
K250K	1, 2, . . . , 250,000 at random
K500K	1, 2, . . . , 500,000 at random

Figure 9.26 Indexed Columns of the BENCH Table

600
only pseudo-random, since they are generated by a simple function. The effect, however, is that each column seems to have random values in the appropriate range. See Figure 9.27 for a tabulation of the indexed columns of the first ten rows of the BENCH table. The random nature of these columns allows us to give a rather precise statistical prediction of the result of many queries. For example, consider the query

```
select count(*) from BENCH where K5 = 2;
```

Since there are five different values for K5, the filter factor for the predicate K5 = 2 is 1/5 = 0.20, and with 1,000,000 rows in the BENCH table we expect to retrieve a number close to 200,000. (The actual number retrieved is 200,637.)

The 13 indexed columns have a total length of 13 * 4 = 52 bytes. To make up the additional 148 bytes of a 200-byte row, the BENCH table has eight character columns that are never used in retrievals: S1 (char 8) and S2 through S8 (char 20). The decision to avoid queries by non-indexed columns is reasonable, considering the resource cost of a tablespace scan, which we will see shortly.

The rows contain 200 bytes of user information but are actually a bit longer because of necessary overhead information. With rows exactly 200 bytes in length, we would expect to be able to fit 20 rows on a 4-KB disk page loaded 100% full. With 1,000,000 rows this would mean 1,000,000/20 = 50,000 pages for data rows. Because of the extra row length and the fact that pages are only 95% full, there are actually 18 rows to a page in **DB2** (version 2.3), and the number of data pages is CEIL(1,000,000/18) = 55,556. See Figure 9.28 for **DB2** statistics on the BENCH table.

All indexes are also loaded 95% full, one for each indexed column (there are no indexes that concatenate different columns), and index names are based on the corresponding column name with the letter X affixed; thus column K100 has index K100X. Indexes with an extremely large number of duplicate values, such as K2 through K100,

KSEQ	K500K	K250K	K100K	K40K	K10K	K1K	K100	K25	K10	K5	K4	K2
1	16808	225250	50074	23659	8931	273	45	4	4	5	1	2
2	484493	243043	7988	2504	2328	730	41	13	4	5	2	2
3	129561	70934	93100	279	1817	336	98	2	3	3	3	2
4	80980	129150	36580	38822	1968	673	94	12	6	1	1	2
5	140195	186358	35002	1154	6709	945	69	16	5	2	3	2
6	227723	204667	28550	38025	7802	854	78	9	9	4	3	2
7	28636	158014	23866	29815	9064	537	26	20	6	5	2	2
8	46518	184196	30106	10405	9452	299	89	24	6	3	1	1
9	436717	130338	54439	13145	1502	898	72	4	8	4	2	2
10	222295	227095	21610	26232	9746	176	36	24	3	5	1	1

Figure 9.27   Indexed Column Values for the First Ten Rows of the BENCH Table

	CARD	NPAGES
BENCH table	1000000	55,556
	COLCARD	INDEX NLEAF
KSEQ	1000000	2080
K500K	432419	2168
K250K	245497	1682
K100K	99996	1303
K40K	40000	1147
K10K	10000	1069
K1K	1000	1053
K100	100	1051
K25	25	1051
K10	10	1051
K5	5	1051
K4	4	1051
K2	2	1051

Figure 9.28 Statistics for the BENCH Table in **DB2** Version 2.3

have index entries averaging about 4 bytes in length because of index compression performed by **DB2**. Thus we should be able to fit about 1000 entries on each leaf page (if the pages were 100% full), and about 1000 index leaf pages would be needed to contain all entries. In Figure 9.28 we provide the actual measured values for the number of disk pages (NLEAF) for each index. For indexes with fewer duplicates, the compression becomes less valuable and the effective length greater, so that more disk pages are needed. There is no compression possible with KSEQ, and compression doesn't help with K500K, so NLEAF is largest for these indexes.

Note in Figure 9.28 that the COLCARD value for each column is what you would expect in all the low-cardinality columns, but it is surprisingly deficient in the large-cardinality columns. For example, K500K has a COLCARD value of only 432,419, a good deal less than the 500,000 values possible. The reason for this becomes immediately apparent if we consider the random generation of column values and picture throwing 1,000,000 darts into 500,000 slots. By formula (7.6.4), the expected number of slots hit is

$$M (1 - e^{-N/M}) = 500,000 (1 - e^{-2})$$

Working this out on a calculator, we get 432,332, close to the actual value observed.

Load Measurements

The measurements reported in what follows were taken running **DB2** version 2.3 on an IBM 9221 model 170 mainframe, with 1200 4-KB memory buffer pages (the buffer space required by the benchmark) and two 3390 disk drives (any number is permitted, but the greatest efficiency comes when one disk drive is used for data pages and one is used for indexes).

	Elapsed time (secs)	CPU time (secs)	Disk MB
LOAD	10,170	3186	
RUNSTATS	5082	1535	
Disk space used			296

Figure 9.29   BENCH Table Load Measurements, **DB2** Version 2.3, IBM 9221 Model 170

The elapsed and CPU times for loading the BENCH table and executing RUNSTATS to gather statistics are given in Figure 9.29, together with the disk storage required to hold the table and indexes.

9.10   Query Performance Measurements

In the following section we present measurements from running suites of queries labeled as Q1, Q2A, Q2B, Q3A, Q3B, Q4A, Q4B, Q5, Q6A, and Q6B. You are again warned to proceed with care, to take the details that follow one at a time. Each suite of queries normally consists of a set of measurements of a single SQL query form, with predicate variation to use a number of different indexed columns and provide a spectrum of filter factor characteristics. (See, for example, Figure 9.30 for query Q1 results.) Paired queries such as Q2A and Q2B have comparable but slightly different SQL forms.

For each query measured we provide the elapsed time in seconds (that is, wall clock time waiting for response), CPU time in seconds, and count of pages requested, broken

KN	Elapsed time (secs)	CPU time (secs)	Get page requests	Random I/O count	Sequential prefetch I/O count	List prefetch I/O count
KSEQ	1.33	0.07	3	3		
K100K	0.59	0.08	3	3		
K10K	0.89	0.07	3	3		
K1K	0.67	0.09	4	4		
K100	0.83	0.19	14	2	2	
K25	1.73	0.58	44	25	3	
K10	2.20	1.34	107	54	5	
K5	3.47	2.55	214	46	9	
K4	5.09	3.13	265	57	10	
K2	7.73	6.17	528	48	18	

Figure 9.30   Q1 Measurements

down into random I/Os, sequential prefetch I/Os, and list prefetch I/Os. (Any two of these I/O counts can be zero.) These numbers are extracted from a standard MVS logging facility by the DB2PM product (**DB2** performance monitor), which is licensed separately and priced in Section 9.11. The random I/Os reported are designated *sync I/Os* in DB2PM reports. Note that all queries reported here are submitted as Embedded SQL statements from a program, and the elapsed and CPU times reported are slightly less than what you would see submitting ad hoc queries from the standard user interface (SPUFI). We also try to make the I/O measurements consistent by flushing the memory buffers in advance of each query suite, so that disk pages to be accessed are not likely to be already resident. The process used to flush the buffers is to perform a long query of a different kind, so some small overlap is possible as in normal use. We explain the results from each query as we progress, in terms of the EXPLAIN results from **DB2**.

Query Q1

Query Q1 has the form

```
For each KN ∈ {KSEQ, K100K, . . . . , K4, K2}
    select count(*) from BENCH where KN = 2;
```

As indicated by the set notation preceding the Select statement, the symbol KN stands for any one of the indexed columns KSEQ, K100K, . . . , K4, K2. Each of these cases represents a query with measures given in Figure 9.30, and together they make up the Q1 query "suite."

Note that Q1 is a typical early query in text retrieval applications (see Example 3.10.7). A user searching for all published journal articles with a specific keyword in the abstract might well start by asking how many articles contain that keyword, and then later refine the search further until the number of articles counted is small enough to retrieve the full abstracts of the documents. Clearly the filter factor of the keyword might vary dramatically and unexpectedly from one keyword to another (keyword = 'experiment%' versus keyword = 'ruthenium'), and this motivates having KN range over various column cardinalities.

The EXPLAIN command applied to all queries in the Q1 suite shows that the appropriate KN index is used (for example, in the case where KN represents K100, ACCESSTYPE = I, and ACCESSNAME = K100X), and also that the query is resolved entirely in the index without recourse to the data (INDEXONLY = Y). Thus in the top row of Figure 9.30, where KN represents KSEQ (we symbolize this in what follows by KN ≡ KSEQ), we see that three random I/Os are performed to access the three levels of the KSEQX index down to the unique entry at the leaf level. Recall that the buffer has been flushed of most useful pages, so the maximum number of I/Os is usually performed.

In all cases with duplicate values, the predicate KN = 2 is resolved in the index by walking down to the leftmost value 2 in the appropriate index leaf level, then progressing from left to right until there are no more entries with value 2. For the predicate K100K = 2, this means that approximately ten entries are traversed; for K10K, 100 entries; and so

604

on. (The precise number of rows retrieved for most queries in the Set Query benchmark is given in Appendix D.) Since nearly 1000 entries fit on each leaf page, we would not expect more than three I/Os for the two predicates just mentioned (the leaf-level traversal will probably not cross pages), and perhaps four for K1K = 2, with 1000 entries (where the traversal is practically guaranteed to cross from one leaf page to another). With the predicate K2 = 2, we would expect to traverse approximately 500,000 entries at the leaf level, and this implies about 526 leaf pages, or half of NLEAF for the K2X index (see Figure 9.28). We see from the number of Get Page requests, G = 528, that these 526 leaf pages and an additional two index pages are accessed. We also see that 18 sequential prefetch I/Os are performed and 48 random I/Os. We can calculate the total number of pages accessed through prefetch as (528 − 48) = 480, and the average number of pages read in each prefetch as (480)/18 = 26.7. Note that **DB2** uses 18 sequential prefetch I/Os of 26.7 pages each, rather than the maximum prefetch size of 32 pages. The reasons for this are technical and are of little interest, but note that short prefetch I/Os of this kind appear on several rows of measurements for Q1.

Most of the elapsed time for the longer queries arises from CPU time, however, rather than I/O wait time. We can roughly calculate the elapsed time for I/O using our rule of thumb. In the K2 case, 480 S at 400 S per second gives 1.20 seconds, and 48 R at 40 R per second gives 1.20 seconds, so the total I/O elapsed time is 2.40 seconds. Adding a CPU time of 6.17 seconds, we come up with 8.57 elapsed seconds. Since the elapsed time was only 7.73 seconds, we conclude that some of the I/O time overlapped with CPU time, a perfectly reasonable effect that we continue to see in queries that follow. The range of CPU time measurements is well predicted by a linear function of the number of leaf-level entries traversed. If the predicted CPU time is represented by T and the number of entries traversed is N, then we can write

```
T = .0000122N + 0.07
```

This linear form has a maximum error of 0.05 seconds across the entire range of measurements. Here the constant 0.07 seconds represents a relatively constant start-up cost, and the constant .0000122 seconds represents the time needed to deal with (that is, count) each leaf-level entry, not counting overhead for I/O and other operations that are less significant. Given that this is a 6.5-MIPS CPU, the actual number of instructions executed for each entry is $(6,500,000)(0.0000122) = 79$, an important improvement over past releases, but still somewhat large when we consider that all that is being done is to count successive entries in a long list. Much more efficient counting methods exist; the original Set Query paper measured performance of a database product known as MODEL 204, which performed Q1 queries 20 to 30 times more efficiently. But most relational database products are not as efficient as **DB2** in terms of CPU.

Query Q2A

Query Q2A has the form

```
For each KN ∈ {KSEQ, K100K, . . . . , K4}
    select count(*) from BENCH where K2 = 2 and KN = 3;
```

The measurements are shown in Figure 9.31a.

Q2A is another typical early query in text retrieval application, searching for journal articles with two properties, one with a low filter factor (date > '65/01/31' and keyword = 'plutonium'). Query Q2A might also be used in direct-marketing applications to estimate the number of prospects with a given pair of qualities (gender = 'M' and hobby = 'tennis'). One of the reasons this query type was included in the benchmark was to measure how well a database product performs in combining RID lists from two separate indexes. As we have learned, the **DB2** product has the capability to combine such RID lists by using the MX type plan explained in Section 9.6. Having combined the two indexes, there is no need to ever access the data rows, since the select list contains only a count(*) function that can be satisfied by counting the final RID list.

However, the EXPLAIN command for this suite of queries shows that an MX plan is never used, and the reason is quite illuminating. Recall that a single RID list can use only 50% of the RID pool, and the RID pool space is half the size of the disk buffer pool. Since there are 1200 pages in the disk buffer pool allowed by the benchmark, the RID pool contains 600 pages worth of space, or about 2400 KB. Now consider the predicate K2 = 2. We expect to find 500,000 rows that satisfy this predicate, and 500,000 RIDs, at 4 bytes each, take up 2000 KB—more than the 50% of the 2400 KB of the RID pool. Therefore the predicate K2 = 2 cannot be extracted in an MX-type plan, and an alternative plan must be used.

The EXPLAIN command for the Q2A suite reveals that **DB2** uses two different plans for different queries. In cases where KN does not represent K4 (KN ≠ K4), **DB2** uses the predicate with the smaller filter factor (KN = 3) in a matching index scan (ACCESSTYPE = I) to retrieve rows from the data, then tests each row to resolve the remaining predicate,

KN	Elapsed time (secs)	CPU time (secs)	Get page requests	Random I/O count	Sequential prefetch I/O count	List prefetch I/O count
KSEQ	0.38	0.08	4	4		
K100K	1.27	0.09	14	4		1
K10K	2.27	0.14	100	4		4
K1K	12.46	0.39	969	7		31
K100	71.33	2.29	9167	17	3	287
K25	108.41	7.59	28,935	45	4	903
K10	125.83	14.35	47,248	47	5	1474
K5	135.19	21.05	54,792	61	8	1706
K4	133.27	26.90	55,559	56	1737	

Figure 9.31a Q2A Measurements

counting the rows that satisfy both conditions. In the case where KN ≡ K4, however, a tablespace scan is used (ACCESSTYPE = R) to solve the query. In the bottom row of Figure 9.31a, where KN ≡ K4, we see 1737 sequential prefetch I/Os and 56 random I/Os performed. The total number of pages read in is 55,559 (note that in Figure 9.28, NPAGES = 55,556). Sequential prefetch I/O reads (55,559 − 56) = 55,503 pages, and we see 55,508/1737 = 32 pages per sequential prefetch. Our rule of thumb says that the elapsed time required for 55,503 S is 55,503/400 seconds = 138.76 seconds, and the 56 R adds a relatively insignificant 1.4 seconds. Obviously this gives a slight overestimate of about 5%—138.76 + 1.4 = 140.16 seconds compared to the measured time of 133.27 seconds. We can assume that the CPU time of 26.90 seconds completely overlaps with I/O during this heavily I/O-limited query.

Now consider the predicates on the other randomly generated columns referenced in suite Q2A, KN = 3, where KN ∈ {K100K, K10K, K1K, K100, K25, K10, K5}. The measurements for random and sequential prefetch I/Os for the corresponding rows of Figure 9.31a correspond to the resources used to scan through the appropriate index and compare quite closely to the INDEXONLY measures of Q1. (For example, the resources to evaluate the predicate K5 = 3 in Figure 9.31a are eight sequential prefetch I/Os and 61 random I/Os. In Figure 9.30, the index I/O resources to evaluate the predicate K5 = 2 are nine sequential prefetch I/Os and 46 random I/Os.) The list prefetch I/Os appearing in Figure 9.31 are used exclusively to access the desired rows. In the case of K100K = 3, there are about ten rows retrieved—probably all on separate disk pages—and there is one list prefetch I/O. A list prefetch I/O can access *up to* 32 pages, but in this case it accesses only about ten. Similarly, in the case K10K = 3, there are about 100 rows retrieved—probably on 100 distinct disk pages—and four list prefetch I/Os. Consider the case where K100 = 3. The number of rows retrieved is about 10,000. To see the number of disk pages retrieved, picture this as the problem of throwing 10,000 darts randomly into 55,556 disk pages and asking how many pages are hit. Formula [8.6.4] gives us

$$E(\text{no. pages hit}) = M\,(1 - e^{-N/M}) = 55{,}556\,(1 - e^{\,(-10{,}000/55{,}556)}) = 9152$$

Now to calculate the number of list prefetch I/Os needed to pick up 9,196 disk pages, we take CEIL(9,152/32) = 286, quite close to the 287 list prefetch I/Os performed.

The fact that an MX-type plan cannot be used for this query suite is a serious problem. If we could combine indexes without going to the data, the maximum elapsed times for Q2A would probably compare best to the Q1 time for K2 plus some other time in Q1 to extract the RID list of KN, a maximum of less than 20 seconds. Instead we see numerous, much larger elapsed times. Note that **DB2** had enough RID pool space in most cases to handle the Q2A queries (the final case might not fit), but an inflexible rule made it impossible to take advantage of this. This is not the behavior we might expect from a query optimizer. Still **DB2** has a good deal of flexibility, and the lesson to take from this is that *the DBA should always plan a buffer pool as large as possible, and order more memory if necessary.*

Query Q2B

Query Q2B has the form

```
For each KN ∈ {KSEQ, K100K, . . . , K4}
    select count(*) from BENCH where K2 = 2 and not KN = 3;
```

See Figure 9.31b for the measurements of this query suite.

Q2B is a variant of Q2A that was suggested when the Set Query benchmark was originally being tested with a group of commercial users. It represents a query type that finds use in cases where it can be efficiently executed (MODEL 204 users can usually get a response to this query in less than a second). In the case of **DB2**, a number of problems arise for efficient indexed use. We would like to see the query optimizer perform a non-matching index scan to extract a RID list for the predicate not KN = 3 and then perform MX processing with the predicate K2 = 2, thus avoiding accesses to all the table rows. However, the RID list for K2 = 2 cannot be extracted, as we saw in the discussion of Q2A, because of the limited size of the RID pool. Even if there were no limitation on the RID pool, another factor rules out MX processing, since **DB2** will not perform a non-matching index scan on KN to extract a RID list (RID pool rule 2 of Definition 9.6.1). With the KN index ruled out, a simple index scan on the predicate K2 = 2 does not have sufficient filtering power to exclude any disk pages from consideration (there are 17 rows per page), so the query optimizer chooses a tablespace scan for all queries of the Q2B suite. Measurements compare to the K4 row of Q2A.

KN	Elapsed time (secs)	CPU time (secs)	Get page requests	Random I/O count	Sequential prefetch I/O count	List prefetch I/O count
KSEQ	142.73	30.07	55,569	56	1737	
K100K	137.83	30.24	55,568	63	1737	
K10K	137.45	30.12	55,569	47	1737	
K1K	140.33	30.42	55,569	59	1737	
K100	141.73	30.17	55,569	59	1737	
K25	144.65	30.25	55,569	60	737	
K10	139.72	29.82	55,569	53	1737	
K5	142.73	30.07	55,569	56	1737	
K4	135.29	29.13	55,562	48	1737	

Figure 9.31b   Q2B Measurements

Query Q3A

Query Q3A has the form

```
For each KN ∈ {K100K, K10K, K100, K25, K10, K5, K4}
    select sum(K1K) from BENCH
        where KSEQ between 400000 and 500000 and KN = 3;
```

Figure 9.32a contains measurements of this query suite.

Query Q3A was created to model a direct-marketing type of application, where rows of a prospects table within a range of zip codes (in a given geographical area) and having some other property (hobby = 'tennis') must be examined in detail. Up until now, all queries considered have been ones that could be satisfied by examining only index information. (Although **DB2**'s rules make this impossible in Q2A and Q2B, MODEL 204 is able to satisfy these queries in index only, with much faster response times.) In the Q3A case, however, the set function sum(K1K) cannot be satisfied in index, since the K1K values do not appear in any index used in the WHERE clause. (Note that Figure 9.32a has no entry for KN ≡ K1K, so the INDEXONLY case is avoided.) Therefore the rows selected must be accessed in order to sum the K1K values. Although Query Q3A retrieves only a single set function value, it does most of the work of a query that retrieves a column value from each row.

The EXPLAIN command reveals that there are two different types of query plans used in performing this suite. For KN ≡ K100K and KN ≡ K10K, a matching index scan is performed on K100K and K10K, respectively, and the predicate on KSEQ is then tested for the rows retrieved. In Figure 9.32a the random I/Os are used to retrieve the index entries, and the list prefetch I/Os are used to retrieve the rows, approximately ten rows with one prefetch in the K100K case and 100 rows with four prefetches in the K10K case. It turns out that with a maximum of 100 rows to retrieve using random I/O, there is no advan-

KN	Elapsed time (secs)	CPU time (secs)	Get page requests	Random I/O count	Sequential prefetch I/O count	List prefetch I/O count
K100K	1.84	0.09	24	8		1
K10K	2.06	0.14	110	8		4
K100	14.43	3.12	5778	200	184	
K25	14.89	3.37	5778	202	184	
K10	15.35	3.73	5778	199	184	
K5	15.07	4.17	5778	208	184	
K4	15.01	4.24	5778	197	184	

Figure 9.32a Q3A Measurements

tage to be gained in performing multiple index access, extracting a RID list from KSEQ to
save some of those row accesses—we have reached the point of diminishing returns seen
in Section 9.6.

For low-cardinality columns, KN ∈ {K100, K25, K10, K5, K4}, the BETWEEN predicate
on KSEQ is used in a matching index scan, and the predicate on KN is tested for the rows
retrieved. For each of these cases, Figure 9.32a shows that 5778 pages are read in. Most
of these represent about 10% of the index leaf pages and 10% of the data pages to evaluate the predicate KSEQ between 400000 and 500000, and we can calculate this from the
statistics of Figure 9.28 as NLEAF/10 + NPAGES/10 = 208 + 5556 = 5764 pages. We see
that 184 sequential prefetch I/Os are used to retrieve 5778 − 200 = 5578 pages (in the
KN ≡ K100 case, relatively representative I/O use for the low-cardinality columns), and
this means that the average number of pages read in sequential prefetch I/Os is about
30.3.

DB2 performs extremely well in this query suite, beating MODEL 204 and all other
current products by a wide margin, because of the unique prefetch I/O capability that is
part of the **DB2** bag of tricks, aided by intelligent disk controllers.

Query Q3B

Query Q3B has the form

```
For each KN ∈ {K100K, K10K, K100, K25, K10, K5, K4}
    select sum(K1K) from BENCH
        where (KSEQ between 400000 and 410000
        or KSEQ between 420000 and 430000
        or KSEQ between 440000 and 450000
        or KSEQ between 460000 and 470000
        or KSEQ between 480000 and 500000)
        and KN = 3;
```

Figure 9.32b lists the measurements of this query.

Query Q3B was created as a variant of Query Q3A after experience with direct-
marketing applications showed that prospects in a given geographical area do not normally fall within a single range of zip codes, but in a union of different ranges. In addition, the query is a good one to evaluate advanced capabilities of the query optimizer.
Note that the BETWEEN predicates, connected by ORs in this query, together make up
60% of the single range covered in Q3A (a total 6% of the KSEQ range and clustered data
range).

The EXPLAIN command shows three different types of query plans used to perform
the Q3B suite. As with Q3A, when KN ≡ K100K or KN ≡ K10K, a matching index scan is
performed on K100K and K10K, respectively, and the predicates on KSEQ are then tested
for the rows retrieved to determine if one of them holds. The measurements for these
cases are very similar to those of Q3A. For the two lowest-cardinality columns, KN ≡ K5
and KN ≡ K4, EXPLAIN shows a plan with ACCESSTYPE = I, ACCESSNAME = KSEQX,

KN	Elapsed time (secs)	CPU time (secs)	Get page requests	Random I/O count	Sequential prefetch I/O count	List prefetch I/O count
K100K	2.01	0.09	17	5		1
K10K	2.23	0.14	109	7		4
K100	7.57	2.48	714	34	12	18
K25	10.66	3.66	1934	57	7	55
K10	14.37	5.93	3068	79	14	88
K5	57.76	47.33	5430	250	173	
K4	57.77	47.58	5430	235	173	

Figure 9.32b Q3B Measurements

and MATCHCOLS = 0; in other words, a non-matching index scan on KSEQ. What seems to be happening is that the KSEQ index values ranging from 400,000 to 500,000 are examined, and for each value the KSEQ predicates are tested to determine that one of them holds. With the resulting RIDs, rows from the BENCH table are read in (sequential prefetch I/O is used, because the data is clustered by KSEQ), and the remaining KN = 3 predicate is tested. We see that a somewhat smaller number of sequential prefetch I/Os are being used in this case than in the Q3A results, since a smaller number of rows is being retrieved. The fact that the reduced number of sequential prefetch I/Os in Q3B exceeds 60% of the number in Q3A is not fully explained. Note that in these two cases, the CPU resources used (and resulting elapsed times) are extremely large compared to the CPU resources used in comparable cases of Q3A. This seems to arise from the necessity to test a number of BETWEEN predicates on all values extracted from the index in the non-matching index scan, and represents a serious resource cost.

For intermediate-cardinality columns, KN ∈ {K100, K25, K10}, MX processing is used to take the union of RID lists from the different BETWEEN predicates on KSEQ, then to intersect the result with the RID list from the predicate KN = 3. For example, the plan for the case KN ≡ K100 is given in Figure 9.33. In Figure 9.32b you should assume that sequential prefetch I/O is being used to access the KN and KSEQ index values, and then list prefetch is being used to access the data pages. The **DB2** query optimizer probably makes a mistake in this query suite using a non-matching index scan in the two cases of lowest-cardinality columns, judging by the large jump in CPU use for these cases. Nevertheless performance is quite good compared with most other products.

Queries Q4A and Q4B

The two variant query suites Q4A and Q4B have the form

```
select KSEQ, K500K from BENCH
    where <constraint with 3 (Q4A) or 5 (Q4B) ANDed predicates>;
```

ACCESSTYPE	MATCHCOLS	ACCESSNAME	PREFETCH	MIXOPSEQ
M	0		L	0
MX	1	K100X	S	1
MX	1	KSEQX	S	2
MX	1	KSEQX	S	3
MU	0			4
MX	1	KSEQX	S	5
MU	0			6
MX	1	KSEQX	S	7
MU	0			8
MX	1	KSEQX	S	9
MU	0			10
MI	0			11

Figure 9.33   EXPLAIN Plan for Q3B, in the Case KN = K100

Queries in suite Q4A have three predicates, and queries in suite Q4B have five predicates chosen from the sequence of ten predicates given in Figure 9.34. The filter factor for each predicate is given in a column on the right.

Predicates used in a query are chosen in sequence within the 1–10 order, with a given starting point and wraparound from predicate 10 back to predicate 1. For example, a query from suite Q4A with three predicates and starting point 5 will have predicates in the range 5–7 (that is, {5, 6, 7}), with the following form:

```
select KSEQ, K500K from BENCH
     where (K25 = 11 or K25 = 19) and K4 = 3 and K100 < 41;
```

No.	Predicate	FF	No.	Predicate	FF
(1)	K2 = 1	1/2	(6)	K4 = 3	1/4
(2)	K100 > 80	1/5	(7)	K100 < 41	2/5
(3)	K10K between 2000 and 3000	1/10	(8)	K1K between 850 and 950	1/10
(4)	K5 = 3	1/5	(9)	K10 = 7	1/10
(5)	(K25 = 11 or K25 = 19)	2/25	(10)	K25 between 3 and 4	2/25

Figure 9.34   Predicate Sequence, with Filter Factors FF, for Suite Q4

A query in suite Q4B with five predicates and starting point 7 will have predicates in the range 7–1 (that is, {7, 8, 9, 10, 1}) and the following form:

```
select KSEQ, K500K from BENCH
    where K100 < 41 and K1K between 850 and 950 and K10 = 7
    and K25 between 3 and 4 and K2 = 1;
```

A query of the kind measured in Q4A and Q4B is representative of a final form query resulting from a document retrieval search (for example, limiting articles by keywords, journal where they appeared, period of appearance, etc.) or direct-mail applications (for example, retrieving name and address for prospects in a given salary range, gender, hobby, geographical location, etc.). The measurements for query suites Q4A and Q4B are given in Figure 9.35a and 9.35b, respectively.

Predicate sequence range	Elapsed time (secs)	CPU time (secs)	Get page requests	Random I/O count	Sequential prefetch I/O count	List prefetch I/O count
1–3	109.04	32.29	17,321	102	14	531
2–4	62.10	26.91	4409	155	22	121
3–5	107.29	16.50	17,112	111	14	525
4–6	134.55	27.02	54,802	72	8	1706
5–7	156.67	39.47	55,834	126	1747	
6–8	127.00	30.42	47,378	73	5	1477
7–9	83.07	14.94	9393	115	11	287
8–10	22.74	10.69	1097	154	16	25

Figure 9.35a   Q4A Measurements

Predicate sequence range	Elapsed time (secs)	CPU time (secs)	Get page requests	Random I/O count	Sequential prefetch I/O count	List prefetch I/O count
1–5	63.17	21.06	4416	127	22	121
2–6	62.06	20.90	4416	165	22	121
3–7	109.02	15.72	17,377	160	24	525
4–8	109.60	15.82	17,613	180	23	532
5–9	84.30	10.48	9658	175	21	287
6–10	22.64	9.59	1092	161	16	25
7–1	22.96	9.71	1090	157	16	25

Figure 9.35b   Q4B Measurements

EXPLAIN tells us that all queries of Suite Q4A use either index scans or MX processing. Certain predicates from the sequence of Figure 9.34 are never used for indexing: predicate (1) with FF = 1/2, predicate (7) with FF = 1/5, and predicate (5) requiring a non-matching index scan, which is not allowed in RID processing, or else an MU step to achieve FF = 2/25. In addition, predicate (6), with FF = 1/4, is only used for the query with predicate range 5–7, where otherwise there would be no indexable predicate (since (5) and (7) are ruled out). Presumably the unused predicates are not used because of diminishing returns, as explained in Section 9.6. All query plans use all other predicates in the given range for indexing. This implies, for example, that the query with predicate range 1–3 performs MX processing on predicates (2) and (3) (predicate (1) is never used); the query with predicate range 5–7 is solved by a matching index scan on predicate (6), the only place where this predicate is ever used, since predicates (5) and (7) are ruled out; and finally, the query with predicate range 8–10 performs MX processing on all three predicates, (8), (9), and (10), since none of these is ruled out.

Knowing the predicates used, it is possible to estimate the number of rows accessed in the table and to confirm the reported number of I/Os. For example, with range 8–10, the product of the filter factors with the number of rows in the BENCH table gives (1/10) (1/10) (2/25) (1,000,000) = 800. This is also the total number of rows retrieved, since no other predicates exist, and from Appendix D we see that the precise number of rows retrieved in this case is 785. Sequential prefetch I/Os are generally used to access index data, and list prefetch I/Os to access data pages. Since the 785 rows to be retrieved lie on (to a first approximation) nearly 785 data pages, they can be brought into memory with CEIL(785/32) = 25 list prefetch I/Os, the number listed in Figure 9.35a for range 8–10.

More predicates are available from among the five used for queries in suite Q4B, so we expect consistent MX processing throughout and much smaller answer sets. EXPLAIN tells us that the queries of suite Q4B all use MX processing with three predicates, and that the predicates used are always the ones with the smallest filter factors, except that predicate (5), requiring a non-matching index scan or MU processing, is never used. Thus for example, the query with predicate range 4–8 performs MX processing on three of the predicates (4), (6), (7), and (8), with FF values 1/5, 1/4, 2/5, and 1/10, respectively, and chooses the three predicates with smallest values, (4), (6), and (8). For another example, we note that the query with predicate range 7–1 has predicates (7), (8), (9), (10), and (1) to choose from, and selects the three predicates with smallest FF values, (8), (9), and (10), the same as the query having predicate range 8–10 in suite Q4A. As a result, the I/Os for these two queries of Q4A and Q4B are nearly identical. The number of rows in the solution set for the Q4B query, however, is reduced from that of the Q4A query (785 from the discussion earlier), as a result of the filter factors of the two additional predicates, (1) and (7), so that the answer set is approximately (1/2) (2/5) (785) = 157. From Appendix D, we see that the exact number of rows retrieved in this Q4B query is 152.

Query Q5

Query Q5 has the form

```
For each pair (KN1, KN2) ∈ { (K2, K100), (K4, K25), (K10, K25) }
    select KN1, KN2, count(*) from BENCH
        group by KN1, KN2;
```

The measurements for query suite Q5 are given in Figure 9.36.

This query suite is representative of an application known as *crosstabs,* used in decision support systems to calculate the effect of one factor on another in a population. For example, a department store might have a table of customers, with columns containing information on hobby and incomeclass, and one giving levels of purchase totals (1–10, like incomeclass) in various store departments—for example, sportsw_purchases in the sportswear department. A crosstabs analysis of type Q5 can be used to see if there is some correlation between hobby and any desired category of purchases:

```
select count(*) from customers
    group by hobby, sportsw_purchases;
```

If some hobbies, such as sailing, show a high concentration of high-level purchases, then this group is a good choice for a mailing announcing a coming sale in the sportswear department.

EXPLAIN shows that queries in suite Q5 are implemented in two-step plans. In the first step (PLANNO = 1), a tablespace scan (ACCESSTYPE = R) goes through all the data pages and extracts the column pairs (KN1, KN2) into a temporary table. Certain I/Os to perform writes into this temporary table are not shown in Figure 9.36, because they are not reported. (Page writes do not generally occur as part of the plan but do occur later as the buffer pool runs out of space and must write changed pages out to disk to make room. The pages for this data are only used temporarily, however, and may escape being written out to disk entirely.) In the second step (PLANNO = 2), a sort step is performed on this temporary table (METHOD = 3, SORTC_GROUPBY = Y) on both columns KN1 and KN2, with the result that all identical terms are collected together, and in the output from this sort the number of pairs (KN1, KN2) of each identical type is counted and put out to the answer set. We see in Figure 9.36 the signature of a tablespace scan, 1735 sequential prefetch I/Os, that we have seen before. The CPU time makes up a large proportion of the elapsed time for these queries.

KN1, KN2	Elapsed time (secs)	CPU time (secs)	Get page requests	Random I/O count	Sequential prefetch I/O count	List prefetch I/O count
K2, K100	242	219	55,896	81	1737	
K4, K25	230	208	55,802	34	1737	
K10, K25	248	223	55,903	87	1737	

Figure 9.36   Q5 Measurements

Query Q6A

Query suites Q6A and Q6B exercise joins of two tables. Q6A has the form

```
For each KN ∈ {K100K, K40K, K10K, K1K, K100}
    select count(*) from BENCH B1, BENCH B2
        where B1.KN = 49 and B1.K250K = B2.K500K;
```

The measurements for query suite Q6A are given in Figure 9.37a.

Although the BENCH table plays two roles in this query, as B1 and B2, there is no advantage gained thereby over the case where two distinct tables exist, except for a very minor improvement in buffer residence. EXPLAIN tells us that all queries of suite Q6A are implemented as two-step plans performing a nested-loop join. In step 1 (PLANNO = 1) we use a matching index scan loop on KN to extract a RID list for rows to be extracted from the outer table (TABNO = 1—that is, rows with B1.KN = 49). For each row retrieved from B1 in the outer loop, the value B1.K250K has a fixed constant value, which we designate by K. In step 2 the nested-loop join (METHOD = 1), assuming a fixed row from the outer table B1, retrieves the count of rows in B2 where B2.K500K = K. A matching index scan on K500K is used for this, and since only a count is retrieved, the step has INDEXONLY = Y. Note that for each row found in the outer table, we expect to find about two rows in the inner table, since B2.K500K = K is true for about two rows of B2, as long as K lies in the range 1, 2, . . . , 500,000; and since K is extracted from B1.K250K this is certainly the case. Thus with KN ≡ K100, for example, we expect to find 10,000 rows in the outer table and a total of about 20,000 rows after the join with matching columns, which determines the total number of rows in the final answer from the inner table. From Appendix D, we see that the precise count retrieved is 19,948.

In this case, KN ≡ K100, approximately 10,000 rows from B1 must be accessed in the outer loop. As we calculated earlier in analyzing Q2A, these lie on approximately 9152 data pages, and the page reads are accomplished with 290 list prefetch I/Os. Most of the remaining I/Os are used to retrieve leaf-level entries from the K500K index to perform the final count.

KN	Elapsed time (secs)	CPU time (secs)	Get page requests	Random I/O count	Sequential prefetch I/O count	List prefetch I/O count
K100K	0.95	0.10	65	12		1
K40K	1.00	0.14	115	7		1
K10K	3.75	0.29	393	22		4
K1K	16.05	1.68	2313	15	36	31
K100	83.31	13.35	111,510	45	48	290

Figure 9.37a   Q6A Measurements

Query Q6B

Query Q6B has the form

```
For each KN ∈ {K40K, K10K, K1K, K100}
    select B1.KSEQ, B2.KSEQ from BENCH B1, BENCH B2
        where B1.KN = 99 and B1.K250K = B2.K500K and B2.K25 = 19;
```

The measurements for query suite Q6B are given in Figure 9.37b.

Query Q6B is similar to Q6A except for the new restriction on table B2 (B2.K25 = 19) and the fact that data, rather than just a count, is retrieved from columns in both tables. The EXPLAIN command shows that the nested-loop join (METHOD = 1) is used for queries in suite Q6B with KN ∈ {K40K, K10K, K1K}, but a merge join (METHOD = 2) is used when KN ≡ K100.

To start with discussion of the nested-loop join processing, the plan is very similar to the one used for all queries in suite Q6A. A matching index scan on KN is used to extract rows from the outer table, with B1.KN = 99. For each row retrieved from B1 we designate the fixed constant value B1.K250K by K. In the inner loop, instead of just retrieving a count from the K500K index, we retrieve rows in B2 where B2.K500K = K. These rows are then qualified by testing that B2.K25 = 19, and the resulting rows are joined with the row from outer table B1. Note that for each row found in the outer table, we expect to find about two rows in the inner table with B2.K500K = K, as explained in the Q6A discussion. This time, however, the resulting row lies in the answer set only if B2.K25 = 19, and so the number of total rows in the join is shrunk by a factor of 1/25. In the case where KN ≡ K1K, we would expect 1000 rows in the outer table B1 and 2000 rows retrieved from B2, but only (1/25)(2000) = 80 rows in the final join. As we see from Appendix D, the precise number is 81 rows. Note that the I/Os for this case in Figure 9.37b are nearly identical to the I/Os that take place in the comparable case for Q6A, except that there are 2827 more random I/Os. We would expect accesses to rows in B2 through the predicate B2.K500K = 19 to require about three I/Os (one index leaf and two data pages) for each of the 1000 rows found in the outer table, and the somewhat smaller number 2827 no doubt arises because of buffer hits on the K500K index leaf pages.

In the Q6B case where KN ≡ K100, a merge join takes place. In step 1, all the rows in B1 with B1.K100 = 99 are selected with an index scan on K100 and projected onto

KN	Elapsed time (secs)	CPU time (secs)	Get page requests	Random I/O count	Sequential prefetch I/O count	List prefetch I/O count
K40K	2.66	0.27	161	97		1
K10K	11.03	0.91	720	418		4
K1K	77.27	6.68	5164	2842	36	31
K100	191.59	27.59	38,646	86	67	1190

Figure 9.37b Q6B Measurements

two column rows, (B1.KSEQ, B1.K250K), placed in a temporary intermediate table IT1. Similarly, the rows in B2 with B2.K25 = 19 are selected with an index scan on K25 and projected onto rows (B2.KSEQ, B2.K500K) in a temporary table IT2. Both tables IT1 and IT2 are sorted, IT1 by sortkey B1.K250K and IT2 by sortkey B2.K500K. Then IT1 and IT2 are joined on B1.K250K = B2.K500K with the forward moving cursor procedure of Figure 9.21. Considering I/O resources, we see that the index scan on B1.K100 requires a sequential prefetch I/O to retrieve the relevant index and then a number of list prefetch I/Os to retrieve approximately 10,000 rows. These 10,000 rows will lie on a number of pages calculated in the discussion of Q2A, $58,824(1 - e^{(-10,000/58,824)})$ = 9196. Thus the number of list prefetch I/Os required to access these rows is CEIL(9196/32) = 288. The index scan on B2.K25 requires about two sequential prefetch I/Os to retrieve the relevant index and then a number of list prefetch I/Os to retrieve approximately 40,000 rows. The approximate number of pages needed to retrieve these rows is $55,556(1 - e^{(-40,000/55,556)})$ = 28,514. This implies that we will need CEIL(28,514/32) = 892 list prefetch I/Os. For a total number of list prefetch I/Os, we arrive at 288 + 892 = 1180, rather close to the measured number, 1190.

9.11 Cost-Performance Assessment

The Set Query benchmark provides a rating for a hardware/software platform in terms of dollar cost per query per minute ($/QPM). Because all platforms are provided with the same data and respond with the same query answers, the dollar cost to provide these answers is considered a fair measure. The QPM rating for the platform is easily calculated. There are 69 queries in the benchmark, all weighted the same. If we say that the elapsed time to measure all the queries of the benchmark is T minutes, then we are running at a rate of 69/T queries per minute. Adding up the elapsed times for all queries of Section 9.10, we get 4492.24 seconds, or 74.87 minutes, so the QPM rating is 69/74.87 = 0.9216 queries per minute.

The dollar cost of the system represents the cost for hardware, software, and maintenance over a five-year period. The platform for the queries measured in Section 9.10 was an IBM 9221 model 170, running **DB2** version 2.3 on the MVS XA 2.2 operating system. The five-year price for this system is based on the retail prices from October 1993 given in Figure 9.38. The DASD (IBM's name for disk) costs are an exception, representing used prices, since the devices are no longer sold by IBM. Note that monthly maintenance costs are free during the first year of hardware ownership, so only 48 months are charged. Software cannot normally be purchased and the first 2 months are free, so prices are for monthly licenses (a small initial fee is charged for the MVS operating system).

The total dollar cost for the **DB2** system measured is $296,705 + $912,300 = $1,209,005. This supports a QPM rate of 0.9216, and we calculate the final rating by dividing the dollar cost by the QPM rating. The final rating for the Set Query benchmark on this platform is therefore $1,209,005/0.9216 = 1,311,854 $/QPM.

Priced item	Purchase price	Monthly charges (5 years)		
		Charges	Months	Total
IBM 9221 model 170	$252,350	$775	48	$37,200
Ancillary hardware				
1 Channel group	$35,450	None		
Rack enclosure	$3820	$4	48	$192
DASD controller 3880-E23	$3000	$158	48	$7584
DASD device 3380-AE2	$1500	$256	48	$12,288
MVS license	$585	$10,662	58	$618,396
DB2 license	None	$3675	58	$213,150
DB2PM license	None	$405	58	$23,490
TOTAL	$296,705			$912,300

Figure 9.38   Price Calculations for **DB2** System Measured

Elapsed Time versus CPU Time Rating

We used an elapsed time measure in the above rating. However, this may not lead to a true estimate of *query throughput* in a multi-user system. Assume for a moment that we require 10 elapsed minutes to run all the queries of the Set Query benchmark on some platform, but use only 1 minute of CPU time in doing so—the longer elapsed time is a result of waiting for I/O. But if we have a lot of users waiting to get queries performed, couldn't we overlap some of those users by time-sharing the CPU so that we get a lot more queries run every minute? The answer is yes, provided we have several disks holding the data, so that disk I/O doesn't become the bottleneck and overlapping queries on the CPU can find overlapping disks to retrieve needed data. Given all of this, it might seem to be more sensible to use CPU time rather than elapsed time in arriving at the rating.

The only problem in taking this step is that the Set Query benchmark has been run as a single-user benchmark. If we were to run multiple simultaneous users with multiple disks on the system, we would be more justified in generalizing in this way, but as it stands we can't be absolutely sure there isn't some kind of system interference between concurrent user queries that makes this sort of multi-user scenario a pipe dream. There isn't any theoretical reason for such interference—there are no exclusive row locks or other complications that we encounter with update transactions in Chapter 10. But we still have to be careful in coming to the conclusion that we can use all the CPU time in the system. For one thing, as the CPU resource comes closer and closer to being 100% utilized, users form longer and longer *queues* waiting for CPU service, and this has a negative effect on response time. We can only hope to use (perhaps) 90% of the CPU on a reasonably balanced production system. Note that if we calculate the elapsed time for the 69 queries of the Set Query benchmark on the **DB2** platform measured in the last few seconds, we arrive at 74.87 minutes, whereas if we calculate the total CPU time, we arrive at 24.77 minutes. This is a gap of about three to one, not large enough to cause a great deal of concern. If concurrent queries can be performed without interference on a multi-user system (and we have reason to believe from other measurements that this is the case with **DB2**), then the multi-user rating might be reduced from 1,311,854 $/QPM to as little as 500,000 $/QPM. At some point it is appropriate to consider a multi-user test, to see if the queries can be effectively overlapped on the CPU.

Customizing the Rating

It is possible to reinterpret the measurements of the Set Query benchmark to estimate the behavior of a tested platform on a specific query workload. The benchmark query suites have been chosen to span most types of query work, so that it should be possible to equate a given custom workload to a specific weighting of queries from the benchmark. Admittedly some sophisticated flexibility is required if the workload to be estimated contains query forms not included in the Set Query suites. A workload of concurrent update transactions with conflicting data accesses cannot be modeled in this way. We will meet a benchmark for a specific workload of update transactions, the TPC-A benchmark, in Chapter 10.

Assume that we can determine a set of weights, W_i, to represent the relative workload frequency of the benchmark query Q_i, where i ranges from 1 to 69, and assume that all weights are non-negative (some may be zero) and sum to 1.0. The rules of the Set Query benchmark say that all query ratings must be reported in detail, so we always have the elapsed time, the CPU time, and the various types of I/O for each query. Now if we assume that query Q_i takes T_i elapsed minutes to complete, we can calculate the weighted elapsed time period by the formula

$$E = \text{elapsed time period for a weighted query} = \sum_i W_i T_i$$

The weights W_i sum to 1.0, so the quantity E can be thought of as the elapsed time in minutes required for a *single* query that sums up the effects of all queries in the benchmark. Therefore the number of queries per minute, Q_m, for this weighting is given by 1/E. If C is the dollar cost for the platform on which the benchmark has been run, then the custom rating in units of $/QPM is arrived at by dividing C by Q_m, or equivalently, multiplying C by E.

$$\text{Final weighted rating} = C * E = \sum_i W_i T_i \text{ (in units \$/QPM)}$$

To test whether this makes sense, note that a *larger* rating represents *inferior* performance, since the cost goes up or the QPM rating goes down. Sure enough, if the cost C of the platform in the final weighted rating goes up, say, because the vendor raises the price of the platform, a larger rating reflects a lower cost-performance value. The same thing happens if a single one of the T_i values with a positive weight increases, indicating that some query now takes longer.

620   Note that all the considerations of replacing elapsed time with CPU time, mentioned in the last subsection, still hold in the custom workload. The advantage of performing a stand-alone set of measurements is that it is possible to customize by using different query weights in a workload. In a multi-user test the usual course is to choose a specific workload and measure the total elapsed time. Individual measures for the different queries are therefore not available, and a custom rating cannot be derived. However, if the hypothesis of non-interference between concurrent queries holds, we can derive an approximate custom multi-user rating under carefully limited circumstances.

Variations in Indexing Use between DB2 and ORACLE

Note that specific limitations on index use vary with each new release of all database products. As of release 7, **ORACLE** could not combine any predicates except equal match and also could not use an index for the predicate C1 is null. In general, it is fair to say that **DB2** version 2.3 had the most advanced bag of tricks for query optimization at that time, but more recent developments could change that.

Suggestions for Further Reading

The standard SQL reference manuals for most database products give little guidance in understanding query optimization. However, the *DB2 Administration Guide* [1] and the *DB2 Applications Programming and SQL Guide* [2] have quite good coverage of the material presented in this chapter. **DB2 UDB** has corresponding (and somewhat different) coverage in [3] and [4]. **ORACLE** has coverage in the *Server Administrator's Guide* [7] and in *Server Tuning* [8]. The Set Query benchmark is presented in more detail in *The Benchmark Handbook* [6]. Goetz Graefe's paper on query evaluation techniques [5] introduces several principles we have not had space for here, principles that in many cases have not yet been implemented in commercial database systems, but which will probably appear in the future.

[1] *DB2 for OS/390 V5 Administration Guide.* See Chapter 2, "Designing a Database," and Chapter 5, "Performance Monitoring and Tuning." Document no. SC26-8957-02. IBM. Available at www.ibm.com/db2.

[2] *DB2 for OS/390 V5 Applications Programming and SQL Guide.* In particular, see Chapter 6, Section 4,"Using EXPLAIN to Improve SQL Performance." Document no. SC-26-8958-02. IBM. Available at www.ibm.com/db2.

[3] *DB2 Universal Database Administration Guide: Design and Implementation.* V6. See Document no. SC09-2840-00. IBM. Available at www.ibm.com/db2.

[4] *DB2 Universal Database Administration Guide: Performance.* V6. In particular, see Chapter 6 "SQL Explain Facility." Document no. SC09-2840-00. IBM. Available at www.ibm.com/db2.

[5] Goetz Graefe. "Query Evaluation Techniques for Large Databases." *ACM Computing Surveys* 25(2), June 1993, pp. 73–170.

[6] Jim Gray, editor. *The Benchmark Handbook for Database and Transaction Processing Systems,* 2nd ed. San Mateo, CA: Morgan Kaufmann, 1993. Available at http://www.benchmarkresources.com/handbook/.

[7] *ORACLE8 Server Administrator's Guide.* Redwood Shores, CA: Oracle. http://www.oracle.com.

[8] *ORACLE8 Server Tuning.* See Chapter 21, "The EXPLAIN PLAN Command." Redwood Shores, CA: Oracle. http://www.oracle.com.

[9] *ORACLE8 Server SQL Reference Manual.* Volumes 1 and 2. Redwood Shores, CA: Oracle. http://www.oracle.com.

Exercises

Exercises with solutions at the back of the book in "Solutions to Selected Exercises" are marked with the symbol •.

In exercises involving elapsed time for I/O, you should generally assume that index directory pages are buffer resident and that index leaf pages are not, unless instructed otherwise. Ignore index I/O in your answers when these sum to less than 10% of the total. However, you should normally be careful to include index I/O calculations, to demonstrate why you consider them insignificant. The following exercises assume **DB2** architecture except as otherwise mentioned—that is, pages of 4 KB, compression at the leaf level of a B-tree, and so on.

[9.1] **DB2** was designed to use sequential prefetch I/O in one part of an index scan (as in reading from the index) and not in another (in reading data pages in the unclustered case of Example 9.3.4 based on the RIDs found in the index). In this problem, we compare the situation where the disk controller does *not* buffer tracks for answering later page requests so that **DB2** flexibility can be utilized, with the case where the buffer *does* read in a full track at a time (which we will take to be 32 disk pages of 4 KB each).

    (a)• Use the values in Figure 9.6 for components making up an I/O to calculate the time required for a 32-page sequential I/O (assume that reading the 32 pages in sequence requires one seek and one rotational wait and extends the transfer time). Write the result in terms of seconds per page under assumptions of sequential I/O. This is what happens when **DB2** sequential prefetch is used *or* when the disk controller reads a single disk page from a new track.

    (b) Calculate the elapsed time taken by the unique match query of Example 9.3.3:

(i)   Assume that the disk controller reads an entire track into disk buffer for each page retrieved. Also assume no buffering savings from one unique match to another, since there are too many different pages for this buffering to help.

(ii)   Assume single-page random I/Os (with all components in Figure 9.6 repeated for each I/O).

(c)• Recalculate the time taken for Example 9.3.5:

(i)   Under assumptions of 8-page prefetch.

(ii)   Under assumptions of single-page random I/Os.

In this case, 8-page sequential I/O helps elapsed time performance.

(d) Consider a WORKLOAD of some number W1 of queries of the kind mentioned in (b) (type (b)), and W2 of queries of the kind mentioned in (c) (type (c)). Type (b) queries have an elapsed time disadvantage when prefetch I/Os are required, and type (c) queries have a disadvantage when random I/Os are required.

(i)   Choose the weights W1 and W2 so that the total elapsed time due to I/Os in the workload is the same for both choices, random I/O or 8-page prefetch. We are assuming that type (b) queries are much more frequent than type (c) queries.

(ii)   Now calculate the total elapsed time for each query when we have flexibility in different queries to choose between prefetch and random I/Os.

[9.2] This problem duplicates the mathematical derivation given in Section 8.6. If you have had a course in elementary probability, you should have no trouble justifying your answers. You have the option to generate your results by doing a program simulation with a random number generator.

(a)• Consider the unique match query of Example 9.3.3, with an employees table that has 100,000 rows of 400 bytes each. Assume that both the data pages and the eidx index (10-byte entries) have PCTFREE = 0, and thus show that there are 10,000 data pages and a depth-2 eidx B-tree index with 250 leaf pages.

Now assume that we have a set of memory buffers that is kept populated by an algorithm that drops a page from buffer when it has not been referenced for exactly 125 seconds. Assume that our WORKLOAD performs two queries of the type in Example 9.3.3 each second, with a *randomly chosen* eid value, and that this is the only query type in the workload that references the employees table or eidx index. Each time one of these queries is performed, the root node of the eidx B-tree is referenced, so the root node clearly stays in buffer. Note that if the eid values referenced were properly selected to circulate uniformly through the `eidx` leaf nodes, then after 125 seconds every one of the 250 leaf nodes would be referenced, and they would all stay in buffers. That's not likely to happen, of course, since the `eid` values are chosen at random.

(b)• (i)   What is the probability, P(leaf), that a given leaf node is referenced on any given query?

    (ii)   Provide a formula for the probability that a given leaf node is *not* referenced by a given query.

    (iii)   Give a formula for the probability that a given leaf node is not referenced by some number N of queries in a row. (Hint: there is a power involved.)

    (iv)   Using a calculator, give the probability that a leaf node from the `eidx` B-tree has not been referenced for the last 250 queries, 125 seconds, and therefore is not present in buffers.

    (v)   What is the expected number of leaf nodes present in buffers?

    (vi)   State this problem in terms of throwing N darts at M random slots, as in Section 8.6. Perform the calculation of the exponential form from that section.

(c) (i)   Repeat all the steps of part (b) for the data pages of the `employees` table.

    (ii)   How many actual database page references take place in the last 125 seconds, counting the index root page and all others? How many references have there been to index leaf pages? To data pages?

    (iii)   Approximately how many index leaf pages have been referenced during that time? How many data pages have been referenced? (Some pages have been referenced two or more times, but count each page only once.)

    (iv)•   Explain why the number of leaf pages remaining in buffer is smaller than the number of data pages.

(d) What is the approximate number of pages, B, that need to be present in buffers, counting both B-tree and data pages, in order to keep all pages referenced in the last 125 seconds buffer resident?

(e) The LRU buffering algorithm, the most common type in use, works with some well-defined pool of P buffer pages: LRU brings each newly referenced page into the pool and makes room for it by discarding the buffer page that has gone the longest time without reference. Provide an estimate of the number of pages P that must be present for queries of the type we have been dealing with so far, in order to guarantee that each page referenced has a life of *approximately* 125 seconds. Explain your answer.

(f)• Assume that a page in buffer results in an I/O cost of 0 (zero) when it is referenced, whereas a page out of buffer results in a cost of 1 (we have to fetch it from disk—simple units here). What is the I/O cost per second resulting from the query WORKLOAD assumed here? (You can estimate this from the results of parts (b) and (c).)

(g) Assume that we extended the lifetime of pages in buffer from 125 seconds to 250 seconds. Calculate how this would affect problems (b) (iv) and (v), (c) (i), (d), (e), and (f). What we are doing here is reducing the I/O (disk arm) cost by purchasing extra memory to hold more buffer pages.

(h)• What would the I/O cost per second be if we had exactly 251 buffer pages and we kept the eidx root page and all eidx leaf pages in buffer and dropped all data pages? Conclude from this that the idea of keeping all pages around a fixed length of time is not optimal.

[9.3] Write programs in C to simulate the buffering situations of Exercise 9.2.

(a) Input a number N of eidx leaf pages and M of employees data pages. (We would use N = 250 and M = 10,000 in the situation of Exercise 9.2.) Now input K to represent the number of seconds a page must go unreferenced before it is dropped from buffer. (Note that this is *not* an LRU approach.) Assume that two queries are performed each second, referencing some leaf page and data page. Define a function to be called for each query that returns the number of distinct leaf pages and data pages that remain in buffer after the query. Use a random number generator to generate random references to a leaf page and a data page for the query. If you average a long sequence of query results (calling the function 100 or so times in a row, once the system is warmed up and pages are being dropped), you should get the same sort of answers you derived in Exercise 9.2(b)(v) and 9.2(c). (Note that the hard part in writing this program would be to perform efficient lookup to see if a new page referenced is already in buffer, and if not, to determine which page should be dropped from buffer. However, it is not necessary to write efficient code for this exercise. The easiest way is to keep reference times for all M + N pages, in two big arrays.) You might consider using database tables to hold this data.

(b) With N and M as in part (a), write a simulation of LRU buffering with a given fixed buffer size input as B. The query function should return the number of pages *not* found in buffer on each new query (values 0, 1, or 2) and the age of the page being dropped from buffer. The caller of the query function should print out the sequence of ages starting when the system is warmed up.

Check the result of Exercise 9.2(e) by looking at this list of ages. Average a long series of returned values to estimate the average I/O cost of a query, and check the calculation of Exercise 9.2(f) and (g).

[9.4] Assume that we have a table T with 100 million rows, each containing 200 bytes, loaded 90% full, but with all indexes loaded 100% full. Assume that we have an index C1234X on T with columns (C1, C2, C3, C4), and that the table T is clustered by this index. We also have an index C5678X on T with columns (C5, C6, C7, C8), and after running EXPLAIN we find that CLUSTERRATIO for C5678X is 20. Assume that *each column*—C1, C2, C3, C4, C5, C6, C7, and C8—is 4 bytes in length.

CARD(C1) = 100, CARD(C2) = 200, CARD(C3) = 50, CARD(C4) = 10,
CARD(C5) = 10, CARD(C6) = 1000, CARD(C7) = 20, CARD(C8) = 5000

Assume that for each column Ck, the values populating the column go from 1 to CARD(Ck) with uniform distribution.

(a) Calculate the following statistics. Explain your reasoning.

    (i) For the table T, CARD and NPAGES.

    (ii) COLCARD, LOW2KEY, and HIGH2KEY for C2, C3, C6, and C7.

    (iii) For each of C1234X and C5678X, FIRSTKEYCARD and your best estimate of FULLKEYCARD (explain your reasoning).

    (iv) Using FULLKEYCARD and reasonable assumptions about **DB2** index compression (*important*), calculate NLEAF for each index, then NLEVELS for each. Please show work.

(b)• Consider the following query.

```
select C10 from T where C1 <= 10 and C2 between 100
    and 110 and C3 = 4;
```

    (i) Give the relevant columns you would see in the plan table after an EXPLAIN of this query.

    (ii) Say explicitly what range of index entries must be retrieved in order to answer the query given in (b). How many leaf pages is this? Can we use sequential prefetch? What is the approximate elapsed time for this step?

    (iii) Calculate the filter factor for the compound predicate for the query in (b).

    (iv) How many rows are retrieved? Explain why these rows are *not* contiguous and why sequential prefetch can *not* be used. What is the elapsed time for this data page access step?

    (v)   Specify (from (ii) and (iv)) the total I/O and elapsed time for this index step.

  (c) Repeat the same steps as in (b) for *each* of two plans that suggest themselves on the two indexes of T, for the query

```
select * from T where C7 = 3 and C1 = 99 and C2 = 55;
```

    Which of these plans is of lower cost in terms of elapsed time for I/O?

[9.5] Consider again the table T and associated indexes and columns of Exercise 9.4.

  (a) Name the matching columns of the following search conditions, and give reasons why the matching stops where it does if all predicates don't match.

    (i)•   `select * from T where C1 = 7 and C2 >= 101 and C3 in (1,5) and C4 in (2,4,7);`

    (ii)   `select * from T where C1 in (1,3,5) and C2 = 6 and C4 = 7;`

    (iii)• `select * from T where C1 <> 6 and C2 in (1,3,5) and C3 = 5;`

    (iv)   `select * from T where C1 in (1,3,5) and C2 = 7 and C3 = 6 and C4 in (3,6,8);`

    (v)•   `select * from T where C1 = 7 and C2 in (1,5) and C3 like '%abc' and C4 in (2,4,7);`

    (vi)   `select * from T where C1 in (1,3,5) and C4 > 3 and C3 = 7 and C2 = 6;`

    (vii)• `select * from T where C1 = C4 + 6 and C2 in (1,3,5) and C3 = 5;`

  (b) Show your work in providing answers to the following questions.

    (i)•   What is the composite filter factor for the matching predicates of the query of part (a)(i)?

```
select * from T where C1 = 7 and C2 >= 101 and C3 in (1,5) and C4 in (2,4,7);
```

    (ii)   What is the filter factor for the *whole* search condition?

    (iii)• What is the number of pages accessed for index lookup for this query? What kind of I/O is performed (R, S, or L)?

    (iv)   What is the number of data pages accessed, assuming that we used the screening predicates? What kind of I/O (R, S, or L)?

    (v)•   What is the total elapsed time to perform these I/Os?

[9.6] In this exercise, assume that the `prospects` table has the indexes `addrx`, `hobbyx`, `agex`, and `incomex`, defined in Figure 9.12 and Example 9.6.1.

  (a)• Explain under what circumstances the predicate `incomeclass = 10` can be a matching predicate for an MX step in a multiple index scan.

(b) Is it possible to use the predicate age = 40 in an MX step for a multiple index scan? Explain.

(c)• Is it possible to use the predicate age between 20 and 39 in an MX step for a multiple index scan?

(d) Is it possible to use the predicate age between 40 and 44 in an MX step for a multiple index scan?

(e)• Explain why it is not possible to use the predicate age in (40, 43, 45) in a single MX step for a multiple index scan.

(f) Is there a way to create a compound predicate with the same effect as the one in (e) that can be used in an MX step sequence?

[9.7] For the following exercise, add the index mailx, defined in Section 9.5, to the indexes considered for Exercise 9.6. Consider the search condition zipcode between 02139 and 03138 and incomeclass = 10 and age = 40.

(a)• Consider a matching index scan on mailx for this compound predicate, and specify relevant column values in the plan table. In particular, what is MATCHCOLS?

(b) What is the filter factor that will result from the scan on mailx

(i) if a RID list is *not* used?

(ii) if a RID list *is* used? Explain why there is a difference.

(c)• In case (b)(ii), we can consider making this scan of mailx an MX scan in a multiple index access. In that case we can use other indexes as well.

(i) Can we perform an MX step on incomeclass = 10?

(ii) Show the plan table for the multiple index steps we can use.

(iii) What is the filter factor for the full search condition in this case?

(d) Calculate the I/O elapsed time for the full plan that is characterized in (b)(i). (You need to calculate index and data page I/O times. Be sure you use the right kind of I/O—random, list prefetch, or sequential prefetch.)

(e)• Calculate the I/O elapsed time for the full plan that is characterized in (c)(ii).

[9.8] Assume that the prospects table has indexes addrx, hobbyx, incomex, genderx (of Example 9.6.3), agex, and mailx.

(a)• Is it possible to have the predicate gender = 'F' in an MX step of a multi-index access plan?

(b) Consider the query

```
select * from prospects where zipcode between 02139
        and 07138 and hobby = 'chess' and age = 20;
```

(i)• It is possible to resolve this query with an index scan of mailx. Name the matching predicates and the screening predicates in the above.

(ii) It is also possible to perform multi-index access. Place the predicates in order by descending filter factor. Then give the plan table that would be used for this MX-type plan, where smallest filter factors come first and we maintain as few RID lists as possible at once.

(iii)• What is the number of rows retrieved in both parts (i) and (ii), and how many data pages are involved? What kind of I/O is used (R, L, or S), and what is the elapsed time for data page access in both cases? Please show work.

[9.9] Assume indexes mailx, hobbyx, incomex, and agex for the following. Consider the query

```
select * from prospects
    where zipcode between 02159 and 04158 and
    (age = 40 or age = 44) and hobby = 'tennis'
    and incomeclass = 7;
```

(a)• Explain why we cannot simply use a matching index scan on mailx to resolve all these predicates. However, we can perform a matching scan with screening predicates figuring into the filter factor. Analyze elapsed time for I/O for such a plan, including index I/O, the number of rows that will be retrieved, and the I/O type for them. Provide the total elapsed time.

(b) Now determine the plan for multiple index access to match as many of the predicates of the query as seems reasonable. Start by placing the predicates in order by increasing filter factor. Calculate the I/O cost of the index for each predicate RID extraction, the filter factor after each predicate is used, and whether the predicate pays for itself. Follow the pattern of Example 9.6.6. At the end of this determination, write the multi-step index plan columns, as in Figure 9.18, that follow the order of evaluation you have calculated and minimize the number of existing RID lists in the stack at any one time. What is the total elapsed time for this multi-step plan?

(c)• Which wins, (a) or (b)? As a general rule, when we have one composite index with a search condition matching only the first column and a group of other single-column indexes on later columns of the composite index, the composite index scan is still the winner. Justify this rule.

[9.10] Consider Examples 9.7.1, 9.7.2, and 9.7.3. We have the same tables TABL1 and TABL2, but we use some new columns and indexes. There are 1 million rows, 200 bytes each, and the columns are 4 bytes long. We also assume that no space is wasted on the index pages or the data pages. We have the query

```
select * from TABL1 T1, TABL2 T2
    where T1.C6 = 5 and T1.C7 = T2.C8
    and T2.C9 = 6;
```

Assume that we have indexes C6X, C7X, C8X, and C9X; FF(T1.C6 = const) = 1/20; FF(T2.C9 = const) = 1/400; the column T1.C7 has values ranging from 1 to 200,000, uniformly distributed; and T2.C8 also has values ranging from 1 to 200,000, uniformly distributed. There is no recognizable correlation between values of T1.C7 and T2.C8 by row number or anything else. They are independently random.

(a)• Derive the expected number of rows retrieved from this query.

(b) There are three possible plans to consider for this query: (i) nested-loop join where T1 is the outer table, (ii) nested-loop join where T2 is the outer table (these are different), and (iii) merge join. Work out the total elapsed I/O time for each case and declare which is the winner. In the case of merge join, where a sort is necessary, assume that a sort of no more than 50 pages will not require disk I/O, but that for more than 50 pages each page must be written out and then read back in, using sequential I/O to write but random I/O to read in again. (The reason for this has to do with the disk sort algorithm.)

[9.11] As in Example 9.8.1, assume a sequence of 2000-byte rows, two to a page, to be sorted in order by the values of the following sequence, which represents the initial order of the rows.

67 12 45 84 58 29 76 7 91 81 39 22 65 96 33 28 77 4 54 13 41 32 1 59

(a)• Perform a two-way merge sort on these numbers, as in Example 9.8.1. Show all intermediate results.

(b) Repeat the sort of part (a), now as a three-way merge sort.

(c) Now assume that the rows given are 4000 bytes in length and, therefore, one to a page. Perform a four-way merge sort on these numbers.

[9.12] Answer the following questions about the Set Query benchmark, referring to **DB2** measurements in all cases. How many rows of the BENCH table would you expect to retrieve with each of the following WHERE clauses?

(a)• K2 = 2 AND K10 = 7.

(b) KSEQ BETWEEN 400000 AND 410000 OR KSEQ BETWEEN 480000 AND 500000.

(c)• Conditions 1 through 4 of the predicate sequence list of Figure 9.34.

(d) (i) In Q1, assuming that all **DB2** prefetch I/Os are sequential prefetch, how long would the I/Os take in the K2 case? In the K10 case?

(ii) Argue that **DB2** is CPU-bound in the K2 case.

(iii) How many pages are being brought into memory in the K10 case? Give details of how many pages *must* be looked at to perform the query plan.

(e)• Consider query Q2A. Some of the cases clearly use sequential prefetch in blocks of 32 pages. Name one such case. How long does sequential prefetch I/O take, and how does that jibe with the rule of thumb we've been using?

(f) Look at query Q4B, detailed in Figure 9.35b.

(i) What indexes are being used in condition sequence 5–9?

(ii) Give the count of rows you expect to retrieve from the table after combining these indexes.

(iii) Using the darts in slots formula to calculate the number of pages on which the rows of (ii) lie, compare this to the number of pages brought into memory as reported in Figure 9.35b.

(g)• In query Q6B, in the K100 case, perform a calculation, explaining your reasoning, to estimate the total number of rows (joined) that will be retrieved. How does this compare to the number actually retrieved? (Where do you find those numbers?)

[9.13] Consider the following query on the BENCH table of the Set Query benchmark.

```
select B1.KSEQ, B2.KSEQ from BENCH B1, BENCH B2
    where B1.K100 = 22 and B1.K250K = B2.K100K and B2.K25 = 19;
```

(a)• Calculate the number of rows that you would expect to see retrieved. Please show your work.

(b)• Calculate the elapsed time for I/O on the *two different nested-loop joins possible*, and declare which plan wins.

[9.14] Consider the following query on the BENCH table of the Set Query benchmark.

```
select B1.KSEQ, B2.KSEQ from BENCH B1, BENCH B2
    where B1.K100 = 22 and B1.K250K = B2.K250K and B2.K100 = 19;
```

(a) Calculate the number of rows that you would expect to see retrieved. Please show your work.

(b) Calculate the elapsed time for I/O with a *nested-loop* join (both are equivalent) and then with a *merge* join. Please show your work and declare which plan wins.

[9.15] Consider the BENCH table and the indexes on it. In the following exercise, assume that the BENCH table and all indexes are loaded with pages 100% full. Use standard assumptions for **DB2** in the calculations that follow, and show your calculations.

(a)• After running RUNSTATS, provide a Select statement to retrieve from the appropriate **DB2** system catalog table the number of data pages on which rows of the BENCH table sit.

(b) Calculate the number of data pages you would expect to find, with the assumption that pages are loaded 100% full.

(c)• Calculate the number of leaf pages you would expect to find in the K2X index with the assumption that pages are 100% full. Don't forget leaf-level index compression.

(d) Assume that we delete the row in BENCH with KSEQ = 300,000. Is it true or not that we can proceed directly to the index entry in K2X for this row in order to delete it? (That is, do we have a way to "look up" the entry in the directory structure?) Give a reason for your answer (if possible, cite a reference in the text).

Update Transactions   **10**

Six thousand years ago, the Sumerians invented writing for transaction processing.
—Jim Gray and Andreas Reuter

I n Section 5.4 we introduced the concept of a *transaction*. We now wish to review the ideas introduced there, starting with a definition.

DEFINITION 10.1 A *transaction* is a means by which an application programmer can package together a sequence of database operations so that the database system can provide a number of guarantees, known as the *ACID properties* of a transaction (explained later in this section). When the operations making up a transaction consist of both reads (that is, Selects) and updates, they represent an attempt by the application programmer to perform a consistent *change of state* in the data; when the operations of a transaction consist only of reads, they represent an attempt at a consistent *view* of the data. ∎

There is no Begin Transaction statement in standard SQL; a transaction begins whenever there is no active transaction in progress and an SQL statement is performed that accesses the data (for example, Select, Update, Insert, Delete, etc.). While a transaction is in progress, any updates it performs are not visible to concurrent users, and data read cannot be concurrently updated. Recall that in standard SQL there are two statements bearing on transactional execution. The first is the *Commit* statement:

```
exec sql commit work;
```

The programmer uses this statement to inform the system that the ongoing transaction has successfully completed; all updates made by the transaction become permanent in the database and visible to concurrent users.

The second statement that bears on transactional execution is the *Rollback* statement:

```
exec sql rollback work;
```

634

This statement indicates that the ongoing transaction has ended unsuccessfully; all data updates made by the transaction are reversed, and prior versions of the data are put back in place and become visible again to concurrent users. A rollback action that ends a transaction, whether initiated by the program or the system, is often referred to as an *abort*.

In Section 5.4 we introduced the concept of a transaction only in sufficient depth to motivate the need for including a Commit or Rollback statement in an application program, and to suggest the need to handle aborts resulting from deadlock in transactional locking. In the current chapter we propose to treat the transaction concept in much greater depth. Even so, this chapter is just an introduction to a complex and important field. Many hardware and software vendors that offer database system products have created a separate development group, sometimes even in a different physical location, to develop transaction system capabilities. The database system features we have been studying in Chapters 8 and 9 to support efficient query processing are extremely far removed from what is needed to support transactions, and you should be prepared to encounter a change of mind-set in this chapter.

Starting in the 1950s, transactions were developed to solve a number of problems that early systems designers faced in writing large database applications. One such application involved banking activities, allowing a large number of bank tellers to simultaneously read and make changes to customer accounts. In dealing with such an application, early developers faced the following problem areas.

1. Creating an inconsistent result. What are we to do about the following situation? Our application is transferring money from one account to another (the accounts are two different records lying, in general, on different disk pages). After the first account has had money subtracted from its balance and this change has been recorded on disk, the system crashes because of a power failure. (Note that one of the two disk updates must always be performed first, and the crash can always occur before the second disk update is performed.) When we bring the machine back up, our application never remembers what logic it was executing (all memory contents have been lost, including program variable values and flow-of-control registers). The only permanent memory is on disk, and the application has destroyed money with the single account record update it made.

2. Errors of concurrent execution. Concurrent (simultaneous) process executions can interfere with one another in a number of ways if no control is placed on records being read and written. One such type of interference is known as *inconsistent analysis*. Assume that teller 1 is transferring money from account A to account B of the same customer, while teller 2 is trying to add up the two account balances to perform a credit check. If the application acting on behalf of teller 1 subtracts the transfer amount from account A and then teller 2 adds up the two account balances before teller 1 can add the transfer amount to account B, then teller 2 sees the customer as having less money than is true in reality. As a result, the customer may fail a credit check that should have been passed.

3. Uncertainty as to when changes become permanent. Recall that we normally buffer popular pages in memory to save on disk I/Os. This means that an extremely popular record, such as the one containing the balance for the bank branch, remains in memory for an extended period. As we mentioned in problem 1, after a crash we can only remember what has been written to disk, so this seems to mean that either we must always write out all buffered records after they change (and thus we are not saving many I/Os by buffering after all) or else updates don't get out to disk very frequently (and this makes us nervous about handing out money for customer withdrawals, for fear the withdrawal won't be recorded before a computer crash occurs). Can we be confident of updates being recorded without performing a disk write for every record change?

To solve these problems, the systems analysts came up with the concept of a transaction (although the idea did not start being formalized until the mid-1970s). With these concrete problems in mind, the analysts defined a *transaction* to be a grouping of a series of reads and updates to a database that is logically one piece—for example, a transfer of money spanning a number of accounts (involving both reads and updates), or a credit check involving a number of accounts (involving a series of reads only). Application programmers decide what set of reads and updates logically make up a transaction, and then the database system makes the following four *transactional guarantees* to solve the problems listed above, known as the *ACID guarantees*, or *ACID properties*. The term *ACID* is an acronym for four properties: Atomicity, Consistency, Isolation, and Durability.

Atomicity. This property guarantees that a set of record updates that are part of a transaction is indivisible (the old meaning of atomic, before atomic fission was discovered). Thus either all updates of a transaction occur in the database, or none of them occurs. This guarantee continues to hold even in the event of a system crash (see "Durability," below). A procedure known as *database recovery* is performed after a crash to bring the disk-resident database to a state where it will reflect either all or none of the row updates for any transaction that was in progress at the time of the crash. Thus problem 1, the problem of creating an inconsistent result, is solved. The system provides this atomicity guarantee by writing notes to itself on disk in advance of any changes made on disk to the actual data. In the event of a crash the system can figure out what it was in the midst of doing and decide to either back out all transactional disk changes (so the database reflects none of these changes), or else apply all transactional changes that didn't make it out to the disk (so the transaction is completed).

Consistency. This is another property commonly named as a transactional guarantee made by the system; it is defined a bit later. We do not give consistency the same prominence as the other ACID properties because consistency is not logically independent. In fact consistency is implied by the existence of the isolation guarantee (following), which seems to be more fundamental.

Isolation. That transactions are *isolated* means that one can only affect another as it would if they were not concurrent, that is, if their operations were not interleaved in time. Another name for this property is *serializability*, meaning that any schedule of interleaved operations permitted by the system is equivalent to some *serial schedule*, where transactions are scheduled one at a time, and all operations of one transaction complete before any operation of another transaction can start. For performance reasons (explained later in the chapter), we need to have interleaved operation schedules, but we want everything to seem as if we were executing transactions in series. This guarantee solves problem 2, errors arising from concurrent execution. As we have already mentioned in Section 5.4, this guarantee is usually accomplished in commercial systems by having transactions lock data items they access to exclude certain concurrent operations on those same data items by other transactions.

Durability. The last property guaranteed by the system is this: when the system returns to the program logic after a *Commit Work* statement, the transaction is guaranteed to be recoverable. At this point, for example, an ATM (automatic teller machine) can disburse money to a customer without fear that the record of the withdrawal will be lost, a solution to problem 3. We name this transactional guarantee *durability*—that is, a transaction that is *durable* is resistant to a crash. The system writes notes to itself on disk to provide durability, as we mentioned already in discussing the atomicity guarantee. At the same time, the number of I/Os to guarantee durability of a large number of record updates is much reduced, because the system can write out a lot of notes at once with a single disk write, involving many record updates on distinct pages, that otherwise would require multiple disk accesses to write out the individual page contents every time a row was updated. In fact, notes such as this are necessary even if disk pages are written out whenever they're updated, as we will explain below.

Clearly the properties of atomicity and durability are trivially satisfied in a read-only transaction, where no updates occur. The only transactional property that has an effect in this case is isolation, and it guarantees that the rows read by a read-only transaction do not contain any data changes made by uncommitted transactions. If reads of uncommitted data were allowed, the problem of inconsistent analysis could arise, where teller 2 adds up the balances of account A (after the still uncommitted transaction of teller 1 has changed it) and account B (which will be changed by teller 1 before its transaction commits). The three transactional guarantees given prominence above—atomicity, durability, and isolation—require a good deal of study, because they interact in complex ways. In Section 10.1 we begin with a study of isolation (also referred to as serializability). Later sections deal with atomicity and durability.

The property mentioned above as being implied by isolation is known as consistency. We alluded to it when we spoke of inconsistent analysis in problem 2. *Consistency* is a logical property based on some consistency rule, such as "Money should neither be created nor destroyed by a banking transaction transferring money between accounts." Such a rule is an injunction to the programmer, for one thing, that the logic of the money transfer program should not make unbalanced updates to accounts within transaction boundaries. Then given that the program logic does what it should (we *always* assume that program logic obeys all consistency rules when acting in isolation), the consistency property says that the system should guarantee that consistency continues to hold during concurrent execution. However, it turns out that the isolation property already guarantees this, since isolation guarantees that transactions acting concurrently affect one another only as they would if their operations were not interleaved in time. Clearly if the program logic acts consistently in isolation, it will continue to do so in concurrent execution given the isolation guarantee, so in what follows we exclude the consistency property from consideration in the list of guarantees offered by a database system. Note, however, that a test of the consistency property in a database system application is a good test that isolation has been properly implemented. We see this in the TPC-A benchmark of Section 10.10.

In the following sections, we take a rather rigorous approach to transaction concepts, with definitions and theorems and so on. We have taken this kind of approach before in Chapter 2, when we introduced the concept of the relational model, and in Chapter 5, when we studied database design. One reason for such an approach is that the concepts being covered are somewhat difficult to grasp, and a rigorous approach is a good pedagogical method to communicate ideas in the most explicit possible way. Another reason is historical: the field of transactional systems, which began in the 1950s, gave rise to a good deal of publishing activity in rigorous computer science journals starting in the mid-1970s. Why transactions developed as they did is rather revealing, and it constitutes an interesting motivation for rigorous development that you may not have heard before.

The transactional systems being planned in the 1950s were expected to generate billions of dollars in hardware and software sales (a bargain for the banks and the millions of bank clerks, chained to the terrible drudgery of keeping account books). Today money spent on transactional systems by industry amounts to nearly 6 *billion* dollars *per year*. Naturally the cost to develop systems sold into these markets was a good fraction of the revenue realized. When computer companies start making this kind of investment in new systems, they want to be sure that the underlying concepts used in program implementation will result in something that will not have any nasty surprises. Top-level management listened carefully to systems programmers and designers for these projects, and asked how they could be sure that the proposed multi-million-dollar development plan would result in a working system that would do what it was supposed to do. Everything was subject to question. Do we know all the problems that can arise (are problems 1–3 above the only ones)? Does the approach solve all the problems that we know about? Are there any other problems we haven't thought of? How can we be sure?

Rigorous proof can be employed to answer just this kind of question, at least in those areas of endeavor where the problems are simple enough to axiomatize. The journal articles didn't come first, of course. An early set of rough-and-ready principles was created and justified, and then the first transactional systems were built. As these principles continued to be developed, a set of founding papers was eventually published, often written by programmers who had not been involved in journal publishing before. These papers founded the transactional field, codifying all the explicit assumptions and problems, and proving the principles that underlay the solutions adopted. Most of these principles are still used today in commercial systems.

10.1 Transactional Histories

The need for the transaction isolation concept is present whenever two or more users can perform interleaved operations of read and write on the database. When we speak of reads and writes, we are referring to the most primitive possible operations, from which the more "set-oriented" SQL statements are constructed. To "read" means to access a *data item*, such as an individual row of a table or an index entry in the database; to "write" means to change or update a data item in the database. We often refer to reads and writes of data items rather than reads and updates, because the term update has a more powerful implication in SQL. (It often implies that a read is performed followed by a write based on what was read.)

Fundamental Atomic Read and Write Actions in the Database

We use the notation $R_i(A)$ to mean that a transaction, given an identification number i by the database system and denoted by T_i, performs a read of data item A. Consider a table T1 with two columns, uniqueid (which uniquely determines the data item) and val (a value commonly read and written in a transaction). Then $R_i(A)$ can usually be pictured as transaction T_i performing the following SQL statement:

```
select val into :pgmval1 from T1 where uniqueid = A;
```

We also use the notation $W_j(B)$ to mean that a transaction T_j performs a write on data item B, and this can be pictured as transaction T_j performing the following SQL statement:

```
update T1 set val = :pgmval2 where uniqueid = B;
```

These examples are a bit simplistic. There is probably more than one data item read by the Select statement above, and the same may be true of the Update statement. In both statements, a WHERE clause predicate has been evaluated to determine the row in T1 with the given uniqueid value. We can picture reading this predicate information (whether through an index or not) as a data item in its own right. In a later section we will see that this observation has important ramifications.

We need to understand a guarantee associated with reads and writes of this kind, that a read by one transaction cannot occur in the middle of a write by another transaction, when the data item value (such as a long character string) might be inconsistent. Similarly two write actions cannot interfere with each other to result in inconsistent changes. We say that the $R_i(B)$ and $W_j(B)$ actions are *atomic*, meaning that they can be pictured as happening in an instant between all other actions in the database. This is not quite the same thing as the atomicity of transactions that was mentioned above.

Note that we are not specifying the actual values read and written with the notation $R_i(A)$ and $W_j(B)$, but if we wish we can expand $R_i(A)$ to be $R_i(A, val1)$ and $W_j(B)$ to be $W_j(B, val2)$. The value read or written is the second argument (the column name val that takes on values val1 and val2 is not mentioned), and we would normally simply specify constants for these values to show what is happening—for example, $R_i(A,50)$ or $W_j(B,80)$.

Predicate Read Actions

The Select and Update statements for $R_i(A)$ and $W_j(B)$ we have just provided are the simplest possible examples. Database reads and writes actually arise in much more complicated situations. For example, instead of reading or updating a single column value of a uniquely identified row, a read or write could involve multiple columns of a row (although there is only one relevant column in our example table T1). Or assume that transaction T_1 were to execute the SQL statement on a set of rows:

[10.1.1]
```
update tbl set val = 1.15*val
    where uniqueid between :low and :high;
```

In this case a large number of different reads and writes might be generated by this one statement. The first operation performed by T_1 would be a *predicate read*, $R_1(PREDICATE)$, meaning that the set of rows satisfying the predicate in the WHERE clause, with uniqueid values between the program variables :low and :high, must be determined by some means, such as an index lookup. The Update statement [10.1.1] running under transaction T_1 would be denoted as follows:

```
R1(predicate: uniqueid between :low and :high)
```

After taking note of the list of rows that fall in the given range, the Update statement of [10.1.1] will perform a sequence of read-write actions, $R_1(uniqueid_k, value_k)$ followed by $W_1(uniqueid_k, 1.15 * value_k)$, for all $uniqueid_k$ values in the :low to :high range.

Transactional Histories with Reads and Writes

In what follows, we assume that each user process performs atomic reads and atomic writes within some transaction. Later we will consider predicate reads as well. As a running application performs these reads and writes, the transaction manager layer of the database system (see Figure 10.1) intercepts the first read or write operation after a prior transaction ends within a process, and assigns a number i to it. For now, we assume that all database activity performed by any transaction can be modeled as a series of reads $(R_i(A))$ and writes $(W_j(B))$, together with commits (C_i) arising from the Commit Work statement and aborts (A_j) arising because of the Rollback Work statement or because of deadlock, which we will explain Section 10.4. We ignore the need for row inserts and deletes until later. In our model, the reads represent all information taken in by the transaction, and the writes represent all update activity the transaction performs.

An "interleaved" series of read and write operations performed by two transactions, T_1 and T_2, might look like this:

[10.1.2] ... $R_2(A)$ $W_2(A)$ $R_1(A)$ $R_1(B)$ $R_2(B)$ $W_2(B)$ C_1 C_2 ...

A sequence of operations such as this is known as a transactional *history*, or sometimes a *schedule*. In the history of [10.1.2], we see that transaction T_2 first reads the data element A, then transaction T_2 writes back a (presumably) new value of A, after which T_1 reads the newer value of A, and so on, with the final operations C_1 and C_2 representing commits by transactions T_1 and T_2, respectively. This history results from a series of calls submitted by simultaneously executing transactions at the application program level (see Figure 10.1) and eventually transformed into the form of [10.1.2] at the level of the database *scheduler*.

To give a hint of what is to come in the next few sections, we intend to show how a database scheduler, as pictured in Figure 10.1, processing a sequence of interleaved operations of the kind we see in the history given in [10.1.2], can act in such a way that the history actually allowed by the scheduler is *equivalent* in effect to some serial schedule. In this way we are always guaranteed that each of the transactions is isolated from the others—that is, we provide the isolation guarantee. The scheduler accomplishes this task by delaying some submitted operations when it sees that allowing them to occur in the order submitted would break the isolation guarantee; in some special cases, the scheduler declares a *deadlock* and (as we saw in Chapter 5) aborts one of the transactions involved. As a matter of fact, the history given in [10.1.2] represents an illegal series of operations from a serializability standpoint, and the database scheduler will not allow it to occur in

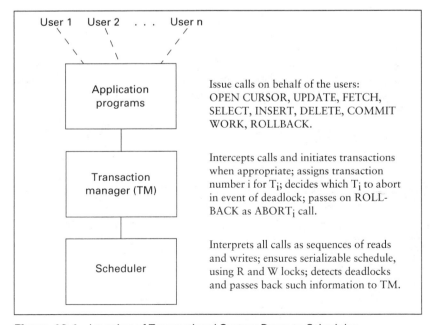

Figure 10.1 Layering of Transactional System Down to Scheduler

this form. The reason this history is illegal is that we can think of a situation in which a series of operations in this order will give an inconsistent result. We call this an *interpretation* of the history.

EXAMPLE 10.1.1

We give an interpretation of the history in [10.1.2], to see how we could arrive at an inconsistent result. To do this, we give specific values to the data items read, postulate an underlying purpose to the logic that determines the values that are written by the transaction based on its input values, and then specify a consistency rule that the series of operations will break. Assume that the data elements A and B are two accounts held by a bank customer, and that their initial values are A = 50 and B = 50. As in Examples 5.4.1 and 5.4.2, the inconsistent analysis example we gave to motivate the need for isolation, transaction T_1 is simply adding up the values in the two accounts and printing out the net worth of the customer who owns these accounts in order to perform a credit check. Transaction T_2 is transferring money from one account to another, moving 30 units from account A to account B. Both transactions operate under the consistency rule that they neither create nor destroy money. However, because the operations of the two transactions are "interleaved" in a way the scheduler should not allow, an inconsistency can arise. Here is a restatement of the history of [10.1.2] with the given value assumptions added.

[10.1.3] ... $R_2(A, 50)$ $W_2(A, 20)$ $R_1(A, 20)$ $R_1(B, 50)$ $R_2(B, 50)$ $W_2(B, 80)$ C_1 C_2. ...

We see in this history that transaction T_1 reads the value of A after transaction T_2 has acted on it (and therefore sees the value 20), but it reads the value of B before transaction T_2 has changed it (and therefore sees the value 50). The sum of the two accounts that T_1 sees is 70, which is incorrect either before or after the updates made by transaction T_2. Such an inconsistent view can clearly lead to an inappropriate failure of a credit check. The reason for the inconsistency is that T_1 has somehow seen "partial" results of the T_2 transaction. The two transactions are not properly isolated from one another. ∎

This viewing of partial results could never have occurred if transaction operations weren't interleaved. Consider the following two "serial" histories, that is, histories in which all the operations of one transaction must be complete before any operations of a different transaction can begin, shown in Figure 10.2.

Note that in both of these serial histories, transaction T_1 gets a consistent view of the data elements A and B. In the first case, T_1 sums 50 and 50 to get 100, and in the second it sums 80 and 20 to get 100. Money has neither been created nor destroyed. It should be clear that if all transaction logic obeys the consistency rule that money is neither created nor destroyed by a transaction, then in any serial execution each transaction starts with a

... $R_1(A, 50)$ $R_1(B, 50)$ C_1 $R_2(B, 50)$ $W_2(B, 20)$ $R_2(A, 50)$ $W_2(A, 80)$ C_2 ...
... $R_2(B, 50)$ $W_2(B, 20)$ $R_2(A, 50)$ $W_2(A, 80)$ C_2 $R_1(A, 80)$ $R_1(B, 20)$ C_1 ...

Figure 10.2 Two Serial Histories for [10.1.2]

642   consistent view: the same amount of total money in the system. However, if money is to be transferred, then it must be created or destroyed at some intermediate point in a sequence of transactional updates, since we can't subtract from one row and add to another row in a single W (write) operation. The problem with viewing partial results of an update transaction, then, is that it may become possible to view an inconsistent state of the data. But if transactions operate only in a serial history, in which all operations of one transaction complete before another transaction can start its operations, then no inconsistencies of the kind shown in [10.1.3] can arise.

In what follows, we use the idea of serial execution as a touchstone for what we consider correct. We say that a history of interleaved transactional operations is *serializable* if it can be shown to have the same effect as some serial history of transactions executing one after another in some possible order; we say that two histories such as this are *equivalent*. But how do we judge whether an *uninterpreted* history like the one in [10.1.2] is equivalent to some serial history? Consider again the reasoning we followed in Example 10.1.1. We say that we created an *interpretation* of a history, H (such as in [10.1.2]), when we specified a consistency rule (money is neither created nor destroyed) and postulated a purpose for the underlying transactions, leading to a sequence of specific values for the reads and writes of H (as in [10.1.3]). When an interpretation of a history, H, can be shown to break the consistency rule (T_1 sees a total balance that cannot exist, despite program logic that guarantees consistency), then it is *not* equivalent to any serial history. We will see a number of such examples in what follows.

At this point it is reasonable to review the four defining properties of a transaction, known as the ACID properties, that we met in the introduction to this chapter. We say that transactions are

Atomic. The set of updates contained in a transaction must succeed or fail as a unit.

Consistent. Complete transactional transformations on data elements bring the database from one consistent state to another. For example, if money can neither be created nor destroyed, then successive states must all have the same balance totals.

Isolated. Even though transactions execute concurrently, it appears to each successful transaction that it has executed in a serial schedule with the others. (Some transactions might be aborted to guarantee isolation, as, for example, in a deadlock situation—they are not successful, but can later be *retried*, as demonstrated in Example 5.4.4.)

Durable. Once a transaction commits, the changes it has made to the data will survive any machine or system failures.

The properties of atomicity, isolation, and durability are all guaranteed by the database system to make the programmer's job easier. The idea of consistency is a logical property that the programmer must maintain in writing the logic for individual transactions acting under isolated circumstances. By guaranteeing the isolation property, the system also guarantees that consistency is maintained, even in the presence of interleaved operations and system failure.

10.2 Interleaved Read-Write Operations

We have just learned that a serial history, in which all operations of one transaction must complete before any operations of another can be executed, is not prey to the inconsistencies arising from interleaved operations of read and write. Why then do we interleave operations from different transactions? Why not execute all transactions in a strict serial schedule? This approach can be thought of as a very simple rule of behavior that the scheduler can impose on an arriving series of transactional operations: after one transaction, T_i, has executed a single data access operation (R_i or W_i) to begin its transaction, we say that T_i is *active*, or *in process*. If another transaction, T_j, operating on behalf of a different user, now submits an initial transactional operation (R_j or W_j) to the scheduler, the scheduler makes transaction T_j WAIT until T_i has completed its sequence of operations—that is, until T_i has either aborted (A_i) or committed (C_i). If more than one transaction is forced to WAIT, then when the scheduler sees that a transaction has completed, it allows the next transaction to begin (execute its first operation), using a first-come-first-served order.

The reason most database systems do not impose a strict serial schedule of transactional operations is simple: interleaved transactional operations offer a chance for greatly improved system performance. The freedom to have several transactions in process at one time means that while one transaction is performing I/O, another transaction can be using the CPU, thus increasing the *throughput* of the system, a measure of the number of transactions that can finish in any given period of time. Since I/O takes a long time, throughput is most enhanced when the system has numerous disk drives and transactions active at once.

EXAMPLE 10.2.1

Assume that a large number of users are awaiting service from a transactional application, and that each transaction uses CPU and I/O resources in the following sequence: (CPU use) $R_i(*)$ (CPU use) $W_i(*)$ C_i, where the operations $R_i(*)$ and $W_i(*)$ represent disk I/O. We assume that the system has a single CPU, that the resource use of the commit action is zero, that each CPU use interval is 5 ms (.005 seconds), and that the I/O to perform $R_i(*)$ or $W_i(*)$ (read or write of some unknown data element) requires a wait time of 50 ms. (As we have seen, an I/O that is immediately serviced requires 12.5 ms, but we assume that a "waiting line" or "queue" is slowing down the service. We begin the following discussion with a single transaction thread, but this is merely a preparation for discussing a situation with a number of concurrent users, where queuing delays are common.) We can picture the sequence of events that occurs when a series of transactions is serviced according to a strict serial schedule with the schematic diagram of Figure 10.3.

In Figure 10.3 the resource use of the system is symbolized by the step function graph, with intervals of resource use alternating between CPU and disk (I/O use). Each disk use is labeled with the transactional access operation being performed, such as $R_1(*)$ or $W_1(*)$. We see that each transaction spends the first 5 ms using CPU, then performs a 50-ms $R_i(*)$, then 5 ms more of CPU and a 50-ms $W_i(*)$. The time to perform C_i is taken to be zero, so the next transaction starts immediately. Each complete transaction therefore takes an interval of 110 ms, and we have a throughput of one transaction every 110 ms, a rate of 9.09 transactions per second (9.09 TPS). The CPU is underutilized with this schedule, active for only 10 ms out of each 110 ms, or 9.09% active, but the disk is rather well utilized, active at least 100 ms out of each 110 ms, and possibly more because of accesses by other processes.

Figure 10.4 shows a schedule in which two transactions interleave operations, but the system still has only one disk. Although we have two labels for CPU and disk on the left, in order to graph resource use for two concurrent transaction processes (also known as transaction threads), the two CPU labels stand for the same thing as do the two disk labels.

In Figure 10.4 we see that the two transaction threads spend most of their time waiting for each other to finish access to the disk so they can get their turn. However, the schedule does succeed in overlapping CPU with I/O. Each transaction requires 100 ms of disk access, and the disk is now fully utilized instead of being unused for 10 ms out of every 110 ms, as it was earlier. In the long run, therefore, since I/O is the gating factor, we have a throughput of one trans-

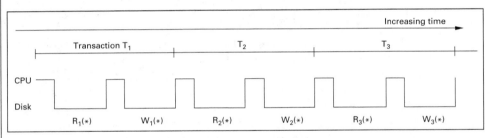

Figure 10.3   Sequence of Events in a Serial Transactional Schedule

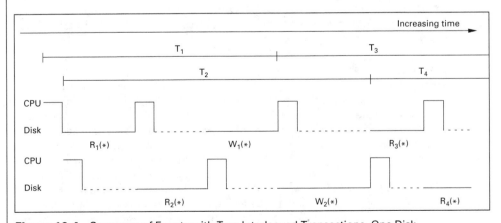

Figure 10.4   Sequence of Events with Two Interleaved Transactions, One Disk

action every 100 ms, or 10 TPS. The specific schedule shown in the figure may be a bit confusing, however, so we work it out in detail. At the very beginning of the example, we see that transaction T_1 uses 5 ms of CPU, then 50 ms for $R_1(*)$, then 5 ms of CPU, waits 45 ms for $R_2(*)$ to complete, then 50 ms for $W_1(*)$, and completes, requiring $5 + 50 + 5 + 45 + 50 = 155$ ms. This is unusually fast because T_1 gets a head start on resource use. From that point on, however, all subsequent transactions T_i spend 5 ms on CPU, wait 45 ms for disk, spend 50 ms for $R_i(*)$, 5 ms for CPU, 45 ms waiting for disk, 50 ms for $W_i(*)$, and complete, requiring $5 + 45 + 50 + 5 + 45 + 50 = 200$ ms. Thus in the long run, each thread runs one transaction every 200 ms, and the two threads together run one transaction every 100 ms, or 10 TPS.

In Figure 10.5 we see two transaction threads interleaving operations, with odd-numbered transactions performing I/O access on disk 1, while even-numbered transactions use disk 2. (Of course, it wouldn't happen so neatly on a real system, but we will consider this point later.) We see that both threads proceed without waits (except in the very first 5 ms, where T_1 uses the CPU and T_2 waits for it). In successive CPU use, the offset established in the beginning ensures that even-numbered transactions never overlap with odd-numbered transactions. (This too is unrealistic for a real system.) Just as in Figure 10.3, each transaction thread performs one transaction each 110 ms, a rate of 9.09 TPS, and the two threads together execute transactions at twice that rate, 18.18 TPS. In this case the CPU is utilized for 10 ms out of each 55, about 18.18% utilized.

In order to increase the utilization of the CPU even further, we add more disks and more transactional threads to overlap operations. Figure 10.6 gives a schematic picture of resource use when 11 disks are available and there are 11 transactional threads, and we assume that resource overlap is perfect. In this case we have 11 threads running at full speed. Each transaction requires 110 ms as in the first case above, but with 11 transactions running simultaneously, we have a throughput of 11 transactions every 110 ms, or 100 TPS. The CPU is 100% utilized because of the unrealistically perfect resource overlap assumed.

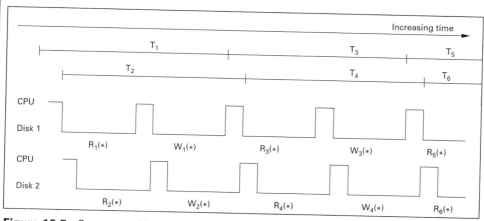

Figure 10.5 Sequence of Events with Two Interleaved Transactions, Two Disks

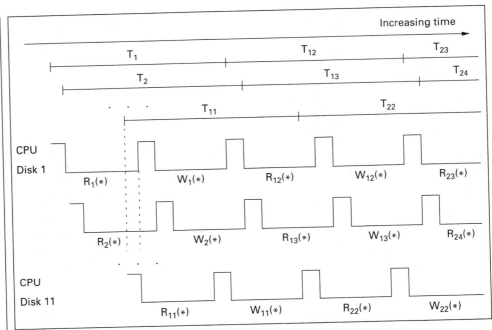

Figure 10.6 Sequence of Events with 11 Interleaved Transactions, 11 Disks

The ratio of 5 ms of CPU use to 50 ms of disk I/O is quite common in transactional systems. As less expensive computers become faster with new advances in technology, the ratio can be expected to become even more extreme, since CPU rates are advancing faster than disk I/O rates. For this reason, many transactional systems will be configured to run with a large number of disks.

Naturally, concurrently executing transactions are not always guaranteed to access distinct disks and to perfectly overlap their CPU time, as they do in Figure 10.6. Let us consider the approach a DBA would normally take to configure for the workload of Example 10.2.1, where each transaction uses 10 ms of CPU and 50 ms of disk. (In the following analysis we consider only the actual utilization of the disk arm, 25 ms per I/O instead of 50 ms, because the decisions we make will affect the waiting time for disk service.) If we pose this problem properly, it is an exercise in a mathematical discipline known as *queuing theory*, a field that incorporates a good deal of hard-won intuition. It is difficult to provide an explanation of the principles involved without the mathematical background, but we try to provide a feel for what happens. A sensible configuration with a ratio of 5 to 1 in I/O elapsed time to CPU time, given above, is to use a good deal more than five disks, say, ten disks, and then run more than ten simultaneous transaction threads, say, 20. The data to be read and written by the transactions should be divided evenly over the disks, so that any $R_i(*)$ or $W_i(*)$ operation of an arbitrarily chosen transaction is equally likely to access any one of them. Clearly as we increase the number of disks there is more and more chance that any thread, as it completes its CPU interval and requires data from disk, will find the data it wants on a disk that is not already occupied seeking data for another thread. Thus it will not have to wait in line, or queue. What we are doing here is shortening the average disk service time in comparison to the CPU time by adding more disks. Although the disk service time was specified as 50 ms in the examples we considered above, the time actually depends on the number of disks available to reduce the queue lengths for a given rate of random service requests. We assume in what follows that it has a lower limit of 25 ms.

Now the DBA also needs to minimize hardware cost by not buying more disks than are required to properly utilize the CPU resource. This means that there will still be a good deal of disk collision, where I/O requests of two different threads are sent to the same disk at nearly the same time; we certainly won't achieve the perfect interleaving that we saw in Figure 10.6. This would be an extremely serious problem if we continued to run only 11 threads, as in that example with an average disk service time of 50 ms, since I/O requests would have to be filled in a nearly perfect interleaved pattern to keep the CPU occupied. But with 20 concurrent threads available, we can conceivably have as many as 20 transactions running in parallel. We can picture at any given instant that some of the transactions are waiting for CPU or running the CPU (these transactions are said to be in the CPU queue), and some transactions are waiting for one of the disks or running one of the disks (these are said to be in one of the different disk queues). In order to achieve high CPU utilization, we merely need to guarantee that the CPU queue rarely becomes empty (whereupon the CPU would have no transaction to execute), and this is achieved if we guarantee a long average CPU queue. Now it should be clear that we can do this if we can keep an average of nearly five out of the ten disks running at all times. It is one of the basic principles of queuing theory that if requesters (transactions) leave one part of the system (the disk part) and make requests of another part (the CPU) faster than they can be serviced, then the queue for the overloaded resource provider will grow arbitrarily long. (Because the disk-to-CPU service time ratio is 25 ms on each disk to 5 ms on the sole CPU, when more than five disks are being kept in service simultaneously on the average, the CPU will be unable to keep up.)

By permitting a large number of threads, we give the system more to do in the event that some subset of disk requests collide. Even though several threads are tied up waiting for disk service, the CPU can run other transactional threads and put out more disk requests. With enough requests, we will be relatively certain to place requests to more than five of the ten disks, and as a result we will keep the CPU heavily utilized. Note that we don't *have* to run 20 simultaneous transactions just because we have that number of threads, and in fact everything we have explained so far is part of a feedback process. As new transactions enter the system, they are assigned to distinct threads, so that up to 20 can run concurrently. However, transactions may run to completion at too high a rate for 20 simultaneous transactions to ever be in existence—the more transactions that run concurrently, the higher the throughput rate, and we shouldn't normally need maximum thread concurrency. We wouldn't normally expect to see 100% CPU utilization either, but rather 90% or 95%. On the other hand, if the CPU utilization falls too low, so that the workload is not being handled at the needed throughput rate, then more transactions enter the system to run concurrently up to the maximum of 20, and this increases the disk and CPU utilization. (Additional transaction starts after the 20 threads are occupied have to wait in another queue to be assigned threads.)

Thus we depend on statistical behavior to increase the CPU utilization as more disks and threads are added. Readers interested in how this sort of process can be numerically balanced should read one of the standard introductory texts on queuing theory. See "Suggestions for Further Reading" at the end of the chapter for a recommendation.

10.3   Serializability and the Precedence Graph

In this section we derive a criterion that allows us to say when a given history of transactional operations (such as the one we saw in [10.1.2]) is *serializable*. This means that the history is *equivalent* (in a sense to be defined below), to some *serial* history, a history where all operations of one transaction must complete before any operations of another can be executed. A serializable history can be accepted by a system scheduler that supports the property of transaction *isolation*. We begin defining what we mean by histories being equivalent with a discussion of when two transactions with interleaved operations in a serial history H are said to have *conflicting operations*. We say that read and write operations by different transactions *conflict* if they reference the same data item and at least one of them is a write (the other can be either a read or a write). This concept is stated with more precise notation in Definition 10.3.1. We will show that when two operations by different transactions conflict in a history, the order in which they occur is important, and we can say that two different histories containing the same transactional operations in a somewhat different order are nevertheless *equivalent* if all pairs of conflicting operations lie in the same order in both histories. With this background, we now define a history to be *serializable* if it is equivalent to some serial history. In Theorem 10.3.4 we demonstrate a criterion for determining when a history is serializable.

To begin to motivate some of these concepts, let us assume that we are given a history H of transactional operations of the kind we saw in [10.1.2]. Now assume that in the history H, one transaction reads a data item A and at a later point in time a second transaction updates (writes) the same data item. Thus the two operations shown in [10.3.1] appear in H, with ellipses (. . .) representing arbitrary intervening operations of the history.

[10.3.1] . . . $R_1(A)$ . . . $W_2(A)$ . . .

When we say that an update is performed by operation $W_2(A)$ in the history H, we simply mean that a new value overwrites the current value of data item A. We are not necessarily implying the kind of update performed by the SQL Update statement, since there is no implied read of the data item A on which to base the new value written. (Of course, there is also nothing saying that there is no such read.) If we had meant to imply a prior read, we would have written . . . $R_2(A)$ . . . $W_2(A)$ . . . in place of . . . $W_2(A)$ . . . .

Now we want to try to come up with an *equivalent* serial history to the history H that contains the two operations of [10.3.1] in the order specified. There may be more than one equivalent serial history, but we denote a representative one by S(H). Then in any equivalent serial history S(H), we claim that all the operations of transaction T_2 must come later in time than all the operations of transaction T_1. This is because transaction T_1 in the history H reads a value for the data item A (say, 50) that existed prior to the write performed by T_2; this write might have changed the value of A, say, to 20. We can certainly construct an *interpretation* where this happens. Since it seems necessary that in an "equivalent" serial history all transactions read the same data as they do in history H, it is obvious that T_2 must follow T_1 in serial order in both cases. We use the notation

$$R_1(A) <<_H W_2(A)$$

to mean that $R_1(A)$ comes before $W_2(A)$ in the history H, and we claim that this means that the same order must be preserved in an equivalent serial history S(H) (there may be more than one). We denote this by

$$R_1(A) <<_{S(H)} W_2(A)$$

More generally, since all operations for a transaction T_i occur together in a serial history, we can denote the set of all operations performed in T_i by the notation T_i itself, and write

$$T_1 <<_{S(H)} T_2$$

Now what we have just been arguing is that if a transaction T_1 reads a value for a data item prior to a write of the same data item performed by T_2, then the two operations cannot be reversed in any equivalent serial history. We now argue that the reverse is also true: if the transaction T_2 updates (writes) a data item B prior to a read of this data item by transaction T_1 in the history H,

$$W_2(B) <<_H R_1(B)$$

then we claim that transaction T_2 must precede T_1 in any equivalent serial history S(H), that is,

$$T_2 <<_{S(H)} T_1$$

What we have determined so far can be stated as follows. Two operations $X_i(A)$ and $Y_j(A)$ by different transactions T_i and T_j in a history H are said to *conflict* if, when one occurs before the other in the history H, the same order must be maintained for the corresponding transactions in any equivalent serial history. The operations $R_i(A)$ and $W_j(A)$ are conflicting operations in a history in whatever order they might occur.

To put it loosely, we have determined that reads conflict with writes. There are only two types of operations and four types of operation pairs, so let us now ask if reads conflict with reads—that is, do $R_i(A)$ and $R_j(A)$ conflict? We maintain that two reads do not

(1) $R_i(A) \rightarrow W_j(A)$ (meaning, in a history, $R_i(A)$ followed by $W_j(A)$)

(2) $W_i(A) \rightarrow R_j(A)$

(3) $W_i(A) \rightarrow W_j(A)$

Figure 10.7 The Three Types of Conflicting Operations

conflict in and of themselves. If we had a sequence . . . $R_i(A)$ . . . $W_k(A)$ . . . $R_j(A)$ . . . in the history H, we could conclude that $T_i \ll_{S(H)} T_k$ and $T_k \ll_{S(H)} T_j$ because of the two pairs of conflicting R-W operations, and thus by transitivity $T_i \ll_{S(H)} T_j$. However, the reads themselves are guiltless: a history H that has $R_i(A) R_j(A)$ and a history H' that has $R_j(A) R_i(A)$ have the same result, as long as no other operations intervene between the two reads.

The pair of operations $W_i(A)$ and $W_j(A)$, on the other hand, *are* conflicting. It should be clear that the order of these two operations is crucial, since if the two writes update the data element A to different values, the final resulting value of data element A will be determined by the specific write that comes last. Clearly two histories cannot be identical that give different final results. Figure 10.7 illustrates the three pairs of conflicting operations we have found.

These three pairs of operations, together with the pair $R_i(A)$ and $R_j(A)$, which we concluded did not conflict, make up all possible pairs of operations between two transactions T_i and T_j that can occur on the same data element. By contrast, any pair of operations on *different* data elements are *not* conflicting: $R_i(A)$ does not conflict with $W_j(B)$, for example, since the order in which these operations are performed doesn't seem to matter. If two different transactions act on totally distinct data items, the order in which they execute is irrelevant. Again as with the $R_i(A)$ and $R_j(A)$ example, we can conceive of a third transaction T_k, which would conflict with $R_i(A)$ and $W_j(B)$ and force a specific order on T_i and T_j by transitivity; but we are claiming that $R_i(A)$ and $W_j(B)$ do not conflict in themselves. To sum up the foregoing discussion, we provide a number of definitions.

DEFINITION 10.3.1 Two operations $X_i(A)$ and $Y_j(B)$ in a history are said to *conflict* if and only if the following three conditions hold. (1) A = B. Operations on distinct data items never conflict. (2) i ≠ j. Two operations conflict only if they are performed by distinct transactions. (3) One of the two operations X or Y is a write, W, while the other may be either an R or a W. ■

This definition of conflicting operations in a history seems like many mathematical definitions at first: we wonder what application it has. To see what we can do with this concept, we need a few examples. Recall the history given in [10.1.2], which we designate as H1.

$$H1 = R_2(A) \, W_2(A) \, R_1(A) \, R_1(B) \, R_2(B) \, W_2(B) \, C_1 \, C_2$$

Also recall that in Example 10.1.1 we gave an interpretation of this history that showed that it was not serializable.

DEFINITION 10.3.2 An interpretation of an arbitrary history H consists of three parts: (1) a description of the purpose of the logic that is being performed by the transactions involved in the history, sufficient to confirm that data values written make sense in terms of data values read; (2) a specification of precise values of data items being read and written in the history; and (3) a consistency rule, that is, a statement of a logical property that we can demonstrate must be preserved by isolated transaction executions of the logic described in (1). In the case where an (interleaved) history is being shown to be nonserializable, we demonstrate that the consistency rule is broken by some transaction in the history, where this is clearly impossible in any serial execution. ∎

EXAMPLE 10.3.1

To repeat the interpretation of Example 10.1.1, we concluded that the given history H1 was not serializable because of the following interpretation. We start with the specification of (2), the precise data items read and written:

$$H1 = R_2(A, 50)\ W_2(A, 20)\ R_1(A, 20)\ R_1(B, 50)\ R_2(B, 50)\ W_2(B, 80)\ C_1\ C_2$$

Here is the specification of (1), the purpose of the logic: T_1 is doing a credit check, adding up the balances A and B, and T_2 is transferring money from A to B (we see here that the amount of money being transferred is 30). Finally the consistency rule (3) is that neither transaction creates or destroys money. But the schedule given here is not serializable because T_1 sees an *inconsistent result,* the sum 70 of the two balances A and B, rather than the balance of 100 that it would see in any serial execution.

The concept of conflicting operations we have introduced gives us a more direct way to check for serializability. Note that the second and third operations in H1 consist of a conflicting pair: $W_2(A) <<H1 R_1(A)$. According to what we have said about conflicting operations, we must therefore have in any equivalent serial history, S(H1), $T_2 <<_{S(H1)} T_1$. At the same time, the fourth and sixth operations of the history H1 give us $R_1(B) <<H1 W_2(B)$, and therefore we see that $T_1 <<_{S(H1)} T_2$. Clearly these two facts lead to a contradiction, since it is impossible to create a serial history where at the same time $T_1 <<_{S(H1)} T_2$, and $T_2 <<_{S(H1)} T_1$. We conclude from this that no equivalent serial history can exist. ∎

If you consider the two facts that led to this conclusion, you will see that Example 10.3.1 supports the reasons we gave that the order of the conflicting operations in an arbitrary history H must be preserved in S(H). The reason for the inconsistency is that (1) T_1 reads the data item A *after* it has been written by T_2, and (2) T_1 reads the data item B *before* it has been written by T_2, two conflicting pairs with opposite orientation. This is precisely the reason that the explicit values appearing in the interpreted history H_1 show that T_1 encounters a sum that could not be produced in any serial execution of the logic: in any proper serial execution, one of the conflicting pairs would be reversed in order.

EXAMPLE 10.3.2
Consider the history H2, given by

$$H2 = R_1(A)\ R_2(A)\ W_1(A)\ W_2(A)\ C_1C_2$$

This is an example of transactional inconsistency known as a *lost update,* or sometimes a *dirty write,* where each transaction reads a data item and then writes it back without realizing that the other transaction is doing the same. As an interpretation, assume that A is a bank balance starting with the value 100 and that T_1 tries to add 40 to the balance at the same time that T_2 tries to add 50. The result would be

$$R_1(A, 100)\ R_2(A, 100)\ W_1(A, 140)\ W_2(A, 150)\ C_1\ C_2$$

and the final value for A is 150. However, going by the intentions of the two transactions, we should have A = 190 in any serial schedule. Therefore this schedule cannot be serializable! In fact, we see that the first operation in this history, $R_1(A)$, conflicts with the fourth operation, $W_2(A)$, giving us $R_1(A) <<_{H2} W_2(A)$, and therefore $T_1 <<_S(H2)\ T_2$. Also the second operation in the history, $R_2(A)$, conflicts with the third operation, $W_1(A)$, giving us $R_2(A) <<_{H2} W_1(A)$, and therefore $T_2 <<_S(H2)\ T_1$. Thus as in Example 10.3.1, there is no equivalent serial history. This example demonstrates that two conflicting pairs, $R_i(A) <<_H W_j(A)$ and $R_j(A) <<_H W_i(A)$ of type (1) from Figure 10.7, are together sufficient to result in the nonserializability that can be demonstrated by interpretation. ∎

EXAMPLE 10.3.3
Consider the history H3, given by

$$H3 = W_1(A)\ W_2(A)\ W_2(B)\ W_1(B)\ C_1\ C_2$$

This example demonstrates that a conflicting pair of type (3), a W-W pair, can cause a history to be nonserializable as well. Clearly since there are no reads involved, conflicting pairs type (1) and (2) cannot be involved. Since the first two operations give $W_1(A) <<_{H3} W_2(A)$, we have $T_1 <<_{S(H3)}\ T_2$. Since the third and fourth operations give $W_2(B) <<_{H3} W_1(B)$, we have $T_2 <<_{S(H3)} T_1$, and so—as in the two previous examples—no equivalent serial history is possible. How would we create an interpretation to demonstrate this fact? Assume that there are two accounts A and B, with balances starting with a sum of 90, and that we are dealing with only one type of transaction in this history that "tops up" the two accounts, resetting the sum of the balances to 100. We have a consistency rule that the sum of the two balances never exceeds 100. Note that a transaction that sets the sum of the two balances need not read the original values—it can simply perform "blind writes" (writes without preceding reads) to A and B so that the two resulting values sum to 100. Now consider the following interpreted history assigning values for H3:

$$W_1(A, 50)\ W_2(A, 80)\ W_2(B, 20)\ W_1(B, 50)\ C_1\ C_2$$

Both of the transactions obey the consistency rules (each one in isolation would give a sum of 100 for the two accounts A and B), but the result of the interleaved schedule gives a sum of 130, and the consistency rule is broken. ∎

The Precedence Graph

To generalize the serializability argument we have seen in these three examples, that certain configurations of conflicting operations are impossible in any serial schedule, we define something called a *precedence graph*. A precedence graph is a structure, created from a history H, that remembers the order of transactions implied by conflicting pairs in the history.

DEFINITION 10.3.3 The Precedence Graph. A precedence graph for a history H is a directed graph denoted by PG(H). The vertices of the precedence graph correspond to transactions that have committed in H—that is, transactions T_i for which the Commit operation C_i exists in the history H. An edge $T_i \rightarrow T_j$ exists in the graph whenever two conflicting operations X_i and Y_j occur in that order in the history H. The edge $T_i \rightarrow T_j$ should be read to mean that T_i comes before T_j in any equivalent history S(H)—that is, that $T_i <<_{S(H)} T_j$. ∎

Whenever a pair of operations conflicts in a history, we can draw the corresponding directed arc in the precedence graph. The precedence graphs for the histories considered in Examples 10.3.1, 10.3.2, and 10.3.3 are all identical, with the structure shown in the following illustration.

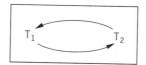

As we can see, this graph has a circuit, and it is for this reason we argue that no equivalent serial history exists. Any serial history would have to place either T_1 or T_2 earlier in time, say, $T_1 <<_{S(H)} T_2$, and then at least one edge of the precedence graph would point backward in time, from T_2 to T_1. Now an edge exists in PG(H) because of conflicting operations between the two transactions, and the direction in which it points is the original order of occurrence in the history H. To have an edge of PG(H) pointing backward in a serial history means that we have reversed the order of two conflicting operations from the original history H, and therefore that the order in the serial history is not equivalent to the original history H. It should be clear then that if PG(H) has a circuit, there can never be a serial history equivalent to H, since at least one edge of PG(H) must always point backward in any serial order of transactions. (The proof of this is given as an exercise at the end of the chapter.) In what follows, we prove that if the precedence graph PG(H) does not have a circuit, then there is a serial execution of the transactions that is equivalent to H.

THEOREM 10.3.4 The Serializability Theorem. A history H has an equivalent serial execution S(H) if and only if the precedence graph PG(H) contains no circuit.

PROOF. We leave the *only if* proof for the exercises at the end of the chapter, and show here that if PG(H) contains no circuit, then there is a serial ordering of the transactions so that no edge of PG(H) ever points from a later to an earlier transaction. Let us assume that there are m transactions involved, and renumber the transactions of PG(H) if necessary, so that they are denoted by $T_1, T_2, \ldots, T_m$. We are trying to find some reordering of these transactions to form a desired serial history $S(H) = T_{i(1)}, T_{i(2)}, \ldots, T_{i(m)}$, where $i(1), i(2), \ldots, i(m)$ is some reordering of the integers $1, 2, \ldots, m$. We start by assuming a lemma, to be proven later, that in any directed graph G with no circuit there is always at least one vertex with no edge entering it. This means that the precedence graph PG(H) has at least one vertex, T_k, with no edge entering it. We choose that transaction, T_k, to be $T_{i(1)}$, the first transaction in the serial history S(H). Notice that it has an important qualifying property, that no other transaction T_m chosen from the remaining vertices of PG(H), which will be placed to the right of $T_{i(1)}$, has an edge in PG(H) pointing backward to $T_{i(1)}$. We now remove the vertex just placed, T_k, from the graph PG(H), as well as all edges leaving T_k, and call the resulting graph $PG^1(H)$, where the superscript 1 means that one vertex has been removed from the original. Note that $PG^1(H)$ also has the property that it contains no circuits (no edges have been added to PG(H), so no circuit could have appeared). By our lemma, this means there is a vertex T_k^1 in $PG^1(H)$ that has no edges entering it in $PG^1(H)$. We choose this vertex to be the second element of S(H), $T_{i(2)}$. Note that there might be an edge from $T_{i(1)}$ to $T_{i(2)}$ in PG(H), but there is no edge entering $T_{i(2)}$ in $PG^1(H)$. That means there will never be an edge going from right to left to point at $T_{i(2)}$ in the serial schedule yet to be determined from the remaining vertices of $PG^1(H)$. Proceeding inductively, we define $PG^{r-1}(H)$ with T_k^{r-1} removed to be $PG^r(H)$, and while $PG^r(H)$ is non-empty, choose T_k^r to be a vertex of $PG^r(H)$ with no edge entering it, setting T_k^r to be element $T_{i(r+1)}$ in S(H). By construction, no edge of PG(H) will ever point backward in the sequence S(H), from $T_{i(m)}$ to $T_{i(n)}$, m > n. The algorithm used to determine this sequence, known as a *topological sort,* is described in a number of algorithmic texts. ∎

To complete the proof of Theorem 10.3.4, we have only to prove the lemma mentioned.

LEMMA 10.3.5 In any finite directed acyclic graph G, there is always a vertex v with no edges entering it.

PROOF. Choose any vertex v_1 from G. Either it has no edge entering it or there is an edge entering it from a vertex v_2. Now v_2 either has no edge entering it or there is an edge entering it from vertex v_3. Continuing in this way, we find that the sequence either ends with some vertex v_m, so that v_m has no edge entering it, or the sequence continues forever. But if the sequence continues forever, then at some point some vertex must be relabeled, since there are only a finite number of vertices in G. Assume that when we label v_n, we find for the first time that this is equivalent to some previously labeled vertex v_i, i < n. But then we have a circuit, $v_n \to v_{n-1} \to v_{n-2} \to \ldots \to v_{i+1} \to v_i = v_n$. We have specified that the graph G is acyclic, so this is impossible. This means that the sequence specified doesn't continue forever and there must be a last vertex v_m with no edge entering it, which is what we wished to show.

■

10.4 Locking to Ensure Serializability

Examine Figure 10.8, which is nearly the same as Figure 10.1, to follow the discussion below.

In a transactional database system there are normally a large number of users trying to get work done at monitors—users who are unaware of such things as transactions or database calls made on their behalf. In the normal course of execution, an application program issues an operation on behalf of some user, and the database initiates a transaction and assigns a number, i, to the transaction. The module of the database system that does this is known as the *transaction manager*, or *TM*, as we see in Figure 10.8. The TM passes on such calls as UPDATE, FETCH, SELECT, INSERT, and DELETE to the scheduler.

It is the job of the *scheduler* to ensure that the "interleaved history" of all the transactional operations is serializable. It does this by forcing some transactional operations to WAIT and allowing others to proceed, so that the resulting history of operations is a serializable one. When a transactional operation is forced to WAIT, the corresponding user is required to wait as well; but since the time period is typically a small fraction of a second, the user will never notice.

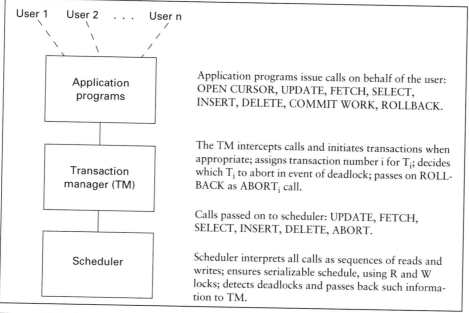

Figure 10.8 Layering of Transactional System Down to the Scheduler

One simple approach we have already mentioned can be used by the scheduler—to impose a strict serial history discipline on the transactional operations, insisting that all operations of one transaction be complete (including a final commit or rollback), before operations from the next transaction are allowed to begin. As we saw in Section 10.2, requiring strict serial execution is usually a very bad idea from the standpoint of performance. In this section we explain how a scheduler that works on the basis of locking can guarantee a serializable schedule with a good deal of interleaving of operations.

The locking discipline used to assure transactional consistency in commercial database systems is known as *two-phase locking*, abbreviated *2PL*, and it is used by most commercial database systems.

DEFINITION 10.4.1 Two-Phase Locking, or 2PL. Three rules determine how locks are taken and released in 2PL.

[1]   When transaction T_i attempts to read a data item, $R_i(A)$, the scheduler intercepts this call and first issues a call on its behalf to *read lock* the data item, $RL_i(A)$. Similarly when T_i attempts to write (update) a data item, $W_i(A)$, the scheduler first issues a call on its behalf to *write lock* the data item, $WL_i(A)$.[1]

[2]   Before granting a lock on a data item, the scheduler requires the requesting transaction to WAIT until no *conflicting lock* on the data item exists. (Conflicting locks occur for what we have been calling conflicting operations, as defined immediately below. Example 10.4.2 shows how such a WAIT affects the history execution.)

Two locks on the same data item are said to *conflict* if and only if they are attempted by different transactions and at least one of the two locks is a write lock.

[3]   There are two phases to locking: the *growing phase,* during which locks are acquired, and the *shrinking phase,* during which locks are released. The scheduler must ensure that after the shrinking phase begins, no new locks are acquired; it is forbidden for a transaction to release a lock and then acquire another lock at a later time.   ∎

The rules for 2PL theoretically allow locks to be released by a transaction before the transaction commits, as long as no new locks will be requested later. Most commercial systems, however, release all locks at once at the last stage of the COMMIT process. We assume that this is what occurs in the discussion that follows except when an unlock action is explicitly performed prior to commit. Two locks by the same transaction never conflict—in particular, a transaction with a read lock on a data item can acquire a write lock so long as no other transaction also has a read lock on the item. A transaction with

---

[1]Although read locks and write locks are logically sufficient, some database systems impose a number of other types of locks, known as *granular locks, multigranular locks,* or *intention locks*, that are outside the scope of this text. See references [1] and [2] at the end of this chapter for a discussion of these.

a write lock on a data item need not acquire a read lock. We say that a read lock is less powerful than a write lock, and the request $RL_i(A)$ on a data item A on which T_i already has a write lock immediately returns successfully.

The definition of conflicting locks is clearly intended to guarantee that two transactions performing conflicting operations will be "serialized," so that a circuit in the precedence graph can never occur. When two transactions have conflicting operations on a data item A, the transaction that accesses the data item first gets a lock and forces the other transaction to "come later" in any equivalent serial history. If the second transaction already holds a lock that the first transaction needs at a later point in its execution, this results in a deadlock, and one of the transactions must abort. The operations of the aborted transaction are then "removed" from the history (and from the precedence graph), so that the result is serializable. Thus the 2PL discipline guarantees a serializable history. We need to deal with the issue of deadlocks before we can show this rigorously.

First, however, we want to demonstrate the importance of locking rule 3 of Definition 10.4.1, which states there must be a growing phase followed by a shrinking phase in locking. This "two-phase rule" is crucial if locking is to have the desired effect of guaranteeing serializability.

EXAMPLE 10.4.1
Recall that history H1 was shown not to be serializable in Example 10.3.1. Here is a reordering of the operations of H1 that we call H1′, a history that is also nonserializable.

$$H1' = R_1(A)\ R_2(B)\ W_2(B)\ R_2(A)\ W_2(A)\ R_1(B)\ C_1\ C_2$$

We now show that if we allow the two-phase rule to be broken in this history, we can perform locking that satisfies all the other rules, but allows the nonserializable history H1′ to execute. In what follows, we add a number of new types of operations to illustrate locking operations in an "extended" history H1′. The operation designated by RL signifies that a read lock is taken, WL signifies that a write lock is taken, RU signifies that an unlock operation is performed to release a read lock, and WU means that an unlock operation releases a write lock. Thus for example, $RL_1(A)$ signifies that transaction T_1 takes a read lock on data item A, and $WU_2(A)$ that transaction T_2 unlocks a write lock on data item A. As usual, all locks held by a transaction are implicitly released at commit time. Here is the extended history H1′:

$$H1': RL_1(A)\ R_1(A)\ RU_1(A)\ RL_2(B)\ R_2(B)\ WL_2(B)\ W_2(B)\ WU_2(B)\ RL_2(A)\ R_2(A)\ WL_2(A)\ W_2(A)$$
$$RL_1(B)R_1(B)\ C_1\ C_2$$

In this extended history each transaction takes the appropriate lock, RL or WL, just before performing the operation R or W, respectively. Thus RULE 1 of 2PL Definition 10.4.1 is obeyed. Furthermore, RULE 2 is obeyed, since there is never a conflicting lock held on the data item by another transaction when a requested lock is granted. The third operation in H1′, $RU_1(A)$, releases the lock that would conflict later with the request of the eleventh operation, $WL_2(A)$, and similarly the eighth operation, $WU_2(B)$, releases the lock that would conflict with the thirteenth operation, $RL_1(B)$. Thus the only rule broken in this extended history is the two-phase rule, since both transactions acquire new locks after they release one. This demonstrates the necessity of the two-phase rule of locking to guarantee serializability. ∎

658   ## The Waits-For Graph

The *waits-for graph* is a directed graph maintained by many transactional locking schedulers, with vertices consisting of all current transactions in process and an edge from vertex T_i to vertex T_j, $T_i \rightarrow T_j$, exactly when T_i is currently waiting for a lock on some data item that is held by transaction T_j. The scheduler keeps a waits-for graph up-to-date as each of the following events occurs: (1) a new transaction starts (a new vertex is added to the graph); (2) a transaction is forced to WAIT (a new edge is added to the graph); and (3) an old transaction commits (a node is deleted, locked data items are released, and the first transaction in the waiting line for each data item is given the lock; this may now result in other transactions being required to wait on the new transaction holding the lock, but the algorithm by which this is done is relatively efficient). We say that a *deadlock* occurs whenever a circuit appears in the waits-for graph.

The scheduler tests for a possible *circuit* (sometimes called a *cycle*) in the waits-for graph at regular intervals after the graph changes. If a circuit is found, the scheduler chooses some transaction in the circuit as a *victim*, and aborts it. The criteria used to select the victim can be of various kinds: abort the youngest transaction first, abort the transaction that has performed the least amount of work, and so on.

EXAMPLE 10.4.2
We refer once again to the nonserializable history H1′ of Example 10.4.1. What will happen when the 2PL discipline is applied?

H1′ = $R_1(A)$ $R_2(B)$ $W_2(B)$ $R_2(A)$ $W_2(A)$ $R_1(B)$ C_1 C_2

History H1′ gives rise to the following sequence of events under the 2PL discipline:

$RL_1(A)$ $R_1(A)$ $RL_2(B)$ $R_2(B)$ $WL_2(B)$ $W_2(B)$ $RL_2(A)$ $R_2(A)$ $WL_2(A)$ (conflict with earlier lock from $RL_1(A)$—T_2 must WAIT) $RL_1(B)$ (conflict with earlier $WL_2(B)$—T1 must WAIT—there is now a circuit in the waits-for graph, so we must abort some transaction—choose T_1 as victim) A_1 (locks by T_1 released, so now $WL_2(A)$, which had been forced to WAIT, is successful) $W_2(A)$ C_2 (assume retry by T_1 code, renamed T_3) $RL_3(A)$ $R_3(A)$ $RL_3(B)$ $R_3(B)$ C_3

The scheduler, by forcing WAITs and aborting one transaction but then executing the retried transaction, has permitted both transactions to eventually succeed.   ■

THEOREM 10.4.2   Locking Theorem. A history of transactional operations that follows the 2PL discipline is always serializable.   ■

Clearly this is an important theorem, since the trust we place in the isolation guarantee of most commercial database systems depends on it. We start by proving a necessary lemma.

LEMMA 10.4.3 Let H be an extended history of transactional operations that follows the 2PL discipline (we call this a 2PL history). If the edge $T_i \rightarrow T_j$ is in the precedence graph for H, PG(H), then there must exist a data item D and two conflicting operations $X_i[D]$ and $Y_j[D]$ in H, such that $XU_i[D] <<_H YL_j[D]$.

PROOF. Since $T_i \rightarrow T_j$, by the definition of precedence graph and conflicting operations, there must exist two conflicting operations $X_i[D]$ and $Y_j[D]$, such that $X_i[D] <<_H Y_j[D]$. By the definition of two-phase locking, there must be locking and unlocking operations on either side of these operations, with $XL_i[D] <<_H X_i[D] <<_H XU_i[D]$ and $YL_j[D] <<_H Y_j[D] <<_H YU_j[D]$. (The unlocking operations might be implicit in commit operations for the two transactions, but we choose to make them explicit in the history H, occurring just prior to the commit operations.)

Now for operations occurring in the range of operations $XL_i[D] <<_H X_i[D] <<_H XU_i[D]$, the X lock is held on D by transaction T_i, and for operations occurring in the range $YL_j[D] <<_H Y_j[D] <<_H YU_j[D]$, the Y lock is held on D. Since X and Y conflict, the locks conflict, and the two intervals cannot overlap. But since $X_i[D] <<_H Y_j[D]$, this means that the locking intervals around these two operations must occur in this order:

$$XL_i[D] <<_H X_i[D] <<_H XU_i[D] <<_H YL_j[D] <<_H Y_j[D] <<_H YU_j[D]$$

and the desired result of the lemma is proved.   ∎

Given this lemma, we can prove Theorem 10.4.2.

PROOF OF THEOREM 10.4.2   We wish to show that every 2PL history H is serializable. But assume for purposes of contradiction that this is not true, so there exists a 2PL history H with a precedence graph PG(H) that contains a cycle $T_1 \rightarrow T_2 \rightarrow \ldots T_n \rightarrow T_1$. By Lemma 10.4.3, for each pair of transactions $T_K \rightarrow T_{K+1}$ in PG(H), there is a data item D_K such that $XU_K[D_K] <<_H YL_{K+1}[D_K]$. We can write this sequence of facts for all K on successive lines, as follows:

1. $XU_1[D_1] <<_H YL_2[D_1]$
2. $XU_2[D_2] <<_H YL_3[D_2]$
        . . .
n–1. $XU_{n-1}[D_{n-1}] <<_H YL_n[D_{n-1}]$
n. $XU_n[D_n] <<_H YL_1[D_n]$

By the two-phase property, all locks must be performed in a transaction T_i before any unlocks are performed. From lines 1 and 2, we see that transaction T_2 locks and unlocks data items D_1 and D_2, and by the two-phase property we know that $YL_2[D_1] <<_H XU_2[D_2]$. But given this, we can conclude from the facts on lines 1 and 2 and transitivity that

$$XU_1[D_1] <<_H YL_3[D_2]$$

In other words, some data item is unlocked by transaction T_1 before some other data item is locked by transaction T_3. We continue to derive conclusions in this way, and by induction through line n, we conclude that

$$XU_1[D_1] <<_H YL_1[D_n]$$

But this contradicts the two-phase property that all locks are performed by transaction T_1 before any unlocks are performed. Since we assume this was a 2PL history, we have arrived at a contradiction, and we conclude that no circuit can exist in PG(H). Therefore H must be serializable. ∎

10.5 Levels of Isolation

Theorem 10.4.2 tells us that a scheduler can guarantee serializable histories by imposing a two-phase locking discipline. This means that before any read or write of a data item, the scheduler attempts to take a read lock or write lock on behalf of the transaction performing the access, and the scheduler retains all locks achieved until it is safe to release them. Property 3 of 2PL assures us that a transaction won't release a lock and later acquire a different lock, so we have to hold all locks until there are no remaining new data item accesses to come. In fact, we are assuming that we hold all locks taken by a transaction until the transaction commits or aborts.

However, scheduling that guarantees perfect serializability can be very intrusive on performance. As we add more threads and concurrent transactions, especially when transactions deal with a large number of data items that are highly popular, transactional accesses begin to overlap on data items, and lock conflicts mean that more and more transactions find themselves in a WAIT state. The number of deadlocks also increases with greater concurrency, and the aborts and subsequent retries of transactional victims that the scheduler chooses seem to waste computer resources. But actually the most serious problem arises because, with large numbers of simultaneously active transactions, more and more transactions go into WAIT because of locking conflicts. This effect is so pronounced that in certain circumstances, if we increase the number of threads for concurrent transactions, we actually *reduce* the number of transactions that are concurrently active and not blocked in WAIT state (the *effective concurrency level*). The performance problem that arises is not because CPU is wasted on abort retries, but rather because the CPU can never be fully utilized, since we never get a high enough effective level of concurrency to keep the CPU busy by overlapping I/Os with transactional logic of active transactions.

Because of this problem, it was suggested a number of years ago that database system schedulers might weaken the rules of two-phase locking to reduce the number of transactional access conflicts that cause WAITs. Presumably this weakening will increase effective concurrency. Of course with weaker rules, we don't have such a strong guarantee of isolation, and it is possible that transactions with overlapped operations will produce effects on one another that wouldn't be possible with strict serial schedules. Nevertheless, various weakened forms of locking are now a fact, with the ANSI SQL-99 standard supporting a feature known as *isolation levels*. (Note that the SQL-99 definition of isolation levels differs in important ways from an earlier definition of *degrees of isolation*, $0°$, $1°$, $2°$, and $3°$, that are still used in some products under different names. See the text by Gray and Reuter [2].)

It is possible in SQL-99 syntax to set the isolation level, immediately before executing an SQL statement that initiates a transaction (any data access), with something
known as a *Set Transaction* statement. Here are the four isolation levels provided by
SQL-99, in increasing restrictiveness and level of isolation guarantee to the programmer:

[1] Read Uncommitted (sometimes known as the "dirty reads" isolation level)

[2] Read Committed (a somewhat weaker form than **DB2**'s "cursor stability")

[3] Repeatable Read

[4] Serializable

The final isolation level, [4] Serializable, is equivalent to the serializability that we
characterized in Theorems 10.3.4 and 10.4.2, while the prior isolation levels, [1], [2],
and [3], are more permissive and therefore give lesser isolation guarantees. The ANSI
SQL-99 Set Transaction statement format follows:

```
SET TRANSACTION {READ ONLY | READ WRITE}
    ISOLATION LEVEL {READ UNCOMMITTED | READ COMMITTED | REPEATABLE READ |
        SERIALIZABLE};
```

A READ ONLY transaction cannot perform any updates as part of its execution
(updates would result in an error message), whereas a READ WRITE transaction can.
The isolation levels and ability to perform updates are normally independently specified,
except that no updates are ever permitted at the READ UNCOMMITTED isolation
level. What we need to do next is discuss each of these isolation levels and indicate how
they differ from one another.

In what follows we will need to understand what is meant by a *short-term lock*. In
practice, a short-term lock on a data item is one that is held just long enough to perform
the access operation associated with the lock: for example, the transaction will perform
the sequence $RL_i(A)$ $R_i(A)$ $RU_i(A)$. This will block other transactions from accessing the
data item only during the time the access attempt is actually in progress, but of course a
transaction that requests even a short-term lock will have to WAIT for the lock to be
granted, meaning that there can be no conflicting locks held by other transactions. Since
most transactions access multiple data items, it should be clear that a transaction that
takes only short-term locks does not obey the two-phase rule, RULE 3 of Definition
10.4.1. Thus non-serializable behavior is possible. But of course this is the whole point of
lower levels of isolation; it is assumed that we use such lower levels in circumstances
where no negative effects will result from a weaker guarantee. The alternative to a short-
term lock is a *long-term lock*, which means that the lock is held until the transaction
commits.

	Write locks on rows of a table are long-term	Read locks on rows of a table are long-term	Read and write locks on predicates are long-term
Read Uncommitted (dirty reads)	No (but it's read-only)	No Read locks at all	No predicate locks at all
Read Committed	Yes	No	Short-term Read predicate locks Long-term Write predicate locks
Repeatable Read	Yes	Yes	Short-term Read predicate locks Long-term Write predicate locks
Serializable	Yes	Yes	Long-term Read and Write predicate locks

Figure 10.9   Long-Term Locking Behavior of SQL-99 Isolation Levels[2]

Figure 10.9 lists which locks should be held long-term for each of the isolation levels of SQL-99. (Locks that are not held long-term are held short-term.) In this figure, we differentiate between taking locks on data items that are rows of tables and taking locks on predicates, such as city = 'Boston', that occur in a WHERE clause and determine what rows are to be read or updated. It is an important point that we need to take locks on predicates as well as data items to guarantee true serializability, and we will discuss this when we cover the Serializable isolation level below. As a short preview of that discussion, we will find that we need predicate locks to avoid certain nonserializable problems known as *phantoms*.

It is possible for a scheduler to support concurrently executing transactions of different isolation levels in the same transactional workload. This is why SQL-99 allows programs to perform Set Transaction statements programmatically, resetting the level of isolation for subsequent transaction executions on a per-execution basis. Different processes executing the code can use different isolation levels, but everything will still work as expected.

The Read Uncommitted Isolation Level

From the first row of Figure 10.9, we see that transactions operating under the isolation level of Read Uncommitted take no data item locks whatsoever. This would seem to mean that the phenomenon of dirty writes can occur (see Example 10.3.2). In the history H2 of that example, restated below with values for the data items, a write by one transaction of a data item A based on an earlier read value of A, can be overwritten by another transaction based on the same earlier read value.

---

[2]Note that the ANSI SQL-99 standard does not use locking behavior to define isolation levels. Instead it presents a number of English-language *phenomena* representing transactional anomalies and characterizes the isolation levels in terms of which phenomena can occur in histories at the various levels. However, this definition of isolation levels was shown to be flawed (see reference [5] at the end of this chapter), and we will provide only a locking definition for isolation levels here. This is not meant to imply that locking is the only way the various isolation levels can be implemented. Locking is the most common method in commercial database systems, but not the only one used.

H2 = R_1(A, 100) R_2(A, 100) W_1(A, 140) W_2(A, 150) C_1 C_2

Thus two concurrent transactions updating an account balance can interfere, so that one increment of 40 is overwritten by the other increment of 50, and the total increment of 90 is lost. However, this turns out not to be a problem in the Read Uncommitted isolation level because a transaction operating at this level in SQL-99 is not permitted to perform updates. If the Set Transaction statement requesting the Read Uncommitted isolation level

```
set transaction isolation level read uncommitted;
```

is given, the update specification of the transactions affected will be READ ONLY by default. (Note that for all other isolation levels, the update specification of the transactions is READ WRITE by default.) Furthermore if the Set Transaction statement

```
set transaction read write isolation level read uncommitted;
```

is given, it will result in an error. A Read Uncommitted transaction cannot update data items. Thus the dirty write of the history H2 above cannot occur.

However, dirty reads certainly do occur. A transaction reading through the accounts and summing up balances in a bank branch ignores all other transaction locks and is able to view uncommitted data. (Note that in Figure 10.9 there are no read locks taken at all in Read Uncommitted, so a transaction acting in this isolation level is never required to WAIT when it encounters a write lock; it simply doesn't notice the lock, because properties [1], [2], and [3] of Definition 10.4.1 are all ignored.) As a result, the balance sum arrived at by a Read Uncommitted transaction is likely to have a value that was never valid at that branch, since it is likely to have read invalid intermediate results. Certainly this will not satisfy an auditor, who wants an accounting that is exact to the penny. But it may satisfy the reporting requirements of the bank manager, who simply wants a rough idea of the branch balances once a week.

The Read Committed Isolation Level and Cursor Stability

In the second row of Figure 10.9, we see that the Read Committed isolation level holds write locks (on rows) long-term, but only short-term read locks. This will make two of the three pairs of conflicting operations (for rows) by concurrently active transactions that we saw in Figure 10.7 impossible: (2) W_i(A) $\rightarrow$ R_j(A) and (3) W_i(A) $\rightarrow$ W_j(A). A transaction at this isolation level cannot read or write rows that have been written by another transaction until that transaction commits. In particular, it cannot read uncommitted dirty data. It can only read data written by transactions that have already committed. This explains the name of this isolation level, "Read Committed," and also the name of the previous level, where reading uncommitted (dirty) updates of data is possible. The only conflicting operation on rows that can occur between concurrently executing transactions with the Read Committed isolation level is (1) R_i(A) $\rightarrow$ W_j(A). What sort of anomalies can a user see with this isolation level that would not occur with strict serial executions? The next two examples illustrate two such anomalies.

EXAMPLE 10.5.1 Nonrepeatable Read Anomaly.

Consider a transaction that opens a cursor on a set of rows, fetches successive rows and reads them, and then later opens the cursor again to read the rows a second time. We find with the Read Committed isolation level that the record values the transaction reads may not be the same the second time through the cursor. In Read Committed, a read lock is held on a row read by a cursor only long enough for the row value to be returned to the user, so it is perfectly possible for some other transaction to update that row in the interval between two different cursor accesses to the row. Here is a value-extended history with a single data item A retrieved through a cursor by T_1 to illustrate this:

$$H4 = R1(A, 50) \; W2(A, 80) \; C2 \; R1(A, 80) \; C1$$

This anomaly is known by the name *Nonrepeatable Read*. ∎

The Nonrepeatable Read anomaly is probably not a problem for most database applications, since it is unusual for an application to read a data item a second time as we see here. We give this example mainly because the next more powerful isolation level is known as *Repeatable Read*, and many textbooks provide the Nonrepeatable Read anomaly of history H4 as the history that differentiates these two levels. However, a much more serious error can occur under the Read Committed isolation level, quite comparable to the Lost Update anomaly of history H2.

EXAMPLE 10.5.2 Scholar's Lost Update Anomaly.

Recall that the Lost Update anomaly was illustrated by the history H2:

$$H2 = R_1(A, 100) \; R_2(A, 100) \; W_1(A, 140) \; W_2(A, 150) \; C_1 \; C_2$$

This history cannot occur under the Read Committed isolation level, not because of any conflicts between reads and writes, but because write locks are held long-term, so the operation $W_2(A, 150)$ could not overwrite the value 140 for A set by T_1. However, consider the following history, H5:

$$H5 = R_1(A, 100) \; R_2(A, 100) \; W_1(A, 140) \; C_1 \; W_2(A, 150) \; C_2$$

Since T_1 commits before T_2 attempts to overwrite A, there is no longer any write lock to keep the lost update from occurring. H5 is a very likely type of error to occur in an application, so it illustrates a serious problem with the Read Committed isolation level. In fact, if the history H2 were to occur in a locking scheduler, H5 would be the result, since when $W_2(A, 150)$ occurs the locking scheduler will force T_2 to WAIT until T_1 commits, and the resulting history will be H5. We call this anomaly the "Scholar's Lost Update" to differentiate it from the lost update of H2. H5 is not really much more subtle than H2, so the term "scholar" is used in a joking way, like the "scholar's mate" example in the game of chess. ∎

DB2 and a number of other products offer an isolation level called *cursor stability*, which is slightly more restrictive than Read Committed. Cursor stability keeps write locks long-term and does not keep read locks long-term, just as Read Committed does, but it prevents the Scholar's Lost Update anomaly of Example 10.5.2 from occurring as long as all updates of data items are performed through cursors (i.e., UPDATE . . . WHERE CURRENT OF CURSOR . . .). The name "cursor stability" comes from the fact that a special type of lock, which is a bit stronger than a read lock, is held on each row fetched through the cursor, even *after* the row has been fetched; the lock is held only until the fetch moves on to the next row of the cursor. (Of course, if an update to the row occurs through the cursor before the fetch moves on, a long-term write lock will be kept on the row.) This locking behavior does not prevent the Nonrepeatable Read anomaly. However, no lost update can occur with the code sequence of Figure 10.10 that gives everyone at the SFBay branch a $10.00 bonus, because a lock is always held on the current row of the cursor.

We can also achieve this update with the single-statement update of Figure 10.11 in a transaction of isolation level Read Committed (or even Read Uncommitted) with no lost update, since an Update statement holds a lock on each row for the duration of the update: *the read and write are performed as an atomic pair, one after the other.*

However, the code sequence of Figure 10.12 to update a single row still might result in a lost update, and even cursor stability doesn't help. This is because no lock is held on the row after it is read by the first statement (it is not read through a cursor) and before it is updated by the second statement.

It does not seem likely that all programmers using the Read Committed isolation level are aware of the anomalies that can arise, since the advantage of cursor stability

```
    exec sql declare cursor deposit for select balance from accounts
        where branch_id = 'SFBay' for update of balance;
    exec sql open c;
    (now loop through rows in cursor, and for each pass do)
        exec sql fetch c into :balance;
        balance = balance + 10.00;
        exec sql update account set balance = :balance
            where current of deposit;
    (end of loop)
    exec sql close deposit;
    exec sql commit work;
```

Figure 10.10   Logic with No Lost Update under Isolation Level Cursor Stability

```
    exec sql update accounts set balance = balance + 10.00
        where branch_id = 'SFBay';
    exec sql commit work;
```

Figure 10.11   Alternate Logic with No Lost Update Even under Isolation Level Read Uncommitted

```
exec sql select balance into :balance from accounts
    where acct_id = 'A1234';
balance = balance + 10.00;
exec sql update accounts set balance = :balance
    where acct_id = 'A1234';
exec sql commit work;
```

Figure 10.12   Logic with Possible Lost Update under Isolation Level Cursor Stability

seems to have been overlooked by the ANSI SQL Committee, and a Read Committed–compliant database system is not necessarily offering cursor stability. It is a good idea for the DBA to test any database system in use to see if the anomaly of Example 10.5.2 can occur when cursors are used.

Repeatable Read Isolation Level

The third row of Figure 10.9 shows that the Repeatable Read isolation level supports all the discipline of two-phase locking on single data items, such as rows; it provides long-term locking for all data items, and short-term locks only for something called *read predicate locks*. Indeed this isolation level solves all the problems we have mentioned up to now that can arise as anomalies. In particular, it solves the problem of Example 10.5.1, that reading row values in a transaction might not be repeatable. This is because long-term read locks are held on rows, so nobody can update a row that has been read by a transaction until the reading transaction commits. Hence the name "Repeatable Read."

True Serializability, the isolation level on row four of Figure 10.9, supplies all the guarantees of Repeatable Read plus the guarantees associated with long-term read predicate locks, which we have not yet discussed. As it turns out, predicate locks allow interleaved transaction executions to avoid isolation anomalies known as *phantoms,* or *phantom updates.* This is a fairly subtle problem, which we deal with in the next subsection.

Serializability and Phantom Updates

We provide an example of an isolation anomaly that can arise in transactions operating under the Repeatable Read isolation level.

EXAMPLE 10.5.3   Phantom Update Anomaly.
Consider a transaction under the Repeatable Read isolation level that opens a cursor on a set of rows from an accounts table at a given branch of a bank, fetches successive rows and sums their balances, then tests that the sum of these balances equals the balance of a special-purpose row in the branch_totals table with branch_id equal to that same branch ID, and prints out an error if it is not. This might be accomplished by the following logic:

```
exec sql select sum(balance) into :total from accounts
    where branch_id = :bid;
```

```
exec sql select balance into :bbal from branch_totals
    where branch_id = :bid;
if (bbal <> total)
    (print out serious error);
exec sql commit work;
```

It seems that we have taken every possible effort in the Repeatable Read isolation level to take long-term locks on data items that are read by this transactional logic or updated by some other transaction that might occur concurrently. However, a different sort of anomaly can occur because of an effect of certain operations that have not been considered up until now: an insert of a new row or an update of an old row that changes the *membership* of the set of rows returned by the WHERE clause of the first Select statement above. Note that this Select statement, which retrieves the SUM of balances for a set of rows, cannot access every row involved all at once. It must determine the set of rows to look at as it goes along, probably by either reading a range of entries in an index or reading through all the rows in the accounts table and qualifying the ones to be selected. Because this takes time, and the process reads through a sequence of information to determine the set of rows retrieved, it is possible for a concurrent Insert or Update to place a new row into this set of rows without this being noticed. The new row could be missed because it is inserted on a page that has already been checked by the WHERE clause qualification, or could have its entry placed in a position that has already been passed in the range lookup. This can lead to an anomaly, as we will see.

We use the terminology $I_i(A)$ to indicate that an insert of data item A has been performed by transaction T_i. When we wish to specify column values for the insert, we do so with a notation of the following sort: $I_i(A, branch = SFBay, balance = 50)$. (Recall that A is taken to be the field value that gives a unique identifier for the row in question, such as acct_id in the accounts table.) Now consider the following history:

R_1(predicate: branch_id = 'SFBay') R_1(A1,100.00) R_1(A2, 100.00)
R_1(A3,100.00) (we assume these are all the rows initially found at this branch)
I_2(A4, branch_id = 'SFBay', balance = 100.00) (a new row that will not be noticed by T_1)
R_2 (branch_totals, branch_id = 'SFBay', 300) W_2 (branch_totals, branch_id = 'SFBay', 400)
C2 (now T2 has updated the branch_totals rows for this branch, a surprise to T1)
R_1 (branch_totals, branch_id = 'SFBay', 400)
(Prints out error message) C_1

In words, what is happening is that transaction T_1 first determines what rows of the accounts table have branch_id equal to 'SFBay', and finds that the rows in question have acct_id values A1, A2, and A3. The three balances of these accounts are read, and they sum to $300.00. At this point another transaction T_2 comes along and creates a new account with acct_id value A4 at the SFBay branch (it certainly needs new accounts, since it only has three to start with). T_2 then updates the branch_totals row with SFBay as acct_id to reflect the added account balance for that branch. But now when T_1 reads the SFBay account balance, it sees an impossible value, $400.00, where the three account balances it had added summed to only $300.00. ∎

There was nothing stopping T_2 from adding this new account A4, and the change it makes to the branch balance for SFBay is necessary to support the consistency rule that the branch balance must equal the sum of the balances of accounts within the branch.

No row locks are ignored by this logic, but an anomaly still arises. The reason is that a new row, A4, comes into the picture after T_1 has evaluated the predicate branch_id = 'SFBay'. T_1 would certainly have taken a lock on A4 if it had been given a chance to notice it, but A4 was added too late.

Does this mean that there is some problem with the serializability theorem, that 2PL does not imply true serializability? No. It only means that we haven't been taking a lock on enough objects, that we cannot restrict ourselves to table rows. Serializability requires that *all* information accessed by a transaction must figure into the precedence graph of Definition 10.3.3. When T_1 reads the predicate branch_id = 'SFBay', a somewhat simplistic predicate locking formulation says that it must take a read lock on that information—that is, on the information consisting of the appropriate set of balance rows, {A1, A2, A3}, that exist at that branch. When T_2 inserts a new row A4 into that branch, it is implicitly taking a write lock on that same predicate, since it is going to change the information available when the predicate is evaluated. Since these two operations on the predicate conflict, such a history will not be allowed when long-term read predicate locks are held. Extending the history of Example 10.5.3 to include the appropriate read and write locks, we get the following:

RL$_1$(predicate: branch_id = 'SFBay') R$_1$(predicate: branch_id = 'SFBay') RL$_1$(A1, 100.00) R$_1$(A1, 100.00) RL$_1$(A2, 100.00) R$_1$(A2, 100.00) RL$_1$(A3, 100.00) R$_1$(A3, 100.00) WL$_2$(A4, branch_id = 'SFBay') (prepare to perform the insert I$_2$(A4, branch_id = 'SFBay', balance = 100.00), but this conflicts with the earlier RL$_1$ on this predicate, so T_2 must WAIT) R$_1$(branch_totals, branch_id = 'SFBay', 300) (sum is correct, no error) C$_1$ (now locks are released, so) I$_2$(A4, branch_id = 'SFBay', balance = 100.00) R$_2$(branch_totals, branch_id = 'SFBay', 300) W$_2$(branch_totals, branch_id = 'SFBay', 400) C$_2$.

The execution is now totally serializable. As we showed in Figure 10.9, the SQL-99 isolation level known as Serializable takes long-term read and write locks on predicates. Thus the Phantom Update anomaly of Example 10.5.3 is avoided, and histories with this locking protocol are totally serializable. The reader should not take the idea of locks on predicates too literally, however. Any type of locking that guarantees that one transaction can't be examining an aggregation of rows based on some predicate while another transaction adds a different row to that aggregation will serve to eliminate phantom updates. Some database systems lock entire tables to achieve this, a coarse locking granularity that unnecessarily reduces concurrency level, but guarantees the Serializable isolation level with simple system logic. The most common technique currently used to provide predicate locks is known as *key-range locking,* the details of which are beyond the scope of our text. For an introduction to this technique, see the text by Gray and Reuter [2] in "Suggestions for Further Reading" at the end of this chapter.

We also mention a rule of SQL-99: if a database system wishes to comply with the standard but doesn't support one of the isolation levels, it must provide one that is *at least* as secure as the one requested in a Set Transaction statement. For example, if the database system doesn't have a Read Committed isolation level, but does have Repeatable Read, then when the following statement is executed—

```
exec sql set transaction isolation level read committed;
```

the system must impose a Repeatable Read isolation level.

10.6 Transactional Recovery

As we have previously pointed out, the data in a database normally resides on disk, which is a *nonvolatile* storage medium. The fact that it is nonvolatile means, for example, that a sudden power loss will not cause the data to be lost. By contrast, data stored in memory disappears when power is lost, and memory storage is therefore termed *volatile*. Several other conditions can also cause memory to become undependable—for example, a system crash resulting from imperfect bulletproofing of an operating system or database system. Bugs like this are thought by most systems designers to be inevitable, and such bugs can make it nearly impossible to trust that memory contents will remain stable over an extended period (months or years). If we could, we would leave data on disk at all times so as not to have to worry about memory volatility.

However, as you will recall from the discussion in Section 9.2, disk access is very slow compared with memory access. We need to read disk pages into memory buffers so the data will be available for high-speed random access by normal computer instructions. Once the page has been read into memory buffer, we make every attempt to keep it there in the hope that it will be referenced again in the near future, and thus we will save on disk I/O. To support buffering we use an approach known as *lookaside*, which allows the system responding to a disk page read request to first try to hash to an entry for that page in the *lookaside table*. If such an entry is found, this tells the system that the page is already in a memory buffer; otherwise it needs to be read in from disk. Naturally the pages we most want to keep in memory buffers are the ones that are the most "popular," and this has historically been achieved with a method known as *LRU buffering* (LRU stands for least recently used). The idea is that database pages that have been read from disk into memory buffers will remain in memory until a new page being read in from disk requires space, and all buffer pages are already occupied. At that point, some page must be dropped from buffer to make room; that will be the page, among all those in buffers, that has not been referenced for the longest time—the least recently used page.

Just as we want to keep popular pages in memory to be read over and over by different transactions, we also don't want to have to write a page back to disk every time it is updated by some transaction. If it is a popular page for update, containing a set of rows with bank branch balances, for example, we might be able to allow hundreds, or even thousands, of updates without writing out the page in question. This is one of the most important optimizations for a common class of transactional applications. To repeat: *we don't want to write out all pages updated by a transaction as soon as the transaction updates them and commits*. Instead we generally allow popular pages to remain in buffer until either they become less popular and *drift out* of buffer on their own because LRU needs their buffer place (note that updated pages must be written back to disk before they can be replaced in buffer), or else we force them to be written back to disk after some period of time has passed. (We will talk about forcing disk pages to be written back to disk a bit later. (Most of the time we don't do this, however—we just depend on LRU. A page in buffer is said to be *dirty* if it has been updated by some transaction since the last time it was written back to disk. We normally allow dirty pages to remain in buffer long after the transaction that originally dirtied them has committed. (We will see some problems in the exercises on buffer page reads and writes under LRU.)

But now we have a problem. Suppose we suddenly lose power or have a system crash. Some of the pages on disk might be terribly out of date because they were so popular that they haven't been written out from buffer during the last thousand updates that took place. But if all those updates existed only in memory, then it would seem this update information is now totally lost. How can we handle this problem, and be able to *recover* these lost updates, without going back to the approach of writing out every update as soon as it happens?

The answer is that as each row update occurs the system writes a note to itself, known as a *log entry,* into a memory area known as a *log buffer.* These log entries contain sufficient information about updates to remind the system how to perform the update again, or to reverse the update if the transaction involved needs to be aborted. At appropriate times the log buffer is written out to disk, into a sequential file known as a *log file,* that contains all the log entries created for some interval of time in the past. In this way, if memory is lost at some point, the recovery process will be able to use the sequential log file to recover updates of rows that are out of date on disk. One reason that this log method is preferable to writing out each update as it happens is that it is more efficient—the system only needs to write the log buffer out to disk at infrequent intervals; it is usually able to batch together a large number of page updates and thus save I/Os.

We also see a bit later that the system needs these notes to itself to perform recovery. Even if all disk page updates were written out to disk as soon as they occurred at no cost in system resources, this would not be sufficient to allow the system to perform recovery properly. If the system were to crash in the middle of a transaction, it could leave the database in an inconsistent state (for example, money has been created or destroyed because the compensating update has not yet been executed), and since we have lost memory contents, we have also lost our place in the program logic that knows how to complete the compensating update. It is important not just to recover every page update on disk, but also to recover a consistent set of updates up through the most recent transaction that committed before the crash. To accomplish this, a log file is definitely needed.

This general introduction to the idea of recovery covers most of the guarantee we have in mind when we refer to the durability of ACID transactions mentioned earlier in the chapter. (One remaining aspect of durability that guarantees against loss of data on stable media such as disks is covered briefly in Section 10.9.) We now proceed to discuss the kinds of notes a normal database system writes to itself in the log file to protect against memory loss, and the way the system uses these notes when it performs a recovery procedure after a system crash.

Consider the following history H5 of operations as seen by the scheduler:

[10.7.1] H5 = $R_1(A, 50)$ $W_1(A, 20)$ $R_2(C, 100)$ $W_2(C, 50)$ C2 $R_1(B, 50)$ $W_1(B, 80)$ C_1 ...

Because of the LRU buffering scheme explained in the previous section, we notice that the updated values of the data elements A, B, and C might not be written out to disk in the order in which the updates occur in this history. If a crash were to occur at some time in the future, we might find the following values on disk: A = 50 (the update $W_1(A, 20)$ was never written out because A was on a popular disk page), C = 100 (the update of C never got out to disk), and B = 80 (the update of B *did* get out to disk). It should be clear that while we depend on the LRU buffering scheme to write out updates in a manner that minimizes disk resource use, we cannot expect consistent results to be on disk as a result of LRU buffering. The bank account withdrawal of $50 carried out by transaction T_2 didn't get out to disk even though the transaction committed and, presumably, the customer walked away with the money. At the same time, the customer who transferred $30 from account A to account B has somehow gained $30 on the deal. (Banks don't like this kind of behavior.)

However, as we mentioned earlier, a system that performs updates to disk as soon as they occur wouldn't solve the problem either. (Even if the system tried to perform all writes to disk at commit time, this would not be a solution.) Assume that we are operating under a discipline where we perform writes to disk as soon as the page is updated in buffer, and that a system crash occurred immediately after operation C_2 in history H5. Then the second update performed by transaction T_1 would not make it out to disk. When we restarted the system after the crash, we would find on disk that A = 20, C = 50, and B = 50. The sum of A and B should be 100, since T_1 never intended to create or destroy money, but instead we see that money has been destroyed. The problem with trying to perform all writes to disk at commit time is that a crash might still occur between one page write and the next, so the same example shows that this approach doesn't solve the problem.

The difficulties we have just raised are addressed by two of the transactional guarantees mentioned at the beginning of this chapter, atomicity and durability. Recall that atomicity guarantees that a set of data item updates that make up a transaction is indivisible; either all updates of the transaction occur in the database or none of them occurs. This guarantee continues to hold even in the event of a system crash, when it is referred to as durability. Durability says that when the system returns to the program logic after a Commit Work statement, the transaction is durable, so that the updates are remembered after a system crash. As we have already mentioned, these guarantees are achieved when the system writes notes to itself in a log file. A procedure known as *database recovery* is performed after a crash, which uses the log entries written earlier and brings the disk-resident database to a state where it will reflect either all or none of the row updates for transactions that were in progress at the time of the crash.

Note an important assumption of recovery that we mentioned in passing in the previous section: *a transactional system, after being restarted following a crash, will never remember the intentions of the transaction logic that was running when memory was lost.* Such program states are considered too subtle to recapture (although there are attempts currently being made to change this). At present, all the recovery process can depend on is that there is information in nonvolatile storage that will allow it to bring the database back to a consistent state. What is the proper consistent state in the case of the system crash we just explained, immediately after operation C_2 in history H5? It is this: since T_2 performed a commit, we should be able to recover the final results of that transaction; but since T_1 failed to perform one of the updates it intended, and therefore certainly did not commit, *all* the updates performed by T_1 should be rolled back! This would give us the results A = 50, C = 50, B = 50, a consistent state.

We now rewrite the operations of history H5 in Figure 10.13, and list beside these operations schematic log entries that are written into the log buffer in memory for the recovery method presented here. (We emphasize that log entries are placed in a *memory-resident* log buffer. The occasions when the contents of this log buffer are written out to the disk-based log file are mentioned as special events in Figure 10.13.) Note that the details presented here are not based on the recovery architecture of any specific commercial database system. Instead we are offering a simplified and easy-to-follow recovery approach that captures the spirit of what recovery is expected to do in most systems. An actual recovery architecture of a commercial database system would be quite complex and detailed by comparison.

Recall that the second operation in Figure 10.13, $W_1(A, 20)$, is assumed to represent an update by transaction T_1, changing the balance column value to 20 for a row in the accounts table with acct_id = A. In the same sense, in the write log (W, 1, A, 50, 20) of Figure 10.13, the value 50 is the before image for the balance column in this row, and 20 is the after image for this column. In more sophisticated log entries, a unique identifier for the row would be used (perhaps the ROWID) and the list of columns changed with all before and after image values. The log entry types appearing in this figure are all that we will consider for now. Log entries also exist for insert and delete operations, for example, but we will simplify our discussion by ignoring them. We see two events in Figure 10.13 where the contents of the log buffer are written out to the sequential log file. The log buffer is normally written out to the log file under only two circumstances in our simple scheme: (1) when some transaction commits; and (2) when the log buffer becomes too full to hold more entries, if that should occur first. (So as not to slow down other work, we expect the system to do a "double-buffered disk write," meaning that it has a second log buffer in memory into which it continues to write log entries, while the first log buffer is being written to disk "asynchronously.")

Now we want to prove to ourselves that there is enough data in these log entries to permit the system to recover after a system crash. We see that two different kinds of problems may have occurred. First, we may have written to disk page updates of transactions that never completed. We say that we need to UNDO updates of this kind on disk, and it is for this reason that we include before images in the log entries. We may also find that some page updates of transactions that have committed never got to disk. We say

Operation	Log entry	Explanation
R_1(A, 50)	(S, 1)	Start transaction T_1 log entry. No log entry is written for a read operation, but this operation is the start of T_1.
W_1(A, 20)	(W, 1, A, 50, 20)	T_1 write log for update of A.balance. The value 50 is the before image (BI) for the balance column in row A, 20 is the after image (AI) for A.balance.
R_2(C, 100)	(S, 2)	Another start transaction log entry.
W_2(C, 50)	(W, 2, C, 100, 50)	Another write log entry.
C2	(C, 2)	Commit T_2 log entry. *(Write log buffer to log file.)*
R_1(B, 50)	No log entry.	
W_1(B, 80)	(W, 1, B, 50, 80)	
C_1	(C, 1)	Commit T_1. *(Write log buffer to log file.)*

Figure 10.13 Operations from History H5 and the Corresponding Log Entries

that we need to REDO updates of this kind, to write the new values out to disk, and it is for this purpose that after images occur in the log entries.

Now assume that a system crash occurs immediately after the operation W_1(B, 80) has completed, in the sequence of events of Figure 10.13. This means that the log entry (W, 1, B, 50, 80) has been placed in the log buffer, but the last point at which the log buffer was written out to disk was with the log entry (C, 2), and this is the final log entry we will find when we begin to recover from the crash. At this time, since transaction T_2 has committed while transaction T_1 has not, we want to make sure that all updates performed by transaction T_2 are placed on disk and that all updates performed by transaction T_1 are rolled back on disk. As we explained just before Figure 10.13, the final values for these data items after recovery has been performed should be A = 50, B = 50, and C = 50.

After the crash the system is reinitialized and the system operator gives a command that initiates recovery. (This is normally known as the RESTART command, and we often refer to the recovery process as RESTART.) The process of recovery takes place in two phases, *ROLLBACK* and *ROLL FORWARD*. In the ROLLBACK phase, the entries in the sequential log file are read in reverse order back to system start-up, when all data access activity began. (We assume here that this system start-up happened just before the first operation, R_1(A, 50), of history H5.) In the ROLL FORWARD phase, the log file is read forward again to the last entry. During the ROLLBACK step, recovery performs UNDO of all the updates that should not have occurred, because the transaction that made them did not commit, and also makes a list of all transactions that have committed. During ROLL FORWARD, recovery performs REDO of all updates that should have occurred, because they were legal updates by transactions that have committed. Recall that we are presenting a simple recovery architecture for purposes of illustration, and in it we assume that the ROLLBACK phase occurs first and the ROLL FORWARD phase afterward. This is the order that was used by IBM's System R, a prototype precursor of **DB2**, but you should be aware that most modern databases perform these phases in the opposite order. This is not important for our illustrative introduction, however.

Log entry	ROLLBACK action performed
1. (C, 2)	Put T_2 into the committed list.
2. (W, 2, C, 100, 50)	Since T_2 is on the committed list, we do nothing.
3. (S, 2)	Make a note that T_2 is no longer active.
4. (W, 1, A, 50, 20)	Transaction T_1 has never committed (its last operation was a write). Therefore system performs UNDO of this update by writing the before image value (50) into data item A. Put T_1 into the uncommitted list.
5. (S, 1)	Make a note that T_1 is no longer active. Now that no transactions were active, we can end the ROLLBACK phase.

Figure 10.14   ROLLBACK Process for History H5, Crashed Just after W_1(B, 80)

Log entry	ROLL FORWARD action performed
6. (S, 1)	No action required.
7. (W, 1, A, 50, 20)	T_1 is uncommitted—no action required.
8. (S, 2)	No action required.
9. (W, 2, C, 100, 50)	Since T_2 is on the committed list, we REDO this update by writing after image value (50) into data item C.
10. (C, 2)	No action required.
11.	We note that we have rolled forward through all log entries and terminate recovery.

Figure 10.15   ROLL FORWARD Process, Taking Place after ROLLBACK of Figure 10.14

Figures 10.14 and 10.15 list all the log entries encountered and the actions taken during these two phases of recovery. Note that the steps of ROLLBACK are numbered on the left. This numbering is continued during the ROLL FORWARD phase of Figure 10.15.

We need to explain the steps taken in these two figures. During ROLLBACK the system reads backward through the log entries of the sequential log file and makes a list of all transactions that did and did not commit. This is easy, because the last operation performed by any such transactions is either a commit or some other operation that indicates that no commit took place, and the system encounters this last operation first. The list of committed transactions is used in the next phase, ROLL FORWARD, but the list of transactions that did not commit is used to decide when to UNDO updates. Since the system knows which transactions did not commit as soon as it encounters (reading backward) the final log entry, it can immediately begin to UNDO write log changes of uncommitted transactions by writing before images onto disk over the row values affected. Naturally disk buffering is used during recovery to read in pages containing rows that need to be updated by UNDO or REDO steps. We see an example of an UNDO write in step 4 of Figure 10.14. Since the transaction responsible for the write log entry did not commit, it should not have any transactional updates out on disk. It is possible that some values given in the after images of these write log entries are *not* out on disk (they never got there), but in any event it is clear that writing the before images in place of these data items can't hurt—we eventually return to the value such data items had before any uncommitted transactions tried to change them. The attention that is paid to the Start Transaction log entries during ROLLBACK is not strictly necessary, because we are guaranteed that when we reach the beginning of the log file, corresponding to system start-up time, no transactions were active. In a slightly more general case, however, ROLLBACK will need to know what transactions were still active in order to decide when to terminate.

During the ROLL FORWARD of Figure 10.15, the system simply uses the list of committed transactions gathered during the ROLLBACK phase as a guide to REDO updates of committed transactions that might not have gotten out to disk. (We see an example of REDO in step 9.)

At the end of this phase the data we find on disk should have the right values. All updates of transactions that committed will be applied, and all updates of transactions that did not complete will be rolled back. Indeed we note that in step 4 of ROLLBACK we write the value 50 to the data item A, and in step 9 of ROLL FORWARD we write the value 50 to data item C. Recall that the crash occurred just after the operation $W_1(B, 80)$ in H5. Since the log entry for this operation didn't get to disk (as we see in Figure 10.13), we cannot apply the before image for B during recovery. We need to depend on the fact that the update for B to the value 80 also did not get out to disk. Basically we need to be sure that if an update of an uncommitted transaction got out to disk, the needed log entry to UNDO that update also got out to disk. We consider this in the next subsection. Given that we can depend on the fact that the new value, B = 80, did not get out to disk, the values for the three data items mentioned in H5 are A = 50, B = 50 (the initial value), and C = 50 (the proper values that recovery was to put in place).

Guarantees That Needed Log Entries Are on Disk

How can we be certain that all the log entries needed for proper recovery are out on disk? To begin with, it is important to realize that the operating system offers a guarantee when data is written out to disk, comparable to the guarantees that ACID transactions offer to application programmers. Writes to disk are carried out in an atomic fashion, meaning that even if a crash occurs while a disk write is in process, later reads of the block that was just written will be able to tell immediately if the write was successful; if so, then the block can be depended on to contain exactly the data that the database system logic intended to write. When a disk write is performed, the I/O subsystem normally tests the resulting disk image by reading it again immediately after it is written, and then performs the write again if there is any error. A serious error return to the operation system occurs if a write is not successful after a given number of retries. Thus the normal logic that continues after a successful disk write will never regain control if there is a write error. For example, if a log file is being written out triggered by a transaction commit, the commit will fail when there is an error return in attempting the disk write. If the write-read retry sequence is interrupted by a crash so that an erroneous block reaches disk to be read after RESTART, the error in the block will be detected when a disk read occurs. Thus we have a guarantee that there will be no undetected error; the guarantee is supported by sensitive "error detection encoding" of the data stored on disk, and a "read after write" protocol in performing disk writes that is built into the disk head. All of this error detection is performed at a very low level of the I/O subsystem, transparent even to the operating system.

The guarantee that there will be no undetected errors for disk writes carries over to situations where no crash occurs. When the system is notified of successful completion of a disk write, this carries a high probability guarantee that future reads of the block will be successful (unless the entire disk is lost, as explained in Section 10.9). Thus when the logic in the database system writes out the log buffer to the log file (it actually does this to two different disks at once on systems with serious recovery concerns, for extra guarantee of durability), it can safely consider the commit that triggered this write to be successful.

Now given that we can trust log writes to disk, we still have to assure ourselves that the logic of recovery is correct, that is, that we will always be able to find needed log entries in the log file to achieve the kind of recovery we have outlined. Recall that we can break down the tasks we need to perform into two kinds, UNDO and REDO. Consider first the need to REDO all updates of transactions that have committed. We know that a commit log is a trigger for writing out the log buffer, and the transaction is not considered to have successfully completed until this log buffer write has been successful. (For example, if the transaction were a bank withdrawal, we would not actually hand out the money until the buffer write was complete.) Since the commit log must get out to disk, clearly all earlier write logs for that transaction are out to disk (they were placed into the log buffer in sequential order, and the commit log came last), so we are assured that the REDO task can be performed successfully.

The second task we need to carry out during recovery is to UNDO all updates of transactions that have not committed in the log file. We have not previously been provided any guarantee that all log entries for updates of uncompleted transactions will get out to disk. For example, the final write log entry in the recovery example of Figures 10.13 through 10.15 (W, 1, B, 50, 80) was written to the log buffer but did not get out to disk before the crash occurred. (We do not write the log buffer out to the log file until the (C, 1) log event in Figure 10.13.) We need to ask ourselves whether any problems could arise as a result of this. Could a needed UNDO not take place during recovery because the associated log entry didn't go out to disk? It should be clear that this could happen only if the page updated drifted out to disk through the LRU buffer before the log buffer containing the associated write log entry was written to the log file. (If this page had not drifted out, the UNDO operation would not be needed in recovery, as we saw earlier in considering the value of data item B.) It seems that the updated data page could beat the associated write log entry to disk, for example, if there were an enormous amount of page read activity of new pages after a page write, without any intervening commits to force the log buffer out. The read activity could eventually force the buffering scheme to reuse the page on which the updated row sits.

This is a perfectly reasonable scenario, and so we need to offer some special guarantee to ensure that it does not happen. One possibility is to subvert LRU page replacement in some way, so that an updated page will not drift out to disk until the transaction that has written on it has committed. Such a buffering scheme has in fact been proposed, where all pages dirtied by a transaction in buffer will remain in buffer until the transaction commits. With this scheme, in fact, no UNDO processing is ever needed at all during recovery, and therefore before images are not needed in the logs. However, in cases where an arbitrarily large number of updates might be performed by a single transaction, we cannot guarantee to keep all pages in memory buffers until the transaction commits (we might run out of memory). A more sophisticated scheme is required, one that allows a transaction to say it is finished with a page before the transaction commits. For example, when a FETCH from a CURSOR on a table finishes with a given page, we can say that the transaction is finished with that page and it need not be kept in buffer. (Of course, a transaction at the Serializable isolation level must retain its lock on any row it has read or updated, whether the row is on a page in buffer or not.)

Thus we come back to the case where an updated page might drift out to disk through the LRU queue before the associated log buffer is written out to disk, leading to a problem in UNDO recovery. To guard against this, the system makes a guarantee that relevant logs will be written out to disk prior to dirty buffer pages reaching disk that might be subject to UNDO recovery at a later time. This is often referred to as the *write ahead log* (WAL) guarantee. To implement it, database systems usually create something called the *log sequence number* (LSN), a sequentially increasing integer value associated with every entry written into the log buffer. We keep track of the smallest LSN of any entry in the log buffer that has been created since the log buffer was last written out to disk; we call this LSN_BUFFMIN. (This is a global value for the database system, if we assume that there is only one system page buffer in memory.) Additionally for every disk page in buffer, we note the most recent LSN of an action that has performed an update on a data item in that page, and call this value LSN_PGMAX. Finally we institute a rule that a disk page cannot be written out to disk from the LRU buffer unless its associated LSN_PGMAX is smaller than the global LSN_BUFFMIN value. This guarantees that the associated page never gets written out to disk until the log buffer with the relevant log entry has been written out to disk, and so solves the UNDO problem. With this definition we have the following theorem, which we offer without proof.

THEOREM 10.7.1 Simple Recovery. Given these guarantees on logs getting to disk, the recovery procedure outlined will perform valid recovery on any transactional history as of a given crash point. The transactions committed as of the time of the crash will have all their updates reflected on disk, and the transactions with partial results that have not yet committed will have all their disk updates backed out. ∎

10.8 Checkpoints

In the recovery example of Section 10.7, we performed ROLLBACK to the time of system start-up. This is an obvious choice, since at that time the database was completely consistent, no dirty pages were sitting in cache buffers, and indeed all transactional data updates lay in the future. We can picture that the ROLLBACK process is attempting to restore the database to this pristine state (except that some updates of transactions committed later remain on disk), and the job of ROLL FORWARD is to go forward from that point and REDO all the changes that were performed by transactions that completed before the system crash.

But the length of time needed to perform recovery grows with the length of the log file that we need to read through in our ROLLBACK-ROLL FORWARD phases. In each phase we have to actually read rows in from disk and update them, and in the worst case this might take just as much elapsed time as it originally did to run the applications that executed the updates in the first place. If we assume that most transactions are relatively short-lived (a few seconds), then the ROLLBACK phase quickly becomes quite efficient as it reads backward through the log file, since we only need to UNDO row updates for transactions that were still active at the time of the crash. ROLL FORWARD, however, entails a large effort through most of the length of the log, since we need to REDO all updates of transactions that have committed (presumably, most of them). The elapsed time to perform ROLL FORWARD might even take longer than the original applications that executed these updates, if the recovery process is naive about using concurrent threads of recovery. What we would like is the ability to reestablish the state we had at system start-up after a reasonable amount of time has passed, so that recovery does not have to ROLL FORWARD all the way from the beginning of time, but only from this new point (which we call a *checkpoint*). Naturally we want to be able to guarantee that recovery will still work, that it will be able to ignore all the transactions and page updates that occurred before this checkpoint.

There are three distinct approaches to creating a recovery checkpoint for a database system. In order of increasing sophistication and complexity, these three methods are known as *commit-consistent checkpointing*, *cache-consistent checkpointing*, and *fuzzy checkpointing*. With the more complex checkpointing methods, the system gains the ability to maintain a smoother flow of transactional throughput, so as users we prefer complex checkpointing schemes if the system designers have been able to implement them properly. No system would have any reason to support two different methods at the same time. We start by describing the simplest type of checkpoint that can be taken in the midst of running a transactional system, a *commit-consistent checkpoint*.

The Commit-Consistent Checkpoint

To begin with, the system makes the decision that it is time to initiate a checkpoint (perhaps because the count of log events since the last checkpoint has exceeded some limit). The system enters a "performing checkpoint state" with the following steps.

DEFINITION 10.8.1 Commit-Consistent Checkpoint Procedure Steps. After the performing checkpoint state is entered, we have the following rules.

[1]   No new transactions can start until the checkpoint is complete.

[2] Database operation processing continues until all existing transactions commit, and all their log entries are written to disk.

[3] The current log buffer is written out to the log file, and after this the system ensures that all dirty pages in buffers have been written out to disk.

[4] When steps 1–3 have been performed, the system writes a special log entry, (CKPT), to disk, and the checkpoint is complete. ∎

Steps 1–3 of Definition 10.8.1 also define the precise process we would use for an orderly shutdown of the system, so that we would not need to perform recovery when we next start up. The final state is equivalent to what we have been thinking of as system start-up, when the log file has zero length. As a result, it should be clear that we can now modify the recovery process of the previous section, so that it rolls back only until it encounters a log entry of the form (CKPT), instead of continuing until nothing earlier is left in the log file. We have a guarantee that there are no transactions running at this point and that all earlier transactions have completed all their operations to disk, so that there are no earlier operations of importance in the log file. The benefit we receive from performing the checkpoint is that we have greatly shortened the length of time needed to perform recovery.

Motivation for Other Kinds of Checkpoints

As we mentioned, the checkpoint procedure given in Definition 10.8.1 requires exactly the same effort as an orderly shutdown of the system. No new transactions can start until the system has been "drained" of active transactions and all dirty pages in buffer have been written out to disk. This may require a long period of time. We tend to think of transactions as being rather short, in the sense that they probably take only a few seconds to complete, but this is not guaranteed at all computer sites. It is perfectly possible on most database systems for transactions to last minutes, or even hours, performing reads and updates throughout this period. While such long transactions are in process a commit-consistent checkpoint is almost impossible, unless we are willing to shut down the system to users for this extended period. (As we said in step 1 of the definition, no new transactions can be accepted while the checkpoint procedure is in process.) To speak of writing out the buffers, consider that if we had 200 MB of memory devoted to disk buffering of 4-KB pages, and half of these pages were dirty and had to be written out, we would have about 100M/4K = 25,000 pages to write out. Since each page takes about 1/40 of a second to write to disk using a single disk arm, the total time required would be 25,000/40 = 625 seconds, divided by the average number of disk arms being kept busy. As memory prices continue to drop, such scenarios will become more common.

To avoid these problems of halting system operations during a checkpoint procedure, more sophisticated checkpoint schemes have been devised. The type of checkpoint we outlined in Definition 10.8.1 is known as a *commit-consistent checkpoint* because all transactions must commit and the dirty cache buffers must be flushed to disk. The next

680   stage of sophistication is known as the *cache-consistent checkpoint*. With this scheme, transactions are allowed to continue active through the checkpoint process, and we only require that all dirty pages in buffer (and associated write log entries) be forced out to disk. Disk buffer space in memory is also known as disk cache, and this explains the name of the checkpoint procedure. While a cache-consistent checkpoint is in process, the transactions that remain active must WAIT; in particular, they can perform no new I/Os. However, this still represents a great advantage over being required to drain the system of active transactions for a commit-consistent checkpoint, which may take a very long time when long-lived transactions are permitted. We next outline the recovery procedure associated with a cache-consistent checkpoint. We simply mention at this point that there also exists a yet more sophisticated type of checkpoint covered below, known as a *fuzzy checkpoint*, which allows a checkpoint to be taken even without forcing out all pages in cache. (This checkpoint is not considered complete until all pages in cache get out to disk, but useful work is allowed to continue in the meantime.)

The Cache-Consistent Checkpoint

Here is the procedure the system follows when a cache-consistent checkpoint has been initiated.

DEFINITION 10.8.2 Cache-Consistent Checkpoint Procedure Steps.

[1]   No new transactions are permitted to start.

[2]   Existing transactions are not permitted to start any new operations.

[3]   The current log buffer is written out to disk, and after this the system ensures that all dirty pages in cache buffers have been written out to disk.

[4]   Finally a special log entry, (CKPT, List), is written out to disk, and we say that the checkpoint is complete. The List in this log entry contains a list of active transactions at the time the checkpoint is taken.   ∎

The recovery procedure when cache-consistent checkpoints are used differs in a number of ways from the procedure when commit-consistent checkpoints are employed.

EXAMPLE 10.8.1 A Log File and Recovery Using a Cache-Consistent Checkpoint.
Here is a new history of events to illustrate the features of cache-consistent checkpointing. We will outline the log entries written to the log buffer and the recovery process performed after a crash during this history. First, the history:

$R_1(A, 10)\ W_1(A, 1)\ C_1\ R_2(A, 1)\ R_3(B, 2)\ W_2(A, 3)\ R_4(C, 5)\ CKPT\ W_3(B, 4)\ C_3$

$R_4(B, 4)\ W_4(C, 6)\ C_4\ CRASH$

Here is the series of log entry events resulting from this history. The operation C_4 does not complete prior to the crash, so the last entry that gets out to disk is the (C, 3) log entry.

(S, 1) (W, 1, A, 10, 1) (C, 1) (S, 2) (S, 3) (W, 2, A, 1, 3) (S, 4)(CKPT,

(LIST = T_2,T_3,T_4)) (W, 3, B, 2, 4) (C, 3) (W, 4, C, 5, 6)

At the time we take the cache-consistent checkpoint, we have these values out on disk: A = 3, B = 2, C = 5. (The dirty page in cache containing A at checkpoint time is written to disk.) We assume that no other updates make it out to disk before the crash, and so the data item values remain the same. The following diagram illustrates the time scale of the various events. Transaction T_k begins with the (S, k) log and ends with (C, k).

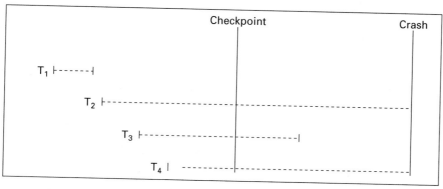

Now we outline the actions taken in recovery, starting with ROLLBACK.

ROLLBACK

1. (C, 3)	Note that T_3 is a committed transaction in active list.
2. (W, 3, B, 2, 4)	Committed transaction, wait for ROLL FORWARD.
3. (CKPT, (LIST = T_2, T_3, T_4))	Note active transactions T_2, T_4 not committed.
4. (S, 4)	List of active transactions now shorter: {T_2}.
5. (W, 2, A, 1, 3)	Not committed. UNDO: A = 1.
6. (S, 3)	Committed transaction.
7. (S, 2)	List of active transactions empty. Stop ROLLBACK.

We see that with a cache-consistent checkpoint, when ROLLBACK encounters the CKPT log entry the system takes note of the transactions that were active, even though we have never seen any operations in the log file. We now take our list of active transactions, remove those that we have seen committed, and have a list of transactions whose updates we need to UNDO. We continue in the ROLLBACK phase until we complete all such UNDO actions. We can be sure when this happens because as we encounter an (S, k) log, rolling backward, we take transactions off the active, uncommitted list. When all such T_k have been removed the ROLLBACK is complete, even though there may be more entries occurring earlier in the log file.

ROLL FORWARD

8. (CKPT, (LIST = T_2, T_3,T_4))	Skip forward in log file to this entry. Committed transactions = {T_3}.
9. (W, 3, B, 2, 4)	ROLL FORWARD: B = 4.
10. (C, 3)	No action. Last entry, so ROLL FORWARD is complete.

In starting the ROLL FORWARD phase, we merely need to REDO all updates by committed transactions that might not have gone out to disk. We can jump forward to the first operation after the checkpoint, since we know that all earlier updates were flushed from buffers. ROLL FORWARD continues to the end of the buffer file. Recall that the values on disk at the time of the crash were A = 3, B = 2, C = 5. At the end of recovery, we have set A = 1 (step 5) and B = 4 (step 9). We still have C = 5. A glance at the time scale figure (and the fact that the (C, 4) log entry was never written) shows that we want updates performed by T_3 and those by T_2 and T_4 to be backed out. No writes performed by T_4 got out to disk, so we have achieved what is necessary for recovery: A = 1, B = 4, C = 5. ∎

The Fuzzy Checkpoint

The aim of a fuzzy checkpoint is to reduce to an absolute minimum the elapsed time needed to perform a checkpoint. A cache-consistent checkpoint, which only needs to flush all dirty buffer pages to disk, is an improvement over a commit-consistent checkpoint, which needs to also allow all transactions in progress time to complete. However, flushing a 40-MB buffer with dirty pages accumulated over several minutes of operation to random positions on disk at 80 writes per second on a small number of disks can still take a good fraction of a minute. Users accustomed to seeing transactional response in a few seconds will be quite sensitive to such a "hiccup," during which no transactional activity can be carried out.

To get around this limitation, fuzzy checkpoint recovery makes use of *two* checkpoint events, the most recent two checkpoints that have been recorded to the log file with the CKPT log notation. The way this works is that each time the system takes a fuzzy checkpoint, $CKPT_N$, it takes note of the set of dirty pages that have accumulated in buffers since the *prior* checkpoint, $CKPT_{N-1}$. The intent is that all of these pages will be written out to disk by the time the *next* checkpoint is taken, $CKPT_{N+1}$. During the period between checkpoints, there is a good opportunity for most of the pages dirty during the first checkpoint to drift out to disk under the normal operation of the buffer manager. When the time for the next checkpoint is close, a background process can be enlisted to force out extremely popular dirty pages before we start the next checkpoint process, so that by the time the checkpoint is performed we have the following guarantee: all the pages that were dirty at the time $CKPT_{N-1}$ was taken have been forced out to disk by the time we complete $CKPT_N$. This allows us to avoid having to do any buffer flushing at the time of $CKPT_N$. We only need to modify the recovery process from the one used with the cache-consistent checkpoint by performing ROLL FORWARD from the time of the *second* most recent CKPT log, $CKPT_{N-1}$, if $CKPT_N$ is the one most recently completed.

DEFINITION 10.8.3 Fuzzy Checkpoint Procedure Steps.

[1] Prior to checkpoint start, the remaining pages dirty as of the previous checkpoint are forced out to disk (but the rate of writes should leave I/O capacity to support current transactions in progress; there is no critical hurry in doing this).

[2] At the start of the checkpoint process, no new transactions are permitted to start. Existing transactions cannot start any new operations.

[3] The current log buffer is written out to disk with an appended log entry, $(CKPT_N, List)$, as in the cache-consistent checkpoint procedure.

[4] The set of pages in buffer that are dirty since the last checkpoint log, $CKPT_{N-1}$, is noted. This will probably be accomplished by special flags on the buffer directory. There is no need for this information to be made disk resident, since it is used only to perform the next checkpoint, not in case of recovery. The checkpoint is now complete.

∎

As explained above, the recovery procedure with fuzzy checkpoints differs from the procedure with cache-consistent checkpoints only in that ROLL FORWARD must start with the first log entry following the *second-to-last* checkpoint log. See the exercises for an illustration.

10.9 Media Recovery

Up to now we have been making the assumption that data in memory might be lost as a result of power failure or a system crash, but data that has gone out to disk is dependable, in the sense that everything on disk will be available after a crash. This is not the whole story. It is possible for a disk unit and all the data it contains to be lost, for example, as a result of a "head crash" where the disk medium is physically scored in the way that an old-fashioned record might be scratched by a phonograph needle. When such an event occurs a special type of recovery, known as *media recovery,* must be performed. We need to take this into account in our general recovery strategy. In this section, we indicate the approach that is taken to solve this problem.

When there is a system crash that does not involve any of the disk media, we perform recovery following the methods outlined in Sections 10.7 and 10.8, where we trust disk media to be correct. If a disk is lost during transactional operations the system will crash, with an advisory to the operator as to which disk has been lost, and it will be clear that there is a need to perform media recovery. The simplest version of media recovery follows. Before system start-up, it is standard practice to perform a bulk copy of all disks being run on a transactional system. The copies are made to duplicate disks or to less expensive tape media, and we refer to *backup copies* of the online disks. When a disk has been lost in a system crash, we replace it with a backup disk (still keeping a backup in case a new problem arises), and run the normal recovery process. During this recovery, however, we perform ROLLBACK all the way to system start-up, since we can't depend on the backup disk to have any updates that were forced out at the last checkpoint. Then we run ROLL FORWARD from that point to the time of system crash. We can simply pretend that the new disk is the same one that just crashed on the system, except that all the data elements on that disk were *very* popular and never drifted out to disk since the time of system start-up. With this viewpoint, it is clear that normal recovery will allow us to recover all updates on this backup disk.

Stable Storage

Now that we know that disk media can fail, the following question arises: What happens if the log file is on the disk that fails? The answer is that we foresee such an eventuality and handle it by writing out two copies of the log file to separate devices (tape is common). This practice is often referred to as *log mirroring*. We attempt to ensure that the two devices receiving mirrored logs have *independent failure modes*; we take pains to ensure that an accident that might cause us to lose data on one of the two devices does not affect the data on the other device. For example, the two devices are on separate power services (or at least have separate power backup), and they are separated so that a physical jolt will not affect both of them at once. Storage that has been duplicated on two independent devices (whether it is used for logs or not) is also referred to as *stable storage*, as compared with *nonvolatile* storage for a single copy on disk and *volatile storage* for memory.

10.10   Performance: The TPC-A Benchmark

Let us review the performance-related issues that have been discussed so far in Chapter 10. In Section 10.2 we explained how high levels of concurrency allow us to overlap operations of different transactions to keep multiple disk arms busy at one time. As a result, we get much better CPU utilization and improved transactional throughput. In Section 10.5 we explained how insisting on perfect transaction serializability could hurt the throughput of a system by reducing the *effective concurrency level* when too many transactions enter WAIT state, and introduced the idea of *isolation levels*, provided by SQL-99. In Section 10.6 we began to deal with durability issues arising from buffering disk pages in memory; of course performance is the motivating factor for buffering to reduce I/O elapsed time and save on disk arm resource requirements.

At the same time, however, we have avoided discussing a number of rather complex implementation issues that have a tremendous influence on transactional performance. The ACID guarantees offered by transactional systems require a good deal of CPU and I/O resource overhead at runtime, to the point where it is almost meaningless to compare a transactional system with a simpler disk access file system that doesn't provide such guarantees. To gain some idea of the runtime overhead, consider the following scenario of a transaction execution.

Assume that a transaction begins with an SQL call that accesses a row through an index. A series of I/O calls are generated and passed to the transaction manager (see Figure 10.8), which must establish a transaction number for this thread and then pass calls along to the scheduler. The predicate for index lookup must be locked by the scheduler, involving a check that this lock doesn't conflict with previous ones in existence, and lookaside must be performed for all I/Os before the actual disk access is performed. Short-term and long-term locks must also be taken on disk pages and rows accessed. If a lock request locates a conflict, a test will sometimes be performed to determine whether a deadlock has occurred. Assuming there is no deadlock, the calling thread must be placed in a WAIT state by the scheduler, and some sort of *process switch* must be performed to change the context of the machine to run a different thread. When a deadlock is detected, a victim transaction must be chosen and aborted, with the effect of reversing all data item updates by updating previously modified rows using before images. Of course each time an update is performed on a row or index in the normal course of the transaction, a log entry must be created with before images and after images of all data affected, and this entry must be placed in the log buffer. When the transaction commits (in the simple system we've been considering), the log buffer contents must be written out to the log file (two copies to two stable media devices with independent modes of failure).

We see that a lot of work needs to be done by systems providing the transactional ACID guarantees, and to perform this work numerous design choices must be made. Historically a number of performance bottlenecks in transactional systems arose from naive design features. As time passed and serious system implementors became more sophisticated about how to design for improved performance, various transactional benchmarks were developed to allow users to compare transactional systems from different vendors. The most famous of these developed into something called the *TPC-A benchmark*. This is a benchmark test that was standardized and carefully specified by the Transaction Processing Performance Council (TPC), an industry consortium of transactional database software and hardware vendors. For several years most vendors would not have tried to market a transactional database product without publishing the results of the TPC-A (or a simpler TPC-B) to meet the information demands of potential customers. The TPC-A benchmark is no longer officially used for benchmarking by vendors. However, the TPC-A benchmark still gives a good idea of the kind of bottlenecks that can arise in a transactional system that can hurt performance, and most vendors still run the benchmark internally to track possible performance problems. A short description of the benchmark follows.

Note that the reason that the benchmark has been so carefully specified is to ensure that all vendors performing the benchmark are making the same test—that there is no looseness in the rules that one vendor might be able to interpret to its own benefit, so as to report unfairly high transactional throughput numbers.

The TPC-A Benchmark Specification

The TPC-A benchmark models a banking application and requires four tables to be defined, specified in Figure 10.16. (Note that the transactional system under test need not be relational, and that instead of a table with a given number of rows, we might speak of a *file* with the same number of *records*. ACID properties are required, however, so we can't perform this benchmark on a simple file system.)

Note that the number of rows specified for each of the first three tables of Figure 10.16, Account, Teller, and Branch, is based on the assumption that the benchmark will result in a transactional throughput of no more than 100 TPS. The number of rows

Table name	Number of rows	Row size	Primary key
Account	10,000,000	100 bytes	Account_ID
Teller	1000	100 bytes	Teller_ID
Branch	100	100 bytes	Branch_ID
History	Varies	50 bytes	(Account_ID, Time_Stamp)

Figure 10.16   Tables Required for the TPC-A Benchmark (Rating ≤ 100 TPS)

required for these tables actually scales linearly up or down with larger or smaller TPS ratings. For example, for a rating of 200 TPS to be valid, Account would need to have 20 million rows, Teller 2000, and Branch 200. A test that resulted in a smaller rating could use a larger number of rows, but the test engineer might wish to reduce the table sizes to see if this would improve performance (because an increased fraction of the data would be memory-buffer resident for I/O).

In general, a large number of transactions are expected to be in process concurrently during the benchmark period, each transaction requested by an emulated *terminal* (a simulated user typing at a simple monitor keyboard). The transactions are all identical in outline, adding a Delta value (presumed withdrawal) to the Balance field of a number of rows identified by values for a specific Account (Account.Account_ID = Aid), Teller (Tid), and Branch (Bid). A History row is also written to a History file during this process. Pseudo-code for the logic executed by all transaction executions is provided in Figure 10.17. Only the parameters Aid, Tid, Bid, and Delta vary from one execution to another.

Note that three row updates are performed for each withdrawal transaction, a form of triple-entry bookkeeping to prevent errors. The Aid, Tid, and Bid values in the sequence of transactions used in the benchmark measurement period are randomly generated before runtime in such a way that all of the rows in the Account table are equally likely to be updated by each transaction, and similarly for the Teller and Branch tables. Note that no test is performed at runtime, to ensure that adding Delta to the Account row balance does not reduce the balance below zero (recall that this is a withdrawal, so Delta is negative), but this is a decision made by the TPC committee and is the same for everyone.

A number of tests given in the full benchmark specification are intended to determine that the ACID properties of atomicity, consistency, isolation, and durability are supported by the system. These tests are not part of the timed benchmark interval. A test of the Isolation guarantee listed in paragraph 2.4.2.1 of the TPC-A Benchmark Specification is given in Figure 10.18. This test has transaction executions using the logic of Figure 10.17. However, it is the responsibility of the test sponsor to demonstrate the full Serializable isolation level of SQL-99 under any mix of arbitrary transactions, not just TPC-A transactions. Tests of durability include causing memory failures in a running system and showing that recovery will recapture changes made by completed transactions up to a consistent point. Durable (stable) media failure recovery is also tested. One important point to note is that the History table mentioned earlier cannot be used for log recovery. Although the History rows seem to have all the necessary information to

```
(Read 100 bytes from the terminal, including Aid, Tid, Bid, and Delta)
(BEGIN TRANSACTION)
    Update Account where Account.Account_ID = Aid
        set Account.Balance = Account.Balance + Delta;
    Insert to History (50 bytes, include column values: Aid, Tid,
        Bid, Delta, Time_Stamp)
    Update Teller where Teller.Teller_ID = Tid
        set Teller.Balance = Teller.Balance + Delta;
    Update Branch where Branch.Branch_ID = Bid
        set Branch.Balance = Branch.Balance + Delta
COMMIT TRANSACTION
Write 200 byte message to Terminal, including Aid, Tid,
    Bid, Delta, Account.Balance
```

Figure 10.17 Transaction Logic of TPC-A Benchmark

```
Start transaction 1. (Logic of Figure 10.17)
Stop transaction 1 immediately prior to COMMIT.
Start transaction 2.
Transaction 2 attempts to update the same account record as transaction 1.
Verify that transaction 2 WAITS.
Allow transaction 1 to complete. Transaction 2 should now complete.
Verify that the account balance reflects the results of both updates.
```

Figure 10.18 Isolation Test for Completed Transactions (Conventional Locking Schemes)

perform recovery, they are under the control of the application, and might be deleted at any time.

Recall that we are emulating a system with a number of different terminals requesting transactions during the timed interval of the benchmark. To specify the frequency and number of transaction executions requested by these terminals during this interval, we need the following definition.

DEFINITION 10.10.1 The time between successive requests to the system from a single terminal is referred to as the *cycle time,* and is made up of two parts—the *response time* (delay by the system) and the *think time* (approximating the time the terminal user spends thinking). ∎

To run a valid TPC-A benchmark, the think times between terminal requests must be randomly generated before the benchmark is run, so that the resulting cycle times average at least 10 seconds. (This is a somewhat difficult problem, because we don't know the precise response time until we perform the benchmark, so we don't know exactly how long the think time should be in order to get a cycle time as close as possible to a 10-second average. We can only determine an accurate think time by a series of approximations.) The point of requiring a cycle time of 10 seconds is that a transactional system that wishes to achieve a rate of 100 TPS must be able to efficiently serve a network of at least 1000 terminals. There is also a condition limiting response time in the benchmark. Most systems measured would give a response time of much less than 1 second when only a single user is being run, but as more and more users are added we begin to see resource queues forming for the disk and CPU, leading to slower response. The official method used to determine the TPS rating of a system is basically this: we start with a given number of terminals and crank up the number, each executing one transaction every 10 seconds, until just before the point where 10% of the transactions executed have a response time of more than 2 seconds. This is the criterion used to ensure that all vendors performing the TPC-A benchmark get approximately the same resource utilization.

DEFINITION 10.10.2 Response-Time Criterion of the TPC-A Benchmark. During the measurement interval of the benchmark, at least 90% of all executed transactions must have a response time of no more than 2 seconds. ∎

To run the test, there is a warm-up period during which the concurrent transaction stream is run, until the system attains a "steady state" with a sustainable TPS rate. The measurement interval in steady state must extend for at least 15 minutes and no longer than 1 hour, and a checkpoint must take place during this interval. We usually assume that enough disks have been provided for the system under test so that the CPU is over 90% utilized, with the resource queues expected under the response-time criterion. How many disks to use is up to the test engineer, but there is an incentive to economize because one of the two major ratings for a system (other than the TPS rating) is the 5-year system cost per TPS ($COST/TPS).

As with the Set Query benchmark (which modeled its $COST/QPM rating on the earlier TPC-A benchmark), the $COST figure is calculated by including all hardware costs (including terminals and network), plus software and maintenance rental for 5 years. (This is a simple sum, without net present value calculations.) To give some idea of the ratings that occur, a small number of reported ratings for randomly selected commercial systems is provided in Figure 10.19. Notice that a TPC-A TPS rating of hundreds of transactions per second is perfectly possible. As a general rule, the $COST/TPS increases with increasing TPS. The UNIFY 2000 rating in Figure 10.19 is an exception.

Database system	Hardware	TPS	$COST/TPS	Date
ORACLE7	VAXcluster 4x 6000-560	425.70	$16,326	5/12/92
UNIFY 2000	Pyramid MIServer 12S/12	468.45	$5971	3/4/92
INFORMIX 4.10	IBM RISC 6000/970	110.32	$2789	7/16/92
SYBASE 4.8.1.1	Symmetry 2000/250	173.11	$2770	3/30/92

Figure 10.19 Some Historical TPC-A Ratings of Commercial Systems

Lessons from the TPC-A Benchmark

Bottlenecks are likely to occur in a number of areas in transactional systems if naive design features are used, and the TPC-A benchmark does an excellent job of making these bottlenecks prominent when they exist. To begin with, we note that the TPC-A transactions interleave very simple CPU tasks, theoretically requiring only a few thousand instructions, with requests for I/O, and a relatively small number of update requests are made before the transactions commit. However, the deceptively simple transaction logic exercises three important bottlenecks in three areas that we consider below: (1) data item locking, (2) writes to the log file, and (3) buffering.

Data Item Locking

We note that the rows of the 100-row Branch table and recent portions of the History table are extremely popular during transaction execution. From Figure 10.16 we see that there is one row in the Branch table for each transaction executed each second, with the assumed 100-TPS rating. This means that each row of the Branch table is locked on the average of once a second, and since there are certain to be a lot of overlaps we will see numerous occasions when a transaction is forced to WAIT. Some of the early systems were very inefficient at taking locks and switching context from one process to another under these circumstances, and transactional throughput was held down as a result. We also note that since nearly 10% of the transactions can spend more than 2 seconds before they commit (response-time criterion), there can be a real problem getting enough access to the Branch rows, at the rate of once a second, to run the full transaction rate. This can be thought of as an added requirement—locks on Branch rows must not be held so long that access to the rows becomes a bottleneck.

Historically many database products have taken locks, not on rows of tables, but on the disk pages that contain those rows. (**DB2** was one such product until recently, and no official TPC-A ratings of **DB2** have been published.) Page locking for rows simplifies the locking logic, since page locks are necessary in any event when rows on a page must be reconfigured. Clearly if a transaction takes a lock on the disk page containing a row, so that another transaction attempting to access any row on the same page runs into a conflict on the page lock and has to WAIT, this excludes conflicting pairs of accesses to the same row just as well as row locking. The only problem is that a lot of additional rows are excluded from access at the same time.

There are two tables in the TPC-A benchmark where page locks can be expected to cause a throughput problem: the Branch table and the History table. With no new row inserts to the Account, Teller, and Branch tables during the measured interval of the TPC-A benchmark, we would expect tables to be loaded 100% full, so that Branch rows of 100 bytes fit 40 on a page in **DB2**. History rows are inserted with every transaction in sequential order, but we would normally want to pack the rows as tightly as possible, so that 50-byte rows in the History table will fit 80 on a page. Since locks on Branch rows are already very critical for the level of concurrent access in TPC-A that will support good throughput, a locking protocol that grabs a lock on an additional 39 Branch rows

690

can be expected to cause a serious bottleneck. Similarly in the case of the History table, each transaction inserts a new History row in sequential order, and this means that new transactions are always making inserts on the last page of the table. We can assume that this page is buffered because of its popularity, but a locking protocol that takes a lock on the containing page will now lock out any concurrent transaction from writing a History row. The lock will be held until the requesting transaction commits, making the system write the log buffer to the log file on disk, and we can expect this to take at least 1/80 of a second (with our rule of thumb for random I/O). As a result, the page-locking protocol can be expected to limit the maximum throughput of a transactional system to 80 TPS.

To get around this sort of bottleneck that arises with page locking, the DBA can do something rather clever, configuring the Branch table and the History table so that in each case only one row falls on each page. There will be a good deal of wasted space as a result, but at least now when the locking protocol takes a lock on the containing page it locks only one row, and presumably the bottlenecks pointed out in the previous paragraph are solved. What this costs us is disk space to hold these relatively empty data pages and memory space to buffer them. The Branch table has only one Branch row for each 1 TPS in the rating, so with 100 TPS we would expect 100 disk pages. This is quite inexpensive in terms of disk cost, and even though all of these popular pages are consistently buffered, it is inexpensive in memory cost as well. By the cost rule of thumb presented in Section 7.2, 100 4-KB pages of disk at $1000 per GB costs approximately $0.40, and 100 pages of memory at $50 per MB costs $20.

With the History table we need to keep only a small number of pages buffered, the most recent pages to receive inserts in sequential order, so the memory cost is minimal. But the disk cost is a different story. There is a rule in the cost calculation for the TPC-A benchmark specification (paragraph 10.2.3.1) that the report must include in the $COST of the system enough online storage (disk) to contain history rows for 90 8-hour days at the published TPS rate. That's $90 * 8 * 60 * 60 = 2,592,000$ rows for each 1 TPS. Assuming one row per 4-KB page, a 100-TPS-rated system must pay for 252,200,000 disk pages, or about 1009 GB of disk, at a cost of about $2 million. This compares with a cost of $25,000 if the History table is stored 80 rows to a table page. Such a large cost for History storage will be sure to adversely affect the $COST/TPS rating of the system, and this is the way the TPC-A specification penalizes the relatively primitive page-locking protocol. The satisfying thing about this is that the requirement for 90 days of online storage for the History table is relatively realistic, and the penalty is one that would probably apply in commercial use.

Writes to the Log File

The log file on disk is normally configured as a sequential file, since recovery must read log entries in temporal placement order. As successive transactions commit and the log buffer contents are written to the log file, there is a "refractory period" after one disk write has been started and before the next write can be successful. The rule-of-thumb rate for random I/O we have been using, 80 I/Os per second, is a reasonable estimate of

how fast we can perform writes to the log file. Since the system must write out the log
buffer to disk with every transaction commit under the simple scheme we have been discussing, this means that we can have only about 80 transaction commits each second, or
a maximum rating of 80 TPS. The TPC-A benchmark, with its extremely simple transaction logic, can be expected to find this a bottleneck. As we saw in Figure 10.19, TPS ratings of hundreds per second are quite common. How are these rates achieved, given the
limitations on log writes?

One possible way to achieve TPS ratings higher than the log file I/O rate is a somewhat sophisticated design alternative known as *group commit*. The idea is that instead of
force-writing the log buffer out to the log file every time a single transaction commits, we
allow a *group* of transactions to commit before we force this write. Of course a transaction commit isn't complete until the log buffer has been written to disk (a bank won't
hand out money for a withdrawal until it has a durable record of the event), and this
means that a transaction that completes must be put in WAIT state until its commit log
entry is written out, even though this won't be done immediately. But there is no need to
worry about long delays here, since what we are trying to do is achieve a high TPS rate.
If it takes a long time for a group of several transactions to complete, then we don't have
to wait on writes to the log file after all. We just have to write slowly enough, a maximum of 80 times a second, so that we don't outrun the disk I/O rate. Basically what this
means is that with group commit the system writes out the log buffer to disk whenever
either of the following two events occurs:

[1]   the log buffer in memory fills up with entries

[2]   1/80 of a second has passed since the last log file write

The log buffer is typically 16 KB or longer, so it should be able to contain enough log
entries for a large number of transactions at high TPS rates before being forced to disk.

Buffering and the 5-Minute Rule

How many real disk I/Os (page requests not found in buffer) for data and index are being
performed in running the transactional logic of Figure 10.17? (We are not counting the
log write here.) Clearly this depends on which index and data are to be found in buffer
once a steady state has been reached in the TPC-A measurement interval. The only thing
restraining us from buying enough memory for buffers to contain all the data in the TPC-
A benchmark is that this will add to the $COST for the system, and even if the TPS rat-
ing is somewhat improved, this could adversely affect the $COST/TPS rating reported. It
turns out to be cost effective to purchase enough memory for I/O buffers so that the
Branch and Teller rows are always buffer resident. However, it is *not* cost effective at
present to keep the entire Account table memory resident.

To make the determination of what data is cost effective to keep buffered in memory
we use the 5-minute rule, introduced by Jim Gray and Franco Putzolu in 1987 [3]. They
pointed out that the reason for buffering disk in memory is to reduce the need for disk
arm movement to perform data accesses that cannot be found in buffer. More memory

buffers reduce the number of disks we need to buy (we assume that we can place the same data on fewer disks), and for this we are willing to invest money to buy more memory for buffering. In this trade-off we are spending more money on memory, keeping more and more popular pages memory resident, and saving on disk cost. With a given workload and known costs for disks and memory, there is a specific point in reduced popularity where we stop investing in new buffer space. Popularity of a disk page is measured in time between accesses: the more frequent the accesses, the more popular the page. What Gray and Putzolu showed was that the time between accesses that characterizes the marginal utility point, where we stop buying more memory for buffers, is about 5 minutes—hence the 5-minute rule. But the time interval was arrived at under slightly different assumptions than we want, and we will derive our own.

EXAMPLE 10.10.1 The 5-Minute Rule.

For simplicity we assume that we buy disks or memory for an unchanging workload over a 5-year period, so we don't have to worry about a rental rate for short time intervals. In purchasing disks, we can achieve a high rate of disk accesses per second, for each page of resident data, by loading a smaller amount of data under each disk arm than would be possible if we used all the capacity of the disk. (Note that some disks have multiple arms serving distinct regions, and it is the capacity served by the arm that is important.) This will cost more, of course. For example, the Account table in a system with a 200-TPS rating for TPC-A contains 20 million rows of 100 bytes each, or 2 GB of data (we ignore the index for now). Commercially available disks at present service about 10 GB with each disk arm, at a maximum access rate of 80 I/Os per second. We assume 10 GB and that the cost of the disk is $500. At 200 TPS we will see 200 read and 200 write I/Os per second to the Account tables. With a nominal rate of 50 I/Os per second for each disk arm (less than the maximum rate of 80 I/Os per second because with 100% utilization the disk queue will grow too long), this implies a need for at least eight disk arms to perform the I/Os to the Account table. Since the Account table contains 2 GB, and the eight disk arms we need sit over 80 GB of disk medium, we see that the capacity of the disks is only about 2.5% utilized. The cost for eight disks to hold the Account table is $4000. If we could buffer this data entirely in memory instead of leaving it on disk, we could reduce the need for disk arms, placing the entire Account table on a single disk, and save $3500 of the disk cost.

The cost to keep 2 GB of data in memory at $4000 per GB is $8000, so it is not appropriate to place the entire Account table into memory to save $3500. But if the price for memory were to go down far enough, say, to $1000 per GB, while the disk price stayed the same, it would be appropriate to keep the Account table on a single disk, at a cost of $2000 for memory, saving $3500 in disk costs. From this it becomes clear that there is a trade-off between disk and memory prices in our decision of how much data to buffer. ∎

EXAMPLE 10.10.2 More about the 5-Minute Rule.

Under the same assumptions as Example 10.10.1, we derive the marginal reference frequency for a disk page, where the price of being buffered in memory is the same as the price of being kept on disk. Assume that this rate is represented by X, in accesses per second for a page, 4 KB of data. The cost of keeping this 4 KB of data in memory at $4000 per GB is about $4000/256,000 (1 GB/4 KB = 256,000) or

Cost for memory residence = $4/256 = $0.015625

On the other hand, we can perform X accesses per second by using a fraction of a disk arm given by X/50, since a disk arm supplies 50 I/Os per second without a long queue. Since the cost of a disk arm is $1000 (using the figures following Figure 8.2), this means that the cost for X accesses per second when the page is on disk is

Cost for disk residence = $1000 * (X/50) = X * $20

At the marginal reference frequency, we see that the cost to keep the page in memory is the same as the cost of keeping it on disk, so we need to solve the following equation for X:

0.015625 = X * 20

The solution is X = .00078125, in references per second, or taking 1/.00078125 we get about 1280 seconds per reference, the *marginal access interval*. Pages that are referenced more frequently than once every 1280 seconds have a larger value for X, and we see that the cost of disk residence goes up while the cost for memory residence remains the same. Thus these more popular pages should remain in memory. The converse is true for less popular pages, referenced less than once every 1280 seconds. ∎

Note that 1280 seconds is slightly more than 21 minutes, so we see that the 5-minute rule has become the 21-minute rule as memory cost has come down faster than disk arm cost since the rule was invented. Memory component cost is still going down faster than disk arm cost, and as memory becomes cheaper relative to disk the marginal access interval for popular pages becomes longer. In another 20 years the marginal access interval will probably be much longer.

In performing buffering for the TPC-A benchmark, it is interesting to note that we are not particularly concerned about response time. Our transactions can take up to 2 seconds, while an additional disk I/O takes only about 50 ms, and for practical purposes we can ignore it. What we are concerned with is good buffering behavior to minimize the $COST of the system. A good transactional system under the TPC-A benchmark displays a real I/O rate to disk reflecting just a bit over two I/Os per transaction for data tables. Hashing should be used for the Account table index if possible, since otherwise the leaf level of a B-tree might not be buffer resident and would increase the I/O to over three per second. The Teller and Branch tables are much more frequently referenced than the Account table and remain in memory buffers for long periods, while being updated with every referencing transaction. Clearly it is important that we do not write pages out to disk whenever they are updated. The History table only needs to be written out to disk about once every 80 transactions, assuming that History rows are packed as fully as possible on the page.

Data that is referenced with high frequency is said to possess *heat*. When data is sufficiently popular that it should be buffered in memory, it is known as *hot* data. The Branch and Teller tables are examples of this. When data should not be buffered, but must be stored on disk in a way that does not use the full storage capacity in order to provide faster disk arm service, we say that it is *warm* data. We saw this behavior with the Account table. Transactional systems commonly deal with warm data. On the other

694   hand, it is often the case with query systems that there are very large storage requirements and relatively low concurrent use requirements, so that storage capacity becomes
the gating factor in cost-performance, and we say that the data is *cold*. The History
table represents cold data, except for the tail that is buffered to receive inserts, because
there are no real-time references to the History records after they are written (at least
none that are modeled in the TPC-A benchmark).

Suggestions for Further Reading

We recommend two texts that contain additional details about transactions. The first is a
text by Bernstein, Hadzilacos, and Goodman [1]. It is out of print but often still available
from second-hand sources, and can be downloaded from the Web in PDF form from
http://research.microsoft.com/pubs/ccontrol/default.htm. This text concentrates mainly
on proofs of correctness for some of the approaches mentioned in the current chapter,
although it goes into some implementation detail on the technique of fuzzy checkpointing. A number of concurrency methods and recovery approaches that were not covered
here are presented in detail, such as multiversion concurrency and shadowing. (These
methods find little current use in commercial systems, but this situation might change in
the future.)

The Gray and Reuter text [2], on the other hand, provides a fascinating compen-
dium of system implementation details needed to support the database features we have
been discussing, as well as myriad others. Proofs are provided, but the main focus is on
how to make database systems work. This is a seminal work, and no serious transactional systems practitioner can afford to be without it.

[1]   P. A. Bernstein, V. Hadzilacos, and N. Goodman. *Concurrency Control and Recovery in Database Systems.* Reading, MA: Addison-Wesley, 1987.

[2]   Jim Gray and Andreas Reuter. *Transaction Processing: Concepts and Techniques.*
San Mateo, CA: Morgan Kaufmann, 1993.

[3]   Jim Gray and Franco Putzolu. "The 5-Minute Rule for Trading Memory for Disc
Accesses and the 10-Byte Rule for Trading Memory for CPU Time." *Proceedings of
the 1987 ACM SIGMOD Conference*, pp. 395–398.

[4]   K. Kant. *Introduction to Computer System Performance Evaluation.* New York:
McGraw-Hill, 1992.

[5]   Hal Berenson, Phil Bernstein, Jim Gray, Jim Melton, Elizabeth O'Neil, and Patrick
O'Neil. "A Critique of ANSI SQL Isolation Levels." *Proceedings of the 1995 ACM
SIGMOD Conference*, pp. 1–10.

Exercises with solutions at the back of the book in "Solutions for Selected Exercises" are marked with the symbol •.

[10.1] For this exercise, assume that each transaction requires 10 ms for each CPU block and 50 ms for each I/O, as a variation from the 5-ms CPU and 50-ms I/O assumed in Example 10.2.1 and the discussion following that example.

(a)• Taking the approach of Figure 10.6, draw the equivalent graph of resource usage with the maximum number of disks and the maximum number of simultaneous transaction "threads" that give optimal throughput with perfect resource overlapping. Recall that each transaction requires two I/Os and two CPU blocks. What is the resulting throughput, in TPS?

(b) Consider the more realistic case where we have statistical allocation of resources, with random allocation of data on 10 disks. Assume 20 concurrent transactions as of a given time, with 5 transactions in queue for CPU and 15 in queue for disk I/O.

(i) With the model of throwing 15 darts at 10 disks, calculate the expected number of disks that do *not* have moving disk arms, and thus the disk utilization (percentage of disks busy). Do not use an approximation.

(ii) With the model that a queue of five transactions for CPU is like an average queue length of five in hashing, calculate the percentage of CPU we expect to be utilized.

[10.2] Draw the precedence graph for the histories

(a)• $W_3(A)\ R_1(A)\ W_1(Z)\ R_2(B)\ W_2(Y)\ W_3(B)\ C1\ C2\ C3$

(b) $W_3(D)\ R_1(D)\ W_1(F)\ W_2(F)\ R_2(G)\ W_3(G)\ C1\ C2\ C3$

[10.3]• Consider the following history:

$R_1(A)\ W_1(A)\ R_2(A)\ R_2(B)\ C_2\ R_1(B)\ W_1(B)\ C_1$

There is a circuit in the precedence graph (draw it), yet we can argue that nothing inconsistent could have occurred if we go by the effect of this history on the database alone. Transaction T_2, it is true, may have seen a partial result of transaction T_1, but it took no action and therefore had no effect on any data in the database. Transaction T_1, on the other hand, has seen only consistent data, since T_2 made no changes. Therefore we ask why we must say that this history is *not* serializable, since the only nonserializable view of data had no effect. (The flaw in this reasoning is that T_2 *might* have taken some other action if it had seen a consistent view of the data.) Explain, and give an interpretation for this history where such an inconsistency can cause problems.

[10.4]   Prove that if PG(H) contains a circuit, there is no ordering of transactions that doesn't have an edge of PG(H) pointing from right to left. (This is the part of the serializability theorem that was left as an exercise.)

[10.5]•   Show how the following series of calls would be handled by the locking scheduler. Take the approach of Example 10.4.2.

$$R_1(A) \; R_2(A) \; W_1(A) \; W_2(A) \; C_1 \; C_2$$

[10.6]   As in the previous exercise, show how the locking scheduler would handle the following sequences of transactional operation requests. Draw the waits-for graph at any point where a deadlock would occur.

(a)• $W_3(A) \; R_1(A) \; W_1(Z) \; R_2(B) \; W_2(Y) \; W_3(B) \; C1 \; C2 \; C3$

(b) $W_3(D) \; W_1(F) \; R_1(D) \; W_2(F) \; R_2(G) \; W_3(G) \; C1 \; C2 \; C3$

[10.7]   We consider cache buffering of disk pages in memory under the assumption that, to begin with, the cache buffer disk pages are empty, and that the maximum number of pages that can be held in cache is four (an unrealistically small number to test understanding). Assume in the history that follows that each of the data items A, B, C, D, E, and F accessed in the history lies on a distinct page.

$$H = R_1(A, 1) \; R_2(B, 2) \; W_1(A, 3) \; R_3(C, 4) \; W_2(B, 5) \; C_2 \; W_3(C, 6) \; R_4(D, 7)$$
$$R_5(E, 8) \; W_5(E, 9) \; R_6(B, 5) \; R_6(A, 3) \; R_3(F, 10) \; W_3(F, 11) \; W_4(D, 12)$$

(a)•   Name the first operation where an existing page in buffer must be dropped in order that another page can be read in.

(b)   Pages in buffer are called *dirty* if they have been updated in buffer but not yet written back out to their place on disk. What are the dirty pages in buffer at the time of the operation named in (a)?

(c)•   Assume that we are using an LRU scheme, and that each page is in use only for the duration of the read or write that accesses it. What page will be dropped from buffer at the time of the operation named in (a)?

(d)   Can we simply drop the page mentioned in (c) at that time, forgetting its value, or must some other event take place first? Why?

(e)•   When C_2 occurs in the history above, does this force out the page with the data item updated by T_2?

(f) List all of the operations above and the set of all data item pages that are in buffer at the conclusion of each operation, together with their values. Also list values of these data items on disk, when they are different. Here is an example of the format you should use:

Operation	Data items in buffer	Different on disk
$R_1(A, 1)$	A = 1	
$R_2(B, 2)$	A = 1, B = 2	
$W_1(A, 3)$	A = 3, B = 2	A = 1

[10.8] In the following histories, assume that there are no prior transactions in existence at the beginning of this history, and that each transaction starts with the first operation listed here, as in Example 10.8.1. For each history, provide the following:

(i) Write down the log entries that this series of operations would create in the log buffer under cache-consistent checkpointing.

(ii) Write down the cache-safe ROLLBACK and ROLL FORWARD sequences, starting from the last entry that would be found in the log file on disk.

(iii) Draw a time scale for the duration of these transactions, as in Example 10.8.1.

(a)• H1 = $R_2(A, 1)$ $R_1(B, 2)$ $W_1(B, 3)$ $R_3(C, 4)$ $W_2(A, 5)$ $W_3(C, 6)$ CKPT R_4 (D, 7) $R_2(E, 8)$ $W_2(E, 9)$ C_2 $R_4(E, 9)$ $W_4(D, 11)$ Crash

(b) H2 = $R_1(A, 1)$ $W_1(A, 3)$ $R_2(D, 2)$ $R_3(B, 4)$ C_1 $W_2(D, 5)$ $W_3(B, 6)$ CKPT $R_3(C, 7)$ $R_2(E, 8)$ $W_2(E, 9)$ C_2 $R_3(F, 6)$ $W_3(C, 11)$ Crash

[10.9]• Here is a time scale for a cache-consistent checkpoint followed by a crash, on which we claim that all possible transaction durations are exemplified. Argue why this is true, then consider each case and explain why the recovery process we have outlined does the right thing for each. This is how you would prove to yourself and others that such an algorithm works.

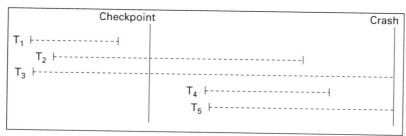

[10.10]   Is it possible for a transaction to continue active through more than one cache-consistent checkpoint? If not, explain why not. If so, explain why recovery will still work.

[10.11]•   Give an example of a serializable history H with operations from at least the three transactions T_1, T_2, and T_3, having the following properties: (1) every operation in T_1 precedes every operation in T_2, which precedes every operation in T_3; (2) in SG(H), we have $T_3 \rightarrow T_2$ and $T_2 \rightarrow T_1$. Write down the equivalent serial history. (Hint: you will need two other transactions, T_4 and T_5, and the ordering in SG(H) is by transitivity.) Note that no locking scheme is specified here, so you are free to design the serializable history independent of the temporal sequencing that a locking scheme would force on the system.

[10.12]   Recall the phantom problem of Example 10.5.3, where a new row is placed in an aggregate collection (account rows with a given branch) by one transaction, and another transaction performing an aggregation on these rows gets an inconsistent result. Explain how predicate locking solves this problem. Assume that T_1 needs to count the employees in the math department and that T_2 needs to add a new employee.

(a)   Show how the phantom problem could occur without predicate locking.

(b)   In predicate locking, what is locked by T_1 and in what mode?

(c)   What is locked by T_2 and in what mode?

(d)   How does this solve the phantom problem?

Parallel and Distributed Databases

11

The control of large numbers is possible, and like unto that of small numbers, if we subdivide them.
—Sun Tze, 5th–6th century B.C.

I n the preceding chapters we introduced most of the concepts that have been developed for traditional database systems, but the discussion of these concepts has been simplified by restricting consideration to a relatively old-fashioned computer environment: a single CPU database system architecture. In this environment we have pictured multiple terminals connected to a powerful computer having a single CPU and a relatively large number of connected disk drives. See Figure 11.1 for a schematic diagram of this architecture. We have not gone into much detail about this, but we have assumed that the single CPU is performing *time-shared* computing, running a number of different terminal processes (or *threads)* in a time-sliced manner to execute independent streams of application logic. Twenty years ago this picture of the standard database environment would have been accurate, but today competing database system architectures are replacing the old standard in most commercial applications. For many reasons, most new systems today operate in an environment where multiple CPUs are working in parallel to provide database services.

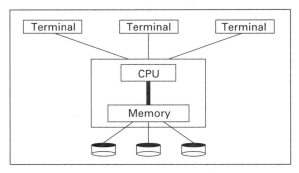

Figure 11.1   A Single-CPU Database System Architecture

In this chapter we briefly describe a number of different types of database system architectures that support multiple CPUs. Some of these architectures assume that CPUs share equal responsibility for database services that are physically close together, in the same building, and communicating at very high speed, while others assume that CPUs are geographically distributed, in different cities, communicating relatively slowly by telephone lines. Database systems with multiple CPUs that are physically close together are generally said to have a *parallel architecture* and to be *parallel systems*, while systems that are geographically distributed are generally said to be *distributed systems*. Architectures can vary in numerous other ways; indeed there are sufficient variations that consistent naming of the different types is becoming a bit of a problem. As we will learn, many of the most basic concepts of database operation are fundamentally dependent on these architectural variations. A thorough coverage of the various architectures is beyond the scope of this text. In the following sections we give a short introduction to the most fundamental concepts, and then list several references that deal with these architectures in more detail.

11.1   Some Multi-CPU Architectures

In this section we delineate three multi-CPU database architectures in which the CPUs bear equal responsibility for database services, and one called *client-server* in which different CPUs have differing responsibilities. New types of systems are still being invented, and our list is nowhere near complete; however, the architectures listed exemplify most of the basic principles.

As explained earlier, database systems with *parallel* architectures have multiple CPUs that are physically close together, while *distributed* systems have multiple CPUs that are geographically far apart. These two types of architecture actually arose from different needs. Parallel systems represent an attempt to construct a faster (and less expensive) centralized computer, while sidestepping the need to always have to construct a faster CPU. As we will see in the next section, it is more economical to purchase several smaller CPUs that together have the power of one large CPU. Distributed systems, on the other hand, arise from the need to offer local database autonomy at geographically distributed locations—for example, local branches of a large company. The distributed database approach developed as it became possible to allow these distributed systems to communicate among themselves, so that data could be effectively accessed among machines in different geographic locations. We start by describing three system architectures, beginning with the most closely coupled CPUs in the parallel architecture category and proceeding along a spectrum to the most loosely coupled distributed systems.

The first type of parallel database system is known as a *shared-memory multiprocessor*, where a computer has several simultaneously active CPUs that share access to a single memory and a common disk interface. See Figure 11.2 for a schematic picture. This is the type of parallel architecture that is closest to the traditional single-CPU processor, and the design challenge is to get N times as much work performed with N CPUs as can

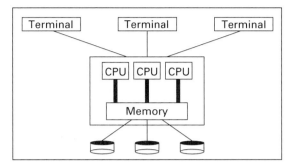

Figure 11.2 A Shared-Memory Multiprocessor Architecture

be performed with a single CPU of the same power. However, the design must take special precautions that the different CPUs have equal access to the common memory, and also that data retrieved by one CPU is not unexpectedly modified by another CPU acting in parallel. Because memory access uses a very high-speed mechanism that is difficult to partition without losing efficiency, these shared-memory access problems become more difficult as the number of CPUs increases. The largest IBM OS/390 mainframe currently has only 12 parallel CPUs. (Another type of architecture, known as *massively parallel,* allows hundreds of CPUs to share access to a common memory, but this requires some special design variations that we do not cover here.)

The second type of system falls in the category of *parallel shared-nothing* architecture, where a number of physically proximate CPUs acting in parallel each have their own memory and disk. We sometimes refer to this generically as a *parallel database system,* when there is no chance of confusion. CPUs sharing responsibility for database services in this type of configuration usually split up the data among themselves and perform transactions and queries by dividing up the work and communicating by messages over a high-speed network, at a communication rate measured in megabits per second. In Figure 11.3 this high-speed network is represented by thick, jagged connecting lines between the different CPU/memory packages, known as *system sites,* or simply *sites,* in what follows.[1] Such high-speed networks are limited in size, because of speed-of-light considerations, and this leads to the requirement that a parallel architecture has CPUs that are physically close together. Such networks are known as *local area networks,* or *LANs.*

The third type of system, a *distributed database system,* is also an example of shared-nothing architecture, since memory, like high-speed networks, cannot be shared between CPUs separated by great distance. Once again, the system database is partitioned between the different autonomous sites, so that queries and other data manipulation statements must be performed independently at the different sites and partial results communicated between the CPUs involved. However, network communication between

---

[1] The term *sites* is more commonly used for the physically removed CPUs and memories of a distributed database system (see the next architecture description), but we find it useful not to differentiate between a distributed system and a parallel shared-nothing system.

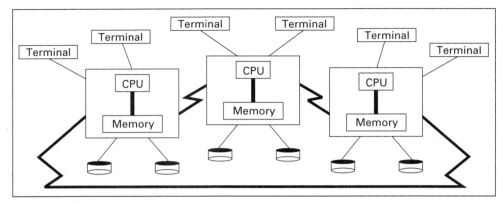

Figure 11.3   Parallel Shared-Nothing Architecture

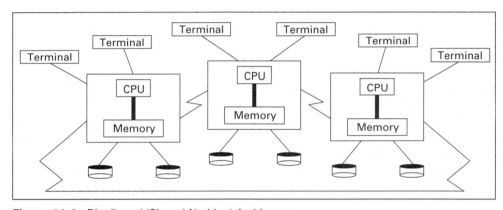

Figure 11.4   Distributed (Shared-Nothing) Architecture

CPUs in different cities is sometimes still limited to medium-speed lines, with a relatively low communication rate measured in megabits per second (on *wide area networks,* or *WANs*). See Figure 11.4, where the jagged connecting lines between CPUs are thin in comparison to those in Figure 11.3. Otherwise, the design of distributed systems and parallel shared-nothing systems is identical.

Parallel database systems are usually designed from the ground up to provide best cost-performance, and they are likely to be quite uniform in site machine architecture. Distributed database systems, on the other hand, often arise out of a need to tie together preexisting systems in different locations. As a result, the different site machines are quite likely to be *heterogeneous,* with entirely different individual architectures: an **ORACLE** system on a Sun Solaris UNIX system at one site, **DB2** on an OS/390 machine at another, and Microsoft SQL server on an NT machine at a third. Such machines often have different systems of data representation (for example, of floating point numbers) as well as **703** varying SQL syntax (motivating the common X/Open syntax when queries must be communicated between sites). Cooperation between site machines in a parallel system is usually achieved at the level of the transaction manager module of a database system (see Figure 10.8), but this is not generally possible in an architecture that combines heterogeneous sites with widely varying database systems. For this reason, a new type of software system known as a *TP monitor* is often used to tie such sites together. The TP monitor sits above the individual database systems on the various sites and uses them locally to provide needed services. The TP monitor provides threads for user execution and *remote procedure calls* (RPCs) to allow application logic to make requests to remote sites; the monitor supplies the needed data representation conversion in the act of communicating parameters of such calls. TP monitors are extremely sophisticated systems that are outside the scope of this text; they are investigated in great detail in the text by Gray and Reuter [5].

In the architectures of Figures 11.2, 11.3, and 11.4, all CPUs pictured are equally responsible for database services delivered by the system. In the shared-nothing architectures, data is partitioned between the disks at the distinct sites, and queries that reference data on multiple sites must have the cooperation of all the CPUs involved, communicating partial results back to the site with the terminal (user) that made the request. Clearly these architectures have important implications for database system design. How is query optimization affected when tables of a database are partitioned on disks in different cities? How are update transactions affected when one CPU doesn't have all the data affected in a transaction under its control? These significant problems are still being investigated by database implementors.

Client-Server Architectures

The motivation for the parallel architectures of Figures 11.2 and 11.3 is the relative economy of small CPUs in comparison to large ones. But there is an alternative to the types of architecture in which the CPUs share responsibility equally for all database services. With the *client-server* architecture, small client CPUs (usually personal computers, costing about a thousand dollars) take responsibility for interaction with the user, providing presentation services and deciding what data is needed to answer user requests. The client machines do not have most of the needed data on local disks, however, and to respond to user needs the client machines pass high-level data requests (SQL-level requests or else programmatic *remote procedure calls)* to a *centralized server* machine, often a shared-memory multiprocessor. It is also possible to have client machines deal with more complex parallel servers, or even multiple servers on a network. The major characteristic of a client-server system is the division of labor between the client CPUs, which take responsibility for presentation services, and the server CPUs, which take responsibility for database services (Figure 11.5).

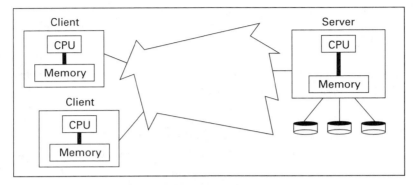

Figure 11.5   Client-Server Architecture

11.2   The Curve of CPU Cost versus Power

We have mentioned that a major motivation for parallel database architectures, pictured in Figures 11.2 and 11.3, is cost-performance. Let us expand on this point.

We define the *$COST* of a specific CPU as the cost in dollars for which one CPU can be purchased at wholesale. Note that most PCs costing over $1000 have CPUs that cost less than $100; the extra cost is for the casing, disk drive, software, and the like. We define the *power* of the CPU as the number of instructions the CPU can execute in 1 second, and assume that this is reported in *millions of instructions per second,* or *MIPS*. It is important to realize that this definition of power is badly flawed; there are a lot of different types of work a CPU can perform (scientific computation, graphics display, various types of commercial database applications), and benchmarks need to be devised to allow us to measure any one kind accurately. Once such benchmarks have been designed, they become targets for partisan vendor representatives performing "benchmarketing." For certain well-known benchmarks, computer designers have created special operations and compiler modifications for the sole purpose of achieving high ratings on that benchmark. In many cases these ratings drop sharply when minor realistic modifications are made in the benchmark logic. Also in many cases the people measuring the performance ratings of a machine are the same ones who want to sell the machine, and this leads to a self-serving inflation of ratings. It is certainly the case that a PC with a 50-MIPS rating is a good deal less powerful than an IBM mainframe with a 50-MIPS rating. IBM has not supported MIPS ratings for some time because of the difficulties just mentioned, among others.

Still everyone likes a simple answer, so in what follows we act as if there is a simple MIPS rating that can be determined for different CPUs, and that this MIPS rating reflects the type of CPU work that needs to be performed in all database system applications. Then the most important fact driving computer architecture for the last 15 years or so is the curve presented in Figure 11.6, representing the relationship between $COST and

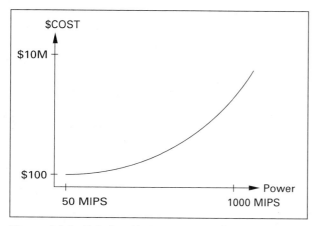

Figure 11.6 Relationship between CPU $COST and Power

power for a range of CPUs. We do not claim that the specific numbers shown are accurate (prices and CPU technology are constantly changing), but the general shape of the curve is valid.

What this curve shows is that $COST is a function of power that grows at a superlinear rate. That is, if 50 MIPS in a single CPU cost $100, then 200 MIPS in a single CPU will cost a good deal *more* than $200. By the time we get to a 1000-MIPS CPU, with power 20 times as great as that of the CPU we started with, the $COST is $10 million, *100,000 times as much as the 50-MIPS CPU!* The reason for this extraordinary growth in cost is basically this: as the CPU speed goes up we are getting closer and closer to the upper limits of the technology, and we have to pay more and more for the sophisticated means needed to gain more speed. It's like the difference between sending a letter to Europe by two-day mail (cheaply) and hiring a courier to fly on the Concorde and deliver it personally. It's faster, but it costs a *lot!*

What is the lesson for the database industry? Simply this: *lots of little CPUs are cheaper than one big CPU*. If a commercial company owns a powerful old-style mainframe machine that is spending most of its time in time-shared mode giving interactive service to a group of terminal users, the company should probably buy a PC for each user to give the needed interactive service. Then it can connect all the PCs as client machines to a central server, and that server can be a much smaller machine, now that it doesn't have to deal with presentation services for a lot of terminals. With this design the server is doing the work that large machines are best at, accessing data on a large number of disks and communicating simple answers to clients. Thus we see that the $COST/power curve of Figure 11.6 is the motivation for the client-server architecture. Indeed it provides the motivation for all the types of multiple-CPU database architectures mentioned above: we need to learn how to make several small CPUs do the work of one big CPU.

It is extremely simple to parallelize certain types of work that are naturally divisible. An example of such a type of work is when word processing is being performed by a group of technical writers who don't need to communicate except by passing printed text to each other for review. In this case the proper solution is to buy all the users PCs and some single-user word processing software. This work environment provides all needed parallelism and an important cost savings over using a time-shared computer for word processing (which was actually done at one time, at extremely high cost).

But with database applications there are numerous requirements for communication that make it less straightforward to run applications on a group of distinct CPUs, even when these CPUs communicate over a high-speed network. A good deal of thought must go into a system architecture that will support database applications, and without great care the communication overhead for such applications can add back the cost that we are saving by using smaller computers. In addition, a database system has a significant investment in online data access devices, such as disk drives (as much as 50% of the cost on modern workstation systems), and a careless approach to storage will also make an architecture uneconomical. Thus we see that CPU cost scalability isn't the only cost factor in a distributed database system. The battle to find the best parallel database system architecture is still being fought, and we try to give some idea of the problems that can arise in the following section.

11.3   Shared-Nothing Database Architecture

The usual idea of a shared-nothing database architecture, as pictured in Figures 11.3 and 11.4, is as follows. For reasons of either cost-performance or geographical distribution, it is not considered feasible to provide all database services on a single mainframe computer, so the data is partitioned and placed on disks of a number of different low-cost computers with separate memories. These different systems (we call them *sites* or *site machines*) must then cooperate to perform database work, and this entails a need to communicate between sites.

EXAMPLE 11.3.1 The TPC-A Benchmark.
The TPC-A benchmark was described in Section 10.10, with no mention of the possibility of implementing the benchmark on a multi-CPU shared-nothing database system. However, such an implementation was foreseen by the benchmark designers (the TPC), and certain rules were laid down to make sure that the benchmark test would be realistic. To run TPC-A on a shared-nothing system, the data must be partitioned on a number of machines. Assume ten site machines and that we are measuring for a 100-TPS rating, resulting in 100 rows in the Branch table. Now each of the tellers and accounts (rows in the Teller and Account tables) is associated with a specific branch: there are ten tellers and 100,000 accounts in each "home" branch. In order to use each of the site machines of the distributed database system equally to support the TPC-A workload, it is necessary to *partition* the tables among the ten sites. The standard way to do this is to give each site its own Branch, Teller, and Account tables, except that the Branch table contains only ten rows at each site (we are dividing, or partitioning, the 100 rows of the Branch table among the ten site machines). The Teller and Account tables are then also partitioned among the ten site machines, and the tellers and accounts belonging to local branches are the only ones that have rows in a local site.

Now to recapitulate the transaction logic for TPC-A, each transaction represents an account holder (Aid) coming into a bank branch (Bid) to some teller (Tid) at random, and making a withdrawal (Delta) from the holder's account balance; this withdrawal is reflected in the Branch balance and Teller balance as well. Where, we wonder, does the communication requirement between the site machines come in? If an account holder enters the local bank branch and makes a withdrawal, there seems to be no need for communication to access data from other sites. Ah, but we have failed to mention another requirement. Of the randomly generated (Aid, Tid, Bid, and Delta) messages, 85% can represent Aid values that belong as home accounts to the Bid listed, but another 15% of the messages must have randomly chosen Aid values from all Account_ID values that are held at *foreign* branches. Since the Bid value determines the local site machine that processes the message, the need for communication now becomes clear. About 15% of the transactions will be drop-in account holders making withdrawals on accounts from foreign branches. Since there are ten branches at each site, about 90% of these foreign branch drop-ins will require communication with a different site. Remember that the transaction needs to add Delta to the Branch balance (local site) and to the Teller balance (local site), but it also needs to add Delta to the Account balance, and this implies an update to an Account row at a different site as part of the same transaction that updates the local Branch and Teller rows. As we will see, this means that we need to revisit our ACID properties to make sure that this *distributed transaction* is properly handled. ■

At first the communication overhead suggested by Example 11.3.1 doesn't appear very serious; it seems that we have to send a message and make an update at a foreign site about 15% of the time. The problem is that different rows to be updated in a single transaction now appear in distinct memories, the locks are held on separate processors, and it is therefore not possible to coordinate the transaction commit as we have done in the traditional centralized database architecture. Presumably we need to start another transaction at that foreign site to make that update, and then coordinate the commits of the two transactions. This is rather vague, but on the whole it seems like a fairly simple requirement. On closer examination, however, it turns out that a number of complex problems arise in executing distributed transactions. We treat several of these in the following subsections.

Two-Phase Commit

Consider the idea mentioned earlier of starting another transaction when a local transaction must suddenly access data at a remote site and become distributed. For example, in TPC-A on a shared-nothing system, consider the situation when an account holder at a branch handled by the site 2 machine drops in on a foreign bank branch handled by the site 1 machine. From the transaction logic of Figure 10.17, we see that the first data access is at site 2, while the teller-terminal interaction is at site 1. Therefore a distributed transaction T_D is immediately initiated and coordinated at site 1, with a local transaction component at site 2, which we call rather simplistically T_2. The second data access to the History table is on the local machine at site 1, so the distributed transaction T_D now also has a local transaction component T_1 at site 1. When the logic of the TPC-A transaction commits, the two transactions T_1 and T_2 must commit in a coordinated fashion to successfully complete the distributed transaction T_D.

In most shared-nothing database systems with homogeneous sites, access to remote data is transparent to the application logic; it is normally handled by the transaction manager (TM) component of the database system, which has a global picture of how the database is partitioned on the various site machines. See Figure 10.8 and the discussion that follows for a schematic picture of the TM and its place in the transactional system. In a shared-nothing architecture, the TM decides which sites should start local component transactions, forwards scheduler calls for data access and manipulation to the appropriate site and awaits replies, and takes responsibility for the distributed transaction commit. The TM might eventually find that when it comes time to commit (or abort), the transaction has read and updated a large number of different data items at several different sites (although the TPC-A transaction is too simple to involve more than two sites).

We say that the site transactions of a distributed transaction are *coordinated* if they are all guaranteed to commit or abort together. Given this coordination, the distributed transaction inherits the ACID properties from its site components. If two-phase locking is used whenever some data item is accessed at any site by a distributed transaction, this provides isolation for all distributed data items accessed as a package. (The locking theorem, 10.4.2, still holds in a distributed transaction.) Isolation then implies consistency, as we explained earlier. As far as the ACID property of durability is concerned, we need to consider what will happen if a single site crashes. A distributed transaction that has committed will have written the Commit log at all local sites (remember we assume that all participating site transactions commit or abort together), and so we conclude that the system will be able to perform REDO recovery when the crashed site comes back to life. Naturally a new level of recovery logic is needed to handle recovery of a distributed transaction when one site out of several crashes, but this presents no difficulty.

The only hard part in all this comes with our assumption that all site transactions of a distributed transaction can be coordinated, so that they all commit or abort together. This can also be thought of as the ACID guarantee of atomicity for the distributed transaction; all updates of the transaction are performed (all sites commit) or none are performed (all sites abort). It turns out to be impossible to coordinate different site transactions in this way with the type of local transactional behavior we have dealt with up to now, which we call *basic transaction* behavior. As we have described it, a basic transaction that has been initiated by a scheduler has only three states in which it can exist. These basic transaction states are as follows:

Active   A transaction becomes *active* on being initiated by the scheduler in response to a data access request by some application thread. A transaction can pass from the Active state to either the Committed or the Aborted state. In the event of a system crash and subsequent recovery, a transaction in the Active state enters the Aborted state.

Committed   An active transaction becomes *committed* as a result of a commit request by the application thread. There is no way to leave the Committed state.

Aborted   An active transaction becomes *aborted* as a result of a rollback request by the application thread or because of various other conditions that can arise in the system, such as transaction deadlock or system crash and recovery. There is no way to leave the Aborted state.

Figure 11.7 gives a schematic picture of the basic transaction states and the possible transitions between them. Note carefully that while an active transaction can enter either the Committed or the Aborted state, once either of these states is entered no further change of state is possible. When a transaction commits, it loses the ability to back out the effects of its data item updates that it possessed as an active transaction. This is because the commit causes locks to be released (we have to let them go sometime), and the effects of the updates become visible to other transactions; with the loss of isolation, we can no longer roll back. At the same time, an abort arising for any reason also causes locks to be released. Finally it is important to understand that the system never has any guarantee that a basic transaction in any other state will enter the Committed state. If the site where the transaction is active crashes, even if recovery is almost instantaneous, an active transaction will have UNDO recovery performed on all its updates and enter the Aborted state. The Aborted state is entered in this case because it is normally impossible for the system to recover enough context to continue the transaction through a successful commit. Only the original application logic can do that by performing a *retry*. Finally we note that in our model there is no way to guarantee against crashes at a given site.

It turns out that this combination of properties of the basic transaction states makes coordination of site transactions (so that they are always guaranteed to abort together or commit together) an impossible task. To see this, assume that as before we initiate two basic transactions on different sites, with the intention of performing the distributed TPC-A logic of Example 11.3.1. Denote by T_1 the action at the "local" branch, site 1, where Delta (a negative number) is added to the Branch and Teller balances, and denote by T_2 the "remote" transaction where Delta is added to the balance of an account at a foreign branch, site 2. Now let us assume that the TM at site 1 acts as a *coordinator,* attempting to schedule the two site transactions so that they commit or abort in lockstep. How is the coordinator to act?

One possibility is for the coordinator to start by committing the local transaction T_1, and after succeeding locally sending a message to commit the remote transaction T_2. But if site 2 has crashed by the time it receives this message, then T_2 will abort when recovery takes place. See Figure 11.8 for an illustration of this series of events.

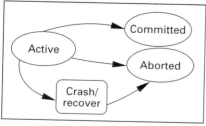

Figure 11.7 Basic Transaction State Transition Diagram

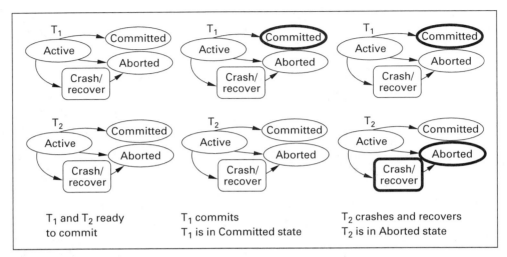

Figure 11.8 Failed Coordination of a Distributed Transaction

After site 2 has recovered, the request to commit T_2 will be unsuccessful since T_2 has irrevocably entered Aborted state. Because T_1 has committed and T_2 has aborted, money has been destroyed in the bank records (it was taken out of the branch and teller by T_1, but not given to the account holder by T_2).

A second possibility (not pictured) is that the coordinator starts by sending a message to site 2 to commit transaction T_2 and after receiving successful return notification attempts to commit T_1. This approach can also go wrong. The commit at site 2 may be successful but then site 1 may crash before it receives the successful return notification so the coordinator can commit T_1. After recovery, T_1 will be aborted and T_2 committed, so the foreign account balance will have money taken out, but there will be no compensating changes in branch and teller (and presumably the account holder has not received any cash). Finally the coordinator could forget about waiting for successful notification and try to perform both commits "at the same time" by sending out both commit requests one after another. But of course it is still possible for either of the two sites to crash, causing an abort, while the other succeeds in committing.

There is no way to get around the fact that an arbitrary site in a distributed transaction can crash at an inopportune time. Our problem with coordination arises when one site transaction aborts and another commits; both site transactions have entered irrevocable states, and these states conflict. In the situations we have been considering, the Aborted state is entered because an active transaction in a crashed site is forced into an Aborted state by recovery. What we need is some new state that has more flexibility than this. We introduce something called the *prepare request* that can be made by a coordinator to cause site transactions to enter a state we call the *Prepared state*. Here is the definition:

Prepared   A transaction becomes *prepared* as a result of a request by a distributed transaction coordinator (a TM) making a *prepare* request.

From a Prepared state, the transaction can enter either the Committed state or the Aborted state. In the event of a system crash and subsequent recovery, a transaction in a Prepared state returns to Prepared state. (Some practitioners refer to this as the *Hardened* state.)

When a prepare request is received at a site for an active site transaction, a process is performed to *make the current flexible Active state durable*. Note that all transactional logic has been completed before prepare is called. Now a *Prepare log* is placed into the log buffer and the buffer is force-written to the log file, after which we say that the transaction has entered the Prepared state. In the event of a crash and subsequent recovery, the current state of the transaction is reconstructed; from this recovered Prepared state, we can still perform either a commit or an abort (see Figure 11.9). In order to maintain this flexibility, we could, after a site crash, REDO all updates of the transaction and maintain all before image log entries in the log file after recovery is complete. All data item locks held by the transaction in its Active state must also be reestablished after recovery.

With this new Prepared state, a distributed transaction coordinator can overcome the problem of inopportune aborts in participating sites. In the example just presented of the distributed TPC-A transaction, symbolized as T_D, with T_1 at site 1 and T_2 at site 2, the coordinator at site 1 can perform the logic of Figure 11.10. The method employed is known as a *two-phase commit* (2PC) protocol, and it is a standard approach used by commercial database systems to achieve a coordinated commit of distributed transactions. Note that the initial request to PREPARE(T_2) in Figure 11.10 may fail for a number of reasons. An abort may occur at the site for some reason, such as to break a deadlock, and in this case a response of "unsuccessful" is returned by site 2. Alternatively, the site might crash or become disconnected from the network, and we treat this in the same way as we treat a return message of "unsuccessful": in every case we presume that T_2 will abort. This is certainly the proper course if a crash occurs, since an active transaction is aborted by recovery. If a network failure has occurred, we make a rule to abort an active transaction after a time-out period. On the other hand, if the PREPARE request did reach site 2 before the site or network failure, we have a more durable state. Since the coordinator got no response, it aborts T_1, writes ABORT T_D to the local log file, and transmits the message to site 2 with an appropriate distributed transaction identifier

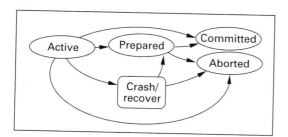

Figure 11.9   Transaction State Transition Diagram with Durable Prepared State

```
BEGIN
    REQUEST PREPARE(T₂)                  /* requires message to site 2          */
    IF RESPONSE IS "UNSUCCESSFUL"        /* site 2 crashed, network failed      */
        ROLLBACK T₁, WRITE "ABORT TD"    /* abort distributed transaction       */
    ELSE IF (T1 is "ACTIVE")             /* T1 hasn't aborted while waiting      */
        COMMIT(T₁, TD)                   /* no going back now                   */
        REQUEST COMMIT(T₂)               /* will succeed eventually             */
    ELSE                                 /* T1 has aborted                      */
        WRITE "ABORT TD"                 /* abort distributed transaction       */
        REQUEST ABORT(T₂)                /* message to site 2                   */
END
```

Figure 11.10   Two-Phase Commit for Two-Site Distributed Transaction

for T_D. We assume that this message is delivered to site 2 when it recovers, so site 2 will know enough to abort T_2, which was a participant in T_D.

On the other hand, if the response from site 2 is "successful," the coordinator commits the local transaction T_1, together with the distributed transaction T_D, writing log entries to the log file. This is the point of weakness in distributed transaction coordination that we explained earlier. After one transaction has committed the other site crashes, and on recovery the other basic transaction has aborted. But that can't happen here, because T_2 has been prepared. If a crash occurs at site 2, this will only mean a delay, since on recovery T_2 will return to the Prepared state. After committing T_D and T_1 locally, the coordinator sends a COMMIT message to site 2, and eventually this will be delivered to an operational site with T_2 in the Prepared state and succeed. If site 1 crashes after T_D is committed, recovery will bring it back up with a list of participating site transactions and another commit message will be sent to site 2 (a second one won't hurt). This sequence of events is pictured in Figure 11.11.

The two-phase commit also works for transactions at more than two sites. An outline of the multi-site 2PC protocol follows.

Phase 1. Coordinator sends messages to all involved foreign sites asking them to prepare site transactions that participate in this distributed transaction.

If any of these sites respond "unsuccessful," then the coordinator rolls back the local site transaction and sends messages to all sites in doubt to tell them to abort as well.

Phase 2. If all prepare requests result in "successful" responses, the coordinator commits the distributed transaction T_D, and the local transaction component, and then starts sending commit messages to each of the participating site transactions. Sooner or later these messages will all be delivered.

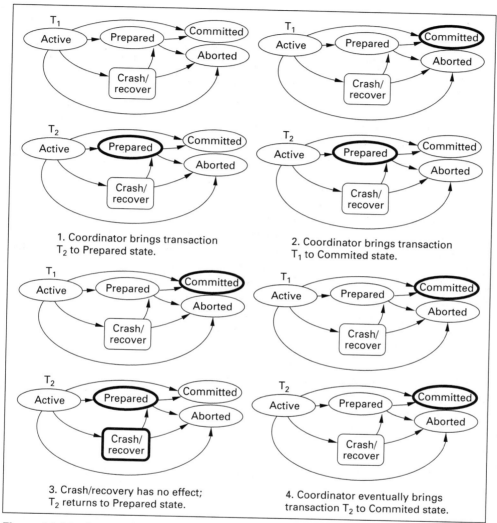

1. Coordinator brings transaction T_2 to Prepared state.

2. Coordinator brings transaction T_1 to Commited state.

3. Crash/recovery has no effect; T_2 returns to Prepared state.

4. Coordinator eventually brings transaction T_2 to Commited state.

Figure 11.11 Sequence of Events in Two-Phase Commit

Further Problems with Shared-Nothing Architecture

The two-phase commit protocol isn't very easy to implement (**DB2** spent several years in its development), and a number of other complexities arise as well. We list some of them below.

Distributed deadlock. Assume that distributed transaction T_{D1} updates data item A on site 1 and then attempts to update data item B on site 2, but finds it locked, and therefore goes into WAIT. Now assume that the lock on data item B at site 2 is held by distributed transaction T_{D2}, which attempts to update data item A at site 1. Clearly this is a deadlock. But how is the deadlock going to be detected? Recall that we are dealing with site CPUs that do not have common memory or any knowledge of locking tables for data items on foreign machines. No single-site machine knows enough to trace a WAITS-FOR circuit that might extend over several sites. The simplest solution to this problem is to give up on deadlock detection and use *time-out abort*. When a distributed transaction is waiting for a lock on a foreign data item so that distribute deadlock is possible, then after a certain waiting period (a few seconds), the transaction aborts and retries. It is important that different transactions choose randomly different time-out periods. That way they don't get into a "chatter" mode of giving up and retrying together so that they run into each other again.

Transaction blocking. A transaction is said to be *blocked* if it must wait for recovery from some sort of long-term failure before it can proceed. Since the blocked transaction might be holding locks on popular data items (12-oz. cans of Pepsi in a soft-drink whole-sale business), this can be a serious problem. Blocking can occur with the two-phase commit protocol we have just presented in the following way. Assume that a coordinator at site 1 makes a prepare request for transaction T_2 at site 2, and then crashes before sending the final message to site 2 that it should commit (or abort if the local transaction T_1 has aborted for some reason). We assume that either outcome is possible and because of this, transaction T_2, which is in the Prepared state, cannot make a choice on its own under the protocol. It must hold itself in readiness for whatever decision the coordinator announces after it recovers. This might take quite some time, however, and if T_2 is holding a lock on the PEPSI_12_OZ row that is normally referenced by 50 orders a second, such an outage is unacceptable. There is no good solution to this. A different protocol known as *three-phase commit* has been designed to avoid blocking under most circumstances, but it involves another round of messages to arrive at a commit, and it has not been commercially adopted. (Remember the fear that communication overhead was going to cost enough to lose the cost advantage of smaller CPUs?)

Replicated data. Leslie Lamport, a well-known researcher, is said to have remarked, "A distributed system is one where the failure of some computer I've never heard of can keep me from getting my work done." The problem, of course, is that we have partitioned the data, and if a lot of transactions need data from several machines (not a problem with TPC-A transactions because they're so simple), this greatly increases the chance of failure. If we have a group of CPUs that individually fail only once a month (assuming 8-hour days and 5-day weeks), and we put a hundred of them into a distributed database, one of them will fail every 1.7 hours! (Added to this is the problem that inexpensive CPU hardware has inferior mean time to failure (MTTF) ratings when compared to large mainframe CPUs.) To overcome this problem, the standard approach is to *replicate* all the data in the database, so that data is not simply partitioned but stored at a minimum of two different sites. The downside of this replication is that any data updates must then be communicated to at least two sites and take place in lockstep. Once again we have the problem of communication and other types of overhead increasing the cost of a distributed database.

Notwithstanding all these complexities with update transactions, shared-nothing database systems are the coming thing. The economies and ease of use that arise are just too compelling for any complexities to daunt the practitioners designing new database systems, and new approaches are being tried constantly.

11.4   Query Parallelism

Up until now we have been concentrating on how to use multiple-CPU architectures to support update transactions, and most of the complexity we have seen has revolved around the need to perform updates. But there are a growing number of application systems where online updates rarely occur, queries are the common requests, and new data is added infrequently in a merge of old data with new that happens off line. For example, large department store chains commonly study past customer buying habits to determine locations to hold sales and customers who should receive mailing announcements. Almost all merchandisers use existing sales data to drive their reordering. The reorders are executed as row inserts, a particularly simple kind of update that can be processed in update transactions at a later time, but the determination of *what* to order is query based. And the queries used can be quite complex, since marketing specialists are not merely reordering what has been purchased before. Careful analysis can determine new products that should be ordered, seasonal items such as snow chains that need to be stocked, or how to change the layout of a store to improve visibility of items that should be selling better. A system like this is known as a *decision-support system* (DSS). A number of large companies (for example, drug wholesalers) provide this kind of analysis as a value-added service to their customers. Systems that support mainly queries in normal use are also provided by libraries, book and audio stores, state license agencies for police inquiries, and so on.

With query-only distributed systems, it is clear that we don't have the problems associated with two-phase commit (there are no updates to coordinate), transaction blocking (there are no write locks), or distributed deadlock. If data is replicated for availability in case of failure, it simply remains in place, and there is no concern about updating multiple copies simultaneously. Our major challenge is to come up with an architecture that allows us to decompose a query into parts that can act in parallel, usually at several different sites. This is sometimes known as *intra-query parallelism*.

Intra-Query Parallelism

Here is a classic picture of a shared-nothing query system. The tables to be queried are partitioned among K different sites, comparable to what we saw with the TPC-A earlier, the Account table being partitioned into Acct1 at site 1, Acct2 at site 2, . . . , AcctK at site K. The site machines do not share memory or disk, but communicate among themselves by messages over a communication network. Now assume that we wish to answer the following query, submitted at site 1, to list the senior citizen account holders:

[11.4.1] `select Account.name, Account.phone from Account`
`        where Account.age >= 65;`

There is no single `Account` table in our architecture, and the straightforward way to accomplish this task is to have the system decompose query [11.4.1] into K different queries Q_J, of the form

```
select AcctJ.name, AcctJ.phone from AcctJ
    where AcctJ.age >= 65;
```

Here J ranges from 1 to K. The query coordinator needs to send messages for each query Q_J, communicating the request to site J. Each site then answers the query from data in its local table `AcctJ` and communicates the answer back to the coordinator, let us say, at site 1. Site 1 has the task of accepting rows from each of the participating sites and putting them together to form the answer.

Note that the query coordinator's job could become somewhat more complicated, for example, if an ORDER BY clause were affixed to query [11.4.1], such as ... `order by Account.name`. The same clause would then be affixed to each of the Q_J queries, so that participating sites would return their rows in the appropriate order, but it is still left to the coordinating site to merge these different streams into a single ordered sequence of rows. As with the queries we have already seen, there might be good reason to limit the materialization of the answer if there is any suspicion that only an early set of rows in the answer will be considered, and this feature creates slightly more complexity for the coordinator. Another alternative arises when we consider a modification to query [11.4.1]:

[11.4.2] `select count(*) from Account where Account.age >= 65;`

This query too will be decomposed into site-component queries, and the coordinator must now know enough to *add* the responses from the various sites to arrive at the final answer.

The most difficult problem of all arises as a result of a query that requires a join to take place between tables at different sites. Consider a design where individuals can have multiple bank accounts at different branches, but one of the accounts is considered to be *primary*. The Account table contains a column named `acct_type` that has value *primary* or *secondary*; rows that are secondary have a column value `Pracct_ID`, which gives the value of `Account_ID` for the corresponding primary account. (Rows that are primary have a null value for `Pracct_ID`.) Now consider the following query to bring together all multiple account balances of multiple account holders:

[11.4.3] `select A1.Account_ID, A1.balance, A2.Account_Id, A2.balance`
`        from Account A1, Account A2`
`        where A2.acct_type = 'secondary'`
`            and A2.pracct_id = A1.Account_ID;`

Consider how this query will be executed in a multi-site database of the kind we have been discussing. We can fragment the query into different queries Q_J for communication to sites J, varying from 1 to K, where secondary accounts are positioned:

[11.4.4]
```
select A1.Account_ID, A1.balance, A2.Account_Id, A2.balance
    from Account A1, AcctJ A2
    where A2.acct_type = 'secondary'
        and A2.Pracct_ID = A1.Account_ID;
```

But we note that the Account table for primary accounts taking part in the join is still multi-site resident. A join between different sites is unavoidable under these circumstances. One possible query execution plan when query [11.4.4] is executed at site J is to retrieve all Account_ID values from AcctJ into a set X:

[11.4.5]
```
select A1.Pracct_ID into X
    from AcctJ A2
    where A2.acct_type = 'secondary';
```

We can now have database site J partition X into sets $X_1, X_2, \ldots, X_K$, where set X_M consists of Pracct_ID values that match with Account_ID values at site M (the system knows where the different rows of the Account table are stored by primary key value). Now site J sends messages to the different sites M asking for solutions to the query

[11.4.6]
```
select A1.Account_ID, A2.balance
    from AcctM A1
    where A1.Account_ID in X_M;
```

When the answers to these queries are returned from the different sites M to the requesting site J, a join can then be performed to answer query [11.4.4]. The results of the various queries of the form [11.4.4] can now be communicated back from the different sites J to answer the original query [11.4.3].

Queries on a multi-site shared-nothing database can have extremely complex query plans, involving multiple levels of intra-site messaging. Clearly a set of distributed sites with slow communication over a wide area net is at a severe disadvantage for plans of this kind, involving *dataflow* between different sites. An excellent overview of shared-nothing queries of this kind is given in a paper by DeWitt and Gray [2].

Suggestions for Further Reading

Distributed database system design, with all the variant problems that can arise, is well presented in the text by Ozsu and Valduriez [7]. The Bernstein, Hadzilacos, and Goodman text [1] provides a good rigorous grounding for distributed transactions, and Gray and Reuter [5] give a superb introduction to the design and implementation issues that arise. The Gray and Reuter text is also the best introduction to TP monitors. The text by Khosafian, Chan, Wong, and Wong [6] is a good basic introduction to writing client-server applications in SQL on a number of systems. Parallel queries are discussed in the paper by DeWitt and Gray [2], the chapter of *The Benchmark Handbook* [4] dealing with the Wisconsin benchmark, and several papers of the Stonebraker text [8], which also reprints founding papers on distributed database systems.

[1]   P. A. Bernstein, V. Hadzilacos, and N. Goodman. *Concurrency Control and Recovery in Database Systems*. Reading, MA: Addison-Wesley, 1987.

[2]   D. J. DeWitt and J. Gray. "Parallel Database Systems: The Future of High-Performance Database Systems." *Comm. of the ACM*, 35(2), June 1992, p. 85.

[3]   Goetz Graefe. "Query Evaluation Techniques for Large Databases." *ACM Computing Surveys*, 25(2), June 1993, pp. 73–170.

[4]   Jim Gray, editor. *The Benchmark Handbook for Database and Transaction Processing Systems*. 2nd ed. San Mateo, CA: Morgan Kaufmann, 1993. See Section 4.3, "Benchmarking Parallel Database Systems Using the Wisconsin Benchmark."

[5]   Jim Gray and Andreas Reuter. *Transaction Processing: Concepts and Techniques*. San Mateo, CA: Morgan Kaufmann, 1993.

[6]   Setrag Khosafian, Arvola Chan, Anna Wong, and Harry K. T. Wong. *A Guide to Developing Client/Server SQL Applications*. San Mateo, CA: Morgan Kaufmann, 1992.

[7]   M. Tamer Ozsu and Patrick Valduriez. *Principles of Distributed Database Systems*. Englewood Cliffs, NJ: Prentice Hall, 1991.

[8]   Michael Stonebraker, editor. *Readings in Database Systems*. 2nd ed. San Francisco: Morgan Kaufmann, 1994. See original research papers: Chapter 7, "Distributed Database Systems," and Chapter 8, "Parallelism in Database Systems."

Exercises

[11.1]• Answer true or false for the following questions and explain your answers.

(a)   Two-phase commit is required in order to guarantee a coordinated transaction on a shared-memory multiprocessor.

(b)   Distributed deadlock is not possible on a shared-nothing DSS system where only queries are performed.

(c)   The server in a client-server architecture cannot be a shared-nothing parallel database system.

(d) According to Figure 11.6, five CPUs with a 60-MIPS rating should cost less than one CPU with a 300-MIPS rating.

(e) A transaction in a Prepared state can still commit after the site machine on which it lives has crashed and later recovered.

Introductory Tutorial   **A**

A.1   Setting Up the CAP Database in ORACLE

This section explains the skills you need to perform Exercise 3.2.1 of Chapter 3, a computer assignment to exercise SQL *data definition statements* to create database tables duplicating the customers-agents-products (CAP) database of Figure 2.2. Specifically you will learn in this tutorial how to enter the database from the operating system, how to load data from an operating system file into the database, and how to deal with the SQL*Plus interactive environment. SQL*Plus has a number of commands that allow you to compose SQL statements, edit them, save them to operating system files, and then read them back and so on. As explained in Section 3.2, you first need to get an account on your operating system—an OS user ID and password to log in to the computer—and an **ORACLE** name and password to enter the database. Your instructor or DBA should be able to advise you on how to do this at your installation.

In **ORACLE** there is usually one monolithic database owned by the database administrator. Unlike **INFORMIX**, individual users in **ORACLE** do not normally create their own databases. In order to keep different users' data separate, the database administrator grants each user access to a private *tablespace* in the database. A tablespace is like a directory that contains a set of tables. We will still informally refer to a group of related tables as a "database"; an example is the customers-agents-products (CAP) database of Figure 2.2.

Creating the CAP Database

To enter **ORACLE**, give the operating system command

[A.1.1] `sqlplus`

ORACLE then prompts you for your database username and password, which your DBA should have given you. If your username and password are accepted, you see a new kind of prompt:

SQL> _

which means that you are now in the SQL*Plus interactive environment. This environment has a number of commands (basically *editor* commands) that are explained in the next subsection, but for now we concentrate on the SQL statements you will want to create. These SQL statements are really *directives* to the **ORACLE** system (rather than to the interactive environment, which you are just using to compose them) that allow you to create tables, load them, pose queries, and so on. As explained in Section 3.2, to create the CUSTOMERS table of the CAP database in **ORACLE**, using the lowercase tablename customers, you would issue the statement

```
SQL> create table customers (cid char(4) not null, cname varchar(13),
    2 city varchar(20), discnt real, primary key (cid));
```

Notice that after pressing Enter on the first line, the system prints out a prompt for the second line, 2. The prompt for the third line would be 3, and so on. There is no limit to the number of lines you can type. The system doesn't attempt to interpret what you have written until you end a line with a semicolon (;).

The result of the Create Table statement is the creation of an empty customers table with the column names (or attributes) cid, cname, city, and discnt. The *type* of each attribute (also known as the *domain* of the attribute) follows each attribute name specified; thus cname is of type varchar(13) (meaning a character string of variable length of up to 13 characters) and discnt is of type real. Refer to Section 3.2 for further explanation and to Section A.3, "Datatypes," for a complete list of **ORACLE** datatypes. **ORACLE** supports the ANSI SQL datatype names integer, real, double precision, and so on, with its own datatypes (number(n), etc.) having at least the required range and precision. We will use the ANSI SQL datatype names instead of the **ORACLE**-specific names to make our SQL statements as portable as possible.

Now that we have a table, we can load data into it. To do this, we leave SQL*Plus by typing exit at the SQL prompt, and then run the SQL*Loader utility.

Using the SQL*Loader

The SQL*Loader is a utility program that reads operating system text files and converts the contents into fields in a table. To do this, it must be told what format it should expect the external data to be in. This description is stored in a control file, which usually has the filename extension ".ctl". For example, the control file custs.ctl should look like this:

```
load data
replace
into table customers
fields terminated by ","
(cid, cname, city, discnt)
```

The data file, typically having the extension .dat, contains the data to be loaded into the table. It should be in the format described in the control file. For example, custs.dat should look like this:

```
c001,Tiptop,Duluth,10.0
c002,Basics,Dallas,12.0
c003,Allied,Dallas,8.00
. . .
```

To run the loader, type the operating system command:

```
sqlldr control=custs.ctl
```

The SQL*Loader then prompts you for your **ORACLE** username and password. If you prefer, you may put these in the command line:

```
sqlldr username/password control=custs.ctl
```

Note that this command assumes that custs.ctl is in the current directory when the command is entered. Otherwise a more complete directory pathname would be needed. For example, in UNIX a file custs.ctl in the poneil user directory, oracle subdirectory would be represented in the Copy command by /usr/poneil/oracle/custs.ctl. In either case, the SQL*Loader requires write permission in the directory containing the control file, so that it can create log files and bad files. Log files, ending with the filename extension .log, contain a detailed report of the loading process. The bad file, ending in .bad, contains any records that could not be properly read. You will need to copy custs.ctl and custs.dat from your instructor or the book's homepage to one of your own directories before you can use them properly; sqlload will fail if it attempts to create the log file and the bad file in your instructor's or DBA's directory, since you are only allowed to read that directory.

Now that you have seen how to create a table and how to load it, you need to know how a table is to be destroyed (deleted from the database, as a file is deleted from a directory). As explained in Section 3.2, for this purpose we use the command

[A.1.2] `drop table tablename;`

All the tables can be created by the use of one file of statements, here named create.sql and provided as input to SQL*Plus as follows:

```
sqlplus username/password @create.sql
```

The file create.sql has the following content. (Note that we drop tables before creating them, in case there are old versions in the database.) The double hyphen marks the rest of a line as a comment, that is, unexecuted text. **ORACLE** also allows the C comment syntax /* ... */, but this is not ANSI standard and thus not portable to other database systems.

```
-- create.sql: SQL script file for table creation

drop table customers;
create table customers (cid char(4) not null, cname varchar(13),
    city varchar(20), discnt real,
    primary key (cid));

drop table agents;
create table agents (aid char(3) not null, aname varchar(13),
    city varchar(20), percent smallint,
    primary key (aid));

drop table products;
create table products (pid char(3) not null, pname varchar(13),
    city varchar(20), quantity integer, price double precision,
    primary key (pid));

drop table orders;
create table orders (ordno integer not null, month char(3),
    cid char(4), aid char(3), pid char(3),
    qty integer, dollars double precision,
    primary key (ordno));
```

Here we are using SQL-92 datatypes, not the **ORACLE**-specific types more commonly used for historical reasons. An **ORACLE**-trained DBA would use number(6) or number(10) for integer quantities, number(10, 2) for money, and float for double precision. Here we are using double precision for money, but other SQL standard datatypes commonly used for it are numeric(10, 2) and decimal(10, 2); these have the advantage of holding pennies exactly and allowing dollars as units, while double precision allows exact pennies only if the unit is a penny, since 1/100 is not a binary terminating fraction.

After the above commands are executed, the tables can be loaded by sqlload at the operating system command level as follows:

```
sqlload username/password control=custs.ctl
sqlload username/password control=agents.ctl
sqlload username/password control=prods.ctl
sqlload username/password control=orders.ctl
```

To automate the job fully, put the sqlplus command and the four sqlload commands in a command file—for example, loadcap.cmd on Windows NT or other systems, loadcap on UNIX—and then the simple command line loadcap does the whole job.

Using SQL*Plus

SQL*Plus is the environment you enter by typing `sqlplus` from the operating system level. To begin with you see this prompt:

```
SQL> _
```

You can type in any SQL statement you want; if it doesn't fit on one line, you may continue onto the next line. SQL*Plus prints the line number of each new line as a prompt at the beginning of the line; for example,

```
SQL> select * from customers
  2 where cname = 'Tiptop'_
```

SQL*Plus won't try to interpret this statement until you terminate it with a semicolon:

```
SQL> select * from customers
  2 where cname = 'Tiptop';
```

After pressing Enter on line 2, SQL*Plus prints out the row that matches this query and returns you to the SQL> prompt. It is also possible to enter a command but not execute it; the usefulness of this feature will become apparent shortly. To terminate a command without executing it, simply enter a completely blank line; you then return to the SQL> prompt. The text of the command (whether executed or not) is saved in the buffer. We can always view the current contents of the buffer by typing the command l or `list`:

```
SQL> l
  1 select * from customers
  2* where cname='Tiptop'
SQL> _
```

SQL*Plus commands that operate on the buffer, such as l, are not saved in the buffer; that would severely limit their usefulness!

In the above example, the star after the 2 indicates the current line in the buffer, which is used by several SQL*Plus commands. To change the current line, simply enter the line number at the SQL prompt:

```
SQL> 1
  1* select * from customers
SQL> _
```

To alter a small part of the current line, rather than retyping the whole thing you may use the c or `change` command, which replaces an old sequence of text with a new sequence of text. For example, in

```
SQL> c /customers/agents
     1* select * from agents
SQL> _
```

the slashes (/) are called *separating characters*. You may use any non-alphanumeric character for separating characters. For example, the command c &customers&agents would be equivalent to the example above. To delete a substring of the current line, simply replace it with an empty string:

```
SQL> c /agents/
     1* select * from
SQL> _
```

To replace the contents of an entire line, type the line number, followed by the new contents:

```
SQL> 1 select * from customers
```

To re-execute the (possibly modified) contents of the buffer, use the command /; the command r lists the contents of the buffer and then executes them.

You can delete the current line in the buffer by using the command del. You can insert lines after the current line in the buffer with the i command. This command can be used in two different ways: you can either insert a single line of text following the i command:

```
SQL> i where cid = 'c001'
SQL> _
```

or, to enter several lines of text, type i with no arguments:

```
SQL> i
     2 where cid
     3 = 'c001';
```

In this mode, SQL*Plus behaves as if you are simply continuing to add to the previous command (or insert after a given line in a large buffer). A terminating semicolon, as in this example, executes the entire buffer contents.

We use these commands to correct a typical spelling error. Assume that you type

```
SQL> sellect * from customers
     2 where cname = 'Tiptop' _
```

and then realize your spelling error. You can correct it by ending command entry (entering a blank line), selecting the line to modify, replacing the misspelled word with the correct spelling, and executing the buffer:

```
SQL> sellect * from customers
     2 where cname = 'Tiptop'
     3
SQL> 1
     1* sellect * from customers
SQL> c /sell/sel
     1* select * from customers
SQL> /
```

This is the equivalent of simply retyping the command, but it requires fewer keystrokes.

The edit command is a trapdoor to your system editor. With no arguments, it invokes the editor on the contents of your buffer; or you can specify a filename to edit.

To execute an SQL command file from within SQL*Plus, use the command @, followed by the command file's name. To simply load a command file into the buffer, use the command get, followed by the filename. To save the contents of the buffer to a file, use the command sav or save, followed by the filename.

To summarize, here is a table of commands available in the SQL*Plus environment:

```
c /old/new       change first occurrence of old string to new string
                 in current line
l                list contents of buffer
del              delete current line from buffer
i new line       insert a new line after current line in buffer
i                begin interactively inserting lines after current
                 line in buffer
/                execute statements in buffer
r                list and then execute statements in buffer
edit filename    edit file using default operating system editor
edit             edit buffer using default operating system editor
@filename        execute SQL statements stored in file named
get filename     load file named into buffer
save filename    save buffer to file with given name (overwrites old)
5 new line       replace line 5
5                set current line to 5
host command     do the operating system command as specified
spool filename   start saving user interaction (user keystrokes and output) to file named
spool off        stop saving user interaction from prior spool command and close file
exit             leave SQL*Plus environment
```

If the edit command does not work, you need to issue the SQL*Plus command define_editor = 'editor_name'. There are automatic start-up files to do such setup, but their description is beyond the scope of this summary.

A.2 Setting Up the CAP Database in INFORMIX

This section explains the skills you need to perform Exercise 3.2.1 of Chapter 3, a computer assignment to exercise SQL *data definition statements* to create database tables duplicating the customers-agents-products (CAP) database of Figure 2.2. Specifically you will learn in this tutorial how to enter the database system from the operating system, how to load data from an operating system file into the database, how to issue SQL statements, and edit them, save them to operating system files, and then read them back and so on. As explained in Section 3.2, you first need to get an account on your operating system—an OS user ID and password to log in to the computer. Your instructor or DBA should be able to advise you how to do this at your installation. Certain environment variables need to be set up as well, such as INFORMIXDIR for UNIX users. Note that the **INFORMIX** interactive menu environment explained below is specific to the UNIX operating system. The Windows operating system uses a different interface, the sqleditor utility. We are planning to make a tutorial on this Windows interface available in the future on Web page http://www.cs.umb.edu/~poneil/dbppp.html.

   In **INFORMIX** (unlike **ORACLE**) it is normal for users to create their own databases. Creating the CAP database involves creating your own database and then creating the CAP tables within that database. If you are using a UNIX system, to enter the **INFORMIX** interactive environment before you have a database, give the dbaccess operating system command.

Creating the CAP Database (in UNIX)

After giving the dbaccess command at the UNIX level, you will see a simple one-line menu:

[A.2.1] DBACCESS: Query-language Connection Database Table Session Exit

   Choose Database by typing d or using the left-right arrow keys to highlight the word and typing RETURN. The next menu will be

[A.2.2] DATABASE: Select Create Info Drop Close Exit

   Choose Create by typing c, and type in a name for the database when it is requested. This name can be based on your username or whatever your instructor specifies, for example, eoneildb. Then when asked for Dbspace, choose the default by typing e for Exit. You will be asked to confirm your database creation with a menu having "Create-new-database" as the default, and you should do this by pressing Enter, then e to Exit the Database menu, and e again if you want to Exit dbaccess. If you should ever become uncertain about what you are doing or get into a loop in the menu tree, you can get help in the menu by pressing Ctrl-W. It is not always the case that a succession of e for Exit characters will get you out of the loop, although this is the first thing to try.

Now that you have a database, the next time you use dbaccess you may specify it on the system command line, as in dbaccess eoneildb. You will see the one-line menu given in [A.2.1] above. Choose the menu item Query-language, the first highlighted choice, by pressing Enter, and in the next menu,

[A.2.3] SQL: New Run Modify Use-editor Output Choose Save Info Drop Exit

choose New in the same way to start a new SQL Editor session for composing SQL statements. In this environment, you will be able to create tables for the CAP database. To begin doing this, type the SQL statement

```
create table test1(col1 int);
```

The top part of the screen should now look like this:

```
NEW:     ESC    = Done editing     CTRL-A = Typeover/Insert      CNTL-R = Redraw
         CNTL-X = Delete character  CTRL-D = Delete rest of line
----------eoneildb@dbserver--------------Press CTRL-W for Help--------------
create table test1(col1 int);
```

Press Esc to return to the higher menu [A.2.3] from editing, and then select Run to execute the statement. You should see "Table created," or similar output at the bottom of the screen.

If your Run command fails, you need to edit your SQL statement text to try again. Simply choose Modify from the Query-language menu, and you will be back in the same SQL Editor environment as you had previously with New, but now your old text will appear in the bottom part of the screen. Edit your text as before and use Esc Enter to execute it.

Now to delete this test table, select New, and type in the SQL statement

```
drop table test1;
```

Then execute it as before.

Now that you know how to execute SQL statements using dbaccess on UNIX (or have mastered the corresponding actions using sqleditor in Windows), we may proceed with UNIX and Windows together. As explained in Section 3.2, to create the customers table of the CAP database, using the lowercase tablename customers, you would issue the following SQL statement:

```
create table customers (cid char(4) not null, cname varchar(13),
    city varchar(20), discnt real, primary key(cid));
```

The result of the Create Table statement is the creation of an empty customers table with the column names (or attributes) cid, cname, city, and discnt. The *type* of each attribute (also known as the *domain* of the attribute) follows each attribute name specified; thus cname is of type varchar(13) (meaning a character string of variable length of up to 13 characters) and discnt is of type real. Refer to Section 3.2 for further explanation and to Section A.3, "Datatypes," for a list of **INFORMIX** datatypes. We will use the SQL standard names for datatypes, and these are fully supported by **INFORMIX.**

Now that we have a table, we can load data into it from a data file that typically has the filename extension .dat. For example, for data on customers we set up a file custs.dat that should look like this:

```
c001,Tiptop,Duluth,10.0
c002,Basics,Dallas,12.0
c003,Allied,Dallas,8.00

...
```

To do the load, we can use the Load statement that **INFORMIX** has added to its SQL language. For example, to load date from the file custs.dat into database table customers, we can use the following SQL statement (entered in SQL Editor the same way as the Create Table statement above):

```
load from 'custs.dat' delimiter ',' insert into customers;
```

Note that this command assumes that custs.dat is in the current directory when the command is entered. Otherwise a more complete directory pathname would be needed. For example, in UNIX a file custs.dat in the poneil user directory, oracle subdirectory, would be represented in the Load command by, for example, /usr/poneil/oracle/custs.dat.

Now that you have seen how to create a table and how to load it, you need to know how a table is to be destroyed (deleted from the database, as a file is deleted from a directory). As explained in Section 3.2, for this purpose we use the SQL statement we have met with before:

[A.2.4]   drop table tablename;

All the tables can be created by the use of one file of SQL statements, for example, file create.sql, which is provided as input to dbaccess for UNIX and the SQL Editor for Windows as follows:

```
dbaccess eoneildb create.sql   (UNIX systems, using local server)
sqleditor /s csdb /d eoneildb create.sql  (Windows systems, using server csdb)
```

The file create.sql has the following content. (Note that we drop tables before creating them, in case there are old versions in the database.) The double hyphen marks the rest of a line as a comment, that is, unexecuted text. **INFORMIX** also allows comments to be enclosed in curly braces, { . . . }, but this is not ANSI standard and thus not portable to other database systems. The following SQL statements are standard SQL (SQL-92 and X/Open).

```
-- create.sql: SQL script file for table creation
drop table customers;
create table customers (cid char(4) not null, cname varchar(13),
    city varchar(20), discnt real,
    primary key (cid));

drop table agents;
create table agents (aid char(3) not null, aname varchar(13),
    city varchar(20), percent smallint,
    primary key (aid));

drop table products;
create table products (pid char(3) not null, pname varchar(13),
    city varchar(20), quantity integer, price double precision,
    primary key (pid));

drop table orders;
create table orders (ordno integer not null, month char(3),
    cid char(4), aid char(3), pid char(3),
    qty integer, dollars double precision,
    primary key (ordno));
```

After the above commands are executed, the tables can be loaded by the following SQL script, named `infload.sql`, short for "Informix load," in recognition of the product-specific extension to standard SQL that is being utilized here.

```
-- load rows from text files into tables already created by create.sql
-- Note that the "load" statement is an INFORMIX extension to SQL
load from 'custs.dat' delimiter ',' insert into customers;
load from 'agents.dat' delimiter ',' insert into agents;
load from 'prods.dat' delimiter ',' insert into products;
load from 'orders.dat' delimiter ',' insert into orders;
```

Then run this SQL script the same way as `create.sql`. To automate the job fully, put the two script-file-execution commands in a command file—for example, `loadcap.cmd` for Windows NT or `loadcap` on UNIX—and then the simple command line `loadcap` does the whole job. You can even put the Create Database statement into the script file, in which case you need to run dbaccess with a - (hyphen) in place of the database name: `dbaccess - createall.sql`. If you would like to see the commands echoed as they are executed, use the `-e` option, as in `dbaccess -e - createall.sql`.

Using DB-Access (UNIX Systems)

DB-Access is the environment you enter by typing dbaccess dbname from the operating system level, once the database has been created as explained above. You will see a simple one-line menu, called the Main menu:

```
DBACCESS: Query-language  Connection  Database  Table  Session  Exit
```

We have seen how to use the Database menu item to create a database. Once that is done, the Query-language menu item is by far the most important. Since it is listed first, a simple Enter selects it and brings you to the Query-language submenu. (Alternatively use the command dbaccess dbname -q to skip the Main menu and go right to the Query-language submenu.) You will then see the Query-language menu screen, with the menu options listed below:

```
SQL: New  Run  Modify  Use-editor  Output  Choose  Save  Info  Drop  Exit
```

Choose New from this menu to start a new editing session (SQL Editor) for composing SQL queries. Alternatively you can specify a system editor (vi, emacs, etc.) via Use-editor.

In SQL Editor you can type in any SQL statement you want. If it doesn't fit on one line, you may continue onto the next line by typing Enter at any convenient point before you reach the right-hand edge. Note that SQL Editor does not do automatic line wrapping. If you make an error, use Enter and the arrow keys to reposition the cursor and then type over the error. You can type Ctrl-A to switch over to "insert mode," which pushes the old characters aside to accommodate the new characters. Another Ctrl-A reverts you to "overstrike mode." The screen looks like the following after a simple Select statement has been entered on two lines:

```
NEW:     ESC   = Done editing      CTRL-A = Typeover/Insert      CNTL-R = Redraw
         CNTL-X = Delete character  CTRL-D = Delete rest of line
-----------eoneildb@dbserver--------------Press CTRL-W for Help---------------
select * from customers
where cname = 'Tiptop';
```

Now press Esc to return to the Query-language menu, where you can choose to Run this statement, return to this editing session by using Modify, or switch over to using a system editor such as vi. You can save the text in a file by choosing Save and entering a filename. If you enter mytest, the file will be mytest.sql in the file system because dbaccess adds on the expected .sql filename extension.

For extensive SQL statements, a system editor is better than the simple editor built into dbaccess. Once a file of SQL statements is constructed by Save or use of any editor in, say, mytest.sql, it can be run from the UNIX command line

```
dbaccess eoneildb mytest.sql
```

Alternatively you can use Choose in the Query-language menu to bring the contents of
mytest.sql into dbaccess memory, where you can Run it, Modify it, or Use-editor to
work on it and eventually Save it again.

In summary, here are the menu commands for the Query-language menu:

```
New          enters new SQL statements using the SQL Editor.
Run          runs the current SQL statements.
Modify       modifies the current SQL statements using the SQL Editor.
Use-editor   uses a system editor to modify the current SQL statements.
Output       send the results of the current SQL statements to a printer, file, or pipe.
Choose       chooses a file that contains SQL statements and makes them current.
Save         saves the current SQL statements in a file so you can use them again later.
Info         displays information about tables in the current database.
Drop         removes a file that contains SQL statement.
Exit         returns to the DB-Access Main Menu.
```

A.3 Datatypes

The datatype for each column in a Create Table statement can be chosen from Figure
A.1.

SQL-99	ORACLE	INFORMIX	DB2 UDB	Range	C equivalent
char(n), n limit not specified	char(n), n <= 4000	char(n), n <= 32,767	char(n), n <= 254	$1 \leq n \leq 254$, X/Open	char array[n+1]
varchar(n), n limit not specified	varchar(n) varchar2(n), n <= 4000	varchar(n), n <= 255	varchar(n), n <= 32672	$1 \leq n \leq 254$, X/Open	char array[n+1]
numeric(6, 0), decimal(6, 0)	numeric(6, 0), number(6)	numeric(6, 0), decimal(6, 0)	numeric(6, 0), decimal(6, 0)	$-10^6 < x \leq 10^6 - 1$	short int, (approx.)
numeric(p, 2), decimal(p, 2)	numeric(p, 2), decimal(p, 2), number(p, 2)	numeric(p, 2), decimal(p, 2), money(p, 2)	numeric(p, 2), decimal(p, 2)	p digits, 2 to right of decimal point, for example.	none
smallint	smallint	smallint	smallint	$-2^{15} \leq x \leq 2^{15} - 1$	short int
integer	integer	integer	integer	$-2^{31} \leq x \leq 2^{31} - 1$	int, long int
real	real	real, smallfloat	real	$-10^{-38} \leq x \leq 10^{38}$ 7-digit precision	float
double precision, float, float(bp)	double precision, number, float, float(bp)	double precision, float	double precision, double, float, float(bp)	$-10^{-38} \leq x \leq 10^{38}$ 15-digit precision, or bp bits precision	double

Figure A.1 Some Important SQL Datatypes

The char(n) datatype contains fixed-length strings of n characters. Thus in [3.2.1] the cid column is defined to have datatype char(4) and is perfect for strings such as 'c001', but a value such as 'c1' (which we do not have in our tables) would be filled in with blanks at the end, c1$\Delta\Delta$, where the symbol Δ represents a blank character. For columns with highly varying string length values, it saves storage space to use a datatype varchar(n). For example, the attribute city has the datatype varchar(20), allowing varying character strings of *up to 20 characters*. Here short character strings don't require long terminal sequences of blank characters, and common short city names such as 'Troy' and 'Austin' use up less storage space than long ones such as 'Oklahoma City' and 'San Francisco'. We would use a smallint datatype in place of an integer for the same reason: to save storage space in cases where the integer value in question will *never* exceed $2^{15} = 32,767$ in absolute value.

SQL-92, SQL-99, and individual database products have additional datatypes not listed in Figure A.1. SQL-92 has date, time, timestamp, (time) interval, and national character strings. SQL-99 (in its named features beyond Core) has LARGE OBJECTs, or LOBs for short, including BLOBs, binary large objects, and the Boolean type, as well as the object-relational, user-defined, structured types and arrays. Core SQL-99 has distinct types, that is, user-specified synonyms for built-in types. The lvarchar datatype in **INFORMIX** allows lengths up to 32,767, and the long datatype in **ORACLE** supports character string values up to 2 GB in length. **ORACLE** implements the smaller SQL numeric types smallint and real with the dynamically sized number(38) and number (i.e., double precision). The information above on the range and precision of the floating point types is simplified; check the manuals for details.

Programming Details   B

B.1   The prompt( ) Function

In this appendix we explain the prompt( ) function used in many examples in Chapter 5 to perform prompted interaction with the user. See the subsection "Prompted User Interaction" after Figure 5.1 for an explanation of its use in the simple case of user input of a single item. In general, the prompt function outputs a string prompt given by its first argument and then inputs a line of text from the user, that is, everything typed by the user up to and including the next end-of-line (newline '\n' to C). It parses this line of text into *tokens* separated by *whitespace*, defined as follows.

Whitespace consists of one or more consecutive blanks (spaces), tabs, or newlines, denoted by ' ', '\t', and '\n', respectively, in C. Tokens are character strings with no embedded whitespace. Multiple tokens in a string are separated by whitespace. Lines of input are separated by newlines. Thus multiple tokens on *one* line of input are separated by whitespace other than newlines. Since users are allowed to edit their input on one line until they enter the newline, one line of input is the natural unit of work for a function for prompted input such as prompt( ).

The prompt( ) function is able to prompt for and read in any specified number of tokens on one line input from the user. The declaration of the prompt function is in the header file prompt.h of Figure B.1. It uses a special form with an ellipsis (. . .) to support a variable number of arguments, but you can think of the function as if the declaration looked like this:

```
int prompt(char prompt_str[],int N, buf1, len1, buf2, len2, . . . , bufN, lenN);
```

The first argument, prompt_str, is a prompt to be printed out to the user; the second argument, N, is the number of tokens to be read from the user input line. The following

```
/* prompt.h: prompted input of one or more tokens on one line of input */
int prompt(char prompt[], int ntokens, . . .);
```

Figure B.1 Prompt Header File prompt.h

variable number of argument pairs—buf1, len1, buf2, len2, . . . , bufN, lenN—have
the following interpretation: bufK, K = 1 to N, is a character array to contain the Kth
token, and lenK is the maximum allowed length of the Kth token. Note that all tokens
will be read into character arrays by the prompt( ) function.

If some of the string array arguments filled in by prompt( ) need to be interpreted as
int or float numbers, this can be accomplished later by using the ANSI standard C library
function sscanf( ) to convert the string arrays to the appropriate types, with the conversion characters %d for int, %ld for long int, %f for float, and %lf for double. Here is some
code from Figure 5.13 that inputs two strings and a number for a C double variable dollars (corresponding to a double precision column value in the database):

```
char acctfrom[11], acctto[11];
double dollars;
char dollarstr[11];

while ((prompt("Enter from, to accounts and dollars for transfer:\n",
    3, acctfrom, 10, acctto, 10, dollarstr, 10)) < 0) ||
    (sscanf(dollarstr,"%lf",&dollars) != 1)) {          /* convert to double     */
    printf("Invalid input. Input example: 345633 445623 100.45\n");
}
```

The & symbols in front of the dollars variable in sscanf( ) is used to create a pointer
to the variable as an argument, so that the called function will be able to modify the variable value. This is the method used in C to allow a non-array variable in a function argument to return a value to the caller.

Use of Numeric Constants in Code Examples

Our programs have one unusual property. Notice that in the examples above, the function calls to prompt contain constants as arguments, such as 4 in the prompt( ) call of
Figure 5.1:

```
while((prompt(cid_prompt, 1, cust_id, 4)) >= 0) {      /* main loop, get cid    */
```

As explained above, 4 represents the maximum-length string that can be placed in the
array cust_id. Normal C programming practice would require the use of a symbolic
constant in this position, rather than the constant 4. At the beginning of the source file,
we would have

```
#define CIDLEN 4
```

Then the call to prompt( ) would be changed to this:

```
while((prompt(cid_prompt, 1, cust_id, CIDLEN)) >= 0) {      /* . . .            */
```

For applications with a large number of uses of the constant CIDLEN, it is much better **737** to have a single definition in an `include` file that can be changed if the number of characters in the `cid` column changes, say, from four to six, with a new table definition. This allows us to make a single edit modification, and not have to perform a context search for the digit 4 in every application by making a logical decision from context whether to change that digit 4 to the digit 6. Having said this, we often decide to break this convention in examples in this text, in order to make the value of a particular constant immediately obvious in context. This usage is not meant to lead you away from good programming practice.

The code for the prompt function is shown in Figure B.2. It uses the capability of ANSI C to handle a variable number of arguments, using the va_list type defined in `stdarg.h`. See Brian Kernighan and Dennis Ritchie, *The C Programming Language*, 2nd ed. (Englewood Cliffs, NJ: Prentice Hall, 1988), section 7.3.

B.2   The print_dberror( ) Function

To obtain the **ORACLE** error message that goes with an SQLERROR condition, we can call the **ORACLE** library function sqlglm( ). Note that the error message is not null terminated, as delivered by sqlglm. We can null-terminate it ourselves using the length returned in errsize, and then print it out with printf, as shown in Figure B.3.

DB2 UDB provides a similar facility. See Figure B.4 for the code. In addition, you will need to change the Connect statement and Disconnect statements to the SQL-92 forms, as explained in Example 5.1.1. See also the Connect and Disconnect statements in Appendix C for full syntax possibilities.

B.3   Building Embedded C Programs

As we mentioned in Chapter 5, a C language compiler won't recognize the syntax of an embedded EXEC SQL statement, so the source file is typically run first through a *precompiler*, which converts such embedded statements into appropriate statements in C. The precompilation/compilation procedure is different for the different systems; two examples follow.

Precompilation and Compilation Procedure Using ORACLE/UNIX

With the **ORACLE** release 7 and 8 product under UNIX, the programmer starts by creating a source file with a name such as main.pc, which contains all the C language statements and Embedded SQL (EXEC SQL) statements of the program; the suffix .pc denotes a source file with Embedded SQL constructs. The **ORACLE** programmer then invokes the precompiler by giving the command

```
/* prompt.c: prompted input of one or more tokens on one line of input    */
#include <stdio.h>
#include <stdarg.h>
#include <string.h>
#include "prompt.h"
#define LINELEN 1000
int prompt(char prompt_str[], int ntokens, . . .)
{
  va_list ap;                        /* type from stdarg.h               */
  char line[LINELEN];                /* buffer for input line            */
  char *token;                       /* token from user input            */
  char *tbuffer;                     /* caller's buffer for token        */
  int maxlen, i;

  va_start(ap, ntokens);             /* start at last named arg          */
  printf("%s", prompt_str);          /* output prompt to user            */
  fgets(line, LINELEN, stdin);       /* get line from user               */
  for (i=0;i<ntokens;i++) {
    /* strtok takes line the first time it's called, 0 after that        */
    if ((token = strtok(i?0:line," \t\n")) == 0)
      return -1;
    tbuffer = va_arg(ap, char *);    /* caller's buffer for string       */
    maxlen = va_arg(ap, int);/       /* and length of that buffer        */
    if (strlen(token) > maxlen) {    /* check length of user token       */
      va_end(ap);
      return -1;                     /* fail: user token too long        */
    }
    strcpy(tbuffer, token);          /* return token to caller           */
  }
  va_end(ap);
  return 0;                          /* success                          */
}
```

Figure B.2   Prompt Function Code, for File `prompt.c`

```
proc iname=main.pc
```

This command results in a new file, main.c, with all EXEC SQL statements replaced by appropriate pure C statements. Consider the Select statement in Example 5.1.1:

```
exec sql select cname, discnt into :cust_name, :cust_discnt
    from customers where cid = :cust_id;
```

```
/* print_dberror()--print database error message, ORACLE case          */
#define ERRLEN 512                        /* max length of an ORACLE error message*/
void print_dberror()
{
    int errlength = ERRLEN;              /* size of buffer                      */
    int errsize;                          /* to contain actual message length    */
    extern sqlglm();

    char errbuf[ERRLEN+1];                /* buffer to receive message           */
    sqlglm(errbuf, &errlength, &errsize);/* get error message from ORACLE       */
    errbuf[errsize] = '\0';               /* make sure it is null terminated     */
    printf("%.*s\n",errsize,errbuff);     /* print it out                        */
}
```

Figure B.3   print_dberror( ) for **ORACLE**

```
/* print_dberror()--print database error message, DB2 UDB case          */
#include <sql.h>
#define MAXERRLEN 512                     /* max length of an error message      */
#define LINEWIDTH 72                      /* max characters desired on a line    */
extern struct sqlca *sqlca;               /* reference global SQLCA struct       */
void print_dberror()
{
    char errbuf[ERRLEN];                  /* buffer to receive message           */
    int errlen;
    if ((errlen=sqlaintp(errbuf, MAXERRLEN, LINEWIDTH, &sqlca)) > 0)
        printf("%*s\n",errlen,errbuff);
    else
        printf("No error message provided. SQLCODE = %d, SQLSTATE = %s\n",
            sqlca.sqlcode, sqlca.sqlstate);
}
```

Figure B.4   print_dberror( ) for **DB2 UDB**

This would be replaced by a series of function calls to the **ORACLE** runtime library. After main.c is created, the following command is used to perform compilation:

```
cc -c main.c
```

This creates a new object file called main.o. A similar command would be used to compile the prompt.c file mentioned earlier, and to create a new file, prompt.o. To link main.o and prompt.o into the same executable file main, we need to do something like this:

```
cc -o main main.o prompt.o $ORACLE_HOME/lib/libsql.a ...<many libraries>
```

In practice, an expert usually creates a makefile that contains rules for each of these steps. With a makefile, you can do the whole build with one command, for example, `make E=main`. The resulting executable file may require a large quantity of disk space, and it is a good rule to try to limit the number of executable files in your directories.

Note that database systems often come with sample programs and build procedures for them. It pays to snoop around in the directories that accompany the executable files needed to run the database system.

Precompilation and Compilation Procedure Using DB2 UDB/UNIX

As we mentioned in Chapter 5, a C language compiler won't recognize the syntax of an embedded `EXEC SQL` statement, so the source file is typically run first through a *precompiler*, which converts such embedded statements into appropriate statements in C. The precompilation/compilation procedure is different for the different systems.

With the **DB2 UDB** release 5 or 6 product under UNIX, the programmer starts by creating a source file with a name such as main.sqc, which contains all the C language statements and Embedded SQL (`EXEC SQL`) statements of the program; the suffix .sqc denotes a source file with Embedded SQL constructs. The first step uses the precompiler `prep` that inputs main.sqc and outputs main.c, with all `EXEC SQL` statements replaced by appropriate pure C statements. Consider the Select statement in Example 5.1.1:

```
exec sql select cname, discnt into :cust_name, :cust_discnt
    from customers where cid = :cust_id;
```

This would be replaced by a series of function calls to the **DB2** runtime library. Prep also creates a bindfile that describes the program at a high level to the database. This bindfile is delivered to the database by another **DB2** command `bind`. These two actions, together with the connection to the database and disconnection at the end, are all accomplished by running one **DB2** script `embprep` that can be found in the samples/c subdirectory in the distribution file system. Using this script, the programmer only needs to supply the right arguments:

```
embprep main [mydbname [username password]]
```

The default database name is "sample," the **DB2**-provided sample database. You may not need to supply the username or password, for certain sites may simply use the operating system's authentication for user identity.

At this point the program itself is still in .c form. The ordinary C compiler is used to compile this into an object file, main.o., as follows:

```
cc -c main.c
```

A similar command would be used to compile the prompt.c file mentioned earlier, and to create a new file, prompt.o. To link main.o and prompt.o into the same executable file main, we need to do something like this:

```
cc -o main main.o prompt.o -L$(DB2INSTANCEPATH)/sqllib/lib -R ...-ldb2
```

In practice, an expert usually creates a makefile for the site that contains rules for each of these steps. The same samples/c directory has a makefile to start from. With a makefile, you can carry out the entire build with one command, for example, make E=main.

Note that database systems often come with sample programs and build procedures for them. It pays to snoop around in the directories that accompany the executable files needed to run the database system.

You can read the embprep script and see that running prep is done by the UNIX command db2 prep main.sqc bindfile. This means that prep is an argument to the UNIX program called db2, not a separate program. Surprisingly enough, db2 leaves a database connection open between runs of the db2 program, so you can use db2 connect mydb, then be back at the UNIX prompt and do some other UNIX commands, and then use db2 select pid from products and see the pids displayed. You finish with db2 connect reset to disconnect. This capability is utilized by the embprep script. If you use db2 alone, you will enter the db2 environment with its own prompt, until you use the quit command.

SQL Statement Syntax

C

This appendix gathers together syntax definitions of standard relational SQL statements and object-relational statements presented in this text. (There are also occasional clauses of the relational SQL statements that deal with object-relational capabilities.) The two statement types are listed separately in Figures C.1 and C.2 but appear intermixed in the text in alphabetical order. In addition to standard SQL, this appendix also contains statements in various product dialects of SQL, some of which were not covered in the main text.

In general, we try to discuss how the statements we cover fit into the common SQL standards: Entry Level SQL-92, Core SQL-99, and X/Open, and often refer to the Basic SQL and Advanced SQL syntax defined in the text, mainly in Chapters 3 and 5.

All of the statements of Figure C.1 can be used in Embedded SQL programs. Only Select has additional capability as an interactive statement: the ability to output multiple rows for display to the user. To process multiple rows in Embedded SQL, you need to use a cursor as explained in Section 5.1. Some statements are normally not used in interactive SQL, such as Commit. These statements have syntax starting EXEC SQL, rather than the bracketed [EXEC SQL] showing optional embedded use.

The object-relational and related user-defined function statements covered in this appendix are listed in Figure C.2. For these, we have not covered the issues involved in embedded programming in C, for example, the process of getting object values into appropriate structured program variables. Thus we do not prefix these statements with [EXEC SQL]. We note that **ORACLE** has a program called the Object Type Translator (OTT), which converts Create Type statements into C struct declarations. It can also provide access from C to nested tables by use of an Array ADT supplied with OCI (**ORACLE** Call Interface). Informix also has an API for accessing data in collections.

Note that the syntax given here for products often omits specialized clauses. See the product SQL manual for full details. These manuals for **ORACLE**, **DB2 UDB**, and **INFORMIX** are listed at the end of Chapter 3. For the cursor and dynamic SQL statements, see the Embedded SQL manuals listed at the end of Chapter 5.

Alter Table	Add or delete columns or constraints on an existing base table
Close Cursor	Close a cursor
Commit	Bring a transaction to a successful conclusion
Connect	Connect to a database
Create Index	Create an index on a base table
Create Schema	Create a schema to hold tables, views, etc.
Create Table	Create a base table (both relational and object-relational)
Create Tablespace	Create tablespace (in **ORACLE, DB2 UDB**)
Create Trigger	Create a trigger
Create View	Create a view table
Declare Cursor	Define a cursor
Delete	Delete rows from a table
Describe	Get information on dynamic prepared columns
Disconnect	Disconnect from a database
Drop	Drop (delete) a table, view, schema, trigger, or index
Execute	Execute a prepared dynamic statement
Execute Immediate	Execute an SQL statement in a host variable character string
Fetch	Advance a cursor and fetch values from the newly current row
Grant	Grant privileges on a table
Insert	Insert rows into a table
Open Cursor	Open a previously declared cursor
Prepare	Prepare a dynamic SQL statement for execution
Revoke	Revoke privileges on a table
Rollback	Bring transaction to an unsuccessful conclusion
Select	Retrieve values from table(s) (both relational and object-relational)
Update	Update values in a table

Figure C.1   Relational SQL Statements Presented in this Appendix

Create Function
Create Row Type
Create Table (both relational and object-relational)
Create Type
Drop Function
Drop (Row) Type

Figure C.2   Object-Relational and User-Defined Function Statements in this Appendix

Alter Table Statement

The Alter Table statement was introduced in Section 7.1, with variant **ORACLE**, **DB2 UDB**, and **INFORMIX** forms in Figures 7.7, 7.8, and 7.9. These forms are duplicated below in Figures C.3, C.4, and C.5. The Alter Table statement allows the DBA to alter the structure of a table originally specified in a Create Table statement, adding or deleting columns of the table, and with many products adding or deleting various constraints as well. This statement is intended to apply to tables that already have existing columns, and this brings up a number of new considerations of disk storage. The Alter Table statement is not provided in Entry SQL-92, and the Core SQL-99 standard provides only the capability to add new columns, not to delete old columns or to add or drop constraints. Full SQL-99 provides ways to add and drop columns and table constraints and to alter column definitions. The X/Open Alter Table statement provides the capabilities of both adding and dropping columns. The syntax for adding columns in all these standards is the same as that used by **DB2 UDB**. Because of the weak standards guidance in this area, there is significant variation by product.

Alter Table Statement in ORACLE, DB2 UDB, and INFORMIX

The **ORACLE** product provides many features, including the capability to change a column that already exists. See the SQL reference manual for the specific product you are working with to determine the exact form of Alter Table statement available.

```
[EXEC SQL] ALTER TABLE [schema.]tablename
    [ADD ({columnname datatype    [DEFAULT {default_constant|NULL}] [col_constr {col_constr...}]
            | table_constr}              -- choice of columnname-def. or table_constr
        {, {columnname datatype
        [DEFAULT {default_constant|NULL}] [col_constr {col_constr...}] | table_constr}
        ...})]                           -- zero or more added columnname-def or table_constr
    [DROP COLUMN columnname | (columnname {, columnname...})]
    [MODIFY (columnname data-type
        [DEFAULT {default_constant|NULL}] [[NOT] NULL]
        {, columnname data-type
        [DEFAULT {default_constant|NULL}] [[NOT] NULL]
        ...})]
    [DROP CONSTRAINT constr_name]
    [DROP PRIMARY KEY]
    [disk storage and other clauses (not covered)]
    [any clause above can be repeated, in any order]
    [ENABLE and DISABLE clauses for constraints];
```

Figure C.3 ORACLE Alter Table Syntax

```
ALTER TABLE [schema.]tablename
    [ADD [COLUMN] columnname datatype
        [DEFAULT {default_constant | NULL}] [col_constr {col_constr...}]
    [ADD table_constr]
    [DROP CONSTRAINT constr_name]
    [DROP PRIMARY KEY]
    [repeated ADD or DROP clauses, in any order]
    [disk storage and other clauses (not covered)];
```

Figure C.4   DB2 UDB Form for Alter Table Syntax

```
[EXEC SQL] ALTER TABLE [schema.]tablename
    [ADD new_col | (new_col {, new_col...})]
    [DROP columnname | (columnname {, columnname...})]
    [ADD CONSTRAINT table_constr | (table_constr {, table_constr...})]
    [DROP CONSTRAINT constraintname | (constraintname {, constraintname...})]
    [repeated ADD or DROP clauses, in any order]
    [disk storage and other clauses (not covered)];
```

The new_col form that constrains a single column value follows:
```
columnname datatype
        [DEFAULT {default_constant|NULL}] [col_constr {col_constr...}]
```

Figure C.5   INFORMIX Form for Alter Table Syntax

C.2   Close Cursor Statement

In all standards and products we cover, the statement to close a cursor has the form

```
EXEC SQL CLOSE cursor-name;
```

This statement closes the cursor so that the active set of rows is no longer accessible. It is always performed from within a program, since cursors are not used in ad hoc SQL. For more information, see Section 5.4 and Figure 5.12.

C.3   Commit Work Statement

In all standards and products we cover, the statement to commit a transaction has the form

```
EXEC SQL COMMIT [WORK];
```

This statement causes the transaction to finish successfully; all row updates made during the transaction become permanent in the database and visible to all users, consistent with database privileges. For more information, see Section 5.4.

C.4 Connect Statement

The Connect statement is usually needed in Embedded SQL for the initial connection to the database system. In interactive SQL, the user interface makes the connection for the user session. Neither the Connect nor the corresponding Disconnect statement are part of Entry SQL-92 or Core SQL-99; this allows vendors freedom in determining what needs to be specified: database server, database, username, password, authorization server, and so on. Full SQL-99 syntax is this:

```
EXEC SQL CONNECT TO target-server [AS connect-name] [USER username];
```

or

```
EXEC SQL CONNECT TO DEFAULT;
```

where `target-server` is implementation defined (vendor defined, not SQL-99 defined). The `connect-name` is an identifier you select for future reference to this connection, especially if it is one of several you have.

The X/Open standard has an additional USING clause:

```
EXEC SQL CONNECT TO target-server [AS connect-name]
    [USER username [USING authentication]];
```

or

```
EXEC SQL CONNECT TO DEFAULT;
```

The basic Embedded SQL statement to connect with SQL in **ORACLE** is

```
EXEC SQL CONNECT :user_name IDENTIFIED BY :user_pwd;
```

Note the colons used to identify the host variables that appear as arguments for this SQL syntax. **DB2 UDB** follows the Full SQL-99 forms and also allows the first form without the USER clause in the case that users are identified by their OS usernames. **INFORMIX** follows the X/Open forms. For more information, see Section 5.1.

C.5   Create Function Statement (UDF)

The only standard specifying user-defined functions (UDFs) callable from SQL is SQL-99. In that standard, the Create Function statement is given many options, the most important of which are shown in Figure C.6. There is a similar Create Procedure statement, for routines with no return values.

There are two kinds of UDFs, *stored procedures* written in a language safe enough to run inside the database server (usually Procedural SQL), and *external functions* written in C or other languages not directly compiled by or stored in the server.

The choice of LANGUAGE SQL in the Create Function statement defines the function as an *SQL function*, with its SQL code stored in the server, thus making it a *stored procedure*. The SQL function has an executable SQL statement as its code. This executable_SQL_statement can be a compound statement in SQL/PSM (persistent stored modules, the Procedural SQL language of SQL-99) of the form BEGIN . . . END, so we could write PSM_code_block instead of executable_SQL_statement, but other single SQL statements are possible there too. For examples of SQL functions, see Section 4.4, where the Procedural SQL language in use is PL/SQL for **ORACLE** and SPL for **INFORMIX**.

On the other hand, the choice of any other language, say, LANGUAGE C, in the Create Function statement defines an *external function,* which then requires an EXTERNAL NAME clause to specify the file (outside the server) containing the code. Note that provisions are made for external functions that access or avoid access (NO SQL) to the database data via SQL. External functions are discussed in Section 4.5.

ORACLE has syntax that is similar to the Core SQL-99 of Figure C.6, with important clauses as shown in Figure C.7. This form can define a PL/SQL function or an external C function in a certain library file. For examples of the former, see Section 4.4.1.

INFORMIX has a slightly different syntax, shown in Figure C.8, to define an SPL function or an external C function. In **ORACLE** and **INFORMIX**, external functions can access database data from the C code, although the simpler ones would not. Java should soon be available for external functions in both of these products.

DB2 UDB has no procedural language, so we can't expect a code_block form. It uses the Create function to declare external C or Java functions. Its syntax is close to SQL-

```
CREATE FUNCTION [schema.]funtionname ([param {, param ...}])
    RETURNS datatype
    [LANGUAGE SQL|C|FORTRAN|COBOL] -- or some others, but not Java (yet)
    [NO SQL|CONTAINS SQL| READS SQL DATA | MODIFIES SQL DATA]
    {executable_SQL_statement              -- for SQL/PSM function
    |EXTERNAL NAME external_function_name}  -- for external function

param ::= [IN|OUT|INOUT] paramname datatype
```

Figure C.6   The Core SQL-99 Create Function Statement Syntax (Partial)

```
CREATE [OR REPLACE] FUNCTION [schema.]funtionname
        ([oparam {, oparam ...}])
    RETURN datatype IS
    {PL/SQL_code_block                              -- for PL/SQL function
    |EXTERNAL LIBRARY libname [NAME ext_functionname]}  -- for external UDF


oparam ::= paramname [IN|OUT|IN OUT] datatype
```

Figure C.7 The **ORACLE** Create Function Statement Syntax (Partial)

```
CREATE [OR REPLACE] FUNCTION [schema.]funtionname
            ([iparam {, iparam ...}])
    RETURN datatype IS
    {PL/SQL_code_block                              -- for SPL function
    |EXTERNAL LIBRARY libraryname [NAME ext_functionname]}; -- for external UDF


iparam ::= paramname [IN|OUT|IN OUT] datatype
```

Figure C.8 The **INFORMIX** Create Function Statement Syntax (Partial)

99's, with NO SQL required because external functions are not allowed to use SQL statements (this is a rather serious limitation). The main use of external functions is to implement operations on a single column value. In addition, a Create Function with RETURNS TABLE instead of "RETURNS datatype" defines a table function. A table function is implemented in C or Java and turns non-database data into a virtual table that can be referenced in SQL.

C.6 Create Index Statement

The Create Index statement was introduced in Chapter 8, with a number of variant forms introduced in Figures 8.1 (X/Open), 8.7 and 8.14 (**ORACLE**; the two figures have identical syntax), and 8.15 and 8.20 (**DB2 UDB**; the syntaxes of these two figures are again identical). The Create Index syntax for these products is repeated below in Figures C.9 and C.10.

Here is the X/Open standard specification of the Create Index statement. (SQL-99 does not cover the Create Index statement.)

```
[EXEC SQL] CREATE [UNIQUE] INDEX [schema.]indexname
    ON tablename (columnname [ASC | DESC] {, columnname [ASC |DESC]...});
```

This standard form is supported in **ORACLE**, **DB2 UDB**, and **INFORMIX**. Each product extends the syntax to specify, for example, where to store the index, what kind of index to build, and how to add disk storage incrementally to the index.

```
[EXEC SQL] CREATE [UNIQUE | BITMAP] INDEX [schema.]indexname ON [schema.]tablename
    (columnname [ASC | DESC] {, columnname [ASC | DESC]})
    [TABLESPACE tblspacename]
    [STORAGE ([INITIAL n [K|M]] [NEXT n [K|M]] [MINEXTENTS n] [MAXEXTENTS n]
        [PCTINCREASE n] ) ]
    [PCTFREE n]
    [other disk storage and transactional clauses not covered]
    [NOSORT]
```

Figure C.9   ORACLE Create Index Statement Syntax

```
[EXEC SQL] CREATE [UNIQUE] INDEX indexname ON [schema.]tablename
    (columnname [ASC | DESC] {, columnname [ASC | DESC]...})
    [INCLUDE (columnname [ASC | DESC] {, columnname [ASC | DESC]...})]
    [CLUSTER]
    [PCTFREE n]
    [MINPCTUSED n]
    [ALLOW REVERSE SCANS];
```

Figure C.10   The **DB2 UDB** Create Index Statement Syntax

Create Index Statement in ORACLE

The **ORACLE** syntax for the Create Index statement appears in Figure C.9. The TABLESPACE clause specifies the tablespace on which the index is to be created. See Figure 8.3 for a schematic picture of **ORACLE** data storage structures. The STORAGE clause options are explained in the text following the Create Tablespace statement syntax of Figure 8.4. The NOSORT option is explained after Figure 8.7. The PCTFREE clause is explained after Figure 8.14.

Create Index Statement in DB2 UDB

The **DB2 UDB** Create Index statement syntax appears in Figure C.10. See the discussion following Figure 8.15 for an explanation of the options in Figure C.10.

Like **DB2 UDB**, **INFORMIX** supports CLUSTER indexes. Like **ORACLE**, it allows placement of indexes on their own disk areas (known as dbspaces in **INFORMIX**, tablespaces in **ORACLE**). Further **INFORMIX** supports indexes with access methods provided by DataBlades, such as two-dimensional indexes for geographic data.

Object-Relational Considerations

ORACLE allows indexes using any object attribute(s) but requires that each column name be specified by a dotted expression starting with the tablename. Indexes on nested tables are also allowed, using the tablename from the Create Table STORE AS clause. **INFORMIX** allows row type columns in a table, and functions of these columns, to be used as index columns. However, **INFORMIX** does not allow fields within row type columns of a table to appear as individual column names in an index. Thus the field fname in the WHERE clause of Example 4.2.23 cannot be indexed as a column because it is a field within a field in the row type definition of Example 4.2.20, thus a field within a column in the table people of Example 4.2.21. Since a primary key must be indexed, a field within a table column cannot be a primary key either.

C.7   Create Row Type Statement (O-R)

User-defined structured types, which are called object types in **ORACLE**, are called *row types* in **INFORMIX** and are created as follows.

```
CREATE ROW TYPE rowtype
    (fieldname datatype [NOT NULL]{, fieldname datatype [NOT NULL] ...})
    [UNDER supertype];
```

See Create Type in this appendix for the corresponding SQL-99 syntax. See Section 4.2.2 for examples and more information on row types.

C.8   Create Schema Statement

A *schema* in Core SQL-99 is a collection of tables, indexes, and other related database objects, typically intended for a single user. The full name of a table within a database catalog is schemaname.tablename (where the schema name is usually a username), and similarly for other named database objects. For more information, see Section 7.4.

The following syntax shows the important parts of the SQL-99 Create Schema statement. It is in Core SQL-99 except for the option to specify an explicit name for the new schema. In Core SQL-99, the DBA can set up a schema for a user with an AUTHORIZA-TION clause, letting the schema name default to the authorization_id, usually the username.

```
[EXEC SQL] CREATE SCHEMA
    {schemaname                      -- to specify explicitly; not Core SQL-99
    | AUTHORIZATION authorization_id}   -- default schemaname is authorization_id
        [{schema_element schema_element ...}];
```

X/Open has the same syntax, with an additional optional clause specifying the character set. The optional schema_elements are SQL statements in Core SQL-99 and X/Open that create database objects: Create Table, Create View, Create Index, and Grant. They are used to provide initial contents for the new schema with appropriate ownership. Of the three products we are covering, only **DB2 UDB** currently allows users to create additional named schemas, with the schema name specified explicitly. All three support the Core SQL-99 syntax.

C.9   Create Table Statement

The general Create Table statement was introduced in Section 7.1, in a Basic SQL form that describes syntax in common among **ORACLE**, **DB2 UDB**, and **INFORMIX**. Figure C.11 shows it again.

This Basic SQL syntax is accepted by **ORACLE**, **DB2 UDB**, and **INFORMIX**, except that **INFORMIX** requires all of the column definitions to precede the table constraint definitions, whereas the Basic SQL syntax allows the column definitions and table constraint definitions to occur in any order. See Section 7.1 for discussion of these clauses.

Create Table Statement in ORACLE

The form of the **ORACLE** Create Table statement shown in Figure C.12 was originally presented in Figures 8.5 (all but the CLUSTER clause) and 8.22 (the CLUSTER clause),

```
[EXEC SQL] CREATE TABLE [schema.]tablename
    ({columnname datatype [DEFAULT {default_constant|NULL}] [col_constr {col_constr...}]
        | table_constr}   -- choice of either columnname-definition or table_constr
    {,{columnname datatype [DEFAULT {default_constant|NULL}] [col_constr {col_constr...}]
        | table_constr}
    ...});                 -- zero or more additional columnname-def or table_constr
```

The col_constr form that constrains a single column value follows:

```
    {NOT NULL |                     -- this is the first of a set of choices
    [CONSTRAINT constraintname]     -- if later choices used, optionally name constraint
        UNIQUE                      -- the rest of the choices start here
        | PRIMARY KEY
        | CHECK (search_cond)
        | REFERENCES tablename [(columnname)]
            [ON DELETE CASCADE]}
```

The table_constr form that constrains multiple columns at once follows:

```
    [CONSTRAINT constraintname]
        {UNIQUE (columnname {, columnname...})        -- choose one of these clauses
        | PRIMARY KEY (columnname {, columnname...})
        | CHECK (search_condition)
        | FOREIGN KEY (columnname {, columnname...})  -- following is all one clause
            REFERENCES tablename [(columnname {, columnname...})]
                [ON DELETE CASCADE]}
```

Figure C.11   Basic SQL Syntax for Create Table

```
[EXEC SQL] CREATE TABLE [schema.]tablename
    ({columnname datatype [DEFAULT {default_constant|NULL}] [col_constr {col_constr...}]
     | table_constr}                -- choice of either columnname-definition or table_constr
    {, {columnname (repeat DEFAULT clause and col_constr list) | table_constr}...})
     {CLUSTER clustername (columnname {, columnname ...})}  --for table in cluster
     |{[ORGANIZATION HEAP | ORGANIZATION INDEX (this has clauses not covered)]
     [TABLESPACE tblspacename]
     [STORAGE ([INITIAL n [K|M]] [NEXT n [K|M]] [MINEXTENTS n] [MAXEXTENTS {n | UNLIMITED}]
          [PCTINCREASE n]) (additional STORAGE options not covered)]
     [PCTFREE n] [PCTUSED n]
     [disk storage and other clauses (not covered)] }
    [AS subquery]
```

Figure C.12   ORACLE Relational Create Table Statement

and it assumes a knowledge of storage allocation clauses explained in the **ORACLE** Create Tablespace statement (given in this appendix). The first four lines just repeat in summary form the Basic SQL syntax.

Note the last line AS subquery. This extension of the standard allows a Create Table statement to also specify rows to be inserted into the new table. The STORAGE clause is explained after Figure 8.4. The PCTFREE and PCTUSED clauses are explained after Figure 8.5.

Create Table Statement in DB2 UDB

The **DB2 UDB** Create Table (Figure C.13) has fewer detailed storage specifications compared with the **ORACLE** form. Like the **ORACLE** Create Table statement, it can specify placement of the table in a named tablespace, and the tablespace can be set up with physical storage specifications; see the Create Tablespace statement in this appendix for more information.

The **INFORMIX** Create Table has a clause IN dbspace where **ORACLE** and **DB2 UDB** have IN tablespace, to specify placement of the table in a particular unit of disk storage. It also allows specification of first and successive extent sizes, that is, the disk allocation unit sizes.

```
[EXEC SQL] CREATE TABLE [schema.]tablename
    ({columnname datatype [DEFAULT {default_constant|NULL}]
        [col_constr {col_constr...}]| table_constr}
    {, {columnname datatype [DEFAULT {default_constant|NULL}]
        [col_constr {col_constr...}]| table_constr}...})
    [IN tblspacename [INDEX IN tblespacename]]
    [NOT LOGGED INITIALLY]
        [disk storage and other clauses (not covered)]
```

Figure C.13   DB2 UDB Create Table Statement Syntax

```
[EXEC SQL] CREATE TABLE [schema.]tablename
                [OF [schema.]typename]                      -- for object tables
    (column_def | table_constr | table_ref_clause
    {, column_def | table_constr | table_ref_clause ...})
    {CLUSTER clustername (columnname {, columnname ...})}    -- not for object tables
    |{ [ORGANIZATION HEAP | ORGANIZATION INDEX]              -- not for object tables
    [TABLESPACE tblspacename]
    [STORAGE ([INITIAL n [K|M]] [NEXT n [K|M]] [MINEXTENTS n]
                [MAXEXTENTS {n | UNLIMITED}] [PCTINCREASE n])]
    [PCTFREE n] [PCTUSED n]
    [NESTED TABLE columnname STORE AS tablename
    {, NESTED TABLE columnname STORE AS tablename...}]
    [AS subquery];


column_def ::=
    columnname [datatype] [DEFAULT {default_constant|NULL}]   --see discussion
                            [col_constr {col_constr...}]
table_ref_clause ::=
    SCOPE FOR (columnname | dotted_expr) IS [schema.]tablename
```

Figure C.14 Create Table Syntax in **ORACLE** with Object-Relational Extensions, as Covered

Object-Relational Syntax

The Create Table statement with object-relational extensions is displayed in Figure C.14. If OF typename is provided after the tablename, the table is an object table. Otherwise it is a relational table. All the important storage clauses available for relational tables are also provided for object tables. The specialized options of membership in table clusters and index-organized are restricted to relational tables. The column_def syntax shows the datatype as optional, but it is required in the cases that otherwise have no datatype specified, that is, for relational tables with no AS Subquery clause. If the datatype has been specified by an object type or a Subquery, it should be dropped from the column_def.

In a Create Typed Table, **INFORMIX** doesn't need the nested table clause or the scoping clause and handles column nulls in the type definition. Other column constraints need to be handled as table constraints, and default values for columns are not available. There are fewer storage specifications as well, making for a much simpler syntax for a typed table, as shown in Figure C.15.

```
[EXEC SQL] CREATE TABLE [schema.]tablename
            OF TYPE row_typename ( table_constr {, table_constr ...})
        [IN dbspace] [EXTENT SIZE n_KB] [NEXT size n_KB]
        [UNDER supertablename];
```

Figure C.15 Create Typed Table Syntax for **INFORMIX**

The Create Tablespace statement is not in any standard. Tablespaces provide a way for a user to override the database defaults and specify how the underlying disk resource is to be used by the database. Figure C.16 (as in Figure 8.4) contains the syntax for the Create Tablespace statement in **ORACLE**. A more complete description of **ORACLE** database storage structure elements is given in Section 8.2, with a diagram of these structures in Figure 8.3.

Figure C.17 contains the corresponding form for Create Tablespace in **DB2 UDB**. **DB2 UDB** supports two kinds of tablespaces, *system managed space* and *database managed space*. The system-managed space is managed by the file system of the operating system, whereas for database-managed space, the database system directly manages the disk, without using the file system. For small databases, system-managed spaces are recommended as simpler to create and maintain, but for high-performance applications, the extra work of setting up database-managed spaces is often called for.

EXTENTSIZE specifies the unit of disk allocation within the tablespace, as in **ORACLE**. The optional OVERHEAD and TRANSFERRATE parameters provide hints to the query optimizer about how fast the disks are. OVERHEAD is the time in milliseconds to begin an I/O operation (seek time, etc.), while TRANSFERRATE is an estimate of the time it takes to read one 4-KB page into memory, once started.

Both **ORACLE** and **DB2 UDB** have Alter Tablespace commands to modify tablespaces already created, most importantly to add more disk storage to them, and Drop

```
[EXEC SQL] CREATE TABLESPACE tblspacename
    DATAFILE 'filename' [SIZE n [K|M]] [REUSE] [AUTOEXTEND OFF
    | AUTOEXTEND ON [NEXT n [K|M] [MAXSIZE {UNLIMITED |n [K|M]}]
    {, 'filename' (repeat SIZE, REUSE, and AUTOEXTEND options) . . .}
    -- the following optional clauses can come in any order
    [ONLINE | OFFLINE]
    [DEFAULT STORAGE ([INITIAL n] [NEXT n] [MINEXTENTS n] [MAXEXTENTS {n|UNLIMITED}]
         [PCTINCREASE n]) (additional DEFAULT STORAGE options not covered)]
    [MINIMUM EXTENT n [K|M]]
    [other optional clauses not covered];
```

Figure C.16 ORACLE Create Tablespace Statement Syntax

```
[EXEC SQL] CREATE TABLESPACE tblspacename
    MANAGED BY
        {SYSTEM USING 'filename' npages            -- system-managed space
         |DATABASE USING {FILE|DEVICE} 'containername'}   -- or database-managed space
    [EXTENTSIZE npages] [OVERHEAD nmillisecs] [TRANSFERRATE nmillisecs]:
```

Figure C.17   DB2 UDB Create Tablespace Statement Syntax (Partial)

Tablespace commands. None of the standards we are covering specify tablespace commands, because they specify how to implement the database, not its services.

    INFORMIX does not have a Create Tablespace command. Instead of tablespaces, it uses a similar unit of disk space known as a *dbspace*. A dbspace may be created through the graphical administrative program ON-monitor, or by a system program "onspaces."

C.11   Create Trigger Statement

Triggers are code sequences that are registered with the database (i.e., held in the database schema) to be executed when certain events occur for a certain table, namely, inserts, updates, or deletes. SQL-92 offered no standardization for triggers. The SQL-99 Create Trigger syntax is given in Figure C.18. Although not in Core SQL-99, it is an add-on feature called *Basic Trigger Capability*, except for the clause FOR EACH STATEMENT, which is given another feature identification as *Extended Trigger Capability*. Since several important database products have implemented triggers following this standard (as it developed in the late 1990s), we cover it here (from Figure 7.10).

    The Create Trigger statement creates an object named `trigger_name`. The name is used in error messages and in a later request to drop this trigger from currency: `Drop trigger_name`. The trigger is *fired* (executed) either before or after one of the events specified (INSERT, DELETE, or UPDATE optionally limited to a set of named columns) takes place to the table given by tablename.

    The **DB2 UDB** Create Trigger statement shown in Figure C.19 (from Figure 7.11) follows the SQL-99 standard quite closely and uses the same corr_name_def forms.

    The **ORACLE** Create Trigger syntax of Figure C.20 (from Figure 7.12) varies more from the SQL-99 standard, but it is important to realize that it was developed before the standard was finalized!

    INFORMIX has a Create Trigger statement with syntax similar to the SQL-99 form.

```
[EXEC SQL] CREATE TRIGGER [schema.]trigger_name {BEFORE | AFTER}
    {INSERT | DELETE | UPDATE [OF columnname {, columnname...}]}
    ON tablename [REFERENCING corr_name_def {, corr_name_def...}]
    [FOR EACH ROW | FOR EACH STATEMENT]
        [WHEN (search_condition)]
        {statement                                    -- action (single statement)
        | BEGIN ATOMIC statement; { statement;...} END}; -- action (multiple statements

The corr_name_def that defines a correlation name follows:
    {OLD [ROW] [AS] old_row_corr_name
    |   NEW [ROW] [AS] new_row_corr_name
    |   OLD TABLE [AS] old_table_corr_name
    |   NEW TABLE [AS] new_table_corr_name}
```

Figure C.18   SQL-99 Create Trigger Syntax

```
[EXEC SQL] CREATE TRIGGER [schema.]trigger_name
    {NO CASCADE BEFORE | AFTER}
    {INSERT | DELETE | UPDATE [OF columnname {, columnname...}]}
    ON tablename [REFERENCING corr_name_def {, corr_name_def...}]
    {FOR EACH ROW | FOR EACH STATEMENT} MODE DB2SQL
        [WHEN (search_condition)]
        { statement
        | BEGIN ATOMIC statement; {statement;...} END};
```

Figure C.19 DB2 UDB Create Trigger Syntax

```
[EXEC SQL] CREATE [OR REPLACE] TRIGGER trigger_name
    {BEFORE | AFTER | INSTEAD OF}
        {INSERT | DELETE | UPDATE [OF columnname {, columnname...}]}
        ON tablename [REFERENCING corr_name_def {, corr_name_def...}]
    {FOR EACH ROW | FOR EACH STATEMENT}
        [WHEN (search_condition)]
        BEGIN statement {statement;...} END;
```

The corr_name_def that provides row correlation names follows:

```
    {OLD old_row_corr_name
    |NEW new_row_corr_name}
```

Figure C.20 ORACLE Create Trigger Syntax

C.12 Create Type Statement (O-R)

In SQL-99, the Create Type statement is used to create user-defined types, of which there are two kinds, structured types and distinct types. A distinct type is created out of ("cloned from") another type but given a user-specified name. The source type can be any built-in type, for example, numeric, string, or BLOB. By "strong typing," an item of distinct type cannot be compared to another item of its source type without a cast. The Core SQL-99 form for creating a distinct type is, in its simplest form,

```
CREATE TYPE distinct_typename AS source_typename FINAL;
```

In **DB2 UDB** and **INFORMIX**, a distinct type can be created by

```
CREATE DISTINCT TYPE distinct_typename AS source_typename;
```

DB2 UDB allows any built-in type as the source type. **INFORMIX** allows any built-in type, row type, or another distinct type. **ORACLE** has no distinct types. Note that distinct types can be used in a natural way with otherwise purely relational database designs.

Structured user-defined types are a named feature extending SQL-99; the syntax in Figure C.21 displays the most important clauses for defining a UDT.

```
CREATE TYPE [schema.]typename [UNDER] typename AS
    (attrname datatype {, attrname datatype ...})   -- attribute list
    {FINAL|NOT FINAL}
    INSTANCE METHOD methodname [(paramname type {, paramname type ...})]
        RETURNS datatype
    {, INSTANCE METHOD methodname [(paramname type {, paramname type ...})]
        RETURNS datatype ...};
```

Figure C.21   SQL-99 Create User-Defined Type (Structured)

```
CREATE [OR REPLACE] TYPE [schema.]typename AS OBJECT
    (attrname datatype {, attrname datatype ...}
    MEMBER FUNCTION methodname [(param type {, param type ...})]
        RETURN datatype,
    {MEMBER FUNCTION methodname [(param type {, param type ...})]
        RETURN datatype, ...}
    PRAGMA RESTRICT_REFERENCES (DEFAULT, RNDS, WNDS, RNPS, WNPS)
);
CREATE [OR REPLACE] TYPE [schema.]typename                  -- incomplete type
CREATE TYPE typename AS TABLE OF datatype;                  -- nested table
CREATE TYPE typename AS VARRAY (max_elements) OF datatype; -- VARRAY
```

Figure C.22   Syntax for **ORACLE** Create Type, as Covered

Here the optional UNDER clause can be used to define a subtype in an inheritance hierarchy. The finality clause, {FINAL | NOT FINAL}, specifies whether or not this type may be used as a supertype in a type hierarchy.

In **ORACLE**, Create Type is used for (structured) user-defined types, called *object types*, as shown in Figure C.22 (from Figure 4.30).

See Section 4.4.1 for more information and syntax for the member function implementations. In **INFORMIX**, the user-defined structured types are called row types and are defined by the Create Row Type statement, also in this appendix.

DB2 UDB provides structured UDTs, but not as general column value types. All UDT values in the database are there as full rows in an object table, while REFs to them may appear in columns. The Create Type syntax follows SQL-99 through the attribute list, but no method definitions are allowed.

C.13   Create View Statement

The complete description of the Basic Create View statement is, as in Figure 7.13,

```
[EXEC SQL] CREATE VIEW [schema.]viewname [(columnname {, columnname...})]
    AS subquery [WITH CHECK OPTION];
```

Recall that a Subquery, first defined in Figure 3.13, includes an optional UNION clause. The Create View command is legal within a program as an Embedded SQL statement; however, the Subquery of the view must not contain any host variables or any dynamic parameters. The optional WITH CHECK OPTION clause is explained after Figure 7.13.

The Basic SQL Create View syntax is supported in **ORACLE**, **DB2 UDB**, **INFORMIX**, Entry SQL-92, Core SQL-99, and X/Open. **ORACLE** has an additional optional WITH READ ONLY clause that prevents updates through the view.

Object-Relational Considerations

ORACLE, **INFORMIX**, and **DB2 UDB** allow view tables to be defined to act like object tables even if the Subquery is working with relational data. In that case, an object type or row type specification replaces the column list in the Create View statement. In **ORACLE**, the simplest syntax is

```
CREATE VIEW [schema.]viewname
    {[(columnname {, columnname...})]               -- relational syntax
    | OF [schema.]objtypename WITH OBJECT OID DEFAULT}  -- simplest object view form
    AS subquery [WITH {READ ONLY | CHECK OPTION}];  -- where the data comes from
```

INFORMIX has a simpler syntax OF [schema.]typename for specifying the object form (an OBJECT OID DEFAULT clause is not needed), while **DB2 UDB** has a more complex syntax. Full SQL-99 has OF [schema.]typename followed by an optional column list, thus allowing the user to alias the effective column names of the user-defined type. The Subquery needs to provide a column for each top-level **ORACLE** or **DB2 UDB** attribute or **INFORMIX** field with matching type. Similarly, views can convert from object to relational tables by using the columnlist form and a Subquery from the object table.

C.14 | Declare Cursor Statement

The full syntax of the X/Open (and Entry SQL-92) Declare Cursor statement is given in Figure C.23, copied from Figure 5.5 of Section 5.3. The Subquery form used in Figure C.23 is defined in the general Select statement syntax of Figure 3.11, repeated in Figure C.27.

Note that a Fetch statement is used to retrieve selected rows from a cursor, but the cursor can only move forward through a set of rows. This limitation disappears if the database has the SQL-99 extended feature called scrollable cursors.

```
EXEC SQL DECLARE cursor_name CURSOR FOR
    Subquery
    [ORDER BY result_column [ASC | DESC] {, result_column [ASC | DESC]...}
    |[FOR {READ ONLY | UPDATE [OF columnname {, columnname...}]}]];
```

Figure C.23   X/Open Embedded SQL Declare Cursor Syntax

```
EXEC SQL DECLARE cursor_name [INSENSITIVE] [SCROLL] CURSOR [WITH HOLD] FOR
    Subquery
    {UNION Subquery}
    [ORDER BY result_column [ASC | DESC] {, result_column [ASC | DESC]...}
    [FOR READ ONLY | FOR UPDATE OF columnname {, OF columnname}];
```

Figure C.24   The SQL-99 Declare Cursor Statement Syntax

Declare Cursor Statement in SQL-99

Full SQL-99 provides important generalizations of the Declare Cursor and Fetch statements. First, the new Declare Cursor statement is given in Figure C.24.

The three new syntax elements are the keywords INSENSITIVE, SCROLL, and WITH HOLD; only WITH HOLD is in Core SQL-99. When the SCROLL keyword is used in a cursor definition, the cursor is said to be *scrollable,* and the corresponding capabilities of the Fetch statement can be exercised. For further information, see Section 5.7.

C.15   Delete Statement

There are two forms of the Delete statement, a *Positioned Delete* that deletes the current row (most recently fetched row) of a cursor, and the *Searched Delete* that has the same sort of form we have already seen in Interactive SQL Delete, in Section 3.10. Here is syntax (also shown in Figure 5.6) that describes the two forms:

```
[EXEC SQL] DELETE FROM [schema.]tablename
    [WHERE search_condition];                    -- searched delete
EXEC SQL DELETE FROM [schema.]tablename
    [WHERE CURRENT OF cursor_name];              -- positioned delete
```

The Positioned Delete statement uses a special CURRENT OF cursor_name syntax. Only one of the two WHERE forms can be used; if neither is used, all rows of the table will be deleted. For more information, see the discussion following Figure 5.6.

The above forms are those specified in X/Open and SQL-92, Entry and Full. The only extension to these forms in Full SQL-99 involves object-relational considerations, as covered below. All major database products support the above forms. In addition, **ORA-CLE** and **DB2 UDB** allow a correlation name to be specified just after the tablename, for use in the WHERE clause.

Object-Relational Considerations

In the case of deletion from a table in a hierarchy based on an object type hierarchy, the form ONLY ([schema.]tablename) can be used instead of [schema.]tablename to restrict deletions to rows that belong to that one table, not to its subtables in the hierarchy. This form appears in Full SQL-99 and is supported by **INFORMIX** and **DB2 UDB**.

C.16 Describe Statement

When the Prepare statement is called to prepare a Dynamic Select statement in an sql-text[ ] string, the compilation process calculates the number and types of the column values to be retrieved. For the program to learn this information, it must now call a new Dynamic SQL Describe statement, which places the information for all columns retrieved into the SQLDA variable struct. Here is the syntax of the Describe statement:

```
EXEC SQL DESCRIBE statement_identifier INTO sqldavar_pointer;
```

Examples of Dynamic Select statements are given in Section 5.6. Note that the SQLDA structures of **INFORMIX** and **ORACLE** are quite different; the **INFORMIX** structure is close to that of **DB2 UDB**. X/Open and SQL-99 avoid the SQLDA structure and instead have more SQL syntax, but this approach is not implemented in **DB2 UDB** or **ORACLE**. **INFORMIX** allows either method, SQLDA or X/Open syntax.

C.17 Disconnect Statement

The Disconnect statement is used in an Embedded SQL program to disconnect from a database. Like the Connect statement, it is not part of Entry SQL-92 or Core SQL-99 and varies in syntax details from vendor to vendor. The SQL Disconnect statement from Full SQL-99 is

```
EXEC SQL DISCONNECT {connectname | CURRENT};
```

The Disconnect statement from X/Open is

```
EXEC SQL DISCONNECT {connectname|ALL|CURRENT|DEFAULT};
```

ORACLE, beginning with **ORACLE** release 7, requires a different statement to perform a disconnect:

```
EXEC SQL COMMIT RELEASE;
```

DB2 UDB follows SQL-99 and, following the standard, requires a Commit or Rollback statement preceding the Disconnect. To do a Commit and Disconnect together in one statement, it provides

```
EXEC SQL COMMIT RESET;
```

For more information, see Section 5.1.

C.18 Drop Function Statement

SQL-99 is the only standard specifying user-defined functions. The Drop Function syntax is as follows:

```
DROP {FUNCTION [schema.]functionname [(paramtype {, paramtype ...})]
     |SPECIFIC FUNCTION [schema.]functionname}
CASCADE|RESTRICT;
```

This syntax is in Core SQL-99 except for the CASCADE option; in Core SQL-99, RESTRICT must be specified explicitly. The form with the parameter datatype list allows the user to drop one of several overloaded functions, that is, functions with the same name but different parameter lists.

INFORMIX and **DB2 UDB** follow the SQL-99 syntax. **ORACLE** has simply

```
DROP FUNCTION [schema.]functionname;
```

ORACLE does not need the form with a parameter list because **ORACLE** does not support overloading of "stand-alone" functions, that is, functions known individually in the schema outside of any package, created with Create Function, and dropped with Drop Function. Member functions and in-package functions can be overloaded. Member functions are dropped together with their object type. Packages are **ORACLE**-specific encapsulated collections of related database objects, not covered in this text.

C.19 Drop Index Statement

X/Open is alone among the standards to standardize the Drop Index statement, as follows:

```
[EXEC SQL] DROP INDEX [schema.]indexname;
```

All major database products support this form. For more information, see Section 8.1.

C.20 | Drop Trigger Statement

The only standard to cover triggers is SQL-99. It provides the syntax

```
[EXEC SQL] DROP TRIGGER [schema.]triggername;
```

This form is supported in all products providing triggers, including **ORACLE**, **DB2 UDB**, and **INFORMIX**. For more information, see Section 7.1.

C.21 | Drop (Row) Type Statement (O-R)

The only standard to cover user-defined types is SQL-99. It provides the syntax

```
DROP TYPE [schema.]typename CASCADE|RESTRICT;
```

Here the CASCADE option is not part of Core SQL-99, leaving RESTRICT as the only, but still required to be explicit, option. The only in-Core use is to drop a distinct type, since user-defined structured types are a named feature extending SQL-99. See Create Type in this appendix for more information on distinct types versus user-defined structured types.

In **ORACLE**, user-defined structured types are called *object types* and are dropped with

```
DROP TYPE [schema.]typename [FORCE];
```

Here the FORCE option is used to drop types that have REF dependencies outstanding. For more information, see the discussion of REF dependencies near the end of Section 4.2.1.

In **INFORMIX**, user-defined structured types are called *row types* and are dropped with

```
DROP ROW TYPE [schema.]typename RESTRICT;
```

For more information on row types, see Section 4.2.2. **INFORMIX** also provides distinct types and uses the Core SQL-99 syntax to drop them (with RESTRICT again required).

In **DB2 UDB**, user-defined structured types and distinct types are dropped with

```
DROP [DISTINCT] TYPE [schema.]
```

	ORACLE	DB2 UDB	INFORMIX	X/Open, Full SQL-92, -99
DROP TABLE tablename. . .	[CASCADE CONSTRAINTS]		[CASCADE |RESTRICT]	{CASCADE |RESTRICT}
DROP VIEW viewname. . .			[CASCADE |RESTRICT]	{CASCADE |RESTRICT}
DROP SCHEMA schemaname. . .	No user-defined schemas	RESTRICT	No user-defined schemas	{CASCADE |RESTRICT}

Figure C.25 Drop Table and Drop View Statement Options in Products and Standards

C.22 Drop {Schema | Table | View} Statement

The Drop statement is used to delete a schema, table, or view definition from the system catalogs and, in the case of a table (or schema), to free up any allocated space. The complete description of the X/Open Drop statement for these objects is

```
[EXEC SQL] DROP {SCHEMA schemaname | TABLE tablename| VIEW viewname}
         {CASCADE|RESTRICT};
```

The tablename or view name may be prefixed with a schema name, if desired. See the discussion of CASCADE and RESTRICT just before Figure 7.14. Surprisingly enough, there is no Drop Table statement required for Entry SQL-92. Full SQL-92 has the same syntax as X/Open, as does Full SQL-99. Core SQL-99 does not require the CASCADE option but still requires the RESTRICT keyword to be used. The products reflect the variability of the standards, as tabulated in Figure C.25 (from Figure 7.14).

When a schema is dropped with the RESTRICT option, it will not succeed unless the schema is empty, that is, contains no tables or other database objects. When it is dropped with the CASCADE option, all the contained tables and other database objects will be dropped. As allowed in Entry SQL-92 and Core SQL-99, users may be given a schema of the same name as their username, when their database account is set up, and no capability to create other schemas. In that case, holding for **ORACLE** and **INFORMIX**, the Drop Schema command it not useful. In **DB2 UDB**, users are given one original schema with the same name as their username, but users are also allowed to create schemas of any other name with Create Schema, and these may be dropped with Drop Schema.

C.23 Execute Statement

After the Prepare statement has been called to prepare a Dynamic SQL statement from an sqltext[ ] string, the Execute statement is used to associate needed parameter values with dynamic parameters in the string and to execute the prepared statement. Here is the syntax of the Execute statement, for all standards and products we cover:

```
EXEC SQL EXECUTE statement_identifier
    USING :host_variable {, :host_variable...};
```

Examples of Execute statement use are given in Section 5.6.

C.24 Execute Immediate Statement

An Execute Immediate statement executes a Dynamic SQL statement contained in a host variable string, without need for a previous Prepare statement. The general form of the Execute Immediate statement is this, in all standards and products we cover:

```
EXEC SQL EXECUTE IMMEDIATE :host_string;
```

Note that no dynamic parameters of the kind handled by the Prepare and Execute statements are needed, since each execution with Execute Immediate is one of a kind. The character string contents of the host_string must represent a valid SQL statement, including any of the following types: Alter Table, Create Table, Delete (either Searched or Positioned), Drop (Table, View, or Index), Grant, Insert, Revoke, and Update (either Searched or Positioned). Other statements may be possible in specific products. For more information, see Section 5.6.

C.25 Fetch Statement

The statement to fetch a row from an active set of an opened cursor (dynamic or not) has the following form, in all products we cover:

```
EXEC SQL FETCH [FROM] cursor_name
    INTO :host_variable {, :host_variable ...}
    | USING DESCRIPTOR :sqldavar_pointer;
```

The sqldavar_pointer is used with a dynamic cursor, and the host_variable list is used otherwise to receive the values retrieved by the Fetch. See Section 5.3 for more information on the static case and Section 5.6 for the dynamic case. The standards use a descriptor name rather than a pointer.

Fetch Statement for SQL-99 Scrollable Cursors

The syntax of a Fetch statement of a nondynamic cursor in SQL-99 (with the scrollable cursors extended feature) is shown in Figure C.26. For more information, see Section 5.7. **INFORMIX** is the only product we cover that supports this feature for Embedded SQL.

```
EXEC SQL FETCH
    [{NEXT | PRIOR | FIRST | LAST
    |{ABSOLUTE | RELATIVE} value_spec} FROM ]
    cursor_name INTO host-variable {, host-variable};
```

Figure C.26   The SQL-99 Fetch Statement Syntax (Advanced SQL)

C.26   Grant Statement

The Grant statement is an SQL command issued by the owner of a table (base table or view table) to authorize various kinds of access (select, update, delete, or insert) to the table by another user or class of users. It is a form of table access security, but column access can also be implemented through views. The other user must already be able to enter the database containing the table, an authorization provided by the database administrator.

The basic form of the Grant command for tables and views in the X/Open and Entry SQL-92 standards is (from Figure 7.16)

```
[EXEC SQL] GRANT {ALL PRIVILEGES | privilege {, privilege ...}}
    ON tablename | viewname
    TO {PUBLIC | user-name {, user-name ...} } [WITH GRANT OPTION]
```

This syntax is accepted by **ORACLE, DB2 UDB,** and **INFORMIX.** X/Open and Full SQL-92 also define Grant on collations, character sets, and translations, not covered in this text, and allow the optional keyword TABLE before the table or view name. Full SQL-99 supports all the X/Open and SQL-92 syntax, plus Grants on user-defined types and function designators. Core SQL-99 supports the above table/view syntax and Grants on unstructured user-defined types (i.e., distinct types) and function designators for SQL-invoked routines.

The Grant command either grants *all* types of access privileges or else a comma-separated list of privileges from the following set (for X/Open and Entry SQL-92):

```
SELECT
DELETE
INSERT
UPDATE [(columnname {, columnname . . . })]
REFERENCES [(columnname {, columnname . . . })]
```

Core SQL-99 has all of these plus EXECUTE for user-defined functions and procedures. **ORACLE, DB2 UDB,** and **INFORMIX** support all of these privileges, plus the ALTER privilege for a table, and additional privileges by product. For more information, see Section 7.3.

The various products also use nonstandard forms of the Grant statement to assign DBA privilege and other privileges of this kind to users. For example, **INFORMIX** has the following syntax:

```
[EXEC SQL] GRANT {CONNECT|RESOURCE|DBA}
    TO user-name {, user-name ...};
```

ORACLE allows the same syntax, but with more than 50 different system privileges, including SYSDBA for DBA privileges. **DB2 UDB** has several forms of Grant statements; the one to confer DBA privileges is the Grant Database Authorities statement.

C.27 Insert Statement

The Insert statement is identical in Embedded and Interactive SQL, presented in Sections 3.10 and 5.3. There are two insert forms, one that inserts a single row with specified values and one that may possibly insert multiple rows, derived from a general Subquery form as specified earlier in this section. The syntax in common between X/Open and Entry SQL-92 is, as previously given in Figure 3.22 (Interactive) and Figure 5.9 (Embedded),

```
[EXEC SQL] INSERT INTO [schema.]tablename [(columnname {, columnname ...})]
    {VALUES (expr | NULL {, expr | NULL...}) | subquery}
```

A newly inserted row usually cannot be placed into a table at a designated position, but only at a position determined by the disk structure of the table.

The difference between X/Open and Entry SQL-92 involves how to explicitly specify the use of the (previously defined) default values for column values. Core SQL-99, like X/Open and Full SQL-92, allows DEFAULT to be specified instead of expr | NULL for any column value in the VALUES clause. However, note that default values are also used if *no* specific value is supplied, so the DEFAULT keyword is not crucial to the capability to install default values in an Insert.

All major database products support the above Basic SQL syntax for Insert. **ORACLE** has an additional form for insertion into a nested table; see Section 4.3.1. Similarly, **INFORMIX** has a special form for insertion into collection-derived tables. Another variation between products and standards occurs because of differing allowed Subquery forms. Full SQL-92 and **DB2 UDB** support the advanced form of Subquery given in Figure 3.10, allowing INTERSECT and EXCEPT operators, and **ORACLE** comes close to this but uses MINUS instead of EXCEPT. X/Open and **INFORMIX** do not allow INTERSECT and EXCEPT in Subqueries (in general), and X/Open does not even allow UNION in an Insert's Subquery, but **INFORMIX** does.

Object-Relational Syntax

ORACLE allows the tablename to be replaced by TABLE (subquery) where the Subquery returns a nested table value, thus allowing inserts of rows to the nested table.

C.28   Open Cursor Statement

The statement to open a previously declared nondynamic cursor has the form, in all standards and products we cover,

```
EXEC SQL OPEN cursor_name;
```

For more information, see Section 5.1.

The statement to open a dynamic cursor (using an SQLDA structure) has the following form in all products we cover:

```
EXEC SQL OPEN cursor_name
    USING :host_variable {, :host_variable...}
    | USING DESCRIPTOR :sqldavar_pointer;
```

The host variables or descriptor values are provided to substitute for dynamic parameters in the WHERE clause of the previously prepared SQL Select string associated with the cursor. For more information, see Section 5.6. The standards use a descriptor name instead of a pointer.

C.29   Prepare Statement

A Prepare statement is used in Embedded SQL to prepare a Dynamic SQL statement contained in a host variable string for execution. (See the Execute statement, as well as the Execute Immediate statement, which combine the effect of the two statements Prepare and Execute.) The Prepare statement has the following form in all standards and products we cover:

```
EXEC SQL PREPARE statement_identifier FROM :host_string;
```

The character string contents of the host_string must represent a valid SQL statement, including any of the following types: Alter Table, Create Table, Delete (either Searched or Positioned), Drop (Table, View, or Index), Grant, Insert, Revoke, and Update (either Searched or Positioned). Other statements may be possible in specific products. See Section 5.6 for more information.

C.30   Revoke Statement

The SQL statement to revoke privileges on a table has the following general form in X/Open and Core SQL-99 (except that support of CASCADE is non-Core):

```
[EXEC SQL] REVOKE {ALL PRIVILEGES | privilege {, privilege ...} }
    ON tablename | viewname
    FROM {PUBLIC | user-name {, user-name ...} }
    CASCADE | RESTRICT;
```

The Revoke statement can revoke a subset of privileges earlier granted by the current user to a specified user. Unlike the Grant statement, the Revoke statement cannot specify specific column names in revoking update privileges. The owner of a table automatically has all privileges, and they cannot be revoked.

Neither **ORACLE** nor **DB2 UDB** implements the CASCADE | RESTRICT clause, and **INFORMIX** does, but allows it to be optional. For more information, see the discussion at the end of Section 7.3.

C.31   Rollback Statement

The Rollback statement is used in an Embedded SQL program when an active transaction must be aborted—that is, terminated unsuccessfully. The Rollback statement has the following form, in all standards and products we cover:

```
[EXEC SQL] ROLLBACK [WORK];
```

When the Rollback statement is executed, all row updates made during the transaction are reversed and the prior version of these rows is put in place and becomes visible again to concurrent users. If neither a Commit nor a Rollback statement is executed for a transaction in progress before a program terminates, a product-dependent default action (Commit or Rollback) is performed. For more information, see Section 5.4.

C.32   Select Statement

The full general form of the Interactive Select statement is given in Figure C.27 (from Figure 3.14 of Section 3.9). The syntax element called subquery above is called a *query expression* in SQL-92 and X/Open. **ORACLE** calls it a subquery. The various clauses and syntactic elements of the Interactive Select statement are described in great detail in Chapter 3, culminating in Section 3.9, where this general form is introduced. Full SQL-92 and Core SQL-99 allow EXCEPT to connect Subqueries in addition to UNION [ALL], and allow Subqueries to be parenthesized. Full SQL-92 and an extended feature of SQL-99 allow INTERSECT [ALL] as well. Both of these capabilities are in what we referred to in Section 3.6 as "Advanced SQL."

```
Subquery ::=
    SELECT [ALL | DISTINCT] { * | expr [[AS] c_alias] {, expr [[AS] c_alias]...}}
        FROM tableref {, tableref...}
        [WHERE search_condition]
        [GROUP BY colname {, colname...}]
        [HAVING search_condition]
    |  subquery UNION [ALL] subquery


Select statement ::=
    Subquery [ORDER BY result_column [ASC | DESC] {, result_column [ASC | DESC]...}]
```

Figure C.27   General Form of the Basic Subquery and the Basic Select Statement

```
Entry SQL-92:
    tableref::= tablename [corr_name]
Basic SQL:
    tableref::= tablename [[AS] corr_name]
X/OPEN:  if JOIN is used, exactly one of NATURAL, ON, and USING must be used
    tableref::= [schema.]tablename [[AS] corr_name]               -- simple form
        |tableref1 [NATURAL] [INNER | {LEFT|RIGHT} [OUTER]] JOIN tableref2    -- join form
            {ON search_condition | USING (colname {, colname ...})}
SQL-99 & Advanced SQL:
    tableref::= [schema.]tablename [[AS] corr_name][(colname {, colname ...})] -- simple form
        |(subquery) [AS] corr_name [(colname {, colname...})]          -- non-Core subquery form
        |tableref1 [INNER | {LEFT|RIGHT} [OUTER]] JOIN tableref2          -- join form
            {ON search_condition | USING (colname {, colname ...})}
```

Figure C.28   Various Forms for `tableref`

Common Syntactic Elements

In Figure C.27, the tableref form within the Subquery was particularly sensitive to which standard we are considering. See Figure C.28. The joined table form for Core SQL-99 or X/Open may optionally be enclosed in parentheses.

X/Open has the same predicates as Basic SQL and Entry SQL-92, shown in Figure C.29 (from Figure 3.19), plus the OVERLAPS predicate of Full SQL-92, which tests if two ranges of time overlap. The "value" may additionally be CURRENT_DATE, CURRENT_TIME, or CURRENT_TIMESTAMP. These useful constructs are considered *pseudo-literals* in X/Open but the more restrictive, non-Entry *datetime value functions* in SQL-92. As in SQL-92, the Subquery in Figure C.29 is not allowed to have UNIONs. In Core SQL-99, the comparison predicate is generalized to expr1 θ expr2, where the expr now is allowed to have the form (subquery). The other forms using (Subquery) remain that way in Core SQL-99, but the Subquery is allowed to have its full syntax, with UNION, EXCEPT, and JOIN. Core SQL-99 has no additional predicates. Predicates can

Predicate	Form
comparison predicate	expr1 θ {expr2	(Subquery)}
BETWEEN predicate	expr1 [NOT] BETWEEN expr2 and expr3
quantified predicate	expr θ [ALL	SOME	ANY] (Subquery)
IN predicate	expr [NOT] IN (Subquery)
	expr [NOT] IN (value {, value})
EXISTS predicate	[NOT] EXISTS (Subquery)
IS NULL predicate	colname IS [NOT] NULL
LIKE predicate	colname [NOT] LIKE pattern-value [ESCAPE escape-char-value]

Figure C.29   Basic SQL Predicates

search_condition
predicate
(search_condition)
NOT search_condition
search_condition AND search_condition
search_condition OR search_condition

Figure C.30   Recursive Definition of search_condition, Entry SQL-92, X/Open, Core SQL-99

be combined into a search_condition as shown in Figure C.30. For the syntax of expressions and other additional information, see Section 3.9.

Embedded SQL Select Statement

A Select statement can be executed in an Embedded SQL program only when no more than one row is to be retrieved (zero or one rows are permitted); otherwise a cursor must be defined. If more than one row is found by an Embedded SQL Select statement, a runtime error is returned. The syntax of this statement in Embedded SQL is given in Figure C.31.

Product Variations

All three products we have been covering support the syntax displayed in Figures C.27 and C.29 through C.31 using the Entry SQL-92 form for the tableref form of Figure C.28. **INFORMIX** and **DB2 UDB** (but not **ORACLE**) allow the optional keyword AS, as shown in the tableref form called Basic SQL. The same products support the syntax

```
EXEC SQL SELECT [ALL | DISTINCT] expression {, expression}
    INTO host-variable {, host-variable}
    FROM tableref {, tableref ...)
    [WHERE search_condition];
```

Figure C.31 Basic Embedded SQL Select Statement Syntax

labeled simple form in the SQL-99 tableref form of Figure C.28, that is, the additional capability of assigning new column names to the FROM table for use in the query. **DB2 UDB** and **ORACLE** allow the non-Core Subquery form, except that **ORACLE** does not allow the column list after the parenthesized Subquery nor the AS keyword there, so its Subquery form is simply (subquery) corr_name. Of the three products, only **DB2 UDB** supports the SQL-99 join forms following the syntax of Figure C.28, except for the less important USING clause. Both **ORACLE** and **INFORMIX** have special forms for left and right inner joins.

Object-Relational Syntax

The object-relational extensions bring a new expression syntax form using dot notation to access parts of structured types, create new instances of these types, and a way to refer to a whole row object (VALUE(t_alias) in **ORACLE**). Object references in **ORACLE** bring new expression forms REF( ) and DEREF( ). **ORACLE** has a new predicate IS DANGLING to detect dangling object REFs; see Section 4.2.1. Simple objects and references mainly extend the types allowed for columns, and since these types do not show up explicitly in Selects (except in CAST expressions), the Select syntax is very little affected by them. The big effects come with collections, since these provide new sources of tables, the main material of queries.

The tableref form has new variants to allow selections FROM collections, as shown in Figure C.32. Here, Figures 4.22 and 4.28 of Sections 4.3.1 and 4.3.2, respectively, are combined, and the ONLY keyword from the end of Section 4.2.2 is added. The ONLY keyword restricts the selection to the rows of the exact table specified, not including rows of its subtables in an inheritance hierarchy. (See the final Select statement of Section 4.2.2, which exemplifies this.) Full SQL-99 has object-relational tableref syntax identical to that of **INFORMIX** with keyword TABLE replaced by UNNEST, and one additional optional clause.

INFORMIX extends the IN predicate to the form IN collection_expression and provides the form CARDINALITY(collection_columnname) to count the elements of a collection column value. **ORACLE** provides a CURSOR( ) expression for interactive Selects that allows display of rows of a nested table for each row in an outer table, and new forms of CAST to convert collection types.

```
ORACLE object-relational tableref
tableref::=    {[schema.]tablename | (rowset_valued_subquery)
               | TABLE(collection_expression)}
               [corr_name]                      -- "AS" keyword not allowed
INFORMIX object-relational tableref
tableref::=    [schema.]tablename               -- no relational (subquery) form
               | TABLE(collection_expression)
               | ONLY ([schema.]tablename)}      -- restriction in table hierarchy
               [[AS] corr_name [(columnname, {columnname...})]]
```

Figure C.32   ORACLE and INFORMIX tableref Syntax, Including Object-Relational Extensions

C.33   Update Statement

As with the Delete statement, there are two versions of the Update statement: a *Searched Update,* a multi-row Update statement that can be executed either interactively or in Embedded SQL, and a *Positioned Update,* which acts through a cursor and can be executed in Embedded SQL only. The format of the Basic Searched Update statement is illustrated in Figure C.33 (from Figure 5.7). The Positioned Update statement has the syntax shown in Figure C.34 (from Figure 5.8). For more information, see Section 5.3.

All major database products support the above Basic SQL syntax for Update, and it conforms to Full SQL-92 and Core SQL-99. However, the X/Open and Entry SQL-92 standards do not have the indicated (subquery) option for the new column value. Since they do not allow (subquery) to qualify as an expression either, this option is not compliant. Full SQL-92 and Core SQL-99 do expand the meaning of an expression to include (subquery). In these cases we can drop the separate mention of the (subquery) option, or note that it is redundant.

```
[EXEC SQL] UPDATE [schema.]tablename
    SET columnname = expr | NULL| (subquery)
        {, columnname = expr | NULL | (subquery)...}
    [WHERE search_condition];
```

Figure C.33   Searched Update Statement Syntax, Basic SQL

```
EXEC SQL UPDATE [schema.]tablename
    SET columnname = expr | NULL| (subquery)
        {, columnname = expr | NULL | (subquery)...}
    WHERE CURRENT OF cursor_name;
```

Figure C.34   Embedded SQL Positioned Update Syntax, Basic SQL

Object-Relational Syntax

ORACLE allows the tablename to be replaced by TABLE (subquery) where the subquery returns a nested table value, thus allowing updates to the nested table rows. In **INFOR-MIX**, the tablename can be replaced by ONLY([schema.]tablename) to restrict updates to rows of the exact table, not rows of some subtable in the table hierarchy.

Set Query Counts ▮ D

The following list shows the number of rows selected (with different values in a few cases) for each of the queries Q1 through Q6B of the Set Query benchmark. This list is an aid to the practitioner attempting to run the benchmark. If the data has been properly generated and loaded on any platform, these numbers should be duplicated.

Query	Case	Row Count
Q1	KSEQ	1
--	K100K	8
--	K10K	98
--	K1K	1003
--	K100	10,091
--	K25	39,845
--	K10	99,902
--	K5	200,637
--	K4	249,431
--	K2	499,424
Q2A	KSEQ	1
--	K100K	5
--	K10K	58
--	K1K	487
--	K100	5009
--	K25	19,876
--	K10	49,939
--	K5	100,081
--	K4	125,262

	Query	Case	Row Count	Sum
776	Q2B	KSEQ	499,423	
	--	K100K	499,419	
	--	K10K	499,366	
	--	K1K	498,937	
	--	K100	494,415	
	--	K25	479,548	
	--	K10	449,485	
	--	K5	399,343	
	--	K4	374,162	
	Q3A	K100K	1	434
	--	K10K	9	5513
	--	K100	991	496,684
	--	K25	3989	1,978,118
	--	K10	9920	4,950,698
	--	K5	20,116	10,027,345
	--	K4	24,998	12,499,521
	Q3B	K100K	1	434
	--	K10K	6	3300
	--	K100	597	299,039
	--	K25	2423	1,209,973
	--	K10	5959	2,967,225
	--	K5	12,000	5,980,617
	--	K4	15,031	7,496,733
	Q4A	1–3	10,059	
	--	2–4	4027	
	--	3–5	1637	
	--	4–6	4021	
	--	5–7	7924	
	--	6–8	10,294	
	--	7–9	4006	
	--	8–10	785	
	Q4B	1–5	161	
	--	2–6	86	
	--	3–7	142	
	--	4–8	172	
	--	5–9	77	
	--	6–10	76	
	--	7–1	152	

Query	Case	Row Count
Q5	K2=K100=1	4962
--	K4=K25=1	9970
--	K10=K25=1	4049
Q6A	K100K	23
--	K40K	55
--	K10K	239
--	K1K	2014
--	K100	19,948
Q6B	K40K	3
--	K10K	4
--	K1K	81
--	K100	804

Solutions to Selected Exercises

Chapter 2 Solutions

[2.1] (a) A and B are both keys, since they are singleton attributes having unique values in each row. No other key can contain either A or B. Neither C nor D distinguishes all rows singly, but as a pair they do. Therefore the three candidate keys for T1 are A, B, and C D.

(c)

A	B	C	D
a1	b1	c1	d1
a2	b1	c1	d1
a1	b2	c1	d1
a1	b1	c2	d1

Clearly D is not a part of any key, and A B C is a superkey. None of the single columns, A, B, or C, can be a key, since in each column we have three equal entries. No pair of columns A B, B C, or C A can be a key because of duplicate entries. Therefore A B C is the only key.

[2.2] (a) The three candidate keys are ssn, name information-no, and name address city zip.

[2.4] (a) (ORDERS where qty >= 1000)[ordno,pid].

The parentheses are necessary because of the high precedence standing of projection.

(c) (ORDERS where dollars < 500 JOIN CUSTOMERS) [ordno,cname].

There is only one attribute in common between ORDERS and CUSTOMERS, so the join matches that one column and extends the ORDERS table to include customer information, of which we project down to just the ordno and cname. Equally well, we could project out the unnecessary ORDERS columns before joining:

```
((ORDERS where dollars < 500)[ordno,cid] JOIN CUSTOMERS)
    [ordno,cname]
```

(e)
```
((ORDERS where month = 'mar' JOIN CUSTOMERS)[ordno,cname,aid]
JOIN AGENTS)[ordno,cname,aname]
```

NOTE: Unlike the previous two exercises, here the first projection is necessary to prevent unwanted matching in the join based on the city attribute: because it appears in (ORDERS where month = 'mar' JOIN CUSTOMERS), and also in AGENTS, only rows with the matching customer city and agent city would appear in the result unless we do the first projection to throw out the city.

(g)
```
(PRODUCTS where city = 'Duluth' JOIN ORDERS
where month = 'mar')[pname].
```

Again, additional projections before the join are harmless unless they remove the pid.

[2.5] (a)
```
(((CUSTOMERS TIMES AGENTS) TIMES PRODUCTS)
where CUSTOMERS.city = AGENTS.city
and AGENTS.city = PRODUCTS.city)[cid,aid,pid]
```

Because the Cartesian product is associative, the following solution that specifies the product of three tables without saying which product goes first is preferable:

```
((CUSTOMERS TIMES AGENTS TIMES PRODUCTS)
    where CUSTOMERS.city = AGENTS.city
    and AGENTS.city = PRODUCTS.city)[cid,aid,pid]
```

(c)
```
((CUSTOMERS TIMES AGENTS TIMES PRODUCTS)
    where CUSTOMERS.city <> AGENTS.city
    and AGENTS.city <> PRODUCTS.city
    and PRODUCTS.city <> CUSTOMERS.city)[cid,aid,pid]
```

Do you see why you need the third condition? $x <> y$ and $y <> z$ do not imply $x <> z$. For example, $x = c$, $y = k$, $z = c$.

(e)
```
(ORDERS JOIN (CUSTOMERS where city = 'Dallas')[cid] JOIN
    (AGENTS where city = 'Tokyo')[aid] JOIN PRODUCTS)[pname]
```

Projection of the CUSTOMERS and AGENTS tables is needed at some point to remove the city columns so they will not be counted in the join. Also we are taking the join of four tables without specifying order with parentheses because JOIN, like the Cartesian product, is associative.

(g)
```
A1 := AGENTS, A2 := AGENTS
((A1 X A2) where A1.city = A2.city and A1.aid < A2.aid)
[A1.aid, A2.aid]
```

This is like the example in the text where we want to list only distinct pairs of agents, exactly once.

(i) This is very hard if you've never seen the trick before. Let
```
C1: = CUSTOMERS, C2 := CUSTOMERS
X(cid1, cid) :=
((C1 TIMES C2) where C1.discnt >= C2.discnt) [C1.cid, C2.cid].
```

Now the answer is exactly those `cid1` values on the left that are paired with *all* `cid` values on the right—that is, with `discnt >= ` *all* `discnt` values—so the answer is

```
X DIVIDEBY C[cid].
```

To find customers who have the smallest discount, change `>=` to `<=` in the above.

(k)
```
(ORDERS where ORDERS.aid = 'a03')[pid]

   -(ORDERS where ORDERS.aid = 'a06')[pid]
```

(m) We can start by finding all the agents T who do not place orders for any product in Newark:
```
T := all agents - agents who order products in Newark
= AGENTS[aid] - (O JOIN PRODUCTS where city = 'Newark')[aid]
```

Now `(T JOIN AGENTS)[aid,aname]` adds on the `aname` information, and we can finally select on those `anames`:

```
(T JOIN AGENTS) [aid,aname] where aname >= 'N' and aname < 'O'
```

The final result is obtained by substitution.

(o) Let P1 = all products ordered by customer c002, that is, `P1 := (ORDERS where cid = 'c002')[pid]`. Then we need the agents who place orders for all of P1. Their `aid`s are

```
ORDERS[aid,pid] DIVIDEBY P1
```

so the answer by substitution is

```
((ORDERS[aid,pid] DIVIDEBY (ORDERS where cid = 'c002')[pid])
   JOIN AGENTS)[aname]
```

Here the double use of ORDERS looks suspicious, but in fact causes no problem: an alias is required only in cases where the two tables' column names are used at the same point in the computation.

(q) Yes, this is the same as part (b). Using JOIN:

```
(CUSTOMERS TIMES AGENTS TIMES PRODUCTS)[cid, aid, pid] - (CUSTOMERS JOIN AGENTS
    JOIN PRODUCTS)[cid, aid, pid]
```

(s)
```
((ORDERS where dollars > 500)[aid,cid] JOIN CUSTOMERS
where city = 'Kyoto')[aid]
```

(u) Let OY := ORDERS and O := ORDERS. Then the solution is

```
O[cid] - ((O X OY) where O.aid <> OY.aid and O.cid = OY.cid)[O.cid]
```

The remaining exercise solutions, 2.6 through 2.15, will contain many relational operators written in keyboard form to demonstrate their use.

[2.6] (b) In Definition 2.7.4, if there are no columns in common, then the columns $B1$ through B_k in the two tables do not exist (k = 0). Thus in the definition of when a row t is in the table R JOIN S, we should ignore references to columns B_i. Then the remainder of the definition reduces to Definition 2.6.4, for the product R TIMES S, with appropriate column-name substitution. Another argument you could give is that in Theorem 2.8.2, which expresses JOIN in terms of other operators, if we remove references to columns B_i, then the first part of the definition reduces to T := R TIMES S. The second part defining T_2 simply renames columns to remove qualifiers.

[2.7] By Exercise 2.6, R JOIN S is identical to R TIMES S when R and S have no attributes (columns) in common. Let r be a row in R. It is enough to point out that row r is paired with *all* rows of S on some row of R TIMES S. This being the case, if we divide by S, we get back the row r. This shows that every row of R is in (R JOIN S) DIVIDEBY S. But if another row u were to show up in (R JOIN S) DIVIDEBY S, this would mean that u must be paired with all rows of S in (R JOIN S)—that is, in (R TIMES S). But by the definition of TIMES, such a row u must be in R because only such rows are paired with rows of S and placed in R TIMES S. A fully rigorous proof would codify the loose meaning of phrases such as "row r is paired with ALL rows of S," by using the form of Definition 2.6.4: "for every pair of rows u and v in R and S, respectively, there is a row t in R TIMES S such that t(R.Ai) = u(Ai) and . . ."

[2.8] (a) Let N_A be the constant table with one row all nulls and a heading consisting of the attributes that are in A but not in B, and similarly let N_B be the table with nulls for attributes of B that are not in A. Then

$$A \bowtie_O B = A \bowtie B \cup N_A \times (B - (A \bowtie B)[\text{Head}(B)]) \cup (A - (A \bowtie B)[\text{Head}(A)]) \times N_B$$

[2.9] (a) With three tables R, S, and T, there are various ways that attributes can be in common between tables: they can be common between R and S, or S and T, or T and S, and some of these could be in common to all three. R JOIN S selects for rows that agree on the attributes in common to R and S. Then (R JOIN S) JOIN T selects among those for rows that also agree on attributes in common between those of T and R JOIN S—that is, between T and R and also between T and S. Clearly the result requires agreement on any of the three sets of attributes in R – S, S – T, and T – S. Similarly R JOIN (S JOIN T) can be shown to require that same agreement. In all cases, the rows are selected from R × S × T, projected to squeeze out duplicated or triplicated columns.

[2.11] The table S where C contains all rows of S that obey condition C. Thus

r is in (S where C) iff r is in S and C is true for r.
r is in ((R where C1) where C2) iff r is in (R where C1) and C2 is true for r.
(R where C1) is the set of rows in R for which C1 is true.
Thus r is in ((R where C1) where C2) iff r is in R and C1 and C2 are true.

Similarly the other expressions can be reduced to the same elementary form.

[2.13] By a previous exercise, the join of compatible tables is just the intersection of the tables. Consider any x in R INTERSECT T. Since R is a subset of S, R INTERSECT T is a subset of S INTERSECT T.

Consider any x in U DIVIDEBY S. This means that (x,s) is in U for all s in S. But then (x,s) is in U for all s in R, since R is a subset of S. Thus x is in U DIVIDEBY R.

Consider any x in R DIVIDEBY V. This means that (x,v) is in R for all v in V. But then (x,v) is in S for all v in V, since R is a subset of S. Thus x is in S DIVIDEBY V.

Consider any x in (R where C). Then x is in R and C is true for x. Then x is in S and C is true for it. Thus x is in (S where C).

[2.15] (b) For any x in $(R \cup S)[H]$, there is some (x,x') in $R \cup S$, so (x,x') is in R or in S. When these are individually projected, x is seen to be in R[H] or in S[H], and thus in their union. Similarly, any x in $R[H] \cup S[H]$ is in R[H] or in S[H], and thus there is some (x,x') in R or in S—that is, in $R \cup S$—with projection x. Thus x is in $(R \cup S)[H]$.

Chapter 3 Solutions

[3.1] (a)
```
select c.cid, a.aid, p.pid
    from customers c, agents a, products p
    where c.city = a.city and a.city = p.city;
```

(c)
```
select c.cid, a.aid, p.pid
    from customers c, agents a, products p
    where c.city <> a.city and a.city <> p.city
    and c.city <> p.city;
```

Note that even if two of these conditions are true, the third one may fail, so an AND of all three conditions is called for.

(e)
```
select pname from products where pid in
    (select pid from orders where
    cid in (select cid from customers where city = 'Dallas') and
    aid in (select aid from agents where city = 'Tokyo'));
```

This demonstrates that we can use two IN conditions in the same WHERE clause. Alternatively, we can do this all with a join.

```
select distinct pname
    from products p, orders o, customers c, agents a
    where p.pid = o.pid and o.cid = c.cid and c.city = 'Dallas'
    and o.aid = a.aid and a.city = 'Tokyo';
```

(g)
```
select a1.aid, a2.aid from agents a1, agents a2
    where a1.city = a2.city and a1.aid < a2.aid;
```

(i)
```
select cid from customers
    where discnt >=all
    (select discnt from customers);
```

```
select cid from customers
    where discnt <=all
    (select discnt from customers);
```

(k)
```
select distinct pid from orders where aid = 'a03'
    and pid not in (select pid from orders where aid = 'a06');
```

(m) The following would appear to suffice:

```
select distinct a.aid, a.aname from agents a, orders o
    where aname like 'N%' and a.aid = o.aid
    and o.pid not in (select pid from products
        where city = 'Newark');
```

But in fact this only lists agents who placed orders. The complete solution is

```
select a.aid, a.aname from agents a where a.aname like 'N%'
    and a.aid not in
        (select o.aid from orders o where o.pid in
        (select pid from products where city = 'Newark'));
```

(o) ```
select distinct aname from agents a where not exists
    (select * from orders x where x.cid = 'c002' and not exists
    (select * from orders y where y.aid = a.aid
        and x.pid = y.pid));
```

(q)  ```
select cid, aid, pid from customers c, agents a, products p
    where c.city <> a.city or c.city <> p.city
    or a.city <> p.city;
```

(s) ```
select distinct aid from customers c, orders o
    where c.cid = o.cid
    and o.dollars > 500 and c.city = 'Kyoto';
```

(u)  ```
select distinct cid from orders o where not exists
    (select x.cid from orders x, orders y
    where x.aid <> y.aid and
    xcid = o.cid and y.cid = o.cid);
```

[3.2] (a) ```
select aid from agents where percent >any
    (select percent from agents);
```

(c) The quoted query returns the same result as (a) only as long as the minimum commission is 5, which may not continue to be true in the future.

This is what we mean when we say that Figure 2.2 represents "the content as of a given moment," and illustrates what was meant in Example 2.7.6 by a content dependency: the fact that two queries have the same result for a table of a given content is not sufficient to guarantee that the two queries are equivalent.

**[3.3]** (a) We know that 'x in y' is the same as 'x =any y', where y is a set of values returned by the Subquery and x is a simple value. Now 'x not in y' is the same as 'not (x in y)', but 'not (x =any y)' is *not* the same as 'x <>any y'. This is because 'x <>any y' is TRUE if there exists a value in y that doesn't equal x, but 'not (x =any y)' is TRUE only if x is not equal to any value of y; this condition is stated by the SQL predicate 'x <>all y'. Thus NOT IN is the same as <>ALL, but not the same as <>ANY.

(c) The query to retrieve exactly those rows not retrieved by the query of Example 3.4.7:

```
select aid from agents where percent >any
    (select percent from agents);
```

[3.4] (a) ```
select distinct cid from orders, agents
    where orders.aid = agents.aid
    and (agents.city = 'Duluth' or agents.city = 'Dallas');
```

(c) `select A₁,..., Aₙ from S, T where S.A₂ = k and`
     `S.A₁ = T.B₁ and T.B₂ = c and T.B₃ = S.A₃;`

[3.6] (a) `INITIALIZE LIST L to EMPTY`
          `FOR T FROM ROW 1 TO LAST OF TABLE T (No alias)`
          `    IF (T.B₂ = c)`
          `        Place B₁ on LIST L;`
          `END FOR T;`
          `FOR S FROM ROW 1 TO ROW LAST OF TABLE S`
          `    IF (A₂ = k and A₁ an element of LIST L)`
          `        Place (A₁,..., Aₙ) on SOLUTION LIST M`
          `END FOR S`
          `PRINT OUT UNIQUE ROWS ON SOLUTION LIST M`

[3.7] (a) `select * from R union select * from S;`

(c) (R UNION S) MINUS T in Full SQL-92:

`select * from ((R UNION S) EXCEPT T).`

(R UNION S) MINUS T in Basic SQL: consider a row w in (R UNION S) MINUS T. It is in R or S but not in T. Suppose it is in R. Then it is in R but not in T. Likewise, if it is in S, then it is in S but not in T. Thus it is in R – T or in S – T; that is, it is in (R – T) UNION (S – T), and this expression can be written in SQL using the results of 3.7(a):

`(select * from R where not exists (select * from T`
`    where R.A₁ = T.A₁and R.A₂ = T.A₂,... and R.Aₙ = T.Aₙ))`
`UNION`
`(select * from S where not exists (select * from T`
`    where S.A₁ = T.A₁and S.A₂ = T.A₂,... and S.Aₙ = T.Aₙ))`

(e) By Theorem 2.8.3,

`R DIVIDEBY S = R[A₁,..., Aₙ] - ((R[A₁,..., Aₙ] TIMES S)`
`  - R)[A₁,..., Aₙ]`

Here R is `select cid, aid from orders` and S is `select aid from agents where city = 'New York'`. HEAD(R) = $A_1...A_n B_1...B_m$ = cid aid and S = $B_1...B_m$ = aid, so we see that n = 1, A_1 = cid, m = 1, B_1 = aid, and R[cid] TIMES S is V defined as follows:

`V = select o.cid,a.aid from orders o, agents a`
`    where city = 'New York'`

We need as a final result R[cid] - (V-R)[cid]. By MINUS of part (d),

```
(V-R) = select o.cid, a.aid from orders o, agents a
    where city = 'New York' and not exists
    (select * from orders x
        where x.aid = a.aid  and x.cid = o.cid)
```

(V-R)[cid] is the same, with a.aid dropped from the selection list. Finally the answer is, using MINUS once more from part (d):

```
select cid from orders y where not exists
    (select o.cid from orders o, agents a
        where city = 'New York'
            and not exists
            (select * from orders x
                where x.cid = o.cid and x.aid = a.aid)
                and y.cid = o.cid);
```

In fact this returns the result duplicated several times, so select distinct is called for.

[3.8] (a) `select cid, max(dollars) as maxspent from orders`
`group by cid;`

[3.10] (a) Clearly this is an outer join. We want to use WHERE C to derive one table of the 10 customers, say, ctab, and then use the right outer join of ctab with sporders. Then sum up the orders by cid. Here are the steps.

1. Set up the derived table ctab:

```
(select cid, cname from customers where C) ctab
```

2. Right join ctab with sporders, yielding a tableref as follows:

```
(select cid, cname from customers where C) ctab
    right join sporders on ctab.cid = sporders.cid
```

3. Use this tableref in the final query:

```
select cid, cname, sum(dollars) as totdoll from
    ((select cid, cname from customers where C) ctab
            right join sporders on ctab.cid = sporders.cid)
    group by cid, cname;
```

Note that we need cname in the GROUP BY list to allow it in the select list. Sometimes it will be null, but that's OK. There are no extraneous cases due to null cnames—there can't be a non-null cname and also a null one! In **ORACLE**, we can use the derived table ctab as a tableref and do a one-sided join. We mark the non-retained side with the (+). Here we are retaining rows in sporders, so we put the (+) on ctab's side.

```
select cid, cname, sum(dollars) as totdoll from
    (select cid, cname from customers where C) ctab, sporders
        where ctab.cid(+) = sporders.cid
    group by cid, cname
```

We can always mimic an outer join with a union of an inner join and the extra rows.

1. Compose the inner join:

```
select cid, cname, sum(dollars) as totdoll from customers c, sporders
        where C and ctab.cid = sporders.cid
        group by cid, cname;
```

2. Express the extra rows of outer join, the ones that are in sporders but not in ctab:

```
select cid, null, sum(dollars) as totdoll from orders
        where cid not in (select cid from customers where C) ctab
```

3. Take the UNION of steps 1 and 2.

[3.11] (a)
```
select aid, pid, sum(qty) from orders group by aid, pid;
```

(c)
```
select a.aid from agents a where not exists
    (select o.* from orders o, customers c, products p
        where o.aid = a.aid and o.cid = c.cid and o.pid = p.pid
        and c.city = 'Duluth' and p.city = 'Dallas');
```

(e)
```
select distinct cid from orders o
    where aid in ('a03', 'a05') and not exists
    (select * from orders x where
        o.cid = x.cid and x.aid not in ('a03', 'a05'));
```

(g)
```
select aid from agents
    where percent = (select max(percent) from agents);
```

(i)
```
update agents set percent = 11 where aname = 'Gray';
select * from agents;
update agents set percent = 6 where aname = 'Gray';
select * from agents;
```

(k)
```
select cid, sum(dollars) from orders where aid = 'a04'
    and cid not in (select cid from orders
    where aid <> 'a04') group by cid;
```

(m)
```
select o.pid from orders o, customers c, agents a
    where o.cid = c.cid and o.aid = a.aid and c.city = a.city;
```

[3.12] (a) `select discnt from customers where city = 'Duluth';`

```
discnt
------
    10
     8
------
(2 rows)
```

`select percent from agents where city like 'N%';`

```
percent
------
     6
     6
     6
------
(3 rows)
```

```
select city from customers where discnt >=all
    (select discnt from customers where city = 'Duluth');
```

```
city
------
Duluth
Dallas
------
(2 rows)
```

```
select city from agents where percent >any
    (select percent from agents where city like 'N%');
```

```
city
-------
Tokyo
-------
(1 row)
```

```
select city from customers where discnt >=all
    (select discnt from customers where city = 'Duluth')
    union
    select city from agents where percent >any
        (select percent from agents where city like 'N%');
```

```
city
-------
Dallas
Duluth
Tokyo
-------
(3 rows)
```

[3.13] (a) By definition, a superkey is any set of columns whose values uniquely identify each row: no two rows have identical values in these columns. Thus if we select columns that include the superkey from a table, our result has no two rows that are identical.

(c) It is false. The query given by

```
select count(*) from table group by <key>;
```

where <key> is a comma-separated list of columns containing any superkey of the table, invariably produces a table of the same length as the original table, with a single column of ones, all identical.

[3.14] (a) `select * from customers where cname >= 'A' and cname < 'B';`

[3.15] (a) In an outer join, a row should appear for an agent who takes no orders, and a row should appear for an order by an aid that has no corresponding aname in the agents table:

```
select a.aname, a.aid, sum(x.dollars) from agents a, orders x
    where a.aid = x.aid group by a.aid, a.aname
union
select aname, aid, 0 from agents
    where aid not in (select aid from orders)
union
select 'null', aid, sum(x.dollars) from orders x
    where aid not in (select aid from agents) group by aid;
```

[3.16] (a) Answer: They form a distinct group. The output is

```
percent
---------
      5
      6
      7

(4 rows)
```

(c) (i) "Get names of agents whose commission is at least as large as all Geneva-based agents' commissions." Comparisons with null return UNKNOWN, so this returns 0 rows. In the case that there are no agents at all in Geneva, the answer would list all agents (see Exercise 3.14). Thus the existence of a null value can greatly change results.

[3.17] (a) This query returns all customer IDs.

[3.18] (a) Using the **ORACLE** floor( ) function:

```
create table buckets (bucket int, primary key(bucket));
insert into buckets select distinct floor(dollars/500) from orders; -- ORACLE
select bucket*500 as "range-start", sum(dollars) from orders o, buckets b
    where floor(o.dollars/500) = b.bucket
    group by b.bucket;
drop table buckets;        -- only needed for query
```

For systems with CAST, use CAST (dollars/500 as int) instead of floor( ).

[3.19] (b) The fact that the median can be calculated is a direct result of the capability of producing a cumulative histogram of data, that is, for each value, a count of values *below that one* (or equal to it) in the data. For the dollars data in orders, a cumulative histogram can be produced with the following Advanced SQL query:

```
select h2.dollars, sum(ct) from
    (select dollars, count(dollars) ct from orders group by dollars) h1,
    (select dollars from orders group by dollars) h2
    where h1.dollars <= h2.dollars       -- over all h1 values <= h2 value
    group by h2.dollars
    order by h2.dollars;                 -- just for reporting
```

The internal Subqueries just condense the duplicated dollars values into counts for that value, to avoid the multiplication effect on duplicated rows in the join. Now symbolize the derived cumulative histogram table as F, with columns dollars and ct. Here ct is the count of dollars values in orders that are at or below dollars, a particular dollars value in orders. For the median, we need the halfway point in ct, the dollars value where ct = max(ct)/2 = count(dollars)/2 in orders. But we are unlikely to get an exact match, so instead we ask for the dollars value at the lowest point in ct that is greater than or equal to count(dollars)/2:

```
select dollars from F
    where ct = (select min(ct1) from F
        where ct1 >= (select count(*)/2 from orders))
```

Substituting F in twice, we get the full query, with two levels of FROM (Subquery) at work:

```
(select dollars from
    (select h2.dollars, sum(h1.ct) ct from
    (select dollars, count(dollars) ct from orders group by dollars) h1,
    (select dollars from orders group by dollars) h2
        where h1.dollars <= h2.dollars group by h2.dollars) F
```

```
        where ct = (select max(ct1) from (select h2.dollars, sum(ct1) ct1 from
            (select dollars, count(dollars) ct1 from orders group by dollars) h1,
            (select dollars from orders group by dollars) h2
                where h1.dollars <= h2.dollars group by h2.dollars) F
            where ct1 >= (select count(*)/2 from orders)));
```

Chapter 4 Solutions

[4.1] (a) `select ssno from people p where p.pname.mi is null;`

(c) `select p1.ssno, p2.ssno from people p1, people p2`
`        where p1.pname = p2.pname and p1.ssno < p2.ssno;`

[4.2] (a) **ORACLE:**

```
create type student_t as object (
    sperson person_t,
    stuid int,
    emailname varchar(30),
    gradyear int
);
create table students of student_t (sperson not null, primary key(stuid));
```

INFORMIX:

```
create row type student_t (
    sperson person_t not null,
    stuid int,
    emailname varchar(30),
    gradyear int
);
create table students of type student_t (primary key (stuid));
```

[4.3] (a, c, g, i, q) These don't involve the orders table and thus cannot use REFs, since all the REFs are in the orders table.

(e) `select distinct o.ordprod.pname from orders o where o.ordcust.city = 'Dallas'`
`        and o.ordagent.city = 'Kyoto';`

(g, i) Do not involve the orders table.

(k) Involves only the orders table, no need for REFs

(m) `select aid, aname from agents a where a.aname like 'N%'`
`        and a.aid not in`
`            (select o.aid from orders o where o.ordprod.city = 'Newark');`

(o) To eliminate agents with no orders at all, we should use "from orders" in the first line:

```
select distinct o.ordagent.aname from orders o where not exist
    (select * from orders x where x.cid = 'c002' and not exists
    (select * from orders y where y.ordagent = ref(a)
                        and y.ordprod = x.ordprod))
```

(s)
```
select aid from orders o where dollars > 500.00 and o.ordcust.city = 'Kyoto';
```

(u)
```
select cid from (select distinct cid, aid from orders) t
    group by cid having count(*) = 1;
```

[4.4] (a) **ORACLE:**
```
select e.dependents from employees e
        where 1 = (select count(*) from table(e.dependents));
```

INFORMIX:
```
select e.dependents from employees e
        where cardinality(e.dependents) = 1;
```

(c) **ORACLE:**
```
select count(*) from phonebook pb
        where 100 in (select * from table(pb.extensions));
```

INFORMIX:
```
select count(*) from phonebook pb
        where 100 in pb.extensions;
```

[4.5] (a) **ORACLE** or **INFORMIX:**
```
select eid from employees e
            where e.eperson.pname.fname in
            (select t.fname from table(e.dependents) t);
```

(c) **ORACLE:**
```
select value(d) from table
(select e.dependents from employees e where e.eid = 100) d
    where d.age =
(select max(age) from table(select e.dependents from
employees e where e.eid = 100));
```

INFORMIX:
```
select d from table
(select e.dependents from employees e where e.eid = 100) d
    where d.age =
(select max(age) from table (select e.dependents from
employees e where e.eid = 100));
```

(e) We could use <SOME and >SOME in a query like Example 4.3.13, but a more natural approach is to apply the condition "where extension is between 800 and 900" in the internal scan of the extensions table. However, in both products, we have the problem that the internal extensions table has no specific column name for its one column. This problem is resolved by very different mechanisms in the two products. In **ORACLE**, the generic name column_value can be used when there is no specific column name. **INFOR-**

MIX supports the SQL-99 syntax allowing specification of new names for columns as well as tables in the `tableref` form (Figure 3.11, top line), so we may provide an appropriate column name *in* the query, for example, ext below.

ORACLE:
```
select pb.phperson.ssno from phonebook pb
        where exists (select * from table(pb.extensions)
            where column_value between 800 and 900);
```

INFORMIX:
```
select pb.phperson.ssno from phonebook pb
        where exists(select * from table(pb.extensions)
                as x(ext) -- column name "ext" added here
            where x.ext between 800 and 900);
```

[4.6] (a) **ORACLE:**
```
select p.x, p.y, count(*) as ct from points p, rects r
        where r.inside(value(p)) > 0
    group by p.x, p.y
    having count(*)>3
    order by count(*);
```

INFORMIX:
```
select p, count(*) as ct from points p, rects r
        where inside(r,p)
    group by p
    having count(*)>3
    order by count(*);
```

(c) **ORACLE:**
```
select value(p) from points p, rects r
    where r.inside(value(p))>0 and r.area()=
        (select max(r.area()) from rects r);
```

INFORMIX:
```
select p from points p, rects r
    where inside(r,p) and area(r)=
        (select max(area(r)) from rects r);
```

[4.7]
```
select value(p), value(r), (r.pt2.x-r.pt1.x)*(r.pt2.y-r.pt1.y) from
            rects r, points p
    where (r.pt2.x-r.pt1.x)*(r.pt2.y-r.pt1.y) =
        (select min((r1.pt2.x-r1.pt1.x)*(r1.pt2.y-r1.pt1.y)) from rects r1
            where p.x >= r1.pt1.x and p.x <= r1.pt2.x and
                p.y >= r1.pt1.y and p.y <= r1.pt2.y)
    and p.x >= r.pt1.x and p.x <= r.pt2.x and p.y >= r.pt1.y and p.y <= r.pt2.y
    order by p.x, p.y;
```

Chapter 5 Solutions

NOTE: Most of the programs use prompt.c and its header file, prompt.h. See Appendix B, "Programming Details," for discussion and code for prompt( ) and print_dberror( ).

[5.2]

```
/* ORACLE version: program to report on product quantities by agent for cid and pid */
#define TRUE 1
#include <stdio.h>
#include <string.h>
#include "prompt.h"
exec sql include sqlca;
main()
{
    exec sql begin declare section;
        char username[20], password[20];
        char cust_id[5], product_id[4], agent_id[4];
        long total_qty;                          /* sum of shorts may need long*/
    exec sql end declare section;
    char promptcidpid[] = "PLEASE ENTER CUSTOMER ID AND PRODUCT ID: ";
    exec sql declare agent_qty cursor for        /* declare cursor          */
        select aid, sum(qty) from orders
            where cid = :cust_id and pid = :product_id
        group by aid;
    strcpy(username. "scott") ;                  /* set up for              */
    strcpy(password. "tiger");                   /* ORACLE login            */
    exec sql connect :username identified by :password; /* ORACLE connect   */
    while (prompt(promptcidpid, 2, cust_id, 4, product_id, 3) >= 0) {
    exec sql whenever sqlerror goto report_error;  /* error trap condition  */
        exec sql open agent_qty;                 /* open cursor             */
        exec sql whenever not found goto fetchdone;
        while (TRUE) {                           /* loop to fetch rows      */
            exec sql fetch agent_qty into :agent_id, :total_qty;
            printf("%s %d\n", agent_id, total_qty); /* display row          */
        }
    fetchdone:
            exec sql close agent_qty;            /* close cursor when fetches done*/
            exec sql commit work;                /* release read locks      */
    }                                            /* end of prompt loop: repeat  */
    exec sql commit release;                     /* ORACLE disconnect from database*/
    return 0;
report_error:
    print_dberror();                             /* print out error message */
    exec sql rollback release;                   /* ORACLE failure disconnect */
    return 1;
}
```

[5.6] (d) If a Commit is done after the reads, those quantities may change before the updates are made and cause just the problems the checks were supposed to prevent—for example, keeping inventory amounts non-negative. No, there are no places here for additional Commits.

[5.10]

```
/* 4.10, DB2 UDB version: Histogram of dollar amounts of orders */
#define TRUE 1
#define RANGE 500.0
#include <stdio.h>
exec sql include sqlca;
main()
{
    exec sql begin declare section;
        double dollars;
    exec sql end declare section;
    double range_start = 0;
    double range_end = range_start + RANGE;
    double range_sum = 0.0;
    exec sql declare dollars_cursor cursor for
        select dollars from orders
            order by dollars;
    exec sql whenever sqlerror goto report_error;
    exec sql connect to testdb;               /* DB2 UDB connect to database    */
    exec sql open dollars_cursor;
    exec sql whenever not found goto fetchdone;
    printf("%-17s %-8s\n", "range", "total orders");
    while (TRUE) {                            /* loop over orders table         */
        exec sql fetch dollars_cursor into :dollars;
        if (dollars <= range_end) {
            range_sum += dollars;             /* point in same old range        */
        } else {                              /* point beyond end of this range */
            while( dollars > range_end) {     /* -- and possibly several ranges */
                printf("%8.2f-%8.2f %8.2f\n",range_start,range_end, range_sum);
                range_sum = 0;
                range_start = range_end;      /* step range                     */
                range_end += RANGE;
            }
            range_sum += dollars;             /* found new range that fits point */
        }
    }                                         /* end while loop on aid values   */
fetchdone:
    if (range_sum)
        printf("%8.2f-%8.2f %8.2f\n",range_start,range_end, range_sum);
    exec sql close dollars_cursor;
```

```
exec sql commit work;                  /* release locks                      */
exec sql disconnect current;
return 0;
report_error:
print_dberror();                       /* print out error message            */
exec sql rollback work;                /* failing, undo work, end locks       */
exec sql disconnect current;           /* Disconnect from database            */
return 1;
}
```

[5.12] (a)
```
exec sql begin declare section;
      char city[21];
   exec sql end declare sections;
```

(b)
```
exec sql declare cc cursor for
   select distinct a.city from agents a, orders x, products p
      where a.aid = x.aid and x.pid = p.pid and p.price < 1.00;
```

An alternative form with Subquery is of course possible. It is a common error to fail to list products at all, using the condition x.dollars < 1.00, but of course this doesn't answer the question posed.

(c)
```
while (1){                         /* or while TRUE, assume TRUE = 1          */
   exec sql whenever not found goto fetchdone;
   exec sql fetch cc into :city;
   printf ("%s", city);
}
fetchdone:  ...
```

[5.13] (a) `if(sqlca.sqlcode == 100) goto error_handle;`

(b) `if(sqlca.sqlcode < 0) goto error_handle;`

[5.14] (a)
```
select c.city, cid, aid, pid from customers c, agents a,
      products p
         where c.city = a.city and a.city = p.city order by c.city;
```

It is a common mistake to write group by c.city, but of course that isn't legal since the other elements of the target list are not single-valued for individual values of c.city. Ordering by c.city assures that rows occur one after another when they are from the same city.

(b) $30 \times 10 \times 20 = 6000$

(c) The idea here is to avoid printing out 6000 lines for New York. We want to print out "New York" and then three simple lists (without repetition) of cid values, then aid values, then pid values for customers, agents, and products that have city = New York. We want to do this for all cities, one after another. We don't have to write perfect C (pseudo-code is OK), but we have to show how to use Embedded SQL to accomplish this. Start by showing the cursors we need, where in pseudo-code we leave out the exec sql.

```
declare cities cursor for select distinct c.city
    from customers c, agents a, products p
    where c.city = a.city and a.city = p.city;
declare cids cursor for select cid from customers
    where city = :city;
declare aids cursor for select aid from agents
    where city = :city;
declare pids cursor for select pid from products
    where city = :city;

open cities;
while ( rows remain in cities); {    /* loop to fetch citynames        */
    fetch cities into :city;        /* city value to open other cursors */
    print cityname header;
    open cids;
        loop to print out cid values of cursor cids;
    open aids;
        loop to print out aid values of cursor aids;
    open pids;
        loop to print out pid values of cursor pids;
}    /* loop while cities remain */
```

It is a common mistake to use a single cursor, something like

```
declare ccs cursor for select c.city, cid, aid, pid
    from customers c, agents a, products p
    where c.city = a.city and p.city = a.city order by c.city;
```

and then use logic of the following kind:

```
open ccs;
fetch first row of ccs into :city, :cid, :aid, :pid;
remember city name as oldcity;
print city name header;
start printing columns of cid, aid, pid values
while (rows from ccs remain) {
    if latest city does not match oldcity{    /* start new oldcity    */
        remember new city name as oldcity;
        print new city name header;
        start printing columns of cid, aid, pid values;
    }
    else {    /* same oldcity name */
        print out new values of cid, aid, pid in columns;
    }
}    /* next row of ccs */
```

But this doesn't accomplish what we want, to restrict the amount of information (number of rows), because there are still 6000 rows to print out. (The problem is that the list of `cid` values for New York, for example, has a *lot of* duplicates.)

[5.15] (a)
```
exec sql declare topsales cursor for
    select pid, sum(dollars) totdollars from orders
    group by pid
    order by totdollars desc;  /* or "order by 2 desc" in some older systems*/
```

(b)
```
int count = 0;                          /* count 10 rows to print out     */
while (1){
    whenever not found goto fetchdone;
    fetch topsales into :pid, :doltot: indicator :dolind;
    if (dolind >= 0){                   /* not a null value, so count it  */
        if(++count >= 10)
            break;                      /* have already printed 10 rows   */
        printf("pid value is %s, total dollar sales is %s ",
            pid, doltot);
    }    /* end if */
}    /* end loop */
fetchdone:
```

[5.16] We don't really need to test for deadlock after the *first* access, since there can't be one (although there's no harm in doing so). The important thing is to drop *all* locks if we run into one. It is a common error to simply loop back and try to make the *second* access again, without doing a rollback.

```
#define DEADABORT ...                   /* fill in for your system        */
exec sql whenever sqlerror continue;    /* we're taking over error handling */
int count = 0;
while (1) {
    exec sql update orders
        set dollars = dollars - :delta
        where aid = :agent1 and pid = :prod1 and cid = :cust1;
    if (sqlca.sqlcode < 0)
        goto handle_err;                /* can't be deadlock yet          */
    exec sql update orders
        set dollars = dollars + :delta
        where aid = :agent1 and pid = :prod1 and cid = :cust1;
    if (sqlca.sqlcode == DEADABORT){
        if(count++ < 2) {
            exec sql rollback;          /* need to drop locks held        */
                        /* here, call OS to wait for a second, sleep(1) on UNIX */
            continue;                   /* try again                      */
        } else {
            exec sql rollback;
            break;                      /* give up entirely               */
        }
    if (sqlca.sqlcode < 0) goto handle_err; /* other error?               */
    exec sql commit work;               /* if not, commit                 */
} /* end of loop of trials */
```

[5.17] (a) **ORACLE:**
```
for (i=0;i<sqlda->N;i++)
        printf("%*s ",sqlda->M[i], sqlda->S[i])
    printf("\n")
```

DB2 UDB:
```
for (i=0;i<sqlda->sqld;i++)
        printf("%*s ", sqlda->sqlvar[i].sqlname.length,
            sqlda->sqlvar[i].sqlname.length);
```

(b) **ORACLE::**
```
if(*(sqlda -> I[1]))
        handle_null();
```

DB2 UDB:
```
if (*(sqlda->sqlvar[1].sqlind))
        handle_null();
```

Note that the condition to detect a null is to test if the indicator sqlind is TRUE, that is, in C, any non-zero value.

Chapter 6 Solutions

[6.1] Of the four possibilities, min-card = 0 or 1, max-card = 1 or N, only two of these are actually constraints: min-card = 1 (we are not allowed to have 0) and max-card = 1 (we are not allowed to have more than 1). If an example breaks such a constraint, then we know that the constraint does not hold universally. Thus in Figure 6.6(a), we can be sure that min-card(E, R) = 0, since this is the case here, and that min-card(F, R) = 0, but we can't be sure about the max-card in either case. In (b), we can be sure that min-card(E, R) = 0 and max-card(E, R) = N, but we can't be sure about card(F, R), because no real constraint is broken. In (c), we see that min-card(E, R) = 0, max-card(E, R) = N, min-card(F, R) = 0, and max-card(F, R) = N; that is, that no real constraints hold, since all possible constraints are broken by the example.

[6.2] See Figure 6.2 for an acceptable E-R diagram. Note that the labeled cardinalities of the attributes are all somewhat arbitrary in the min-card value, except for the primary keys that must be labeled (1, 1). We try to place the entity E that relates to F by a verb relation to the left or above the entity F; thus Orders ships Products and Orders are to the left, Agents places Orders and Agents are above.

[6.4] (a) Legal.

(c) Violates (3).

[6.5] Let us start by considering FDs with a single attribute on the left. In addition to the identity functional dependencies, we have the following. (a) All values of the A column are the same, so it can never happen for any other column X that $r_1(X)$ = $r_2(X)$ while $r_1(A) \neq r_2(A)$. Thus we see that B → A, C → A, and D → A. At the same time, no other column X is functionally dependent on A since they all have at least two distinct values, and so there are always two rows r_1 and r_2 such that $r_1(X) \neq r_2(X)$ while $r_1(A) = r_2(A)$. Thus $A \nrightarrow B$, $A \nrightarrow C$, and $A \nrightarrow D$. (b) Because the C values are all different, in addition to $C \rightarrow A$, above, we also have $C \rightarrow B$ and $C \rightarrow D$. At the same time, C is not functionally dependent on anything else since all other columns have at least two duplicate values: $B \nrightarrow C$ and $D \nrightarrow C$ are the new FDs derived. (c) We have $B \nrightarrow D$ (because of rows 1 and 2) and $D \nrightarrow B$ (because of rows 1 and 3). Therefore we can list all FDs with a single attribute on the left (with a letter in parentheses keyed to the items above that give us this fact).

(a) $A \nrightarrow B$	(a) $B \rightarrow A$	(a) $C \rightarrow A$	(a) $D \rightarrow A$
(a) $A \nrightarrow C$	(b) $B \nrightarrow C$	(b) $C \rightarrow B$	(c) $D \nrightarrow B$
(a) $A \nrightarrow D$	(c) $B \nrightarrow D$	(b) $C \rightarrow D$	(b) $D \nrightarrow C$

This gives us nontrivial FDs: (1) $C \rightarrow A\,B\,D$, (2) $B \rightarrow A$, and (3) $D \rightarrow A$. Now consider pairs of columns on the left. (d) Since C determines all other columns, clearly any pair of columns containing C also determines all others, but these are all trivial results. (e) The column A, combined with any other column X on the left, still functionally determines only those columns already determined by X (because no new row pairs are different when A is added). Now the only pair that does not contain A or C is B D, and since B D has distinct values on each row (see the table T again), we have that $B\,D \rightarrow$ everything. We already know from nontrivial FD (2) that $B \rightarrow A$, and it is trivial that $B\,D \rightarrow B\,D$, so the only new FD that comes out of this is (4) $B\,D \rightarrow C$. If we consider now triples of columns, it is clear that any triple that does not contain C (and therefore functionally determines all other columns) must contain B D (and therefore functionally determines all columns). The complete list of nontrivial FDs follows:

(1) $C \rightarrow A\,B\,D$, (2) $B \rightarrow A$, (3) $D \rightarrow A$, (4) $B\,D \rightarrow C$

[6.7] (a) No, the last row never figures in the discussion and can be dropped.

[6.9] Union rule: If $X \rightarrow Y$ and $X \rightarrow Z$, then $X \rightarrow Y\,Z$. $X\,X \rightarrow Y\,X$ by given $X \rightarrow Y$ and augmentation. But $X\,X = X$, so $X \rightarrow X\,Y$. Similarly augment $X \rightarrow Z$ by X and get $X \rightarrow X\,Z$.

Next augment by Y, obtaining $X\,Y \rightarrow X\,Y\,Z$. Then $X \rightarrow X\,Y$ and $X\,Y \rightarrow X\,Y\,Z$ give $X \rightarrow X\,Y\,Z$. But Y Z is a subset of X Y Z, so by inclusion $X\,Y \rightarrow Y\,Z$, and by transitivity $X \rightarrow Y\,Z$.

Pseudotransitivity: If $X \rightarrow Y$ and $W\,Y \rightarrow Z$, then $X\,W \rightarrow Z$. $X \rightarrow Y$ gives $X\,W \rightarrow Y\,W$ by augmentation, and this with $W\,Y \rightarrow Z$ gives $X\,W \rightarrow Z$ by transitivity.

[6.11] (a) Suppose that X^+ does not equal X. Then there is an attribute A in X^+, not in X, such that $X \rightarrow A$ (otherwise we can never leave X by following FDs). This

FD must be covered by F, so A is contained in the right-hand side of some element of F, with left-hand side X_i. Since X does not contain any of these left-hand sides, there is some nontrivial set B of attributes in X_i but not in X. Then $X_i = B X$, $B X \rightarrow A$, and also $X \rightarrow A$. But this means that X_i is not minimal; specifically, B can be dropped in step 3 of the minimal cover algorithm. Contradiction.

[6.12] Here is a list of Armstrong's Axioms and results of Theorem 6.6.8 for use in proving the desired results. Let W, X, Y, and Z be arbitrary sets of columns.

[1] Inclusion: If Y is a subset of X, then $X \rightarrow Y$.

[2] Augmentation: If $X \rightarrow Y$, then $W X \rightarrow W Y$.

[3] Transitivity: If $X \rightarrow Y$ and $Y \rightarrow Z$, then $X \rightarrow Z$.

[4] Union: If $X \rightarrow Y$ and $X \rightarrow Z$, then $X \rightarrow Y Z$.

[5] Decomposition: If $X \rightarrow Y Z$, then $X \rightarrow Y$ and $X \rightarrow Z$.

[6] Pseudotransitivity: If $X \rightarrow Y$ and $W Y \rightarrow Z$, then $X W \rightarrow Z$.

(a) $D \rightarrow A B C D$

Steps numbered. (1) By reflexivity, since D is a subset of D (both singleton sets), $D \rightarrow D$. (2) Since $D \rightarrow A B C$ (by FD (3) given) and $D \rightarrow D$, by union, $D \rightarrow A B C D$.

[6.14] (a) Step 1. H = {$A \rightarrow B$, $C \rightarrow B$, $D \rightarrow A$, $D \rightarrow B$, $D \rightarrow C$, $A C \rightarrow D$}.

Step 2.

1. $A \rightarrow B$. J = $H - \{A \rightarrow B\}$, X^+ under J: X[0] = A, X[1] = A, X^+ = A, not containing B, so keep $A \rightarrow B$; that is, H remains the same.

2. $C \rightarrow B$. J = $H - \{C \rightarrow B\}$. X[0] = C, X[1] = C, so X^+ = C, not containing B, so H remains the same.

3. $D \rightarrow A$. J = $H - \{D \rightarrow A\}$. X[0] = D, X[1] = D B X, X[2] = D B X, so X^+ = D B X, not containing A, so H remains the same.

4. $D \rightarrow B$. J = $H - \{D \rightarrow B\}$, X[0] = D, . . . , X^+ = D A B C, containing B, so drop this FD.

New H = {$A \rightarrow B$, $C \rightarrow B$, $D \rightarrow A$, $D \rightarrow C$, $A C \rightarrow D$}.

5. $D \rightarrow C$. J = $H - \{D \rightarrow C\}$. X^+ = D A B, not containing C, so H remains the same.

6. $A C \rightarrow D$. J = $J - \{A C \rightarrow D\}$. X^+ = A C B, not containing D, so H remains the same.

Resulting H = {$A \rightarrow B$, $C \rightarrow B$, $D \rightarrow A$, $D \rightarrow C$, $A C \rightarrow D$}.

Step 3. Only A C → D could possibly be reduced on the left-hand side. Loop over B in its left-hand side:

1. B = A, Y = C, J = {A → B, C → B, D → A, D → C, C → D}. (Y^+ under J) = C B D A, (Y^+ under H) = C B, not same, so keep H the same.

2. B = C, Y = A, J = {A → B, C → B, D → A, D → C, A → D}. (Y+ under J) = A B D C, (Y^+ under H) = A B, not same, so keep H the same.

Note how the proposed (but rejected) changes make too many attributes reachable in the closure.

Step 4. M = {A → B, C → B, D → A C, A C → D}.

[6.15] Let Y^+_H stand for Y^+ determined under H. Then we need to show that $Y^+_H = Y^+_J$ implies $H^+ = J^+$. Here J = (H − {x → A}) UNION {Y → A}, and Y = X − {B}. J has the same FDs as H except for one FD that has one less attribute on the left-hand side, making it imply more than the one it replaces, so clearly H^+ is a subset of J^+. We claim that if they are actually different, then Y → A, clearly in J^+, is not in H^+. For if Y → A is in H^+, then all FDs in J are in H^+ by its definition, so that H^+ covers J, and thus covers J^+, so J^+ is a subset of H^+. But we already know that H^+ is a subset of J^+, so $H^+ = J^+$. Contradiction.

So far we have shown that if H^+ and J^+ differ, then Y → A is not in H^+. But if Y → A is not in H^+, then A is not in Y^+_H, and we know that Y → A is in J^+; that is, A is in Y^+_J, so the sets Y^+_H and Y^+_J are different. The contrapositive is the desired result.

[6.19] (b) Since there are no FDs for T, B ↛ A and B ↛ C, Head(T1) ∩ Head(T2) does not functionally determine either Head(T1) or Head(T2). In such a case, the theorem, by its "only if" statement, ensures the decomposition is not lossless, that is, there is some content for which T <> T1 ⋈ T2. We have shown such content.

[6.20] (b) Here we will work independently of part (a) until we actually need its results to explain things. A slightly neater approach would be to use the results of (a) from the start. We start with the table T = (A, B, C, D, E, F, G). What is the primary key for this table? B and C are not on the right-hand side of any FD and therefore must be in any key, since a key functionally determines all other columns. Now given B C, we get A (from (1) and (5)); E (from (2)); and since we have A, by transitivity we get F (by (3)). Then (4) gives us G, and (5) gives us D. So we have (accumulating from the left) B C, A, E, F, G, and D, which is all of them. Thus B C is a superkey for T, and since B and C must be in any key, B C is the key. All the given FDs lie in this one table.

Now D is not fully functionally dependent on B C, but dependent on C alone, making C → D a proper key subset FD. Therefore even for 2NF we need to factor out a table, and we have two tables: T_1 = (B, C, A, E, F, G) and T_2 = (C, D), with keys B C and C, respectively. T_1 contains all the given FDs except (5), which lies in T_2, and (1), which appears to cross tables. However, if we adopt the minimal cover FD set computed in part (a), we see that all but one are contained entirely in T_1 and one is contained entirely in T_2. FDs A → F and F → G are transitive dependencies. Thus T_1 and T_2 form a 2NF decomposition.

(d) Algorithm 6.8.8 with F = {B C → A E, A → F, F → G, C → D}

S = nullset. Loop through all FDs in F:

B C → A E. Nothing is S yet, so nothing can contain B C A E, so add it to S: S = {{B C A E}}.

A → F. A F is not contained in B C A E, so add it to S: S = {{B C A E},{A F}}.

F → G. F G is not contained in either set so far, so add it: S = {{B C A E}, {A F},{F G}}.

C → D. C D is not contained in any set so far, so add it: S = {{B C A E}, {A F},{F G},{C D}}.

Here the only candidate key is B C, and it is contained in B C A E, so the second loop does not add anything to S. The resulting table design is the same as we had before.

[6.22] FDs for banking problem: each account has a unique type, balance, and branch, so we have acctid → acct_type acct_bal bno. Each branch has a city and each customer has a name, so the set is

```
acctid -> acct_type acct_bal bno
bno -> bcity
ssn -> clname cfname cmidinit
```

T = (acctid, acct_type, acct_bal, bno, bcity, ssn, clname, cfname, cmidinit). Since ssn and acctid appear only on the left of the FDs, they must be in any key, and in fact all the other attributes are in the closure of {ssn, acctid}, so this is in fact the key of T. Now the first and third FDs are key-subset dependencies, and the second one is a transitive dependency, but since the normal level of decomposition is 3NF, we don't really care about this difference and just decompose three times—for example, as follows:

1. T1 = (acctid, acct_type, acct_bal, bno, bcity), T2 = (acctid, ssn, clname, cfname, cmidinit).

2. T1 = (acctid, acct_type, acct_bal, bno), T2 = (bno, bcity), T3 = (acctid, ssn, clname, cfname, cmidinit).

```
3. T1 = (acctid, acct_type, acct_bal, bno), T2 = (bno, bcity), T3 = (ssn, clname,
cfname, cmidinit), T4 = (acctid, ssn) Final result, in 3NT form.
```

Note that along the way we have extracted all the non-key attributes from T, leaving T4 = (acctid, ssn) as a skeletal remains of the original universal table. But in fact it represents an important fact about this design: there is a true binary relationship between accounts and customers. This design is the same as the second proposed design in Exercise 6.3. We can now justify that second design, over the first one, with more confidence. Design 1 of Exercise 6.3 is not fully factored. Look at its result:

```
accounts = (acctid, acct_type, acct_bal)
branches = (bno, bcity)
customers = (ssn, clname, cfname, cmidinit)
has_account_at = (ssn, acctid, bno)
```

We have asserted that acctid –> bno, and this means that the last table has a key-subset dependency and is not even 2NF.

Chapter 7 Solutions

[7.1] (a)
```
create table agents (aid char(3) not null,
    aname varchar(13), city varchar(20),
    percent integer check(percent >= 0 and percent <= 10),
    primary key (aid));

create table products (pid char(3) not null,
    pname varchar(13), city varchar(20),
    quantity integer check(quantity > 0),
    price real check(price > 0.0)), primary key (pid);
```

[7.3] See Figure 7.2 for most of them. There should be exactly one product for each line item, but possibly many line items, or none at all, for each product, so the connection between for_prod and Products should be labeled (0, N), and the connection between for_prod and Line_items should be labeled (1, 1).

As in Section 6.4, we start with tables for the entities and then add foreign keys and/or relationship tables to complete the relational design.

Starter entity tables, using just what we see in Figure 6.11, plus entity IDs, for simplicity:

```
customers = (cid)
orders = (ordno)
agents = (aid)
line_items = (ordno, lineno)
products = (pid)
```

The relationship requests is N − 1, with orders on the many side, and thus is implemented with a foreign key:

```
orders = (ordno, cid)
```

Similarly places is also N − 1, so orders becomes

```
orders = (ordno, cid, aid)
```

Finally for_prod is also N − 1, so line_items becomes

```
line_items = (ordno,lineno, pid);
create table customers (cid char(4) not null, primary key (cid));
create table orders (ordno integer not null, cid char(3) not null references
    customers, aid char(3) not null references agents,
    primary key (ordno));
create table agents (aid char(3) not null, primary key (aid));
create table products (pid char(3) not null, primary key (pid));
create table line_items (ordno integer references orders, lineno integer not null,
    pid char(3) not null references products, primary key (ordno, lineno));
```

[7.4] (a) No.

(c) No.

[7.5] (b)
```
create view agentview (aid, aname, city, percent)
        as select aid, aname, city, percent from agents
            where percent >= 0 and percent <= 10 with check option;
```

(d)
```
create view vproducts as
        select pid, pname, city, quantity from products;
grant select, update (city, quantity) on vproducts to beowulf;
```

[7.6] (a) False by the definition of the primary key clause in Definition 7.1.3.

(c) False. No subquery is allowed in the CHECK clause in X/Open.

[7.7] (a) CASCADE or the default NO ACTION by all three products, RESTRICT, CASCADE, SET NULL, as well as the default NO ACTION in **DB2 UDB**.

[7.8] (a)
```
create table customers1 (cid not null, cname, city,
        discnt constraint discnt_max check(discnt <= 15.0)),
        primary key (cid)) as select * from customers;
```

(c) The Create Table statement will give an error because of a primary key violation (on the cid primary key). The solution is to use a Select UNIQUE Subquery.

[7.10] (a) The view referred to, agentords, is identical except for name to the one given in Example 7.2.1:

```
create view agentords (ordno, month, cid, aid, pid, qty,
    charge, aname, acity, percent)
        as select ordno, month, cid, a.aid, pid, qty, dollars,
            aname, city, percent
            from orders o, agents a where o.aid = a.aid;
```

The view agentords would not be updatable in X/Open by the rules of Figure 7.15 (and similarly in SQL-92, but **ORACLE** allows updates in more circumstances). In general, inserts, updates, and deletes on agentords rows can be thought of as the same operations on orders rows with which agentords rows are in one-to-one correspondence. Agents rows are generally in correspondence with many rows of agentords, but it is defensible to argue that updates to the agents table should also be allowed to take place as long as they make sense.

Insert with a new aid value. It looks like we are inserting a new agent row and a new orders row, both at the same time: the order refers to the new agent. We allow this. Of course all existing integrity constraints must still hold, so, for example, the order must refer to an existing product pid, and the ordno cannot duplicate one that already exists.

Insert with an old aid value. This is an insert of a new order with an existing aid. The only thing that could go wrong is if this insert specifies an existing aid with the "wrong" values for other agents columns, such as aname. Since aid is supposed to be the primary key for agents, aid functionally determines all other columns, and giving a different aname value, for example, would break an integrity constraint, and thus the inserts should fail. It seems reasonable to allow an insert with dependent agents columns left unspecified, with the default being the functionally determined values.

Machine Assignments

[7.14] ORACLE case—

```
SQL> select * from user_constraints;
... many lines of output
SQL> alter table customers add constraint discntmax check (discnt <= 12.0);
ERROR at line 1:
ORA-02293: cannot enable ... check constraint violated
SQL> update customers set discnt = 10.0 where cid = 'c001';
1 row updated.
SQL> alter table customers add constraint discntmax check (discnt <= 12.0);
Table altered.
SQL> update customers set discnt = 16.0 where cid = 'c001';
ORA-02290: check constraint ... violated
```

```
SQL> select * from customers;
...see discnt = 10.0 for c001.
SQL> alter table drop constraint discntmax;
Table altered.
SQL> update customers set discnt = 16.0 where cid = 'c001';
1 row updated.
SQL> select * from customers;
...see discnt = 16.0 for c001.
SQL> exit
Now run loadcap as explained in Appendix A.
```

[7.15] (a) **ORACLE** case—

```
SQL> insert into orders values (1031, 'jul', 'c001', 'a01', 'p01', 1000, 450.0);
1 row inserted.

SQL> create view returns (ordno, month, cid, aid, pid, qty, dollars,
2    discnt, percent, price)
3    as select ordno, month, o.cid, o.aid, o.pid, qty, dollars,
4        discnt, percent, price
5    from orders o, customers c, agents a, products p
6        where c.cid = o.cid and a.aid = o.aid and p.pid = o.pid;

SQL> select view_name from user_views;
view_name
------------
returns
SQL> select column_name from user_tab_columns where table_name = 'RETURNS';

column_name
--------------
ORDNO
MONTH
CID
PID
QTY
DOLLARS
DISCNT
PERCENT
PRICE
```

(c) `select ordno, qty, dollars, discnt, percent, price,`
`    qty * price - (discnt / 100) * price * qty from returns;`

[7.20] To find the row types in use by table people (as column types), we need a triple join, as follows:

```
select typ.name from syscolumns c, systables t, sysxtdtypes typ
    where t.tabid = c.tabid and t.tabname = 'people'
        and c.extended_id = typ.extended_id;
```

```
select typ.name from syscolumns c, systables t, sysattrtyps a, sysxtdtypes typ
    where t.tabid = c.tabid and t.tabname = 'people'
            and c.extended_id = a.extended_id
            and a.xtd_type_id = typ.extended_id;
```

Chapter 8 Solutions

[8.1] (a) Since minextents is 3, 3 * 20,480 = 61,440 bytes.

(b) Since maxextents is 8, 8 * 20,480 = 163,840 bytes.

[8.2] (a) We have 2048 bytes in a page, and for 512 slots we would need 512 * 2 = 1024 bytes for the row directory. This leaves 2048 − 1024 = 1024 bytes for rows, and we have 1024 /512 = 2 bytes for each row.

(c) We can allow 2^{23} = 8,388,608 pages/table.

[8.4] (a) We need about 100 bytes per row (including 2 for the directory offset) and we have nearly 0.75 * 2000 = 1500 usable bytes/page. Now 1500 bytes/page/ 100 bytes/row = 15 rows/page. 200,000 rows/15 rows/page = 13,334 pages.

(d) We will need one disk access for the root of the index, and one for the next level directory. We are searching through 10,000 leaf-level entries, and at 148 entries/page this means about CEIL(10,000/148) = 68 accesses for leaf-node pages. Since the rows are not clustered and assuming buffering is negligible, retrieving 10,000 rows will take 10,000 disk I/Os. Therefore the number of disk I/Os is (1 + 1 + 68 + 10,000) = 10,070 disk accesses. At 40 accesses/ second, we require about 252 seconds. At 80 I/Os/second, we need only 126 seconds.

(f) To *count* the number of rows, the query optimizer only needs to count the number of entries, rather than go down and pick up the rows themselves. Thus the number of accesses is (1 + 1 + 68) = 70, and at 40 I/Os/second, this is 1.75 seconds.

[8.6] (a) (i)   False for **DB2 UDB** (but **DB2 UDB** v6 does allow 32 K byte pages)

(iii) True. See Example 8.3.2.

(v)   True. There will be 1000 pages in the buffer, out of 1,000,000, so 1 in 1000 will be in the buffer.

[8.7] (b) 75% of 2000 is 1500 bytes usable on a page. The entry contains the rowid, 6 bytes; the keyval, here 7 bytes; and 1 byte of overhead, for a total of 14 bytes. Then 1500/14 = 107 entries/page, and 400,000 entries/(107 entries/ page) = 3739 leaf-level pages.

(e) With a clustered index, the same number of index pages is used, but the 20,000 data rows are adjacent on disk, in 20,000/8 = 2500 pages. Thus the total is only 2689 disk-page I/Os.

[8.9] (a) Here N = 128 and M = 10,000. $E(S) = 10,000 * (1 - .9999^{128})$

$.9999^{128} = .9999^{2*2*2*2*2*2*2} = ((((((.9999^2)^2 \ldots^2) = .9873$

$E(S) = 10,000 * .0127 = 127$

Using [8.6.4], $10,000 * (1 - \exp(-128/10,000)) = 10,000(1 - .9873) = 127$

Yes, both show that only one collision is expected.

[8.10] (a) The probability that all the darts will be in different slots, for 2 darts, is 364/365, because the first dart can go into any slot and the second dart must miss the first in 364 out of 365 ways. Then for 3 darts the probability is (364/365) * (363/365). For N darts, it is $364 * 363 * \ldots * (365 - N + 1)/365^{N-1} = .5$ at the desired value of N. $(1 - 1/365)(1 - 2/365) \ldots (1 - (N - 1)/365) = .5$. Expanding the product and neglecting terms with multiple factors of 365 in the denominator, we have approximately $1 - (1 + 2 + 3 + \ldots + (N - 1))/365 = .5$, or $1 + 2 + \ldots + (N - 1) = 365/2$. The sum of the numbers is about $(N - 1)^2/2$, so $(N - 1)^2 = 365$ or N = 20, approximately. By doing it numerically, we find that N = 23 comes the closest to .5, at .493, so the neglected terms have some effect.

Chapter 9 Solutions

[9.1] (a) Seek time .008 seconds + rotational latency .004 seconds + transfer time .004 seconds (32 times .0005) = .028 seconds.

(c) (i) In this case, sequential prefetch of 8 pages at a time *helps*. To read in 5000 index pages in P8 blocks, we calculate 5000/8 = 625 blocks, so about 625 * 0.016 seconds elapsed time, or 10 seconds. (We have no rule of thumb here, as in the case where we say that sequential prefetch proceeds at a rate of 800 I/Os per second, so we need to calculate more carefully.) We also have 50,000 clustered data pages, and 50,000/8 = 6250, 6250 * 0.016 = 100 seconds. So total elapsed time is 10 + 100 = 110 seconds.

(ii) In the case where random I/Os are used, 50,000 R + 5000 R takes 55,000/80 seconds, or 687.5 seconds.

[9.2] (a) With PCTFREE = 0, we can fit 10 rows of 400 bytes each on a 4-KB disk page. Thus 100,000 rows require 100,000/10 = 10,000 data pages. The eidx index, with 10-byte entries, fits 400 entries on a leaf page; thus with 100,000 entries at the leaf level, there are 100,000/400 = 250 leaf pages. At the next level up, with entries the same size, we fit 400 entries per page, and the 250 entries needed clearly fit in a single page, a root.

(b) (i) P(leaf) = 1/250.

(ii) (1 − P(leaf)) = 249/250.

(iii) Call this event NOT-leaf-N. We require a conjunction of N independent events, each with probability 249/250. P(NOT-leaf-N) = (249/250)^N (Nth power).

(iv) (249/250)^{250} = 0.367. (You might be interested to note that this is a good approximation to exp(−1), 0.368 since the formula we are calculating is (1 − 1/x)^x, for a large x, and in the limit as x approaches infinity this formula approaches exp(−1).)

(v) A fraction 0.367 will have fallen out of buffers because they were not referenced in the last 125 seconds, so the number we expect to see remaining in buffers is (1 − 0.367) * 250 = 158.25. (You can recast this in terms of the definition of "expectation" if you want. For each specific leaf, P(leaf in buffer) = 1 − 0.367 = 0.633. Expected number of leaves remaining in buffer = number of leaves * 0.633 = 158.25.)

(vi) Here we have N = 250 darts and M = 250 slots, so the expected number of slots hit is approximately E(S) = M(1 − e$^{-N/M}$) = 250(1 − e^{-1}) = 158.

(c) (iv) From part (b) we see that 250 data page references in the 125-second period yielded 247 pages in buffer at the end. Thus ignoring double rereferences, only three of these references hit pages already referenced, so only three pages were rereferenced. On the other hand, 250 index page references in the period yielded only 158 pages in the buffer at the end, so 250 − 158 = 92 index leaf pages were rereferenced. Since there are fewer leaf pages than data pages, they are rereferenced more often. Thus fewer *different* index leaf pages were referenced in the period and remain in the buffer.

(f) Here we have two queries per second. The fraction of the data pages not available in buffer (10,000 − 247)/10,000 = .975, so we have an I/O cost of 2 * 0.975, or 1.950. A root page is never out of buffer. The leaf pages have a probability 0.367 to be out of buffer (from part (b)), and so this adds an I/O cost for two queries, or 0.734. Total I/O cost is then 1.950 + 0.734 = 2.684 per second.

(h) I/O cost would be 2, for the data pages. Clearly this is a superior strategy to LRU, since we use less memory and have a lower I/O cost.

[9.4] **(b)** **(i)** ACCESSTYPE = I, ACCESSNAME = C1234X, MATCHCOLS = 1, (INDEXONLY = N).

(ii) We must retrieve all index entries with C1 having values from 1 to 10. This is 1/10 of the whole range of C1234X, which has NLEAF = 150,151, so the number of leaf pages retrieved is 15,015. Sequential prefetch can be used, so elapsed time is 15,015/800 = 18.8 seconds.

(iii) The filter factor for this compound predicate is (1/10)(1/20)(1/50) = 1/10,000.

(iv) The number of rows retrieved is (1/10,000)(100,000,000) = 10,000. Rows of T are contiguous by the index C1234X. Here there are 10 values of C1 selected, each subdivided into 200 regions of C2 values, of which we select 10 adjacent. But each of these 10 is further subdivided into 50 regions of various C3 values, of which we select one. Thus there are 100 separate regions of the index in use here, separated by parts of the index not in use. The 10,000 rows are distributed across these 100 ranges, so there are about 100 rows that are contiguous in each range, but the whole set is far from contiguous. But DB2 cannot take advantage of these little contiguous ranges, because it will find them while processing screening predicates. (List prefetch will not be used either, because no filtering is allowed in extracts into a RID list.) Therefore elapsed time is 10,000/80 = 125 seconds.

(v) 15,015 S + 10,000 R, with elapsed time 18.8 + 125 = 143.8 seconds.

[9.5] **(a)** **(i)** C1 and C2 are matching columns. The matching stops at C2 because of part 3 of Definition 9.5.4.

(iii) No columns are matching, because C1 <> 6 is not an indexable predicate.

(v) C1 and C2 are matching columns. The matching stops before C3 because C3 like '%abc' is not indexable.

(vii) No columns are matching because C1 = Expression is not indexable.

(b) **(i)** FF(C1 = 7) = 1/100 = .01, FF(C2 >= 101) = 100/200 = .5, so the composite FF = .01 * .5 = .005.

(iii) .005 * 100,000,000 = 500,000 index entries. Recall that all columns are 4 bytes in length. For C1234X, the key value length is 16 bytes. There is a certain amount of compression at the leaf level, with each block of duplicates containing 1 key value (16 bytes), 4 bytes of block overhead, and 10 RIDs of 4 bytes each; this means a total of 60 bytes for 10 entries, or 6 bytes per entry. We can fit FLOOR(4000/6) = 666 entries per page. Thus there are CEIL(500,000/666) = 751 pages at leaf level, and these can be read by sequential prefetch (S). The index has another level above the leaf level, but only one page of it is accessed on the original lookup of the very first access. This page would require random access (R).

(v) 751 S + 6000 R = 751/800 + 6000/80 = 75.95 seconds.

[9.6] (a) Here we have 50 million rows and FF(incomeclass = 10) = 1/10, so this RID-list extraction from incomex will result in 5 million RIDs, below the absolute maximum of 16 million. Five million RIDs require 20 million bytes, and this must be below 50% of the RID pool, so the RID pool must be at least 40 million bytes. Since the RID pool is half the size of the buffer pool, this means the buffer pool must be at least 80 million bytes. Thus the system must have enough memory to accommodate 120 million bytes for buffer and RID pools.

(c) FF(AGE between 20 and 39) = 2/5: there will be .4 * 50 million = 20 million agex index entries, above the absolute maximum for RID lists, so it is not possible.

(e) It is not possible because of RULE 3 of Definition 9.6.1, excluding in-list predicates.

[9.7] (a) ACCESSTYPE = I, ACCESSNAME = mailx, MATCHCOLS = 1. We stop matching columns left-to-right with the zipcode component for two reasons: (1) the next column in mailx, hobby, is not matched; and (2) we always stop matching when we come to the BETWEEN predicate.

(c) (i) Yes, under the memory conditions found in Exercise 9.6(a), we can use an MX step on incomeclass = 10, using the incomex index.

(ii)

ACCESS TYPE	MATCH COLS	ACCESS NAME	PRE FETCH	MIXOP SEQ
M	0		L	1
MX	1	mailx	S	2
MX	1	agex	S	3
MI	0			4
MX	1	incomex	S	5
MI	0			6

Note that the predicates are ordered from smaller to larger by filter factor, and intersection takes place as often as possible to avoid having more than one RID list at once on the imaginary stack. Other orders are also usable.

(iii)   1/50,000.

(e)   As in (d), start with index scan of mailx to extract RID list for zipcode predicate, taking 3.12 seconds. Then extract the RID list for age predicate from agex with NLEAF = 50,000, so (1/50)(50,000), I/O cost is 1000 S, and elapsed time, 1000/800 = 1.25 seconds. Finally extract RID list for the income predicate from incomex with NLEAF = 50,000, so (1/10)(50,000), I/O cost is 5000 S, and elapsed time, 6.25 seconds. Finally 1000 rows on 1000 data pages, but this time we can use list prefetch, 1000 L, and elapsed time 1000/200 = 5 seconds. Total elapsed time: 3.12 + 1.25 + 6.25 + 5 = 15.62 seconds. The fact that they come out the same is an accident.

[9.8] (a) No. It would have 25,000,000 RIDs, and thus over the absolute maximum.

   (b) (i)   zipcode between 02139 and 07138 is matching, and the rest are screening.

      (iii)   For either method, we expect FF * 50,000,000 = .01 * .02 * .05 * 50,000,000 = 500 rows, not clustered. For method (i), the RIDs are found during screening, and thus entail random I/O, at 500 R = 500/80 = 6.25 seconds. For method (ii), we obtain a RID list and thus can use list prefetch, for 500L = 500/200 = 2.5 seconds.

[9.9] (a) The only matching column is zipcode, because by Definition 9.5.4[3], a BETWEEN predicate terminates the search for matching predicates. The index I/O we perform for the zipcode BETWEEN predicates will scan (2000/100,000)(250,000 leaf pages) = 5000 leaf pages, with sequential prefetch used, and 5000 S requires an elapsed time of 5000/800 = 6.25 seconds. The combined filter factor for all predicates, including screening predicates, in order by predicate clauses as they appear is (2000/100,000)(1/50 + 1/50 − (1/50)(1/50))(1/100)(1/10) = (1/50)(1/25)(1/100)(1/10) = 1/1,250,000. With 50,000,000 rows in prospects, this means that we expect to retrieve (1/1,250,000) (50,000,000) = 40 rows. With random I/O (we can't use list prefetch because we didn't extract a RID list, since we used screening predicates), 40 R takes an elapsed time of 40/80 = .5 seconds. The total elapsed time is 6.75 seconds.

   (c) (a) wins with 6.75 seconds elapsed time, versus (b) with 11.37 seconds. The reason for this general rule is that the matching scan of the first column, in the case where screening predicates are used, must be duplicated in the case of MX retrieval, along with other index scans as well, so the MX case pays more for index I/O. It is *just possible* that this deficit will be made up at the end by the fact that the MX approach allows list prefetch in data page retrieval.

[9.10] (a) With T1.C6 = 5, we limit the 1,000,000 rows of T1 down to 1/20 as many, or 50,000 rows. Now for each value of T1.C7, we wish to match values of T2.C8, and for each of the 50,000 rows selected in T1, we have a constant value K for T1.C7. We ask how many rows in T2 match—that is, what is the selectivity of T2.C8 = K? Clearly the answer is 1/200,000, and there are (on the average) 5 rows that match. Therefore each of the 50,000 rows in T1 matches 5 rows in T2, and we have 250,000 rows in the join so far. Now we have to limit T2.C9 = 6, with filter factor = 1/400, and the resulting number of rows in the join is (1/400)(250,000) = 625.

[9.11] (a) After pass 1:

12 45 67 84 | 7 29 58 76 | 22 39 81 91 | 28 33 65 96 | 4 13 54 77 | 1 32 41 59

After pass 2:

7 12 29 45 58 67 76 84 | 22 28 33 39 65 81 91 96 | 1 4 13 32 41 54 59 77

After pass 3:

7 12 22 28 29 33 39 45 58 65 67 76 81 84 91 96 | 1 4 13 22 41 54 59 77

After pass 4:

1 4 7 12 13 22 28 29 32 33 39 41 45 54 58 59 65 67 76 77 81 84 91 96

NOTE: Below this point we are using old disk speeds S = 1/400, L = 1/100, and R = 1/40 second.

[9.12] (a) (1/2)(1/10)(1,000,000) = 50,000.

(c) For K100 > 80, 1/5. For K10K between 2000 and 3000, 1000/10,000 = 1/10. For K5 = 3, 1/5. So (1/5)(1/10)(1/5)(1,000,000) = (1/250)(1,000,000) = 4000.

(e) As explained in the text, a tablespace scan is being used in the K4 case, and 1737 prefetch I/Os gives 1737 * 32 = 55,584 pages. Recall that the BENCH table has 55,556 pages, so this is very close. Our rule of thumb would mean that 55,584 S takes 55,584/400 = 138.96 seconds. In fact, we see 133.27 seconds elapsed, so we are reading in a bit faster than that. Note that the CPU time of 26.90 seconds does not get subtracted from 133.27 seconds before we start timing the I/Os: I/O and CPU overlap, so basically all of the elapsed time has I/O taking place.

(g) We use a nested-loop join as the basis for calculation, as in Exercise 9.4(a). Limit B1 by B1.K100 = 99, so 10,000 are rows retrieved. For each one of these, B1.250K is a constant K, and we ask how many rows in B2 have B2.500K = K? Average 2. Thus we now have 20,000 rows in the join. Now limit with B2.K25 = 19, FF of 1/25, and (1/25)(20,000) = 800. The actual number retrieved (Appendix D) is 804.

[9.13] (a) B1.K100 = 22 selects for 10,000 rows of B1, and for each of these, B1.K250K is a constant between 1 and 250K, so that B1.K250K = B2.K100K selects for nothing at all if the constant is over 100K, and 10 rows of B2 if it is not over 100K. This happens 40% of the time. Of the 10 rows, only 1/25, or .4 on average, are selected by B2.K25 = 19. Thus we expect .4 * .4 * 10,000 = 1600 rows in the join.

(b) B1 the outer table: Here the 10,000 value-22 index entries of the K100 index are read into a RID list, allowing list prefetch of the 10,000 rows of B1 needed to determine B1.K100K and B1.KSEQ; this data page access has I/O cost 10,000 L. The index entries represent 1% of the K100 index or, using Figure 9.28, 1% of 1051 pages, or about 11 pages, accessible by sequential prefetch at I/O cost 11 S. Then for each of the 10,000 rows the inner loop accesses either about 10 rows of B2 (40% of the cases), using list prefetch, or 0 rows (60% of the cases), depending on whether B1.K250K is below or above 100,000 in value. The 10 rows are further resolved by the B2.K25 = 19 predicate after the rows are retrieved, resulting in .4 rows in the join. But this happens only in 40% of the 10,000 cases—that is, in 4000 cases, so the I/O cost is 4000 * 10 L = 40,000 L. The total I/O cost is then 10 S + 50,000 L = 50,000/100 = 500 seconds.

B2 the outer table: Here the 40,000 value-19 index entries of the K25 index are read into a RID list, allowing list prefetch of the 40,000 rows of B2 needed to determine B2.K100K and B2.KSEQ; this data page access has I/O cost 40,000 L. The index entries are all duplicates, so they take 4 bytes each, or 160,000 bytes, or 40 pages, accessible by sequential prefetch at I/O cost 40 S. Then for each of the 40,000 rows, the inner loop accesses about 4 rows of B1 via the match on B1.K250K = B2.K100K (all cases, since here the B2.K100K value is always in range for K250K). The match also involves a lookup using the K100K index with I/O cost 1 R for each row, or 40,000 R total. Now a count of 4 rows is a bit small for list prefetch, but we have been allowing it, so we count this as 40,000 * 4L = 160,000 L. These rows are further screened by predicate B1.K100 = 22. The total I/O cost is 40 S + 200,000 L + 40,000 R = 3000 seconds.

[9.15] (a) `select npages from systables where name = 'BENCH';`

(See Figure 9.13.)

(c) The K2X index is almost all duplicates, so there are 4 bytes/entry, or about 1000 entries/page. There are 1,000,000 entries and therefore 1000 pages at leaf level.

Chapter 10 Solutions

[10.1] (a) There are six transactions in 120 ms (2 I/Os and 2 CPU blocks), or 50 TPS.

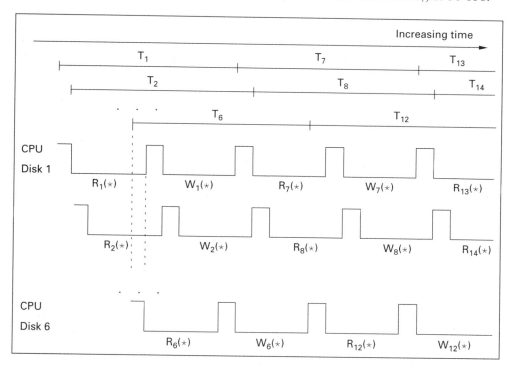

[10.2] (a) $T2 \rightarrow T3 \rightarrow T1$

[10.3]

	$R_1(A)$	$W_1(A)$	$R_2(A)$	$R_2(B)$	C_2	$R_1(B)$	$W_1(B)$	C_1
Operation number:	1	2	3	4		5	6	

Operations 2 and 3 give $T_1 \rightarrow T_2$, and operations 4 and 6 give $T_2 \rightarrow T_1$. The precedence graph is

To answer the second part of the question, assume that A and B are accounts that normally see only deposits, and that T_1 has the job of seeing that account A doesn't get over 100—if A is over 100, T_1 brings the value of A down to 50 and moves the excess, adding it to account B. We assume that the job of T_2 is to check the sum of accounts A and B, and if the sum is more than 200 to bring the sum down to 150 by subtracting from A and B and adding the excess to a third balance, C. Now assume to start that A = 120 and B = 140. Since T_1 doesn't change the sum of A and B, we see that any serial execution will have T_2 subtracting from A and B and adding to C. However, what we see instead is

$R_1(A, 120)$ $W_1(A, 50)$ $R_2(A, 50)$ $R_2(B, 140)$ C_2 $R_1(B, 140)$ $W_1(B, 210)$ C_1

We note that T_2 sees A + B as *at most* 50 + 140 = 190. Since that is less than 200, T_2 makes no changes. This could not have occurred in any serial schedule.

[10.5] This is the "dirty write" example, where each transaction writes back a new value for A that fails to take the other's update into account. The locking scheduler translates this into the following sequence of events:

$RL_1(A)$ $R_1(A)$ $RL_2(A)$ $R_2(A)$ $WL_1(A)$ (conflict with earlier $RL_2(A)$ – T_1 must WAIT) $WL_2(A)$ (conflict with earlier $RL_1(A)$ – circuit in WAITS-FOR Graph— choose T_2 as victim) A_2 ($WL_1(A)$ now successful) $W_1(A)$ C_1 (T_2 now retries as transaction T_3) $RL_3(A)$ $R_3(A)$ $WL_3(A)$ $W_3(A)$ C_3

We see that the operations for T_1 and T_2 (renamed T_3) occur in serial order.

[10.6] (a) $WL_3(A)$ $W_3(A)$ $RL_1(A)$ (conflict with earlier $WL_3(A)$ – T_1 must WAIT for T_3) $RL_2(B)$ $R_2(B)$ $WL_2(Y)$ $W_2(Y)$ $WL_3(B)$ (conflict with earlier $RL_2(B)$ – T_3 must wait for T_2) C_2 (releases lock on B, so $WL_3(B)$ is successful) $W_3(B)$ C_3 (releases lock on A so $RL_1(A)$ is successful) $R_1(A)$ $WL_1(Z)$ $W_1(Z)$ C_1

$W_3(A)$	$R_1(A)$	$W_1(Z)$	$R_2(B)$	$W_2(Y)$	$W_3(B)$	C1 C2 C3
Operation number: 1	2	3	4	5	6	

Note from operations 1 and 2 that $T_1 \rightarrow T_3$ in the waits-for graph. Next, from 4 and 6, we have $T_3 \rightarrow T_2$. No other pairs of operations act on identical data elements. Therefore there are no other conflicting pairs, and the waits-for graph never has a cycle, so there is no deadlock. The waits-for graph after operation 6 follows:

$T_1 \rightarrow T_3 \rightarrow T_2$

[10.7] (a) $R_5(E, 8)$, since before this the pages with A, B, C, and D have been accessed and fill the four pages of the cache buffer.

(c) The page with data item A will be dropped by the LRU scheme, since it has the longest interval since reference.

(e) No, it only forces out the log data on this transaction. The actual dirty page may linger in the buffer until a convenient time to write it.

[10.8] (a) (i)   Here is the series of log entries written as a result of this history:

(S, 2) (S, 1) (W, 1, B, 2, 3) (S, 3) (W, 2, A, 1, 5) (W, 3, C, 4, 6) (CKPT, LIST = T1, T2, T3) (S, 4) (W, 2, E, 8, 9) (C, 2) (W, 4, D, 7, 11)

(ii)   The last write will not get out to the log file, since no Commit forces it. Now we outline the actions taken by recovery:

Rollback

1.	(C, 2)	Place T_2 as committed on active list.
2.	(W, 2, E, 8, 9)	No action.
3.	(S, 4)	No action.
4.	(CKPT, LIST = T1, T2, T3)	Active list = (T1(NC), T2(C), T3(NC)).
5.	(W, 3, C, 4, 6)	UNDO: C = 4.
6.	(W, 3, A, 1, 4)	UNDO: A = 1.
7.	(S, 3)	Active list = (T1(NC), T2(C)).
8.	(W, 1, B, 2, 3)	UNDO: B = 2.
9.	(S, 1)	Active list = (T2(C)), only committed, end of rollback.

Roll forward (jump to first log entry after checkpoint)

10.	(S, 4)	No action. Active committed transactions: T2.
11.	(W, 2, E, 8, 9)	REDO: E = 9.
12.	(C, 2)	No action. No more active committed transactions. End of roll forward.

(iii)

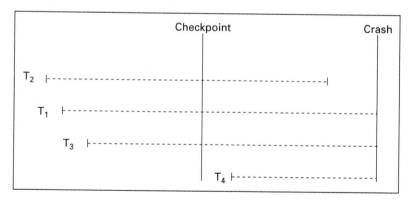

[10.9] First we argue why these are all possible cases of transaction durations. Every transaction must start and stop, start must come before stop, and there are three times possible: (1) before the final checkpoint taken (in the next exercise we show that there is no difference if it started two checkpoints ago); (2) after the final checkpoint and before the crash; and (3) at the time of the crash (at least a stop can happen at this time). Therefore the set of start-stop times that cover all possibilities would seem to be (1–1), (1–2), (1–3), (2–2), (2–3), and (3–3). But (3–3) is really impossible, and each of the other cases is covered by one of the transactions T_1 through T_5, in that order.

Now we argue that each of these cases is appropriately recovered by the recovery process with cache-consistent checkpointing.

(1–1) Both the start and stop for the transaction took place before the last checkpoint. In recovery we don't perform any UNDO or REDO of any of these data items, since the transaction was not active at the time of the checkpoint and of course performed no write operations after the checkpoint took place. In fact, all update operations for this transaction took place before the last checkpoint, and that checkpoint forced every "dirty" data item out to disk. Thus all updates from this transaction are out to disk, and we don't do anything to change them in recovery.

(1–2) The transaction started before the last checkpoint and ended after the last checkpoint. Note that we see the Commit log entry first during ROLLBACK, and therefore perform no action on write logs until ROLL FORWARD. With ROLL FORWARD, starting after the checkpoint, we REDO all write log entries for this transaction to data items on disk. Any updates that occurred before the checkpoint are already out to disk.

(1–3) The transaction started before the last checkpoint and ended as a result of the crash. Since the transaction aborted, we should UNDO all writes that it performed. Note that during ROLLBACK, we will either start by seeing a write log (and not a Commit) or by seeing at the time of the last checkpoint that the transaction was still active (and since we saw no Commit log, it was uncommitted). We must UNDO all write entries for the transaction. If a write log entry occurred after the last checkpoint, we see that it is an uncommitted transaction immediately, and are able to UNDO the action for that same log entry. If it leaves no trace with a write log entry after the checkpoint, we will still see that it was active at the time of the checkpoint, and will continue ROLLBACK until we see the transaction Start log; UNDO will be performed for all write logs back to that point.

(2–2) The transaction started after the last checkpoint and ended after the last checkpoint. Note that we see the Commit log entry first during ROLLBACK, and therefore perform no action on write logs until ROLL FORWARD. With ROLL FORWARD, starting after the checkpoint, we REDO all write log entries for this transaction to data items on disk. This is just what is desired.

(2–3) The transaction started after the last checkpoint and ended as a result of the crash. Since the transaction aborted, we should UNDO all writes that it performed. Note that during ROLLBACK we will start by seeing a write log (and not a Commit), and since we saw no Commit log, it was uncommitted. When we see a write log entry, we see that it is an uncommitted transaction immediately, and are able to UNDO the action for that same log entry, and all other write log entries back to the Start log.

There is one final point to consider. Is it possible that we perform two different actions on the same data element, UNDO-UNDO, UNDO-REDO, or REDO-REDO, which interfere with one another, so that the wrong data element eventually ends up in place? If we consider performing an UNDO action first, we see that this action occurs during rollback, because the transaction that performed an update on the data item never completed and must now abort. By locking, if we assume we hold all locks until Commit, we see that no other transaction could have updated this data item at a later temporal point. Further UNDO actions could only be performed by the same transaction and ultimately put in place the earliest value this transaction saw. Any future REDO actions on the data item (if there are any) must occur earlier in time, and it is clear that the last REDO action (if there is one) will leave the same value in place that the earliest UNDO action put in place. Therefore all committed transactions have completed their updates on this data item (there can only be one) and any uncommitted transaction has had no effect. If we consider performing a REDO action first, by locking we see that there can be no earlier UNDO action; therefore the final REDO action has put into place the final value. We depend on the serializability of histories under the locking discipline to see that this was the right value.

[10.11] $H = W_4(A) R_1(A) C_1 W_2(B) R_4(B) W_5(C) R_2(C) C_2 W_3(D) R_5(D) C_3 C_4 C_5$

$$T_4 \rightarrow T_1 \qquad T_2 \rightarrow T_4 \qquad T_5 \rightarrow T_2 \qquad T_3 \rightarrow T_5$$

$$PG(H) = T_3 \rightarrow T_5 \rightarrow T_2 \rightarrow T_4 \rightarrow T_1$$

Thus PG(H) contains no circuits, and H is serializable by Theorem 10.3.4. The equivalent serial history S(H) is

$$W_3(D) C_3 W_5(D) C_5 W_2(B) R_2(C) C_2 W_4(A) R_4(B) C_4 R_1(A) C_1$$

(Note that locking would put T_1, then T_4, T_2, and T_5 into WAITs, so only T_3 would be running at the time of C_3, which would release T_5, and so on.)

Chapter 11 Solutions

[11.1] (a) False. The master lock table and master transaction table can be in shared memory, so locks and transaction states are system-wide synchronous and two-phase commit is not needed.

(b) True, assuming that the queries take only read locks. No other read-only process needs to wait for such locks.

(c) False. The server can carry out a service via messages to the various processors.

(d) True. A CPU of 60 MIPS would have a point on the graph and the 300-MIPS CPU would be a point five times farther out on the horizontal axis. Five 60-MIPS CPUs would be a point on the ray through the origin and the first point, extended until it reaches the 300-MIPS mark. Since the curve bends up more and more, the 300-MIPS CPU would be the higher point.

(e) True. See Figure 11.9, where the Crashed state feeds back into the Prepared state.

Index